# Production and Operations Management

## Text and Cases

**FIFTH EDITION**

Ray Wild
*Henley Management College*

CASSELL

Cassell
Wellington House
125 Strand
London WC2R 0BB

215 Park Avenue South
New York
NY 10003



This edition first published 1995

**British Library Cataloguing-in-Publication Data**

A catalogue record for this book is available from the British Library.

ISBN 0-304-33077-9

Design, illustration and typesetting by Hardlines, Charlbury, Oxford
Printed and bound in Great Britain by Bath Press

# Contents


Preface vii
Preface to the Fifth Edition vii

**Part 1 Operating Systems and Operations Management** 1

1 The nature of operating systems and operations management 4

**Part 2 The Context of Operations Management** 29

2 Business and operations policy 33
3 Operations management and other business functions 52
4 Operations economics and costs 76

**Part 3 The Arrangement of Facilities** 87

5 Location of facilities 91
6 The layout of facilities and materials handling 122

**Part 4 Work and Work Systems** 153

7 Work and work methods 159
8 Work measurement and work standards 180
9 Workplaces, technology and jobs 210
10 Payment and incentives 239

**Part 5 Capacity Management** 259

11 Capacity management 263

**Part 6 Operations Scheduling** 293

12 Activity scheduling 303
13 Project management and network scheduling 352
14 Scheduling for batch processing 402
15 The design and scheduling of flow processing systems 436

**Part 7 Materials Management** 477

16 Materials management and supply chains 483
17 Inventory management 504

**Part 8 The Control of Operating Systems** 545

18 Operations control principles 557
19 Management of quality 570
20 Quality control and reliability 600
21 Maintenance and replacement 650
22 Performance measurement 680

**Part 9 International Case Studies** 701

**Appendices** 841

I Linear programming 842
II Forecasting techniques 860
III Computer simulation 879
IV Answers to odd-numbered analytical questions 888

Author index 905
Subject index 907

# Preface

This is a book about production and operations management. The production and operating functions within business are concerned with the processes which provide goods and/or 'services'. Production and operations managers are responsible for these processes. This book is concerned with the management of both goods-producing and service-producing processes.

The definitions and ideas presented later in this book are based on a wide view of production and operations management. This approach views the production/operations function as the core – the essential part – of any business. Furthermore, taking this view it will be shown that we are all production and operations managers. All types of business depend on production or operating systems and therefore require good production/operations management. Our subject, therefore, is of importance to *all* managers, whatever their title and whatever their job.

The book introduces some theories, ideas and concepts. It deals also with principles, procedures and techniques. It is intended as a teaching text.

The book is intended as an economic, straightforward volume. Unnecessary words have been kept to a minimum and 'padding' has been avoided. The result, I hope, provides maximum value for minimum effort, for both student and teacher.

## PREFACE TO THE FIFTH EDITION

As an author of a textbook one needs to know about how a subject is taught and studied. As the origins of this book go back almost 25 years, and as it is used (to the best of my knowledge) by students in over 70 countries, I have had plenty of opportunity to get to know my customers. In preparing the fifth edition of the book the needs and views of lecturers and students have been very influential. They have also been a source of considerable frustration for me – because it is impossible to do what everybody wants. My customers are involved in engineering, business and management courses, at undergraduate, postgraduate and post-experience levels. They are pursuing many qualifications, e.g. Bachelors, MSc, MBA and DBA degrees as well as certificates and diplomas and many professional qualifications. They are involved in full-time, part-time and modular-taught courses, supported distance-learning programmes, flexible-study programmes, correspondence courses, etc. They are a very heterogeneous and international community.

I have been asked to devote more space in this edition to technology, human/organizational matters, strategy, advanced manufacturing, service operations, computing and IT, Japanese 'methods', analytical methods, leadership, the management of change, quality, international operations, supply chains, etc. Not only is it not possible to do all of these things, but also to do some would prejudice or contradict others. Not surprisingly therefore I have compromised – but I have, again, stuck closely to certain key principles, e.g.

1. This is a book about operations, broadly defined, in which I try to deal with the subject as a whole. I have, in particular, tried to avoid separate treatment of production/manufacture and service operations. I have tried throughout to ensure that everything relates to both 'aspects'. I have tried to bring things together — to integrate, not differentiate. So, wherever it has been necessary for me to write a separate section in a chapter dealing specifically with service systems, and how they differ from production, or vice versa, I judge myself to have failed!
2. This is a book for anybody. It is not specifically for engineers or those with a technical background. It is not aimed specifically at those with analytical skills/interests, nor at those who are already in production/operations management jobs. All such people, but also all others with an interest in the subject, will I hope find it valuable — but nothing, by way of background, experience, skills, etc., is presupposed.
3. The 'incremental change' approach has, again, been used. I take the view that lecturers do not want new editions of books which they use to be massively different. They do not want to start again with them. They do, however, want to think that adapting to a new edition is worthwhile, so they want to see some changes. In short, they value familiarity but of course want to be up to date in the interests of both their own and their students' development. Within this framework, several significant changes have been made. Coverage of policy/strategic aspects has been increased and extended; the treatment of work systems has been restructured; the section on quality has been changed substantially; there is new material on the location of facilities, workplaces, technology, payment systems, materials management, batch processing and many other areas. The inclusion of a large number of international case studies in Part 9 is a major change. Also, more case examples are used throughout the text.

However, the overall structure remains the same — even though the format, size, presentation, and a significant part of the content have changed.

Finally, and of interest to tutors only, the introduction of a major *Tutor's Guide* is a new development. It contains all of the additional information that should be required by those who are using this text as a core teaching text. It is available, free of charge, to tutors who adopt the text. To obtain the *Tutor's Guide*, tutors should write to the publishers, on their university/college letterhead, also enclosing their business card.

## ACKNOWLEDGEMENTS

As already indicated I am grateful to the many users of the previous edition of this book, worldwide, who have offered comments, advice and suggestions. I hope that they will find the fifth edition to be of value.

I am grateful, on this occasion, to several people from around the world, who have helped me put together the set of international case studies contained in Part 9. Their contributions are acknowledged, individually, in that section. I am grateful also to Drs Bin Wu and Roy Snaddon for their advice on Appendix III and Chapter 21 respectively, and to Joan Walker for her assistance with parts of the manuscript.

Ray Wild
Henley-on-Thames
January 1995

# PART 1

# Operating Systems and Operations Management


Introduction to Part 1

Chapter 1 The nature of operating systems and operations management

## INTRODUCTION TO PART 1

This part of the book is the principal foundation for subsequent chapters. Here we take a broad view of operations management. Definitions are developed, a categorization of types of operating system is provided and operations objectives are identified. The major problem areas, or decisions required of operations managers, are considered and three principal problem areas are identified. A model is presented to identify the factors influencing the operations manager's decision-making and role. And finally we consider the operations management decision-making process.

The chapter introduces several concepts and ideas, and aims to encourage the reader to think about the fundamental nature of operating systems and the role of the operations manager.

## TOPIC MAP

| | Related topics in other chapters | | |
|---|---|---|---|
| **Topics in this Part** | **Chapter** | **Topic** | **Comments/aspects** |
| Chapter 1 | | | |
| Nature of operating systems | | | |
| Nature of operations management | | | |
| Operations management objectives | 2 | Business policy<br>Operations policy | Relationship with operations<br>Competitive advantage<br>Business growth |
| | 3 | Marketing | Influence of marketing decisions |
| | 4 | Operations economics | Economies of scale |
| | 5 | Location of facilities | Factors influencing location choice |
| | 6 | Layout of facilities | Objectives of layout |
| | 7 | Methods of work | Impact of efficiency of operating system |
| | 8 | Work measurement | |
| | 9 | Job design | |
| | 10 | Payment by results | |
| | 11 | Capacity management | Influence of operations objectives on strategies for managing these functions |
| | 12 | Scheduling | Influence of operations objectives on strategies for managing these functions<br>Impact on efficiency and resource utilization |
| | 13 | Scheduling | |
| | 14 | Scheduling | |
| | 15 | Scheduling | |
| | 16 | Materials management | |
| | 17 | Inventory management | |

## TOPIC MAP

| Topics in this Part | Chapter | Related topics in other chapters: Topic | Comments/aspects |
|---|---|---|---|
| *Chapter 1 continued* | 19 | Management of quality | Impact on customer service |
| | 20 | Quality control | |
| | 21 | Maintenance | |
| | 22 | Performance management | Objectives |
| | | Measurement and control | Measurement of achievement against objectives |
| | | Audit | |
| | | Benchmarking | |
| Structure of operating systems | 9 | Work systems | |
| | 11 | Capacity management | Influence of systems structure on strategies for managing these functions |
| | 12 | Scheduling | |
| | 13 | Scheduling | |
| | 14 | Scheduling | |
| | 15 | Scheduling | |
| | 16 | Materials management | |
| | 17 | Inventory management | |
| Operations problems and decisions | 5–21 | Operations management problem areas | |
| Operations management decision-making | 5–21 | Operations management problem areas | |

Chapter 1

# The nature of operating systems and operations management

## ISSUES

What is an operating system?
What is the function or purpose of operations?
What is the role of operations management?
What are the basic operations management objectives?
Why is the structure of operating systems important?
What are the seven basic operating system structures?
What are the main problem areas for operations management?
How do operations managers set out to make decisions?

We must, necessarily, begin by tackling one of the more controversial aspects of our subject. We must provide definitions. Since the structure of this book to some extent reflects a particular view of the nature of operating systems and operations management, that view must be explained. Bookshop browsers are advised to scan this chapter before deciding whether to buy. Those who have omitted this simple precaution are advised to reconsider their decision when they have read this chapter. All serious readers, including those who have no choice but to use this book, are advised to study this chapter before plunging into the remainder of the book.

*Throughout this book we will, for brevity, use the terms 'operations management' and 'operating systems'. They will be defined below.*

## THE NATURE OF OPERATING SYSTEMS

*Definition:*

An operating system is a configuration of resources combined for the provision of goods or services.

Bus and taxi services, motels and dentists, tailors and mines, fire services and refuse collectors, retail organizations, hospitals and builders are all operating systems. They all, in effect, convert inputs in order to provide outputs which are required by a customer. Physical inputs will normally predominate, and hence operating systems convert physical *resources* into outputs, the *function* of which is to satisfy customer wants, i.e. to provide some utility for the customer.

## Resources in operating systems

Operations managers are principally concerned with the use of physical resources; therefore we shall take a physical view of operating systems and concentrate on the physical resources used by the system, which for convenience will be categorized as follows:

(a) ***Materials,*** i.e. the physical items consumed or converted by the system, e.g. raw materials, fuel, indirect materials.

(b) ***Machines,*** i.e. the physical items used by the system, e.g. plant, tools, vehicles, buildings.

(c) ***Labour,*** i.e. the people who provide or contribute to the operation of the system, without whom neither machines nor materials are effectively used.

## Functions of operating systems

Given this definition a large range and variety of systems may be considered as operating systems. The examples above illustrate this variety. Some form of categorization of such systems would be of value, if only for descriptive purposes. If we distinguish between goods-producing and service-producing systems we have a simple categorization of operating systems. However, a more useful categorization is afforded by a consideration of system function.

The function of an operating system is a reflection of the purpose it serves for its customer, i.e. the utility of its output to the customer. Four principal functions can be identified:

(a) ***Manufacture,*** in which the principal common characteristic is that something is physically created, i.e. the output consists of goods which differ physically, e.g. in form or content, from those materials input to the system. Manufacture therefore requires some physical transformation, or a change in form utility of resources.

(b) ***Transport,*** in which the principal common characteristic is that a customer, or something belonging to the customer, is moved from place to place, i.e. the location of someone or something is changed. The system uses its resources primarily to this end, and such resources will not normally be substantially physically changed. There is no major change in the form of resources, and the system provides primarily a change in place utility.

(c) ***Supply,*** in which the principal common characteristic is that the ownership or possession of goods is changed. Unlike in manufacture, goods output from the system are physically the same as those input. There is no physical transformation and the system function is primarily one of change in possession utility of a resource.

(d) ***Service,*** in which the principal common characteristic is the treatment or accommodation of something or someone. There is primarily a change in state utility of a resource. Unlike in supply systems, the state or condition of physical outputs will differ from inputs by virtue of having been treated in some way. (N.B. It should be noted that this definition is somewhat narrower than that normally implied by this term.)

Many organizations comprise several systems with different functions. For example, an airline will depend on operating systems the purposes of which are transport, supply and service, and a typical manufacturing organization will have internal transport and service systems. In fact, except in very small organizations, we are likely to be able to identify all four functions provided we consider small enough parts of the total system. For this reason the description of a complex organization as a manufacturing system, or transport system, etc., provides only a very general indication of its *overall* or principal purpose. A more detailed description necessitates the consideration of parts, or subsystems, of the whole. These four principal functions can together be used in describing all operating systems and their subsystems. They provide a basic language for operations management and permit the development of a slightly more detailed definition of an operating system.

*Redefinition:*[1]

An operating system is a configuration of resources combined for the function of manufacture, transport, supply or service.

Each of these four basic functions is considered briefly, with examples below.

## Manufacture

This is perhaps the principal functional category of operating systems. Most texts on operations management focus implicitly on manufacture, and, while we shall try to avoid undue bias, it is pertinent here to consider the nature of manufacture and, in particular, the types of manufacturing system which might be encountered.

Considering businesses or organizations as a whole, a tailor, coal mine and builder would be categorized as manufacturing systems since their *overall* purpose is that of creating goods. Manufacture is the principal purpose of motor-vehicle firms such as Ford, and within such an organization most factories will be involved primarily in manufacture. Whether we consider large systems and therefore describe their function in overall terms, or whether we consider much smaller systems and therefore take account of more detail, will depend on our purpose. However, whatever our level of description, in general it should be possible to identify different types of manufacturing system, such categorization again being of value mainly for description. We can divide manufacture in two traditional ways.

Firstly we can identify continuous, repetitive and intermittent manufacture. Theoretically a *continuous* process will run for 24 hours per day, 7 days per week and 52 weeks per year. In practice, however, while this degree of continuity is often the objective, it is rarely achieved. Examples of this type of manufacture are steelmaking and petrochemicals. A *repetitive* process is one in which the product (or products) is processed in lots, each item of production passing through the same sequence of operations, as, for example, in the assembly of motor vehicles. An *intermittent* process is one in which very small lots, or even single products, are made in response to separate customer orders.

The second and similar classification divides manufacturing into process (or mass), batch and jobbing. *Process* manufacture involves the continuous production of a commodity in bulk, often by chemical rather than mechanical means. *Mass* production (or manufacture) is conceptually similar to process manufacture except that discrete items such as cars and domestic appliances are usually involved. A single item or a very small range of similar items is manufactured in very large numbers. *Batch* production occurs where the number of discrete items to be manufactured in a period is too small to enable mass production to be used. Wherever possible, similar items are manufactured together in batches. Finally, *jobbing* manufacture, although strictly consisting of the manufacture of different products in unit quantities, in practice corresponds to the intermittent process mentioned above.

Each of these types of manufacture is characteristic of several different industries, but nevertheless no industry consists exclusively of any one type of manufacture. Increasing demand for products at

[1] This, deliberately, is a wide definition. The approach employed throughout this book is equally wide. It derives from the belief that operating systems are at the centre of all types of enterprise and that running all types of enterprise can be seen to be the task of operations management.

present manufactured by means of a jobbing-type arrangement may enable a form of batch production to be introduced; and, similarly, increased demand for products at present manufactured in batches may indicate the desirability of mass production. It is, however, quite unrealistic to consider these types of manufacture in a strict or absolute sense, since they are only parts of a production continuum the ends of which do not, except in theory, exist.

### Transport

The principal function of transport systems is that of changing the location of someone or something. Taxi or bus services, ambulance services, furniture removers and refuse disposal systems can be categorized as transport systems. Within manufacturing organizations, transport systems may be employed for moving work-in-progress between manufacturing departments, removing waste materials, etc.

### Supply

The principal function of supply systems is to change the ownership or possession of item(s) which are otherwise physically unchanged. At an organization level, a retail shop, warehouse, petrol station and broker may be seen to have the principal function of supply. Within organizations, supply systems may be evident as internal stores, etc.

### Service

Dentists, fire services, lauderettes, hospital wards and motels may be considered to have the principal function of service, i.e. the function of treating or accommodating something or someone. Within organizations a similar function may be performed by systems such as welfare departments and rest rooms.

No such categorization can be watertight: inevitably there will be overlap, and such an approach is of value only for descriptive purposes. Descriptionsof this kind indicate something about the purpose of and reason for systems, but we must develop a somewhat different approach if we are to explore the nature of operating systems from an operations management viewpoint. We must consider the *structure* of operating systems.

## THE NATURE OF OPERATIONS MANAGEMENT

Again, it must be emphasized that we are taking a broad view of operations management. We see it as central to any type of enterprise.

> *Definition:*
>
> Operations management is concerned with the design and the operation of systems for manufacture, transport, supply or service.

Operations managers are 'decision-takers'. Without the need for decisions there would be less need for managers. Operations managers are no exception. The need for decisions implies the existence of problems. Operations managers must deal with a host of problems. The number of chapters in this text is testimony to that. Some problems are 'one-offs' or infrequent, while others are recurrent. Many are interrelated. Most are important.

We will consider the nature of operations problems and decisions later in this chapter. For the present it is sufficient to note that several key problem areas exist. They are inescapable. Tackling these problems, and making decisions in these areas, is central to the job of the operations manager.

This decision-making, and therefore the job of the operations manager, is influenced by three major factors:

1. What should be achieved?
2. What can be done?
3. What would we like to do?

These are the *desirability*, *feasibility* and *preference* factors of operations management. Desirability is associated with *objectives*. Feasibility is associated with the nature of the operating *system*. Preference is associated with the *manager*.

Putting these factors together provides us with our basic model for operations management. It is outlined in Figure 1.1 and discussed below.

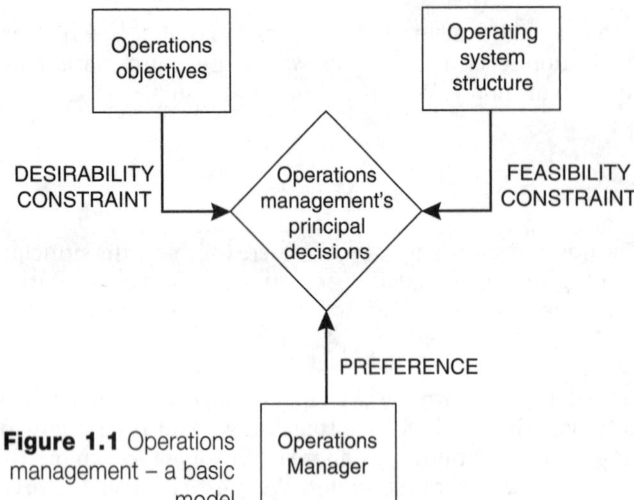


**Figure 1.1** Operations management – a basic model

The way in which the operations manager tackles certain key or principal problems, i.e. their decision-making strategy, will be greatly influenced by the need to achieve given objectives. Those objectives may have been determined for the operations manager by others, or jointly, or largely by the operations manager. Whatever their origin, their influence on the operations manager and their job will be great. How the operations manager tackles certain problems must also reflect what is possible. That, in turn, may be influenced by the nature of the system which the manager must run. The magnitude of these two constraints will largely determine the scope that the operations manager has to exercise choice, i.e. the 'freedom of movement'. Given a choice, the manager will almost certainly have preferences about the way in which things are done. Methods that have been used before, and found to be successful, may be attractive. Familiarity will be a factor. The perceived expectations of others, e.g. supervisors, may lead operations managers to choose a particular strategy for tackling certain problems. Habit, training, and even personality may predispose the manager to do things in particular ways. The greater the desirability and feasibility constraints, the less the choice, and the tougher the job – and vice versa.

So, the nature of the operations manager's job is normally influenced by the objectives and the system. To some extent these two factors may be 'given', i.e. beyond the total and/or direct control of the operations manager. Given the influence of these two factors, we now need to have some better understanding of them.

# OPERATIONS MANAGEMENT OBJECTIVES

## Customer service

The first objective of operating systems is the conversion of input for the satisfaction of customer wants. Customer service is therefore a key objective of operations management.

Customers should want the particular outputs of the operating systems; this is the primary condition for their being customers. In other words the system must provide something to a *specification* which can satisfy the customer. Other considerations, however, will exist and for simplicity these can be considered in terms of *costs* and *timing*. Thus, using the classic marketing phrase, one objective of operations management is to ensure customer satisfaction by providing the 'right thing at the right price at the right time'.

These three aspects of customer service – specification, cost and timing – are summarized in Table 1.1 and described in a little more detail for the four functions in Table 1.2. They are the principal sources of customer satisfaction and must therefore be the principal dimensions of the customer service objective for operations managers.

**Table 1.1 The three aspects of customer service**

| Primary consideration | Other considerations |
|---|---|
| To satisfy customers in respect of *specifications*, i.e. to provide what customers want or expect or will accept | To satisfy customers in respect of *costs*, i.e. to minimise the cost to the customer<br>*and*<br>To satisfy customers in respect of *timing*, i.e. to provide goods or services when required or expected (and in the case of service and transport with an acceptable duration) |

**Table 1.2 Aspects of customer service**

| Principal function | Principal customer wants | |
|---|---|---|
| | **Primary considerations** | **Other considerations** |
| Manufacture | Goods of a given, requested or acceptable specification | *Cost*, i.e. purchase price or cost of obtaining goods<br>*Timing*, i.e. delivery delay from order or request to receipt of goods |
| Transport | Movement of a given, requested or acceptable specification | *Cost*, i.e. cost of movement<br>*Timing*, i.e. (1) duration or time to move (2) wait, or delay from requesting to its commencement |
| Supply | Goods of a given, requested or acceptable specification | *Cost*, i.e. purchase price or cost of obtaining goods<br>*Timing*, i.e. delivery delay from order or request to supply, to receipt of goods |
| Service | Treatment of a given, requested or acceptable specification | *Cost*, i.e. cost of treatment<br>*Timing*, i.e. (1) duration or time required for treatment (2) wait, or delay from requesting treatment to its commencement |

Generally an organization will aim reliably and consistently to achieve certain standards, or levels, on these dimensions, and operations managers will be influential in attempting to achieve these standards. Normally an organization will not aim to maximize customer service in all three areas. Particular emphasis will be placed on some and less on others, and in this way an organization will distinguish itself from others in the market-place. So, an operations manager in one organization will not necessarily be working to the same mix of customer service objectives as a colleague in another organization. But in all cases, this objective will influence the operations manager's decisions since the actions the manager takes must be designed to achieve the required customer service.

## Resource utilization

Given infinite resources any system, however badly managed, might provide adequate customer service. Many organizations have gone bankrupt despite having loyal and satisfied customers. The problem for operations management arises from the fact that operating systems must satisfy multiple objectives. Customer service must be provided simultaneously with the achievement of efficient operation, i.e. efficient use of resources. Either inefficient use of resources or inadequate customer service is sufficient to give rise to the 'commercial' failure of the operating system.

Using conventional definitions, i.e. 'the ratio of useful output to input', efficiency would take a value between 0 and 1. Although this measure might be of relevance in essentially physical activities, it is inappropriate for organizations as a whole, since in many cases the objectives will be to output *more* than is input, i.e. the concept of profit or 'value added'. For this reason the term 'effectiveness' might be preferred, since it suggests perhaps the extent or degree of success in the achievement of given ends. Operations management is concerned essentially with the utilization of resources, i.e. obtaining maximum effect from resources or minimizing their loss, under-utilization or waste. The extent of the utilization of the resources' potential might be expressed in terms of the proportion of available time used or occupied, space utilization, levels of activity, etc. Each measure indicates the extent to which the potential or capacity of such resources is utilized. We shall refer to this as the objective of *resource utilization*.

Again we should note that few organizations will aim to maximize the utilization of all resources. Different emphasis will be placed on materials, machines and labour. But in all cases this objective, whatever the balance, will influence the operations manager's decisions, since the actions the manager takes must be designed to achieve the required utilization of resources and thus satisfy this part of the 'desirability' requirement or constraint.

## The conflict of objectives

Figure 1.2 summarizes the twin objectives of operations management. Operations management is concerned with the achievement of both satisfactory customer service and resource utilization. Operations managers must attempt to balance these two basic objectives. They will be judged against both, and the relative importance attached by any organization to each may be influenced by them. An improvement in one will often give rise to a deterioration in the other. Often both cannot be maximized, and hence a satisfactory performance must be achieved on both and sub-optimization must be avoided. All of the activities of operations management must be tackled with these two objectives in mind, and it is from this 'conflict' that many of the problems faced by operations managers derive.

## The balance of objectives

The type of balance established both between and within these two basic objectives will be influenced by market considerations, competition, the strengths and weaknesses of the organization, etc. The operations manager should make a contribution when these objectives are set, but such decisions rarely rest entirely within the operations function.

**Figure 1.2** The twin (often conflicting) objectives of operations management.

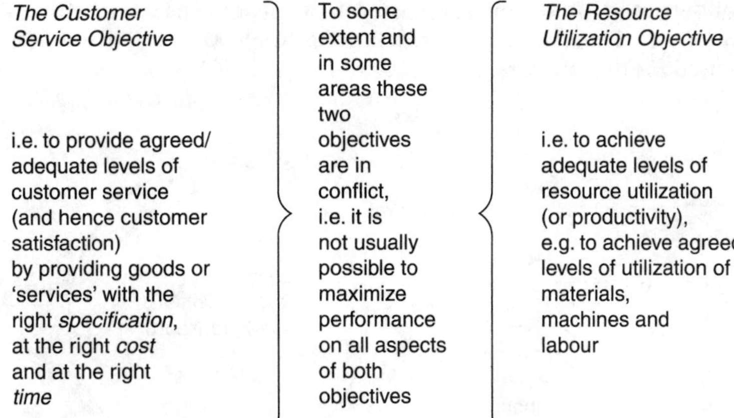


This balance will generally differ between organizations (and may change over time). The fact of this difference is one reason why the operations management job is not the same in different organizations.

A comparison for two organizations with the same function is given in Figure 1.3.

**Figure 1.3** Operations objectives for two organizations

| | Resource Utilization | | | Customer Service | | |
|---|---|---|---|---|---|---|
| | Machines[1] | Materials[2] | Labour | Specification | Cost[3] | Timing |
| Luxury Goods Shop | | | | ✓ | | ✓ |
| Mail Order Co. | ✓ | ✓ | ✓ | | ✓ | |

Notes:
1. Display areas and equipment, check-out facilities, etc.
2. 'Intermediate' materials, e.g. wrappings etc. (not the goods themselves)
3. Maximizing customer service on cost, i.e. minimizing cost

✓ = Relatively important

# THE STRUCTURE OF OPERATING SYSTEMS

Our original categorization of systems by function (manufacture, transport, supply and service) tells us something about their scope and purpose, but little about their nature. The categorization by function is an external perspective. It enables us to describe systems as seen by the customer. Given that the nature of the system influences how operations managers tackle problems, we need a managerial perspective as a way of categorizing operating systems which enables us to distinguish between them from an internal, managerial viewpoint. One way to achieve this is to consider the structure of systems.

Using simple systems terminology all operating systems may be seen to comprise inputs, processes and outputs in the manner of Figure 1.4. This simple system structure can represent any operating system at any level of detail, e.g. an organization as a whole, or some part of it. As a descriptive device it is limited, so we must examine system structure in slightly more detail. The terminology of Figure 1.5 will be used for this purpose.

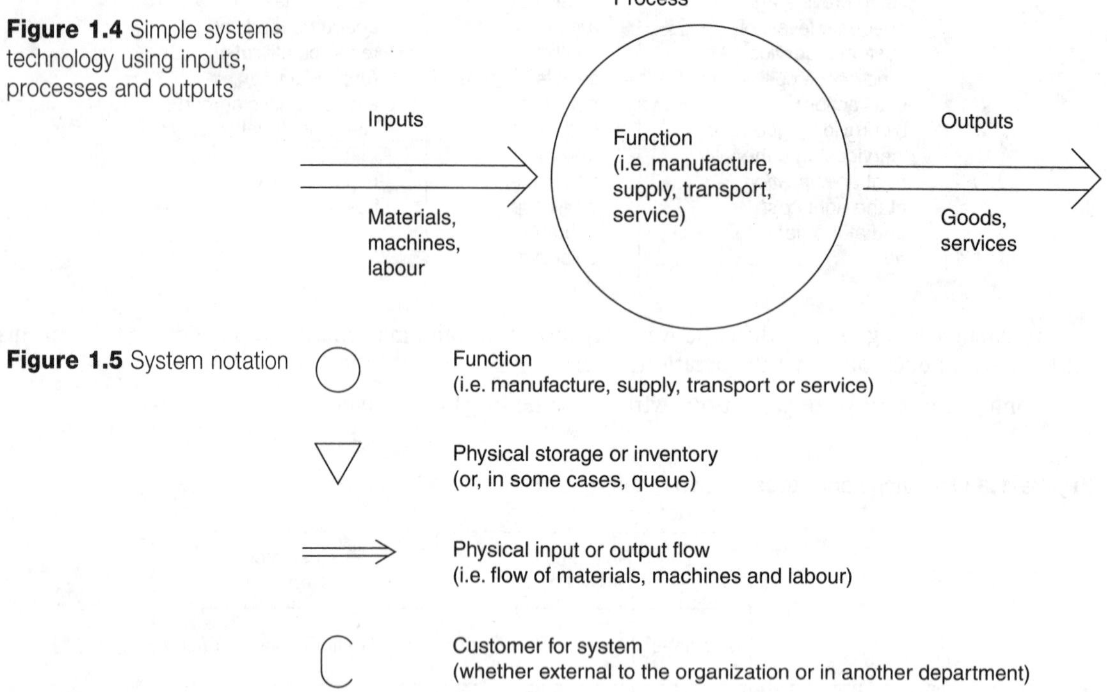


**Figure 1.4** Simple systems technology using inputs, processes and outputs

**Figure 1.5** System notation

With this simple approach we can identify four simple structures for operating systems:

(a) ***'Make from stock, to stock, to customer'***, i.e. all input resources are stocked and the customer is served from a stock of finished goods.

(b) ***'Make from source, to stock, to customer'***, i.e. no input resource stocks are held, but goods are produced to stock.

(c) ***'Make from stock, direct to customer'***, i.e. all input resources are stocked but goods are made only against and on receipt of customers' orders.

(d) ***'Make from source, direct to customer'***, i.e. no input resource stocks are held and all goods are made only against and on receipt of customers' orders.

Each structure shows how a system will provide for future output. Structure (d), for example, indicates that, in order to provide the next output for a customer, resources must first be acquired, whereas in (c) the next customer order will be satisfied through the use of already existing resources.

Now considering supply systems in a similar manner, by substituting 'supply' for 'make' in the above list, we may recognize the validity of these four simple structures. Both structures (a) and (b) require function in anticipation of order, i.e. structure (a) depicts 'supply from stock, to stock, to customer' and structure (b) depicts 'supply from source, to stock, to customer'. Neither case is common in supply operations, but both can exist. More commonly structures (c) and (d) will exist. Structure (c) depicts 'supply from stock direct to customer'. These four basic structures for manufacture and supply systems are shown in Figure 1.6.

**Figure 1.6** Basic system structures for manufacture and supply

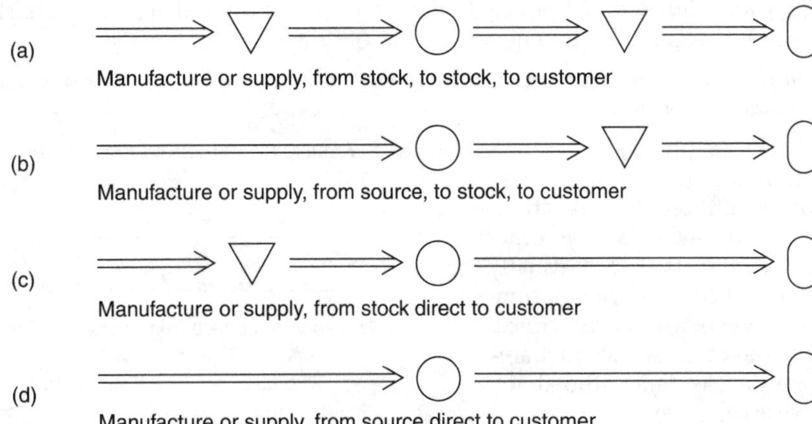


A slightly different situation applies in both transport and service. Those structures which require function in anticipation or in advance of receipt of a customer's order are not feasible, since no physical output stock is possible. Consider transport. A taxi service cannot satisfy a customer's relocation or movement requirements before receiving the customer. Similarly, an ambulance, refuse collection or furniture removal service cannot build up a stock of outputs to satisfy future customer demands. Nor can a bus service perform its function of transporting individuals before those individual customers arrive. The bus can, and often does, move from stop to stop along its route even though no customers have arrived. In doing so, however, it has not performed its function of changing the location of customers. In fact it has simply remained as an unutilized stocked resource, in need of customers. Nor can service systems, such as fire services, launderettes, hospitals and motels, build up a stock of outputs to satisfy future customer orders.

One further important structural difference is evident in the case of transport and service systems. Since the function of transport and service is to 'treat' the customers (whether a thing or a person), the customer is a resource input to the system, *i.e. the beneficiary of the function is or provides a major physical resource input to the function.* Thus transport and service systems are dependent on customers not only taking their output and in some cases specifying what that output shall be, but also for the supply of a major physical input(s) to the function without which the function would not be achieved. For example, in transport, a taxi, ambulance or bus service moves customers or something supplied by them, e.g. pieces of luggage. In service systems, e.g. hospitals or motels, the customer is treated in person, while launderettes and fire services treat items which might themselves be considered as customers (e.g. burning houses) or whose supply is controlled by the customer.

In other words, unlike manufacture and supply, transport and service systems are activated or 'triggered' by an input or supply. The customers exert some 'push' on the system. In manufacture and supply the customers act directly on output: they 'pull' the system, in that they pull goods out of the system whether direct from the function (structures (c) and (d)) or from output stock (structures (a) and (b)). In transport and service the customers push the system: they act directly on input. In such systems, therefore, some part of the resource input is not directly under the control of operations management. In these 'push' systems the customers control an input channel, and we must therefore distinguish this channel when developing models of systems.

Somewhat different structures are therefore required to represent transport and service systems. Three structures would seem to exist, as illustrated in Figure 1.7.

(e) ***'Function from stock, and from customer'***, i.e. input resources are stocked, except in the case of customer inputs where no *queuing* exists.

(f) ***'Function from source, and from customer queue'***, i.e. no input resources are stocked although customer inputs accumulate in a queue (or stock).

(g) ***'Function from stock, and from customer queue'***, in which all inputs are stocked and/or allowed to accumulate in stocks.

Customer queues are physical stocks in the customer input channel, although they cannot be utilized by operations management in the same way as other resource stocks, for they are usually beyond their direct control. Queues comprise those customers who have 'arrived' at the system and await service or transport. They are the customers who at any one time have asked to be 'treated' by the system. The queue therefore represents known and committed future demand.

In total, therefore, we have seven basic structures for operating systems. They are listed in Figure 1.8. They are simple system descriptions. For example, they deal only with single channels for outputs and only with physical flows. However, this type of approach can be used to describe more complex systems. Furthermore, these basic system models can be used to describe operating systems at any level of detail – the organization, a division, a department, a section, etc. – depending on our particular focus.

The principal differences between these basic system types derive from the location and existence of stocks. The presence or absence of output stocks and customer queues is a straightforward aspect, but input stocks can comprise materials, machines and labour (our three types of physical resource). We can consider an input stock of resources to exist if some or all of the necessary resources are available. If any of the required resources are not available in stock awaiting use then in effect the system cannot operate, for no capacity exists, and for our purposes we can consider stock to be absent. It is for this reason that we can regard certain types of builder or broker as having a system structure which operates from source.

**Figure 1.7** Basic system structures for transport and service

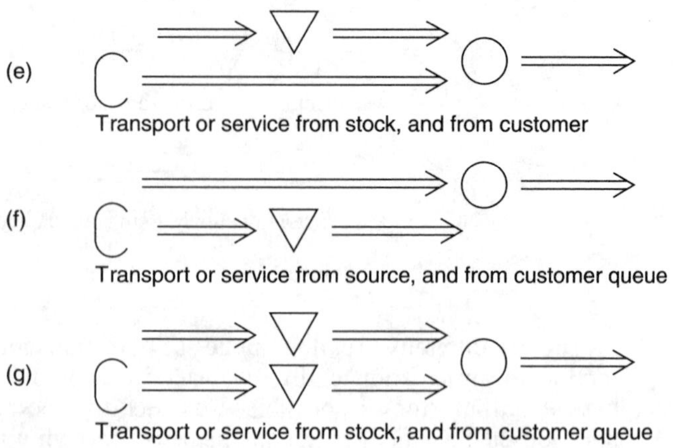

(e) Transport or service from stock, and from customer

(f) Transport or service from source, and from customer queue

(g) Transport or service from stock, and from customer queue

**Figure 1.8** Seven basic operating system structures

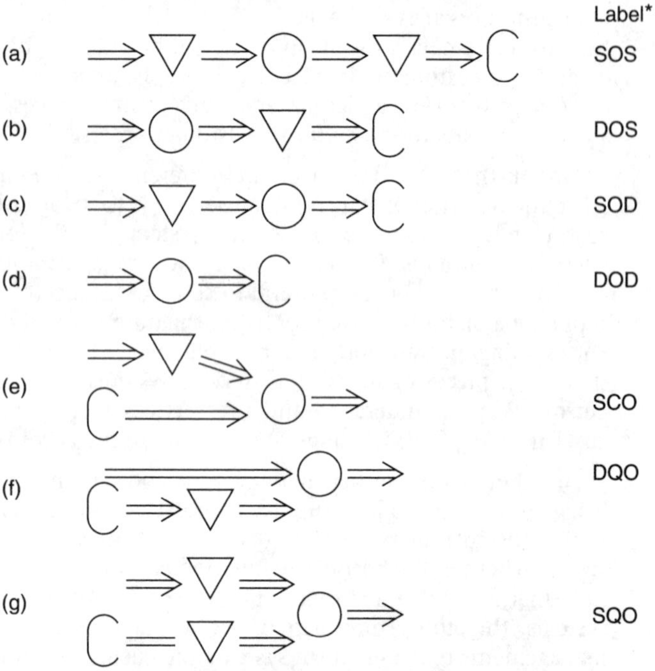

| | Label* |
|---|---|
| (a) | SOS |
| (b) | DOS |
| (c) | SOD |
| (d) | DOD |
| (e) | SCO |
| (f) | DQO |
| (g) | SQO |

* It is sometimes convenient to have a 'label' for each structure, so as not to have to refer to diagrams. In these labels, O = operation, S = stock, D = direct, Q = customer queue, C = customer direct input.

## Examples of system structures

At their simplest level, i.e. described as a single system, we might model operations in the manner shown in Figure 1.9. We could go into more detail and describe operations comprising certain subsystems. Figure 1.10 is an example. The amount of detail will depend upon our purpose. If we aim to understand the nature of single operation, managed by a single operations manager, then a simple model will suffice. If there are identifiable subsystems, each with its own operations manager, we will need more detail. Whatever the level, being able to identify the type of system in this way will help us understand how that system must be managed. For this reason structure is important to the operations manager. Simply knowing the function is not enough.

| BASIC STRUCTURE | EXAMPLES OF NORMAL STRUCTURES |
|---|---|
| ⇒ ▽ → O → ▽ → C | Electronics manufacture |
| ⇒ ▽ → O ⇒ C | Tailor (made-to-measure)<br>Retail shop |
| ⇒ O ⇒ C | Builder (e.g. 'one-off' houses)<br>Broker (e.g. commodities) |
| ⇒ ▽ →<br>C ⇒ O ⇒ | Hospital accident ward<br>Fire service |
| ⇒ ▽ →<br>C ⇒ ▽ → O ⇒ | Dentist<br>Refuse removal |

**Figure 1.9** Some examples of basic operating system structures

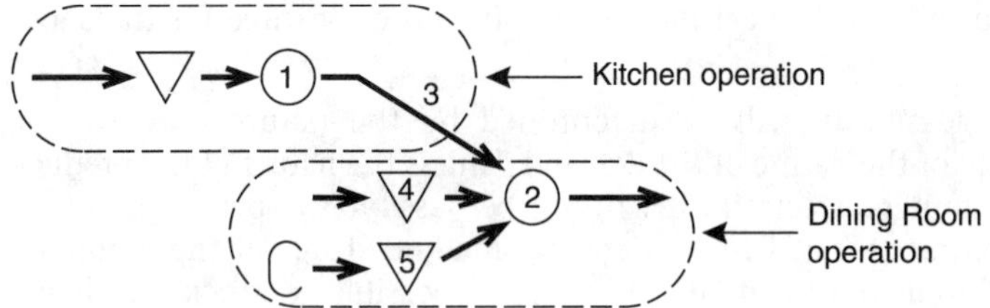


**Figure 1.10** Operating systems structures for a restaurant

Notes:
1. Kitchen function = manufacture
2. Dining room function = service
3. Output from kitchen = meals
4. Dining room resources
5. Customer queue (i.e. waiting). N.B. Might be 'concealed' by a bar operation

*Overall structures*
Kitchen = SOD
Dining Room = DQO (Because whilst some resources are stocked, not all are, i.e. meals, hence no capacity exists, in advance, to serve customers)

## The choice of system structure

Operations managers may have some choice of system structure or be able to change structures, but only within certain constraints. The system structure which exists at a particular time is determined by both internal and external factors. External factors – largely beyond the direct control of operations management – will determine whether a system structure is appropriate and feasible, while internal factors – largely or partly under their direct control – will influence operations management's choice of system structure. Figure 1.11 indicates the manner in which such factors influence system structure and is explained further below.

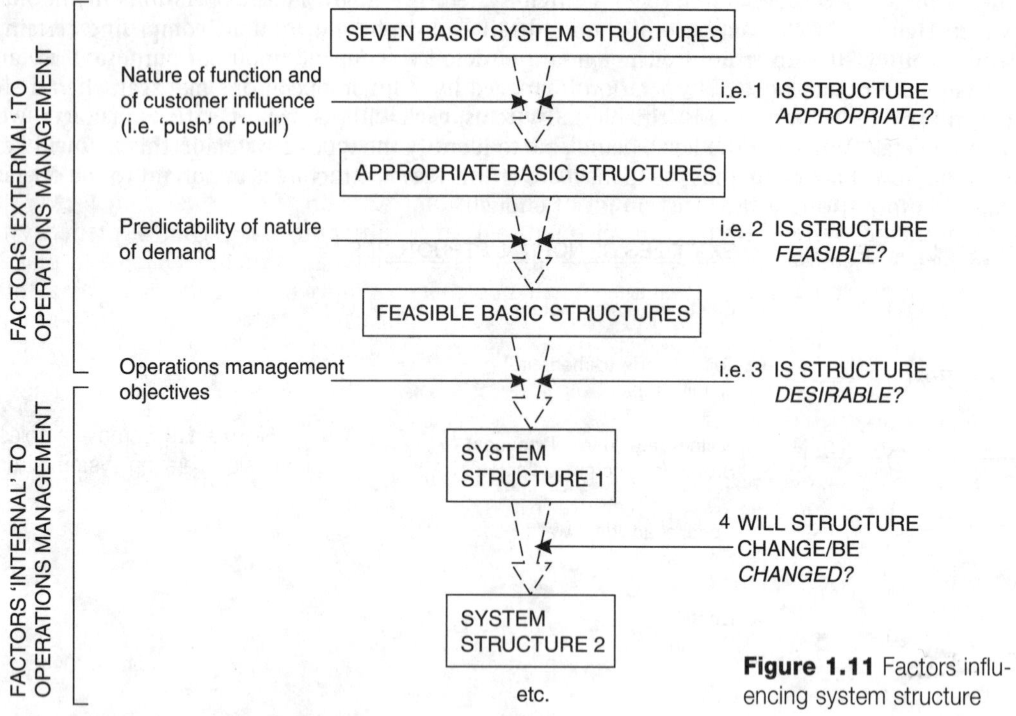


**Figure 1.11** Factors influencing system structure

(a) ***Appropriateness.*** The function of the system and the nature of customer influence (i.e. whether customers 'push' or 'pull') will determine the appropriateness of the structure. (For example, there will be only four appropriate structures for manufacture and supply and only three for transport and service situations).

(b) ***Feasibility.*** Given appropriateness, feasibility will be determined by the nature of customer demand, in particular the predictability of the nature of the demand. Unless the nature of the product which will be required by future customers is certain, it will not be possible to operate in anticipation of demand and to provide output stocks. Unless there is some knowledge of the nature of the items which will be required by customers, it may even be impossible to stock resources. Similarly, unless the general nature of the service or transport required by customers is known, certain structures may not be feasible.

(c) ***Desirability.*** The function of the system, the influence of customers on the system, and the predictability of the nature of demand are all factors which are normally beyond the direct control of operations managers, so we can consider these to be the *external* influences on system structure. Operations management may choose only from feasible system structures. This choice will reflect the desirability of each of the feasible system structures, desirability in turn being influenced by objectives which are partly influenced by operations management. One particular structure may be desirable given the relative importance of customer service *vis-à-vis* resource productivity. For a different balance of importance between these two objectives a different structure may be considered to be more desirable.

(d) ***Change.*** Once adopted, a system structure may be changed by operations management usually through changes in capacity, schedules or inventories. The question of structure change leads us to consider the influence of *time*. System structure can change over a period of time, and for this reason we should consider the structure of systems at a given point in time. If a system is designed to have, or if it must normally have, a certain structure, the strategies adopted by management should reflect the needs and constraints of that system structure. If the structure changes, for whatever reason, either the approach to the management of the system will remain basically unchanged or the approach will be changed. It is likely that in the case of temporary structure changes the approach to management will not change, but in the case of long-term change a corresponding management change will be desirable. Clearly a system may not always exist or work as it is intended to. For example, all customers must ultimately be prepared to wait or queue in a 'push' system. Even an emergency ambulance service may on occasion require customers to wait. However, it may be inappropriate or unnecessary to consider changing the system structure every time such a queue forms. The length of time customers are prepared to wait may be too short to permit the system to be run or managed in a different way. The way the system is managed, therefore, may not change at all, despite a temporary structure change. In practice the manner in which a dentist manages will not change simply because the non-arrival of a few patients causes the system structure to change temporarily. Short-term structure changes may affect customer services or resource productivity, but little else.

In certain cases different 'parties' may see systems in different ways. Customers may consider queues to exist, while operations managers may perceive a different structure. It is the latter which is of importance for us. The operations manager's perception of a system will influence his or her behaviour. We must therefore consider the normal, intended or actual system structure – whichever is appropriate – and consider system structure from the operations manager's viewpoint.

## Operations problems and decisions

Having established the type of context in which operations decisions are taken, we should now identify, and catalogue, the decisions with respect to the problem areas which must be dealt with by operations managers.

**Table 1.3 The scope of operations management**

| | **Problem areas** |
|---|---|
| **Design and planning** | Involvement in design/specification of the goods/services |
| | Design/specification of process/system |
| | Location of facilities |
| | Layout of facilities/resources and materials handling |
| | Determination of capacity/capability |
| | Design of work or jobs |
| | Involvement in determination of remuneration system and work standards |
| **Operation and control** | Planning and scheduling of activities |
| | Control and planning of inventories |
| | Control of quality |
| | Scheduling and control of maintenance |
| | Replacement of facilities |
| | Involvement in performance measurement |

The scope of the operations manager's job is indicated by the list of problem areas or fields of activity given in 'life-cycle' order in Table 1.3. Operations management will normally be responsible for the management of inventories, quality, the maintenance and replacement of facilities, and the scheduling of activities. Such responsibilities will be discharged in respect of an operating system, the nature, location, layout, capacity and staffing of which will have been determined largely by operations management. Managers working in this function will also normally have some influence on the design or specification of the goods or services,[2] processes, staffing policies and performance measurement.

## Principal problem areas *(see also Chapters 11–17)*

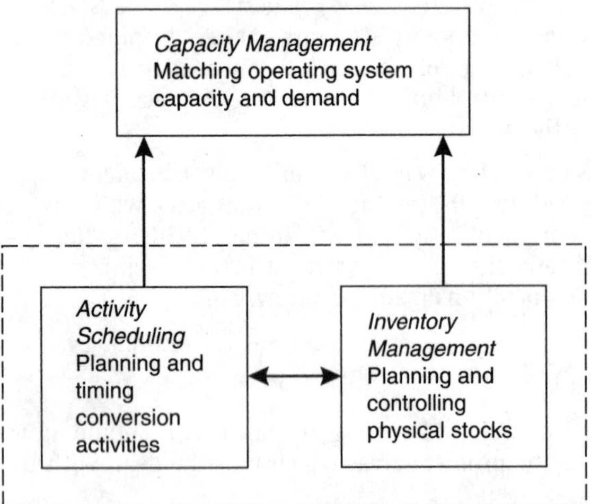


**Figure 1.12** The relationship of the three principal operations management problem areas

Although each of these problem areas is important in the effective planning and operation of the system, we can identify *three areas* which have a particular significance for operations management. These are the principal problem areas of operations management mentioned in Figure 1.12. They will influence the nature of operations management. They are the problems of capacity management, scheduling and inventory management. The type of problem faced by operations management in each of these three principal problem areas will be influenced by the operating system structure. These are the distinguishing or characteristic problem areas; in others, the nature of the problems faced by operations management is largely unaffected by system structure. Each basic system structure will have distinguishing characteristics because of the nature of the problems which occur in these three principal problem areas. Furthermore, decisions in each of these areas may affect system structure. Operations managers working in different situations will probably have to use different strategies and techniques in tackling problems in the three principal problem areas. In contrast, when making decisions in other areas, operations managers may be able to rely on the same types of strategy and technique in different situations. For this reason, in discussing decision-making techniques in the remainder of this book we must, when considering the principal problem areas, ensure that we consider the appropriateness of techniques, while in considering other problem areas the matter of appropriateness is less of an issue.

These three principal problem areas are closely related. Indeed it might be argued that the major problem is that of capacity management, and that inventory and scheduling decisions are subordinate to that decision and provide means of implementing capacity management plans.

## Inventory management

The problem of managing physical stocks or inventories is influenced by the system structure, if only because certain structures provide for the existence of stocks while others do not. The location of inventories is a function of structure, as is the nature of the inventory management problem. If we define inventory management as the planning and control of physical stocks, both aspects of the problem may be affected by structure and may also affect structure. The structure of an operating system

[2] Throughout we shall use the term 'goods and services' to include all outputs from operating systems, i.e. items, transports and the services defined at the beginning of the chapter.

will largely reflect the nature and location of inventories, and the management of such inventories will influence both resource productivity and customer service. The existence of output stocks may facilitate the provision of high customer service, at least in terms of availability or 'timing'. However, their existence may be costly. The provision of input resource stocks may benefit customer service, yet resource productivity may be adversely affected because more resources are idle. Few organizations can exist entirely without stocks of raw materials, work-in-progress or, where appropriate, output goods. The planning of inventory levels, the control of inventories and the maintenance of such stocks are expensive but necessary. Inventories will normally tie up considerable amounts of capital, so there is a balance to be struck between obtaining the benefits of inventories such as flexibility, high customer service and insulation against demand fluctuations on the one hand, and minimizing the costs of such stocks on the other.

## Scheduling

The nature of some aspects of scheduling in operations management is influenced by the system structure, and decisions made in scheduling can affect the structure. Scheduling is concerned with the timing of occurrences. *Operations scheduling* in its widest sense may therefore be considered to be concerned with the specification in advance of the timing of occurrences within the system, arrivals to and departures from the system including arrivals to and departures from inventories within the system. Thus we can consider the inventory management problem to be a part of a wider operations scheduling problem. The nature and extent of this overall scheduling problem will therefore be influenced by the presence and location of inventories and the relationship between the customer and the system, all of which are characteristic of system structure. As with all characteristic problems, the procedures and methods deployed in scheduling may be influenced by structure, and the effectiveness of scheduling may in turn affect structure. If we consider operations scheduling to relate to the physical flow or transfer of resources or goods, then the nature or extent of the overall scheduling problem is clearly influenced by the number of stages involved in the system, and therefore by structure. Where output stocks exist, customer demand will be met by scheduled output from stock, such stocks being replenished by scheduled inputs. In the absence of such stocks customer demand will be met by scheduling output from the function, which in turn will necessitate the scheduling of resource inputs either from input stock or direct suppliers. Conventionally we take a narrower view of the scheduling problem. We normally focus on *activity scheduling*, which is concerned only with activities directly related to the function.

## Capacity management

The determination and adjustment of *capacity* in an operating system is an important problem area, since decisions made here may intentionally or inadvertently change the structure of the system and/or affect the efficiency of operation of a particular system. Equally, decisions not made, or wrong decisions, may also result in structure changes and/or loss of efficiency, as for example following the failure to adjust system capacity to match customer demand changes. The planning and control of capacity is both important and complex, and furthermore the nature of the problem will often be affected by structure. In other words, for a given system structure the capacity management problem may differ from that facing management in a different structure. Since structure affects the nature and complexity of the capacity planning problem, the methods, procedures and techniques appropriate for tackling the problem may also be influenced by structure. In all respects, therefore, we can consider capacity management to be a principal problem area, the nature of which is characteristic of system structure. The management of system capacity is of crucial importance in operations management. The determination of capacity is the key system planning or design problem and the adjustment of capacity is the key problem area in system control. Capacity decisions will have a direct influence on system performance in respect of both criteria, i.e. resource utilization and customer service. It is difficult to see how any organization can operate effectively without good capacity management. Excess capacity inevitably gives rise to low resource productivity, while inadequate capacity may mean poor customer service. Decisions made in other areas are unlikely to offset errors in this area. The capacity problem is often of a medium- to long-term nature. Since system capacity is a reflection of the nature and amount of resources available in the system, short-term adjustments are often impossible. Capacity management is concerned primarily with the matching of resources to demand. It is concerned, therefore, with the levels of resources and demand.

One factor adding considerably to the complexity of inventory, capacity and scheduling problems is their close interdependence. Decisions made in one will have a direct impact on performance in the others. Such interdependence is less evident in the other problem areas, a fact which tends to underline the central importance of these three problem areas in the management of operations. In many respects the problems of inventory management and scheduling are subsidiary to the problem of capacity management. Capacity management decisions will determine how the operating system accommodates customer demand level fluctuations. Capacity management decisions will provide a context within which inventories and activities will be both planned and controlled. They will to some extent reflect operating policy decisions, while inventory and scheduling problems might be considered as more tactical issues.

## **Common problem areas** *(see also Chapters 4–10 and 18–21)*

Certain problems which face operations managers have much the same 'appearance' and require much the same approach in each type of operating system. They are also important, but they do not differentiate different types of operating system. Since we are dealing here specifically with the relationships of Figure 1.1, our description of these 'common problem areas' should be regarded as parenthetical.

## Goods/services design and specification

The design of the goods/services will often be the responsibility of a separate function within the company or even a separate company. A major contribution will often be made by both operations and marketing functions, since it is their responsibility to provide the offering. In all the cases the nature and specification of the goods/services will reflect the policy or strategic objectives of the organization, and thus those responsible within the organization for determining the detailed goods/services specification will, in most cases, be working within fairly clearly defined terms of reference and towards clearly specified objectives.

## Process/system design and specification

Operations managers will have considerable influence in determining or influencing the nature, i.e. the structure, of the system which they are to manage. Additionally they will in most situations be largely responsible for specifying the 'hardware' of that system. In many large organizations this process/system design responsibility will be allocated to a separate department, but in some organizations, including some large organizations, the responsibility for system design will lie with those responsible for the operation of the system, i.e. the operations managers.

## Location of facilities

The location of the organization, or the static parts of the organization, must be determined internationally, nationally and locally. In some cases the international location question will be of relatively minor importance. However, in most cases, locational choice within a country or within a particular area will constitute a real problem, and of course the solution to this problem will influence the subsequent operation of all aspects of the organization and its operating systems.

## Layout of facilities resources and materials handling

Decisions on the arrangement of departments and the resources within these departments must be made with the objective of enabling given goods or services to be provided at minimum total costs. The nature of the layout of the system and within the system will determine the extent of movement, handling, materials flow, etc.

## The design of work and of jobs

Effective methods of working are essential for the efficient design of an operating system and some control of work is necessary in order for adequate use of resources to be achieved and in order for management to determine the times necessary for all operations. The development and implementation of 'optimum' work methods frequently necessitates the study and design of workplaces and work equipment, the consideration of ergonomic factors and the training of workers, all of which will often be regarded as a principal responsibility of operations management. Control is achieved by means of performance standards, which are obtained after exhaustive investigation of work methods and are subsequently used for the planning of operations and as a basis for incentive payment systems and other remuneration schemes.

## Remuneration system design

It follows from the above that the operations manager has some direct responsibility in the operation, if not the design, of the remuneration system, especially where a payment-by-results scheme is used and where work standards are obtained through, for example, work measurement or similar calculations. In most cases the nature of the remuneration system will be closely related to the nature of the work undertaken by workers, their job designs and the work organization. In this area, therefore, operations managers are likely to share responsibility with functions such as personnel management and industrial relations.

## Operations control

Operations control is the complementary activity to operations and activity scheduling and, simply stated, involves the implementation of operations schedules. The problem is most severe in intermittent activities, where, because of the variety of jobs undertaken and services provided, accurate planning is frequently impossible. In repetitive situations, whether in manufacture, transport, supply or service, the planning process is likely to be a good deal more precise simply because of the availability of more accurate information, and thus the problem of control is minimized.

## Quality control and reliability

Rarely, if ever, are the resources employed in operating systems likely to be capable of operating continually at a specified level and in a specified fashion without breakdown or failure, and the need for replacement, repair or adjustment. Thus variations in the quality of the goods or services provided, such as changes in dimension, content, appearance, duration, performance and so on, will result either from assignable causes, such as wear or loss of efficiency in operating resources, or for reasons of pure chance. The ability of resources to operate at a desired level of accuracy in a specified fashion must be established and procedures installed to minimize the number of faulty operations and to ensure that substandard goods produced are identified and not passed on to the customer.

## Maintenance and replacement

None of the resources used within operating systems, whether human or inanimate, can work continually and effectively without maintenance and repair. Some of the problems and decisions involved in the maintenance and repair of equipment are as follows:

(a) Should maintenance consist of repair only, as necessary, or service plus repair?

(b) What should be the timing of service or preventive work in order to involve minimum effort and cost, yet minimize the probability of breakdown of resources?

(c) How should repair work be conducted?

(d) What should be the size of maintenance teams?

(e) How should information be gathered to enable the above questions to be answered?

## Performance measurement

Some measurement and monitoring of performance within organizations is essential. Since the operating systems are likely to be a major component of any organization, the measurement of the performance of such systems is an essential aspect of any total performance measurement. Measurement of the extent to which resources are utilized and measurement of the level of service provided are ingredients of such performance measurement. They are, if not the principal responsibilities of operations managers, the means by which the performance of operations managers is assessed by others, and thus are matters of considerable importance to such managers.

# OPERATIONS MANAGEMENT IN ACTION

The brief example below will help bring together the points discussed in this chapter.

**EXAMPLE**

### *A dentist*

In setting up a new dental practice the dentist, as operations manager, will be influenced by the following factors:

(a) The *operating system structure* will probably be of type (e) (Figure 1.7) in which the resources required for the dental practice are in stock, but where customers are able to gain direct access to those resources without queuing. This situation will be the direct result of the fact that, as yet, the dentist has been unable to create sufficient demand to necessitate customer queuing or the use of a customer appointments system.

(b) The *operations management objectives* must provide for some emphasis on high customer service. Thus the operations manager (i.e. the dentist) will wish to ensure that, even when demand increases, customer waiting times are not excessive either when waiting for an appointment or when waiting for attention after arriving at the surgery at the time required by the appointment.

(c) The nature of the operating system will give rise to certain *system problem characteristics* as regards: (i) the management of capacity; (ii) the scheduling of activities; and (iii) the management of inventories. For example, in managing capacity it will not be possible to rely on the use of output stocks. In scheduling activities, because of the existence of the queue of customers in the appointments book, it will be possible to some extent to schedule activities in order to ensure a fairly high resource utilization. (For example, it may be possible to ensure that customers with particular types of problems or in need of particular types of treatments are timetabled to arrive sequentially on the same day.)

The objectives being pursued and the problem characteristics of the system will necessitate the use of particular *strategies*. For example, in managing capacity it will not be possible, in the short term, to vary capacity to match demand changes, e.g. those caused by the effects of holidays. It will be necessary, therefore, to tolerate some under-utilization of capacity at times of relatively low demand, and some temporary increases in the size of the customer waiting list at times of high demand.

The use of such strategies, together with the type of operating system being employed, will influence the *role* of the operations manager. In these circumstances the operations manager, attempting to provide customer service and relatively high resource utilization, will find it necessary to work to a strict timetable. Since a dentist is unable to subcontract work easily, he or she must try to ensure that facilities are continually available, with no breakdowns, illness, etc. The job will be a somewhat 'relentless' one, with relatively little opportunity for interruptions and little scope for changes in routine.

## OPERATIONS MANAGEMENT DECISION-MAKING

Operations managers must solve problems in the areas identified above on a regular or 'as required' basis. Not only will it be necessary to decide on the problem-solving procedure, but also in many cases it will be necessary to decide between alternative solutions. We have made a distinction between what have been called the 'principal' or 'characteristic' problems which necessitate the problem-solving procedure being tailored to the particular circumstances, and the 'common' problems which may yield to the same type of problem-solving approach each time they are encountered. Much of the remainder of this book is about problem-solving in these areas and therefore about operations management decision-making. Before beginning to discuss the problem-solving strategies, procedures, techniques, etc., we can pull together some of the points made in the previous sections, and develop an overview of the operations manager's decision-making process. This will give a foundation for our discussion in the next part of the book, where we shall deal with operations management in the business policy context and the relationships between operations management and other functions within the organization.

For the purposes of this discussion we define the *operations management decision-making process* as 'the formulation of overall strategies for operations, typically involving interrelated areas of responsibility within operations management, and the making of decisions in these areas in pursuit of these strategies within the broader business context'.

Figure 1.13 provides a simple model of the operations management decision-making process. It is derived from our discussion above, in particular from Figure 1.1. The figure shows the decision-making process as a 'contingency' model. It suggests that operations managers' decisions about (a) the formulation of strategies for the solution of problems, and (b) particular problem-solving procedures are not free, unconstrained processes. It suggests, naturally, that operations managers' decisions are contingent upon other factors, and, deriving from our discussion above, suggests that the three sets of *contingent factors* or constraints might be categorized as follows:

(a) ***Feasibility***. The feasibility of choosing a particular course of action in the principal decision-making area of operations management (i.e. capacity management, scheduling and inventory) will be influenced largely by the nature of the operating system, which in turn will be a function of the demand situation, the processes and outputs involved and the system's function.

We have seen that the predictability of the nature of demand (i.e. whether or not it is known what future customers want) will influence the feasibility of the existence of output stocks created in anticipation of demand, and ultimately the use of input stocks of particular resources. For example, an operating system established to satisfy demand which is totally unpredictable in nature will contain neither output stocks nor stocks of specialized input resources, e.g. specialized materials, equipment, etc.

The types of processes and outputs involved may influence the nature of the system. For example, in electrical power generation, even though the nature of future demand is known (i.e. for electricity of a particular voltage, etc.), it will not normally be possible to provide substantial output stocks.

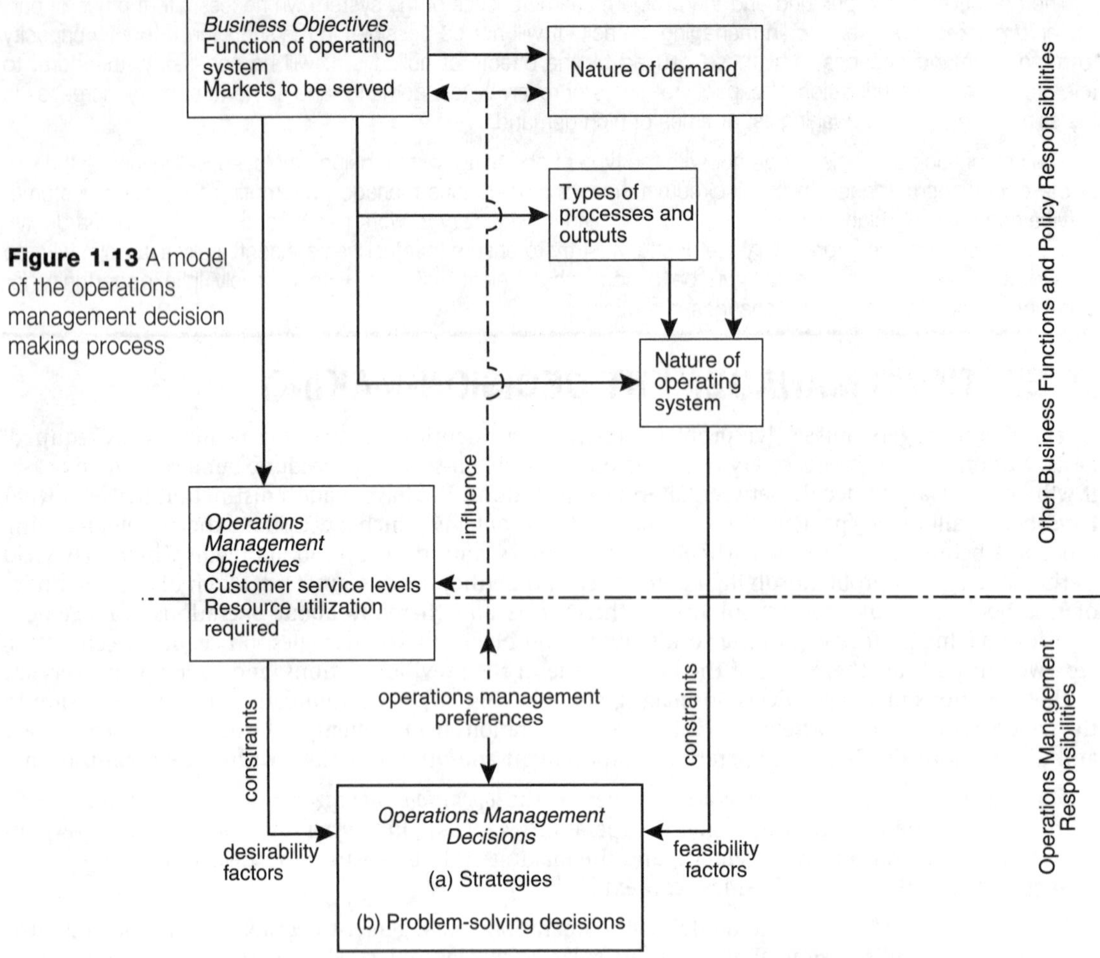


**Figure 1.13** A model of the operations management decision making process

The function of the system will also influence its nature, since the configuration of transport and service systems will differ from that of supply and manufacturing systems, as in both the former cases the customers or some physical item provided by the customers will be a direct input to the process.

Thus the nature of demand, process and outputs, and system function, and their relationship with the customer will influence the nature of the system, which in turn will have a major feasibility influence on the approaches adopted by operations management for the management of such systems.

(b) ***Desirability.*** The desirability of pursuing a particular approach in managing the system will be influenced largely by the operations manager's perceptions of desired outcomes, which in turn will be associated with explicit or implicit business objectives. Thus, considering the twin operations management objectives of providing customer service and achieving high resource utilization, an emphasis on the former will possibly encourage the adoption of particular strategies in capacity management, scheduling, etc., while an emphasis on resource utilization may encourage a different approach. For example, given feasibility, an emphasis on customer service will encourage the use of output stocks and possibly the maintenance of excess capacity, while an emphasis on resource utilization may militate against the use of output stocks and lead to a reduction in capacity. Although in general the operations manager's basic strategies may be seen as a function of the given or required balance between customer service and resource utilization, other objectives, e.g. labour policies and pricing policies, will also have some influence. Most of these factors will be beyond the direct and total control of the operations manager. We can consider them to be policy-level decisions to which the operations manager will make some contribution.

(c) ***Preference.*** Given feasibility and desirability, we would expect operations managers to have certain preferences. For example, the operations manager may prefer a situation in which his or her activities are in some way 'buffered' or protected from demand uncertainties. This, for example through the use of output inventories, permits the 'core' of the operating system to be in some way protected from uncertainties and thus to be run in a steady and efficient manner. In a labour-intensive situation the operations manager may prefer to minimize the amount of change in the labour force, hours worked, etc., thus minimizing the risk of labour/industrial relations problems. Or the operations manager may prefer to schedule work in such a way as to avoid the need to schedule each activity against a particular customer's 'requirement' date. All such approaches provide the operations manager with a far greater choice of strategies, etc., but the extent to which this approach might be employed is of course a function of both feasibility and desirability.

The operations manager who, for whatever reason, has greater 'power' within the organization is likely to be able to exercise his or her preferences to a greater extent than might otherwise be the case. Such power may be informal or formal. It may have been acquired, have evolved, or simply exist because of the broader circumstances, e.g. the existence of minimum feasibility and desirability constraints. This view associates 'power' with the scope, freedom of action and breadth of choice of the operations manager given certain feasibility and desirability constraints. This, however, is largely an internal perspective. We must recognize that such power, perhaps rather more broadly defined, may be exercised by the operations manager in seeking to influence both feasibility and desirability constraints which operate on him or her. Thus in certain circumstances the operations manager may be able to influence product/service design and/or marketing policy in order to make feasible the provision of output stocks of uncommitted goods. Further, he or she may seek to retain an overriding commitment to customer service and a tolerance of low resource utilization. Thus the extent to which the operations manager contributes to and influences these policy-level decisions will at least ensure that such decision-making takes into account the needs, constraints and abilities of the operations function, and at best ensure that constraints are minimized, thus enabling maximization of preference. This mechanism ensures that operations managers who are unable, or unwilling, to influence their policy-level decisions within the organization can be required to operate in highly undesirable situations, seemingly having to meet conflicting objectives while using resources in a diverse range of activities in a continually changing situation. In such circumstances the power of the operations manager clearly approaches zero: no preference is exercised, and the operations manager's decision-making process is entirely constrained by 'external factors'.

Summarizing, we can view the operations management decision-making process as a constrained process where outcomes are influenced by feasibility, desirability and preference factors. Such a view is presented in the simple model in Figure 1.13. The recognition of these relationships and the adoption of a suitable decision-making process are the prerequisites for effective operations management, and the solution of particular operations management problems must be seen as a subsidiary part of this decision-making process. The operations manager's responsibility within the broader business context must include the recognition of the fact that decisions in other functions will limit his or her own decisions, but, equally important, the operations manager must also seek to influence those factors which give rise to feasibility and desirability constraints on his or her decisions in the light of, and in order to exercise, his or her particular preferences.

In the next part of the book we shall look more closely at the policy decision-making context for operations management and the relationships of operations managers with those in other functions within the business.

## CHECKLIST FOR CHAPTER 1

### The nature of operating systems

Definition: operating system
Resources in operating systems
- Materials
- Machines
- Labour

Functions of operating system
- Manufacture
- Transport
- Supply
- Service

Redefinition: operating system

### The nature of operations management

Definition: operations management
Basic model for operations decision-making
- Desirability factors
- Feasibility factors
- Preference factors

Operations management objectives
- Customer service
- Resource utilization

Conflict of objectives
Balance of objectives

### The structure of operating systems

Manufacture and supply
- Function from stock to stock to customer
- Function from source to stock to customer
- Function from stock direct to customer
- Function from source direct to customer

Service and transport
- Function from stock and from customer
- Function from source and from customer queue
- Function from stock and from customer queue

Choice of system structure
Appropriateness
Feasibility
Desirability
Change

### Operations managers' problems

Principal problem areas
- Inventory management
- Capacity management
- Scheduling

Common problem areas
- Goods/service specification
- Process design
- Location } of facilities
- Layout }
- Work and job design
- Remuneration
- Operations control
- Quality control and reliability
- Maintenance and replacement
- Performance measurement

### Operations management in action

Operations management decision-making process
- Feasibility factors
- Desirability factors
- Preferences
- Power

## FURTHER READING

There are many good books on operations and production/operations management. As the major emphasis in our first chapter is on systems, basic concepts, etc., readers may wish to compare our approach with that adopted by other writers. Given that Chapter 1 has offered a basic framework for the subject, i.e. something on which to build, readers will wish to feel comfortable with this. Comparison with other approaches may therefore be valuable.

**Waters, C. D. J. (1991)** *An Introduction to Operations Management,* Chapter 1. Wokingham: Addison-Wesley.

**Meredith, J. R. (1992)** *The Management of Operations: A Conceptual Emphasis,* 4th edn, Chapter 1. Chichester: Wiley.

**Foggarty, D. W., Hoffman, T. R. and Stonebraker, P. W. (1989)** *Production and Operations Management,* Chapter 1. Cincinatti: South Western.

## QUESTIONS

1.1 'Operations management is the "heart" of any business, and we are all operations managers.' Discuss.

1.2 How far is it possible for the operations function within the organization to operate independently of the other main functional areas? Which functions, in particular, must have a close relationship with operations management, and why?

1.3 Describe the principal types of manufacture. What are the prerequisites for each of these types of manufacture and what are the principal operations management problems associated with each type? Illustrate your answers by describing actual cases with which you are familiar.

1.4 Identify seven basic operating system structures and give examples of each, making the simplifying assumption, if necessary, of single-channel outputs.

1.5 Using the basic operating structures, in series and/or in parallel, with multiple input and output channels if necessary, describe (i.e. model) the following operating systems:

(a) a typical 'take-away' or 'fast food' shop (e.g. a hamburger house);

(b) a taxi service.

Identify and explain any assumptions you make.

1.6 Table 1.4 identifies the main resources, customers, objectives and activities associated with an ambulance service. Prepare similar tables containing appropriate details for:

(a) a motel;

(b) a take-away food shop.

1.7 Using the concepts summarized in Figure 1.13 illustrate, using hypothetical or real examples, how and why the decisions of an operations manager in a service organization (e.g. a hotel, hospital or entertainment centre) are influenced by feasibility and desirability factors and preference considerations.

1.8 To what extent is predictability of the nature of demand a prerequisite for the existence of each of the seven basic structures shown in Figure 1.8?

**Table 1.4 Function: Transport. Example: Ambulance service**

| | | Operations management | | |
|---|---|---|---|---|
| | | **Objectives** | **Activities to achieve objectives** | |
| **Physical resources** | Ambulances and auxiliary vehicles<br>Drivers and attendants<br>Maintenance facilities and spare parts<br>Garaging facilities<br>Communications equipment<br>Medical equipment<br>Control staff<br>Maintenance staff | Resource productivity<br><br>e.g. relating to:<br>staff utilization<br>equipment utilization | Design/ planning | Design of equipment<br>Location of vehicles<br>Design of communications system<br>Determination of staffing levels<br>Number of vehicles<br>Staffing of vehicles<br>Work shifts<br>Routeing of vehicles |
| | | | Operation/ control | Stock control<br>Secretarial services<br>Maintenance and replacement of equipment |
| **Customers** | Individual members of public | Customer service<br><br>e.g. relating to<br>waiting time<br>speed of service | | |

**CASE STUDIES** (from Part 9)

The topics covered in this chapter are relevant in the following (see Introduction to Part 9 and Table C.1 for further details):

| No. | Name | Country |
|---|---|---|
| 1 | Carreras SL | Spain |
| 8 | Malcolm Seal | UK |
| 14 | Prince Philip Dental Hospital | Hong Kong |
| 17 | La Patisserie – A | UK |

# PART 2

# The Context of Operations Management


Introduction to Part 2

Chapter 2 Business and operations policy

Chapter 3 Operations management and other business functions

Chapter 4 Operations economics and costs

## INTRODUCTION TO PART 2

Here we consider the business context of operations management. As we take the view that the operating system and operations management are the heart of any enterprise, we must recognize that there must be relationships with other functions in the business. Here we look at business policy decision-making, the nature of its influence on operations management, and the nature of the influence of operations management on it. We look at operations policy formulation, and then consider the nature of the relationships between operations management and marketing, organizational, financial control and design decision. Throughout we shall concentrate on basic concepts and ideas, so that the nature of and reasons for these relationships are clear. Similarly in Chapter 4 we look at some basic aspects of operations economics and costs.

## STRATEGIC CONTEXT

This part of the book sets the strategic (or policy) context for the following parts. The basic aspects are outlined in Chapter 2, where the stages of strategy/policy formulation and implementation are identified and then related to operations management. Policy options are considered and their impact on operations discussed.

In the introduction to subsequent parts of the book we will remind ourselves of these topics in order that we might be aware of the strategic context within which operations managers must work and act, in most of what they do.

## TOPIC MAP

| | Related topics in other chapters | | |
|---|---|---|---|
| **Topics in this Part** | **Chapter** | **Topic** | **Comments/aspects** |
| Chapter 2 | | | |
| Business policy | 1 | Operations management objectives | Influence of business policy on operations objectives |
| Operations policy | 1 | Operations management objectives | |
| Chapter 3 | | | |
| Marketing | 1 | Operations management objectives | Influence on operations management objectives |
| Organization | 9 | Technology and work | Influence of technology on organization structure |
| | | Job design | Relationship of job and organization design |

## TOPIC MAP

| Topics in this Part | Related topics in other chapters: Chapter | Topic | Comments/aspects |
|---|---|---|---|
| *Chapter 3 continued* | 10 | Payment systems | Influence of organization design on payment system |
| | 16 | Materials management | Influence of organization design on materials management organization |
| | 18 | Operations control | Influence of organization design on type of controls |
| | 19 | Management of quality | Need for appropriate organization design for effective total quality management |
| Finance/accounting | 4 | Cost controls | Need for use of appropriate accounting procedures |
| | 10 | Payment systems | |
| | 21 | Performance management | |
| Product/service design | 6 | Layout of facilities | Appropriate design to facilitate processing/operations |
| | | Materials handling | |
| | 7 | Work methods | |
| | 8 | Learning | |
| | 9 | Job design | |
| | 19 | Management of quality | Appropriate design to achieve/ sustain adequate quality and reliability |
| | 20 | Quality controls | |
| | 21 | Maintenance | Design to facilitate maintenance and/or repair |
| | | Repair | |
| Chapter 4 | | | |
| Operations costs | 5 | Location of facilities | Factors affecting location choice |
| | 6 | Layout of facilities | Factors affecting layout design |
| | 7 | Work methods | Factors influencing labour costs |
| | 8 | Work standards | |
| | 9 | Job design | |
| | 10 | Payments | |
| | 17 | Inventory management | Costs of inventories |
| | 19 | Management of quality | Quality costs |
| | 20 | Maintenance | Maintenance/repair/replacement costs |
| | 21 | Performance management | Management of costs |

## TOPIC MAP

| Topics in this Part | Related topics in other chapters: Chapter | Topic | Comments/aspects |
|---|---|---|---|
| *Chapter 4 continued* | | | |
| Operations economics | 1 | Operations management objectives | Influence of economies of scale on resource utilization |
| | 6 | Layout of facilities | Types of layout/breakeven comparisons |
| | 10 | Payment systems | Incentive payments |
| Cost control systems | 3 | Finance/accounting | Cost controls |
| | 10 | Payment by results | Bonus calculations |
| | 16 | Purchasing and supply | Purchase costs |
| | 17 | Inventory management | Inventory costs |
| | 19 | Quality management | Quality cost |
| | 21 | Maintenance Repair<br>Repair<br>Replacement | Decisions on when/whether to maintain/repair replace |
| | 22 | Performance management<br>Performance audit<br>Benchmarking | Measurement of costs in performance measurement/ monitoring |

Chapter 2

# Business and operations policy

## ISSUES

How are business policies formulated?
How do business policies impact on operations?
What are business policy 'options'?
How do these options relate to operations objectives?
What are the key elements of operations policy?
What are the main operations policy decisions?
How is operations policy implemented?

The importance of the business context to operations managers was discussed in Chapter 1. Although operations managers will have a considerable degree of control over decisions within their own area of responsibility, they will not, in general, be able or wish to ignore the actions of others. There exists an external 'framework' for their actions, and marketing, financial, personnel and other decisions are the components of this framework. In a small organization most of these areas will be the sole and direct responsibility of one person, and so co-ordination is easy. In larger organizations, however, some formal co-ordination is necessary. Traditionally this is provided through the hierarchical or pyramid-type structure of most organizations; thus, ultimately, at the apex of the pyramid someone has some knowledge of, and responsibility for, all areas. At this level decision-making will be long-term, strategic and concerned with the business as a whole. This business policy decision-making provides purpose and co-ordination throughout the organization and therefore largely creates the framework within which each function works.

Before considering operations management decision-making we must consider the manner in which this policy mechanism works, for it is essential that we are aware of those factors which influence operations decisions and the manner in which influence is exerted. This chapter will therefore consider business policy and its influence on operations management, while Chapter 3 will examine some particularly important components of the framework for operations management decisions. Initially we shall take a broad approach, since the principal objective is to indicate the nature of the relationship between business policy and operations management decision-making. Then we shall consider the type of policies business might pursue, the policy options, and thus the type of policies available for operations.

# BUSINESS POLICY

## The nature of business policy

Planning occurs in all functions of an organization, but, alone, such plans are an inadequate basis for decisions about the future of the organization. The effectiveness of each function within the organization is dependent on effective planning, but all such planning must start and end with business policy, which is long-term, takes an organization-wide perspective and is concerned with the role, purpose and success of the business as a whole and thus with the *total* resources of the organization.

Business policy planning is a continuous and systematic activity aimed not only at identifying purposes for the organization but also at defining procedures and organizing efforts to achieve these purposes and measuring results against expectations through systematic feedback of information. It is a systematic approach to both the formulation and the implementation of total business plans.

Formal systematic planning is essential, since detailed forecasts and action plans are required to allow co-ordinated action throughout the organization and adequate evaluation of performance. Such planning necessitates co-operation between functional specialists, subdivisions, etc., and therefore brings about a degree of co-ordination and a perspective which might not otherwise have existed within the organization. The existence of detailed plans facilitates delegation and permits the establishment of relatively autonomous divisions, while ensuring that overall control remains. It provides a set of goals and criteria for assessing the merits of new opportunities and proposals, whether for concentration or diversification of the business.

Two important and interrelated aspects are evident in the business policy process: *formulation* (or planning) and *implementation.*

## Formulation of business policy

Classically, four steps must be taken in formulating a business policy:

1 the identification of ***opportunities*** for, and threats to, the organization, together with the estimation of the degree of risk associated with each;

2 the assessment of the organization's present and potential ***strengths*** and ***weaknesses,*** particularly in respect of its material, financial, technical and personnel resources, i.e. its potential capacity to pursue identified opportunities and/or to deal with threats;

3 consideration of the personal ***values*** and aspirations of the organization's major stakeholders and its managers;

4 clarification and acknowledgement of the major social ***responsibilities*** and objectives of the organization.

Consideration of (1) and (2) above can give rise to the development of a rational *economic policy* for an organization through the matching of opportunities to capabilities. This is rarely the total perspective for the development of business policy, for it will often be necessary to consider personal aspirations and preferences (3). It will be necessary to identify what an organization will 'want to do' as distinct from, or as a subset of, what it 'can or might do'. Finally, the inclusion of (4) above – a largely non-economic dimension – raises the question of what the organization 'should do', i.e. having regard to its responsibilities and social objectives. This four-part perspective is illustrated in Figure 2.1, which identifies the economic and non-economic aspects of the process.

The culmination of this policy formulation stage is the statement of policies on:

I the nature of the goods or services to be provided by the organization;

II the nature of the markets/demand to be served;

III the manner in which these markets are to be served.

These are all aspects of considerable direct significance to operations management.

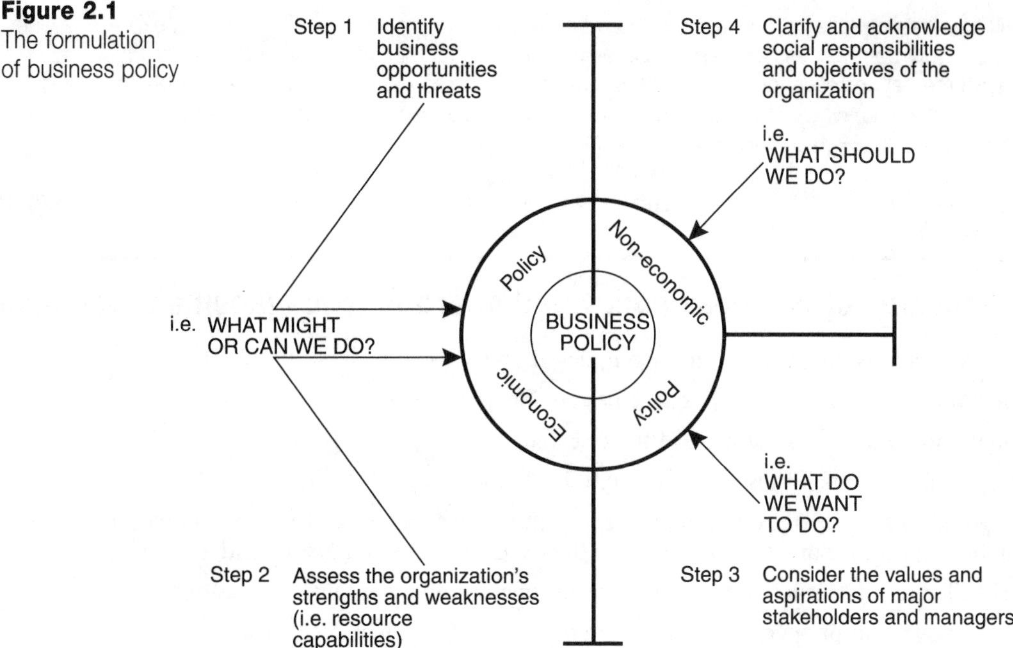


**Figure 2.1**
The formulation of business policy

## Implementation of business policy

Implementation of an agreed policy is concerned with the acquisition and mobilization of resources, the creation of appropriate structures and processes, and monitoring and control. Again four aspects can be identified:

1 use of physical resources, e.g. equipment, machinery and labour, and the development of appropriate technology;

2 the creation of appropriate organization structures and relationships, e.g. the roles and responsibilities of individuals, departments and functions, and the use of appropriate information systems, etc.;

3 organizational processes and behaviour, e.g. the development of individuals, their motivation and rewards, performance measurement, and the establishment of standards;

4 top leadership, i.e. the provision, monitoring and updating of overall objectives, inter-function and inter-division co-ordination, overall resource allocation, etc.

It is through the effective implementation of an appropriate business policy that an organization will 'make its mark'. Success or failure derives from these decisions and actions, and the whole nature of management in and of the organization, including operations management, is influenced by and reflects the policies of the organization.

### *Federal Express v. UPS*

Federal Express (Fed Ex), the company that practically invented overnight delivery service in the USA, found that its formula did not work in Europe. In the spring of 1992, it began dismantling and selling off most of its operations. However, at about the same time, United Parcel Service (UPS) announced its fifteenth European acquisition and predicted its European operations would soon be in profit.

Seeking to replicate its US success, Fed Ex went straight into the international overnight express business in Europe. UPS, in contrast, rather than risking all on the express market, focused on the far bigger market for two-day, three-day (or even longer) guaranteed deliveries. It also established itself and developed business in one country at a time, whereas Fed Ex faced two competitors already established in the European express market: DHL Worldwide Express and TNT Express Worldwide.

Source: Jacobs, J. (1992) Flash! Tortoise beats hare: UPS outlasted Federal Express in Europe . . . *International Business*, **5** (7), pp. 18–19.

## Relationships of business policy and operations management decisions

Given that business policy decisions largely determine:

I the nature of the goods or services to be provided;

II the nature of the markets/demand to be served;

III the manner in which these markets are to be served;

their significance for operations management is clear. We will look at the general relationship of business policy and operations here, and certain details later. Here we must consider:

(a) the influence of business policy decisions on operations management decisions;

(b) the contribution of operations management to business policy decisions.

## Influence of business policy on operations management decisions

Figure 1.13 in fact suggests the means by which business policy decisions influence operations management. Policy decisions on the nature of the market/demand to be served and hence the *predictability of the nature of demand* will influence system structure feasibility. The manner in which markets are to be served influences *operations management objectives*, which in turn must influence the choice or desirability of system structure and the choice of management strategies.

Thus policy decisions on the nature of the goods or services to be provided, the nature of the markets/demand to be served and the manner in which these markets are to be served will influence:

A operations management's choice of operating structure;

B the formulation of operations management objectives;

C operations management's choice of strategies.

The way in which these influences are exerted is shown diagrammatically in Figure 2.2 and is discussed below.

### *Business policy influence on operating system structure decisions and the formulation of operations management objectives*

The structure of the operating system influences the role and problems of operations management; however, operations managers are unlikely to have a free *choice of system structure,* since the nature of the function and the customers' influence on the system are major external factors influencing the appropriateness of a system structure. For example, we have indicated that one fundamental feature of transport and service systems is their dependence on inputs controlled by the customer. In practice an organization may have some scope for influencing the customer, and thus the 'pull' or 'push' on the operating system. Such influence may derive from advertising and marketing activities, pricing, product policies, etc. An organization may therefore have some influence on the structure of the operating system, but such influence will normally be external to the operations manager. From the operations

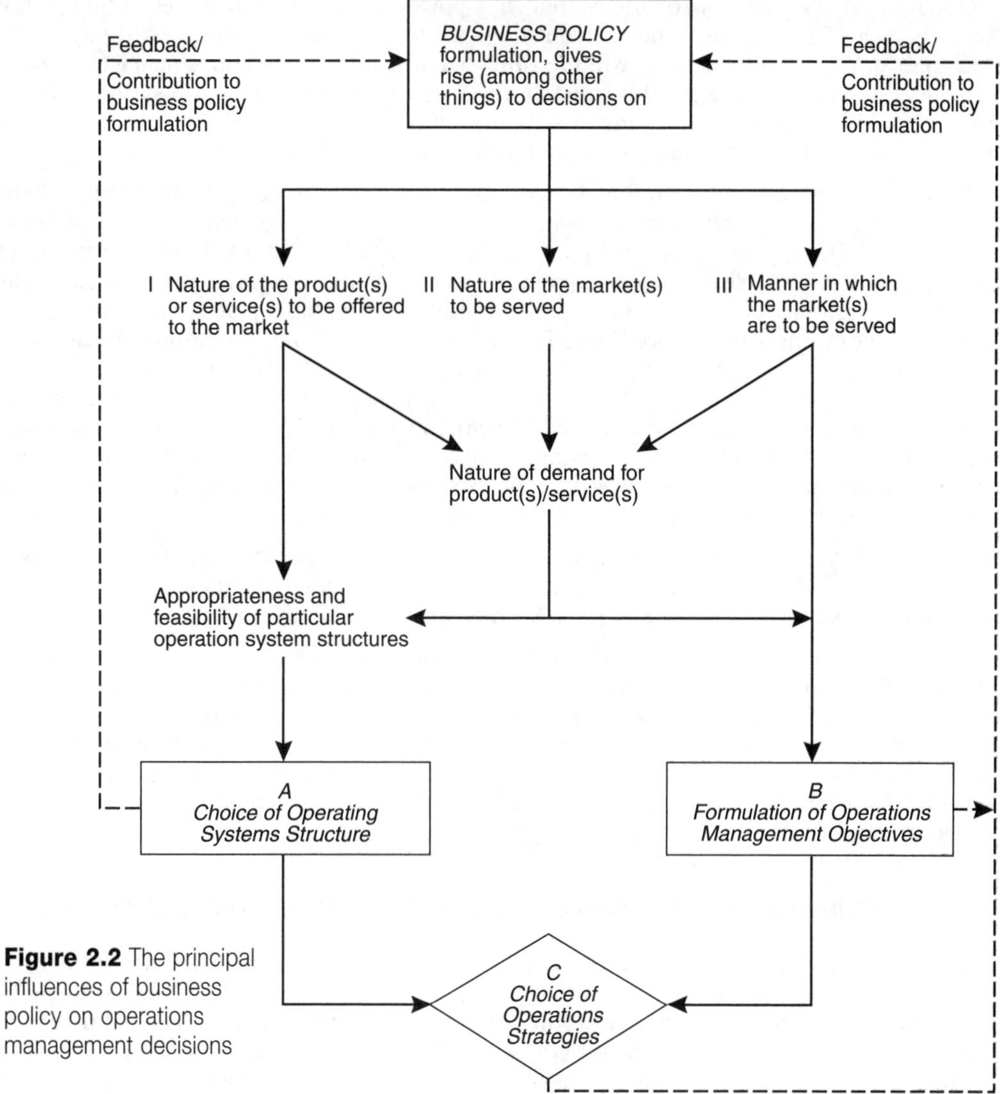


**Figure 2.2** The principal influences of business policy on operations management decisions

manager's point of view the nature of the function and the customer influence on the system are constraints, deriving in part from decisions relating to the nature of the product or service and the nature of the market, i.e. the goods/services and market/demand characteristics determined through business policy decisions.

To take a slightly different viewpoint, the operations manager will recognize that in some circumstances certain system structures cannot be adopted, i.e. they are infeasible, since the factors which permit their existence are absent. There are certain prerequisites for the existence of an operating system structure. Certain factors will permit, and in exceptional conditions cause, one or more of the structures to exist. Such prerequisites or enabling factors are essentially of an external nature and, as we saw in Chapter 1, are mainly related to the predictability of the nature of demand. The feasibility of system structures is dependent on the predictability of the nature of the demands of the customer on the system. Such predictability is an enabling factor, and hence it does not follow that the existence of predictable customer demand will necessarily give rise to the existence of a certain structure. For example, the nature of the demand for the output of a power station is known, yet output is not stocked. This condition is, however, one prerequisite – a further external factor – without which certain structures cannot in reality exist. It will limit the extent to which operations management can choose, or change, structures, and again this constraint will be largely influenced by decisions relating to the nature of the product or service and the nature of the market, i.e. the goods/market and market/demand characteristics determined through business policy decisions.

Given the feasibility of certain operating system structures, the choice between them will be influenced by the *objectives of operations management.* These will reflect management's view of what the customer wants or will be prepared to accept by way of service, and the need within this constraint to maximize resource utilization. While the general objectives of operations management are clear, the manner in which those objectives are pursued, and certainly the emphasis placed on each, may be influenced by broader business policy decisions. To some extent, therefore, operations management will be required to pursue a stipulated policy as effectively as possible. Policy on customer service may be influenced to some considerable degree by broader business policy considerations. Although a mail order firm, a luxury store and a supermarket are all concerned with the function of supply, they each have a different approach to the objective of customer service, so operations management will not be required to achieve the same standards of service in each case. Often standards or objectives for customer service will be influenced by other functions in the organization.

Management can change structures by changing capacity, can allow changes to occur by not adjusting capacity to balance demand-level changes, or can avoid structure changes by manipulating capacity to maintain a balance with a changing demand level. Such changes may result from changed objectives.

There are therefore both indirect and direct influences of business policy on operating system structure. Goods/service characteristics determine the nature of the function and the influence of the customer, which in turn determine which of the seven basic structures are appropriate. Both goods/ service and market/demand characteristics determine the predictability of the nature of demand, which in turn influences system structure feasibility. Business policy will also influence the importance to be attached to customer service and resource productivity objectives, which affects the choice from among feasible structures.

### *Business policy influences on the choice of operations management strategies*

In Chapter 1 we considered how system structure and operations management objectives influenced the strategies and role of operations management (see Figure 1.1). Each system structure is likely to have different problem characteristics in each of the three principal problem areas. The nature of the problems to be tackled by operations management is therefore influenced by system structure. The manner in which these, and other, problems are tackled will also be influenced by the objectives which exist. In other words, a problem may be tackled in a particular manner in order to achieve a particular outcome given one set of objectives, and in a different manner for a different end given a different set of objectives. Thus the strategies adopted for the management of a given system, i.e. the general approaches employed, will be influenced by the nature of the problems which exist and the objectives which are to be pursued. The selection of strategies is therefore influenced by business policy decisions in two ways: through the influences on the selection of system structure in the manner discussed above, and through the influence on operations management objectives.

## Contribution of operations management to business policy decisions

The principal means by which operations management contributes to or influences business policy decisions is through the provision of information on:

(a) the existing operating system structure, objectives and strategies;

(b) the implications for operations management of the goods/service and market/demand characteristics which are proposed or being considered by the business policy makers.

In 'change' situations, both (a) and (b) are relevant, whereas in the establishment of entirely 'new' systems only (b) is appropriate. Change situations may occur when a change or modification of the existing goods or service(s) is under consideration and/or when new markets are being investigated. In such situations an operating system is in existence and changes are being considered which might affect or necessitate a change of system objectives and strategies. Clearly some knowledge of the nature of the existing system, its characteristics and performance will be of value in making business policy considerations in such circumstances. The alternative is the 'greenfield' situation, in which business policy decisions will lead to the establishment of new operating systems. Here operations management must interpret alternative goods/services and market/demand strategies into implications for operations management, since the nature of the system structure, operations management objectives and strategies required to meet given goods/services and market/demand characteristics will influence the choice between alternatives.

Whatever the situation, operations management is, in effect, using the same type of information in seeking to influence business policy decisions. The main factor in both cases is the need to match operating system structures, operations management objectives and strategies to given goods or service and demand conditions, or vice versa. If it is intended to change goods or service and/or demand specifications, then a knowledge of the characteristics and capabilities of the existing operating system, existing operations management objectives and strategies, and the effectiveness of existing systems and strategies is important. Equally, it is important when considering alternative goods or service and/or demand specifications to know what system structures, objectives and strategies will be required for effective operation.

## Business policy for competitive advantage

One aspect of business policy formulation is of particular relevance to operations management. It relates primarily to decisions on the manner in which markets are to be served, and has implications especially for the formulation of operations objectives.

## Policy options

In determining its policy a business will normally be seeking to secure some competitive advantage(s). In other words a business will be aiming to put itself in a position in which it will be able to serve its customers more effectively than its competitors are able to do. Frequently this will involve an organization in identifying its distinctive competencies, in order to deploy them, whilst also avoiding its weaknesses. In all cases 'what the customer wants' must be an important factor.

In some cases the competitive advantage(s) may be obvious. Proximity to customers may offer advantages in terms of timing, i.e. how quickly items or services might be made available to customers. Possession of a particular technology or technique (e.g. protected by patent rights) may ensure that something can be made available to customers which is not available from any other source. Economic factors may ensure that costs are low, e.g. compared to those of competitors in another country, so an organization may have a price advantage.

Generally there is no single, obvious source of sufficient competitive advantage, so businesses must consider the *policy options* available to them in order to construct a policy which when taken as a whole gives some competitive strength. Figure 2.3 identifies some of these options, and their interrelationships. They are explained below.

An organization may choose to seek competitive advantage by means of any of the following:

(a) ***Flexibility***. The ability to supply customers with different types of goods or service, to offer

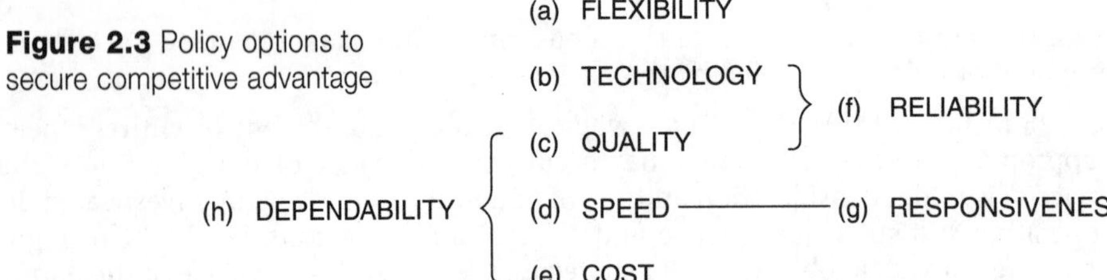


**Figure 2.3** Policy options to secure competitive advantage

different variants on a basic portfolio, to customize, adapt and tailor, can be a major strategic advantage. This capability may help build long-term, more secure relationships with customers, whose needs may change over time. Such flexibility may enable organizations to command a higher price, to secure more profitable sectors of a business, etc.

(b) ***Technology.*** Organizations with strong research and development will often be in a position to market products/services which are more advanced, more sophisticated or more capable than others. They may be able to get such items to the market earlier than their customers, create new markets and win large market shares. In some sectors technological superiority may be a critical success factor (e.g. aerospace, health care). The ability to compete by innovating provides advantages which might be secured through patent protection. For some it is a major strength, and an advantage beyond that available to organizations that seek to exploit, or are able only to exploit, existing, established technologies.

(c) ***Quality.*** For most organizations product/service quality is important. Few customers will willingly acquire low-quality items or services. However, the ability to provide products or services at outstanding quality, when compared to competitors, can afford a major strategic advantage. Quality is a variable. It is often related to price. Having the organizational capabilities to deliver high quality can be a major source, or one source, of competitive advantage.

(d) ***Speed.*** Doing things quickly can mean quicker delivery to customers, shorter queuing or waiting time for customers, and quicker processing of customers than can be achieved by competitors. 'Speed is of the essence' for many customers. The ability to satisfy a customer now, rather than tomorrow, can be a major strength in manufacturing, transport, supply and service businesses.

(e) ***Cost.*** Some organizations choose to compete on cost, i.e. the price to the customer. High-volume operations providing a limited range of goods or services may have a cost and price advantage.

(f) ***Reliability.*** The fact that something, whether product or service, is always available, serviceable and satisfactory – doing what it was intended to do and in the intended manner – can be a major attraction to certain customers in certain circumstances. The ability to provide outputs having such high reliability gives considerable competitive advantage to organizations in industries such as aerospace, motor vehicles, health care, emergency services, etc. The factor relates in some ways to quality, the two often being interdependent, and technology.

(g) ***Responsiveness*** is to do with speed. Advantage may be secured by an organization which is able to respond quickly to changes in customer requirements, e.g. the need for new types of product or service, and which can most quickly satisfy those needs. Getting new 'offerings' to the market-place can put an organization in an advantageous position. Responsiveness is also associated with an ability to detect and/or understand a customer's need, even to anticipate it, and a willingness to seek ways to satisfy it.

(h) ***Dependability.*** To have a record and a reputation as a dependable supplier can count for a great deal. The ability to provide, time after time, what is required when it is required and at the expected price is not something everyone can achieve. Such dependability alone, even for the supply of goods or services which are available from others, and at the same price, can be a considerable strength. It is not the same as speed. It is to do with consistency and repeatability on three of the other dimensions – quality, speed and cost.

## Focus and position

The determination of the competitive stance of the organization, which of the above options to concentrate on, or which combination, will give a focus to the organization's efforts and character to the organization. An organization which has chosen to compete on flexibility, quality and responsiveness will neither behave nor feel like one that is competing on speed and cost. Each will have positioned itself in the market. Each will have sought to differentiate itself from others in the eyes of the customer.

The management roles in each, not least the roles of operations managers, will be different, for among other things the operations objects will be different. Certainly the weight attached to the three customer service objectives for operations will be different.

# Business policy for growth and development

Business policy formulation often reflects certain beliefs about the growth and development of an organization. The tacit objective of growth may be questioned or qualified yet it must be a legitimate and major consideration in business policy formulation. The formulation of an appropriate policy for an organization requires an understanding of how organizations grow and decline. Further, the operations manager must appreciate the nature of business growth and decline in order to understand the consequences for the operations function. Certainly where a business pursues a policy of growth it must be expected that the nature of the business may change, and hence the nature of the operations function and its management may change.

We can consider such changes in respect of: (a) the goods/services provided by the organization and their markets; and (b) the nature of the organization as a whole.

## Growth and decline: products/services and markets

There is considerable evidence to show that goods, services and technologies have a 'life', i.e. they are introduced, grow, mature and decline. Technologies have a 'switch-over point', when the new takes over from the established technology. Figure 2.4 shows a typical life-cycle for a product or service: demand grows slowly during the 'incubation' or introduction period, rapidly during a period of growth, followed by a period of steady demand as the product or service matures in the market, prior to its decline. The product life-cycle is discussed in greater detail in Chapter 3.

Large markets are rarely homogeneous, and should therefore be viewed as a collection of smaller segments, distinguished perhaps according to customer usage or the distribution channels used for geographical location. Since segments vary in attitude and sophistication, products may reach their point of decline in one market yet have considerable potential in others. Because of this segmentation a product or service with a distinct life-cycle might be introduced over a period of time in different markets in order to give a relatively stable overall demand.

**Figure 2.4** A life-cycle for a product/service

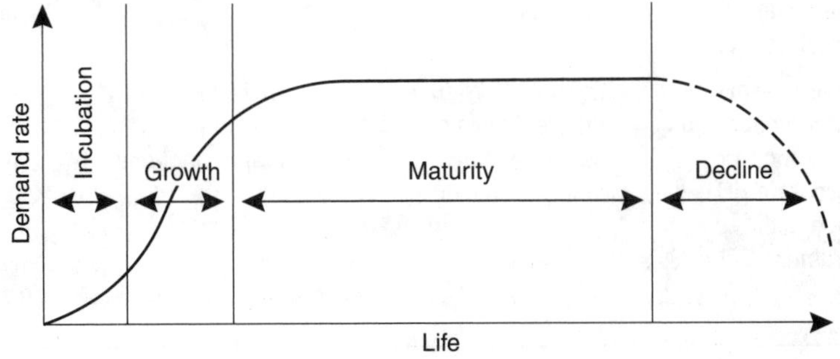

## Growth and decline: organizations

Some evidence points towards a type of life-cycle for the development of organizations. Typically it is suggested that organizations tend to pass through four distinctive stages of development. These are:

(a) the owner-entrepreneur with a single product/service and an informal organization;

(b) a single unit with delegated control to departmental managers, e.g. engineering production, sales and service;

(c) a divisional organization with a number of semi-autonomous businesses based on different goods/services;

(d) a diversified organization with central management working through an industrial holding company and regarding the business largely as investments.

Table 2.1 summarizes these four stages of corporate development, and identifies their characteristics. Growth, as a means of avoiding goods/service obsolescence, is implicit in these stages, and is indeed a central concept in business policy. Consideration of growth needs and opportunities gives rise to the concept of the 'business of the firm'. Increased market penetration, the development of new markets, the development of new products or services, and diversification are therefore principal directions for growth. These are illustrated in the manner of a product/service and market/demand matrix shown in Figure 2.5.

**Table 2.1 Four possible stages in corporate development**

| Stage | Organization structures | Goods/service and market characteristics | Management | Measurement of performance |
|---|---|---|---|---|
| 1. | Single unit managed by a sole proprietor | Small scale, single line of related goods/service for one market, one distribution channel | One-person operation, very little task differentiation | Very few, personalized, not based on formal criteria |
| 2 | Single unit managed by a team | Large scale, single line of related goods/service for one market, one distribution channel | Responsible for single functions, e.g. operations, sales, finance | Operating budgets for each function |
| 3 | Several regional units reporting to a corporate HQ each with structure 1 or 2 | Each region produces same line for single market, multiple channels | Regional units performing several functions | Operating budget, return on sales, return on investment |
| 4 | Several semi-autonomous units reporting to corporate HQ each with structure 1, 2 or 3 | Each unit produces different lines for separate markets, multiple channels | Divisions performing all major functions | Return on sales, return on investment |

**Figure 2.5** Directions for growth. (Adapted with permission from Ansoff, H. I. (1970) *Corporate Strategy*. Harmondsworth: Penguin.)

| | | Markets/Demands | |
|---|---|---|---|
| | | Present | New |
| Goods/ Services | Present | Increase market penetration | Develop new markets |
| | New | Develop products or services | Diversify (markets and products) |

# OPERATIONS POLICY

## Achieving competitive advantage

Operations managers will aim to influence the policy options chosen by business in its pursuit of competitive advantage. Once these decisions are made the nature of one part of the operations objectives to be pursued by operations managers is fixed, for the policy options followed by a business will largely determine the customer service objectives of operations managers. This relationship is illustrated by Figure 2.6, which is simply a reworking of Figure 2.3. We should also remind ourselves of one other point made in our discussion of objectives in Chapter 1, i.e. that customers will have some interest in the reliability of operations in delivering goods and services to agreed specification, cost and timing. So the 'dependability' and 'reliability' options (Figure 2.3) also relate to the customer service objectives of operations.

**Figure 2.6** The relationship of policy options and operations objectives

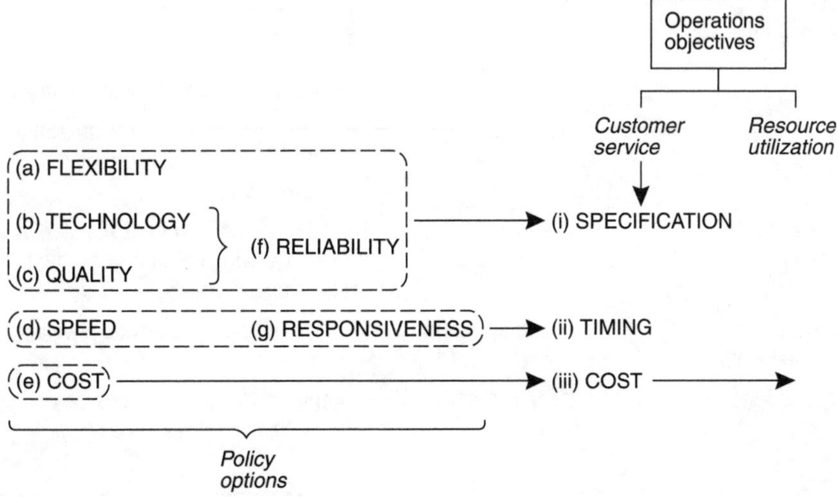

## Policy implications for operations

Pursuit of each of the policy options will have implications for operations managers. They will need to achieve certain things in order that the business policy is achieved. The implications are outlined in Table 2.2. Notice that they relate largely to resources and the manner in which the operating system must be used. For example, to achieve competitive advantage on cost, the operation must be highly productive, intensive and efficient. To achieve flexibility the operating system must be versatile, readily changed and adaptable. To compete on speed, there must be fast throughput, low in-process inventories, short lead times, etc. In each case a policy option can be perceived as a customer service objective, from

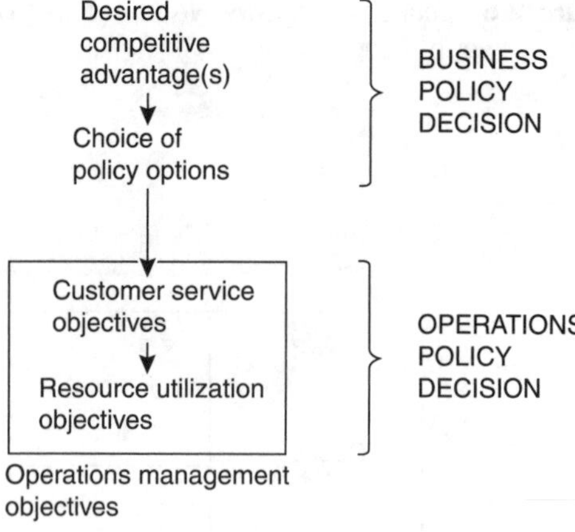


**Figure 2.7** Relationship of policy options and operations policy

**Table 2.2 Policy options and operations implications**

| Competitive advantage | Policy option | Typical operations |
|---|---|---|
| Products/services to satisfy a wide range of customer needs | Flexibility | Versatile facilities and labour<br>Rapid change-overs<br>Broad range<br>Flexible work systems |
| Most sophisticated and advanced products/services | Technology | High process and product technology<br>Substantial R&D<br>Good new-project management |
| High-quality products/services | Quality | Error-free processes and systems<br>Substantial quality assurance/control<br>Adequate systems capability |
| Fastest delivery or service with minimum waiting time | Speed | Fast throughput<br>Adequate capacity<br>Short queues<br>Dedicated/specialized work systems |
| Lowest price | Cost | High productivity/resource utilization<br>Limited range/standardization<br>Low inventories |
| Unfailing serviceability of products/services | Reliability | Good systems/resources maintenance<br>Rapid 'de-bugging' of new products/services<br>High process quality |
| Fastest response to new customer requirements | Responsiveness | Rapid new product/service development |
| Consistently good service | Dependability | High repeatability of processes and systems<br>High reliability of resources |

which certain resource utilization objectives are evident. So, business policies aimed to achieve competitive advantage which influence the way in which the business serves its markets must be translated into customer service objectives for operations – which therefore is one critical aspect of operations policy decision-making (Figure 2.7).

**EXAMPLE**

## *Sleep Inn*

### *Case*

Choice Hotels International wanted to return to the days of no-frills rooms at bargain prices. The company also needed to find a way to deal with the unexpected labour shortages and declining employee productivity in the service industry. The solution was the 'labour-lean' Sleep Inn, which won *Personnel Journal*'s 1991 Human Resources Award in the 'competitive advantage' category. Sleep Inns are less expensive to operate and require half as many employees as a comparable budget hotel. The rooms are smaller and designed for cleaning efficiency, enabling housekeepers to service them in two-thirds of the time it takes to clean the average room. This strategy, with its prime objective of labour-saving and efficiency, resulted in profit margins 10% better than the average budget hotel. A Choice Hotels study shows that 97% of Sleep Inn guests rated their stay either excellent or good, while 99% indicated that the rooms had high value for the price paid.

### *Analysis*

Here the business priorities are to achieve competitive advantage in the market, and also to minimize labour needs and increase labour efficiency, so the strategy of providing a low-cost service for a market which attaches importance to cost, reliability and dependability is established. From an operations viewpoint this can be interpreted as implying an emphasis on:

*Customer service:*

| | |
|---|---|
| Specification | low but reliable and consistent |
| Cost | low |
| Timing | rapid |

The implication for operations management is the need to achieve the following:

(a) High labour productivity, e.g. through
efficient work scheduling
flexible labour
good training
appropriate facilities design

(b) Consistent and dependable quality, e.g. through
standardized work procedures
appropriate quality controls
good maintenance of facilities and equipment
error-free work

(c) Short cycle-time operations, e.g. through
close facilities monitoring
adequate materials stocks
good labour supervision and control

*Source*: Schember, J. (1991) Sleep Inn wakes up to new labour. *Personnel Journal,* **70** (8), pp. 71–73.

## Dealing with growth

Clearly, if product/service life-cycles are evident, the level of demand for a particular product/service will change over time. For operating systems which provide few products/services, such demand changes will have particular importance. Systems providing a range of products/services, perhaps launched at different times with different life-cycle patterns, may benefit from a relatively smooth aggregate demand. The development and provision of a set of products/services with complementary product life-cycles, and perhaps also complementary seasonal demand patterns, may be a major objective in both business and operations policy.

If a pattern of corporate development exists, whether growth (as in Table 2.1) or decline, then it will be reasonable to suppose that these 'structural changes' within the organization will be matched by structural changes within the operating system. Certainly it can be argued that the structure of operating systems may change in some predictable fashion during business growth, and equally during business decline. Similarly, it can be argued that the strategies employed in the management of operations must also change to reflect the changing nature of the organization during growth or decline, and of course the objectives of the operations manager will be affected by the 'state' of the business, i.e. differing where business is in a state of positive growth from where the business is in a defensive contraction state.

It will not be appropriate to speculate on these notions at this stage, but we must note that as business policy formulation is an on-going process, often designed to achieve growth, it follows that both the policies and the nature of the organization in which they are to be implemented will change; hence operations managers' policies must also change and constantly be under review.

## Operations policy decisions

We can now consider policy for the operations function in the business. First we will identify the general framework for operations policy based on our previous discussion in this chapter. Then we will look at policy implementation for operations.

### The nature of operations policy decisions

We have seen that three major operations management decisions are influenced by prior business policy decisions, i.e.

A selection/choice of system structure;

B selection/formulation of operations management objectives;

C selection/formulation of strategies for the management of the operating system.

These are key operations management decision areas. They are all concerned with planning. Operations management must determine system structure and objectives and contribute to the determination of objectives before anything can be manufactured, supplied, transported or serviced. They are key decisions, since wrong decisions in these areas will inevitably affect the performance of the system and the organization. Together they will determine the nature and character of the operating system. They are in fact operations management *policy* decisions. The choice of operating system structure, the objectives of the system, and the strategies which will be employed in the management of the system are the principal ingredients in the formulation of an operations management policy.

We have seen that operations management contributes to business policy decisions by providing information on:

(A) the existing system structure, objectives and strategy, in order that the characteristics and capabilities of the system might be considered in the selection/change of goods or service and demand characteristics;

(B) the implications of proposed or alternative goods or service and demand characteristics for system structure, objectives and strategy.

This contribution of operations management to business policy decision-making therefore derives from the three operations management policy decision areas. In fact, therefore, as would have been expected, it is principally the policy decisions of operations management which both are influenced by and contribute to business policy decisions.

**EXAMPLE**

### *The 'Big Fry-up'*

#### *Case*

The 'Big Fry-up' is an established town centre 'steak house' type restaurant with a single dining room and adjacent bar. It has a frontage onto the main shopping street and a small car park at the side.

Recently the restaurant owner has become concerned that, in the middle of a recession when his trade has been flat, a new burger restaurant and take-away has opened nearby, and there is talk of another pizza restaurant opening soon. He has now decided to add a take-away facility to the existing Big Fry-up.

#### *Analysis*

This decision, and the consequences of it, are set out in Figure 2.8. The major policy decision – to set up the Take Away Rapid Service facility – inspires certain decisions on (I) products, (II) market and (III) the manner in which these markets are to be served. These three decisions, whether explicit or implicit, give rise to certain requirements for (A) the operating system structure, and (B) operations objectives. These in turn have implications for operations strategies, i.e. how capacity, schedules and inventories are to be managed. (A), (B) and (C) are the major policy-related decisions of operations (see also the model in Figure 2.2).

From this analysis it is clear that (A), (B) and (C) for the new system are likely to differ substantially from those of the restaurant, so the owner and the manager are faced with the decision as to whether the two operating systems are compatible and, if not, whether anything can be done to make them more compatible, or whether they must be operated as separate systems.

## Implementing operations policies

To achieve operations policies managers must make decisions and take action in particular areas. It is these decisions and subsequent actions which link operations policies to the day-to-day running of the operation. The principal 'linkages' are listed in Table 2.3. Decisions such as these will determine the character of operations, e.g.[1]

1 *Cost minimizers*
   (a) Standard product design and specifications for services
   (b) Low price/cost minimization
   (c) High-volume/low-cost operations
   (d) Emphasis on customer service through 'cost' and 'timing'
2 *Customizers*
   (a) Emphasis on adaptation of designs
   (b) Emphasis on low prices
   (c) Emphasis on flexibility
   (d) Low-volume operations
3 *Technological service people*
   (a) Emphasis on design

[1] Richardson, P. R., Taylor, A. J. and Gordon, J. R. M. (1985) A strategic approach to evaluating manufacturing performance. *Interfaces* **15**(6), pp. 15–27.

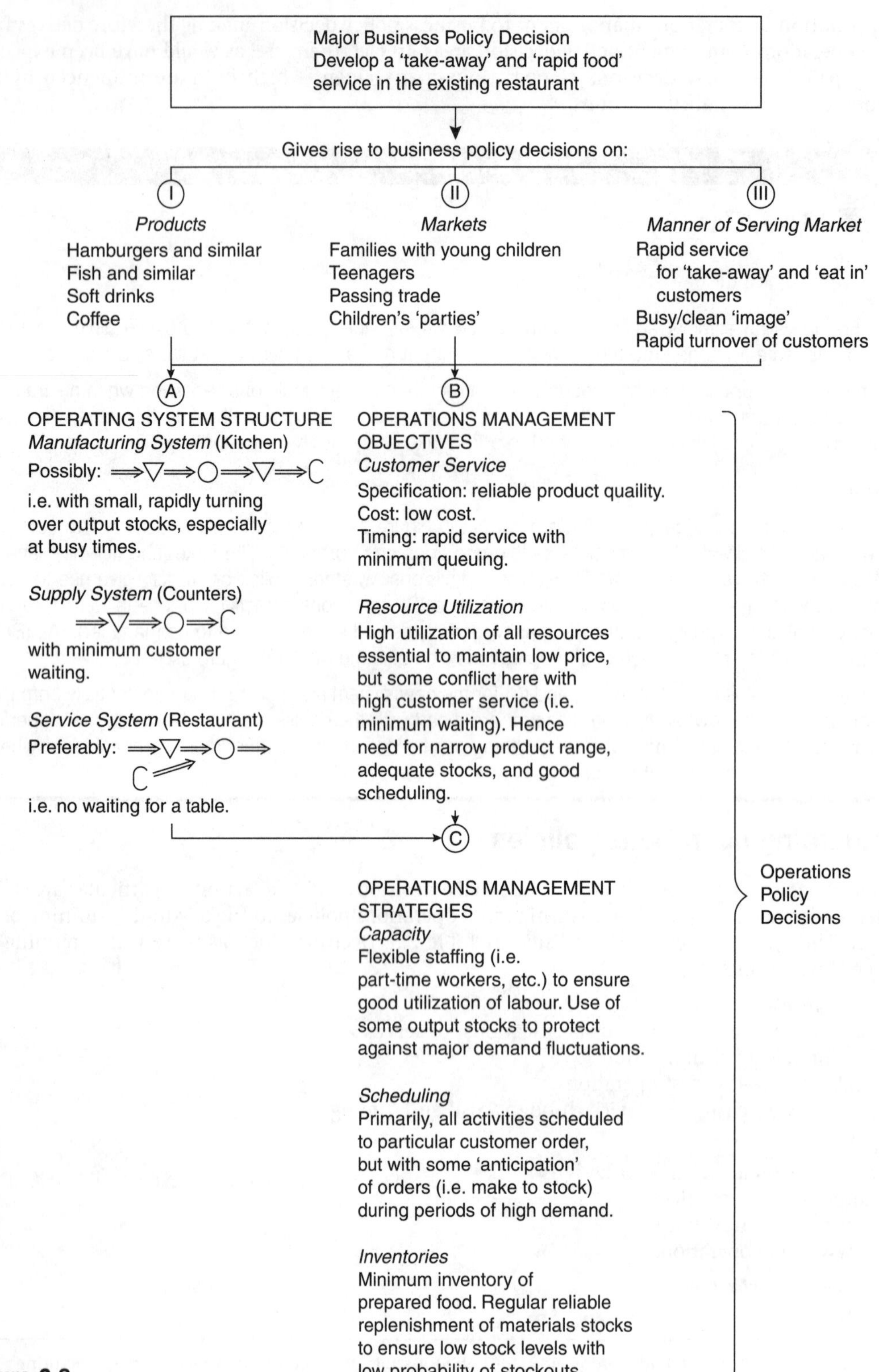
Major Business Policy Decision
Develop a 'take-away' and 'rapid food' service in the existing restaurant
Gives rise to business policy decisions on:
I
Products
Hamburgers and similar
Fish and similar
Soft drinks
Coffee
II
Markets
Families with young children
Teenagers
Passing trade
Children's 'parties'
III
Manner of Serving Market
Rapid service for 'take-away' and 'eat in' customers
Busy/clean 'image'
Rapid turnover of customers
A
OPERATING SYSTEM STRUCTURE
Manufacturing System (Kitchen)
Possibly:
i.e. with small, rapidly turning over output stocks, especially at busy times.
Supply System (Counters)
with minimum customer waiting.
Service System (Restaurant)
Preferably:
i.e. no waiting for a table.
B
OPERATIONS MANAGEMENT OBJECTIVES
Customer Service
Specification: reliable product quaility.
Cost: low cost.
Timing: rapid service with minimum queuing.
Resource Utilization
High utilization of all resources essential to maintain low price, but some conflict here with high customer service (i.e. minimum waiting). Hence need for narrow product range, adequate stocks, and good scheduling.
C
OPERATIONS MANAGEMENT STRATEGIES
Capacity
Flexible staffing (i.e. part-time workers, etc.) to ensure good utilization of labour. Use of some output stocks to protect against major demand fluctuations.
Scheduling
Primarily, all activities scheduled to particular customer order, but with some 'anticipation' of orders (i.e. make to stock) during periods of high demand.
Inventories
Minimum inventory of prepared food. Regular reliable replenishment of materials stocks to ensure low stock levels with low probability of stockouts.
Operations Policy Decisions

**Figure 2.8**

(b) Adaption of sophisticated products/services
(c) Emphasis on quality

4 *Innovators*
(a) Emphasis on research, design and development
(b) High product/service quality
(c) High product/service innovation
(d) Rapid rate of new product/service introduction
(e) Sophisticated products/service

5 *Technology exploiters*
(a) Emphasis on design and development
(b) Exploitation of new technologies
(c) Exploitation of products/services through to 'maturity' stage
(d) Emphasis on quality
(e) Emphasis on cost reduction
(f) Emphasis on delivery and availability

**Table 2.3 Principal 'linkage' decision areas for operations**

1. **Capacity and facilities:** Amount and location of resources
2. **Scheduling and control:** Methods for planning and controlling flows
3. **Inventories:** Locations and quantities
4. **Technology:** Types of processes, degree of automation
5. **Workforce:** Skills, payment
6. **Organization:** Structure, roles, authority
7. **Integration:** Links with suppliers, etc.

Given alternatives, operations managers will often need to choose between different ways of implementing business policy through operations. It will be necessary therefore to have some means of evaluating alternatives. Two principal criteria for evaluation are evident: consistency and contribution.[2] They are outlined in Table 2.4.

**Table 2.4 Criteria for evaluating an operations policy**

1. **Consistency (internal and external):**
   Between the operations strategy and the overall business strategy
   Between the operations strategy and the other functional strategies within the business
   Among the decision categories that make up the operations strategy
   Between the operations strategy and the business environment (resources available, competitive behaviour, governmental restraints, etc.)
2. **Contribution (to competitive advantage):**
   Making trade-offs explicit, enabling operations to set priorities that enhance competitive advantage
   Directing attention to opportunities that complement the business strategy
   Promoting clarity regarding the operations strategy throughout the business unit so its potential can be fully realized
   Providing the operations capabilities that will be required by the business in the future.

[2] Hayes, R. H. and Wheelwright, S. C. (1987) Strategic planning for manufacturing. In White, J. A. (ed.) *Production Handbook*, 4th edn, Chapter 1.2. New York: Wiley.

## CHECKLIST FOR CHAPTER 2

The importance of the business context to operations management

### Business policy

Formulation of business policy

Implementation of business policy

### Relationship of business policy and operations management decisions

Influence of business policy on operations management decisions

- Choice of system structure
- Formulation of objectives
- Choice of strategies

Contribution of operations management to business policy

### Business policy for competitive advantage

Policy options

- Flexibility
- Technology
- Quality
- Speed
- Cost
- Reliability
- Responsiveness
- Dependability

Focus and position

### Growth and development of businesses

Growth and decline of products and services

Product/service life-cycle

Growth and decline of organizations

### Operations policy

Achieving competitive advantage

Policy implications for operations

Dealing with growth

Operations policy decisions

A general framework

Implementing operations policies

## FURTHER READING

In other books, much of the material in the area covered in this chapter focuses specifically on manufacture. Some of it is relevant also to service, transport and supply systems, but there is little written specifically on policy for operations.

**Berry, W. L. and Hill, T. (1992)** Linking systems to strategy. *International Journal of Operations and Production Management*, **12**(10), pp. 3–15.

**Garvin, D. A. (1992)** *Operations Strategy – Text 2 Cases*. London: Prentice-Hall. Despite the title, largely about manufacturing.

**Harrison, M. (1993)** *Operations Management Strategy*. London: Pitman. Despite the title the book has a strong manufacturing emphasis.

**Slack, N. (1991)** *The Manufacturing Advantage*. London: Mercury. Discusses achieving competitive advantage in manufacture, by reference to five 'options' – quality, speed, dependability, flexibility, cost.

**Voss, C. A. (1992)** *Manufacturing Strategy – Process and Content*. London: Chapman & Hall. An edited book, comprising material previously published as well as new material.

## QUESTIONS

2.1 Show, by modifying and developing Figures 1.1 and 1.13, how business policy decisions might influence the principal decision areas of operations management.

2.2 Discuss the relationships of operating system structure and:

(a) the characteristics of the goods or services provided by the system;

(b) the nature of demand for those products or goods.

Show, by reference to examples, how changes in (a) and/or (b) give rise to changes in the operating system structure.

2.3 Show by means of a diagram similar to that in Figure 2.8 how the following business policy decision might affect the operations manager's decisions:

*Organization*: A large hotel adjacent to city airport.

*Major policy decision*: In addition to airline passenger and airport staff trade, to develop trade associated with business conferences, seminars, exhibitions, etc.

2.4 Discuss how the growth of an organization in the manner described in Table 2.1 might affect the job of the most senior person responsible for managing the operating system. If appropriate use a hypothetical case study on which to base/to illustrate your answer.

2.5 In what circumstances might an operations manager wish to seek to reverse, or promote further discussion on, recent business policy decisions? How might that influence be exercised, and what would be an appropriate role for the operations manager in such discussions with colleagues of equal status from other functional areas?

2.6 Give examples of companies which correspond to the five types (1–5) listed on pages 47 and 49. What aspects of operations objectives might be emphasized and what type of systems structures might be used by companies pursuing these five missions?

2.7 The establishment of surgical recovery centres attached to hospitals illustrates the trend away from inpatient stays and towards outpatient days. One such recovery centre in California shows promise in many areas, including: (1) reducing the length of stay and daily room charges for certain types of surgical procedures; (2) releasing acute care beds in markets where there is a shortage; and (3) creating bottom-line profits. Opponents say that early available evidence is still mixed and that it is far too early to make any such projection. However, more hospitals are now planning to establish recovery centres, encouraged by the growing interest on the part of employers, consumers and insurers in lowering health care costs. Recovery centres do not have the capital overhead of an acute care hospital; this, proponents say, makes the recovery centre promising as a hospital service function and threatening as potential competition.

Discuss this strategic development from the point of view of a hospital administrator whose hospital is about to set up such a centre, which will be run as a separate unit.

## CASE STUDIES (from Part 9)

The topics covered in this chapter are relevant in the following (see Introduction to Part 9 and Table C.1 for further details).

| No. | Name | Country |
|---|---|---|
| 15 | The Textile Machinery Co. | UK |
| 16 | America Burger and Pasta | Brazil |
| 18 | La Patisserie – B | UK |
| 24 | Winterthur non-life commercial insurance | Netherlands |
| 27 | Food Concept Sdn. Bhd. | Malaysia |

Chapter 3

# Operations management and other business functions

### ISSUES

What is the relationship between operations and marketing?
How do marketing decisions affect the operations manager?
Is organization structure important to operations?
What is the relationship of operations with finance and accounting?
How are design decisions related to operations management?

Following our examination of the business policy context of operations management in Chapter 2, we can now look more closely at the relationships of the operations function with other functions in the business. We shall consider relationships with marketing, personnel, finance and design, but concentrate on marketing, which is perhaps the most important relationship for operations management. We shall look for the nature of these relationships – at basic factors. The aim is to map out the main relationships of operations with other functions and to provide a sufficient description of each.

## OPERATIONS MANAGEMENT AND MARKETING

Chapter 2 showed that certain decisions which are largely 'external' to the operations function have a considerable influence on decisions within the function. These external, policy-related decisions are largely concerned with the organization's relationship with its market(s).

Three market-related policy decisions have been shown to be of particular importance, i.e.

A the nature of the goods or services to be provided by the organization, i.e. the goods/service(s) characteristics;

B the nature of the markets to be served, i.e. the market demand characteristics;

C the manner in which these markets are to be served.

### The marketing function

Marketing managers will have a major influence on these policy decisions, since the marketing function is primarily concerned with decisions on the nature of the 'offering' (i.e. the good or service(s) to be provided to customers) and the methods by which the 'offering' is made. These marketing decisions are usually referred to as the four aspects of the *marketing mix,* i.e. goods or services, cost, distribution and promotion. Although all businesses must make decisions on each of these four aspects, different types of businesses will employ different 'mixes'. For example, companies involved in providing consumer goods might emphasize promotion (e.g. advertising), while companies providing a specialist service might emphasize cost or price. Decisions on these four factors, outlined below, may be considered to be the deliberate *market decisions* of the organization.

1 ***Goods/service***, i.e. goods/service characteristics – the actual item, transport or service provided to the customer, its attributes and characteristics, the features and provisions surrounding it and the essential benefits it provides.

2 ***Cost***, i.e. the purchase price of the goods or service and any additional costs or allowances.

3 ***Distribution***, i.e. the location of the market, channels of distribution, outlets, territories, etc. involved in the provision of the offering to the customer.

4 ***Promotion***, i.e. the publicity, selling and advertising practices employed to bring the goods or services to the notice of the intended customer.

These market decisions influence, but do not determine, the nature of the demand faced by the organization, i.e. the demand felt by the operating system. In addition, other factors only partially influenced by the organization will influence demand, i.e.

(a) ***environmental variables*** – factors (largely beyond the control of the enterprise) that have broad effects on demand, e.g. the economic situation, public policy and culture;

(b) ***competitive variables*** – factors under the control of competitors.

**Figure 3.1** Factors influencing demand and operations management

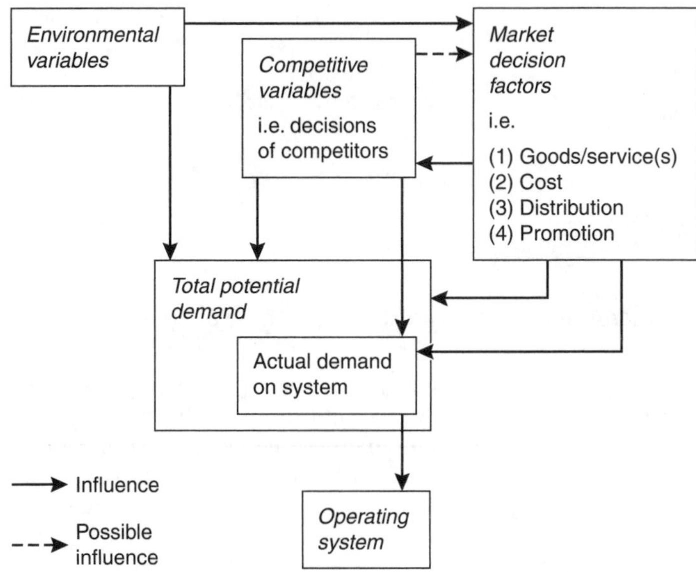


Figure 3.1 indicates the manner in which environmental, competitive and market decision factors influence demand. The introduction of a new product or service by an organization may affect the total potential demand for products or services of that type and will also help secure a part of that total. Environmental variables, the action of competitors and the market decisions of the enterprise may all affect the total potential market. Certain actions of competitors, e.g. advertising, price changes, etc., may affect the potential market, and of course market decisions by an organization, particularly promotion decisions, will directly affect market share.

The nature of the environment will be known and therefore may influence market decisions. The actions of competitors will be uncertain but nevertheless may be considered by an enterprise when making decisions on goods/services, cost, promotion and distribution.

Within this framework we shall focus on the market decision factors, i.e. those decisions required of the business. In so doing we shall be looking more closely at the three market-related policy decisions identified at the beginning of this section in order to try to identify how these decisions, which directly influence operations management, are made, and thus to identify the means by which operations managers might influence them.

## Decisions on goods/service characteristics

The nature of the 'offering' is, from the operations manager's viewpoint, an important market decision. We shall identify some of the factors that influence this decision.

Growth is a common corporate objective. Goods/service(s) decisions are an important part of the four policies for growth identified in Chapter 2, i.e.

(a) ***Market penetration*** is the expansion of sales of existing offerings in existing markets by selling more to existing customers, and/or gaining new customers in existing markets.

(b) ***Market development*** is the creation of new markets by discovering new applications for existing offerings.

(c) ***Product development*** is the launching of new offerings onto existing markets.

(d) ***Diversification*** or lateral integration is the development of new offerings for new markets.

Many enterprises will offer a range of goods and/or services. This market decision may therefore require consideration of a particular offering or the number and mix of the whole range of offerings. It may be concerned with the addition, change or abandonment of one offering or one group of offerings from the whole range, and/or the nature, consistency and mix of the whole range. Three notions are of importance in this context:

(a) A small part of the range often provides a relatively large part of the profits of the enterprise. It follows, therefore, that this group of offerings must be closely managed and monitored.

(b) The upper limit of revenue is influenced by the nature of the range of offerings. Eight categories of offering have been identified for most ranges:

 1. yesterday's 'breadwinners' (or yesterday's profit-makers)
 2. today's 'breadwinners'
 3. tomorrow's 'breadwinners'
 4. products/services needing too many repairs
 5. unnecessary specialities
 6. undesired specialities
 7. investments in management ego
 8. 'Cinderellas'.

 An enterprise's profit capacity can be improved by regularly abandoning those offerings which cost more to retain than to drop (e.g. (4) and (8)).

(c) Most offerings have a sales curve or life-cycle. In the course of this cycle the offering progresses through a number of logically interrelated stages in which sales and profitability vary. For most enterprises, since offerings must pass through a distribution channel (see below), the maximum sales level is reached before the maximum consumption level. Furthermore, profits tend to reach their maximum level while sales are still increasing.

### *Life-cycles*

Four stages in the life-cycle of offerings can be identified, i.e. 'incubation', 'growth', 'maturity' and 'decline'. Life-cycles may be practically unnoticeable for some offerings and obvious for others, such as consumer durables. The span of the life-cycle may be determined by such factors as:

(a) the degree of technological progress;

(b) changes in customer habits;

(c) ease of entry to the market.

Different actions or market decisions may be required at each stage of a life-cycle. Price decisions will be required before or at the launch time, while during the incubation period the emphasis will be on promotion. Distribution is all-important during the growth period. The maturity period may see the introduction of price changes or changes in specifications to prevent decline and/or the introduction of new offerings.

### *The development process*

Goods/service development involves the search for new offerings as well as the improvement of the existing. Since the number of entirely new offerings is normally small, development is largely concerned with the introduction of variants through adaptations and improvements.

At least six stages of development can be identified. These are:

(a) exploration, including research, i.e. the continual search for new ideas;

(b) systematic, rapid screening to eliminate less promising ideas;

(c) business analysis, including market research and cost analysis;

(d) development of the remaining possibilities;

(e) testing the offerings developed;

(f) launching on a commercial scale.

Development, testing and launching ((d), (e) and (f)) are the most time-consuming and most costly stages. Few new ideas are eventually launched, and of these only a small proportion succeed. For these reasons enterprises may adopt contrasting *philosophies on development*, resulting in:

(a) some enterprises assuming market leadership because of their strong research and development base; or

(b) some enterprises seeking to react quickly to the innovations of others and therefore joining the competition during the growth stage; or

(c) some enterprises joining in at a later stage, just before market saturation sets in, by adapting the offerings to the needs of special market segments; or

(d) some enterprises not wishing to be excluded from new markets but relying on their ability to provide on a mass scale and offer very competitive prices.

### *Market policies*

Three main methods are available to the enterprise to exploit the market: market aggregation, market segmentation and production differentiation.

***Market aggregation*** is the penetration of the market to the greatest possible width and depth with a single offering or a very limited range. This approach relies on a uniform pattern of consumption and an appeal to the needs which customers have in common in order to win sales.

***Market segmentation*** is concerned with placing an extensive range of offerings each of which is suited to the needs of a different submarket or market segment. Here a conscious search is made to determine the essential differences between buyer groups so that they can be clearly separated into different segments, each varying in size, buying power and buyer behaviour.

***Production differentiation*** is the deliberate attempt to encourage demand to adjust itself to the manner in which supply has been segmented. Unlike market segmentation, product differentiation may be employed where segments are not clearly defined and where segments must therefore be created by emphasizing the presence of product differences between the enterprise's own offerings and those of competitors, in particular by emphasizing product differences which promote a social/psychological segmentation of the market favouring the product concerned.

### Quality, brand and brand policy

Quality is the extent to which an offering satisfies a need. Improving the quality of an offering is known as 'trading up', and the reverse as 'trading down'. Quality may be changed. For example, it may be appropriate to adjust the range in response to economic developments such as the trade cycle and/or to raise or lower both the quality and the price of offerings in the range. Trading up or down in the long term may help the enterprise to gain access, from its traditional market position, to other higher or lower segments of the market.

A brand is used to identify and distinguish offerings from those of competitors. For brand policy to be successful the offering must lend itself to differentiation, to facilitate advertising and promotion. The aim of branding is to facilitate, improve and simplify control of the market process. A successful brand image will help to secure a market. A brand suggests consistency in the quality and origin of the offering.

## Decisions on cost, distribution and promotion

Here we shall consider the three remaining market decision variables, since all three directly influence market and demand characteristics. The operations manager will, of course, have some interest in these decisions and will wish to make some contribution to them. He or she will wish to influence decisions on the market which is to be pursued, to measure or estimate demand, and to predict future demand, in order to facilitate his or her own decision-making on capacity, schedules and inventories.

### Cost

We shall concentrate on the *price* of the product/service, which is normally the most important but not the only cost factor.

Price is clearly important as a regulator of demand and a component of customer service. It:

(a) regulates sales volume;

(b) determines revenue;

(c) influences the rate of return on investment through its influence on sales profitability;

(d) has an impact on unit costs.

Thus price policy has several major objectives:

(a) a sales target;

(b) a profit target;

(c) a liquidity target;

(d) meeting competition;

(e) maintaining price and margin stability in the distribution chain;

(f) discouraging potential competitors;

(g) eliminating existing competitors.

Reactions to pricing decisions can be expected from:

(a) resellers, i.e. intermediaries in the distribution channel;

(b) final customers.

The principal decisions in pricing derive from four main problems, discussed in order below.

(a) How should the relative importance and the relative emphasis of price and non-price variables within marketing decisions be determined?

(b) To which pricing policy is a particular price geared? Pricing policy, in a broad sense, should answer two questions:
   1. What are the objectives for pricing?
   2. How will these objectives be attained?

(c) How should prices (i.e. price levels) for offerings be determined (and redetermined)?

(d) How should pricing policy, e.g. the timing and extent of price changes and deviations such as discounts, be implemented?

### *Relative importance of price and non-price variables*

Competition on price may be an attractive proposition to an enterprise provided:

1. total demand for the offering in the market as a whole is price elastic (or sensitive to price);
2. the enterprise's (lower) price is based on a more or less lasting advantage, e.g. a cost advantage based on a technological lead.

Without these conditions any enterprise relying on the price variable may discover that the price of its offerings will never be low enough, and hence competitive advantages derived from one of the other marketing decisions will probably be preferred.

### *Pricing policy*

Two main pricing policy alternatives are available in marketing policy, i.e.

(a) an ***active*** pricing policy in the case of
   1. a new product service
   2. changes in cost levels (inflation)
   3. changes in the level of demand (product cycle)
   4. discounts;

(b) a ***passive*** pricing policy in the case of
   1. non-price competition
   2. pricing agreements
   3. price cartels
   4. leasing
   5. price leadership

An active pricing policy may take any one of a broad spectrum of different forms:

(a) skimming the market – a skimming price, often temporary in nature;
(b) sliding gradually down the demand curve;
(c) maintaining a margin above the current market price – a price premium;
(d) setting a price fractionally below the current market price;
(e) a penetration price for penetrating the market quickly and within a short period;
(f) an expansion price for accelerating the penetration process;
(g) stay-out pricing – a warning to potential competitors;
(h) put-out pricing – the elimination of competitors.

In the case of a new offering, the enterprise may choose between a skimming price and a penetration price. A skimming price may be used:

(a) if sales are insensitive to price changes;

(b) if the offering is difficult to imitate;

(c) if the market is gradually expanding – with the aid of successive price reductions, more new, lower market/income segments are tapped;

(d) if competition is expected to increase considerably and the enterprise wants to build funds for promotional activities in the later phases of the life-cycle;

(e) if it is suspected that a new offering's lifespan is likely to be short.

A penetration price may be used:

(a) if, from the beginning, sales are price sensitive;

(b) if a large market share is essential to compete in the market;

(c) if the enterprise expects to achieve short-term economies of scale.

Implementing pricing policy involves:

(a) timing price changes to coincide with various factors such as a particular stage of the life-cycle;

(b) defining a policy on price variations, i.e. where there should be departures from pricing policy.

Objectives of price variations include:

(a) encouraging customers to better their performance by granting performance discounts for reaching certain targets, e.g. quantity rebates, turnover bonuses, discounts for prompt payment, etc.;

(b) keeping certain distribution channels open long-term by means of functional discounts, e.g. to wholesalers;

(c) meeting competition in the short run;

(d) offsetting short-run fluctuations in demand;

(e) promotional objectives such as sharing the costs of dealer campaigns, supplying advertising material, etc.;

(f) ensuring operations at a high level of plant capacity.

### Distribution

Two aspects of decision-making for distribution can be identified: distribution channel decisions and physical distribution management decisions. The latter are more likely to influence operations management directly. The former will be described briefly in the interests of comprehensiveness, and a more detailed treatment of the subject will be provided in Chapter 16.

The channels through which items flow to the customer or through which the customer flows to the organization will range from the simplest, i.e. a system dealing directly with the final customer, to the complex, in which several intermediaries intervene in the distribution process. The nature of the channel(s) employed will depend largely on the nature of the organization and on the number and location of final customers. The more diverse the points of contact with customers the longer and more complex the distribution channel.

The management of physical distribution or customer channels is normally termed *physical distribution management* (PDM). Three principal PDM decision areas can be identified, the last two of which are of particular relevance to operations management as sources of influence on customer service and demand:

(a) channel design;

(b) service-level decisions;

(c) inventory decisions.

High customer service, in terms of short delivery delays or a lower probability of stockouts, incurs higher cost through the need for a larger number of stock holdings, higher stock levels, more and frequent stock replenishments, etc. Distribution service levels conflict with distribution costs, and hence enterprises must determine economic service or delivery levels for distribution systems.

Service-level decisions are intimately related to inventory decisions.[1] There are two basic approaches to inventory control:

(a) ***the reorder level system***, in which stock is replenished (usually with a fixed quantity) or a replenishment order is made when stock falls to a fixed reorder level;

(b) ***the reorder interval system***, in which stock is replenished or a replenishment order is made such that the stock level returns to a fixed maximum level at fixed intervals.

Whichever approach is adopted, the variable rate of stock depletion which normally exists, plus possibly the uncertain delays between placing a replenishment order and receiving items into stock, necessitates the use of a buffer or safety stock designed to ensure a required customer service level. For example, use of the reorder level system will normally necessitate the adoption of a reorder level which is high enough to ensure that in most, if not all, cases a replenishment order is received into stock before the stock level falls to zero. Given information on the variability of both demand and replenishment lead time, a reorder level can be established to provide a required service level (e.g. a maximum probability of stockout).

Decisions on reorder levels, reorder quantities, etc. at various stages in the distribution channel affect both customer service and the nature of demand, and are therefore of some importance to operations management.

## Promotion

Promotion is concerned primarily with persuasion, aimed largely at securing and increasing the share of the market. Four promotional activities can be identified.

(a) ***advertising*** – any paid form of non-personal presentation and promotion of products or services by an identified sponsor;

(b) ***personal selling*** – oral presentation to one or more prospective purchasers for the purpose of making sales;

(c) ***publicity*** – non-personal stimulation of demand for a product or service, by planting commercially significant news about it in a published medium or obtaining favourable presentation of it that is not paid for by the sponsor;

(d) ***sales promotion*** – those marketing activities, other than personal selling, advertising and publicity, that stimulate consumer purchasing and dealer effectiveness, such as displays, shows and exhibitions, demonstrations and various non-recurrent selling efforts not in the ordinary routine.

An enterprise must decide how much promotional effort to make and the relative mix or importance of each of the above within that total effort. The importance of promotion will depend, among other things, on the merits of alternative, non-promotional expenditure, the nature of the product or service offered by the enterprise and its competitors, and the stage in the product or service life-cycle.

---

[1] Discussed in detail in Chapter 17.

Promotion is one way to secure and stimulate demand. Given limited resources, promotion competes for funds with the other three market decision variables. The more impersonal the method of distribution and the greater the similarity to the products or services offered by competitors, the greater is the need for promotional effort. Products and services which are at an early stage in their life-cycle, where exposure and customer awareness are important, may also need relatively high promotion.

Figure 3.2 suggests the relative importance of the four elements of the promotional mix in respect of the four stages of promotion, i.e. customer awareness of, interest in, desire for, and acquisition of the offering. We shall concentrate on advertising and personal selling, which are normally the most important elements of the promotional mix.

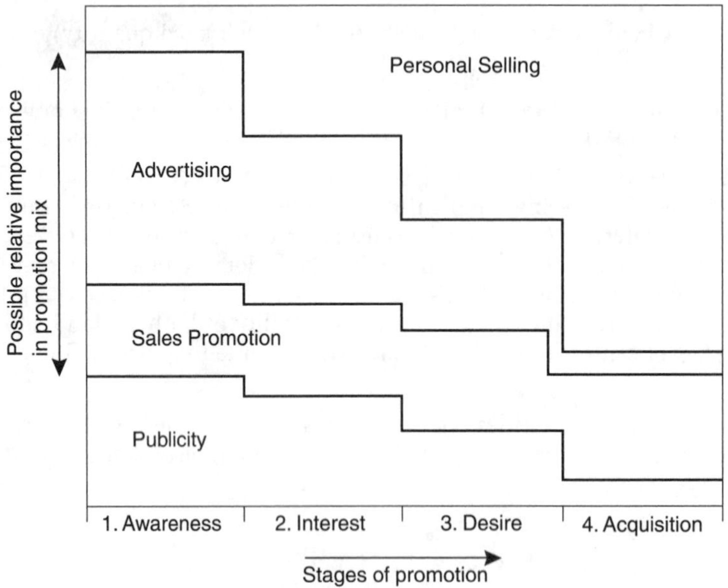


**Figure 3.2** Promotion mix and the 'stages' of promotion

## *Advertising*

In general, the demand-related objectives of advertising are to attract new customers both from the actual market (i.e. competitors' customers) and from the potential market (i.e. previously 'non-users'), to increase the existing customers' rate of consumption and to control demand patterns. The persuasion process through which these objectives are pursued involves the enterprise sending 'messages' (or ideas) via various 'media' to a 'target group' (or audience), the effectiveness of the whole being subject to some form of assessment through feedback.

Ultimately enterprises require some positive net effect of advertising on revenues and profits. Simply to increase demand is not enough if the additional sales increase is more than offset by the cost of attracting it. Advertising at the beginning of a life-cycle may enable an enterprise to gain time by achieving quicker market penetration and an earlier breakeven. In the longer term, advertising may be used to secure a market share to combat the effects of any external influences on demand (e.g. environmental and competitive variables), to combat seasonal variations, etc., the latter being concerned more with the control of demand patterns than with the change of long-term demand levels.

The major decisions required in advertising are:

(a) the amount of advertising (the advertising budget);

(b) the scheduling of advertising effort;

(c) the advertising message(s);

(d) the advertising media;

(e) the procedures for control and evaluations.

Decisions (a) and (b, in particular, may affect the nature of demand. Both, therefore, may influence operations management, and vice versa.

Pragmatic methods are commonly employed in determining advertising budgets. For example, methods based on a fixed amount of advertising (cost) per unit of product or service to be sold, a fixed percentage of turnover or parity with competitors have some 'rule of thumb' value. Quantitative decision models, however, have the advantage of indicating the nature of the sales response to advertising and the likely effects of changes in variables.

The scheduling of advertising is of relevance to the operations manager since, if the advertising effort can affect the level of demand, the timing of such efforts will affect the demand pattern. Here we are concerned not so much with short-cycle scheduling problems, such as the timing or frequency of advertisements on a TV or radio station, which may not affect the pattern of demand 'felt' by the operating system, but rather with the longer-term or macro scheduling which customers frequently acquire when competitors adopt a similar strategy, when the offering is similar to that of competitors, and when, without such action, the pattern of demand would be unacceptable to the enterprise. Advertising to counteract seasonal fluctuations, fiscal changes, the actions of competitors, etc. is common practice at all stages of the product or service life-cycle. They are attempts to smooth the demand patterns rather than to affect long-term needs.

Similarly, scheduling decisions are required in order to ensure favourable overall demand patterns, appropriate advertising schedules being a function of factors such as the nature of customer behaviour.

### *Selling*

Personal selling, with advertising, is the normal form of promotion, at least for consumer offerings. Personal selling is directed at individuals. It involves direct contact, offers direct feedback, is time-effective, flexible and adaptable, but time-consuming and expensive.

The major decisions affecting the nature and extent of personal selling as a promotional activity are:

(a) the size of the sales force;

(b) the sales force design (e.g. territories);

(c) the management of sales staff (e.g. recruitment, training, remuneration);

(d) the evaluation of selling.

## The relationships of operations management and marketing decisions

Marketing managers are primarily responsible for the four 'marketing mix' decisions discussed above. These decisions are of substantial interest to operations managers, for they will determine the products/services to be provided by the operating system and the nature of the demand for those outputs. Operations managers will, at least, wish to monitor all the decisions which influence them. In most cases they will wish to exercise some influence on these decisions, and in some cases they may need to ensure that marketing managers do not make decisions which give rise to circumstances which operations managers cannot adequately accommodate. For example, they will wish to avoid situations in which, as a result of decisions over which they had no influence, they feel obliged to deal with a great diversity of products/services, each with too small quantities, with unacceptable deadlines or delivery dates, too high a quality and too low a cost. This is an extreme situation, but operations managers must seek to avoid the impossible by emphasizing the feasible. It would be appropriate for them, therefore, to have in mind a 'checklist' of those decisions which influence the nature of the product/service, the market for that 'offering' and the manner in which that market is to be satisfied. Table 3.1 provides such a checklist.

**Table 3.1 A checklist of some marketing decisions which influence operations management**

| Product/service characteristics: | Cost: |
|---|---|
| The development philosophy | Pricing policy |
| Market policy | The price of the offering |
| The nature and quality of the product/service | Price variations |
| **Distribution:** | **Promotion:** |
| Level of service | Advertising – amount |
| Inventory decisions | – scheduling |
| | Selling – size of sales force |

Operations managers will also need to measure, estimate or forecast demand. We saw in Chapter 1 that, in certain types of operating systems, resources are stocked in anticipation of their being needed at a future date. Similarly, some systems rely on the provision of output stocks from which customers are supplied direct.

In all such systems the level of both resource and output stocks provided must be influenced by the level of demand which is expected to exist at some future date. In such cases, therefore, the estimation or prediction of demand is of importance.

Existing demand levels can be measured, and this is of significance in the management of operating systems which require resources to be obtained directly to meet demand from particular customers. It should be noted, however, that even given this need, and given the ability to measure demand levels, errors may be introduced. Rarely is it possible to measure directly the amount of resources required to satisfy particular customer orders. Normally, since orders will probably differ (otherwise resources will probably have been stocked), it will be necessary to estimate the resource requirements of a particular customer order. Thus for all types of operating systems the translation of either known or expected demand into required resources will be susceptible to error through:

(a) demand estimation/forecasting errors; and/or

(b) errors in the estimation of the resource requirements associated with customer orders/demand.

Procedures appropriate for demand estimation and forecasting are discussed in some detail in Appendix II; our purpose here is simply to note that operations management must employ such procedures in order adequately to accommodate this externally influenced factor and ensure realistic internal decision-making on problems such as capacity and inventory management and activity scheduling.

In demand forecasting, the length of the forecast period will depend largely on the nature of system resources and the nature of the market. For example, capacity planning may involve periods in excess of five years where there is sufficient stability or predictability of the nature of demand. A long-term view may be essential where there is a long lead time on the provision or replacement of resources. Examples might include:

(a) manufacture – steel manufacture, electricity generation and supply, oil production;

(b) transport – airlines, rail systems;

(c) service – hospitals, telephone service.

In contrast, a shorter-term view would be appropriate where the nature of demand is less stable or less predictable, and where resources are more readily provided or replaced, or where the manner in which the function is accomplished may change, e.g. through technological change. Examples might include:

(a) manufacture – fashion goods, consumer durables;

(b) supply – retail shops, mail order;

(c) transport – bus service, taxi service, road delivery service;
(d) service – secretarial services, security service.

## OPERATIONS MANAGEMENT AND ORGANIZATION

The 'technology' in an organization will inevitably have some impact on its employees. For example, the type of equipment used will inevitably affect the nature of the jobs and the working conditions of employees. Further, the type of technology employed within an organization may affect its structure or shape. Here we shall consider briefly the relationship between technology and job/organizational factors, with particular reference to the role of the operations manager. We shall in effect be looking at some aspects of the relationship between operations management decisions and the decisions of those responsible for personnel/organizational matters.

### Technology and organization

Early research suggested a relationship between technology and the nature (or shape) of the organization. In considering different types of production systems Woodward found relationships between the type of technology employed and organizational factors such as the length of the chain of command, the span of managerial control, and the ratio of direct to indirect labour. This research gave rise to a considerable amount of study aimed at clarifying the relationships between technology and such organizational factors. Over a period of time new definitions emerged, and eventually the research began to focus on the relationships of the types of factors defined in Table 3.2. This research resulted in a series of general conclusions which can be summarized as follows:

(a) ***Task uncertainty***. The greater the routineness or repetitiveness of tasks and the less the task variability, complexity and uncertainty, then the less the degree of participation in organization decision-making and the greater the formalization of roles, procedure and practices.

(b) ***Task interdependence***. The greater the interdependence of tasks, roles and activities and the less the rigidity of workflows, then the greater the participation in decision-making and the less formalized the authority structures, procedures, etc.

(c) ***Workflow uncertainty***. The less the variability, complexity or uncertainty of workflow, and the greater the standardization of inputs and outputs, then the more formalized and centralized the management, the greater the vertical integration and departmentalization, and the more sophisticated the control procedures.

(d) ***External uncertainty***. The less the rate of change in products/service specifications and ranges, the less the rate of programme/demand change, the less the market uncertainty and the greater its homogeneity, then the more mechanistic the management of the organization, the greater the formalization and centralization of management, and the more structured the organization.

Taken together these conclusions suggest a negative relationship between the extent of uncertainty in and around an organization and the degree of structuring and concentration of authority and decision-making of that organization. We might expect this type of relationship to exist at different levels within the organization. For example, the uncertainty of tasks, their interdependence, the uncertainty of workflows and the demands placed on a department and the workgroups within that department will be reflected in the organization of both the department and its workgroups. At the organizational level, a high degree of structuring and concentration may be evident through functional divisions, staff/line relationships, reporting and control mechanisms, etc., while at the workgroup level a similar organizational structure or style may be evident through detailed job descriptions, work procedures, closeness of supervision and high division of labour. At the organizational level, low structuring and concentration may be evident through the use of 'matrix'-type structures, project or task group

**Table 3.2 'Technology' and 'organization' factors or measures**

| ***Technology factors*** **(relating mainly to the nature of the work or tasks performed within the organization)** | | ***Organizational factors*** **(relating to the nature and shape of the organization and the manner in which decisions are made)** |
|---|---|---|
| ***Task uncertainty***, comprising<br>(a) task difficulty, as indicated by the extent to which there are known and adequate procedures for performance, and the amount of time required for solving task problems.<br>(b) task non-routineness, indicated by the amount of variety in and/or the number of changes in the task over a period of time<br>(c) task unmanageability, as indicated by the extent to which the task and any changes in it are understood by the worker.<br>***Task interdependence***<br>as indicated by the need for active self-initiated collaboration and co-operation between workers.<br>***Workflow uncertainty***, comprising<br>(a) workflow variability, as indicated by the number of possible or alternative sequences of activities available for each item<br>(b) workflow complexity, as indicated by the difficulty of determining the appropriate sequence or next stage of activity for each item.<br>***External uncertainty***<br>as indicated by the rate of change of product of service characteristics, or demand, and the heterogeneity of demand. | ? Relationships between these factors | ***Specialization*** refers to the division of labour within the organization. One aspect is the number of specialisms as indicated by a count of those functions that are performed by specialists. The degree of 'role' specialization is a further aspect and is concerned with the differentiation of activities within each function. It refers to the specificity of the tasks assigned to any particular role. Other relevant aspects are the level of specialist operation in terms of technical complexity and the relevant status and influence of particular specialisms as exemplified by their level in the line hierarchy for which the top person in the function is responsible.<br>***Standardization*** can be considered as two aspects. Standardization of procedures is a basic aspect of organizational structure and may cover decision-making procedures, information-conveying procedures and procedures for operating or carrying out decisions. Procedures are standardized when there are rules or definitions that cover all circumstances and that apply invariably. Standardization of roles is concerned with the degree to which the organization prescribes the standardization of role definition and qualifications for office, role performance measurement, titles for offices, symbols of role status, and rewards for role performance.<br>***Centralization*** concerns the focus of authority to make decisions affecting the organization. Two types of authority can be identified: formal or institutional authority stemming essentially from ownership, and real or personal authority stemming from knowledge and experience. Factors affecting centralization include: the location of the actual decision-making function at particular points in the authority structure, the promulgation of rules for decisions which limit the discretion of subordinates, the frequency and thoroughness of review procedures and control systems, and the legitimate availability of relevant information.<br>***Configuration.*** The relationships between positions or jobs, described in terms of the authority of superiors and the responsibility of subordinates, are commonly expressed in the form of an organization chart. Various aspects may be distinguished, including vertical and lateral spans of control and numbers of positions (or jobs) in various segments. |

arrangement, working parties, an emphasis on informal communications, frequent role or job changes and transfers. At the workgroup level such an approach may be evident as job rotation, worker control of workflow, absence of formal supervision, the use of semi-autonomous workgroup arrangements, informal training procedures, broadly defined jobs, and absence of specialist and technical functions.

## Technology factors and operations management

The existence of a particular technology (as defined above) can, as we have seen, influence the nature of people's work. It follows, therefore, that if operations managers, through their decisions, influence the nature of this 'technology' then their decisions can influence the nature of individuals' work, and the structure of the organization. (Equally, if the existence of a particular organizational structure and particular job arrangements obliges or encourages the adoption of a particular technology, this is of interest to operations managers, since it may affect their decisions or limit their courses of action.)

Operations managers do influence 'technology', both indirectly and directly.

All organizations must deal with some uncertainties in the external environment, e.g. uncertainties in demand. Operations managers, perhaps working with marketing personnel, are largely responsible for determining the extent to which these external uncertainties are allowed to give rise to internal uncertainties. For example, an organization might protect itself against uncertainties in demand by the use of output stock, etc., but if it chooses to operate directly in response to individual customer orders then external uncertainties will be communicated directly into the organization. Thus decisions about the way in which capacity is managed, the way in which activities are scheduled and the deployment of inventories will affect the extent to which uncertainties external to the organization are reflected in internal uncertainties. It will be appreciated that operations managers, therefore, through their decisions, can mediate the effect of external uncertainties on the organization. In this manner, therefore, *indirectly* their decisions may affect the 'technology' (as defined above) within the organization and thus the nature of the work which must be undertaken and the nature of the organization, which will be appropriate to such circumstances.

Equally, operations managers may choose *directly* to use their resources, including their workers, in a particular way. We shall see in Chapters 7 to 10 that they are responsible for the design of the jobs and the tasks undertaken by workers. It is for these reasons that operations managers' decisions have some relevance to those concerned with the management of labour, the design of jobs, and the design and structuring of the organization. For just these reasons operations managers must be aware of any limitations on their actions resulting, perhaps, from the existence of a particular organizational structure.

These relationships are outlined in Figure 3.3 and illustrated by the following example.

**EXAMPLE**

### *A taxi company*

In this company the operations manager is responsible for obtaining, maintaining and deploying adequate resources for the company to operate an effective taxi service within an urban area. *Until recently* the company has operated in a fairly stable environment. There were few external (e.g. demand) uncertainties and much of the company's custom was regular and repeat business. The operations manager aimed to provide high customer service while also attempting to achieve at least 75% utilization of the cars and drivers. Her major decisions gave rise to the operation of a system with a 'function from stock, and from (a small) customer queue' structure, using a capacity management strategy which maintained a small quantity of excess resources (spare cars and drivers) and necessitated customer queuing during times when demand exceeded capacity. Wherever possible customers were asked to pre-book taxis, and special price discounts were given for pre-booked customers using regular services. The decisions by the operations manager, taken in the light of the external uncertainties facing the organization, gave rise to the existence of fairly repetitive, routine and predictable jobs within the company and therefore the opportunity to operate in a fairly centralized, routine and structured fashion.

*Recently* major changes have taken place which have now begun to affect this company. Other taxi companies have begun to compete and the nature of other local transport has changed, so that it is no longer possible to predict demand accurately or to be certain about the types of journeys likely to be made by the majority of customers. It has now become necessary, in order to retain an adequate part of a somewhat uncertain market, to place more emphasis on customer service, particularly in terms of minimizing delays, etc., and to accept, hopefully for a short period only, a lower utilization of resources. This in turn has given rise to the operations manager adopting a somewhat different strategy for the management of the system, i.e. the use of more variable capacity through the use of part-time drivers and vehicles, subcontracting arrangements, etc., and trying to maintain an operating system structure which does not oblige customers to queue. These decisions in turn have given rise to the existence of quite different types of jobs within the organization. No longer is it possible for work to be organized on a routine and predictable basis. Drivers now have to be given far more discretion and the size of the labour force now varies. Much more initiative and authority has been delegated to drivers, and there is far less of a dependence on routines, rules and procedures. Thus the tasks and jobs of the drivers and maintenance crews are no longer quite so predictable, and the organizational structure is now more decentralized, with a far greater delegation of authority and decision-making.

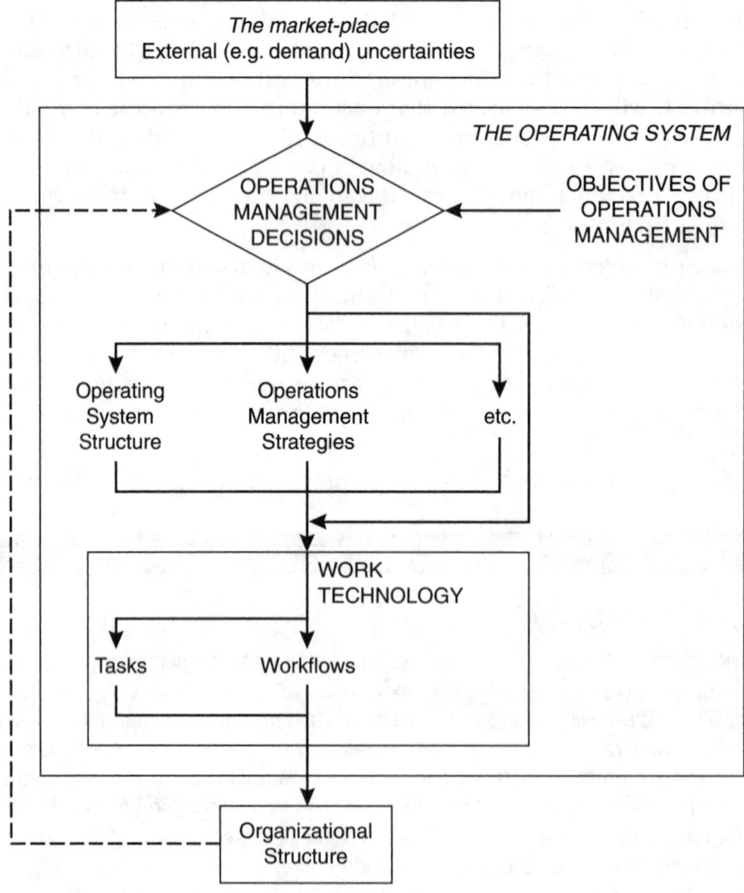


**Figure 3.3** Operations management decisions and their influence on work and organization structure

# OPERATIONS MANAGEMENT AND THE FINANCE/ACCOUNTING FUNCTION

Many of the relationships between these two functions are obvious. For example, in the acquisition of capacity (e.g. physical facilities for the operating system) a capital investment will be required, so the finance manager will have some interest in the operations manager's decision. Also, the finance manager will have some interest in the operations manager's inventory decisions, since inventory represents tied-up capital. Equally, the relationship is clear in respect of the operations manager's decisions about facilities maintenance, the payment of incentives, etc. All these aspects are dealt with later in the book. Here we shall concentrate on one somewhat different aspect of the relationship between operations and finance managers, namely that involving financial control.

## Managerial and financial controls *(see also Chapters 18 and 22)*

The top management of any organization will seek to exercise some control over the constituent parts of that organization and hence over the managers responsible for those parts. Such control will seek to measure progress and compare it with plans or intentions, in order to facilitate correction where necessary. Such controls may take several forms, but will often involve financial measures, and thus involve finance managers and accountants.

The purpose of such management controls on operations management must be to ensure that operations managers achieve agreed objectives. This, as will be clear from our discussion of objectives in Chapter 1, must recognize operations managers' objectives in respect of the achievement of adequate levels of customer service and resource productivity.

It has been pointed out that two basic types of control mechanism exist: (a) behaviour control and (b) output control. The differences are identified in Figure 3.4. With a 'behaviour' control mechanism the behaviour of the system which is to be controlled is monitored and compared to a standard or objective in order that corrective action can be applied to the system if necessary. With an 'output' control system the output from the system is observed and compared to a standard in order that the system itself can be adjusted if necessary. The distinction between the two types of control, therefore, is the point at which the system is monitored, i.e. the system itself or the output of the system.

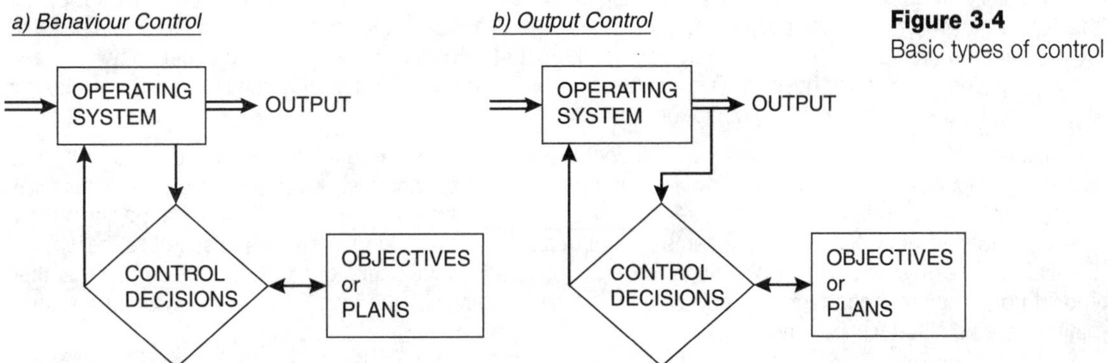


**Figure 3.4**
Basic types of control

In some cases the use of either of these two types of control will ensure adequately comprehensive control of the operating system for senior managers. In many cases, however, in order that the performance of the operating system can be monitored against *both* objectives, i.e. customer service objectives and resource utilization objectives, both types of control mechanism must be employed. It can be shown that the need to use both mechanisms in order to control performance against both objectives is mainly a function of operating system structure, the type of scheduling strategy, and the location of inventories.

For example, if the scheduling of activities within an operating system is undertaken primarily to satisfy internal (e.g. machine-loading) requirements, and does not take direct account of individual customers' delivery-date requirements, then it will be difficult to monitor customer service solely by monitoring the internal working of the operating system. In these circumstances an 'output' control measure will be needed to check on customer service, since a 'behaviour' control measure will monitor only resource utilization. Similarly, where an inventory or queue exists between the operating system and the customer, then what happens within the system is not necessarily directly linked to what happens for the customer at the same time. In these circumstances also both types of control must be employed if the performance of the operating system against both objectives is to be controlled. It follows that operations managers must seek to ensure that appropriate and adequate controls are applied to them, otherwise they will be assessed only on the achievement of one of their twin objectives, which in time can lead to a distortion of their behaviour with too much emphasis on that objective and consequent neglect of the other.

It can be argued that, in general, financial/accounting controls are primarily of the 'behaviour control' type. For example, budgetary control methods based on the calculation of cost variances, etc. are essentially a form of 'behaviour control'. It can be argued, therefore, that in many situations such controls in themselves are an inadequate means of providing management control over the operations function. In such circumstances, unless some other form of managerial control is employed, the operations manager's performance will be assessed largely in terms of productivity, with insufficient emphasis on customer service. It is for this reason that the operations manager must at least establish a close relationship with the finance manager, who will need to understand the nature, method of operation, strategies, etc. of the operating function in order to be able to implement comprehensive system managerial controls.

We shall look again at the use of management controls in dealing with performance measurements in Chapter 22.

**EXAMPLE**

## A private hospital

A small private hospital exists in an urban area. It is part of a larger company and it is run on a commercial basis. The hospital provides treatment and care for certain types of ailment. The operations manager is responsible for the administration of the entire hospital. She must achieve an annual profit, and her performance is monitored by the parent organization. The existing management controls monitor primarily the bed occupancy rates and length of patient stays in the hospital. The number of patient bed days per month is compared with the number of staff days worked, as a measure of labour productivity.

Patients are referred to the hospital by local doctors. They are placed on a waiting list and are admitted as soon as an appropriate bed becomes available in one of the small specialist wards. However, the admissions policy is not strictly on a 'first come first served' basis, since the hospital will often admit at the beginning of a week several patients who all need the same type of treatment, thus making it possible to schedule the work of the staff more easily. The lengths of waiting lists vary, but the hospital operations manager is anxious that they should not grow too long, as clearly one objective must be to satisfy the local doctors by ensuring that their patients are admitted without undue delay.

The operations manager is anxious that the management controls which are applied to her are adequate to measure her performance against her two objectives of resource utilization and customer service. She is aware that the present controls are largely of a 'behaviour control' type. She realizes that they focus on the 'internal' operations of the hospital, and is concerned that they over-emphasize performance related to productivity and resource utilization. She feels that in these circumstances such controls cannot monitor customer service, and intends therefore to persuade the parent organization that additional controls of the 'output control' type must be employed, aimed at collecting, directly from customers, information relating to customer service. She plans to put up specific proposals for additional measures which she hopes the parent company will use in controlling the hospital. (N.B. This case is further developed in Chapter 22.)

## OPERATIONS MANAGEMENT AND THE DESIGN OF PRODUCTS/SERVICES

The nature of the 'offering', i.e. the product or service for the market, was discussed in Chapter 2. We know there is a need for offering(s) with potential competitive advantages. We considered pricing, promotion, quality and other market-related issues earlier in this chapter. Here we will look briefly at the process by which such offerings are designed, for operations managers must contribute to that process if only to ensure that the final design or specification can be delivered or achieved in practice.

### The design process

While some of the procedures and techniques in this area have been evolved primarily in connection with product design, the basic ideas that we shall discuss apply equally to products and services.

Figure 3.5 outlines the steps involved in the traditional design process. These steps – from initial design concept through to *provision* by the operating system – traditionally involve several functions or departments in the organization. This can be a long process – several years in many industries – so it is often difficult to get new products or services quickly to market, and thus achieve competitive advantage on 'responsiveness' or 'speed'. We will return to this issue later but for the moment consider the processes covered by Figure 3.5.

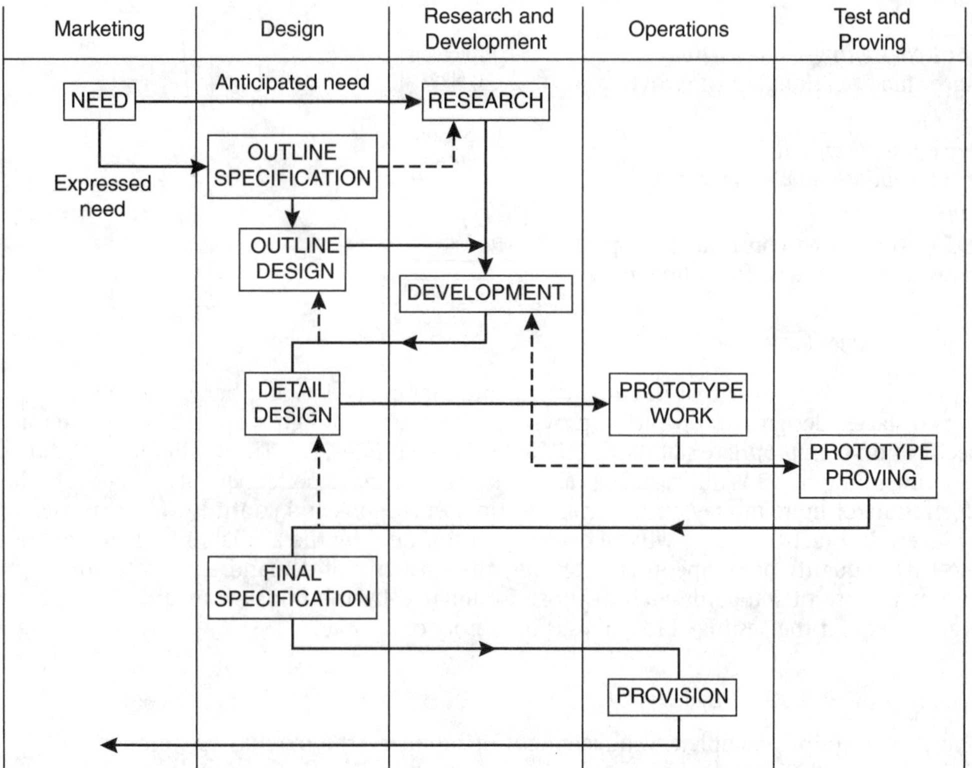


**Figure 3.5** The design process – *traditional model*

Figure 3.6 takes another look at the 'design to provision' process. It shows also that initial ideas, usually numerous, can be lost at each stage, and so the number surviving the whole process is very small. An outline description of the stages in the design process is given in Table 3.3.

## The role of operations

Operations has a contribution to make in stages 2, 3, 4, 5, 6 and 7 of Figure 3.6, for there is little benefit in conceiving a product which cannot efficiently, fully or economically be provided. Hence operations must enter into the design dialogue as follows:

***Stage 2: Screening and selection***
Can the product/service be provided by the operating system?
Do we have the processes, technology and skills?
Do we have the capacity?

***Stage 3: Initial design***
What is the most appropriate design for providability, at the required quality and probable cost required?

***Stage 4: Economic analysis***
How much would it cost to make the appropriate volumes, and at the required quality?

***Stage 5: Prototype testing***
Check providability through operating system

***Stage 6: Redesigning/modification***
Introduce modifications to improve providability

***Stage 7: Final specification***
Ensure appropriate quality specifications
Begin process specification

In making the above contribution, operations must have regard to the following.

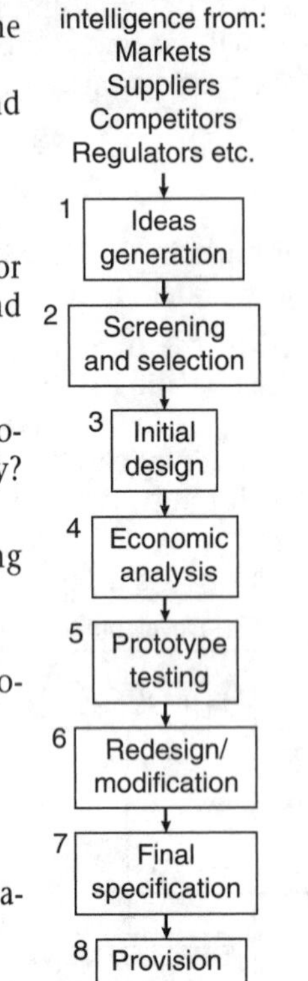


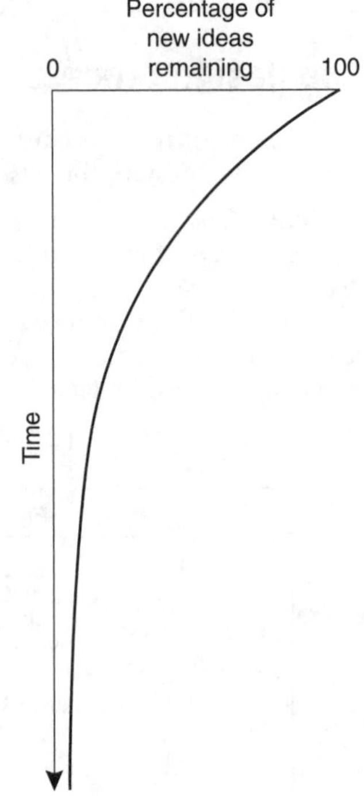


**Figure 3.6** The 'design to provision' process and the progress of ideas

### **Quality** *(see also Chapter 19)*

In Chapter 19 we shall show that the quality of a product or service, and hence reliability, is invested during two stages: design and operation/provision. During the design stage quality is determined by the specification of appropriate standards on dimensions, content, etc. The quality level obtained is, of course, a function of cost. While nothing can be designed to have perfect quality or perfect reliability, the expenditure of more money on materials, testing, operations and control will, of course, improve quality levels. In practice quality will be determined not only by the availability of suitable resources but also by the quality of competitors' offerings, the elasticity of demand and the planned price. In many cases the use of standards such as those formulated by the British Standards Institution or the American Society for the Testing of Materials is obligatory or advisable.

### **Purchasing** *(see also Chapter 16)*

Since no organization is completely independent of suppliers, the purchasing function will influence design. The new design will depend not only on the ready availability of certain purchased items but on the redesign, i.e. modification, replacement or improvement, of existing items. The purchasing

**Table 3.3 Stages in the design process**

1. **Ideas generation**
   Market- or technology-oriented ideas
   New concepts or incremental developments
   Internally or externally generated
2. **Screening and selection**
   Market analysis test
   Technological feasibility
   Competitive advantage
   Risk assessments
3. **Initial design**
   Specification of major aspects/features
   Initial model/'mock-up'
4. **Economic analysis**
   Estimate of development cost
   Estimate of provision cost, thus:
   Estimate of final cost
   Estimate of price
5. **Prototype testing**
   Performance/function testing
   Consumer tests
   Test of 'providability'
6. **Redesign/modification**
   Improvements, corrections and modifications
   Retesting if necessary
   Approval for final design
7. **Final specification**
   Full detailed specification of content, structure, function and performance

department will play an important part because of its knowledge of such factors in the development of new or improved items and services.

## *Make or buy decision* (see also Chapter 16)

Theoretically, every item or service which is currently purchased from an outside supplier is a candidate for internal provision and vice versa. In reality the problem is not quite so extensive as this, since there will always be many things which it would just not be in our interest to provide ourselves. Similarly, there will always be many things which it would not be in our interest to purchase. By making an item or providing a service ourselves we reduce our dependence on other companies, we are able to determine our own quality levels and we preserve our trade secrets. Conversely, to purchase rather than provide ourselves may enable us to obtain them more quickly, and to obtain the benefits of a continual development programme which we ourselves could not sustain. Additionally, purchase instead of self-provision may reduce costs such as those associated with storage, handling, paperwork, etc. as well as releasing our facilities for jobs on which they might be more suitably and profitably employed.

## *Standardization*

Specifications provide details of product or service requirements in terms of content, performance, and so on, while standards are rules, models or criteria against which comparisons can be made. Standardization is therefore concerned with the concept of variety, and, more specifically, with the control of necessary variety. Company standardization begins to operate once unnecessary variety has been eliminated. The elimination of unnecessary variety (variety reduction) can be defined as 'the process of eliminating the unnecessary diversity' which frequently exists in the various stages from design to provision and is undertaken in anticipation of obtaining some or all of the following advantages:

(a) increased interchangeability of items or services;

(b) provision of goods/services, or parts of them, in larger quantities, with better resource utilization;

(c) staff training is simplified;

(d) record-keeping and inventory control is simplified;

(e) greater flexibility is possible;

(f) reduced cost and price.

## Simultaneous development

Many companies, particularly in manufacturing industries such as the automotive, electronics and domestic appliance industries, have discovered that their competitors can get new items into the market far quicker than they are able to do. In other words they cannot compete on 'responsiveness'. 'Time to market', i.e. to get a totally new product/service through from concept to the customer, has for certain outstanding companies often been less than half that of the average company. This was evident in comparisons of Japanese motor-vehicle manufacturers compared to those in Europe and the USA. Especially in high-technology sectors, this competitive advantage was considerable – it enabled those organizations to be able to continually demonstrate technological superiority in the market-place, even though they may have had no greater access to new technology than their slower competitors. In order to improve 'time to market', organizations have sought to 'streamline', and thus speed up, the design/development process by achieving simultaneous rather than sequential activity.

'Simultaneous development' aims to optimize the design to provision process, to achieve reduced lead times, improved quality and cost, by integrating the stages of the process through maximum parallelisms of working practices. Critical elements of this revised process include:

(a) the use of multi-disciplinary/multi-departmental task forces or project teams in design and development;

(b) improved communications between functions/disciplines;

(c) simultaneous development of the product/service, the progress quality control and marketing processes;

(d) design for 'providability' and performance.

Figure 3.7 provides a comparison between the traditional and simultaneous approaches, highlighting the problems of the transition from one to the other.

**Figure 3.7** Comparison: design/development processes

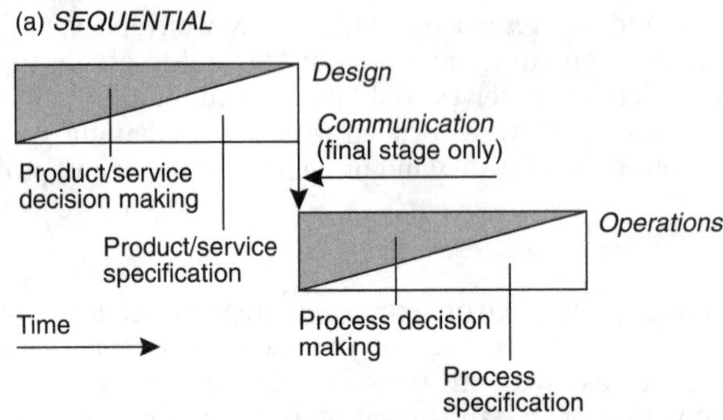


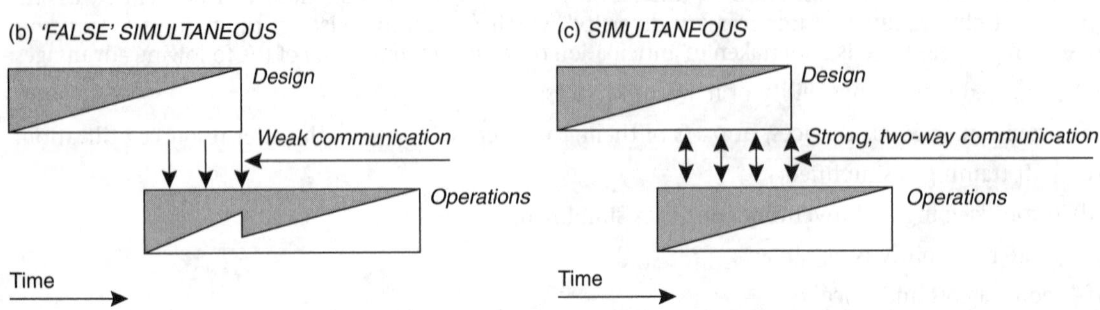

**EXAMPLE**

### *Sun Microsystems*

Known as the business team, the Sun Microsystems approach to concurrent or simultaneous engineering is used during the introduction of new products. The business team consists of representatives from design engineering, manufacturing, customer service, finance and marketing. The team creates a formal plan that is submitted to an executive-level committee within the corporation. This plan, known as the product approval form, is essentially a product-specific business plan. Once the team has an approved PAF, the next step is the establishment of tactical implementation teams and the construction of the programme's communications infrastructure. Through the cross-functional deployment of manufacturing and engineering staff under the business team organization, Sun achieves rapid and on-time delivery at cost, with high quality and no major engineering changes.

Source: Siegal, B. (1991) Organizing for a successful CE process. *Industrial Engineering*, **23**(12), pp. 15–19.

## Designing 'services' – the differences

All of the concepts, etc. outlined above apply to the 'design through to provision' process for goods and services. However, there are some distinctive aspects in 'service' design which should be noted. These will be of particular relevance to those involved in supply, transport and service-type operations as defined in Chapter 1.

The first thing to note is that, as far as the customer is concerned, there is no physical product involved in transport and service systems. That is not to say that no products are used, but rather that they are the products of other organizations, acquired and used by the system rather than being designed and provided by it. Supply systems do bring products into contact with customers, but again they are the products of other organizations and are designed by them.

In general, in designing the offerings of supply, transport and service systems, more emphasis will be placed on the process, i.e. the operation itself, in which the customer takes some part. Thus the relative effort required and the time devoted to initial idea generation are less. The main task is to design the process which delivers the service idea. For this reason, operations managers will probably be more involved, and from an early stage. However, there will still exist opportunities for achieving economies through simultaneous development.

The provision of supply, transport and service will usually be a labour-intensive process, so labour will be a critical factor in evaluating whether a system can deliver services at adequate quality, etc.

The lead time for the design and development of such offerings will often be shorter than for product design and development. 'Prototype' testing will often be more difficult to achieve, and of course such offerings, when finalized, cannot be protected with patents.

The equivalent to a design 'blueprint' for a service is usually a flow chart, which shows, in detail, the processes through which a customer will pass. Examination of that flow chart will often show that there are some activities which, whilst esssential for the delivery of the offering, are nevertheless separated from the customer – a type of technical core which for the customer remains in the background. Often, securing efficiency and effectiveness in supply, transport and service systems involves separating that core, or decoupling it from the 'up-front' system, so as to be able to operate an efficient repetitive high-volume activity, whilst exposing the customer to the minimal actual contact with the organization to deliver the required benefit. The 'behind the scenes' activities in freight companies, hospitals, etc. are good examples.

Finally, we might note that, as with product design and development, it is often the customer who specifies the design through an expressed need. Nevertheless, in all types of operation there is always the possibility of developing something entirely new which customers will be found to want, even though they could not express a prior need.

## CHECKLIST FOR CHAPTER 3

### *Operations management and marketing*

The marketing function
- Four market mix decisions
- Environmental variables
- Competitive variables

Decisions on goods/service characteristics
- Growth policies and product/service decisions
- Life-cycles
- The development process
- Market policies
- Quality, brand and brand policy

Decisions on cost
- Price decisions
- Relative importance of price and non-price variables
- Pricing policy

Decisions on distribution
- Distribution channels
- Physical distribution management

Decisions on promotion
- Advertising
- Selling
- Publicity
- Sales promotion

The relationships of operations management and marketing decisions
- Demand considerations
- Forecasting

### *Operations management and organization*

Technology and organization
- Technology factors: definitions
- Organization factors: definitions
- Relationships of technology and organization factors

Technology factors and operations management
- Influence of operations management decisions on work technology
- Influence of operations management on organization structure

### *Operations management and the finance/accounting function*

Managerial and financial controls
- Types of control
  - Behaviour control mechanism
  - Output control mechanism
  - Need for controls on operations management
  - Financial control as a control mechanism
  - Need for dual controls on operations management

### *Operations management and the design of products/services*

The design process
- The traditional model – design to provision
- The role of operations
- Quality factors
- Purchasing issues
- Make/buy decisions
- Standardization

Simultaneous development
- Comparison – design/development processes
- Requirement of simultaneous development
- Design services – the differences

## FURTHER READING

For a more detailed description of the functions covered in this chapter see, for example:

**Cannon, T. (1995)** *Basic Marketing*, 4th edn. London: Cassell.

**Khandwalla, P. N. (1977)** *Design of Organizations*. London: Harcourt Brace Jovanovich.

**Lovelock, C. (1992)** Seeking synergy in service operations – seven things marketing needs to know about service operations. *Euro Management Journal*, **10**(1), pp. 22–29.

The following deals specifically with design/development and 'simultaneous engineering':

**Clark, K. and Fujimoto, T. (1993)** Product development performances: strategy, organization and management in the world auto industry. *Interfaces*, Jan./Feb., pp. 140–141.

'Behaviour' and 'output' controls are discussed in the following:

**Guehi, W. G. (1977)** The relationship between organisational structure and organisational control. *Administrative Science Quarterly*, **22**(i), pp. 95–113.

## QUESTIONS

3.1 In what way can 'marketing mix' decisions influence the customer demand on the operating system?

3.2 How does the performance of the operating system influence decisions on the 'marketing mix' variables? In other words, to what extent and in what way does the success with which the operations manager achieves his or her objective influence any one, or all four, of the marketing mix variables, i.e. product/service characteristics, cost, distribution and promotion?

3.3 Identify and discuss the principal considerations and factors which will be taken into account in determining the nature of the goods or services to be provided by the organization.

3.4 What factors or variables can be manipulated in order to create particular market/demand conditions and how might decisions on these factors/variables be made?

3.5 How might the operations manager's decisions on operating systems structure affect the nature of jobs within the organization and the manner in which the organization must operate?

3.6 A particular organization has a high degree of task uncertainty and workflow uncertainty. Comment on the manner in which decisions might be made within the organization, the nature of the roles, procedures and practices within that organization, and the authority structures.

3.7 Appropriate management control procedures are to be introduced in order to ensure that the operating system achieves its twin, and equally important, objectives. For each of the seven basic types of system structure, indicate whether an output control mechanism alone, or a behaviour control mechanism alone, or both mechanisms, will be necessary if performance of both objectives is to be monitored.

3.8 Select a particular type of service, and describe how a 'simultaneous development' approach might shorten the time required to develop a replacement service, and get that service to the market.

## CASE STUDIES (from Part 9)

The topics covered in this chapter are relevant in the following (see Introduction to Part 9 and Table C.1 for further details):

| No. | Name | Country |
|---|---|---|
| 11 | St John's Church | UK |
| 27 | Food Concept Sdn. Bhd. | Malaysia |

Chapter 4

# Operations economics and costs

## ISSUES

What are operations costs?
What factors influence operations costs?
What are economics of scale and 'scope'?
What is a 'breakeven' point?
How are costs controlled?

The transformation process within any business adds value and cost to the goods or service output from the system. In a manufacturing system the cost of physical conversion, e.g. materials processing and assembly, will often represent a major part of the total cost of the products produced. In transport, the cost of moving the customer, comprising the cost of the equipment used (e.g. the vehicles and service equipment) and the cost of the labour employed, as well as any overheads, will often be a major ingredient determining the total cost of the transport to the customer. Similarly, in supply and service systems the operations function, which is the responsibility of the operations manager, will add significant cost to the total cost of the items or service provided for the eventual customer. Given this responsibility for 'cost contribution', the operations manager must be familiar with the factors contributing to the cost of operations, the factors influencing these costs, and the means available for the measurement and control of the cost of operations.

Without venturing into a detailed discussion of either microeconomics or cost accounting, we must here devote some time to a consideration of the nature of the costs associated with operations and the means available for the control of such costs.

## OPERATIONS COSTS *(see also Chapter 22)*

The components of operations costs may be direct or indirect. *Direct costs* (or the prime cost) comprise those which may be identified separately for each good or service produced, e.g. the cost of the direct materials consumed or incorporated and the cost of the direct labour involved in the provision of output items or services.

*Indirect costs* (or operations overheads) are all other expenses which cannot be charged specifically to particular output items, services or transports. Indirect costs include the cost of indirect materials, indirect labour and all other charges involved in operating the system where such charges cannot be allocated realistically or accurately to particular goods or services, e.g. administration costs.

**Figure 4.1** Operations and total cost

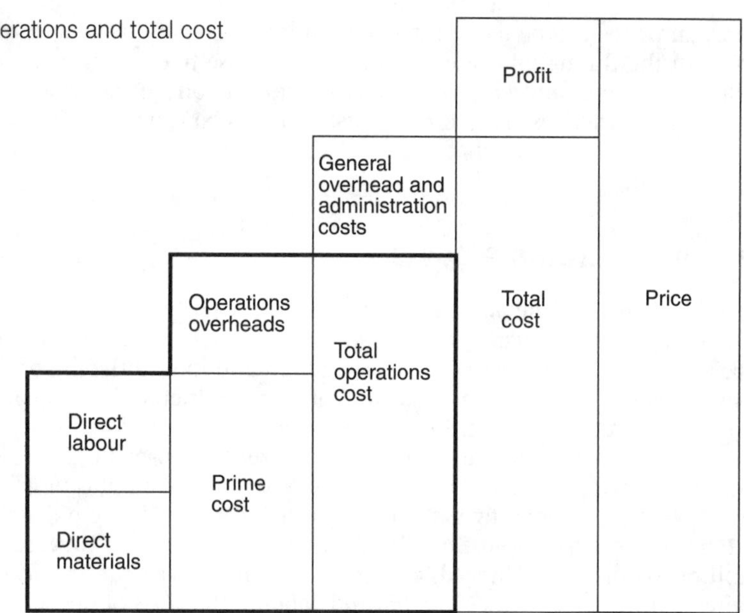


Together these costs might be seen, sequentially, to build up to the *total operations cost* and thus, with the general and administrative costs and the profit, to the total cost to the customer, i.e. the selling or purchase price, in the manner shown in Figure 4.1. It will be noticed that while the prime cost is normally considered to comprise the sum of direct labour and materials, no provision is made for direct costs associated with the third of the major resource inputs to the operating system, i.e. the machinery employed. The assumption here, as is usually the case in practice, is that machinery is used for multiple purposes and its costs therefore cannot normally be seen as a direct charge; they must be allocated as part of the overheads associated with the operation. Although in some cases expenses other than those associated with labour and materials can be charged directly to particular outputs, other expenses are normally seen as part of the operations overheads. The operations overheads can, in turn, be subdivided into material, labour and other expenses in the manner outlined in Table 4.1.

**Table 4.1 Operations overheads**

| | | Other expenses | |
|---|---|---|---|
| **Indirect materials** | **Indirect labour** | **Standing costs** | **General costs** |
| Tools | Supervision | Rent | Management |
| Consumed materials | Technical services | Depreciation | Welfare costs |
| | Transport | Insurance | Planning |
| | Quality control | Rates | Services |
| | Operations control | | Power |
| | | | Maintenance |

Operations managers are responsible for the total operations cost. They will be interested in the components of this cost, and will also be interested in the distinction between *fixed* and *variable* costs. Over a fairly short period of time certain of the organization's costs, in particular those associated with the operating system, can be seen to be fixed; they will not be affected by changes in the scale of the operation, i.e. changes in the throughput rate or output rate. These fixed costs will include many of the operations overheads, e.g. rent and rates on premises, depreciation on significant items of equipment, and insurance. Certain other costs, e.g. direct costs, in particular wages and the cost of consumer materials, will vary in the short term in that they will increase roughly in proportion to increased throughput or output, and vice versa.

## Factors influencing operations costs

Clearly the objectives established for the operating system will have fairly substantial cost implications. For example, in a manufacturing system the need to produce high-quality items may necessitate different manufacturing methods, the use of different materials and indeed the use of different labour from what would have been the case in the manufacture of a similar item of lower quality. The cost of manufacturing to this higher quality, other things being equal, will therefore be higher. It follows that the specification of the item to be produced, or in the case of non-manufacturing systems the specification of the service or transport to be provided, has significant implications for the cost of operations. The way in which the operating system is managed, e.g. the choice of batch sizes and the scheduling of operations, must also have cost implications. The productivity of the resources employed will clearly affect unit operations costs. Indeed, taking an economist's view of operations and considering the principal prerequisites to be 'land', 'capital' and 'labour', the costs of operations may depend on the nature of the mix of these ingredients. In certain industries the value added to inputs is very much greater. Such differences cannot be attributed solely to the productivity of the various operations resources, but rather to the nature and mixture of these resources. For example, the greater the quantity of machinery the lower the labour charges per unit of output. Thus where labour charges are high there will be some benefit in substituting machinery for labour, despite the fact that the additional machinery incurs depreciation, maintenance and other costs. Comparisons between industries will provide the opportunity only for long-term control and not enough opportunity for day-to-day control of costs within the operations function. For this reason certain budgeting and cost control systems must be employed (see below).

It should also be noted that certain scale factors are associated with the cost of operations, so that with increasing throughput or output rates unit costs might be reduced. These are discussed in the following section.

# OPERATIONS ECONOMICS

Figure 4.2 illustrates some aspects of the relationship between operations cost and output (or throughput) rate. Over a short period certain of the operations costs can be seen to be fixed while others, the variable costs, will increase as output or the scale of operations increases. Initially this increase will be fairly rapid, then will become more stable, and eventually become rapid as the maximum possible output or throughput rate is reached, and as bottlenecks are experienced and overtime working/subcontracting, etc. becomes necessary. The sum of the fixed variable costs is shown in Figure 4.2 as the total operations costs.

Also shown in Figure 4.2 is a curve representing revenue, i.e. the income generated from customers in payment for the goods or services provided by the operating system, and a curve representing the profit associated with that output, i.e. revenue less total costs. Total revenue rises as the organization is able to expand its scale of operations and thus its sales, although eventually revenue will reach a maximum point as price is lowered in order to stimulate further sales. The profits are maximized at a point where the difference between the total revenue and total cost curve is greatest. Notice that in most cases this profit maximization point occurs at a lower level than the point of maximum revenue, which in turn occurs at less than maximum output/sales.

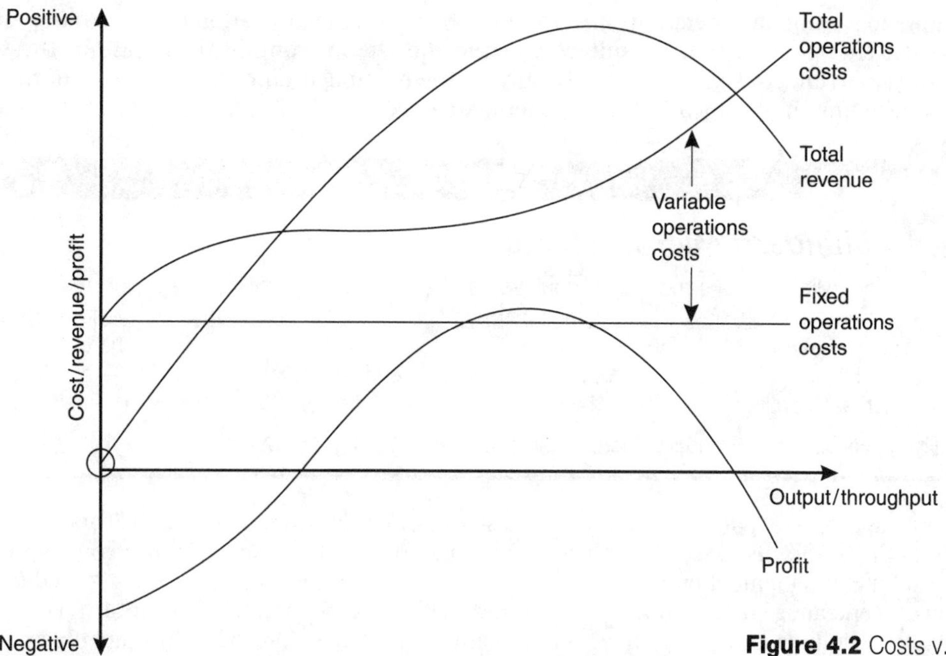


**Figure 4.2** Costs v. output

The relationship which will be of particular interest to the operations manager is that between the cost per unit throughput or output and the level or scale of throughput or output. In the short term the operations manager might seek to alter output byvarying the amount of variable factors employed, e.g. materials and labour, whereas in the longer term all factors can be varied. In the short term the unit cost structure might appear as in Figure 4.3. As fixed costs remain the same, the fixed cost per unit will fall as output or throughput increases. The variable cost per unit will fall at first and then rise as further variable factors are employed in order to expand output or throughput. Figure 4.4 shows the long-run average total cost–output relationship. Superimposed on this long-run average total cost curve is an average total cost curve for a short-run period. Thus while in the short term increasing output or throughput from $Q_1$ to $Q_2$ will give rise to a U-shaped curve representing falling unit total cost followed by increasing total costs, in the long run, since the 'fixed' factors can also be varied, the unit total cost curve should continue to fall. Thus in the long term, since all the factors can be considered variable, increasing output should result in economies of scale reflected in reduced unit costs.

**Figure 4.3** Short-term unit cost–output relationship

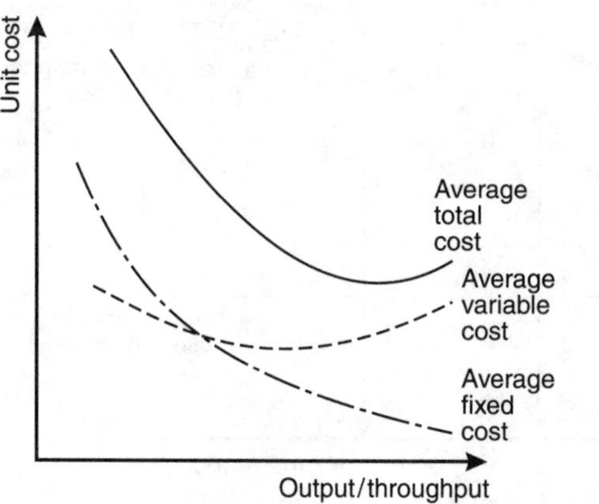


**Figure 4.4** Long-term unit cost–output relationship

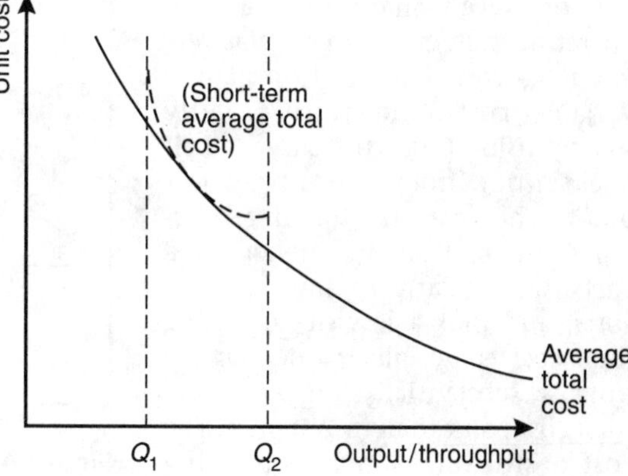

It follows that while the operations manager might, by clever combination of the resources at his or her disposal, effect a reduction in unit cost in the short term, continued increase in the scale of operations can be undertaken economically only by the manipulation of the mix of all of the factors involved, including those which in the short term are fixed.

**EXAMPLE**

### Standard Microsystems

In 1991, Standard Microsystems more than doubled its size with the acquisition of a major product line from another company. The focus, now, of the combined operations is on devices supplied to the fast-growing field of local area networks. As a result of the acquisition, Standard greatly expanded its market share, got into newer technologies and lowered its cost through economies of scale and vertical integration. The acquisition enabled Standard to increase earnings substantially by the end of 1992, and reverse the previous loss-making situation.

Source: Byrne, H. S. (1992) Standard Microsystems. *Barron's*, **72**(32), pp. 35–36.

This is an appropriate point at which to contrast economies of *scale* and of *scope*. Economies of scale derive from the factors discussed above. The achievement of such economies has been one of the objectives behind the development of operations in many sectors. In other words, the drive for reduced costs has tended to encourage organizations to try to deal with larger volumes, which in turn has tended to reduce variety. Volume and variety have traditionally been seen as somewhat incompatible.

Market pressures on organizations to provide a variety of types of output or service, at competitive cost, and with minimum delay, have focused attention on how best to achieve economies of *scope*. This has led to the development of operating systems which are efficient and flexible. We will consider this again in Chapter 14. In fact the real basis for achieving such economies differs little from that of economies of scale, i.e. the possibility of spreading fixed costs over a larger output. The only fundamental difference is how this larger output is achieved. In the case of economies of scale it is achieved through repetition, while in the case of economies of scope it is achieved by making the processing requirements of non-identical items as similar as possible, which in turn requires careful design, process planning, and facilities design.

## Breakeven point

A breakeven point chart also shows the relationship between output or throughput on the one hand and cost on the other. Figure 4.5 shows two breakeven charts. A chart for operating system A shows relatively low fixed costs but fairly substantial variable costs and thus a fairly steeply rising total cost curve, albeit one starting from a relatively low point. The cost structure for operating system B shows higher fixed costs with relatively low variable costs, and thus a less steeply rising total cost curve, albeit one starting from a substantially higher initial total cost point than in system A. The cost structure for operating

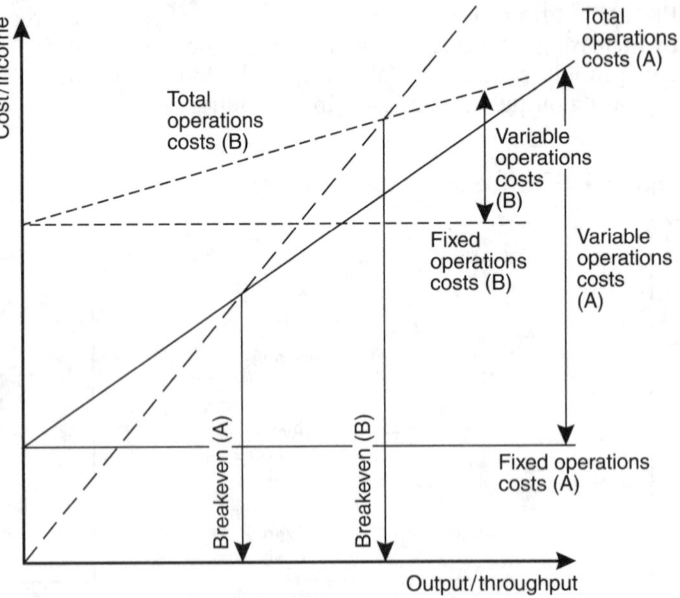


**Figure 4.5** Breakeven charts

system B might reflect the higher capital investment of that system, whereas operating system A may be more dependent on the use of overtime work, double staffing, etc. to achieve increased outputs. Notice that because of the differing cost structures the breakeven point, i.e. the point at which income begins to exceed total costs, is lower for operating system A than it is for B but that the excess of income over total cost increases less rapidly beyond the breakeven point in the case of operating system B. A point worth noting, therefore, is that for systems dependent on greater fixed costs, greater output must be achieved before a breakeven point is reached but that, thereafter, rewards are likely to increase at a greater rate.

**EXAMPLE**

*Breakeven calculation*

Current costs and sales @ 100% capacity:

Annual sales = £200 000
Fixed costs = £80 000
Variable costs = £100 000

What is current breakeven capacity now, and how would this change if fixed costs increased to £90 000 while variable costs fell to £65 000?

| Calculations (£000) | | Percentage capacity used 0% | 100% |
|---|---|---|---|
| *Present situation* | Sales | – | 200 |
| | Fixed costs | 80 | 80 |
| | Variable costs | – | 100 |
| | Profit | –80 | +20 |
| *New situation* | Sales | – | 200 |
| | Fixed costs | 90 | 90 |
| | Variable costs | – | 65 |
| | Profit | –90 | +45 |

**Figure 4.6**

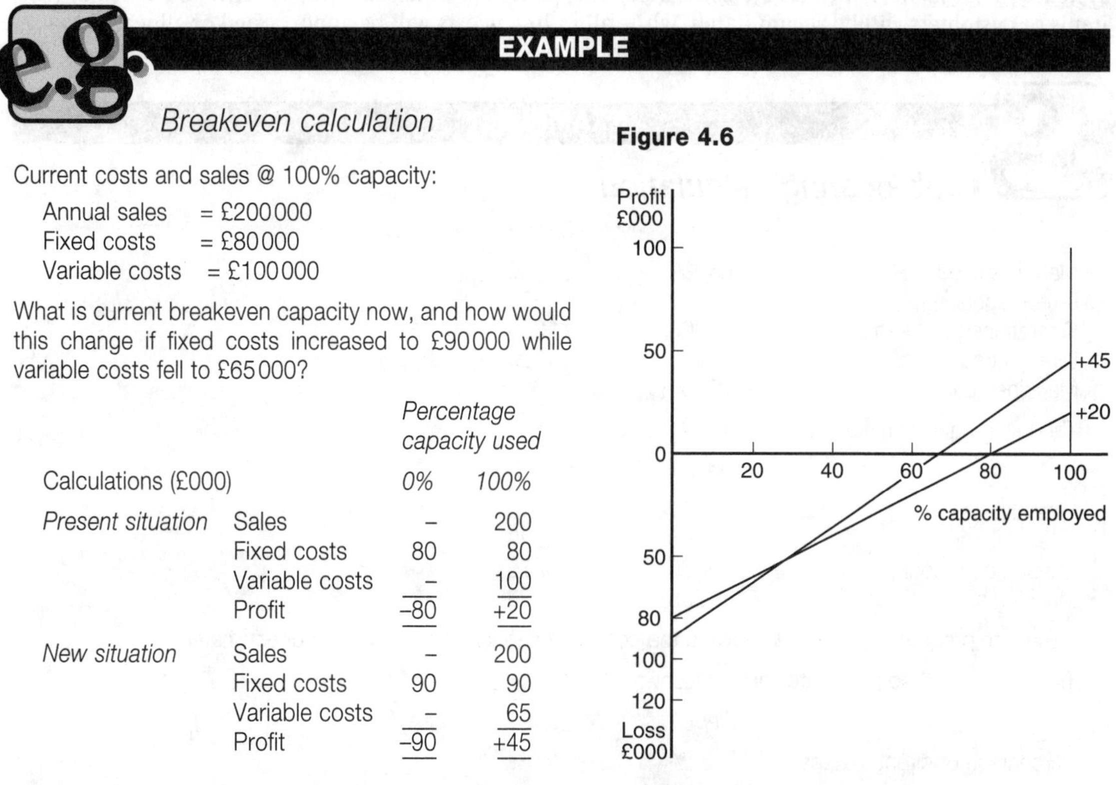


From Figure 4.6: breakeven capacity = present situation, 80%; new situation, 68%.

## COST CONTROL SYSTEMS *(see also Chapters 3 and 21)*

Some form of cost accounting or cost control system will be essential within an organization and will be of considerable importance to the operations manager. As with all such managerial control systems the operations manager will seek to employ the cost control mechanisms to sustain and improve the efficiency of the operating system, whereas his or her superiors will use the same cost information, albeit analysed somewhat differently, as a means of establishing objectives for and maintaining control over the operations manager.

From the operations manager's viewpoint, therefore, the cost control mechanism provides a means of assessing the efficiency of the operating system, noting significant variations from normal or budgeted performance, assessing the efficiency of new operating methods, determining the relative allocation of resources, determining the capacity required, etc. The cost control or cost accounting system adopted by an organization, and thus by the operations manager, will depend largely on the scale and nature of the organization, in particular on the type of operating system employed and the type of goods/services provided. Basically, two types of costing system can be identified: job costing and process costing.

## Job costing

Job costing is often employed by organizations which produce goods or provide services, transport, etc. to the specific requirements of the customer. In job costing, items or customers passing through the system remain identifiable and are associated with particular costs. All costs specific to particular jobs, items or customers will be accumulated, while all indirect costs will be apportioned or allocated to jobs so that on completion the total cost of each job is ascertained.

**EXAMPLE**

### *Job costing calculation*

| | *Dept 1* | *Dept 2* |
|---|---|---|
| Materials used | £6000 | £500 |
| Direct labour | £3000 | £1500 |
| Operations overheads | £1800 | £1200 |
| Direct labour hours | 12000 | 5000 |
| Machine hours | 10000 | 2000 |

The following information relates to job A:

| | *Dept 1* | *Dept 2* |
|---|---|---|
| Materials used | £120 | £10 |
| Direct labour | £65 | £25 |
| Direct labour hours | 265 | 70 |
| Machine hours | 255 | 25 |

We are to prepare a statement showing the cost for job A as a percentage of direct material.

The overhead absorption rates are as follows:

| | *Dept 1* | *Dept 2* |
|---|---|---|
| Percentage of direct material | 30% | 240% |

Cost of job A:

| | *Dept 1* £ | *Dept 2* £ | *Total* £ |
|---|---|---|---|
| Material | 120 | 10 | 130 |
| Direct labour | 65 | 25 | 90 |
| Prime cost | 185 | 35 | 220 |
| Operations overheads | 36 | 24 | 60 |
| Total cost | 221 | 59 | 280 |

(Based on Sizer, J. (1979) *An Insight into Management Accounting*. Harmondsworth: Penguin.)

## Process costing

Process costing is used by organizations engaged in more repetitive activities, i.e. where the operating system is devoted to the provision of a relatively small variety of goods, services or transport on a fairly repetitive basis. Since in such situations it is not practical to identify separate items of throughput, unit costs are determined by dividing the total costs of each process by the number of units, i.e. goods or customers output or throughput, making allowances for items partially completed or customers partially serviced at the beginning and the end of the costing period.

## Budgeting

The long-range plans formulated for the organization must be translated into detailed short-term plans or budgets for individual departments. The performance of departments, including the operating system, will be evaluated against these departmental budgets. The operations budget will specify the output or throughput required as well as the planned direct and indirect costs, broken down into appropriate detail. Preparation of this budget will involve apportioning or allocating operations overheads on some equitable basis between departments and/or 'jobs'. Overheads might be apportioned in proportion to the direct wages or direct materials costs, etc. The budget will make a distinction between current costs and revenue items and capital expenditure items. The former comprise such things as wages, salaries and materials costs. The latter group includes expenditure on equipment and building.

Once budgets have been established and the periods to which they relate have commenced, the actual costs incurred during each period must be collected for subsequent comparison.

## Standard costing

Standard costing is widely used in industries where rapid cost feedback information is required, i.e. where operations take place on a relatively short cycle time. In such circumstances costs are estimated and compared with actual costs on a month-by-month basis. The estimate is referred to as the 'standard cost'. Standard costs for items or services are established by category, e.g. labour, materials and overheads, based on predicted prices, labour rates and other expenses for the given period. Variations from predicted costs can be assessed and the necessary action taken to prevent their recurrence without having to wait for the end of the costing period, e.g. one year, before the necessary cost control information is available.

## Marginal costing

Accurate standard costs necessitate the use of realistic means and bases for the apportionment of overhead costs to departments, cost centres, jobs, etc., and accurate pre-estimation of throughput or output volumes as bases for establishing cost rates. The use of marginal costing avoids these problems. After distinguishing direct from overhead costs, marginal costing divides overheads into those which vary with output and those which are fixed. Direct costs are also divided into the categories 'variable' and 'fixed'. All variable costs are then related to units of throughput/output while fixed costs are not charged to separate units but kept as a single block to be set against revenues earned by the throughputs of the system. Thus with marginal costing the cost of unit throughput or output is considered to comprise direct material, direct labour and direct expenses plus their variable overheads only, the total being the variable cost per unit output/throughput. This variable cost is in fact the marginal cost, since it is the amount by which total cost would increase as a result of the processing of one extra unit. Marginal costing provides a convenient way of assessing the effects of volume on profits and can be used in conjunction with the breakeven chart approach.

## Activity-based costing

An activity-based costing (ABC) system generates costs by relating consumption of resources to activities, with greater discrimination than does a system of traditional accounting methods such as those described above. The system accomplishes this by identifying and differentiating the various types of activities that support operations. It is based on the premise that outputs consume activities, activities consume resources, and resources consume cost. There are two types of activities in an ABC system:

1. direct or conversion activities, which are consumed directly at the point of operation; and
2. indirect or sustained activities, which support operations but are not directly consumed by the process. An ABC system must be designed for a specific operations environment. It is partly this custom approach which gives ABC its strength.

**EXAMPLE**

## *ABC in manufacture*

A \$100m per annum plumbing fixture manufacturer had a vertically integrated 720 000-ft$^2$ factory. The firm sold a very large number of products. There was a large overhead structure that amounted to almost 60% of the cost of goods sold. When the company began losing money, it decided to conduct a study to reduce costs and improve profitability. The firm could not be competitive in all of the many manufacturing processes it performed, and its current labour and depreciation-based cost allocation system would not adequately support 'make or buy' decision-making. The manufacturing operations had to be recosted. An ABC system was developed. Overhead allocations were accumulated into two groups:

1. elements driven by volume, and
2. elements driven by transactions.

The impact of different manufacturing options was estimated using the cost database and actual data from similar case studies. The company succeeded in implementing both product-line reductions and manufacturing configuration changes.

Source: P'Guin, M. (1990) Focus the factory with activity-based costing. *Management Accounting*, **71**(8), pp. 36–41.

## CHECKLIST FOR CHAPTER 4

### Operations costs

Price = Profit + Total cost

Total cost = General and administration costs + Total operations costs

Total operations costs = Operations overheads + Prime cost

Prime cost = Direct labour + Direct materials

Factors influencing operations costs

- Quality
- Mix
- Volume
- Economics of scale and scope

### Operations economics

Cost v. output, long term

Cost v. output, short term

Breakeven point

### Cost control systems

Job costing

Process costing

Budgeting

Standard costing

Marginal costing

Activity-based costing

## FURTHER READING

**Blank, L. T. and Tarquin, A. T. (1989)** *Engineering Economy*, 3rd edn. New York: McGraw-Hill.

**Drury, C. (1990)** *Costing – an Introduction*, 2nd edn. London: Chapman & Hall.

**Horngren, C. T. (1990)** *Cost Accounting*, 7th edn. Hemel Hempstead: Prentice-Hall.

**Kaplan, R. S. (1992)** In defense of activity-based cost management. *Management Accounting*, **74**(5), pp. 58–63.

## QUESTIONS

4.1 Within organizations overheads are usually divided between operations overheads and general and administrative overheads and costs (including administrative overheads and selling and distribution overheads). Explain why this distinction is made and suggest methods by which each class of overhead can be absorbed or allocated to units of throughput/output.

4.2 The following data relate to a company:

Total capacity, 75 000 units
Fixed costs, £12 000 per annum
Variable expenses, 75p per unit
Sales prices, up to 4000 units £1.50 per unit and then over 4000 units £1.00 per unit

Draft a breakeven chart incorporating these data.

4.3 Throughput volumes (or output volumes) can affect unit operating costs. In addition, batch volumes can affect unit costs. Both output/throughput volumes and costs are related to profits. Outline the nature of these relationships, illustrating your answer with simple graphs.

4.4 How, in the long term, might a transport organization seek to reduce unit total operations costs beyond the level available in the short term?

4.5 You plan to go into the mail order business. You will advertise and sell (cash with order) personal stationery. The following two alternatives are available to you depending on the quality of the product:

| | | £ |
|---|---|---|
| Option 1 | Cost, to you, of product | 8.00 |
| | Cost of processing each order | 1.25 |
| | Cost of advertising | 220.00 |
| | Overhead: 100% of product cost | |
| Option 2 | Cost, to you, of product | 6.75 |
| | Cost of processing each order | 1.20 |
| | Cost of advertising | 350.00 |
| | Overhead: 100% of product cost | |

Compare the two options on a breakeven analysis. Which option would you employ if you expected sales of 30 products?

## CASE STUDIES (from Part 9)

The topics covered in this chapter are relevant in the following (see Introduction to Part 9 and Table C.1 for further details):

| No. | Name | Country |
|---|---|---|
| 6 | Bourg Breton | France |
| 18 | La Patisserie – B | UK |

PART 3

# The Arrangement of Facilities

Introduction to Part 3
Chapter 5 Location of facilities
Chapter 6 The layout of facilities and materials handling

## INTRODUCTION TO PART 3

This part deals with locational and layout decisions. We look at the relatively rare problem of locating internationally an entirely new facility. We also deal with the problem of locating an additional new facility for an organization, to provide access to existing facilities, suppliers and markets. In Chapter 6 we look at layout decisions – themselves a form of layout problem – and at materials handling. We look at the problem of arranging an entirely new layout for a facility, and consider also the modification of existing facilities and the addition of new departments or items of equipment to existing facilities. Throughout we consider the nature of the problems involved and introduce some relevant procedures and techniques. We emphasize computer-based techniques, for this is an area in which numerous alternative solutions exist and where there is considerable merit in obtaining some alternative solutions quickly and economically.

## STRATEGIC CONTEXT

The operations issues, problems and decisions considered in this part of the book exist within the broader strategic context of the organization. The main relationships are set out here, as a preface to the details which follow.

### Influences of business policy decisions (see Chapter 2, Figure 2.2)

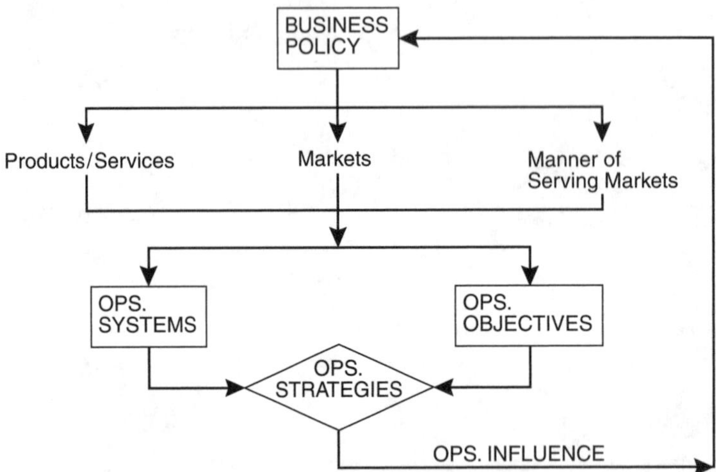


Location decisions are essentially to do with placing an operation relative to those who supply it with inputs and those who benefit from its services or outputs. The nature of these two groups and the relationships which are required with them will be influenced by strategic/policy issues.

Therefore, any business policy requirements which emphasize speed of service to customers, or ease of access by customers, will be reflected in the operations objective of customer service or timing and will, in turn, encourage the choice of locations close to markets. Any business policy requirements which stress cost may influence the structures of the operation, e.g. by encouraging the reduction

– even elimination – of input resource stocks, which will in turn encourage proximity to suppliers. An emphasis on both speed and cost will encourage a locational choice with proximity to both suppliers and customers.

For an existing location, operations managers will be accustomed to handling input and output relationships, and will have views on what can be achieved with the given location. They will therefore wish to influence or inform any prospective business policy decision which might depend, for its implementation, on achieving particular relationships with suppliers (e.g. frequency, reliability and cost of supplies), or proximity to customers (e.g. accountability).

The influence of business policy on layout decisions is not evident but not absent. The nature of the product or service to be provided may influence the operating system structure and thus the layout requirement. For example, the need to accommodate input and output stocks will be an important consideration in layout design. The provision of a small range of products/services in high volumes will have different implications for layout design than, for example, the need for flexibility in order for the organization to be able to offer a range of products/services through the same facility. Policy requirements relating to cost and timing (e.g. speed of processing customers in a service system) may also influence layout design.

Again, for an existing layout, operations managers will be aware of capabilities or limitations on flexibility/variety, cost, speed, etc. and will wish to influence/inform any potential business policy decisions which will have implications in these areas.

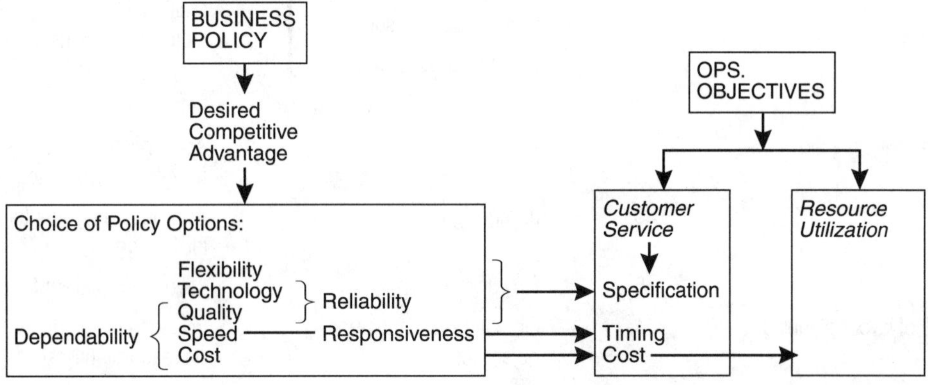


## Competitive advantage (see Chapter 2, Figures 2.6 and 2.7)

The diagram above in effect shows some of the detail behind the previous diagram, for it sets out more precisely the relationship between business policy decisions relating especially to the 'manner of serving markets' and operations objectives relating to customer service. Some of the points made above can therefore be illustrated here.

Where business policy decisions emphasize speed or responsiveness in relationships with customers, there will be a need for a location which provides good access to or by customers in order that the customer service objective of timing might be achieved. Further, service systems with fast throughput, with short queues, will be required. This in turn will influence layout decisions. A business emphasis on cost may place emphasis on proximity to suppliers for low inventories, as well as layouts which afford low work-in-progress inventories or short customer queues, and relatively specialized, i.e. low-variety, processing. A business emphasis on flexibility or quality will be reflected in the importance attached to customer service or specification. This may influence the relationship and hence proximity required with suppliers, and will almost certainly influence layout decisions, for it will be desirable to be able to accommodate greater variety and consequently flexible systems, rapid change-overs, etc.

## TOPIC MAP

| Topics in this Part | Chapter | Related topics in other chapters: Topic | Comments/aspects |
|---|---|---|---|
| Chapter 5 | | | |
| Need for locational choice | 16 | Supply chain management<br>Purchasing and supply | Proximity to suppliers |
| | | Distribution and logistics | Proximity to customers |
| Factors influencing locational choice | 1 | Operations management objectives | Customer service considerations |
| | 4 | Operations costs | Costs of location |
| | 7 | Learning | Availability of appropriate skills |
| | 8 | Learning curve | |
| | 16 | Supply chain management<br>Purchasing and supply | Proximity to suppliers |
| | | Distribution and logistics | Proximity to customers |
| Types of location problems | 16 | Supply chain management<br>Purchasing and supply<br>Distribution and logistics | Multi-facility location problems |
| Chapter 6 | | | |
| Need for layout planning | 7 | Work methods | Appropriate layouts for efficient work methods |
| | 9 | Job design | Appropriate layouts for effective job design |
| | 15 | Flow line principles | Layout for efficient flow |
| Objectives of layout planning | 1 | Operations management objectives | Influence of layout on resource utilization |
| | 7 | Work methods | Layout for efficient work methods and job design |
| | 9 | Job design | |
| Layout problems | | | |
| Types of layout | 4 | Operations economics | Breakeven analysis |
| Layout planning methods | 7 | Work methods | Work flows and process charts |
| Modifying layouts | 5 | Types of location problems | Addition of a location |
| Planning other types of layout | | | |
| Materials handling | 7 | Work methods | Flow processes and process charts |
| | 9 | The worker | Ergonomics safety |
| | 16 | Materials management | |
| Automated storage and retrieval | 9 | Technology and work | Automation |
| | 17 | Inventory management problems | |

Chapter 5

# Location of facilities

## ISSUES

Why and when do we need to select a location?
What factors will influence that decision?
What are the different types of location choice problems?
How are locations evaluated and chosen?

## NOTATION USED IN THIS CHAPTER

$O_{i_m}$ Cost, score, etc., associated with factors 1, 2, 3, . . . *m*, for location *i*
$W_m$ Weight attached to factors 1, 2, 3, . . . *m*,
$L$ Total transport cost
$T_i$ Transport cost/unit distance/unit quantity between facility and location *i*
$Q_i$ Quantity to be transported between facility and location *i*
$D_i$ Distance between facility and location *i*
$n$ Number of locations ($i = 1 \ldots n$)

The facilities location problem is of major importance in all types of business. Whether we are concerned with manufacture, supply, transport or service we must consider the problem of where to base our operations. Certainly the location problem for a transport operation is slightly different, since, by definition, transport moves. However, even in such cases there will normally be a 'home base' or centre of operations at which certain facilities are provided. Throughout this chapter, when referring to facilities we mean the collection of *geographically static resources* required for the operation.

Having decided the nature and specification of the goods/services to be provided, the location of the business facilities is often the next major problem to be considered. At times, however, the two decisions may be quite unconnected. For example, a company intending to manufacture ships will be restricted to comparatively few locations, unlike a company intending to manufacture scientific electronic instruments; the location of ferry services will be relatively restricted compared with the location of furniture removers; and the location of a holiday hotel or an airport hotel will be relatively limited compared with the location of a retail store.

## THE NEED FOR LOCATIONAL CHOICE

We can consider the location problem as applying in two basic situations, i.e. the case of the entirely new business and the case of the existing business.

The choice of location is a vital decision for any new business; indeed, there are numerous examples of new businesses which have had brief and troubled lives solely because of their disadvantageous location. The existing firm will seek new facility locations either in order to expand capacity or to replace existing facilities. An increase in demand, if it is to be satisfied by the organization, gives rise to one or more of three decisions:

(a) whether to expand the present capacity and facilities;

(b) whether to seek locations for additional facilities;

(c) whether to close down existing facilities in favour of larger premises elsewhere.

Replacement of existing facilities may be occasioned by one or more of the following occurrences:

(a) the movement of markets, i.e. changes in the location of demand;

(b) changes in the cost or availability of local labour;

(c) changes in the availability of materials;

(d) demolition or compulsory purchase of premises;

(e) changes in the availability or effectiveness of transport;

(f) relocation of associated industries or plants;

(g) national legislation.

**Figure 5.1** Pressures for change in space (which must give rise to the need to select a facility location). Adapted with permission from Townroe, P.M. (1969) Locational choice and the individual firm. *Regional Studies*, **3**(1), pp. 15-24

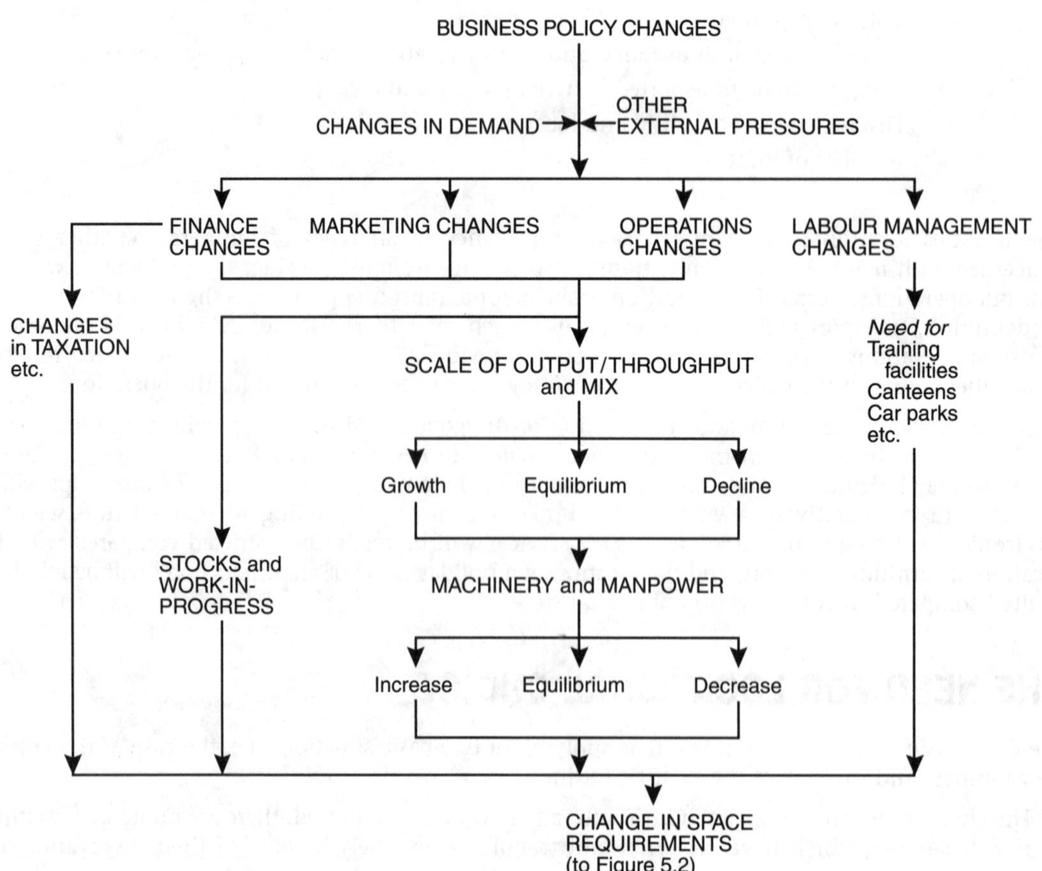

For our purpose in discussing the facility location problem, it makes little difference whether we consider the problem as applying to a new business or to an existing one. However, since the latter tends to be the more complex, we shall focus on it. An increase in demand will, unless associated with increased productivity, inevitably result in pressure for additional capacity; the only alternatives to an expansion of the existing facilities or the acquisition of additional facilities are a reduced share of the market or an increased amount of subcontracting. On the other hand, a reduction in demand will often result in the under-utilization of existing capacity and encourage a move to smaller premises. Figure 5.1 outlines some of the forces within a company which give rise to the pressure for either an increase or a decrease in the amount of space available. While the main forces are associated with demand, and hence with the operations and marketing functions, it is worth noting that both finance and labour management might also be instrumental. Changes in interest rates may affect the cost of holding stock and cause a change in stock-holding policy, which in turn may affect space requirements.

Legislation relating to investment allowances, employment tax, depreciation, etc. may influence company financial policy enough to affect the scale or the nature of the undertaking; similarly, legislation relating to labour may necessitate a change in the nature or extent of facilities, e.g. the addition of extensive training facilities and welfare facilities. Scientific discoveries or developments, new fields

**Figure 5.2** Pressures for a new location. Adapted with permission from Townroe (1969), as for Figure 5.1

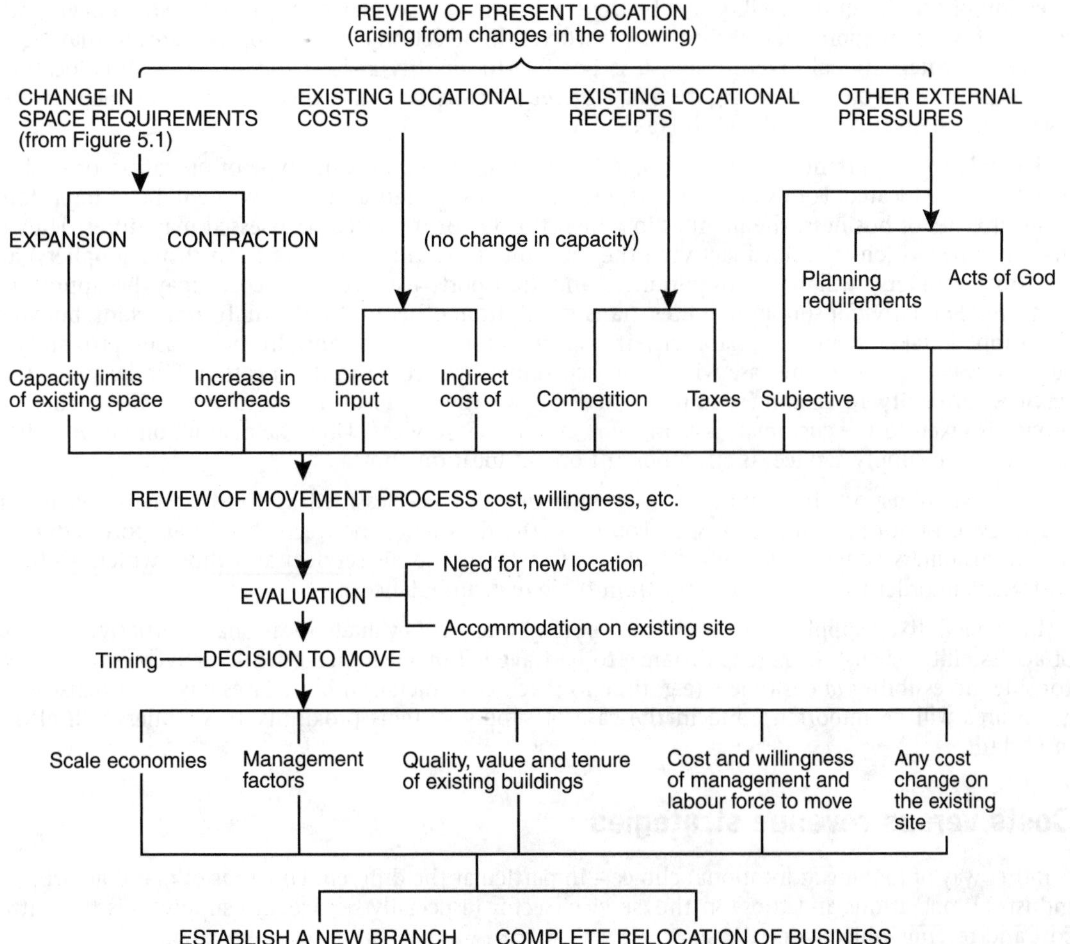

of technology, increasing competition, licensing or patent arrangements all may affect company research and development effort, which in turn will influence space requirements, as will changes in operations technology, obsolescence of equipment, etc.

A change in space requirements is only one of several possible reasons for the need to consider the acquisition of an additional facility location. Figure 5.2 identifies other forces which may give rise to such a decision. The need to seek smaller or larger premises may arise without the occurrence of a change in demand and thus capacity. For example, the cost associated with the present location may change through increases in the cost of labour caused, perhaps, by increasing employment opportunities in the area. The price of raw materials or indirect materials may change through changes in the cost of transport or changes within associated industries. Indirect costs such as those associated with communications, education, housing, etc. may change. Also new competition or changes in local taxation may prompt the decision to seek alternative premises as may other external pressures such as labour disputes. These forces may prompt the consideration of a complete move or the acquisition of an additional site(s).

## FACTORS INFLUENCING LOCATIONAL CHOICE

Theoretically, both new and existing businesses have a vast range of alternative new locations. The selection of the site of the facility will be the final stage of a sequence of decisions which begins with the selection of an appropriate region, then involves the selection of an appropriate area in that region, etc. For an international organization, it is possible to identify at least four stages in this locational choice process, as outlined in Figure 5.3. Different factors will influence decisions at each of these levels, and these also are outlined in Figure 5.3.

The relative importance of some of these factors will depend on the type of operation or business which is to be located. For example, whilst proximity to suppliers and customers will be of importance in most types of business, the manner in which this factor is viewed or assessed may differ. Thus for manufacture, which is a 'fixed' activity, the movement or transport of items in (from suppliers) and out (to customers) will be of importance, and transport distances and costs may be appropriate measures. Similarly, for supply activities, transport in from other locations will be important, but when the supplier takes items to customers, transport out is unimportant. In such cases proximity to customers is to do with the ease with which customers can come to the location. Similarly, for fixed services proximity to customers is likely to focus on their ease of access to the facility, when the service is taken to the customers – as in some emergency services. Thus the distinction between fixed and delivered supply/services is an important one in location choice.

Although transport, by definition, moves, it can also be classified as fixed or delivered for the purposes of locational choice. This, of course, is the distinction between those transport systems to which customers come to start their journeys (e.g. ferry and air service) and those which go to the customers in order to start the journey from there (e.g. ambulances).

In general, fixed supply, service and transport systems will evaluate locational alternatives in terms of accessibility *by* customers (e.g. distance to be travelled by customers), while delivered systems will consider accessibility *to* customers (e.g. time to reach customers). In both cases customer density in a given area will be important, and in the case of supply systems proximity to suppliers will also be important.

### Costs versus revenue strategies

Another way of looking at locational choice – in particular the different concerns of manufacturing (or industrial) operations and those in the 'service' sector (especially service and supply) – is to contrast cost and revenue objectives.

**Figure 5.3** Facility location decision levels (an international example)

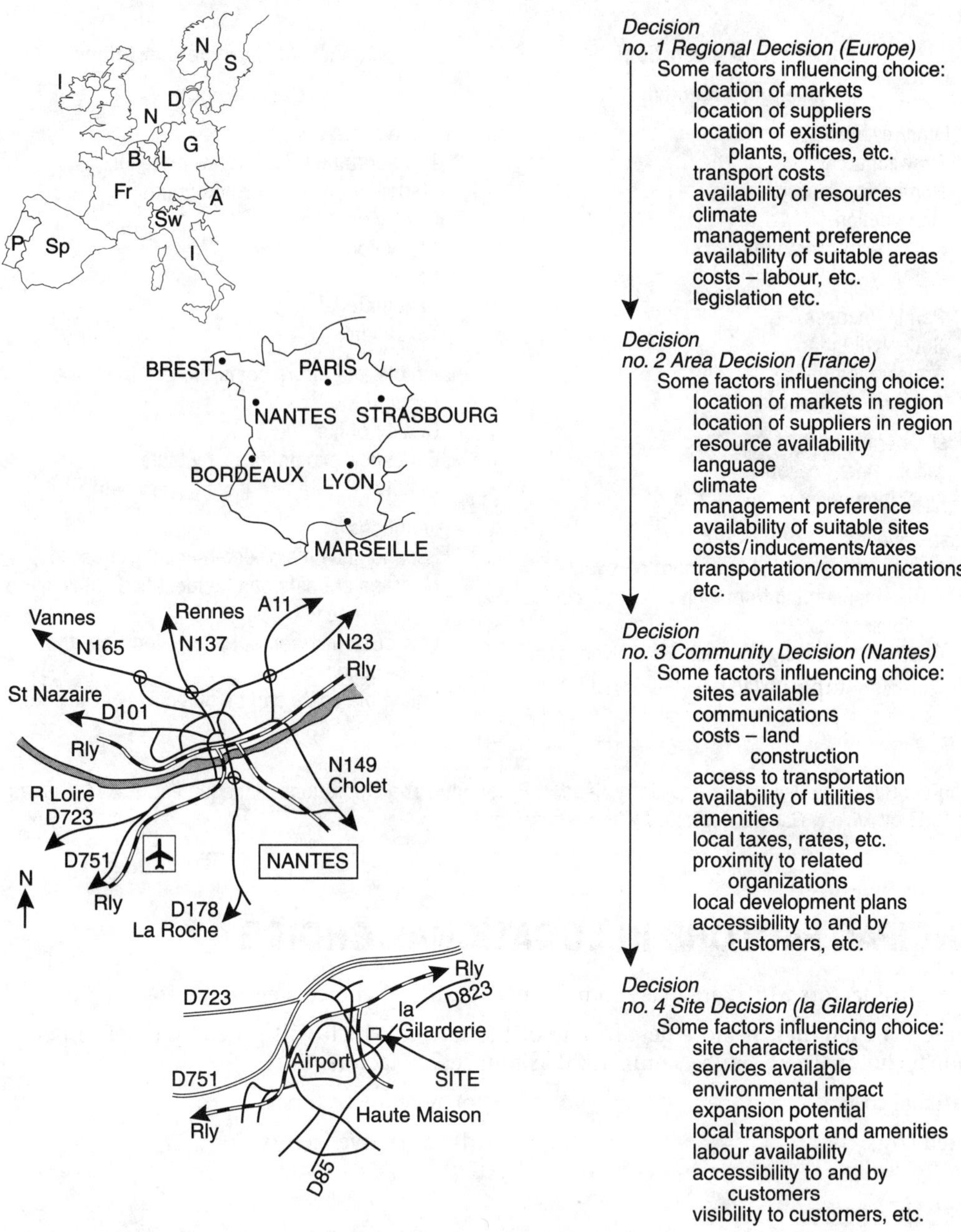


Manufacturing-type operations tend to focus on cost minimization in making location decisions, but revenue maximization is of equal, if not greater, concern for many 'service'-type operations. The reason for this difference in focus, which is summarized in Table 5.1, is that costs can differ significantly between locations for manufacturing or industrial operations, but may differ little for 'service'-type operations. The latter, therefore, may tend to focus on revenue-related factors, e.g. the likely volume of business.

**Table 5.1 Location strategies: 'service' versus manufacture operations**

| 'Service'-type operations | Manufacturing-type operations |
|---|---|
| **Revenue: Objective** | **Cost: Objective** |
| Volume/revenue<br>Drawing area<br>Purchasing power<br>Competition<br>Advertising/promotion/pricing | Tangible costs<br>Transportation cost of raw material<br>Shipment cost of finished goods<br>Energy cost<br>Utility costs<br>Labour<br>Raw material<br>Taxes, etc. |
| Physical quality<br>Parking/access<br>Security/lighting<br>Appearance/image<br>Associated business | Intangible and future costs<br>Attitude towards union<br>Quality of life<br>Education expenditures by state<br>Quality of state and local government |
| Cost determinants<br>Management calibre<br>Operation policies | |
| Assumptions<br>Location is a major determinant of revenue<br>Issues manifesting from high customer contact dominate<br>Costs are relatively constant for a given area: therefore, the revenue function is critical | Assumptions<br>Location is a major determinant of cost<br>Most major costs can be identified explicitly for each site<br>Low customer contact allows focus on the identifiable costs<br>Intangible costs can be objectively evaluated |

Source: *Based on Jay Heizer and Barry Render*, Production and Operations Management, *p. 344. Copyright © 1988 by Allyn & Bacon. Reprinted with permission.*

## PRINCIPAL FACTORS IN LOCATIONAL CHOICE

The principal factors which are likely to influence locational choice are summarized in Table 5.2.

Figure 5.4 examines in more detail some of the factors which will generally be of importance in locational choice. These can be summarized as four sets of factors:

(a) variable costs;
(b) fixed costs;
(c) revenue factors;
(d) subjective factors.

### Variable costs

Perhaps the main factor here is the 'accessibility' of the proposed location in terms of both inputs and outputs. As regards input, accessibility to labour is important; not merely sufficient labour, but labour of the correct type and at a correct price. Accessibility of raw materials, sub-assemblies and components is important, the cost of such input being mainly a function of transport. Access to technical advice and to other services such as warehousing and maintenance is often essential. With regard to output, a location must clearly have easy access to adequate markets, as well as public services and associated industries.

**Table 5.2 Principal factors influencing locational choice**

| Type of operation/ organization | Principal factors | |
|---|---|---|
| Manufacture | Movement/transport of items (e.g. goods, materials) from suppliers and to customers (possibly including other facilities within the organization) | |
| Supply | Accessibility by and visibility to customers (e.g. distance from markets)<br>Accessibility from suppliers<br>Market density in area | Accessibility to markets (e.g. time to reach customers)<br>Accessibility from suppliers<br>Market density in area |
| Service | Accessibility by and visibility to customers (e.g. distance from markets)<br>Market density in area (e.g. no. of potential customers in area) | Accessibility to markets (e.g. time to reach customers)<br>Market density in area (e.g. no. of potential customers in area) |
| Transport | Accessibility by customers (e.g. distance from markets)<br>Market density in area (e.g. no. of potential customers in area) | Accessibility to markets (e.g. time to reach customers)<br>Market density in area (e.g. no. of potential customers in area) |
| | 'Fixed' operation | 'Delivered' operation |

## Fixed costs

These are associated with the provision and maintenance of facilities. The design of buildings and the layout of facilities will influence such costs. The cost of erecting and maintaining buildings, the cost of access roads, the cost of transportation of machinery, rates, rent and so on will all influence the choice of location. We should also consider as fixed costs the cost of inventories of materials and finished items which may depend on the plant location.

It will be seen from Figure 5.5, which compares fixed and variable costs for four possible new facility locations, that volume considerations can influence the selection of a site.

## Revenue factors

Often the principal economic differences between alternative locations for a 'service'-type operation relate to revenues rather than costs. Proximity to customers/potential customers, accessibility, usability, etc. are all likely to influence demand, and therefore revenue, by influencing either the number of customers, and/or the extent to which each makes use of the service.

## Subjective factors

These may also influence the decision. Individual preferences, congeniality of the district, attitudes of present employees, etc. will all be important. National and regional data relating to the various factors influencing the facility location decision are available from a variety of sources. Data on population change, average wage levels, unemployment, industrial disputes, absenteeism, labour turnover, etc. may be of relevance and will often be available.

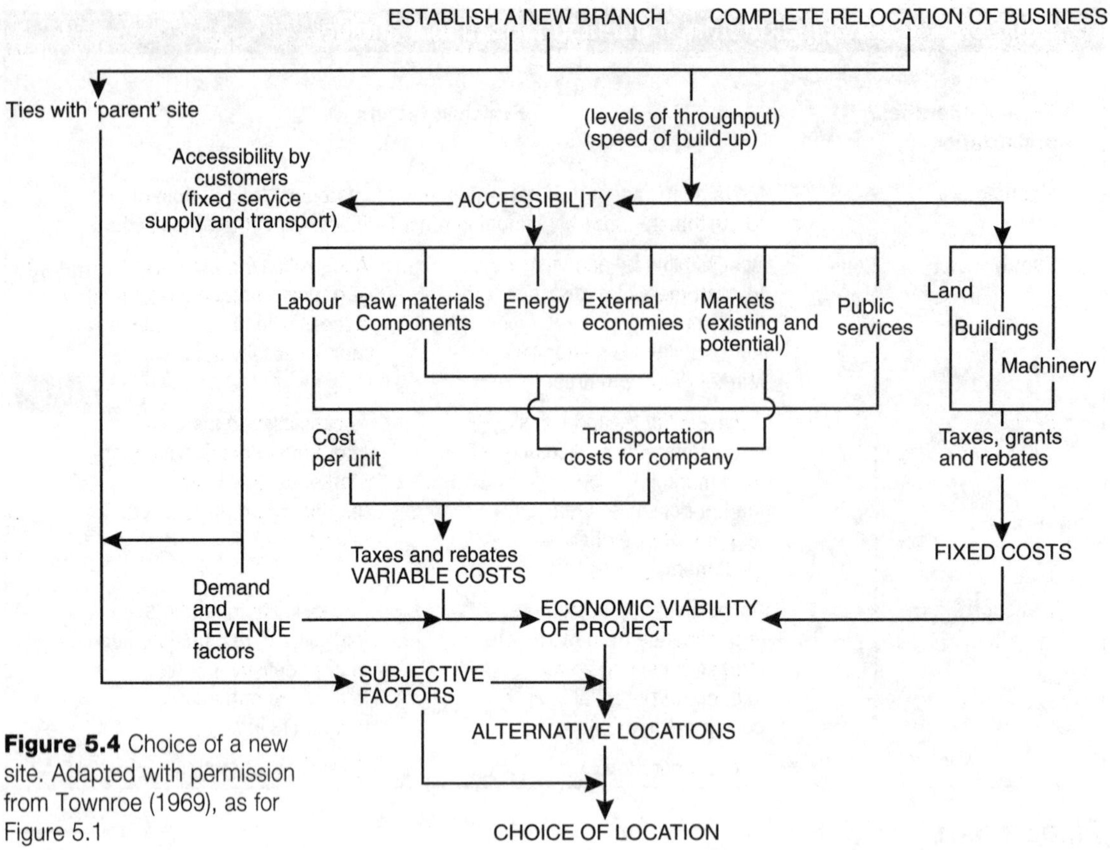

ESTABLISH A NEW BRANCH
COMPLETE RELOCATION OF BUSINESS
Ties with 'parent' site
(levels of throughput)
(speed of build-up)
Accessibility by customers (fixed service supply and transport)
ACCESSIBILITY
Labour
Raw materials Components
Energy
External economies
Markets (existing and potential)
Public services
Land
Buildings
Machinery
Cost per unit
Transportation costs for company
Taxes, grants and rebates
Taxes and rebates VARIABLE COSTS
FIXED COSTS
Demand and REVENUE factors
ECONOMIC VIABILITY OF PROJECT
SUBJECTIVE FACTORS
ALTERNATIVE LOCATIONS
CHOICE OF LOCATION

**Figure 5.4** Choice of a new site. Adapted with permission from Townroe (1969), as for Figure 5.1

A further factor which will influence the choice of location is the *time factor*, i.e. the urgency of acquiring the facility compared with the time required to make it available, the latter being influenced by the necessity for planning permission, preparation of plans, purchase of land, availability of building labour, provision of services, electricity, water, roads, etc.

**Figure 5.5** Fixed and variable cost relationships for four possible new facility locations

$ Fixed 20 000 p.a.
$ Variable 4/unit
Darwin
AUSTRALIA
$ Fixed 10 000 p.a.
$ Variable 8/unit
Perth
$ Fixed 40 000 p.a.
$ Variable 1/unit
Sydney
Melbourne
$ Fixed 30 000 p.a.
$ Variable 3/unit
Annual operating cost ($ 000)
70
60
50
40
30
20
10
Perth
Darwin
Melbourne
Sydney
Locate at Perth
Locate at Darwin
Locate at Sydney
1 2 3 4 5 6 7 8 9 10
Volume throughput units (000)

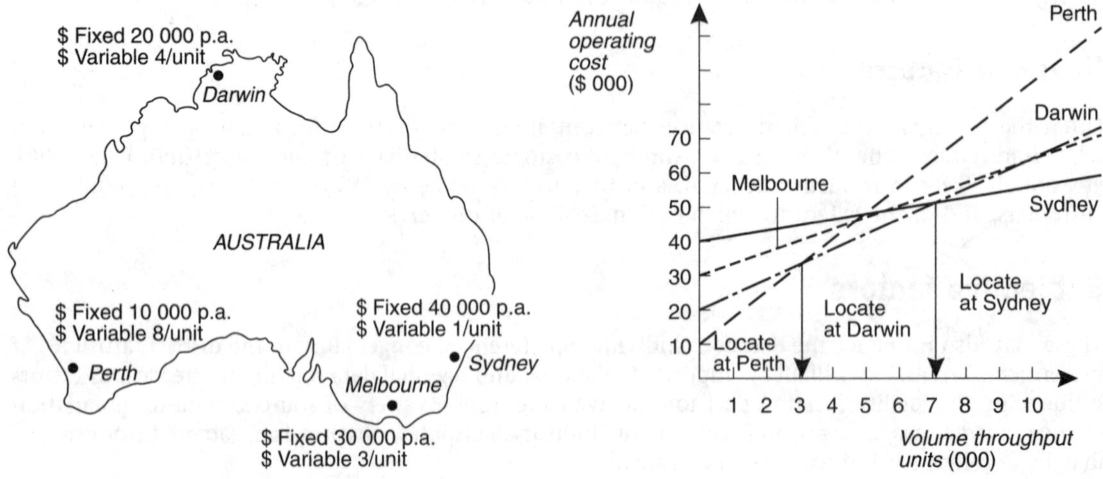

The role of central and local government and the influence of legislation and incentives can be of importance in locational choice, especially for manufacturing organizations. There may be several reasons for government concern with the location of companies and industry, e.g. regional unemployment costs associated with the congestion of major conurbations, problems of environmental pollution, and population drift from rural areas.

There are often substantial incentives to encourage companies to establish facilities in certain parts of a country designated for industrial and economic development. Furthermore, with the growth of multinational firms and the increasing importance of the international dimension in locational choice, e.g. in industries such as motor vehicles and chemicals, similar factors at an international level (e.g. within Europe) are of considerable significance.

**EXAMPLE**

### *Locating an ATM*

Usage is a key factor when considering the deployment of an automated teller machine (ATM). One bank thoroughly analysed potential usage when deploying its eighth ATM. As a result, the machine's first full month of operation generated transaction volumes that significantly exceeded the average machine use within the entire network. Population density was the most important aspect and one of the easiest to examine. Where people live and how they move around within the area provided the best placement information. By applying basic knowledge of local street systems, it was possible to devise a general traffic flow pattern. As consumers viewed convenience as their top concern, ingress–egress as well as traffic flow had to be considered. Further, when ATM users have to leave their cars to use a machine, safety becomes a primary concern.

Source: Adams, P. (1991) Choosing a choice ATM site: ATM buyer's guide. *Credit Union Management*, **14**(3), pp. 15–20.

## TYPES OF LOCATION PROBLEMS

As we have seen, the need to select a location or site for a facility can arise for many reasons. The cause is perhaps less important to the operations manager than the nature of the locational choice problem. For example, if it is necessary to select the location of a new single-facility business which is entirely self-contained, with no dependence on suppliers, the problem will be relatively straightforward and the choice wide. In contrast, in the choice of a site of a new facility for a company that has several existing facilities which have some supply interdependence and which together supply a particular market, the problem will be more complex and the choice more limited.

In order to understand how best to try to solve locational choice problems we must first appreciate the range of types of problems which might be encountered. Some of the common types of locational choice problems are identified in Table 5.3, and of course combinations of these basic types can exist. In discussing procedures for tackling location problems in the remainder of this chapter we shall refer back to this simple classification of problem types.

### The single-facility location problem *(Table 5.3, categories A1, 2, 3 and 4 and B1, with relevance also to B2, 3 and 4)*

Here we are concerned with the location of a single business facility, e.g. the new single-plant firm or single-facility service organization, or the location of a new facility for a larger organization where the facility has no significant dependence on or relationship with the other facilities in the business (e.g. Table 5.3, category B1).

**Table 5.3 Some types of location problems**

| Type of problem | | Example – location of: |
|---|---|---|
| A. Single facility | | |
| 1. Single facility with *no* connections to other locations | Locate a self-contained facility to serve a local community | Single new cinema for a small community |
| 2. Single facility with connections *in* from other locations | Locate a facility to serve a local community taking into account the need for the facility to be supplied from elsewhere | Single new retail shop for a small community |
| 3. Single facility with connections *out* to other locations | Locate a facility to serve customers elsewhere | Market garden to serve an area of several towns |
| 4. Single facility with connections *in* from and *out* to other locations | Locate a facility to serve customers elsewhere, with supplies also being received from elsewhere | Single new manufacturing plant; single new wholesale distributor or warehouse |
| B. Multi-facility | | |
| 1. Addition(s) to an existing 'set' of facilities, with *no* connections to others in the set or to other locations | Effectively, as A1 | Additional new cinema for a small community, but part of a national chain |
| 2. Addition(s) to an existing set of facilities, the 'set' having connections *in* from other locations | Effectively, as A2 (but possibly with the need to consider the distribution of capacity within the set) | Additional new retail shop for a small community, but part of a national chain |
| 3. Addition(s) to an existing set of facilities, the set having connections *out* to other locations | Effectively, as A3 (but with need to consider the distribution of capacity within the set) | Additional market garden for national organization |
| 4. Addition(s) to an existing set of facilities, the set having connections *in* and *out* with other locations | Effectively, as A4 (but with the need to consider the distribution of capacity within the set) | Additional manufacturing plant for a company, where there is no flow between plants |
| 5. Addition(s) to an existing set of facilities with connections *in* from within the set | Effectively, as B2 | Retail shop for company to sell items supplied from elsewhere within the company |
| 6. Addition(s) to an existing set of facilities with connections *out* to elsewhere in the set | Effectively, as B3 | Additional market garden for a company to supply goods to other company locations, e.g. for packaging or processing |
| 7. Addition(s) to an existing set of facilities with connections *in* and *out* within the set | Effectively, as B4 | Additional manufacturing plant for a company, to be supplied from other plants in the company and to supply items for other company plants |

Note: In many cases combinations will exist, particularly B2 and 5, B3 and 6, and B4 and 7.

Unlike the multi-facility location problem, the existing or future locations of other facilities within the business will be of little relevance. Here, therefore, we are *not* concerned with the type of locational problems encountered in businesses with interdependent facilities (as in the car industry, in which different parts of final products are made in different facilities, or specialized hospitals and clinics in a regional health service). Procedures for tackling the single-facility location problem may, however, be of relevance in multi-facility organizations in which there is no specialization or interdependence of facilities, e.g. supply organizations comprising several similar outlets servicing different areas. Some procedures are discussed below.

## Checklists

Given a choice of possible locations, perhaps the simplest but least rigorous means for decision-making involves their comparison against a checklist of relevant factors. Such a checklist is shown in Table 5.4, which also gives some indication of the relevance of each factor at each of the four 'levels' of decision-making discussed earlier. If not an adequate means of decision-making, such a checklist at least provides a means of initially narrowing down the range of alternative regions and/or areas and/or communities and/or sites.

**EXAMPLE**

### *Sonic Industries*

At Oklahoma-based Sonic Industries Inc., a chain of 1043 fast food drive-ins, hunting for a superior location used to be unscientific. To choose a site today, Ted Kergan, Sonic franchisee, studies demographic data to find neighbourhoods that fit the profile of his best customers, blue-collar workers who earn \$11 000–22 000 a year, drive a pickup truck, and have no more than an hour to eat their lunch. Once a business knows who its best customers are, it should start looking for neighbourhoods where many of them live. The quest can be begun at the local chamber of commerce, city planning commission, economic development agency, or local office of the US Census Bureau. Ideally, a location should be sought that includes the maximum number of choice neighbourhoods within the trade area's radius. Chosen properties should be ranked according to basic real estate criteria, including: (1) cost versus value; (2) access and traffic patterns; and (3) leasing terms.

Source: Wang, P. (1991) Finding the right location for your business. *Money*, Summer, pp. 26–33.

## Location factor comparisons

Most locational decisions will at some stage involve the preparation of tabular comparisons of the type shown in Table 5.5. In some cases it will be possible and appropriate to draw up such comparisons entirely in cost terms, in which case addition of columns provides a means of comparing alternatives and therefore of choosing a location. Frequently, however, it will be necessary to consider cost and non-cost factors, and some of the latter may be represented only as 'yes' or 'no'. This ensures that the use of this type of approach, while providing a means of summarizing the factors to be considered, or providing a checklist against which to assess alternatives, must normally be employed along with more rigorous procedures of the type discussed below.

## Dimensional analysis

Even if we are able to identify the various factors influencing locational choice, the problem of quantification remains. How, for example, do we determine, for various potential locations, the cost of moving or the cost of labour? Furthermore, having quantified such factors, what weight or importance do we attach to each? Do we, for example, consider the subjective factors as being of equal importance

## Table 5.4 Checklist: some factors influencing locational choice

| | Of region (international) | Of area (national) | Of community (city) | Of site |
|---|---|---|---|---|
| Political stability | √ | | | |
| Relevant legislation, e.g. industrial relations | √ | | | |
| Unionization of labour | √ | | | |
| Industrial relations 'climate' | √ | | | |
| Feasibility of joint operations | √ | | | |
| Capital restrictions | √ | | | |
| Transfer of earnings restrictions | √ | | | |
| Taxation for foreign firms | √ | | | |
| Currency restrictions | √ | | | |
| GNP trends | √ | | | |
| Foreign investment trends | √ | | | |
| Restrictions of foreign labour/staff | √ | | | |
| Climate | √ | | | |
| Language | √ | | | |
| Management preference | √ | √ | √ | ? |
| Location of company's existing facilities | √ | √ | √ | ? |
| Availability of 'suitable' areas | √ | | | |
| Cost of living | √ | | | |
| Standard of living | √ | | | |
| Location of markets/customers | √ | √ | √ | |
| Location of suppliers | √ | √ | √ | |
| Proximity to related industries | √ | √ | √ | |
| Labour/staff availability and skills | √ | √ | √ | |
| Unemployment, turnover and absenteeism | ? | √ | √ | |
| Pay levels and scales | ? | √ | √ | |
| Planning and development restrictions | ? | √ | √ | ? |
| Tax structures and incentives | ? | √ | ? | |
| Environmental (e.g. pollution) controls | ? | √ | ? | |
| Communications: international | √ | | | |
| national | | √ | | |
| local | | | √ | |
| Transport: air | √ | √ | √ | |
| rail | √ | √ | √ | |
| road | √ | √ | √ | |
| other | √ | √ | √ | |
| Availability of suitable communities | | √ | | |
| Land availability and costs | | √ | √ | |
| Availability of premises | | √ | √ | |
| Cost of land | | √ | √ | |
| Cost of building | | | √ | |
| Rents for premises | | √ | √ | |
| Cost of services | | | √ | |
| Zoning and planning restrictions | | √ | √ | |
| Availability of utilities | | √ | √ | |
| Availability of amenities | | | √ | |
| Availability of education and training | | √ | √ | |
| Community attitudes and culture | | | √ | |
| Energy availability | | √ | √ | |
| Energy costs | | √ | √ | |
| Impact on environment | | | √ | |
| Development plans | | | √ | |
| Availability of subcontractors | | | √ | |
| Availability of suitable sites | | | √ | |
| Site characteristics | | | | √ |
| Availability of adjacent space | | | | √ |
| Transport access | | | | √ |
| Parking space | | | | √ |
| Local transport provisions | | | | √ |
| Facilities for waste disposal | | | | √ |

**Table 5.5 Comparison of factors for three possible locations for a retail shop**

| Location factor | Location A | Location B | Location C |
|---|---|---|---|
| Site rental per year | £1 000 | £1200 | £800 |
| Car parking spaces within 1/2 km | 110 | 30 | 205 |
| Shop frontage | 4m | 3m | 4m |
| Cost of services per year | £750 | £275 | £800 |

to the fixed-cost factors? Indeed, we may even find that we are unable to attach cost figures to some of the important factors.

Consider a simple example in which we are faced with two possible locations. We have decided that the choice between these locations will be made on the basis of the following factors:

(a) the cost of land;

(b) the cost of buildings;

(c) the cost of labour (fixed investment cost for the total required labour force for a location).

We have further found that the cost associated with each of these three factors for each of the possible locations is as shown in Table 5.6.

**Table 5.6**

| Factor | Location A<br>£ | Location B<br>£ |
|---|---|---|
| Land | 10000 | 15000 |
| Buildings | 25000 | 30000 |
| Labour | 15000 | 10000 |

We might compare the relative merits of the two locations merely by summing the relevant costs, i.e.

Total for A = £50000
Total for B = £55000

Using this method of comparison we would choose location A, since it is the cheaper of the two. This method assumes that each of the factors is of equal importance, which may be far from true. For example, suppose we decide that, while the costs of land and buildings are equally important to our decisions, the cost associated with labour is twice as important as the two other costs. Then we may assess the alternatives by introducing this weighting factor:

| | £ | | £ |
|---|---|---|---|
| Location A: | 10000 | Location B: | 15000 |
| | 25000 | | 30000 |
| | +2(15000) | | +2(10000) |
| | = £65000 | | = £65000 |

Now it appears that each location is equally attractive.

Let us take this type of argument a little further by introducing two more factors into our examination of the two locations. Now, as well as the costs associated with land, buildings and labour, we need to consider the influence of community relations and the cost of moving. We find it difficult to place an accurate cost on either of these factors for the two locations, so we settle for a system of rating using a scale 1 to 100. A rating of 1 indicates that a location scores very highly, i.e. it is the best possible result, whereas a rating of 100 is the worst possible result.

Suppose the five factors for the two locations are quantified as shown in Table 5.7; then we might again compare locations by adding together the figures to obtain the totals shown in Table 5.7. This comparison would lead us to select location A.

**Table 5.7**

| | Location A | Location B |
|---|---|---|
| Land (cost) | 10000 | 15000 |
| Buildings (cost) | 25000 | 30000 |
| Labour (cost) | 15000 | 10000 |
| Community relations (score) | 60 | 30 |
| Cost of moving (score) | 80 | 40 |
| Total | 50140 | 55070 |

However, this type of analysis is quite wrong, because we have indiscriminately mixed together two dimensions: cost and ratings. To illustrate the inadequacies of the procedure, suppose we alter the scale of the first three factors and perform our calculations in £000s rather than £s, i.e.

| Location A | | Location B | |
|---|---|---|---|
| | 10 | | 15 |
| | 25 | | 30 |
| | 15 | | 10 |
| | 60 | | 30 |
| | 80 | | 40 |
| | 190 | | 125 |

Such an analysis would lead us to select location B, since the change of scale has distorted our analysis.

So that such an anomaly does not occur, we must take care to treat multidimensional analysis in a more satisfactory manner. Such a method was developed by Bridgeman,[1] and is referred to as dimensional analysis. Using the following notation:

$O_{i_1}, O_{i_2}, O_{i_3}, \ldots O_{i_m}$ = costs, scores, etc. associated with factors 1, 2, 3, . . . $m$, for location $i$

$W_1, W_2, W_3, \ldots W_m$ = the weight to be attached to factors 1, 2, 3, . . . $m$

The merit of the various locations should be assessed as follows:

$$\text{For location } i, \text{ merit} = (O_{i_1})^{W_1} \times (O_{i_2})^{W_2} \times (O_{i_3})^{W_3} \ldots \times (O_{i_m})^{W_m}$$

In the case of two possible locations the merit might be compared as follows:

$$\frac{\text{Merit of A}}{\text{Merit of B}} = \left(\frac{O_{A_1}}{O_{B_1}}\right)^{W_1} \times \left(\frac{O_{A_2}}{O_{B_2}}\right)^{W_2} \ldots \times \left(\frac{O_{A_n}}{O_{B_n}}\right)^{W_m}$$

If > 1, select B.

If < 1, select A.

[1] Bridgeman, P. W. (1963) *Dimensional Analysis*. New Haven, Conn.: Yale University Press.

EXAMPLE

### *A retail shop*

Several factors are identified as being important in choosing one of two available locations for a new retail shop. Wherever possible the factors have been costed; otherwise a score from 1 to 10 has been given, 1 representing the best possible result and 10 the worst possible. The factors are of different importance, so they have been weighted from 1 to 10 (weight of 1 indicating least importance and 10 most importance).

| Factor | | Location A | Location B | Weight |
|---|---|---|---|---|
| Cost | = | £10000 | £15000 | 1 |
| Score | = | 3 | 7 | 2 |
| Score | = | 6 | 2 | 3 |
| Cost | = | £1500000 | £1000000 | 4 |
| Score | = | 4 | 7 | 4 |
| Score | = | 5 | 5 | 3 |

The merit of location A is represented by:

$$(10000)^1 \times (3)^2 \times (6)^3 \times (1500000)^4 \times (4)^4 \times (5)^3$$

and that of location B by:

$$(15000)^1 \times (7)^2 \times (2)^3 \times (1000000)^4 \times (7)^4 \times (5)^3$$

To simplify the calculations we can change the scales for the cost factors for both locations.

Merit of A: $(1)^1 \times (3)^2 \times (6)^3 \times (150)^4 \times (5)^3$

Merit of B: $(1.5)^1 \times (7)^2 \times (2)^3 \times (100)^4 \times (7)^4 \times (5)^3$

$$\therefore \quad \frac{\text{Merit of A}}{\text{Merit of B}} = 1.79$$

Such an analysis indicates that location B is superior on the basis of the six factors considered.

In this example we have considered only factors which should be minimized, i.e. costs. An analysis might also be undertaken even where some factors are to be maximized (e.g. profits, revenue) while others are to be minimized. In such a case the powers would be positive for factors to be minimized and negative for factors to be maximized.

EXAMPLE

### *A cinema*

Compare the merit of two locations X and Y on the basis of factors with different weights, i.e.

| | Cinema location X | Cinema location Y | Weight |
|---|---|---|---|
| Costs (£) | 10000 | 12000 | 4 |
| Benefits (score, 1–10) | 8 | 6 | 3 |

$$\frac{\text{Merit of X}}{\text{Merit of Y}} = \frac{(10\,000)^4(8)^{-3}}{(12\,000)^4(6)^{-3}}$$

$$= \frac{(10)^4(8)^{-3}}{(12)^4(6)^{-3}}$$

$$= 0.203$$

∴ Select location X for the cinema

## Minimization of transport costs

It is clear from our previous discussion that many factors other than transport costs are likely to affect locational choice. Nevertheless, minimization of transport costs may provide a suitable first solution which might then form a basis for further discussion, analysis and modifications. This approach might be relevant in selecting the location of a warehouse relative to its principal customers or markets, or a manufacturing plant relative to its suppliers and customers.

Employing such an approach we would seek to minimize the sum of all transport costs, i.e. minimize:

$$L = \sum_{i=1}^{n} n\ T_i Q_i D_i$$

where

$L$ = Total transport cost to and from the facility to be located

$T_i$ = Transport cost per unit distance per unit quantity for movement between the facility and existing location $i$

$Q_i$ = Quantity to be transported between the facility and existing location $i$

$D_i$ = Distance between the facility and existing location $i$ for $n$ locations

Considering movement between the facility and the supplier/customer locations to be in a rectangular pattern, and using Cartesian co-ordinates to indicate locations, distances $D_i$ may be represented as follows:

$$D_i = |x - x_i| + |y - y_i|$$

where $x_i$ and $y_i$ indicate the existing location of a supplier or customer $i$, and $x$ and $y$ give the location of the facility. Hence:

$$L = \sum_{i=1}^{n} T_i Q_i |x - x_i| + \sum_{i=1}^{n} T_i Q_i |y - y_i|$$

Our task now is to develop a procedure to identify values for $x$ and $y$ which minimize $L$, and this can be done independently for the $x$ and $y$ dimensions. In fact the location required is given by the *median* point for each dimension.[2] A simple example will illustrate the procedure.

**EXAMPLE**

### *A warehouse*

Square Deal Ltd wish to establish a new warehouse in the UK from which to supply a new line of building products to existing customers in Manchester, Liverpool, Birmingham and London. The locations of the customers are shown in Figure 5.6 and transport details are given in Table 5.8.

[2] The median is the mid-point in a frequency distribution, i.e. the point below which 50% of observations fall and above which the other 50% fall.

**Table 5.8 Transport details for Square Deal Ltd**

| Customer | $Q_i$ Annual delivery quantities (kg) | $T_i$ Transport cost (per kg km) |
|---|---|---|
| Manchester | 80000 | £0.0001 |
| Liverpool | 40000 | £0.0001 |
| Birmingham | 90000 | £0.0001 |
| London | 50000 | £0.0001 |

Multiplying $T_i$ by $Q_i$ and summing gives:

$$\sum_{i=1}^{4} T_iQ_i = (8 + 4 + 9 + 5)$$

$$= 26$$

In this situation the median point is taken as the value where the sum of the *TQ*s below the point equals the sum of the *TQ*s above the point.

Now to find the value of $x$ which minimizes $\sum_{i=1}^{4} T_iQ_i|x - x_i|$ we work from west to east and find the existing location $x_i$ which corresponds to the median value of $T_iQ_i$. With the sum of the *TQ*s equal to 26 the median value occurs at the 13th unit. To find the value of $x$ which minimizes $L$ we calculate the cumulative *TQ* total from west to east as follows:

| | Cumulative total | |
|---|---|---|
| Liverpool $T_iQ_i = 4$ | 4 | |
| Manchester $T_iQ_i = 8$ | 12 | |
| Birmingham $T_iQ_i = 9$ | 21 | Includes the 13th unit |
| London $T_iQ_i = 5$ | 26 | |

Now the 13th unit is associated with Birmingham, so the value of $x$ which minimizes $L$ occurs at the Birmingham $x$ co-ordinate.

Similarly, to find the value of $y$ which minimizes $\sum_{i=1}^{4} T_iQ_i|y - y_i|$ we work from south to north and find the existing location which corresponds to the median value of $T_iQ_i$ as follows:

| | Cumulative total | |
|---|---|---|
| Liverpool $T_iQ_i = 5$ | 5 | |
| Manchester $T_iQ_i = 9$ | 14 | |
| Birmingham $T_iQ_i = 4$ | 18 | Includes the 13th unit |
| London $T_iQ_i = 8$ | 26 | |

Again Birmingham corresponds to the median value. Hence the preferred location for the warehouse is to be found on the $x$ co-ordinate corresponding to Birmingham and on the $y$ co-ordinate corresponding to Birmingham, i.e. at Birmingham.

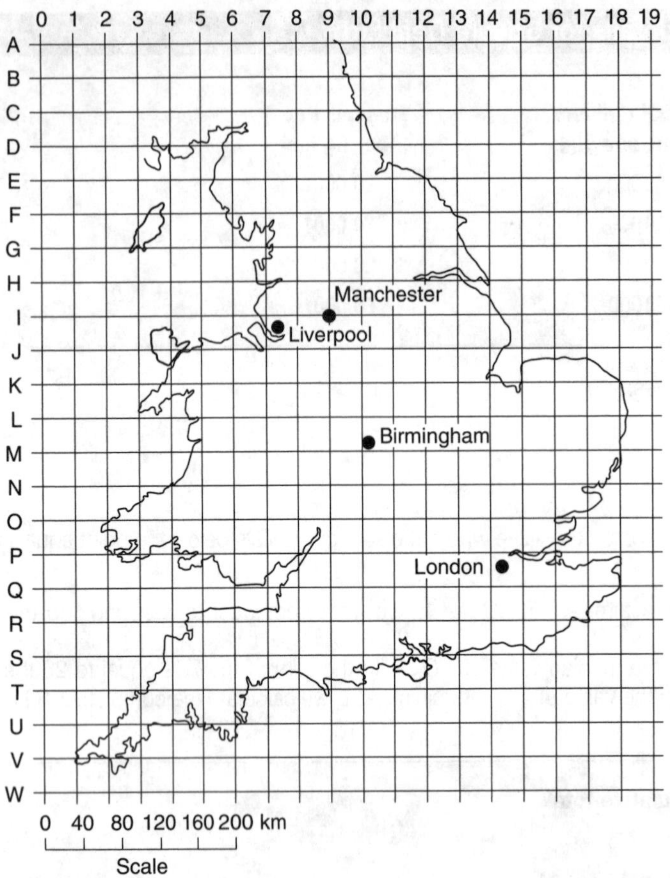


**Figure 5.6** Location of customers for warehouses for Square Deal Ltd (UK).

The total transport cost for this warehouse location can be found by substituting values $x$, $x_i$, $y$ and $y_i$ into the equation for $L$, i.e. taking approximate distances from Figure 5.6:

| | $T_iQ_i\,\lvert x - x\rvert$ | | $T_iQ_i\,\lvert y - y\rvert$ |
|---|---|---|---|
| For Manchester | 8(40) | + | 8(140) |
| For Liverpool | 4(120) | + | 4(120) |
| For Birmingham | 9(0) | + | 9(0) |
| For London | 5(150) | + | 5(160) |
| | $L$ = £1550 | + | £2400 = £3950 |

In fact this is an approximate procedure. It does not, theoretically, apply when transport between points is direct, but can be used to provide a solution which in most cases is near to the least transport cost location.

The simple example above involved the same unit transport cost between the warehouse and each customer location. In practice, however, unit transport costs may differ. For example, in a suppliers/warehouse/customers situation, transport to the customer will often be more expensive than transport from the supplier, if only because of the smaller quantities which are normally involved between warehouse and customer. In the not unusual case of a single plant supplying a warehouse, which in turn supplies several customers, if the unit cost of transport from the plant to the warehouse equals the unit cost of transport between the warehouse and the supplier, it will normally be appropriate to locate the warehouse and plant together.

## The multi-facility location problem *(Table 5.3, categories B2, 3, 4, 5, 6 and 7)*

The multi-facility locational choice problem will occur wherever there is a need to establish a new multi-facility organization, e.g. a new choice of retail shops. This is relatively uncommon. The problem is more likely to be encountered with an existing business where there is a need for an additional facility.

### Number of facilities

One question which must be asked at some stage is how many separate facilities should exist. Would it be better, for example, to have three separate facilities each capable of dealing with a throughput of 100 units per year, or two capable of dealing with 150 each? Consideration of economies of scale would suggest that fewer, larger facilities might be desirable, but consideration of transport costs, etc. might suggest that more facilities closer to their respective suppliers and/or markets might be more attractive. In fact, as is often the case, in this situation there are certain counter-directional costs to consider. One set of costs will increase as the number of facilities increases, e.g. cost of equipment, building, etc., while another set of costs will decrease as the number of facilities increases, e.g. transport costs. The point at which the total of these two sets of costs is minimized indicates the (least cost) number of facilities to employ.

### Facility capacity

The need to decide on the distribution of capacity between facilities where several facilities are undertaking, or are able to undertake, similar activities is a related problem. If an organization currently has the capacity to deal with 1000 units per year, yet demand is sufficient to encourage the company to expand to a throughput of 1200 units per year, then this expansion in capacity can be provided by the addition of a new facility capable of dealing with 200 units per year, or the expansion of one or more of the existing sites, or the addition of a larger site coupled with the closure of or reduction in some of the existing facilities.

To consider locational choice and capacity simultaneously would necessitate the use of extremely complex procedures. In many cases, therefore, the two aspects are treated separately. Again, the procedures which are available apply equally to problems involving the location of manufacturing facilities, supply establishments, etc. We shall again consider the latter. We shall deal only with the simple case in which there are a finite number of locations with fixed and known capacities.

**EXAMPLE**

### *A distribution company*

A company has two warehouses both handling the same range of goods. They are located in the United Kingdom at Cambridge and Bradford. Both distribute goods to five major centres: London, Bristol, Birmingham, Manchester and Hull. Because of an increase in demand the company is anxious to establish another warehouse, and the choice has been narrowed to two possible locations, Nottingham and Crewe, both of which are within easy reach of all major customer locations (Figure 5.7).

The unit distribution costs and the capacities of the existing warehouses are shown in Table 5.9. The forecast unit distribution cost and the capacities of warehouses at the two possible new locations together with forecast demand for the five distribution centres, are shown in Table 5.10.

Clearly we are faced with the problem of selecting one of the two possible situations:

(a) Warehouses at Cambridge, Bradford and Nottingham;

(b) Warehouses at Cambridge, Bradford and Crewe.

In order to make this choice we must investigate the costs associated with each of the two situations. Considering situation (a), we can rearrange our data in the manner shown in Table 5.11. This table shows the total distribution cost/unit moved from each of the warehouses to each of the customer locations. The total capacity of the three warehouses is sufficient to satisfy the total demand, but in order to be able to evaluate the merit of this situation we must find the minimum cost allocation of goods between warehouses and customer locations.

This is now a straightforward linear programming problem which can be solved quite easily using the transportation method, or algorithm.[3] This method of obtaining an optimal solution to allocation problems of this type is described in detail in Appendix I. Using this technique, a minimum cost allocation of goods from warehouses to destinations as shown in Table 5.12 can quite easily be found.[4]

The total distribution cost associated with this situation and with the choice of this location is found as follows (referring to Tables 5.11 and 5.12).

9000 × 1.6
1000 × 1.7
2000 × 1.7
4000 × 1.7
8000 × 1.6
7000 × 1.4
6000 × 1.5
Total = £57 900

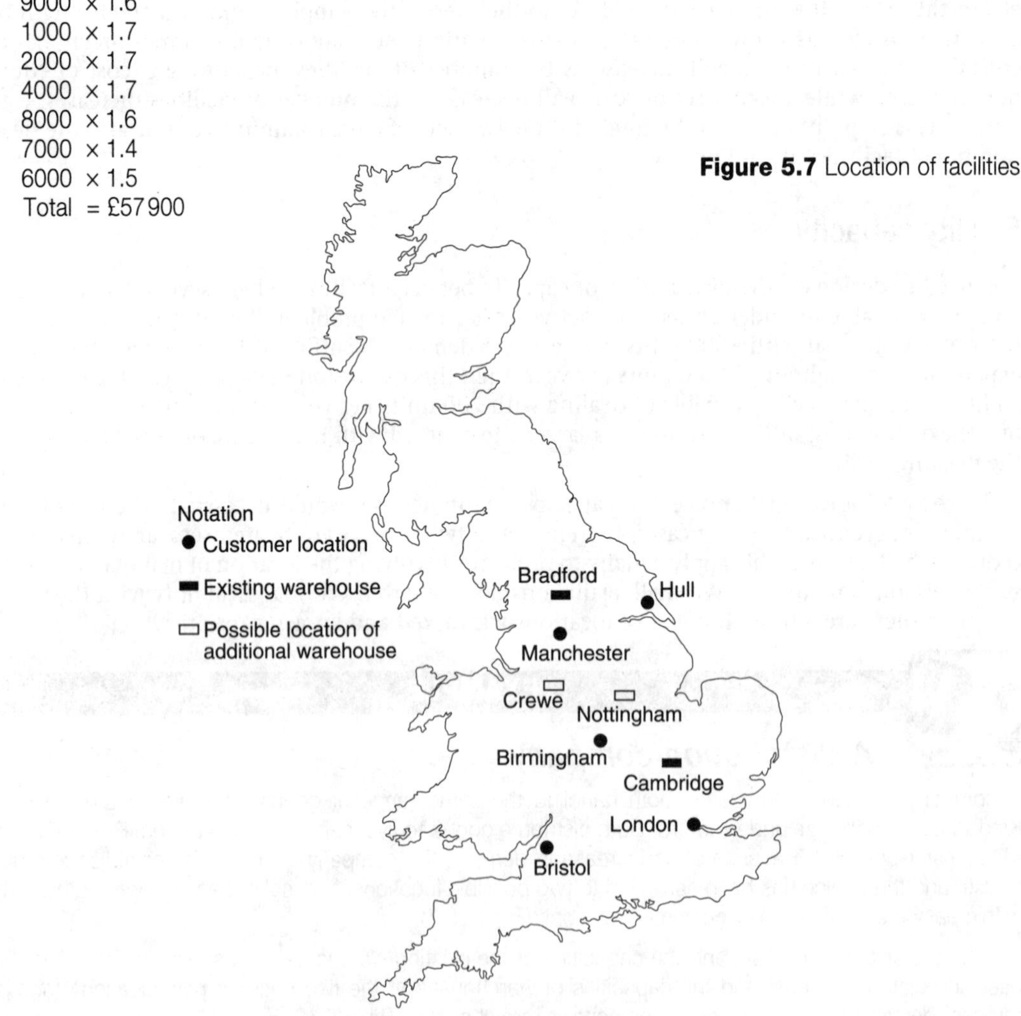


**Figure 5.7** Location of facilities

[3] An algorithm is an iterative solution procedure, i.e. a procedure which, by means of a defined sequence of steps or calculations, converges on a solution.

[4] You may wish to read Appendix I at this point. Having become familiar with the transportation method, you will be able to solve the problem shown in Table 5.11.

**Table 5.9 Distribution costs data for existing warehouses**

| Warehouse \ Customer location | London | Bristol | Birmingham | Manchester | Hull | Unit distribution cost | Monthly capacity |
|---|---|---|---|---|---|---|---|
| **Cambridge** | 0.3[a] | 0.4[a] | 0.4[a] | 0.5[a] | 0.6[a] | 1.3[a] | 10000 |
| **Bradford** | 0.5[a] | 0.5[a] | 0.4[a] | 0.2[a] | 0.3[a] | 1.2[a] | 15000 |

[a] Additional £/unit distributed from warehouse to a particular customer

**Table 5.10 Forecast demand and distribution cost data for each of possible warehouses**

| Warehouse \ Customer location | London | Bristol | Birmingham | Manchester | Hull | Unit distribution cost | Monthly capacity |
|---|---|---|---|---|---|---|---|
| **Nottingham** | 0.3[b] | 0.3[b] | 0.2[b] | 0.2[b] | 0.3[b] | 1.4[a] | 12000 |
| **Crewe** | 0.4[b] | 0.3[b] | 0.2[b] | 0.2[b] | 0.4[b] | 1.3[a] | 12000 |
| **Forecast monthly demand** | 9000 | 7000 | 8000 | 7000 | 6000 | | |

[a] £/unit distributed from warehouse to any customer
[b] Additional £/unit distributed from warehouse to a particular customer

**Table 5.11 Total unit costs associated with situation (a) (£/unit)**

| Warehouse \ Customer location | London | Bristol | Birmingham | Manchester | Hull | Capacity |
|---|---|---|---|---|---|---|
| **Cambridge** | 1.6 | 1.7 | 1.7 | 1.8 | 1.9 | 10000 |
| **Bradford** | 1.7 | 1.7 | 1.6 | 1.4 | 1.5 | 15000 |
| **Nottingham** | 1.7 | 1.7 | 1.6 | 1.6 | 1.7 | 12000 |
| **Requirements** | 9000 | 7000 | 8000 | 7000 | 6000 | |

**Table 5.12 Minimum cost allocation of goods for situation (a)**

| Warehouse \ Customer location | London | Bristol | Birmingham | Manchester | Hull | Capacity |
|---|---|---|---|---|---|---|
| **Cambridge** | 9000 | 1000 | | | | 10000 |
| **Bradford** | | 2000 | | 7000 | 6000 | 15000 |
| **Nottingham** | | 4000 | 8000 | | | 12000 |
| **Requirements** | 9000 | 7000 | 8000 | 7000 | 6000 | |

Now consider the alternative situation (b). Table 5.13 shows the total unit costs associated with the delivery of goods from each of the warehouses to each of the customer locations. (Only the third line, the costs associated with the additional location, differs from Table 5.11.) We can again use the transportation method of linear programming to obtain an optimum allocation of goods as shown in Table 5.14. The quantities allocated from the three warehouses to the five centres are the same as in the previous case, but for this situation the total cost is as follows:

9000 × 1.6
1000 × 1.7
2000 × 1.7
4000 × 1.6
8000 × 1.5
7000 × 1.4
6000 × 1.5
Total = £56700

Since this cost is less than the minimum obtained for situation (a), then on a basis of the criterion considered here, *i.e. cost of distribution*, we would select situation (b), i.e. Crewe, as the location of our additional warehouse.

**Table 5.13 Total unit costs associated with situation (b) (£/unit)**

| Warehouse \ Customer location | London | Bristol | Birmingham | Manchester | Hull | Capacity |
|---|---|---|---|---|---|---|
| **Cambridge** | 1.6 | 1.7 | 1.7 | 1.8 | 1.9 | 10000 |
| **Bradford** | 1.7 | 1.7 | 1.6 | 1.4 | 1.5 | 15000 |
| **Crewe** | 1.7 | 1.6 | 1.5 | 1.5 | 1.7 | 12000 |
| **Requirements** | 9000 | 7000 | 8000 | 7000 | 6000 | |

**Table 5.14 Minimum cost allocation of goods for situation (b)**

| Warehouse \ Customer location | London | Bristol | Birmingham | Manchester | Hull | Capacity |
|---|---|---|---|---|---|---|
| **Cambridge** | 9000 | 1000 | | | | 10000 |
| **Bradford** | | 2000 | | 7000 | 6000 | 15000 |
| **Crewe** | | 4000 | 8000 | | | 12000 |
| **Requirements** | 9000 | 7000 | 8000 | 7000 | 6000 | |

It should of course be remembered that distribution costs are rarely the sole criterion considered during the determination of plant locations; however, this type of analysis is often used if only as a means of providing a first solution. It should also be noted that the factors influencing location decisions are liable to change. The logical location at present may, at a later date, appear quite inferior because of change in one of the many factors which influenced the original choice.

Conceptually, the problem of the location of facilities abroad does not differ from the problems discussed in this chapter. In practice, however, such a problem will often be more complex and will assume greater proportions, if only because more investment may be involved. In such situations the identification and quantification of factors may be more difficult; nevertheless, the decision is amenable to the type of technique discussed earlier.

## COMPUTER METHODS

Location decisions and the related logistics and transportation problems are areas in which computer-based methods are invaluable. As we have seen, even the simplest locational choice problem can necessitate detailed and lengthy calculations. More realistic problems involving multiple facilities, alternative locations and constraints may be impossible to examine quantitatively without the use of a computer. Further, location decision-making is often not a 'one-off' problem-solving situation. Circumstances (costs, etc.) may change and alternatives must be re-examined. 'What if . . .' type questions may need to be asked and the merits of several alternatives quickly evaluated. These types of situation are ideal candidates for computer analysis.

Three basic types of computer application in location decision-making can be identified.

### Analytical models

Certain particular and well-defined locational choice problems can be expressed mathematically. A mathematical model can be set up, data inserted, calculations performed, and an answer (normally an optimal solution) found. The last two problems covered above fall into this category. In each case an objective can be stated and the best solution found, given the assumptions and simplifications implicit in the mathematical approach. There are other location problems that can be tackled in this way. One categorization of such problems is as follows:

(a) ***planar location problems***: where one or more new locations are to be chosen anywhere in a given area;

(b) ***network location problems***: where one or more new locations are to be chosen from among a limited number of alternatives, on a given network, e.g. from among the available *nodes* on a transportation or distribution network;

(c) ***discrete location problems***: similar to (a) above, but with possible locations limited to a discrete set of available 'sites'.

Mathematical models or algorithms exist for solving at least some types of problems in these categories. Computer programs have been written for these algorithms since otherwise the amount of calculations would have prevented this type of approach except for the simplest of cases.

## Simulation *(see also Appendix III)*

Computer simulation involves the establishment of a model of a real system on a computer to permit experiments to be performed. This enables inferences to be drawn about the behaviour of real systems without the need for actual experiments on them. A computer simulation of, say, a national distribution system comprising supply points, warehouses, distribution routes and customer destinations could be used to evaluate the effects of increased/decreased loads, changed costs, changed demands, etc. Such investigations may lead to decisions on the relocation of facilities. Simulations of hypothetical systems will enable alternatives to be compared and locational choices to be made.

This type of approach has been possible for many years but has become more valuable with the availability of user-friendly general-purpose simulation software offering animation capabilities, etc.

## Decision support and expert systems

Decision support systems (DSSs) allow managers to select and manipulate information to aid decision-making. Three basic components exist:

(a) ***a database management system***, comprising several databases (with facilities to add, delete or modify data), and a means to handle these data;

(b) ***a model management system***, comprising facilities to model systems, add and integrate models, and interact with the database(s);

(c) ***a dialog management system***, comprising facilities to interact with users, present data, etc.

Sophisticated DSSs offer a modelling capability (in the manner of a simulation package – see above), analysis capability, forecasting and statistical facilities, data management, communication and reporting facilities, all in a user-friendly manner.

MICRO-LMS (Logistics Modelling System) is a proprietary microcomputer-based DSS for logistics planning.[5] This DSS helps managers tackle questions such as:

(a) the number, size, location and type of facilities;

(b) supply relationships with customers;

(c) the allocation of customer orders to facilities;

(d) the effect of changes in costs, capacities and customer demands;

(e) customer service versus cost trade-offs.

---

[5] Optimal Decision Systems Inc.,10921 Reed Hartman Hory, Cincinatti, Ohio 45242, USA.

At the policy level, MICRO-LMS may be used to evaluate hypothetical facility locations such as new plants or warehouses. At a lower level, it can be used to consider the effects of changing costs, capacities and customer orders to production and distribution facilities, subject to available capacity and customer service restrictions. It can also be employed to determine the best allocation of customer orders to a facility within given capacity and customer service restrictions. Thus the system provides the manager with the capability to evaluate alternatives and choose the best configuration.

A DSS, such as that described, is basically a *responsive system*. It will simulate, process and analyse in response to a user request. It has little or no expertise of its own – no intelligence. In contrast, a computer *expert system* offers some measure of artificial intelligence (AI) and can therefore make decisions for, or at least offer decisions to, its user. An expert system can be defined as a tool which has the capability to 'understand' problem-specific knowledge, and use domain knowledge intelligently to suggest alternative paths of action.[6] Expert systems can be constructed to combine the knowledge of experts in a particular area, coupled with a set of rules (an inference engine) and procedures to deploy and develop such expertise in developing solutions to given problems. Expert systems – a short yet significant step from DSSs – will surely have an important role to play in locational choice and logistics decision-making.

---

6 Kumara, S. and Lehtihet, A. L. (1989) in Wild, R. (ed.) *International Handbook of Production and Operations Management*. London: Cassell.

## CHECKLIST FOR CHAPTER 5

### The need for locational choice

Expansion/contraction
Replacement
Pressures for change of space
Pressures for a new location

### Facilities location decisions

- Facility location decision levels
  - Region
  - Area
  - Community
  - Site
- 'Fixed' and 'delivered' services

Factors influencing decisions

The choice of a new site
- Costs: fixed
- Costs: variable
- Volume considerations in location choice
- Timing
- Subjective assessments
- Government inducements

### Types of location problem

Single-facility
- No connections
- Connections IN
- Connections OUT
- Connections IN and OUT
- Multi-facility
  - Set with no connections
  - Set with connections IN
  - Set with connections OUT
  - Set with connections IN and OUT
  - Addition to set with connections IN from other set locations
  - Addition to set with connections OUT
  - Addition to set with connections IN and OUT
- Combinations

Single-facility location problems
- Checklists of factors
  - Regional
  - Area
  - Community
  - Site
- Location factor comparisons
- Dimensional analysis
  - With weightings
- Minimization of transport costs

Multi-facility location problems
- Number of facilities
- Capacity of facilities
- The transportation algorithm

### Computer methods

Analytical models
Simulation
Decisions support and expert systems

## FURTHER READING

**Francis, R. L. and White, J. A. (1987)** *Facilities Layout and Location: An Analytical Approach.* Englewood Cliffs: Prentice-Hall.

**Love, R. F. *et al.* (1986)** *Facilities Location: Models and Methods.* Amsterdam: Elsevier.

The above are major texts dealing in detail with many of the topics covered in this chapter.

**Bridgeman, P. W. (1963)** *Dimensional Analysis.* New Haven, Conn.: Yale University Press.

**Domschke, W. and Drexl, A. (1985)** *Location and Layout Planning*. Berlin and Heidelburg: Springer-Verlag. Deals with the topics of this and the next chapter.

**Haigh, R. W. (1980)** Selecting a US plant location: the management decision process in foreign companies. *Columbia Journal of World Business*, **25**(3), pp. 22–31.

## QUESTIONS

5.1 Briefly, what changes might result in the need for additional space for a service operation (of your own choice)? Under what circumstances might such changes lead to the need for an entirely new site, and what would influence the choice of such a site?

5.2 Galvanated Decorations (Sales) Ltd is a family business situated in the heart of the UK Midlands, i.e. at Birmingham. The company distributes ornamental lamp-posts to agents in London, Newcastle and Manchester. The lamp-posts are obtained from a manufacturer in Liverpool. The tables below show the annual quantities involved, the distances and the transport cost per item per 40 km travelled. What maximum total transportation cost benefit would Galvanated Decorations Ltd obtain by relinquishing its Birmingham premises for a warehouse elsewhere, and where should this new warehouse be located?

| Product | Annual quantity | Transportation cost per unit per 40 km |
|---|---|---|
| Lamp-posts from Liverpool | 13000 | 0.4 |
| Lamp-posts for London | 7000 | 0.8 |
| Lamp-posts for Newcastle | 3000 | 0.65 |
| Lamp-posts for Manchester | 2400 | 0.65 |

**Table of distances (km)**

| | London | Manchester | Birmingham | Liverpool | Newcastle |
|---|---|---|---|---|---|
| London | – | | | | |
| Manchester | 306 | – | | | |
| Birmingham | 177 | 129 | – | | |
| Liverpool | 322 | 61 | 145 | – | |
| Newcastle | 475 | 217 | 290 | 241 | – |

*Note*: See Figure 5.6. Birmingham, shown; Liverpool, shown; London, shown; Newcastle, Ref. 10C: Manchester shown.

5.3 Incredible Chemicals Ltd intends to establish a plant solely for the blending of Formula X14, which is a composite of X9 and X5 and is used by the company in the manufacture of agricultural fertilizer.

X9 is imported by Incredible Chemicals and is to be transported from London docks, while X5 is obtained from a subsidiary company at Hull.

Formula X14 is to be used at three other Incredible Chemicals works at Manchester, Bristol and Newcastle, where the requirements are 40, 30 and 50 tonnes per week respectively. Equal quantities of X9 and X5 are required to blend Formula X14, but because of atmospheric contamination 15% of the tonnage of Formula X14 is wasted and has to be burnt.

Incredible Chemicals transports all products and materials by road, the cost per tonne per kilometre being £0.016. There is, however, an additional charge associated with imported items which effectively increases transportation costs to £0.018 per tonne per kilometre. Considering only transportation costs, where should the new Incredible Chemicals blending plant be situated?

**Table of distances (km)**

| | Manchester | Bristol | Newcastle | London | Hull |
|---|---|---|---|---|---|
| Manchester | - | | | | |
| Bristol | 257 | - | | | |
| Newcastle | 217 | 483 | - | | |
| London | 306 | 193 | 475 | - | |
| Hull | 121 | 290 | 193 | 322 | - |

*Note*: See Figure 5.6. Manchester, shown; Bristol, Ref. P9; Newcastle, Ref. 11D; London, shown; Hull, Ref. H13.

5.4 In the interests of public health, Incredible Chemicals Ltd decides not to burn the 15% of Formula X14 which is wasted by atmospheric contamination during blending. (See previous question.) After careful consideration and research the company decides to sell this 'waste' product to a company in London which intends to use it in a patent weed-killer.

How does this decision affect the choice of site for the new Formula X14 blending plant, and what is the total weekly transportation cost difference between the previous choice of site and the new choice of site?

5.5 Micro Software Labs is anxious to establish a UK HQ. Although in theory the choice of location is wide, in practice the choice is limited to two government-designated development areas centred on Sunderland and Birkenhead. One of the economists employed by MSL has evaluated both of these locations and has completed the following information. Which location should the company choose?

| Factor | Sunderland £ | Birkenhead £ | Weighting factor[b] |
|---|---|---|---|
| Cost of land | 10000 | 12500 | 4 |
| Cost of buildings | 30000 | 35000 | 4 |
| Cost of labour | 7500 | 10000 | 3 |
| Transport cost p.a. | 6000 | 2000 | 3 |
| Industrial relations[a] | 50 | 80 | 5 |
| Labour training needs[a] | 75 | 60 | 2 |
| Community benefits[a] | 70 | 30 | 1 |

[a] Because of the difficulty of costing these factors, a score (1 to 100) has been given where 1 is equivalent to a low cost and 100 to a high cost.

[b] This weighting factor indicates the importance of each factor; 1 is of least importance and 10 is of most importance.

5.6 After several years' successful trading in Europe, Euro Design Consultants Ltd has decided to establish a subsidiary in North America. The possible locations for the American HQ have been reduced to three: Chicago, Seattle and Detroit.

The following information has been provided by the company's accountants and marketing people. All other things being equal, which location should the company adopt for its American distribution operations?

| Factor | Chicago | Seattle | Detroit |
|---|---|---|---|
| 1 Cost of buildings | $50 000 | $45 000 | $38 000 |
| Cost of land | $9 000 | $8 000 | $7000 |
| Distribution costs | $7 000 | $10 000 | $12 000 |
| 2 Initial labour training and recruitment costs | $4 000 | $6 000 | $7 000 |
| 3 Percentage annual labour turnover expected | 10% | 20% | 35% |
| 4 Recreational attractions[a] | 1 | 2 | 3 |
| Availability of housing[a] | 2 | 1 | 3 |
| 5 Suitability of site for subsequent expansion[b] | 5 | 7 | 10 |

[a] Ranking: 1 = most attractive: 3 = least attractive
[b] Rating on ten-point scale provided by managing director: 1 = most attractive; 10 = least attractive

As a means of evaluating the alternatives, the managing director considers that factors 1 and 3 above have twice the importance of factors 2 and 4 and three times the importance of factor 5.

5.7 Company Z manufactures the same product at two existing factories located at A and B, and distributes them to three retail outlets at L, M and O. Because of an expected increase in demand for the product the company is considering opening an additional factory at *either* C or D. The tables below and at the top of p. 120 show:

(a) the unit production costs, the unit distribution costs and the monthly production capacity associated with the present situation, i.e. factories at A and B distributing to L, M and O;

| (a) | Outlet L | Outlet M | Outlet O | Unit production cost | Monthly production capacity |
|---|---|---|---|---|---|
| Factory A | 0.2 | 0.4 | 0.3 | 1.0 | 4000 |
| Factory B | 0.3 | 0.3 | 0.2 | 1.2 | 6000 |

(b) the unit production costs, the unit distribution costs and the monthly production capacities

| (b) | Outlet L | Outlet M | Outlet O | Unit production cost | Monthly production capacity |
|---|---|---|---|---|---|
| Factory C | 0.3 | 0.2 | 0.4 | 1.2 | 3500 |
| Factory D | 0.2 | 0.3 | 0.5 | 1.0 | 3000 |

associated with each of the possible additional factories;

(c) the forecasted monthly product demands for each of the three retail outlets.

| Outlet | Forcasted monthly demand |
|---|---|
| L | 3800 |
| M | 4500 |
| O | 4500 |

Where should the additional factory be established?

5.8 Referring to the previous question, how does the inclusion of *both* of the following modifications affect the choice of location?

(a) The cost per unit associated with the under-utilization of production capacity is 0.1 for factories A and C and 0.12 for factories B and D. (For example, if the required output from factory A is 3500 units per month compared with its production capacity of 4000 units per month, a cost of (4000 – 3500) × 0.1 is incurred.)

(b) The forecasted monthly demand for outlet L is 4000 units.

5.9 A company rents three warehouses at A, B and C, from which it supplies timber to two builders, P and Q. The profit (£) per tonne supplied, the annual demands of the builders and the supplies available from the warehouses are shown below.

The company is unhappy at not being able to meet the total annual demand of the builders, and for this reason is considering replacing warehouse C with a warehouse rented at D whose annual supply capacity would be 5000 tonnes, the use of which would give a profit of £6 and £5 per tonne of timber distributed to P and Q respectively. The additional cost of renting warehouse D in place of C would be £5000.

| | P | Q | Supply (000 tonnes) |
|---|---|---|---|
| A | 3 | 4 | 4 |
| B | 2 | 3 | 4 |
| C | 5 | 4 | 3 |
| Demand (000 tonnes) | 6 | 6 | |

(a) Should the company replace warehouse C?

(b) If warehouse C were replaced, at which warehouse would the excess supply capacity be stored assuming that storage is possible at A, B or D at negligible cost?

5.10 The map on p. 121 shows, to scale, the location of four cities in the eastern United States of America. The Moonshine Corporation is to locate three new facilities at Cleveland, Memphis and Jacksonville. One facility is the primary process, which is to supply each of the two other facilities, both of which supply a single customer at Richmond. The total annual output from the two secondary processes is 10000 units per year. The maximum size of either facility is 7000 units per year. The annual demand from Richmond is 10000 units per year.

The primary process facility has sufficient capacity to satisfy the two secondary processes.

The transportation costs are shown in Table 5.15. Assume direct movement between cities. Where should the three facilities be located, and what should the size of the two secondary process facilities be?

[a]Whether of 'primary' or 'secondary' outputs.

**Figure 5.8** Eastern USA

**Table 5.15** $ movement cost/unit[a]/mile

| From \ To | M | C | R | J |
|---|---|---|---|---|
| M | | 0.1 | 0.2 | 0.15 |
| C | 0.8 | | 0.25 | 0.2 |
| R | – | – | | – |
| J | 0.13 | 0.15 | 0.31 | |

**CASE STUDY (from Part 9)**

The topics covered in this chapter are relevant in the following (see Introduction to Part 9 and Table C.1):

| No. | Name | Country |
|---|---|---|
| 12 | FotoPrint Pronto | Italy |

Chapter 6

# The layout of facilities and materials handling

## ISSUES

What types of layout planning problems can occur?
What are the objectives in planning a layout?
What methods and procedures are available?
How can we evaluate alternative layouts?
Why is transport and handling important?
What methods are there for moving things and people?

## NOTATION USED IN THIS CHAPTER

$n$ Number of facilities
$L$ Cost value of a point (direct movement)
$x_i$ Co-ordinate of point $i$
$y_i$ Co-ordinate of point $i$
A Closeness rating: essential
E Closeness rating: very important
I Closeness rating: important
O Closeness rating: ordinary close
U Closeness rating: unimportant
X Closeness rating: undesirable

The layout problem is to do with the arrangement of facilities in a given space. It is important, common and complex. All types of organization will face this problem, to some extent and at some time. Objectives will differ. Even simple situations can result in much complexity. There are no simple, sufficient procedures for solving such problems.

Materials handling is to do with movement within the layout. Providing efficient and safe movement is important. Further, the need for such movement is often an important consideration in planning a layout.

## THE NEED FOR LAYOUT PLANNING

We often tend to think in terms of *planning complete layouts* and designing entirely new *sets of departments*, but although such occasions undoubtedly do arise the following are the types of problems we are much more likely to encounter.

### Enlarging or reducing existing departments

The addition or removal of facilities, the trading of areas between departments, or a complete relayout may be necessary because of increases or decreases in demand for goods or services, changes in the nature of goods and services, or changes in the scope or capability of processes.

### Movement of a department

The need to move a department because of a change in the specification or nature of the goods or services, or because of changes in demand or operating processes, may constitute a simple exercise. Alternatively, if the existing layout is inadequate, it may present the opportunity for a major change, the extent of which bears little relationship to the primary cause.

### Adding or removing a department

Adding a department may be the result of a desire to undertake work never before done on the site, or the desire to centralize work previously undertaken in several separate departments. Conversely, the removal of a department which is no longer required may facilitate or obviate the need for a rearrangement of other departments.

### Replacing equipment and adding new equipment

Frequently, even equipment designed to perform exactly the same function as its predecessors is physically different and its installation necessitates a certain amount of reorganization.

## OBJECTIVES IN LAYOUT PLANNING

Some of the advantages of good facilities layouts and hence some possible objectives in planning layouts are as follows.

### Cost of movement

In most operating systems there will be physical flows. The extent and cost of these flows will be affected by the layout of facilities. In manufacturing, the handling and movement of materials, components and the finished product, as well as the movement of labour, are primarily dependent on the location of the production and service facilities. The movement of customers in a retail store or in a service system such as a hotel or restaurant will be influenced by the layout of facilities. Improved layout will result in a reduction in the distance moved by items and/or customers and the time consumed, and hence in the cost of such movement whether to the organization or to the customer.

### Congestion and delay

The objective of most operations is to add to the value of inputs. This is achieved by subjecting inputs to some form of processing. No value is added and nothing is contributed to profits by delays or storage during operations. Although the extent of work-in-progress is also determined by the effectiveness of operations scheduling and the nature of the operations process, poor facilities layout may necessitate high work-in-progress and hence increase throughput time. Time spent by the customer waiting in a system generates no turnover, and the turnover of a supply system is adversely affected by delays in obtaining items for customers, so in all such cases an objective will be to minimize congestion and delay and thus provide for the more intensive use of facilities and the more efficient use of capacity.

### Utilization of space, facilities and labour

The cost of space is high. Wasted space may be eliminated and the total area required minimized by adequate facilities layout. Effective arrangement of facilities may reduce idle time and cut down investment in both direct (e.g. plant) and indirect (e.g. support) equipment. Adequate layout also facilitates operation, maintenance, service and supervision, and therefore permits a better utilization of resources. We have identified the importance of movement and flows and thus the handling of physical items and/or customers as factors or criteria in layout planning. Much of our discussion of layout planning techniques will reflect the importance of minimizing physical movement and handling. We have also referred to *capacity*, one objective of layout planning being the maximization of capacity utilization. When planning a new layout we must know the extent or quantity of each type of facility to be provided; we must know what capacity is to be provided. Layout planning is therefore contingent on capacity planning, which is discussed in Chapter 11.

## FACILITIES LAYOUT PROBLEMS

There are three levels of layout planning problem. Layout planning begins after the solution of the site location problem and then moves through these three levels:

(a) the layout of 'departments' within the site;

(b) the layout of 'facilities' within the 'departments';

(c) the layout of individual 'workplaces'.

In this chapter we are concerned explicitly with level (a) but implicitly the discussion relates to level (b) also, since they are the large-scale and small-scale levels of the same problem. Level (c), being concerned with ergonomics and work study, is dealt with in Chapters 7, 8 and 9. We shall use the term 'department' to mean an area containing several (perhaps interrelated) facilities. A 'facility' will be considered as a single (perhaps large and complex) piece of equipment, while a 'workplace' can be seen as the work area of one person or a work team.

Examples of the types of layout planning problems which might occur in different types of operating systems are given in Table 6.1.

## BASIC TYPES OF LAYOUT

### Manufacture

There are, classically, three main systems of manufacturing layout, each with individual characteristics and each appropriate to some form of manufacture, depending on the output rate and the range of products involved. Although each system is normally associated with a particular type of production, none is exclusive to any one industry. We shall examine each of these basic systems in turn, identifying the nature of production and the characteristics of each.

### Layout by process (or functional layout) *(see Figures 6.1 and 6.4(a))*

In a process or functional layout all operations of a similar nature are grouped together in the same department or part of the factory.

**Table 6.1 Facilities layout problems: examples**

| Type of operating system | Examples of operating system | Examples of a facilities layout planning problem | Basic type (or cause) of problem | Possible objectives |
|---|---|---|---|---|
| Manufacturing system | Kitchen of a large restaurant | Because of building changes elsewhere in the restaurant, the locations of drains have been changed, and it is now necessary to relocate dish washing and drying. | Movement of a department | 1. Maximize space utilization<br>2. Minimize amount of movement of crockery and/or people in kitchen |
| Supply system | Supermarket | It has been decided to provide a petrol station in or adjacent to the car park, to provide fuel for customers' cars and for others who choose to call. | Adding a department | 1. Ease of access (minimum distance for customers)<br>2. Space utilization<br>3. Prominence |
| Transport system | Passenger transport within an airport terminal building | The transport system comprises elevators (lifts), escalators and moving walkways. There is a need to replace the main set of four (adjacent) elevators with eight rapid elevators. They cannot be located in the present elevator area. | Enlarging a department | Minimum passenger congestion |
| Service system | Reception area in a large hotel | Information for residents (e.g. weather reports, local entertainments, bus, rail and flight times, etc.) was displayed on a notice-board. This is to be removed and a computer data terminal is to be installed to provide a complete information service for customers. | Replacing a facility | 1. Minimize customer congestion<br>2. Maximize space utilization<br>3. Maximize utilization |

Layout by process is appropriate where small quantities of a large range of products are to be manufactured, perhaps the best example being jobbing production. The nature of the layout permits flexibility in production, i.e. complex products requiring processing in every one of the functional departments may be made alongside simple products requiring processing in only a few departments. Such a situation would be difficult to accommodate in either of the other two systems of layout. This flexibility, however, brings disadvantages. Process layouts normally operate with a comparatively high level of work-in-progress, and throughput time is high. Specialist supervision is possible and the grouping of employees of similar type and skill within the same department promotes cohesiveness and enables individual bonus schemes to be used. The provision of services is simpler than in other forms of layout, but the cost of materials handling is high.

## Layout by product *(see Figure 6.2)*

Layout by product is appropriate for the production of a small range of products in large quantities. Ideally, only one standardized product is involved and processing should be continuous. Facilities are arranged according to the needs of the product and in the same sequence as the operations necessary for processing. Such layouts are relatively inflexible. Enough stable demand to ensure a high utilization of equipment is essential, as is a regular supply of the right quantities of materials and components.

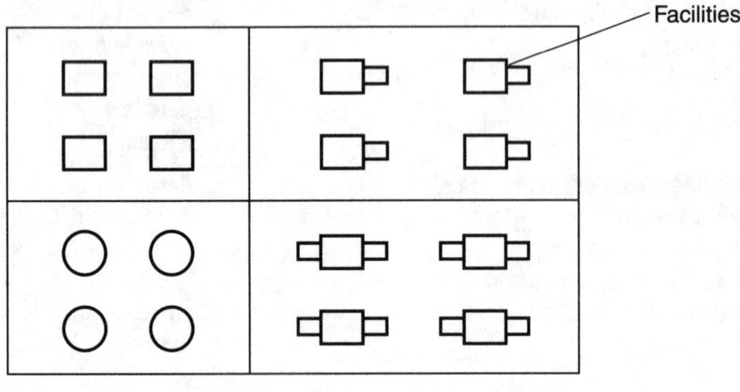


**Figure 6.1** Process or functional layout with four departments

The provision of services is difficult, since different pieces of equipment with different characteristics and requirements may be located adjacent to one another. A mixture of skills and tasks often occurs, resulting in difficulties in payment and supervision, but usually little specialized supervision is required, since the work performed is often highly rationalized. Minimum floor space is required, work-in-progress is minimized and the throughput is high. The requirements for handling materials are small and facility utilization is high.

**Figure 6.2** Product type layout – Mamma Mia Pasta House (see also case example in Chapter 15)

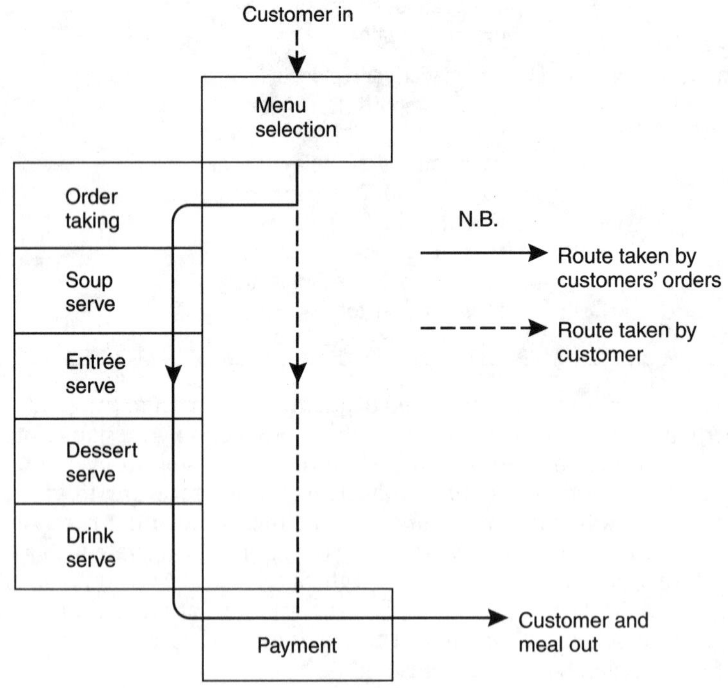

## Layout by fixed position *(see Figure 6.3)*

In the two previous layout systems the product moves past stationary production equipment. In this case the reverse applies. In the extreme case, e.g. civil engineering, neither the partly completed nor the finished product moves. Alternatively, as in ship building, the product remains stationary only until it is completed.

Historically a large proportion of production was undertaken in this manner by artisans in their own homes. Layout by fixed position is comparatively unimportant, except where civil engineering and large items such as ships and aircraft are concerned.

## Group layout (or cell) *(see Figure 6.4(b))*

Process, product and fixed-position layouts are the traditional forms in manufacturing industry. Recently, however, in batch production, configurations known as group layouts have begun to emerge as distinctive arrangements. In effect, group layout is a hybrid form which provides a type of product arrangement of facilities for the manufacture of similar items, each of which, if taken individually, would normally be manufactured through a process configuration. This approach is used as a means of achieving some of the benefits of layout by product in the batch manufacture of products. Groups of similar items are formed using group technology classification procedures of the type described in Chapter 3. Given a large enough group it is practical to arrange in one area all the facilities required for their production. Group layouts differ from layouts by product, therefore, in that they are used for the manufacture of similar (but not the same) items required for the batch manufacture of final products. In most cases all items passing through a group layout will not require the use of all facilities, so flow patterns will differ, but because of the similarity of items utilization will be high. Figures 6.4(a) and (b) show flow patterns for alternative arrangements, the group layout having been designed to accommodate items A to H as groups I to IV. The most advanced application of group-type layouts can be found in computer-controlled flexible manufacturing systems.

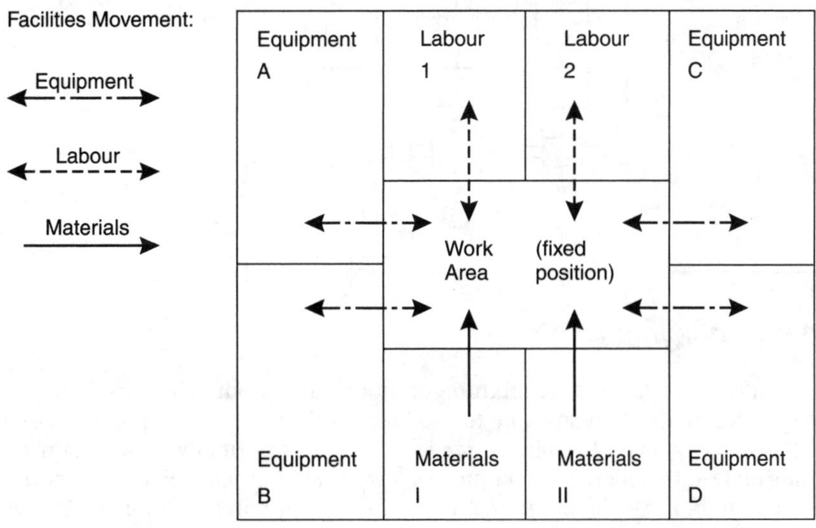


**Figure 6.3** Layout by fixed position

**Figure 6.4(a)** Workflow in a functional layout (with four 'departments')

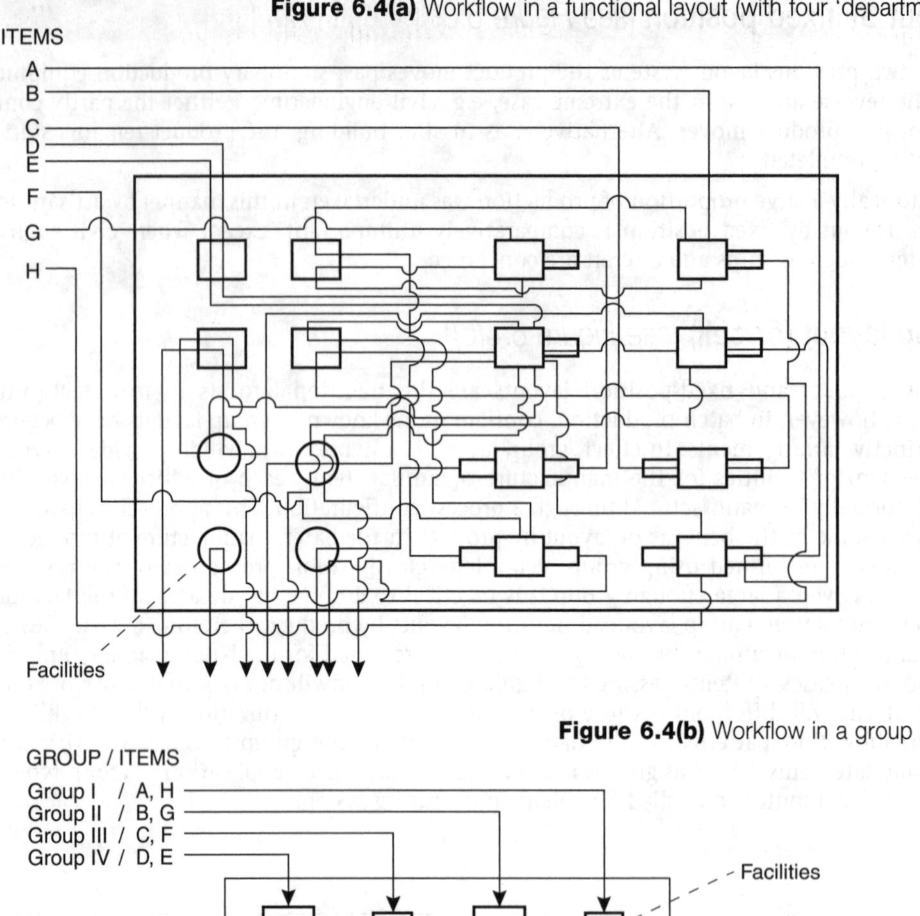


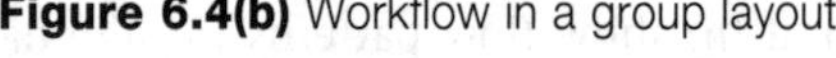

**Figure 6.4(b)** Workflow in a group layout

## Hybrids and mixed layouts

Most practical manufacturing layouts are mixtures of process and product layouts. Rarely are companies in the enviable situation where they are able to produce continuously large quantities of an absolutely standard product. Similarly, even the largest range of products normally uses certain common components, and firms obliged to concentrate on process layouts are normally able to support some product layouts as well. A common mixed layout in manufacture would involve an arrangement which was predominantly by process, but with subsidiary areas arranged by product or as group layouts. Such an arrangement might exist in engineering production where, although products differ substantially, it has been possible to identify a group of similar sub-assemblies or components which taken together permit the use of a more specialized layout with adequate volume throughput.

**Table 6.2 Comparison of process and product layouts**

| | **Layout by process** | **Layout by product** |
|---|---|---|
| Nature | All similar facilities grouped together | Sequence of facilities derived from needs of product |
| Application | Low quantity throughput<br>Large range of items | Large quantity throughput<br>Only a few items |
| Characteristics | Permits specialist supervision | Little specialized supervision required |
| | High work-in-progress | Minimum work-in-progress |
| | High materials handling cost | Minimum materials handling cost |
| | Ease of provision of services | Difficult to provide services |
| | | Minimum space required |
| | Can tolerate breakdowns | Single breakdown stops all machines |
| | Easy to incorporate inspection | Difficult to incorporate inspection |
| | Individual bonus possible | Group bonus |
| | Flexibility, variety and product changes possible | Little variety possible |
| | Possibility of loss or neglect of some jobs/items | |
| | Maintenance easy | Maintenance out of production hours |
| | Control complex | Control simple |
| | Planning simple | Planning complex |
| | | Accurate work measurement essential |
| | Long throughput time | Low throughput time |

## Comparison of layout types

The characteristics of layout by product and by process are listed and contrasted in Table 6.2. Figure 6.5 shows a breakeven point analysis of three types of production, indicating the relative cost benefits first of process layout, then of product layout as output increases.

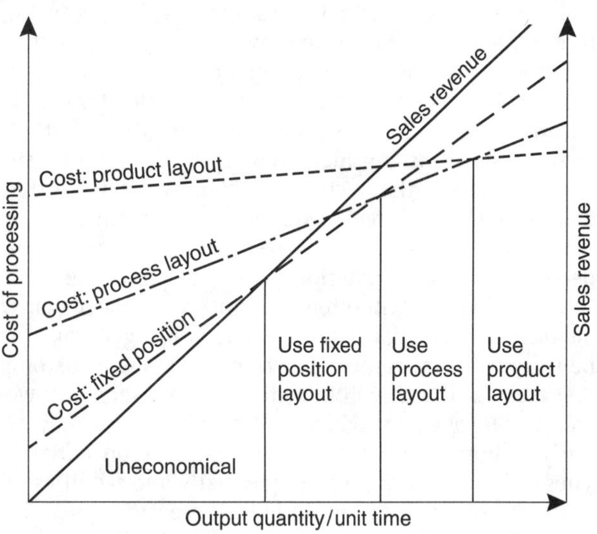


**Figure 6.5** Breakeven analysis showing economic advantage of various types of layout for the same product at different output levels

## Non-manufacturing systems

The four types of layout described above also exist in non-manufacturing situations. With the exception of transport systems, these four layout types encompass most of what will be encountered in planning the layout of non-manufacturing systems. Some examples are given in Table 6.3. Mixed layouts are also used, e.g. in service systems such as restaurants (layout by product for buffets, and layout by process for waiter service dining).

Table 6.3 Types of layout: examples

| Type of operating system | Type of layout | | | |
|---|---|---|---|---|
| | **Process layout** | **Product layout** | **Fixed-position layout** | **Group layout** |
| Service systems | 1. Hotel<br>2. Reference library | 1. Automatic carwash<br>2. Medical screening and diagnosis | Hospital operating theatre | - |
| Supply systems | 1. Supermarket<br>2. Warehouse | 1. Restaurant self-service | Restaurant dining room | - |
| Manufacturing systems | 1. Jobbing production<br>2. Small batch production | 1. Motor-vehicle assembly line<br>2. Chemical process plant | 1. Shipyard<br>2. Civil engineering | Batch production of components for a variety of products |
| Transport systems | See text | See text | - | - |

## Supply and service systems

Similar configurations can be identified in supply and service systems. In supply the principal flows and movements will resemble those of manufacturing systems, since again goods are involved. In service systems the principal flows may involve people, often customers. In a warehouse, for example, a functional layout may be employed in which particular areas are used for the storage of particular product lines or goods. In such situations flow patterns will be relatively simple in that goods will be received into the warehouse and placed into storage, from where eventually they will be transferred to customers. In such cases therefore there will be little flow or movement between areas, and thus the layout problem is considerably simplified. A similar situation may exist in a retail store. In these situations, however, the 'picking' problem will exist in that warehouse or counter staff may be required to collect together all items required for a particular customer by travelling between the appropriate areas within the facility. Thus movement problems are of importance and minimization of movement becomes a relevant criterion for layout planning. In service systems such as hospitals, the process or functional layout will often be found, since particular wards and particular parts of the hospital will be devoted to particular types of activity, e.g. general surgery, medicine, geriatrics. Here again there may be substantial movement between areas, since customers, i.e. patients, may need attention from several areas, and staff will have to move between and work in several of these areas. In certain medical facilities layout by product or flow-type layout may be used. For example, in certain cases a series of fairly elaborate medical tests will be made on patients as part of screening or diagnostic procedures. These tests may be arrange sequentially and facilities provided to minimize throughput time and maximize resource utilization. In both these functions it is possible to envisage a layout by fixed position, particularly in the service sector, where facilities might be brought to a customer; for example, in the case of a road accident, medical facilities would be brought to the injured patient.

Thus the three traditional layouts may exist in supply and service organizations and the movement and flows of items and people between areas within the layout may be a principal feature in determining the configuration.

### Transport systems

The essential feature of transport systems is movement. In many such systems the principal facilities employed are mobile. In this chapter we are concerned with the arrangement of essentially static facilities, so a somewhat different situation applies as regards facilities layout for transport systems, since in this context we are concerned only with the arrangement of a portion (perhaps in a way the least important portion) of the facilities of the system, namely the fixed facilities, e.g. garage, service bays. Given this, however, much the same situation might be found, and again it will be possible to identify at least two of the three traditional configurations, namely layout by process and by product. As with manufacture, supply and service, movement and physical flows may again be seen to be the principal criteria in establishing the layout.

## LAYOUT PLANNING PROCEDURE

The planning of an entirely new layout is the most comprehensive problem and although such occasions are comparatively rare we shall consider this case in order to cover the subject adequately.

We are proposing to establish a new set of facilities in one location. It is assumed that the precise nature of the goods or services to be provided and the demand for them either are known or may be determined. Given this information, the required capacity and hence the number and nature of facilities can be determined (see Chapter 11).

Facilities required = $f$(nature of goods or services and demand)

In addition to the principal facilities, other equipment will be needed; hence additional space must be provided. Storage space will be required. Departments such as personnel, etc. must be accommodated.

Space required = $f$(nature of facilities and nature of additional facilities required)

The layout planning procedure therefore involves consideration of demand, capacity, work methods and standards, resource requirements, handling and movement, and space requirements, among other factors. We will consider these factors below.

### Demand

Normally, an operation will be established to meet an existing demand. If we are building a new hospital ward to increase the total throughput of patients and reduce waiting lists, then the extent of the demand for that type of treatment will be known. If we are building a new warehouse to supply a particular area with existing items we will again know something of expected demand. Otherwise we will rely on market research to help determine the capacity required.

### Capacity

The determination of capacity requires not only the estimation of steady-state or average demand levels but also decisions on how best to deal with demand level fluctuations. In Chapter 11 it will be seen that the accommodation of demand fluctuations may necessitate the provision of 'storage' space for goods or customer over-capacity, etc.; thus detailed capacity planning is essential before layout planning is begun.

### Work methods and standards

Method study (see Chapter 7) will establish the sequence of operations to be performed and the types of equipment to be used. Given work methods, work measurement (see Chapter 8) will be used to establish work content.

### Resource requirements

Given an estimate of capacity, and work content, it will be possible to calculate resource requirements in terms of both labour and equipment. Some allowance must be made for breakdowns, holidays, stoppages, etc.

### Handling and movement

The nature of any handling equipment must be known. The equipment required to provide movement and handling will itself require space both for operation and for maintenance, repair, etc. Furthermore, in certain industries movement and handling may be achieved only in particular ways because of the particular requirements of the process.

### Space requirements

In addition to the space necessary to accommodate the machinery and materials required for the operation, allowances must be made for the movement of personnel and for service and repair, etc.

### Other factors affecting layout

Even more factors affect layout; for example, the removal, reprocessing or use of waste materials; noise; safety legislation; customer areas; anticipated developments and the necessity for change. Consequently, the stages above can be considered only as a general procedure for the generation and collection of basic data which, along with other considerations peculiar to the particular circumstances, enable us to begin to plan the layout.

### Layout planning method

When we have considered the factors above we can begin to plan the layout. The method which we shall adopt will depend on our objectives and circumstances. Some common methods are outlined below.

## TRADITIONAL LAYOUT PLANNING METHODS

Traditional layout planning procedures appear quite mundane beside current theory, but nevertheless these procedures are proven, accepted and valuable. Visual aids play an important part. Some form of scale representation, e.g. scale drawing, templates, three-dimensional models, is often used. Frequently, movement patterns are shown on drawings or models. String diagrams are a familiar method of showing movement, coloured cord being attached to diagrams or models to indicate the paths taken by different products.

The main criticism of such methods is that they are unstructured and depend on the knowledge, experience and insight of the planner. This same fact, however, can be interpreted as their main advantage, for it is possible, while planning the layout, to take into account all relevant constraints. Their merit, therefore, is the breadth of their approach rather than their rigour.

If we attempt to develop analytical methods of layout planning we must determine precisely what our objective is. The common concern in all layouts, whether in manufacturing, supply, service or transport, is the need for efficient movement. Thus the need to minimize movement is usually the first consideration, and only after an initial layout has been obtained are additional objectives allowed to intervene. Each movement operation normally involves pick-up, movement and put-down, the distance usually being the main variable factor.

## General requirements of a layout planning procedure

To be of general value, a layout planning procedure must:

(a) take as its objective(s) something of prime, if not sole, importance, e.g. total movement cost;

(b) 1. be capable of producing several good layouts, from which we might choose the best or most appropriate, or which can be modified to take into account additional objectives and/or constraints; *or*

2. work in such a way that the development of one layout, or a set of alternative layouts, is undertaken interactively, with the layout designer being given the opportunity to modify, adapt or select alternatives at each stage in the development of the layout(s);

(c) 1. be capable of dealing with the situation in which an entirely new layout, or a set of alternative layouts, is to be developed from a set of data: *or*

2. cope with the situation in which an existing layout is to be improved, modified or changed in some way.

Additionally we also often need a procedure which can accommodate:

(d) different floor areas for departments;

(e) a wide variety of flow patterns among departments;

(f) different costs of movement;

(g) the fact that certain departments may need to remain in a given position;

(h) the fact that, in certain circumstances, certain departments must have a given relationship with one another;

(i) the use of more than one floor.

## Cross and relationship charts

These are traditional procedures in layout planning. They satisfy few of the above requirements. They provide no solutions, but simply help organize data in order to help in the layout planning process. One deals with movement. The other is only a way of expressing relative location preferences.

The pattern and extent of movement or handling which is known to take place, or expected to exist, is often summarized on some form of chart, which can then be used to assist in layout planning.

The *cross chart* shown in Figure 6.6 indicates the pattern and amount of movement of items among ten departments in a small factory. In the case of a new layout the routeing will have been obtained from routeing instructions, e.g. flow process charts, and the quantities from output/throughput requirements. The figures in the matrix are the number of items or loads which in a given period of time must move from one department to another. In the case of the existing layouts this information may be obtained by sampling of the activity taking place within the factory.

Notice that the row and the column totals are not necessarily equal. Where some of the items are consumed or combined, row totals may be less than column totals.

Absence of any figures below the diagonal means that none of the items backtrack between departments, but the scatter above the diagonal indicates a varied movement pattern characteristic of the processing of several types of product or customer. Some of the items follow a path through from department 1 to department 10, but, to judge from these data alone, a 'product layout' seems impractical.

**Figure 6.6** Cross chart showing the nature and extent of the movement of items between departments over a given period of time

| FROM Dept no. \ TO Dept no. | 1 | 2 | 3 | 4 | 5 | 6 | 7 | 8 | 9 | 10 | TOTAL |
|---|---|---|---|---|---|---|---|---|---|---|---|
| 1 | | 15 | | | | 12 | 8 | 5 | | | 40 |
| 2 | | | 10 | 5 | | | | | | | 15 |
| 3 | | | | 10 | | | | | | | 10 |
| 4 | | | | | 5 | 7 | | 3 | | | 15 |
| 5 | | | | | | 5 | | | | | 5 |
| 6 | | | | | | | 12 | | | | 12 |
| 7 | | | | | | | | 12 | 8 | | 20 |
| 8 | | | | | | | | | 12 | 8 | 20 |
| 9 | | | | | | | | | | 20 | 20 |
| 10 | | | | | | | | | | | |
| TOTAL | | 15 | 10 | 15 | 5 | 24 | 20 | 20 | 20 | 28 | |

Various elaborations on the cross chart have been suggested, but the simple principle remains the same. For example, a *weighted cross chart* may on occasions offer sufficient advantages to justify the extra effort. Here, unlike the procedure of Figure 6.6, the movements of items between departments are not given equal weight, but each movement is weighted according to that item's importance, e.g. in terms of its contribution to profit. An alternative approach either with a weighted or with an unweighted cross chart is to consider only the principal goods or services.

Cross charts are a means of collecting and presenting information from which preferable departmental relationships can be obtained. This information can then be summarized on a *relationship chart.* For example, the relationship chart shown in Figure 6.7 is partly derived from the cross chart (Figure 6.6).

The required closeness of departments summarized by a relationship chart may reflect needs other than the minimization of movement; indeed, a relationship chart can be used to summarize proximity requirements where the minimization of movement is not of overriding importance.

**Figure 6.7**

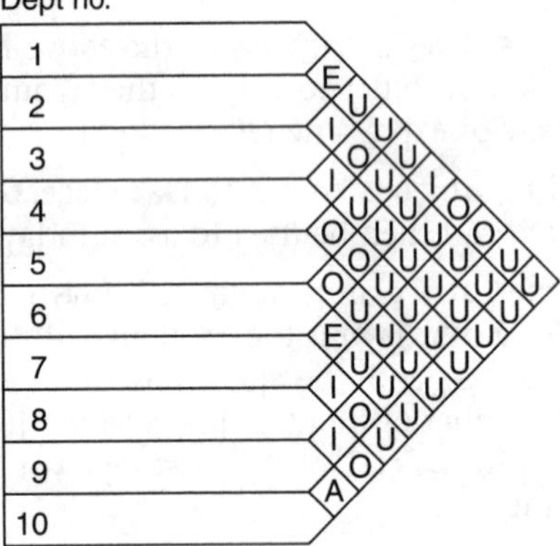


| Code | Closeness |
|---|---|
| A | Essential |
| E | V. important |
| I | Important |
| O | Ordinary close |
| U | Unimportant |

## COMPUTER-AIDED LAYOUT PLANNING

In all but the simplest of situations, layout planning 'by hand' can be a long and tedious process. It is partly for this reason that computer-based approaches have been developed. There are, however, other benefits of this type of approach, notably:

1. Alternative layouts can be generated quickly for comparison and evaluation.
2. An interactive design procedure can be used, allowing a designer to influence the development of a layout during the design process, rather than waiting to see what is produced and then having to modify it, to accommodate practical requirements, etc.
3. Computer-based layout planning procedures can be linked with computer-based procedures for planning materials handling, maintenance, services management, etc.

The first computer programs for layout planning were developed in the early 1960s. Much has changed since then, but these origins are important, because many current software packages are direct descendants. For example, one of the most widely used is based on a methodology first developed in 1963. Another popular approach today can be traced back to a program developed in 1967.

There are two basic methodologies behind most of today's computer-based layout planning procedures:

1. Proximity maximization.
2. Movement minimization.

## Proximity maximization

This approach derives directly from the methodology of the relationship chart, as in Figure 6.7. Required or desired interdepartmental closeness ratings or codes, usually expressed numerically, are one input to the program, along with department sizes and overall building dimensions or constraints. The procedures used by such programs are often based on those first developed for either CORELAP[1] (Computerized Relationship Layout Planning ) or ALDEP[2] (Automated Layout Design Program). The former has the more complex procedure, which is basically as follows:

(a) Place first in the layout the department which has the highest total closeness rating (using numerical values for the closeness codes).

(b) Add other departments in descending order of total closeness rating so that they achieve, as far as possible, proximity to those departments with which they have a high closeness rating.

This, of course, is all done subject to overall space/dimension limitations, and various rules are used to determine the order in which departments are placed into the layout, and to ensure appropriate relationships between pairs of departments, etc. The overall object is to maximize the total closeness score.

The ALDEP procedure also utilizes a closeness/proximity rating approach. The program either generates a series of largely random layouts and selects that with the best total closeness score, or generates one lay-out and then seeks movementally to improve on it by moving/exchanging departments.

**EXAMPLE**

### *COMLAD II*

COMLAD II is a microcomputer-based layout design program, developed from COMLAD and based on a methodology developed by Sule. The program aims to place into the layout first those departments with the strongest 'closeness' relationships with others, before placing the departments with weaker relationships. Up to 20 departments can be dealt with. Besides developing an efficient layout, COMLAD II has useful features that allow fixing departments, changing the shape of departments, and changing the length and width dimensions of the overall layout. After the layout has been generated it is evaluated by computing a score that represents

---

[1] Lee, R. C. and Moore, J. M. (1967) CORELAP – Computerized Relationship Layout Planning. *Journal of Industrial Engineering*, **18**(3), pp. 195–200.

[2] Seehof, J. M. and Evans, W. O. (1967) Automated Layout Design Program. *Journal of Industrial Engineering*, **18**(12), pp. 690–695.

the total 'closeness' rating. The score not only is a function of the relative position of each department but also is influenced by their shape. The designer can modify the layout and the resultant closeness score is calculated.

Source: Ziai, M. R. and Sule, D. R. (1991) Computerized facilities layout design. *Computers in Industrial Engineering*, **21**(1–4), pp. 385–389.

## Movement minimization

The proximity (closeness maximization approach), built on the relationship chart concept, will often take account of the need to minimize interdepartmental movement or traffic, because the required closeness ratings or codes will often take account of movement alongside other factors. The movement minimization approach, however, deals primarily with this criterion. It aims to minimize total interdepartmental movement, e.g. the total number of journeys over a period of time, or the total traffic density (i.e. journeys × loads), or the total cost of movement.

Most of the more widely used computer procedures are based on CRAFT[3], first developed in 1963. An outline of the basic procedure is given below.

The procedure requires an initial layout to be input at the beginning. It can therefore be considered as an 'improvement' or 'modification' *procedure*; however, it is in fact intended for the design of new layouts, since the initial layout can be an arbitrary one. A simplified flow diagram for the program is shown in Figure 6.8.

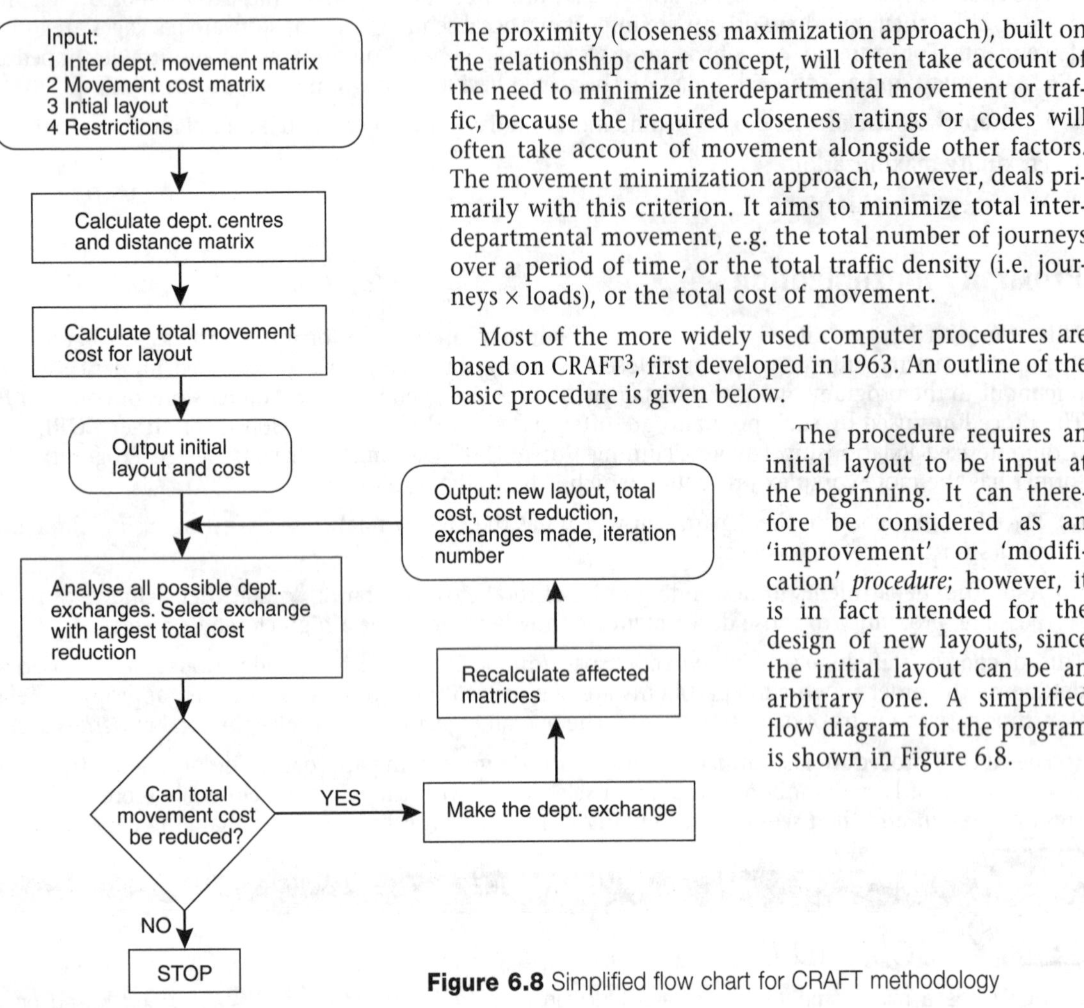


**Figure 6.8** Simplified flow chart for CRAFT methodology

The necessary input is:

(a) interdepartmental flow matrix, which gives the number of unit loads moving between all departments over a given period of time;

(b) interdepartmental movement cost matrix, giving the cost per unit distance of movement between all departments;

[3]Armour, G. C. and Buffa, E. S. (1963) A heuristic algorithm and computer simulation approach to the relative location of facilities. *Management Science*, **9**(1), pp. 294–309.

(c) initial layout configuration showing the size of departments;
(d) any restrictions, i.e. fixed departments which cannot be moved.

The procedure then seeks to improve on the initial layout by interchanging pairs of departments. Every pair of departments is examined and the effect of their interchange on the total movement cost for the layout is calculated. The pair change giving the greatest reduction in total movement cost is effected and the process is repeated until no further interchange of departments will provide any additional reduction in the total movement cost associated with the layout.

The algorithm by which the program operates is as follows:

(a) Determine which pairs of departments may be interchanged. Departments are considered for interchange when they are adjacent, of equal area, or bordering on a common third department.
(b) Calculate the distance between departments, the distances being taken as those between the centres of the departments.
(c) Calculate the reduction in total movement costs resulting from the interchange of all possible pairs of departments.
(d) Interchange the two departments which provide the greatest saving in total movement costs.
(e) Calculate the total movement cost and print out the revised layout.

This procedure is repeated until no further cost saving is possible, and then the final layout is printed.

Several of the better-known software packages embody the CRAFT methodology – often enhanced or extended for specific types of application. Some of these developments are listed below:

(a) SPACECRAFT[4]
A development of CRAFT, specifically for use in the planning of three-dimensional layouts.

(b) FACLO[5]
The program uses the CRAFT-type procedure to obtain the best relative location of areas and obtain a high-level layout. A user interface creates the data file required. With the interface, the user, who need not be expert in the program, can analyse layouts, perform sensitivity analyses, create a layout using graphics, etc.

(c) MOCRAFT[6]
This is a full 40-department CRAFT-type layout development program. It can utilize cost/flow and relationship chart type data and accommodate constraints between points and departments in the layout.

## Combination procedures

The 'proximity' approach is more general since it can take account of several factors – provided they can be taken together and expressed on a single 'closeness' rating. The 'movement' approach, whilst narrower, offers advantages, for it focuses on real criteria, and lends itself to a quantitative approach.

Recently, procedures have been developed which accommodate both approaches. MOCRAFT, described above, is one such 'combination' program. It allows the user to develop a layout using movement or relationship data, and permits either criterion to 'switch' either of these into the objective function – even to mix them, giving different weights to each. There are other procedures which aim to do this, the emphasis usually being on the provision of an interactive procedure through which a designer works with a computer-based procedure to develop a layout, and/or to manipulate that layout.[7]

---

[4] Johnson R. (1982) SPACECRAFT for multifloor layout planning. *Management Science*, **28**(4), pp. 407–417.

[5] Allenbach, R. and Werner, M. (1990) Facility Layout Program. *Computers and Industrial Engineering*, **19**(1–4), pp. 290–293.

[6] Svestka, J. A. (1988) An interactive microcomputer implementation of CRAFT with multiple objectives and side constraints. *Computers and Industrial Engineering*, **15**(1–4), pp. 264–271.

## Computer-aided design (CAD) and interactive graphics

Computer-aided design (CAD) procedures were developed initially for electronic and mechanical engineering applications. The use of CAD systems transformed the ways in which integrated circuits, printed circuit boards, complex structures, etc. were designed. They are also widely used in structural and civil engineering and in architecture. Using a CAD system a designer can call up previous designs, details, specifications, etc., design items on his VDU screen, manipulate them, store them, print out details, and interface with other systems, e.g. for computer-aided manufacturing.

CAD is now being used in layout planning. Linked with layout planning algorithms such applications provide[8] powerful tools for the facilities designer for manufacturing plant, offices, etc.

Computer simulation is discussed in Appendix III. Visual interactive modelling (VIM) has its roots in simulation. It provides a pragmatic, 'what-if' type of approach through which the designer can interact with colour graphics models generated by a microcomputer, to develop, modify and manipulate layouts.[9]

EXAMPLE

### FactoryFLOW

FactoryFLOW is a microcomputer-based iterative, interactive program that integrates the graphics of a CAD system with the analysis of plant layout and materials handling systems. In addition to analysing materials handling and workcentre/storage locations, FactoryFLOW computes operator–machine–workcentre utilizations. This analysis shows users the effect of routeing and layout changes on the workload of all of the machines, workcentres and operators included in the analysis. The data input for the program is provided by the user in three files: (1) the products file, which includes the product names, their production volumes, and a unique colour selected to represent a product's material flow paths in the subsequent flow diagrams; (2) the parts file, which contains routeing and production information for all parts in all products; and (3) the materials handling file, which contains the materials handling system names and each system's type, quantity, fixed cost and other variables.

Source: Tamashunas, V. M., Labban, J. and Sly, D. (1990) Interactive graphics offer an analysis of plant layout and materials handling systems. *Industrial Engineering*, **22**(6), pp. 38–43.

## Modifying existing layouts

Most of the computer-based procedures described above are of value in modifying existing layouts. Modification may be required for the types of reason given at the beginning of ths chapter (pp. 122–123).

One qualitative approach, concerned essentially with the addition of new facilities, is outlined below.

### Level curves

Suppose we wish to position one additional facility in an existing single-floor layout. Adopting the same movement cost objective, and knowing the facilities to and from which the new facility will send and receive material or customers, we can calculate for every point in the layout a numerical value

[7] Houshyar, A. (1991) Computer aided facilities layout: an interactive multi-goal approach. *Computers and Industrial Engineering*, **20**(2), pp. 177–186.

[8] Chen, Chiu-Stveng and Kengskool, K. (1990) An AutoCAD-based expert system for plant layout. *Computers and Industrial Engineering*, **19**(1–4), pp. 299–303. Russo, T. J. and Tortorella, A. J. (1991) Plant layout – Part 3. The contribution of CAD. *Chemical engineering*, **99**(4), pp. 97–101.

[9] Bright, J. G. and Johnston, K. J. (1991 Whither VIM – a developer's view. *European Journal of Operational Research*, **54**(3), pp. 357–362.

[10] Indicates that the value contained is taken to be a positive value only.

which represents the total cost of movement to and from that point. For example, for an existing layout consisting of one facility, a position 5 m away will be twice as attractive as one 10 m away. Where we can calculate the cost of several points in the layout and then join up these points of equal cost we can produce an *isocost* curve. These curves we shall call level curves, since they can be considered as analogous to contour lines on maps. For a single-facility, straight-line movement example, the level curves are shown in Figure 6.9.

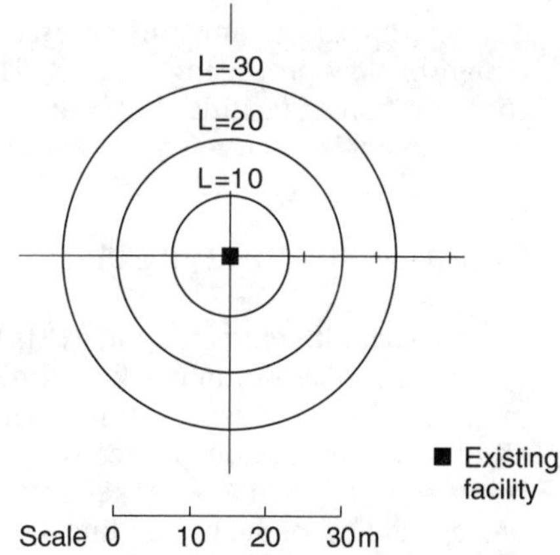


**Figure 6.9** Level curves for single existing facility layout, assuming straight line movement

Where $L$ equals the cost value of a point, and $x$ and $y$ are co-ordinates of existing facilities,[10]

$$L = \left|\sqrt{x^2 + y^2}\right|$$

In the case of $n$ facilities existing at positions $x_1y_1$; $x_2y_2$; $x_3y_3$; . . . $x_ny_n$, the $L$ value for any point $x$, $y$ is given by:

$$L = \sum_{i=1}^{n} \left|\sqrt{(x - x_i)^2 + (y - y_i)^2}\right|$$

For example, Figure 6.10 shows the level curves for a layout with four existing facilities.

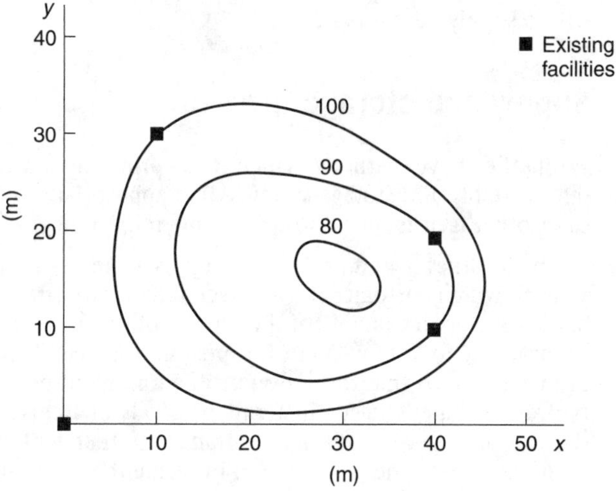


**Figure 6.10** Level curves for the location of the facility among four existing facilities

Two disadvantages of this method are evident. First, where the problem involves the positioning of several facilities in an extensive layout, the construction of level curves becomes rather long and tedious. However, in practice a limited number of possible locations are usually available, which reduces the extent of the calculations. Second, we have assumed that movement between facilities is via the shortest direct route. However, with a more complex formula it is possible to deal with movements which are 'rectangular', as would be the case where trucks, etc. are confined to a series of orthogonal aisles. We have further assumed throughout this section that movement between all facilities is equally important, whereas in the previous sections we used a product of the distance and the number of items or customers moving as our criteria; however, it is possible to apply a weighting to the distances in the equations.

# PLANNING OTHER TYPES OF LAYOUT

## Product layout

The approaches discussed above are concerned primarily with minimizing movement, whether of materials or of people. They are of particular relevance in planning functional/process layouts, and can be used for planning layouts in which facilities are organized on a product or group basis. As such, therefore, they are relevant in certain types of manufacturing and non-manufacturing situations. The planning of product-type layouts, whether in manufacture or service systems (e.g. flow or assembly lines, or flow-processing customers through specialist service systems), may require a somewhat different approach, and this is discussed in some detail in Chapter 15, which deals solely with the design of flow processing systems. The approaches described there are concerned not only with the configuration of facilities but also with the balancing of the resources within each of those facilities. The problem is often referred to as that of 'line balancing'.

## Fixed-position layouts

A somewhat different situation exists in the planning of fixed-position layouts. Here the principal item or customer does not move, but all necessary parts and facilities move to and from it. Such a situation might be visualized as several fixed departments or areas within a site, one of which is the customer of all others. This 'customer' area is the fixed location of the item being manufactured or the customer being serviced, while all other areas are the permanent locations of the facilities required in this process. For example, in building a ship, the construction area is fixed, and around it are located areas in which plating work is carried out, stern gear is manufactured, engines are prepared, etc. The layout problem therefore involves the arrangement of these areas around the main construction area. Again, movement cost can be important, so it will be desirable to place close to the construction areas those departments which must supply heavy items and/or large quantities of items, while areas providing smaller quantities of smaller or lighter items might be located further away. Taking this approach the problem may be tackled by one of the methods outlined above, since in effect we are planning a process-type layout in which the flow pattern is largely one in which all departments communicate with a supply department.

## Supply and storage layouts

While the above methods, which focus primarily on movement, may be relevant in planning the layout of supply and storage systems, it is appropriate to consider such systems separately, since in these cases other factors may also be of some importance.

The facilities layout problem in supply systems often involves the location of display and/or storage areas to which customers have direct access. The arrangement of display and shelving areas in a supermarket is a good example of the type of problem often encountered. In such cases there will be a need to minimize total movement for most customers. Thus the procedures referred to above will be of relevance provided that those responsible for layout planning have some data concerning the average or typical customer's needs in terms of goods or items to be acquired. If this information is available, shelving and passageways can be arranged so that, with a knowledge of the layout, customers may collect their goods with the minimum of movement. Other factors, however, are of relevance in the planning of the layout and should be introduced at this point. For example, the arrangement of displays and storage in supply systems such as supermarkets is also a function of display-type considerations. It is, for example, well known that 'traffic' patterns in supermarkets follow a particular form, with most customers preferring, initially at least, to travel around the edges of the area rather than along intermediate aisles and passageways. It is known that goods displayed at the end of the aisle tend to sell better than those placed in the middle of an aisle and that goods stored in such a way that they can be seen from the entrance or through windows attract the customer to the store. Thus it might be argued that the arrangement of such facilities must take into account certain customer-oriented factors rather than simply concentrating on retail-oriented factors such as maximum use of space, minimum transport, etc.

The arrangement of storage areas such as warehouses also necessitates the consideration of factors other than movement. In such cases there is often a conflict between the need to obtain maximum space utilization and the need to minimize the cost of movement. For example, maximum space utilization often involves high stacking, whereas the storage of items in this manner often necessitates the use of expensive materials handling equipment and therefore gives rise to high movement costs. The arrangement of passageways is also of considerable importance, while the possibility of future expansion, the need to accommodate new items which may have different dimensions or different weight, the need to locate items associated with one another in the same area, the need to provide secure areas for other items, etc. are all of some importance in layout planning.

## EVALUATION OF ALTERNATIVE LAYOUTS

The comparison of alternative layouts is a necessity in many of the procedures described above. The emphasis there was on movement criteria, and it will be appropriate here to look at this need from a broader perspective.

Determining which of many alternative layouts to adopt is often a very difficult problem. If we consider all the possible features and characteristics then our list is likely to be very long indeed. If, on the other hand, we consider only the problem of movement and evaluate the alternative layouts only in this light, we shall very probably neglect certain quite important considerations and be guilty of sub-optimization. One factor should be common to whatever considerations we adopt: *cost*. We must, as a rule, aim to minimize the total cost involved in establishing and using the layout. Muther, referring specifically to manufacturing systems, has suggested that layouts should be evaluated on the basis of the following costs:

(a) Investment:

1. Initial cost of new facilities of all kinds:
   - (i) *buildings
   - (ii) *construction
   - (iii) *machinery
   - (iv) *equipment.
2. Accessory costs:
   - (i) tools, jigs, fixtures
   - (ii) *handling equipment
   - (iii) *containers
   - (iv) benches and chairs
   - (v) timeclocks, water coolers, etc.
   - (vi) *shelves, bins, racks
   - (vii) wiring and lighting
   - (viii) piping and ducting.
3. Installation costs:
   - (i) *building changes
   - (ii) *machinery and equipment
   - (iii) *services and supporting facilities
   - (iv) *auxiliary service lines.
4. Depreciation and obsolescence costs.

(b) Operating costs:

1. Material:
   - (i) production
   - (ii) scrap and waste
   - (iii) supplies and packing
   - (iv) maintenance parts and materials.
2. Labour:
   - (i) direct
   - (ii) overtime or extra-shift premium
   - (iii) idle or waiting time

(iv) efficiency variation
(v) clerical
(vi) maintenance
(vii) inspection
(viii) *handling and storerooms
(ix) other indirect labour
(x) supervision.

3. General:
(i) *floor space
(ii) power
(iii) fuel
(iv) taxes
(v) insurance
(vi) rentals
(vii) interest on investment.

This is not the most comprehensive list that could be suggested, but even so it is a little difficult to appreciate how certain of these items will vary with different layouts, or to understand how some depend on layout at all. We would suggest that in the majority of cases cost items marked with an asterisk will be the most important. Nevertheless, in certain circumstances many of the other costs will merit consideration. The comparison and evaluation of designs for completely new layouts is a difficult problem, and, while such factors as movement, cost of equipment, space required, etc. are normally the principal components of comparison, they are by no means the only components.

The evaluation or rearrangement of parts of factories or departments constitutes an easier problem only because of the relative lack of size of the layouts, and not because fewer factors need be considered.

## MATERIALS HANDLING

The fact that we have considered the minimization of total movement cost as one principal objective in planning facilities layout is sufficient evidence of the importance of efficient handling and the efficient management of movement in most operating systems. Although we have adopted the title 'materials handling' we should emphasize that the management, i.e. the efficient planning and control of movement in all types of systems, is of considerable importance, whether that movement relates to raw materials, finished goods, customers or indirect materials. Movement of materials, work-in-progress and finished goods is of crucial importance in all manufacturing operations. The movement of customers and goods is clearly of ultimate importance in transport systems, while the handling, i.e. the organization of the movement of customers and items, is of considerable importance also in supply and service systems. Here, therefore, we are concerned with the movement of customers or items (whether materials or finished goods) into or out of stores, during processing, into the operating system, and from the operating system to the final customer.

Efficient materials handling (i.e. the movement of items or customers) can bring considerable cost benefit to operating systems. Work-in-progress might be reduced; accidents or losses might be reduced; the capacity of the operating system might be increased; speed of processing, i.e. the throughput time, might be improved; level of service to customer, e.g. the waiting time and the number of stockout situations, might be improved; total space required by the operation might be reduced; etc. Naturally there are equally substantial costs involved in designing, installing, staffing and maintaining an efficient system, including both recurrent and capital costs, so the design and planning of the system must be undertaken with a full awareness of, and therefore after detailed analysis of, movement needs, conditions, requirements and constraints, both present and future.

**Table 6.4 Principles of efficient materials handling**

1. Eliminate need for handling/movement (e.g. by eliminating unnecessary movement and by suitable arrangement of processes)
2. Combine processing and movement
3. Plan layout of operations together with planning of materials handling to minimize handling/movement
4. (In general) use mechanical handling where regular high-volume movement is required or where safety hazards exist
5. Arrange handling/movement to minimize number of 'pick-up/put down' movements
6. Use unit loads and use pallets and containers to avoid damage, reduce subsequent handling, etc.
7. Avoid mixing items/materials which subsequently need to be separated
8 Use straight line movement

## Materials handling objectives

The principles of efficient materials handling are listed in Table 6.4, from which it will be seen that an early objective should be the elimination of the need for handling or movement, or, failing that, a reduction in the need for such handling or movement. This might be achieved by more appropriate layout of the operating facilities, by combining operations with movement, etc. The *necessary* handling/movement should be organized in as efficient a manner as possible. This will often involve the minimization of 'pick-up/put-down' movements, the use of unit loads and pallets, the use of straight line movement, the use of mechanical rather than manual movement, and the separation of items which require subsequent separate processing.

## Methods for materials handling

We cannot discuss the details of materials handling technology here. However, some consideration of the *types* of handling equipment and their applications will be appropriate.

Table 6.5 identifies the principal classes of materials handling equipment and suggests some of the normal applications for such equipment. In this table the applications are considered in terms of the type of movement required, i.e. whether predominantly overhead, vertical, a combination of vertical and horizontal, or largely horizontal (having a fixed route, or with a variable, i.e. non-fixed, route). Certain types of equipment conventionally operate at a constant speed, although often on an intermittent basis. Conveyors normally fall into this category. Other types of equipment, e.g. trucks, cranes, are able to operate at variable speeds.

The selection of appropriate materials handling equipment will be determined by the types of applications required as well as by factors of the type listed in Table 6.5. Principal among these (see Table 6.6) are the types of materials/items/customers to be moved, their volume or weight, the frequency and regularity of movement and of course the extent to which this movement requirement is temporary or 'permanent'. The movement route, particularly whether fixed or variable, and the extent to which this route is influenced by existing constraints such as the location of equipment, the shape of buildings, etc. will be of considerable importance. In certain cases the speed of movement is determined; for example, the handling of hot items may require a speed of movement differing from that needed for the handling of fragile items. In certain cases the speed of movement required is low, since some form of processing is associated with the movement; for example, in the brewing industry, movement, storage and maturing often occur simultaneously. The type of storage employed, both before and after movement, will influence the type of materials handling equipment envisaged, as will considerations of safety and the needs of concurrent and subsequent processes.

| Table 6.5 Methods for materials handling and their applications | | | | | | | |
|---|---|---|---|---|---|---|---|
| **Class of equipment** | **Type of equipment** | **Speed (v = variable; c = constant)** | **Normal applications (type of movement)** | | | | |
| | | | **Overhead** | **Vertical** | **Vertical/horizontal** | **Horizontal fixed route** | **Horizontal non-fixed route** |
| Cranes | Gantry | v | √ | √ | √ | | |
| | Mobile (e.g. truck) | v | √ | √ | √ | | |
| | Revolving | v | √ | √ | √ | | |
| Lifts | Elevator | v | | √ | | | |
| | Escalator | v | | √ | | | |
| | Bucket | c | | √ | | | |
| Trucks | Fork | v | | | | | √ |
| | Hand | v | | | | | √ |
| | Tractor | v | | | | | √ |
| | Sideloader | v | | | | | √ |
| | Platform | v | | | | | √ |
| | Pallet | v | | | | | √ |
| | Straddle | v | | | | | √ |
| Conveyor | Belt | c | | | | √ | |
| | Roller | c | | | | √ | |
| | Flight | c | | | √ | √ | |
| | Pneumatic | c | | | √ | √ | |
| | Screw | c | | | | √ | |
| | Slatted | c | | | | √ | |
| | Vibrating | c | | | | √ | |
| | Drag chain | c | √ | | | √ | |
| Towing | Overhead chain | c | √ | | | √ | |
| | Overhead monorail | v | √ | | | √ | |
| | Floor | c | | | | √ | √ |
| Chute | Gravity | c | | | √ | √ | |
| | Spiral lift | c | | √ | | | |

A recent development in materials handling in industry is the use of 'unit load procedures'. The use of pallets, containers and other unit load handling is often associated with unit load storage procedures. Such an approach might be considered as a form of batch materials handling in situations in which larger quantities of identical or similar items are collected together into a container, pallet or other device for convenience in storing and handling. Alternatively, unit load procedures are used as a form of 'kit' handling and storage where a variety of different yet complementary items are collected together so that the entire unit or 'kit' contains all the necessary items for a particular purpose, e.g. for the manufacture or assembly of a particular item.

**Table 6.6 Factors influencing selection of materials handling equipment**

| | |
|---|---|
| **Materials/items** | to be moved<br>i.e. size, weight, nature (e.g. fragility or hazards) |
| **Volume/rate** | of movement<br>i.e. frequency of movement<br>volumes to be moved<br>regularity of movement<br>temporary or 'permanent' need |
| **Route of movement** | i.e. whether fixed or variable, or complex (or straight line) and whether influenced by building layouts, etc. |
| **Speed of movement required** | i.e. speed required/necessary (e.g. fast for hot items, slow for fragile items) |
| **Storage** | method employed (for storage before and after movement)<br>i.e. how and where stored (e.g. pallets, unit loads, loose, packed, etc.) |
| **Safety/hazards** | involved<br>e.g. fire hazards, spillage risks, etc. |
| **Concurrent processing** | involved or possible<br>e.g. whether movement can be combined with processing |

# AUTOMATED STORAGE AND RETRIEVAL

Systems which provide for the automated storage of items, and automated retrieval of items from stock, are now commonplace in manufacturing, distribution and supply systems. Automated storage and retrieval (ASR) enables organizations to provide for better space utilization, and to offer greater flexibility and responsiveness in the management of stocks. ASR systems are of importance therefore in the context of flexible manufacturing, and just-in-time manufacture. They are also found in mail order organizations, food warehouses (especially where low temperatures must be maintained), and in large retail organizations where rapid stock turnover and rapid replenishment of retail shelf space from an adjacent warehouse is important. Certain types of automated car-parking are, in effect, a form of ASR. Automated storage and retrieval systems are used alongside assembly activities in the electronics industry, and are of value in holding and managing parts stocks in maintenance organizations.

## The nature of ASR systems

Whilst the size of such systems varies considerably, the same four basic components are to be found in most applications, namely:

(a) storage area(s);
(b) storage and retrieval machine(s);
(c) conveying devices;
(d) control computers.

These are shown diagrammatically in Figure 6.11 and are discussed briefly below.

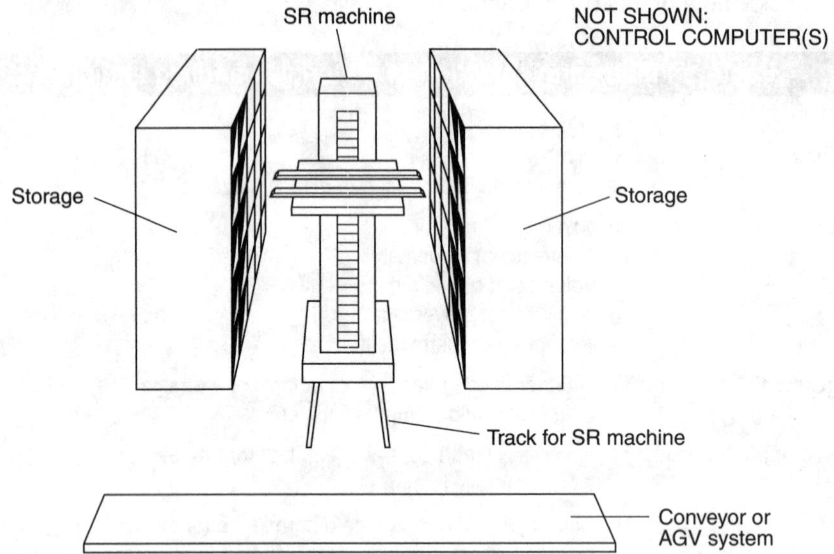


**Figure 6.11** Elements of an automated storage and retrieval system (two storage areas with a single SR machine)

## Storage

The most common type of ASR is the *unit load system* where a unit load is regarded as a pallet or standard container for items. Unit loads are stocked in specific locations in a storage structure which may be up to 500–600 metres long and 50–100 metres in height. Individual locations in the structure may be arranged to accommodate one or more unit loads, often with access from both sides – one side for replenishment and the other side for retrieval.

## Storage and retrieval (SR) machines

The SR machine is used for transporting, storing and retrieving loads within the ASR system. Such machines operate at speeds of up to 100 metres per minute, typically travelling over a fixed track. They comprise, in effect, sophisticated fork-lift-type arrangements.

One machine may operate in one or more aisles serving storage systems on one or both sides of each aisle. One or more SR machines may be used to place items in a storage system, whilst others may be used to retrieve items. Alternatively each machine may be used for storage and retrieval.

## Conveying devices

A conveyor system is used to transport items beyond the reach of the SR machines. It transports items to a deposit station for placement/storage by an SR machine, and out from the station after retrieval by the SR machine. Gravity or powered conveyors may be used, and in more sophisticated installations automated guided vehicle (AGV) systems will be employed. The latter are more flexible than fixed conveyors and provide for the distribution of items to more remote locations without the need for the installation of bulky semi-permanent machinery.

### Control computer

Computer control of ASR systems is often achieved by the use of two 'levels' of control computer. Individual SR machines and AGVs may have their own 'on-board' computer to control and monitor functions, and to interact with a main computer used, perhaps, for the control of all activities within the warehouse or manufacturing area. The main computer will often perform scheduling and routeing tasks and download placement, retrieval and movement instructions to the 'on-board' SR and AGV computers.

## Operating policies for ASR systems

The performance of an ASR can be measured by the delay time of storing or retrieving items, the throughput rate or the average cost per storage or retrieval operation, or by the total time required to store or retrieve a batch comprising several individual items. The latter is widely used as a performance measure.

Against this measure, the performance of an ASR is determined by several factors, especially the operating policies employed and the physical design of the system. The more important managerial decision is to do with *operating policies*. The physical design of the system, i.e. the size and arrangement of the storage facilities, the number and nature of SR machines, types of conveyor, etc., will, in turn, be influenced by operating policy. Some of the questions which must be answered in establishing an operating policy are as follows.

### Storage policy

The principle employed in allocating items to space in the storage structure(s) is perhaps the main storage policy decision. Four factors are of relevance:

(a) compatibility;

(b) complementarity;

(c) popularity;

(d) space.

The *compatibility* of types of item suggests that they can be stored next to each other without fear of spoilage or contamination. *Complementarity* of items suggests the need for proximity in storage since the need for one may often imply the need also for the other. The *popularity* of a product is measured by the demand for it, and will influence the extent to which items are stored close to the point of access, i.e. with minimum travel distance and time for the SR machine. The *space* required by items affects the storage space required, which may influence the storage policy. The location of items in the storage structure will be a function of these four factors. Mathematical treatments are available to allocate items to a storage structure given a measure of these four factors.

Basically two storage policies are available: *dedicated* and *randomized* storage. With a dedicated storage policy particular storage locations are reserved for particular types of item. In this case items are always found in the same location. This is sometimes known as a 'fixed slot' storage policy. With a randomized storage policy, products are located in the closest available location. Thus a particular item, at any time, may be located in several storage 'slots'. With this policy items are usually retrieved on a first in/first out basis and the system of course provides not only for memory of the location of items, but also the date/time when such items were placed. The main advantage of a randomized storage policy is that less space is required to meet the same demand requirements than with dedicated storage policy. However, the sophistication of the randomized system, in particular of the control system, is greater.

## Order storage/retrieval policy

An *order* comprises a set of items consecutively to be placed in or retrieved from storage. To help improve the efficiency of the system such orders may be *batched.*[11] A batch comprises several orders to be dealt with together, so that, for example, the SR machine can deal with all of a particular type of item for all orders in the batch before moving on to deal with another type of item for all orders in the batch. A batching procedure can only be used if some procedure is available for grouping retrieved items into batches at the deposit station or vice versa. Whether to batch orders, and which to put together, is one aspect of a storage/retrieval policy.

## SR machine routeing

Another decision relates to the *routeing* of the SR machine, i.e. determining the routeing of the machine, to place or retrieve all items in an order, or batch of orders, such that the total travel time is minimized.

Algorithms are available to solve the routeing problem, giving either optimal or near optimal solutions.[12]

**EXAMPLE**

### *Terumo Medical*

An $11m automated materials handling system was installed at Terumo Medical Corp. for raw materials, work-in-progress, and finished products. The system consists of an automated storage and retrieval system and two automatic guided vehicle systems. In the summer of 1988, this system helped in tripling Terumo's manufacturing capacity for syringes, medical tubing, and blood collection test kits. By 1989 the company's six-aisle 10 000-plus storage location ASRs handled approximately 100 putaways/retrievals daily. Bar-coded pallets travel by AGV to a sizing station before being put away in the ASRs. The central computer then calls raw materials out of the ASRs when they are needed for delivery to the assembly and sterilization areas by the 12-vehicle AGVs.

The combination of bar code labels and sophisticated inventory tracking software ensures that unsterilized loads are not shipped.

Source: Forger, G. (1989) How an AS/RS and two AGV systems saved the day at Terumo. *Modern Materials Handling*, **44**(14), pp. 44–46.

---

[11] Elsayed, E. A. and Stern, R. G. (1983) Computerised algorithms for order processing in automated warehouse systems. *International Journal of Production Research*, **21**(4), pp. 571–586.

[12] Han, M. H. *et al.* (1987) On sequencing retrievals in automated storage/retrieval systems. *IEE Transactions*, **19**(3), pp. 56–66.

## CHECKLIST FOR CHAPTER 6

### The need for layout planning

Enlarging/reducing departments
Moving a department
Adding a department
Replacing/adding facilities

### Objectives in layout planning

Movement
Turnover
Space and resource utilization

### Facilities layout problems

(a) Departments
(b) Facilities in departments
(c) Workplaces
Examples of (a)

### Basic types of layout

Manufacture
- (a) Process/functional
- (b) Product
- (c) Fixed position
- (d) Group
- (e) Hybrids and mixed layouts
- Comparison of (a) and (b)
- Breakeven comparison of (a), (b) and (c)

Non-manufacturing
- Supply and service
- Transport
- Examples

### Layout planning procedure

Demand
Capacity
Work methods and standards
Resource requirements
Handling and movement
Space requirements
- Other factors
- Layout planning method

### Layout planning methods

Traditional methods
General requirements
Cross and relationship charts

### Computer-aided layout planning

Proximity maximization methods
Movement minimization methods
Combined objectives
CAD and interactive graphics

### Modifying existing layouts

Level curves

### Planning 'product' layouts

Line balancing

### Planning 'fixed position' layouts

### Planning supply and storage layouts

### Evaluating alternative layouts

Investment
Operating cost

### Materials handling

Objectives
Principles
Methods
Factors influencing selection of methods

### Automated handling and storage

## FURTHER READING

**Brown, J. (1989)** AGVs in action. *Plant Engineering and Maintenance,* **12**(5), pp. 24–27.

**Domschke, W. and Drexl, A. (1985)** *Location and Layout Planning.* Berlin and Heidelburg: Springer-Verlag.

**Ketcham, R. L., Malstrom, E. M. and McRoberts, K. L. (1989)** A comparison of three computer assisted facilities design algorithms. *Computers and Industrial Engineering,* **16**(3), pp. 375–386.

**Savsar, M. (1991)** Flexible facility layout by simulation. *Computers and Industrial Engineering,* **20**(1), pp. 155–165.

**Sule, D. E. (1988)** *Manufacturing Facilities – Location, Planning and Design.* Boston, Mass.: PWS-Kent Publishing.

**Ziai, M. R. and Sule, D. R. (1989)** Computerized materials handling and facility layout design. *Computers and Industrial Engineering,* **17**(1–4), pp. 55–60.

## QUESTIONS

6.1 The following cross chart has been constructed by means of observations of all movement between the seven production departments of a factory over a typical one-month period. In addition to these seven production departments, there are three other departments: the general office, the drawing office and the personnel department. The general office should preferably be close to the assembly department but not close to the test department. The drawing office should preferably be close to assembly stores and the general office, but must not be close to the test area. The location of the personnel department is comparatively unimportant; however, it should not be too far away from any of the production departments. The relative location of the production departments depends on materials flow only, as shown in the figure.

| | R | S | T | M | G | A | T |
|---|---|---|---|---|---|---|---|
| Receiving | | 40 | | | | 3 | 3 |
| Stores | | | 20 | 20 | | | |
| Turning | | | | 18 | 2 | | |
| Milling | | | | | 18 | 20 | |
| Grinding | | | | | | 10 | 10 |
| Assembly | | | | | | | 38 |
| Testing | | | | | | 5 | |

Construct a relationship chart showing the desirable relative locations of each of these ten departments. Use an appropriate notation to indicate the desired proximities.

6.2 'Visual or graphical minimization is the only satisfactory and practical method of designing facility layouts, and the minimization of total movement costs is the most appropriate objective function during layout planning.' Discuss.

6.3 Determine a rectangular layout consisting of the 11 departments of a hospital included in the table overleaf.

6.4 What are the fundamental differences between the methods of layout planning adopted in the methodologies of CRAFT (computerized relative allocation of facilities technique) and CORELAP (computerized relationship layout planning)?

**Table for question 6.3**

| Department | A | B | Part C | D | E | Department area ($m^2$) |
|---|---|---|---|---|---|---|
| 1 | 2 | 2 | 2 | 2 | 2 | 500 |
| 2 | 3 | 7 | 3 | 4 | 3 | 400 |
| 3 | 5 | | 4 | | 4 | 200 |
| 4 | | | 7 | 6 | 7.7 | 600 |
| 5 | 7 | | | | | 200 |
| 6 | 9 | 9 | | 10 | 4 | 500 |
| 7 | 6 | 8 | 8 | | 8.9 | 1000 |
| 8 | | 6 | 9 | | 6 | 500 |
| 9 | 10 | 10 | 10 | | 10 | 800 |
| 10 | 11 | 11 | 11 | 11 | 11 | 500 |
| 11 | | | | | | |
| | **A** | **B** | **C** | **D** | **E** | |
| **Loads/month** | 50 | 100 | 250 | 100 | 100 | |

6.5 What factors, other than the cost of movement, need to be considered during the planning of a new layout, and how is the consideration of these factors included in the whole layout planning procedure?

6.6 Evaluate the comparative merits of locating an additional facility at points A, B and C in the four existing facility layouts shown in Figure 6.12. You may assume that all movement between the new facility and each existing facility is equally costly, and that movement is by the shortest direct route.

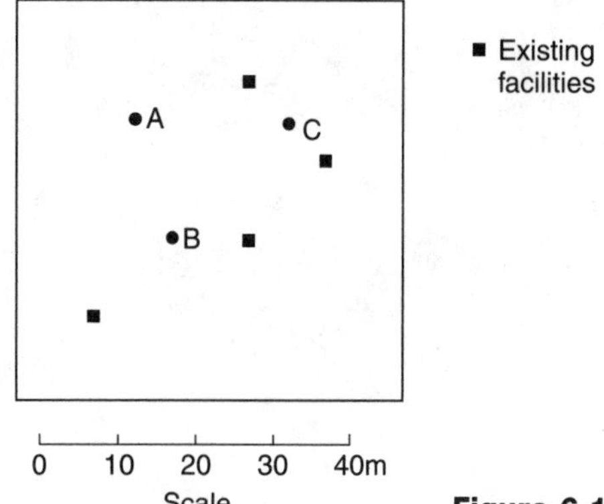


**Figure 6.12**

6.7 Discuss the requirements of the handling systems and identify appropriate types of handling equipment for the following applications:

(a) the handling of passengers' baggage (other than hand baggage) in an airport terminal;

(b) the movement of metal waste from the machine shop of a mass-production engineering company;

(c) the movement of goods from the goods receiving department through stores, onto shelves, and to customers in a large supermarket.

## CASE STUDIES (from Part 9)

The topics covered in this chapter are relevant in the following (see Introduction to Part 9 and Table C.1 for further details):

| No. | Name | Country |
|---|---|---|
| 5 | The Sahil Tea Garden | Turkey |
| 7 | Pokhara Weavers | Nepal |
| 10 | Airport building project | India |

PART 4

# Work and Work Systems

Introduction to Part 4
Chapter 7 Work and work methods
Chapter 8 Work measurement and work standards
Chapter 9 Workplaces, technology and jobs
Chapter 10 Payment and incentives

## INTRODUCTION TO PART 4

In this part of the book we concentrate on work systems. We focus on human work, i.e. the execution of tasks by people within the operating system, and in so doing we look at some traditional and established areas of responsibility of operations management as well as at some newer topics. We shall look at work methods, work standards, the rewards for work, the problems of learning, people's attitudes to work, the design of the workplace, health and safety considerations, etc. All these topics are interrelated. For our purposes we can perhaps identify four sets of considerations which must be taken into account in the design of work systems.

(a) The design of the ***work*** itself, i.e. the specification of the tasks to be performed – the work content, the determination of appropriate methods of executing these tasks and the establishment of standards of performance for this work.

(b) The ***conditions*** in which people work, i.e. the design of the workplace, the ergonomics of the workplace, and health and safety considerations.

(c) The ***workers*** themselves – workers' needs, motives, expectations and attitudes, their skills, abilities, the need to learn, etc.

(d) The nature and design of the ***organization*** in which the work is to be undertaken, the reward or payment system for such work, etc.

These four sets of considerations are examined in the following chapters. No one set of considerations is more important than any other. All must be taken together.

## STRATEGIC CONTEXT

The operations issues, problems and decisions considered in this part of the book exist within the broader strategic context of the organization. The main relationships are set out here, as a preface to the details which follow.

### Influences of business policy decisions *(see Chapter 2, Figure 2.2)*

The nature of the work required within the operating system must, necessarily, be a function of the purpose, and therefore policies, of the organization. Work content and the technology employed will be influenced in large part by the nature of the products or services to be provided.

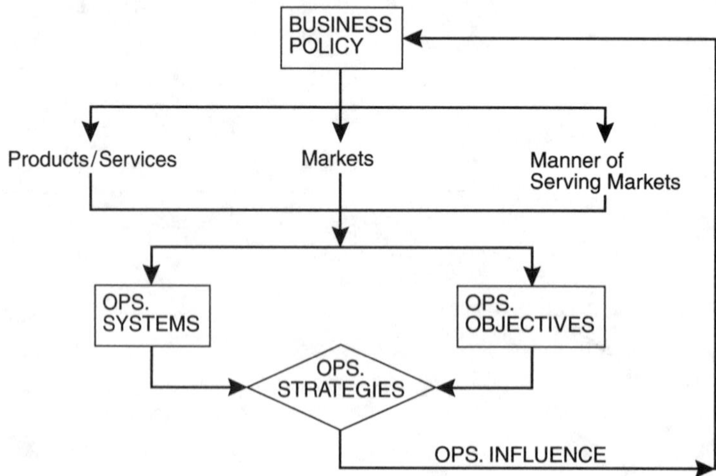

Given the nature of the work required, then the work methods, the nature of the workplaces, and payments systems employed will also be influenced, so policy decisions on products/services will influence, if not determine, the requirements of the operating system. Further policy decisions on the way in which markets are to be served, e.g. the importance of cost, will influence operations objectives, in turn influencing the way in which work is done in the system.

The existence of a work capability, e.g. as represented by worker skills and capabilities, available technology, work organization, etc., will lead operations managers to wish to influence/inform any proposed business policy decisions which might depend for their implementation on the work capabilities of the operations, e.g. the achievement of particular levels of performance on cost, quality, flexibility or reliability.

Inasmuch as business policy also sets requirements for human resources (HR), policy decisions may also have an impact on job design and work organization and payment systems. Again, the nature of existing work systems must be allowed to influence HR policy objectives and certainly the speed with which any new HR objectives are to be achieved – thus operations managers will wish to participate also in business policy decision-making in these areas.

## **Competitive advantage** *(see Chapter 2, Figures 2.6 and 2.7)*

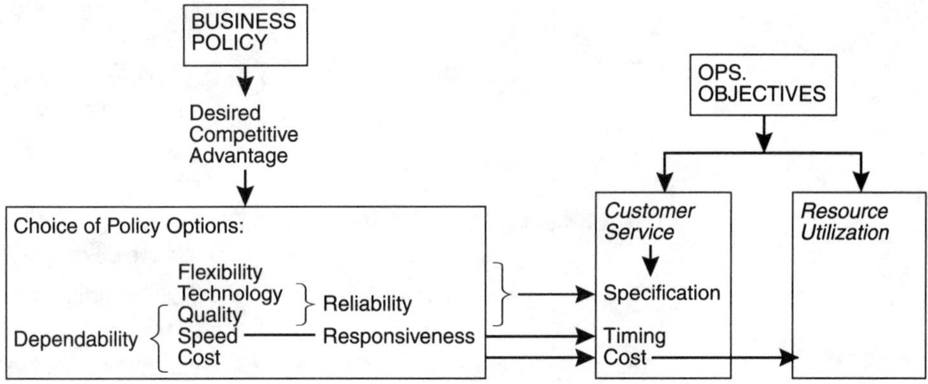


Reference to the above model, which focuses on the link between policy objectives for the manner in which markets are to be served, and operations objectives on customer service, reveals the following possible business policy/work system design relationships.

Given a policy emphasis on flexibility, quality and reliability, operations managers will be concerned to ensure that: work systems deploy versatile and skilled labour; work methods are flexible; work standards do not constrain workers' flexibility; flexible technology is employed; jobs are designed to encourage workers' responsibility for quality; and, if used, payments-by-results systems encourage flexibility and reward high, reliable and consistent quality.

If, however, policy objectives emphasize cost, then operations may be more concerned to establish dedicated/specialized work systems with high emphasis on repetition and low variety, and with rationalized work systems, dedicated technology and different types of payment system.

These two approaches for the implementation of particular policy objectives contrast, and might even be considered as extremes. A policy emphasis on flexibility and cost, coupled with quality and speed, places a far more demanding set of requirements on operations. In these circumstances, no longer uncommon, operations will seek to establish work systems without tightly prescribed work methods but with demanding standards. They will seek to deploy multi-skilled workers, flexible technology and participatory job designs, and will seek efficiency through rapid change-overs, job rotation, group payments schemes, etc.

## TOPIC MAP

| Topics in this Part | Related topics in other chapters<br>Chapter | Topic | Comments/aspects |
|---|---|---|---|
| Chapter 7 | | | |
| Work study | 8 | Work measurement | |
| | 9 | Job design | |
| | 10 | Payment systems | Job evaluation |
| | 19 | Quality – behaviour and organization factors | Worker contribution to quality assurance |
| | 20 | Process capability | Worker skills and capability |
| Method study | 1 | Operations management objectives | Impact of work method on efficiency |
| | 3 | Product/service designs | Consideration of work method in design |
| | 4 | Operations costs | Influence of work method on labour cost |
| | 6 | Layout planning<br>Objectives of layout planning | Consideration of work methods in planning layouts |
| | 8 | Work measurement | Use of work times in the study methods |
| | 9 | Job design | Appropriate methods for effective job design |
| | 15 | Flow line principles | Work rationalization in mass production |
| | 19 | Quality – behaviour and organization factors | Appropriate work methods for quality assurance |
| Learning | 4 | Operations costs | Learning effects on labour costs |
| | 5 | Locational choice | Availability of appropriate labour skills |
| | 8 | Learning curve | |
| Chapter 8 | | | |
| Work measurement procedure | 4 | Operations costs | Work times and standards and labour costs |
| | 7 | Method study | Use of work times in work study |
| | 10 | Payment systems | Job evaluation |
| | | Payment by results | Use of work standards |
| | 11<br>12<br>13<br>14 | Operations planning<br>Scheduling<br>Network scheduling<br>Batch scheduling | Need for work times for USP in scheduling and work and allocation |

## TOPIC MAP

| Topics in this Part | Related topics in other chapters: Chapter | Topic | Comments/aspects |
|---|---|---|---|
| *Chapter 8 continued* | | | |
| | 15 | Flow process design | Need for work times for USP in scheduling and work and allocation |
| | 21 | Maintenance/repair | |
| | 22 | Performance/measurement | Measurement of performance against standard times |
| Learning curve | 4 | Operations costs | Effect on labour costs |
| | 7 | Learning | |
| | 10 | Payment systems<br>Payment by results | Recognition/reward of improvement |
| | 11 | Operations planning | Need to allow for improvement factor in scheduling/planning work activities |
| | 12 | Scheduling | |
| | 13 | Network scheduling | Need to allow for improvement factor in scheduling/planning work activities |
| | 14 | Batch scheduling | |
| | 15 | Flow process design | |
| | 21 | Maintenance/repair/replacement | |
| Chapter 9 | | | |
| Working conditions | 5 | Location of facilities | Potential work conditions as a factor in location choice |
| | 6 | Layout planning | Need for adequate workplace design |
| | 7 | Work methods | Need for methods to fit working circumstances and conditions |
| | 8 | Work measurement | Allowances for conditions, fatigue, etc. |
| | 10 | Payment | Compensation for working conditions and factors |
| | 19 | Management of quality | Need for good working conditions in context of TQM |
| | 21 | Maintenance/reliability/repair | Need for workplace maintenance |
| Technology and work | 2 | Competitive advantage | Technology in output/services and processes |
| | 6 | Layout facilities | Flexible processing technology, handling and storage |

## TOPIC MAP

| Topics in this Part | Related topics in other chapters<br>Chapter | Topic | Comments/aspects |
|---|---|---|---|
| *Chapter 9 continued* | | | |
| | 7 | Work methods | Impact of process technology on work content and methods |
| | 8 | Work measurement | Work pacing factors |
| | 14 | Batch processing | Flexible processing systems |
| | 15 | Flow processing | Automation of processing |
| | 19 | Management of quality | Automation of quality controls |
| The workers/job design | 6 | Layout of facilities | Workplace design |
| | 7 | Work methods | Work standardization and job satisfaction problems |
| | 15 | Flow processing | Complexity of job design in repetitive work |
| | 19 | Management of quality | Responsibilities for quality |
| Chapter 10 | | | |
| Payment and payment systems | 3 | Organizations | Payment and remuneration factors in job and organization design |
| | | Finance | Labour cost factors |
| | 4 | Operations economics | Labour cost factors |
| | 8 | Work standards | Need for standards for payments by results |
| | 19 | Management of quality | Workers' role in quality management |
| | 22 | Performance measurement | Payment by results |
| Payment by results | 8 | Work standards | Need for standards for payment by results |
| | 19 | Management of quality | Workers' role in quality management |
| | 22 | Performance measurement | Payment by results |

Chapter 7

# Work and work methods

## ISSUES

Is manual work still important?
Why study work methods and procedures?
What is the objective of method study?
What are the main steps involved in developing a good work method?
How can a work method be described and recorded?
How can work methods be improved?
How do we deal with leaving?

## NOTATION USED IN THIS CHAPTER

| | |
|---|---|
| D | Delay |
| □ | Inspection |
| O | Operation |
| ▽ | Storage (or hold) |
| ⇨ | Transportation |
| MTM | Methods time measurement |
| PMTS | Predetermined motion time system |
| SIMO | Simultaneous motion |

The development and use of robotics, automation and information technology has influenced and will continue to influence the number of people employed and the nature of their work. The need for people to work in hazardous conditions, and the need for manual work in information storage and retrieval, etc. are reducing, but people still work in large numbers in most types of business. Production workers, dentists, surgeons, typists, agricultural workers, etc. spend a considerable part of their time in manual activities. Such human work must be specified and designed. Tools, equipment and workplaces must be designed. In many cases estimates of the time required to undertake particular tasks must be obtained for scheduling, capacity planning, training or payment purposes. Even the work of a robot must be designed and measured.

Thus the study of work is a subject of some importance. In this chapter, after a brief discussion of work study, we will concentrate on the design of work methods. Chapter 8 will focus on the measurement of work, and later chapters on other related topics.

# WORK STUDY

## The nature of work study

Work study is concerned primarily with human manual work. Specifically, it deals with the efficient design and execution of manual work, and with the establishment of standards of performance. Work study is practised extensively in manufacturing, services, transport and supply industries. Some of the major developments in the subject took place in the service sector, e.g. in hospitals, and in transport. It has been a controversial subject. The principles were laid down many years ago; they still exist and are applied, but not without criticism. The work study practitioner, in whatever industry, will now be concerned with applying these principles in a sensitive and adaptable way, in particular taking into account work conditions, the characteristics of workers, and behavioural and organizational factors. Their application is relevant in most industrial and business sectors. Some examples are given in Table 7.1.

In planning the layout of facilities and methods and procedures for the handling of materials, etc., it will often be necessary to conduct some form of work study investigation. Wherever it is necessary to obtain estimates for the duration of activities for the purposes of scheduling, capacity management, work/worker allocation, incentive payments, etc., some form of work measurement will be needed. The study of work methods will be necessary for the development of training plans, for the design of workplaces, for the design of equipment, and in satisfying health and safety requirements at the workplace.

## The structure and purposes of work study

Throughout these chapters we shall use the British terminology and, where possible, the British Standard definitions. The British Standards Institution defines work study as 'a generic term for those techniques, particularly method study and work measurement, which are used in the examination of human work in all its contexts, and which lead systematically to the investigation of all the factors which affect the efficiency and economy of the situations being reviewed, in order to effect improvements'.

The aims of work study are, by analysis of work methods and the materials and equipment used, to:

(a) establish the most economical way of doing the work;

(b) standardize this method, and the materials and equipment involved;

(c) establish the time required by a qualified and adequately trained worker to do the job, while working at a defined level of performance;

(d) install this work method as standard practice.

Work study, then, is a comparatively low-cost way of either designing work for high productivity or improving productivity in existing work by improving current work methods and reducing ineffective or wasted time. In each case the design or improvements are sought within the context of existing resources and equipment; consequently work study is an immediate tool and is not dependent on the redesign of goods or services, research and development of operating processes, or extensive rearrangement of facilities.

We must apply the technique in circumstances from which we expect maximum returns. The economic results of the study, whether they are increases in throughput, reduction in waste, improved safety, reduction in training time, or better use of equipment or labour, should outweigh the cost of the investigation. To ensure this we should consider:

(a) the anticipated life of the job;

(b) whether manual work is an important part of the job, e.g. (1) the wage rate for the job, (2) the ratio of machine time to manual time in the work cycle;

**Table 7.1 Some examples of the applications of work study (method study and work measurement)**

| Type of operation | Examples | Applications of method study | Applications of work measurement (other than to obtain standards for examples in previous column) |
|---|---|---|---|
| Transport systems | Road freight | Devise most appropriate method of loading and unloading vehicles | To obtain standard times for certain vehicle repair/service/refuel operations |
| | Passenger bus | Devise best method of fare collection and ticket issuing for 'one-person' operated buses | To obtain standard journey times |
| | Passenger airline | Devise best method of emergency evacuation of airline on ground | To obtain standard times for flight deck pre-flight checks |
| Service systems | Hotel | Devise most appropriate procedure for customer check-in, registration, key issue, etc. | To obtain standard time for cleaning a bedroom |
| | Dentist | Devise best layout of equipment and work procedure for filling a tooth | To obtain standard time for a 'clean and polish' |
| | Hospital | Devise most appropriate procedure for routine patient screening/testing | To obtain standard time for specific medical activities, e.g. eye test, blood test, pathological analysis, etc. |
| Supply systems | Post office | Devise most appropriate allocation of different activities to tellers/counters (e.g. change, traveller's cheques, pensions, etc.) | To obtain standard time for opening a new account |
| | Supermarket | Devise most appropriate layout and work method at check-out desks | To obtain standard time for replenishing shelves |
| | Mail order | Devise most appropriate procedure for filling an order, e.g. 'picking and packing' goods | To obtain standard time for processing a telephoned order |
| Manufacturing systems | Motor-vehicle production | Devise best method for an operation on an assembly line | To obtain standard time for the service of a piece of equipment |
| | Construction | Devise best method and layout of equipment for brick-laying | To obtain standard time for tiling roofs (e.g. per square metre) |
| | Brewing | Devise most appropriate method of packing bottles into crates and/or stacking crates | To obtain standard time for a line change-over, i.e. from one product to another |

(c) utilization of equipment, machines, tools, etc., the cost of such equipment, and whether the utilization is dependent on the work method;

(d) the importance of the job to the company.

We should distinguish between work study of existing jobs and that of proposed or anticipated jobs. Whenever new products or services are to be provided or new equipment used, jobs must be designed. Consequently the question is to what extent work study should be used and how much effort is justified by the importance of the job. Some investigation may be necessary on existing jobs, not necessarily because they were inadequately designed in the first place, but perhaps because there has been a slight change in the product or service, new equipment is being used, or wage rates or incentives are to be altered. Examinations of existing work methods could also result from low machine utilization, excessive labour overtime or idle time, complaints from the workers, inadequate quality, high scrap or wastage rate, etc.

Figure 7.1 shows the structure of work study. Two aspects exist: first, *method study*, concerned with establishing optimum work methods; and second, *work measurement*, concerned with establishing time standards for those methods.

Method study is normally conducted before work measurement. Apart from the possible need to compare the times for old work methods with the times for new methods, work measurement conducted before method study is poor practice.

**Figure 7.1** The structure of work study

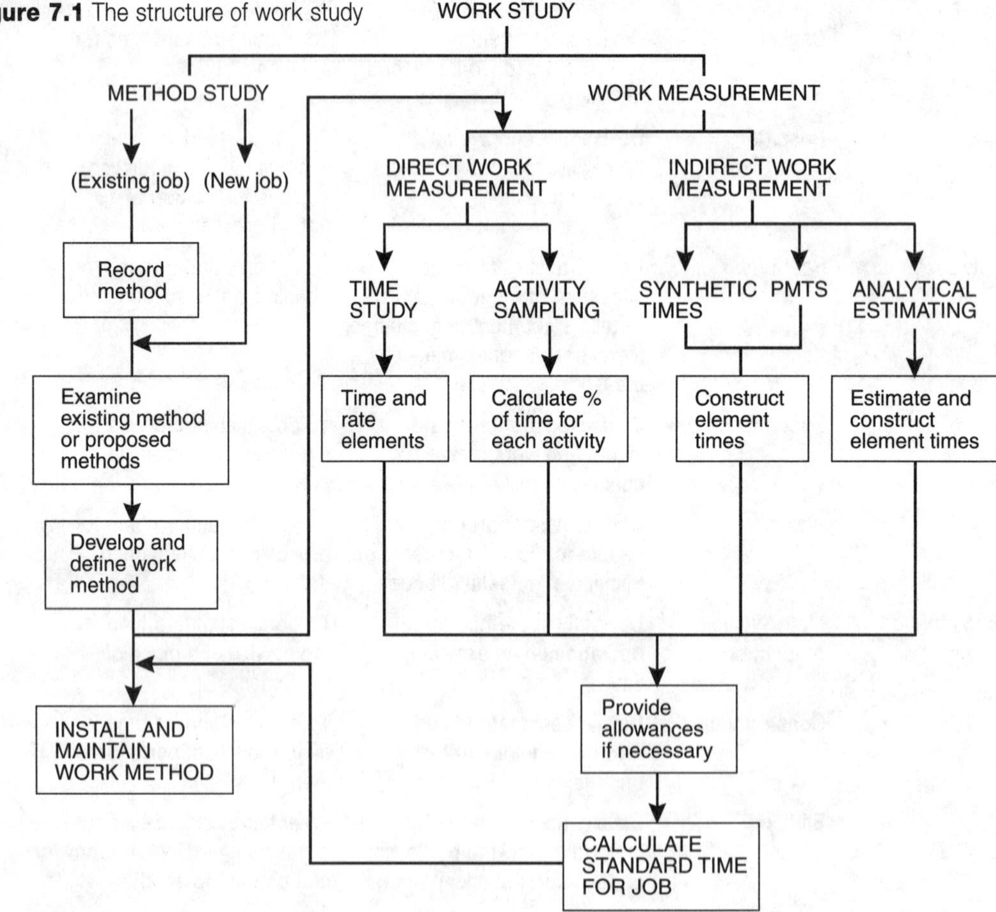

## METHOD STUDY

Method study is the systematic recording and critical examination of existing and proposed ways of doing work, as a means of developing and applying easier and more effective methods and reducing costs. Method study procedure, when applied to an existing job, consists of a maximum of seven steps:

1. Select the work to be studied (existing jobs only).
2. Record the existing work method and all other relevant facts.
3. Examine the method.
4. Develop the most efficient or optimum method of doing the work.
5. Define the method.
6. Install this method as standard practice.
7. Maintain this practice.

Table 7.2 summarizes the purpose of each step in the procedure for both existing and new jobs. The steps are discussed in more detail below.

**Table 7.2 Method study procedure**

| Method study step | Purpose: in the case of existing jobs | Purpose: in the case of new jobs |
|---|---|---|
| 1. Select | Select jobs appropriate for study, i.e. jobs likely to produce significant savings as a result of study | |
| 2. Record | Make a record in sufficient detail of present work method together with all relevant information | Using charts and diagrams, etc., show in sufficient detail each of the alternative methods under consideration |
| 3. Examine | Study the record(s) critically with a view to improving method | Study these alternatives critically with a view to selecting best or improving upon them |
| 4. Develop | Develop the most practical, economic and efficient work method available in given circumstances | ditto ⟵ |
| 5. Define | Using charts, lists, etc., describe the method to be used in sufficient detail | ditto ⟵ |
| 6. Install | Get the method adopted, retain workers, provide equipment, test method, improve, etc. | ditto ⟵ |
| 7. Maintain | Ensure that the method is used in the manner intended. Check complaints and check improvements in productivity, etc. | Ensure that the method is used in the manner intended. Check complaints and measure productivity |

*Source: Wild, R. (1980)* Management and Production, *2nd edn. Harmondsworth: Penguin. Reproduced with permission*

## Step 1: Select the job to be studied

Maximum potential cost benefit is the normal objective. Direct cost of labour, materials and equipment is certainly the main component of total cost, but indirect cost, such as the cost of supervision, training, recruitment and welfare, is also relevant. Although work methods may affect each of these costs there is a tendency to emphasize direct costs, and to develop work methods which minimize the cost of labour, machinery and materials. This approach can be criticized by those who are concerned with the human or behavioural implications of work design (Chapter 9). They point out that factors such as labour absenteeism and labour turnover may result from the nature of the work, and that work design should be evaluated in a broad manner.

## Step 2: Record the work method

The objective here is to obtain a record of the work method for subsequent examination. We must discuss two interrelated aspects:

(a) the type of record which is to be obtained (the principal distinction between the different types being the amount of detail provided);

(b) the procedure by which this record is to be obtained, e.g. by direct observation or subsequent examination of films, video tapes, etc.

## Types of records

We shall begin by considering records which provide relatively little detail of the work method: such records might be appropriate for a preliminary investigation of a work method. Later we shall look at more detailed records which might be appropriate for detailed critical examination of existing work methods with a view to improvement and/or where a subsequent objective is to establish a work standard for the method. In the latter context it is worth noting that the subsequent use of the record may determine the type of record and the type of notation which will be employed. For example, if a work standard is to be developed using a predetermined motion time system (PMTS) (see Chapter 8) then the record of the method must be in sufficient detail, and must employ the same terminology as the appropriate PMTS system.

**Figure 7.2** Flow diagram (for the process shown in Figure 7.4). N.B. for notation see Table 7.4 for flow process charts.

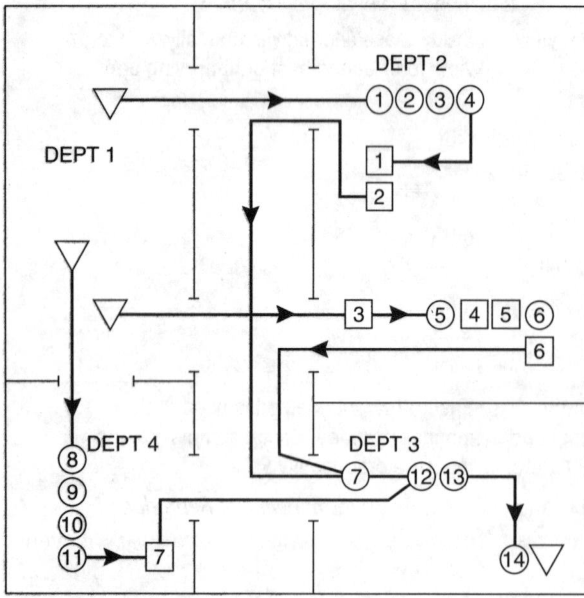


The principal types of records are listed in Table 7.3 (on pages 166–7). The more common methods or those needing most detailed descriptions are outlined below.

### Flow diagrams

Three types of flow diagram are in general use. A *flow diagram* (see Figure 7.2) shows the location and sequence of the activities carried out by workers and the routes followed by materials, components or (in the case of service and transport systems) customers, etc. A *string diagram* is a scale diagram (or model) on which coloured thread wrapped around pins or pegs is used to indicate the paths taken during a sequence of activities. String diagrams are a useful means of recording when complex movement patterns are involved and/or when the objective is to record and illustrate the movement of numerous items or workers. They can, like flow diagrams, be used to record movements throughout large areas, such as entire departments or buildings, or movement throughout smaller areas, such as individual workplaces. The *travel chart*, sometimes called the cross chart, is a slightly more sophisticated instrument for recording patterns of movement and the extent, e.g. volume, of movement between areas. Further details are given in the discussion of facilities layout planning in Chapter 6.

## Multiple activity charts

This type of record is of value where the activities of one or more workers and/or pieces of equipment are to be examined. The activities and their duration are represented by blocks or lines drawn against a time-scale. It is not usually possible to include much detail on such charts, but colour or shading is often used to distinguish between:

(a) independent work (worker working independently of equipment, e.g. reading instructions, preparing material, etc., or equipment working independently of worker);

(b) combined work, where both worker and equipment work together, e.g. setting up, adjusting;

(c) waiting time, by either worker or equipment.

Figure 7.3 shows a multiple activity chart for the operation of five identical pieces of equipment in a small office. The cycle of work consists of setting up the equipment, locating the job in it and finally performing an operation. A certain amount of idle or waiting time is also involved.

Multiple activity charts are also of value in studying maintenance jobs where workloads are varied and uneven and where several products and machines are to be attended by one worker.

**Figure 7.3** Multiple activity chart

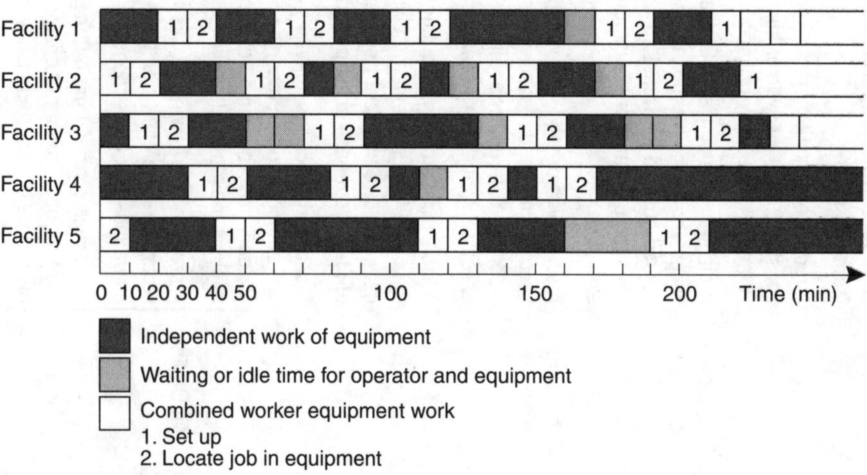


## Process charts

These are certainly the most familiar of the method study recording procedures. The sequence of events is represented by a series of symbols which are basically the same for each type of chart. They are shown in Table 7.4.

**Table 7.3 Types of recording**

| Type of record | | Definition (where appropriate from BS 3138) | Amount of detail | Applications |
|---|---|---|---|---|
| 1. Diary | | A record of a work method, normally constructed by the worker himself or herself, in the form of a diary or list of activities. | Usually very little, e.g. often just a diary of activities or movements. | To establish amount of time devoted to particular jobs, etc. |
| 2. Flow diagrams | (a) Flow diagram | A diagram or model substantially to scale which shows the location of specific activities carried out and the routes followed by workers, materials or equipment in their execution. | Shows location with respect to departments, etc. and sequence of principal activities. | Particularly useful as a means of studying layout. |
| | (b) String diagram | A scale plan or model on which a thread is used to trace and measure the paths of workers, materials or equipment during a specified sequence of events. | Shows only extent and nature of movement between areas. | Particularly useful as a means of studying layout. |
| | (c) Travel chart | A tabular record for presenting quantitative data about the movement of workers, materials or equipment between any number of places over any given period of time. | Gives in quantitative terms extent of movement between areas. | Particularly useful as a means of studying layout. |
| 3. Multiple activity charts (activity analysis) | | A chart on which the activities of more than one subject (worker, machine or equipment) are each recorded on a common time-scale to show their interrelationship. | Difficult to record more than a limited number of types of activity, e.g. working, idle, delay, etc. | As a preliminary investigation, or to study extent of occurrence of particular activities. |
| 4. Process charts | (a) Outline | A process chart giving an overall picture by recording in sequence only the main operations and inspections. | Shows principal elements only, i.e. operations and inspections. | As a preliminary investigation. |
| | (b) Flow process chart for worker | A process chart setting out the sequence of the flow of a product or customer, or a procedure by recording all events under review using the appropriate process chart symbols. This chart gives a record of all events associated with the worker. | Operations, inspections, movements and delays associated with the worker. | Normally used as the principal means of recording work methods. |

Table 7.3 continued

| Type of record | | Definition (where appropriate from BS 3138) | Amount of detail | Applications |
|---|---|---|---|---|
| | (c) Flow process chart for material | A process chart setting out the sequence of the flow of a product or customer, or a procedure by recording all events under review using the appropriate process chart symbols. This chart gives a record of all events associated with the material. | Operations, inspections, movements, delays and storage of material. | Ditto |
| | (d) Flow process chart for worker and material | A process chart setting out the sequence of the flow of a product or customer, or a procedure by recording all events under review using the appropriate process chart symbols. This chart gives a record of all events associated with worker and material. | Operations, inspections, movements, delays and storage. | |
| | (e) Flow process chart for equipment | A process chart setting out the sequence of the flow of a product or customer, or a procedure by recording all events under review using the appropriate process chart symbols. This chart shows how equipment is used. | Ditto | Ditto |
| | (f) Two-handed (or operator) | A process chart in which the activities of a worker's hands (or limbs) are recorded in relationship to one another. | Shows work method in same detail as above for each hand of operator at a given workplace. | Operations at a workplace. To provide greater detail than other types of process chart. |
| 5. SIMO (simultaneous motion chart) | | A chart, often based on film analysis, used to record simultaneously on a common time-scale the Therbligs or groups of Therbligs performed by different parts of the body of one or more workers. | Equivalent to above but gives much more detail, i.e. in terms of 'work elements'. | Where considerable detail is required, or as convenient record of film analysis. |
| 6. Memomotion | | A form of time-lapse filming or video which records activity at any instant in time at given intervals. The time intervals usually lie between ½ second and 4 seconds. | Little detail but condenses activities occurring over a long period of time into shorter periods, through a form of activity sampling. | For studying jobs with long cycle times, or jobs involving many people and movement over a large area. |

*Source: Based on Wild, R. (1980)* Management and Production, *2nd edn. Harmondsworth: Penguin. Reproduced with permission*

**Table 7.4 Process chart symbols**

| Symbol | Type of process chart | | | |
|---|---|---|---|---|
| | Outline | Flow process chart | | Two-handed (or operator) |
| | | Worker type | Material type | |
| ○ | Operation | Operation | Operation | Operation |
| ⇨ | - | Transportation | Transportation | Transportation |
| □ | Inspection | Inspection | Inspection | - |
| ▽ | - | - | Storage | Hold |
| D | - | Delay | Delay | Delay |

Note. Operation indicates the main steps in a process method or procedure. Usually the part, material or customer in the system or product concerned is modified or changed during the operation.

Transportation indicates the movement of workers, materials, customers or equipment from place to place.

Storage indicates a controlled storage in which the user or customer is received into or issued from stores under some form of authorization, or an item is retained for reference purposes.

Delay indicates a delay in the sequence of events, for example work waiting between consecutive operations, or any object or customer laid aside temporarily without record until required.

Inspection indicates an inspection for quality and/or a check for quantity.

Hold indicates the retention of an object in one hand, normally so that the other hand may do something to it.

An *outline process chart* (Figure 7.4) is a record of the main parts of the process only (i.e. the operations and the inspections). It is often used as a preliminary step prior to more detailed study. Alternatively, outline process charts are often used to record basic information for use during the arrangement or layout of plant, during the design of the product or specification of the service, or even during the design of equipment for the system. It is a simple record of the important 'constructive' and essential steps in a process, omitting all ancillary activities.

A *flow process chart* may be concerned with either *materials* (or customers in the system) or *workers* or both. It is an amplification of the outline process chart and shows, in addition, the *transportations*, *storages* and *delays* which occur. In material flow process charts, *operations* occur when an object is intentionally changed in any way; *transportations* when an object is moved, except where such movement forms part of the operation; *inspections* when an object is examined; *storage* when an object is deliberately kept or protected against unauthorized removal; and *delay* when conditions do not permit the performance of the next activity. Figure 7.5 shows a simple worker-and-material flow process chart.

A *two-handed* or *operator process chart* is the most detailed type of flow process chart, in which the activities of the worker's hands are recorded in relation to one another. Unlike the previous recording methods, the two-handed process chart is normally confined to work carried out at a single place. The

**Figure 7.4** Outline process chart

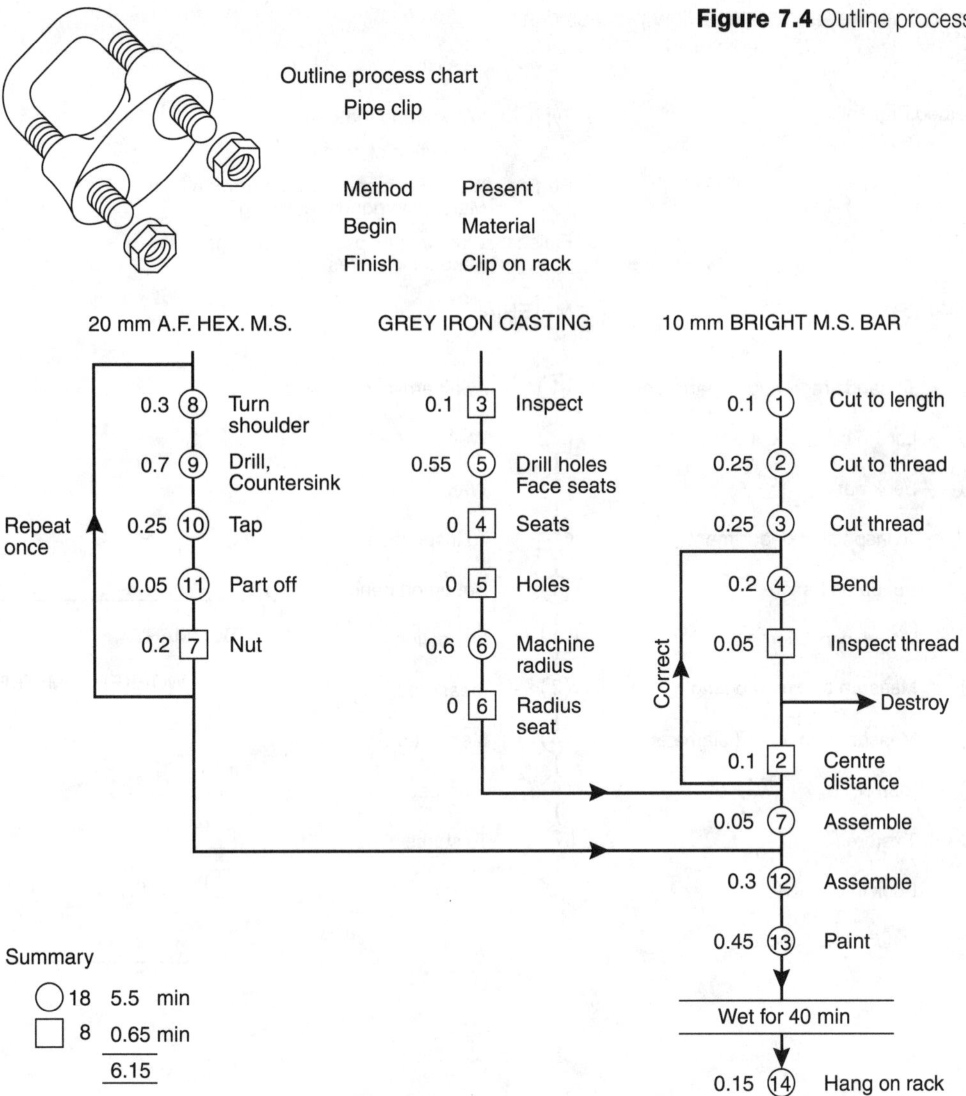


ordinary symbols are used, except *inspection* is omitted since this can be represented by movements of the hands, and the *storage* symbol is now taken to mean *hold*. A two-handed process chart for a simple job is shown in Figure 7.6.

## SIMO (simultaneous motion cycle) charts

When it is necessary to study work in more detail than is possible using two-handed or flow process charts, a different notation and a different type of record are required. The recording method most frequently used is the SIMO chart which shows in detail the work method, usually for the worker's left and right hands. Two types of notations are available: 'Therbligs' and 'PMTS' notation.

Frank Gilbreth was responsible for identifying and defining the 17 elementary or fundamental movements which together constitute all types of manual work. These Gilbreth called *Therbligs* (almost the reverse of his own name). Since then one additional element has been added to the original list and new symbols have been introduced to identify these basic movements for use in SIMO charts.

**Figure 7.5** Worker-and-material flow process chart

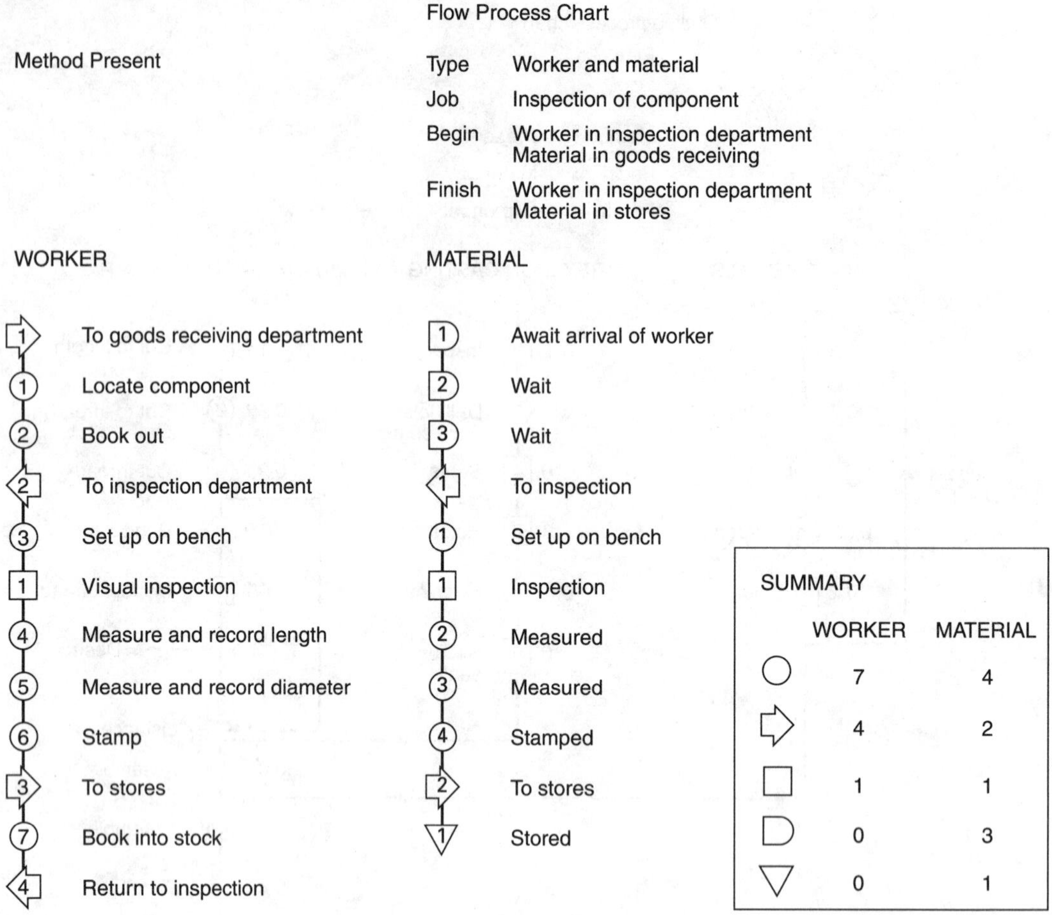

Flow Process Chart

Method Present

| | |
|---|---|
| Type | Worker and material |
| Job | Inspection of component |
| Begin | Worker in inspection department<br>Material in goods receiving |
| Finish | Worker in inspection department<br>Material in stores |

| WORKER | | MATERIAL | |
|---|---|---|---|
| ⇨ 1 | To goods receiving department | D 1 | Await arrival of worker |
| ○ 1 | Locate component | D 2 | Wait |
| ○ 2 | Book out | D 3 | Wait |
| ⇦ 2 | To inspection department | ⇦ 1 | To inspection |
| ○ 3 | Set up on bench | ○ 1 | Set up on bench |
| □ 1 | Visual inspection | □ 1 | Inspection |
| ○ 4 | Measure and record length | ○ 2 | Measured |
| ○ 5 | Measure and record diameter | ○ 3 | Measured |
| ○ 6 | Stamp | ○ 4 | Stamped |
| ⇨ 3 | To stores | ⇨ 2 | To stores |
| ○ 7 | Book into stock | ▽ 1 | Stored |
| ⇦ 4 | Return to inspection | | |

SUMMARY

| | WORKER | MATERIAL |
|---|---|---|
| ○ | 7 | 4 |
| ⇨ | 4 | 2 |
| □ | 1 | 1 |
| D | 0 | 3 |
| ▽ | 0 | 1 |

As an alternative to the use of the Therblig notation various predetermined motion time system (PMTS) notations are available. PMT systems classify motions and provide codes to identify each type and class of motion. They are of particular value in developing work standards, since each type and class of motion has a known standard time. The PMTS notation can be used in recording and describing the method, especially where it is intended to use the record subsequently to determine a standard time for the job (see Chapter 8).

## Recording procedure

The type of record to be obtained, in particular the level of detail to be incorporated, will in part determine the recording procedure to be used. For example, a 'self-recording' procedure will be feasible for obtaining a diary-type record. The construction of a record of a work method by the worker himself or herself may also be feasible for some of the less detailed flow diagrams or process charts, but in general work method records will be obtained by an independent 'observer' adopting one or more of the procedures outlined below.

**Figure 7.6** Two-handed process chart

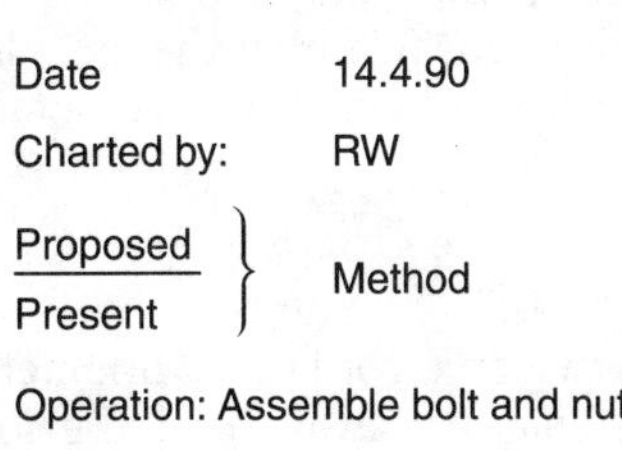


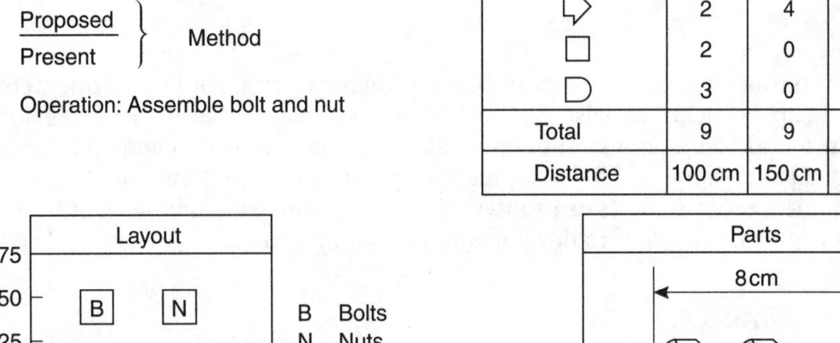

| Summary per 1 pieces | Present L.H. | Present R.H. | Proposed L.H. | Proposed R.H. |
|---|---|---|---|---|
| ○ | 2 | 5 | | |
| ⇨ | 2 | 4 | | |
| □ | 2 | 0 | | |
| D | 3 | 0 | | |
| Total | 9 | 9 | | |
| Distance | 100 cm | 150 cm | | |

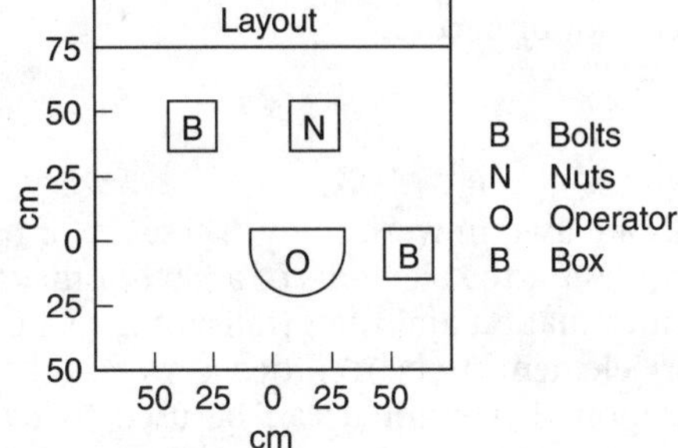


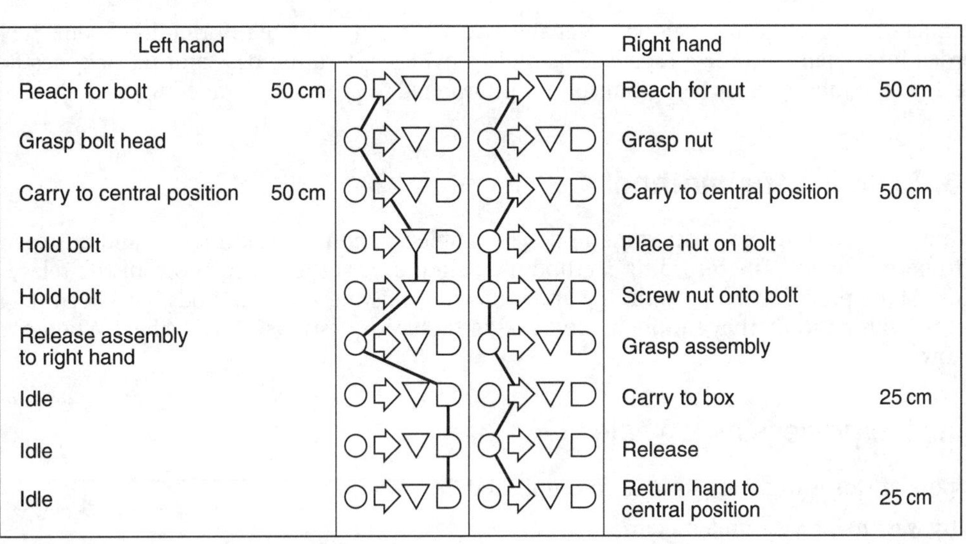

| Left hand | | Right hand | |
|---|---|---|---|
| Reach for bolt | 50 cm | Reach for nut | 50 cm |
| Grasp bolt head | | Grasp nut | |
| Carry to central position | 50 cm | Carry to central position | 50 cm |
| Hold bolt | | Place nut on bolt | |
| Hold bolt | | Screw nut onto bolt | |
| Release assembly to right hand | | Grasp assembly | |
| Idle | | Carry to box | 25 cm |
| Idle | | Release | |
| Idle | | Return hand to central position | 25 cm |

## *Direct visual observation*

Direct observation of a work method will permit the development of any one of the records listed in 2 and 4 of Table 7.3, but when more detail is to be obtained, e.g. in two-handed and SIMO charts, the observer will need to watch several repetitions of the task. It may, therefore, take some considerable time to develop a process chart for even a short cycle-time task. Similarly, in developing a multiple activity chart several complete work cycles must be observed. Direct visual methods can be used without too much difficulty in developing outline process charts, etc.

### *Recollection/memory*

For simple tasks and for the development of records with little detail, it may be possible to describe a task, i.e. to prepare a method record directly from memory. The extent to which the recorder is familiar with the task will, of course, affect the accuracy and the level of detail which can be obtained.

### *Video*

Video filming is of considerable use in method study. A film or video record of a work method permits a permanent record to be held and also facilitates method analysis 'away from the job'. Such an approach has been found to be time saving, up to 30% time saving being claimed in many cases for method analysis of a job or subsequent development of the time standard for a method. If a video film of a method is obtained, process charts can subsequently be developed in any level of detail, or 'frame-by-frame' analysis can be undertaken to develop a micromotion record.

### *Electronic procedures*

Increasingly, electronic portable 'data capture' terminals are used in work study. These are of particular use in time study, where the objective is to record the times for the elements of a job in order to determine the time required. The terminals will store such information and then transmit it to a computer for analysis. Some such terminals allow the type of work elements to be recorded as well as the elapsed time. With the use of an alphanumeric code the keys on the terminal can be used to record the sequence of (predefined) work elements in a job for subsequent examination (see Chapter 8).

Techniques have also been developed to enable the observer to dictate information about the job to be recorded into a tape recorder. *Tape date analysis* provides a 'terminology' and set of codes for this purpose, the tape subsequently being transposed/interpreted to provide a detailed work method record.

## Step 3: Examine the method

The purpose of recording the existing method is to enable subsequent examination and criticism with a view to improvement. The recording method used should be sufficient to show all the relevant information. Many procedures for examining and criticizing existing work methods have been suggested and adopted, but basically they simply involve asking six basic questions: Why? What? Where? When? Who? How?

## Examine the process as a whole

The purpose of this is to define what is accomplished, how and why:

Why was the process undertaken?

What purpose does it serve?

Where is it accomplished and why?

When is it accomplished and why?

Who is involved and why?

How is it accomplished and why?

The aim is to determine the effectiveness of the process as a whole, and identify whether any of the following major changes could be beneficial:

(a) changes in material used;

(b) changes in the design of the product or service;

(c) changes in the nature or design of the process.

## Examine aspects and parts of the process

The activities in the process belong in one of two categories. Those in each category must be examined and considered for elimination or change. First are those in which something is happening to the material, product or customer, i.e. it is being moved, inspected or worked on. Second are those in which nothing constructive is happening, i.e. delays or storages.

The first category can be further divided into *make ready, do* and *put away. Make ready* activities are required to prepare the material, workpiece or customer and set it in position ready to be worked on; *do* activities occur whenever there is change in shape, condition or composition; and *put away* activities occur when the material, product or customer is moved away from the machine or work area.

It is obviously beneficial to have a high proportion of *do* activities during the process and a low proportion of the others, since it is only *do* activities which carry things towards completion, and it is only during these activities that value is added.

Examination of these activities will question purpose, place and sequence, the person undertaking the activity and the means by which it is performed, in order to establish useful alternatives which subsequently can be examined and perhaps incorporated in an improved work method.

## Step 4: Develop and improve the work method

Now a *process improvement formula* which consists of four steps – eliminate, combine, sequence, simplify – is applied to each separate activity in the job, i.e. to each meaningful group of work elements.

Complete *elimination* of unnecessary activities is the most important step that can be taken in developing an improved work method. An activity may have been retained because of custom, history, inertia, inadequate communications or even ignorance. Changes in materials, product/service design, process design, tools or the workplace may facilitate the elimination of activities. If elimination is not possible, then combination of activities should be considered. In many processes two or more activities may be usefully *combined.*

Changes in the *sequence* of activities is the next possibility, and this may then facilitate elimination or combination. Should none of these three steps succeed in eliminating or combining the activity then the last, more expensive step should be considered, i.e. attempting to *simplify* the activity by reducing the number of operations, reducing or eliminating delays and storage, or minimizing transportation. It may become necessary to conduct a more detailed motion study to obtain enough information to enable activities to be simplified, and again consideration should be given to changes in materials and to product/service and process design. The object of simplifying the activity is to permit the worker to complete the job more quickly and easily. The principles of motion economy shown in Table 7.5 provide a means of developing efficient work methods.

## Step 5: Define the new method

It will be necessary to describe the work method to be adopted in sufficient detail for others to be able to install it or for subsequent use in training and instruction, etc. This definition comprises a statement of the nature of the work method and may be used subsequently in the case of any disputes or misunderstandings. It may be referred to when work method changes are contemplated or when changes are considered to have taken place.

**Table 7.5 Principles of motion economy: use of the worker's body and design of the workplace, tools and equipment**

**Use of the worker's body**

1. It is easier and more natural to work with two hands rather than one.
2. The two hands should begin and complete their movements at the same time.
3. The motion of the arms should be in opposite directions and should be made simultaneously and symmetrically.
4. Hands and arms naturally move smoothly in arcs, and this is preferable to straight-line movement.
5. Hand, arm and body movements should be confined to the lowest classification with which it is possible to perform the work satisfactorily, e.g. Gilbreth's classification of hand movements:
   (a) fingers
   (b) fingers and wrists
   (c) fingers, wrists and forearm
   (d) fingers, wrists, forearm and upper arm
   (e) fingers, wrists, forearm, upper arm and shoulder.
6. Work should be arranged to permit natural and habitual movements.
7. Movements should be continuous and smooth with no sharp changes in direction or speed.
8. The two hands should not, except during rest periods, be idle at the same time.
9. Whenever possible, momentum should be employed to assist the work and minimized if it must be overcome by the worker.
10. Ballistic movements are faster, easier and more accurate than controlled (fixation) movements.
11. The need to fix and focus the eyes on an object should be minimized and, when this is necessary, the occasions should occur as close together as possible.

**Arrangement of the workplace**

1. There should be a definite and fixed position for all tools, equipment and materials.
2. All tools, equipment and materials should be located as near as possible to the workplace.
3. Drop deliveries of materials (and even tools and equipment) should be used whenever possible.
4. Tools, equipment and materials should be conveniently located in order to provide the best sequence of operations.
5. Illumination levels and brightness ratios between objects and surroundings should be arranged to avoid or alleviate visual fatigue.
6. The height of the workplace and the seating should enable comfortable sitting or standing during work.
7. Seating should permit a good posture and adequate 'coverage' of the work area.
8. The workplace should be clean and adequately ventilated and heated.
9. Noise and vibration, both local and general, should be minimized.

**Design of tools and equipment**

1. Wherever possible, clamps, jigs or fixtures rather than hands should be used to hold work.
2. Wherever possible, two or more tools should be combined.
3. Wherever possible, tools and equipment should be pre-positioned.
4. The loads should be distributed among the limbs according to their capacities.
5. Wheels, levers, switches, etc. should be positioned to enable manipulation with the minimum movement of the body.

## Step 6: Install the new method

Clearly the first stage is to gain acceptance of the method from management, supervisors and workers. Then a programme for the installation of the method should be developed showing the main steps, those responsible for carrying them out, and the timetable involved. This will include time for training and learning and the rearrangement of equipment, tools, workplaces, etc.

## Learning

In installing the work method, appropriate training must be provided, and a period of learning expected.

We cannot examine this complex subject here in depth and it will be sufficient for our present purposes to consider learning as the process by which an individual acquires skill and proficiency at a task which, in turn, has the effect of permitting increased productivity in his or her performance of that task. Here we shall be concerned only with worker task learning, the speed at which a task can be executed, the extent to which the learning can increase this speed, and the influence of various factors on the learning phenomenon. We shall consider the nature of the learning curve (sometimes called the improvement curve or the progress function), but will discuss the use of the curve in the next chapter.

### *The learning curve (see also Chapter 8)*

The learning curve of the type shown in Figure 7.7 reflects three factors:

(a) The time required to complete a task or unit of work will reduce with repeated performance of that task.

(b) The rate of reduction will decrease over time.

(c) This reduction in time will follow a general pattern.

The learning curve shown in Figure 7.7 represents a 75% rate of improvement. The curve shows a performance improvement resulting from learning equivalent to a constant rate of improvement of 75%, i.e. the first performance of the task requires 1 hour and thereafter every doubling of the number of performances or number of repetitions shows a 75% improvement. Thus the second performance requires $1 \times 0.75$, i.e. 0.75 hours, the fourth performance requires $0.75 \times 0.75$, i.e. 0.56 hours, etc.

**Figure 7.7** 75% learning curve

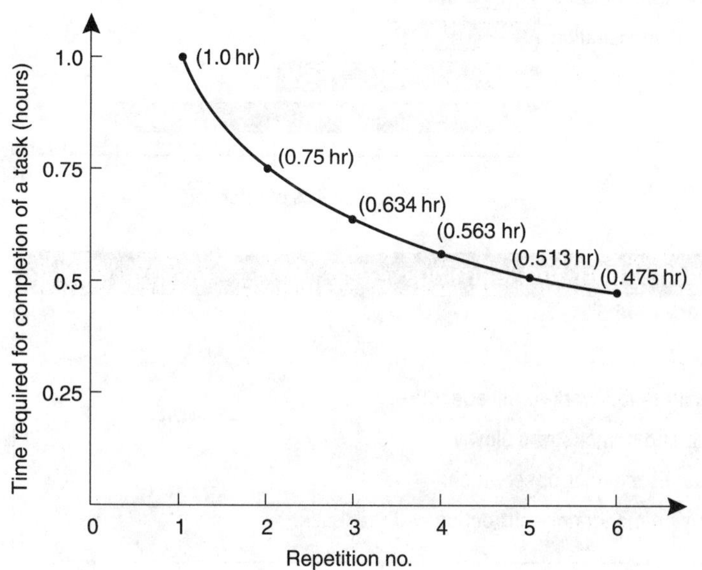


### *Factors influencing learning*

Task learning is influenced by numerous factors. The most important for our purposes are as follows:

(a) Task length, i.e. the longer the task, in general the slower the learning, not only in terms of the total time required to reach a particular level of performance, but also in terms of the number of repetitions required to reach that level of performance.

(b) Task complexity.

(c) The capability or skill of the worker and his or her familiarity with the type of work to be learned.

(d) Task similarity, i.e. the extent to which the task being learned is similar to that undertaken previously by the worker.

(e) Worker motivation and personal characteristics.

(f) External influences, e.g. physical conditions, etc.

(g) Learning methods and circumstances.

### Principles of learning

Item (g) above deserves closer consideration. How a task is learned will influence the rate of learning and the level of proficiency achieved. It follows that there are appropriate learning methods and circumstances, which in turn reflect the application of basic learning principles.

'Learning' *(noun)* – defined as the extent to which an individual retains and is able to apply job-related skills and information – may be influenced by the type of instruction employed, as illustrated in Figure 7.8. This suggests the need to employ appropriate procedures, based on a sound framework of the type shown in Table 7.6. The extent (rate and level) of learning may also be influenced by the motivation of the learner and the rewards achieved. These are two related factors. Thus, motivation may be influenced by:

(a) the extent of understanding of the work to be done;

(b) the level of understanding between instructor and learner;

(c) the knowledge of results and good job performance;

(d) the extent of experience of learning.

## Step 7: Maintain the new method

Finally, once the method is installed, a period of maintenance is required. Unnecessary changes to the work method should not be allowed, and periodic reviews/ checks should be carried out to ensure that the method is satisfactory, that disputes do not arise, that earnings are maintained and that related activities do not compromise the work method.

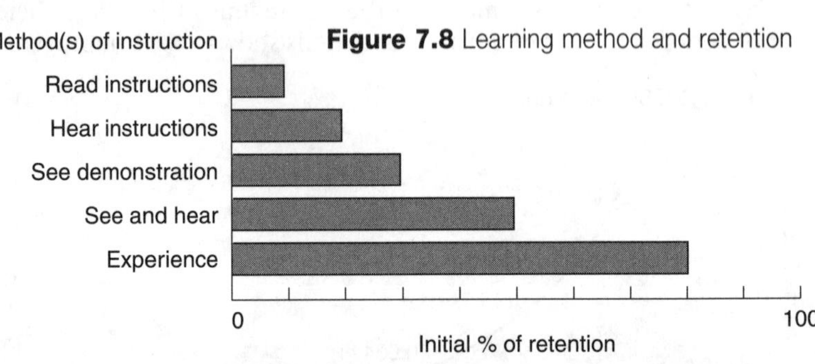


**Figure 7.8** Learning method and retention

**Table 7.6 Framework for instruction and learning**

| Basic element | Learning 'step' |
|---|---|
| 1. Instruction | 1. (a) Demonstrate job/work at full speed. |
| | (b) Explain and demonstrate slowly. |
| 2. Practice | 2. Learner practises under observation. |
| 3. Reinforcement | 3. Follow-up with monitoring, correction and feedback. |

## COMPUTER APPLICATIONS

Computer methods are now widely used in work study. They permit the rapid recording and analysis of data, storage of data for subsequent use, etc., and such applications benefit all aspects of work study, i.e. method study and work measurement. We shall look at some of these applications in the next chapter, but here we consider some uses *specifically related to method study*. Such applications fall into one of three categories: methods development and analysis; methods description; and data storage and retrieval. In all cases the use of computers in method study will be justified more easily if computer-based work measurement is also to be employed.

### Methods development and analysis

Several programs are available to assist in the development or analysis of work methods. Typically, information relating to the work required, the layout of the workplace and the tools or equipment employed is input, from which the program determines the most appropriate work method and provides a detailed workplace layout. This is useful not only for automatic development of work methods but also for a rapid comparison of alternative work methods. For example, by varying the input slightly different methods can be developed and compared.

### Methods description

Less ambitious than methods development programs are those which seek only to provide detailed methods descriptions. These require as input a description of a work method in at least outline and coded form. Then, using stored information from which detailed element descriptions can be obtained, and using one of the PMTS notations, the program generates a description in, for example, SIMO chart format of the job (usually with element and operation times). In this type of application the computer is taking over the detailed, often time-consuming task of preparing printed work method descriptions in a usable format, often also drawing upon filed data for standard or commonly used elements or sequences of elements.

### Data storage and retrieval

Most of the computerized work study programs provide a facility to store information on work elements, sequences of work elements and complete work methods together with information on tools, equipment, layouts and time standards. Such data will be of particular relevance in the development of work standards for jobs, and this will be discussed in the following chapter. Additionally, in developing and specifying work methods for new jobs, it may be possible to 'build up' a method simply by fitting together appropriate sequences, etc. from the data file. With this type of facility it is possible to reduce considerably the time required to develop and specify the new work method. The method study analyst need only identify the major parts of the total job, and the computer program can then construct detailed methodology using the filed data.

## CHECKLIST FOR CHAPTER 7

### Work study

The nature of work study
Applications of work study
Structure and purposes of work study
- Aims of work study
- Which jobs to study

### Method study

Definition
Seven steps of method study – purpose of each step – existing jobs – new jobs

1. Select job to study
2. Record work method
   - Type of record
     - Flow diagrams
       - Flow diagrams
       - String diagrams
       - Travel chart
     - Multiple activity charts
     - Process charts
       - Symbols
       - Types
       - Outline
       - Flow process
         - Worker
         - Material
         - Worker and material
         - equipment
         - Two-handed
       - SIMO chart
   - Recording procedure
     - Direct visual
     - Recollection/memory
     - Video and cine
     - Electronic
3. Examine the method
4. Develop improved method
   - Process improvement formulae
   - Principles of motion economy
     - Body
     - Workplace
     - Tools and equipment
5. Define the new method
6. Install method
   - Learning
   - The learning curve
   - Factors influencing learning
   - Principles of learning
7. Maintain method

Computers in method study
- Method development and analysis
- Methods description
- Data storage and retrieval

## FURTHER READING

**British Standards Institution (1992)** *Glossary of Terms Used in Work Study and Organisations* (BS 3138). London: BSI.

**Currie, R. M. (1986)** *Work Study*. Revised edition by Faraday, J. E. London: Pitman.

**Doty, L. A. (1989)** *Work Methods and Measurements for Management*. Albany, NY: Delmar.

**Niebel, B. W. (1988)** *Motion and Time Study*. Homewood, Ill.: Irwin.

## QUESTIONS

7.1 Describe, with examples, the method study techniques you would use to investigate the work of:

(a) a team of six workers in a hotel reception/cashier area;

(b) a single worker on a short-cycle repetitive task.

7.2 The Gobust Co. packs 'nick-nacks'. They are imported and weighed out in lots of $^1/_2$ kg. There are 12 'nick-nacks' to the kg, on average. The 'nick-nacks' must be inserted in a jar, to which a portion of 'nick-nack' juice is added. The jar is then sealed with a twist cap.

(a) Analyse the job. Develop a good sequence of work elements.

(b) Sketch the process flow and layout.

(c) Use an operation chart to detail the work involved.

7.3 An electric pump is to be assembled manually in large quantities. Describe the plug and then develop a method of assembling the components of the plug and sketch the workplace layout. Use a two-handed process chart to indicate your method. You may approximate the element times.

7.4 Develop a method for manually assembling the pipe clip shown in Figure 7.4. Sketch the workplace layout and approximate the element times.

7.5 Draw up a micromotion analysis of the two-handed operation shown in Figure 7.6, using a SIMO chart and Therbligs.

7.6 What are the six important steps involved in performing a method study? Describe very briefly the principal techniques available for the execution of the second of these steps, and describe also the logical sequence or 'formula' which constitutes step 4.

7.7 Discuss the problems in human relations which are likely to occur during a method study exercise and indicate how they might be minimized. In your answer show how the problems differ at various stages of the investigation.

## CASE STUDIES (from Part 9)

The topics covered in this chapter are relevant in the following (see Introduction to Part 9 and Table C.1 for further details):

| No. | Name | Country |
|---|---|---|
| 5 | The Sahil Tea Garden | Turkey |
| 7 | Pokhara Weavers | Nepal |
| 10 | Airport building project | India |

Chapter 8

# Work measurement and work standards

## ISSUES

Why do we need to measure work?
What type of work do we measure?
What are the basic work measurement procedures?
What procedures are involved?
How accurate and objective is such measurement?
How do we deal with human differences?
What is the effect of the 'learning curve'?

## NOTATION USED IN THIS CHAPTER

| | |
|---|---|
| BM | Basic minute |
| $L$ | Required limits of accuracy |
| MOST | Maynard operation sequence technique |
| MTA | Motion time analysis |
| MTM | Methods time measurement |
| $N$ | Actual number of observations |
| $N^1$ | Required number of observations for given confidence level and accuracy |
| $p$ | Percentage of total time occupied by activity under consideration |
| PMTS | Predetermined motion time system |
| SM | Standard minute |
| TMU | Time measurement unit (0.0006 min) |
| $x$ | Observed element time |
| $a$ | Work hours for first unit or task repetition |
| $x$ | Number of completed units or task repetitions |
| $y$ | Cumulative work hours for $x$ repetitions |

Work measurement is defined in British Standard 3138 as the 'application of techniques designed to establish the time for a qualified worker to carry out a specified job at a defined level of performance'. Work times are necessary for the comparison of work methods, for operations scheduling, for capacity planning, and for use in 'payment-by-results' schemes.

The allocation of work to a single worker and the even distribution of work among members of a team cannot be accomplished without estimates of the duration of all operations. The output of flow process systems depends, to a large extent, on the output of the workers with the longest work cycle; consequently the balanced allocation of work is essential.

Standard times for jobs, once established, may be used to set labour standards for payment purposes, to determine the operating effectiveness of equipment, workers, groups of workers, departments or factories, and to determine standard costs of operations for pricing or estimating purposes. Figure 8.1 outlines some of the uses of work time estimates.

**Figure 8.1** Use of work time estimates and standards

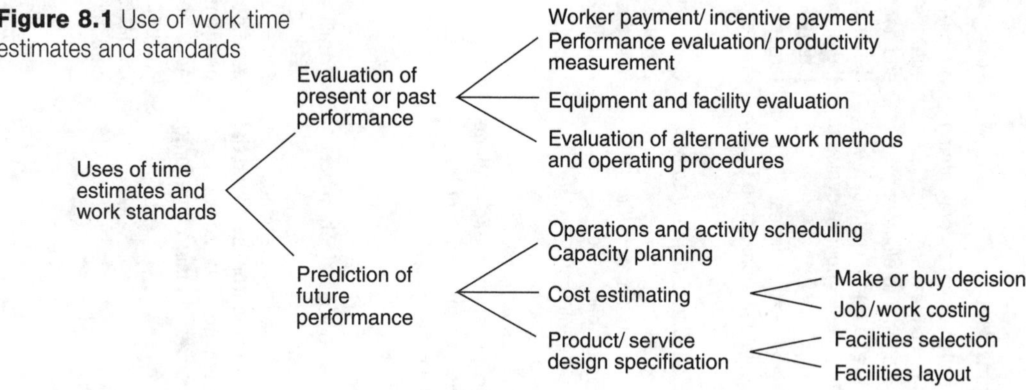


There is normally little difficulty in measuring machine work, since machine times are usually a function of machine speeds, etc. However, even where human manual work is highly rationalized and repetitive, there is a need for most workers to exercise some mental ability. As far as work study and work management are concerned, mental work is often too difficult to measure directly. Part of the process of establishing standard times for a job involves the adoption of allowances, i.e. provision of additional time to compensate for atmospheric conditions, contingencies, etc. Mental effort is dealt with in precisely the same way, i.e.

(a) physical human work is measured;

(b) machine work is calculated;

(c) mental human work is allowed for.

## WORK MEASUREMENT PROCEDURES

There are two categories of work measurement procedures (see Figure 7.1). Direct time study is the traditional timing procedure. Indirect methods are often either desirable or necessary. In the case of a new job it is impossible to conduct direct studies and, where jobs are to be undertaken for a comparatively short period of time, there may not be enough time to conduct direct work measurement. With the exception of analytical estimating, the indirect methods are of more recent origin. They have many advantages in terms of consistency and accuracy, and possibly additional developments may increase their future scope and value.

Table 8.1 summarizes the conventional procedures for work measurement, which are discussed in more detail below.

**Table 8.1 Procedures for work management**

| | Technique | Definition (BS 3138) | Steps involved | Accuracy detail | Applications |
|---|---|---|---|---|---|
| Direct work measurement | 1. Time study | A work measurement technique for recording the times and rates of working for the elements of a specified job carried out under specified conditions, and for analysing the data so as to obtain the time necessary for carrying out the job at a defined level of performance. | 1. Get all information concerning job to be measured<br>2. Divide job into *elements.*<br>3. Time and rate the elements.<br>4. Determine number of cycles to time<br>5. Determine allowances.<br>6. Calculate standard time for job. | Amount of detail is determined by step 2 and accuracy is determined largely by the process of *rating* (step 3), which is largest subjective area of time study. | Widely used, particularly for direct work. May be used as a preliminary to generating synthetic data. |
| | 2. Activity sampling | A technique in which a large number of instantaneous observations are made over a period of time of a group of machines, processes or workers. Each observation records what is happening at that instant and the percentage of observations recorded for a particular activity or delay is a measure of the percentage of time during which that activity or delay occurs. | 1. Get all details of job(s) to be measured<br>2. Divide job into activities.<br>3. Conduct pilot study to:<br>(a) determine number of observations;<br>(b) check method.<br>4. Conduct study; make readings.<br>5. Calculate proportion of time for each activity. | Gives information about proportion of time spent on each activity only. | Intermittent work. Long cycle times. As a preliminary investigation. |
| Indirect work measurement | 1. Synthetic timing | A work measurement technique for building up the time for a job at a defined level of performance by totalling element times obtained previously from time studies on other jobs containing the elements concerned, or from synthetic data. | 1. Get all details of job to be measured.<br>2. Divide job into elements.<br>3. Select time from synthetic data.<br>4. Determine allowances.<br>5. Calculate standard time for job. | Usually as much detail as time study, since data have been obtained from prior time studies. Accuracy depends on amount of data available and care in application. | Where adequate data have been gathered usually provides a sufficiently accurate and rapid method of determining times, often without recourse to stopwatch, and prior to starting job. |

Table 8.1 (continued)

| | | | | |
|---|---|---|---|---|
| 2. Pre-determined motion time systems | A work measurement technique whereby times established for basic human motions (classified according to the nature of the motion and the conditions under which it is made) are used to build up the time for a job at a defined level of performance. | 1. Get all details of the job to be measured.<br>2. Determine amount of detail required.<br>3. Construct time for job.<br>4. Determine allowances.<br>5. Calculate standard time for job. | Systems are available to provide various levels of detail. Consistency is ensured, and accuracy with many systems is greater than that of time study. | Where consistency and accuracy are important. Detailed systems are time consuming to apply. Later systems forfeit detail for speed of application. Suitable for use on indirect workers and for intermittent work. |
| 3. Analytical estimating | A work measurement technique, being a development of estimating, whereby the time required to carry out elements of a job at a defined level of performance is estimated from knowledge and practical experience of the elements concerned. | 1. Get all information concerning job to be measured.<br>2. Divide job into elements.<br>3. (a) Apply synthetic data where available.<br>(b) Estimate or time element durations.<br>4. Determine allowances.<br>5. Calculate standard time for job. | Uses synthetic data supplemented by either time studies or estimates. Slightly less accurate and consistent than synthesis. | Where insufficient synthetic data are available. Rapid method, suitable for intermittent work, e.g. maintenance. |

*Source: Wild, R. (1980)* Management and production, *2nd edn. Harmondsworth: Penguin. Reproduced with permission*

## Direct work measurement

### Time study

As with method study, we can break down time study procedure into a series of simple, logical steps, as follows.

#### *Obtain all necessary information*

The objective in work measurement is to determine the time required for a job carried out under specified conditions. It is necessary to have a record of these conditions in case the exercise is referred to or used at a later date. This recording requires information about the worker, machine, material, layout, output, method, quality standard, etc.

#### *Divide the job into elements*

This is necessary for the following reasons:

(a) to provide a better understanding of the nature of the job;

(b) to break a time study exercise up into manageably sized 'pieces';

(c) to permit a more accurate study;

(d) to distinguish different types of work;

(e) to enable 'machine' elements, i.e. machine-paced work, to be isolated from 'worker' elements;

(f) to enable detailed job descriptions to be produced;

(g) to enable time standards to be checked or modified;

(h) to enable times for certain common or important elements to be extracted and compared.

Jobs may consist of constant or variable, manual or machine, repetitive or occasional elements. Constant elements are of identical specification and have the same duration whenever performed, unlike variable elements, the times of which vary according to characteristics such as weight, size, distance, etc. Machine elements are often constant while worker elements are often variable. Occasional elements do not occur in every cycle but nevertheless are an essential part of the job.

The ease with which the study is conducted, as well as the data obtained, is dependent on the definition of the job elements. Fortunately, there are some general rules which can be used:

(a) The elements selected will be timed separately and repeatedly; consequently it is essential that clearly defined beginning and ending points should be available to identify the element.

(b) Elements should be as short as possible yet not too short to be conveniently timed.

(c) Elements should be as unified as possible. Whenever possible, elements consisting of a logical sequence of basic motions should be used.

(d) Worker and machine elements should be separated.

(e) Regular and irregular elements should be separated.

(f) Elements involving heavy or fatiguing work should be separated out.

(g) Finally, constant elements should be separated from variable elements.

## Timing elements

A variety of devices are available to assist in the timing of work elements. Traditionally, analogue stopwatches were used. Digital stopwatches are more common now. In both cases, the watches are usually mounted on an observation board to which are clipped record sheets on which the observer writes the element, reserve time, ratings, etc.

More sophisticated electronic equipment is used in element timing. A variety of types of 'event recorder' are available which combine ease of use with accuracy and versatility. Electronic data capture terminals are also used.[1] They are in effect alphanumeric keyboard devices with some internal storage and a small LCD display. They can be programmed to 'prompt' the observer with element descriptions in code form so that times can be recorded and then stored within the device. Summary calculations can be performed, and in some cases by interfacing the device directly with a printer, a list of element times can be printed out for editing and for checking for missing observations, etc. In most cases such devices provide for interfacing with the computer so that the stored information can be 'downloaded' to the computer for subsequent analysis.

There are also a variety of 'proprietary' devices to provide specific facilities. Electronic 'time study boards' are available with keys marked with work study terminology. Other boards are available with 'built-in' electronic clocks and one or more displays.

Some methods of timing elements involve filming. A video film can be made of the operation for subsequent analysis 'off the job'. The filmed record can incorporate a clock so that detailed timings can be obtained, or the film can be run at a known and constant speed.

### The number of cycles to be timed

We must take enough readings to be reasonably confident of an accurate result. Direct time study is a sampling process, and the accuracy of the sample as a measure of the elements themselves is determined by the variability of the elements and the size of the sample. The number of observations to be taken depends on:

(a) the variation in the times of the element;

(b) the degree of accuracy required;

(c) the confidence level required.

A 95% confidence level and an accuracy of ± 5% or ± 10% are usually adopted. This means that the chances are at least 95 out of 100 that the mean or average we obtain from the observations will be in error by ± 5% or ± 10% of the true element time.

Before the number of observations necessary to fulfil this requirement can be calculated, we must establish the variability of the element time by conducting a brief 'pilot' study. We can then use one of the following formulae to calculate the required number of observations.

95% confidence ± 5% accuracy:

$$N^1 = \left( \frac{40 \sqrt{N \Sigma x^2 - (\Sigma x)^2}}{\Sigma x} \right)^2$$

95% confidence ± 10% accuracy:

$$N^1 = \left( \frac{20 \sqrt{N \Sigma x^2 - (\Sigma x)^2}}{\Sigma x} \right)^2$$

---

[1] Watson, I. J. (1988) Electronic time study. *Management Services*, **32**(10), pp. 18–19.

where $N^1$ = required number of observations for given confidence and accuracy
$N$ = actual number of observations taken in pilot study
$x$ = each observed element time from the pilot study.

## Rating the worker

So far we have been concerned only with the observed or actual times required by a worker to perform elements of work, but the object of work measurement is to determine not how long it *did* take to perform a job or elements of a job, but how long it *should* take. It is necessary, therefore, to compare the actual rate of work with a standard rate so that the observed times can be converted to basic times, i.e. the time required to carry out an element of work at standard performance. So, every observation we make must be rated and the appropriate rating factor recorded.

Performance rating is the comparison of an actual rate of working against a defined concept of a standard rate. The standard rate corresponds to 'the average rate at which qualified workers will naturally work at a job, provided they know and adhere to the specified method, and provided they are motivated to apply themselves to their work'. On the British Standard Performance Scale, standard rating is equal to 100, i.e. a rating of 50 is equal to half the standard rate of working. However, standard rate is really only a concept. In practice the standard rate of working is a function of the situation, e.g. the physical conditions, the type of labour, company policy, and may differ greatly between companies. Consequently, the company must train the time study analyst to recognize what the company or industry regards as standard performance.[2]

Several systems of rating have been developed. *Effort rating* is concerned primarily with work speed, the worker being rated according to the speed of movement, with adjustments being made for the perceived difficulty of the job. *Objective rating* is similar, depending on the consideration of two factors: speed and difficulty. The operator is rated first according to the speed of movement, irrespective of the nature of the job. After this rating an adjustment is made depending on the nature of the job, particularly:

(a) how much of the body is used;
(b) the use of foot pedals;
(c) the need for bimanualness;
(d) eye–hand co-ordination;
(e) the handling requirements;
(f) the weight of objects handled.

The Westinghouse Company devised a system in which four characteristics were considered: the skill used, the effort required, the conditions prevailing and the consistency required. A numerical scale is attached to each of these characteristics (Table 8.2). Unlike the two systems above, this is used to rate a job rather than the separate elements of the job. For this reason it is sometimes referred to as a *levelling system* rather than a rating system. A separate rating for each element is made for each area and the sum of the four figures represents the final rating factor for each element, e.g.

Observed (actual) element time = 0.45 minutes

Element rating = + 0.06 (skill)
+ 0.12 (effort)
+ 0.00 (conditions)
+ 0.01 (consistency)
+ 0.19

[2] See, for example, Das, B. (1988) The application of Das's programmed learning method to operation performance rating training in industry. *MTM Journal*, **14**, pp. 39–43.

Table 8.2 Factors and point values in performance rating

| Skill | | | Effort | | | Conditions | | | Consistency | | |
|---|---|---|---|---|---|---|---|---|---|---|---|
| +0.15 | A1 | Superskill | +0.13 | A1 | Excessive | +0.06 | A | Ideal | +0.04 | A | Perfect |
| +0.13 | A2 | | +0.12 | A2 | | +0.04 | B | Excellent | +0.03 | B | Excellent |
| +0.11 | B1 | Excellent | +0.10 | B1 | Excellent | +0.02 | C | Good | +0.01 | C | Good |
| +0.08 | B2 | | +0.08 | B2 | | 0.00 | D | Average | 0.00 | D | Average |
| +0.06 | C1 | Good | +0.05 | C1 | Good | −0.03 | E | Fair | −0.02 | E | Fair |
| +0.03 | C2 | | +0.02 | C2 | | −0.07 | F | Poor | −0.04 | F | Poor |
| 0.00 | D | Average | 0.00 | D | Average | | | | | | |
| −0.05 | E1 | Fair | −0.04 | E1 | Fair | | | | | | |
| −0.10 | E2 | | −0.08 | E2 | | | | | | | |
| −0.16 | F1 | Poor | −0.12 | F1 | Poor | | | | | | |
| −0.22 | F2 | | −0.17 | F2 | | | | | | | |

$$\text{Basic time for element} = 0.45 \times (1.00 + 0.19)$$
$$= 0.54 \text{ minutes}$$

Whichever one of these or other methods of rating or levelling is used, the basic time corresponds to the observed time after rating, i.e.

$$\text{Basic time for element or job} = \text{Observed time} \times \frac{\text{Rating \%}}{100}$$

## *Allowances*

It may be necessary now to provide allowances to compensate for fatigue, personal needs, contingencies, etc. The basic time does not contain any allowances and is merely the time required by the worker to perform the task at a standard rate without any interruptions or delays. Allowances are normally given as a percentage of the basic element times and usually include:

(a) Relaxation allowances:

1. fatigue allowances to give the workers time to recover from the effort (physiological and psychological) required by the job;
2. personal needs – to visit toilets, washrooms, etc.

(b) Contingency allowances given to compensate for the time required by the workers to perform all necessary additional and periodic activities which were not included in the basic time because of infrequent or irregular occurrence and the difficulty of establishing the times.

(c) Tool and machinery allowance to compensate the worker for the time necessary for adjusting and setting up equipment, and so on.

(d) Reject allowance, necessary where a proportion of defective items must necessarily be produced.

(e) Interference allowance to compensate for time unavoidably lost because of the stoppage of two or more machines, attended by one worker, at the same time.

(f) Excess work allowance to compensate for the extra work necessary because of unforeseen or temporary changes in the standard conditions.

Total allowances are often of the order of 15–20%, so inaccuracies are of some consequence. Nevertheless, whilst different methods are available, practice is again very much a function of the situation.[3]

### Calculate standard time

The standard time for an element or a job is calculated as follows:

$$\text{Standard time} = \left(\text{Observed time} \times \frac{\text{Rating \%}}{100}\right) \times \frac{\text{Per cent total allowance}}{100}$$

For example, where the worker is observed to be working at greater than the standard rate the three element times may bear a relationship to one another as shown in Figure 8.2.

**Figure 8.2** Breakdown of the standard minute

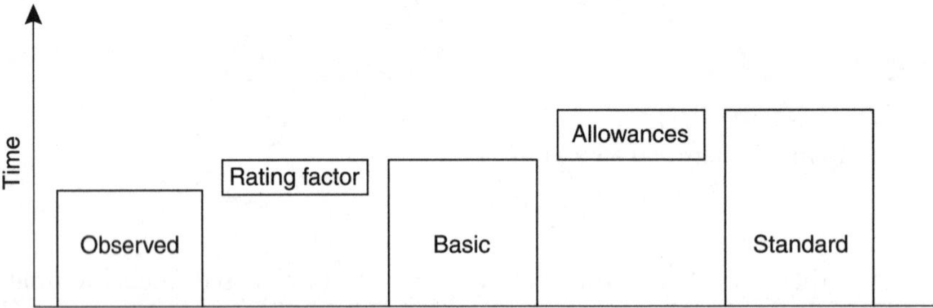


The *standard minute* is the unit of measurement of work, consisting partly of work and partly of relaxation. It represents the output in one minute if the work is performed at the standard rate. By means of work measurement we can express the work content of the jobs in terms of single units – standard minutes (SMs) – irrespective of the differences between the jobs themselves.

Note that an SM is a measure of *work* and not a measure of time. It is connected with time only in that one SM of work will take one minute of time at 100 performance. SMs can therefore be used in calculating wages and performance. For example, performance can be measured by:

$$\frac{\text{Output of work in SMs}}{\text{Total labour time in minutes}}$$

## Activity sampling

Direct time study, as above, is appropriate where we are concerned with short-cycle repetitive work. If, however, it is necessary to establish work standards in situations where long, irregular-cycle work is conducted, or where many different jobs are performed, these techniques may be quite inappropriate.

It may be necessary to study the activities of several workers on several machines in order to establish the proportion of time each worker spends on various activities, or to determine the utilization of resources, space, etc., and in such cases some form of sampling procedure is invaluable.

[3] See, for example, Das, B. (1990) Personal, unavoidable delay, and fatigue allowances for setting performance standards. *International Journal of Operations and Production Management*, **10**(5), pp. 62–70.

The accuracy of our sample as a measure of the actual activity is dependent on the number of observations we take. If we are willing to take many observations, our confidence in the result can be high, but this will have been obtained only at higher cost.

Again, we must decide what confidence level and accuracy we require before we can decide how many observations to take. Furthermore, a pilot study must be conducted to establish the frequency of occurrence of the activity being studied; then for a confidence level of 95% the formula to determine the number of observations required is:

$$N^1 = \frac{4p\,(100 - p)}{L^2}$$

where $N^1$ = number of observations needed

$p$ = percentage of total time occupied by the activity with which we are concerned, as obtained from a pilot study

$L$ = required limits of accuracy (expressed as a percentage).

Activity sampling is normally used to determine the percentage of the total time that a person or machine spends on certain activities. In the simplest case, the requisite number of random observations is taken to determine the percentage of total time spent by either a worker or a machine in working or not working.

## Rated activity sampling

Occasionally it is practical to sample activities at regular rather than random intervals because of the random nature of the activities concerned. In such circumstances it is possible to use an extension of activity sampling known as *rated activity sampling* or *rated systematic sampling*.

**EXAMPLE**

### *A photocopier*

A photocopier is either working or not working. A series of observations is made at regular 1-minute intervals to determine the proportion of the total time devoted to each of these activities. The table gives the results of the survey; each of the marks in the table has resulted from an observation.

| Observation number (1-minute intervals) | Machine running | Machine not running |
|---|---|---|
| 1 | 1 | |
| 2 | 1 | |
| 3 | 1 | |
| 4 | | 1 |
| 5 | 1 | |
| 6 | 1 | |
| 7 | | 1 |
| 8 | 1 | |
| 9 | 1 | |
| 10 | 1 | |
| Total | 8 | 2 |

If the production of items from this machine during the period observed was 25, and if we assume standard performance, then the *basic minutes* (BM) for each product is given as follows:

$$\text{BM/product} = \frac{8}{25} = 0.32$$

**EXAMPLE**

## *An office job*

A worker is performing an office job which has an irregular cycle and consists of a maximum of three elements of work. Observations are made at regular intervals of 0.1 minute; the number of items processed during the period of the study is determined and the operator is rated at each observation. Determine the *basic minutes* for each element and for each item produced.

The table shows the results of the sampling. The figures in the columns indicate not only which element was being performed on each observation, but also the performance rating for that element at that time.

The throughput during this two-minute study was ten items.

| Observation number (0.1-minute intervals) | Element 1 | Element 2 | Element 3 | Idle |
|---|---|---|---|---|
| 1 | 100 | | | |
| 2 | | 100 | | |
| 3 | 95 | | | |
| 4 | | | 110 | |
| 5 | 95 | | | |
| 6 | | | | 100 |
| 7 | | 100 | | |
| 8 | 95 | | | |
| 9 | 100 | | | |
| 10 | | | 105 | |
| 11 | | 100 | | |
| 12 | | | | 100 |
| 13 | | 100 | | |
| 14 | 95 | | | |
| 15 | | 100 | | |
| 16 | 110 | | | |
| 17 | | 110 | | |
| 18 | | | 95 | |
| 19 | | | | 100 |
| 20 | 100 | | | |
| Total (00) | 7.9 | 6.1 | 3.1 | 3.0 |

The basic minutes for each element per product can be calculated using the following formula:

$$\text{BM/Element} = \frac{\text{Sum of all ratings}}{100} \times \frac{\text{Observation interval}}{\text{Output}}$$

i.e. For element 1:
BM = 7.9 × 0.1/10
= 0.079

For element 2:
BM = 6.1 × 0.1/10
= 0.061

For element 3:
BM = 3.1 × 0.1/10
= 0.031

The total basic minutes for each item is of course the sum of the above figures, i.e. 0.171.

## Indirect work measurement

### Synthetic timing

As time studies are completed, the 'elemental' data are coded and stored. Periodically these data are examined to determine whether there is any consistency between times for similar elements. When enough consistent data have been gathered the information can be compiled for future use as a database.

The generation of data for 'machine' elements normally involves comparatively little trouble, since such times are often either constant or the functions of known variables. Similarly, constant 'worker' elements provide little difficulty, since an equal time will be required whenever the job or element is performed.

It is more difficult to deal with variable elements. First, we must examine the variations in time which occur in our accumulated data to establish whether the variation is a result of a difference in the nature of the element itself, or whether it results from the action of one or more variables. If the variations are particularly large there may be fundamental differences in the nature of the elements, in which case the data cannot be assembled together. The remaining variation can usually be attributed to variables such as distance, size and weight, and graphs or tables can then be constructed.

Such 'synthetic' data are reliable and consistent, since normally they have resulted from many studies over a period of time. They can be used to establish time standards for short-run work on which there would be insufficient time to conduct a direct time study, and to construct time standards for jobs not yet begun. It is normal to synthesize basic times to which allowances must be added. The need to rate the job under consideration is avoided and, since the synthetic data will probably have been derived from numerous studies, the consequence of inaccuracies in the original studies is reduced.

### Predetermined motion time systems (PMTS)

PMTS can be defined as 'a work measurement technique whereby times established for basic human motions (classified according to the nature of the motion and the conditions under which it is made) are used to build up the time for a job at a defined level of performance'. A PMT system therefore consists of a list of all motions that a worker can use in doing a task, together with time values for these motions at a specified level of performance and in specified circumstances.

## MTM–1

*Methods time measurement* (MTM) is the oldest and best-known PMTS, and also the basis for many other PMTSs.

The first MTM system (MTM–1) provided times for basic motions, the argument being that, because such motions approximated to the 'lowest common denominators' of all work, it was possible, theoretically at least, to construct time standards for all jobs from a set of tabular data.

MTM–1 classifies all hand motions into basic units as follows:

| | |
|---|---|
| *Reach* (R) | The basic element employed when the predominant purpose is to move the hand to a destination or general location. |
| *Move* (M) | The basic element employed when the predominant purpose is to transport an object to a destination. |
| *Turn* (T) | A movement which rotates the hand, wrist and forearm. |
| *Apply pressure* (AP) | The element employed whenever pressure is applied. |
| *Grasp* (G) | A hand or fingers element employed when an object is required for further operation. |
| *Position* (P) | The basic element employed to align, orient or engage one object with another, when motions used are minor and do not justify classification as other basic elements. |
| *Release* (RL) | The basic elements employed to relinquish control of an object by the fingers or hand. |
| *Disengage* (D) | The basic element employed to break contact between objects. |
| *Eye travel and eye focus* (ET, EF) | |
| *Body, leg and foot motions* | |

The times for various subgroups of each of these units, and under various conditions, are shown in Figure 8.3. In addition Table 8.3 shows how the MTM–1 notation is constructed, and Figure 8.4 indicates the ease or difficulty with which simultaneous motions are achieved.

The time units used in MTM are 'time measurement units' where:

1 TMU = 0.0006 min

It should be noted that because MTM–1 was developed in America, TMU values do not necessarily correspond to 100 on the BS rating scale. It has been suggested that for all practical purposes job times derived using MTM values should be accepted as equivalent to a BSI rating of 83.

## MTM–2

MTM–2 was synthesized from MTM–1 data and consists of nine motions: Get; Put; Apply pressure; Regrasp; Eye action; Crank; Step; Foot motion; Bend and arise. Only Get and Put have variable categories, so the MTM–2 data card has only 39 time standards. As with MTM–1, the motions and their various sub-categories are closely defined and precise rules govern their use.

| | |
|---|---|
| *Get* (G) | A motion with the predominant purpose of reaching with the hand or fingers to an object, grasping the object, and subsequently releasing it.<br>Class A – no grasping motion required. |

**Figure 8.3** MTM–1 application data in TMUs. Reproduced with the permission of the MTM Association of the UK

TABLE I – REACH – R

| Distance Moved Inches | Time TMU A | Time TMU B | Time TMU C or D | Time TMU E | Hand in motion A | Hand in motion B | CASE AND DESCRIPTION |
|---|---|---|---|---|---|---|---|
| 3/4 or less | 2.0 | 2.0 | 2.0 | 2.0 | 1.5 | 1.6 | A Reach to object in fixed location, or to object in other hand or on which other hand rests |
| 1 | 2.5 | 2.5 | 3.6 | 2.4 | 2.3 | 2.3 | |
| 2 | 4.0 | 4.0 | 6.9 | 3.8 | 3.5 | 2.7 | |
| 3 | 5.3 | 6.3 | 7.3 | 5.3 | 4.5 | 3.6 | B Reach to single object in location which may vary slightly from cycle to cycle |
| 4 | 6.1 | 6.4 | 8.4 | 6.8 | 4.9 | 4.3 | |
| 5 | 6.5 | 7.8 | 9.4 | 7.4 | 6.3 | 5.0 | |
| 6 | 7.0 | 8.6 | 10.1 | 8.0 | 5.7 | 5.7 | |
| 7 | 7.4 | 9.3 | 10.8 | 8.7 | 6.1 | 6.5 | C Reach to object jumbled with other objects in a group so that search and select occur |
| 8 | 7.9 | 10.1 | 11.5 | 9.3 | 6.5 | 7.2 | |
| 9 | 8.3 | 10.8 | 12.2 | 9.9 | 6.9 | 7.9 | |
| 10 | 8.7 | 11.5 | 12.9 | 10.5 | 7.3 | 8.6 | |
| 12 | 9.6 | 12.9 | 14.2 | 11.8 | 8.1 | 10.1 | |
| 14 | 10.5 | 14.4 | 15.6 | 13.0 | 8.9 | 11.5 | D Reach to a very small object or where accurate grasp is required |
| 16 | 11.4 | 15.8 | 17.0 | 14.2 | 9.7 | 12.9 | |
| 18 | 12.3 | 17.2 | 18.4 | 15.5 | 10.5 | 14.4 | |
| 20 | 13.1 | 18.6 | 19.8 | 16.7 | 11.3 | 15.8 | |
| 22 | 14.0 | 20.1 | 21.2 | 18.0 | 12.1 | 17.3 | E Reach to indefinite location to get hand in position for body balance or next motion or out of way |
| 24 | 14.9 | 21.5 | 22.5 | 19.2 | 12.9 | 18.8 | |
| 26 | 15.8 | 22.9 | 23.9 | 20.4 | 13.7 | 20.2 | |
| 28 | 16.7 | 24.4 | 25.3 | 21.7 | 14.5 | 21.7 | |
| 30 | 17.5 | 25.8 | 26.7 | 22.9 | 15.3 | 23. | |

TABLE II – MOVE – M

| Distance Moved Inches | Time TMU A | Time TMU B | Time TMU C | Hand in Motion B | Wt Allowance: Wt (lb) Up to | Wt Allowance: Fact–or | Wt Allowance: Con–stant TMU | CASE AND DESCRIPTION |
|---|---|---|---|---|---|---|---|---|
| 3/4 or less | 2.0 | 2.0 | 2.0 | 1.7 | 2.5 | 1.00 | 0.0 | A Move object to other hand or against stop |
| 1 | 2.6 | 2.9 | 3.4 | 2.3 | | | | |
| 2 | 3.6 | 4.6 | 5.2 | 2.9 | 7.5 | 1.06 | 2.2 | |
| 3 | 4.9 | 5.7 | 6.7 | 3.6 | | | | |
| 4 | 6.1 | 6.9 | 8.0 | 4.3 | 12.5 | 1.11 | 3.9 | |
| 5 | 7.3 | 8.0 | 9.2 | 5.0 | | | | |
| 6 | 8.1 | 8.9 | 10.3 | 6.7 | 17.5 | 1.17 | 5.6 | |
| 7 | 8.9 | 9.7 | 11.1 | 6.5 | | | | |
| 8 | 9.7 | 10.6 | 11.8 | 7.2 | 22.5 | 1.22 | 7.4 | B Move object to approximate or indefinite location |
| 9 | 10.5 | 11.5 | 12.7 | 7.9 | | | | |
| 10 | 11.3 | 12.2 | 13.5 | 8.6 | 27.5 | 1.28 | 9.1 | |
| 12 | 12.9 | 13.4 | 15.2 | 10.0 | | | | |
| 14 | 14.4 | 14.6 | 16.9 | 11.4 | | | | |
| 16 | 16.0 | 15.8 | 18.7 | 12.8 | 32.5 | 1.33 | 10.8 | |
| 18 | 17.6 | 17.0 | 20.4 | 14.2 | | | | |
| 20 | 19.2 | 18.2 | 22.1 | 15.6 | 37.5 | 1.39 | 12.5 | C Move object to exact location |
| 22 | 20.8 | 19.4 | 23.8 | 17.0 | | | | |
| 24 | 22.4 | 20.6 | 25.5 | 18.4 | 42.5 | 1.44 | 14.3 | |
| 26 | 24.0 | 21.8 | 27.3 | 19.8 | | | | |
| 28 | 25.5 | 23.1 | 29.0 | 21.2 | 47.5 | 1.50 | 16.0 | |
| 30 | 27.1 | 24.3 | 30.7 | 22.7 | | | | |

TABLE III – TURN AND APPLY PRESSURE – T AND AP

| Weight | | Time TMU for Degrees Turned | | | | | | | | | | |
|---|---|---|---|---|---|---|---|---|---|---|---|---|
| | | 30° | 45° | 60° | 75° | 90° | 105° | 120° | 135° | 150° | 165° | 180° |
| Small | 0 to 2 lb | 2.8 | 3.5 | 4.1 | 4.8 | 5.4 | 6.1 | 6.8 | 7.4 | 8.1 | 8.7 | 9.4 |
| Medium | 2.1 to10 lb | 4.4 | 5.5 | 6.5 | 7.5 | 8.5 | 9.6 | 10.6 | 11.6 | 12.7 | 13.7 | 14.8 |
| Large | 10.1 to 35 lb | 8.4 | 10.5 | 12.3 | 14.4 | 16.2 | 18.3 | 20.4 | 22.2 | 24.3 | 26.1 | 28.2 |
| APPLY PRESSURE CASE 1 16.2 TMU APPLY PRESSURE CASE 2 10.6 TMU | | | | | | | | | | | | |

**Figure 8.3** continued

TABLE IV – GRASP – G

| Case | Time TMU | DESCRIPTION |
|---|---|---|
| 1A | 2.0 | Pick Up Grasp – small, medium or large object by itself, easily grasped |
| 1B | 3.8 | Very small object or object lying close against a flat surface |
| 1C1 | 7.3 | Interference with grasp on bottom and one side of nearly cylindrical object. Diameter larger than1/2" |
| 1C2 | 8.7 | Interference with grasp on bottom and one side of nearly cylindrical object. Diameter 1/4" to 1/2" |
| 1C3 | 10.8 | Interference with grasp on bottom and one side of nearly cylindrical object. Diameter less than 1/4" |
| 2 | 5.6 | Regrasp |
| 3 | 5.6 | Transfer grasp |
| 4A | 7.3 | Object jumbled with other objects so search and select occur. Larger than 1" × 1" × 1" |
| 4B | 9.1 | Object jumbled with other objects so search and select occur. 1/4" × 1/4" × 1/2" to 1" × 1" × 1" |
| 4C | 12.9 | Object jumbled with other objects so search and select occur. Smaller than 1/4" × 1/4" × 1/2" |
| 6 | 0 | Contact, sliding or hook grasp |

TABLE V – POSITION – P

| CLASS OF FIT | | Symmetry | Easy to Handle | Difficult to Handle |
|---|---|---|---|---|
| 1 – Loose | No pressure required | S | 5.6 | 11.2 |
| | | SS | 9.1 | 14.7 |
| | | NS | 10.4 | 16.0 |
| 2 – Close | Light pressure required | S | 16.2 | 21.6 |
| | | SS | 19.7 | 25.3 |
| | | NS | 21.0 | 26.6 |
| 3 – Exact | Heavy pressure required | S | 43.0 | 48.6 |
| | | SS | 46.5 | 52.1 |
| | | NS | 47.8 | 53.4 |

*Distance moved to engage – 1 or less

TABLE VI – RELEASE – RL

| Case | Time TMU | DESCRIPTION |
|---|---|---|
| 1 | 2.0 | Normal release performed by opening fingers as independent motion |
| 2 | 0 | Contact release |

TABLE VII – DISENGAGE – D

| CLASS OF FIT | Easy to Handle | Difficult to Handle |
|---|---|---|
| 1 Loose. Very slight effort, blends with subsequent move | 4.0 | 5.7 |
| 2 Close. Normal effort, slight recoil | 7.5 | 11.8 |
| 3 Tight. Considerable effort, hand recoils markedly | 22.9 | 34.7 |

TABLE VIII – EYE TRAVEL TIME AND EYE FOCUS – ET AND EF

Eye Travel Time = $15.2 \times \frac{T}{D}$ TMU, with a maximum value of 20 TMU

where T = the distance between points from and to which the eye travels
D= the perpendicular distance from the eye to the line of travel T

Eye Focus Time = 7.3 TMU

**Figure 8.3** continued

TABLE IX – BODY, LEG AND FOOT MOTIONS

| DESCRIPTION | | | SYMBOL | DISTANCE | TIME TMU |
|---|---|---|---|---|---|
| Foot motion | | Hinged at ankle<br>with heavy pressure | FM<br>FMP | Up to 4" | 8.6<br>19.1 |
| Leg or foreleg motion | | | LM | Up to 6"<br>Each add 1 inch | 7.1<br>1.2 |
| Sidestep | Case 1 | Complete when leading leg contacts floor | SS-C1 | Less than 12"<br><br>12"<br>Each add 1 inch | Use REACH or MOVE Time<br>17.0<br>6 |
| | Case 2 | Lagging leg must contact floor before next motion can be made | SS-C2 | 12"<br>Each add 1 inch | 34.1<br>1.1 |
| Bend, stoop or kneel on one knee<br>Arise<br>Kneel on floor both knees<br>Arise | | | B,S, KOK<br>AB, AS, AKOK<br>KBK<br>AKBK | | 29.0<br>31.9<br>60.4<br>76.7 |
| Sit<br>Stand from sitting position<br>Turn body 45 to 90 degrees –<br>Case 1 – Complete when leading leg contacts floor<br>Case 2–Lagging leg must contact floor before next motion can be made | | | SIT<br>STD<br>TBC1<br><br>TBC2 | | 34.7<br>43.4<br><br>18.6<br>37.2 |
| Walk<br>Walk<br>Walk | | | W-FT<br>W-P<br>W-PO | Per foot<br>Per pace<br>Per pace | 5.3<br>15.0<br>17.0 |

**Table 8.3 Examples of MTM–1 notation**

| Motion | Code | Meaning and TMU value |
|---|---|---|
| Reach | R7A | Reach, path of movement 17.5 cm, class A. Hand not in motion at beginning or end (7.4 TMU) |
| Move | M6A | Move, 15 cm, class A, object weighs less than 1.1 kg (8.9 TMU) |
| Turn | T90M | Turn, 90° object weighing 0.95 to 4.5 kg (8.5 TMU) |
| Grasp | G1C1 | Grasp, case 1C1 (7.3 TMU) |
| Position | P2NSE | Position, close fit, non-symmetrical part. Easy to handle. (21.0 TMU) |
| Release | RL1 | Release, case 1 (2.0 TMU) |
| Disengage | D1D | Disengage, loose fit, difficult to handle (5.7 TMU) |
| Eye travel | ET10/12 | Eye travel, between points 25 cm apart, line of travel 30 cm from eye (12.7 TMU) |

**Figure 8.4** Simultaneous motions. Reproduced with the permission of the MTM Association of the UK

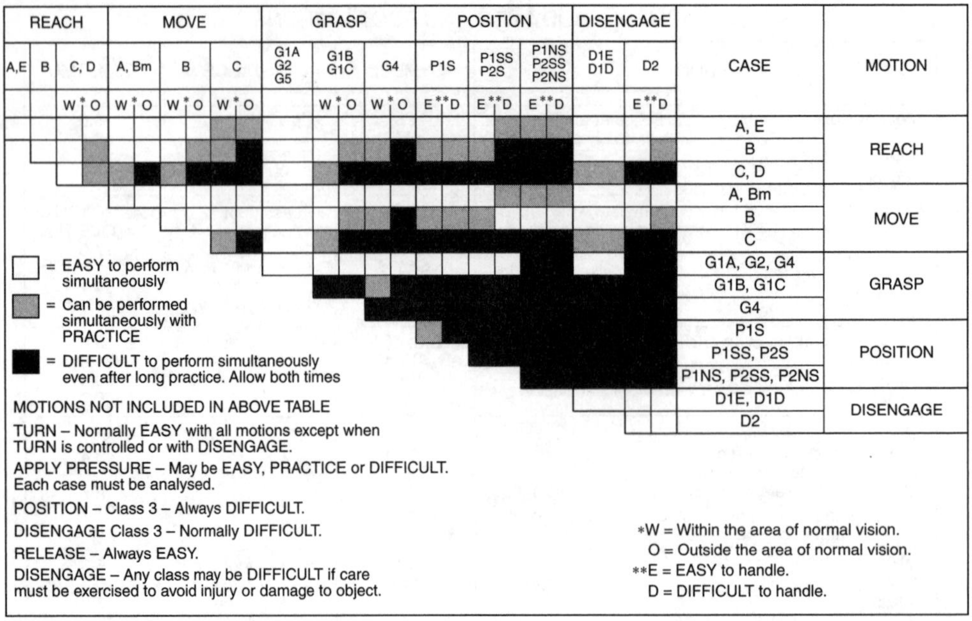

| REACH | | | MOVE | | | GRASP | | | POSITION | | | DISENGAGE | | CASE | MOTION |
|---|---|---|---|---|---|---|---|---|---|---|---|---|---|---|---|
| A,E | B | C, D | A, Bm | B | C | G1A G2 G5 | G1B G1C | G4 | P1S | P1SS P2S | P1NS P2SS P2NS | D1E D1D | D2 | | |
| | | W * O | W * O | W * O | W * O | | W * O | W * O | E ** D | E ** D | E ** D | | E ** D | | |
| | | | | | | | | | | | | | | A, E | REACH |
| | | | | | | | | | | | | | | B | |
| | | | | | | | | | | | | | | C, D | |
| | | | | | | | | | | | | | | A, Bm | MOVE |
| | | | | | | | | | | | | | | B | |
| | | | | | | | | | | | | | | C | |
| | | | | | | | | | | | | | | G1A, G2, G4 | GRASP |
| | | | | | | | | | | | | | | G1B, G1C | |
| | | | | | | | | | | | | | | G4 | |
| | | | | | | | | | | | | | | P1S | POSITION |
| | | | | | | | | | | | | | | P1SS, P2S | |
| | | | | | | | | | | | | | | P1NS, P2SS, P2NS | |
| | | | | | | | | | | | | | | D1E, D1D | DISENGAGE |
| | | | | | | | | | | | | | | D2 | |

☐ = EASY to perform simultaneously

▒ = Can be performed simultaneously with PRACTICE

■ = DIFFICULT to perform simultaneously even after long practice. Allow both times

MOTIONS NOT INCLUDED IN ABOVE TABLE

TURN – Normally EASY with all motions except when TURN is controlled or with DISENGAGE.

APPLY PRESSURE – May be EASY, PRACTICE or DIFFICULT. Each case must be analysed.

POSITION – Class 3 – Always DIFFICULT.

DISENGAGE Class 3 – Normally DIFFICULT.

RELEASE – Always EASY.

DISENGAGE – Any class may be DIFFICULT if care must be exercised to avoid injury or damage to object.

*W = Within the area of normal vision.
O = Outside the area of normal vision.
**E = EASY to handle.
D = DIFFICULT to handle.

| | |
|---|---|
| | Class B – grasping involving closing of the hand or fingers with one motion.<br>Class C – complex grasping motion.<br>Class W – *get weight,* the action required for the muscles of the hand or arm to take up the weight of an object. |
| *Put* (P) | A motion with the predominant purpose of moving an object to a destination with the hand or fingers.<br>Class A – continuous smooth motion.<br>Class B – discontinuous motion, but without obvious correcting motion (i.e. unintentional stop, hesitation or change in direction).<br>Class C – discontinuous motion with obvious correcting motions.<br>Class W – *put weight,* in an addition to a put action depending on the weight of the object moved. |
| *Apply pressure* (A) | An action with the purpose of exerting muscular force on an object. |
| *Regrasp* (R) | The hand action performed with the purpose of changing the grasp of an object. |
| *Eye action* (E) | The action with the purpose of either (a) recognizing a readily distinguishable characteristic of an object, or (b) shifting vision to a new viewing area. |
| *Crank* (C) | A motion with the purpose of moving an object in a circular path more than 180° with hand or fingers. |
| *Step* (S) | Either (a) a leg motion with the purpose of moving the body or (b) a leg motion longer than 30 centimetres. |
| *Foot motion* (F) | A short foot or leg motion the purpose of which is *not* to move the body. |
| *Bend and arise* (B) | Bend, stoop or kneel on one knee and subsequently arise. |

**Figure 8.5** The MTM–2 data card. Reproduced with the permission of the MTM Association of the UK

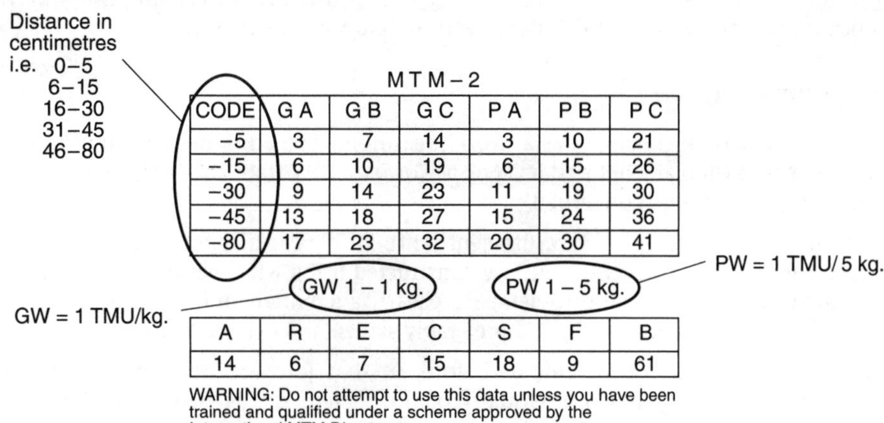


MTM – 2

| CODE | G A | G B | G C | P A | P B | P C |
|---|---|---|---|---|---|---|
| –5 | 3 | 7 | 14 | 3 | 10 | 21 |
| –15 | 6 | 10 | 19 | 6 | 15 | 26 |
| –30 | 9 | 14 | 23 | 11 | 19 | 30 |
| –45 | 13 | 18 | 27 | 15 | 24 | 36 |
| –80 | 17 | 23 | 32 | 20 | 30 | 41 |

| A | R | E | C | S | F | B |
|---|---|---|---|---|---|---|
| 14 | 6 | 7 | 15 | 18 | 9 | 61 |

WARNING: Do not attempt to use this data unless you have been trained and qualified under a scheme approved by the International MTM Directorate.

The time standard, in TM units, for each of the motions is easily obtained from the MTM–2 data card (Figure 8.5). The values for the seven motions without variable categories are given at the bottom of the card, while the remaining figures on the card relate to Get and Put. The time standard for both of these is determined by the category of the motion and the distance involved. The left-hand column gives distance in centimetres. The time standards for GW and PW are shown on the card; in the case of the former, a time value of 1 TMU per kilogram applies, and in the case of the latter 1 TMU per 5 kilograms, i.e. the TMU associated with 'Getting' an object of effective net weight 10 kg (GW 10) is 10 TMU, whereas the time standard for PW 10 is 2 TMU.

## *Other MTM-derived PMTS*

### *MODAPTS*

MODAPTS (modular arrangement of predetermined time standards) and MODAPTS PLUS is now one of the best-known systems for computer application.

### *4M*

There are many other MTM-based PMTS. The 4M DATA system was developed specifically for use in a computerized PMTS.

### *MOST*

The MOST (Maynard Operations Sequence Technique) was derived with the objective of simplifying and accelerating application without loss of accuracy. MOST identifies eight key activities which occur in three fixed sequences. Index numbers ascribed to the variables for each activity reflect the relative simplicity or complexity of the sequence or move. Thus the 'compression' of a single activity into a short formula is achieved, enabling MOST to be used (it is claimed) up to 40 times faster than MTM–1 and up to 15 times faster than MTM–2.

### *Clerical PMTS*

Most of the PMTS described above are of value in the study of most types of manual work. However, some systems, also derived from MTM, have been developed specifically for use with office/clerical jobs. For example, PADS was developed around 1989. It is a simplified, predetermined method time system that analyses the sequences of manual actions performed in clerical work and assigns to each performance of the sequence. PADS is a three-level data system consisting of: (1) simplified MTM data; (2) common office motion sequences; and (3) application data for specific tasks.[4]

### Analytical estimating

Analytical estimating may be described as a 'work measurement technique whereby the time required to carry out elements of a job at a defined level of performance is established from knowledge and practical experience of the elements concerned'.

In some circumstances there are often insufficient synthetic data available to allow time standards to be established, and consequently standards must be constructed using whatever data are available, plus estimates of the basic times for the remaining elements. Clearly a requirement in analytical estimating is that the estimator is completely familiar with, and preferably skilled and experienced in, the work concerned.

The procedure used is much the same as before, in that jobs are first divided into appropriate elements, synthetic data being used for as many of those elements as possible while basic times are estimated for the remainder. Rather than applying allowances to individual elements, relaxation and contingency allowances are applied as overall or blanket figures for the whole job.

## COMPUTER APPLICATIONS IN WORK STUDY *(see also p. 177)*

We referred to computer applications in method study in Chapter 7. Now we can bring those comments together with the above, and consider computer applications which serve both aspects. Many broad-based systems are available.[5] They provide for the following:

(a) preparation of detailed work methods descriptions;

(b) methods development and analysis (and workplace layout);

(c) storage and retrieval of data on work methods and times;

(d) development of workplace layout;

(e) analysis of direct time study data;

(f) determination of time standards;

(g) computerized PMTS.

## THE LEARNING CURVE

We noted in Chapter 7 the need to provide training and to allow a period of learning following introduction of a work method. We looked also at the nature of the learning curve. Now we must look again at this topic, for often it will be necessary for us to be able to calculate learning time, and performance during learning.

### Learning curve calculations

A 75% learning curve was shown in Figure 7.7. The same curve is shown, with others, on a logarithmic scale in Figure 8.6. This type of presentation clearly shows one of the important characteristics of the learning effect – predictability. Tables of learning coefficients are also available (Table 8.4).

---

[4] Willis, D. (1989) A new multi-level MTM based system for clerical evaluation. *Management Services*, **33**(9), pp. 30–33.

[5] Wygant, R. M. (1989) A comparison of computerized predetermined time systems. *Computers and Industrial Engineering*, **17**(1–4), pp. 480–485.
Genaidy, A. M., Agrawal, A. and Mital, A. (1990) Computerized predetermined motion time systems in manufacturing industries. *Computers and Industrial Engineering*, **18**(4), pp. 571–584.

**Table 8.4 Learning curve coefficients**

| Unit number | 70% | | 75% | | 80% | | 85% | | 90% | |
|---|---|---|---|---|---|---|---|---|---|---|
| | Unit time | Total time | Unit time | Total time | Unit time | Total time | Unit time | Total time | Unit time | Total time |
| 1 | 1.000 | 1.000 | 1.000 | 1.000 | 1.000 | 1.000 | 1.000 | 1.000 | 1.000 | 1.000 |
| 2 | .700 | 1.700 | .750 | 1.750 | .800 | 1.800 | .850 | 1.850 | .900 | 1.900 |
| 3 | .568 | 2.268 | .634 | 2.384 | .702 | 2.502 | .773 | 2.623 | .846 | 2.746 |
| 4 | .490 | 2.758 | .562 | 2.946 | .640 | 3.142 | .723 | 3.345 | .810 | 3.556 |
| 5 | .437 | 3.195 | .513 | 3.459 | .596 | 3.738 | .686 | 4.031 | .783 | 4.339 |
| 6 | .398 | 3.593 | .475 | 3.934 | .562 | 4.299 | .657 | 4.688 | .762 | 5.101 |
| 7 | .367 | 3.960 | .446 | 4.380 | .534 | 4.834 | .634 | 5.322 | .744 | 5.845 |
| 8 | .343 | 4.303 | .422 | 4.802 | .512 | 5.346 | .614 | 5.936 | .729 | 6.574 |
| 9 | .323 | 4.626 | .402 | 5.204 | .493 | 5.839 | .597 | 6.533 | .716 | 7.290 |
| 10 | .306 | 4.932 | .385 | 5.589 | .477 | 6.315 | .583 | 7.116 | .705 | 7.994 |
| 11 | .291 | 5.223 | .370 | 5.958 | .462 | 6.777 | .570 | 7.686 | .695 | 8.689 |
| 12 | .278 | 5.501 | .357 | 6.315 | .449 | 7.227 | .558 | 8.244 | .685 | 9.374 |
| 13 | .267 | 5.769 | .345 | 6.600 | .438 | 7.665 | .548 | 8.792 | .677 | 10.052 |
| 14 | .257 | 6.026 | .334 | 6.994 | .428 | 8.092 | .539 | 9.331 | .670 | 10.721 |
| 15 | .248 | 6.274 | .325 | 7.319 | .418 | 8.511 | .530 | 9.861 | .663 | 11.384 |
| 16 | .240 | 6.514 | .316 | 7.635 | .410 | 8.920 | .522 | 10.383 | .656 | 12.040 |
| 17 | .233 | 6.747 | .309 | 7.944 | .402 | 9.322 | .515 | 10.898 | .650 | 12.690 |
| 18 | .226 | 6.973 | .301 | 8.245 | .394 | 9.716 | .508 | 11.405 | .644 | 13.334 |
| 19 | .220 | 7.192 | .295 | 8.540 | .338 | 10.104 | .501 | 11.907 | .639 | 13.974 |
| 20 | .214 | 7.407 | .288 | 8.828 | .381 | 10.485 | .495 | 12.402 | .634 | 14.608 |
| 21 | .209 | 7.615 | .283 | 9.111 | .375 | 10.860 | .490 | 12.892 | .630 | 15.237 |
| 22 | .204 | 7.819 | .277 | 9.388 | .370 | 11.230 | .484 | 13.376 | .625 | 15.862 |
| 23 | .199 | 8.018 | .272 | 9.660 | .364 | 11.594 | .479 | 13.856 | .621 | 16.483 |
| 24 | .195 | 8.213 | .267 | 9.928 | .359 | 11.954 | .475 | 14.331 | .617 | 17.100 |
| 25 | .191 | 8.404 | .263 | 10.191 | .355 | 12.309 | .470 | 14.801 | .613 | 17.713 |
| 26 | .187 | 8.591 | .259 | 10.449 | .350 | 12.659 | .466 | 15.267 | .609 | 18.323 |
| 27 | .183 | 8.774 | .255 | 10.704 | .346 | 13.005 | .462 | 15.728 | .606 | 18.929 |
| 28 | .180 | 8.954 | .251 | 10.955 | .342 | 13.347 | .458 | 16.186 | .603 | 19.531 |
| 29 | .177 | 9.131 | .247 | 11.202 | .338 | 13.685 | .454 | 16.640 | .599 | 20.131 |
| 30 | .174 | 9.305 | .244 | 11.446 | .335 | 14.020 | .450 | 17.091 | .596 | 20.727 |
| 31 | .171 | 9.476 | .240 | 11.686 | .331 | 14.351 | .447 | 17.538 | .593 | 21.320 |
| 32 | .168 | 9.644 | .237 | 11.924 | .328 | 14.679 | .444 | 17.981 | .590 | 21.911 |
| 33 | .165 | 9.809 | .234 | 12.158 | .324 | 15.003 | .441 | 18.422 | .588 | 22.498 |
| 34 | .163 | 9.972 | .231 | 12.389 | .321 | 15.324 | .437 | 18.859 | .585 | 23.084 |
| 35 | .160 | 10.133 | .229 | 12.618 | .318 | 15.643 | .434 | 19.294 | .583 | 23.666 |
| 36 | .158 | 10.291 | .226 | 12.844 | .315 | 15.958 | .432 | 19.725 | .580 | 24.246 |
| 37 | .156 | 10.447 | .223 | 13.067 | .313 | 16.271 | .429 | 20.154 | .578 | 24.824 |

**Table 8.4 continued**

| Unit number | 70% Unit time | 70% Total time | 75% Unit time | 75% Total time | 80% Unit time | 80% Total time | 85% Unit time | 85% Total time | 90% Unit time | 90% Total time |
|---|---|---|---|---|---|---|---|---|---|---|
| 38 | .154 | 10.601 | .221 | 13.288 | .310 | 16.581 | .426 | 20.580 | .575 | 25.399 |
| 39 | .152 | 10.753 | .219 | 13.507 | .307 | 16.888 | .424 | 21.004 | .573 | 25.972 |
| 40 | .150 | 10.902 | .216 | 13.723 | .305 | 17.193 | .421 | 21.425 | .571 | 26.543 |
| 41 | .148 | 11.050 | .214 | 13.937 | .303 | 17.496 | .419 | 21.844 | .569 | 27.111 |
| 42 | .146 | 11.196 | .212 | 14.149 | .300 | 17.796 | .416 | 22.260 | .567 | 27.678 |
| 43 | .144 | 11.341 | .210 | 14.359 | .298 | 18.094 | .414 | 22.674 | .565 | 28.243 |
| 44 | .143 | 11.484 | .208 | 14.567 | .296 | 18.390 | .412 | 23.086 | .563 | 28.805 |
| 45 | .141 | 11.625 | .206 | 14.773 | .294 | 18.684 | .410 | 23.496 | .561 | 29.366 |
| 46 | .139 | 11.764 | .204 | 14.977 | .292 | 18.975 | .408 | 23.903 | .559 | 29.925 |
| 47 | .138 | 11.902 | .202 | 15.180 | .290 | 19.265 | .405 | 24.309 | .557 | 30.482 |
| 48 | .136 | 12.038 | .201 | 15.380 | .288 | 19.552 | .403 | 24.712 | .555 | 31.037 |
| 49 | .135 | 12.173 | .199 | 15.579 | .286 | 19.838 | .402 | 25.113 | .553 | 31.590 |
| 50 | .134 | 12.307 | .197 | 15.776 | .284 | 20.122 | .400 | 25.513 | .552 | 32.142 |
| 51 | .132 | 12.439 | .196 | 15.972 | .282 | 20.404 | .398 | 25.911 | .550 | 32.692 |
| 52 | .131 | 12.570 | .194 | 16.166 | .280 | 20.684 | .396 | 26.307 | .548 | 33.241 |
| 53 | .130 | 12.700 | .192 | 16.358 | .279 | 20.963 | .394 | 26.701 | .547 | 33.787 |
| 54 | .128 | 12.828 | .191 | 16.549 | .277 | 21.239 | .392 | 27.094 | .545 | 34.333 |
| 55 | .127 | 12.955 | .190 | 16.739 | .275 | 21.515 | .391 | 27.484 | .544 | 34.877 |
| 56 | .126 | 13.081 | .188 | 16.927 | .274 | 21.788 | .389 | 27.873 | .542 | 35.419 |
| 57 | .125 | 13.206 | .187 | 17.144 | .272 | 22.060 | .388 | 28.261 | .541 | 35.960 |
| 58 | .124 | 13.330 | .185 | 17.299 | .271 | 22.331 | .386 | 28.647 | .539 | 36.499 |
| 59 | .123 | 13.453 | .184 | 17.483 | .269 | 22.600 | .384 | 29.031 | .538 | 37.037 |
| 60 | .122 | 13.574 | .183 | 17.666 | .268 | 22.868 | .383 | 29.414 | .537 | 37.574 |

The following formula may also be used for calculating performance times:

$$y = ax^b$$

where $y$ = time for $x$th repetition

$x$ = number of repetitions

$a$ = time for first repetition

$$b = \frac{\text{log of \% improvement rate/100}}{\text{log of 2}}$$

For example, the time required for the tenth repetition of a task which initially required 1 hour, given a 75% learning effect, would be:

$$1 \times 10^{-0.416} = 0.385 \text{ hours}$$

The following examples illustrate further types of learning curve calculations in which the coefficients in Table 8.4 are used.

**Figure 8.6** Learning curves (75–90%)

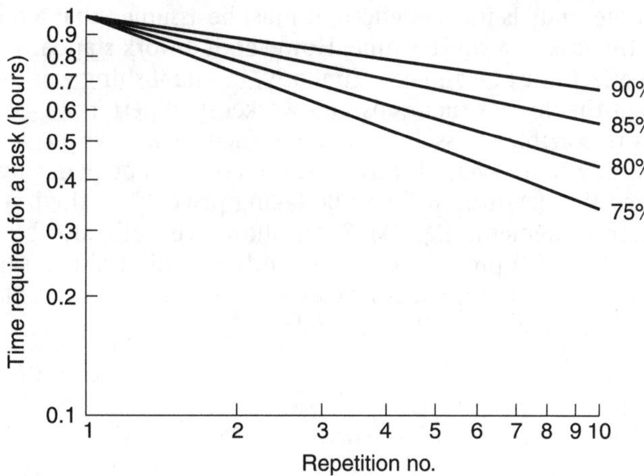


## EXAMPLES

1. A worker is to repeat a job 20 times. It is estimated that the first time the job is done it will take 1.5 hours. It is estimated that an 80% learning effect will exist. How long will it take to finish all 20 jobs?

   *Answer*. For 20 units at 80% learning, total time = 1.5 (10.484) = 15.73 hours

2. It is known that the average time for a job over a 'run' of 15 identical jobs is 3 hours. What is the time required for the first and the last jobs if the learning rate is 75%?

   *Answer.* Total time for 15 units (for an initial time of 1 hour) = 7.319

Average time for 15 units (for an initial time of 1 hour) = $\frac{7.319}{15}$ = 0.4879 hours

Hence:

Time for first unit $\frac{3}{0.4879}$ = 6.149 hours

Time for last unit 0.325 (6.149) = 1.998 hours

In certain circumstances, particularly where work has begun on a particular task, it will be possible to estimate the learning percentage and thus to predict, using the formula above, the time required to complete a task or the performance level at some future date. Thus it will be possible to predict the relatively steady state performance, i.e. the work standard for a particular task. In other circumstances, especially where work has not begun on a particular task, it will be necessary to estimate the learning percentage in order to predict the 'relatively steady state' work standard. Prediction might be undertaken either by comparing the task to be completed with similar work undertaken in similar circumstances or by analysing the nature of the task by comparison with other tasks.

Because of this learning phenomenon it will be unrealistic to assume that a constant time is required for the completion of particular tasks, i.e. that a particular work standard will always apply. Thus in direct time study it will be necessary to take some account of the level of learning accomplishment of the worker in order to 'correct' the work standard based on the observed time. Thus if the worker being observed during direct time study is inexperienced, it must be assumed that a more experienced worker will be able to perform the task in a shorter time. However, if a work standard is being determined for a new job, the learning effect must be allowed. Similarly, in establishing work standards for jobs some account must be taken of the 'life' of such jobs. If a worker is to perform a job for some considerable length of time then it is reasonable to assume that he or she will achieve a level of performance equivalent to the relatively steady state level. If, however, the task is to be performed for a relatively short time it might be assumed that learning will still be taking place when the last cycle is completed. In applying indirect work measurement, e.g. PMTS, an allowance must also be made for the learning effect. In general, PMTS times will provide work standards for fully trained, skilled and accomplished workers, i.e. steady-state learned performances. Some allowances must be made in such times to provide for the learning effect during the start-up period.

## CHECKLIST FOR CHAPTER 8

Definition of work measurement (BS 3138)
Use of work standards
  Evaluation of present and past performance
  Prediction of future performance
Measurement of what?
  Manual work
  Machine work
  Mental work

### *Work measurement procedures*

Direct work measurement
  Time study
    Obtain all necessary information
    Divide job into elements
    Time elements
      Number of cycles to be timed
    Rate the worker
    Allowances
    Calculate standard time
Activity sampling
  Rated activity sampling

Indirect work measurement
  Synthetic timing
  PMTS
  MTM–1
  MTM–2
  Other MTM-based systems
    MODAPTS
    4M
    MOST
    Clerical PMTS
    PADS
  Analytical estimating

### *Computer applications*

Computers in work measurement
Analysis of time study data
Computerized PMTS
Computers in work study

### *The learning curve*

Learning curve calculation

## FURTHER READING

**Hall, M. (1991)** Computer work measurement systems. *Management Services*, **35**(2), pp. 30–35.

**Whitmore, D. A. (1987)** *Work Measurement*, 2nd edn. London: Heinemann.

See also Further Reading as follows for Chapter 7.

**British Standards Institution (1992)**
**Currie (1986)**
**Doty (1989)**

## QUESTIONS

8.1 The figures below are the observed times obtained during 25 observations of a single element of a manual task. Have sufficient observations of this element been made to provide an accuracy of ± 5% with a confidence interval of 95%?

| Observation number (*N*) | Time for element (in 1/100 min) | Observation number (*N*) | Time for element (in 1/100 min) |
|---|---|---|---|
| 1 | 40 | 14 | 41 |
| 2 | 45 | 15 | 43 |
| 3 | 43 | 16 | 44 |
| 4 | 42 | 17 | 46 |
| 5 | 45 | 18 | 43 |
| 6 | 47 | 19 | 42 |
| 7 | 40 | 20 | 42 |
| 8 | 48 | 21 | 44 |
| 9 | 47 | 22 | 43 |
| 10 | 42 | 23 | 40 |
| 11 | 40 | 24 | 42 |
| 12 | 39 | 25 | 45 |
| 13 | 42 | | |

8.2 The Westinghouse method of rating (see Table 8.2) was used to rate the performance of the element for which the observed times given in the previous question were also obtained. The rating is to be made on a basis of the following:

| | |
|---|---|
| Skill | C1 |
| Effort | B2 |
| Conditions | E |
| Consistency | D |

Calculate the standard time for the element if a personal allowance of 5% is given.

8.3 Using the data given on the sheet shown opposite calculate the output of a worker at standard performance for an 8-hour shift.

8.4 The following task relates to a series of four time studies which were taken of a worker assembling an electric plug which had two identical terminal pins.

The worker removes a completed plug from a jig and sets it aside; he takes a base for a new plug and fits this in the jig. He then takes two terminal pins and inserts these through the base, and a lid is placed on top of the base. When pressure is exerted on the lid a mechanical screwing device, situated under the jig, automatically fastens the base and the lid together. The cycle then starts again.

After every 1000 plugs assembled, the screwdriver blade in the mechanical screwing device has to be resharpened.

Four studies were made of this operation and the results tabulated as on p. 206.

**Table for Question 8.3**

| Study | Worker | Times | Date | Sheet |
|---|---|---|---|---|
| | Male | 1/10 min | | 1 |

| Element number | Rating | Observed time | Ineffective time | Basic time | Element number | Rating | Observed time | Ineffective time | Basic time |
|---|---|---|---|---|---|---|---|---|---|
| 1 | 110 | 0.45 | | | 1 | 105 | 0.45 | | |
| 2 | 100 | 0.70 | | | 2 | 110 | 0.70 | | |
| 3 | 110 | 0.35 | | | 3 | 115 | 0.40 | | |
| 1 | 105 | 0.50 | | | 1 | 100 | 0.45 | | |
| 2 | 110 | 0.65 | | | 2 | 100 | 0.80 | | |
| 3 | 105 | 0.40 | | | 3 | 90 | 0.50 | | |
| 1 | 100 | 0.45 | | | 1 | 95 | 0.52 | | |
| 2 | 100 | 0.72 | | | 2 | 100 | 0.75 | | |
| 3 | 100 | 0.42 | | | 3 | 110 | 0.45 | | |
| | | | | | 1 | 100 | 0.45 | | |
| – | | | 3.80 | | 2 | 100 | 0.75 | | |
| | | | | | 3 | 100 | 0.40 | | |
| 1 | 100 | 0.47 | | | 1 | 110 | 0.52 | | |
| 2 | 90 | 0.85 | | | 2 | 100 | 0.75 | | |
| 3 | 110 | 0.50 | | | 3 | 100 | 0.38 | | |
| 1 | 100 | 0.45 | | | | | | | |
| 2 | 100 | 0.75 | | | | | Adjust jig every 25 cycles | | |
| 3 | 110 | 0.48 | | | | | | | |

Allowances: Fatigue 5% Personal 10% Delay 2%

Note: (a) BM in each case is the total basic time in 1/10 min (i.e. the observed time adjusted for rating) spent on that element during the study.

(b) A relaxation allowance of 10% is appropriate for all the elements except the occasional element. For this element a relaxation allowance of 15% should be given.

Determine the standard time for assembling one plug.

8.5 Assume that after the application of appropriate work simplification techniques you have taken a direct time study and, after subtraction, you get the results (time in minutes) tabulated overleaf:

(a) Elements 2 and 4 are machine paced.

(b) You have a decision rule which states that any reading which varies by more than 25% from the average of all readings for an element will be considered 'abnormal'.

**Table for Question 8.4**

| | Study number | 1 | 2 | 3 | 4 |
|---|---|---|---|---|---|
| | *Repetitive elements* | | | | |
| A | Remove complete plug and fit new base in jig (BM) | 1.61 | 3.31 | 2.55 | 1.72 |
| | Number of occurrences | 20 | 40 | 30 | 20 |
| B | Inset one terminal pin through base (BM) | 2.11 | 4.06 | 3.31 | 2.05 |
| | Number of occurrences | 40 | 80 | 60 | 40 |
| C | Locate lid on base and fix with mechanical device (BM) | 1.96 | 3.92 | 3.05 | 2.04 |
| | Number of occurrences | 20 | 40 | 30 | 20 |
| | *Occasional elements* | | | | |
| D | Remove, sharpen and refit screwdriver blade (BM) | 7.60 | - | - | 7.30 |
| | Number of occurrences | 1 | - | - | 1 |
| | *Contingencies* | | | | |
| E | (BM) | 1.3 | - | 0.9 | - |
| | Number of occurrences | 2 | - | 1 | - |

(c) The operator is rated at 120%.

(d) Allowances have been set at (for an 8-hour shift):

| | |
|---|---|
| personal time | 30 minutes |
| unavoidable delay | 36 minutes |
| fatigue | 5% |

(e) The operator, who is paid on a straight time rate, receives 50p per hour.

(f) Material costs are 3p per piece.

(g) Overhead costs are calculated at 80% of the sum of direct labour and material costs.

How many pieces per shift should each operator produce and what is the production cost per piece? Discuss the appropriateness of these estimates for planning purposes.

**Table for Question 8.5**

| Cycle number | Element number 1 | 2 | 3 | 4 | 5 |
|---|---|---|---|---|---|
| 1 | 0.15 | 0.62 | 0.33 | 0.51 | 0.23 |
| 2 | 0.14 | 0.58 | 0.20 | 0.50 | 0.26 |
| 3 | 0.13 | 0.59 | 0.36 | 0.55 | 0.24 |
| 4 | 0.18 | 0.61 | 0.37 | 0.49 | 0.25 |
| 5 | 0.22 | 0.60 | 0.34 | 0.45 | 0.27 |

8.6 'The principal benefit in using predetermined motion time systems to develop work standards is the avoidance of performance rating, and hence the avoidance of undue dispute over the resultant standards.' Discuss.

8.7 Discuss the function of performance rating in the determination of work standards. Compare stopwatch study and work sampling in the determination of work standards. You have obtained the following work sample from a study during a 40-hour work week:

| | |
|---|---|
| Idle time | 20% |
| Performance rating | 135% |
| Total parts produced | 280 |

The allowance for this particular type of work is 10%. Determine the standard time per part.

8.8 Activity sampling has been used as a convenient means of studying the activities of a worker and a printing machine. The following figures have been calculated from the results of such a survey, in which the sampling interval was a constant 5 minutes and in which the total non-stop duration of the survey was 3 hours.

| | |
|---|---|
| Percentage of total time operator idle | 30% |
| Percentage of total time operator adjusting machine | 40% |
| Percentage of total time operator cleaning workplace | 10% |
| Percentage of total time stacking printed sheets | 20% |

What is the percentage accuracy of each of these figures at a 95% confidence interval?

8.9 'Inherent worker variability invalidates conventional time study.' Discuss.

8.10 The table overleaf gives details of the data obtained during a rated activity sampling or rated systematic sampling exercise. The observations were made at 0.4-minute regular intervals, and the figures in the columns are the performance ratings (on the BS scale) for each of the elements during particular observations. (Notice that each element does not necessarily occur during each work cycle.)

If a total allowance of 15% of the basic time is to be provided, what is the standard time in SM for the assembly of one product?

Number of assemblies produced during this 8-minute exercise = 12.

8.11 The technique of rated activity sampling is used to study the activities of three workers employed on an assembly line. The first two workers on the line have two elements to perform on each item, whereas the third worker has one element of work for each item.

At the beginning of the study the line is empty. Sufficient parts to enable the assembly of ten items are then provided, and observations are taken at 0.1-minute intervals as follows:

| Time | Observed worker | Time | Observed worker |
|---|---|---|---|
| 0.1 | A | 0.2 | B |
| 0.2 | B | 0.3 | C |
| 0.3 | C | etc. | etc. |
| 0.1 | A | | |

These observations result in the ratings shown in the table on p. 209.

What are the basic times for each of the five work elements and for each of the three workers?

**Table for Question 8.10**

| Observation number | Assembly element numbers 1 | 2 | 3 | 4 | Idle |
|---|---|---|---|---|---|
| 1 | 100 | | | | |
| 2 | | 100 | | | |
| 3 | 105 | | | | |
| 4 | | 95 | | | |
| 5 | | | | | 100 |
| 6 | | | | 100 | |
| 7 | | | 95 | | |
| 8 | 90 | | | | |
| 9 | | 105 | | | |
| 10 | 95 | | | | |
| 11 | | | 90 | | |
| 12 | | | | | 105 |
| 13 | 100 | | | | |
| 14 | | | | | 100 |
| 15 | | 110 | | | |
| 16 | | | 105 | | |
| 17 | 110 | | | | |
| 18 | | | | 105 | |
| 19 | 95 | | | | |
| 20 | | 90 | | | |

8.12 What are the basic objectives of work measurement? Describe briefly the main techniques and give in detail the situations suitable for one particular technique. Measured work standards are frequently used as a basis for operations scheduling and control. Comment briefly on the required accuracy of the work standards.

8.13 You are to determine the standard time for a manual job which has not previously been studied, and for which there is no detailed work method record. A computer-based work study system has been made available to you for the first time. You have a 'Microfin'-type device and a micro-computer in your office equipped with a VDU, line printer and hard disc storage. You are led to believe that all the necessary computer programs are available. How would you expect to collect information on the job to be studied, and use the computer? What output would you want to obtain from the computer?

8.14 (a) An 80% learning effect is known to exist in a situation in which the first performance of a manual task takes 100 hours. What is the average performance time for the task after 32 task repetitions?

(b) How many hours are required for the eighth performance of the task?

**Table for Question 8.11**

| Observation number | | | Worker A | | | Worker B | | | Worker C | |
|---|---|---|---|---|---|---|---|---|---|---|
| A | B | C | El 1 | El 2 | Idle | El 3 | El 4 | Idle | El 5 | Idle |
| 1 | 2 | 3 | 80 | | | | | 100 | | 100 |
| 4 | 5 | 6 | | 110 | | 90 | | | | 100 |
| 7 | 8 | 9 | | 100 | | | | 100 | 75 | |
| 10 | 11 | 12 | | 90 | | | 80 | | 85 | |
| 13 | 14 | 15 | | | 100 | | | 100 | 90 | |
| 16 | 17 | 18 | 110 | | | | | 100 | | 100 |
| 19 | 20 | 21 | | 100 | | 100 | | | | 100 |
| 22 | 23 | 24 | | | 100 | 100 | | | 100 | |
| 25 | 26 | 27 | | 75 | | | 85 | | 110 | |
| 28 | 29 | 30 | 120 | | | 110 | | | 100 | |
| 31 | 32 | 33 | | | 100 | 85 | | | 120 | |
| 34 | 35 | 36 | | | 100 | | | 100 | | 100 |

(c) How many repetitions of the task are required before a target performance level of 41 hours is achieved?

8.15 What factors might be expected to influence the learning, i.e. the rate of performance improvement, of a worker operating a new piece of office machinery? How might the standard performance for such a task be determined for operations scheduling purposes, and what factors would influence the procedure employed?

## CASE STUDY (from Part 9)

The topics covered in this chapter are relevant to the following (see Introduction to Part 9 and Table C.1 for further details):

| No. | Name | Country |
|---|---|---|
| 8 | Airport building project | India |

Chapter 9

# Workplaces, technology and jobs

## ISSUES

How do we design an efficient 'worker–machine' system?
What are the requirements of a well-designed workplace?
How do we design a VDU workplace?
How does technology impact on work?
How should tasks be divided between people and machines?
What are the latest views on job design?
What is a satisfying job?
What is semi-autonomous group working?

In this chapter we concentrate on work and working conditions. The topics covered complement those in Chapters 7 and 8. They relate largely to the 'behavioural' dimensions in the design of work and work systems. Three main topics are covered:

(a) Working conditions – the design of the workplace.
(b) Technology and work – the impact of technology on the nature and organization of work.
(c) The worker – the design of jobs and workgroups.

## WORKING CONDITIONS

### Ergonomics

In this section we focus on people at work, and particularly with the design of workplaces and equipment. Interest in these subjects developed during the two world wars, when the focus was on working conditions, fatigue, accuracy, vigilance, etc. Many studies focused on factory workers, aircrews, military personnel, etc. Working hours, workplace layouts, the design of equipment, etc. were all studied in detail.

It was during this period that the term 'ergonomics' was coined in Britain, while in America the phrases 'human engineering' and 'human factors engineering' were in use to describe basically the same activities.

## The worker–machine system

Despite increasing automation, people are still essential in most operating systems. Certainly the worker's role is changing, the worker being relieved of many routine and/or hazardous tasks. This trend will continue, but there will always be a need for some people. The emphasis will, increasingly, be on the design and management of worker–machine systems. Here we look briefly at the nature of worker–machine systems as a preliminary to further considerations of ergonomics. (NB. Throughout, our use of 'machine' implies equipment of all types.)

Consider the situation in which worker and machine are interdependent, in which neither can work effectively or continually without the other. When a worker uses a machine, a loop or closed system results. The worker will receive certain information from the machine, either from displays, etc. designed for that purpose, or by observation of the machine itself. He or she will process this information and make decisions on what action, if any, to take and may then manipulate controls or attend to the machine in some other way so as to affect its behaviour in the desired manner. This worker–machine system is depicted diagrammatically in Figure 9.1.

The efficiency with which the worker functions depends on environmental factors, on his or her own characteristics, such as motivation, training and experience, and on the efficiency with which the machine provides the information feedback and accepts control measures.

If we accept, for our present purposes, that workers and their characteristics are largely fixed, this leaves us with only three aspects of the worker–machine system to discuss:

(a) design of information displays;

(b) design of controls;

(c) environmental factors.

### *Design of information displays*

The most common means of displaying or communicating information is visual. We can identify two categories of visual display: analogue and digital. Analogue methods, such as the circular graduated scale, are in common use, but this is mainly due to expediency rather than functional merit. The use of digital displays is a more recent phenomenon.

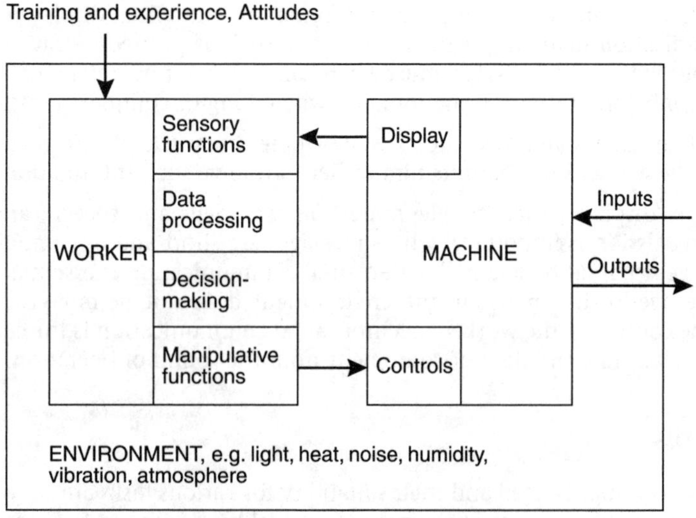


**Figure 9.1** Simplified worker–machine system

We can further classify visual displays as follows:

(a) Displays used without controls:

1. for quantitative measurement, e.g. clocks or meters, the purpose of which is to determine whether the correct value exists, or whether corrective action is necessary;
2. for check reading, i.e. to determine the proximity of a characteristic to a desired value, and not for obtaining a precise measurement;
3. for comparison, e.g. to compare the readings on two dials;
4. for warning; although warning systems often include audible devices, lights are also frequently used.

(b) Displays used with controls:

1. for controlling, i.e. to extract information and measure the effect of corrective action;
2. for setting, i.e. to use a control and display to ensure that a correct value is obtained, e.g. setting the running speed of an engine after starting up;
3. for tracking, i.e. to use a control continuously to correct movement or to compensate for external factors, e.g. keeping two indicators synchronized, or on target, by means of a control.

There are many sources of 'standards' and design data for visual displays. They are not identical in their recommendations, but the following cover most of the important points:

(a) Instruments should enable the worker to read information as accurately as necessary, but not more so.

(b) The scale used should be both simple and logical, using the minimum number of suitable divisions.

(c) The scale should provide information in an immediately usable form, and no mental conversions should be necessary.

(d) Scales that must be read quantitatively should be designed so that workers need not interpolate between marks.

(e) Vertical figures should be used on stationary dials and radial figures used on rotating dials.

(f) Scales should not be obscured by the pointer.

Also in the visual category are written or printed information and visual display units (VDUs). Visual methods of communication involving permanent copies, such as printed output from computers, are particularly valuable where the message must be retained for future reference, where there is no urgency in the transmission of the information, and where long or complex messages are involved.

Instruments such as gauges and dials are of value where many sets of information are to be transmitted, and where the worker's job permits him or her to receive such information when it arrives.

Aural information 'displays', such as telephones, buzzers, bells and speech, are more appropriate where speed of transmission is important, where messages are short and uncomplicated, and where a record of the message need not be retained. Often aural communication is essential in industry, where visual channels are overloaded or where the environment does not permit visual communication. However, within the context of the worker–machine, aural communication is infrequent, except where workers are able to determine the state of equipment from the sound of operation.

### Design of controls

The types of controls commonly used and their suitability for various tasks are shown in Table 9.1. The first and most important step is to select the type of control best suited to the requirements. This will involve answering the following questions:

**Table 9.1 Suitability of various controls for different purposes**

| Type of control | Speed | Accuracy | Force | Range |
|---|---|---|---|---|
| Cranks | | | | |
| small | Good | Poor | Unsuitable | Good |
| large | Poor | Unsuitable | Good | Good |
| Handwheels | Poor | Good | Fair/Poor | Fair |
| Knobs | Unsuitable | Fair | Unsuitable | Fair |
| Levers | | | | |
| horizontal | Good | Poor | Poor | Poor |
| vertical (to–from body) | Good | Fair | *Short* Poor; *Long* Good | Poor |
| vertical (across body) | Fair | Fair | Fair | Unsuitable |
| Pedals | Good | Poor | Good | Unsuitable |
| Pushbuttons | Good | Unsuitable | Unsuitable | Unsuitable |
| Rotary selector switch | Good | Good | Unsuitable | Unsuitable |
| Joystick selector switch | Good | Good | Poor | Unsuitable |

*Source: Adapted from 'Ergonomics for Industry No. 7, Ministry of Technology, 1965, by permission of the Controller, HMSO*

(a) What is the control for?

(b) What is required, e.g. in terms of precision, force, speed, number of settings?

(c) What information must be displayed by the control, i.e. must the control be identified from the others, must it be picked out in the dark, and should the worker be able to tell how the control is set?

(d) How do environmental conditions affect or limit the use of the control?

After selection of the most appropriate types of controls to use, they should be logically arranged, clearly marked and easily accessible. They should suit the capabilities of the operator and should be positioned to distribute the loads evenly among them. Functionally similar controls may be combined, as for example in the combined sidelights, headlights and flasher switch on cars; also, as far as possible, controls should 'match' the changes they produce in the machine or the system (e.g. clockwise rotation to 'increase' something, etc.). There should be consistency in the direction of movement of controls and they should be close, and identifiable with, their associated displays.

## *Environmental factors*

The provision of good workplace lighting, heating, ventilation, etc. is often a statutory requirement, and is necessary, though insufficient, to motivate workers and provide job satisfaction.

### *Lighting*

Good lighting is not achieved merely by adding extra lights, since the type of lighting should depend on the type of work being performed, the size of objects, the accuracy, speed and duration of the work, etc. An adequate lighting system should provide:

(a) sufficient brightness;

(b) uniform illumination;

(c) a contrast between brightness of job and of background;

(d) no direct or reflected glare.

Although a considerable amount of research has been conducted to establish optimum levels of illumination for various jobs, there is little agreement on the subject, and American recommendations in particular differ from British in suggesting higher levels of illumination.

Lighting should be arranged to avoid 'flicker' and to provide an acceptable amount of shadow. Notice that freedom from shadow is not always desirable, since in certain circumstances, e.g. inspection, shadows can be used to improve the visibility of details by accentuating surface details.

### Noise

We can make the obvious distinction between continuous and intermittent noise, both of which are to some extent inevitable; both can have detrimental effects on behaviour and may even cause physical damage to the worker.

Noise levels and the effect on workers can be reduced by controlling noise at its source, by putting barriers between the worker and the source of noise, by providing protective devices for the workers, or by modifying work processes to reduce workers' exposure to noise. Prolonged exposure to continuous noise levels in excess of 90 dB (decibels) is likely to result in hearing loss; 40 dB is an acceptable maximum level for comfort.

Sudden noises greatly in excess of the background noise level can produce a reaction, shock or startling effect which could have disastrous consequences for workers employed on or close to machinery. Regular intermittent noise is a common feature in industry where, for example, automatic machines such as presses are involved, but there is a danger of underestimating its effect by assuming an eventual adjustment by the worker to the situation.

### Temperature and ventilation

Figure 9.2 shows that the type of work and its duration determines the individual's tolerance to heat, and Table 9.2 indicates the relationship between space requirements and ventilation.

**Figure 9.2** Tolerance to heat. From Woodson, W. S. and Conover, D. W. (1964) *Human Engineering Guide for Equipment Designers*. Berkeley: University of California Press. Reproduced with permission

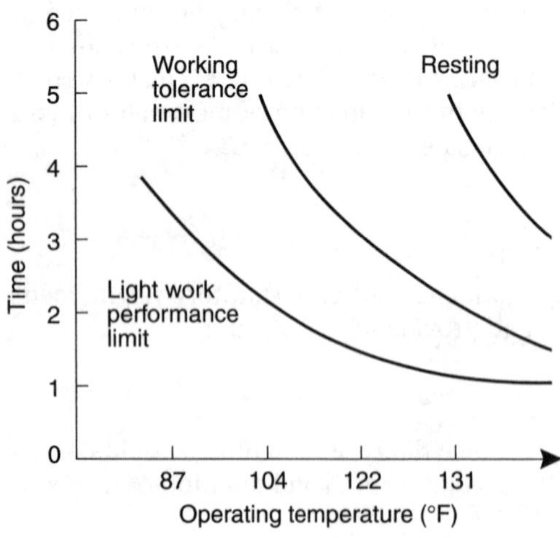


## Workplace design

The design of workplaces and equipment was mentioned in Chapter 7. All the comments made there are relevant here.

In many jobs the worker has to remain sitting or standing for long periods of time while performing a given series of tasks. Inadequate design of workplaces will inhibit the ability of the worker to perform his or her tasks and may result in injuries, strain or fatigue, or a reduction in quality or output.

Determination of workplace requirements will involve an examination of the work elements which constitute the work cycle and an examination of the body measurements, reach and movement capacities of the worker.

**Table 9.2 Relationship between space requirements and ventilation**

| Net volume of space (cubic feet)<br><br>Fresh air supply (cubic feet per minute) | Volume of space required per person (cubic feet) |
|---|---|
| 1000 | 500 |
| 600 | 450 |
| 400 | 400 |
| 200 | 300 |
| 100 | 200 |
| 60 | 150 |
| 35 | 100 |
| 22 | 65 |

*Source: Fogel, L. J. (1963)* Biotechnology: Concepts and Applications. *Englewood Cliffs, NJ: Prentice-Hall. Reproduced with permission*

## Anthropometric data

Figure 9.3 and Table 9.3 give anthropometric data, in terms of mean dimensions in centimetres, for western adult males and females. The dimensions for males given in Table 9.3 correspond to a 'nude' height of 175 cm, and those for females to a height of 162 cm. Corrections for different heights can be made by increasing or decreasing the given dimensions in proportion to the different heights.

Figures 9.4 and 9.5 give the normal working areas. The data given in these figures are offered *for guidance purposes only*. They have been extracted from several specialist books (see Further Reading) each of which provides more detailed information should this be required.

## VDU (visual display unit) and keyboard work

A substantial proportion of workers in offices and factories work with VDUs and keyboards. Such situations are commonplace in all types of office work, in retailing, banking and insurance, and in many aspects of factory work. Such is the importance of this technology that the design of VDU-dominated working environments merits special reference in this chapter.

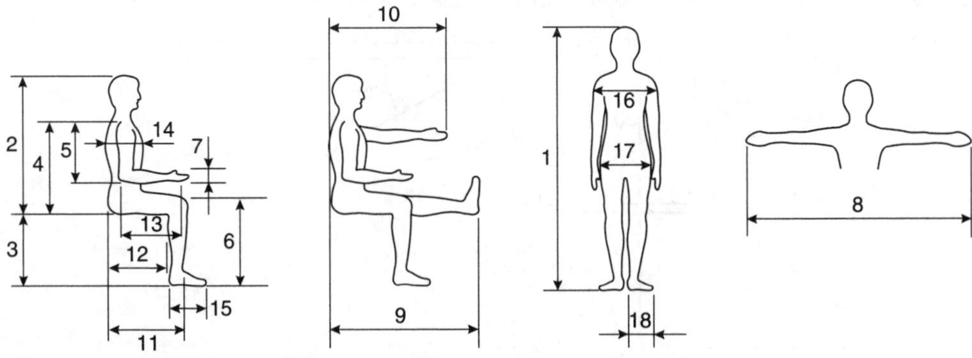


**Figure 9.3** Anthropometric data (for dimensions see Table 9.3)

**Table 9.3 Anthropometric data (mean dimensions, adult males and adult females) used in Figure 9.3**

| Measurement | Adult male (mean dimension, cm) | Adult female (mean dimension, cm) |
|---|---|---|
| 1 | 175 | 162 |
| 2 | 90 | 85 |
| 3 | 48.5 | 45.5 |
| 4 | 58 | 55.5 |
| 5 | 36 | 34 |
| 6 | 55 | 51 |
| 7 | 9 | 8.5 |
| 8 | 178 | 162 |
| 9 | 107 | 101.5 |
| 10 | 87 | 79 |
| 11 | 59.5 | 56 |
| 12 | 47.5 | 46.5 |
| 13 | 47 | 43 |
| 14 | 22.8 | – |
| 15 | 27.5 | 24.5 |
| 16 | 44.5 | 39.5 |
| 17 | 33 | 34.5 |
| 18 | 9 | 8.8 |

**Figure 9.4** Space for normal seated work (cm) male/female

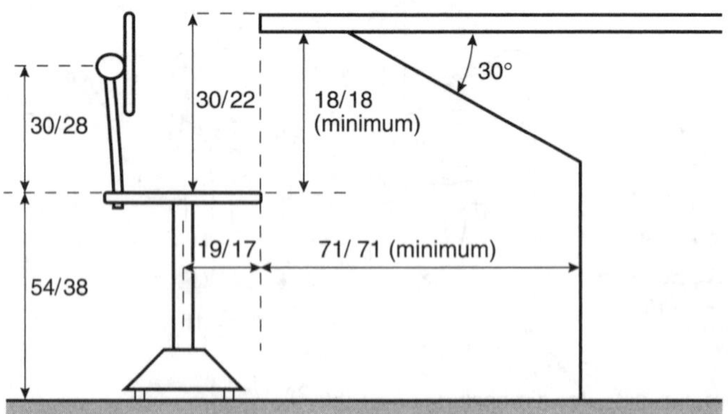

**Figure 9.5** Normal horizontal work area (cm) male/female

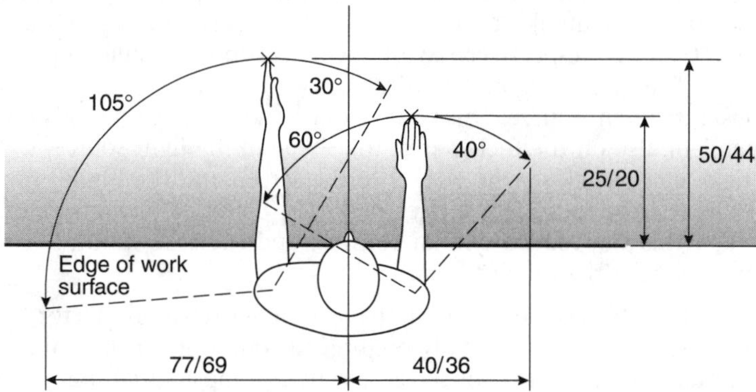


There is evidence of VDU work giving rise to physical discomforts, especially relating to visual fatigue, headaches, back and shoulder ache, etc. Clearly, adequate ergonomic design of a VDU-dominated workplace is essential. Much of the previous discussion is also relevant in this context, but here there are additional factors which in some countries have given rise to regulations or guidelines governing VDU work, e.g. covering the provision of anti-glare arrangements, requirements for movable, adjustable display screens, the provision of an appropriate level of workplace illumination, recommendations in respect of operators who wear spectacles, and the provision of rest periods, etc.

**EXAMPLE**

### European Community directive

The directive passed by the Council of the European Commission in May 1990 deals with the minimum safety and health requirements for work involving visual display units (VDUs). European Community member states were required to introduce the changes necessary to comply with the directive by 31 December 1992, and to report to the commission every five years on the implementation of the provision, giving the points of view of both employers and workers. The directive applies to employees who habitually use VDUs for a significant part of their normal work. Employers must analyse work stations to evaluate the safety and health conditions to which workers are exposed. In particular, risks to eyesight, physical problems and mental stress must be considered. Minimum requirements were established with regard to: (1) the equipment; (2) the environment; and (3) the operator–computer interface.

The sections below outline some of the major considerations in the design of VDU-dominated work environments.[1]

## Visual conditions

A major problem in designing VDU workplaces is the distribution of luminescences (light emissions) at the workplace. A compromise must be found between the low luminescence required of the display screen and the high luminescence required for reading the keyboard and printed documents.

Symbols on the VDU are produced by an electron beam which excites an emission of light in the phosphor coating of the screen. There is a choice of different phosphors, and this influences not only luminous intensity but also colour, flicker and the life of the screen. The legibility of symbols on the

[1] See also other sources of design information, e.g. Lyon, B. R. (1992) Video display terminal ergonomics, *Professional Safety*, **37**(6), pp. 32–39.

screen depends on the contrast, and it has been suggested that a contrast of 10 : 1 is near optimum, while the maximum and minimum values are 15 : 1 and 2.5 : 1 respectively. Depending on the level of illumination in the room, the symbol luminescence of 90 cd/m$^2$ is near optimum, with maximum and minimum values of 160 and 20 respectively. Symbol colour is not considered to be of critical importance; however, 'flicker' is a major factor. A 'critical flicker frequency' is that at which the individual can just detect a flicker in a light source. This varies from person to person but is normally in the range 20–60 Hz. It is dependent also on the flicker area, the shape of the light source, its illumination, location in the visual field, etc. The closer the worker to the screen and the higher the luminescence, the higher the critical flicker frequency. The surface of VDUs, being convex and glossy, can reflect surrounding features, and this can reduce symbol contrast and increase strain. Such reflections can be muted by surface treatment or the use of filters.

The cabinet surrounding the VDU tube should have a higher reflection factor than the screen itself to provide a smooth transition to the normally brighter surroundings. The luminescence of keyboards should not differ substantially from that of screens, which in most situations will necessitate the use of a dark-coloured keyboard. Concave keys can result in reflections.

Normally the level of illumination required for reading a manuscript will be higher than that required for other aspects of VDU work. However, substantial contrast with the level of illumination at the workplace is undesirable, so in most cases 'manuscript illumination' will be lower than provided for normal office work; hence legibility must be good. Printed character size, character colour and paper colour will affect legibility.

Ambient lighting conditions in working environments where VDUs exist will often be influenced by the needs of other workers on different types of work. In such cases VDUs must be positioned and oriented to prevent glare and to minimize the contrast between screen, keyboard and manuscript illumination, and levels of background illumination. It has been suggested that the area surrounding the VDU workplace should have a horizontal illumination of 300 lx and a background luminescence of 20–40 cd/m$^2$.

## Heat and noise

The power delivered to the VDU and associated equipment is partly converted to heat and can result in a higher temperature than is desirable unless adequate local ventilation is provided. The largest contributor to local heat production will be the control unit for the VDU; the heat output of such units, typically in the range 75–100 W, must be considered in determining the thermal balance for working environments. Convection effects which might produce draughts and humidity requirements must also be considered.

Several sources of noise are associated with the operation of a VDU: mechanical ventilation of a VDU can add considerably to the local noise level, and keyboard noise and the noise caused by printers can be substantial. A recommended noise level below 55 dB(A) has been recommended, while VDU tasks requiring high levels of mental concentration might be adversely affected by background noise levels greater than 45 dB(A).

## Ergonomic considerations

The checklists below deal specifically with a VDU working environment comprising VDU screen, keyboard, manuscript or printed material (being read) and operator.

### Terminal desk

(a) Adjustable desk height is desirable. A height indicator to facilitate adjustment by different workers is beneficial.

(b) The desk top should be large enough to allow for all items used by the operator and for readjustment/repositioning of those items. The VDU, keyboard and documents should all be included in a range of 50–70 cm from the eyes.

(c) The desk top should consist of one piece with no gaps, joints, etc.

(d) The desk top should have a non-reflecting surface and a pleasant (not a cold) feel.

### *Keyboard*

(a) The thickness/height of the keyboard should not exceed 20 mm including the second row of keys and it should be as narrow as possible.

(b) Keyboards with a height greater than 30 mm should be sunk into the desk (although this reduces the possibility of relocation, etc.).

(c) It should be easy to push or turn the keyboard.

(d) The keyboard should stand firmly.

(e) The keyboard should not be attached to the screen unit.

(f) The slope of the keyboard should be between 5° and 15°.

(g) The keyboard should not have more keys than are needed for the work in question.

(h) It will often be better to change from one keyboard to another to accommodate different types of work rather than have a comprehensive, over-large keyboard to accommodate all requirements.

### *Keys*

(a) The force required to press a key should be 0.25–1.5 N.

(b) The distance of travel in key depression should be 3–4.8 mm.

(c) The length of a square key should be 12–15 mm.

(d) The distance from centre to centre of adjacent keys should be 18–20 mm.

(e) The function keys should be larger than, and perhaps a different colour from, other keys.

(f) The symbols should be engraved in the key surface or printed below a non-reflecting transparent cap.

(g) The keys should be concave but only enough to match the convexity of fingers and not so much as to cause undue reflection.

(h) Guide keys should be marked with a small raised dot for easier location in touch typing.

### *Screen unit*

(a) It should be possible to adjust the height of the screen unit and to tilt (–3° to +20°) or turn it without tools.

(b) It should be possible to push the screen unit backwards and forwards on the desk. Distance markers will facilitate readjustment.

(c) The screen unit should stand firmly and not be too heavy to move.

### *Documents*

(a) A manuscript stand should be stable and adjustable in height and sideways. It should also tilt (+15° to +20° when at side of VDU, and +60° to +75° between VDU and keyboard).

(b) The best position for the documents is at the same distance from the eyes as the screen, and as close to the screen as possible. Abrupt changes in luminescence and reflection must be avoided.

### Work schedules

Views on the definition of fair rest periods for VDU workers are numerous and varied. Recently, collective agreements in industry have envisaged short breaks after rather long periods, e.g. 15 minutes minimum after two hours' work at a VDU. Clearly the 'relaxation' allowance provided (see Chapter 8) in VDU work will be significant in most situations. This is an area in which legislation and collective agreements will undoubtedly have considerable impact.

## Health and safety

Our discussion of working conditions and job design leads us to consider issues relating to health and safety at work – important aspects for operations managers who in many cases are legally responsible for the health and safety of their subordinates. Employees are of course required to carry responsibility for the safety of themselves and their colleagues through both the observance of safety practices and the adoption of those working methods in which they have been instructed. The employer or manager is required to provide an overall working environment, including adequate training, so that it is safe and healthy for employees to undertake their jobs. In effect, therefore, the safety of workers becomes the individual responsibility of managers responsible for departments as well as the responsibility of the employing organization.

In considering health and safety we are concerned in effect with the prevention of accidents or ill health. Such subjects should of course be considered in a preventive rather than a remedial sense, since it is in the interests of all parties to prevent the occurrence of illness or accidents, but in order to indicate the magnitude of the problem it will be appropriate to remind ourselves of the effects of accidents and the extent to which accidents have occurred in industry and commerce in the past.

### Industrial accidents

In most industrialized countries statistics reveal that accidents are one of the most significant causes of lost working days – and this despite the fact that in many countries an accident is defined as something which 'causes disablement for more than three days', plus the possibility that many, even severe, accidents are not reported.

In general, at least in factories, the major source of accidents is concerned with the handling of goods, e.g. lifting, placing, movement, etc. at the workplace and between workplaces. Falls, and accidents caused by machinery, are the next most important source of accidents. Most severe accidents occur as a result of individuals becoming 'involved' with machinery, while accidents occurring during the handling of goods comprise a major proportion of those accidents causing lesser or shorter periods of disablement. Fires and explosions are also a major source of accidents.

The economic implications to the employer resulting from an accident include:

(a) working time lost by the employee;

(b) time lost by other employees who choose to or must of necessity stop work at the time of or following the accident;

(c) time lost by supervision, management and technical staff following the accident;

(d) proportion of the cost of employing first aid, medical staff, etc.;

(e) cost of disruption to the operation;

(f) cost of any damage to the equipment or any cost associated with the subsequent modification of the equipment;

(g) cost of any compensation payments or fines resulting from legal action;

(h) costs associated with increased insurance premiums;

(i) reduced output from the injured employee on return to work;

(j) cost of reduced morale, increased absenteeism, increased labour turnover among employees.

This is just one side of the equation, since the injured person, his or her dependants, colleagues, etc. also incur some cost. Certainly it would be socially, morally and probably legally unacceptable to consider accidents only in terms of direct and indirect cost to the employers.

### Preventive action

The prevention of illness and accidents requires efforts on the part of employees and management, the latter including those responsible for the design of the operating system and its staffing. Some of the steps which might be taken to reduce the frequency and severity of accidents are as follows:

(a) developing a safety awareness among all staff;

(b) developing effective consultation between management, workers and unions so that safety and health rules and procedures can be agreed and followed;

(c) giving adequate instruction in safety for new and transferred workers, or where working methods are changed;

(d) minimizing materials handling, and designing as far as possible for safe working and operation;

(e) ensuring a satisfactory standard for all equipment;

(f) good maintenance of all equipment;

Fire prevention and control represent a further area for preventive action. The main causes of fire tend to be associated with electrical appliances and installations. Smoking is a major source of fires in business premises. The Fire Protection Association (of the UK) suggests the following guidelines for fire prevention and control:

(a) Management should accept that fire prevention policies and practices must be established and reviewed regularly.

(b) Management should be aware of the possible effects and consequences of fires in terms of loss of buildings, plant and output, damage to records, effects on customers and workers, etc.

(c) Fire risks should be identified, particularly as regards sources of ignition, presence of combustible materials, and the means by which fires can spread.

(d) The responsibility for fire prevention should be established.

(e) A fire officer should be appointed.

(f) A fire prevention drill should be established and practised.

As for other sources of illness and accidents, there are detailed guidelines for fire prevention and checklists for use in assessing the adequacy of existing procedures and in designing new procedures.

## TECHNOLOGY AND WORK

We have noted that, because of technological developments, workers' roles are changing. It is appropriate now, in all types of operating systems, to look more closely at the nature and effects of such change. We will do so by focusing on automation.

### The nature of mechanization and automation

One attempt to overcome some of the problems of defining 'automation' suggests that, in general, 'automation' means something significantly more automated than that which existed previously.

Hence 'automation' in one type of business or industry may contrast both in level of development and in characteristics with automation elsewhere. Other authors have taken the view that the elimination of direct manual involvement *in control* is the key feature of automation. In other words, mere elimination of work tasks (i.e. 'doing' tasks) is not automation, but simply mechanization. It is reasonable, therefore, to view automation as a trend rather than a state. Mechanization is an aspect of, or component part of, automation; it is concerned with activities, while automation also implies the use of control procedures which are also largely independent of human involvement. The two terms will be used in this manner throughout the remainder of this chapter.

We can identify four basic components of operations in order to aid examination of the nature and effects of automation:

(a) power technology – sources of energy used;

(b) processing technology – equipment used in operations performed on materials or customers (in service systems);

(c) handling technology – transfer of materials, items or individuals (in service systems) between processes

(d) control – regulation of quality and quantity of output and throughput.

It has been suggested that the process of automation usually occurs in the order: processes, handling and control. Thus a hierarchy of levels of automation such as that shown in Table 9.4 might be envisaged. In each case level 1 is fully manual work, while levels 2, 3 and 4 are the intermediate steps to the achievement of level 5, where fully automatic work is obtained.

## The impact of automation

The relationships between technology and work are complex. Technological change, such as increasing automation, has both direct and indirect impacts on work. We will look firstly at the broad context,[2] and then at specific 'cause and effect' type relationships.

**Table 9.4 Dimensions of automation**

**Automation of process**

Level 1. Use of hand and handtool
2. Use of powered handtool
3. Use of machine – hand controlled
4. Use of machine – automatic cycle – hand activated
5. Use of machine – automatic

**Automation of handling**

Level 1. Use of hand and handtool
2. Use of powered handtool
3. Use of machine – hand controlled
4. Use of machine – automatic cycle – hand activated
5. Use of machine – automatic

**Automation of control** (i.e. (a) activation, (b) monitoring, (c) regulation and (d) rectification and maintenance of processes and handling)

Level 1. Manual (a), (b), (c) and (d)
2. Product activated or timed with manual (b), (c) and (d)
3. Automatic (a), (b); manual (c), (d)
4. Automatic (a), (b), (c): manual (d)
5. Fully automatic

[2] Wild, R. (1991) Technology, work and workplaces. *Management Decision*, **29**(8), pp. 32–37.

The technological capability available to an organization will influence the strategy of that organization, i.e. what it seeks to do, and how it aims to do it. This must influence the nature of the operations which are established, and thus the whole context, organization, arrangement and nature of the work associated with that operation. Technology is therefore an enabling factor, making possible certain competitive strategies for organizations (see Chapter 2). It also makes possible certain types of work systems and different forms of work, and working contexts. This is the biggest impact that technological change has on work. It is an indirect impact – and it opens up possibilities for the nature of jobs that might not have existed before.

But technology, and technological change such as automation, also has a direct impact on work at the more micro level. It can directly and immediately change the nature of the tasks which are undertaken, work cycles, skill requirements, the interaction of workers with one another and with others, etc.

**EXAMPLE**

## Teleworking

Telework (telecommuting, teletravel, etc.) is a dramatic technology/work development. Individuals or groups work at a distance from what might otherwise be their workplace, using computing/information/communications technology in their work and also to reduce/eliminate the effect of 'distance'. Here, clearly, we have new work practices coupled with the use of new (office) technologies.

Without the technology such work would not exist, but there is no general direct cause–effect relationship. The main reasons for the introduction of telework have been identified as follows:

1. politico-economic – for decentralization, and for revitalization of geographical areas;
2. work rationalization and organization – improve performance, cut operating costs, improve flexibility, etc.;
3. social – improving 'quality of working life'.

Thus, in effect, a new 'work ecology' is being created (i.e. the location, form and organization of work) for largely strategic reasons, and made possible by the capability of new technologies.

Source: Wild, R. (1991) Technology, work and workplaces. *Management Decision*, **29**(8), pp. 32–37.

**EXAMPLE**

## Banking

New technology in banking is readily evident to the customer (automatic dispensers of cash, statements, etc.; automatic in-payments, telephone/computer banking, etc.). There are associated new technology developments 'within' the banks and the banking system. Technology-related changes in the nature of the work of employees are also evident – and have been studied. Some of the principal findings of such studies for clerical-type jobs in banking and insurance are as follows:

| Work level | Changes | |
|---|---|---|
| *Micro*<br>i.e. tasks and jobs performed | Increased load and complexity<br>More stress<br>Problems with workplace ergonomics | Less control over work and work pace<br>Changed skill requirements<br>Less scope for decision-making |

| | |
|---|---|
| *Macro*<br>i.e. work systems and relationships between jobs | Integration of previously separate tasks/jobs<br>Increased 'technical' communication between workers<br>Reduced face-to-face/social contact between workers |
| *Ecology*<br>i.e. contact, form and organization of work | Less contact with customers<br>Changing working patterns (shifts, hours)<br>Changing employment patterns (fewer female full-time jobs – more part-time work – more female part-timers. |

Source: Wild, R. (1991) Technology, work and workplaces. *Management Decision*, **29**(8), pp. 32–37.

This is, perhaps, the level of the relationship of technology and work which is of greatest, and most immediate, interest to us here, so it will be appropriate to summarize some of the findings of studies of the impact of automation on work.

With increasing automation, jobs tend to become more demanding, varied, interesting and challenging for many workers, although in some cases such changes may be of a temporary nature – a result of a 'start-up' situation. Technical know-how tends to become more important and workers may expect increased job content together with increased demands on skills, knowledge and training. In general, greater job complexity and responsibility, and therefore greater intrinsic rewards, are associated with work in automated systems, but often at the expense of increased worker inactivity.

A further consideration is that of social interaction. Often the greater distance between workers in automated systems results in reduced social interaction. However, as full automation is approached, the central grouping of controls gives rise to grouping of workers. Up to a certain level, therefore, automation increases the ratio of working space to people and therefore inhibits social relationships. The relationship of workers and their supervisors is also affected by automation, the general view being one of increased contact and improved worker–supervisor relations. An increased separation of workers from both operations and their outputs is often found. Increased training needs are often associated with the wider responsibilities of automated jobs, while emphasis on vigilance and monitoring duties, the importance of minimizing process disruption, the consequences of breakdowns, and the comparative inactivity of workers are considered to lead occasionally to increased stress.

The above comments relate mainly to situations approaching full automation. The effects of lower levels of automation have received less attention; however, we can conclude tentatively that such developments tend to give rise to:

(a) the increasing isolation of workers and hence a reduction in social interaction;

(b) a reduction in the amount of physical effort required, largely due to reduced handling requirements;

(c) a loss of worker control of work pace and worker independence from the machine cycle;

(d) improved working conditions and increased safety;

(e) increased use of shift working.

In conclusion, therefore, although the manner and characteristics of the development of automation can be affected by various factors, in general, at higher levels of automation, work becomes more varied and demands greater use of skills and knowledge, offset to some degree by physical inactivity coupled with the need for vigilance, which could give rise to a stressful situation. Equally, it is clear that what has generally been referred to as mechanization, because of continued dependence on manual intervention in control, offers few of these job characteristics.

## Worker–machine systems

Full automation obviates the need for direct human intervention, except perhaps in a supervisory capacity, but semi-automation, or advanced mechanization, requires some human contribution in, for example, control. Semi-automation is commonplace. In these situations there is some sharing of work between people and machines. Such worker–machine situations are found in most types of organization. The design and operation of such systems raises some difficult and distinctive problems. Two particularly important aspects are dealt with in this section. Since they are general problems not confined to particular situations, types of work or technology, we shall examine them in a general manner, and then, as an illustration, we shall consider the design of worker/robot work systems.

## The allocation of functions

A work system, whether manual, automated or a combination of both, will be established to fulfil certain job requirements. Certain tasks or activities must be performed. One requirement in the design of the system, therefore, is the allocation of these tasks to the active parts of the system, i.e. their division between worker and machine. This allocation of functions must reflect the abilities of worker and machine, i.e. their skills, capabilities and limitations, and, where a choice exists, the relative cost of performing a task by worker and machine.

A general procedure for the allocation of functions is outlined below:

Step 1: ***Job or task analysis*** – identify jobs/tasks which must be undertaken by the work system.

Step 2: ***Skills analysis*** – identify the skills/abilities of the component parts of the work system, i.e. the worker(s) and the machines.

Step 3: ***Allocation of tasks*** – allocate tasks from 1 to the component parts of the system as far as possible to match 2.

A general skills statement for worker and machines is given in Table 9.5.

**Table 9.5 Skills and abilities of man and machines**

| Functional area | Man | Machine |
|---|---|---|
| Data sensing | Can monitor low-probability events not feasible for automatic systems because of number of events possible. | Limited program complexity and alternatives; unexpected events cannot be handled adequately. |
| | Absolute thresholds of sensitivity are very low under favourable conditions. | Generally not as low as human thresholds. |
| | Can detect masked signals effectively in overlapping noise spectra. | Poor signal detection when noise spectra overlap. |
| | Able to acquire and report information incidental to primary activity. | Discovery and selection of incidental intelligence not feasible in present designs. |
| | Not subject to jamming by ordinary methods | Subject to disruption by interference and noise. |
| Data processing | Able to recognize and use information, redundancy (pattern) of real world to simplify complex situations. | Little or no perceptual constancy or ability to recognize similarity of pattern in spatial or temporal domain. |
| | Can make inductive decisions in new situations; can generalize from few data. | Virtually no capacity for creative or inductive functions. |

**Table 9.5 (continued)**

| Functional area | Man | Machine |
|---|---|---|
| Data processing (continued) | Reasonable reliability in which the same purpose can be accomplished by different approach (corollary of reprogramming ability). | High reliability may increase cost and complexity; particularly reliable for routine repetitive functioning. |
| | Computation weak and relatively inaccurate; optimal game theory strategy cannot be routinely expected. | Can be programmed to use optimum strategy for high-probability situations. |
| | Channel capacity limited to relatively small information throughput rates. | Channel capacity can be enlarged as necessary for task. |
| | Can handle variety of transient and some permanent overloads without disruption. | Transient and permanent overloads may lead to disruption of system. |
| | Short-term memory relatively poor. | Short-term memory and access times excellent. |
| Data | Can tolerate only relatively low imposed forces and generate relatively low forces for short periods. | Can withstand very large forces and generate them for prolonged periods. |
| | Generally poor at tracking though satisfactory where frequent reprogramming required; can change to meet situation. Is best at position tracking where changes are under 3 radians per second. | Good tracking characteristics over limited requirements. |
| | Performance may deteriorate with time, because of boredom, fatigue or distraction; usually recovers with rest. | Behaviour decrement relatively small with time; wear maintenance and product quality control necessary. |
| | Relatively high response latency. | Arbitrarily low response latencies possible. |
| Economic properties | Relatively inexpensive for available complexity and in good supply; must be trained. | Complexity and supply limited by cost and time; performance built in. |
| | Light in weight, small in size for function achieved; power requirement less than 100 watts. | Equivalent complexity and function would require radically heavier elements, enormous power and cooling resources. |
| | Maintenance may require life support system. | Maintenance problem increases disproportionately with complexity. |
| | Non-expendable; interested in personal survival; emotional. | Expendable; non-personal; will perform without distraction. |

*Source: Beishon, J. and Peters, G. (eds)* Systems Behaviour. *London: Harper & Row. Reproduced with permission*

## Working conditions

One reason for the automation of work is the desire to remove workers from unsatisfactory working environments. So, if the tasks which must be performed are dangerous or require excessive physical effort, or are in any other way associated with bad working conditions, such tasks are candidates for automation. However, in designing semi-automated work systems, technological consideration can sometimes dominate so that inadvertently the work and the working conditions given to workers can be compromised. It is necessary, therefore, to have some means to check the acceptability or appropriateness of working conditions. This will enable existing work systems to be checked in order to establish whether there is the need for change. Similarly, new work system design can be checked for acceptability/appropriateness before implementation.

Checklists can be drawn up to cover the topics discussed earlier in this chapter. In this way working conditions can be checked for acceptability against ergonomic and workplace design criteria. Failure to satisfy any requirement should lead to an existing work system being redesigned with perhaps some changes in the allocation of functions, or a proposed design being rejected. Whilst a detailed quantitative evaluation will not normally be feasible, the checklist approach should be a sufficient 'design tool' for most circumstances.

Examples for checklists intended for use in these cases are given in Tables 9.6 and 9.7.[3]

**Table 9.6 Working conditions checklist and relative weighting factors**

| Checklist criteria for working conditions | | Weighting factor for criteria |
|---|---|---|
| A | - Risk of accidents | 5 |
| B | - Monotony of work<br>- Noise | 4 |
| C | - Exposure to dirt and dust<br>- Exposure to high or low temperatures<br>- Muscular strain | 3 |
| D | - Exposure to oil or grease<br>- Exposure to wetness, acids and alkalis<br>- Exposure to gases and vapours<br>- Exposure to intense or inadequate light<br>- Risk of catching cold | 2 |
| E | - Vibrations<br>- Need to wear protective clothing | 1 |

[3] Based on material from *Robots in Manufacturing* (*c.* 1987) (Chapter 5), a document produced for a project sponsored by the Commission of the European Communities by the Institute for Manufacturing and Automation (IPA), Stuttgart, West Germany.

**Table 9.7 Example of evaluation of human working conditions of a proposed robot/manual work system**

| Criteria | Weight | Evaluation of human working conditions (proposed) | | | | Score | |
|---|---|---|---|---|---|---|---|
| | | Small 0 | Low 1 | Medium 2 | High 3 | Actual* | Maximum |
| A. Accidents | 5 | | | | √ | 15 | 15 |
| B. Monotony | 4 | | √ | | | 4 | 12 |
| Noise | 4 | | √ | | | 4 | 12 |
| C. Dirt/dust | 3 | | √ | | | 3 | 9 |
| Temperature | 3 | | √ | | | 3 | 9 |
| Muscular strain | 3 | | √ | | | 3 | 9 |
| D. Oil/grease | 2 | √ | | | | 0 | 6 |
| Wet/acid/alkali | 2 | √ | | | | 0 | 6 |
| Gas/vapour | 2 | | √ | | | 2 | 6 |
| Light | 2 | √ | | | | 0 | 6 |
| Cold | 2 | | √ | | | 2 | 6 |
| E. Vibrations | 1 | | | √ | | 2 | 3 |
| Protective clothing | 1 | | | | | 3 | 3 |
| Total | | | | | | 41 | 102 |

*Any criterion with maximum score is unacceptable – redesign/reallocation required.

Total score: < 34 System acceptable
34–67 Redesign/reallocations required
> 67 System unacceptable

**EXAMPLE**

## *Impact of automation on workers*

Employee survey data were used to examine the impact of a Canadian firm's automation programme on employee skill levels, workplace organization, and employee–management relationships. The majority of workers had been significantly affected by the introduction of automated materials handling systems and computerized process controls. Approximately half of them indicated that their jobs had either been eliminated or changed by the technological developments.

Source: Chaykowski, R. P. and Slotsve, G. A. (1992) The impact of plant modernization on organizational work practices. *Industrial Relations*, **31**(2), pp. 304–329.

# THE WORKER

## Job design and work organization

No longer is the design of work and jobs simply to do with the application of method study, work measurement and ergonomics. There is a need to consider the behavioural aspects of work and job design.

Views about how work and jobs should be designed have changed considerably during this century. Initially the design or specification of work made few assumptions about the capability of workers – beyond considering them as 'machines'. The 'scientific management' approach therefore was concerned with identifying the single best way of working. Concern with working environments, and with fatigue and performance, focused concern on workers' psychology, especially as a consequence of the results of experiments conducted at the Hawthorne works of the Western Electric Company in Chicago. Then interest in the social aspects of the workplace grew, to be replaced by a focus on worker motivation. Soon after, predominantly in Europe, the industrial democracy or workplace autonomy approach began to influence thinking about job design. At about the same time there was considerable interest in the redesign of jobs, to introduce greater sources of job satisfaction. All of this provides the foundation for present thinking, which as yet cannot be characterized by a single term or title.

This historical development of views about work and job design is summarized in Figure 9.6. (For further details see Further Reading.)

**Figure 9.6**

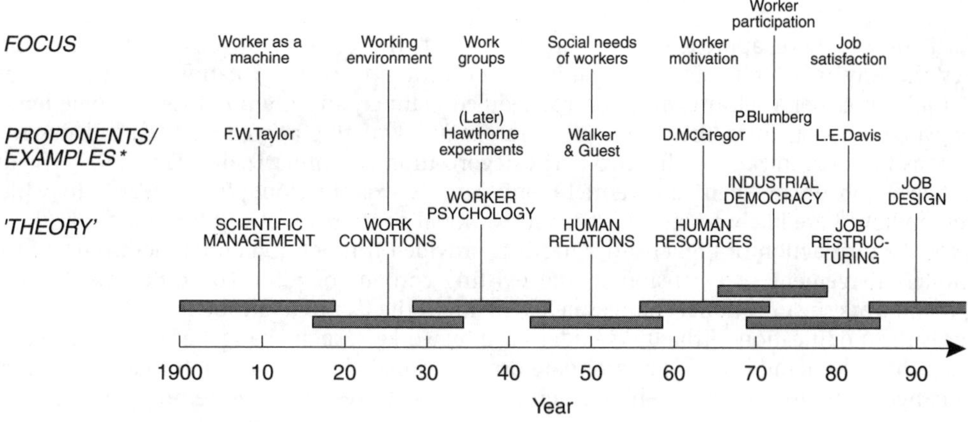


* See Further Reading at end of chapter.

We will pick up on this development from the job restructuring 'movement', which aimed to rectify some of the inadequacies of work and job design – which were seen as the consequences of the scientific management/work study approaches – by redesigning into jobs more rewarding and satisfying ingredients.

## Job restructuring

The job restructuring 'experiments' which were undertaken in the 1970s involved one or both of two basic approaches, i.e. the *enlargement* of work content through the addition of one or more related tasks, and job *enrichment,* involving the increase in the motivational content of jobs through, for example, the addition of different types of tasks or the provision of increased worker involvement

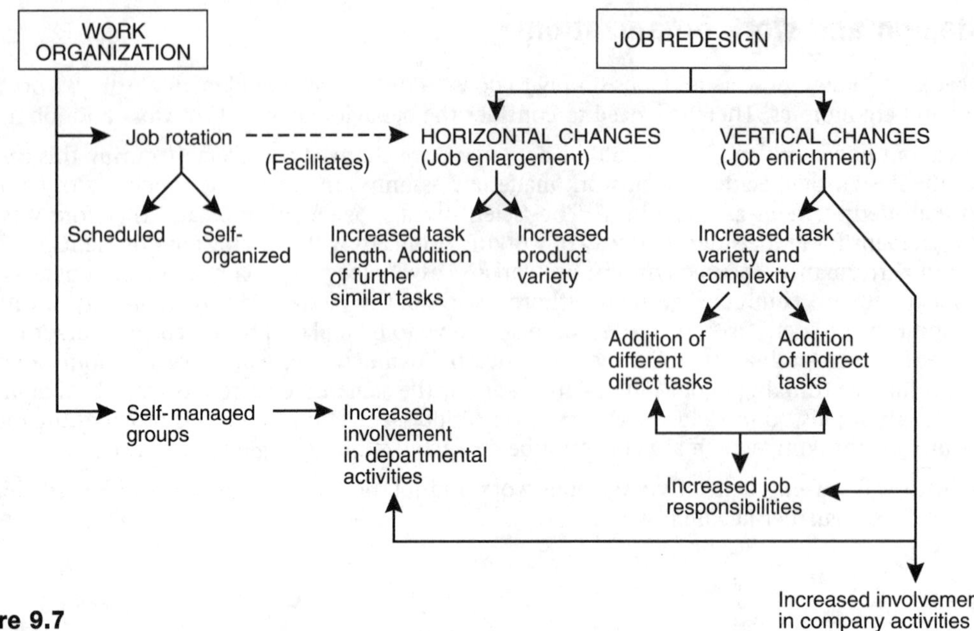


**Figure 9.7**

and participation. Both approaches are concerned with the content of jobs. A different approach involves the way in which jobs are organized. The provision of job rotation, i.e. workers moving between jobs in either a self-organized or a scheduled manner, and the provision of some opportunities for workers to organize their own jobs are examples of this approach. We shall describe this approach as work organization. This two-part categorization is summarized in Figure 9.7. The distinction between job enlargement and enrichment permits examination of the degree to which the changes employed are likely to increase the motivational content of jobs. It is argued that the opportunity for the satisfaction of higher-order needs is provided through job enrichment but not through the simple enlargement or extension of the existing content of jobs. The difference between job redesign and work organizational changes helps highlight the fact that, although the objective of many changes is the modification of the tasks undertaken by workers, such changes are often dependent on, or perhaps brought about only by, appropriate organizational change. Thus job rotation, an organizational change, may provide for job enlargement, and some degree of worker self-organization may give rise to, or be a necessary prerequisite for, certain types of job enrichment.

## An approach to job design

We can now build on this framework to specify a general approach to the design of jobs[4] to satisfy behavioural considerations – the focus of this chapter – whilst also being compatible with efficiency considerations – the focus of the previous two chapters.

---

[4] The approach outlined here focuses on job enrichment and worker autonomy. It is sometimes referred to as the 'motivational' approach. For a survey of approaches to job design see: Campion, M. A. and Thayer, P. W. (1989) How do you design a job? *Personnel Journal*, **68**(1), pp. 43–46.

For an alternative but similar approach to that presented here see: Kelly, J. (1992) Does job re-design theory explain job re-design outcomes? *Human Relations*, **45**(8), pp. 753–774.

Table 9.8 identifies most of the desirable job characteristics which have been advocated by authors, i.e. those characteristics which are considered to give rise to job satisfaction and worker motivation. These are further considered below.

**Table 9.8 Desirable characteristics of jobs (for job satisfaction and motivation)**

1. Work content
   - A 'Closure', i.e. complete module of work
   - B Obvious relationship between tasks
   - C New and more difficult tasks added
   - D Increased variety of tasks
   - E Make use of workers' valued skills and abilities
   - F Include some auxiliary and preparatory tasks
   - G Individual inspects own work
   - H Worker repairs defective items
   - I Operator sets up machines
   - J Operator responsible for cleanliness of work area
   - K Operator responsible for maintenance
   - L Perceived contribution to product's utility
   - M Work content such that job is meaningful and worthwhile
2. Work method
   - A No machine pacing
3. Work organization
   - A Give worker some choice of method
   - B Worker discretion
   - C Operator plans own work
   - D Operator organizes own work
   - E Self-regulation
   - F Worker responsible for controlling own work
   - G Operator sets own performance goals
   - H Subgoals to measure accomplishment
   - I Individual accountable for own work
   - J Job responsibilities (generally)
   - K Worker autonomy
   - L Operator involved in solving problems
   - M Workers participate in design and improvement of own job
   - N Workers involved in decision-making concerning work
   - O Workers receive performance feedback at regular intervals
4. Job opportunity
   - A More than minimum required training provided
   - B Worker able to learn new things about process
   - C Promotion prospects for worker
   - D Specific or specialized tasks enable worker to develop expertise
   - E Increased challenge for worker
5. Social conditions/relations
   - A Conversation either easy or impossible
   - B Facilitates workers' movement about factory

### Work content and method

Examination of the nature of the 14 job characteristics listed in Table 9.8 reveals a three-level structure, i.e.

(a) ***Tasks:***
new and more difficult tasks to be added;
inclusion of some auxiliary and preparatory tasks.
The characteristics listed also provide some examples of the above, i.e.
inspect own work;
repair defects;
set up machines;
responsibility for cleanliness of work area;
responsibility for maintenance.

(b) ***Task relationships:***
'closure' – perform complete module of work;
obvious relationship between tasks.

(c) ***Work attributes:***
perceivable contribution to product utility;
increased task variety;
use of workers' valued skills and abilities;
meaningful and worthwhile job.

These three levels might be seen to have cause and effect relationships, i.e. it might be advocated that tasks (a) should be structured so that the tasks done bear a holistic relationship (b) in order to provide certain work attributes (c).

### Work organization

Examination of the work-organization characteristics listed in Table 9.8 reveals a possible two-level structure: work organization and work attributes.

(a) Work organization:
worker has some choice of work method;
worker plans/organizes own work;
worker controls own work/self-regulation;
workers set performance goals;
regular performance feedback;
worker participates in job design/improvement;
worker involved in work problem-solving.

(b) Work attributes:
worker discretion/decision-making;
worker accountability/responsibility;
worker autonomy.

Group (a) above may be seen to give rise to the attributes of (b) and, further, some work method characteristics may be seen as prerequisites for certain organizational characteristics.

### Job opportunity

Of the five cited characteristics, four relate to personal development while one relates to job advancement. Worker involvement in the organization (involvement, identity, feelings of importance) and self-actualization (growth and advancement, self-development and pride) are given as consequences of opportunities for worker development, but no specific effects are associated with opportunities for promotion. It could be argued that personal development, e.g. increase in skills, abilities and accomplishment, will give rise to openings in employment and hence promotion opportunities, although it is not clear whether authors advocating development characteristics had this consequence in mind.

### Social conditions

Both characteristics in this section relate to ease of social interaction. We would suggest that a job should facilitate social interaction in the interests of job satisfaction, although it is recognized that complete lack of verbal contact may be preferable to contact with difficulty.

The above analysis suggests a breakdown of the listed job characteristics into two groups: first, work and job attributes, and second, those characteristics (tasks, task relationships, work methods and organization) which in some combination provide for the existence of such attributes. It appears that it is largely the provision and manipulation of these latter characteristics which give rise to the existence of work and jobs with the desired attributes. This 'model' is summarized in Figure 9.8, in which certain additions have been made. It does not necessarily provide a complete checklist. However, it is of value in that it helps to distinguish between those aspects of jobs which might be manipulated and those job attributes which might then be achieved.

**EXAMPLE**

### *Work reorganization in contract cleaning*

| | |
|---|---|
| Jobs: | Factory and office cleaners |
| Original arrangement: | Contract workers do all cleaning |
| Problem: | Poor standard of work of contract cleaners |
| New arrangement: | Groups of cleaners established (employed by company)<br>Groups given specific areas of responsibility<br>Groups responsible for organizing their own work in each area<br>Groups plan and control own work schedules<br>Groups given training in work simplification |
| Results: | Cleanliness improved<br>71 personnel used in place of 120<br>Turnover of staff substantially reduced<br>Saving $103 000 p.a. |

**EXAMPLE**

### *Job enlargement in assembly work*

The previous method of assembly of a type of office equipment involved the use of two parallel, non-mechanical-type flow lines staffed by both male and female workers. Each line was divided into five main sections and staffed by approximately 65 workers working at a cycle time of 3 minutes. The sections at the beginning of the line had the more complex tasks, those towards the end being concerned with simpler assembly tasks prior to quality checks and rectification work. Each section had a supervisor. The payment system employed consisted of a base rate plus an individual bonus which accounted for as much as 25% of the total earnings.

Following the redesign the cycle time of the new operations is now 20 minutes and the layout of the line has been rearranged to facilitate greater interpersonal contact. The groups are given responsibility for checking quality and fault rectification. The piecework scheme has been replaced by a monthly time rate. Social areas have been provided adjacent to each of the lines and workers arrange their own breaks among themselves, with the freedom to rearrange work methods if they so desire. Improvements include a 35% increase in output, a cheaper cost for the desired product quality, less floor space required, better worker–management relations and an increase in production flexibility.

**Figure 9.8** Model relating the characteristics and attitudes of work and jobs

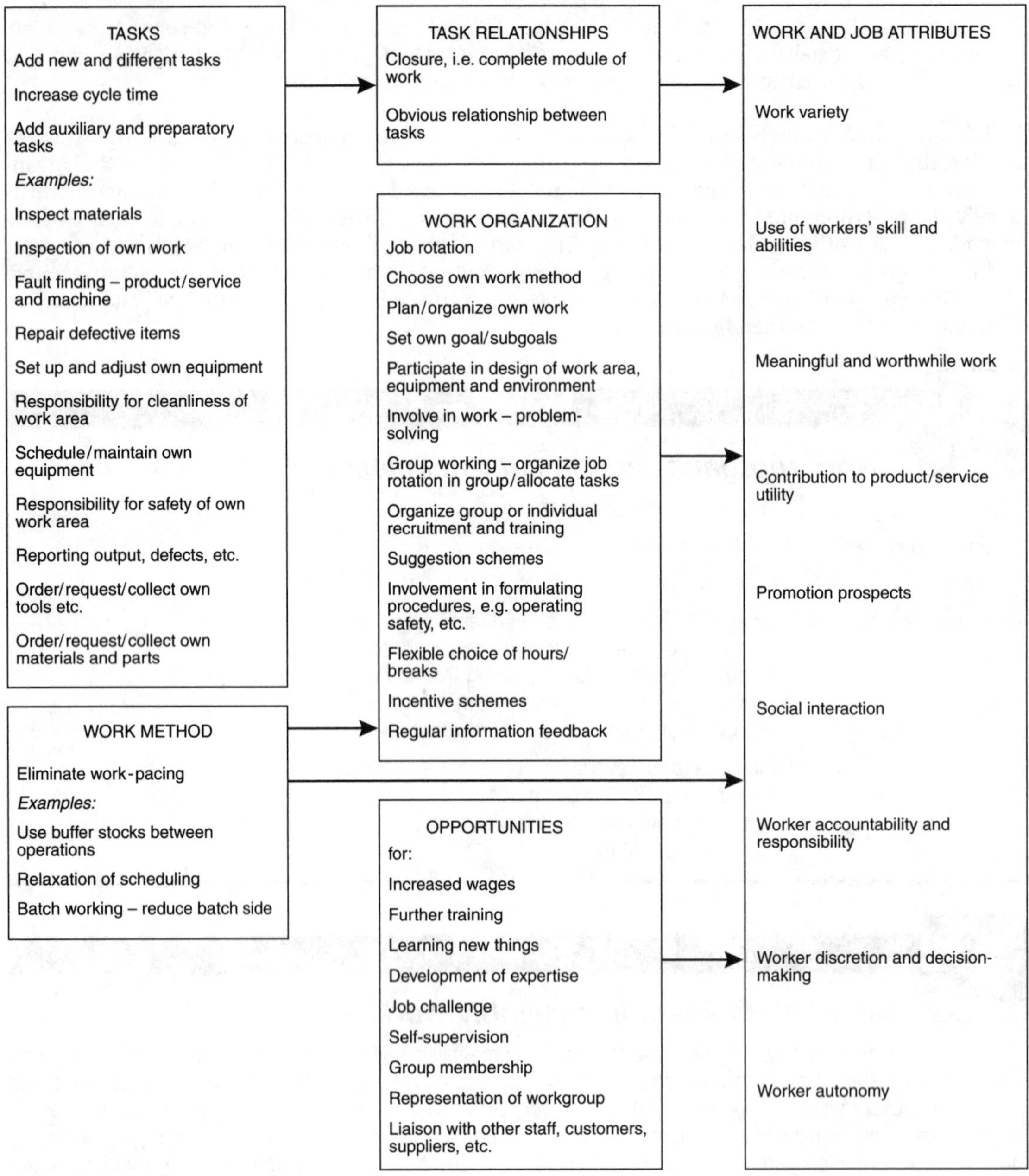


## Group working

The use of the approach to job design outlined above, with its emphasis on work organization and autonomy, will in many situations give rise to the creation of semi-autonomous working groups. Such groups are usually relatively small and composed of interdependent workers, together taking responsibility for most of the activities required for delivering a service or providing a product. The use of such groups is increasing, as organizations seek satisfactory solutions to job design problems, in increasingly technology-dominated workplaces, and in situations where organization-wide approaches are being used to ensure total quality operations (see Chapter 19).[5]

Thus, some of the benefits of this approach, first popularized in the 1970s, are:

(a) increased employee satisfaction;

(b) reduced absenteeism and turnover;

(c) increased flexibility;

(d) increased productivity;

(e) improved quality;

(f) decreased need for supervision.

The critical prerequisites for the successful implementation of this approach include:[6]

1. management support;
2. training and development;
3. evaluation of job candidates;
4. adequate/appropriate structuring of work.

**EXAMPLE**

### *Patient care jobs*

Redesigning work patterns and jobs is becoming an important activity in nursing administration. Striking a balance between adapting jobs to people and adapting people to jobs is considered to be the best approach. There is increasing interest in the use of the sociotechnical systems approach, which provides a framework, logic and method. It aims at work designs which neither compromise the integrity of people in order to achieve work efficiency, nor compromise productivity to satisfy people. Rather than seeking to reduce immediate tensions and errors, the approach encourages a broader perspective oriented toward the enterprise's long-term purpose. This helps designers see nursing as an integral part of the total patient care delivery system and to blend clinical and economic case management.

Source: Tonges, M. C. (1992) Work designs: sociotechnical systems for patient care delivery. *Nursing Management*, **23**(1), pp. 27–32.

## JOB DESIGN AND ORGANIZATION DESIGN

We should now reflect on certain points made in Chapter 3. There we noted a relationship between aspects of job design – i.e. the tasks to be performed, their relationships, and the workflows – and aspects of organization design. It should be clear to us now that the creation of certain types of job, e.g. the establishment of a semi-autonomous group working within an organization, will depend for their success and indeed viability on the existence of an appropriate organization structure, i.e. one which permits the delegation of authority and responsibility down the organization and therefore facilitates decentralized decision-making. Equally, the existence of this type of organization will tend to encourage such forms of job design and work organization and may tend to militate against the existence of a highly structured work situation.

[5] Schuring, R. (1992) Reasons for renewed popularity of autonomous work groups. *International Journal of Operations and Product Management*, **12**(4), pp. 61–62.

[6] Satem, M., Lazarus, H. and Cullen, J. (1992) Developing self managed teams: structure and performance. *Journal of Management Development*, **VII**(3), pp. 24–32.

## CHECKLIST FOR CHAPTER 9

### Working conditions

Ergonomics and workplace design
The worker–machine system
Design of information displays
- With controls
- Without controls

Design of controls
- Suitability of controls

Environmental factors
- Lighting
- Noise
- Temperature and ventilation

Workplace design
Anthropometric data
Working areas and space
VDU work
- Visual factors
- Temperature and noise
- Ergonomic factors
- Work patterns

Health and safety
- Industrial accidents
  - Economic implications
- Preventive action
  - Six steps
  - Fire prevention
    - Six steps

### Technology and work

Nature of automation
Mechanization
Impact of automation
Worker–machine systems
- Allocation of functions
- Working conditions

### The Worker

Job design and work organization
- Theories of job design
- Nature of job redesign and work organization
  - Job enlargement
  - Job enrichment
- An approach to job design
  - Desirable job characteristics

Learning
Group working
- Benefits
- Requirements

### Job design and organization design

The importance of the business context to operations management

## FURTHER READING

**Pugh, D. S. and Hickson, D. J. (1989)** *Writers on Organizations*, 4th edn. Penguin. Refers to many of the developments identified in Table 9.4.

**Safizadeh, M. H. (1991)** The case of workgroups in manufacturing operations. *California Management Review*, **33**(4), pp. 61–82.

**Salvendy, G. (ed.) (1987)** *Handbook of Human Factors*. New York: Wiley.

**Wild, R. (1990)** *Technology and Management*. London: Cassell.

For a discussion of job design issues in a traditionally repetitive work situation, motor-vehicle assembly, see the following (N.B. also relevant to Chapter 15).

**Kapstein, J. (1989)** Volvo's radical new plant: the death of the assembly line? *Business Week*, 28 August, pp. 92–93.

**Rehder, R. R. (1992)** Building cars as if people mattered: the Japanese lean system vs. Volvos's Uddervalla system. *Columbia Journal of World Business*, **27**(2), pp. 56–70.

## QUESTIONS

9.1 State, discuss and compare the principal requirements of displays used for the following purposes:

(a) indicating road speed of car to driver;

(b) indicating domestic oven temperature required and actual temperatures;

(c) indicating time of day in an airport departure lounge.

9.2 State, discuss and compare the principal requirements of controls used for the following purposes:

(a) setting temperature required for a domestic oven;

(b) emergency 'off' control for metal-cutting lathe;

(c) controls for a hi-fi stereo radio receiver.

9.3 Outline and justify the ambient conditions required for the following working environments:

(a) an engineering design office;

(b) an electronic instrument assembly workshop;

(c) a hospital operating room.

9.4 How might anthropometric data be used in the design of the following items:

(a) an adult's cycle;

(b) a VDU worker's chair;

(c) the driver's seat and controls of a car?

9.5 Discuss and compare the nature of the manual jobs likely to be associated with a moving-belt, fixed-item assembly line for small products (see Chapter 15) and a toolroom grinding machine.

9.6 How might the following jobs be enriched:

(a) word processor operator;

(b) bank teller;

(c) domestic appliance service repair worker?

Indicate any assumptions made about the jobs and their circumstances.

## CASE STUDIES (from Part 9)

The topics covered in this chapter are relevant in the following (see Introduction to Part 9 and Table C.1 for further details):

| No. | Name | Country |
|---|---|---|
| 5 | The Sahil Tea Garden | Turkey |
| 25 | European Foundation – Group Work | Netherlands, Portugal |
| 26 | Open Polytechnic of New Zealand | New Zealand |

Chapter 10

# Payment and incentives

## ISSUES

What are the ingredients of remuneration?
What should a good payment system achieve?
How are jobs evaluated?
What is payment by results?
What are the basic payment-by-results schemes and how do they work?
What are 'gainshare' payments systems?

## NOTATION USED IN THIS CHAPTER

$E$ Earnings for a given period
$H$ Hours worked
$N$ Number of pieces/units
$P$ Piece rate
$R$ Base pay rate
$S$ Standard hours allowed for job ( $= s \times N$)
$s$ Standard hours allowed for each piece/unit
$X$ Performance level at which incentive participation begins
$Y$ Extent of gearing of an incentive payment system
VA Value added
PBR Payment by results

This chapter completes our examination of factors which are relevant in the design of jobs and work systems. Here we look at remuneration, payment systems and incentives.

## PAYMENT AND PAYMENT SYSTEMS

In Chapter 8 we looked at work measurement – one application of which is in the design and operation of payment systems. Here we review the principles of payment and reward systems. We consider the context and objectives of payment systems, and look in more detail at job evaluation and at 'payments by results'.

## Nature of remuneration

All work undertaken in the context of employment will be associated with some form of remuneration, the major element of which will be financial. We shall focus on financial rewards, which might be classified as follows:

(a) wages, i.e. payment received by employees on a periodic basis, e.g. weekly or monthly;

(b) bonuses, e.g. lump sum awards, often provided on an annual basis;

(c) benefits, e.g. insurance benefits, pensions, allowances, non-monetary rewards such as the use of company cars, etc.;

(d) long-term rewards, i.e. lump sum rewards over a long period of time, typically five years and/or on termination of contract or on completion of contract employment period.

Our focus here will be on wages and wage-related factors, in particular the establishment of wage payment systems and structures, and forms of incentive wage payment.

Adequate wages and acceptable wage systems are matters of importance to most working people. We must, however, distinguish between those factors which encourage an individual to work and those factors influencing satisfaction at work. Financial reward is undoubtedly a major factor in the former, although beyond a certain level and in certain circumstances job satisfaction may be influenced largely by factors other than wage. Certainly in many countries in recent years there has been a growing interest in non-wage aspects of remuneration, and increasing importance is now attached to such factors. However, without adequate wages and without the use of an acceptable and equitable wage payment system such interest would decline. Adequate wage levels and an acceptable wage payment system may therefore be seen as a foundation or 'platform' upon which other aspects of remuneration might be built and without which other aspects might not exist.

Needless to say, payment of wages represents a major cost source in many organizations. Not only do companies compete with one another as regards wage levels, but also their competition in the market-place, in which price is a factor, is affected by wages as one factor affecting price and margins. The value added during operations is influenced by wage levels, and the ability to recruit and retain labour is also influenced by wage levels and the nature of payment systems. In these respects, therefore, the design and administration of wage payment systems are of relevance to the operations manager.

## Payment structure and systems

The objectives of any payment system are numerous and might include the following:[1]

(a) to enable the employee to earn a good and reasonable salary or wage;

(b) to pay equitable sums to different individuals, avoiding anomalies;

(c) to be understandable and acceptable to the employees and their seniors;

(d) to reward and encourage high-quality work;

(e) to encourage employees to accept transfers between jobs;

(f) to encourage employees to accept changes in methods of working;

(g) to discourage waste of materials or equipment;

(h) to encourage employees to use their initiative and discretion;

(i) to encourage employees to develop better methods of working;

(j) to reward and encourage high levels of output;

(k) to discourage and lead to a decrease in overtime working.

---

[1] See Bowey (1975) (Further Reading).

The design of a wage payment system to meet some or all of the above objectives will require some consideration of (a) pay structure and (b) pay systems.

The development of an adequate pay structure will require some consideration of the pay to be provided and the differentials between various jobs, i.e. the establishment of the 'relative worth' of different jobs in different circumstances. In most cases it will be necessary to establish some scale or grading of jobs based on some objective assessment and to relate jobs measured on this scale to pay rates or levels in the manner shown in Figure 10.1. The establishment of such a scale will often provide some form of career or job structure for employees.

**Figure 10.1** A pay/job structure

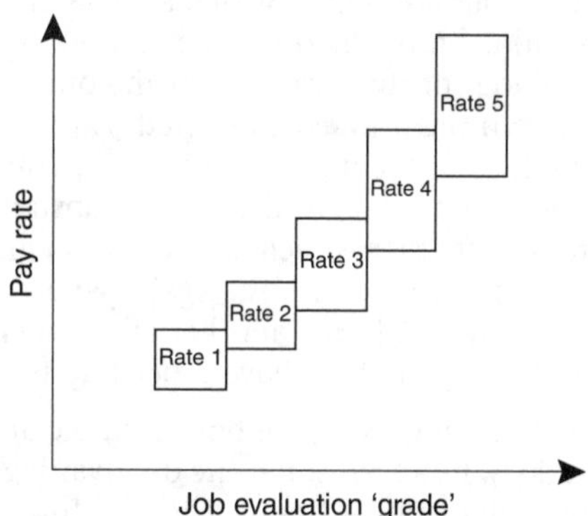


Various job evaluation schemes are available for the establishment of such structures; however, it should be remembered that in many cases the establishment of pay levels or pay bands for particular jobs will be a matter of negotiation between employees (often represented by trade unions) and employers. In some cases, of course, there will be national agreements between employers or employers' associations and trade unions. Such agreements may stipulate pay bands or minimum pay levels for particular jobs and conditions of service, etc.; in supplementing such national agreements there may be certain local negotiating and bargaining machinery to establish pay and wage structures at local or company level.

Other factors, e.g. government intervention, may constrain companies; however, in most situations it will be appropriate to aim to develop and employ some consistent method of job evaluation if differentials are to be recognized and wage drift is to be avoided.

The design of the wage payment system will require the consideration of questions such as: 'To what extent will the wage be paid through some form of incentive payment system? How might such an incentive payment system operate? How will standards of performance be established and what control system will be introduced to monitor payment levels, earnings, etc.?' In many cases some form of incentive payment system will be employed, although, as we have noted, in recent years there has been a move towards the introduction of non-financial incentives.

Job evaluation and incentive schemes are now examined in more detail.

## Job evaluation

This is a term used to cover a number of methods of systematically measuring the relative worth of jobs, using yardsticks which are derived from the content of the jobs. A job evaluation scheme will enable new jobs to be placed in a proper relationship with existing jobs by the use of easily explained and acceptable facts and principles. Thus the principal purpose of job evaluation is to rank jobs as a basis for a pay structure. It aims, therefore, to compare all jobs under review using common criteria, to define the relationship of one job to another. It is essentially concerned with establishing relationships and not with absolutes. In comparing jobs it is the job content which is considered, and job evaluation is used primarily for establishing basic pay levels or wage bands.

The four main methods of job evaluation are described below.

### Job ranking

This is perhaps the simplest method. Job descriptions are prepared for each job to identify the duties, responsibilities and qualifications necessary for the job. Such descriptions may be developed jointly by management and worker representatives, and should certainly be agreed by both parties. In some cases 'key' jobs are chosen which adequately cover the whole range of jobs and these are compared with one another in order to produce a ranking of jobs. Where few jobs exist it will be possible to develop a ranking for the entire list at the outset. Given this ranking of jobs on the basis of difficulty, importance to the firm, etc., job grades are established through an examination of the relative importance or merit of adjacent jobs on the scale. Thus grade boundaries may be established between jobs in the ranking which are agreed to have substantially different importance or difficulty ratings. Pay levels or ranges are then attached to each job grade. A somewhat more sophisticated approach involves the use of 'paired comparisons'. Again, where many jobs exist, key jobs will be chosen and each pair of jobs compared with one another by a panel of judges. This process will enable a ranking to be established and thereafter the above procedure is followed.

The job ranking method is simple and straightforward. It is relatively cheap to install and is flexible. It does, however, suffer the disadvantage of relying heavily on judgement and having a relatively minor objective or quantitative content. In the use of this job ranking system there is a tendency to rank jobs to reflect current pay systems. Furthermore, the resultant ranking of jobs reflects only their rank order importance and does not provide for the quantitative assessment of differences between jobs.

## Job classification

Using this procedure a number of job grades are first determined and then the existing jobs are allocated to these predetermined grades. Each grade will normally have recognizable characteristics, taking into account features such as the skill required in jobs, and their responsibilities. Each grade may be represented by a 'benchmark' job, which, taking into account the majority of factors, is most representative of the job grade. The job descriptions are then prepared for each of the existing jobs or each of the jobs to be allocated to the job structure. These jobs are then allocated to the existing grades through a process of comparison with the job grade descriptions or with the predetermined 'benchmark' jobs. Thus the procedure is much the same as in job ranking, except that jobs are allocated against an existing or required job structure. In both cases whole jobs may be treated and in both systems jobs may be evaluated on a variety of factors as agreed or as considered important within the particular circumstances. Skill and responsibilities are usually considered, and job difficulty and jobholder qualifications are also usually of some importance.

## Points evaluation

This is one of the most popular job evaluation schemes. Unlike the others, it relies on the identification and comparison of job factors rather than the whole job. Factors, e.g. skill, effort, responsibility and working conditions, are selected which are common to all or most of the jobs within the organization. These *compensatable* factors are defined. Each is then broken down into sub-factors which are again defined.

A typical set of factors is given in Table 10.1. Here each of the four general factors are subdivided in a manner suitable for two different types of job.

In evaluating jobs a weighting is attached to each of the general factors, i.e. those which apply throughout the organization. This represents the maximum points score achievable for that factor. This weight/score is then broken down amongst the sub-factors to indicate their relative importance. Then job descriptions are prepared for each job to be evaluated, and each job *(not* the worker carrying out that job) is scored against the relevant list of sub-factors.

This evaluation, or scoring, will normally be carried out by a committee which is responsible for examining all jobs in a department. A typical evaluation is given in Table 10.2.

The total points score represents the evaluation of 'merit' of that job. Jobs are finally ranked according to points score. Job grades are established and pay scales or ranges are agreed.

**Table 10.1 Factors for job evaluation (points evaluation)**

| General factor | Sub-factor: For clerical/office work | Sub-factor: For physical work |
|---|---|---|
| A. Skill | Education<br>Experience<br>Initiative | Training<br>Experience<br>Initiative |
| B. Effort | <br>Mental<br>Visual | Physical<br>Mental<br>Visual |
| C. Responsibility | Equipment<br><br><br>Subordinates<br>Environment<br>Financial<br>Customers | Equipment/process<br>Material/product safety of others<br>Work of others<br>Environment |
| D. Conditions | Surroundings<br>Work hours | Working conditions<br>Work hours<br>Noise<br>Hazards |

Unlike the above systems, the points evaluation system provides a semi-objective means of job evaluation. Because of the detail which might be introduced through the identification and definition of sub-factors, the scheme might be employed consistently and agreement may be achieved relatively easily. The use of this scheme provides not only a means of establishing job rankings and a job structure but also a way of quantitatively identifying differentials between jobs and grades.

## Factor comparison

This method is an extension of points evaluation and uses five factors:

(a) mental effort required in the job;

(b) skills required for the job;

(c) physical effort required for the job;

(d) responsibility of the job;

(e) job conditions.

A number of key jobs are selected and then a panel of 'experts' determines the proportion of the total wage paid for each constituent factor. Each factor is given a monetary value for the key jobs. This allows a scale to be established for each factor and other jobs can then be compared with them, factor by factor, to yield a ranking of all jobs. Since the initial exercise is carried out in terms of monetary values, interpolation will yield wage rates for all jobs. This method is more complex and difficult both to describe and implement because it uses, in one process, job evaluation and the allocation of monetary values.

Table 10.2 Points evaluation of job: telephone 'help-line' operator for a computer software company

| Factors | Points | | |
|---|---|---|---|
| | Weighting (i.e. maximum) for group | Normal maximum for factor | Actual for job |
| A. Skill | (60) | | |
| 1. Education | | 15 | 10 |
| 2. Experience | | 20 | 15 |
| 3. Initiative | | 25 | 20 |
| B. Effort | (40) | | |
| 1. Mental | | 20 | 15 |
| 2. Visual | | 20 | 5 |
| C. Responsibility | (70) | | |
| 1. Equipment | | 10 | 5 |
| 2. Subordinates | | 10 | 0 |
| 3. Environment | | 10 | 0 |
| 4. Financial | | 20 | 5 |
| 5. Customers | | 30 | 25 |
| D. Conditions | (30) | | |
| 1. Surroundings | | 15 | 5 |
| 2. Working hours | | 15 | 10 |
| | (200) | | 115 |

**EXAMPLE**

## *Equal pay*

A city school district set out to investigate teachers' pay with a view to ensuring or implementing pay equality for men and women. A job evaluation approach was used. The approach emphasized reaching a consensus between employees and the supervisors filling out the job evaluation questionnaire. Major features of the job evaluation questionnaire included areas of supervision, contacts with others, and budget responsibilities. The new questionnaire described jobs in terms of instruction or training, with the lowest degree being service or support operations. Two other categories were added, one dealing with the amount of exposure to the risk of physical harm and the other relating to the employee's flexibility. To the usual categories of direct or indirect supervision were added ultimate authority, functional supervision and consultative supervision. Salaries fixed as a result of this exercise were then examined and no gender or race inequalities were found.

Source: Gray, M. W. (1992) Pay equity through job evaluation: a case study. *Compensation and Benefits Review*, **24**(4), pp. 46–51.

# PAYMENT BY RESULTS (PBR)

We shall not comment directly on the merits of PBR schemes, but it is appropriate to describe some of the more popular schemes so that their basic principles are understood. We shall deal with two types of scheme: individual and group incentives.

## Individual incentives

### 100% participation or one-for-one schemes

This is one of the simplest and most widely used incentive payment systems. Under this system, increases in performance above a certain level lead to directly proportional increases in wages. In its simplest form, incentive payment is provided for throughput or output above 100 performance, there being a guaranteed payment of the base rate for performances at 100 or less (see Figure 10.2). In other words, earnings are calculated on a time basis as follows:

$E = RH + R(S - H)$

where $E$ = earnings for a given period

$R$ = base pay rate

$H$ = hours worked

$S$ = standard hours allowed for job

= standard hours for each unit[2] ($s$) × number of units ($N$) output or throughput

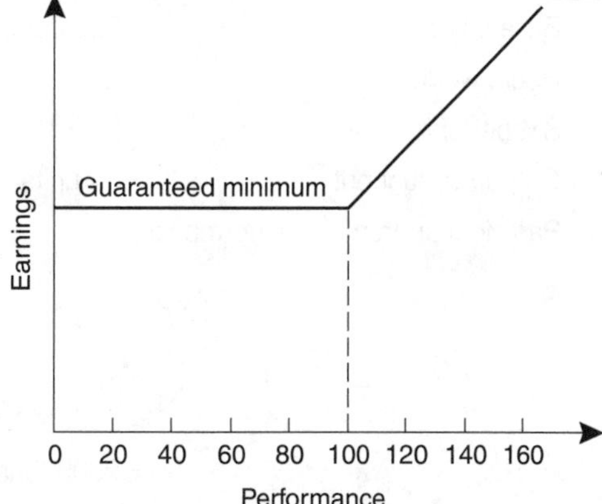


**Figure 10.2** 100% participation incentive payment scheme beginning at 100 performance

**EXAMPLE**

| | |
|---|---|
| Base pay rate | = 250 pence per hour |
| Hours worked | = 8 |
| Standard minutes (SM) per unit | = 20 |
| Output/throughput | = 30 units |

$$E = 250(8) + 250\left[\left(\frac{20}{60} \times 30\right) - 8\right]$$

[2] Each unit processed or produced, e.g. item produced, customer dealt with.

$$= 2000 + 250(10 - 8)$$

$$= \underset{\text{(base pay)}}{2000} + \underset{\text{(incentive pay)}}{500}$$

$$= 2500 \text{ p (total pay)}$$

Often 100% participation or 'one-for-one' schemes begin at a level less than 100 performance, i.e. incentive payment is offered to workers who exceed a performance of perhaps 75 or 80. As with the previous scheme, it is usual to guarantee minimum base rate earnings. In this case earnings are calculated as follows:

$$E = RH + R\left(\frac{100S}{X} - H\right)$$

where $X$ = the performance at which participation begins, e.g. 75 or 80.

**EXAMPLE**

| | |
|---|---|
| Base pay rate | = 250 pence per hour |
| Hours worked | = 8 |
| SM per unit | = 20 |
| Output/throughput | = 30 units |
| Participation from 80 performance | |

$$E = 250(8) + 250\left(\frac{100 \times 20 \times 30}{60 \times 80} - 8\right)$$

$$= 2000 + 250(12.5 - 8)$$

$$= 2000 \text{ (base pay)} + 1125 \text{ (incentive pay)}$$

$$= 3125 \text{ p (total pay)}$$

## Less than 100% participation or geared schemes

A large number of schemes have been developed which differ from those described previously in that they do not offer 100% increases in payment for 100% increases in performance. Such schemes differ mainly in the extent to which workers participate as a result of increased performance. Figure 10.3 illustrates a 50/50 scheme in which earnings increase by 0.5% for every 1% increase in performance beyond 100. The main benefit of such incentive payment schemes is that they provide some measure of safeguard for management in circumstances where allowed times may have been inaccurately estimated. An additional safeguard can, of course, be provided by applying an upper limit to incentive earnings.

**Figure 10.3** 50/50 geared incentive schemes

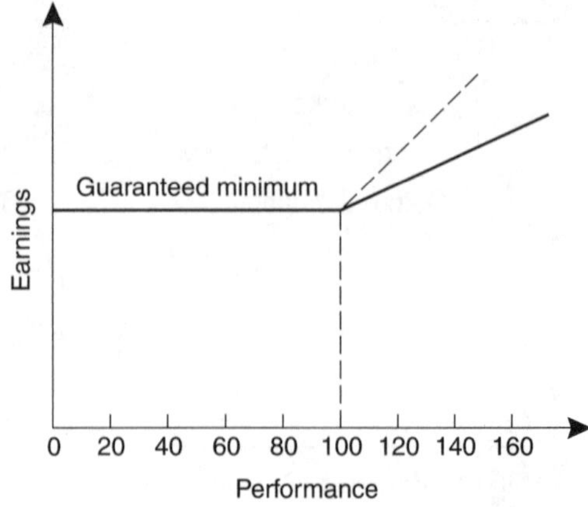

The formula for calculating earnings for geared schemes without an upper earnings limit, and starting at a performance level of 100, is as follows:

$$E = RH + YR(S - H)$$

where $Y$ = the extent of the gearing, e.g. 0.5 for a 50/50 plan.

e.g. **EXAMPLE**

| | |
|---|---|
| Base pay rate | = 250 pence/hour |
| Hours worked | = 8 |
| SM per unit | = 20 |
| Output/throughput | = 30 units |
| Gearing | = 50/50 |

$$E = 250(8) + 0.5(250)\left(\frac{20 \times 30}{60} - 8\right)$$

$$= 2000 + 125(10 - 8)$$

$$= 2000 \text{ (base pay)} + 250 \text{ (incentive pay)}$$

$$= 2250 \text{ p (total pay)}$$

As before, participation may begin at a level below 100, in which case earnings are calculated by the following formula:

$$E = RH + YR\left(\frac{100S}{X} - H\right)$$

## Piecework

This is one of the oldest methods of incentive payment, under which workers are paid a fixed amount for each unit processed. In fact the piecework system is very similar to the 100% participation or one-for-one system previously described, the principal difference being that in piecework the standard is described in terms of money and not time. As with the previous systems, it is usual to operate the incentive payment system in conjunction with a guaranteed minimum payment level.

The piece-rate ($P$) is defined as follows:

$$P = Rs$$

Consequently, earnings ($E$) over a period of time are calculated by means of the following simple equations:

$E = RsN$ (where performance is above 100)

$E = RH$ (where performance is below 100)

**EXAMPLE**

Base pay rate = 250 pence per hour

Hours worked = 8

SM per unit = 20

Output/throughput = 30

Piece-rate = $Rs$

$$= 250 \times \frac{20}{60}$$

$$\text{Performance} = \frac{\text{Standard hours produced}}{\text{Hours worked}} \times 100$$

$$= \frac{\frac{20}{60} \times 30}{8} \times 100 = 125$$

$\therefore$ Earnings ($E$) = $RsN$

$$= 250 \times \frac{20}{60} \times 30 = 2500 \text{ p}$$

It should be noted that certain practical complexities must be accommodated during the operation of any incentive payment method. For example, a certain amount of waiting time will be incurred throughout most working periods and, in addition, unmeasured work may be undertaken. It is usual to pay both of these at base rate or at day-work rate and, consequently, care must be taken to include them in the wage calculations.

**EXAMPLE**

Base pay rate = 250 pence per hour

Total hours worked = 9½

Hours worked on unmeasured work = ½

Waiting hours = 1

SM per unit for measured work = 20

Output/throughput of measured work = 30 pieces

Using a 100% participation system above a 100 performance,

$$E = 250(9\tfrac{1}{2}) + 250\left[\left(\frac{20}{60} \times 30\right) - (9\tfrac{1}{2} - 1\tfrac{1}{2})\right]$$

$$= 2375 + 500 \text{ (incentive pay)} = 2875 \text{ p (total pay)}$$

## Measured day work

The use of the measured day-work system avoids some of the problems normally encountered in the design and administration of the type of incentive wage systems described above. It avoids the need for continual measurement of performance and adjustment of wage levels based on such performance, yet it provides a form of incentive wage system. Measured day work offers a fixed rate of pay for a defined standard of performance. Work measurement is used to establish standard times for various jobs and to negotiate the pay rate for such jobs at different levels of performance. Workers are then guaranteed a regular weekly wage if they are able consistently to achieve a given level of performance. Having demonstrated the ability to maintain a level of performance over a minimum period, they are paid an appropriate wage. Subsequent failure to achieve this level of performance results first in some form of discipline or review by management, and subsequently in a reduction to a lower wage level. Measured day work therefore incorporates elements of normal incentive pay with some other benefits of a straight time rate system, in that wage levels do not fluctuate as much as in incentive pay, yet an incentive element remains.

**EXAMPLE**

### *Computer data input*

A bank operates a measured day-work scheme for computer terminal operators in a particular department. Four pay rates exist: £50, £55, £60 and £65 a week. Based on clerical work measurement there are four performance standards: ≤ 80, 80–100, 100–120 and ≥ 120 BSI. New employees are paid at £50 a week during a four-week training period. Thereafter their performance is measured weekly. If they are able to perform at ≥ 80 BSI for four consecutive weeks they are upgraded to £55 a week. If thereafter, at any time for four consecutive weeks, they can perform at ≥ 100 BSI they are then upgraded to £60 a week, etc. Subsequent failure to achieve the appropriate performance level leads after two consecutive weeks to a formal review which can be followed, after a further two consecutive weeks of performance less than target, by a reduction of the weekly wage to the next lowest category. Certain wage premiums (e.g. for length of service, skill level, etc.) are paid to some workers on top of the weekly wage, whatever the level.

## Premium payment scheme

The approach here is similar to that of measured day work, but the time-scale is often extended so that performance reviews take place at long intervals; hence stability is high.

## Multi-factor incentives

Increasingly, incentive payment schemes are based on multiple performance or achievement criteria. In particular such schemes take into account factors other than the output-related or throughput-related criteria used in the schemes described above. At the simplest level, multi-factor schemes will also provide for the reward of quality, attendance and timekeeping achievements. At this level they can readily be applied to individuals, but in general multi-factor schemes are more appropriate for group incentive payment (see below). In these cases, factors such as output (or throughput) quality, resource utilization and customer service criteria can be accommodated. With this approach a high base rate is supplemented by an 'incentive' earning usually calculated on a 'points' basis, points being awarded for a level of achievement on each factor. Factors may carry different weightings to reflect their relative importance in the particular situation, and the total incentive earning may be obtained by adding the weighted points achievements for each factor and converting the total to a money equivalent, to be added to the base pay.

Such schemes offer the following benefits:

(a) The incentive has a broad base and can be designed more readily to reflect the organization's needs.

(b) Overall performance/achievement is rewarded, and the risk of high achievement on one factor at the expense of another is reduced.

(c) The setting and weighting of factors offer opportunities for the participation of all groups involved.

(d) Flexibility can be built into the scheme by allowing for changes in factor weighting.

## Group PBR schemes

The schemes described above are *primarily* applied to individuals. Derivatives of them (in particular measured day work, premium payments and multi-factor schemes) may be applied to small groups of people employed in related tasks in a particular area, but in general other types of schemes, with a distinctive philosophy, are used to provide incentive pay to groups of workers. Many such schemes exist, ranging from those developed for a particular application to those based on general principles, which are relevant in a variety of organizations. Such group incentive schemes might be applied to small groups of workers engaged together on a task and working interdependently, to departments, and in some cases to entire organizations. In general the larger the group involved in such incentive pay the greater the problem of designing a scheme which has perceived *relevance* and *immediacy*. In other words, the larger the group and the more 'remote' the criteria for determining the amount of incentive pay, the greater the likelihood that individuals will see the factors which influence their incentive pay as being beyond their direct influence, and the greater the risk that the time lag in providing the incentive pay will limit the development of individuals' motivation. These, therefore, are the principal motivational obstacles of such schemes, but on the other hand such schemes do emphasize the sharing of achievements and productivity gains, and with that the need for team working, and perhaps the development of some greater identification with organizational goals, etc.

Group PBR schemes are being used, increasingly, in all types of business, whilst individual PBR schemes are seen to be of diminishing importance. Amongst the main reasons for this trend to group schemes are:

1. the increasing need for people to work together, e.g. as teams, rather than individually and independently;
2. the reducing importance of direct labour costs as a part of total costs;
3. the increased emphasis being placed on organizational approaches to improving efficiency and effectiveness, e.g. the use of total quality control (see Chapter 18);
4. the increasing importance of non-price and therefore non-cost factors in achieving competitive advantage (see Chapter 2).

These trends make it increasingly difficult to build effective and appropriate PBR schemes from simple, single criteria (e.g. time to do a job or task) for individual workers, so organizations have begun to pursue different means to link pay and performance.[3]

Basically, group PBR schemes aim to achieve the following:

1. to encourage employees working together continually to improve productivity/efficiency and effectiveness, i.e. to improve organizational 'performance';
2. to secure measurable financial benefits from increased performance, and to share these between employees and the organization.

---

[3] See, for example: Solano, M. S. (1992) Making pay for performance work in the 1990s. *Journal of Compensation and Benefits*, **8**(2), pp. 24–31; Grossmann, J. (1992) Pay, performance and productivity, *Small Business Reports*, **17**(10), pp. 50–59.

The principal prerequisites for a successful scheme include:

1. The scheme should be relatively straightforward, and should be readily understandable by all concerned.
2. There should be commitment to the scheme from all concerned.
3. There should be a clear measure of 'performance'.
4. Performance measurement, feedback on performance, and reward should be rapid and frequent.
5. There should be substantial and general management commitment.
6. Training, instruction and education programmes are required for all involved.
7. The scheme should be introduced, and then maintained, in a participatory manner – not unilaterally.

**EXAMPLE**

### *Southern Company Services*

Southern Company Services has organized a team incentive programme to improve productivity through better use of labour and materials. It is a group-based incentive programme that encourages employees to improve productivity through efficient use of labour, capital, materials and energy. The value of the increased productivity is determined, and the dollar amount is split between the company and the team. In this way, the company and its stockholders see tangible benefits for their investment, and the employees receive bonuses for their work. Specifically organized around natural workgroups and not individuals, the programme is administered by a steering committee composed of 7 staff personnel and 11 management personnel. The amount of money allocated is based on gains over target rates and achievements related to system performance service-level objectives. Eligible participants receive payments equal to a certain percentage of their total annual wages.

Source: Davidson, R. L. (1988) 'Gainsharing' incentive spurs productivity. *Transmission and Distribution*, **40**(12), pp. 42, 44.

## Types of group PBR scheme

Traditionally, there are considered to be two types of scheme, although the distinction between them now is blurred:

(a) ***team profit sharing*** – through which groups of employees and the organization share the financial benefits of increased profits;

(b) ***team 'gainsharing'*** – through which groups of employees and the organization share the financial benefits of reduced costs.

Figure 10.4, which uses the cost structure introduced in Chapter 4 (see Figure 4.1), compares the 'coverage' of these two approaches by reference to the total cost base of an operation. We see that profit sharing schemes tend to relate to total costs, whereas gainshare schemes relate to labour costs, or, in the case of broader schemes, to operation costs. The difference, of course, is the range of costs covered. The broader the range, the more likely it is that the scheme will be seen to be related substantially to profit.

In practice the term 'gainshare' is now generally used to cover the full range of schemes.

## Implementation and operation

The essential steps in designing and introducing a gainshare scheme are:

1. Identify the measure of performance.
2. Identify the size/scope (i.e. membership of the group/s) to be covered by the scheme.

**Figure 10.4** Operations costs, and the 'coverage' of group PBR schemes

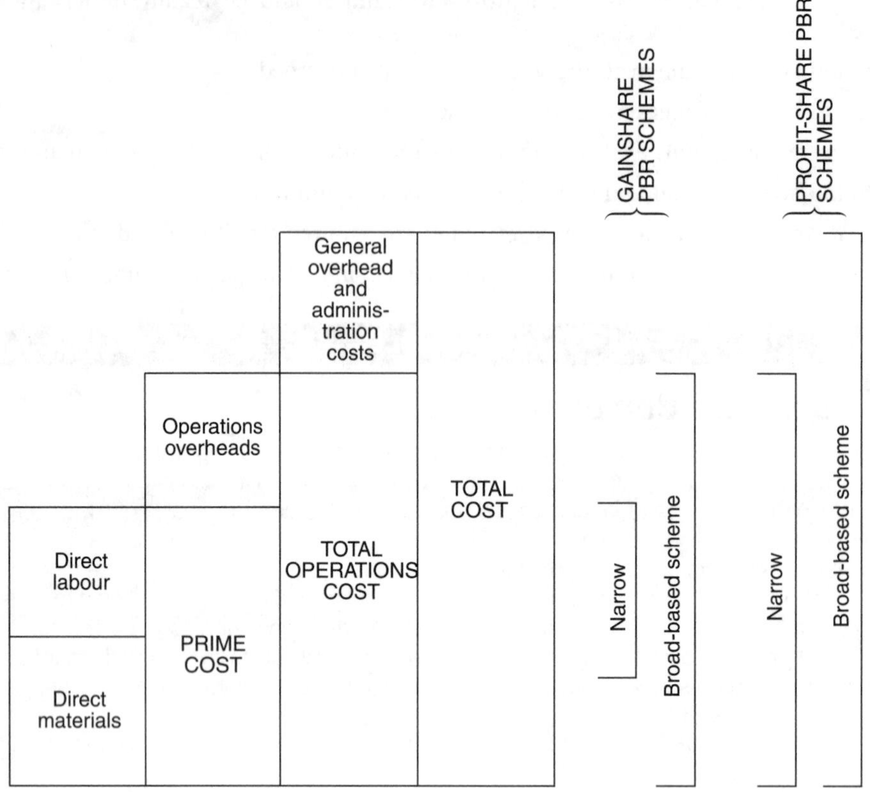


3. Establish a representative and consultative process (to cover management, employees involved, and specialist personnel) through which to define and introduce the scheme.
4. Design and define the scheme – and if appropriate incorporate it in collective bargaining agreements.
5. Train and educate all involved and affected.
6. Establish a representative committee to run the scheme.
7. Establish a representative review/monitoring procedure.
8. Establish a communications procedure to provide information on bonuses paid, sizes of bonus 'pools', trends, etc.

## Some gainshare schemes

Some of the pioneer group PBR schemes are now considered to be examples of gainshare. The Scanlon scheme, first developed in 1978, and the Rucker scheme (1952) are both examples of profit share systems. Scanlon is better known than the Rucker scheme, which is proprietary. It utilizes two basic steps.[4]

1. Management and employee representatives form committees to run the scheme.

[4] Description and example based on Dar-El, E. M. (1989) Incentive and reward through 'gainsharing' schemes. In Wild, R. (ed.) *International Handbook of Production and Operations Management*. London: Cassell.

2. Bonus payment made monthly or bi-monthly based on positive changes in ratio of total labour costs to total value of output/throughput, over given time periods.

   The total bonus for the period is divided, usually as follows:

   75% for immediate payment, of which:

   75% goes to participants

   25% to organization

   and 25% for reserve, which is retained to cover defects in future periods (but if the accumulated reserve reaches a given amount the excess is distributed immediately). Distribution of the 'reserve' is in the proportions given above.

Table 10.3 gives an example of a bonus calculation under this scheme.

*IMPROSHARE* (Improved Productivity Sharing) is another proprietary system.[5] It is a widely used, straightforward productivity/cost group share scheme, with little provision for employee involvement. It is easy to install – provided employee participation in design and installation is not required.

**Table 10.3 Bonus calculations for a gainshare PBR scheme**

Assume that in the 12-month base period the payroll cost of each pound's worth of throughput value was 32.84p. This establishes a productivity norm or ratio of 32.84 percent against which to measure the performance in each month of the following year, governing the bonus distribution.

| | |
|---|---|
| Assume that during the month of June the value of throughput | £1 125 750 |
| If performance had been no better during this month than the average for the base period, the allowed payroll would have to amount to (1 125 750 × 0.3284): | £ 369 696 |
| Assume, however, the actual payroll for June amounted to: | £ 327 488 |
| This would mean an improvement over the norm amounting to (this is the overall *bonus*): | £ 42 208 |
| Setting aside 25% of the bonus pool as a reserve: | £ 10 552 |
| Leaving for immediate distribution the sum of: | £ 31 656 |
| Deducting the company's share (25%): | £ 7 914 |
| Making the employees' share (75%): | £ 23 742 |
| As a percentage of the actual payroll, the share for the employee is: {(23 742 ÷ 327 488) × 100}: | £ 7.25% |

An individual employee's pay record for the month of June may be as follows:

| Name | Total hours worked | Including overtime hours | Hourly rate | Total pay | Bonus % | Bonus | Total earnings |
|---|---|---|---|---|---|---|---|
| A. N. Other | 200 | 20 | £10 | £2 200 | 7.25 | £160 | £2 360 |

[5] Fein, M. (1982) *Improshare – an Alternative to Traditional Managing.* Atlanta: IIE Publications.

*SHRED* (Shared Reductions in Cost)[6] is broader than IMPROSHARE, and resembles Scanlon and Rucker in focusing on profit performance rather than direct costs. Like them it requires a comprehensive involvement/participation process. SHRED provides two plans. Plan A is a scheme through which there is profitability showing up to a previously agreed ceiling, beyond which a different formula applies. Plan B is based on target bonuses.

Value added PBR schemes deserve mention here, for they are types of gainshare. They focus on costs – specifically labour cost, for they aim to reward improvements in value added to input materials. They are of particular relevance in manufacturing operations.

Added value (AV) can be defined as 'the value added to input materials', i.e. the difference between the value of output (e.g. sales) and the costs of the materials used in creating those sales. From this added value must be paid all the other costs incurred in the operation, e.g. wages, administrative costs, capital charges. Hence (see Figure 22.1):

$$\text{AV} = \text{Sales revenue } \textit{less} \text{ Total external purchases}$$

$$\text{AV productivity} = \frac{\text{Added value}}{\text{Labour costs} + \text{Capital charges}}$$

$$= \frac{\text{Added value}}{\text{Internal expense}}$$

The major benefits of using the AV productivity measure as an indication of the overall performance of a unit and a basis for incentive payment include:

(a) It clearly demonstrates that increases in wages must be met from increases in the value of outputs, not simply from sales or turnover (which might result from non-profitable activity).

(b) Value can be increased in numerous ways, e.g. rationalization of activities (eliminating low-value work), increased capital expenditure, improved resource utilization, modified pricing; thus the AV productivity criterion emphasizes overall effort, not simply output and worker-controlled factors.

(c) The comparison of the performance of different units or organizations is easier, since AV (unlike profit measure) is not influenced by depreciation, etc.

(d) The measurement of AV productivity requires consideration of the whole organization's activities and therefore demands meaningful participation and negotiation within the organization.

One method of calculating AV-based incentive bonus is described in the example below.

**EXAMPLE**

## *AV bonus scheme*

*Step 1* Agree a value added/employee cost ratio, e.g. average of annual for past five years:

| | £ |
|---|---|
| Net sales revenue | 10 000 000 p.a. |
| Total external purchases | 3 000 000 p.a. |
| VA | 7 000 000 p.a. |

[6] Dar-El, E. M. (1986) *Productivity Improvement – Employee Involvement and Gainsharing Plans*. Amsterdam: Elsevier.

which is represented by:

| | £ |
|---|---|
| Labour costs | 5 000 000 |
| Capital charges | 1 000 000 |
| Profits | 1 000 000 |
| | 7 000 000 |

Hence:

$$\frac{\text{Value added}}{\text{Employee cost}} = \frac{7\,000\,000}{5\,000\,000}$$

$$= 1.4$$

*Step 2* Agree basis for sharing of VA/employee cost improvement, e.g. 50% to company, 50% to employees (subject to 50% payment to reserve for uses in periods where no improvement is obtained).

*Step 3* Calculate periodic results, e.g. monthly:

| | | £ |
|---|---|---|
| Net sales revenue for period | = | 1 000 000 |
| Total external purchases for period | = | 400 000 |
| VA for period | | 600 000 |
| which includes labour costs | | £400 000 |

Hence:

$$\frac{\text{VA for period}}{\text{Employee cost}} \quad \frac{600\,000}{400\,000}$$

$$= 1.5$$

*Step 4* Determine bonus payment:

Agreed employee labour cost for given VA

$$= \frac{600\,000}{1.4} \quad £\ 429\,000$$

| | £ |
|---|---|
| Allocation to the company | 214 500 |
| Available as bonus | 214 500 |
| Less payment to reserve | 107 250 |
| ∴ Available for bonus payment this period | 107 250 |

EXAMPLE

## Mosier Industries

Mosier Industries of Brookville, Ohio implemented a gainsharing programme in an effort to involve employees in improving company performance. A committee of three company officers monitors company performance and has full authority to resolve any issues connected with the 'efficiency reward program'. At the end of each six-month bonus period, the committee allocates an amount of money that varies according to performance to the efficiency reward fund. Eligible employees earn efficiency points based on seniority, job classification and co-operation. Employees receive a cash award based on their number of efficiency points and the total amount in the fund. In the 18 bonus periods that have occurred since the programme was implemented, awards totalling nearly $250 000 have been paid out over only six bonus periods. The company has tied wage increases to the bonus formula to prevent workforce letdown at the end of a bonus period when it becomes apparent that a bonus will not be achieved.

Source: Owens, T. (1988) Case history – making gainsharing work. *Small Business Reports*, **13**(10), pp. 29–32.

## Experience with gainshare schemes

Organizations which introduced gainshare-type group PBR schemes have reported significant initial profit and productivity improvements. Figures around 5–15% in the first year and 25–35% overall (i.e. when a steady state is achieved) are typical.[7] Other reported benefits include:[8]

(a) greater employee involvement in decision-making;

(b) greater/better ideas generation;

(c) higher morale;

(d) improved absenteeism and reduced labour turnover.

7 See, for example, Paulsen, K. M. (1991) Lessons learned from gainsharing. *HR Magazine*, **36**(4), pp. 70–74.

8 See, for example, Owens, T. (1991) Gaining from gainsharing. *Small Business Reports*, **16**(8), pp. 51–60.

## CHECKLIST FOR CHAPTER 10

### *Payment and incentives*

Nature of remuneration
- Significance of wages

Payment systems and structures

Job evaluation
- Job ranking
- Job classification
- Points evaluation
- Factor comparison

### *Payment by results*

Individual schemes
- 100% or 'one-for-one' systems
- Less than 100% or 'geared' systems
- Piece-work
- Measured day work
- Premium payment schemes
- Multi-factor schemes

Group PBR schemes
- Reasons for use
- Aims
- Pre-requisites
- Types of scheme
  - Profit sharing
  - Gainsharing
- Implementation and operation
- Examples
  - Scanlon
  - IMPROSHARE
  - SHRED
  - Value added schemes
- Experience with gainshare schemes

## FURTHER READING

**Bowey, A. (ed.) (1975)** *Handbook of Salary and Wage Systems*. Epping: Gower.

**Friedman, B. (1990)** *Effective Staff Incentives*. London: Kogan Page.

**Gowen, C. R. (1996)** Gainsharing programs: an overview of history and research. *Journal of Organizational Behaviour Management*, **11**(2), pp. 77–79.

## QUESTIONS

10.1 Refer to Question 8.3. The worker on that job produces 2600 pieces during an 8-hour working shift. He is working on a 10% participation incentive scheme, in which the basic rate is £3 per hour and in which incentive payment is given for outputs in excess of 75. What are the worker's total gross earnings for the shift?

10.2 Show how any two of the job evaluation schemes described in this chapter could be used to evaluate:

(a) the job of a supermarket check-out worker;

(b) your job.

10.3 A worker is capable of giving a regular 125 performance over a working week of 40 hours. If she is employed on testing work and if the standard hour (SH) per item tested is 0.75, what would the gross total pay per week be on a base rate of 270 pence per hour under the following systems of payment:

(a) 100% participation with incentive payment for performances over 100;

(b) 100% participation with incentive payment for performances over 75;

(c) 50/50 scheme with incentive payment for performances over 100;

(d) 50/50 scheme with incentive payment for performances over 75?

What piece-rate must be paid to the worker if her gross total weekly earnings under a piecework system are to equal the largest gross total weekly earnings provided by one of the above incentive schemes?

10.4 In order to monitor the performance of an organization, and as a basis for a value added PBR scheme, calculate some value added ratios for each of the following, using whichever of the given data are relevant. Explain your ratios and comment on the results.

| ***Case*** | ***A*** | ***B*** | ***C*** |
|---|---|---|---|
| **Number of employees** | **216** | **202** | **195** |
| | **£** | **£** | **£** |
| Net sales (including changes in stocks) | 2 562 100 | 2 884 600 | 3 600 500 |
| Cost of materials | 1 000 000 | 1 000 500 | 1 000 750 |
| Wages and salaries | 800 500 | 750 750 | 1 100 000 |
| Profit | 250 000 | 175 000 | 300 000 |
| Fixed assets | 3 000 000 | 2 000 100 | 1 500 000 |
| Current assets | 1 500 000 | 500 000 | 575 000 |

10.5 What are the principal benefits, disadvantages and applications of a gainshare payment scheme?

## CASE STUDY (from Part 9)

The topics covered in this chapter are relevant in the following (see Introduction to Part 9 and Table C.1 for further details):

| No. | Name | Country |
|---|---|---|
| 25 | European Foundation – Group Work | Netherlands, Portugal |

PART 5

# Capacity Management


Introduction to Part 5

Chapter 11 Capacity management

## INTRODUCTION TO PART 5

In this chapter we deal in some detail with what is perhaps the most difficult, and certainly the most important, problem and decision area for operations management. Unless the capacity of the operating system is managed effectively, the operations manager is unlikely to achieve his or her twin objectives. Good decision-making and effectiveness in other areas are unlikely to compensate for or conceal poor capacity management.

This is one of the 'principal' problem areas of operations management as defined in Chapter 1. The strategies which might be adopted for the management of capacity can be: (a) limited by feasibility constraints (associated mainly with the structure of the operating system) and (b) influenced by desirability factors (deriving from the objectives of the organization and operations managers).

## STRATEGIC CONTEXT

The operations issues, problems and decisions considered in this part of the book exist within the broader strategic context of the organization. The main relationships are set out here, as a preface to the details which follow.

### Influences of business policy decisions *(see Chapter 2, Figure 2.2)*

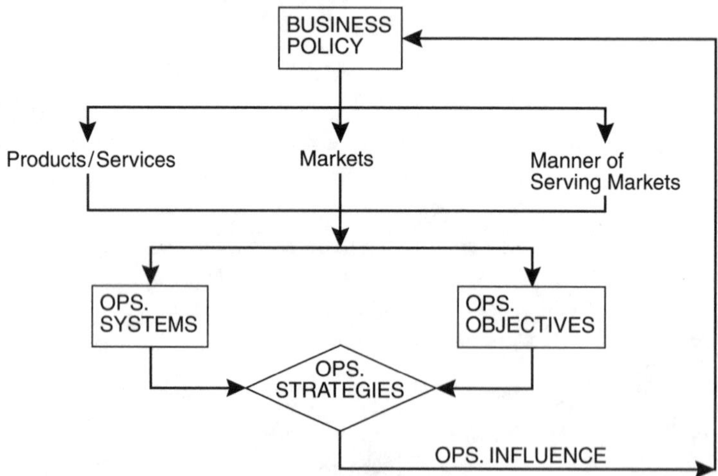


The management of capacity is one of the principal or key problem areas of operations management. The manner in which capacity must be managed will be influenced both by operations objectives, which determine what must be achieved, and also, probably, by the operating system structure, which may influence what is feasible. The model above indicates that both of these factors are in turn influenced by business policies.

For example, if the outputs to be offered by the system and the markets for which they are intended make it possible to create them in advance for stock, then a particular type of operating system may exist (i.e. with output stocks) which in turn makes possible certain strategies for managing capacity.

Similarly, if the services to be provided, and the nature of the markets, makes possible the use of customer input queuing, then again the operating system structure which is created makes possible certain approaches for managing capacity. If business policy emphasizes certain distinctive means for serving markets, e.g. speed or cost, then these will be reflected in operations objectives and will probably have a major influence on the way in which the capacity of the system is managed.

Conversely, if well-established procedures exist for managing capacity, and since effective capacity management is critically important in achieving customer service and/or resource utilization objectives, operations managers will wish to try to ensure that when business policies are established they are consistent with the capabilities of operations, i.e. that operations can in fact implement the business policies which are formulated.

## Competitive advantage *(see Chapter 2, Figures 2.6 and 2.7)*

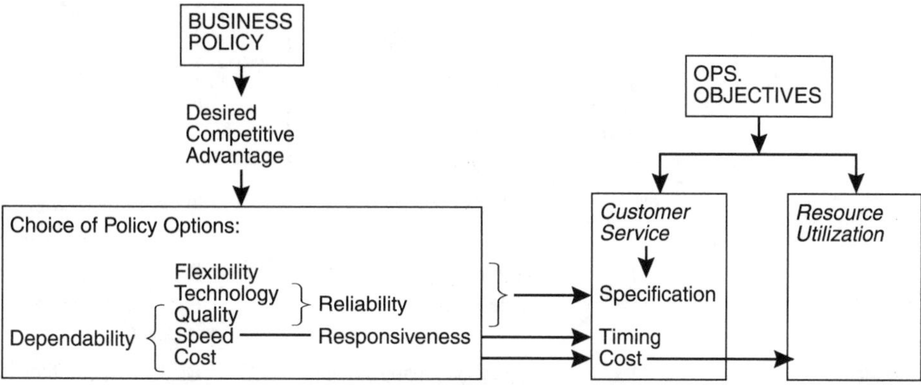


The model above focuses on the relationship of business policy options and their implementation/achievement as operations objectives in customer service. If we recall the discussion of policy options in Chapter 2 (e.g. Table 2.2), it is evident that the following main relationships will exist:

| An emphasis on business policy option: | Places importance on capacity management through: |
|---|---|
| Speed | Need to have adequate (e.g. spare) capacity and/or means for rapid adjustment of capacity, to avoid queues/waiting |
| Cost | Need for high capacity utilization, e.g. minimization of spare capacity |
| Flexibility | Difficulty of having output stocks of goods |
| Technology | Need to ensure high utilization of expensive facilities |
| Reliability | Need for reliable resources, and therefore the difficulty of relying on effective capability flexibility through subcontracting, changes in the labour force, etc. |

## TOPIC MAP

| Topics in this Part | Related topics in other chapters: Chapter | Topic | Comments/aspects |
|---|---|---|---|
| Chapter 11 | | | |
| Operations planning and control | 1 | Operations management objectives | Influence of objectives on operations planning |
| | 8 | Work measurement | Need for work times in planning |
| | | Learning curve | Need to allow for learning in operations planning |
| | 11 | Operations control | Relationship of planning and control |
| | 12 | Activity scheduling | Scheduling decisions as an aspect of operations planning |
| | 13 | Project scheduling | |
| | 14 | Batch scheduling | |
| | 15 | Flow process scheduling | |
| | 17 | Inventory management | Implications of inventories on planning and vice versa |
| | 21 | Maintenance and replacement | Reliability and availability of resources influences capacity available |
| Capacity management | 1 | Operations management objectives | Objectives, and their influence on capacity management strategies |
| | | Operating system structures | Influence of system structure on capacity strategy |
| | 8 | Work methods | Influence on available capacity |
| | | Learning effects | |
| | 12 | Activity scheduling | Implementation of capacity strategies through scheduling decisions |
| | 13 | Project scheduling | |
| | 14 | Batch scheduling | |
| | 15 | Flow process scheduling | |
| | 17 | Inventory management | Implementation of capacity strategies through inventory decisions |

Chapter 11

# Capacity management

## ISSUES

Why is the management of capacity a major strategic issue?
What is the capacity of a system?
How do we determine the future capacity required?
How do we deal with uncertainty – especially variations in demand?
What are the basic strategies for managing capacity?
How do capacity decisions relate to operations objectives?
What capacity planning procedures are available?

## NOTATION USED IN THIS CHAPTER

$C_I$ Cost of storage/unit/period
$C_O$ Cost of overtime production/unit/period
$C_R$ Cost of regular production/unit/period
$I_i$ Inventory level at end of period $i$
$t$ Average number of units in system
$L_q$ Average number of units in queue
$O_i$ Maximum overtime production in period $i$
$p$ Throughput rate
$P_n$ Probability of $n$ units in system (i.e. queue + one being serviced)
$R_i$ Maximum regular time production in period $i$
$S_i$ Sales for period $i$
$W$ Average time units spend in system
$W_q$ Average time units spend in queue
$\lambda$ Average arrival rate (units/period of time)
$\mu$ Average service rate (units/period of time)
$\rho$ $\lambda/\mu$

Planning and managing the capacity of an operating system is the most important area of responsibility of operations management. Capacity management is the critical, strategic decision area of operations. Decisions on how to match the capacity of the operating system to the levels of demand which are to be met by that system will influence many other decisions, yet no other decisions can rectify wrong decisions in this area. The capacity of an operating system is a measure of the usable resources available to that system. Acquiring the wrong levels of resource must have direct consequences for either customer service or resource utilization – the twin objectives of operations management. The reverse also applies, i.e. the importance to be attached to customer service or to resource utilization will influence the way in which capacity is managed, i.e. the capacity management strategy. We noted in Chapter 1 that this is the *desirability* constraint on capacity management. Also, the strategy used for capacity management will be influenced by the structure of the operating system. As we saw in Chapter 1, this is the *feasibility* constraint on capacity management.

In this chapter we look, in detail, at strategies, and then procedures for capacity management. To set an appropriate context, we first consider the nature of operations planning and control.

## OPERATIONS PLANNING AND CONTROL *(see also Chapter 12)*

In this book we treat operations planning and operations control separately. We regard operations planning as a *pre*-operating activity, i.e. the determination of the facilities needed to provide the required goods or services and the construction of a schedule by means of which this will be achieved. Operations control we consider to be a *during*-operating activity involving the implementation of operations planning decisions. Our definition of the two areas is, therefore:

> Operations planning is concerned with the determination, acquisition and arrangement of all facilities necessary for the future operations.
>
> Operations control is concerned with the implementation of a predetermined operations plan or policy and the control of all aspects of operations according to such a plan or policy.

Notice, however, that operations planning and control are closely linked and interdependent. Decisions during planning will determine the problems, and often the nature, of control, and experiences during control will influence future planning.

### The stages in operations planning and control

Figure 11.1 outlines the main stages in operations planning and control and identifies the area of responsibility of capacity management. They are described below:

#### Demand estimation or measurement

A prerequisite of any purposeful planning is a statement of the demand which is to be satisfied. In most cases this will involve estimation or forecasting. Rarely will it be possible to measure future demand. Demand forecasting is discussed in more detail later in this chapter whilst some of the techniques are covered in Appendix II.

#### Aggregate capacity planning

Here the objective is to develop a medium- to long-term statement of capacity requirements in aggregate terms, i.e. a plan indicating the amount of facilities needed to satisfy total expected demand, period by period.

**Figure 11.1** Principal stages in operations planning and control

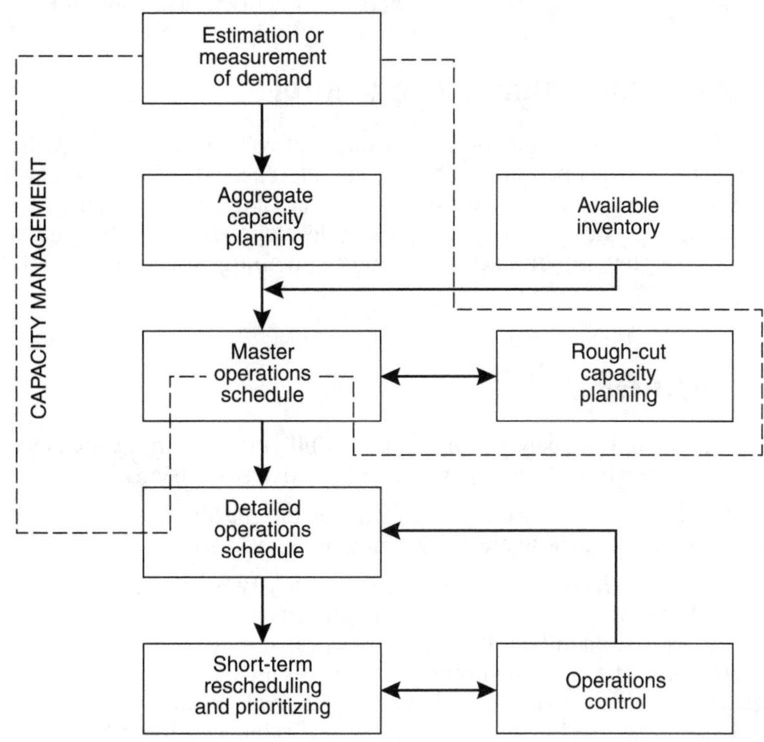


## Master operations schedule (MOS)

The master operations schedule is developed from the aggregate capacity plan. It is a breakdown of the aggregate plan showing when the major operations required for each expected item of demand are to be undertaken. Unlike the aggregate capacity plan, the MOS is time-phased, and identifies each major resource category and individual orders.

## Rough-cut capacity planning

This involves the analysis of the MOS in order to identify time-phased capacity requirements for major resources or operations. It is, in effect, a means to test the feasibility of the MOS. If the rough-cut plan reveals that inadequate capacities are available for any major resource during any period, the MOS will be recalculated.

## Detailed operations schedule (DOS)

Given a feasible MOS, the next requirement is the development of a detailed schedule for all operations for all jobs or orders to be completed in the planning period. The time horizon here will be less than that for the MOS.

## Short-term rescheduling and prioritizing and control

Some short-term rescheduling will be necessary to accommodate changes in capacity demands or availabilities. For example, particular operations may require more time than anticipated or equipment may be unavailable through breakdown. The operations control activities will monitor such changes and modify the DOS.

### Computer systems for planning and control

Until recently the above aspects of operations planning and control have been dealt with by separate systems. For example, the master operations schedule has often been developed and maintained by using a computer-based materials requirement planning system (see Chapter 12). Recently, attempts have been made to integrate these separate systems. Mostly these developments have focused on manufacturing operations and one such system is manufacturing resource planning (also known as MRP II – see Chapter 12).

## CAPACITY MANAGEMENT

The management of capacity is the key planning responsibility of operations managers. All other operations planning takes place within the framework set by capacity decisions.

*Capacity management is concerned with the matching of the capacity of the operating system and the demand placed on that system,* i.e. those areas identified in Figure 11.1.

A system has capacity if it has at least some of *each* of the types of resources which are needed to perform its function. For example, a taxi service has capacity to transport a person if it has a vacant cab, a driver, fuel, etc., and a manufacturing system has capacity to produce if it has equipment, raw materials, labour, etc. Some of *each* of the necessary resources must exist if capacity is to exist. However, in measuring capacity we shall often refer only to the principal, or most costly, or most greatly used, or most commonly used resource in the operating system. Table 11.1 identifies some of the resources and some of the measures which might be used to describe the capacity of different types of systems.

One approach to the capacity management problem is to try to plan the capacity required and then manipulate that capacity so that it matches the changing demands placed on it. If insufficient capacity is provided it will be possible to meet only some of the demand, and so some customers must wait or go elsewhere. If too much capacity is provided there will be some under-utilization of resources. Another approach is to try to manipulate demand to match the available capacity. Demand might be increased through advertising, increased promotion, lower prices, etc., and this might help avoid under-utilization of available capacity. However, if there is insufficient capacity available, demand may be allowed, or even encouraged, to fall.

In most cases an organization will seek to match capacity and demand by a combination of these two approaches. However, operations managers will be concerned mainly with the former, and in most cases they will see their task as that of trying to ensure that a forecast or given demand can be satisfied. From the operations manager's viewpoint, one of the major problems is uncertainty of demand. The existence of a stable and known demand would simplify the problems of capacity management considerably, and changing demand can be accommodated relatively easily provided changes can be predicted accurately. However, the expectation of changing demand levels without the possibility of accurate prediction gives rise to extremely complex capacity problems. We should note that this uncertainty of demand level may be caused by:

(a) uncertainty about the number of 'orders' to be received; *and/or*

(b) uncertainty about the amount of resources required for the satisfaction of customer orders.

Capacity management will involve the study of likely demand patterns for the medium to long term, the determination of the capacity required to meet such demand, and the development of strategies for the deployment of resources, in particular for accommodating changes in demand levels. Capacity management will involve the examination of alternative strategies. For example, it will be

**Table 11.1 The capacity of operating systems: measures of capacity**

| Operating system | Measures of capacity |
|---|---|
| *Manufacture* | |
| Electricity generation | Megawatt capacity |
| Steel manufacture | Number of mills or blast-furnaces |
| Craft manufacture | Labour force |
| *Transport* | |
| Airline | Number of seats |
| Taxi service | Number of cabs |
| Telecommunications | Number of lines |
| *Service* | |
| Hospital | Number of beds |
| Library | Number of books/journals |
| Restaurant | Number of tables |
| *Supply* | |
| Warehouse | Volume |
| Retail shop | Shelf area |
| Petrol station | Number of pumps |

necessary to examine alternative methods of meeting demand-level fluctuations. Can and should the amount of resources (e.g. labour) be varied? Is it desirable to maintain a steady level of activity and, if so, how can this be achieved? Can customers be expected or required to wait? What is the role of inventories and should the system attempt to meet all potential demand?

An objective of capacity management is the determination of the quantity of each resource required. Notice that some resources (e.g. labour and machines) may be stocked, used and re-used, while others (e.g. materials) will be acquired, i.e. input, and consumed. For the former a decision must be made about the amount of each resource to have in stock, whilst for the latter the input rate must be determined. In many cases such decisions will reflect assessment of the *average* demand rate expected over a period of time. If resources are available to satisfy average demand, and if fluctuations about this level can be accommodated, then capacity is satisfactory. In some cases, periods during which demand exceeds average may be offset against periods below average. In others, demand above expectation may be lost, so there may be some justification in providing capacity in excess of expected requirements as a form of safeguard. In most cases demand levels lower than expected will give rise to either an under-utilization of capacity and/or a build-up of resources beyond expectations. Failure to satisfy either resource utilization and/or customer service criteria can therefore result from inaccurate assessment of average demand levels and hence the provision of too little or too much capacity, or failure to provide for adequate capacity adjustment.

For example, in many systems an overestimate of demand will lead to an under-utilization of resources, while an underestimate of demand may, sooner or later, affect customer service – sooner in the case of systems without output stocks and later where output stocks exist.

**Table 11.2 Examples of capacity planning problems**

| Examples of operating systems | Types of capacity planning problem |
|---|---|
| *Manufacture*: Builder (of 'one-off' houses to customer order) | Houses are built as, when, how and where required by particular customers. Resources must be obtained for each job but, since each house is different, it will not be possible to predict exactly how many resources are needed. The builder must complete the houses on time and therefore must provide excess resources or be able to subcontract. |
| *Supply*: Wholesaler | The wholesale business supplies retailers in an area with goods. They need to provide a good service, but don't want to hold too much stock. They will try to forecast demand, in particular to identify seasonal variations. They will then have to decide how much of each item to stock, and what to do if stocks are insufficient at any time. |
| *Transport*: Furniture removal | The furniture remover will want to give a good service, and in particular will not want customers to wait too long. However, it is known that demand will fluctuate. The business doesn't want to have too many spare, unused vans, drivers, etc., so will hope to have enough resources to deal with most demand most of the time. |
| *Service*: Fire service | A fire service cannot keep its customers waiting; nor can demand be forecast accurately. It will probably be necessary to have enough capacity (e.g. vehicles, staff, etc.) to deal with most situations, but also to arrange for other facilities to be 'on call', e.g. from other towns. |

Although it is convenient to consider capacity management as occurring in two stages – determination of normal capacity required and planning for meeting variations about this level – these two aspects are clearly interdependent. The capacity provided may be influenced by the manner in which adjustments may be made. Constraints on adjustment, particularly limitations on ability to accommodate short-term excess demand, may necessitate provision of 'excess' capacity.

Examples of capacity planning in different types of operating systems are given in Table 11.2. The next section considers in more detail the two major decision areas of capacity planning, the normal capacity required and dealing with demand fluctuations.

## THE NORMAL CAPACITY REQUIRED

The objective here is to determine the normal capacity required for the medium to long term. The decision will be based on demand forecast.

When forecasting future demand for capacity planning purposes, fluctuations will be expected – but to some extent ignored. The aim will be to get a general picture of future demand. Short-term fluctuations will usually be dealt with later. Take as an example the forecast demand pattern shown in Figure 11.2. The average

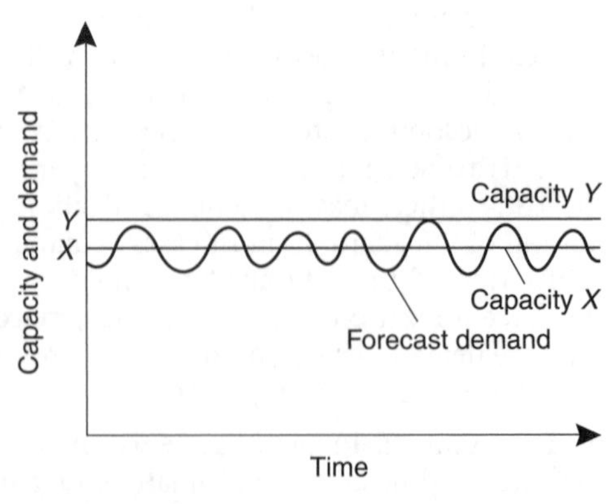


**Figure 11.2** Demand forecast

demand is stable at $X$, but some variations about this level are expected. In this case, when planning future capacity, a capacity level of $X$ could be established, with the expectation that some means would be available to deal with the short-term variations. However, if it was known in advance that this was not possible, then a higher level of capacity, e.g. $Y$, might be fixed. So, knowing whether and how demand fluctuations might be dealt with will influence the normal capacity, which is fixed given the forecast of future demand.

## Demand forecasting *(see also Appendix II)*

In most situations the first step in capacity planning will be demand forecasting.

The length of the forecast period will depend largely on the nature of system resources and the nature of the market. Capacity plans may involve periods in excess of five years where there is sufficient stability or predictability of the nature of demand. A long-term view may be essential where there is a long lead time on the provision or replacement of resources. In contrast, a shorter-term view would be appropriate where the nature of demand is less stable or less predictable, where resources are more readily provided or replaced, or where the manner in which the function is accomplished may change, through, for example, technological advances.

Some of the more important forecasting techniques are described briefly in Appendix II, and here we shall confine ourselves to a brief discussion of the subject.

A very large area of forecasting and many forecasting techniques depend on a formal analysis of past data for a prediction or forecast of the future. The objective of such techniques is to assess past demands, and to determine a trend which might then be used to forecast future demand. Such procedures are applied with varying degrees of sophistication. One of the simplest methods of identifying trends is the use of *moving averages*. Figure 11.3 shows how a four-period moving average has been used to indicate the trend in a series of sales figures. This figure also shows the results obtained by an alternative method, *exponential smoothing*, which, as compared with the previous method, places more weight on recent data.

Another approach involves the use of *economic indicators* or *associative predictions*. Many companies have found that there is a close relationship between the sale of their goods or services and certain of the indices of economic conditions produced by the government or by trade associations. Where such relationships exist a change in the index or indices might usefully be regarded as an indication of a likely change in demand. The objective, therefore, is to find one or more indices whose fluctuations are *afterwards* reflected in changes in demand.

**Figure 11.3** Sales trends plotted by four-period moving average and exponential smoothing methods

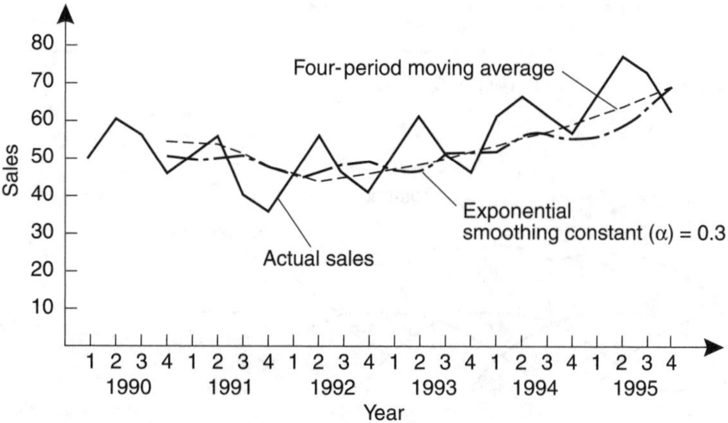

To develop forecasting techniques based on associative predictions can be a rather lengthy business which usually involves an extensive examination of the statistical relationship of past sales data and various likely indices. The closeness of the statistical association of variables can be measured by calculation of a *correlation coefficient*. Once indices bearing a close correlation with historical data have been found, this relationship can be used for forecasting. The relationship is expressed mathematically by means of a *regression equation*.

Each of these techniques and terms will be discussed more fully in Appendix II.

## The demand life-cycle

In forecasting demand for goods or services it is appropriate to recognize that in many cases demand is a function of age. The classic life-cycle curve shown in Figure 11.4 illustrates this relationship. This curve will normally apply in the case of goods or services consumed directly by the public (e.g. domestic appliances, sport and leisure facilities). The time-scale will depend on the nature of the product or service. While there is a tendency to assume continued growth for goods and services such as raw materials, basic services and transport (e.g. steel, fuel, medical care, rail and air transport), a similar life-cycle relationship may in fact exist, although the time-scale may be considerable.

Various policies might be employed for the provision of capacity to satisfy such demand. At one extreme, sufficient capacity to meet all expected demand might be provided from the outset, with attendant benefits of economies of scale in ordering, acquisition, training, etc. Alternatively, capacity might be matched to demand by incremental change over time, with benefits in utilization, etc. Systems providing several outputs from common resources might, despite the life-cycle characteristics, expect relatively steady total demand. Figure 11.5 illustrates this.

**Figure 11.4** A life-cycle curve for a single good or service

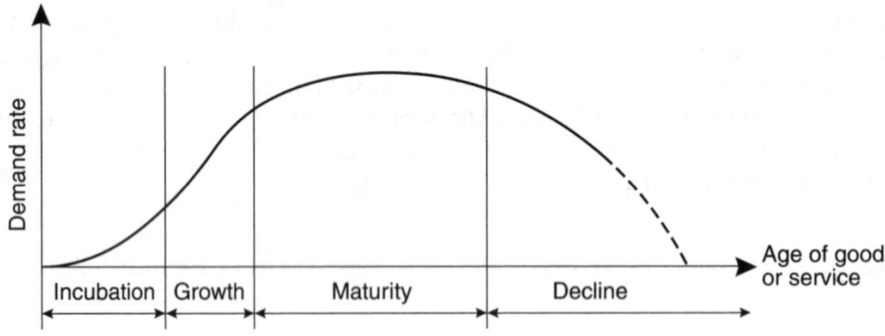


**Figure 11.5** Combination of individual demand curves

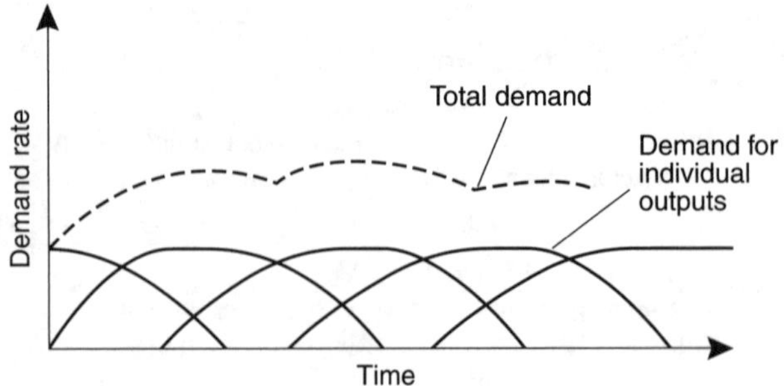

## Some factors affecting the capacity of resources

Given a forecast of demand for a future period, the next step in capacity planning is to decide what overall or general level of capacity to provide for that period.

Before proceeding further we must recognize that a given quantity of resources does not necessarily provide a fixed level of capacity. For example, in one situation a labour force of ten people may provide a greater capacity than in another. The absence of a fixed relationship between a quantity of physical resources and capacity is a result of a variety of factors, including those discussed below.

Figure 11.6 shows a typical *learning* or *improvement* curve. Clearly the effect of such learning is to increase the capacity of a given quantity of labour resource. Such capacity change effects may be of considerable importance in capacity planning.

It should also be noted that the capability, or capacity, of a given set of resources might also change with time. The *reliability* of machinery might change (Figure 11.7 shows a typical reliability curve) and so might the 'reliability' of people.

**Figure 11.6** A learning curve

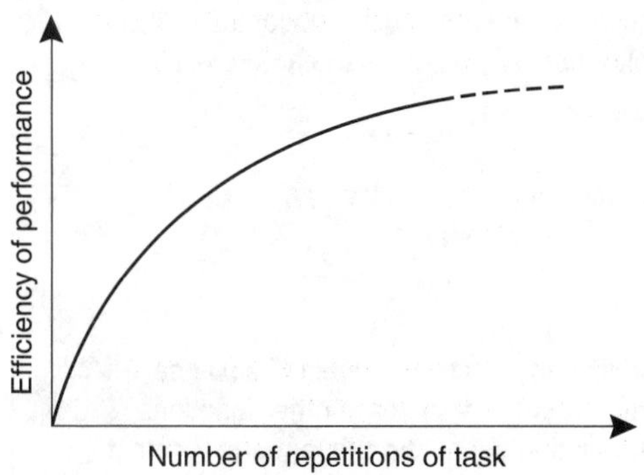


**Figure 11.7** A reliability curve

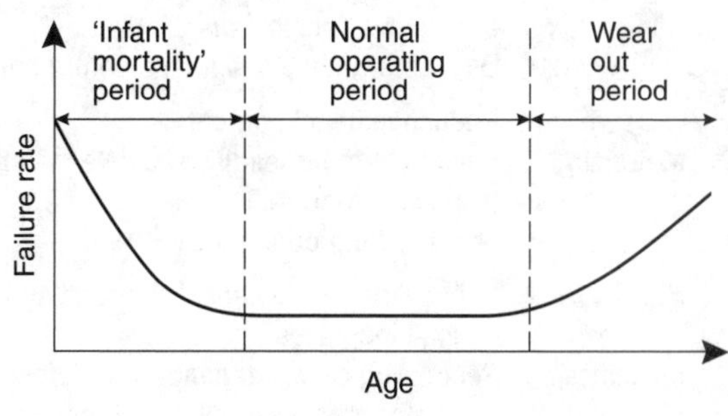


# DEALING WITH DEMAND FLUCTUATIONS – CAPACITY MANAGEMENT STRATEGIES

Faced with fluctuating and uncertain demand levels there are two basic capacity planning strategies which might be employed: (1) providing for efficient adjustment or variation of system capacity; and (2) eliminating or reducing the need for adjustments in system capacity.

## Strategy 1: Provide for efficient adjustment or variation of system capacity

In most situations it will be both possible and desirable to adopt this strategy. Usually system capacity can be changed within certain limits, perhaps not instantaneously but certainly with little delay. Temporarily, more useful capacity might be created by providing more resources and/or providing for their more efficient or intense utilization. Temporary reductions in capacity might be achieved through the transfer of resources to other functions or of course the temporary reduction in the resources on hand or the input rate of resources consumed.

In *supply* systems, e.g. supermarkets, such a strategy is employed as the principal means of accommodating inevitably fluctuating demand levels. Consider the supermarket check-out system. In periods of low demand some of the resources, i.e. the staff, can be transferred to other functions such as restocking shelves. During periods of high demand, staff resources may be increased temporarily by transfer from other functions to provide 'double-staffing', e.g. operation of cash register and wrapping and loading, in turn providing for more intensive utilization of the other resources, i.e. the cash register and the counter. Similarly in certain *manufacture* systems capacity released during periods of low demand might be employed on rectification or service work, while peak demand periods might be accommodated by temporary increase in resource levels through, for example, overtime working and more intensive use of equipment, perhaps through deferral of maintenance work. In some cases capacity might effectively be increased by subcontracting work. To some extent this strategy might be appropriate in the management of *transport* and *service* systems. In both cases maintenance and service work might be scheduled for periods of low demand, and flexible work shift patterns might be employed, overtime working introduced, etc.

Table 11.3 lists some of the means available for the adjustment of system capacity.

**Table 11.3 Means available for capacity adjustment (capacity strategy 1)**

| Resources | Capacity increases | Capacity reductions |
|---|---|---|
| *All* | Subcontract some work<br>Buy rather than make (manufacture only) | Retrieve some previously subcontracted work<br>Make rather than buy (manufacture only) |
| *Consumed* Material | Reduce material content<br>Substitute more readily available materials<br>Increase supply schedules<br>Transfer from other jobs | Reduce supply schedules<br>Transfer to other jobs |
| *Fixed* | Scheduling of activities, i.e. speed and load increases | |
| Machines | Scheduling of maintenance, i.e. defer, hire or transfer from other functions | Scheduling of maintenance, i.e. advance<br>Subcontract or transfer to other functions |
| Labour | Hours worked, i.e. overtime<br>rearrangement of hours, shifts, holidays | Hours worked, i.e. short time rearrangement of hours, shifts, holidays |
| | Workforce size, i.e. staffing levels<br>temporary labour<br>transfer from other areas | Workforce size, i.e. layoffs, transfer to other areas |

## Strategy 2: Eliminate or reduce the need for adjustments in system capacity

In some cases it may be impossible, undesirable or time-consuming to provide for temporary adjustment in system capacity. In general it will be difficult to provide for temporary capacity adjustments in systems which employ large quantities of a large variety of resources, without incurring considerable expense and/or delay. Complex process plants which normally work around the clock present little scope for capacity adjustments to meet temporary demand increases, while reductions in demand will often give rise to under-utilization of major resources. Similarly, in systems which use highly specialized resources such as skilled labour, it may be desirable to avoid the need for temporary capacity adjustments.

In such situations a strategy of minimizing the need for system capacity adjustments will be more appealing. The adoption of such a strategy might involve the provision of excess capacity and therefore the acceptance of perhaps considerable under-utilization of resources, in order to increase the probability of being able to meet high or even maximum demand. Such an approach might be desirable where there is little possibility of providing temporary increases in capacity, and where customer service is of paramount importance. Examples of such situations might include an emergency ambulance service, power station or hospital emergency ward. The provision of some excess capacity, yet insufficient to meet maximum demand, necessitates the acceptance that during periods of peak demand either customers will be lost or they must wait or queue until demand levels fall. In practice such an approach is frequently adopted, for in many cases very considerable excess resources must be provided to ensure that peak demand can be satisfied.

In systems where output stocks can exist, the provision of inventories of goods is a conventional strategy for the smoothing of demand. Such inventories not only insulate the function from fluctuations in demand levels and thus facilitate the use of relatively stable resource levels and high utilization, but also enable customers to be provided with goods with little delay. Many systems operate in this fashion, e.g. the production of domestic appliances, vehicles, building materials, etc. The manufacture of Christmas cards, fireworks and goods subject to seasonal demand fluctuations is often undertaken on this basis, especially where resources cannot readily be used for other purposes. A similar situation exists where customer waiting or queuing is feasible. In such cases, despite a fluctuating demand rate, the rate at which customers are dealt with, i.e. the system capacity, might remain fairly stable. Bus and rail services are frequently intended to operate in this manner. Similar situations might exist at times of peak demand in both manufacture and supply, e.g. the bespoke tailor and the retail shop.

To summarize:

(a) It is possible to eliminate the need for adjustments in capacity if sufficient capacity is provided to deal with all future demand.

(b) It is possible to reduce the need for adjustments in capacity if:

  (i) the capacity level which is provided will be sufficient to cope with most demand situations, but, when that capacity is insufficient, one or both of the following situations is accepted:

    loss of trade

    customer queuing/waiting

  (ii) output stocks are provided to absorb demand fluctuations.

This strategy for capacity management is outlined in Table 11.4. These four approaches can be used individually or in combination.

Notice that only 2b(i) with customer queuing and 2b(ii) will enable us to deal with demand reductions without reducing resource utilization. Notice also that the provision of excess capacity alone is rarely a sufficient basis for accommodating demand fluctuations. In most cases it will be necessary to take some action aimed at reducing or smoothing the *effect* of fluctuations on the function, i.e. approaches 2b(i) and 2b(ii).

## Factors influencing the choice of strategy

### Operating system structure and function (feasibility factors)

In many cases organizations would prefer to have demand-level fluctuations eliminated or reduced. To some extent they may be able to smooth demand by offering inducements or by requiring customers to wait. Failing or following these efforts to reduce the effects of demand-level fluctuations, operations managers will seek to accommodate fluctuations by adjusting capacity. However, the opportunities (or indeed the need) to adopt these strategies for capacity planning will be influenced or limited by the structure of the system. We only need to consider those structures in which resource stocks are maintained, since capacity planning as outlined above is needed only where resources are acquired in

**Table 11.4 Methods for eliminating or reducing the need for capacity adjustment (strategy 2)**

| Method | Relevance for: Dealing with demand increases | Relevance for: Dealing with demand decreases |
|---|---|---|
| (a) *Eliminate adjustment by:* Maintaining sufficient excess capacity | Yes | Not directly relevant |
| (b) *Reduce/minimize adjustment by:* | | |
| (i) Some excess capacity, together with: | | |
| Loss of trade *and/or* | Yes (ignore some demand) | Not directly relevant |
| Customer queuing | Yes (increase queue) | Yes (reduce queue) |
| (ii) Output stocks | Yes (reduce stock) | Yes (increase stock) |

anticipation of requirements. In these cases capacity planning will aim to deal with uncertainty about the number of orders to be received and perhaps also uncertainty about the resources needed to satisfy the orders received. The feasibility of each strategy for each of the four structures is outlined in Figure 11.8 and discussed below.

Operating systems which provide for output stocks permit accommodation of fluctuations in demand level through the use of physical stocks, which not only protect the function against unexpected changes in demand level but also permit a relatively stable level of function activity and thus high resource utilization. The stock levels employed will often reflect the variability of demand and the 'service level' to be provided.

Systems which are unable to operate with output stocks will in most cases have relatively fixed capacity, and hence during temporary high-demand periods they will either require customer waiting or suffer loss of trade. Since some excess capacity will normally be provided, capacity utilization will often be low, especially when demand is highly variable.

Transport and service systems do not permit function in anticipation of demand, so either a relatively fixed capacity will be under-utilized despite efforts to maximize the ability of the system to adjust, or customer queuing will be required. The queue size will depend on relative levels and variabilities of demand and function capacity, and in some cases, through the use of scheduling (e.g. appointment) systems, customer queuing can be planned.

## Operations management objectives (desirability factors)

In Chapter 1 we identified the 'twin' objectives of operations management as providing customer service and achieving resource utilization. The emphasis given to these objectives will vary, and this relative emphasis will influence the approach employed in capacity planning. For example, the need to provide high customer service even at the expense of resource utilization will encourage the provision of excess capacity and/or output stocks. The influence of objectives on capacity planning is illustrated

**Figure 11.8** Capacity planning strategies for systems with resource stocks. From Wild, R. (1977) *Concepts for Operations Management*. New York: Wiley. Reproduced with permission

| STRATEGY / STRUCTURE | 1. PROVIDE FOR EFFICIENT ADJUSTMENT OF SYSTEM CAPACITY | 2. ELIMINATE OR REDUCE NEED FOR ADJUSTMENT OF SYSTEM CAPACITY | | | |
|---|---|---|---|---|---|
| | | (a) Maintain sufficient excess capacity | (b) Reduce or smooth effect of demand level fluctuations | | |
| | | | (i) Capacity limit with effect of | | (ii) Use stock to absorb demand fluctuations |
| | | | Loss of trade | Customer queuing/waiting | |
| ⇒▽⇒○⇒▽⇒C | Feasible and often desirable to supplement strategy 2b (ii) | Feasible, but not necessary | Feasible, but not normally necessary | Waiting feasible, but not normally necessary | Feasible and normally adopted |
| ⇒▽⇒○⇒C | Feasible and often desirable to supplement strategy 2b (i) | Feasible and may be necessary in conjunction with or instead of 2b(i) | Feasible and normally adopted | Waiting feasible and normally adopted | Not feasible |
| ⇒▽⇒<br>C⇒ ○⇒ | Feasible and desirable in conjunction with 2a | Feasible and normally adopted | Might be feasible depending on nature of function | Not feasible | Not feasible |
| ⇒▽⇒<br>C⇒▽⇒ ○⇒ | Feasible and often desirable to supplement strategy 2b(i) | Feasible, but not necessary | Feasible and might be adopted | Queuing feasible and normally adopted | Not feasible |

in the following cases, while Figure 11.9 provides a 'decision tree' type of approach to the selection of capacity management strategies and suggests the relationship of these strategies to the two basic operations management objectives.

## EXAMPLES

The types of approach which may be used in capacity planning in three contrasting cases are summarized in Table 11.5 and outlined below.

### Building (of 'one-off' houses to customer order)

Here we shall consider the special 'one-off' house builder who neither has a permanent labour force nor owns much equipment. In effect, on receipt of an order from a customer the builder acquires all the resources necessary for the satisfaction of the order. In this case the capacity management problem is relatively simple. The determination of the capacity needed is a straightforward problem, since no capacity (i.e. no resources) is provided prior to receipt of the customer's order. There is therefore no need to attempt to forecast demand. Demand is in effect measured and sufficient capacity is then provided to meet that demand, i.e. to satisfy that order. Theoretically at least, the development of a strategy for the utilization of resources is straightforward, since there is never the need to provide for efficient adjustment of capacity or the need to eliminate or reduce the need for such adjustment. In practice, however, since in such situations all orders will be different, it may be difficult to determine exactly how much of each resource is required. For example, the quantity of each type of building material can only be estimated and the amount of labour required will depend on a variety of factors. In practice, therefore, there will be a need *either* to ensure that further capacity can be provided if enough is not obtained initially *and/or* to eliminate or reduce the need for adjustment in system capacity by the provision of excess capacity. Hence the capacity planning strategy adopted will often consist of:

**Figure 11.9** 'Decision tree' type approach to the selection of capacity management strategies. Derived from an original by B. Melville, University of Waikato, New Zealand

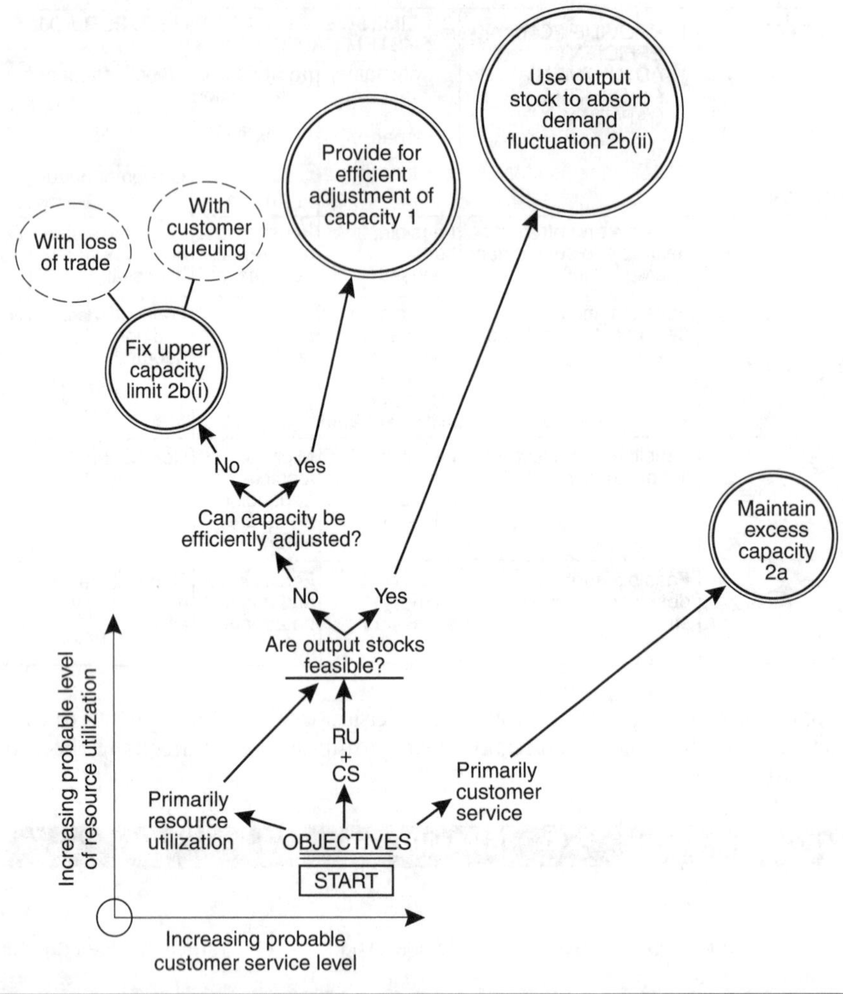


(a) provision for efficient adjustment of system capacity through, for example, subcontracting, transferring material, labour and machinery from other jobs, increasing hours worked and/or labour force; and/or

(b) eliminating or reducing the need for adjustment in system capacity by providing excess capacity.

Customer service will be one principal objective in determining and managing capacity in such systems. Apart from price, which in part will be influenced by the resource utilization expected, delivery or completion time will be the main variable affecting the probability of receiving orders. The customer service objective will therefore be manifest in attempts to minimize building time. In addition the building operations manager will of course seek to ensure that resource productivity is high, so that costs can be kept down, and will therefore seek to satisfy a partly competing objective by ensuring that equipment, labour and materials are all sufficiently highly utilized. Therefore strategy 2b(i) above may be favoured when requirements are being planned.

## Fire service

In this case we can consider the normal system structure to provide input resource stocks but no input queue of customers, since it will usually be the intention of the fire service to ensure that appliances, etc. are 'standing

**Table 11.5 The nature of capacity management: examples**

| Example | Operating system structure | Capacity management: Determination of capacity required | Capacity management: Capacity planning strategy (see Figure 11.8) | Principal objectives |
|---|---|---|---|---|
| Builder (of 'one-off' houses) | →○→C | Demand is measured. Capacity is provided to meet each demand. | 1 and/or 2b(i), i.e. provide for capacity adjustment and/or some excess capacity. | Maximum customer service (in particular through minimizing completion time) + Maximum utilization of (consumed) resource |
| Fire service | →▽→○→, C→○ | Expected demand is forecast. Capacity is provided to meet maximum or near maximum demand. | 2a with some possibility of 1, i.e. eliminate or reduce need for adjustment in system by providing excess capacity with further possibility of providing some capacity adjustment. | No customer queuing + High resource productivity |
| Furniture removal | →▽→○→, C→▽→○ | Expected demand is forecast. Capacity is provided to meet average or 'sufficient' demand. | 2b(i) (with customer queuing and possibly loss of trade), with possibility of 1, i.e. eliminate or reduce need for adjustment in system capacity by smoothing effect of demand-level fluctuations through fixing upper capacity limit and accepting loss of trade with the further possibility of providing some capacity adjustment. | Minimum customer queuing and/or loss of trade + High resource productivity |

by' for calls. There will, of course, be situations, such as major disasters, in which all available resources are committed and hence new customers must wait, but here we shall consider the capacity management problem for the normal, i.e. the intended, situation.

Expected demand will be forecast and enough capacity will doubtless be provided to meet substantially more than average demand. In effect, therefore, capacity planning strategy 2a, i.e. eliminate or reduce the need for adjustment in system capacity through the 'provision of excess capacity', is adopted. Undoubtedly the emphasis will be on this approach.

However, there may also be some possibility of providing for some degree of capacity adjustment (i.e. strategy 1) through, for example, subcontracting work (to neighbouring fire services), transferring resources from other jobs (e.g. maintenance, practices, etc.) and temporary yet rapid increases in the labour force or hours worked (use of standby labour, etc.).

The principal objective in capacity planning will be the maintenance of the system structure, i.e. to ensure that no customer queuing occurs, coupled of course with reasonably high capacity utilization. In practice the customer service criterion will often be satisfactorily attained at the cost of poor resource productivity.

### *Furniture removal*

This differs from the above example in offering a far wider range of alternative approaches to capacity management. Here input resources will be stocked and will be utilized on jobs drawn from an available queue.

Again expected demand will be forecast and on this basis a certain capacity will be provided. Unlike in the case of the fire service, there will be no necessity to meet high demand and in practice capacity will be provided which is sufficient to meet near average demand or 'sufficient' demand – 'sufficient' being defined by management as that proportion of available demand which management choose to seek to satisfy. Having established a normal capacity in this way, the operations manager must choose whether, and if so how, to provide for efficient capacity adjustment (strategy 1) and/or whether, and if so how, to eliminate or reduce the need for such adjustments (strategy 2). Both strategies are feasible and might be implemented as follows:

(a) provision for efficient adjustment of system capacity, through for example subcontracting work, transfer of resources from other jobs, rescheduling activities, temporary changes in staffing or hours;

(b) eliminating or reducing the need for adjustment in system capacity through

  (i) providing excess capacity (although this is normally neither necessary nor adopted)

  (ii) reducing or smoothing the effect of demand level changes by fixing an upper capacity limit and normally requiring customers to queue, and in some cases accepting some loss of trade.

The principal objective in capacity planning here will be the provision of an acceptable level of customer service by minimizing average waiting time or queue length and thus minimizing the loss of customers, coupled with providing for high resource productivity, i.e. utilization of resources.

## CAPACITY PLANNING PROCEDURES

In this section we shall describe some of the procedures which may be used in capacity planning. Before going into detail two general points will be made.

### Aggregation

The term *aggregate planning* is often employed in the capacity context (see Figure 11.1). The implication is that such planning is concerned with *total* demand, i.e. all demands collected together. This is of relevance in operating systems where different goods or services are provided. In such cases capacity planning will seek to estimate or measure all demands and express the total in such a way as to enable enough of all resources (or total capacity) to be provided. Demand for all outputs must therefore be expressed in common capacity-related units such as the number of resources or resource hours required (see for example, Table 11.1). An operating system may, for example, provide three types of service, or service three types of customer. The estimated demand for each source expressed in, for example, hours per unit time (e.g. week) required for each type of resource must be identified and totalled. Given this aggregate demand, an overall capacity plan can be developed to cope with all demands.

### Economic operating levels *(see also Chapter 4)*

Figure 11.10 shows the relationship between the unit cost of processing and the throughput rate for a hypothetical situation. It will be evident from the figure that the economic throughput rate is $p^1$ since this is the rate at which the unit cost is least. The use of a higher throughput rate involves higher unit

**Figure 11.10** Unit cost/volume relationship

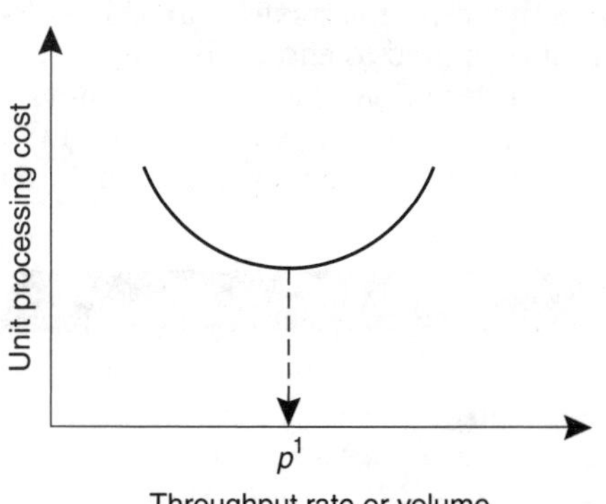


**Figure 11.11** Unit cost/volume relationships

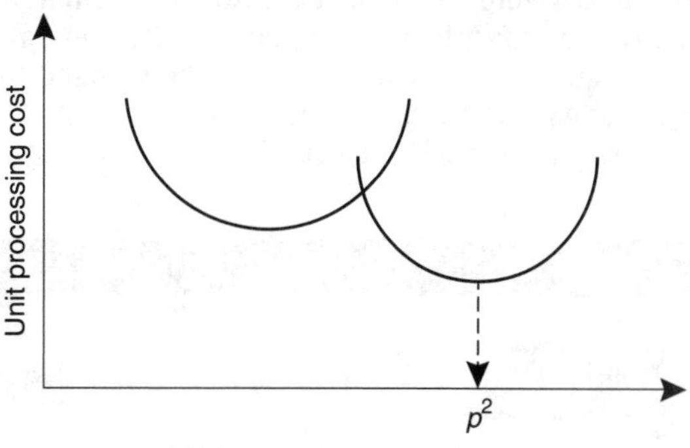


costs, as does a lower throughput rate. Such a situation will often exist, especially where an operating system has been designed specifically to process items or customers at a particular rate. For example, in a flow processing system involving a series of interdependent facilities, the entire system must be designed to provide a particular output or throughput rate. If the output rate is reduced, then costs will increase because of facility idle time, etc., and if the output rate is increased, then subcontracting, overtime work, duplicate facilities, etc. will be required, all of which will contribute to the unit output costs.

If it is now considered appropriate to increase the level of resources in order to provide for a greater throughput rate, then it may be possible to shift the entire curve as shown in Figure 11.11. This implies that the facilities have been rearranged or set up in a different manner so that the intended rate is now $p^2$. Again, departures from this throughput rate $p^2$ can incur increased unit costs.

This concept of an 'economic operating level' is relevant in many situations and is of value in capacity planning since, where curves such as those shown in Figure 11.10 and 11.11 are available or can be approximated, the cost of changing capacity through the adoption of capacity planning strategy 1 can be established for different magnitudes of change.

Notice that in some situations the cost–throughput rate relationship is not a 'smooth' one. For example, in some situations a throughput rate can be increased only incrementally. However, whatever the nature of the relationship, provided it is known or can be approximated, the economic level of operations can be found and the cost of capacity changes above or below a particular level can be obtained.

In the remainder of this chapter we shall look at capacity (or aggregate) planning procedures. We shall consider only a few of the many procedures which are available, the intention being to illustrate the types of approach which might be employed.

Most of the available procedures are relevant only in particular situations and deal only with particular types of capacity planning problems. In introducing each of the procedures below we shall first try to indicate where the approach might be employed and for what particular purpose.

## Cumulative graphs

This is a procedure for comparing alternative capacity plans for a period, particularly where there is a need to balance the costs of changing capacity against cost of insufficient or extra capacity. The capacity provided to satisfy estimated demand will, as shown above, be influenced by the strategy employed for meeting demand fluctuations. The use of cumulative graphs is a method of examining alternatives.

Table 11.6 gives the estimated monthly demand for a one-year period. The figures are plotted cumulatively in Figure 11.12, which also shows three possible cumulative capacity curves. Curve 1 corresponds to a capacity of 37.5 resource hours per day – the minimum required to ensure that capacity is always equal to or in excess of expected demand for this period. The adoption of a strategy of providing sufficient excess capacity to eliminate the need for capacity adjustment (strategy 2a) would lead to the provision of such capacity. The provision of approximately 30 resource hours per day (curve 2)

**Table 11.6 Estimated monthly demand**

| Month | Working days | Cumulative days | Estimated demand (in resource hours) | Cumulative estimated demand |
|---|---|---|---|---|
| Jan. | 20 | 20 | 500 | 500 |
| Feb. | 18 | 38 | 650 | 1150 |
| Mar. | 22 | 60 | 750 | 1900 |
| Apr. | 18 | 78 | 900 | 2800 |
| May | 21 | 99 | 700 | 3500 |
| June | 20 | 119 | 500 | 4000 |
| July | 20 | 139 | 300 | 4300 |
| Aug. | 10 | 149 | 300 | 4600 |
| Sept. | 20 | 169 | 450 | 5050 |
| Oct. | 21 | 190 | 500 | 5550 |
| Nov. | 20 | 210 | 550 | 6100 |
| Dec. | 18 | 228 | 300 | 6400 |

**Figure 11.12** Cumulative demand and capacity curves

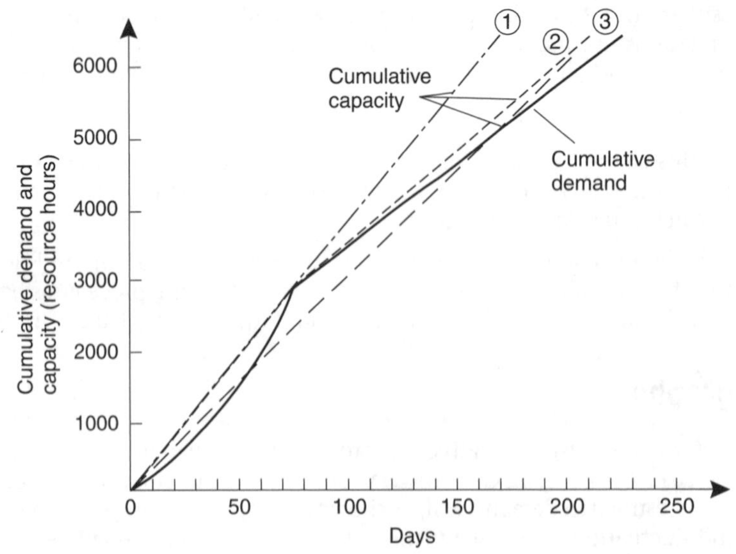

might result from the adoption of a different strategy for the use of resources (strategy 2b(i)). Such an arrangement would mean either increasing output stock or reducing customer waiting time during the period up to day 50 and after day 160, when capacity exceeds demand. Day 50 to day 160 would see:

(a) stock diminishing or depleted; and/or

(b) increased customer waiting time; and/or

(c) loss of trade

Both curves 1 and 2 require no capacity adjustment during this period. The adoption of an approach relying wholly on or involving the strategy of providing for efficient adjustment in capacity (strategy 1) might give rise to the provision of capacity in the manner of curve 3, in which one capacity adjustment is made (at day 75) and which provides for the satisfaction of all forecast demand without the use of output stocks, customer queuing or loss of trade, yet with better capacity utilization than curve 1.

It will be possible to cost these three (and other) alternative strategies if the cost of changing capacity and the costs of having insufficient capacity (e.g. cost of lost customers) and extra capacity (e.g. cost of stock) are known.

*Note*: In practice the use of cumulative graphs in capacity planning must take into account the lead time normally required between the use of capacity or resources and the satisfaction of customers. For example, the expected customer demand in April equivalent to 900 resource hours (Table 11.6) would necessitate the provision of appropriate capacity at an earlier period. Hence the capacity curves in Figure 11.12 should in fact be displaced forward by the amount of this lead time. Similarly, the use of such curves must take into account the situation which exists at the start of the planning period. For example, if an output stock exists at day 0 then any cumulative capacity curve must start above point 0 on the *y* axis.

## Linear programming *(see also Appendix I)*

This approach provides a means of allocating available capacity and inventories against a forward demand in such a way as to balance these costs and smooth the level of operations. This is relevant only where strategy 2b(ii) is possible alongside other strategies.

Various linear programming methods have been used in this context. Here we shall concentrate on the use of the 'transportation' algorithm. The 'transportation' method of linear programming provides a means of minimizing a combination of capacity and inventory costs. Various alternative means of providing capacity are recognized, typically normal working, overtime working and subcontracting. The use of the method requires that demands for each of several periods are satisfied from inventory and/or from the use of normal plus, if necessary, additional capacity in such a manner that total costs are minimized. The approach has one major disadvantage in that it is static, i.e. it is a method for formulating policy for a given period assuming no changes in circumstances, etc. during that period. Repeated recalculations for a forward period will overcome this to some extent, but there is a danger of sub-optimization.

For the sake of easy illustration let us consider a manufacturing situation in which planning is necessary for only four sales and production periods ($n = 4$). The sales demand during each of these periods is represented by $S_1$, $S_2$, $S_3$ and $S_4$ and this demand may be met from one of the following:

(a) stock;

(b) 'regular' production during the normal shifts;

(c) overtime production.

The costs associated with each of these are:

(a) storage – $C_I$ – cost of storage per unit per period;

(b) regular production – $C_R$ – cost of production per unit per period;

(c) overtime production – $C_O$ – cost of production per unit per period.

**Table 11.7 Matrix of costs associated with production, stock and demand during four periods**

| Production period | | Sales period 1 | 2 | 3 | 4 | Final stock | Total capacity |
|---|---|---|---|---|---|---|---|
| 0 | Opening stock | 0 | $C_I$ | $2C_I$ | $3C_I$ | $4C_I$ | $I_0$ |
| 1 | Regular production | – | $C_R$ | $C_R + C_I$ | $C_R + 2C_I$ | $C_R + 3C_I$ | $R_1$ |
| | Overtime production | – | $C_O$ | $C_O + C_I$ | $C_O + 2C_I$ | $C_O + 3C_I$ | $O_1$ |
| 2 | Regular production | – | – | $C_R$ | $C_R + C_I$ | $C_R + 2C_I$ | $R_2$ |
| | Overtime production | – | – | $C_O$ | $C_O + C_I$ | $C_O + 2C_I$ | $O_2$ |
| 3 | Regular production | – | – | – | $C_R$ | $C_R + C_I$ | $R_3$ |
| | Overtime Production | – | – | – | $C_O$ | $C_O + C_I$ | $O_3$ |
| Total demand during period | | $S_1$ | $S_2$ | $S_3$ | $S_4$ | | |

*Notation* $I_i$ = stock level at end of *i*th period

$R_i$ = max. no. of units that can be produced on regular time during *i*th period

$O_i$ = max. no. of units that can be produced on overtime during *i*th period

We might further assume that items produced during one period are not available to the customer until the following period; consequently some initial stock must be available to satisfy demand for sales period 1. We can now represent the unit costs as a 'transportation' matrix as shown in Table 11.7.

Notice that certain cells contain dashes, since these represent impossible routes. (The production from one period cannot be used to satisfy demand for an earlier period. In order to ensure that these cells do not feature as part of the solution it is conventional to allocate extremely high cost values to them.) To indicate how this table has been constructed consider period 2. Sales during this period may be satisfied from stock which has incurred cost associated with storage for one period, i.e. $C_I$, or from production which was undertaken during the previous period at cost $C_R$ for regular production and $C_O$ for overtime production. The case shown in Table 11.7 deals only with one product; however, this method can easily be extended to cover production planning for two or more products merely by constructing two or more columns for each of the sales periods and for final stock.

Furthermore, it is not necessary that the costs of production, $C_R$ and $C_O$, or the costs of storage, $C_I$, should be the same for each period or each product.

**EXAMPLE**

Two very similar products, A and B, are to be manufactured. The total demand for each for three future periods is:

Period 1 A = 100 B = 50

Period 2 A = 70 B = 105

Period 3 A = 50 B = 125

It is estimated that the stock of products at the beginning of period 1 will be:

A = 150

B = 75

The cost of stockholding per product per period, $C_I$, is £2. The costs of production are as follows:

For production during period 1:

| | |
|---|---|
| Product A | $C_R$ = £1 per product |
| | $C_O$ = £2 per product |
| Product B | $C_R$ = £1 per product |
| | $C_O$ = £2 per product |

For production during period 2:

| | |
|---|---|
| Product A | $C_R$ = £2 per product |
| | $C_O$ = £3 per product |
| Product B | $C_R$ = £2 per product |
| | $C_O$ = £3 per product |

The production capacity per period is as follows.

| | |
|---|---|
| Period 1 | regular production = 125 units (of either type) |
| | overtime production = 50 units (of either type) |
| Period 2 | regular production = 125 units (of either type) |
| | overtime production = 50 units (of either type) |

**Table 11.8 Costs associated with a three-period production plan for three products**

| Production period | | Sales period | | | | | | Final stock | | Total capacity (both products) |
|---|---|---|---|---|---|---|---|---|---|---|
| | | 1 | | 2 | | 3 | | | | |
| | | Product | | Product | | Product | | Product | | |
| | | A | B | A | B | A | B | A | B | |
| 0 | Opening stock | 0 | 0 | 2 | 2 | 4 | 4 | 6 | 6 | 225 |
| 1 | Regular production | | | 1 | 1 | 3 | 3 | 5 | 5 | 125 |
| | Overtime production | | | 2 | 2 | 4 | 4 | 6 | 6 | 50 |
| 2 | Regular production | | | | | 2 | 2 | 4 | 4 | 125 |
| | Overtime production | | | | | 3 | 3. | 5 | 5 | 50 |
| Total demand during period | | 100 | 50 | 70 | 105 | 50 | 125 | | 75 | (575) |

What is the optimal production plan and what is the cost associated with satisfying the above demands?

The cost matrix is shown in Table 11.8. Using the transportation methods of linear programming described in Appendix I, the solution shown in Table 11.9 can easily be obtained. The cost associated with this production plan is as follows:

$$\begin{aligned} &100(0) + 50(0) + 70(2) + 5(2) \\ &+100(1) + 25(3) \\ &+ 25(4) + 25(4) \\ &+100(2) + 25(4) \\ &+ 50(5) \qquad = £1075 \end{aligned}$$

**Table 11.9 Three-period production plan for two products**

| Production period | | Sales period | | | | | | Final stock | Total capacity (both products) |
|---|---|---|---|---|---|---|---|---|---|
| | | 1 | | 2 | | 3 | | | |
| | | Product | | Product | | Product | | Product | |
| | | $A_0$ | $B_0$ | $A_2$ | $B_2$ | $A_4$ | $B_4$ | $A+B_6$ | |
| 0 | Opening stock $_0$ | $100_0$ | $50_0$ | $70_2$ | $5_2$ | 4 | 4 | 6 | 225 |
| 1 | Regular production $_{-1}$ | | | 1 | $100_1$ | $25_3$ | 3 | 5 | 125 |
| | Overtime production $_0$ | | | 2 | 2 | $25_4$ | $25_4$ | 6 | 50 |
| 2 | Regular production $_{-2}$ | | | | | 2 | $100_2$ | 25 4 | 125 |
| | Overtime production $_{-1}$ | | | | | 3 | 3 | 50 5 | 50 |
| Total demand | | 100 | 50 | 70 | 105 | 50 | 125 | 75 | |

Notice that in this solution a proportion of both regular and overtime production during production period 2 is delivered to stock. This is necessary because production capacity during this period is in excess of demand. If, however, the total production capacity in any period need not be used then our solution would have involved the production of 100 of product A during regular production in period 2. This would result in a saving of 25(4) + 50(5), i.e. £350, during this period, but of course no opening stock would be available for the next period.

## Heuristic methods

These methods are largely concerned with workforce or capacity smoothing. They may be of relevance where there is a need to balance costs of capacity change with costs of inventories, i.e. strategies 1 and 2b(ii). A 'heuristic' method provides a good, but not necessarily the best, solution. In reality most operations management decisions are heuristic or, more colloquially, 'rules of thumb'.

The *management coefficients* model uses a simplified version of the workforce production level decision rules incorporated in the *linear decision rule* method. Coefficients for these rules are determined by regression analysis on historical performance, i.e. managers' actual past behaviour. The equation is then used to indicate the future decisions as with the linear decision rules.

An alternative approach involves a *search* of feasible solutions to establish the coefficients for the linear decision rule method. The coefficients are established to minimize total cost and the two equations are then used for planning purposes. Two approaches have been developed. The parametric production planning model deals with inventory, workforce changes, overtime costs and customer queuing. The search decision rule is of a similar nature.

## Queuing theory methods

Such approaches may be of relevance in determining the capacity required in service and transport systems and/or in deciding levels of utilization of capacity and customer service levels. Transport and service systems depend on an input provided by the beneficiary of the service and 'processing' cannot take place until that is available. Because of this time dependence, capacity planning is constrained and such systems cannot usually achieve the same levels of resource productivity as manufacture or supply systems. However, some such systems improve utilization by scheduling inputs, i.e. by controlling them (e.g. appointments systems for GPs, dentists, etc., and certain types of transport system). In other situations (e.g. roads, hospitals, shops), since there is little control of input arrival rate, adequate capacity must be provided to meet peak demand without excessive 'customer' waiting time (strategy 2a and 2b). Outside peak demand periods, low utilization must be tolerated unless alternative services can be provided. Queuing theory may be used in capacity planning in such situations.

Although input 'arrivals' may follow specific patterns, the overall pattern in many cases is random. This gives rise to queuing situations. The methods used to describe and analyse queuing situations depend on the form of the system, in particular:

(a) number of servicing units;

(b) configuration of servicing units, i.e. whether in parallel or in series;

(c) queue discipline;

(d) distribution of arrival times;

(e) distribution of service times.

The simplest case is shown in Figure 11.13.

Let:

$P_n$ = probability of $n$ units in system (i.e. queue + one being serviced)

$L$ = average number of units in system

**Figure 11.13** Simple queuing situation

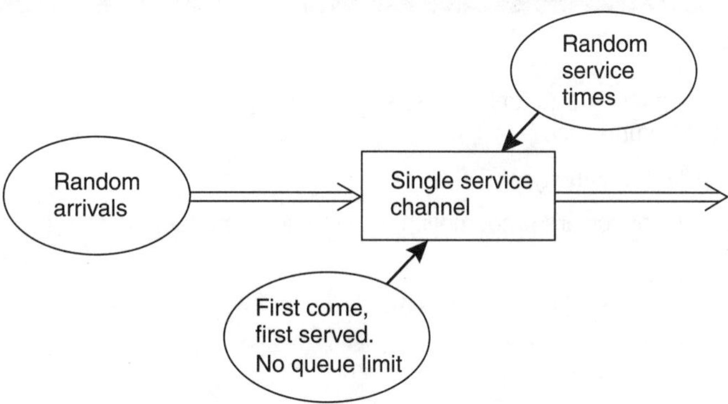

$L_q$ = average number of units in queue
$W$ = average time units spend in system
$W_q$ = average time units spend in queue

where:

$\lambda$ = average arrival rate (units/period of time)
$\mu$ = average service rate (units/period of time)

$\rho$ = utilization parameter = $\dfrac{\lambda}{\mu}$

$\mu > \lambda$

If there are $\lambda$ arrivals/h and the system has a capacity of $\mu$/h, the system will be busy $\dfrac{\lambda}{\mu}$ proportion of time and idle $\left(1 - \dfrac{\lambda}{\mu}\right)$ proportion of time. Thus:

$P_0$ (probability of no units in system)

$$= 1 - \frac{\lambda}{\mu}$$

It can also be shown that:

$$L = \frac{\lambda}{\mu - \lambda}$$

$$L_q = \frac{\lambda^2}{\mu(\mu - \lambda)}$$

N.B. $L_q$ does not equal $L - 1$ since for some of the time the service channel is empty; the average number being served $\neq 1$.

$$W = \frac{1}{\mu - \lambda}$$

and $W_q = \dfrac{\lambda}{\mu(\mu - \lambda)}$

**EXAMPLE**

A new hospital is to be designed. If one ambulance is provided, what will be its utilization and what will be the average waiting time for the ambulance?

Taking data from a similar community:

1. Emergency calls for ambulances are random with an average of one per hour (half due to accidents and half due to various illnesses).
2. Time required for ambulance round trip is random with an average of ½ hour (i.e two per hour).

Hence $\lambda = 1$

$\mu = 2$

$$W_q = \frac{1}{\mu(\mu - \lambda)} \quad = ½ \text{ hour}$$

$$P_0 = 1 - \frac{\lambda}{\mu} \quad = ½$$

$$L_q = \frac{\lambda^2}{\mu(\mu - \lambda)} \quad = 0.5$$

i.e. for one ambulance, average waiting time = ½ hour, but the ambulance is busy only half of the time.

## CHECKLIST FOR CHAPTER 11

Capacity management as a strategic operations decision area

### *Operations planning and control*

Operations planning: definition
Operations control: definition
The stages in operations planning and control

### *Capacity management*

Nature of capacity management
Capacity management: definition
Nature of capacity
Measures of capacity
Examples of capacity planning problems

### *The normal capacity required*

Forecasting
- Moving averages
- Exponential smoothing

Life-cycles
Factors affecting capacity
Learning and improvement
Reliability

### *Dealing with demand fluctuations*

Strategies for use of capacity
- Strategy 1: adjustment
- Strategy 2: smoothing

Means of implementing strategies
Factors influencing capacity management
- Operating system structure and function
- Operations management objectives

Case examples of capacity management
- Builder
- Fire service
- Furniture removal

### *Capacity planning procedures*

Aggregation
Economic operating levels
Cumulative graphs
Linear programming
- Transportation method

Heuristic methods
- Management coefficients
- Search

Queuing theory

## FURTHER READING

**Eilon, S. (1975)** Five approaches to aggregate production planning. *AIIE Transactions*, **7**(2), pp. 118–131.

**Jarrett, J. (1991)** *Business Forecasting Methods*, 2nd edn. Oxford: Basil Blackwell.

**Vollman, T. E., Berry, W.L. and Whybark, D. C. (1988)** *Manufacturing Planning and Control Systems*. Homewood, Ill.: Irwin.

## QUESTIONS

11.1 A small company is engaged in the manufacture of automatic 'gigglecocks' for three principal customers, Smith, Brown and Jones. These three customers are in the habit of placing their orders for a four-week period three weeks in advance; a set of orders has just been received by the company and is shown on the right.

Given the following information, determine the optimal production plan and the cost associated with the satisfaction of these orders for automatic gigglecocks according to such a plan.

| **Customer** | **Quality to be delivered during week number** | | | |
|---|---|---|---|---|
| | **26** | **27** | **28** | **29** |
| Smith | 10 | 14 | 20 | 15 |
| Brown | 14 | 20 | 25 | 17 |
| Jones | 7 | 9 | 10 | 7 |
| Total | 31 | 43 | 55 | 39 |

| | |
|---|---|
| Stockholding cost per gigglecock per week | = £1 |
| Production cost per gigglecock | = £10 during normal shift work |
| | = £15 during night-shift work |
| 'Free' stock of gigglecocks at end of week 25 | = 35 |
| Production capacity each week | = 35 gigglecocks in normal shifts |
| | = 15 gigglecocks in night shifts |

No stock is required at the end of week 29.

11.2 What are the two basic capacity planning strategies? Describe with examples the use of each and their use together.

11.3 Table 1 shows the number of each of two products, A and B, which have recently been ordered from company X for delivery to customers during the four months May to August.

Each of the two products consists of two sub-assemblies (I and II or II and III) as shown in Table 2. Table 2 also gives the work hours of production for each sub-assembly.

The company works a three-shift system. The production capacity in work hours per shift is shown in Table 3.

The company is in the habit of planning production for several months ahead, each additional customer order being included in the production plan when it is received. The production plan prior to the receipt of the recent orders is shown in terms of work hours of production capacity required in Table 4.

Table 5 shows the unit production costs for each sub-assembly for each shift, while Table 6 gives the unit storage cost per sub-assembly per month.

Assume: (a) that the details of the existing

**Table 1 Demand from new orders**

| **Product** | **May** | **June** | **July** | **August** |
|---|---|---|---|---|
| A | 20 | 40 | 25 | 40 |
| B | 30 | 25 | 50 | 32 |

**Table 2 Sub-assemblies/product, and work hours/sub-assembly**

| **Product** | **Number of sub-assemblies per product** | | |
|---|---|---|---|
| | **I** | **II** | **III** |
| A | 1 | 1 | – |
| B | | 1 | 1 |
| Work hours production | 5 | 7 | 5 |

production plan cannot be altered; (b) that sub-assemblies manufactured during one month enable the products of which they are a part to be delivered to customers no later than the last day of the same month; (c) that there will be no sub-assemblies in stock at the end of April.

Formulate this planning problem as a linear programming problem; arrange the data in a manner which permits a linear programming algorithm to be used, but do not solve the problem. Comment on any important characteristic of the solution which is evident from the initial formulation.

**Table 3** Production capacity (work hours)/month

| | March to July inc. | August |
|---|---|---|
| Shift 1 | 400 | 400 |
| Shift 2 | 400 | 300 |
| Shift 3 | 400 | 300 |

**Table 4** Work hours committed to previous orders

| | March | April | May | June | July | August |
|---|---|---|---|---|---|---|
| Shift 1 | 300 | 250 | 250 | 200 | 150 | 100 |
| Shift 2 | 300 | 200 | 200 | 100 | 100 | 50 |
| Shift 3 | 300 | 200 | 200 | 50 | 100 | 50 |

**Table 5** Unit production cost (£)/sub-assembly

| | Sub-assembly | | | | | |
|---|---|---|---|---|---|---|
| | I | | II | | III | |
| Shift 1 | 5 | 6 | 6 | 7 | 4 | 5 |
| Shift 2 | 7 | 8 | 8 | 9 | 6 | 7 |
| Shift 3 | 7 | 8 | 8 | 9 | 6 | 7 |
| | March–July | August | March–July | August | March–July | August |

**Table 6** Unit storage cost/month

| Sub-assembly | £/month |
|---|---|
| I | 0.5 |
| II | 0.6 |
| III | 0.5 |

11.4 Identify and discuss the relevance of the various approaches available for the adjustment of capacity. Indicate what factors or considerations might encourage or prevent the use of each.

11.5 A company has decided to set up an interior design consultancy. It will provide a service for individuals and organizations on the design of rooms, offices, furnishings, decoration, etc. What type of capacity planning problems might be encountered (i.e. deciding the types and quantities of resources to be provided)?

## CASE STUDIES (from Part 9)

The topics covered in this chapter are relevant in the following (see Introduction to Part 9 and Table C.1 for further details):

| No. | Name | Country |
|---|---|---|
| 1 | Carreras SL | Spain |
| 4 | Qormi Post Office | Malta |
| 8 | Malcolm Seal | UK |
| 11 | St John's Church | UK |
| 17 | La Patisserie – A | UK |
| 19 | K&S (Israel) Ltd | Israel |
| 20 | TAARUP Farming Machines Ltd | Denmark |

PART 6

# Operations Scheduling

Introduction to Part 6
Chapter 12 Activity scheduling
Chapter 13 Project management and network scheduling
Chapter 14 Scheduling for batch processing
Chapter 15 The design and scheduling of flow processing systems

## INTRODUCTION TO PART 6

Here we deal with the scheduling (or planning or timing) of the conversion activities of the operating system. We try first to identify the different types of scheduling problems which can be encountered in different types of operating systems, and then consider some techniques for their solution. The techniques and the types of problems which are of particular importance are dealt with in depth in Chapters 13, 14 and 15.

The scheduling of the activities within the operating system is another principal problem area of operations management, as defined in Chapter 1. As with capacity management (see Introduction to Part 5), the strategies employed in activity scheduling will again be influenced by:

(a) feasibility constraints (influenced mainly by the operating system structure);

(b) desirability factors (influenced mainly by the organization's and operations manager's objectives).

The nature of the activity scheduling problem will be influenced by the operating system structure, but equally, activity scheduling decisions can change that structure. Further, the objectives being pursued by the operations manager, in particular the relative importance of resource utilization and customer service, will influence the selection of an activity scheduling strategy but, given some freedom of choice, the operations manager may prefer to employ an approach which insulates the operating system from external uncertainties, e.g. demand changes.

## STRATEGIC CONTEXT

The operations, issues, problems and decisions considered in this part of the book exist within the broader strategic context of the organization. The main relationships are set out here, as a preface to the details which follow.

### Influences of business policy decisions *(see Chapter 2, Figure 2.2)*

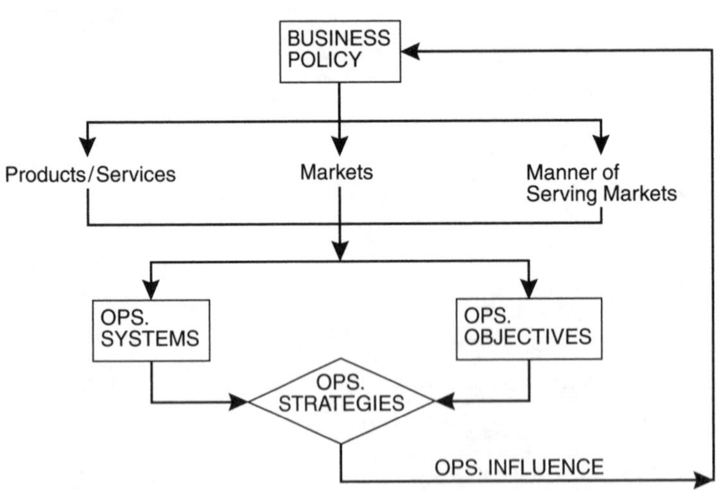


Like capacity management, scheduling decisions form one of the principal or key problem areas of operations management. Scheduling decisions – indeed the strategies employed in scheduling activities in and through operations – will, to a large extent, influence whether customer service objectives or resource utilization objectives are achieved.

How operations are scheduled – i.e. the broad approaches taken, not the particular scheduling techniques – will probably be influenced by operations objectives (which influence what should be achieved in customer service or resource utilization) and operating system structures (which may influence what is feasible – through, for example, the nature of the relationship with the customer). These two factors will in turn be influenced, if not determined, by business policies. If the policy of the business requires the provision of goods of a predetermined nature for certain markets, then the scheduling of operations must differ from what would have been required had it been the intention to provide goods to individual customers' specifications. The same situation applies in the provision of services – further, if customers on arrival at a service system must be dealt with immediately, the scheduling of activities will inevitably differ from that which would be possible if customer queues were expected. The latter may be influenced by policy objectives on customer service or indeed cost. Thus what a system provides, the nature of the markets, and the manner in which those markets are to be served will influence the strategies used in scheduling through their influence on operations objectives and systems structures.

Conversely, the existence of well-established and effective scheduling practices in operations should be allowed to influence the nature of any new business policies, as otherwise policy implementation may be ineffective, impossible, costly, or slow.

## **Competitive advantage** *(see Chapter 2, Figures 2.6 and 2.7)*

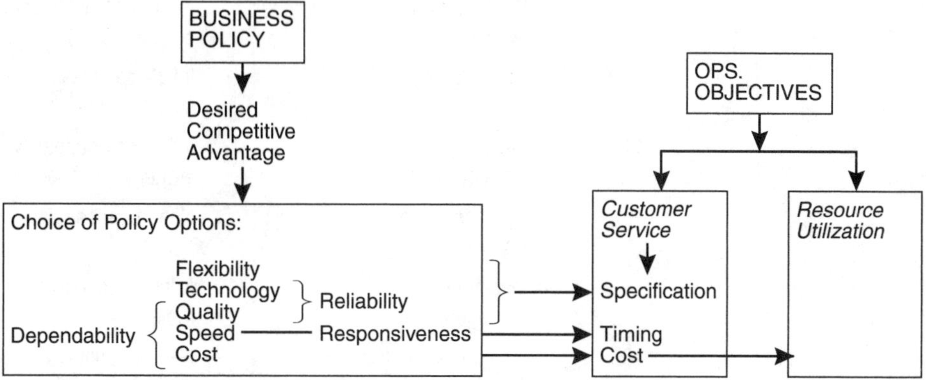


If we recall our discussion of policy options in Chapter 2 (e.g. Table 2.2), from which we derived the above model, it will be evident that a business policy which attaches importance to certain policy options must have a major impact on the requirements of scheduling. For example:

| **An emphasis on the following policy options** | **Gives rise to the following scheduling considerations** |
|---|---|
| Speed | Need to schedule service systems so that customers can be dealt with on arrival, without the need to queue |
| | Desirability of scheduling goods output in advance of requirements if possible, e.g. 'make to stock' rather than 'to order' |
| Cost | Need to ensure that activities are scheduled so as to achieve high resource utilization |
| Flexibility | Need to avoid fixed, long-term schedules |
| Responsiveness | Need to schedule operations so that total throughput times are minimized |

Naturally, given these major interdependencies, operations managers will wish to avoid a situation in which incompatible requirements are placed on existing scheduling systems, so they will wish to avoid a situation in which business policy changes require major changes in scheduling strategies for their implementation, unless the nature, cost and delays involved in such changes are understood. Further, they will wish to avoid a situation in which mixed and conflicting requirements are placed on scheduling, e.g. through the need to process items or customers for which there are differing cost, timing, etc. requirements.

## TOPIC MAP

| Topics in this Part | Related topics in other chapters: Chapter | Topic | Comments/aspects |
|---|---|---|---|
| Chapter 12 | | | |
| Strategies for scheduling | 1 | Operations management objectives<br>Structure of operations systems | Influence on scheduling strategies |
| | 8 | Work standards | Need for times/standards in scheduling |
| | | Learning effects | Influence of learning on scheduling times |
| | 11 | Capacity management | Influence of capacity strategy on scheduling |
| | 16 | Purchasing and supply | Need to schedule system inputs |
| | 17 | Inventory management | Need to schedule stock replenishment |
| | 18 | Operations control | Need to control operations against schedules |
| | 20 | Reliability | Effect of reliability on schedules |
| | 21 | Maintenance and replacement | Need to schedule |
| | 22 | Performance measurement | Need to measure performance against schedules (e.g. due dates) |
| Just in time | 2 | Operations policy | JIT as a policy for operations |
| | 4 | Operations economics | Effects of JIT on costs |
| | 6 | Facilitation layout<br>Materials handling | Effects of JIT on layouts, inventories and handling |
| | 7 | Technology | Technology (e.g. FMS) for JIT implementation |
| Types of scheduling problem | 1 | Operations objectives | Influence of service objectives |
| | 2<br>3 | Operations policy<br>Operations and marketing | Influence on nature of scheduling |

## TOPIC MAP

| Topics in this Part | Related topics in other chapters: Chapter | Topic | Comments/aspects |
|---|---|---|---|
| *Chapter 12 continued* | | | |
| Managing demand uncertainty | 3 | Operations and marketing | Effects of marketing decisions on demand |
| Activity scheduling techniques | 13 | Project planning | Network techniques |
| | 14 | Scheduling batches | Batch scheduling and sequencing |
| | 15 | Scheduling flow processes | Line balancing |
| | 17 | Inventory decisions | Scheduling batch processes |
| | 18 | Operations control | Kanban |
| | 21 | Maintenance and reliability | Interference |
| Balancing scheduling and control | 18 | Operations control | |
| Effectiveness of scheduling | 18 | Operations control | Effectiveness of scheduling and the need for control |
| | 22 | Performance measurement | Measurement of scheduling effectiveness |
| Chapter 13 | | | |
| Project management | 1 | Operations management systems | Types of operation |
| Project scheduling and control | 1 | Operations management objectives | Influence on scheduling strategies |
| | | Operating system structures | Influence on scheduling strategies |
| | 8 | Work measurement | Need for times/durations for schedules |
| | | Learning curve | Need to allow for learning in scheduling |
| | 11 | Operations planning and control | Scheduling decisions as an aspect of planning and control |
| | | Capacity management | Implementation of capacity strategy through scheduling |

## TOPIC MAP

| Topics in this Part | Related topics in other chapters<br>Chapter | Topic | Comments/aspects |
|---|---|---|---|
| *Chapter 13 continued* | | | |
| | 12 | Strategies for scheduling | Implementation of scheduling strategy |
| | | Scheduling techniques | Network scheduling as a technique |
| | 14 | Sequencing | Dispatching rules |
| | 18 | Operations control | Control of project systems |
| Chapter 14 | | | |
| Dealing with batches and avoiding them | 2 | Operations policy | Policy options |
| | 4 | Operations costs | { Economies of scale and scope<br>Costs of inventories |
| | 9 | Technology | Flexible programming systems |
| | 11 | Operations planning | JIT |
| | 12 | Scheduling | Batch sizes and sequences |
| | 15 | Flow process systems | Flow processing to avoid batching |
| | 16 | Materials management | Reducing batch sizes in purchasing and supply |
| | 17 | Inventory management | Batch size economics |
| | 18 | Operations control | Kanban |
| | 22 | Performance measurement | Work-in-progress levels |
| Managing batch processing | 1 | Operations objectives<br>Operating system structures } | Influence on batch scheduling strategies |
| | 8 | Work measurement | Need for job times in scheduling |
| | | Learning curve | Need to allow for learning in scheduling |
| | 11 | Operations planning | Scheduling decisions as an aspect of planning |
| | | Capacity management | Implementing capacity strategies through scheduling |
| | 12 | Scheduling techniques | Batch scheduling techniques |
| | 13 | Project scheduling | Scheduling batches in project work |

## TOPIC MAP

| Topics in this Part | Related topics in other chapters: Chapter | Topic | Comments/aspects |
|---|---|---|---|
| *Chapter 14 continued* | | | |
| | 15 | Flow processes | Mixed- and multi-model flow line scheduling and sequencing |
| | 16 | Purchasing and supply | Batch supplies |
| | 17 | Inventory management | Batch size calculations |
| | 18 | Operations control | Control of batch flow systems |
| | 20 | Quality control | Batch inspection and sampling |
| | 21 | Maintenance/repair<br>Replacement | Batch replacement policies |
| Reducing batch sizes | 2 | Operations policy | Policy options |
| | 4 | Operations costs | Economies of scale |
| | 11 | Operations planning and scheduling | JIT |
| | 17 | Inventory management | Economic batch sizes |
| Flexible processing systems | 2 | Operations policy | Flexibility |
| | 3 | Marketing | Flexible service and customer satisfaction |
| | | Product/service design | Design for flexibility in provision |
| | 4 | Operations economics | Costs of flexibility |
| | 6 | Layout planning | Layouts for flexibility and change |
| | | Materials handling | Flexible movement |
| | | Automated storage and retrieval | FMS-type systems |
| | 9 | Technology | Automation for flexibility |
| | 10 | Payments | Payment by results |
| | 11 | Capacity management | Capacity strategies dependent on flexibility |
| | 12 | Scheduling strategies | Flexibility through scheduling |
| | | JIT | JIT to achieve flexibility in outputs |
| | | Managing demand uncertainty | Need for flexibility |
| | 13 | Project management | Flexibility to deal with uncertainties |

## TOPIC MAP

| Topics in this Part | Related topics in other chapters: Chapter | Topic | Comments/aspects |
|---|---|---|---|
| *Chapter 14 continued* | | | |
| | 15 | Flow systems | Changes in model mix |
| | 20 | Reliability | Need for flexibility to deal with unreliability and failures |
| | 21 | Maintenance/repair<br>Replacement | Need for flexibility to deal with unreliability and failures |
| Chapter 15 | | | |
| Nature of flow processing | 2<br>3 | Operations policy<br>Marketing<br>Organization | Flow processing and the provision of flexibility, speed, variety, cost, etc.<br>Work rationalization and organization design |
| | | Product/service design | Design for flow processing |
| | 4 | Operations economics | Economies of scale |
| | 6 | Layout | Product layouts |
| | 7 | Work methods | Work rationalization |
| | | Learning | Learning of repetitive jobs |
| | 8 | Learning curve | Learning of repetitive jobs |
| | 9 | Working conditions | Workplace design |
| | | Technology | Process automation |
| | | Job design | Job enrichment, enlargement and rotation |
| | 10 | Incentive | Performance-related pay |
| | 12 | Scheduling | JIT |
| | 16 | Materials management | Importance of supplies |
| | 17 | Purposes of inventory | Buffer stocks |
| | | Inventory costs | Buffer stocks |
| | 18 | Operations control | Kanban and JIT |
| | 19 | Management of quality | Quality assurance<br>Behavioural and organization factors<br>TQM principles |
| | 20 | Quality control | Inspection<br>Control charts<br>Acceptance sampling |

## TOPIC MAP

| Topics in this Part | Related topics in other chapters: Chapter | Topic | Comments/aspects |
|---|---|---|---|
| *Chapter 15 continued* | | | |
| | 21 | Maintenance and replacement | Important, to ensure continuity of operation |
| Flow line principles | 6 | Layout planning | Layouts for efficient flow |
| | 7 | Method study | Work rationalization and repetitive work |
| | 11 | Capacity management | Capacity management strategies and flexibility of systems |
| | 12 | Scheduling | Scheduling strategies |
| | 17 | Inventories | Use of stocks in flow systems; Output inventories; Batch processing |
| | 19 | Quality | Ensuring quality in repetitive work |
| | 21 | Maintenance | Need to avoid breakdowns and stoppages |
| Design of simple lines | 4 | Operations economics | Line balance and efficiency and operations cost |
| | 6 | Layout of facilities | Layout for efficient flow |
| | | Materials handling | Need for efficiency in process handling and movement |
| | 11 | Capacity management | Balance and balancing loss |
| | 17 | Inventories | Role and need for interstation buffer |
| | 19 | Quality | Need for process quality assurance and outgoing controls |
| | 21 | Maintenance | Importance of system reliability |
| Design of complex lines | 4 | Operations economics | Line balance and efficiency and operations cost |
| | 6 | Layout of facilities | Layout for efficient flow |
| | | Materials handling | Need for efficiency in process handling and movement |
| | 11 | Capacity management | Balance and balancing loss |
| | 17 | Inventories | Role and need for interstation buffer stocks |

## TOPIC MAP

| Topics in this Part | Related topics in other chapters | | Comments/aspects |
|---|---|---|---|
| | Chapter | Topic | |
| *Chapter 15 continued* | | | |
| | 19 | Quality | Need for process quality assurance and outgoing controls |
| | 21 | Maintenance | Importance of system reliability |
| | 7 | Work methods<br>Learning | Worker reliability and system loss |
| | 8 | Work measurement<br>Learning curve | Work variability and system loss |
| | 9 | Technology | Work time variability for workers versus machines |
| | 11 | Capacity | System loss effects on capacity |
| | 12 | Scheduling | Scheduling and sequencing, mixed- and multi-model systems |
| | 17 | Inventories | Role of buffer stocks and buffer capacity |
| | 19 | Quality management | Human and behavioural factors in complex flow systems |

Chapter 12

# Activity scheduling

## ISSUES

What is the purpose of activity scheduling?
Are there different types of scheduling problems?
What are the basic strategies for scheduling?
What is the relationship with, and the influence of, the customer?
Are there relevant techniques and where can they be used?
To what extent should we use a mathematical approach?
How practical is it to try to get optimal schedules?
How do scheduling decisions link with capacity and inventory decisions?

## NOTATION USED IN THIS CHAPTER

| | |
|---|---|
| $a$ | Concurrent facility and operator time/cycle |
| $a_i$ | Processing time for $i$ |
| $A_i$ | Set-up and processing time for job $i$ on facility A |
| $A_n$ | Ashcroft number |
| $b$ | Operator independent time/cycle |
| $C_o$ | Cost of operator/h |
| $C_m$ | Cost of facility/h |
| $E$ | $C_o/C_m$ |
| $f_i$ | Delay or contingency allowance |
| FCFS | First come first served |
| $I$ | Index no. |
| $i_o$ | Operator idle time/cycle |
| $i_m$ | Operator independent time/cycle |
| LIO | Longest imminent operation |
| LOB | Line of balance |
| $L_q$ | Average queue length |
| $m$ | Number of facilities ($j = 1 \ldots m$) |

| | |
|---|---|
| MRP | Materials requirements planning |
| $n$ | Number of jobs ($i = 1 \ldots n$) |
| $n$ | Number of facilities assigned |
| $n1$ | Ideal number of facilities for one worker |
| $N$ | Number of remaining operations |
| $Q_i$ | Order quantity for item $i$ |
| $S$ | Job slack |
| SIO | Shortest imminent operation |
| $t$ | Facility independent activity time/cycle |
| $t_0$ | Scheduled completion date |
| $t_1$ | Present date |
| $T$ | Total throughput time |
| $x_i$ | Time at which $i$ must begin |
| $Y_n$ | Cost/unit of processing with $n$ facilities |
| $\lambda$ | Mean arrival rate |
| $\mu$ | Mean service rate |
| $\rho$ | $\lambda/\mu$ |
| $\Delta pq$ | Interval between end of $p$ and start of $q$ |

Activity scheduling is an aspect of operations management which has considerable strategic importance. Decisions in this area will be influenced by business strategy, and will in turn influence performance and effectiveness of the business – as regards both service to customers and resource utilization. Whilst in capacity management the problem was to deal with uncertain demand levels in scheduling, here the problem is to deal with uncertain demand timing.

The nature of the scheduling problems faced by operations managers will be influenced by the structure of the operating system. The system structure influences what operations managers can, feasibly, do in scheduling activities. Also, the nature of the problems is influenced by operations objectives – these influence what, desirably, the manager should achieve.

Within these constraints of what can be done, and what should be achieved, the operations manager will have preferences – i.e. a wish to deal with scheduling problems in particular ways.

This framework for decision-making was set out in Chapter 1. Within this framework the operations manager must decide what general approach or strategy to use in dealing with activities scheduling, and then identify the most appropriate procedures to follow to implement that strategy. This two-stage approach will be used in this chapter. Firstly, we examine the nature of scheduling problems and the strategies that are available, and then we examine scheduling procedures.

## STRATEGIES FOR ACTIVITY SCHEDULING

Here we are dealing with the activities which take place *within* the operating system. An activity schedule will show the times (or dates) at which all of the activities are to be undertaken. The fixing of such times determines the manner in which items or, in the case of service and transport systems, customers will flow through the operating system. The activity scheduling problem is concerned with the fixing of these times in advance. The manner in which the problem is tackled will depend largely on the situation in which activity scheduling is undertaken. For example, if an operating system is working in anticipation of demand, the scheduling problems will differ from those in an operating system which is working specifically to satisfy individual customers' 'due date' requirements. Other factors will influence the nature of the activity scheduling problem and therefore the techniques which might be appropriate for the solution of that problem. In order better to understand the nature of the activity scheduling problem we shall first consider two factors:

(a) whether scheduling is to be 'internally' or 'externally' oriented;

(b) whether demand is 'dependent' or 'independent'.

## Internally and externally oriented scheduling

Activity scheduling is concerned with the timing of activities, but these times must be fixed in relation to some other requirements. Consider as an example a situation in which products are manufactured against a specific customer order. Each customer order specifies exactly what is to be produced and when it is required – the 'due date'. Here the internal activities which create end products (e.g. the manufacture of components and sub-assemblies) must all be scheduled so that each end product is available on the required 'due' or delivery date. A similar situation can exist in non-manufacturing organizations. Here those activities which are necessary to satisfy a particular service or transport requirement must be performed in time to satisfy a particular customer's request. In all such cases the customer has a *direct* influence on the timing of activities within the operating system, so activity scheduling can be seen to be *externally* oriented in that the timing of all activities is fixed to satisfy *particular* external customer timing requirements.

In contrast, consider a situation in which items are manufactured for stock in anticipation of future customer orders. Here there need to be no *direct* influence from a particular customer on the internal activity schedule. Customers are satisfied from stock and the need to replenish this stock gives rise to the need to schedule activities within the operating system. A similar situation can exist in service and transport systems, where a system is 'buffered' from its customers by an input queue. In these circumstances the activity scheduling can be mainly *internally oriented*, and in such cases there can be more freedom in activity scheduling, so schedules can be fixed more easily to maximize resource utilization, etc.

Thus the nature of the activity scheduling problem can in part be defined by the *orientation* of scheduling.

## Externally oriented scheduling strategy

An externally oriented strategy involves the scheduling of activities within an operating system specifically to satisfy particular customer timing requirements. This will normally involve due date considerations. One approach to externally oriented scheduling is shown in Figure 12.1, which illustrates the due date scheduling procedure in chart form. Three particular cases are considered:

(a) An operating system in which there is a 'function from stock, direct to customer order' (see Chapter 1). Here the customer due date is fixed and activity scheduling involves subtracting from this date the duration of the function which must be undertaken to satisfy the customer's requirements. This reverse scheduling process gives rise to a start date for the function.

(b) An operating system in which there is a 'function from source, direct to customer'. Here a similar situation exists but in this case it is necessary, by reverse scheduling, to establish a start date for the function, and then the order date for the acquisition of resources for that function.

(c) An operating system in which there is a 'function from stock and from customer'. In this situation the customer's due date is the date on which the customer *arrives* into the system. This in fact is the start date for the function, the end date of which is found by adding the function duration to the start date.

This is a simple scheduling technique. Others are also available for tackling the externally oriented scheduling problem, and these will be described in this and subsequent chapters.

**Figure 12.1** 'Due date' activity scheduling

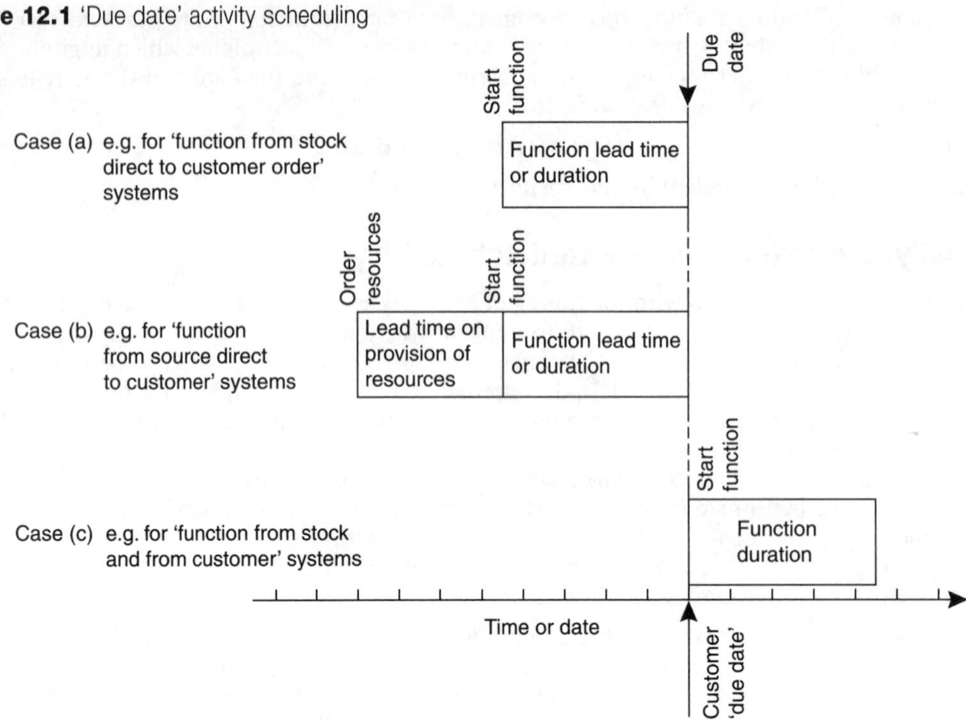


## Internally oriented scheduling strategy

With this approach the activities within the operating system are scheduled without direct reference to individual customers' due date requirements. Such a situation can exist where there are stocks between the activities and the customer. In these circumstances there is a greater opportunity to schedule activities to provide for efficient flow, high resource utilization, economic batching, etc. within the operating system. The emphasis therefore may be on the maximization of resource utilization, with relatively little direct concern for individual customers' due date requirements. Several techniques may be appropriate for tackling the internally oriented activity scheduling problem.

Clearly, the structure of the operating system will have some influence on the choice of a scheduling strategy. In some cases an internal scheduling strategy seems likely to be more appropriate. In other cases it seems likely that an external strategy will be employed. It is a matter not only of feasibility, but also of desirability. In fact it is feasible to employ an internal strategy in all situations but clearly, in some cases, the consequences of doing so, for customer service or timing, will make that type of approach quite unattractive. Those system structures which have a goods stock between the function and the customer, and those in which there is a customer queue (i.e. system structures SOS, DOS, DQO and SQC – using the notation from Chapter 1) permit the use of an internal scheduling strategy without risking customer service on timing.

In contrast, for the other system structures – in which there is no buffer between demand and the function – the adoption of an internal scheduling strategy, whilst feasible, seems likely to give rise to relatively poor customer service on timing. So, when customer service on timing is unimportant compared to resource utilization, the use of an external scheduling strategy is likely.

As with capacity management, the choice of an appropriate strategy for activity scheduling will depend on the balance of importance of resource utilization and customer service (in this case on 'timing').

Table 12.1 outlines some typical situations.

**Table 12.1 Scheduling strategies – some typical situations**

| Example | Function | System structure | Operations objectives | Scheduling strategy | Comments |
|---|---|---|---|---|---|
| Routine surgery ward in a large public hospital | Service | SQO | Resource utilization and customer service on specification | Internal | Waiting lists of patients will exist, and appointments will be given to ensure full use of facilities |
| Ambulance service | Transport | SCO | Customer service on timing and specification | External | Resource utilization will be low as ambulances stand by for emergencies |
| Bank cash machine or 'Auto Teller' providing 24-hour service | Supply | SOD | Customer service on specification and timing | External | The aim is to enable customers to be supplied on demand Utilization of the machine will be low |
| Domestic appliance manufacturer | Manufacturer | SOS | Resource utilization and customer service on timing (and cost or specification) | Internal | Goods are made in anticipation of future orders, and held in stock in the distribution 'channel' |

## 'JUST IN TIME' – EXTERNALLY ORIENTED SCHEDULING AND ITS IMPLICATIONS

The just in time (JIT) concept is simple, but its adoption has widespread implications. JIT is the application of an externally oriented approach to scheduling, but its implementation also has an impact on inventory management and other areas. Successful JIT requires a broad management commitment to a distinctive operations policy. The concept is introduced here, not only as an illustration of externally oriented scheduling, but also to remind us of the interrelationships of capacity management, scheduling and inventory management. Several aspects of JIT will also be discussed in later chapters (especially Chapters 16 and 17).

### The philosophy

JIT was developed by companies in Japan – notably Toyota. It was adopted by manufacturing organizations in the USA and Europe and quickly became one of the most widely advocated, copied and popular manufacturing philosophies, especially in large-volume, repetitive manufacturing environments such as the motor industry. Virtually all that has been written on the subject is concerned with manufacture. However, since JIT is essentially a general approach, many of the basic principles are of relevance, and could be implemented for other types of operating systems.

JIT has been defined as involving 'the production of the necessary items in the necessary quantities at the necessary time'. In other words, with this approach, the materials and items required by a process are made available at that process as and when they are required, and not before. This seemingly simple idea in fact contrasts markedly with practice in many operating systems which depend upon substantial inventories. Thus, with the JIT approach, queues awaiting processing at an operation are minimal. Work-in-progress, therefore, is low. Throughput times are reduced, space requirements are reduced, and flow through the system is virtually continuous. Considerable managerial effort is required to bring about and sustain such a situation. It is not the normal 'steady-state' arrangement for an operating system, since with JIT there is an absence of 'buffers' and safety measures. Given the uncertainty which exists in most operating systems, e.g. uncertainties of demand, the processing times of particular operations, scrap and loss rates, etc., it has been quite common to build inventories into the system to provide some degree of safety and to 'decouple' processes. If an inventory exists between two processes then the failure of one does not immediately impact on the activities of the other. An inventory might also exist so that increases in demand can be met without the immediate need to change the rate at which the operating system works. Inventories of output items, work-in-progress and materials are commonplace in industry for these reasons. The JIT approach, however, completely reverses this principle. In JIT inventories are minimized, and work is not done until required. Items are not processed until required at the next process, and processes are interdependent.

The principal feature of the JIT approach, therefore, concerns the management of inventories. JIT aims to create a zero or low inventory operating system. It is argued that the reduction in inventory is of considerable benefit in its own right, e.g. to reduce space requirements, reduce the amount of tied-up capital, reduce the risk of loss and damage and reduce handling requirements. In addition, the elimination of inventories is considered to have considerable managerial benefits. If, as is often the case, inventories have grown up in order to protect an operating system against uncertainties, then it can be argued that such inventories serve to conceal the real problems, whilst JIT aims to reveal them in order that they can be tackled at source. Thus for low-inventory operation, problems must be identified and solved. If input stocks of materials have been held in order to protect an organization from disruptions in supply, then the use of JIT requires that those problems be overcome through, for example, the use of different vendors, and/or the establishment of different arrangements with suppliers. If work-in-progress stocks have been held to protect against the breakdown of equipment, the introduction of JIT requires that the causes of breakdown be identified and eliminated. Thus JIT has both system and managerial advantages.

## Elements of the JIT policy

There are six characteristics of JIT:

### 'Demand call'

The entire system is led or pulled by demand. The need to serve or supply a customer triggers activities throughout the operating system. Thus, where a customer places an order for a manufacturing operation, that order requirement flows back through the system, triggering each stage of the overall process. This contrasts with the practice in many manufacturing systems where work is begun when materials become available. (This might be regarded as an input 'push' system.)

### Reduced set-up times and smaller batch sizes

Except in systems where only one type of product or service is provided, it will be necessary to 'set up' processes in order that they can deal with a particular type of item. This is a basic characteristic of a batch processing system. The JIT aim of processing items only as and when required necessitates the processing of small batch sizes. It will be shown in Chapter 14 that reducing the cost of set-ups, which in turn is related to set-up time, reduces the economic batch size. JIT, therefore, is associated with small batch sizes and short, economical set-ups.

## Efficient flow

The need for rapid throughput and the avoidance of substantial work-in-progress and thus the need for space necessitates – and enables – efficient flow systems to be established. The rapid movement of items between processes is an essential prerequisite. Rationalization of flows is therefore a requirement.

These three aspects are the essential characteristics of a JIT system. They are the necessary characteristics. However, in practice, because of the manner in which JIT is normally pursued, there are three additional characteristics:

## Employee involvement

The interdependence of operations, the rapid flow and the absence of buffers necessitate smooth and efficient control. In practice this has been found to necessitate the active participation of all employees. In this way, possible disruptions can be seen and avoided, and operations scheduling and control improved also. In practice, however, in the introduction of JIT improved communications and participation is also one of the principal aims. It is pursued because of its intrinsic benefits. JIT in effect provides the opportunity to achieve participation in matters such as quality control, problem-solving work, etc. (See the discussion of quality circles in Chapter 19.)

## Kanban

Kanban is a device used in the scheduling of activities in JIT systems. It is a Japanese name for 'card'. The Kanban system, and its derivatives, has become the standard means for achieving production control with JIT. This aspect will be considered in detail in Chapter 18.

## Visibility

One of the principal objectives of JIT is simplicity. One means to achieve and sustain a simple system is by ensuring visibility, e.g. one of our objectives is to ensure that stocks are visible. The ability to see what is happening is an important characteristic of JIT.

## Benefits of JIT

From the above, it will be clear that the benefits of JIT include:

(a) reduced inventories and work-in-progress;

(b) reduced space requirement;

(c) shorter throughput times;

(d) greater employee involvement, participation and motivation;

(e) smoother work flows.

To these can be added the following, also normally sought and achieved in good JIT systems:

(f) greater productivity;

(g) improved product/service quality;

(h) improved customer service;

(i) more uniform loading of facilities.

These benefits derive in part from the systems efficiencies of JIT, and also from the managerial/organizational benefits. Some are direct benefits whilst others are indirect.

## Prerequisites for effective JIT

1. Low variety of items being processed.
2. Demand stability.
3. Vendor reliability (to ensure reliable supply).
4. Defect-free materials (to avoid disruptions).
5. Good communications (to help ensure continuous operation and minimum disruption).
6. Preventive maintenance (to avoid disruption).
7. Total quality control.
8. Management commitment.
9. Employee involvement.
10. Worker flexibility.

**EXAMPLE**

### *Cummins Engines*

Cummins Engines (UK) found itself falling behind its Far East competitors. At that time, Japanese competitors had 80% lower inventory levels, more responsiveness to customers, and almost no scrap or rework. Cummins decided to implement JIT manufacturing, which involves reducing non-value-added activities. At its Darlington plant, $25 million was invested in JIT tools, including automated assembly, automated guided vehicles, and a computerized assembly information-management system. JIT reduced overhead costs by 70%, reduced lead time dramatically, lowered labour cost by 30%, reduced floor space required by 31%, and reduced work-in-progress by 97%. Batch sizes were reduced from 25 to 6, and time spent on large machine tools was reduced by up to 80%. A kanban system helped decrease inventory from a 29-day supply to an 8-day supply and eliminated some material shortages.

Source: Mullins, P. (1989) JIT's competitive edge. *Production*, **101** (7), pp. 62–64.

## Dependent and independent demand

Another way of describing the activity scheduling situation is to consider the relationship between demand for the outputs of the operating system (i.e. the products or services) and the need to perform the various activities which take place within the operating system. Consider as an example the manufacture of a complex product consisting of several components, parts, sub-assemblies, etc.

If in this case we know the parts and components which are required to produce a particular end product, and if we know the demand for that product, then we can, for a particular period of time, calculate exactly what activities must be performed within the system to satisfy that demand. Thus there is a completely *dependent* relationship between demand, which is known, and the activities required within the operating system. A similar situation can exist in the non-manufacturing organization where the satisfaction of a particular customer requirement, e.g. a service or transport, requires the performance of particular activities within the system and where demand for that service is known and hence the particular activities which must be performed can be calculated and known with certainty.

Thus we can describe a *dependent activity demand situation* as one in which a knowledge of customer demand in terms of both *what* is required and *when* it is required permits us to calculate what activities must be performed within the operating system in a particular period of time. Notice that in most cases we shall be concerned with a particular scheduling period, i.e. the need to schedule particular activities to be performed within a particular period. This will often correspond to the planning period, or the period for which demand is forecast.

It will be appreciated that, in many respects, the scheduling of activities in a dependent activity demand situation is relatively straightforward, since there are few uncertainties. All that is required is that a known amount of work is scheduled to take place so that known customer requirements are satisfied by particular times or dates. In addition to this objective it will, of course, be appropriate to try to schedule these activities to take place, within these constraints, in such a manner that resource utilization is maximized.

In contrast, an *independent activity demand situation* exists where it is impossible to calculate exactly what activities are required within the operating system in a particular period of time. Such a situation can exist *either* where there is not enough knowledge about demand, i.e. customers' orders are not known in advance or there is a good deal of uncertainty about future customer orders, *or* where there is no clear relationship between the nature of the product, service, transport, etc. required by the customer and the nature of the activities which must be performed by the operating system to satisfy that customer requirement. In an independent activity demand situation, therefore, the activity scheduling problem is more complex since there are more uncertainties. In this type of situation it will often be necessary to estimate or forecast in some way the amount of activities required to satisfy some future, as yet unknown, demand, and then to schedule those activities to take place so that the end products are available at what is expected to be the right time, or so that the service or transport is available when customers arrive.

## TYPES OF SCHEDULING PROBLEM

The distinction between the internal and external orientation of scheduling, and that between dependent and independent activity demand, are relevant in identifying different types of activity scheduling situations. These two factors are *interrelated* and normally those responsible for the scheduling of activities will find themselves dealing with a situation in which there is either dependent activity demand and externally oriented scheduling or, in total contrast, independent activity demand and internally oriented activity scheduling. These are the two normal and distinctive activity scheduling situations but a third situation is possible, as outlined in Table 12.2. These three situations are described in more detail below.

### Externally oriented activity scheduling with dependent activity demand

Here the nature of the customers' demand on the system is known, whether for goods, services or transport. The customers have been identified and their requirements determined in terms of both the nature of the things required and the time when those things are required. There is a known relationship between the nature of products or services provided by the organization and the types of activities which must be performed within the organization so that these outputs or services are available. Thus given the knowledge of demand and given this relationship, the activities required by the operating system and the dates by which these activities must be completed can be calculated. Here the activity scheduling problem is that of determining when to do given activities such as to satisfy given customer due date requirements, while also satisfying certain internal requirements, e.g. capacity requirements.

Appropriate scheduling techniques for this type of activity scheduling situation will include:

(a) materials requirements planning (see this chapter);

(b) OPT (see this chapter);

(c) network analysis using scheduled project completion dates (see Chapter 13);

(d) line of balance (see Chapter 14);

(e) reverse or forward scheduling (see this chapter).

## Internally oriented activity scheduling with independent activity demand

Here we have little information about customer demand. It is not possible to calculate actual activity requirements, so the nature and quantity of the activities which must be performed within the operating system will be obtained by direct forecasting of activity requirements. The activity scheduling problem in this situation therefore involves the timing of an estimated activity requirement in order to satisfy a period's estimated needs while also satisfying internal, e.g. capacity, requirements. In this situation there are no known customers and no definite due dates.

Appropriate techniques for use in this type of situation might include:

(a) network analysis without the use of schedule end dates (see Chapter 13);

(b) sequencing (see this chapter);

(c) dispatching (see this chapter);

(d) assignment (see this chapter);

(e) forward scheduling (see this chapter);

(f) batch scheduling (see Chapter 14);

(g) flow scheduling (see Chapter 15);

(h) timetabling (see this chapter).

## Internally oriented activity scheduling with dependent activity demand

This situation will not occur often. However, it is possible to envisage such an approach where, even though knowledge of customer demand permits the calculation of the activities required within the system in terms of quantity, nature and due dates, it is nevertheless intended that scheduling of these activities is undertaken primarily to satisfy internal requirements. The situation therefore differs from (1) in Table 12.2 in that the scheduling problem is not specifically concerned with due date requirements. It differs from (2) in Table 12.2 in that the activities which are to be performed during a particular period of time are known with certainty rather than being a result of the estimates.

Such a situation might occur where it is necessary to manufacture goods against specific customer orders without a due date requirement, or where items are to be supplied to particular customers without any due date or dates being imposed by such customers. In transport or service industries such a situation may exist where it is necessary to deal with particular customers and their requirements over a period of time, but where the timing of this provision is not imposed by customers.

The scheduling techniques which might be appropriate in this situation are similar to those for (2) in Table 12.2.

# MANAGING DEMAND UNCERTAINTY

At the beginning of this chapter we noted that one purpose of scheduling was to deal with demand uncertainty, i.e. with uncertain timing of demand. Our initial analysis of scheduling strategies has shown that in some cases it is feasible to adopt an approach which enables schedules to be fixed without direct reference to individual customers' timing requirements. This internal strategy eliminates the need to deal directly with timing uncertainties. An 'external strategy', however, brings operations managers face to face with the problem. This is often unavoidable – especially where output stocks of items or input queues of customers cannot or may not exist. In such situations attempts can be made to reduce scheduling problems by managing demand uncertainty. Rarely can this be done to such an extent as to eliminate all uncertainty about timing but often something can be done – sufficient, that is, to influence the way in which we schedule the activities of the operating system.

## The problem of 'random arrivals'

In many situations, demand from individual customers is entirely random. Individuals may arrive at a transport or service system, or customers may arrive at a manufacture or supply system at random intervals. The only way to deal with such arrivals, if waiting is to be avoided, is by external scheduling coupled with the use of 'total' excess capacity (strategy 2a for capacity management - Chapter 11).

We dealt with this type of approach when considering queuing theory in Chapter 11. In practice, since it will not often be possible to have excess capacity on all occasions, some customer waiting will often occur.

A complementary approach is to try to reduce the randomness of the arrival pattern. If this can be done, arrivals can be anticipated, capacity requirements may be reduced and scheduling made easier.

## Appointments and reservations

This is the normal way to manage demand uncertainty. It is employed extensively in service systems such as hospitals, dentists, professional services, etc. It makes arrival times and thus the arrival rate of customers more certain. If the 'work content' of customers, i.e. the extent of the demand that they will place on the system, is also known, it also makes the level of demand more certain. By giving appointments to customers, i.e. obliging them to arrive at the system at particular times, an internal scheduling strategy is, in effect, made possible where otherwise an external approach would have been employed. Similarly, by offering reservations, i.e. pre-committing activities to customers, the same is achieved. Such an approach is often used in conjunction with the timetabling of activities (dealt with later in this chapter).

# ACTIVITY SCHEDULING TECHNIQUES

The discussion above has identified which types of scheduling techniques might be appropriate in different activity scheduling situations. A third factor will influence which type of technique is employed in a particular situation: this factor is concerned with the nature of the process involved within the operating system. Let us take as an example a system in which the operating system provides services to satisfy different customer requirements. No two customers ever come to the system with precisely the same requirements, so the operating system must respond to quite different customer needs. This is a form of 'one-off' situation. A similar situation can exist in the manufacturing industry where items are to be manufactured against specific customer orders and where such orders are never repeated. In the manufacturing context this will be referred to as project production.

In contrast, there are manufacturing systems which produce one type of item only to satisfy the needs of a particular set of customers; this might be a form of repetitive production. A similar situation can exist in service or transport industries where an operation system exists solely to provide one particular service or transport for customers who require or are prepared to accept that service or transport. There are also intermediate situations in which jobbing or batch processes are employed.

The type of scheduling technique used in a particular situation will depend on the factors outlined in Table 12.2, and in addition on whether the activities are to be scheduled in a project, jobbing, batch or repetitive manner. This distinction is rather simplistic, since there are areas of overlap between the four categories; however, it is sufficient for our present purposes, Table 12.3 lists the activity scheduling techniques previously introduced in Table 12.2. Each technique is described briefly and some indication is given of whether the technique will be appropriate for project and/or jobbing and/or batch and/or repetitive processes.

**Table 12.2 Activity scheduling situations**

| | **Externally oriented activity scheduling** | **Internally oriented activity scheduling** |
|---|---|---|
| Dependent activity demand | ① *Situation* Customer demand known in terms of what is required, quantities and due dates. Hence the activities required to satisfy this demand can be calculated.<br>*Activity scheduling problems* Determine when known activities must be done to satisfy given customer due dates while also satisfying internal requirements.<br>*Appropriate techniques* MRP (Chapter 12). OPT (Chapter 12). 'Reverse' network analysis, i.e. with scheduled project completion dates (Chapter 13). Line of balance (Chapter 14). Reverse scheduling (Chapter 12) for production and supply. Forward scheduling (Chapter 12) for service and transport. | ③ *Situation* Customer demand known in terms of what is required, quantities and due dates, but due dates not taken into account *or* demand stated only in terms of what is required and the quantities (i.e. no due date requirement). The activities which are needed can be calculated.<br>*Activity scheduling problems* Determine when known activities must be done to satisfy internal requirements.<br>*Appropriate techniques* Forward network analysis (i.e. without scheduled project completion dates) (Chapter 12). Sequencing (Chapter 12). Batch scheduling (Chapter 14). Dispatching (Chapter 12). Assignment (Chapter 12). Forward scheduling for production and supply (Chapter 12). Flow scheduling (Chapter 15). Timetabling (Chapter 12). |
| Independent activity demand | ④ Does not normally exist | ② *Situation* Activities to be completed in a given time period must be *estimated.*<br>*Activity scheduling problems* Determine when activities must be done to satisfy the estimated overall requirements for the period while satisfying internal requirements.<br>*Appropriate techniques* Forward network analysis (i.e. without scheduled project completion dates) (Chapter 12). Sequencing (Chapter 12). Dispatching (Chapter 12). Assignment (Chapter 12). Forward scheduling for production and supply (Chapter 12). Batch scheduling (Chapter 14). Flow scheduling (Chapter 15). Timetabling (Chapter 12). |

Reference to Tables 12.2 and 12.3 will indicate which scheduling technique might be appropriate for a given situation. Some of the main techniques are described in the remainder of this chapter. We start with straightforward procedures and then introduce more sophisticated techniques, which also have relevance for areas such as capacity and inventory management.

**Table 12.3 Activity scheduling techniques for project, jobbing, batch and flow systems**

| Scheduling technique | Brief description | Project | Jobbing | Batch | Flow | See Chapter: |
|---|---|---|---|---|---|---|
| A Reverse scheduling (Gantt charts) | A technique by which the durations of particular activities are subtracted from a required completion date, i.e. the schedules for all the activities required for the satisfaction of some particular customer requirements are determined by scheduling in reverse from the required due date. | √ | √ | √ | | 12 |
| B Forward scheduling (Gantt charts) | The opposite of reverse scheduling, where the scheduled times for a particular set of activities are determined by forward scheduling from a given date in order ultimately to obtain a date for completion of a particular set of activities or project. | √ | √ | √ | | 12 |
| C Sequencing | The determination of the best order for processing a known set of jobs through a given set of facilities in order, for example, to minimize total throughput time, minimize queuing, minimize facility idle time, etc. | | √ | ? | | 12 |
| D Dispatching | A technique by which it is possible to identify which of an available set of jobs to process next on an available facility in order to minimize, over a period of time, throughput times, lateness, etc. | | √ | ? | | 12 |

**Table 12.3 continued**

| Scheduling technique | Brief description | Project | Jobbing | Batch | Flow | See Chapter: |
|---|---|---|---|---|---|---|
| E Assignment | A technique by which it is possible to assign or allocate an available set of jobs against an available set of resources (where each job may be undertaken on more than one resource), in order to minimize throughput time, maximize resource utilization, etc. | ? | √ | ? | | 12 |
| F Timetabling | Techniques resulting in the development of a schedule, timetable or rota indicating when certain facilities or resources will be available to those wishing to use them. | | | | √ | 12 |
| G OPT (optimized production technology) | A scheduling technique which concentrates on flows through 'bottleneck' operations. | ? | ? | √ | √ | 12 |
| H Materials requirements planning (MRP) | A technique by which known customer demand requirements are 'exploded' to produce 'gross' parts, components or activity requirements. These 'gross' requirements are compared with available inventories to produce 'net' requirements which are then scheduled within available capacity limitations. MRP is for scheduling and also for inventory management and capacity management. | ? | ? | √ | | 12 |
| I MRP II | A development of MRP, but far broader in concept and application. | ? | √ | √ | ? | 12 |
| J Network analysis (or critical path analysis) | A technique by which the various interrelated and interdependent activities required in the completion of a complex project can be scheduled, with any slack or free time being identified. The technique can be used in scheduling activities from a start date (forward NA) or by working backwards from a required completion date (backward NA). | √ | ? | ? | | 13 |

Table 12.3 continued

| Scheduling technique | Brief description | Project | Jobbing | Batch | Flow | See Chapter: |
|---|---|---|---|---|---|---|
| K Batch scheduling | A technique involving the determination of optimum batch sizes and a schedule for the completion of such batches on a set of facilities. The batch sizes are determined by comparing set-up (or change) costs with holding or inventory costs. The schedule is determined by reference to these batch sizes. The technique is concerned with both scheduling and inventory management. | | | √ | ? | 14 |
| L Line of balance (LOB) | A technique which permits the calculation of the quantities of the particular activities or parts and components which must have been completed by a particular intermediate date, in order that some final delivery schedule might be satisfied. It is therefore a scheduling and a control technique. | | | √ | | 14 |
| M Flow scheduling | A technique for establishing appropriate facilities for the processing of items and customers where each item or customer passes through the same facilities in the same order. The technique is concerned primarily with meeting certain output requirements in terms of cycle time and balancing the use of the resources within the system. | | | ? | √ | 15 |

## REVERSE SCHEDULING

External due date considerations will directly influence activity scheduling in certain structures. The approach adopted in scheduling activities in such cases will often involve a form of reverse scheduling of the Gantt chart type illustrated in Figure 12.1(a) and (b).

One major problem with such reverse of 'due date' scheduling is in estimating the total time to be allowed for each operation, in particular the time to be allowed for waiting or queuing at facilities. Some queuing of jobs (whether items or customers) at facilities is often desirable since, where processing times through facilities are uncertain, high utilization is often achieved only by the provision of some queue.

Operation times are often available, but queuing times are rarely known initially, and can only be estimated.

Schedules of this type are usually depicted on Gantt or bar charts. The advantage of this type of presentation is that the load on any facility or any department is clear at a glance, and available or spare capacity is easily identified. The major disadvantage is that the dependencies between operations are not shown. Notice that, in scheduling the processing of items or customers, total throughput time can be minimized by the batching of similar items to save set-up time, inspection time, etc.

## FORWARD SCHEDULING

For a manufacturing or supply organization a forward scheduling procedure will in fact be the opposite of that illustrated in Figure 12.1(a) and (b). This approach will be particularly relevant where scheduling is undertaken on an internally oriented basis and the objective is to determine the dates or times for subsequent activities, given the times for an earlier activity, e.g. a starting time.

In the case of transport organizations the forward scheduling procedure will be as illustrated in Figure 12.1(c). Here the objective will be to schedule forward from a given start date, where that start date will often be the customer due date, e.g. the date at which the customer arrives into the system. In these circumstances, therefore, forward scheduling will be an appropriate method for dealing with externally oriented scheduling activities.

## SEQUENCING

Sequencing procedures seek to determine the best order for processing a set of jobs through a set of facilities.

Two types of problems can be identified: first, the static case, in which all jobs to be processed are known and are available, and in which no additional jobs arrive in the queue during the exercise; and second, the dynamic case, which allows for the continuous arrival of jobs in the queue. In the static case the problem is merely to order a given queue of jobs through a given number of facilities, each job passing through the facilities in the required order and spending the necessary amount of time at each. The objective in such a case is usually to minimize the total time required to process all jobs: the throughput time. In the dynamic case the objective might be to minimize facility idle time, to minimize work-in-progress or to achieve the required completion or delivery dates for each job.

### Sequencing: two facilities and *n* jobs (static)

This example[1] considers the situation where $n$ jobs are to be processed on each of two facilities (A and B) with the same order (A, B) and no passing.

Let $A_i$ = set-up time + processing time for job $i$ on facility A ($A_i > 0$; $i = 1 \ldots n$)

$B_i$ = the same for facility B

[1] For a review and comparison of methods, see Ho, J. C. and Chang, Y. L. (1991) A new heuristic for the $n$-job, $M$-machine flow shop problem. *European Journal of Operations Research*, **52**(2), pp. 194–202.

Objective: to minimize $T$ (total throughput time) for all $n$ jobs

Solution procedure:

(a) List information as shown in Table 12.4.
(b) Select shortest time (or remaining time).
(c) If this is $A_i$ put that job first (or nearest first).
(d) If this is $B_i$ put that job last (or nearest last).
(e) Delete this job from the table.
(f) Return to (a).

**Table 12.4**

| $i$ | $A_i$ | $B_i$ |
|---|---|---|
| 1 | $A_1$ | $B_1$ |
| 2 | $A_2$ | $B_2$ |
| 3 | $A_3$ | $B_3$ |
| ↓ | ↓ | ↓ |
| $n$ | $A_n$ | $B_n$ |

**EXAMPLE**

A two-facility, six-job sequencing problem and its solution using this procedure are shown in Table 12.5 and Figure 12.2.

**Table 12.5**

| $i$ | $A_i$ | $B_i$ | Order |
|---|---|---|---|
| 1 | 5 | 1 → | 6th |
| 2 | 4 → | 5 → | 3rd |
| 3 | 6 | 5 → | 5th |
| 4 | 7 | 6 | 4th |
| 5 | 2 → | 6 → | 1st |
| 6 | 3 → | 4 → | 2nd |

**Figure 12.2** Program to minimize $T$ ($T$ = 29)

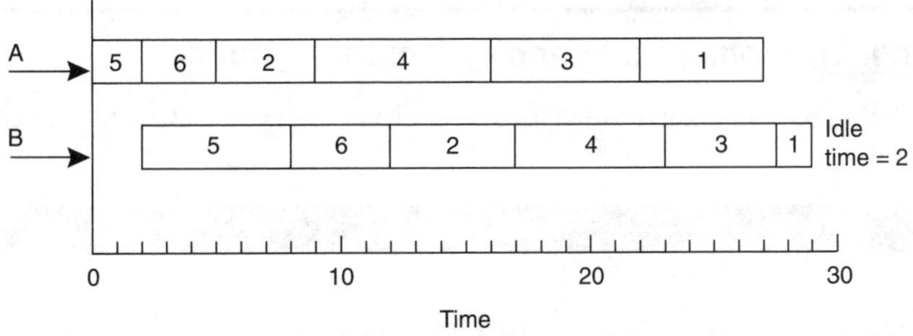


## Sequencing: special case of *m* = 3 (A, B, C) (static)

This considers the situation where $n$ jobs are to be processed on each of three facilities (A, B and C) with the same order (A, B, C) and no passing.

Let $A_i$ = set-up time + processing time for job $i$ on facility A ($A_i > 0$; $i = 1 \ldots n$)

$B_i$ = the same for facility B

$C_i$ = the same for facility C

Either one or both of the following requirements must be satisfied:

(a) min. $A_i \geq$ max. $B_i$

(b) min. $C_i \geq$ max. $B_i$

Objective: to minimize $T$ (total throughput time) for all $n$ jobs.

**EXAMPLE**

The example shown in Table 12.6 satisfies requirement (b) above (min. $C_i$ = max. $B_i$).

Solution procedure:

(a) Calculate $(A_i + B_i)$ and $(B_i + C_i)$.

(b) Proceed as before (Table 12.5) using two 'imaginary' facilities whose processing times are $(A_i + B_i)$ and $(B_i + C_i)$ as shown in Table 12.7.

**Table 12.6**

| $i$ | $A_i$ | $B_i$ | $C_i$ |
|---|---|---|---|
| 1 | 6 | 5 | 5 |
| 2 | 8 | 3 | 7 |
| 3 | 4 | 2 | 8 |
| 4 | 3 | 2 | 11 |
| 5 | 5 | 5 | 9 |

**Table 12.7**

| $i$ | $A_i + B_i$ | $B_i + C_i$ | Order |
|---|---|---|---|
| 1 | 11 | 10 → | 5th |
| 2 | 11 | 10 | 4th |
| 3 | 6 — | 10 → | 2nd |
| 4 | 5 — | 13 → | 1st |
| 5 | 10 — | 14 → | 3rd |

Solution: 4, 3, 5, 2, 1 or 4, 3, 5, 1, 2. $T$ = 45.

## Sequencing: Two jobs ($n$ = 2) and $m$ facilities (static)

A graphical solution procedure can be used for the problem where two jobs are to be processed on each of $m$ facilities but in different orders.

**EXAMPLE**

Consider the example shown in Table 12.8 where there are five facilities, A, B, C, D and E. The solution is shown in Figure 12.3. The graph shows job 1 plotted on the $x$ axis and job 2 plotted on the $y$ axis. Co-ordinates (0, 0) represent the time at which the programme begins and co-ordinates (13, 12) the time the programme finishes. Because each facility can process only one job at a time the shaded rectangular areas represent unfeasible areas. The problem is, therefore, to travel from (0, 0) to (13, 12) by the shortest route (to minimize $T$) using only vertical (processing job 2) or horizontal (processing job 1) or 45° lines (processing jobs 1 and 2). The graph shows two possible solutions. The minimum throughput time ($T$) is 15 hours.

**Table 12.8**

| Job (*i*) | 1 | | 2 | |
|---|---|---|---|---|
| | Order | Time (hours) | Order | Time (hours) |
| First operation | $A_1$ | 4 | $A_2$ | 2 |
| Second operation | $B_1$ | 3 | $D_2$ | 2 |
| Third operation | $C_1$ | 1 | $C_2$ | 4 |
| Fourth operation | $D_1$ | 3 | $B_2$ | 2 |
| Fifth operation | $E_1$ | 2 | $E_2$ | 2 |

**Figure 12.3**

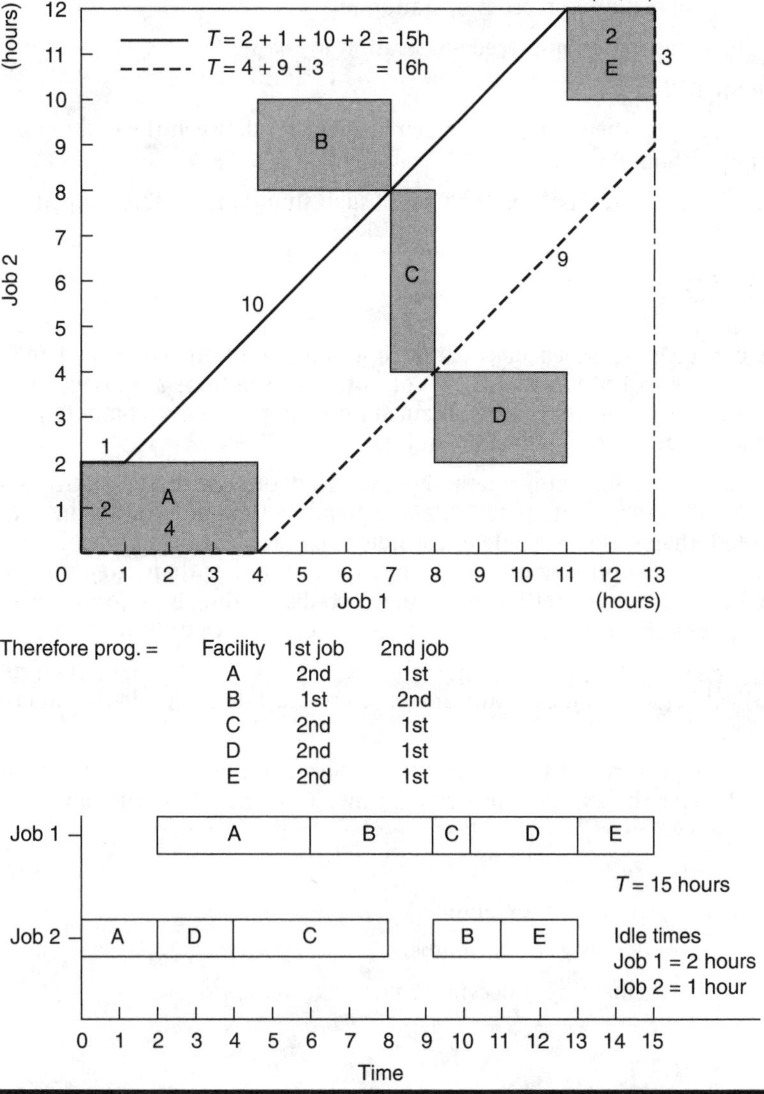

## Sequencing by linear programming (static)

With a little ingenuity the sequencing of jobs on facilities can be represented by a series of linear equations or inequalities, e.g.

let $x_i$ = time at which operation $i$ must begin

and $a_i$ = processing time for operation $i$

Then, since each facility can process only one job at a time, one job must precede the other by an interval equal to or greater than its processing time.

Either $x_2 - x_1 \geq a_1$ (job 1 precedes job 2) or

$x_1 - x_2 \geq a_2$ (job 2 precedes job 1)

Additional requirements can be represented in a similar manner, e.g.

(a) Order requirements:

$x_l + a_l \leq x_m$ (operation $l$ precedes operation $m$)

$x_m + a_m \leq x_n$ (operation $m$ precedes operation $n$)

(b) Delay requirements:

$x_p + a_p + \Delta_{pq} = x_q$ (there must be a given interval $\Delta_{pq}$ between the end of operation $p$ and the start of operation $q$)

Linear programming is a method of solving a set of such simultaneous linear equations or inequalities.

# DISPATCHING

Many of the techniques described above offer optimum solutions to sequencing problems, but a question that should be asked is whether or not optimum solutions are necessary or even desirable. Clearly, if a solution to a problem can be obtained only after excessive computation or through over-simplification then there is little to recommend it.

Furthermore, all of the foregoing methods have dealt only with the static problem. When the dynamic situation arises there is no practical and general method of ensuring an optimum solution. If this fact is accepted, then it is reasonable to consider such problems in simpler 'dispatching' terms, i.e. considering the immediate priority of jobs on one facility, rather than attempting explicitly to consider several facilities at once. The efficiency with which dispatching is performed determines to a large extent the overall operations efficiency, since it can affect resource utilization, etc.

The principal procedure for 'dispatching' is the use of priority rules. Many such rules exist, some of which are described below. In all cases the aim is to use the rule to decide the order in which waiting jobs will be processed.

1. ***Job slack*** (*S*). Give priority to the jobs with least 'job slack' , i.e. the amount of contingency or free time, over and above the expected processing time, available before the job is completed at a predetermined date, i.e.

   $$S = t_0 - t_1 - \Sigma a_i$$

   where $t_0$ = future date (e.g. week number)

   $t_1$ = present date (e.g. week number)

   $\Sigma a_i$ = sum of remaining processing times (e.g. weeks)

Where delays are associated with each operation, e.g. delays caused by interfacility transport, this rule is less suitable, and hence the following rule may be used.

2. ***Job slack per operation.*** $(S/N)$, where $N$ = number of remaining operations. Therefore where $S$ is the same for two or more jobs, the job having the most remaining operations is processed first.
3. ***Job slack ratio***, or the ratio of the total remaining time to the remaining slack time, i.e.

$$\frac{S}{t_0 - t_1}$$

In all the above cases, where the priority index is negative the job cannot be completed by the required date.

4. ***Shortest imminent operation*** (SIO), i.e. process first the job with the shortest processing time.
5. ***Longest imminent operation*** (LIO). This is the converse of (4).
6. ***Scheduled start date***. This is perhaps the most frequently used rule. The date on which operations must be started so that a job will meet a required completion date is calculated, usually by employing reverse scheduling from the completion date, e.g.

$$x_i = t_0 - \Sigma a_i$$

$$\text{or } x_i = t_0 - \Sigma(a_i + f_i)$$

where $x_i$ = scheduled start date for an operation

$f_i$ = delay or contingency allowance

Usually some other rule is also used, e.g. first come, first served, to decide priorities between jobs with equal $x_i$ values.

7. ***Earliest due date***, i.e. process first the job with the earliest due or completion date.
8. ***Subsequent processing times***. Process first the job that has the longest remaining process time, i.e. $\Sigma a_i$ or $\Sigma(a_i + f_i)$.
9. ***Value***. To reduce work-in-progress inventory cost, process first the job which has the highest value.
10. ***Minimum total float***. This rule is the one usually adopted when scheduling by network techniques (see Chapter 13).
11. ***Subsequent operation***. Look ahead to see where the job will go after this operation has been completed and process first the job which goes to a 'critical' queue, i.e. a facility with a small queue of available work, thus minimizing the possibility of facility idle time.
12. ***First come, first served*** (FCFS).
13. ***Random*** (e.g. in order of job number).

Rules 12 and 13 are random since, unlike the others, neither depends directly on job characteristics such as length of operation, value, etc.

Priority rules can be classified further, as follows:

(a) ***Local rules*** depend solely on data relating to jobs in the queue at any particular facility.

(b) ***General rules*** depend on data relating to jobs in the queue at any particular facility and/or data for jobs in queues at *other* facilities.

Local rules, because of the smaller amount of information used, are easier and cheaper to calculate than general (sometimes called *global*) rules. All the above, with the exception of rule 11, are local rules.

One further classification of rules is as follows:

(a) ***Static rules*** are those in which the priority index for a job does not change with the passage of time, during waiting in any one queue.

(b) ***Dynamic rules*** are those in which the priority index is a function of the present time.

Rules, 4, 5, 6, 7, 8, 9, 10, 11, 12 and 13 above are all static, whereas the remainder are dynamic.

A great deal of research work has been conducted in an attempt to evaluate the merits of these rules. Several criteria have been used, e.g.

(a) *Due date criteria*, e.g.

1. *Mean of the completion distribution*. The completion distribution shows the relative frequency with which jobs are completed early, on time and late. The mean of the distribution represents the average dispatching efficiency. Early completion is assumed to offset late completion.
2. *The variance of the completion distribution.* The variance is a measure of the dispersion of values or the spread of a distribution; hence the variance of the completion distribution is a measure of the consistency of dispatching results.
3. *Mean lateness*. If we consider that only the *late* completion of a job is detrimental, then the mean lateness is a measure of dispatching efficiency.
4. *The number of jobs late.*

(b) Criteria related to *throughput*, or *waiting time* and the *congestion* of jobs, e.g.

1. mean throughput time;
2. throughput time variance;
3. mean number of jobs in process;
4. variance of number of jobs in process.

Perhaps the most effective rule according to such research is the SIO rule, and more particularly various extensions of this rule. Simulation studies have shown that of all 'local' rules, those based on the SIO rule are perhaps the most effective, certainly when considered against criteria such as minimizing the number of jobs in the system the mean of the 'completion distribution' and the throughput time. The SIO rule appears to be particularly effective in reducing throughput time, the truncated SIO and the two-class SIO rules being perhaps the most effective derivatives, having the additional advantage of reducing throughput time variance and lateness.

The 'first come, first served' priority rule has been shown to be particularly beneficial in reducing average lateness, whereas the 'scheduled start date and total float' rule has been proved effective where jobs are of the network type.

## ASSIGNMENT *(see also Appendix I)*

Sometimes, when the operations manager is attempting to decide how orders are to be scheduled onto available facilities, there are alternative solutions. For example, many different facilities may be capable of performing the operations required on one customer or item. Operations management must then decide which jobs are to be scheduled onto which facilities in order to achieve some objective, such as minimum cost or minimum throughput time. We shall look at two methods of tackling this problem.

### The index method

This simple, rapid, but approximate method of facility/job assignment is best described by means of an example.

EXAMPLE

## A laboratory

A laboratory must analyse five samples in a period of time. Each in effect requires several very similar tests, and each can be run on any one of three facilities A, B and C. Table 12.9 gives the operation time for each sample test on each of the available facilities.

**Table 12.9 Operation time per sample test on each facility**

| Sample no. (i) | No. of tests for sample ($Q_i$) | $x_{ij}$ Operation time per test on facility $j$ (min.) | | |
|---|---|---|---|---|
| | | A | B | C |
| 1 | 30 | 5.0 | 4.0 | 2.5 |
| 2 | 25 | 1.5 | 2.5 | 4.0 |
| 3 | 45 | 2.0 | 4.0 | 4.5 |
| 4 | 15 | 3.0 | 2.5 | 3.5 |
| 5 | 10 | 4.0 | 3.5 | 2.0 |

The available capacity for these facilities for the period in question is:

A = 100 minutes

B = 80 minutes

C = 150 minutes

The index number for a facility is a measure of the time disadvantage of using that facility for processing, and is obtained by using this formula:

$$I_j = \frac{x_{ij} - (x_i \text{ minimum})}{(x_i \text{ minimum})}$$

where $I_j$ = index number for facility

$x_{ij}$ = operation time for test $i$ on facility $j$

$x_i$ min. = minimum operation time for test $i$.

For order 1:

$$I_A = \frac{5.0 - 2.5}{2.5} = 1.0$$

$$I_B = \frac{1.0 - 2.5}{2.5} = 0.6$$

$$I_C = \frac{2.5 - 2.5}{2.5} = 0$$

Table 12.10 shows the index numbers for all facilities and samples. Using Table 12.10 and remembering that the index number is a measure of the time disadvantage of using that facility, we can now allocate samples to facilities. The best facility for sample 1 is C ($I_C = 0$): the processing time for that sample (75 minutes) is less than the available capacity. We can, therefore, schedule the processing of this sample on this facility. Facility A is the best facility for sample 2, but also the best for sample 3. Both cannot be accommodated because of limitations on available capacity, so we must consider the possibility of allocating one to another facility. The next best facility for sample 2 is facility B ($I_B = 0.67$) and for sample 3 the next best facility is also facility B ($I_B = 1$). Because the time disadvantage on B is less for order 2, allocate order 2 to B and 3 to A. The best facility for sample 4 is B but there is now insufficient capacity available on this facility. The alternatives now are to reallocate order 2 to another facility or to allocate sample 4 elsewhere. In the circumstances it is better to allocate sample 4 to facility C. Finally sample 5 can be allocated to its best facility, C.

Table 12.10

| | | Facility A | | Facility B | | Facility C | |
|---|---|---|---|---|---|---|---|
| **Sample no.** | **No. of tests** | **Index no.** | **Processing time for test (min)** | **Index no.** | **Processing time for test (min)** | **Index no.** | **Processing time for test (min)** |
| 1 | 30 | 1.0 | 150 | 0.6 | 120 | 0 | 75 |
| 2 | 25 | 0 | 37.5 | 0.67 | 62.5 | 1.67 | 100 |
| 3 | 45 | 0 | 90 | 1.0 | 180 | 1.25 | 202.5 |
| 4 | 15 | 0.2 | 45 | 0 | 37.5 | 0.4 | 52.5 |
| 5 | 10 | 1.0 | 40 | 0.75 | 35 | 0 | 20 |
| Capacity | | | 100 | | 80 | | 150 |
| (% utilization) | | | (90) | | (78) | | (98) |

The disadvantages of this method are readily apparent. First, with problems involving more jobs and facilities than the one used here, the allocation and reallocation of jobs might be very tedious. Second, we have not considered the possibility of splitting a job.

## Linear programming method

The problem of assigning jobs to available facilities can also be solved by linear programming. The objectives and the constraints can be formulated as a set of linear inequalities which might then be solved using, say, the Simplex method described in Appendix I. Let us assume, for the sake of simplicity, that the operating costs of the facility are not dependent on the type of job assigned to them and that, unlike previously, individual orders may be assigned to more than one facility. Consider our previous three-facility, five-order problem (Table 12.11).

**Table 12.11**

| No. ($i$) | No. of jobs in order ($Q_i$) | Throughput per minute per facility (jobs) | | |
|---|---|---|---|---|
| | | A | B | C |
| 1 | 30 | 0.20 | 0.25 | 0.40 |
| 2 | 25 | 0.67 | 0.40 | 0.25 |
| 3 | 45 | 0.50 | 0.25 | 0.22 |
| 4 | 15 | 0.33 | 0.40 | 0.29 |
| 5 | 10 | 0.25 | 0.29 | 0.50 |
| Capacity available (mins) | | 100 | 80 | 150 |
| Operating cost (£/min) $C_j$ | | 1.00 | 0.75 | 0.85 |

We can represent the assignment of items to facilities by using the following notation:

$Q_{i,j}$ where $i$ = order no.

$j$ = facilities

i.e. $Q_{1,A}$ = quantity of order 1 assigned to facility A

$Q_{1,B}$ = quantity of order 1 assigned to facility B

Our objective is to obtain the least-cost assignment of jobs to facilities; we must therefore minimize the following objective function:

$$\text{Total cost} = C = 1.0\left(\frac{Q_{1,A}}{0.20}+\frac{Q_{2,A}}{0.67}+\frac{Q_{3,A}}{0.50}+\frac{Q_{4,A}}{0.33}+\frac{Q_{5,A}}{0.25}\right)$$

$$+\ 0.75\left(\frac{Q_{1,B}}{0.25}+\frac{Q_{2,B}}{0.40}+\frac{Q_{3,B}}{0.25}+\frac{Q_{4,B}}{0.40}+\frac{Q_{5,B}}{0.29}\right)$$

$$+\ 0.85\left(\frac{Q_{1,C}}{0.40}+\frac{Q_{2,C}}{0.25}+\frac{Q_{3,C}}{0.22}+\frac{Q_{4,C}}{0.29}+\frac{Q_{5,C}}{0.50}\right)$$

Since the number of jobs allocated to facilities must not exceed the quantity in the order, the following constraints must be observed:

$Q_{1,A} + Q_{1,B} + Q_{1,C} = 30$

$Q_{2,A} + Q_{2,B} + Q_{2,C} = 25$

$Q_{3,A} + Q_{3,B} + Q_{3,C} = 45$

$Q_{4,A} + Q_{4,B} + Q_{4,C} = 15$

$Q_{5,A} + Q_{5,B} + Q_{5,C} = 10$

Also:

$$Q_{i,j}\begin{pmatrix} i = 1, 2, 3, 4, 5 \\ j = \text{A, B, C} \end{pmatrix} \geq 0$$

These inequalities may be solved simultaneously and the objective function minimized by using the Simplex method of linear programming. The situation in which facility operating cost is dependent on the type of job being processed may be formulated in the same manner.

## Interference

When more than one facility is assigned to a single worker, a phenomenon known as facilities interference may occur. For example, if one operator attends three facilities, when one stops (either at the end of its operating cycle or for any other reason, e.g. breakdown) then the operator will attend to it. If, however, while the operator is attending to it one of the other facilities stops, then, since he or she is unable to attend to both, a certain amount of facility idle time must result. This is known as interference.

The assignment of two or more facilities to one operator is a common feature in many industries, and, of course, the nature of the work being done on such facilities will determine the amount of attention required from the operator. This, in turn, will determine the optimum number of facilities to assign to the operator. This worker–facility assignment, since it determines the system capacity, is of considerable importance during operations planning.

The mathematical treatment of multi-facility assignments has been attempted by many authors, but the problem is a particularly complex one, especially when the operators have duties other than simply attending to the facility and when the characteristics of the facilities differ. In this section we will confine ourselves to a simple deterministic case in which facilities, all of which are the same, behave in some predictable manner.

We can identify three types of activity:

(a) ***Independent activities*** performed by either facility or operator without the need for the services or attention of the other.
   1. Facility-independent activity time per cycle = $t$.
   2. Operator-independent time per cycle = $b$.

(b) ***Concurrent activities*** which must be performed by operator and facility together = $a$.

(c) ***Idle time***, when either operator or facility is waiting for the other.
   1. Operator idle time per cycle = $i_o$.
   2. Facility idle time per cycle = $i_m$.

For example, if an operator attended only one facility the situation in Figure 12.4 might result.

Unless the operator is able to perform other duties during the period in which the facility operates independently, a great deal of operator idle time must result. In such a case the operator might reasonably be asked to attend to more than one of these facilities. (In the example in Figure 12.4 he or she could attend to at least two facilities.)

The ideal number of facilities to allocate to one operator ($n^1$) can be calculated using this formula:

$$n^1 = \frac{a + t}{a + b}$$

**Figure 12.4** Cycle for operator attending one facility

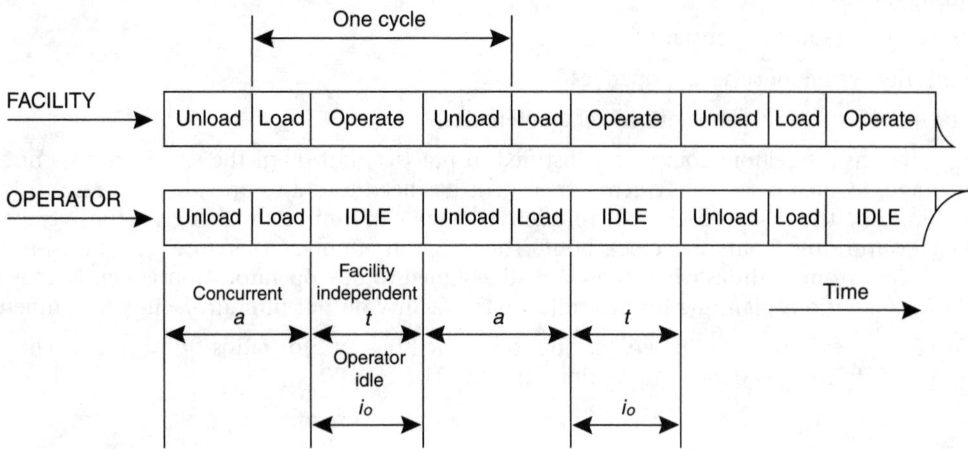


Unless we are particularly fortunate, $n^1$ will not be a whole number, but as it is usually possible to assign only whole facilities to operators we must decide whether to allocate the next whole number smaller than $n^1$ and hence incur operator idle time, or the next whole number larger than $n^1$ and incur facility idle time, i.e.

$$(n) < n^1 < (n + 1)$$

This decision, of course, will depend on the relative cost of operator and facility idle time.

If

$C_o$ = Cost of operator/h

$C_m$ = Cost of facility/h

and

$$E = \frac{C_o}{C_m}$$

then the best multi-facility assignment can be found by using the formula:

$$\frac{Y_n}{Y_{(n+1)}} = \frac{E + n}{E + n + 1} \times \frac{n^1}{n}$$

$Y_n$ is the cost per unit of processing with an assignment of $n$ facilities, and $Y_{(n+1)}$ likewise for an assignment of $n + 1$ machines.

If $Y_n/Y_{(n+1)}$ is greater than 1, then $n + 1$ facilities should be used, and if $Y_n/Y_{(n+1)}$ is less than 1, then $n$ facilities should be used.

When the facility-independent time ($t$) and the concurrent activity time ($a$) per cycle are constant, then we can calculate, as above, the assignment arrangement to avoid interference; but when either or both of those times vary the problem is considerably more difficult.

One of the best-known treatments of this complex, queuing-type situation was presented by Ashcroft over thirty years ago. He made the following assumptions:

(a) The probability of a facility requiring service by the operator is independent of the time it has been running hitherto.

(b) All service times ($a$) are constant.

(c) No priority system of servicing operates.

(d) All facilities have similar operational characteristics.

Such assumptions are seldom completely justified in practice, but often the situation does not differ too much and, in such cases, the Ashcroft treatment has been found to provide good results. Using a statistical queuing theory approach, Ashcroft derived a table of numbers which gives the average number of facility running hours per clock hour. The Ashcroft number, therefore, is a measure of the expected output from facilities when these are all assigned to one operator. Consequently they are of value during operations planning for determining the facility output in multi-facility assignments.

Table 12.12 gives Ashcroft numbers for one to ten facilities and for ratios ($p$) of concurrent service time ($a$) to facility-independent running time ($t$) from 0.01 to 1.00.

**EXAMPLE**

### *A laundry*

An operator must attend to several washing machines. Determine the efficiency in terms of average running hours/clock hour for different operator/machine assignments if service time (unload and load machine)/complete cycle (i.e. $a$) = 5 minutes and unattended machine running time/cycle (i.e. $b$) = 10 minutes.

$$p = \frac{a}{t} = 0.5$$

| No. of washing machines ($n$) | Ashcroft no. $A_n$ | Efficiency (%) $\frac{A_n}{n} \times 100$ |
|---|---|---|
| 1 | 0.67 | 67 |
| 2 | 1.24 | 62 |
| 3 | 1.67 | 56 |
| 4 | 1.90 | 48 |
| 5 | 1.98 | 40 |

In fact, to determine the best assignment, operator and facility costs must be taken into account. The cost per clock hour is the cost of one operator per hour, plus $n$ times the cost of a facility per hour:

$$Y = C_o + nC_m$$

The best assignment is that which minimizes the ratio:

$$\frac{Y}{A_n C_o}$$

which can also be expressed as:

$$\frac{1 + (nC_m/C_o)}{A_n}$$

## Table 12.12 Ashcroft numbers

| *p* | *n* = 1 | *n* = 2 | *n* = 3 | *n* = 4 | *n* = 5 | *n* = 6 | *n* = 7 | *n* = 8 | *n* = 9 | *n* = 10 |
|---|---|---|---|---|---|---|---|---|---|---|
| 0.00 | 1.00 | 2.00 | 3.00 | 4.00 | 5.00 | 6.00 | 7.00 | 8.00 | 9.00 | 10.00 |
| 0.01 | 0.99 | 1.98 | 2.97 | 3.96 | 4.95 | 5.94 | 6.93 | 7.92 | 8.91 | 9.90 |
| 0.02 | 0.98 | 1.96 | 2.94 | 3.92 | 4.90 | 5.88 | 6.85 | 7.83 | 8.81 | 9.78 |
| 0.03 | 0.97 | 1.94 | 2.91 | 3.88 | 4.84 | 5.81 | 6.77 | 7.74 | 8.70 | 9.66 |
| 0.04 | 0.96 | 1.92 | 2.88 | 3.84 | 4.79 | 5.74 | 6.69 | 7.64 | 8.58 | 9.52 |
| 0.05 | 0.95 | 1.90 | 2.85 | 3.79 | 4.74 | 5.67 | 6.61 | 7.53 | 8.45 | 9.37 |
| 0.06 | 0.94 | 1.88 | 2.82 | 3.75 | 4.68 | 5.60 | 6.51 | 7.42 | 8.31 | 9.19 |
| 0.07 | 0.93 | 1.86 | 2.79 | 3.71 | 4.62 | 5.52 | 6.42 | 7.29 | 8.15 | 8.99 |
| 0.08 | 0.93 | 1.85 | 2.76 | 3.67 | 4.56 | 5.44 | 6.31 | 7.16 | 7.89 | 8.76 |
| 0.09 | 0.92 | 1.83 | 2.73 | 3.62 | 4.50 | 5.36 | 6.20 | 7.01 | 7.78 | 8.50 |
| 0.10 | 0.91 | 1.81 | 2.70 | 3.58 | 4.44 | 5.28 | 6.08 | 6.85 | 7.57 | 8.21 |
| 0.11 | 0.90 | 1.79 | 2.67 | 3.53 | 4.38 | 5.19 | 5.96 | 6.68 | 7.33 | 7.89 |
| 0.12 | 0.89 | 1.77 | 2.64 | 3.49 | 4.31 | 5.10 | 5.83 | 6.50 | 7.08 | 7.55 |
| 0.13 | 0.88 | 1.76 | 2.61 | 3.44 | 4.24 | 5.00 | 5.69 | 6.31 | 6.81 | 7.19 |
| 0.14 | 0.88 | 1.74 | 2.58 | 3.40 | 4.18 | 4.90 | 5.55 | 6.10 | 6.53 | 6.83 |
| 0.15 | 0.87 | 1.72 | 2.55 | 3.35 | 4.11 | 4.80 | 5.40 | 5.90 | 6.25 | 6.48 |
| 0.16 | 0.86 | 1.71 | 2.52 | 3.31 | 4.04 | 4.70 | 5.25 | 5.68 | 5.97 | 6.14 |
| 0.17 | 0.85 | 1.69 | 2.50 | 3.26 | 3.97 | 4.59 | 5.10 | 5.47 | 5.70 | 5.82 |
| 0.18 | 0.85 | 1.67 | 2.48 | 3.22 | 3.90 | 4.48 | 4.94 | 5.26 | 5.44 | 5.52 |
| 0.19 | 0.84 | 1.66 | 2.44 | 3.17 | 3.83 | 4.37 | 4.79 | 5.05 | 5.19 | 5.24 |
| 0.20 | 0.83 | 1.64 | 2.41 | 3.12 | 3.75 | 4.26 | 4.63 | 4.85 | 4.95 | 4.99 |
| 0.21 | 0.83 | 1.62 | 2.38 | 3.08 | 3.68 | 4.15 | 4.48 | 4.66 | 4.73 | 4.75 |
| 0.22 | 0.82 | 1.61 | 2.35 | 3.03 | 3.61 | 4.04 | 4.33 | 4.47 | 4.53 | 4.54 |
| 0.23 | 0.81 | 1.59 | 2.33 | 2.98 | 3.53 | 3.94 | 4.18 | 4.30 | 4.34 | 4.34 |
| 0.24 | 0.81 | 1.58 | 2.30 | 2.94 | 3.46 | 3.83 | 4.04 | 4.13 | 4.16 | 4.16 |
| 0.25 | 0.80 | 1.56 | 2.27 | 2.89 | 3.39 | 3.72 | 3.90 | 3.98 | 4.00 | 4.00 |
| 0.26 | 0.79 | 1.55 | 2.24 | 2.85 | 3.31 | 3.62 | 3.77 | 3.83 | 3.84 | 3.84 |
| 0.27 | 0.79 | 1.53 | 2.22 | 2.80 | 3.24 | 3.52 | 3.65 | 3.69 | 3.70 | 3.70 |
| 0.28 | 0.78 | 1.52 | 2.19 | 2.75 | 3.17 | 3.42 | 3.53 | 3.56 | 3.57 | 3.57 |
| 0.29 | 0.77 | 1.51 | 2.16 | 2.71 | 3.10 | 3.33 | 3.42 | 3.44 | 3.45 | 3.45 |
| 0.30 | 0.77 | 1.49 | 2.14 | 2.67 | 3.03 | 3.23 | 3.31 | 3.33 | 3.33 | 3.33 |
| 0.31 | 0.76 | 1.48 | 2.11 | 2.62 | 2.97 | 3.14 | 3.21 | 3.22 | 3.22 | 3.22 |
| 0.32 | 0.76 | 1.46 | 2.09 | 2.58 | 2.90 | 3.06 | 3.11 | 3.12 | 3.12 | 3.12 |
| 0.33 | 0.75 | 1.45 | 2.06 | 2.53 | 2.84 | 2.98 | 3.02 | 3.03 | 3.03 | 3.03 |
| 0.34 | 0.75 | 1.44 | 2.03 | 2.49 | 2.77 | 2.90 | 2.93 | 2.94 | 2.94 | 2.94 |
| 0.35 | 0.74 | 1.42 | 2.01 | 2.45 | 2.71 | 2.82 | 2.85 | 2.86 | 2.86 | 2.86 |
| 0.40 | 0.71 | 1.36 | 1.89 | 2.25 | 2.43 | 2.49 | 2.50 | 2.50 | 2.50 | 2.50 |
| 0.45 | 0.69 | 1.30 | 1.78 | 2.07 | 2.19 | 2.22 | 2.22 | 2.22 | 2.22 | 2.22 |
| 0.50 | 0.67 | 1.24 | 1.67 | 1.90 | 1.98 | 2.00 | 2.00 | 2.00 | 2.00 | 2.00 |
| 0.55 | 0.64 | 1.19 | 1.57 | 1.76 | 1.81 | 1.82 | | | | |
| 0.60 | 0.62 | 1.14 | 1.48 | 1.63 | 1.66 | 1.67 | | | | |
| 0.65 | 0.61 | 1.10 | 1.40 | 1.51 | 1.54 | 1.54 | | | | |
| 0.70 | 0.59 | 1.05 | 1.32 | 1.41 | 1.43 | 1.43 | | | | |
| 0.75 | 0.57 | 1.01 | 1.25 | 1.32 | 1.33 | 1.33 | | | | |
| 0.80 | 0.55 | 0.97 | 1.19 | 1.24 | 1.25 | 1.25 | | | | |
| 0.85 | 0.54 | 0.94 | 1.13 | 1.17 | 1.17 | 1.18 | | | | |
| 0.90 | 0.53 | 0.91 | 1.07 | 1.11 | 1.11 | 1.11 | | | | |
| 0.95 | 0.51 | 0.87 | 1.02 | 1.05 | 1.05 | 1.05 | | | | |
| 1.00 | 0.50 | 0.84 | 0.98 | 1.00 | 1.00 | 1.00 | | | | |

*Source: O'Connor, T. F. (1952)* Productivity and Probability. *Manchester: Emmott & Co. Ltd. Reproduced with permission*

**EXAMPLE**

## A 'super' laundry

Find the best machine assignment.

In this case:

$p = 0.1$

$C_o = £2$

$C_m = £6$

Hence:

| No. of machines/ operator ($n$) | $A_n$ | $\frac{1 + nC_m/C_o}{A_n}$ |
|---|---|---|
| 1 | 0.91 | 4.40 |
| 2 | 1.81 | 3.87 |
| 3 | 2.70 | 3.71 |
| 4 | 3.58 | 3.63 |
| 5 | 4.44 | 3.61 |
| 6 | 5.28 | 3.60 ← best assignment = 6 machines/operator |
| 7 | 6.08 | 3.62 |
| 8 | 6.85 | 3.65 |

**EXAMPLE**

## Another 'super' laundry

Find the best machine assignment.

In this case:

$p = 0.26$

$\frac{C_m}{C_o} = 2.0$

| $n$ | $A_n$ | $\frac{1 + (nC_m/C_o)}{A_n}$ |
|---|---|---|
| 1 | 0.80 | 3.75 |
| 2 | 1.56 | 3.21 |
| 3 | 2.27 | 3.08 ← best assignment = 3 machines/operator |
| 4 | 2.89 | 3.11 |
| 5 | 3.39 | 3.24 |
| 6 | 3.72 | 3.50 |

# TIMETABLING

The timetabling of activities is of particular relevance for repetitive functions. Bus, train and air services usually operate to a timetable. Similarly, the activities of certain service systems, e.g. cinemas, are timetabled. These are 'customer push' systems, so customers have to take advantage of the function at predetermined times. The function is not performed at other times, so customers arriving at the wrong time must wait, and, of course, if there are no customers at the time selected for the performance of the function, or if not enough customers are available to utilize fully the facilities provided, there will be under-utilization of capacity. In many situations timetables are necessary, since common resources are deployed to provide a variety or series of functions. In many transport systems, for example, vehicles travel a set route, providing movement for individuals between points along that route. In certain service systems, e.g. hospitals, common resources such as medical specialists provide a service in a variety of departments, or for a variety of types of customers, in a given period of time. Certain out-patient clinics operate in this fashion. In all such cases a timetable will normally be developed and made available to customers. Much the same situations may apply in 'customer pull' systems, where functions occur at given times. It follows that in all such cases the nature of demand must be predictable since, in effect, function is undertaken in anticipation of demand. In fact, in such cases, the absence of (sufficient) customers at the time selected for the performance of the function may give rise to the creation of output stock. Alternatively, output may be lost or wasted. The timetabling of such activities is an exercise in internally oriented scheduling, since no direct account is taken of individual customers' demands. The development of timetables will take into account the time required for, or the duration of, activities, and in many cases (e.g. transport systems) the required or preferred order or sequence.

Few quantitative techniques are relevant in the development of such timetables. 'Routeing', flow planning and vehicle scheduling procedures are of relevance in timetabling transport systems. In some cases the problem will resemble that of sequencing outlined above, while in others it may be convenient to use Gantt charts and simulation procedures in both the development and the evaluation of timetables.

# OPT (OPTIMIZED PRODUCTION TECHNOLOGY)

OPT is a proprietory computer 'package' which aims to schedule flows through batch working and demand dependent/externally oriented systems so that output is maximized. The principal distinguishing feature of the OPT approach is the focus on 'bottleneck' operations. In fact OPT is based on a set of rules which have some general applicability, so it is also of interest here as an approach to scheduling.

At its simplest, OPT is a method for scheduling work through bottlenecks. More broadly, the OPT approach is a system for planning, scheduling and inventory management. We will consider both aspects and in so doing compare OPT to MRP.

## Scheduling bottleneck operations

The nine basic 'rules' of OPT are given in Table 12.13. The example below illustrates the significance of several of these rules.

**Table 12.13 OPT rules**

1. Balance flow, not capacity.
2. The level of utilization of a non-bottleneck is not determined by its own potential but by some other constraint in the system.
3. Activation and utilization of a resource are non-synonymous.
4. An hour lost at a bottleneck is an hour lost for the total system.
5. An hour saved at a non-bottleneck is a mirage.
6. Bottlenecks govern both throughput and inventories.
7. The transfer batch may not, and often should not, be equal to the process batch.
8. The process batch should be variable, not fixed.
9. Schedules should be established by looking at all of the constraints simultaneously. Lead times are the result of a schedule and cannot be predetermined.

**EXAMPLE**

A three-stage processing system, through which two types of item A and B are to be processed, is shown in Figure 12.5.

**Figure 12.5**

Stage X — X
Inventory
Stage Y — Y
Inventory
Stage Z — Z
Customer

The relevant data for the three stages are given in Table 12.14.

The bottleneck operation is Y. If all three operations work continually, processing a single type of item, inventory will build up after X, and idle time will occur at Z when the inventory after Y is eliminated and Z becomes starved of work. If the capacity of X or Z is increased there will be no increase in the output of the system. If the capacity of Y is increased, system throughput and output is increased. Whilst the cost of increasing throughput in this way is only related to the cost incurred at Y, the value of the increased output is a function of the value added by all three stages. Conversely, a reduction in throughput at Y reduces system throughput, whilst a reduction at Y and Z will, initially, have no such effect (Rules 4, 5 and 6).

Consider now the processing of items in batches. The economic batch size (see Chapter 14) has been calculated for each process and is shown in Table 12.14. It is intended that an operation be set up, the 'economic batch' be processed, and then the operation be re-set for the processing of the other types of item. For X this would mean that we would spend 2 hours setting up the operation and then 40 hours processing a batch of 200. For Y, a set-up time of 1 hour would be followed by a run of 25 hours to process 100 items, etc. However, as Y is the bottleneck we need to try to increase the throughput rate at this operation. Although the processing rate is fixed (4/hour) the total number processed over a period of time can be increased if less time is given to set-ups, which means fewer set-ups and larger processing batches. Notice also that if the number of set-ups is increased, and batch sizes reduced at X and Z, this does not affect system throughput. So, in practice, the concept of fixed processing batch sizes for each operation may be inappropriate (Rule 8).

Table 12.14

| Stage | Processing time | Set-up time for process for A and B | Batch size for A and B |
|---|---|---|---|
| X | 0.2 hours | 2 hours | 200 |
| Y | 0.25 hours | 1 hour | 100 |
| Z | 0.15 hours | 2.5 hours | 250 |

Even if a batch of 100 items were to be processed at Y, since Z is likely to be held up or starved, it would be inappropriate to wait for the completion of the whole batch before transferring items to Z. So the 'transfer' batch size could differ from the 'processing' batch (Rule 7).

This example illustrates also the first rule of OPT, that is, the desirability of ensuring a steady flow through the system, i.e. balanced flow, rather than seeking to keep all resources busy. Rule 9 indicates that throughput times are variable, not fixed. They are dependent on schedules, so in managing a system the whole system should be considered simultaneously.

### The OPT approach

The OPT approach, whilst based on the use of these simple rules, also involves the modelling and analysis of the complete processing system. In fact the software package comprises four parts:

(a) ***System modelling***. The program creates a network model of the operating system using information on processing and set-up times, the routeings of items through the system, bills of materials, inven-tories and sales forecasts.

(b) ***Bottleneck identification***. The operation of the system is simulated to identify bottlenecks.

(c) ***Division of system***. The network model is divided into two parts – critical and non-critical. The bottlenecks and all operations that follow these are included in the critical part of the network. The remaining portion of the network includes non-critical operations.

(d) ***Scheduling***. The operations in the critical portion of the network are scheduled. This includes determination of processing and transfer batch sizes, and the timing of operations for each item for the bottleneck operations.

## MATERIALS REQUIREMENTS PLANNING (MRP)[2]

*(see also Chapter 17)*

The principal applications of MRP[2] are in manufacture, particularly batch manufacture. In this context it has some similarities with the line of balance technique (see Chapter 14). There are also similarities

[2] MRP is an open-loop system. It deals only with a part of the planning and scheduling problem for demand-dependent systems. If, in the same computer system, we were able also to take account of some of the other decisions required in planning, scheduling and controlling activities and workflow in an operating system (e.g. the areas covered by Figure 11.1), we would have a more comprehensive, closed-loop system for operations planning and control. MRP II was developed for this purpose. Whilst its origins are in MRP, it is not just an extension of MRP but rather a computer-based system of which MRP is just one part. It was developed for use in manufacturing situations and is also known as manufacturing resource planning (see later in this chapter).

with group technology (see Chapter 14) and the reverse scheduling method (see this chapter). MRP is, however, in principle, of relevance in other situations, both in manufacture and in service operations. Where an MRP approach is appropriate it will often provide the framework within which all scheduling and also inventory decisions are made (see Chapter 17).

## The principles of MRP

Materials requirements planning is concerned primarily with the scheduling of activities and the management of inventories. It is particularly useful where there is a need to produce components, items or sub-assemblies which themselves are later used in the production of a final product or, in non-manufacturing organizations, where the provision of a transport or service for a customer necessitates the use or provision of certain subsystems. For example, it may be used when a customer orders a motor vehicle from a manufacturing organization, which must first manufacture or obtain various components which are then used in the final assembly of that vehicle for that customer. Similarly, in treating a patient in a hospital, e.g. for a major operation, the hospital must, in order to satisfy this service requirement, provide accommodation for the patient, diagnostic tests, anaesthetics and post-care facilities as well as surgical facilities so that the patient's total requirements are satisfied. In these two cases the product or service requested by the customer can be seen to be the 'final' output of the system, which derives from certain lower-level provisions. These lower-level provisions are considered to be *dependent* on the customer's final requirement. Given a measure or forecast of the total number of customers, the demand at lower levels can be obtained. The materials requirements planning technique is used for precisely this purpose. It takes as one of its inputs the measured or forecast demand for the system's outputs. It breaks down this demand into its component parts, compares this requirement against existing inventories, and seeks to schedule the parts required against available capacity. The MRP procedure produces a schedule for all component parts, if necessary through to purchasing requirements, and where appropriate shows expected shortages due to capacity limitations. The basic procedure is illustrated in Figure 12.6. The procedure will be undertaken on a repetitive basis, the

**Figure 12.6** Basic MRP structure

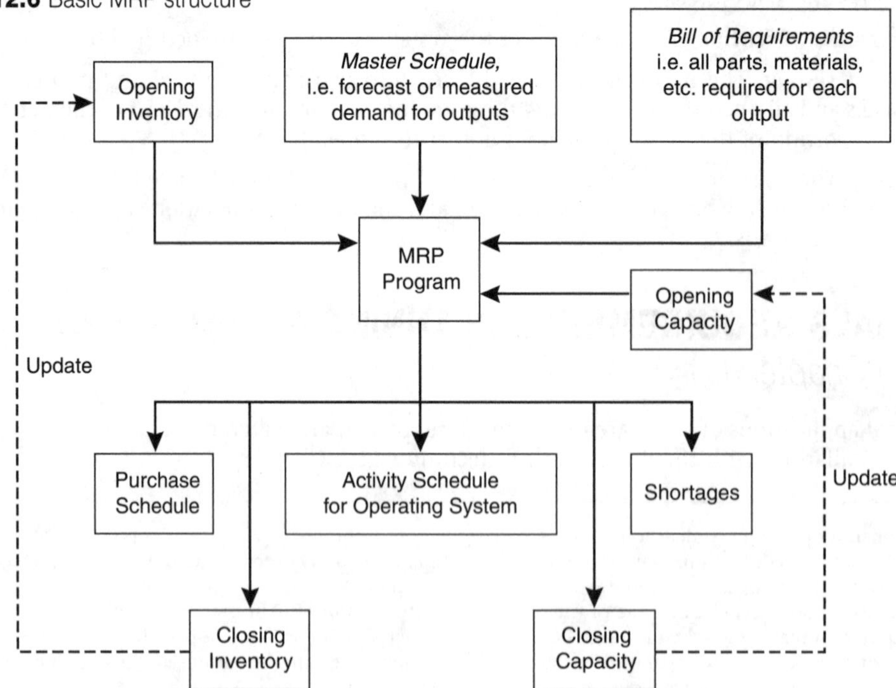

'explosion' and scheduling procedure being repeated at regular intervals, perhaps corresponding to the intervals at which demand forecasting is undertaken or as and when required as a result of changes in known demand. The use of this procedure involves considerable data processing, even for relatively simple outputs. The popularity of the MRP technique and its extensive use have resulted largely from the availability of cheap computing power within organizations.

## The use of MRP

The manner in which MRP operates will be described by reference to a manufacturing situation. The principal *inputs* to the MRP process are as follows:

(a) The ***bill of requirements***. This, in effect, identifies the component parts of a final output product. At each 'level' the different components, materials or sub-assemblies are shown, so the bill of requirements shows not only the total number of sub-parts but also the manner in which these parts eventually come together to constitute the final product. The lead time between levels is also shown. The arrangement is shown diagrammatically in Figure 12.7. There are several different methods of structuring the bill of requirements data. In general, however, the final product level will be referred to as level zero. Below this, at level 1, are the principal sub-assemblies, etc. which

**Figure 12.7** Bill of requirements structure (five levels)

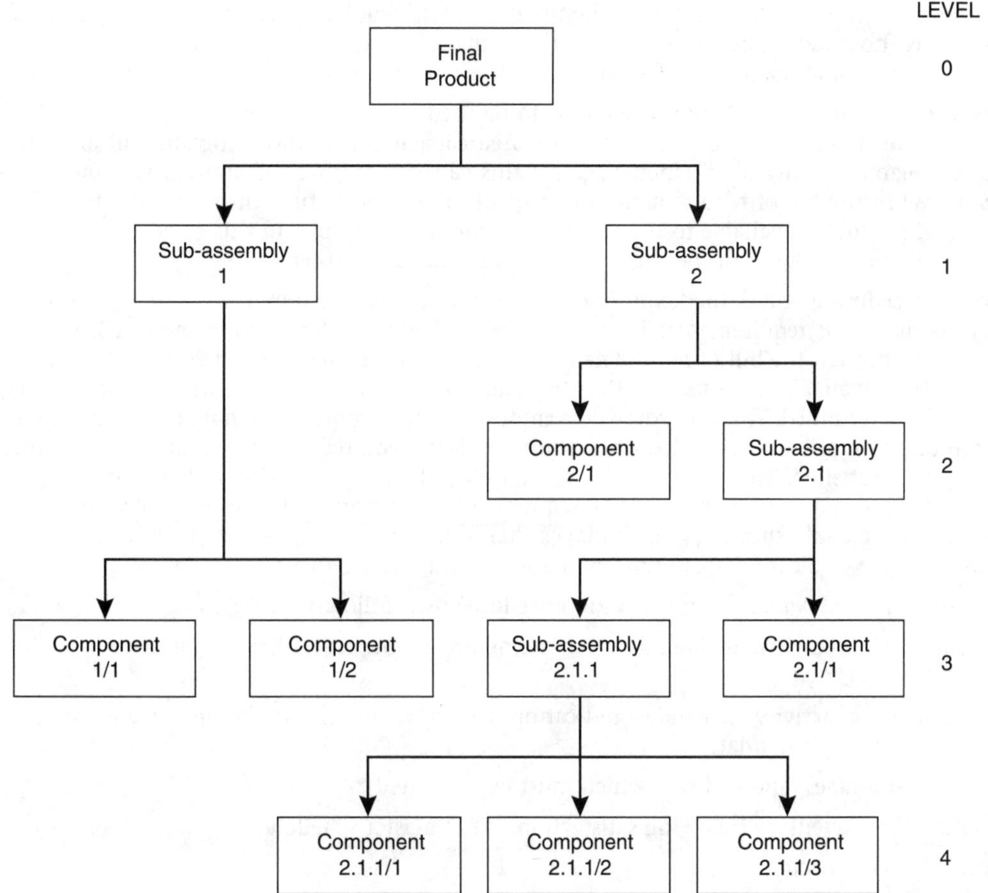

together make up the final product. At level 2 are the components, etc. of the principal sub-assemblies, and so on through as many levels as appropriate to reach the level of raw materials or bought-in items. Each item is assigned to one level only, and each item at each level has a unique coding. The different levels and/or branches may correspond to different design or manufacturing responsibilities. Where complex end products may be made in several different possible configurations from a large number of parts or sub-assemblies which may be assembled in different ways, it is common to use a 'modular' bill of requirements structure. When this approach is being used, even though there may be a very large range of end products differing in detail from one another, it will not be necessary to have a large number of different, unique bill of requirements structures, but sufficient to specify those modules from a composite bill of requirements structure which together constitutes the required end product.

(b) The ***master production schedule*** is based on known or forecast demand for a specified future period. The schedule shows how much of each end item is wanted and when the items are wanted. It is in effect the delivery or the 'due date' schedule for each product expressed in terms of both quantity and timing. The period over which this demand is expressed will depend on the type of product concerned and the capacity planning procedures used by the organization. In general, however, the time period should allow enough time for the acquisition of all materials, the manufacture of all components, parts and sub-assemblies, and the assembly of the final product.

(c) ***Opening inventory***. This record will show the available inventories of all materials, components, sub-assemblies, etc. required for the manufacture of the end product. In general the file will show both total and free (i.e. unallocated) inventory. The latter is more important in the context of MRP, since the objective is to compare component or parts requirements against available stock (i.e. excluding those items already committed to the manufacture of other products), in order to determine purchase and manufacture requirements for items for a particular delivery schedule.

(d) ***Opening capacity***. If the MRP procedure is to be used to provide a production schedule it will be necessary to have available information on free capacity. The MRP program will allocate component manufacturing requirements against this capacity so that the appropriate components at each level in the bill of requirements are available at an appropriate time, in order to ensure that the final product is available to the customer at the required time. In this respect the procedure is very similar to that used in the line of balance technique (Chapter 14).

The basic procedure involves the 'explosion' of the final product requirements into constituent component and materials requirements. This procedure (sometimes referred to as 'netting') is performed level by level through the bill of requirements. The gross requirements for each item at each level are compared with available inventory so that the outstanding parts, components or materials requirements can be determined. This procedure determines how many units of each item are required to meet a given production schedule and also when those units are required, in order that manufacturing lead times might be satisfied. The result of this procedure will be the production of a schedule of purchase requirements, a schedule of manufacturing requirements (i.e. manufacturing activity schedule) and, if appropriate, a schedule showing the shortages that will occur as a result of there being insufficient capacity available to meet component/item manufacturing requirements.

Thus the principal *outputs* from the MRP procedure are as follows:

(a) purchase requirements, including which items are to be ordered, at what time, and in what quantities;

(b) manufacturing activity schedules indicating which items are to be manufactured, in what quantities and by what date;

(c) expected shortages (and/or items which must be expedited);

(d) resultant free inventory following satisfaction of the master schedule;

(e) available free capacity.

The above procedure will be undertaken repetitively. Basically there are two types of approach available. Using the *regenerative* approach the entire MRP procedure, as described above, is repeated periodically. The time period between repetitions will normally conform to the time period between demand forecasts, the two usually being undertaken on a regular basis, e.g. once a month. The approach using the regenerative system is in effect to undertake an entirely new MRP calculation on each occasion, i.e. to undertake each set of calculations as if there had been no previous MRP study. In such cases the inventory inputs to the system will assume that all current stocks are free and that none of the available capacity is committed. Thus each MRP repetition takes into account all known demand for the schedule period, and, from the demand, bill of requirements, inventory and capacity data, calculates a new schedule. Such an approach may be appropriate where the output schedule changes to a relatively small extent. In such circumstances the amount of computation may not be too great and the differences between the schedules produced for successive calculations may not be substantial. An additional advantage of the regenerative approach is that data errors are not repeated or compounded.

Where there is considerable change in the output schedule, or where forecasts are subject to large margins of error, or where the bill of requirements details change, e.g. as a result of design changes, it may be more appropriate to adopt a *net change* approach to materials requirements planning. When this procedure is used only the alterations to the master schedule and/or the other input data are taken into account as and when necessary. These changes are considered and the effects on purchase and manufacturing schedules, inventories, capacity factors, etc. are considered. While the regenerative approach might be useful in a relatively stable situation, in a volatile situation the net change approach might be more appropriate. The net change system requires more processing and will not normally be used when the volumes are high.

## Other factors in the use of MRP

### Batch sizes

The operation of an MRP procedure as described above results in the purchase and/or manufacture of items in the quantities required when they are required. But this takes no account of the need to purchase and manufacture economic batch sizes (see Chapters 14 and 16) which balance ordering or set-up costs against the holding costs. If these economies are to be obtained the MRP procedure must accommodate an economic batching procedure. One method of achieving this is to issue an order, whether a purchase or a manufacturing order, for a fixed (i.e. most economic) quantity of an item whenever there is a requirement for that item. Items surplus to requirements are then placed in stock, and when at a later date an item is required again, stock is depleted or a further economic batch quantity is manufactured. In fact the need for inventories of items over a period of time results mainly from the need to manufacture items in economic batches unless there are safety stock considerations at these levels.

### Safety stock

Where an MRP procedure is used against forecast end-product demand there is a risk that the forecast may be inaccurate and therefore that on occasions more end products are required than had been anticipated for a given period. To protect against such a situation it would be necessary to hold some safety stocks. Where customer requirements are concerned exclusively with end products rather than also being expressed in terms of components or parts (e.g. for spares or replacement purposes) such safety stock is best held at the higher levels within the bill of requirements structure, e.g. at final sub-assembly or final product assembly levels. In these circumstances the MRP procedure itself tends to protect against shortage of lower-level items by producing them in time to meet the final master production schedule. Hence safety stock is normally held only at lower levels where customer demand can be expressed in terms of component parts as well as finished products.

## MRP – comparisons

### MRP and OPT

OPT has some similarities with MRP, of which it can be considered an extension. MRP can be used to form the basis of a system for computer-aided scheduling and inventory control, to which can be added the OPT approach for the identification of bottlenecks and the maximization of throughputs. MRP and OPT are compared further in Table 12.15.

**Table 12.15 Comparison of OPT and MRT**

| OPT | MRP |
|---|---|
| 1. Balance flows, not capacity. | 1. Balance capacity, maintain flows. |
| 2. Bottlenecks are result of other constraints. | 2. Manpower potential is self-determined. |
| 3. Utilization/activity of resource are not same. | 3. Utilization and activity are same. |
| 4. Time lost at bottleneck is totally lost. | 4. Impact is not realized. |
| 5. Time saved at non-critical event is not critical. | 5. System is limited by bottlenecks. |
| 6. Bottlenecks decide inventory throughput. | 6. Little impact on inventories, temporarily on throughput. |
| 7. Transfer not equal to lot size. | 7. Lot splitting should be discouraged. |
| 8. One lot (process batch) can be in several stages of manufacture (transfer batches) at the same time. Process batch (lot size) should vary. | 8. Lot sizes should be fixed. |
| 9. Schedule should be determined by simultaneous input of all constraints. Lead times cannot be predetermined and are variable. | 9. Predetermine lot size; calculate lead time; assign priorities schedule by lead time; adjust capacity by above steps. |

*Source: Jacobs, R. F. (1984) OPT uncovered.* Industrial Engineering *(October)*

### MRP and JIT

MRP was developed as a computer-based system for scheduling activities in dependent demand situations. It enables decisions to be made for each stage of an operating system in a co-ordinated fashion, i.e. so that activities at one stage satisfy the requirements of subsequent stages. It is a demand-driven system, a characteristic which it shares with JIT. There are, however, significant differences between MRP and JIT which are outlined in Table 12.16.

## MRP and capacity, inventory and scheduling decisions

In the above, the relationship between the MRP procedure and capacity planning is clear. MRP, where used, can be seen as the next logical step after that of capacity planning as described in Chapter 11. As most capacity planning is undertaken in aggregate terms, and as activity scheduling requires the development of detailed schedules for particular items or particular processes, the MRP procedure can be seen as a logical intermediate step. Where MRP is used the activity schedule will be an outcome of MRP, and likewise where an MRP procedure is adopted, inventory management will be an integral part of it except for the need, separately, to accommodate batch requirements, etc. Clearly also, the use of MRP has considerable implications in purchasing (see Chapter 17).

Table 12.16 Principal differences between JIT and MRP

| Feature | JIT (with Kanban) | MRP |
|---|---|---|
| Principal objectives | Low inventory | Scheduling activities |
| | Low throughput times | Reduced throughput times |
| | Low WIP | |
| | Organizational change | |
| Time-scale | Short-term | Medium-term |
| Batch sizes | Standard 'bucket' or container sized processing batches | Variable |
| Bill of materials (BOM) | Final operation (e.g. assembly/BOM used) | Detailed and accurate BOM essential |
| Operations control | Normally daily | Usually longer cycle time |
| Inventories | Mostly held as WIP and at workcentres | Off-line stocks normally necessary |
| Vendors | Schedule vendors as extension to own system | Purchase orders with due dates |
| Initiation of work | Kanban cards | Computer-prepared workcentre schedules for a given period |

## MRP II (manufacturing resource planning)

Now that we have broadened our discussion to take in matters relating to but beyond scheduling, we can take the opportunity to note a further development of MRP.

Manufacturing resource planning was developed from and incorporates MRP, but is a much broader concept. MRP II aims to provide a computer-based procedure for dealing with all of the planning and scheduling activities outlined in Figure 11.1 together with procedures for dealing with purchasing, cost accounting, inventory and maintenance decisions and records.

An outline of the elements of an MRP II system is given in Figure 12.8. Those elements not already described at the beginning of Chapter 11 are summarized below.

### Inventory control *(see also Chapter 17)*

(a) Maintain inventory records.

(b) Record all transactions.

(c) Originate purchase requirements.

(d) Allocate available stock against manufacturing orders.

(e) Allocate available stock against customer orders.

(f) Maintain work-in-progress files.

**Figure 12.8** Principal stages in operations planning and control (MRP II)

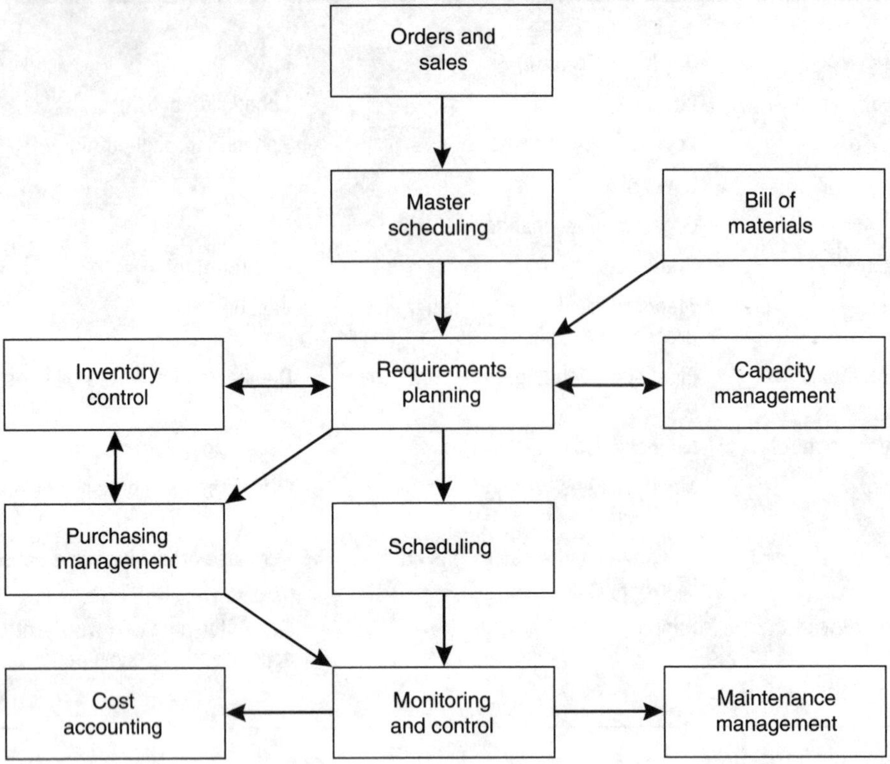

## Purchasing *(see also Chapter 16)*

(a) Place purchase orders.
(b) Record receipts.
(c) Maintain vendor register and monitor vendor performance.

## Orders and sales

(a) Record customer orders and deliveries.
(b) Monitor status of orders.
(c) Maintain customer records.

## Maintenance *(see also Chapter 20)*

(a) Maintain equipment records.
(b) Schedule preventive maintenance.
(c) Maintain repair records.
(d) Maintain spare parts inventory records.
(e) Maintain repair staff records.

### Cost accounts

(a) Monitor plant performance.

(b) Collect manufacturing costs.

(c) Calculate cost variances.

MRP II is a comprehensive top-down approach which provides a means for planning, control and co-ordination for all important aspects of manufacturing in the context of business planning. It is a 'closed-loop' system and virtually self-contained planning and control system for demand-dependent situations.

A computer-based approach is essential, because the data handling requirements are considerable. Numerous software packages are available, each differing in detail, but all the same in principle.

## MRP and MRP II compared

MRP II is comprehensive, but demanding to install and apply. MRP is narrower, and sufficient in some circumstances. It is not a choice between these two that must be made by operations managers, but rather a choice of where to be on a continuum. Satisfactory procedures can be implemented at any point, providing the approach adopted is consistent with the objectives to be achieved. Failure, or problems, are just as likely to result from attempts to implement a system which is too sophisticated, or too large, for what is actually required, as from the pursuit of unrealistically ambitious objectives.

EXAMPLE

### *Publishers Equipment Corp.*

Publishers Equipment Corp. implemented MRP II to meet two objectives: higher customer service and better manufacturing effectiveness. The system was a modular database system organized to effectively supply information to various parts of the organization for decision-making purposes. Major components of the system included material requirements planning (MRP), accounting, and purchasing databases. Integration of the MRP II system was accomplished in four separate phases:

1. The foundation was laid for the implementation by reviewing data for accuracy, loading the computer system, and interfacing the material requirements planning with other systems.
2. A test-run of the MRP II system was conducted to identify any errors in programming or logic.
3. The order-entry and master-production-scheduling software were brought on-line.
4. Each work station was operated according to schedule priorities, and shop-floor controls tracked and updated all operations.

Source: Ormsby, J. G., Ormsby, S. Y. and Ruthstrom, C. R. (1990) MRP II implementation: a case study. *Production and Inventory Management Journal*, **31**(4), pp. 77–81.

## THE EFFECTIVENESS OF SCHEDULING

Criteria or measures of effective activity scheduling and control might include the following:

(a) the level of finished goods or work-in-progress (for systems with output stocks);

(b) percentage resource utilization (all systems);

(c) percentage of orders delivered on or before due date (for function to order systems only);

(d) percentage stockouts/shortages (for systems with output stocks only);

(e) number of customers dealt with (all systems);

(f) down time/set-ups, etc. (all systems);

(g) customer queuing times (for systems in which customers wait or queue).

In virtually all cases there will be a need to avoid sub-optimization. It may be easy in most cases to satisfy each of the above criteria individually, but the objective of operations management, and therefore of activity scheduling, is to obtain a satisfactory balance between customer service criteria (e.g. c, d, g) and resource utilization criteria (e.g. b, f).

## BALANCING SCHEDULING AND CONTROL

In many situations it will not be feasible, and in some cases not desirable, to attempt to develop optimum activity schedules. In these situations there will be a need to control activities as they happen. The relative importance attached to scheduling (planning ahead) or control (dealing with activities as they happen) will depend to some extent on the type of situation and particularly the type of system structure.

In general, scheduling will be more complex in 'function to order' situations where scheduling decisions will be required to absorb external (i.e. demand) fluctuations directly. Furthermore, in such situations the degree of repetition may be less, and therefore the need for control may be greater. In contrast, in 'function to stock' situations, scheduling may be somewhat easier, and therefore the need for control less.

Demand levels may also influence the relative complexity and importance of scheduling and control activities. In general, high demand levels will be associated with function repetition and the provision of special-purpose resources together with product or service specialization. In contrast, relatively low demand levels may be associated with relatively low function repetition, high product or service variety and the use of general-purpose resources, and hence scheduling may be complex and there will be a relatively greater dependence on control. In situations where predictability of the nature of demand permits the provision, i.e. stocking, of resources, and where demand levels are high, the provision of special-purpose equipment may give rise to an emphasis on the provision of balance, the avoidance of interference and consideration of learning or improvement effects. In such situations much of the internally oriented scheduling will be built into the system. In contrast, in situations where demand predictability is low and where demand levels are also low, accurate scheduling will be impossible, and hence low equipment utilization, high work-in-progress and/or customer queuing will be evident. In these situations the use of local dispatching rules, resource smoothing, allocation of jobs etc., together with an emphasis on control, will be evident.

## CHECKLIST FOR CHAPTER 12

*The strategic importance of scheduling*

*Strategies for activity scheduling*

Internally and externally oriented scheduling
- JIT as an example of external scheduling

Dependent and independent demand

*Types of scheduling problem*

External/dependent
Internal/independent
Internal/dependent

*Managing demand uncertainty*

Appointments and reservations

*Activity scheduling techniques*

Reverse scheduling
Forward scheduling
Sequencing
- Two facilities and *n* jobs
- Three facilities and *n* jobs
- *m* facilities and two jobs

Dispatching
- Priority rules
- Local/general rules
- Static/dymanic rules
- Criteria
- Effectiveness of dispatching rules

Assignment
- Index method
- Linear programming
- Machine interference

Timetabling
OPT
- Bottleneck operations
- Nine OPT rules
- Process and transfer batches
- The OPT approach

MRP
- Procedures
- Inputs
- Regenerative/net change
- MRP compared to OPT
- MRP compared to JIT
- MRP II

The effectiveness of scheduling
Balancing scheduling and control

## FURTHER READING

**Department of Trade and Industry (UK) (1989)** *Managing into the 90s: Just-in-Time: Manufacturing Resource Planning; Computer Integrated Manufacturing; Optimised Production Technology*. Department of Trade and Industry.

**Fox, R. E. (1983)** OPT vs MRP: throughware versus software. *Inventories and Production*, **3**(6), Nov/Dec.

**Green, A., Costello, R. and Loizeaux, E. (1992)** MRP II: out with the old . . . *Computerworld*, **26**(23), pp. 73, 77–9, 82–5.

**Harrison, A. (1992)** *Just in Time Manufacturing in Perspective*. Hemel Hempstead: Prentice-Hall.

**Landvater, D. V. and Gray, C. D. (1989)** *MRPII Standard System*. Essex Junction, Vt.: Oliver Wight Publications.

**Morris, B. and Johnson, R. (1987)** Dealing with inherent variability: the difference between manufacturing and service? *International Journal of Operations and Production Management*, **7**(4), pp. 13–22.

**Vollman, C. E., Berry, W. L. and Whybark, D. C. (1989)** *Manufacturing Planning and Control Systems*, 2nd edn. Homewood, Ill.: Irwin.

## QUESTIONS

12.1 Five patients, 1, 2, 3, 4 and 5, must be examined on each of three hospital diagnostic tests, A, B and C, in that order. Process times are given in the table. Determine the best sequence for the five patients and use a Gantt chart to show an optimum schedule.

**Table of process times (hours)**

| | Patients | | | | |
|---|---|---|---|---|---|
| | **1** | **2** | **3** | **4** | **5** |
| Test A | 5 | 4 | 9 | 7 | 6 |
| Test B | 3 | 2 | 4 | 3 | 1 |
| Test C | 8 | 3 | 7 | 5 | 2 |

12.2 Distinguish between the sequencing and the dispatching problems. How important is the sequencing problem in activity scheduling and how useful in practice are the various algorithms which can be used to provide optimal solutions to such problems?

12.3 Solve the following sequencing problems, the objective in each case being to minimize the throughput time of all customers.

(a) Two facilities: A, B (see table, right).

Seven customers: 1, 2, 3, 4, 5, 6, 7.

Each customer to be processed on each facility in order A–B.

No overtaking of customers.

**Table of process times (hours)**

| | Facility | |
|---|---|---|
| **Customer** | **A** | **B** |
| 1 | 8 | 5 |
| 2 | 6 | 7 |
| 3 | 3 | 10 |
| 4 | 7 | 8 |
| 5 | 6 | 4 |
| 6 | 5 | 10 |
| 7 | 7 | 7 |

(b) Two facilities: X, Y (see left-hand table opposite).

Six customers: 1, 2, 3, 4, 5, 6.

Customers to be processed on each facility in order X–Y.

No overtaking of customers.

Customer 4 process on facility Y only.

Customer 1 process on facility X only.

(c) Three facilities: X, Y, Z (see right-hand table opposite).

Four customers: 1, 2, 3, 4.

**Table of process times (hours)**

| Customer | Facility X | Facility Y |
|---|---|---|
| 1 | 5 | – |
| 2 | 7 | 6 |
| 3 | 5 | 9 |
| 4 | – | 8 |
| 5 | 7 | 4 |
| 6 | 9 | 3 |

**Table of process times (hours)**

| Customer | Facility X | Facility Y | Facility Z |
|---|---|---|---|
| 1 | 4 | 3 | 3 |
| 2 | 2 | 4 | 2 |
| 3 | 4 | 4 | 4 |
| 4 | 6 | 2 | 4 |

Each customer to be processed on each facility in order X–Y–Z.

No overtaking of customers.

12.4 Two cars (1, 2; see table below) must be serviced on all of five garage facilities (A, B, C, D, E). The servicing times and the order of the operations for each car are given below. Draw a bar chart showing the minimum throughput time programme for the servicing of the two cars.

| Operation number | Car 1 Facility | Car 1 Time (hours) | Car 2 Facility | Car 2 Time (hours) |
|---|---|---|---|---|
| 1 | A | 4 | A | 5 |
| 2 | D | 3 | C | 7 |
| 3 | E | 5 | D | 4 |
| 4 | B | 6 | B | 3 |
| 5 | C | 4 | E | 5 |

12.5 Ten jobs are waiting to be run through a medical analysis process.

(a) Given the information in the table overleaf, arrange these jobs in priority order (the one with highest processing or dispatching priority first) according to the following priority rules:

1. job slack;
2. job slack per operation;
3. job slack ratio;
4. shortest imminent operation;
5. longest imminent operation;
6. scheduled start date;
7. earliest due date;
8. subsequent processing time;
9. first come, first served.

| Job | Schedule completion date (week no.) | Sum of remaining processing times (weeks) | Number of remaining operations | Duration of operations on this process | Arrival order at this process |
|---|---|---|---|---|---|
| 1 | 17 | 4 | 2 | 1 | 1 |
| 2 | 15 | 6 | 3 | 2 | 10 |
| 3 | 17 | 3 | 4 | 1 | 2 |
| 4 | 16 | 5 | 1 | 3 | 4 |
| 5 | 19 | 7 | 2 | 0.5 | 9 |
| 6 | 21 | 4 | 5 | 2 | 3 |
| 7 | 17 | 2 | 4 | 0.5 | 5 |
| 8 | 22 | 8 | 3 | 3.5 | 8 |
| 9 | 20 | 6 | 2 | 2 | 6 |
| 10 | 25 | 10 | 1 | 2 | 7 |

N.B. The present date is week no. 12.

(b) Use the 'first come, first served' (FCFS) priority rule to resolve 'ties' given by the above rules.

12.6 Describe some of the activity scheduling problems which may occur and the techniques available for their solution in the following situations:

(a) an emergency ward in a hospital;

(b) a furniture removal company;

(c) a take-away food shop (e.g. a hamburger shop).

12.7 Holdtight Company Ltd have just received orders from four customers for quantities of different 'expanderbolts'. Each order is to be manufactured over the same very short period of time, during which three machines are available for the manufacture of the bolts.

The table below shows the manufacturing time in hours/bolt for each of the three machines and the total available hours' capacity on each for the period in question.

| Order no. | Number of expanderbolts | Manufacturing time (hours/bolt) | | |
|---|---|---|---|---|
| | | *M/c* A | *M/c* B | *M/c* C |
| 1 | 50 | 4 | 5 | 3 |
| 2 | 75 | 3 | 2 | 4 |
| 3 | 25 | 5 | 4 | 3 |
| 4 | 80 | 2 | 5 | 4 |
| Total capacity (hours) | | 175 | 275 | 175 |

Assuming that each order is to be manufactured on one machine only, how should orders be allocated to machines?

12.8 Five orders are received by a company, each order being for a quantity of one type of agricultural bucket. Each type of bucket can be made on any of the five machines which happen to have available production capacity. The table below gives details of the numbers of buckets in each order, the manufacturing time (in hours/bucket) for each machine, and the total hours of production capacity available on each machine.

Using the index method described in this chapter, determine the optimum allocation of orders to machines, assuming (a) that orders cannot be split between several machines, and (b) that individual orders can be manufactured on a maximum of two machines.

| Order no. | No. of products | Machine | | | | |
|---|---|---|---|---|---|---|
| | | A | B | C | D | E |
| 1 | 30 | 2.0 | 2.5 | 3.0 | 4.0 | 3.5 |
| 2 | 25 | 3.0 | 3.0 | 3.5 | 4.0 | 2.5 |
| 3 | 40 | 4.0 | 5.0 | 2.0 | 3.0 | 2.5 |
| 4 | 25 | 3.5 | 2.0 | 3.5 | 2.5 | 3.0 |
| 5 | 30 | 4.0 | 2.0 | 2.5 | 3.0 | 4.0 |
| Total hours available | | 175 | 150 | 130 | 120 | 120 |

12.9 If the hourly operating costs of each of the three machines described in Question 12.7 are as shown to the right, express the allocation problem given in Question 12.7 as a set of equations or inequalities suitable for solution using the Simplex method of linear programming.

| Machine | Operating cost/hour (£) |
|---|---|
| A | 2.0 |
| B | 3.0 |
| C | 2.5 |

12.10 Demand forecasting is an essential prerequisite of capacity planning for certain types of operating systems. Which systems and why?

12.11 Products A and B can be produced at factories I and II. The production time required per product unit is one hour for A and two hours for B – the same at both factories.

The demand for A and B, the time available at each factory, and production costs and inventory holding costs per product unit are given for the forthcoming two months in the tables right and overleaf.

| Product | Demand (product units) | |
|---|---|---|
| | May | June |
| A | 100 | 110 |
| B | 150 | 190 |

| | Time available (hours) | | Cost per product unit (£) | |
|---|---|---|---|---|
| | May | June | Product A | Product B |
| Factory I | | | | |
| Normal time | 200 | 200 | 3.0 | 6.2 |
| Overtime | 40 | 10 | 3.6 | 6.8 |
| Factory II | | | | |
| Normal time | 250 | 200 | 3.1 | 6.4 |
| Overtime | 60 | 40 | 3.9 | 7.2 |
| | Inventory holding costs (£ per product unit per month) | | | |
| Factory I | 0.6 | | | |
| Factory II | 0.4 | | | |

Determine an optimum production plan that will meet demand at minimum cost. What is the total cost of this optimum programme?

12.12 A worker is required to attend to one or more semi-automatic machines. The cycle of operations for each machine is as follows:

Worker loads/unloads machine: 5 minutes

Machine operates without requiring attention of worker: 12 minutes

Repeat

During this cycle the worker must stack up the items which he has unloaded from the machine. This takes him 2 minutes.

What is the ideal number of such identical machines to allocate to one worker, given the following additional information?

Total cost associated with each machine = £50/h

Total cost associated with each worker = £5/h

12.13 A telephonist is required to deal with (i.e. answer and then monitor) incoming calls only, on four telephone lines. Each call for each line takes an average of three minutes of the operator's time, and after each call each line is silent for an average of ten minutes. (During this period the operator is not required to perform any work.) The total hourly cost associated with each line, which is independent of the proportion of time the line is idle, is five times the total hourly cost associated with the telephonist.

(a) What is the efficiency of each line in terms of the percentage of total time devoted to operation?

(b) How many should be allocated to a telephonist?

(c) What assumptions have you made in arriving at your answer?

12.14 Explain why and how the type of procedure used in MRP might be of relevance in activity scheduling in the following situations:

(a) a major hotel which, nightly, provides large formal dinners for different companies, business societies, clubs, etc.;

(b) an advertising agency which prepares TV advertisements for a large range of different types of customer.

12.5 Identify the key prerequisites for the effective use of a comprehensive computer-based operations planning and control system such as MRP II.

12.6 Outline in more detail than in Figure 12.8 the functions which must be undertaken by an MRP II system in one of the following areas:

(a) purchasing;

(b) maintenance.

Refer to the appropriate chapter for details on either of these two activities.

## CASE STUDIES (from Part 9)

The topics covered in this chapter are relevant in the following (see Introduction to Part 9 and Table C.1 for further details):

| No. | Name | Country |
|---|---|---|
| 1 | Carreras SL | Spain |
| 4 | Qormi Post Office | Malta |
| 8 | Malcolm Seal | UK |
| 11 | St John's Church | UK |
| 17 | La Patisserie – A | UK |
| 19 | K&S (Israel) Ltd | Israel |
| 20 | TAARUP Farming Machines Ltd | Denmark |

Chapter 13

# Project management and network scheduling

## ISSUES

What is a project?
How are projects managed?
What is the distinctive role of project managers?
What are the success factors in project management?
How are projects scheduled and controlled?
What is network planning and how is it done?
What is PERT, and how is it used?
How are resources and costs managed?

## NOTATION USED IN THIS CHAPTER

| | |
|---|---|
| $a$ | Optimistic estimate of activity duration |
| $b$ | Pessimistic estimate of activity duration |
| $\sigma$ | Standard deviation } of duration distribution |
| $\sigma^2$ | Variance } of duration distribution |
| CPM | Critical path method |
| $d$ | Activity duration |
| $EF$ | Earliest finish date |
| $ES$ | Earliest start date |
| GERT | Generalized evaluation review technique |
| $LF$ | Latest finish date |
| $LS$ | Latest start date |
| $m$ | Most likely duration of activity |
| PERT | Programme evaluation review technique |
| $s$ | Schedule date |
| $t$ | Expected time or mean duration |
| $TF$ | Total float |
| $x$ | Standardized value |

We shall concentrate in this chapter on the scheduling of project-type activities, i.e. scheduling of non-repetitive work. We shall deal in detail with network scheduling, but it will be appropriate, initially, to set this discussion in a broader context.

# PROJECT MANAGEMENT

## The nature of projects and project management

A project can be defined as an activity with a specific goal occupying a specific period of time. A project is a finite activity, not only in time, but also in the use of resources.

Project management, therefore, is concerned with the pursuit of a specific goal, using given resources over a defined time period. This will often require the planning and establishment of an operating system, the acquisition of resources, the scheduling of activities and evaluation/review of the completed activity. Project management is a distinctive activity requiring a different type of approach to that of managing ongoing repetitive operations.

The management of finite projects is a need not only in the engineering and construction industries – the focus of much of the literature on this subject – but also in areas such as:

(a) ***Transport***: planning and executing a major transport project, e.g. deploying military resources, major explorations and missions.

(b) ***Supply***: planning and executing projects such as the distribution of aid, the sale and distribution of equities during privatizations, etc.

(c) ***Service***: managing projects such as emergency and disaster relief, mass immunizations, and major consultancy projects.

In many cases the focus, as above, will be upon major projects – often involving considerable resources, cost and time. Scale, however, is not a part of our definition. Projects may be large or small.

Figure 13.1 outlines a typical project three-phase life-cycle. Some of the managerial activities associated with the seven stages are discussed below.

**Figure 13.1** Typical project life-cycle

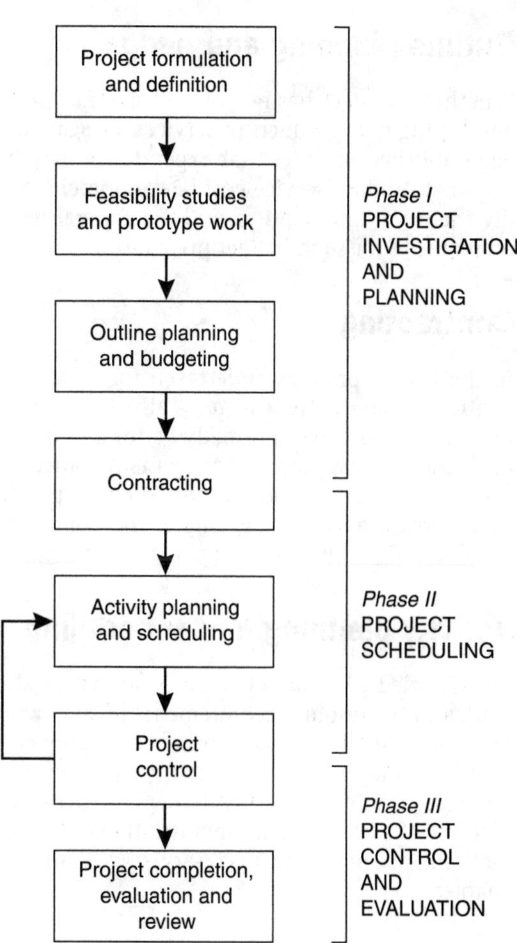


## Project formulation and definition

In managing a research and development activity within an organization, decisions will be required on the selection of projects for further work. Whilst the number of possible projects, e.g. those projects on which some initial exploratory work has been done, may be large, only a few of these may qualify for further development through prototype work to ultimate product development and marketing. Project selection, in such circumstances, is of crucial importance. The corporate objectives, in particular product/market policy (see Chapter 3), the availability of appropriate skills and resources, financial implications, and development cost estimates will be among the 'checklist' of items that might be used in an initial test of project feasibility or in the ranking of possible projects.

In contrast, in those types of organization which operate essentially in response to customer enquiries or tender requests, project selection may be unimportant. The emphasis here will be upon the interpretation, definition and formulation of project requirements. The interpretation of tender conditions, the development of outline specifications, initial evaluation of alternatives and discussions with customers should lead to an agreed project formulation in sufficient detail to permit further work.

## Feasibility studies and prototype work

Except in the case of small projects or activities undertaken by organizations against known customer requirements, further feasibility studies, possibly culminating in prototype work, will be required. Such work may, itself, be covered by a contractual arrangement between an organization and its customer. In the case of organizations involved in the development of projects in anticipation of demand, e.g. development of new products or services, prototype development may be required not only to test feasibility and performance, but also as a means to determine initial market reaction through pilot or test marketing exercises.

## Outline planning and budgeting

Whether a project has been undertaken as part of a company R&D programme with the intention of developing new products or services, or against a specific customer requirement, a project budget must be established in order that expenditure may be controlled, and so that an estimate may be made of the final product/service cost. Development of outline plans for the execution of the project indicating the total time required and the general level of resources to be committed to the project will be a prerequisite for such budget preparation.

## Contracting

In the case of projects undertaken for a particular customer, the preparation and completion of legal contracts is an essential stage. Whilst the legal form and details differ throughout the world, the essential requirements will normally be for a written, legal contract, covering details of specification, documentation, costs, project management, cancellation, modification, completion and delivery. A type of contracting may also be involved even for projects undertaken within an overall R&D framework within an organization. For example, the commissioning of projects from specific departments and the involvement of subcontractors may necessitate contractual arrangements.

## Activity planning and scheduling

The detailed plan or schedule of activities showing estimated start and finish times for all major work and the resource requirements of such work is an essential prerequisite at the start of any project. By definition all or a major part of any project will be new. Thus in developing a plan or schedule the project manager faces uncertainty. The amount of time required to complete jobs, the amount of resources required and the interdependence of jobs are all uncertain. The planning procedure must take account of such risk, and opportunities for modification/revision of schedules or the use of alternative methods/resources are necessary. We shall deal with activity scheduling in the remainder of this chapter.

## Project control

This, together with planning and scheduling, is the major ongoing task for project management. Since, by definition, planning cannot be exact, some emphasis must be placed upon project control. A principal characteristic of project management situations is the need for close monitoring and control of activities, for comparison of progress against plans, subsequent modification of schedules, redeployment of resources, and redirection of effort. Here, also, the project manager will be concerned with the management of project teams, the provision of leadership for such teams and the management of personnel. Team working is characteristic of project-type work and considerable attention must be given to the selection, training and development of individuals, the creation of effective teams and the management of workgroups.

## Project completion, evaluation and review

On project completion, final outcome costs will be calculated and compared to budget, the effectiveness of the project will be assessed, and project teams will be 'wound down'. The evaluation and review of the project provides information and opportunities for improvement in the management of subsequent projects, and permits the development of a database (e.g. of resource requirements, activity durations, learning times, etc.) to facilitate future project planning and control.

# ROLE OF PROJECT MANAGEMENT

It is the role of the overall project manager to take responsibility for this whole project life-cycle. Thus, frequently, project managers must operate within a matrix-type organization, being responsible for co-ordinating specific activities across functions, each of which is headed by its own function manager. The success of a project – e.g. completion on time, to specification and to cost – is very dependent on effective project management.

Successful project management has been found to depend upon the adoption of an appropriate strategy designed to ensure:[1]

1. There exists an attitude for success.
2. The objectives by which success are to be measured are defined.
3. There is a procedure for achieving objectives.
4. The environment is supportive.
5. Adequate and appropriate resources are available.

Within such a strategy the most appropriate approach, or style, for project management, will normally involve the following:[1]

(a) manage through a structured breakdown – the management system is built around a structured breakdown of the facility delivered by the project into intermediate products or results;

(b) focus on results – what to achieve, not how to do it; i.e. the deliverables, not the work for its own sake;

(c) balance the results between different areas of technology; and between technology and people, systems and organizational changes;

(d) organize a contract between all the parties involved, defining their roles, responsibilities and working relationships;

(e) adopt a clear and simple management approach.

[1] Turner, J. R. (1993) *The Handbook of Project Based Management.* London: McGraw-Hill.

# PROJECT SCHEDULING AND CONTROL

In the remainder of this chapter we deal in detail with the use of network techniques in activity scheduling and control. The topic was introduced in Chapter 12, where it was noted that this approach provides a means of establishing schedules for sequentially interdependent activities. It is useful for internally or externally oriented scheduling. The technique is of wide relevance, is used extensively in the scheduling of complex projects, and merits consideration in detail. Our description throughout will refer to projects, the planning of projects, etc., and it should be noted that such projects might relate to manufacture, supply, service or transport (see also Chapter 12).

The rudimentary steps in operations planning by network analysis are as follows:

(a) Construct an arrow or network diagram to represent the project to be undertaken, indicating the sequence and interdependence of all necessary jobs in the project.

(b) Determine how long each of the jobs will last and insert those times on the network.

(c) Perform network calculations to determine the overall duration of the project and the criticalness of the various jobs.

(d) If the project completion date is later than required, consider modifying either the network and/or the individual job durations so that the project may be completed within the required time.

This is the extent of the planning phase of simple network analysis; there are, however, subsequent steps concerned with the control of the operation and these will be dealt with later. Furthermore, this simple description of the procedure has omitted all considerations of costs and resources, and these will be dealt with later in this chapter.

# THE CONSTRUCTION OF NETWORK DIAGRAMS

Any project may be represented by means of an arrow diagram[2] in which the arrangement of arrows indicates the sequence of individual jobs and their dependence on other jobs. Arrow diagrams consist of two basic elements: *activities* and *events*.

An activity is a time-consuming task and is represented by an arrow or line. An event is considered as instantaneous, i.e. a point in time. An event may represent the completion or the commencement of an activity and is represented by a circle. A sequence of events is referred to as a *path*.

Unlike with bar charts, the scale to which activities are drawn has no significance. The length of an activity arrow on a network diagram is unrelated to the duration of that activity. It is normal to number events as in Figure 13.2 so that paths within the network can easily be described but, other than for identification, event numbers have no significance. Also for convenience we shall identify each activity with a letter and/or description.

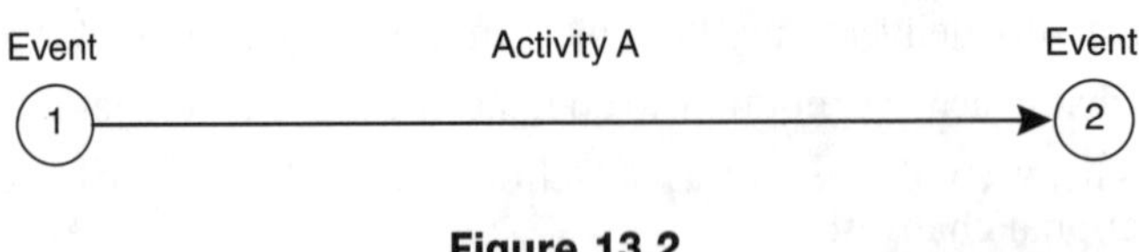


**Figure 13.2**

[2] Throughout the *main text* in this chapter we shall employ one particular approach in the construction of networks, i.e. the *activity on arrow* method. This is the most widely used method. In some situations, however, the alternative approach – *activity on node* – may be preferred; this approach is used throughout this chapter in the footnote sections. Those wishing to adopt this approach should first read the Appendix to this chapter.

The network diagram is constructed by assembling all activities in a logical order. For example, the networks shown in Figures 13.3 and 13.4 relate to a decorating job. No activity may begin until all the activities leading to it are completed. In Figure 13.3 only after the walls have been cleaned can they be painted. In Figure 13.4 starting to paper the walls is dependent not only on the old paper having been removed but also on the new paper being available.

**Figure 13.3**

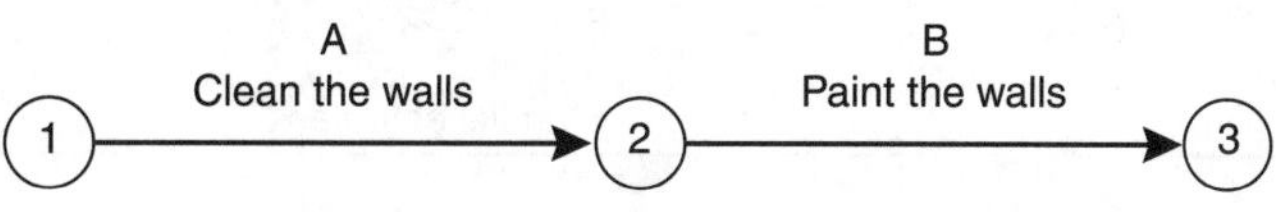


**Figure 13.4**

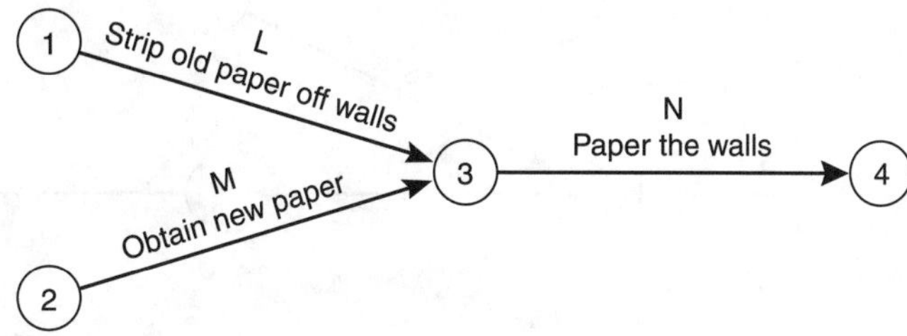


Activities occurring on the same path are *sequential* and are directly dependent on each other. *Parallel* activities on different paths are independent of one another (Figure 13.5).

The convention in drawing networks is to allow time to flow from left to right and to number events in this direction so that events on the left of the diagram have smaller numbers than, and occur before, events on the right of the diagram.

It is not usually possible to use network diagrams in which 'loops' or 'dangles' occur; a loop such as that in Figure 13.6 may be a perfectly legitimate sequence of operations where, for example, a certain amount of reprocessing of materials or rectification takes place but, because of the calculations which must later be performed on the diagram, it cannot be accepted in network analysis.

Although there are certain computer programs which will accept multiple-finish and multiple-start events on networks, it is not normally possible to leave events 'dangling' as in Figure 13.7.

## Dummy activities

The activities discussed above represent some time-consuming operation or job to be performed during the project. Dummy activities consume no time; they are of zero duration and are used solely for convenience in network construction. Dummy activities, represented by dotted lines, may be necessary on the following occasions:

---

*Activity on node diagrams*

An activity is a time-consuming task and is represented here by ⬭. Arrows are used to join activities, to show the precedence relationships of activities. Thus the activities in the network are represented by the *nodes* of the network (not the arrows).

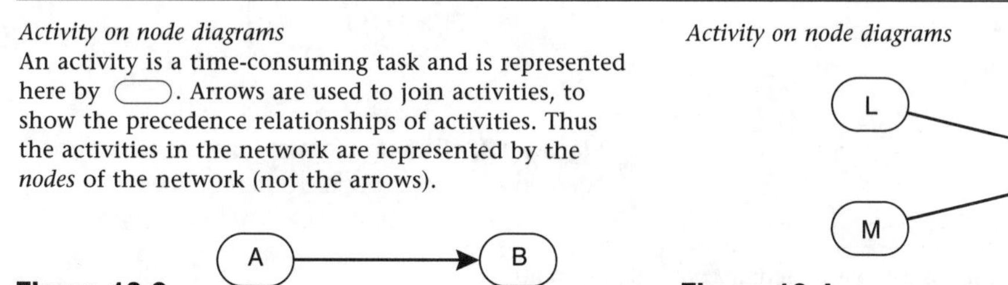


**Figure 13.3**

*Activity on node diagrams*



**Figure 13.4**

**Figure 13.5**

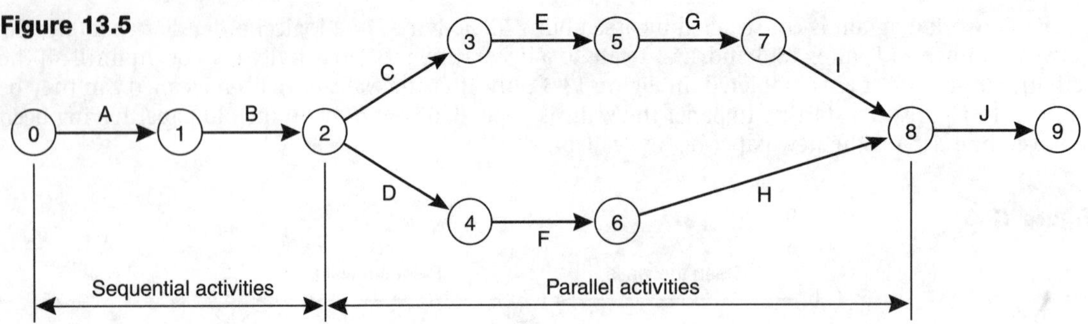


**Figure 13.6**

**Figure 13.7**

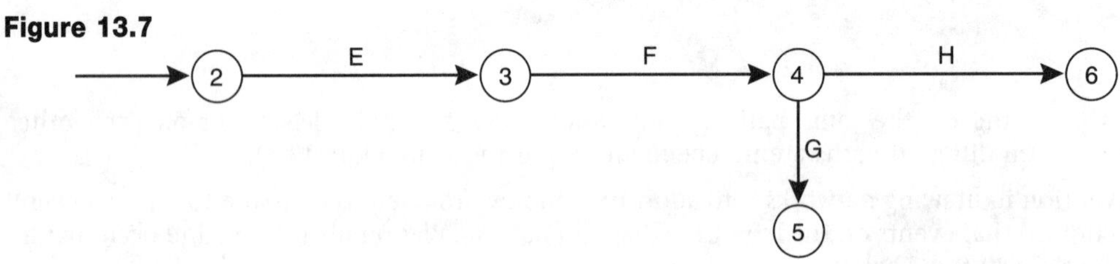


*Activity on node diagrams*

**Figure 13.5**

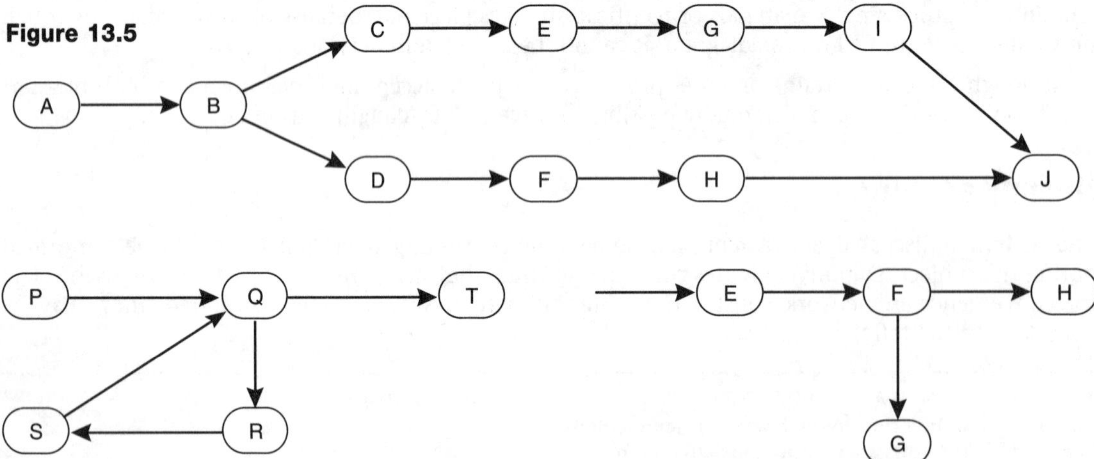


**Figure 13.6**

**Figure 13.7** The problem of 'dangles' does not occur in activity on node diagrams

*Dummy activities*
There is no need to use dummy activities in activity on node diagrams.

(a) To provide the correct logic in the diagram. In Figure 13.8 the completion of activities C and D is necessary before either E or F may begin. If, in practice, only activity E depends on the completion of both activities C and D, and activity F depends on D alone, to represent this logic a dummy activity is required (Figure 13.9).

**Figure 13.8**

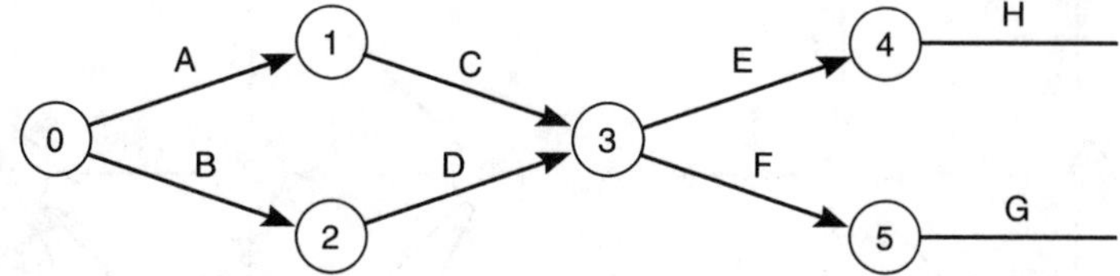


**Figure 13.9**

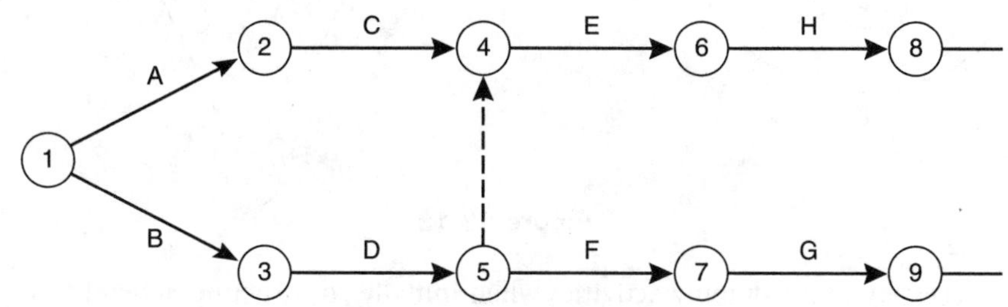


(b) To avoid having more than one activity with the same beginning and end event (Figure 13.10). It is not usually possible to represent activities in this manner since activities B and C would be described from their event numbers as 3–4, so a dummy activity is necessary (Figure 13.11).

**Figure 13.10**

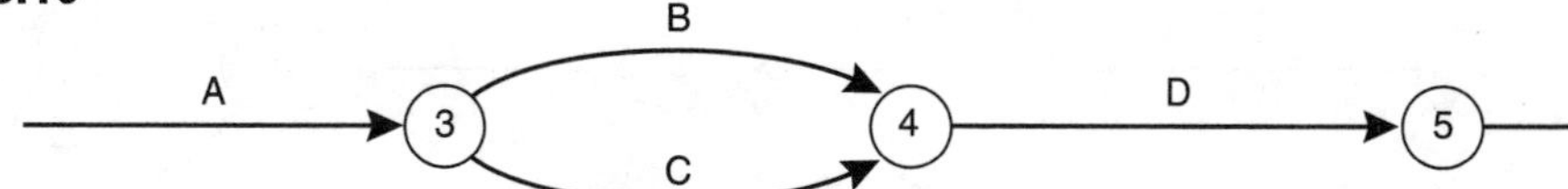


**Figure 13.11**

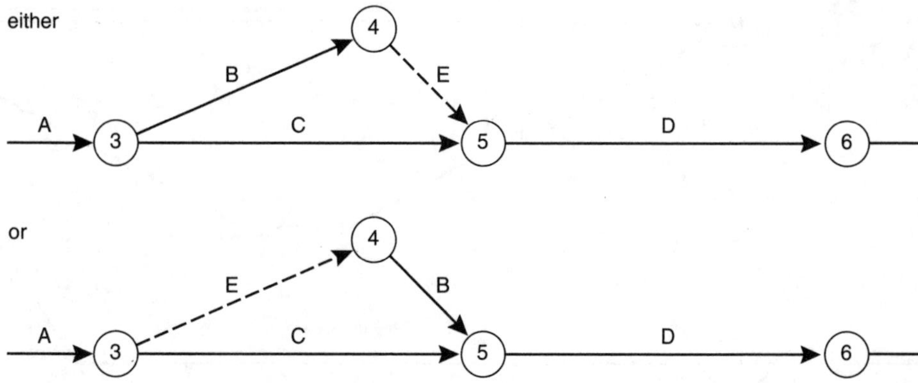

(c) For convenience in drawing. The two networks in Figure 13.12 are equivalent, but the use of dummy activities facilitates representation. This is often necessary in complex networks.

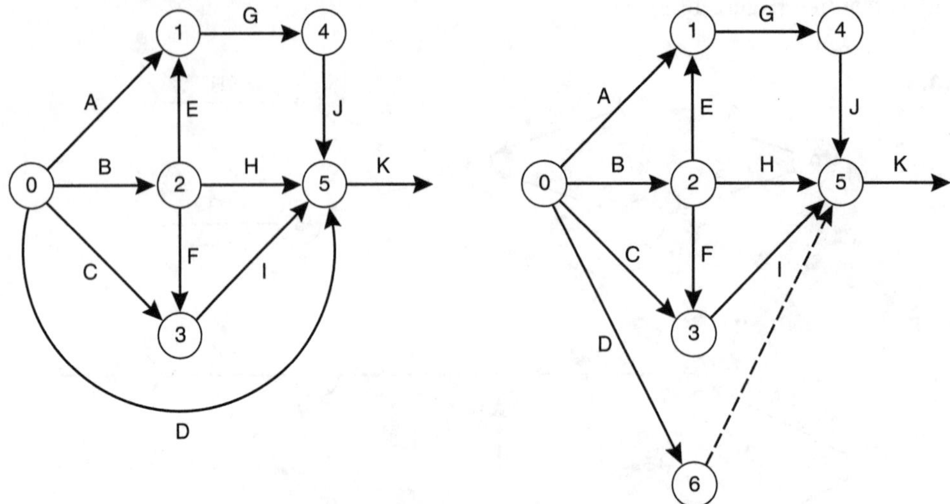


**Figure 13.12**

It may be necessary to use dummy activities when initially constructing networks to avoid complicated and untidy diagrams. Nevertheless, since the amount of subsequent analysis is dependent on the number of activities in a diagram, redundant dummies should be eliminated in order to save calculation time.

In drawing large networks for projects with many activities we have often found it to be easier to begin from the end of the project and work backwards. It is often helpful to consider large projects in

---

*Activity on node diagrams*

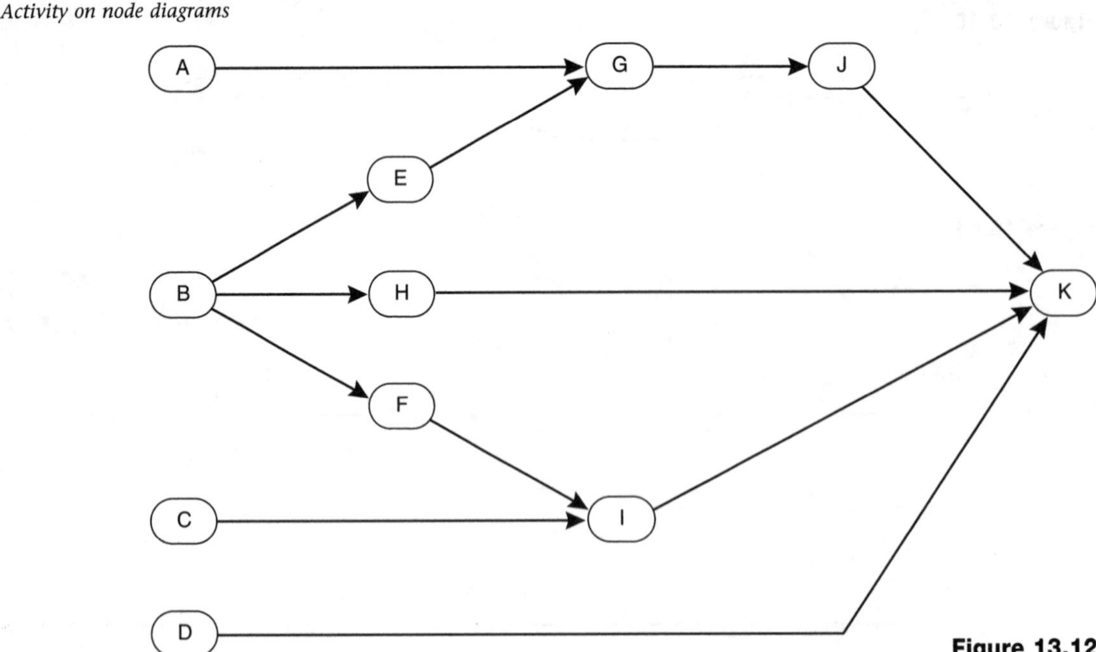


**Figure 13.12**

separate parts, i.e. certain sections of the project or, if more appropriate, certain periods during the project, and then to piece together several smaller networks rather than try to construct the complete network from scratch. For example, the manufacture of a large water turbine could be divided into rotating parts (impeller, shafts, etc.) and stationary parts (housing, ducting, etc.). Alternatively it may be considered in terms of two time periods, the first covering the cutting, forming and welding of the parts, and the second the machining and assembling.

Except in the case of simple projects it is usually beneficial to construct the network around the important activities. Identify the important or major parts, locate the important activities on the diagram, then attach all the other, secondary activities to construct the complete network.

# NETWORK CALCULATIONS

## Dates

The objective of initial network calculations is to determine the overall duration of the project so that either a delivery date can be given to the customer or we can consider what alterations are necessary for the project to be completed on or before a date to which we are already committed.

To perform the network calculations two things are required: first, an *activity network* representing the project, and second, the durations of all the activities in that network. Network analysis is only a tool: its value depends entirely on the way in which it is used and the information on which it is based. Consequently, the collection of activity durations from records or the estimation of durations is an important part of the exercise.

If the activities have been performed previously then, assuming the use of the same resources and procedures, the durations may be obtained from records. On occasions some form of estimation is necessary. For the time being we shall ignore the possibility of using multiple estimates of activity durations and consider only the case in which each activity is given one duration.

### Earliest start date for activities (*ES*)

The earliest start date for each activity is calculated from the *beginning* of the network by totalling all preceding activity durations (*d*).

Where two (or more) activities lead into one event the following activity cannot begin until both of the preceding activities are completed. Consequently the last of these activities to finish determines the start date for the subsequent activity.

In Figure 13.13 the earliest start date for activity I is day 17 (assuming the projects starts at day 0), since the start date for activity I will depend on the completion of the later of the two activities G and H, which is H.

Therefore, when calculating *ES* dates, work from the *beginning* of the network and use the *largest* numbers at junctions.

### Latest finish date for activities (*LF*)

This is calculated from the *end* of the project by successively subtracting activity durations (*d*) from the project finish date.

Where two (or more) activities stem from one event the earliest of the dates will determine the latest finish date for previous activities.

In Figure 13.14 the latest finish date for activity A is day 3, since activity B must start on day 3 if the project is not to be delayed.

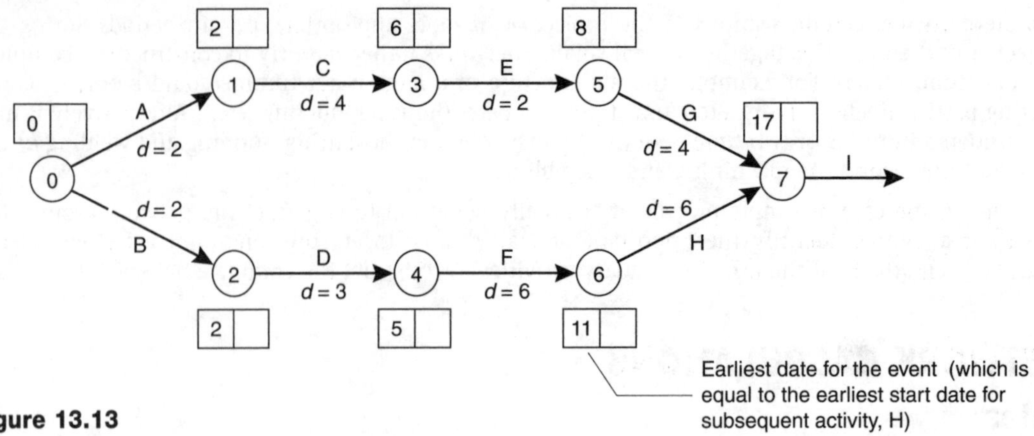


**Figure 13.13**

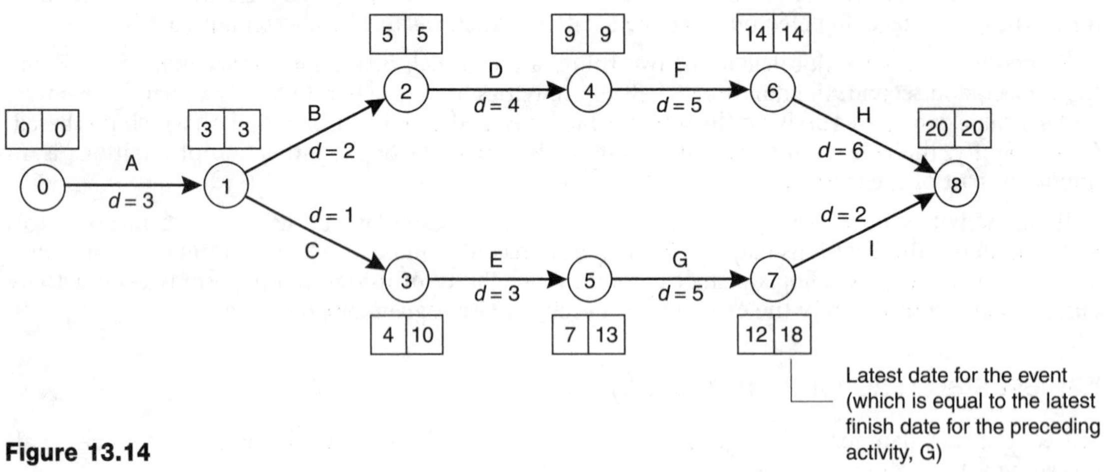


**Figure 13.14**

*Activity on node diagrams*

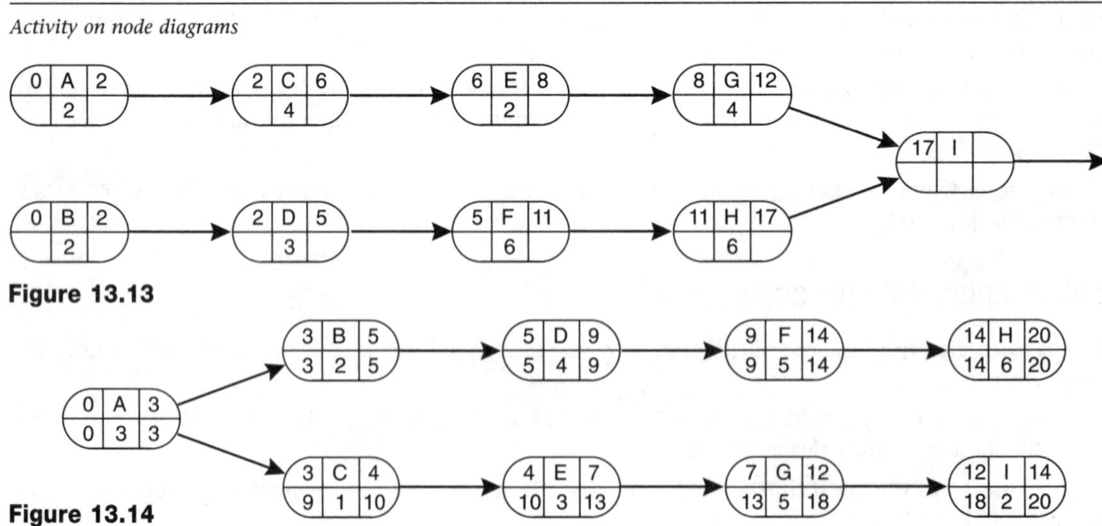


**Figure 13.13**

**Figure 13.14**

Therefore, when calculating *LF* dates begin from the *end* of the network and use the *smallest* numbers at junctions.

## Earliest finish date for activities (*EF*)

The earliest finish date for any activity cannot normally be read directly from the diagram, and should be calculated from that activity's earliest start date and its duration, i.e. for any activity: $EF = ES + d$.

## Latest start date for activities (*LS*)

The latest start date for any activity cannot normally be read directly from the diagram, and should be calculated from that activity's latest finish date and its duration, i.e. for any activity: $LS = LF - d$.

# Float

In the previous example the earliest completion date for the project, i.e. the date of event 8, is determined by the *EF* dates for activities H and I. Activity I could finish on day 14 (the *EF* date for activity I is $ES + d = 12 + 2$), but activity H cannot finish until day 20 and it is this activity which determines the finish date for the project. In fact, it is path ABDFH which determines the project's earliest finish date rather than path ACEGI.

The earliest finish date for any project is determined by the longest path through the network; consequently, it follows that the shorter paths will have more time available than they require. The difference between the time available for any activity and the time required is called the *total float* (*TF*).

In Figure 13.14 the time required for activity I is 2, but the time available is 8 and hence the *TF* on activity I is 6.

| | | |
|---|---|---|
| Time available | = | $LF - ES$ |
| Time required | = | $d$ |
| Total float | = | $LF - ES - d$ |

i.e. for any activity (say G), using our notation the *TF* can be expressed as in Figure 13.15.

Total float is a characteristic of a path and not a characteristic of a single activity. For example, in Figure 13.14 the total float on activities A, C, E, G and I is 6. If the total float is used up at any time by delays or lateness in one of the activities then it is no longer available to any of the other activities on that path.

**Figure 13.15**

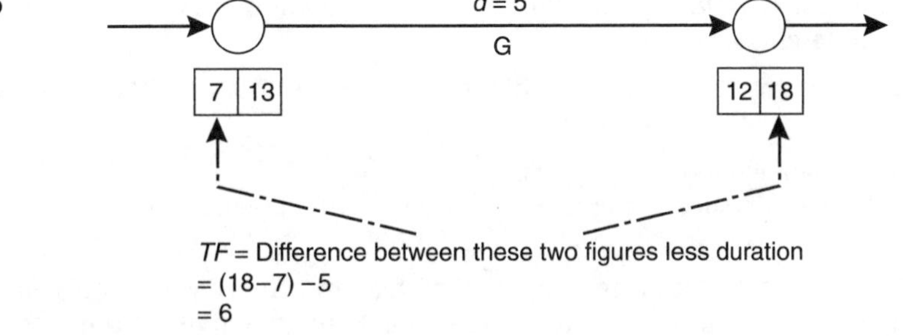


*Activity on node diagrams*

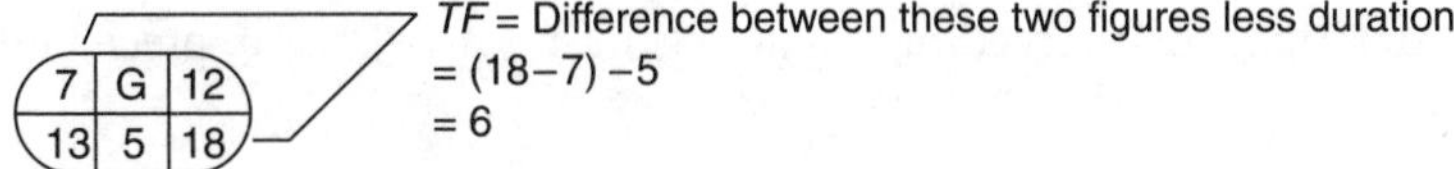

## The critical path

The *critical path* is the longest path through the network and is, therefore, the path with minimum total float (zero *TF* in the above example). Any delay in the activities on the critical path will delay the completion of the project, whereas delay in activities not on the critical path will initially use up some of the total float on that path and not affect the project completion date.

## Slack and other types of float

This is perhaps an appropriate point at which to mention two additional items. The term 'slack' is sometimes used with reference to network analysis. It is often taken as equivalent to float but, strictly speaking, whereas float relates to activities, slack relates to events. So far we have mentioned only total float, but two further types of float exist, i.e. *free float* and *independent float*. In this chapter we shall be concerned only with total float but, for the sake of completeness, free float is the difference between the time required for an activity and the time available for that activity if both preceding and succeeding activities occur either as early or as late as possible (free float early and free float late respectively). Independent float is the difference between the time required for an activity and the time available for that activity without affecting any other activities; i.e. it is the spare time available when the preceding activity occurs as late as possible and the succeeding activity as early as possible.

These four principal types of float are compared below.

(a) ***Total float***. The maximum free time available for an activity if preceding and succeeding activities are as far apart as possible:

Total float for an activity
= Latest start date of succeeding event – Earliest finishing date of preceding event – Activity duration

Unlike (b) and (c) below, total float will be identical for activities which are in series. Total float is shared for such activities.

(b) 1. ***Free float/early***. The amount of free time available for an activity when every activity occurs at the earliest possible point in time:

Free float/early for an activity
= Earliest start date of succeeding event – Earliest start date of preceding event – Activity duration

Free float is not a shared float in the sense that the calculation does not cause the same float to be shown on different activities.

2. ***Free float/late***. This is the amount of free time available to an activity when every activity occurs at the latest possible point in time.

Free float/late for an activity
= Latest start date for succeeding event – Latest start date for preceding event – Activity duration

(c) ***Independent float***. The amount of free time available to an activity without displacing any other activity, i.e. the maximum amount of free time available to an activity if the preceding and succeeding activities are as near together as possible.

Independent float on an activity
= Earliest start date of succeeding event – Latest start date of preceding event – Activity duration

## EXAMPLE 13.1

The following table lists all the activities which together constitute a small project. The table also shows the necessary immediate predecessors for each activity and the activity durations.

(a) Construct an activity network to represent the project.

(b) Determine the earliest finish date for the entire project, assuming the project begins at day 0.

| Activity | Immediate predecessors | Activity duration (days) |
|---|---|---|
| A | – | 2 |
| B | A | 3 |
| C | A | 4 |
| D | A | 5 |
| E | B | 6 |
| F | CD | 3 |
| G | D | 4 |
| H | B | 7 |
| I | EFG | 2 |
| J | G | 3 |

*Answer*

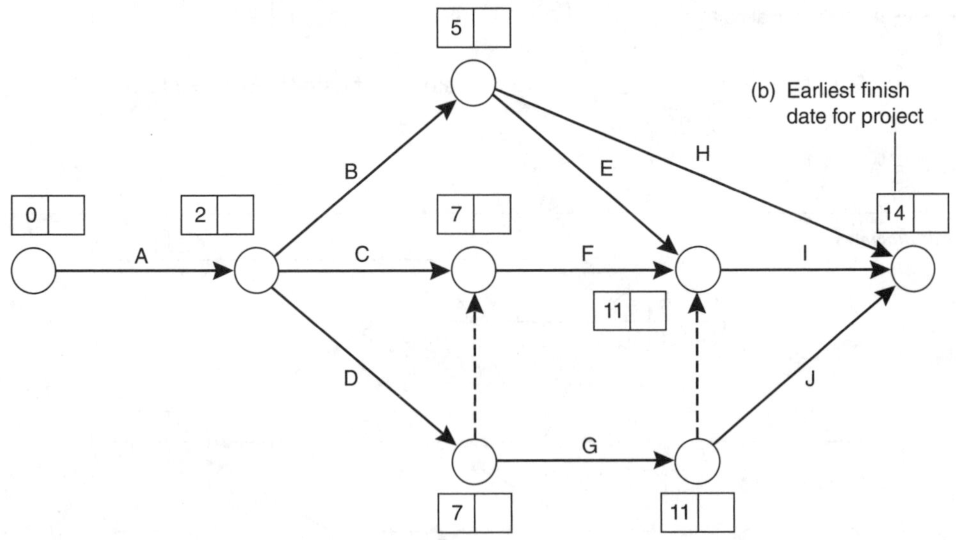

## EXAMPLE 13.2

For the project described in Example 13.1 determine:

(a) the total float on each activity;

(b) the critical path;

(c) the latest start date for activity B;

(d) the earliest finish date for activity F;

(e) the effect on the project duration if activity I were to take three days.

(f) the effect on the project duration if activity F were to take six days.

*Answer*

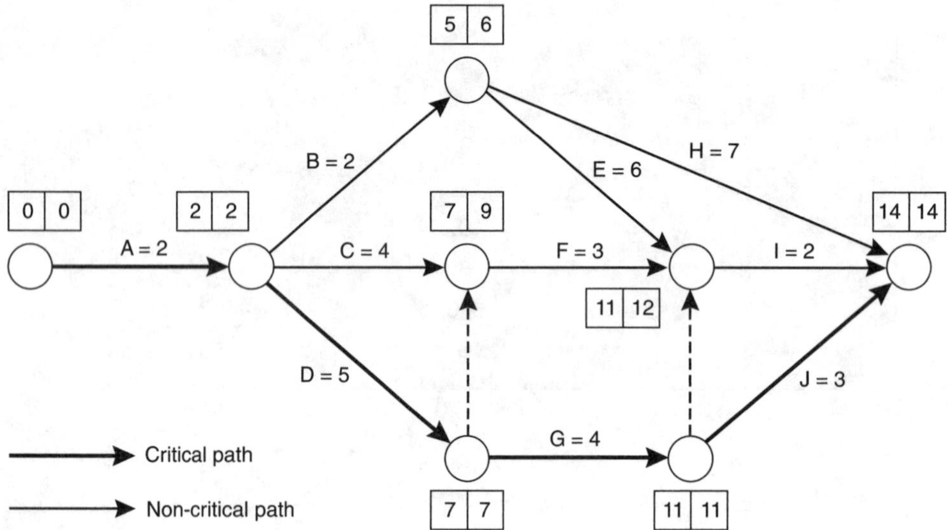


(a) *Activity* A B C D E F G H I J

*TF* 0 1 3 0 1 2 0 2 1 0

(b) Critical path = A D G J

(c) Latest start date for B = *LF* – duration
= 6 – 3
= day 3

*Activity on node diagrams*

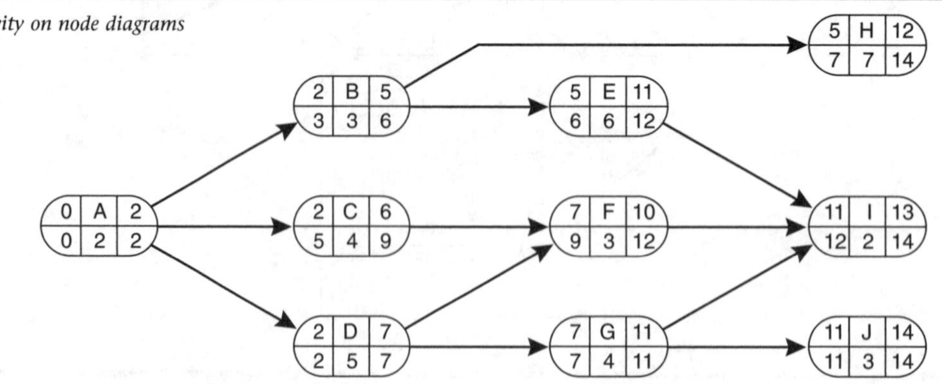

(d) Earliest finish date for F = *ES* + duration
= 7 + 3
= day 10

(e) No effect, but since increase in duration is equal to the total float on the activity, this activity would become critical.

(f) Project would be delayed by one day since only two days' *TF* are available on the activity.

## Schedule dates

At the beginning of this section we indicated that one approach in network calculations is to calculate the earliest completion date for the project and if necessary compare this with the desired completion date. (This is what we referred to as 'forward' NA in Chapter 12.) However, we may be committed to complete a project by a certain date and, if the calculated earliest finish date for the project occurs after this scheduled finish date, it will be desirable to try to reduce the project duration. If we had used the schedule completion date in the calculations and worked backwards from this date ('reverse' NA) then we would have obtained negative total float values, the greatest negative values occurring on the critical path and indicating the minimum amount by which the project would be late unless some alterations were made. Schedule dates may also be placed on intermediate events. If it is necessary to complete one of the intermediate activities by a given date, e.g. so that the customer or the main contractor may inspect or test the partly completed product, then an *intermediate schedule date/late* may be used. If this date is earlier than the *LF* date for that activity it would be used in the network calculations instead of the calculated *LF* date. If one of the intermediate activities cannot be started until a given date for some reason, e.g. because of the delivery of materials, then an *intermediate schedule date/early* may be used. If this date is later than the *ES* date for that activity it would be used instead of the calculated *ES* figure.

In the example in Figure 13.16 the final schedule date, day 20, is earlier than the calculated finish date for the project and therefore replaces the calculated *LF* date. The same applies to the intermediate schedule date/late for the completion of activity C. The intermediate schedule date/early for the start of activity J has no effect, since this date is earlier than the calculated *ES* date for that activity.

Using schedule dates it is possible to obtain not only negative values of total float but also different values along the critical path. In the example in Figure 13.16 the *TF* on activities A and C is – 2, and on E and I it is –1, but all four activities form a critical path.

## The matrix method

The two figures which are written at each event on the network are sometimes called *event dates*. The first figure, which we have obtained by considering the earliest finish date for the activities, is referred to as the earliest event date or time, while the second one is referred to as the latest event date or time.

To facilitate the network calculations the *matrix* method is sometimes preferred. Any network diagram can be represented as a matrix; for example, the matrix shown in Figure 13.17 represents the network diagram in Figure 13.18. The event numbers are listed across the top of the matrix and also down the left-hand side. The figures in the cells are the durations of the activities connecting pairs of events. For example, event 1 is connected to event 2 by an activity of duration 4, i.e. event 1 is the initial event for activity A, and 2 is the ending event for that activity. Similarly, event 2 is connected to event 3 by an activity of duration zero, i.e. a dummy. Because the network shown in Figure 13.18 has events numbered sequentially, all the entries in the matrix are above the diagonal. However, this situation will not always occur; for example, if the direction of the arrow for activity E had been reversed, then an entry would have occurred below the diagonal in the matrix.

The earliest times ($E$) for each of the events are calculated as follows. The earliest time (zero) for initial event 1 is entered opposite 1 in the column on the right of the matrix. Now referring to initial event 2, move along the second row of the matrix until the diagonal is reached. Read the figure(s) from above the diagonal in this column (i.e. 4), add them to the $E$ values for their rows (i.e. 0) and enter the largest answer as $E$ for initial event 2. Similarly, for initial event 3 move along the third row to the diagonal, read the figures from above the diagonal in this column (3 and 0), add them to the $E$ values for their rows (0 and 4) and enter the largest answer as $E$ for initial event 3 (i.e. 4).

For initial event 4 there is only one figure above the diagonal (7); add this to the $E$ values for that row (4) and enter the answer (11) as the earliest time for initial event 4.

The latest times are calculated in the reverse manner. First the latest time for the last event is entered. In this case the last event is 9 and the latest time is the same as the earliest time; hence 23 is

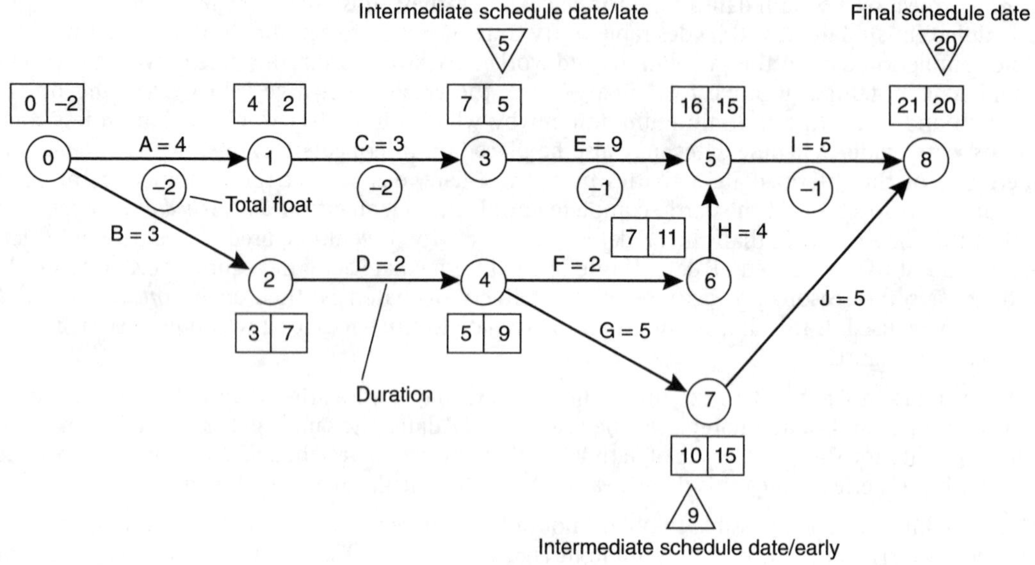


**Figure 13.16**

*Activity on node diagram*

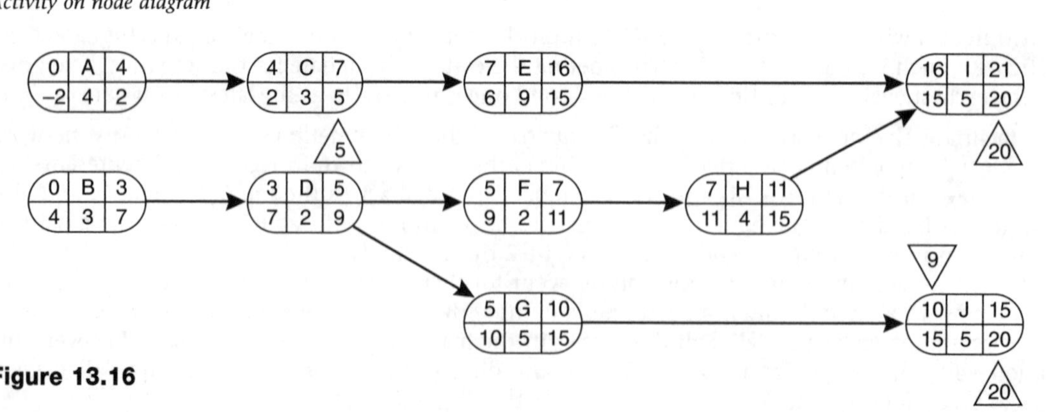

**Figure 13.16**

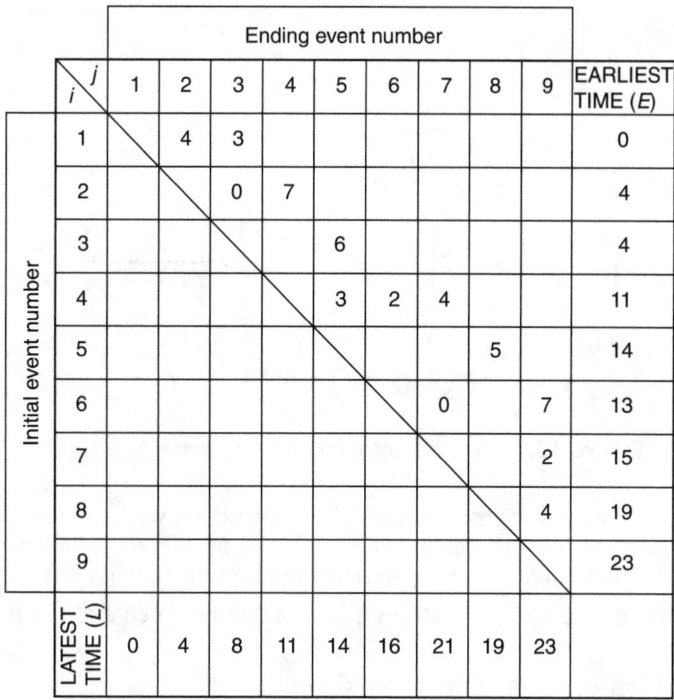

Ending event number

| i \ j (Initial event number) | 1 | 2 | 3 | 4 | 5 | 6 | 7 | 8 | 9 | EARLIEST TIME (*E*) |
|---|---|---|---|---|---|---|---|---|---|---|
| 1 | | 4 | 3 | | | | | | | 0 |
| 2 | | | 0 | 7 | | | | | | 4 |
| 3 | | | | | 6 | | | | | 4 |
| 4 | | | | | 3 | 2 | 4 | | | 11 |
| 5 | | | | | | | | 5 | | 14 |
| 6 | | | | | | | 0 | | 7 | 13 |
| 7 | | | | | | | | | 2 | 15 |
| 8 | | | | | | | | | 4 | 19 |
| 9 | | | | | | | | | | 23 |
| LATEST TIME (*L*) | 0 | 4 | 8 | 11 | 14 | 16 | 21 | 19 | 23 | |

**Figure 13.17** Matrix equivalent of network in Figure 13.18

entered under ending event 9 in the *L* row. Now move to ending event 8; move up the column to the diagonal, read the figure(s) to the right of the diagonal in this row (i.e. 4), subtract them from the *L* values for those columns (23) and enter the smallest answer as the latest time for ending event 8. Similarly, the calculation of the latest time for ending event 7 is as follows:

$L = 23 - 2 = 21$

For ending event 6 there are two figures to the right of the diagonal, and hence the calculation of *L* is as follows:

$L = 21 - 0$ or $23 - 7$

*L* for ending event 6 is 16

The matrix method of calculating dates gives precisely the same results as the method used previously. It is perhaps preferable in that it is a simple, routine procedure, but, of course, unlike the previous method, it gives no indication of the reasons for, or the logic of, the calculations. For this reason it is preferable first to master the original method. In this example calculations by either method reveal that the critical path for the network is 1 2 4 5 8 9.

## MULTIPLE TIME ESTIMATES (PERT)

We have previously assumed that a single time can be given for the duration of every activity. There are many occasions, however, when the duration of activities is not certain or when some amount of variation from the average duration is expected. For example, in maintenance work unexpected snags may occur to increase the activity duration, or failures may be found to be less serious than had been

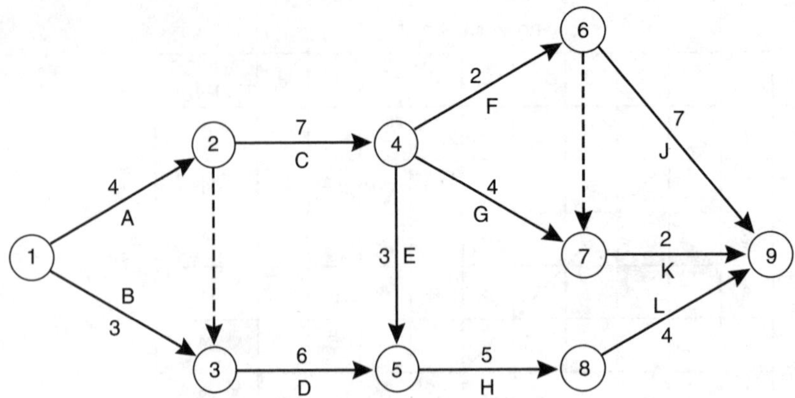


**Figure 13.18** Network diagram from matrix in Figure 13.17

expected and the activity duration is thus reduced. In construction work, jobs may be delayed because of unfavourable weather, etc. In such cases it is desirable to be able to use a time distribution rather than a single time for activity durations to represent the uncertainty that exists.

In network analysis uncertainty in durations can be accommodated and the following notation is usually used:

$m$ = the most likely duration of the activity

$a$ = the optimistic estimate of the activity duration

$b$ = the pessimistic estimate of the activity duration

These three estimates can be used to describe the distribution for the activity duration. It is assumed that the times are distributed as a 'beta' distribution (Figure 13.19) where

$t$ = the expected time (the mean of the distribution)

$\sigma$ = the standard deviation (which is a measure of the spread of the distribution)

$\simeq$ the range between the extreme values divided by 6

$$\equiv \frac{b-a}{6}$$

*Activity on node diagrams*

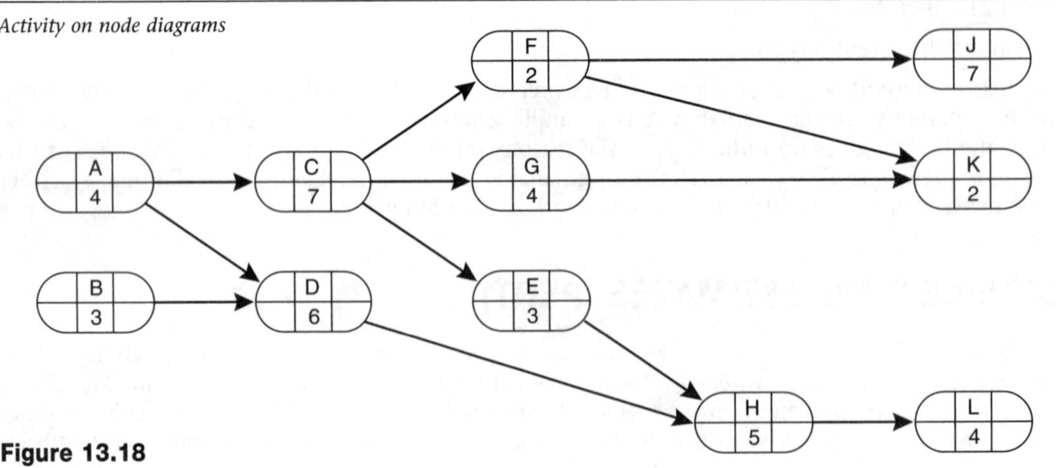


**Figure 13.18**

**Figure 13.19**

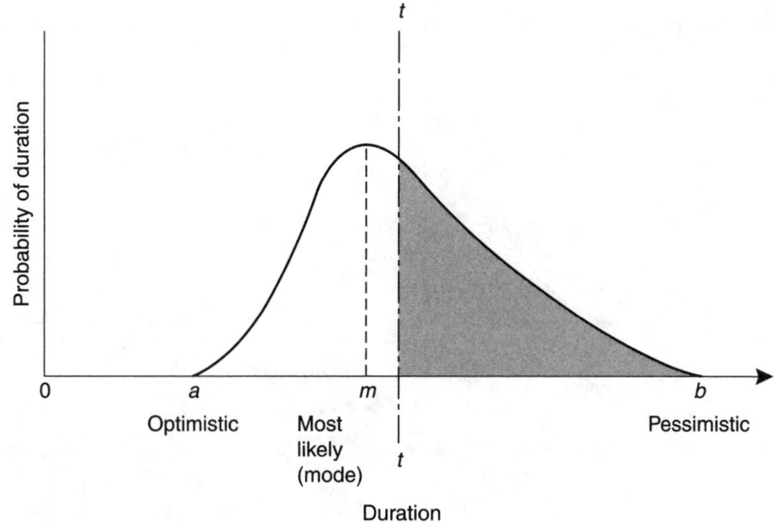


If certain assumptions are made about the distribution, the mean ($t$) and the variance ($\sigma^2$) can be expressed as follows:

$$\text{Mean (the expected time) } t = \frac{a + b + 4m}{6}$$

$$\text{Variance} \qquad \sigma^2 = \frac{(b - a)^2}{36}$$

## Probability of achieving scheduled dates

Suppose we have two sequential activities, A and B, for which the durations are:

| | |
|---|---|
| $a_A = 0.5$ days | $a_B = 4$ days |
| $b_A = 3.5$ days | $b_B = 12$ days |
| $m_A = 2$ days | $m_B = 8$ days |

Using these formulae, for activity A the expected duration $t_A$ is 2 days and the variance $\sigma^2 = 0.25$ days, and for activity B the expected duration $t_B$ is 8 days and variance $\sigma^2{}_B = 1.75$ days. Assuming activity durations to be independent, the expected duration for the pair of activities is 10 days and, since the variances may be added together, the variance for the pair is 2 days. It is usually assumed that the distribution for the duration of a series of activities corresponds to the 'normal' probability curve; consequently, in this case, the probability that the two activities will be completed in a minimum of 10 days is 50%, since the normal distribution is symmetrical about the mean (Figure 13.20) and consequently the probability is given by the proportion of the area to the left of the mean of 10 days (50%).

Suppose we have three activities which represent the critical path in a network, as in Figure 13.21. If we assume that these durations are independent, i.e. that the duration of activity A does not affect that of B and so on, and that the normal distribution applies for the project duration, then we can calculate the probability that the project will be completed on or before the required schedule date.

**Figure 13.20**

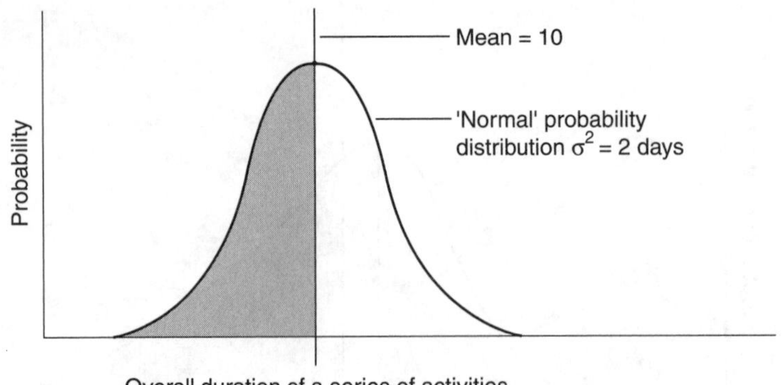


**Figure 13.21**

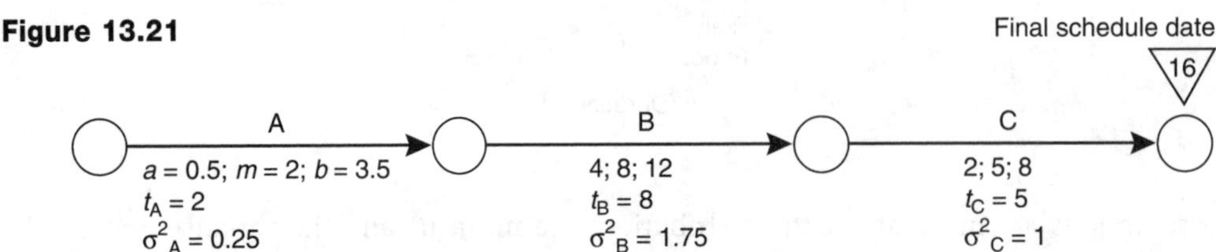


$$\text{Expected project duration} \quad (t) = 2 + 8 + 5 = 15$$
$$\sigma^2 = 3$$

In the distribution shown in Figure 13.22 the probability of meeting the schedule date is represented by that portion of the area under the curve to the left of the 16-day ordinate. This area can be obtained from normal distribution tables if the diagram is first converted to a standardized scale.[3] In this case the probability of completing the project by day 16 is 0.72, since the area to the left of the 16-day ordinate is 72% of the total area.

The assumptions underlying the use of probabilities in this way in network analysis are, to say the least, of doubtful validity. The assumptions that the distribution for each activity duration corresponds to a 'beta' distribution and that the distribution of the duration of a sequence of activities can be regarded as 'normal' are not based on thorough research and should be regarded only as empirical rules which, over a period of time, have been found to work. Furthermore, in calculating the probability on project end dates only the critical path is used, but where the duration of each activity in the network is uncertain any path through the network has a certain probability of being critical and we should perhaps examine more than one path.

Suppose that in a network in which most of the activities' durations are uncertain, the critical path has an expected duration of 16 days and a standard deviation of 1 day. In the same network there is a path of expected duration 15 days with a standard deviation of 3 days. According to the usual practice

*Activity on node diagrams*

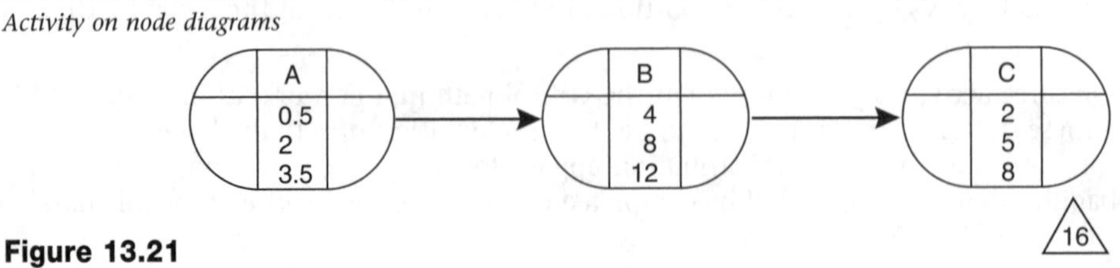


**Figure 13.21**

we ought to consider only the critical path in calculating our probabilities, but to do so in this case would mislead us, since there is a possibility that it will be the second path which will determine the project duration (Figure 13.24).

Had our scheduled completion date been day 19 then, considering the critical path only, we would be almost certain of meeting it, but the probability would be less if we considered the sub-critical path since, although the expected duration of this path is shorter, it is subject to greater variance.

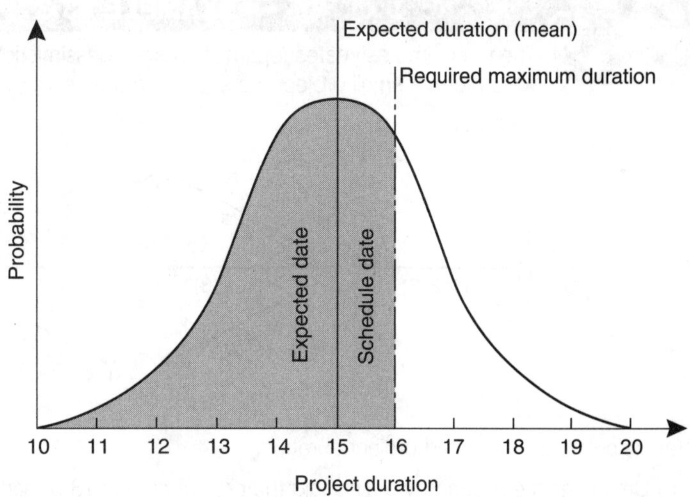


**Figure 13.22**

**Figure 13.24**

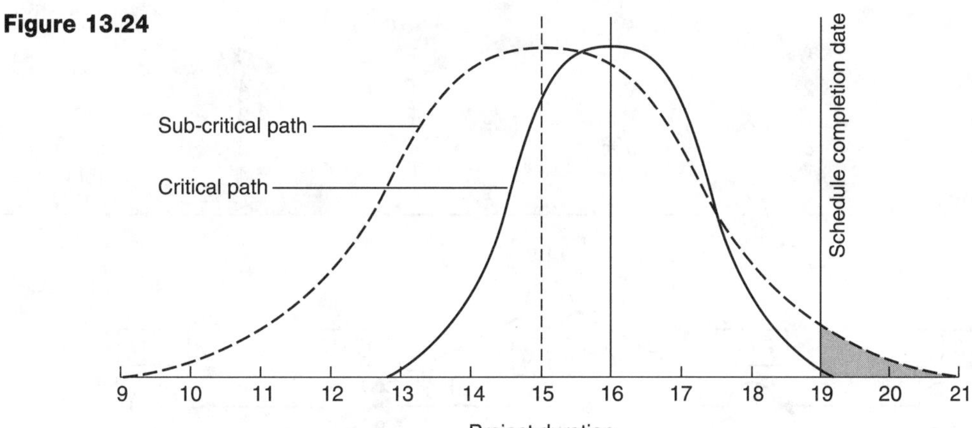


[3] The standardized scale is used solely for convenience. The standardized normal distribution has a total area of 1.00, a mean value of 0, and variance of $\sigma^2$ of 1 (Figure 13.23(a)):

where $s$ = schedule date
$t$ = expected date
$\sigma$ = standard deviation
$x$ = standardized value for the ordinate required, i.e. the schedule date

$$x = \frac{s-t}{\sigma} = \frac{16-15}{\sqrt{3}} = 0.58$$

When this value is located in normal distribution tables (Figure 13.23(b)) the area to the left of this value is found to be 72%.

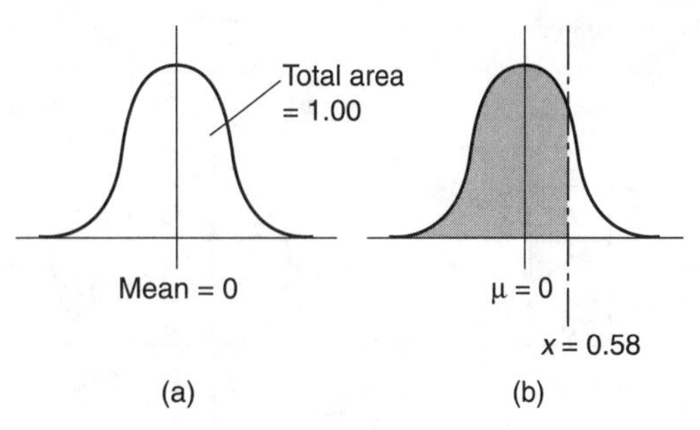


**Figure 13.23**

## EXAMPLE 13.3

The three time estimates (optimistic, likely, pessimistic) for the duration of the individual activities which form a small project are shown on the network diagram below.

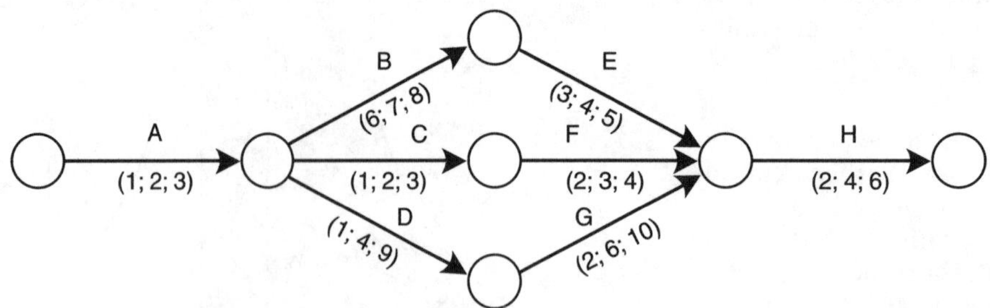


(a) Calculate the expected project duration.

(b) Determine the probability of finishing the project by day 18 or earlier.

*Answer*

(a)

| Activity | $t$ days | $\sigma^2$ | Activity | $t$ days | $\sigma^2$ |
|---|---|---|---|---|---|
| A | 2 | 4/36 | E | 4 | 4/36 |
| B | 7 | 4/36 | F | 3 | 4/36 |
| C | 2 | 4/36 | G | 6 | 64/36 |
| D | $4^1/_3$ | 64/36 | H | 4 | 16/36 |

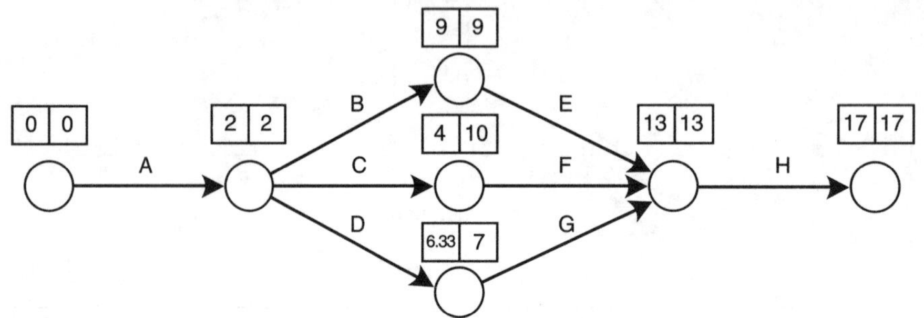


*Activity on node diagrams*

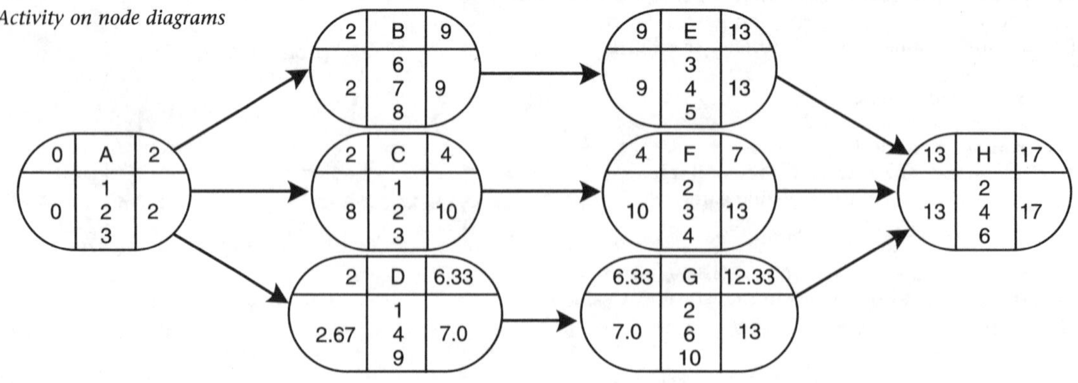

Expected project duration = 17 days.

(b) Considering critical path ABEH:

$$t = 17$$

$$\sigma^2 = 4/36 + 4/36 + 4/36 + 16/36$$

$$= 0.777$$

$$x = \frac{s - t}{\sigma} = \frac{18 - 17}{\sqrt{0.777}}$$

$$x = 1.14$$

From normal probability tables $x = 87.3\%$

Considering sub-critical path ADGH:

$$t = 2 + 4.33 + 6 + 4$$

$$= 16.33$$

$$\sigma^2 = 4/36 + 64/36 + 64/36 + 16/36$$

$$= 4.1$$

$$x = \frac{s - t}{\sigma} = \frac{18 - 16.33}{\sqrt{4.1}}$$

$$x = 0.825$$

From normal probability tables $x = 79.6\%$

---

In using three activity duration estimates to calculate the probabilities of completing projects or parts of projects on or before given scheduled completion dates, it is important to consider sub-critical paths. This is particularly important when the length of such a path approaches the length of the critical path, and also where the duration of the activities on such a path is subject to comparatively large variance.

Unless jobs have been done before, it is often difficult to obtain accurate estimates of activity durations. One advantage of using multiple estimates is that it encourages people to commit themselves to estimates when they might be reluctant to give a single estimate. But if this method is used principally for this reason, then there is little to be said for using these figures and subsequently calculating project durations and probabilities to several places of decimals. In such cases it may be enough merely to take advantage of the three estimates; in fact many computer programs provide this facility.

## RESOURCES

Our treatment of network analysis so far has assumed that only time is important in executing tasks. There are certainly many situations where time is indeed the only or the most important factor, but in the majority of cases other factors affect our ability to do the job. We have assumed, for example, that the correct facilities have been available and in the correct quantities. The availability of such facilities as labour, plant, etc. determines not only our ability to do the job but also the time required to do it. Estimates of activity duration will rely implicitly on our capability to undertake those activities, so it is a little unrealistic to speak of activity durations in the abstract. An estimate of the duration of an activity may differ substantially depending on the time at which the activity is undertaken. When very little other work is being undertaken an activity duration is likely to be shorter than when facilities are already heavily loaded or committed.

Each estimate of duration is based on the assumed use of a certain amount of resources, and consequently, when the project duration is calculated initially, we may also calculate the forward resource utilization, e.g. Figure 13.25.

**Figure 13.25**

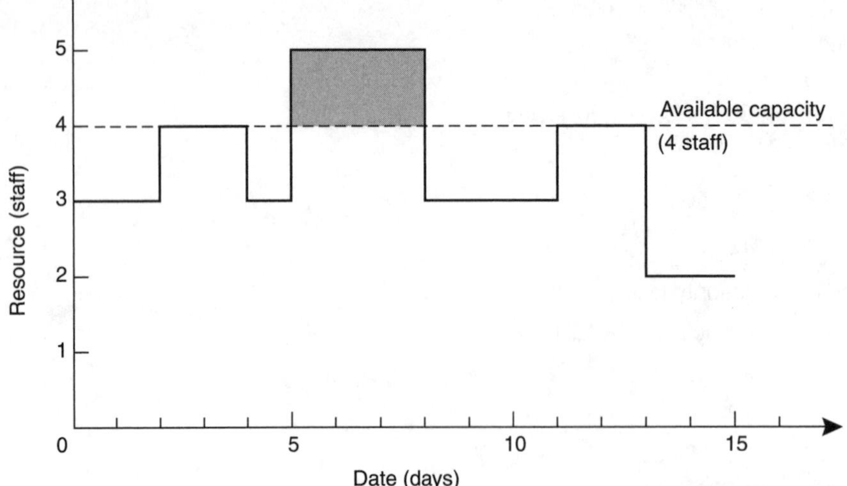


In this example an overload occurs from day 5 to day 8; consequently, unless we arrange either to subcontract this work or obtain additional resources, we cannot expect to meet our project completion date. The only remaining alternative is to reschedule some of the jobs which constitute this overload. We can, for example, delay three work-days of work from this period until days 8 to 11 and avoid overloading the resources.

Consider the part of a network shown in Figure 13.26. To be completed in four days, activity C requires six workers and four machines; activity D requires eight workers and five machines for three days. The total resources available are eight workers and six machines, so activities C and D cannot occur together. The solution is to:

(a) subcontract one of the activities; or

(b) obtain additional resources; or

(c) reschedule one or both of the activities.

Solutions (a) and (b) are particularly suitable where large overloads would occur and where this can be predicted well in advance. Often, rescheduling is undertaken, and certainly where the overload is small and has occurred unexpectedly this is perhaps the only solution. The question is, how can we reschedule the project to avoid overloading the resources and yet incur a minimum delay in completion? Activity D is on the critical path (it has a total float of 0) and the total float of activity C is three days so activity D should be undertaken before C and this results in no additional project delay (Figure 13.27).

**Figure 13.26**

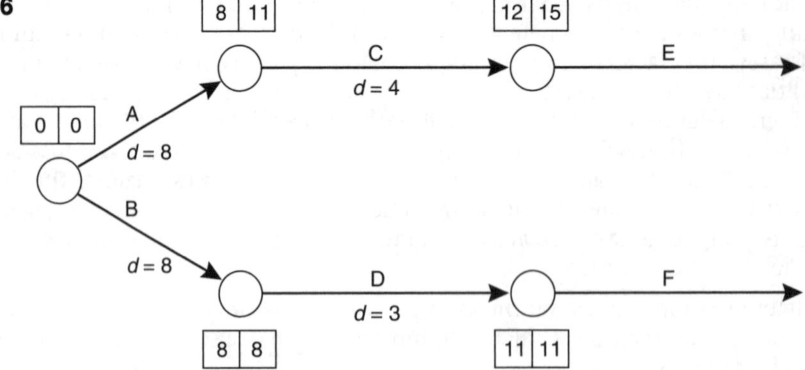

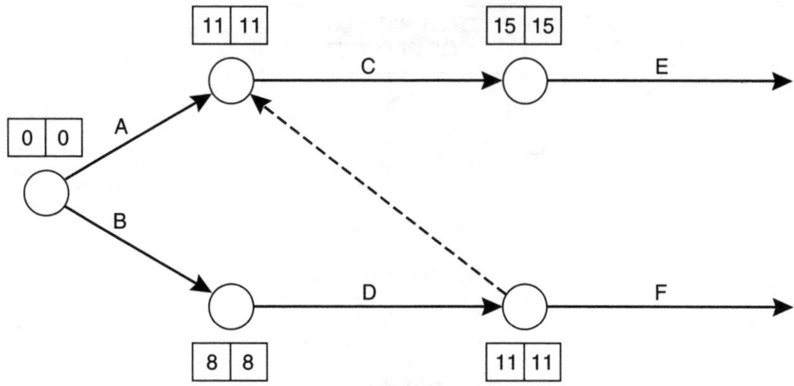


**Figure 13.27**

This is, in effect, a *resource levelling* procedure (see also Chapter 11) concerned with the allocation of resources to activities in order to level or smooth the resource requirement for a project for which an initial network has been constructed and activity dates calculated. This levelling approach is used where it is not possible, because of resource limitations, to perform all activities according to the original dates. In other words it is a method for modifying either the initial network logic (as in Figure 13.27) and/or the activity dates to take resource limitations into account. The example above used the 'priority rule': total float, to reschedule activities. This is the normal approach and is the basis of many computer-based resource allocation/levelling procedures for network planning (see later in this chapter). If such an approach is used a straightforward procedure such as that described in Figure 13.28 can be employed. Notice, however, that other priority rules are available, some of which are listed below:

(a) Reschedule first the activity with least total float (as above).

(b) Reschedule first the activity with shortest duration.

(c) Reschedule first the activity with the earliest *ES* date.

(d) Reschedule first the activity which has the smallest sum of duration and total float.

Resource aggregation, i.e. calculating the total resources necessary in any period to complete the project, is a straightforward job, but resource allocation can involve extensive computation for a large project. Networks involving more than a few hundred activities are normally processed on a computer, but the use of one of the numerous computer/network analysis programs is still economic for networks of fewer activities if resource allocation is to be undertaken. Although methods of resource allocation suitable for manual processing are available, in practice almost all resource allocation/levelling in network analysis occurs during computer processing.

---

*Activity on node diagrams*

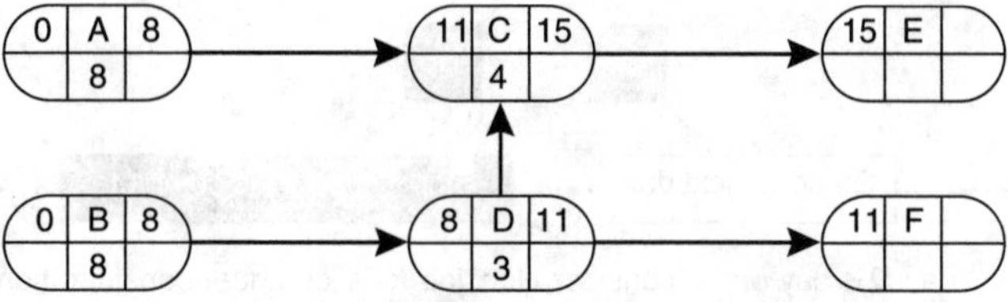


**Figure 13.27**

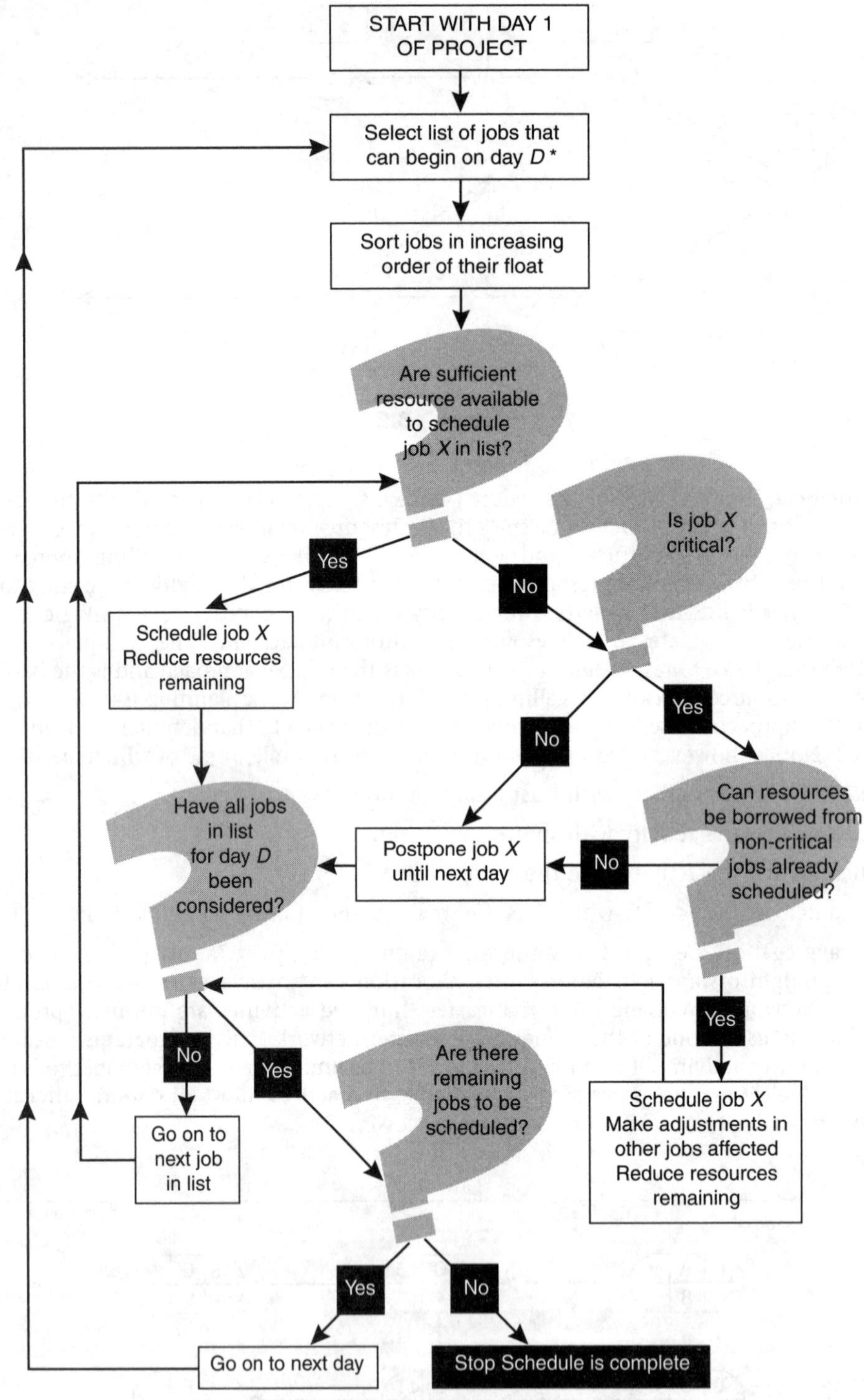


**Figure 13.28** Heuristic program for resource allocation. From Weist, J. D. (1966) Heuristic programs for decision-making. *Harvard Business Review*, **44**(5), pp. 129–143. Reproduced with permission.

# COSTS

The duration of an activity depends on the quantity of resources allocated to it. At additional cost more resources can usually be acquired and the activity duration decreased. In many cases this additional expenditure can be justified by the earlier completion of the activity and of the project. If a heavy penalty clause applies for late completion of the project, or if the project must be completed by a given date so that it can begin earning revenue (e.g. a hotel ready for the beginning of the holiday season), then additional expenditure during manufacture may be economically justifiable. In network analysis it is assumed that cost is linearly related to activity duration, and that as duration decreases the cost increases (Figure 13.29).

**Figure 13.29**

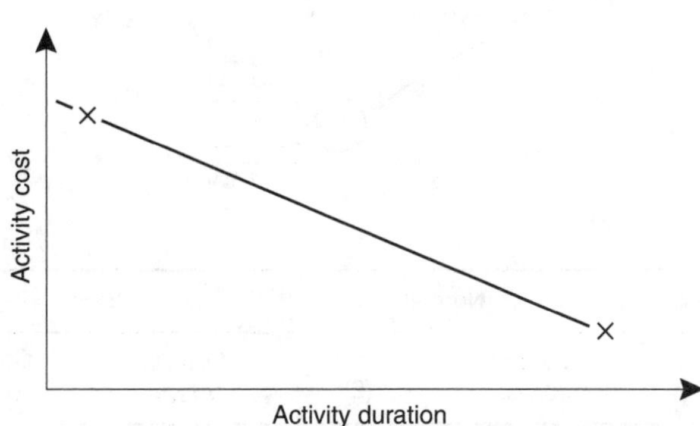


When it is possible to reduce an activity duration by engaging extra resources at additional cost, two extreme cases are assumed to exist:

(a) ***Normal*** activity duration at normal cost, utilizing the normal quantity of resources.

(b) A shorter ***crash*** activity duration at crash cost, utilizing additional resources.

Where the difference between normal and crash durations results from the use of a different method or process, no intermediate duration may be possible. For example, an estate of houses built by conventional techniques may require 50 days and cost £200 000, but an estate of 'industrialized' buildings may require 25 days and cost £330 000. Since two entirely different sets of resources are used no compromise state exists on the same cost/duration function, whereas where the difference between normal and crash duration results from the use of additional similar resources, the two extremes may be interpolated, as in Figure 13.29.

The total cost of a project is determined not only by variable costs such as production resources, but also by fixed or overhead costs such as rent for buildings, insurance, power, administration, etc. Consequently the project duration involving minimum total cost is not necessarily the duration with minimum cost of resources.

The network diagram for a small construction project, activity cost data and network dates is shown in Figure 13.30(a). Only the activities on the critical path affect the project duration, so reduction in project duration must be sought on the critical path and from those activities offering time savings at least cost. Initially there are two critical paths – ABE and ADE – and the least cost time saving is two days from both activities B and D. After activities B and D have been reduced from five to three days all three paths are critical and, since no further reduction is possible on activity D, savings must be obtained from activities A and E. Activity A can be reduced by one day at a cost of £10, then activity E by one day at a cost of £15. This procedure for reducing the project duration is given in the table in Figure 13.30(b), which also shows the construction of the total cost/project duration curve. The least cost project duration is nine days.

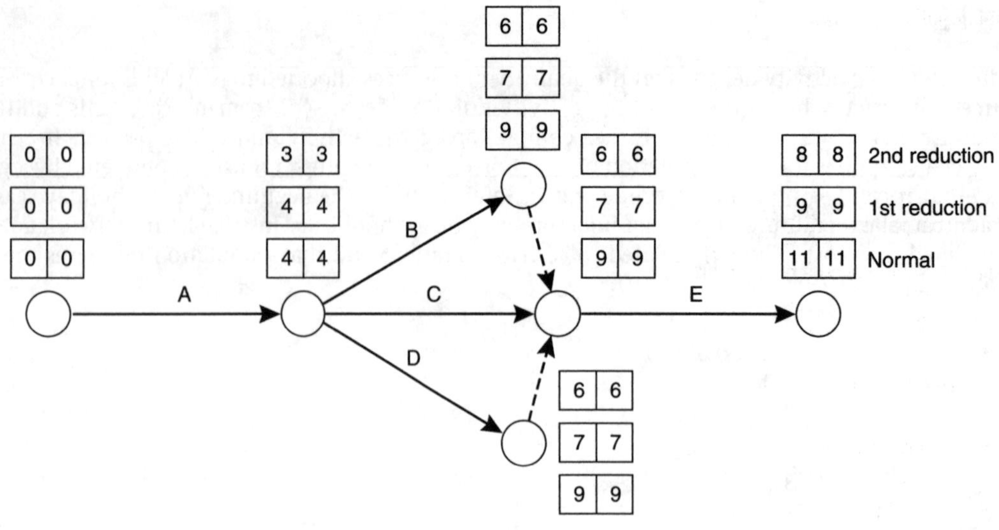


| Activity | Normal | | Crash | |
|---|---|---|---|---|
| | Duration (days) | Cost (£) | Duration (days) | Cost (£) |
| A | 4 | 30 | 3 | 40 |
| B | 5 | 12 | 2 | 18 |
| C | 3 | 10 | 2 | 20 |
| D | 5 | 10 | 3 | 12 |
| E | 2 | 15 | 1 | 30 |
| | | Total 77 | | |

N.B. Indirect fixed cost – £5/day.

**Figure 13.30(a)** Network diagram and comparison between cost of normal and crash activities

Before ending our discussion of costs we must draw attention to a rather interesting 'twist' or variation of the procedure followed in the preceding example. Again we shall consider a simple example in order to explain the variation. Consider the simple project represented by Figure 13.31. Let us calculate the total cost associated with the completion of this project in first one and then two days less than the normal duration.

The normal duration of the project is 32 days at a normal cost of £1620. Under those conditions the critical path is 0 1 4 3 5 6 (see Figure 13.31 and Table 13.1). To reduce this duration by one day, one of the jobs on the critical path must be reduced by one day. The cheapest reduction is available on job 1–4 (£15), and consequently a project duration of 31 days is achieved at a cost of £1635.

There are now three critical paths (0 1 4 3 5 6, 0 2 4 3 5 6 and 0 1 3 5 6), and consequently a reduction of the project duration by a further day is achieved by reducing each of these paths by one day. Job 1–4 cannot be reduced any further, and hence the cheapest direct method of reducing the project duration from 31 to 30 days is reducing by one day the duration of job 1–3 (thereby reducing critical path 0 1 3 5 6) and the duration of job 4–3 (thereby reducing the duration of *both* paths 0 1 4 3 5 6 and 0 2 4 3 5 6). Thus the additional cost incurred is £40 and the total cost for a project duration of 30 days is £1675. Notice that although three critical paths were involved, job 4–3 was common to two of those and it was necessary only to alter the duration of two jobs.

Normal duration = 11 days
Normal cost = £77

| Job | Cost/day saved | Reduction (days) | Total reduction (days) | Additional cost (£) | Duration (days) |
|---|---|---|---|---|---|
| Initial critical paths = { ABE, ADE } | | | | | 11 |
| Least cost saving occurs on B and D | | | | | |
| B, D | 2 + 1 | 2 | 2 | 6 | 9 |
| Now three critical paths = { ABE, ACE, ADE } | | | | | |
| Least cost saving on A | | | | | |
| A | 10 | 1 | 3 | 16 | 8 |
| Least cost saving on E | | | | | |
| E | 15 | 1 | 4 | 31 | 7 |

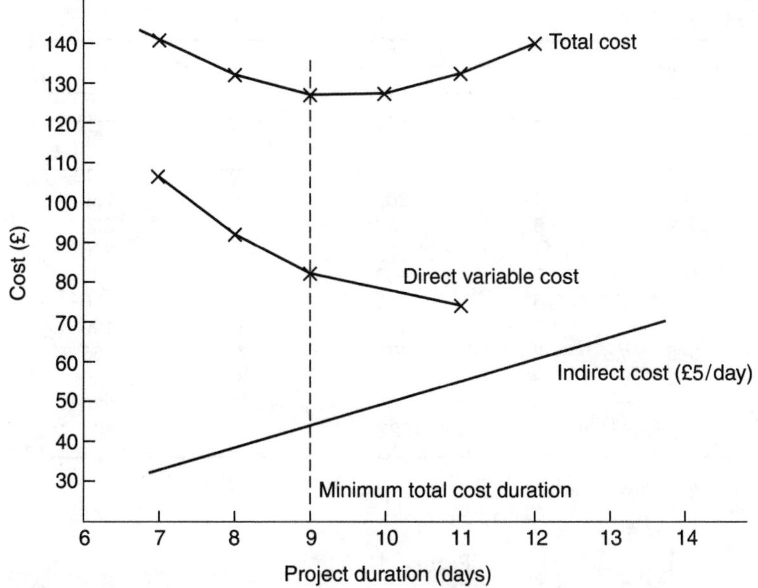


**Figure 13.30(b)** Activity variable cost/duration relationships for Figure 13.30(a)

Job 0–1 is also common to two critical paths and we could therefore have reduced the duration of this job and that of either job 0–2 or 2–4 to reduce the duration of the project, but such a solution would have been more expensive than that outlined previously. One further means of reducing the duration of the project would have been to reduce the duration of jobs 0–1 and 4–3. This again would have been a more expensive solution than the original. Notice, however, that both jobs 0–1 and 4–3 are common to two paths. Reduction of job 0–1 would reduce both path 0 1 3 5 6 and path 0 1 4 3 5 6, while reduction of job 4–3 would reduce path 0 1 4 3 5 6 and path 0 2 4 3 5 6. The reduction of both of these jobs by one day would reduce path 0 1 4 3 5 6 by two days, and hence an alternative method

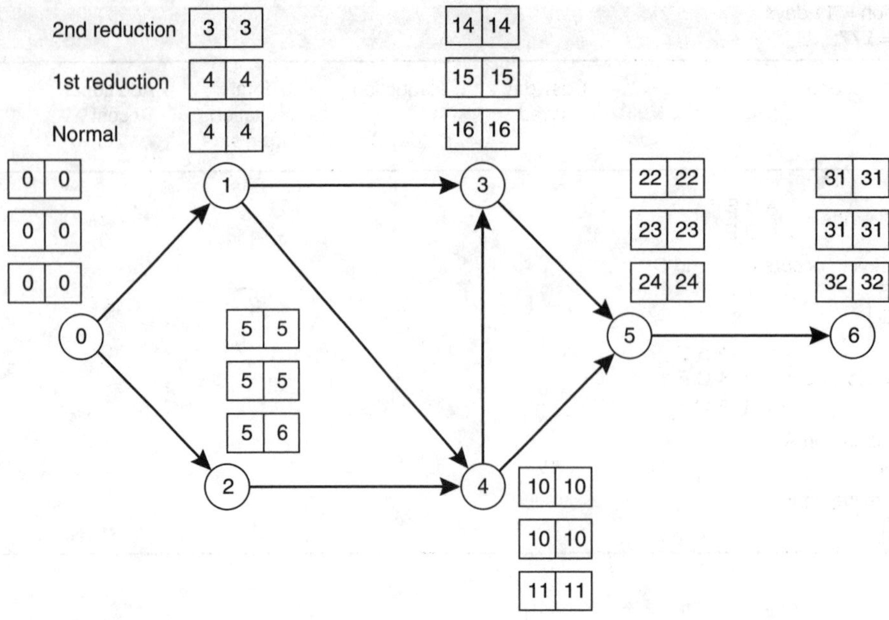


| Activity | Normal | | Crash | |
|---|---|---|---|---|
| | Duration (days) | Cost (£) | Duration (days) | Cost (£) |
| 0–1 | 4 | 200 | 3 | 230 |
| 0–2 | 5 | 180 | 4 | 200 |
| 1–3 | 11 | 200 | 9 | 240 |
| 1–4 | 7 | 150 | 6 | 165 |
| 2–4 | 5 | 150 | 4 | 170 |
| 4–3 | 5 | 170 | 4 | 190 |
| 3–5 | 8 | 170 | 7 | 265 |
| 4–5 | 8 | 200 | 8 | 200 |
| 5–6 | 8 | 200 | 8 | 200 |
| | | Total 1620 | | |

N.B. Indirect fixed cost considered to be zero.

**Figure 13.31**

of obtaining a reduced project duration is to reduce, by one day, jobs 0–1 and 4–3 and to *increase* by one day job 1–4. In fact this alternative is cheaper than the previous one, the cost of the reduction being 30 + 20 – 15, i.e. £35 compared with the £40 cost of the previous method.

This interesting twist occurs only infrequently; nevertheless it is worth while keeping a lookout for this type of solution when the analysis involves more than one critical path, and when two or more reducible activities are common to these paths which themselves contain previously reduced activities.

Table 13.1

| Job or activity | Cost/day saved | Reduction | Total reduction | Additional cost | Duration |
|---|---|---|---|---|---|
| Critical path 0 1 4 3 5 6 | | | | | 32 |
| Least cost reduction occurs on path 1–4 | 15 | 1 | 1 | 15 | 31 |
| Critical paths { 0 1 4 3 5 6, 0 2 4 3 5 6, 0 1 3 5 6 } | | | | | |
| *Method 1* | | | | | |
| 1–3 } 4–3 } | 20 + 20 | 1 | 2 | 55 | 30 |
| *Alternative method* | | | | | |
| 0–1 } 4–3 } 1–4 } | 30 + 20 −15 (increase duration) | 1 | 2 | 50 | 30 |

## RESOURCES: AGGREGATION AND ALLOCATION

Resource *aggregation* is a comparatively simple procedure and the output consists of either lists or histograms showing the total requirements per resource per period. There are occasions where such information might be of value.

For example, an allocation (or levelling) aggregation of resources will indicate which periods and which resources are overloaded. It is then possible either to reschedule the activities using these resources during the overload periods to obtain extra resources or subcontract some of the work.

Unless the system is working considerably under capacity, some form of resource *allocation* is normally necessary, and a procedure often adopted in computer-based network analysis is as follows:

(a) Aggregate resources.

(b) Identify periods of overload.

(c) Reschedule activities during these periods as follows:

1. delay activities in order of decreasing total float by a period up to the allowed maximum delay;
2. if overload still occurs use additional resources available;
3. if overload still occurs allow overload to stand.

This is an imperfect procedure, for no attempt is made to overcome resource overloads by moving activities forward, nor is any attempt made to compare the cost of extra resources with the cost of either delay or subcontracting. To deal with the resource allocation problem in this, more comprehensive, manner, and to be able to do so routinely, necessitates the use of a computer-based approach. Software for such applications is considered later in this chapter.

## MULTI-PROJECT OPERATIONS PLANNING

Network analysis was originally developed for use on large single projects and this still remains the most important application of the technique. Recently, however, greater use has been made of network planning procedures for simultaneous manufacture of several items. This type of application is best dealt with by computer.

Perhaps the main thing to avoid is compromise. Network analysis is such an effective planning procedure that, unless all the projects in any particular situation are planned in this way, there is a very real danger that those to which network analysis is applied will progress at the expense of the remainder. One of the important advantages of this procedure is that it highlights critical activities and encourages those responsible to make a real effort not only to meet the required finish dates but also to 'get off the critical path'. Under this sort of influence there is little incentive to worry unduly about other projects which do not appear in the limelight.

To use network analysis on several projects the following additional information is required:

(a) The activities in each network must be separately identifiable, either by using different event numbers or by the use of a prefix letter to identify the project.

(b) In addition to responsibility codes to identify which department is responsible for the activities, a further code must be used to identify the project so that the output for each project and each department can be collected together if necessary.

One of the difficulties in using this method for multi-project planning is to define the relative importance of each project. For example, if three projects are running concurrently and at any time one department is responsible for processing an item from each and each item has the same total float and start date, which is the most important? To some extent this problem can be overcome by deciding on the order of priority of the projects and communicating this to all concerned; alternatively, schedule dates may be used to indicate priorities. Nevertheless, this assumes first that priorities remain constant and that decisions about activities will necessarily be resolved in relation to the priority of the overall projects, whereas there may be occasions when it is preferable to do jobs from less important projects first (when, for example, the set-up cost of a facility is substantially less if two or more jobs are done in this order rather than in order of project priority).

## THE USE OF GANTT (BAR) CHARTS

It will often be useful to represent the activities of a project diagrammatically against a time-scale. The normal network diagram has no time-scale, but it is possible to use a form of Gantt or bar chart. The use of Gantt charts to represent activities, their start dates, etc. will be appropriate when using network techniques to develop schedules which must then be communicated to others and/or displayed for easy reference. Gantt charts are easily read and can be used to show the progress of work on activities or projects. They can easily be updated and changed, and various proprietary 'kits' are available for the construction of such charts, with colour coding for different types of resources, etc. However, the main problems with this approach are that: (a) it is difficult to show the interdependence of activities; and (b) it is difficult to show all the dates for each activity, which are determined from the network calculations. The first problem can be overcome with ingenuity. The second problem is normally overcome by showing only earliest start and finish dates.

Figure 13.32 is a Gantt chart representation of the project previously described in network form in Example 13.2. This chart also shows the resource requirements for the activities. Figure 13.33 shows how this type of representation can be used to develop a resource aggregation for this project.

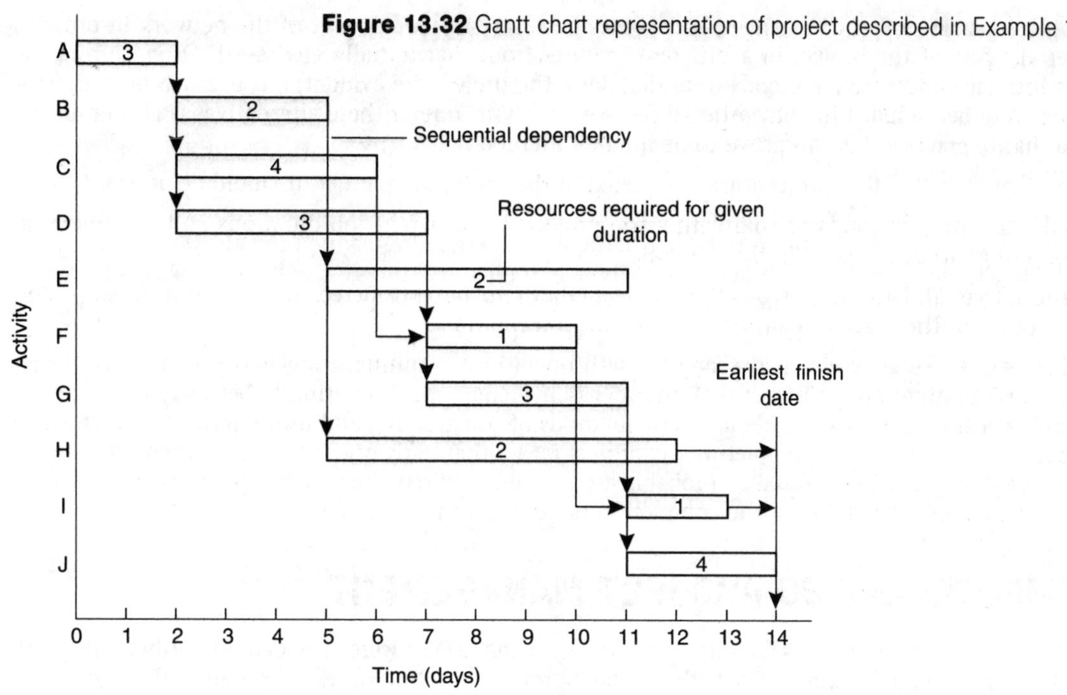


**Figure 13.32** Gantt chart representation of project described in Example 13.2

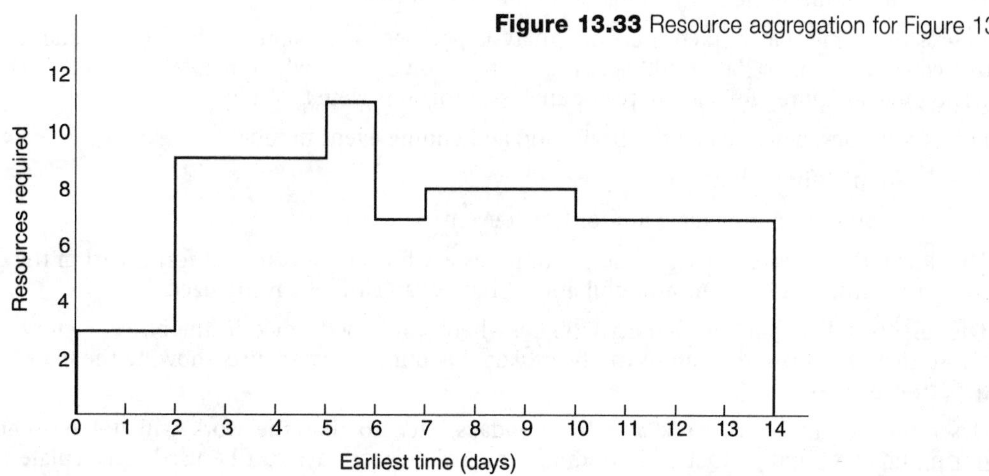


**Figure 13.33** Resource aggregation for Figure 13.32

## PROBABILISTIC NETWORKS

In the past, network analysis has been criticized because of the difficulty of altering the network construction in the light of experience or circumstance during the actual performance of jobs. In other words, it has been suggested that there is inadequate connection between the planning stage, during which the network is constructed, and the usage stage, during which the network and the activity start and finish dates are used to schedule and control the overall project.

In some cases, particularly when concerned with new or novel projects never before undertaken, the initial network drawn up during the project planning stages proves either impractical or disadvantageous in use. In many cases, e.g. because of a delay in certain parts of the project or because of unforeseen snags and circumstances, it becomes necessary to modify part of the network in order to undertake part of the project in a different manner from that initially envisaged. Often during the planning stage alternative methods of undertaking the project are evident, but because such alternatives cannot be included in conventional network analysis, one of these alternatives is chosen in the hope that in practice this will prove to be the best method.

In order to ensure that projects are completed in the optimum manner, it would be necessary for:

(a) all alternative methods of completing the project, i.e. different job durations and technological orderings, to be included in the network;

(b) the effects and the merits of alternative methods to be considered at the planning stage and throughout the usage or control stage of the project.

In this chapter we are concerned primarily with operations planning using network analysis; nevertheless, it is pertinent to point out that, in order to overcome the discontinuity between planning and control, attempts have been made to devise methods of constructing and using networks which show the several possible ways of completing the project rather than only one method. This type of network can be described as a generalized or probabilistic network and has the merit of permitting alternative methods to be evaluated during the completion or control of the project.

## COMPUTER-BASED PROJECT MANAGEMENT

Most of the early software packages for use in project management were provided primarily for network construction and analysis, together with schedule production. Procedures for resource allocation, and for dealing with multi-project situations, were then developed.

These early, somewhat limited, network analysis packages were valuable for project planning and control when more than 200 or 300 activities were involved, and where regular updating was necessary. The inputs required for such network analysis programs were typically:

(a) List of activities, described by the beginning and ending event number.

(b) The duration(s) for each activity.

(c) Schedule dates on intermediate and/or finish events.

(d) The description of each activity. This is not necessary for the program but forms part of the output so that the information is meaningful and activities can easily be recognized.

(e) The responsibility code for each activity, i.e. whether it is performed in the office, factory, and so on, so that, if desired, the output can be broken down into separate lists showing the plan for each department or area.

(f) Description of the work week and the holidays, etc., so that the work will not be scheduled during holidays and so that activity durations in hours or days can be used to calculate project durations in weeks or months.

(g) The resource levels normally available, i.e. normal work and machine hours per week.

(h) Additional resources available due to overtime, etc.

(i) Maximum activity delay which, if necessary, can be tolerated because of the rescheduling of activities to conform to resource availability.

(j) Computer run parameters, e.g. customer's name, name of project.

(k) Output parameters to determine the type of output required, etc.

Many more comprehensive and sophisticated software packages for project management are now available. Current estimates suggest that there are about 250 on the market. A list of just a small number of them is given in Table 13.2. Table 13.3 provides a categorization of such software and outlines capabilities/features.

**Table 13.2 Some software packages for project management**

| Name | Source/Details (for addresses see list at end of chapter) |
|---|---|
| Project Scheduler | Scitor Corp. |
| SAS System | SAS |
| Project/2 | Project Software & Development |
| Super Project Expert | Computer Associates |
| Artemis | Lucas Management Systems (see also *Project Manager Today*, Feb. 1992, pp. 42–45) |
| Project Manager Workbench | Hoskins |
| Open Plan | Welcome Software |
| Primavera | Primavera Systems |
| Trackstar | Cosar Project Management |
| Plantrac | Computerline |
| Promis-PMS (based on Artemis) | (see *Project Manager Today*, Nov./Dec. 1992, pp. 30–33) |
| Project Guide | Deepak Sareen |
| Power Project | Asta |
| PC Project 3 | (see *Project Manager Today*, Oct. 1992, pp. 34–36) |

**Table 13.3 Types and capabilities of computer software packages**

| | |
|---|---|
| **1. Simple:** | Single-project planning<br>Limited analysis (e.g. no rescheduling)<br>Simple, easy to use and understand |
| **2. Single:** | Single-project management (planning, scheduling control, monitoring)<br>Comprehensive analysis (with progress reports, rescheduling, etc.) |
| **3. Multiproject:** | Multiproject management (planning, scheduling control, monitoring)<br>Comprehensive analysis and reports<br>Uses common database |

**Typical capabilities**

1. Formats (activity on arrow or on node)
2. Bar or Gantt chart displays/outputs
3. Schedule dates
4. Updating (e.g. with revised durations, schedule dates, etc.)
5. Sorting (i.e. listing of activities with dates, by department)
6. Resource aggregation and allocations
7. Cost controls and calculations
8. Calendar dates (i.e. internal calendar used to apply calendar dates to activities)
9. Reports (i.e. choice of report formats)
10. PERT calculations
11. Cost/duration comparisons
12. 'What if?' calculations (e.g. calculate effects of changes in durations, resources, etc.)

## EXAMPLE

Gibraltar Savings installed a microcomputer-based project management system to manage the conversion from one manufacturer's computer system to another, following acquisition of another savings company. The project management system created a conversion schedule detailed to task level. It was used to schedule the execution of the weekend-long conversion, indicating at what points the conversion process should stop for data verification and when to undertake full-production file testing, etc. Because of the success in this application the system was adopted by Gibraltar as a standard for major conversions and for regular operations.

Source: Skylar, J. (1988) Macro project, micro manager. *Computer Decisions*, **20**(11), pp. 76.

## CHECKLIST FOR CHAPTER 13

### Project management

Nature of projects and project management
Definition of a project
Project phases and stages
Role of project management
- Success factors

### Project scheduling and control

Construction of network diagrams
- Dummy activities

Network calculations
- Dates (EF, LF, ES, LS)
- Float
- The critical path
- Slack
- Free and independent float
- Schedule dates
- Event dates
- Matrix method of calculation

Multiple time estimates (PERT)
- Probability of achieving scheduled dates

Resources
- Aggregation
- Allocation and levelling

Costs
- Cost v. activity duration
- Minimum total variable cost durations

### Operations planning with network analysis

### Resource aggregation and allocation

### Multi-project operations planning

### Gantt (or bar) chart representations

### Probabilistic networks

### Computer-based project management

## FURTHER READING

**British Standards Institution (1987)** *Glossary of Terms Used in Project Network Techniques* (BS 4335). London: BSI.

**East, E. and Kirby, J. (1990)** *A Guide to Computerized Project Scheduling*. New York: Van Nostrand Reinhold.

**Fawcette, J. E. (1984)** Choosing project management software. *Personal Computing*, **8**(10), pp. 154–167.

**Kerzner, H. (1992)** *Project Management: A Systems Approach to Planning, Scheduling and Control*. New York: Van Nostrand Reinhold.

**O'Neal, K. R. (1987)** Project management software buyers' guide. *Industrial Engineering*, **19**(1), pp. 53–63.

**Turner, J. R. (1993)** *The Handbook of Project Based Management*. London: McGraw-Hill.

**Wood, L. (1989)** A manager's guide to computerized project management. *Manufacturing Systems*, **7**(8), pp. 18–24.

## SOFTWARE SOURCES

Asta Development Corp.
5 St Andrews Court
Wellington St
Thame
Oxfordshire OX9 3WT
UK

Computerline Ltd
Tavistock House
319 Woodham Lane
Woodham
Weybridge
Surrey KT15 3PB
UK

Cosar Project Management
Dovetail House
Wycombe Road
Stokenchurch
Bucks HP14 3RQ
UK

Deepak Sarren Associates
Bydell House
Sudbury Hill
Harrow on the Hill
Middlesex HA1 3BR
UK

Hoskins Group
PMW Centre
95 Wandsworth Road
London SW8 2LX
UK

Lucas Management Systems
Metier House
23 Clayton Road
Hayes
Middlesex UB3 1AN
UK

Primavera Systems Inc.
International Business Park
Europa Building
TH160 Archamps
France

Project Software and Development Inc.
20 University Road
Cambridge
MA 02138
USA

SAS Institute Inc.
Software Sales
SAS Campus Drive
Cary
NC 27513-2414
USA

Scitor Corp.
343 Vintage Park Drive
Suite 140
Foster City
CA 94404
USA

Welcome Software
South Bank Technopark
90 London Road
London SE1 6LN
UK

## QUESTIONS

13.1 Construct a network diagram for the following activities:

| Activity | A | B | C | D | E | F | G | H | J | K | L | M | N | O |
|---|---|---|---|---|---|---|---|---|---|---|---|---|---|---|
| Necessary preceding activities | – | – | A | AB | C | C | D | D | E | EF | GH | H | JK | LM |

13.2 Redraw the following network diagram so that the logic is retained and dummy activities are used correctly.

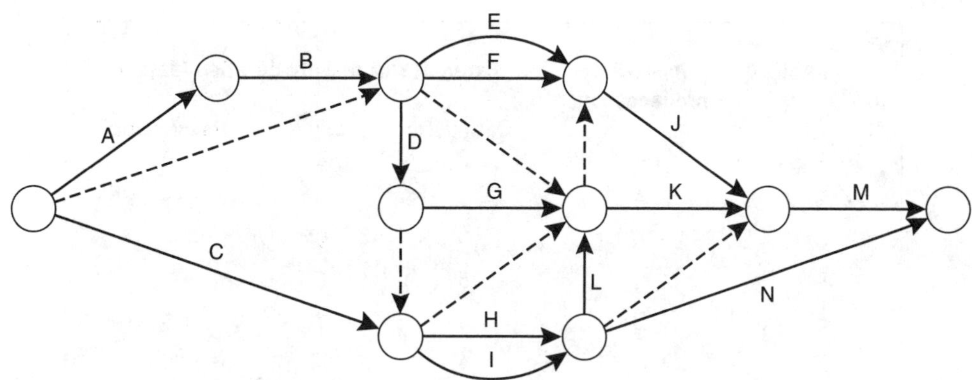


13.3 Draw an activity network for the following activities. Assuming that the project starts at day 0, calculate the earliest start and latest finish dates for all activities, and the project earliest completion date. Calculate also the total float on all activities and identify the critical path.

| Activity | A | B | C | D | E | F | G | H | I |
|---|---|---|---|---|---|---|---|---|---|
| Immediate predecessors | – | – | A | AB | BC | CD | CD | EF | EGF |
| Activity duration (days) | 3 | 5 | 6 | 2 | 4 | 7 | 3 | 4 | 5 |

13.4 In the following network, assuming that the project starts at day 0, what is the probability that the project will be completed by day 26?

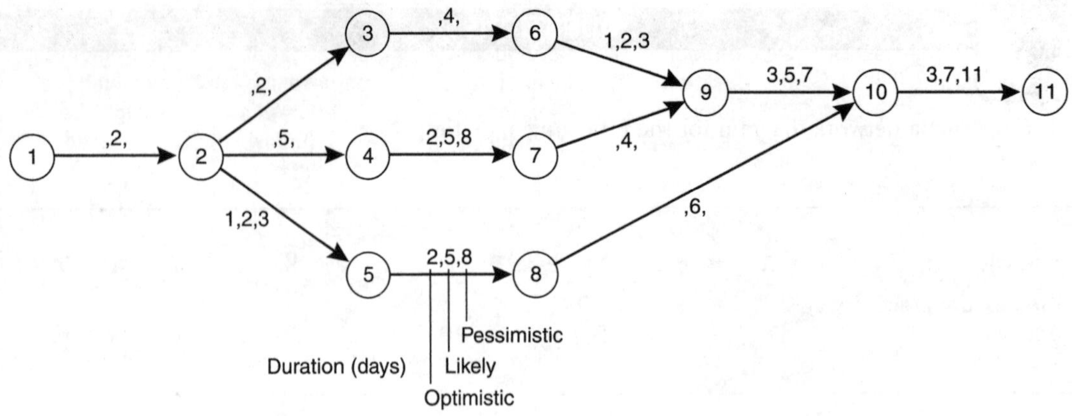


13.5 The following table describes the various activities of a small project. What is the probability that the project will be completed in $22^1/_2$ days or less?

| Activity | Immediate predecessor(s) | Estimates of activity duration (days) | | |
|---|---|---|---|---|
| | | Optimistic | Likely | Pessimistic |
| A | – | 2 | 4 | 6 |
| B | A | 1 | 5 | 9 |
| C | A | – | 9 | – |
| D | C | 5 | 6 | 7 |
| E | B | 5 | 7 | 9 |
| F | B | 4 | 10 | 16 |
| G | DE | – | 7 | – |
| H | F | 6 | 9 | 12 |

13.6 A service operation in a garage involves 12 separate jobs (A–L inclusive). The table opposite gives the normal durations of these jobs. The necessary dependencies of the jobs on one another are also shown in the table. It is possible to reduce the normal duration of many of the jobs if additional money is spent on resources.

The normal total cost of the project would be £1500, which includes a fixed cost of £200 and indirect costs which are charged at £25 per day.

What is the minimum duration of the project irrespective of cost and what is the least cost duration? Draw a curve of total cost versus project duration.

Notice that, because of unavoidable constraints on the delivery of the materials, job H cannot start before the seventh day, and because of further constraints job B must on no account be finished later than day 14.

| Job | Predecessors | Normal duration (days) | Number of days by which job may be reduced | Cost of shortening job duration (£/day) (days) | Increments by which job might be reduced |
|---|---|---|---|---|---|
| A | - | 4 | 3 | 50 | 1 |
| B | - | 8 | 0 | - | - |
| C | - | 3 | 1 | 100 | 1 |
| D | A | 6 | 3 | 50 | 2 |
| E | C | 5 | 2 | 80 | 1 |
| F | D | 8 | 3 | 100 | 1/2 |
| G | D | 2 | 1 | 75 | 1 |
| H | E | 6 | 2 | 75 | 1 |
| I | E | 2 | 1 | 60 | 1 |
| J | F | 1 | 0 | - | - |
| K | GBH | 6 | 3 | 50 | 1 |
| L | 1 | 5 | 2 | 35 | 2 |

13.7 A publishing project consists of 15 activities and can be represented by the network diagram below.

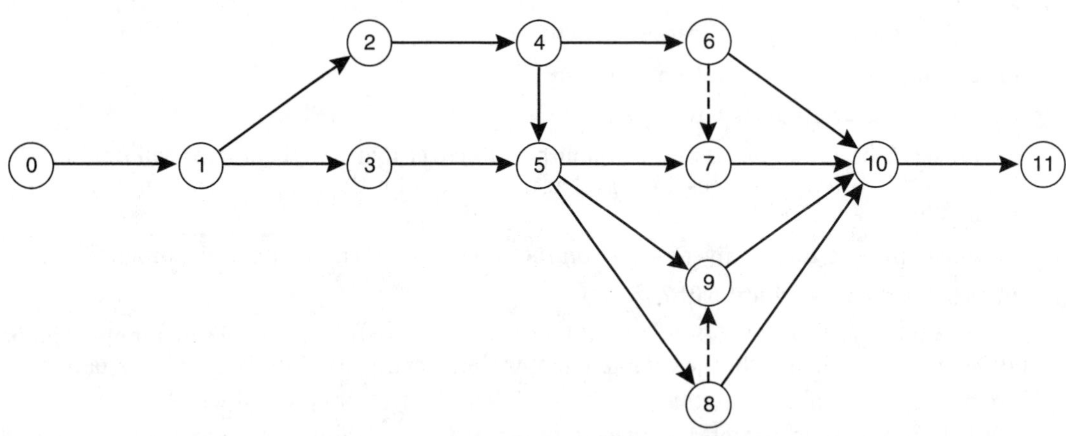


The duration of each of the activities is as follows:

| Activity | | Duration (days) |
|---|---|---|
| Begin event | End event | |
| 0 | 1 | 10 |
| 1 | 2 | 5 |
| 1 | 3 | 6 |
| 2 | 4 | 3 |
| 3 | 5 | 4 |
| 4 | 5 | 3 |
| 4 | 6 | 8 |
| 5 | 7 | 4 |
| 5 | 8 | 5 |
| 5 | 9 | 9 |
| 6 | 7 | Dummy |
| 6 | 10 | 7 |
| 7 | 10 | 2 |
| 8 | 10 | 3 |
| 9 | 8 | Dummy |
| 9 | 10 | 6 |
| 10 | 11 | 9 |

(a) If the project is to start at, say, day 0 and is to end as soon as possible, calculate the total float (TF) on each activity and identify the critical path.

(b) Activity 3–5 is 'copy edit the manuscript'.

Activity 6–10 is 'check book cover design'.

The project is begun on day 0 but the publishers discover that the manuscript will not be delivered from the author until week 18, and that the artwork for the book cover will not come from the artist until week 24.

(i) What effect do these deliveries have on the earliest completion date of the project?

(ii) What is the new critical path?

13.8 If certain multiple time estimates are used for the duration of individual jobs in a project, probabilities may be calculated for the completion of the project or part of the project by certain schedule dates.

What are the basic assumptions necessary for such calculations, and how justified are such assumptions in practice?

Under what circumstances is this procedure likely to be beneficial, and in what circumstances are the results likely to be either inaccurate or unrealistic?

Wherever possible, construct numerical examples to illustrate your answer.

13.9 The network diagram shown below has been drawn up by a project planner. The diagram represents the sequence of jobs which will be undertaken during the service of a large component which must be completed by day 35. Using the estimates of the job durations given by the managers of the various departments, the project planner has calculated event dates which indicate that the project will be completed one day before the scheduled completion date.

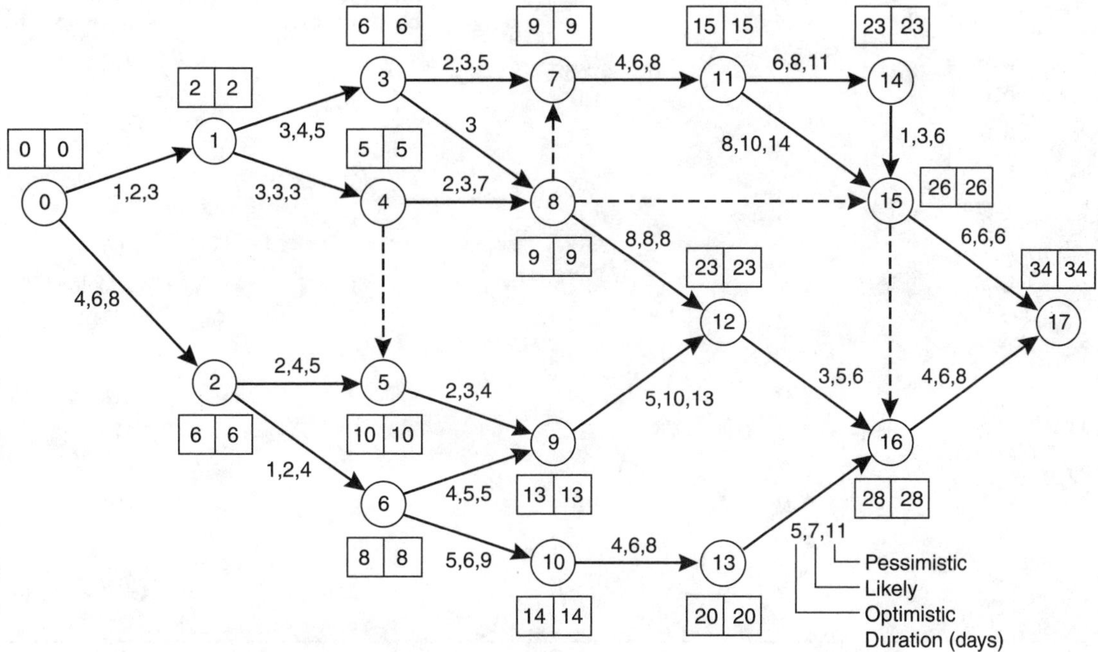


The information given on the diagram has been submitted to you, the project executive, for approval prior to being distributed to the various departments. What are your reactions and why?

13.10 The table overleaf gives the durations of the individual jobs in a complex project and shows the sequential relationship between the jobs. The activities are not listed in order of occurrence and the letters refer to events. It is possible to reduce the durations of some of the jobs to the extent shown in column (4) at an incremental cost per week saved as shown in column (5).

The target time for completing the project is 23 weeks, and the benefits of completion before the target date are estimated at £160 per week saved.

Find the most economical duration for the whole project and the corresponding durations for individual jobs.

13.11 From the information given overleaf construct a network diagram.

(a) Neglecting resource considerations, what is the earliest finish date for the project?

(b) Assuming that each activity begins as early as possible, construct a graph showing the amount of resources used during each period.

(c) The maximum number of resources available is 10 workers. Again, assuming that activities are begun as soon as possible, redraw the network so that the resources used at any time do not exceed 19 workers and so that a minimum project delay is incurred.

(d) What project delay is incurred through this adherence to the resource limit?

## Table for Question 13.10

| (1) Job designation | (2) Prior job(s) | (3) Duration of job (weeks) | (4) Number of weeks by which job can be shortened | (5) Cost of shortening job by 1 week (£) |
|---|---|---|---|---|
| P–L | – | 5 | 2 | 120 |
| P–D | – | 10 | 0 | – |
| P–M | – | 9 | 2 | 80 |
| L–Z | P–L | 7 | 2 | 100 |
| Z–D | L–Z | 0 | 0 | – |
| Z–Y | L–Z | 5 | 3 | 50 |
| D–Y | L–D<br>P–D<br>M–D<br>Z–D | 6 | 3 | 80/week for first week, thereafter 100/week |
| Y–R | Z–Y<br>D–Y | 3 | 1 | 170 |
| M–R | P–M | 10 | 2 | 30 |
| M–D | P–M | 2 | 0 | – |
| L–D | P–L | 4 | 3 | 100 |

## Table for Question 13.11

| Activity | Immediate predecessor | Duration (days) | Number of workers used |
|---|---|---|---|
| A | – | 8 | 4 |
| B | – | 7 | 8 |
| C | A | 6 | 5 |
| D | B | 8 | 4 |
| E | B | 4 | 8 |
| F | B | 8 | 6 |
| G | CD | 5 | 5 |
| H | E | 6 | 4 |
| I | F | 6 | 5 |
| J | GHI | 10 | 6 |

N.B. Because of the nature of the work, jobs cannot be interrupted and must be finished once begun.

13.12 Unit Construction Ltd is a small company engaged in the manufacture of high-class furniture. About once a year a new product is added to the already extensive range. In the past some difficulty has been experienced in co-ordinating the various activities involved in introducing the new product, so this year it has been decided to draw up an activity network for the entire job. The managing director of the company has described the entire design and 'launching' process as follows, and this information is to be used in constructing the activity network.

Basic designs are prepared by our furniture design department, following which detailed drawings are produced and several prototypes made. The prototypes are tested in the laboratories, after which it is usually necessary to make minor design modifications.

Preliminary market research is normally begun after the detailed drawings have been produced, but of course full-scale market research cannot be started until after the prototypes have been made. Incidentally, customer reactions uncovered during the full-scale market research are normally included in the final design along with modifications resulting from prototype laboratory testing. The main purpose of full-scale market research is to establish: (1) the likely demand for the product – information which is required before we can begin to tool up for production or lay out the factory for manufacture; and (2) the nature of press adverts and TV commercials (we always do both).

Final design details are required before these two types of advertisement can be designed. Following the preparations of the TV film and the press copy, both sets of advertisements are approved by myself, then released. Copies of the press adverts are sent to the showroom for point-of-sale advertising.

Once a final design has been established, the prototypes are modified and sent to our showroom where displays are established. When these displays are established and copies of the press adverts have been received, the showroom manager designs the final display. The display material is made by the showroom artists and should, of course, be ready in time for the delivery of the products to the showroom.

13.13 The diagram given below shows the sequence and interdependence of the 11 activities (A–K) which together are necessary in the launch of a new product. Each of the circles represents an activity and the arrows show the interdependence of these activities. This type of diagram is known variously as an *activity* on *node, precedence* or *circle and link* diagram and is sometimes adopted in preference to the more usual *activity on arrow* diagram when using network analysis.

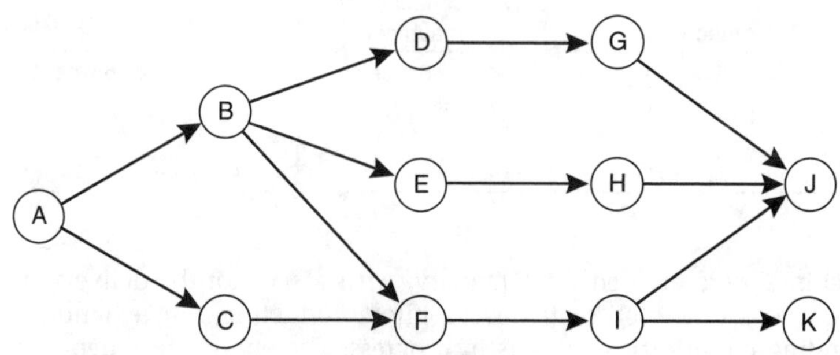


The durations (in days) of each of the activities are given in the table. Also given are the numbers of workers required to complete each activity in the given time.

(a) Either using the type of diagram given or redrawing the diagram in the conventional form, calculate the earliest completion date for the project, identify the critical path and calculate the total float on each activity. (Assume that the project is begun at day 0.)

| Activity | Duration (days) | Workers required |
|---|---|---|
| A | 2 | 4 |
| B | 4 | 3 |
| C | 3 | 6 |
| D | 5 | 5 |
| E | 6 | 7 |
| F | 3 | 4 |
| G | 4 | 6 |
| H | 7 | 8 |
| I | 6 | 3 |
| J | 8 | 7 |
| K | 4 | 10 |

(b) Assuming (i) that each activity is begun as soon as possible, and (ii) that each activity once begun cannot be interrupted, draw a table to indicate the labour requirements for each day during the project.

(c) What are the advantages of the *activity on node* type of network construction over the more conventional method?

13.14 This morning the following information collected by the previous company network analyst on the installation of new operations facilities was presented to you. Make a full analysis and propose a work schedule for the project. Report on what actions may be necessary to ensure that the facilities are ready for the September/October production peak this year.

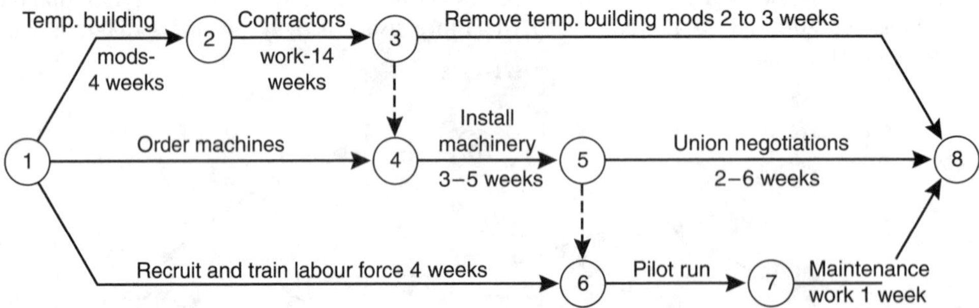


The machines were ordered on 1 January, with a six months delivery promise. The plant manager requires a one-week or two-week pilot production run, extending to at least three weeks if building modification work is in progress. The engineering department is to produce sub-nets for the temporary building modification and their removal, and machine installation. Approximate durations which assume that these three jobs do not overlap are given, together with other durations on the skeleton network.

13.15 Construct an activity on node network from the following data, and then draw a Gantt chart equivalent to the network, using earliest dates. Show any float which exists on activities on the Gantt chart.

| Activity | Predecessors | Duration (hours) |
|---|---|---|
| A | – | 7 |
| B | A | 4 |
| C | A | 5 |
| D | B, E | 3 |
| E | C | 8 |
| F | C | 9 |
| G | F | 2 |
| H | C, D | 6 |

## CASE STUDIES (from Part 9)

The topics covered in this chapter are relevant in the following (see Introduction to Part 9 and Table C.1 for further details):

| No. | Name | Country |
|---|---|---|
| 13 | K&S (Israel) Ltd | Israel |
| 21 | Linden Christian Nursery School – A | South Africa |
| 22 | Linden Christian Nursery School – B | South Africa |
| 23 | Williams' College | UK |
| 26 | Open Polytechnic of New Zealand | New Zealand |

Appendix to Chapter 13

# 'Activity on node' diagrams

Throughout this chapter we concentrated (in the main part of the text) on one particular method of constructing network diagrams: the method in which activities or jobs are represented by arrows, i.e. the *arrow diagram* or *activity on arrow* method. An alternative approach represents activities or jobs by circles or nodes, and is known variously as the *activity on node, precedence* or *circle and link* method. For example, the two arrow diagrams shown in Figure A13.1 can be redrawn as the activity on node diagrams shown in Figure A13.2.

The advantages of this type of network construction, which nevertheless is not generally adopted (except in flow process design – see Chapter 15), are:

(a) The diagrams are simpler both to construct and to interpret, mainly because it is unnecessary to use dummies.

(b) The diagrams are easy to modify.

(c) Description of activities by a single number rather than a pair of numbers is possible.

Network calculations are performed in much the same manner as described in the main part of the text. For example, consider the simple network shown in Figure A13.2(a). Given the duration of each of the activities, the earliest and latest start and finish dates can be calculated as in Figure A13.3.

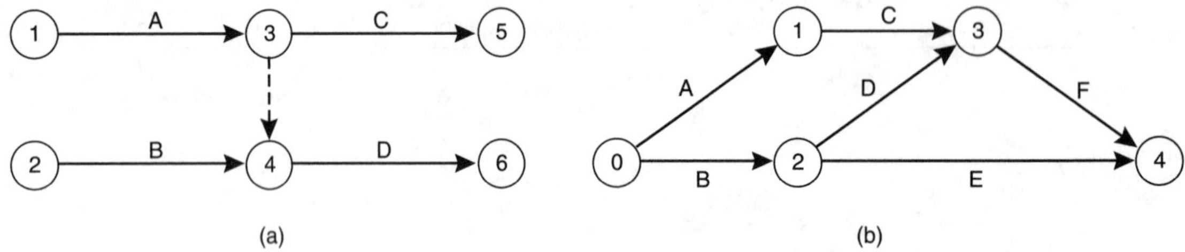


**Figure A13.1** Arrow diagrams

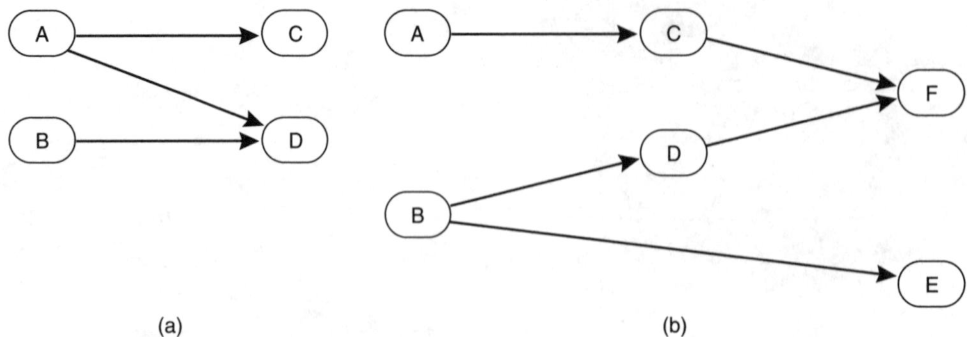


**Figure A13.2** Activity on node diagrams

Notice that with activity on node networks there is often no single point on the network to represent the start or the finish point. For example, in Figure A13.3 the project is complete when C and D are finished. C can be finished by date 9, but D cannot be finished before date 13. Date 13 is therefore the earliest finish date for the project, and also becomes the latest finish date for activity C (assuming the need to finish the project as soon as possible and in the absence of an earlier schedule completion date). In this case, therefore, we have to remember to transfer a date calculated for activity D to the other ending activity for the network, i.e. activity C. In order that we might be reminded of this need it is helpful to show all ending activities in a final column, as shown in Figure A13.2(a) and (b). Similarly, it is helpful to show only the starting activities in the first column.

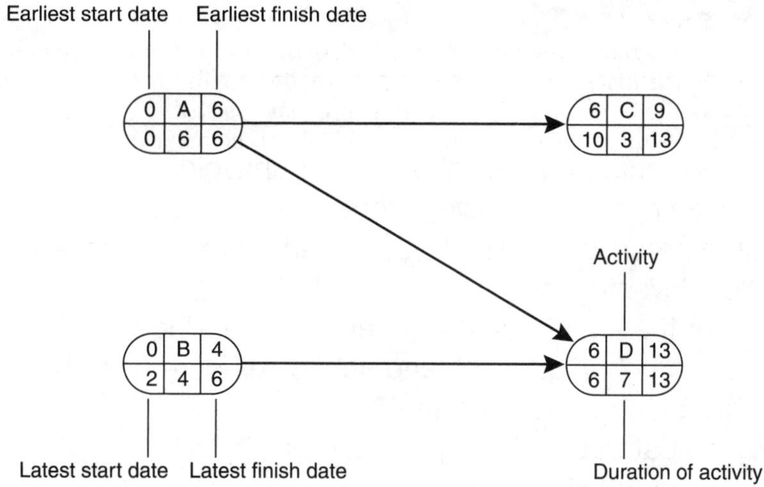


**Figure A13.3** Network calculations for activity on node diagrams

The activity on node diagram approach is used throughout this chapter in footnotes to the main text. Those wishing to employ this approach can follow the main text by substituting the material from the footnotes (particularly the figures) where appropriate.

Chapter 14

# Scheduling for batch processing

## ISSUES

Is batch processing desirable, or just unavoidable?
How does batch processing work?
Is batch processing still relevant when there is a desire to operate with low inventories?
What are the key decisions in batch processing?
How are batch sequences and schedules determined?
Why are batch sizes important?
How can batch processing be avoided?
What is group technology?
What is an FMS and what does it achieve?

## NOTATION USED IN THIS CHAPTER

| | |
|---|---|
| $B$ | Buffer stock |
| $c$ | Allowable increase (proportion) of $C$ over $C^*$ |
| $C$ | Total cost of set-up and holding |
| $C_1$ | Stock-holding cost/item/unit of time |
| $C_2$ | Shortage cost/item/unit of time |
| $C_{1i}$ | Stock-holding cost/item $i$/unit of time |
| $C_s$ | Set-up or preparation cost/batch |
| $C_{si}$ | Set-up cost/batch item $i$ |
| $C^*$ | Minimum total cost |
| GT | Group technology |
| LOB | Line of balance |
| $N$ | Number of complete processing cycles |
| $q$ | Processing rate |
| $q^1$ | Actual batch size/$Q^*$ |
| $q_i$ | Processing rate for item $i$ |
| $Q$ | Batch size |

$Q^*$ Optimum batch size

$Q_i$ Batch size for item $i$

$Q_i^*$ Optimum batch size for item $i$

$r$ Consumption rate

$r_i$ Consumption rate for item $i$

$t$ Processing cycle time

$t^*$ Optimum processing cycle time

$T_p$ Processing period for a batch

In the previous chapter we discussed planning in relation to project or 'one-off' types of operation. In the next chapter scheduling for repetitive operations will be discussed. Both types of systems are comparatively easy to describe, since in both cases, reference can be made to their *pure* forms, i.e. the processing of unit quantities of different types of items or customers, and the continual processing of a single type of item or customer respectively. Here we are going to deal with the situation which exists between these two extremes. It is more difficult to envisage and describe. It is unlike flow processing, since the operating system must deal with a variety of types of items or customers and the processing rate is not normally equal to the demand rate; and it is unlike project systems since a greater variety of types of items or customers must be dealt with. For convenience we will use the traditional terminology, and refer to this as the 'batch' processing situation.

# DEALING WITH BATCHES AND AVOIDING THEM

There are two parts to this chapter. Firstly we will discuss how batches are dealt with, and secondly we will look at how to minimize, or even avoid, the problems of batch processing.

## Batches and inventories

Typically, if items or customers are processed through systems in batches, inventories will exist. For example, in processing a batch of items to meet subsequent demand we often build up an output stock. That stock is used to satisfy demand during a period in which that item is not being processed. Also, stock is usually created 'in process' as batches await completion at individual operations in the complete process. Batch processing of customers in a service or transport system usually necessitates input queues (i.e. stocks) of customers.

We have noted in Chapter 2 that organizations are now seeking to reduce, even to eliminate, inventories, e.g. through the use of just-in-time systems. The effect of this is to reduce batch sizes, since lower batch sizes involve lower inventories. With this approach the ideal is to operate with batch sizes of one.

We will see that batch size is, in effect, a function of two costs: inventory holding costs, which increase with increased batch sizes, and set-up costs, which reduce with increased batch sizes. So the use of small batch sizes – perhaps approaching unity – in order to minimize in-process inventory would be justified where unit holding costs were high, and where process set-up costs were low. In practice, therefore, in seeking to implement low inventory, operations management will seek to reduce set-up costs. This can be achieved in two ways: by reducing the difference between the processing requirements of the items which are being dealt with (i.e. increasing their processing similarity) and by improving the inherent flexibility or adaptability of processing equipment. The processing similarity of items might be improved through design changes and the use of common parts. Additionally, families of similar items might be identified, and processing systems set up to deal with each such family. This is the group technology approach discussed later in this chapter. Improvements in the inherent flexibility of processes can be achieved through the use of standard tooling, changes in equipment design, or the use of more sophisticated equipment which provides for automated set-up/reconfiguration. This latter is the principal characteristic of the flexible manufacturing systems (FMS) which are now being introduced into traditional batch manufacturing situations.

We will look at these means to reduce batch sizes in the second part of this chapter. Firstly, however, we will look at how batch processing is managed.

# MANAGING BATCH PROCESSING

## Examples of batch processing

Batch processing can exist in all four types of operations, i.e. supply, service, transport and manufacture.

A batch flow system might exist in *supply* in that the function might seek to transfer items from input stock to customers in batches rather than in unit quantities. For example, where the cost of supply, i.e. transfer from input stock to customer, is high there may be some benefit in dealing with several customers at one time, given the possibility of accumulating 'customers' for particular types of item. Equally, in supply systems which operate without input stocks, i.e. in which items are acquired for particular customers, there may be benefits in operating on a batch processing system.

In *service* systems customers may be processed in batches. For example, certain entertainment services operate in this way in that the service is provided when a given number or minimum number of customers are available. Such a situation might exist in systems in which resources are stocked, as in certain entertainment facilities or in situations which must acquire resources to satisfy customer needs.

Likewise certain *transport* systems might operate on a batch processing arrangement. Transport, for example, might be available only when a certain number of customers have presented themselves. Thus a function might be triggered by the growth of the queue of customers to or beyond a certain minimum limit.

In *manufacture*, batch processing might be employed in systems which have output stocks, i.e. batches of items are produced in anticipation of demand. Also, the batch processing method might be employed in the manufacture of items to order, provided, of course, orders are received for sufficiently similar items.

Normally, batch processing involves the use of inventories or queues. It was for this reason that we drew attention to low-inventory systems above. In manufacture, batch processing often, but not always, gives rise to output stocks.

For transport and service systems it is likely that batch processing can be employed only where customer input queues exist, since it is unlikely that batches of customers will present themselves to the organization but rather that they will be allowed to accumulate over time. In these cases the use of batch processing at the expense of the customer waiting or queuing time is feasible only in certain market situations. However, the use of batch processing to provide a stock of items in anticipation of demand will be appropriate in circumstances where customer waiting or queuing is to be minimized.

The main benefit of batch processing is higher resource utilization than might otherwise be possible.

## Batch processing decisions

In general the planning of batch processing[1] requires the solution of three problems:

(a) batch sequencing, i.e. the determination of the order in which batches of different items (or customers) will be processed;

---

[1] Much of what will be discussed in this chapter will relate to and overlap with that introduced in Chapter 17 on inventory management. Many of the problems of planning for batch processing are similar to those involved in inventory management, and in general, detailed treatments, particularly of more sophisticated aspects, will be covered in Chapter 17.

(b) the determination of batch sizes, i.e. the quantity of each type of item (or customer) to be processed at one time;

(c) batch scheduling, i.e. the timing of the processing of batches of items (or customers).

Table 14.1 gives examples of batch processing in manufacture, supply, transport and service systems. The common features of all such batch processing situations are: (a) the processing of different types of items (or customers) on a common set of facilities; and (b) a processing rate for each type of item (or customer) which is greater than the demand or usage rate. The table also indicates where each of the three basic batch processing decisions will be required. Notice that in all cases the batch size decision will be needed.

Figure 14.1 illustrates the manner in which batch processing systems can operate. Consider first Figure 14.1(a)(1), which shows changes in an output stock over a period of time. At time 0 the processing of a batch begins and items are delivered continually into the output stock. Simultaneously, items are consumed from that output stock, but since the processing rate is greater than the consumption rate the stock builds up to a level $X$. At time 1 processing finishes, the batch having been completed. During period 1–2, consumption only occurs, so the stock is depleted to time 2, at which point the processing of a further batch must begin. This type of situation might exist in manufacture where items are made in predetermined quantities for output stock. In Table 14.1, this type of situation might describe examples AI and AII and the less common examples BI and BII.

**Table 14.1 Examples of batch processing**

| Operating system function | Examples of batch processing situation | Planning/scheduling problems: (a) Determine sequence of batches | (b) Determine batch sizes | (c) Determine schedule for batches |
|---|---|---|---|---|
| A Manufacture and<br>B Supply | I Make (or supply) several items, each in predetermined quantities for output stocks, to satisfy future customers' demands. | Yes | Yes | Yes |
| | II Make (or supply) several items, each in predetermined quantities, for known customers, but only when enough customers have been obtained (i.e. without output stocks). | Probably | Yes | Probably |
| C Transport and<br>D Service | I Transport (or service) customers in predetermined quantities, each batch drawn from a larger number of customers in a queue. | Probably | Yes | Probably |
| | II As I, but taking an entire queue when it reaches the predetermined quantity. | No | Yes | No |

Refer now to Figure 14.1(b)(1). Here at time 1 a complete batch of items is delivered into stock, and then from time 1 to time 2 only consumption takes place and thus stock is depleted to a level at time 2 at which a further batch must be delivered. Unlike the situation in Figure 14.1(a)(1), processing takes place instantaneously. This is less likely to exist in practice, but could describe a situation (Table 14.1) similar to examples AI, AII, BI and BII where the batch of items is processed instantaneously, or where no items are released from the process until the entire batch is completed.

Both the above cases apply to situations in which items are processed for an *output stock*. In transport and service, customers exist on the input side of the function. Here input stocks of customers may build up, and then be depleted as batches are processed through the system. If we take, for example, Figure 14.1(a)(2), in the period 0–1 the input stock, i.e. the waiting queue of customers, falls, since during this period customers or items are being taken from the queue to be processed at a greater rate than that at which they arrive. From 1 to 2 the processing stops and the input queue of customers builds up. Such a situation might exist in examples CI, CII, DI and DII (Table 14.1), where items or customers are taken from stock continually during the processing of a given quantity or batch of items. Where items are taken from the input queue in a complete batch for processing, the situation shown in Figure 14.1(b)(2) will exist. Here during period 1–2 the queue will build up, since no processing is taking place. Instantaneously at time 2 an entire batch of customers is taken from the queue for processing, so the queue falls by that batch quantity, only to build up again during period 2–3.

Clearly, in each of the situations shown in Figure 14.1, there will be some need to determine the *size of the batch* to be processed. The size of the batch will influence the average stock level. Thus, for example, in Figure 14.1(b) the maximum stock level shown is in fact equal to the batch quantity. Thus for larger batch sizes the average stock level will increase, and be equal to the batch processing size divided by two. In Figure 14.1(a) the maximum stock quantity is less than the batch processing size, since consumption takes place simultaneously with processing. Nevertheless, an increase in batch size will increase the stock level. Thus the principal penalty of processing larger batches is the need to hold larger stocks and thus incur larger stock-holding costs, whether these be the costs of output stocks or the costs of customer input queues. However, in processing larger batches, for a given demand fewer batches must be processed over a given period of time. Since the processing of one batch will incur certain

**Figure 14.1** Types of batch processing

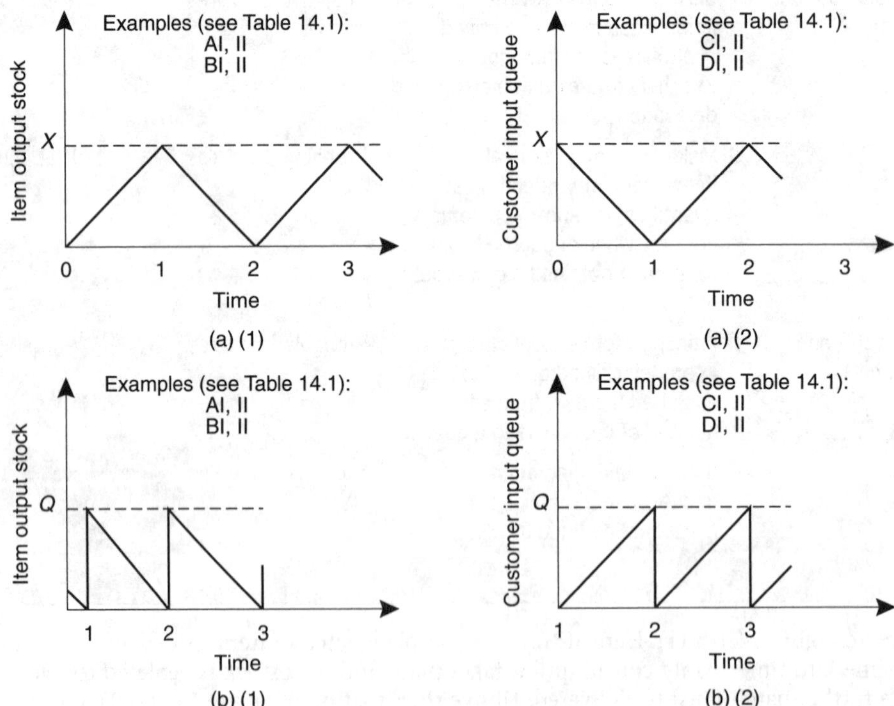

set-up costs, the use of larger batches will incur lower set-up costs over a period of time. In other words, the problem of determining the batch size is that of determining the best balance to strike in the cost of stock-holding and the cost of set-up.

In a typical batch processing situation several different types of items or customers are to be processed on one set of facilities. In these circumstances a batch set-up cost may be influenced not only by the type of item which is to be processed, but by the type of item which the facility was previously set up to process. Thus the set-up cost may be a function of batch sequence. In these circumstances it will be appropriate to try to determine the sequence which minimizes the total cost of set-up over a period of time. Where this situation exists, the batch sequence must be determined *before* determining batch sizes, since not until the batch sequence is determined can the cost of set-up be found, and the cost of set-up is required in order to determine the batch size (see above).

Also, in most cases it will be necessary to determine the timing for the processing of batches of different items, i.e. the time at which each batch process is to begin. This problem is also related to that of batch size determination, since with a larger batch size, for a given demand, fewer batches must be produced, so the intervals between processing will be greater. Conversely, for a smaller batch size, with a given demand, the intervals between the processing of batches will be smaller.

We shall deal with these three interrelated problems in the following sections. We shall deal first with the problem of batch sequencing before considering the determination of batch sizes and the batch scheduling problem. Throughout we shall concentrate on the types of situations shown in Figure 14.1(a)(1) and 14.1(b)(1). These are the more common batch processing situations; however, the formulae which we shall develop will also be relevant to the types of situations shown in Figure 14.1(a)(2) and 14.1(b)(2).

## Batch sequencing *(see also Chapter 15)*

It is possible that the cost of setting up, i.e. preparing, a set of facilities for the processing of a batch of items (or customers) will depend not only on the type of items or customers to be processed in that batch, but also on the type in the batch which was previously processed on the same facilities.

In these circumstances total set-up cost is also a function of the sequence of items, and it is appropriate to try to determine the appropriate sequence in order to minimize set-up cost. Thus if four types of item, A, B, C and D, are to be processed in batches on a common set of facilities, and the set-up cost for each batch is influenced by the type of item which was previously processed, where that cost is known an optimum sequence of batches can be determined.

The assumption here, of course, is that each batch must be processed the same number of times, i.e. that a repetitive sequence involving one batch of each item can be established. This is the normal situation, and a solution can often be found using the assignment method of linear programming, which is described in Appendix I. (The problem is identical to that of determining the optimum sequence for batches of items to be processed on a mixed-model repetitive/flow processing system. This is described in Chapter 15.)

## Processing 'families' of items

A situation might exist in which several different types of item (or customers) each require a similar, but not identical, set-up.

In this situation those items may be seen as a 'family' of similar items. It will be sensible when setting up the facilities to process a batch of any one of the items in the family to take advantage of that set-up and process a batch of all the other items within the family, especially where the cost of the set-up is relatively high.

For example, in the situation shown in Table 14.2, the set-up costs incurred between the processing of items B, C and D are small whereas the cost of setting up the process between either A or E and any of the family B, C and D is relatively high. In this case, therefore, there will be some merit in processing the 'family' of items B, C and D in succession (possibly in the order C, B, D) with the other two items produced at another time (possibly in the order A, E). In fact the sequencing problem shown in Table 14.2 is an example of the type of situation which *cannot* be solved using the assignment method referred to above: this is because of the configuration of the cost within the matrix. In such cases, particularly where a 'family' of items exist, an alternative approach will be required.

One approach to the solution of the 'family' sequencing problem is as follows:

(a) Identify the items within a 'family'.

(b) Determine the 'processing cycle' for these items (i.e. the time interval between the successive processings of the family) together with the batch quantity for each item.

(c) Determine the optimum sequence for the remaining items and process these items as required between families.

The procedure for determining the optimum processing cycle for a set of items is given later in this chapter.

(Notice that the 'family' processing problem has some similarities with the approach discussed in the section on group technology later in this chapter.)

**Table 14.2**

| Preceding item | Succeeding item | | | | |
|---|---|---|---|---|---|
| | A | B | C | D | E |
| A | 0 | 100 | 90 | 110 | 60 |
| B | 105 | 0 | 10 | 5 | 60 |
| C | 95 | 20 | 0 | 25 | 70 |
| D | 100 | 15 | 10 | 0 | 80 |
| E | 70 | 75 | 80 | 75 | 0 |

## Determination of batch sizes *(see also Chapter 17)*

The normal approach here is to try to determine the batch sizes which minimize total cost. Certainly other approaches exist, e.g. maximization of profits, but the cost minimization approach is the most important, and is the only approach which will be dealt with here.

For given costs, batch quantities which are too large will result in high stock levels and cause a large amount of capital to be tied up in stock which might otherwise be invested elsewhere. Additionally, unduly high stock levels will incur other costs, such as the cost of stock-keeping, insurance and depreciation. On the other hand, batch quantities which are too small will result in the need for a large number of batches to be processed for a given period of time and thus incur large set-up costs. In practice batch sizes are rarely constant. It will often be appropriate to 'split' batches during processing and/or to use a batch size which differs from the theoretical optimum. Our discussion of batch sizes should be taken in this context and the formulae which are developed should be used with discretion rather than rigidly.

Smaller batch sizes can be justified if set-up costs can be reduced, so the implementation of the 'low-inventory' processing systems associated with JIT requires low set-up cost. If set-up costs are very low and if the cost of holding inventory is high, batch sizes approaching unity can be justified. Often this is a matter of policy. Since the full cost of stock cannot be quantified, if the non-quantifiable aspects are judged to be high, then lower batch sizes can be justified.

Figure 14.2 shows the relationship of these costs to batch size. Clearly the problem is to determine the batch size which minimizes total variable costs. Our aim is to determine the economic batch size $Q^*$ associated with minimum total variable cost $C^*$.

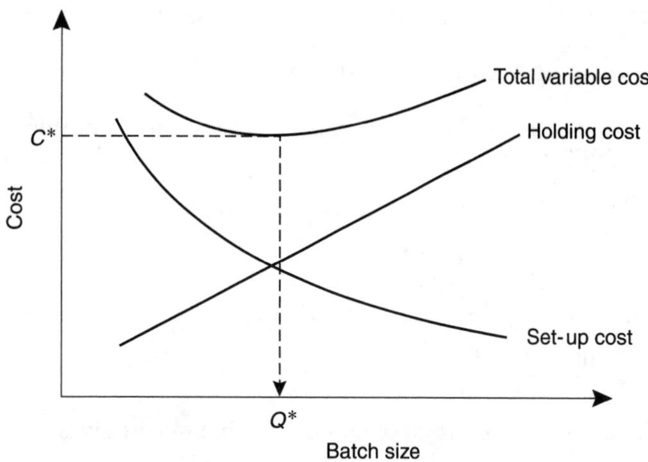


**Figure 14.2** Economic batch size

We shall deal first with *deterministic* situations in which demand, etc. is considered to be known and to be constant. We shall deal with three such situations, as shown in Figure 14.3.

**Figure 14.3** Batch size models

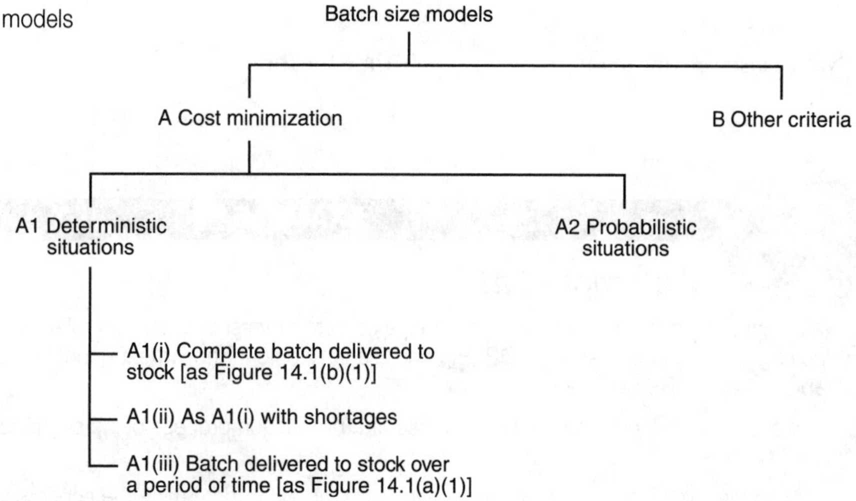

Batch size models

A Cost minimization

B Other criteria

A1 Deterministic situations

A2 Probabilistic situations

A1(i) Complete batch delivered to stock [as Figure 14.1(b)(1)]

A1(ii) As A1(i) with shortages

A1(iii) Batch delivered to stock over a period of time [as Figure 14.1(a)(1)]

## A1: Deterministic situations

### *A1(i): Complete batch delivered to stock, as Figure 14.1(b)(1)*

Our notation is as follows:

$Q$ = Process batch quantity

$C_s$ = Set-up or preparation cost/batch

$C_1$ = Stock-holding cost/item/unit of time
$r$ = Consumption rate
$q$ = Processing rate

Then:

Average stock level $= Q/2$
Stock-holding cost/unit of time $= C_1(Q/2)$

Set-up of cost per unit of time $= \frac{C_s r}{Q}$

To determine the optimum batch size we need consider only those costs which vary according to batch size.

Total cost of set-up and holding:

$$C = C_1(Q/2) + \frac{C_s r}{Q} \quad (1)$$

Differentiating with respect to $Q$:

$$\frac{dC}{dQ} = \frac{C_1}{2} - \frac{C_s r}{Q^2}$$

Equating this to zero to obtain the minimum cost gives:

$$\text{Minimum cost batch size} = Q^* = \sqrt{\frac{2C_s r}{C_1}} \quad (2)$$

Substituting (2) into (1) gives the total cost per unit of time associated with this processing policy, i.e.

$$C^* = \sqrt{2rC_sC_1} \quad (3)$$

Notice also the optimum processing cycle time for this item:

$$t^* = \frac{Q^*}{r}$$

**EXAMPLE**

### Watertight Ltd

Watertight Ltd are the manufacturers of a range of plastic overshoes. The complete range consists of 14 different types (i.e. sizes and styles). Type BB (Big and Black) is sold in the largest quantities, demand being reasonably stable at 4500 pairs per month.

All overshoes are manufactured in batches, the production process being such that the entire batch is completed at the same time.

(a) Given the following information, use the formulae above to determine the economic batch production quality:

Machine set-up cost per production batch = £150
Stock-holding cost per pair = £3.75 per annum

(b) The present production policy is to manufacture BB overshoes in batch sizes of 3000 pairs at regular intervals. How does the actual production cycle time compare with the optimum production cycle time?

*Answer*

(a) $r$ = 4500 per month
$C_s$ = £150

$$C_1 = 3.75 \times \frac{1}{12} = £0.313 \text{ per month}$$

$$\therefore\; Q^* = \sqrt{\frac{2C_s r}{C_1}} = \sqrt{\frac{2 \times 150 \times 4500}{0.313}}$$

$$= 2077 \text{ pairs}$$

(b)

$$t^* = \frac{Q^*}{r} = \frac{2077}{4500}$$

$$= 0.46 \text{ months}$$

$$\text{Actual } Q = 3000 \text{ pairs}$$

$$\therefore\; \text{Actual } t = \frac{Q}{r} = \frac{3000}{4500}$$

$$= 0.67 \text{ months (46\% longer interval than optimum policy)}$$

## *A1(ii): As A1(i) with shortages*

We can extend the simple model above to include the possibility of stock shortages or 'stockouts'. This introduces an additional cost factor: the cost of shortages, $C_2$. The model, which still assumes known and constant demand, is depicted in Figure 14.4. The areas below the horizontal axis, i.e. periods $t_2$, represent demand which would have been satisfied had adequate stock been available. The cost of such shortage in terms of loss of profit, etc. must be introduced into the formula, since it will influence the choice of batch size.

**Figure 14.4** A stock/batch processing model allowing shortages

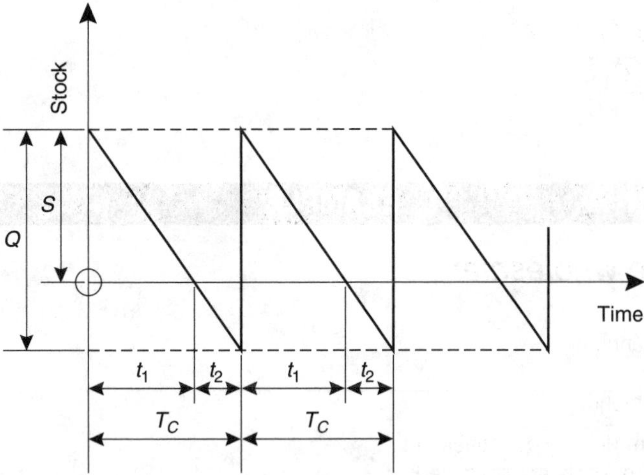


Using the previous notation, plus $C_2$ = shortage cost/item/unit of time:

$$\text{Stock-holding cost per unit of time} = \frac{S}{2}\left(\frac{t_1}{t_1 + t_2}\right)C_1$$

$$= \frac{C_1 S}{2}\left(\frac{S}{Q}\right)$$

$$= \frac{C_1 S^2}{2Q}$$

$$\text{Shortage cost per unit of time} = C_2 \frac{(Q-S)}{2}\left(\frac{t_2}{t_1+t_2}\right)$$

$$= \frac{C_2(Q-S)^2}{2Q}$$

$$\text{Set-up cost per unit of time} = \frac{C_s r}{Q}$$

Total set-up, holding, shortage cost/unit time:

$$C = \frac{C_1 S^2}{2Q} + \frac{C_2(Q-S)^2}{2Q} + \frac{C_s r}{Q} \qquad (1)$$

Differentiating with respect to $S$:

$$\frac{dC}{dS} = \frac{SC_1}{Q} - \frac{(Q-S)C_2}{Q}$$

$= 0$ for maximum or minimum

$$\therefore S^* = \frac{QC_2}{C_1 + C_2} \qquad (2)$$

Differentiating with respect to $Q$:

$$\frac{dC}{dQ} = \frac{-S^2 C_1}{Q^2} + \left[\frac{4Q(Q-S) - 2(Q-S)^2}{4Q^2}\right]C_2 - \frac{C_s r}{Q^2}$$

$= 0$ for maximum or minimum

$$Q^* = \sqrt{\frac{2rC_s}{C_1}}\sqrt{\frac{C_1 + C_2}{C_2}} \qquad (3)$$

Substituting (3) into (1):

$$C^* = \sqrt{2rC_1C_s}\sqrt{\frac{C_2}{C_1 + C_2}} \qquad (4)$$

**EXAMPLE**

### *A shoe wholesaler*

$r$ = 9500 per month
$C_1$= £5 per item per annum
$C_s$= £1 250
$C_2$= £2 per item per month

(a) Compare the optimum delivery quantities for:
(i) a policy in which stockouts are permitted;
(ii) a policy in which stockouts must not occur.

(b) What is the maximum set-up cost per batch which can be accepted under policy (ii) if the total cost per month associated with this policy is not to exceed the total cost per month of policy (i)? (Assume all other data above to apply except $C_s$ for policy (ii).

*Answer*

(a) (i) $$Q^* = \sqrt{\frac{2C_s r}{C_1}}\sqrt{\frac{C_1 + C_2}{C_2}}$$

$$= \sqrt{\frac{2 \times 1\,250 \times 9500}{5/12}}\sqrt{\frac{5/12 + 2}{2}}$$

$= 7550 \times 1.1$

$= 8305$

(ii) $Q^* = \sqrt{\dfrac{2C_s r}{C_1}}$

$= 7550$

(b) (i) $C^* = \sqrt{2rC_1C_s}\sqrt{\dfrac{C_2}{C_1 + C_2}}$

$= \sqrt{\dfrac{2 \times 9500 \times 5 \times 1250}{12}}\sqrt{\dfrac{2}{5/12 + 2}}$

$= 3146 \times 0.910$

$=$ £2863 per month

(ii) £2863 $= \sqrt{2rC_sC_1}$

$C_s = \dfrac{2863^2}{2rC_1}$

$= \dfrac{2863^2 \times 12}{2 \times 9500 \times 5}$

Maximum $C_s =$ £1035

---

## *A1(iii): Batch delivered to stock over a period of time, as Figure 14.1(a)(1)*

Now instead of considering the total processing batch to be delivered into stock at the same time, we shall consider a situation in which the items that constitute the batch are delivered into stock continuously throughout the process period (see Figure 14.5).

Maximum stock level $= X$

$= \dfrac{Q}{q}(q - r)$

Average inventory $= \dfrac{Q}{2}[1 - (r/q)]$

$\therefore$ Stock-holding cost per unit time $= C_1\left[\dfrac{Q}{2}(1 - (r/q))\right]$

Total cost of set-up and holding per unit of time:

$$C = \frac{C_1Q}{2}[1 - (r/q)] + \frac{C_s r}{Q} \quad (1)$$

**Figure 14.5**

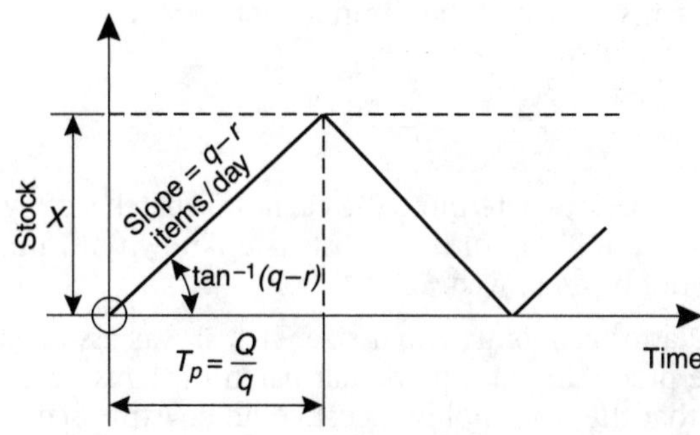

Differentiating with respect to Q:

$$\frac{dC}{dQ} = \frac{-C_s r}{Q^2} + \frac{C_1}{2}[1 - (r/q)]$$

Equating this to zero gives the maximum or minimum point of the function. Hence:

$$\text{Minimum cost batch size} = Q^* = \sqrt{\frac{2C_s r}{C_1[1 - (r/q)]}} \qquad (2)$$

The total cost per unit of time associated with this processing policy is given by substituting equation (2) into equation (1):

$$C^* = \sqrt{2rC_s C_1}\,\sqrt{1 - (r/q)} \qquad (3)$$

**EXAMPLE**

### *Express Drinks Company (1)*

A product is sold at a constant rate of 600 per day, the processing rate for the item being 2000 per day. It is known that set-up costs are £10 per batch and that stock-holding costs, including notional loss of interest on capital, are £0.5 per item per year. What is the minimum cost processing batch quantity?

*Answer*

$C_s = £10$

$q = 2000$

$r = 600$

Assuming that there are 250 working days per year:

$$C_1 = \frac{0.5}{250} = £0.002 \text{ per item per day}$$

$$Q^* = \sqrt{\frac{2 \times 10 \times 600}{0.002[1 - (6/20)]}}$$

$Q^* = 2928$

## A2: Probabilistic situations – dealing with uncertainty

The above discussion assumed an entirely deterministic situation, i.e. the assumption was made that all the relevant information for the determination of batch sizes was known with certainty. It was assumed, for example, that the demand rate was known and that it would not change from that known quantity. It was assumed that the production or processing rate was known and was not subject to any variation. Clearly this highly simplified situation may not exist in practice. We must be able to deal with situations in which demand rate varies, production rate varies, and costs are uncertain. These sources of uncertainty are discussed below, their implications are identified, and ways in which they might be dealt with are considered.

### *Uncertainties in costs*

The procedures described above seek to determine the economic batch size by balancing the cost of set-up and the cost of stock-holding. If either of these costs is unknown or cannot be estimated accurately then these procedures cannot be employed.

In determining the formula for economic batch size, etc., it was assumed that the set-up cost, i.e. the cost of preparing for the processing of a particular batch of items, was independent of the batch size. It was further assumed that the stock-holding cost could be expressed as cost per item per unit of time, irrespective of inventory level. In practice, both these assumptions may be invalid. It is possible, however, through modifications of the above procedures, to determine the economic batch size where a set-up cost is not constant and where the stock-holding cost is a function of stock quantity. One of these approaches is discussed in Chapter 17.

Rarely will $C_s$ and $C_1$ be known with certainty. In most cases they must be estimated. Since the objective of the economic batch size procedure is to determine the batch size which corresponds to the minimum total variable cost it will be of interest to identify to what extent the total variable cost is sensitive to change in batch sizes, etc. This is considered later in the section entitled 'The Production (or Processing) Range'.

## Uncertainties in usage or consumption rate (only)

Consider the situation in which only the usage rate is uncertain. We will look at the effect that this single source of uncertainty might have on the stock position as shown by diagrams such as those in Figure 14.1.

For example, in Figure 14.1(a)(1), the processing of a batch is finished at time 1 and the processing of the next batch is not due to commence until time 2. If the demand between times 1 and 2 is greater than expected then stock will fall to zero before time 2, and a stockout situation will exist. A similar situation might exist in the type of batch processing shown in Figure 14.1(b)(1). A complete batch is delivered to stock at time 1 and the next batch is due to be delivered at time 2. If demand between times 1 and 2 is greater than expected then again a stockout situation can exist. The equivalent situations can exist for customer input queue situations, as shown in Figures 14.1(a)(2) and 14.1(b)(2).

One way of protecting against the risk of stockouts resulting from higher than expected demand is through the use of a buffer stock. Figure 14.6 shows the use of a buffer stock in the type of batch processing situation shown in Figure 14.1(a)(1). The buffer stock quantity $B$ is a measure of the degree of protection provided against increases in demand. A large buffer stock reduces the risk of a stockout but of course increases the stock-holding cost, while a lower buffer stock quantity $B$ provides less protection against stockouts but incurs less stock-holding cost. Whatever the buffer quantity, the economic batch size can be determined in the same manner as described above and will be unaffected by the value $B$. However, the use of a buffer stock together with the economic batch size approach which employs a formula assuming constant demand should be employed with caution (see below).

For the batch processing system shown in Figure 14.6:

Total cost of set-up and stock-holding/units of time, $C$

$$= C_1B + \frac{C_1Q}{2}\left[1-\left(\frac{r}{q}\right)\right]+\frac{C_sr}{Q} \qquad (1)$$

**Figure 14.6** The use of buffer stocks (in the type of batch processing shown in Figure 14.1 (a)(1))

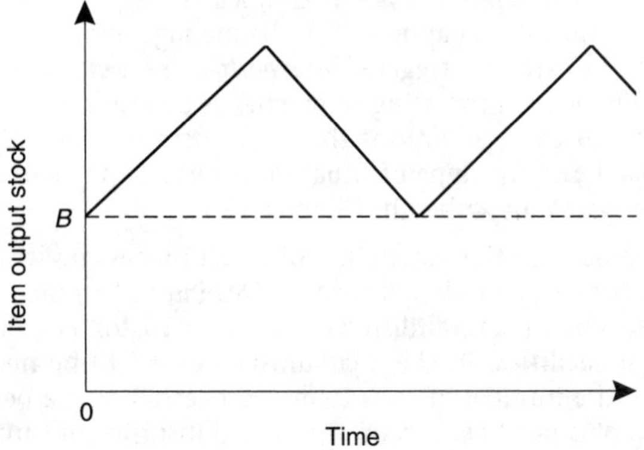

Differentiating with reference to $Q$:

$$\frac{dC}{dQ} = \frac{-C_s r}{Q^2} + \frac{C_1}{2}\left[1 - \left(\frac{r}{q}\right)\right]$$

hence:

$$Q^* = \sqrt{\frac{2C_s r}{C_1\left[1 - \left(\frac{r}{q}\right)\right]}} \qquad (2)$$

(as before). But substituting (2) into (1) gives:

$$C^* = \sqrt{2rC_s C_1}\sqrt{1 - \left(\frac{r}{q}\right)} + C_1 B$$

Similarly, a buffer stock can be used to protect against fluctuations in demand or usage in the type of batch processing in which complete batches of items are delivered to stock (Figure 14.1(b)(1)), and again if the economic order quantity is determined using the previous approach, it is not influenced by $B$ but, of course, the minimum total variable cost associated with this batch size is increased by the cost of the buffer quantity multiplied by the holding cost ($C_1B$).

Where a buffer stock is used the buffer quantity will be determined by the reference to two factors:

(a) the extent of the variation in demand or usage, possibly expressed as a standard deviation about a mean demand;

(b) the degree of protection required in stockouts, possibly expressed as the maximum probability or risk of stockout which can be tolerated.

It may be possible, however, to protect against uncertain demand without having to use a buffer stock. For example, if arrangements can be made for stock to be replenished immediately the stock level falls to zero then no buffer stock is required even though the rate at which stock is depleted is unknown. Quite often it will not be possible to arrange for stock to be replenished, or for stock replenishment to begin, at a given time. For example, there may be a delay (or lead time) between the making of a decision to replenish stock and the time at which the first items or the complete batch are received into stock. If that lead time is known then it may be possible to accommodate uncertainties in demand without the use of buffer stocks, but more often the lead time will be uncertain. In these circumstances we must protect against uncertain demand and lead time. In this, the normal situation, the problem is that of accommodating *uncertain lead time usage.* Again a buffer stock approach will be appropriate, and this approach is discussed in detail in Chapter 17.

We have seen that buffer stocks can be used to protect against usage variations and variations in lead time without the need to modify the batch quantity. Remember, however, that the determination of batch quantity assumes a known usage rate. If the variation in usage about a mean rate is not great, and there is no overall trend towards increasing or reducing usage, it is still possible, without introducing substantial errors, to determine the batch size as discussed above for the deterministic situation and to use in conjunction with that approach a buffer stock strategy to protect against demand/lead time uncertainties. This will be the normal approach in the management of batch processing where the need to begin the processing of a batch is 'triggered' *at a particular inventory level.* In other words, where the scheduling, i.e. the timing, of the processing of batches is determined by the inventory level, this approach will be appropriate. In these situations therefore there will be no fixed or regular interval between the processing of batches. (This type of situation is directly analogous to the reorder level (or perpetual) inventory control system described in Chapter 17.)

There is an alternative approach to the scheduling of batch processing which relies on the processing of batches of items or customers at predetermined or *fixed intervals of time.* This approach will often be necessary where the processing of several different items (or customers) on common facilities uses most of the capacity of those facilities. In these circumstances it will be necessary to plan ahead in order to ensure that the requisite number of each item is processed over a period of time without the penalties of under-utilization of capacity at certain times, and insufficient capacity and hence the need to subcontract at other times. (Such an approach is directly analogous to the reorder interval (or periodic) method of inventory control described in Chapter 17.) For this type of system a somewhat different approach will be required to accommodate demand uncertainties since, in the circumstances, it may not be possible to determine a fixed optimum batch quantity for each item being processed. This situation is discussed in detail in Chapter 16.

### *Processing rate uncertainties*

One type of batch processing involves the processing and consumption of items simultaneously over a period of time (Figure 14.1(a)(1) and (2)). In determining the economic batch size for this situation it was assumed not only that usage was constant, but also that the processing rate was known and constant. Such a 'simple' situation may not exist in practice because, as we have seen, usage may be uncertain, but also because the processing rate may be affected by the breakdown of equipment, wastage rates or the need for reprocessing. In general the level of uncertainty associated with the processing rate will be less than that associated with usage. However, it can be an additional source of uncertainty. Hence there can be a risk that a stockout situation might occur or be aggravated because less than the expected quantity of items were delivered to stock. Equally, a variation in processing rate may offset a variation in usage rate.

A similar situation may exist in batch processing situations in which complete batches of items are delivered into stock. In these cases there may be some uncertainties in the delivered quantity; thus, for example, stock may be replenished to a lower level than had been expected, and therefore a stockout situation can occur or be made worse.

Both these situations can again be accommodated along with or in the absence of uncertainties in usage by using a buffer stock type of approach as outlined above.

## The production (or processing) range

Given the difficulty of accurately establishing costs such as $C_1$ and $C_s$ it is fortunate that the total cost curve (see Figure 14.2) is fairly flat at the point of minimum cost, since this means that the total variable cost is not very sensitive to deviations from optimal batch size. It is possible, therefore, to adopt a batch size which differs slightly from the optimal without incurring substantially increased costs. This feature of the total cost curve gives rise to the 'production range' concept. Batch quantities within this range are considered as acceptable. In Figure 14.7 the production range is between $Q_1$ and $Q_2$, corresponding to a maximum increase in cost from the minimum $C^*$ to $C$.

**Figure 14.7**

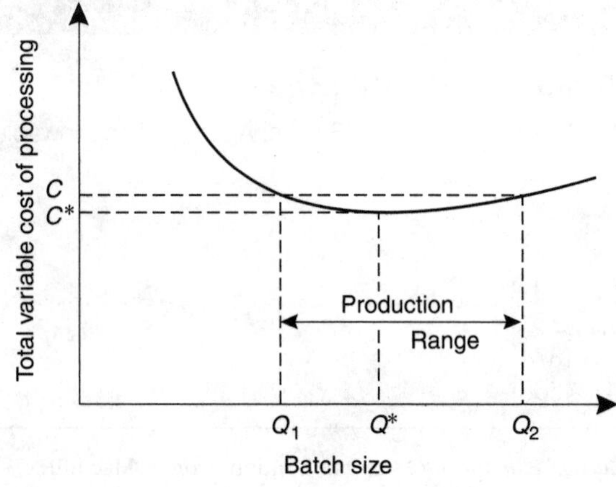

Eilon[2] developed a procedure for the determination of an acceptable processing range which is dependent on knowing the allowable increase in the total variable costs of production, $c$. Thus:

$$c = \frac{\text{Actual variable costs per unit}}{\text{Minimum variable costs per unit}}$$

and let:

$$q^1 = \frac{\text{Actual batch size}}{\text{Minimum cost batch size}}$$

It can be shown that:

$$q_1 = c \pm \sqrt{c^2 - 1}$$

and thus the two limits of 'production ' range are:

$$Q_1 = Q^* (c - \sqrt{c^2 - 1}) = Q^* q^1{}_1$$
$$Q_2 = Q^*(c + \sqrt{c^2 - 1}) = Q^* q^1{}_2$$

The values of $q^1{}_1$ and $q^1{}_2$ can be found by using formula (1) or from the curve given in Figure 14.8, and the production range can then be calculated.

**Figure 14.8**

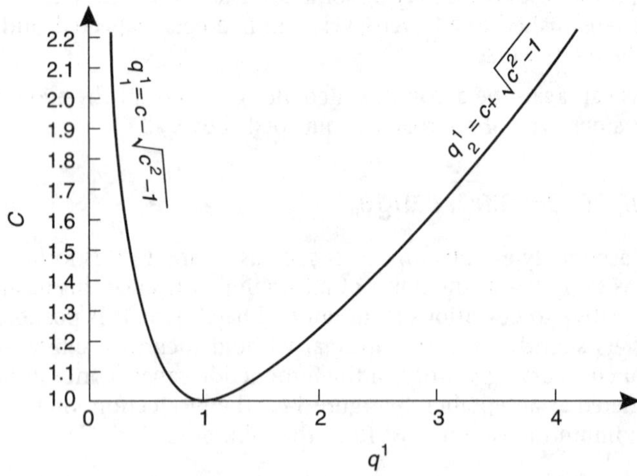


## EXAMPLE

### Express Drinks Company (2)

In our previous example the optimal batch size was 2928 units. A policy of an allowable increase in cost per unit of 10% has been adopted, i.e. $c = 1.1$.

*Answer*

From Figure 14.8,

$q^1{}_1 = 0.64$
$q^1{}_2 = 1.56$
$Q_1 = Q^* q^1{}_1 = 2928\ (0.64) = 1874$
$Q_2 = Q^* q^1{}_2 = 2928\ (1.56) = 4568$

---

[2] Eilon, S. (1969) *Elements of Production Planning and Control.* London: Collier-Macmillan.

## Scheduling for batch processing *(see also Chapter 12)*

Having now decided the batch size for each item which is to be processed on a common set of facilities, and the sequence or order of processing, we must consider the timing of the processing of these batches.

Given the processing batch size Q and the consumption rate $r$, the processing cycle time $t$ can be determined as follows:

$$t = \frac{Q}{r}$$

Thus for a batch size of 100 items with a production rate of 400 items/month the processing cycle time will be 1/4 month (i.e. approximately 1 week). Therefore a batch of size 100 must be manufactured each week.

In fact, as shown previously, the processing cycle time for the optimum batch quantity $Q^*$ can be determined directly and can be shown, for the three situations which were dealt with in this chapter, to be as follows, where $t^*$ = optimum.

Processing cycle time (i.e. interval between starting the processing of successive batches of one type of item):

$$\left.\begin{aligned} &\text{A1(i) } t^* = \sqrt{\frac{2C_s}{rC_1}} \\ &\text{A1(ii) } t^* = \sqrt{\frac{2C_s}{rC_1}}\sqrt{\frac{C_1 + C_2}{C_2}} \\ &\text{A1(iii) } t^* = \sqrt{\frac{2C_s}{rC_1\left[1 - \left(\frac{r}{q}\right)\right]}} \end{aligned}\right\} \text{assuming deterministic situation (e.g. see Figure 14.3)}$$

The schedule for the processing of batches of items can be determined in this manner but the approach takes each item separately. No consideration is given to the fact that because of limited capacity on a set of facilities, there may, for example, not be enough time available to process each item in the optimum batch quantity at the optimum production cycle. Where there is considerable excess capacity such an approach may be appropriate, but where capacity is limited a somewhat different approach will be necessary, since in these situations the multi-batch schedule problem occurs.

As an illustration of the batch scheduling problem consider a situation in which only two items (A and B) are to be processed successively on the same equipment. The economic (minimum cost) batch quantity for each item has been calculated by use of one of the previous formulae and the processing schedule is shown in Figure 14.9. In this case there is no idle time on the equipment and the optimum and individually calculated processing policies for the two batches do not clash, so we must think ourselves particularly lucky. Quite easily we could have found ourselves in a difficult situation in which, for example, the sum of the processing times for the batches of items was either greater or less than the time available. Alternatively a situation might have resulted in which processing of successive batches of one item was constrained to take place at greater than the desired interval and consequently stocks of that item would fall to a level below the desirable safety or buffer stock level. Any of these situations is quite likely to arise if, in a multi-item situation, we attempt to calculate batch sizes and processing cycles for items individually and without reference to their effect on one another.

Very often the sequence in which the different items are to be processed will be determined either by the process itself or by the setting-up or preparation requirements for each item. For example, in a paint-manufacturing process it is desirable to manufacture lighter colours first and darker colours later. In the manufacture of engineering components, the order in which batches of items are manufactured is often determined by the change-over costs of jigs and tools. In such cases the only problems to be solved are the desirable length of the complete manufacturing cycle (i.e. the time required to manufacture one batch of all the products) and the frequency of the cycles.

The problem is to find the most economical cycle, i.e. that which minimizes set-up and holding or inventory costs. As before, the set-up costs increase and the holding costs decrease as the number of cycles increases.

**Figure 14.9** Successive processing of batches A and B on the same equipment: ideal situation

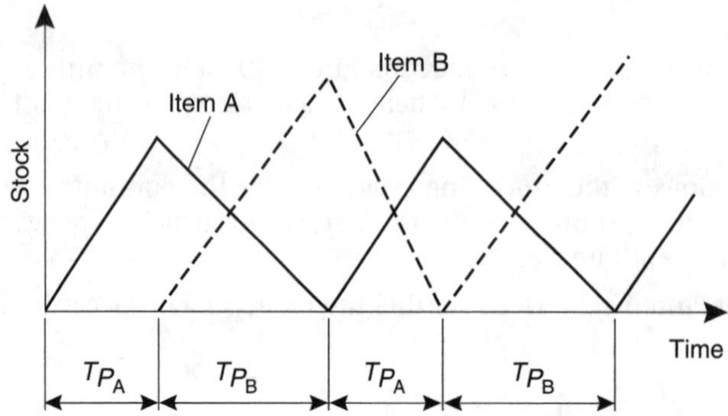


It is clear that to obtain a satisfactory solution the cycle time for all items must be set simultaneously. Furthermore, the processing and consumption rates for each item in the sequence must be expressed in common units. The unit normally used is 'hours of processing'; hence consumption is expressed as 'hours of processing used per unit of time'. Of course, when this convention is used the process rate for all items will be the same.

When a number of items are to be processed successively, and when processing is of the type shown in Figure 14.9, the total number of complete cycles per unit time, $N$, is given by the following formula:[3]

$$N = \sqrt{\frac{\sum_i C_{1i} r_i \left[1 - \left(\frac{r_i}{q_i}\right)\right]}{2\sum_i C_{si}}}$$

where $N$ = number of complete processing cycles per unit time, each consisting of the processing of a batch item

$r_i$ = consumption rate for item $i$

$q_i$ = production rate for item $i$

$C_{1i}$ = holding cost/unit of time for item $i$

$C_{si}$ = set-up cost for batch of item $i$

Furthermore, since:

$$Q_i = \frac{r_i}{N}$$

$$Q_i = \sqrt{\frac{2r_i^2\ 421\sum_i C_{si}}{\sum_i C_{1i} r_i \left[1 - \left(\frac{r_i}{q_i}\right)\right]}}$$

[3] For another approach see Davis, S. G. (1990) Scheduling economic lot size production runs. *Management Science*, **36**(8), pp. 985–998.

e.g.

## EXAMPLE

Four items, A, B, C and D, are to be processed successively in batches on the same facility. The consumption and process rates, batch set-up and item holding costs for each product are shown in Table 14.3. To use the formula, the processing and consumption rates for all items must be expressed in common units. The unit used will be 'days of processing per year'. If there are 250 working days per year, then the new consumption rates can be calculated; for example, for item A, with a processing rate of 250/day, 40 days' processing are needed per year to satisfy an annual consumption of 10 000.

Notice also that the holding cost must also be related to 'days of processing', e.g. for item A, $C_1$ is 250 × 0.005 = 1.25, i.e. the holding cost for a day's processing of item A per year. The process rate for each item is the same, since, in each case, it requires one day to process one unit of each (i.e. one day's processing). The rescaled figures are shown in Table 14.4.

Table 14.3

| Item | Consumption per year | Processing rate per day | Holding cost per item per year (£) | Set-up cost of batch (£) |
|---|---|---|---|---|
| A | 10 000 | 250 | 0.005 | 10 |
| B | 5 000 | 100 | 0.005 | 5 |
| C | 8 000 | 200 | 0.010 | 8 |
| D | 12 000 | 300 | 0.008 | 6 |

Table 14.4

| Item | $r_i$ | $q_i$ | $C_1$ | $C_s$ |
|---|---|---|---|---|
| A | 40 | 250 | 1.25 | 10 |
| B | 50 | 250 | 0.50 | 5 |
| C | 40 | 250 | 2.00 | 8 |
| D | 40 | 250 | 2.40 | 6 |

The consumption rate ($r_A$) for item A is 40 in the new units because 40 days at 250 per day are necessary to process 10 000. Similarly:

$$r_B = \frac{5000}{100} = 50, \text{ etc.}$$

Referring now to the formula for $N$:

Table 14.5

| Item | $\frac{r_i}{q_i}$ | $1-\frac{r_i}{q_i}$ | $C_1r_i$ | $C_1r_i\left[1-\left(\frac{r_i}{q_i}\right)\right]$ | $C_{si}$ |
|---|---|---|---|---|---|
| A | 0.16 | 0.84 | 50 | 42 | 10 |
| B | 0.20 | 0.80 | 25 | 20 | 5 |
| C | 0.16 | 0.84 | 80 | 67.2 | 8 |
| D | 0.16 | 0.84 | 96 | 80.6 | 6 |
| | | | | $\Sigma C_1r_i\left[1-\left(\frac{r_i}{q_i}\right)\right]$ = 209.8 | $\Sigma Cs_i$ = 29 |

Hence:

$$N = \sqrt{\frac{209.8}{2 \times 29}}$$

$$N = 1.9 \text{ cycles/year}$$

Consequently, for minimum cost, 1.9 complete runs per year should be made. Each complete cycle will consist of four batches as follows:

$$Q_A = \frac{r_A}{N} = \frac{10000}{1.9} = 5250 \text{ items}$$

$$Q_B = \frac{r_B}{N} = \frac{5000}{1.9} = 2630 \text{ items}$$

$$Q_C = \frac{r_C}{N} = \frac{8000}{1.9} = 4220 \text{ items}$$

$$Q_D = \frac{r_D}{N} = \frac{12000}{1.9} = 6300 \text{ items}$$

and each complete run lasting

$$t_A = \frac{5250}{250} = 21.0 \text{ days}$$

$$t_B = \frac{2630}{100} = 26.3 \text{ days}$$

$$t_C = \frac{4220}{200} = 21.1 \text{ days}$$

$$t_D = \frac{6300}{300} = 21.0 \text{ days}$$

$$\text{Total} = 89.4 \text{ days}$$

Since the process rate for each product is such that total annual consumption or demand can be satisfied by substantially less than one year's processing, unless consumption is increased or additional items are manufactured, equipment will spend some time idle each year.

## The line of balance technique

Our discussion has taken for granted the fact that batch processing proceeds in a series of steps. For example, we have assumed that in a process consisting of several operations, 1, 2, 3, etc., the entire batch is completed on operation 1 before being passed to operation 2, and so on. This type of situation is attractive, since it provides easier operations control. On the other hand, there are disadvantages in this iterative type of procedure. For example, the throughput time for any batch will be high, the work-in-progress will be high and, consequently, a large amount of storage space will be required. Ideally, therefore, we must look for a procedure in which batches of items might be divided, i.e. processing begun on subsequent operations before the complete batch has been processed on previous operations, and yet a procedure which enables adequate control of operations to be exercised. Such a situation might be desirable in manufacture, supply or service systems in certain conditions.

When batches are kept complete during processing and when an activity schedule for each batch on each operation is available, it is an easy matter to determine whether processing is proceeding according to plan. If the dividing of batches[4] is allowed then the situation is more complex and it is often

[4] Sometimes called 'lot-streaming'. See, for example, Baker, K. R. and Pyke, D. F. (1990) Solution procedures for the lot-streaming problem. *Decision Sciences*, **21**(3), pp. 475–491.

quite difficult both to establish an activity schedule and to determine whether progress is satisfactory or not. It is difficult, for example, to determine whether, at a given time, sufficient items have completed sufficient operations.

For example, consider the completion schedule shown in Table 14.6. Twelve finished items must be completed at the end of week 1, another 14 at the end of week 2, and so on. It is clear from this that, at the end of the fifth week, 40 items should have completed the final operation. What is not clear, however, is how many items should have passed through the previous operations at this date so as to ensure completion of the required quantity of items in later weeks.

Table 14.6 Job completion requirements

| Week no. | Delivery of finished items required | Cumulative completions required |
|---|---|---|
| 0 | 0 | 0 |
| 1 | 12 | 12 |
| 2 | 14 | 26 |
| 3 | 8 | 34 |
| 4 | 6 | 40 |
| 5 | 10 | 50 |
| 6 | 12 | 62 |
| 7 | 14 | 76 |
| 8 | 16 | 92 |
| 9 | 18 | 110 |
| 10 | 22 | 132 |

The 'line of balance' technique was developed to deal with precisely this type of situation. It deals only with the important or crucial (exceptional) operations in a job, establishes a schedule or plan for them and attracts attention to those which do not conform to this schedule (those about which something must be done if the progress of the entire job is not to be jeopardized). It is particularly useful where large batches of fairly complex items requiring many operations are to be delivered or completed over a period of time.

The technique can be regarded as a slightly more sophisticated form of the Gantt chart, the objective being to study the progress of jobs at regular intervals, to compare progress on each operation with the progress necessary to satisfy the eventual delivery requirements, and to identify those operations in which progress is unsatisfactory.

We can best describe the technique by means of a simple example. Two pieces of information are required, first the completion requirements and second an operation programme, i.e. the sequence and duration of the various operations. Four stages are involved in the use of the technique:

(a) the completion schedule;

(b) the operation programme;

(c) the programme progress chart;

(d) analysis of progress.

## The completion schedule

Construction of the completion schedule is the first step. The cumulative complete requirements must be calculated and presented either as a table (Table 14.6) or, and this is more useful later, as a graph (Figure 14.10), which may also be used to record deliveries in the manner shown.

**Figure 14.10** Cumulative completions

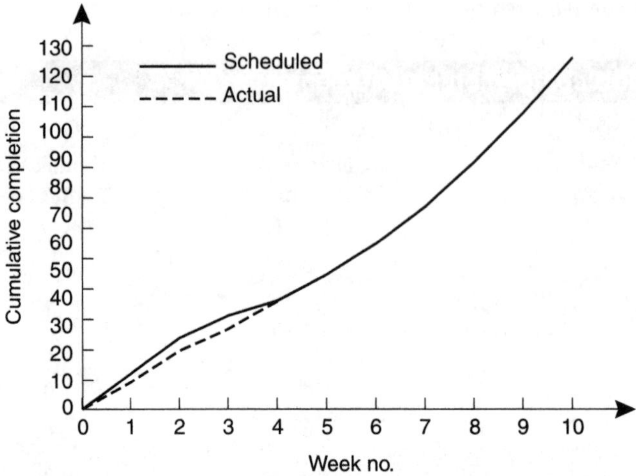


## The operation programme

The operation programme depicts the 'lead time' of the various operations, i.e. the length of time prior to the completion of the final operation by which intermediate operations must be completed.

In a simple job it is possible to show such information for *all* operations in the job, but in more complex jobs we concern ourselves only with those operations which are important or critical to the progress of the job and the satisfaction of the schedule.

The operation programme is best depicted as a chart, with the final delivery date as zero. Figure 14.11 is such an operation programme. The final completion date (completion of operation 15) is zero and the time-scale runs from right to left. This programme shows that items B and C must be combined (operation 14) two days before completion. Item C, prior to this combination, undergoes two conversion operations; the second must be finished five days before final completion, and the first two days before that. Purchase of the material for item C must be completed ten days before final combination. The item with longest lead time, 17 days, is B.

These two pieces of information – completion schedule and operation programme – are prerequisites for use of the line of balance technique. They need to be constructed only once for any job, unlike the following documents, which must be constructed each time the schedule and progress are examined.

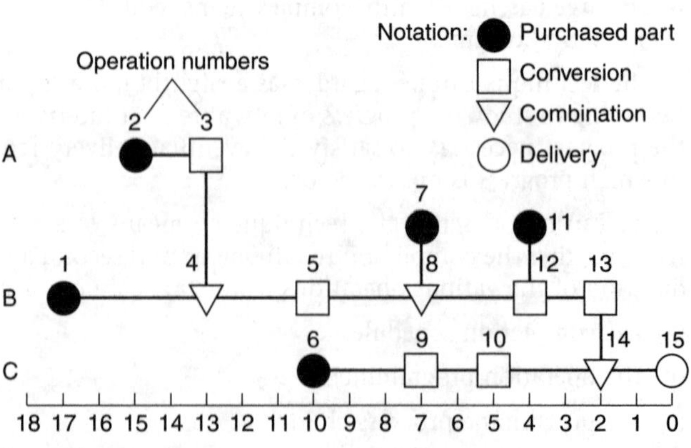


**Figure 14.11** Operation programme

## The programme progress chart

This chart shows the number of items which have been finished at each of the critical or important operations at a given date. Suppose, for example, the review date is week 4, by which, according to the completion schedule, 40 items should have been completed, i.e. 40 items should have passed operation 15 of the operation programme. The number of items that have completed this and each of the other operations can be obtained simply by checking inventory levels. The results can then be depicted by means of a histogram. Figure 14.12 shows the programme performance at week 4.

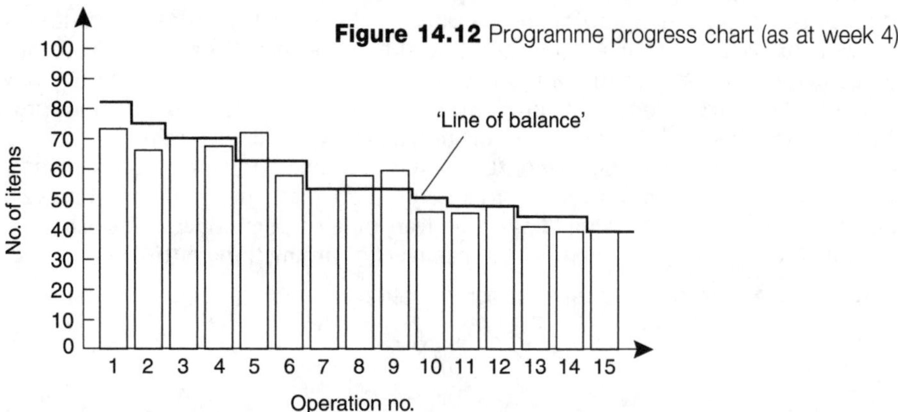


**Figure 14.12** Programme progress chart (as at week 4)

Since the object is to compare actual progress with the scheduled progress, the information given in Figure 14.12 must be compared with required progress. This is done by constructing a line on the programme progress chart which shows the number of items that should have been finished at each operation at the time of review. This line – the line of balance – can be constructed analytically or graphically. The line of balance shows the total number of items which should have been finished at each operation. Since a cumulative completion of 40 items is required for week 4, a total of 40 items must have completed operation 15 by this date. Operation 14 has a lead time of two days, so at week 4 enough items must have completed operation 15 to ensure that completion requirements two days later are satisfied. From the completion schedule the delivery for week 4 plus two days is 44 units (assuming five working days per week). The longest lead time, operation 1, is 17 days, so at week 4 enough items to satisfy the delivery requirements for week 4 plus 17 days, i.e. 82 units, should have been finished. The graphical procedure shown in Figure 14.13 is a convenient way of performing these calculations.

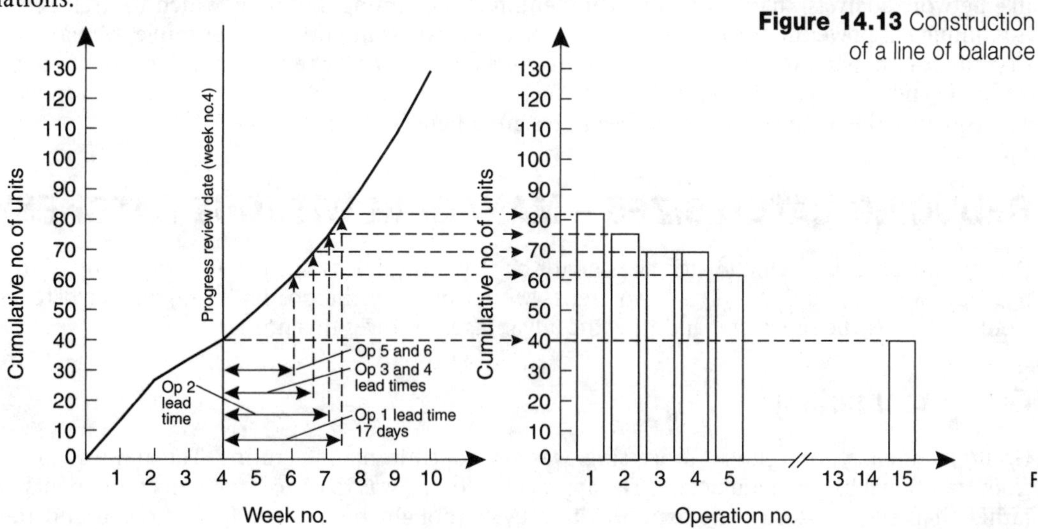


**Figure 14.13** Construction of a line of balance

## Analysis of progress

In comparing required with actual progress it is again convenient to work backwards, beginning with the last operation (15). From Figure 14.12 it is clear that the required number of completed items have been delivered to the customer (operation 15 = 40), a fact which is reflected by the actual performance line on the completion schedule. Clearly there is a shortage on both operations 13 and 14 and, unless processing can be expedited in some way, completion during the next week may fall short of requirements. When shortages occur we must obviously attempt to ascertain the reasons. If operations other than those considered as critical are the cause of shortages then those operations must be included in subsequent versions of the progress and line of balance chart. As an aid to control, colour codes might be used for the 'bars' on the progress chart to depict responsibility: alternatively, additional charts might be constructed containing progress information on operations in various processing areas. Figure 14.14 shows three additional programme progress charts, each containing one type of operation. From these it is clear that performance on the purchasing operations may well jeopardize future deliveries. We must therefore attempt to ensure that items, particularly on operations 1 and 2, are purchased more quickly, or failing this we should alter the lead time on these operations. Charts such as these might be issued to and used by departmental managers or production controllers.

**Figure 14.14** Additional programme progress charts

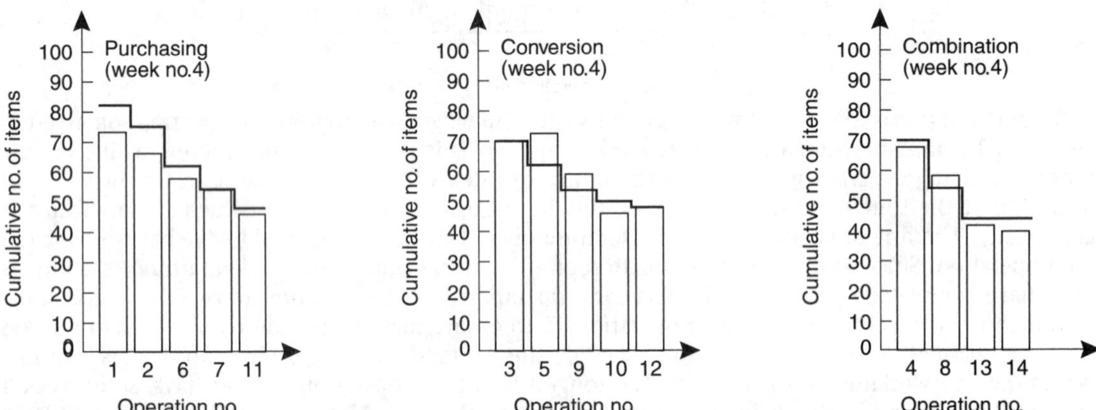


The line of balance is a simple and useful planning and control technique, its main advantage being, like network analysis, that it formalizes and enforces a planning discipline which in itself is useful. It is a simple but powerful procedure which relies on several assumptions. For example, we have assumed that the lead times shown in Figure 14.11 are constant, and that the type and sequence of operations are independent of production quantities. Such assumptions are very often justified in practice and consequently the technique as it has been presented here is of direct value.

# REDUCING BATCH SIZES - MANAGING WITHOUT BATCHES?

We identified ways in which batch sizes might be reduced towards unity at the beginning of the chapter. Now we look more closely at two tactics which promise the possibility of smaller batches than would otherwise be necessary, and thus the advantages of lower inventories.

## Group technology

Group technology, or 'cellular' processing, was developed in manufacturing. The aim was to get away from traditional batch manufacture. The approach adopted was to concentrate on components or parts rather than end products. The logic was that even though the end products differed and therefore could not be processed through common facilities and at the same time, some of the component parts were often quite similar, and if grouped together they could be put through the same facilities together – so avoiding the need for batch processing and the change of facility set-up between batches.

In conventional batch processing work, batch sizes and sequences are determined from the information available to the appropriate manager. Such information normally derives directly from the sales order or works order documents; consequently batch sizes are usually related directly to customer order sizes. The net result of this type of situation is that similar parts are often passed through widely differing sequences of operations and usually constitute different processing batches. This situation leads directly to low efficiency because of frequent machine set-ups and high work-in-progress.

Adopting a group technology method, the following stages are achieved:

(a) The parts of each of the items processed are examined and placed into logical classes or families and the operations sequence for each class of parts is determined and specified.

(b) Groups of facilities suitable for the processing of these classes of parts are specified using the operations planning details and forecasted demand for the items and hence the components.

(c) The sequencing of each class of parts for each group of facilities.

For purposes of implementing group technology, two types of family or group and three methods of processing can be identified. The two types of family are:

(a) ***Type A***, consisting of parts which are similar in shape and which have all or the majority of processing operations in common.

(b) ***Type B***, consisting of apparently dissimilar parts which are related by having one or more processing operations in common.

The three methods of processing using group technology are therefore as follows:

(a) ***Method 1*** – processing of a type-A family on a group of different conventional machines.

(b) ***Method 2*** – processing of a type-A and/or type-B family on one or more similar and conventional machines.

(c) ***Method 3*** – processing of a type-B family on a group of different machines.

In conventional terms the processing of a large quantity of type-A parts by method 1 corresponds to flow processing, which is of course an efficient method since it maximizes machine utilization. It is the object of group technology, by identifying common features in parts, to extend this type of application and to obtain increased efficiency in processing by adopting one of the three methods described above.

## Formation of parts families

Clearly an important decision influencing both the nature and the success of group technology is the classification of parts. Some of the approaches which might be employed are discussed below.

On occasions the selection of the parts for inclusion in a family may be relatively simple so the use of one of the more rigorous techniques will be unnecessary. Such a situation may occur when the item range is fairly static, when there are large numbers of parts with similar shapes, and when several obviously exclusive categories of parts exist.

*Classification* in this context refers to the assignment of parts into predefined groups or classes, while *coding* is the allocation of identities to these groups. The type and amount of information contained in the code depend on the potential uses of the system. A designer may wish to retrieve designs to obtain relevant information and to utilize existing parts in new items, while retrieval is also necessary in connection with costing, planning, variety reduction, etc. For this reason the design of a classification and coding system is normally a compromise that attempts to satisfy as many potential demands as possible.

The demands made on the system require not only that it should establish what types of parts are being processed, but also that it should facilitate the arrangement of parts into groups suitable for manufacture by the group method. The size of some groups formed will be such that their process is not economically feasible, but by merging such groups together their group processes may become economic.

A different type of approach relies on the classification of operation or process routes for parts to identify families which use the same group of facilities, or which can be readily re-routed to do so. In production flow analysis a progressive form of analysis is used, consisting of three basic steps as follows:

(a) ***Factory-flow analysis***. The objective of this is to identify the best division of facilities into departments. The operations routeings for all parts (obtained from route cards) are coded to indicate the department visited by each item and then sorted by this code to create groups of parts with the same interdepartment routeings.

(b) ***Group analysis***. The route cards for all parts processed in each department are analysed to identify the best division into groups. This is achieved by sorting cards into packs containing items with the same operation routeing, these packs then being combined to form viable facility/operation groupings.

(c) ***Line analysis***. The objective here is to obtain the best sequence of facilities in groups through study of the flow patterns within these groups. This is the layout problem in group technology, which will be discussed more fully in the next section.

## Facilities grouping

The facilities necessary to perform all operations on the parts family and the expected load on each piece of equipment can be listed for each family identified. It may be necessary at this stage to eliminate certain parts from families or to add others to avoid low or uneven machine utilization. Rarely, however, will it prove possible to achieve full utilization of all machines in a group, and some flexibility of labour is probably required – a characteristic which distinguishes group technology from classic flow processing.

Several techniques suitable for assisting in the determination of the arrangement of facilities in a group technology system have been developed. Singleton[5] outlined a simple method for determining a layout sequence for a number of operations or machines through which a variety of parts are processed, each part having a particular route through the operations. This method involves converting the process or operation sequence for each part to a common length scale of 100 units, the spacing of operations on this scale being equal to $100/N$, where $N$ is the number of operations for that part. Histograms are plotted for each operation, showing its placing on the percentile scale for each part, the occurrences being weighted by the processing quantity for each part. These distributions are then ranked in order of their means to give a suitable sequence of operations, i.e. the operation with the lowest mean is placed first on the line and the one with the highest mean is placed last. Backtracking or bypassing of operations by parts is indicated by the overlapping of the distributions, while distributions with a large spread or range might suggest that alternative operations routeing for parts be examined to improve part flow.

*Travel or cross charts* are of some value in developing layouts (see Chapter 6). Such a chart can show the nature of inter-operation movements for all parts for a given period of time. The row totals on the

---

[5] Singleton, W. T. (1962) Optimum sequence of operations for batch production. *Work Study and Industrial Engineering*, **3**, pp. 100–110.

chart show the extent of movement from an operation, and the column totals show movement to an operation. Each cell of the chart shows the relative frequency of movement between two operations; an ideal movement pattern suitable for use on a flow line is indicated when all the entries in the matrix appear in the cells immediately above the diagonal. Such travel charts can be used to help develop a sequence of operations. For example, operations with a low 'to/from' ratio (i.e. row-total/column-total ratio) receive parts from relatively few sources but distribute work to a large number of destinations. Hence, if in-sequence movement is to be maximized and backtracking is to be minimized, such operations should be placed at the beginning of the sequence of operations. Conversely, operations with a high 'to/from' ratio should be placed towards the end of the sequence, since they receive work from a large number of sources but distribute to comparatively few destinations. This heuristic approach is simple and attractive, and clearly has considerable practical merit.

## Sequencing

The determination of the sequence in which batches of parts are loaded onto a group technology cell or 'line' will be influenced by the desire to reduce setting-up costs and minimize throughput time. The problem is entirely congruent with the multi-model line batch sequencing problem and can be approached in the same way (see Chapter 15). If component batching is not adopted, individual components will be launched into the cell in much the same manner as in mixed-model line production. However, in this case, launch discipline and model sequence are unlikely to be important because of the far greater throughput time and component idle time.

## Flexible processing systems

If the inherent flexibility of the individual processes in a system and the linkages between these processes can be increased, then smaller batch sizes can be justified, since set-up costs are in effect reduced. This type of approach in manufacture has led to the development of flexible manufacturing systems (FMS) and the 'low-inventory' processing associated with just-in-time (JIT). In practice, attempts to increase inherent process flexibility will go hand in hand with attempts to minimize the differences between the processing requirements of the types of item which the system is required to deal with. Thus the implementation of design changes, the use of common items and the grouping of similar items into families for processing through a 'common' system are also associated with the use of flexible FMS.

Here we shall deal only with the nature of FMS, and specifically with manufacturing situations, although FMS principles are also evident in other types of operation.

## FMS principles

A flexible manufacturing system can be described as a computer-controlled arrangement of work stations, each with automated load and unload facilities, connected by an automated materials handling system, supplied by, and supplying to, an automated storage area. The essential ingredients of an FMS are therefore:

(a) computer-controlled work stations with automated load/unload facilities;

(b) automated materials handling system;

(c) automated storage facilities;

(d) control computers.

Such a system is shown in diagrammatic form in Figure 14.15.

**Figure 14.15** FMS layout

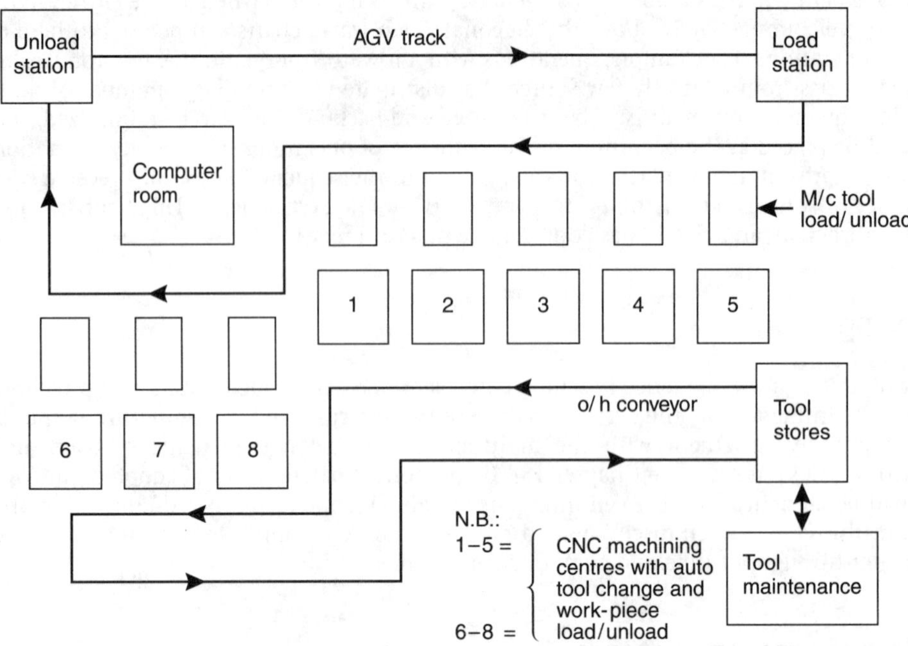


A true FMS will operate largely as an unmanned facility, requiring intervention only for maintenance and repair work. It will be capable of processing a range of different types of item in unit batch quantities and in random sequence. Work-in-progress, throughput times, queuing time at facilities and machine and facility idle time will all be low. The capital investment required in such facilities is, however, substantial.

In a manufacturing application, complex 'machining centres' will be the principal components of an FMS. These will be served by automatic tool change facilities and automatic pallet loading and unloading of components to be machined. Such facilities will be linked by automated conveyors, or by AGVs (automatically guided vehicles). A supervisory computer will schedule work through an FMS comprising up to a dozen such machines, and provide also for instructions for tool changes at machines, etc. Automated inspection and measurement will be incorporated as well as the monitoring of machines to detect tool wear and tool breakage. A tool supply system will schedule the delivery of cutting tools to each machine, and an automated swarf and waste removal system will be in use. The FMS will be linked into an overall scheduling and inventory control system, and such an arrangement might operate, essentially unmanned, for 24 hours per day, so that with a sophisticated FMS 'lights out' operation is feasible with minimum human intervention.

Most FMS installations have limited flexibility. Many have been established to deal only with a limited range or family of components, and virtually all systems are concerned with machining work. For these an adequate volume requirement for a limited range of similar items is the prerequisite condition. However, more sophisticated systems are being employed, providing for a combination of machining and assembly work, and themselves forming part of a more extensive computer-integrated manufacturing (CIM) environment. In such applications data drawn directly from a computer-aided design database will be used to configure and equip machines for the manufacture of particular items which will automatically be checked against design specification before being passed on for subsequent operations. A CIM system will also handle design changes, scheduling and inventory control, order book details, quality control and quality records, and machine performance monitoring.

## Robotics

Robots are often used in FMS for load/unload operations. An industrial robot can be defined as a device to perform a variety of handling and movement tasks in response to programmed instructions and/or sensory inputs. The flexibility of such a device is beneficial in two respects.

### *Short-term flexibility*

The industrial robot can be programmed to handle a variety of different types of item. Thus, for example, in a mixed-model processing system such as an FMS, industrial robots can be programmed to handle or perform operations on a succession of different types of item where the sequence of items is known. Alternatively, input devices can be provided, e.g. bar code readers, or visual systems can be used to enable a robot to recognize a type of item presented to it and thus perform the operations necessary on that item. The loading or unloading of different types of item at a machining centre in an FMS, performing movement or processing tasks on a mixed-model assembly line, and removing items or placing them into store, are examples of the use of this 'short-term' flexibility.

### *Long-term flexibility*

Robot installations can be justified even when no such short-term flexibility is required. For example, the installation of a reprogrammable device may be appropriate for a facility intended to deal only with a single type of item, where that facility is intended to have a relatively short lifespan. Such situations exist in the motor industry where an assembly line is set up for the manufacture of a particular product for a known period of time. When that product is replaced by its successor, a new facility will be established, and the programmable devices from the former can be transferred for use in the replacement facility. In this way expensive industrial robots can be justified and installed in the manufacturing system with the intention that they later be transferred for use in a system concerned with the manufacture of a different or replacement product.

## CHECKLIST FOR CHAPTER 14

*The nature of batch processing*

*Low-inventory operating systems*

*Examples of batch processing*

- In supply
- In service
- In transport
- In manufacture
- System structures for batch processing

Batch processing decisions

*Managing batch processing*

Models of batch processing

Batch sequencing

- Processing families of items

Determination of batch sizes

The economic batch size

A1 Deterministic situations

- (i) Complete batch from/to stock
- (ii) As (i) with shortages
- (iii) Batch from/to stock over period of time

A2 Probabilistic situations

- Uncertainties in costs
- Uncertainties in usage or consumption rates
- Buffer stocks
- Processing rate uncertainties
- The production (processing) range

Scheduling for batch processing

- Optimum processing cycles
- Scheduling for multiple items

Line of balance

- The completion schedule
- The operation programme
- The programme progress chart
- Analysis of progress

*Reducing batch sizes*

Group technology

- Formation of families
- Facilities grouping
- Sequencing

Flexible manufacturing systems (FMS)

- Definition
- FMS as a means to achieve JIT
- The component parts of an FMS
  - FMS for fully automated production
- Industrial robots
  - Definition
  - Use in FMS
  - The flexibility of robots

## FURTHER READING

For books on techniques, particularly analytical techniques related to batch sizes, schedule, etc., see Further Reading, Chapter 17.

**Lumsden, N. P. (1972)** *Line of Balance Method*. Oxford: Pergamon.

**O'Grady, P. and Byrne, M. (1989)** Adaptive lot sizing. *Engineering Costs and Production Economics*, **15**, pp. 397–404.

**Snead, C. S. (1989)** *Group Technology*. New York: Van Nostrand Reinhold.

**Voss, C. (1989)** Managing manufacturing technology. In Wild, R. (ed.) *International Handbook of Production and Operations Management*. London: Cassell.

**Zygmont, J. (1986)** Flexible manufacturing systems. *High Technology*, October, pp. 22–27.

## QUESTIONS

14.1 What circumstances necessitate the use of batch processing in manufacture, supply, transport and service systems? What are the principal characteristics of this method of processing and what are the principal managerial problems involved?

14.2 (a) Calculate:
(i) the optimum processing batch quantity;
(ii) the processing cycle time, given the following information

| | |
|---|---|
| Set-up cost per batch | = £17 |
| Stock-holding cost per item per month | = £0.05 |
| Buffer stock required | = 25 items |
| Demand rate per year | = 12 000 (stable) |
| Process rate per month | = 1500 |
| Processing cost per item | = £25 |

The process is such that all items in a batch are completed at the same time.

(b) Because of deterioration in the processing facilities, the processing rate per month drops from 1500 to 900. How does this change affect the economic batch quantity?

14.3 Experimental Brewers Ltd are the sole manufacturers of 'Instant Beer'. Because of the market potential for this new style of beverage an entirely new manufacturing facility has been established, the capacity of which is 5000 litres (equivalent) per day. At the moment demand for 'Instant Beer' is stable at 3000 litres (equivalent) per day. The product is manufactured intermittently, set-up costs for the facility being £250 and storage costs per day per 10 000 litres (equivalent) being £100.

The company is prepared to tolerate the occasional stockout, which it estimates to cost £500 per 10 000 litres (equivalent) per day.

In what batch quantities should 'Instant Beer' be manufactured?

14.4 Pizza is made at a rate of 240 pieces per hour by an automatic cooking machine. The pizza is sold (cold) through a shop on the same premises at a rate of 100 per hour (virtually constant). The cost of setting up the machine for production of the pizza is £15. (The same machine is also used to produce other items.) The cost of stocking cold pizza is £1 per 1000 per hour.

What is the optimum batch production quantity and how frequently should such batches ideally be produced (neglecting limitations caused by the need to produce other items)?

14.5 Refer to the situation faced by Experimental Brewers Ltd (Question 14.3). The company decides to adopt a policy of allowing a variation in production batch quantities equivalent to a variation of plus or minus 8% of the cost associated with the economic batch quantities.

What is the 'production range' in such circumstances?

14.6 A hospital uses a certain medication at a rate of 200 units per day. The medication is prepared in the hospital's own laboratories in batches. The set-up cost is £100. The processing cost is £5 per unit, and the refrigerated storage is £0.1 per unit per day.

If the management is prepared to tolerate an increase of up to 1% in the minimum total cost per unit, what flexibility does this give in the choice of batch quantities and what is the total cost per unit of the cheapest solution if, for chemical reasons, processed batches are restricted to multiples of 50 units?

14.7 Assuming processing of equal batch sizes at regular intervals and given the following, calculate the processing cycle time:

(a) $C_s = £150$
$C_1 = 50p$ per item per annum
$r = 5000$ per month

(b) $C_s = £150$
$C_1 = 50p$ per item per annum
$r = 5000$ per month
$C_1 = £1$ per item per month

(c) $C_s = £150$
$C_1 = 50p$ per item per annum
$r = 5000$ per month
$q = 50\,000$ per month

14.8 Discuss the advantages, disadvantages and limitations of the line of balance planning and control technique.

Compare and contrast it with any other planning and control technique, such as network analysis, with which you are familiar.

14.9 Ornamental Doorknobs Ltd assemble four types of door knocker – Elizabethan, Victorian, Georgian and Modern – in batches on the same equipment. The following table gives the annual demand, the assembly rate and the inventory cost per item per annum for each type of knob. A change in the equipment set-up is necessary whenever there is a change in the type being assembled. This set-up cost is £10 irrespective of the type of change. Assume a working year of 250 days.

Calculate the processing batch sizes for each type of knocker and how many complete runs of all four types should be made per year.

| Knocker | Demand (per year) | Assembly rate (per day) | Inventory cost (per item p.a.) |
|---|---|---|---|
| Elizabethan | 7000 | 150 | 0.008 |
| Victorian | 10000 | 250 | 0.006 |
| Georgian | 15000 | 300 | 0.005 |
| Modern | 5000 | 100 | 0.007 |

14.10 The delivery schedule of items and the operations programme for the making of these items are given below.

| Week no. | Delivery required | Cumulative delivery | Week no. | Delivery required | Cumulative delivery |
|---|---|---|---|---|---|
| 0 | 0 | 0 | 7 | 15 | 89 |
| 1 | 12 | 12 | 8 | 10 | 99 |
| 2 | 15 | 27 | 9 | 27 | 126 |
| 3 | 12 | 39 | 10 | 15 | 141 |
| 4 | 20 | 59 | 11 | 20 | 161 |
| 5 | 5 | 64 | 12 | 17 | 178 |
| 6 | 10 | 74 | | | |

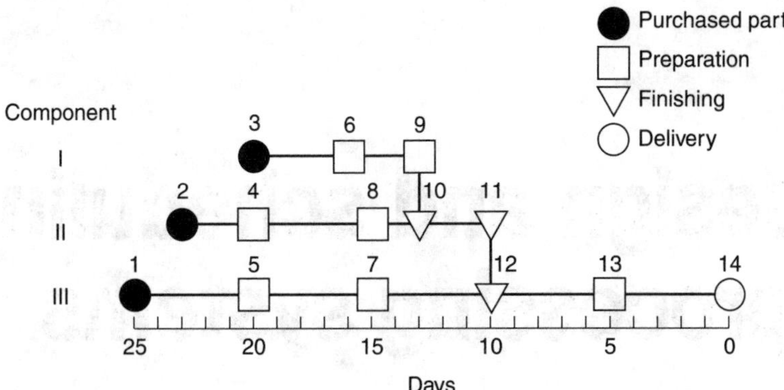


Construct the line of balance for weeks 3, 6 and 10. Indicate how you would use the line of balance to analyse progress in the several different departments involved in the making of the items.

14.11 What is group technology and what benefits are likely to be obtained by introducing group technology, if appropriate, into a company?

What steps would be followed during an investigation to determine whether group technology is appropriate in a given manufacturing situation?

Describe briefly the principal methods of component classification, designed for use in group technology.

14.12 'The pursuit of JIT in mixed-model engineering manufacture will lead to the implementation of FMS.' Discuss.

14.13 Refer to the concept of economic batch quantities. Show how low work-in-progress might be justified on economic grounds, and comment on the role of FMS in achieving this.

Chapter 15

# The design and scheduling of flow processing systems

## ISSUES

What is 'flow planning'?
What is a flow-line?
Are flow lines used only in manufacturing?
How do we design a simple flow line?
Can flow lines cope, efficiently, with different items?
What are the distinctive characteristics of manual lines?
How do we deal with worker variability?

## NOTATION USED IN THIS CHAPTER

| | |
|---|---|
| $C$ | Cycle time |
| $C_i$ | Cycle time for unit $i$ |
| $C_j$ | Cycle time for model $j$ |
| $C_n$ | Cycle time for $n$ ($n = 1 \ldots i$) |
| COMSOAL | Computer method for sequencing operations for assembly lines |
| $\bar{c}$ | Average work station time |
| $K$ | Constant |
| $L_1$ | Unit inventory cost/unit time |
| $L_2$ | Idle facilities cost/unit time |
| $N$ | Number of items to be produced |
| $N_j$ | Total number of model $j$ required |
| $n$ | Number of work stations |
| $n_{min}$ | Minimum number of work stations |
| PW | Positional weight |
| RPW | Ranked positional weight |
| $T$ | Production time period |
| $T_F$ | Feed interval |
| $T_T$ | Tolerance time |

| | |
|---|---|
| $t$ | Element time |
| $\bar{t}$ | Mean work time for element |
| $X$ | Optimum buffer capacity |
| $x_i$ | Time of launching unit $i$ |
| $Z$ | Cumulative work station time |
| $\gamma$ | Regular item launch interval |
| $\alpha$ | Time interval between successive stations starting work on any one unit |
| $\sigma$ | Standard deviation of normally distributed work times |

In this chapter we concentrate on the design and scheduling of flow processing systems, which because of their importance deserve individual attention. There is perhaps a temptation to think that such systems exist only in manufacturing. This is not the case. Certainly flow processing and flow technology was first developed, in a sophisticated way, for mass production, and our discussion here will make some reference to that, but we should note that the basic principles have far wider relevance.

## THE NATURE OF FLOW PROCESSING

Fundamentally, most types of operating system provide a form of flow processing, i.e. customers, materials or products arrive into the system and proceed through several departments or facilities before emerging from the end of the system. For example, each of the following could be considered as a form of flow processing:

(a) passage of paperwork through an office;

(b) passage of patients through a hospital;

(c) passage of children through classes and schools in an educational system;

(d) passage of a car down a vehicle assembly line.

The manner and nature of 'flow' in these cases differ. In some cases items or customers will flow through a system by different routes, i.e. visiting different departments or facilities (e.g. (a) and (b) above). In some cases the flow rate will be low and/or the throughput time high (e.g. (b) and (c) above). In some cases the consistency of routes, the flow routes and the desire to minimize throughput times will justify a 'product'-type arrangement of facilities, e.g. as a 'line' (as in (d) above), but in others a functional/process layout will be appropriate.

We will be concentrating on those types of system in which the flow characteristics form a distinguishing feature. So, some consistency of routeing through the system and a relatively high flow rate will usually exist, whether the things which are flowing are products, or customers being treated. The classic example is the manufacturing flow line, but even that will be evident in different 'guises'.

**EXAMPLE**

### *Mamma Mia Pasta*

This pasta restaurant can be found at 160 Michigan Ave, Chicago. The manner in which it operates is best described by considering the passage of a customer through the system.

On entering the restaurant the customer first sees a large menu giving the day's selection for starters, main course and desserts. The customer then enters the serving process. The arrangement is shown in the diagram in Figure 15.1. Customers place their order at the start of the 'line', i.e. they specify their full meal requirement. This is entered onto a form (by checking certain boxes) by a member of staff, and the form is placed on a tray which is then dispatched down the line. Customers move through their queueing area at the same speed as

**Figure 15.1** Layout of Mamma Mia pasta restaurant

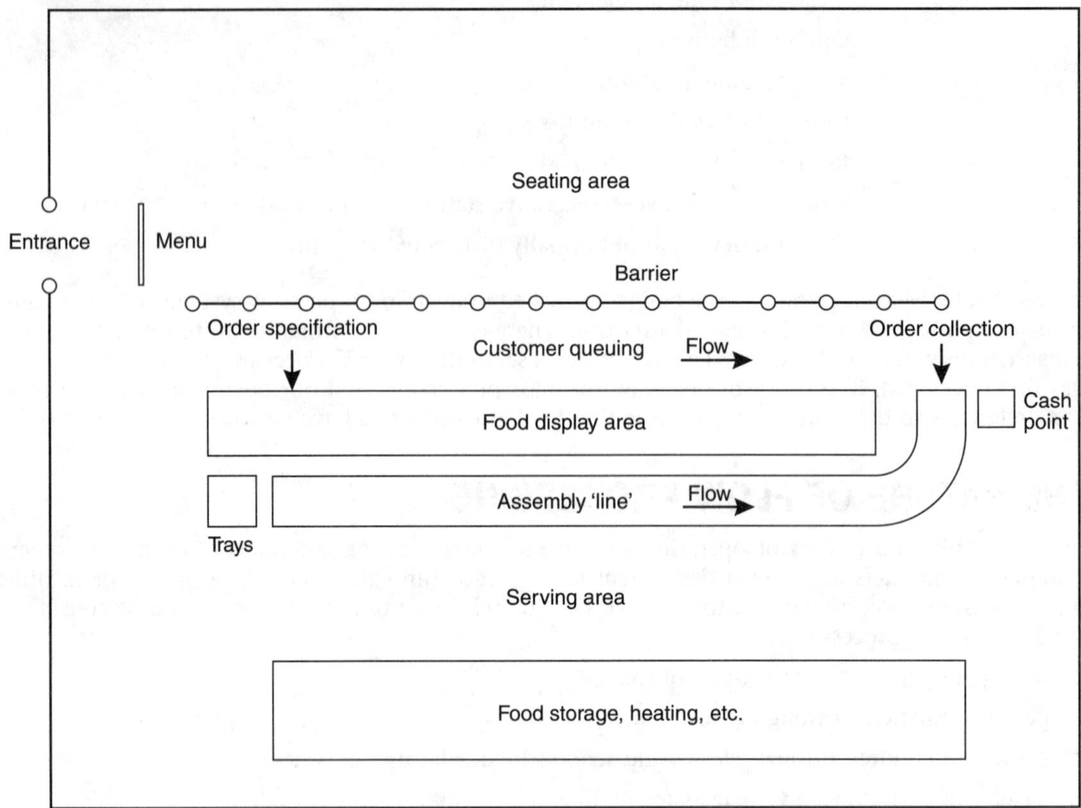


their trays. As the trays are moved along the 'assembly' line, the required meal is assembled by staff, each 'manning' one or two adjacent 'stations' concerned with a particular type of menu item. The trays are pushed through all stations but receive items at only some of them. Occasionally serving staff interact with customers, e.g. to identify the required size of portions (e.g. dressing, sauces, etc.) When both the fully assembled tray and the customer reach the end of the line, the meal is paid for, collected and taken away.

---

We will focus on the manufacturing 'flow line', as in (d) above, and in the case example. This provides a good basis for an examination of the most important aspects of flow processing system design and operation.

## FLOW LINE PRINCIPLES

Although details differ, the basic flow line principles remain the same – items are processed as they pass through a series of work stations along a line. Generally, raw materials, items or components are fed in at the beginning of, and at certain points along, the line, and goods are delivered from the end of the line.

Flow lines which are engaged, essentially, in product assembly are often referred to as *assembly lines*, while those which use automatic material transfer between the automatic machining 'stations' are normally referred to as *transfer lines*. Transfer lines are fully automated. The degree of automation on assembly lines will differ.

**Table 15.1 Classes and varieties of flow line**

| Flow line description: Class | Variety | Number of products | Product changes | Flow of items | Setting of equipment and allocations of work |
|---|---|---|---|---|---|
| Transfer line | Single model | 1 | None | Regular | No changes required |
| | Multi-model | >1 | Batch changes | Regular batches | Changes of equipment setting and/or work allocation required on change of batch |
| Assembly line | Single model | 1 | None | Irregular[a] | No changes required |
| | Multi-model | >1 | Batch changes | Irregular[a] | Changes of equipment setting and/or work allocation required on batch change |
| | Mixed model | >1 | Continual[c] | Irregular | Changes of equipment setting and/or work allocation normally required[b] |

[a] Because of variable work station times – characteristic of manual flow lines.
[b] Alternatively, as in 'group technology', tools and equipment might be permanently allocated a specific group of components.
[c] At any time the line contains a mixture of product types.

Given the two classes of flow line, we can now identify various subdivisions (Table 15.1). Both classes of flow line can be used for the processing of one or more products. The processing of one product or model on either class of line can be accomplished without the need to alter the 'set-up' of the line, i.e. without the need to change tools or work allocations, etc. The processing of more than one product, however, gives rise to more complex situations. In such cases two alternative strategies are available:

(a) The processing of the two or more products in separate batches. This we shall refer to as the multi-model situation, and it necessitates the rearrangement of the flow line between batches.

(b) The processing of the two or more products simultaneously on the line. This we shall call the mixed-model situation, which gives rise to rather complex design problems and will be discussed in some detail later (Mamma Mia Pasta was a simple example of a mixed-model line).

Whichever strategy is adopted, if more than one model or product is to be processed on the line, these products must have similar work contents. The greater the similarity, the easier it will be to provide either multi-model or mixed-model processing. More flexibility is normally available on assembly lines; consequently in certain circumstances it may be possible to design such lines for either multi-model or mixed-model operation. For example, many car assembly lines work on the mixed-model principle, different 'builds' of the same vehicle, and occasionally different types of vehicle, being produced simultaneously on the line. The use of reprogrammable or flexible tools, such as industrial robots, facilitates this flexibility. In contrast, transfer lines are far less flexible. They are normally confined to single-model, or occasionally large-batch multi-model, operation.

## THE DESIGN OF 'SIMPLE' FLOW LINES

We must begin by considering the nature and design of 'simple' flow lines. The reason for the use of the term 'simple' will become apparent later in the chapter, and here it is sufficient to recognize that certain simplifying assumptions will be made.

A simple flow line consists, essentially, of a series of work stations. The total work content of the product or item, i.e. the total time required to complete the item, is divided among these stations so that, as the item travels down the line, it becomes incrementally more complete at each station.

One objective in designing flow lines is to attempt to allocate equal mounts of work to each station, i.e. to divide the total work content of the job as evenly as possible between the stations. This is known as *line balancing*. Without such balance, a certain amount of inefficiency or loss must inevitably occur, since some stations will have more work to perform than others, but all stations will normally be required to process the same number of items within a given period of time.

The time required to complete the work allocated to each station is known as the *service time*. The time available at each station for the performance of the work is known as the *cycle time* – the cycle time normally being longer than the service time. The cycle time at a station is the time interval between the completion or the starting of work on successive items, and therefore includes both productive and non-productive work as well as any idle time. Non-productive work will include the transfer of the product between stations, and may also include a certain amount of handling, movement, etc. (Figure 15.2).

**Figure 15.2**

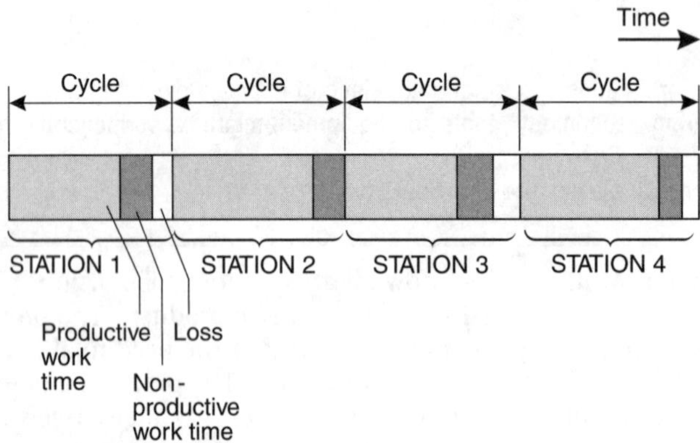


$$\text{Cycle time} = \text{Service time} + \text{Idle time or loss}$$

$$= \frac{\text{Productive}}{\text{work time}} + \frac{\text{Non-productive}}{\text{work time}} + \text{Idle time or loss}$$

The total work content of the job consists of the total productive work plus the total non-productive work.

Total work content = Total productive work + Total non-productive work

The manner in which work can be allocated to stations on the line is influenced by certain constraints. Each job will consist of certain work elements, and normally the order in which some of these elements of work can be performed will be influenced by technological or *precedence* constraints, e.g. one operation must be completed before another can be started. Such precedence constraints will limit the ability to achieve balance in allocating work (i.e. work elements) to stations.

The allocation of elements to stations may also be limited by *zoning* constraints. Such constraints will necessitate or preclude the grouping of certain work elements at certain stations. For example, it may be essential that two work elements are not allocated to the same station if they might in some way interfere with one another. Such a constraint is known as a negative zoning constraint. In contrast, a positive zoning constraint necessitates the grouping of two or more work elements at one station, as might be the case when the maximum utilization of a single expensive piece of equipment is to be achieved.

Because of such constraints, perfect line balance is rarely achieved in practice, and a certain amount of *balancing delay* or *balancing loss* is inevitable. Balance delay is the difference between the total time available for completion of the job and the total time required. For example, at any one station the balance delay is the difference between the cycle time and the service time. The percentage balancing loss for any station is given by the difference between the cycle time and the service time, expressed as a percentage of the cycle time. Similarly, the balancing loss for a complete line is given by the difference of the total time available (e.g. the sum of the cycle times) and the total time required (i.e. the sum of the service times), expressed as a percentage of the total time available.

## Line balancing

The cycle time can be calculated, at least theoretically, from the required output. For example, if $N$ items are to be produced in $T$ minutes, then the cycle time ($C$) should be:

$$C = \frac{T}{N}$$

Furthermore, given these two figures and knowing either the total work content or each of the element times ($t$), the minimum number of work stations ($n_{\text{min.}}$) can be calculated.

$$n_{\text{min.}} = \frac{N\Sigma t}{T}$$

In fact, since we must have a whole number of work stations, $n_{\text{min.}}$ will be the integer equal to or greater than $N\Sigma t/T$.

The average work station time ($\bar{c}$) is simply the total work content ($\Sigma t$) divided by the actual number of stations, $n$:

$$\bar{c} = \frac{\Sigma t}{n}$$

Almost invariably, this figure is less than the cycle time ($C$). Hence:

$$\text{Balancing loss (\%)} = \frac{C - \bar{c}}{C} \times 100$$

$$\text{or (\%)} = \frac{n(C) - \Sigma t}{n(C)} \times 100$$

In practice, when designing lines we cannot normally achieve the perfect balance shown in Figure 15.3. A situation such as the one shown in Figure 15.4(a) will result if we are lucky, but often it will be as shown in Figure 15.4(b), in which neither the work station times are balanced nor is the maximum work station time equal to the desired cycle time.

**Figure 15.3** Perfectly balanced five-station flow line

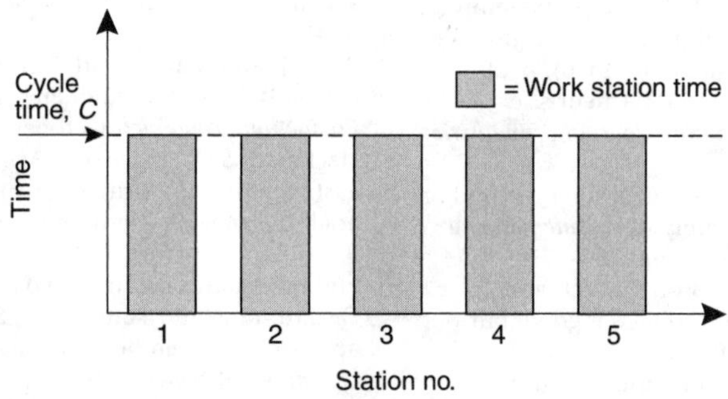

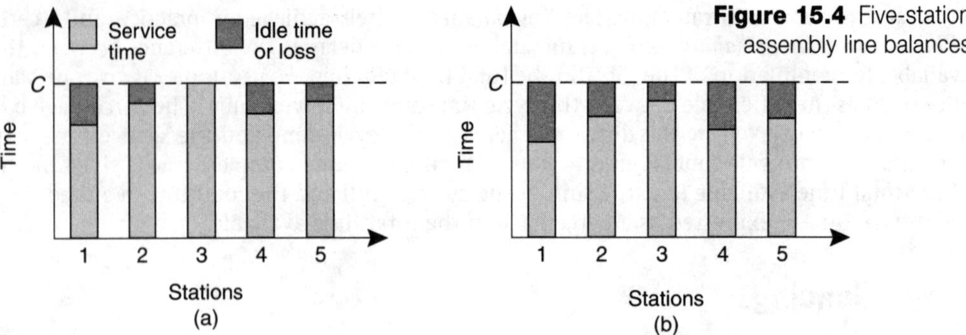


**Figure 15.4** Five-station assembly line balances

Although we have spoken of and depicted idle time resulting from imperfect line balance, in practice periods of idleness caused by the difference between cycle times and work station times may not exist because the work to be done may be undertaken more slowly in the time available. Nevertheless, the consequences are precisely the same because an under-utilization will result.

The objective of line balancing is that, given a desired cycle time or output rate, the minimum rational work elements and their standard times and other constraints, one should attempt to assign work elements to work stations in order to:

(a) minimize idle time or balancing loss;

(b) minimize the number of work stations;

(c) distribute balancing loss evenly between stations;

(d) avoid violating any constraints.

## Methods of simple line balancing

The first analytical treatments of the line balancing problem were developed in the 1950s. They aimed to secure optimal solutions and depended on many simplifying assumptions. Because of the nature of the problem and the inadequacy of these treatments, several authors have developed 'heuristic' methods of assembly line balancing, those suggested by Helgerson and Birnie,[1] Kilbridge and Wester[2] and Arcus[3] being perhaps the best known. Whilst other approaches are available,[4] these three methods only will be dealt with here.

## The Kilbridge and Wester method

This simple heuristic method of assembly line balancing is best described by means of an example.

---

[1] Helgerson, N. B. and Birnie, D. P. (1961) Assembly line balancing using the ranked positional weight technique. *Journal of Industrial Engineering*, **11**(6), p. 394.

[2] Kilbridge, K. and Wester, L. (1961) A heuristic method of assembly line balancing. *Journal of Industrial Engineering*, **11**(4), p. 292.

[3] Arcus, A. L. (1966) COMSOAL – a computer method of sequencing operations for assembly lines. *International Journal of Production Research*, **4**(4), pp. 259–277.

[4] For example, procedures based on 'branch and bound' algorithms (capable of producing good, but not necessarily optimal solutions):
Hoffman, T. R. (1992) Eureka: a hybrid system for assembly line balancing. *Management Science*, **38**(1), pp. 39–47.
Betts, J. and Mahomoud, K. I. (1989) A method for assembly line balancing. *Engineering Costs and Production Economics*, October, pp. 55–64.
Hackman, S. T., Magazine, M. J. and Wee, T. S. (1989) Fast effective algorithms for simple assembly line balancing problems. *Operations Research*, **37**(6), pp. 916–924.
and procedures based on 'goal programming':
Deckro, R. F. and Rangachari, S. (1990) A goal approach to assembly line balancing. *Computers and Operations Research*, **17**(5), pp. 509–521.

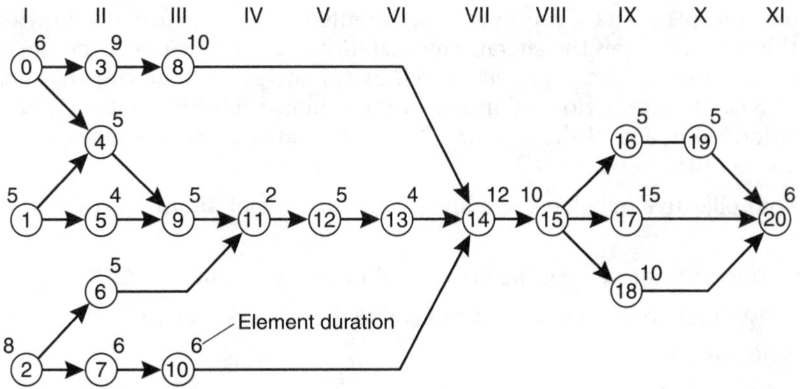


**Figure 15.5**

Assembly of a simple component requires the performance of 21 work elements which are governed by certain precedence constraints, as shown in Figure 15.5. This precedence diagram shows circles representing work elements placed as far to the left as possible with all the arrows joining circles sloping to the right. The figures above the diagram are column numbers. Elements appearing in column I can be started immediately, those in column II can be begun only after one or more in column I have been completed, and so on.

**Table 15.2 Tabular presentation of data in Figure 15.5**

| Column no. in precedence diagram (a) | Element no. (b) | Transferability of element (c) | Element duration (d) | Duration for column (e) | Cumulative duration (f) |
|---|---|---|---|---|---|
| I | 0 | | 6 | | |
| | 1 | | 5 | | |
| | 2 | | 8 | 19 | 19 |
| II | 3 | III–V (with 8) | 9 | | |
| | 4 | | 5 | | |
| | 5 | | 4 | | |
| | 6 | III | 5 | | |
| | 7 | III–V (with 10) | 6 | 29 | 48 |
| III | 8 | IV–VI | 10 | | |
| | 9 | | 5 | | |
| | 10 | IV–Vi | 6 | 21 | 69 |
| IV | 11 | | 2 | 2 | 71 |
| V | 12 | | 5 | 5 | 76 |
| VI | 13 | | 4 | 4 | 80 |
| VII | 14 | | 12 | 12 | 92 |
| VIII | 15 | | 10 | 10 | 102 |
| IX | 16 | | 5 | | |
| | 17 | X | 15 | | |
| | 18 | X | 10 | 30 | 132 |
| X | 19 | | 5 | 5 | 137 |
| XI | 20 | | 6 | 6 | 143 |

The data shown on this diagram can now be represented in tabular form as shown in Table 15.2. Column (c) of this table describes the lateral transferability of elements among columns; for example, element 6 can be performed in column III as well as column II without violating precedence constraints. Element 8 can also be performed in any of the columns IV to VI, as can element 10. Element 3 can also be performed in any of the columns III to V provided element 8 is also transferred, as can element 7.

Suppose it is our objective to balance the line for a cycle time of 36. In this case we would proceed as follows:

1. Is there a duration in column (f) of the table equal to the cycle time of 36? *No.*
2. Select the largest duration in column (f) less than 36, i.e. 19 *for column 1.*
3. Subtract 19 from 36 = 17.
4. Do any of the elements in column II, either individually, or collectively, have a duration of 17? *No, the nearest is 16 for elements 4, 6 and 7, which will give a work station time of 35 for station 1.*
5. Select the smallest duration from column (f) which is larger than 36, *i.e. 48 for columns I and II.*
6. Can one or more of the elements in columns I and II be transferred beyond column II so as to reduce the duration as near as possible to 36? *No, but element 3 (with 8) plus 6 can be transferred to give a work station time of 34.*

**Table 15.3**

| Column no. in precedence diagram (a) | Element no. (b) | Transferability of element (c) | Element duration (d) | Duration for column (e) | Cumulative duration (f) |
|---|---|---|---|---|---|
| I | 0 | | 6 | | |
| | 1 | | 5 | | |
| | 2 | | 8 | | Station 1 |
| II | 4 | | 5 | | |
| | 6 | | 5 | | |
| | 7 | | 6 | | (35) |
| III | 3 | III–V (with 8) | 9 | | |
| | 5 | | 4 | | |
| | 9 | | 5 | | |
| | 10 | IV–VI | 6 | 24 | 24 |
| IV | 8 | V–VI | 10 | | |
| | 11 | | 2 | 12 | 36 |
| V | 12 | | 5 | 5 | 41 |
| VI | 13 | | 4 | 4 | 45 |
| VII | 14 | | 12 | 12 | 57 |
| VIII | 15 | | 10 | 10 | 67 |
| IX | 16 | | 5 | | |
| | 17 | X | 15 | | |
| | 18 | X | 10 | 30 | 97 |
| X | 19 | | 5 | 5 | 102 |
| XI | 20 | | 6 | 6 | 108 |

**Table 15.4**

| Column no. in precedence diagram (a) | Element no. (b) | Transferability of element (c) | Element duration (d) | Duration for column (e) | Cumulative duration (f) | |
|---|---|---|---|---|---|---|
| | 0 | | | | | Station 1 |
| | 1 | | | | | |
| | 2 | | | | | |
| | 4 | | | | | |
| | 6 | | | | | |
| | 7 | | | 35 | (35) | |
| III | 3 | | 9 | | | Station 2 |
| | 5 | | 4 | | | |
| | 9 | | 5 | | | |
| | 8 | | 10 | | | |
| | 10 | | 6 | | | |
| IV | 11 | | 2 | 36 | (36) | |
| V | 12 | | 5 | 5 | 5 | |
| VI | 13 | | 4 | 4 | 9 | |
| VII | 14 | | 12 | 12 | 21 | |
| VIII | 15 | | 10 | 10 | 31 | |
| IX | 16 | | 5 | | | |
| | 17 | X | 15 | | | |
| | 18 | X | 10 | 30 | 61 | |
| X | 19 | | 5 | 5 | 66 | |
| XI | 20 | | 6 | 6 | 72 | |

7. Select the next largest duration from column (f), i.e. 69 *for columns I, II and III.*
8. Can one or more of the elements in columns I, II and III be transferred beyond column III so as to reduce the duration to 36? *No, the nearest are elements* 3, 7, 8 *and* 10, *which would give a duration of* 38, *which is too large.*
9. Will an improved allocation of elements for this station be obtained by considering a large duration from column (f)? *No.*
10. Adopt the best allocation found previously, i.e. step 4, which gave a work station time of 35.
11. Rewrite the table to show this allocation and calculate new cumulative figures for column (f) (Table 15.3).
12. Is there a duration in column (f) of the new table equal to 36? *Yes, for columns III and IV.*
13. Allocate the elements in these columns to the second work station and redraw the table showing new figures for column (f) (Table 15.4).
14. Is there a duration in column (f) of the new table equal to the cycle time of 36? *No.*

**Table 15.5**

| Column no. in precedence diagram (a) | Element no. (b) | Transferability of element (c) | Element duration (d) | Duration of column (e) | Cumulative duration (f) | |
|---|---|---|---|---|---|---|
| | 0 | | | | | Station 1 |
| | 1 | | | | | |
| | 2 | | | | | |
| | 4 | | | | | |
| | 6 | | | | | |
| | 7 | | | 35 | (35) | |
| | 3 | | | | | Station 2 |
| | 5 | | | | | |
| | 9 | | | | | |
| | 8 | | | | | |
| | 10 | | | | | |
| | 11 | | | 36 | (36) | |
| V | 12 | | 5 | | | Station 3 |
| VI | 13 | | 4 | | | |
| VII | 14 | | 12 | | | |
| VIII | 15 | | 10 | | | |
| IX | 16 | | 5 | 36 | (36) | |
| IX | 17 | | 15 | | | |
| | 18 | | 10 | 25 | 25 | |
| X | 19 | | 5 | 5 | 30 | |
| XI | 20 | | 6 | 6 | 36 | |

15. Select the largest duration in column (f) which is less than 36, *i.e.* 31 for *columns V, VI, VII and VIII.*
16. Subtract 31 from 36 = 5.
17. Does one or more of the elements in the next column (IX) equal 5? *Yes, element* 16.
18. Allocate the columns concerned and that element to the work station and redraw the table (Table 15.5).
19. Is there a duration in column (f) of the new table equal to 36? *Yes, for columns IX, X and XI.*
20. Allocate the elements in these columns to the work station.

All 21 elements have now been assigned to four work stations in the manner shown in Figure 15.6, the balancing loss involved being:

$$\frac{n(C) - \Sigma t}{n(C)} \times 100$$

$$= \frac{4(36) - 143}{4(36)} \times 100$$

$$= 0.7\%$$

**Figure 15.6** Allocation of 21 elements to four work stations

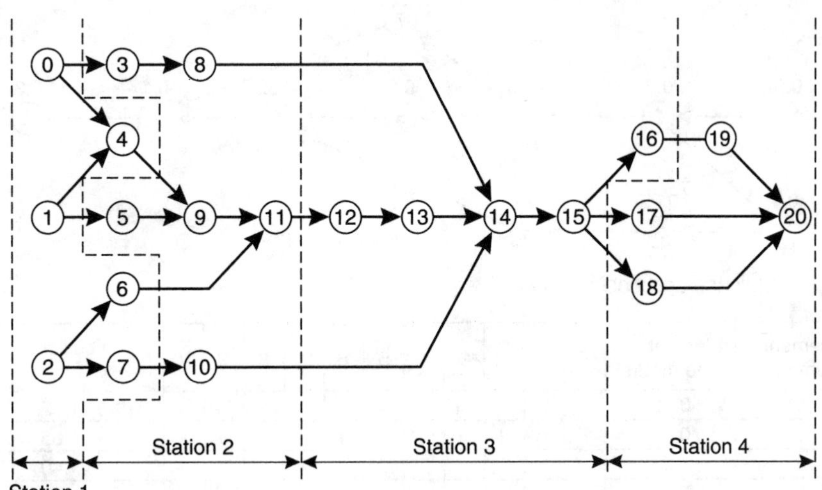


As can readily be seen from the example, this heuristic method is rapid, easy and often quite efficient. The allocation of elements is basically determined by precedence relationships, lateral transferability of elements being used to aid allocation when necessary. The originators of this method offer the following comments to aid in the application of the method.

(a) Permutability within columns is used to facilitate the selection of elements (tasks) of the length desired for optimum packing of the work stations. Lateral transferability helps to deploy the work elements (tasks) along the stations of the assembly line so they can be used where they best serve the packing solution.

(b) Generally the solutions are not unique. Elements (tasks) assigned to a station which belong, after the assignment is made, in one column of the precedence diagram can generally be permuted within the column. This allows the line supervisor some leeway to alter the sequence of work elements (tasks) without disturbing optimum balance.

(c) Long-time elements (tasks) are best disposed of first, if possible. Thus, if there is a choice between the assignment of an element of duration, say 20, and the assignment of two elements of duration, say 10 each, assign the larger element first. Small elements are saved for ease of manipulation at the end of the line.

(d) When moving elements laterally, the move is best made only as far to the right as is necessary to allow a sufficient choice of elements for the work station being considered.

In view of point (c) above, the *ranked positional weight* (RPW) method of line balancing, described next, might be considered a logical extension of the present method, since in the RPW method a heuristic procedure is used which allocates elements to stations according to both their position in the precedence diagram and their duration.

## *Ranked positional weights*

The ranked positional weight procedure (developed by Helgerson and Birnie) is a rapid, but approximate, method which has been shown to provide acceptably good solutions quicker than many of the alternative methods. It is capable of dealing with both precedence and zoning constraints. The procedure is best illustrated by considering a simple example.

**Figure 15.7** Element precedence diagram

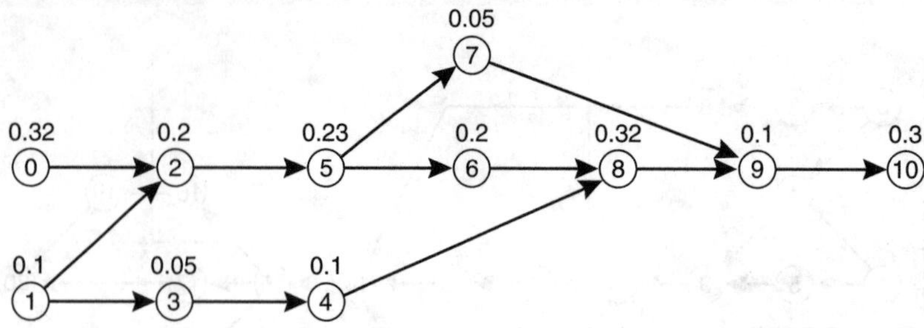


**Figure 15.8** Precedence and positional weights

| Element number | Element time (hours) | 0 | 1 | 2 | 3 | 4 | 5 | 6 | 7 | 8 | 9 | 10 | Positional weight |
|---|---|---|---|---|---|---|---|---|---|---|---|---|---|
| 0 | 0.32 | | | I | | | + | + | + | + | + | + | 1.72 |
| 1 | 0.1 | | | I | I | + | + | + | + | + | + | + | 1.65 |
| 2 | 0.2 | | | | | | I | + | + | + | + | + | 1.40 |
| 3 | 0.05 | | | | | I | | | | + | + | + | 0.87 |
| 4 | 0.1 | | | | | | | | | I | + | + | 0.82 |
| 5 | 0.23 | | | | | | | I | I | + | + | + | 1.20 |
| 6 | 0.2 | | | | | | | | | I | + | + | 0.92 |
| 7 | 0.05 | | | | | | | | | | I | + | 0.45 |
| 8 | 0.32 | | | | | | | | | | I | + | 0.72 |
| 9 | 0.1 | | | | | | | | | | | I | 0.40 |
| 10 | 0.3 | | | | | | | | | | | | 0.30 |

Assembly of a very simple component involves 11 minimum rational work elements. There are constraints on the order in which these elements are to be undertaken, but there are no zoning constraints. Figure 15.7 is a precedence diagram in which the circles depict work elements. Element 2 must follow elements 0 and 1 and must precede element 5, etc. The standard element times (hours) are also shown in Figure 15.7. In Figure 15.8 this same information is listed: in the first column the element number is given, and in the second its standard time. The middle of the table shows the element precedences; for example, element 0 is immediately followed by element 2, which in turn is followed by 5, which is followed by 6 and 7, and so on. A single mark indicates the element which follows immediately and crosses indicate elements which follow because of their relationship with other elements. The final column of the table gives the *positional weight* (*PW*) for each element. This is calculated by summing the element's own standard time and the standard time for all following elements. Thus, in the case of element 0:

$$
\begin{aligned}
\text{PW} = \text{element } & 0 = 0.32 \\
+ \text{element } & 2 = 0.20 \\
+ \text{element } & 5 = 0.23 \\
+ \text{element } & 6 = 0.20 \\
+ \text{element } & 7 = 0.05 \\
+ \text{element } & 8 = 0.32 \\
+ \text{element } & 9 = 0.10 \\
+ \text{element } & 10 = 0.30 = 1.72
\end{aligned}
$$

The positional weight is therefore a measure of the size of an element and its position in the sequence of elements.

In Table 15.6 the elements, their times and the immediate predecessors are given in order of decreasing positional weights.

**Table 15.6 Elements in order of positional weights**

| Element no. | 0 | 1 | 2 | 5 | 6 | 3 | 4 | 8 | 7 | 9 | 10 | Total |
|---|---|---|---|---|---|---|---|---|---|---|---|---|
| Element time | 0.32 | 0.1 | 0.2 | 0.23 | 0.2 | 0.05 | 0.1 | 0.32 | 0.05 | 0.1 | 0.3 | 1.97 |
| PW | 1.72 | 1.65 | 1.4 | 1.2 | 0.92 | 0.87 | 0.82 | 0.72 | 0.45 | 0.40 | 0.30 | |
| Predecessors (immediate) | - | - | 0, 1 | 2 | 5 | 1 | 3 | 4, 6 | 5 | 7, 8 | 9 | |

We are required to design a line with the minimum number of stations to provide a cycle time of 0.55 hours (i.e. an output of 1.82 per hour). Using Table 15.6, elements are allocated to work stations in order of decreasing positional weights and without violating precedence constraints. Element 0, with the highest PW of 1.72, is allocated first to station 1. This allocation is acceptable because element 0 has no immediate predecessors, and furthermore its element time is less than the spare time available in station 1 (see Table 15.7).

**Table 15.7 Element allocation for cycle time of 0.55 hours**

| Work station | Element | PW | Immediate predecessor | Element time | Cumulative station time (Z) | Unassigned station time (C − Z) |
|---|---|---|---|---|---|---|
| 1 | 0 | 1.72 | - | 0.32 | 0.32 | 0.23 |
| | 1 | 1.65 | - | 0.1 | 0.42 | 0.13 |
| | 3 | 0.87 | 1 | 0.05 | 0.47 | 0.08 |
| 2 | 2 | 1.4 | 0, 1 | 0.2 | 0.2 | 0.35 |
| | 5 | 1.2 | 2 | 0.23 | 0.43 | 0.12 |
| | 4 | 0.82 | 3 | 0.1 | 0.53 | 0.02 |
| 3 | 6 | 0.92 | 5 | 0.2 | 0.2 | 0.35 |
| | 8 | 0.72 | 4, 6 | 0.32 | 0.52 | 0.03 |
| 4 | 7 | 0.45 | 5 | 0.05 | 0.05 | 0.50 |
| | 9 | 0.4 | 7, 8 | 0.1 | 0.15 | 0.40 |
| | 10 | 0.3 | 9 | 0.3 | 0.45 | 0.10 |

C = 0.55

$$\text{Balancing loss} = \frac{4(0.55) - 1.97}{4(0.55)} \times 100 = 10.4\%$$

Element 1 is the next to be allocated since it has the next highest PW. It is acceptable in station 1 since no precedence constraints are violated and there is sufficient unassigned cycle time left to accommodate it.

The next highest PW belongs to element 2, but this cannot be assigned to station 1, even though its immediate predecessors have been assigned, because the unassigned station time remaining (0.13) is less than the element time (0.2).

Element 5 cannot be allocated because it must follow element 2; nor is there enough time available.

Element 6 cannot be allocated to station 2 for the same reasons.

Element 3 can be allocated to station 1 since its immediate predecessor is already allocated and there is enough time available.

Of the remaining elements only 7 is short enough for accommodation in station 1, but it cannot be allocated here because it must follow element 5.

The same procedure is now repeated for the remaining stations.

Four work stations are required for this line, and the initial allocation gives a balancing loss of 10.4%. Notice that there is unassigned time at each station, the largest work station time of 0.53 hours occurring at station 2. In fact we now have a situation similar to the one depicted in Figure 15.4(b).

For the specified output required (1.82 per hour) there is no better solution than the one given above, but, if other considerations permit, the cycle time could be reduced to 0.53 hours with a corresponding increase in output to 1.89 per hour and a reduction of balancing loss to 7%. A reduction of the cycle time to less than 0.53 hours would necessitate the use of five work stations.

There is really little point in retaining a cycle time of 0.55 hours in this case, since to do so is merely to introduce inefficiency into the system for the sake of obtaining a given output. Here, as in many cases of line balancing, it is desirable to modify output in order to minimize balancing loss. In this case, therefore, the line balancing procedure would be first to seek a balance for a given cycle time $C$, and then to minimize the cycle time for the same number of work stations. A flow diagram for such a procedure using the ranked positional weight (RPW) technique is shown in Figure 15.9.

Very many refinements of this basic RPW method have been proposed, and many computer programs are available.

## COMSOAL

An interesting method of line balancing called COMSOAL (computer method of sequencing operations for assembly lines) was developed by Arcus. COMSOAL uses a computer to sample data and simulate possible line balances. The simulation follows the following comparatively simple basic procedure:

(a) Consider the job in terms of a precedence diagram of minimum rational work elements of the type shown in Figure 15.7. Construct a list (List A) showing, in one column, all work elements and, in an adjacent column, the total number of elements which *immediately precede* them in the precedence diagram. (Such a list based on Figure 15.7 is shown in Table 15.8).

(b) Construct a list (List B) showing all elements which have *no* immediate predecessors (i.e. elements with a zero in the second column of List A (Table 15.9)).

(c) Select at random one element from List B, say element 0.

(d) Eliminate the selected element from List B and move all elements below the selected element up one position.

(e) Eliminate the selected element from the precedence diagram and update List A.

(f) Add to List B those elements which immediately follow the selected element and now have no immediate predecessors.

This simple procedure is then repeated until a sequence containing all elements has been constructed. The elements (in this order) are then assigned to station 1, 2, 3, etc., the cycle time at each station being diminished until no further elements can be accommodated, at which stage the next element is assigned to the next station. The number of stations used in the balance is counted, and compared with the previous best balance. If there is an improvement the new balance is stored in the computer and the previous best discarded; thus by generating a fairly large set of possible solutions a good assembly line balance can be obtained.

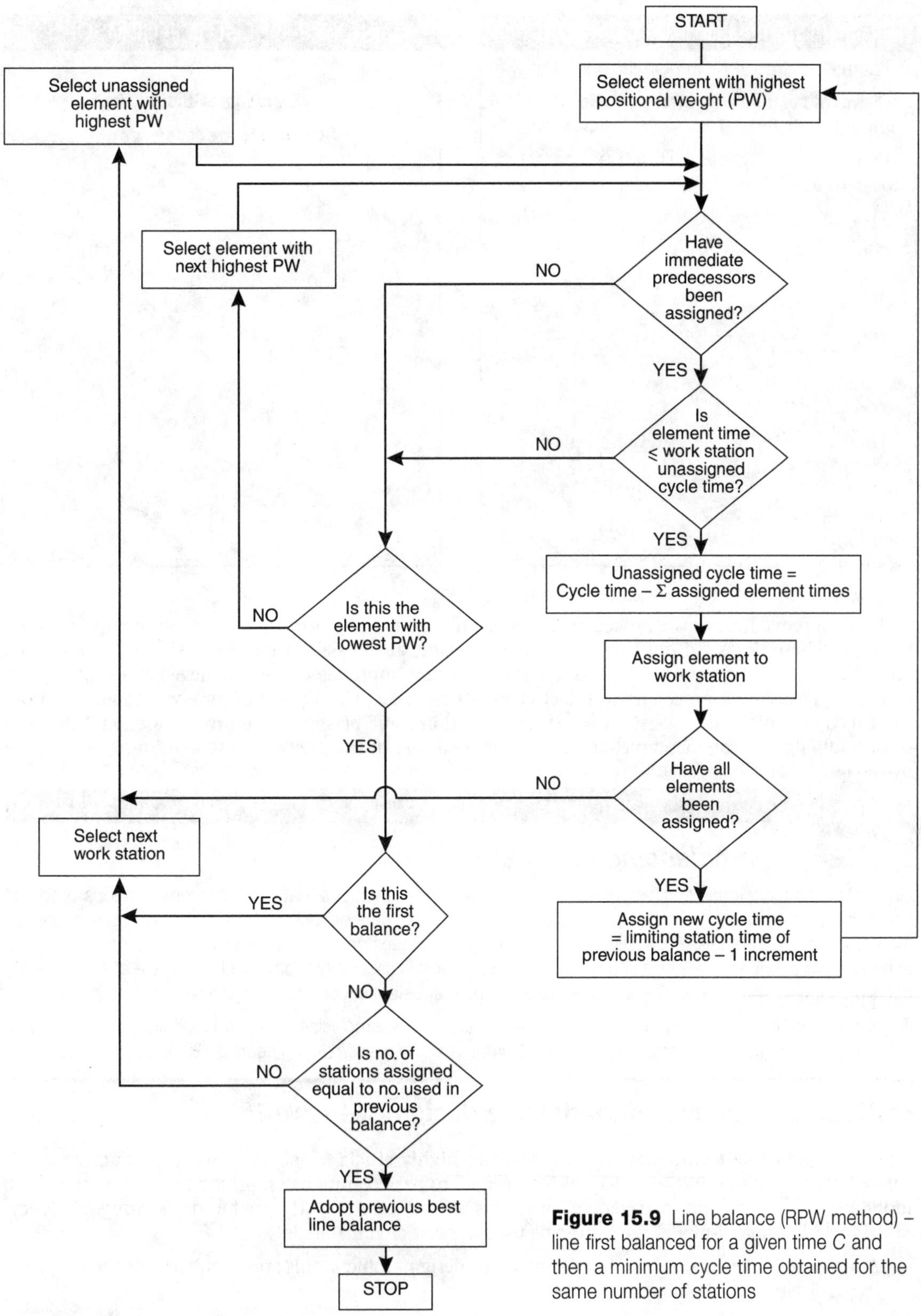


**Figure 15.9** Line balance (RPW method) – line first balanced for a given time *C* and then a minimum cycle time obtained for the same number of stations

**Table 15.8 List 'A' – COMSOAL**

| Element no. | No. of immediate predecessors |
|---|---|
| 0 | 0 |
| 1 | 0 |
| 2 | 2 |
| 3 | 1 |
| 4 | 1 |
| 5 | 1 |
| 6 | 1 |
| 7 | 1 |
| 8 | 2 |
| 9 | 2 |
| 10 | 1 |

**Table 15.9 List 'B' – COMSOAL**

| Elements without immediate predecessors |
|---|
| 0 |
| 1 |

Arcus improved this basic procedure by extracting from List B a further list, C, consisting of those elements whose times did not exceed the time available at the station under consideration, and then selecting elements randomly from this new list. A further improvement was achieved by using a biased or weighted sampling procedure to select elements from List C, in place of purely random selection. Arcus also incorporated a procedure by which a solution could be aborted before completion if the total station idle time of the incomplete solution exceeded that of the previous best solution.

**EXAMPLE**

### *Line balancing in a bank*

Line balancing techniques can be applied to bank processing functions that produce homogeneous products having fairly deterministic demand and processing time. An example of such a processing function is an installment lending documentation operation. Line balancing techniques are used to determine the optimal staff level and job assignment scheme for this operation. In this case, the assembly line balancing module of a proprietary decision support software package is used to show how substantial cost savings can result.

Source: Levary, R. R. and Renfro, M. D. (1991) Application of assembly line balancing techniques to installment lending operations of commercial banks. *Computers and Industrial Engineering*, **20**(1), pp. 105–109.

## Multi-model and mixed-model line design *(see Table 15.1)*

The use of flow line techniques certainly leads to highly efficient operation when product variety is small, but any increase in the variety of the product to be accommodated on the line not only leads to more complex design and management problems but will often result in reduced operating efficiency. Multi-model or mixed-model lines must be used in such circumstances.

(a) ***Multi-model line***. Again assuming a simple line design problem, this approach requires the following major decisions to be made:

1. How will the line be 'balanced'?
2. What will be the batch sizes of the models?
3. In what order will the batches be processed? (The batch sequencing problem.)

(b) ***Mixed-model line.*** Here the major decisions are:
1. How will the line be balanced?
2. In what order will the models be launched into the line? (The model sequencing problem.)

## Multi-model lines

The several models processed in batches on a multi-model line may be either different items or different versions of the same item, but in either case the different models or products will have similar, though not identical, processing requirements, since otherwise there would be little justification in dealing with them on the same basic line.

In practice, in running a multi-model line, the line is set up for one model, then adjustments are made to the line prior to the processing of a batch of the second model, and so on. We can therefore consider the line design problem as being a succession of separate line design problems, and hence decisions (1) and (2) above may be considered in the manner outlined previously. Decision (2), batch sizes, was dealt with in detail in Chapter 14, so we shall be concerned here only with decision (3), the batch sequencing problem.

| Cost ↗ | | Succeeding model | | | |
|---|---|---|---|---|---|
| | | A | B | C | D |
| Preceding model | A | 0 | 100 | 150 | 80 |
| | B | 50 | 0 | 100 | 75 |
| | C | 80 | 40 | 0 | 110 |
| | D | 115 | 100 | 60 | 0 |

**Figure 15.10** Setting-up cost associated with pairs of models

The optimum sequence for the batches of different models is influenced by the cost of setting up the line. The total cost of setting up the line comprises the cost of tool and machine changeovers, tool and machine re-setting, machine and labour idle time, etc., and is clearly influenced by the nature of the preceding and succeeding models. The problem, therefore, is to determine the sequence order of the model batches to minimize the total setting-up cost over a given period of time.

One attractive and simple technique which will *often* give a solution to the batch sequencing problem is the assignment method of linear programming. The matrix shown in Figure 15.10 shows the setting-up cost associated with pairs of models, i.e. the figures in the matrix are the costs of changing the line from a set-up suitable for processing of the 'preceding' model to one suitable for processing of the 'succeeding' model. The zeros appear in the diagonal of this matrix, because these batch sequences involve no changes in the line set-up; however, since our objective is to determine the least cost of changes, we must ensure that the diagonal elements do not feature in the solution by attaching very high cost values to them (in this case a cost of 1000).

| Cost ↗ | | Succeeding model | | | |
|---|---|---|---|---|---|
| | | A | B | C | D |
| Preceding model | A | 920 | 20 | 70 | [0] |
| | B | [0] | 950 | 50 | 25 |
| | C | 40 | [0] | 960 | 70 |
| | D | 55 | 40 | [0] | 940 |

N.B. A cost of 1000 was allocated to the diagonal elements

**Figure 15.11** Least cost solution to the assignment problem in Figure 15.10

The solution to this assignment problem, which is shown in Figure 15.11, indicates that for minimum setting-up cost, model D must follow model A, model A must follow model B, B must follow C, and C must follow D. In other words, starting with model A, the model batch sequence would be as follows:

A–D–C–B–A–D–C and so on.

## Mixed-model lines

The advantage of this type of processing is that, unlike with multi-model lines, a steady flow is produced in order to meet demand requirements, theoretically without the need for large stocks of finished goods. The major disadvantages arise from the differing work contents of the models, resulting in the uneven flow of work and consequent station idle time and/or congestion of semi-finished products.

This type of line undoubtedly presents the most complex design and operating problems; we will summarize the issues involved and describe briefly some of the solutions that have been used. We shall deal mainly with the line balancing and the model sequencing problems, the latter being the more complex.

## Balancing

Line balancing for mixed-model lines might be considered merely as several single-model balancing problems, i.e. each model could be considered separately and the total work content divided as equally as possible between the work stations. Consider a case where a line is built for the processing of two similar models of a product, A and B. The work elements of model A are allocated to the work stations so that during the periods in which A is being processed, balancing loss is minimized. Similarly, the work elements of B are allocated to work stations in order to minimize balancing loss during the processing of model B. Such a procedure is fairly satisfactory when the models to be processed are of a similar nature, i.e. when the processing of each model involves similar work elements to be undertaken in a similar order or when the processing of all models merely involves the repetition of similar work elements. When such circumstances apply, each station will be required to do the same type of work irrespective of which model is being produced. If, on the other hand, basically dissimilar models are to be processed, then independent line balancing for each will often result in dissimilar work elements being allocated to each station. In circumstances such as these, balancing should be undertaken in such a way as to ensure that similar work elements are allocated to the same work stations or groups of stations, irrespective of which model is being processed. A method by which this might be achieved is to assign elements to stations on a total time rather than a cycle time basis.

Consider the case mentioned above, Two models, A and B, are to be processed on the same line. Model A is the product we considered previously (Figure 15.7) and model B is dissimilar but nevertheless has several work elements in common with Model A.

The precedence relationship of the elements of both models is shown in Figure 15.12 (elements 1, 3, 4, 7, 8 and 9 are common to both models). The output requirements are: model A, 200 per week; model B, 100 per week. Table 15.10 gives all the details that we shall require for balancing the line. Column (b) gives the element duration. Column (e) shows the number of times the work element must be performed during the week to satisfy the output requirements of both models. The total time required for each work element per week is given in column (f) (total time/week = b × e).

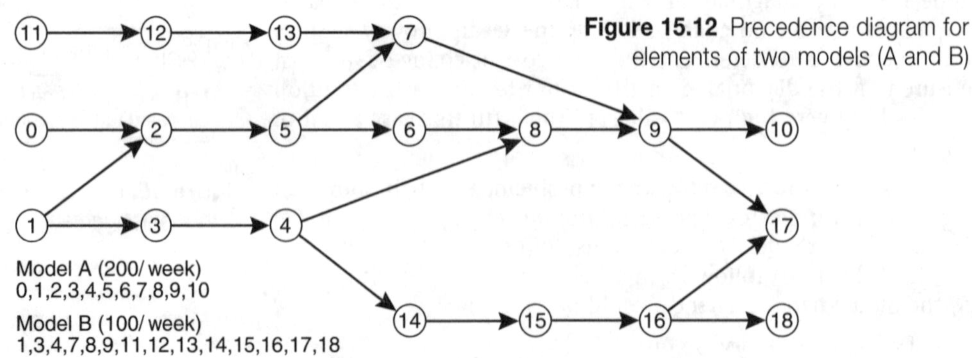


**Figure 15.12** Precedence diagram for elements of two models (A and B)

The line balance is obtained using the ranked positional weights technique, but instead of calculating positional weights by summing element times, they are found by summing total times.[5] All that now remains is to allocate elements to work stations. The available time per station per week is considered to be 40 hours (five eight-hour days) and the element allocation is shown in Table 15.11. Balancing loss is 5.1% but it has been necessary to combine several work stations because the total time for four elements (0, 5, 8 and 10) is greater than the available 40 hours.

These figures indicate that, in respect of one week's production, we have achieved quite a respectable line balance. Notice, however, that such a method of line balancing is justified *only* when production is truly *mixed*-model. Had there been a tendency to send models through the line in batches rather than individually, a quite unsatisfactory situation would have resulted. If a batch of model A is being processed, stations 1, 8, 9, 10, 11, 13, 14 and 15 will be under-utilized and incur a great deal of

**Table 15.10 Data for two-model line balancing problem**

| (a) Element no. | (b) Element duration (h) | (c) No. of times elements must be performed | (d) | (e) | (f) Total time/wk (h) | (g) Positional weight (using total times) |
|---|---|---|---|---|---|---|
| | | A | B | Total/wk | $\Sigma = 569$ | |
| 0 | 0.32 | 200 | 0 | 200 | 64 | 411 |
| 1 | 0.1 | 200 | 100 | 300 | 30 | 463 |
| 2 | 0.2 | 200 | 0 | 200 | 40 | 347 |
| 3 | 0.05 | 200 | 100 | 300 | 15 | 292 |
| 4 | 0.1 | 200 | 100 | 300 | 30 | 277 |
| 5 | 0.23 | 200 | 0 | 200 | 46 | 307 |
| 6 | 0.2 | 200 | 0 | 200 | 40 | 246 |
| 7 | 0.05 | 200 | 100 | 300 | 15 | 125 |
| 8 | 0.32 | 200 | 100 | 300 | 96 | 206 |
| 9 | 0.1 | 200 | 100 | 300 | 30 | 110 |
| 10 | 0.3 | 200 | 0 | 200 | 60 | 60 |
| 11 | 0.1 | 0 | 100 | 100 | 10 | 167 |
| 12 | 0.15 | 0 | 100 | 100 | 15 | 157 |
| 13 | 0.17 | 0 | 100 | 100 | 17 | 142 |
| 14 | 0.08 | 0 | 100 | 100 | 8 | 61 |
| 15 | 0.07 | 0 | 100 | 100 | 7 | 53 |
| 16 | 0.13 | 0 | 100 | 100 | 13 | 46 |
| 17 | 0.2 | 0 | 100 | 100 | 20 | 20 |
| 18 | 0.13 | 0 | 100 | 100 | 13 | 13 |

[5] Other approaches are available, typically aiming to balance the time for average, or for the worst situation, e.g. Milas, G. H. (1990) Assembly line balancing – let's remove the mystery. *Industrial Engineering*, **22**(5), pp. 31–36. Berger, I., Bourjolly, J. M. and Laporte, G. (1992) Branch and bound – algorithms for the multi-product assembly line balancing problem. *European Journal of Operations Research*, **58**(2), pp. 215–222.

**Table 15.11 Two-model assembly line balance**

| Station no. | Element no. | Total time per week for element (h) | Time remaining from 40-hour (h) |
|---|---|---|---|
| 1 | 1 | 30 | 10 |
| | 11 | 10 | 0 |
| 2, 3 | 0 | 64 | 16 |
| | 3 | 15 | 1 |
| 4 | 2 | 40 | 0 |
| 5, 6 | 5 | 46 | 34 |
| | 4 | 30 | 4 |
| 7 | 6 | 40 | 0 |
| 8, 9, 10 | 8 | 96 | 24 |
| | 12 | 15 | 9 |
| | 14 | 8 | 1 |
| 11 | 13 | 17 | 23 |
| | 7 | 15 | 8 |
| | 15 | 7 | 1 |
| 12 | 9 | 30 | 10 |
| 13, 14 | 10 | 60 | 20 |
| | 16 | 13 | 7 |
| 15 | 17 | 20 | 20 |
| | 18 | 13 | 7 |

balancing loss, and while the batch of model B is being processed stations 2, 3, 4, 5, 6, 7, 13 and 14 will be under-utilized. Only if Model A and model B are processed concurrently on the line, and particularly if the line has been designed to include buffer stocks between stations, will a satisfactory situation result from the allo-cation shown in Table 15.11. In other words, this method of 'combined' line balancing for a shift's or a week's production of all models is beneficial where:

(a) models are to be processed concurrently on the line, and not in batches;

(b) dissimilar work elements are involved and it is desirable to ensure that work of a similar nature is allocated to separate stations or groups of stations.

## Sequencing

The efficient design and operation of mixed-model lines depend on the solution of two problems: first, the line balancing problem just discussed, and second, the model sequencing problem. The latter problem is concerned both with the time interval between the 'launching' or starting of models onto the

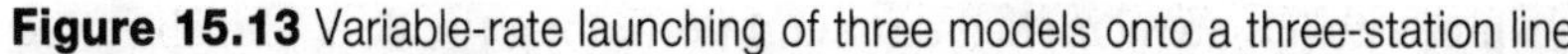

**Figure 15.13** Variable-rate launching of three models onto a three-station line

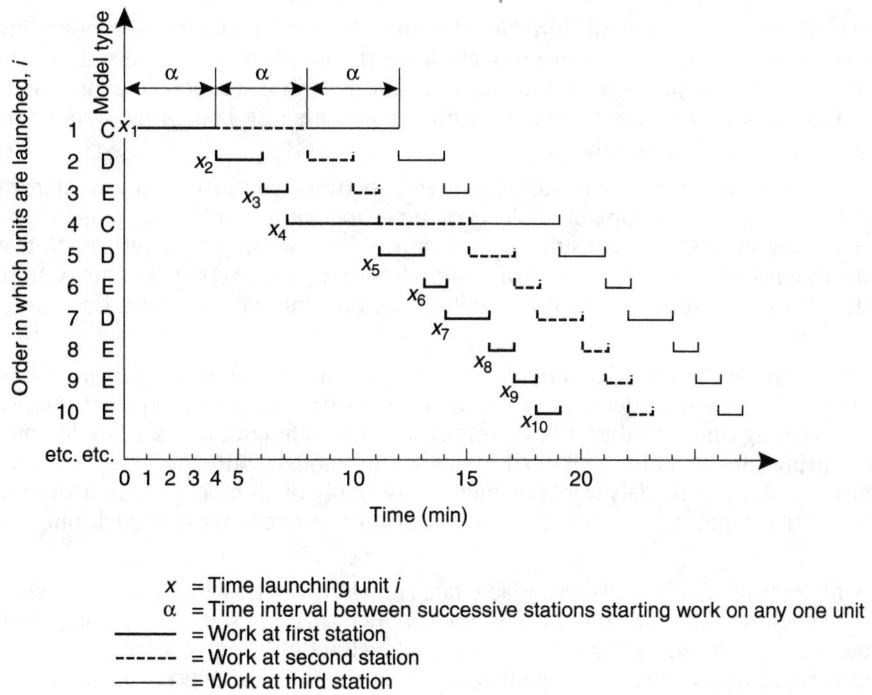


**Figure 15.14** Increase in item waiting time after launch of model C with longer cycle time

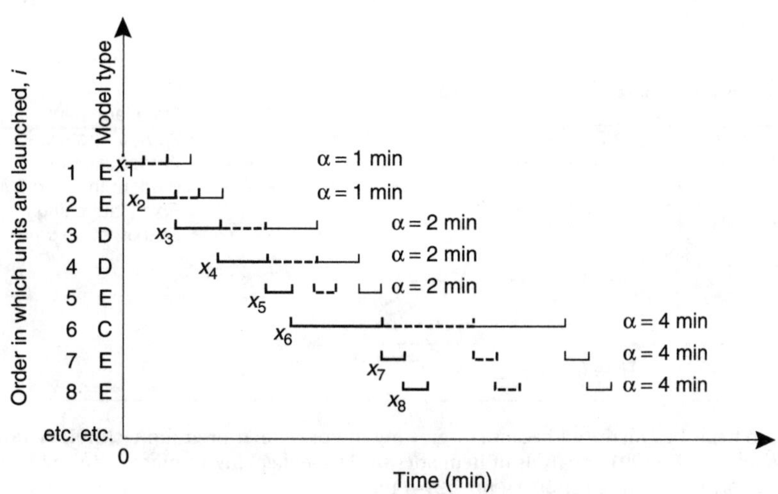

line, and also with the *order* in which models are launched onto and flow along the line. The objective of such sequencing is to provide for the best utilization of the line, high utilization being associated with minimum station idle time and minimum congestion of work along the line (item waiting).[6]

Two systems of launching are used: *variable rate* and *fixed rate*. In variable-rate launching the time interval between the starting of successive models down the line is equal to the station cycle time of the leading model. For example, if three models, C, D and E, whose station cycle times are 4, 2 and 1 minutes respectively, are to be assembled on a line, a variable-rate launching system such as that shown in Figure 15.13 might be used.

It is quite clear from this figure that the time interval between successive stations starting work on any one model ($\alpha$) is equal to the longest model cycle time, and consequently, when models with shorter cycle times are being processed, a considerable amount of item waiting time results. Notice also that this same idle time results even when none of the models with the longer cycle time is present on the line. (After the 19th minute there are no model Cs on the line, yet the time interval is still four minutes.)

There is little that can be done by way of model sequencing to minimize this item waiting time, since, assuming that for each model the cycle time remains constant, and is equal at each station, the amount of item waiting time will always be determined by the difference in model cycle times. A reduction in item waiting time would be obtained by launching models with shorter cycle times first, but unless complete batching of models were possible, i.e. assembly of all model Es, then all model Ds and finally model Cs, the improvement would last only until it was necessary to launch one model C (see Figure 15.14).

An important practical disadvantage of variable-rate launching occurs where there is a need for related activities to be synchronized with the line, e.g. the supply of materials at points along the line or the joining of two or more lines. In such a case these related activities must be carefully planned and controlled to synchronize with the variable launching on the line. In such circumstances a system of fixed-rate launching may be preferable, in which units are launched or started on the line at regular intervals ($\gamma$).

It is clear from Figure 15.15 that the fixed launching interval must not be greater than the time of the first unit or model launched, otherwise station idle time will result, i.e.

**Figure 15.15** Fixed-rate launching system for three-station assembly line

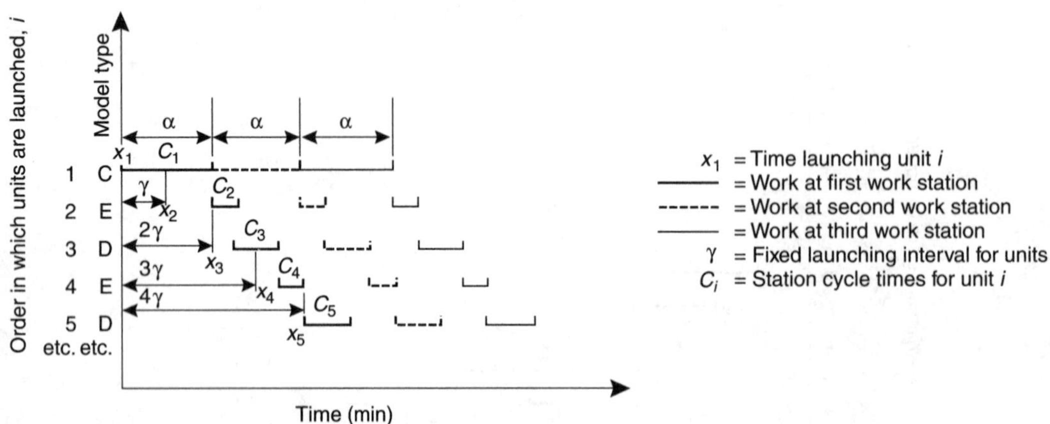


[6] Interest in these problems has increased because of growing use of cellular or group technology principles, e.g. Park, T. and Streudel, H. J. (1991) Analysis of heuristics for job sequencing in manufacturing flow line work cells. *Computers and Industrial Engineering*, **20**(1), pp. 129–140.

$$\gamma \leq C_1$$

Similarly:

$$2\gamma \leq C_1 + C_2$$
$$3\gamma \leq C_1 + C_2 + C_3$$
$$4\gamma \leq C_1 + C_2 + C_3 + C_4$$

We can rewrite these requirements as follows:

$$\gamma \leq C_1$$

$$\gamma \leq \frac{C_1 + C_2}{2}$$

$$\gamma \leq \frac{C_1 + C_2 + C_3}{3}$$

$$\gamma \leq \frac{C_1 + C_2 + C_3 + C_4}{4}$$

$$\vdots \qquad \vdots$$

$$\gamma \leq \frac{C_1 + C_2 + C_3 + C_4 + \ldots + C_m}{m}$$

where $m$ = total number of units to be produced.

Each of the requirements must be satisfied simultaneously if station idle time is to be avoided.

From Figure 15.15 it can also be seen that $\alpha$, the time interval between successive stations starting work on any one unit, must ideally be equal to the longest station cycle time:

$$\alpha_{\text{optimum}} = \text{Max. } C$$

and it can be shown that the optimum value for $\gamma$ is equal to the average of the station cycle times for all units:

$$\gamma_{\text{optimum}} = \frac{\Sigma N_j C_j}{\Sigma N_j}$$

where $N_j$ = total number of model $j$ required
$C_j$ = cycle time for model $j$.

In order to avoid both operator idle time and the congestion of work on the line, the following double inequality must be satisfied each time a unit is launched onto the line:

$$0 \leq \left(\sum_{h=1}^{i} C_h\right) - i\gamma \leq \alpha - \gamma$$

where $C_h$ = cycle time.

It is usually impossible, unless both models and station times are very carefully chosen, to avoid both station idle time and work congestion, but, by careful ordering of the models, both of these inefficiencies can be minimized. To select the correct order a decision must be made every time a unit is launched onto the line, i.e. every step $i$. For example, in order to avoid station idle time and minimize work congestion, models should be launched onto the line so that for every launching or step $i$, the following function is minimized:

$$\left(\sum_{h=1}^{i} C_h\right) - i\gamma$$

**EXAMPLE**

Three models, A, B and C, of a particular product are assembled concurrently on an assembly line.

The quantities required over a given period and the model cycle times are as follows:

| Model | No. of units required | Model cycle time |
|---|---|---|
| $j$ | $N$ | $C_j$ |
| A | 60 | 0.5 |
| B | 110 | 0.6 |
| C | 55 | 0.8 |

Calculate the fixed interval at which units must be launched onto the line, and show how the sequence of models might be determined in order to avoid station idle time:

*Answer*

$$\gamma = \frac{\Sigma N_j C_j}{\Sigma N} = \frac{30 + 66 + 44}{60 + 110 + 55}$$

$$= 0.62$$

Units must be launched onto the line in such a way that multiples of the launching interval (ig) are less than, but as nearly equal as possible to, the sum of the model cycle times,

$$\left(\sum_{h=1}^{i} C_h\right)$$

Such a method of launching is illustrated in Table 15.12.

Notice that in this example the optimum sequence of models results from the repeated launching of models in the order: C–A–B–B–B, but notice also that the continual launching of units in this order would not lead to the assembly of the required number of each model in the given time period (too many of model B and too few of models A and C would be completed). Consequently, in practice it would be necessary to depart from this optimal procedure to some extent in order to satisfy manufacturing requirements. Had the figure in the final column ($\Sigma C_h - i\gamma$) been greater than $\alpha - \gamma$ (0.18) at any time, this would have indicated that the operator would have been forced out of his or her work station in order to complete the work on the particular unit, or alternatively that the unit would continue to the next station incomplete.

# THE DESIGN OF 'COMPLEX' FLOW LINES

## Human aspects of assembly line design *(see also Chapter 9)*

The major assumption in our discussion of simple flow line design was that elements of work require a given constant time – the standard element time. In the chapters on work design the validity of the assumption that there was a single best method of doing a job and consequently a single time for the job was questioned. But even assuming this to be the case, or assuming that for some other reason a worker continually adopts the specified work method, it still does not follow that the time required will be constant. Many things may affect the time required to complete the operation, e.g. availability of materials.

**Table 15.12 Fixed-interval launching of units onto an assembly line**

| Unit $i$ | $i\gamma$ | Model | Model cycle time $C_i$ | $\sum_{h=1}^{i} C_h$ | $\left(\sum_{h=1}^{i} C_h\right) - i\gamma$ |
|---|---|---|---|---|---|
| 1 | 0.62 | C | 0.8 | 0.8 | 0.18 |
| 2 | 1.24 | A | 0.5 | 1.3 | 0.06 |
| 3 | 1.86 | B | 0.6 | 1.9 | 0.04 |
| 4 | 2.48 | B | 0.6 | 2.5 | 0.02 |
| 5 | 3.10 | B | 0.6 | 3.1 | 0.00 |
| 6 | 3.72 | C | 0.8 | 3.9 | 0.18 |
| 7 | 4.34 | A | 0.5 | 4.4 | 0.06 |
| 8 | 4.96 | B | 0.6 | 5.0 | 0.04 |
| 9 | 5.58 | B | 0.6 | 5.6 | 0.02 |
| 10 | 6.20 | B | 0.6 | 6.2 | 0.00 |
| 11 | 6.82 | C | 0.8 | 7.0 | 0.18 |
| 12 | 7.44 | A | 0.5 | 7.5 | 0.06 |
| 13 | 8.06 | B | 0.6 | 8.1 | 0.04 |
| 14 | 8.68 | B | 0.6 | 8.7 | 0.02 |
| 15 | 9.30 | B | 0.6 | 9.3 | 0.00 |
| 16 | 9.92 | C | 0.8 | 10.1 | 0.18 |
| 17 | 10.54 | A | 0.5 | 10.6 | 0.06 |
| 18 | 11.16 | B | 0.6 | 11.2 | 0.04 |
| 19 | 11.78 | B | 0.6 | 11.8 | 0.02 |
| 20 | 12.40 | B | 0.6 | 12.4 | 0.00 |
| 21 | 13.02 | C | 0.8 | 13.2 | 0.18 |
| 22 | 13.64 | A | 0.5 | 13.7 | 0.07 |
| ... | ... | ... | ... | ... | ... |
| etc. | etc. | etc. | etc. | etc. | etc. |

This phenomenon of variability is the fundamental difference between lines involving human operators and those depending exclusively on 'machines'. It is not invalid to assume that machines at stations require a constant time for elements of work, but it is unrealistic to make the same assumption about human beings. The procedures described above are adequate by themselves for the design of fully automated/mechanical lines, but insufficient for the design of lines involving workers.

It has been found that unpaced work time distributions (the time taken by workers to perform elements of work or operations) are usually unimodal and positively skewed, i.e. the distributions have a single peak, and a long 'tail' to the right of the peak.

Consider the work time distribution shown in Figure 15.16. This is the distribution which would result in the absence of any pacing influence or imposed work time. If a line is designed in which there is *rigid pacing* and in which the worker is allowed the mean time only to complete the task, then on some occasions he or she may be unable to complete the task, and the product would pass on down the line partially completed, later to be rejected. On the remaining occasions the worker would have more time available than required, and while idle time may not necessarily result, there would certainly be an under-utilization of the worker.

This phenomenon is referred to as *system loss* and often occurs where workers on lines are subject to some form of pacing. In practice, rigid pacing rarely occurs but some degree of pacing, involving a tolerance about a given time, often occurs.

**Figure 15.16** Unpaced work time distribution

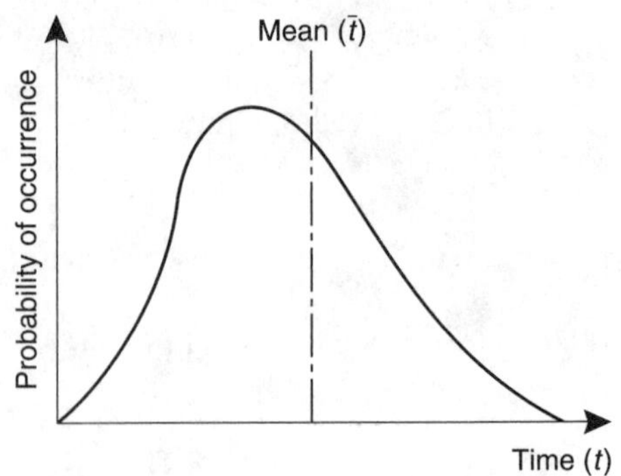


## System loss

It has been found that the differences in average operation times of workers on lines are not primarily a result of differences in standard or work station times, but largely a result of differences in the speed at which workers work. In other words, it appears that the losses resulting from workers' variable operation times (system loss) are perhaps more important than the losses resulting from uneven allocation of work to stations (balancing loss). Consequently the problem of line design is not primarily the equal division of work between stations but the adaptation of tasks to the speed of the workers.

There are three ways in which we might attempt to overcome the problem of system loss, or at least reduce it. One solution often suggested involves an increase in the cycle time. If a cycle time longer than the mean unpaced work cycle time is adopted then fewer occasions will arise on which the worker has insufficient time to complete the operation. This is, however, quite unsatisfactory since there are now more occasions on which the worker could complete the operation in less than the time available. There may be some marginal benefit in increasing the cycle time if the cost of faulty or incomplete items is particularly high, but in general such a 'solution' does not reduce total system loss.

A better approach is to eliminate or reduce the cause of the problem, i.e. the pacing effect. There are two ways in which we can attempt to do this; both involve making the items available to the worker for a longer period of time. Take, for example, a line consisting of workers located at a bench above which jobs travel by means of a conveyor belt with suspended baskets. The worker must take a job off the belt, perform the operation and replace it on the belt, which carries it to the next station. Jobs spaced at 5 m intervals on a belt moving at 5 m/min will produce an output of 60 products/hour. The same output will result from a spacing of 10 m and a belt speed of 10 m/min, or a spacing of 2.5 m and a belt speed of 2.5 m/min. But each of these different arrangements has different consequences for the worker, who can reach only a certain distance either side of the work station. If the worker can reach 2.5 m either way, then in the first case each job will be within reach and available for one minute only, in the second case for half a minute, and in the last case two minutes. Clearly the greater the time the job is available to the worker the lower is the pacing effect, and system loss is reduced.

On lines where jobs pass directly from one worker to the next, every worker, except the one at the first station on the line, is dependent on the previous worker. Under such conditions the work must be strictly paced in order to avoid excessive labour idle time. If, e.g. because of faulty material, a worker at one station takes longer than the cycle time to complete the operation, then the worker at the next station on the line will have to wait for work (unless coincidentally he or she also has exceeded the cycle time for his or her operation). This coupling or interdependence of stations necessitates pacing, but if the stations could be decoupled in some way the pacing effect, and also system loss, could be reduced.

## Buffer stocks *(see also Chapter 17)*

The way in which this is done is to introduce buffer stocks of jobs between stations, so that temporary hold-ups or delays at stations do not immediately result in idle time at subsequent stations. There are certain disadvantages in using buffer stocks on lines. Work-in-progress stock and hence tied-up capital will be increased, and additional space will be required. In fact, in some cases, because of the size of the items, it may be quite unrealistic to consider using buffer stocks. However, in many situations buffer stocks are an important feature of assembly line operation.

Figure 15.17, showing the performance of perfectly balanced lines of various lengths, indicates that the use of buffer stocks of only one item has a significant effect on system loss and, furthermore, that system loss increases as the number of stations increases.

**Figure 15.17** System losses related to length and layout of line

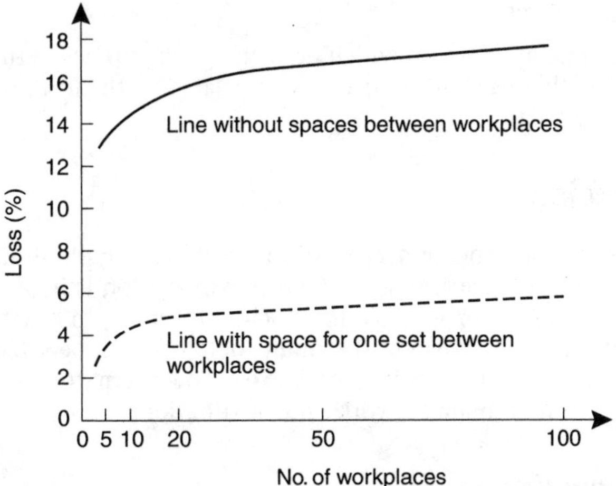


It is possible using queuing theory to calculate the effect of inter-station buffer stocks on line efficiency. In order to be able to use the conventional formulae, one must assume that work time distributions conform to the negative exponential distribution. Furthermore, using this approach it is difficult to treat lines of more than two stations. Despite these assumptions the results of such calculations merit examination. If we assume that an infinite stock is available for the first station and that no stock is allowed between the stations, then the utilization of the line is only 67%, whereas the introduction of buffer stocks between the stations increases utilization as follows:

| Buffer stock | Utilization (%) |
|---|---|
| 2 | 75 |
| 3 | 80 |
| 4 | 83 |
| 8 | 90 |

Some research work has been undertaken in an attempt to determine the optimum inter-station buffer stock capacity (i.e. the maximum amount of buffer stock to allow between stations) under more practical conditions. This research has again depended on assumptions about the nature of work time distribution and also on the assumption of a 'steady state', i.e. that the line has been operating for a sufficient time to allow a stable condition to arise at each station. Young,[7] using a model which assumes steady-state conditions and the normal work time distribution, developed a formula for the optimum buffer stock capacity, as follows:

$$X = \frac{KL_2\sigma^{0.61}}{L_1}$$

where $X$ = optimum buffer capacity at stages in a balanced production line
$L_2$ = idle facilities cost per unit time
$L_1$ = unit inventory cost per unit time
$\sigma$ = standard deviation of the normally distributed work times
$K$ = a constant which depends on the number of stations, e.g.
$K$ = 0.39 for four stages
0.43 for six stages
0.47 for eight stages

Young used a computer to simulate lines (in which no machine maintenance time was required) to test the above formula. He found that the buffer capacities calculated by the formula were very close to the simulated optimum buffer capacities.

## Complex line balancing

Our previous description of line balancing dealt with the relatively simple situation where work times were assumed to be constant. We have seen now that this assumption is invalid. We should therefore consider the problem of balancing for variable (or stochastic) times. In practice, lines will often be balanced in the manner described above, and the results obtained will be satisfactory for all practical purposes, especially where inter-station buffer stocks exist. The alternative is to use a heuristic[8] or a simulation[9] approach using real or assumed work time distributions.

## Types of manual flow lines

When discussing the simple lines above it was unnecessary to distinguish between different methods of line operation since, in the simple case, there is really only one logical operating method, i.e. all stations have the same fixed cycle time, and workflow along the line is regular, since the transfer or movement of items, between all stations takes place at the same time. In practice not only is the manner in which manual flow lines operate more complex than that described above, because of the characteristic work element and service-time variability, but there are also many possible methods of operation.

We can first identify two basic types of manual flow line:

(a) ***Non-mechanical lines***, consisting of lines which do not use a moving belt or conveyor (e.g. the Mamma Mia case) for the transfer of work along the line or between stations. Such lines, although probably making use of power and hand tools, are essentially manually operated.

(b) ***Moving-belt lines***, consisting of all those types of lines which use a continually moving belt or conveyor for the transfer of items along the line and/or between stations.

---

[7] Young, H. H. (1967) Optimization models for production lines. *Journal of Industrial Engineering*, **XVIII**(1), pp. 70–78.

[8] For example, Shin, D. and Min, H. (1991) Uniform assembly line balancing with stochastic task times in just in time manufacturing. *International Journal of Operations and Productivity Management*, **11**(8), pp. 23–34.

[9] See Appendix III.

Moving-belt lines can be broken down into two further categories:

(a) items are removable from the belt;

(b) items are fixed to the belt.

The second of these two categories can be further divided to give a total of five types of line. The five types are described briefly below and their characteristics are summarized in Table 15.13.

## Non-mechanical lines

If all the stations on the flow lines are able to retain items until they have been completed and are able to pass items to the next station on completion, there is a variable-cycle-time situation in which, because there is no maximum limit, incomplete items should not be produced. Furthermore, if such a method of operation were used, there should be no under-utilization of stations or idle time, since the cycle time would always be equal to the service time. In practice, it is not normally possible to operate a line in this manner because of the interdependence of stations. Whilst it is possible to avoid the output of incomplete items, idle time cannot be avoided, and will occur for two reasons:

(a) because, on occasions, stations will be starved of work, i.e. once an item has been passed to the next station, a delay will follow before another item becomes available from the previous station;

(b) because, on occasions, a worker will be prevented from passing a completed item to the next station because that station is still engaged on its work on the previous item, i.e. the station which has completed its work is blocked by the subsequent station.

In practice, if stations operating in this manner are not decoupled by the provision of space for buffer stocks of items between stations, idle time caused by both starving and blocking will be considerable. Thus, in practice, it is normal for this type of line to incorporate buffer stocks. A buffer stock can be defined, therefore, as 'items located between stations to reduce the probability of station starving or blocking'.

This method of line operation involves no work pacing, since there is no maximum cycle time or, theoretically, a limit to the minimum cycle time.

Since the cycle time on this type of line is variable, the flow of work along the line is irregular. Because this type of line does not depend on the use of a moving belt or conveyor, a fixed feed rate does not exist, except perhaps at the first station.

## Moving-belt lines

### *Items removed from line*

There are several types of line in which item movement is by means of moving belts. Perhaps the most complex type of line is the one in which workers at stations remove an item from the line to perform their work, placing it back on the line on completion of the work before picking up the next item. If we consider any one station on such a line, we can identify the following possibilities:

(a) Idle time or station under-utilization may occur if, on completion of one item, the subsequent item is not available to the operator, i.e. idle time may occur because of starvation at the station. The possibility of blocking does not arise because of the continuous movement of the belt and because:

(b) Items may pass a station without being worked on at the station. If a worker finds it necessary to spend considerably more time than usual working on a particular item, it is possible that, during this time, the moving line may carry the next item past the station. Thus, on this type of line, the production of incomplete items is a possibility.

**Table 15.13 Types of manual flow lines and their characteristics**

| | | Moving-belt lines | | | |
|---|---|---|---|---|---|
| | | | | Items fixed to line | |
| | | | | No station overlap possible | |
| | **Non-mechanical lines** | **Items removed from line** | **Station overlap possible** | **More than one item available to station ($T_F < T_T$)** | **Only one item available to station ($T_F \geq T_T$)** |
| Cycle time | Variable | Variable | Variable | Variable | Fixed (determined by station length and feed rate) |
| Work flow | Irregular | Irregular | Regular | Regular | Regular |
| Buffer stocks | Would reduce idle time | Would reduce number of incomplete items and idle time | Physical stocks not possible | Physical stocks not possible | Physical stocks not possible |
| Feed rate (interval = $T_F$) | None, except perhaps for first station | Fixed for first station only | Fixed | Fixed | Fixed |
| Limits on maximum service time | None | None | Determined by station length, feed rate and previous station | Determined by station length and feed rate | Maximum service time = cycle time |
| Tolerance time ($T_T$) | Does not apply | Yes | Yes | Yes | Yes |
| Mechanical pacing | None | With margin | With margin | With margin | With margin |
| Incomplete items | None | Possible | Possible | Possible | Possible |
| Station idle time – through blocking | Possible | Not possible | Not possible | Not possible | Possible because of fixed cycle time (can be considered as either 'blocking' or 'starving') |
| Station idle time – through starving | Possible | Possible | Possible | Possible | |

*Source: Wild, R.(1972)* Mass Production Management. *New York: Wiley*

On such lines there is likely to be a fixed *feed rate* for the first station, since items will probably be fed to the moving line at regular intervals. However, for subsequent stations the fixed rate is likely to be irregular and dependent on the service time of preceding stations. Workflow, therefore, is irregular, and line output is determined by the average feed rate or the fixed feed rate of the first station. The cycle time on these lines is variable, and since there is (theoretically, at least) no maximum cycle time, there is no work pacing, at least not in a mechanical sense. (Notice, however, that on both this and the previous type of line there may be a psychological pacing factor, since excess time spent on one item will result in either the accumulation of large buffer stocks or the production of incomplete items.)

Buffer stocks may be introduced into these lines if workers at stations remove items from the line rather than letting them pass by while completing work on a previous item. Even so, station blocking will not occur, since, when such buffer stocks reach the maximum level, provided the stock is off the line, it will always be possible for the previous station to place items on the line.

On such lines the *tolerance time* is an important concept. The tolerance time is the time period during which an item is available to be taken from the line, and therefore it is determined by the belt speed and the length of the station through which it passes.

## Items fixed to line

### Station overlap possible

Very often, on a flow line in which a moving belt is used, the items on which work is to be performed are, in effect, fixed to the line. By this we mean that they are attached to the line or, because of their weight or other characteristics, cannot be removed from the line. The latter situation exists in motor-vehicle assembly lines. In this type of line the work must be performed at each station while the item is in motion. This requires worker facilities at stations to move with the line to complete their work. In such cases, depending on the physical nature of the line, it is possible for some overlapping of stations to occur, the extent of the possible overlap being determined by the spacing, reach or permitted movement.

On lines of this type the workflow is regular and the cycle time is variable.

Since there will be a limit to either the reach or the permitted movement of workers in either direction, the cycle time is subject to a maximum limit, and thus the work is paced with margin. The maximum cycle time available for an item at a station will be determined by the time at which it is completed by the previous station, the line speed, and the maximum permitted reach or movement of the station down the line. It will be possible for incomplete items to pass from stations because of the limit on cycle times. Idle time may also occur because of work starvation at stations, but blocking is not normally possible, and neither is it possible to introduce physical stocks of items (i.e. buffer stocks) onto such lines. Notice that the term 'tolerance time' is useful in describing this type of line.

### No station overlap possible

On occasion, the class of line described above is used without the facility for station overlap, although this is perhaps less usual than the previous case. Depending on the spacing of the items on the belt and the length of work stations, two alternatives are available:

(i) lines on which more than one item is available to the station;

(ii) lines on which only one item is available to each station.

Alternative (i) is the more usual case, and we shall examine this first. The characteristics of such lines are very similar to fixed item/station overlap lines in that:

(a) the cycle time is variable with a maximum determined by the length of the station and the line speed and item spacing; thus

(b) work is paced with margin;

(c) workflow, as in all lines with fixed items, is regular; and

(d) the feed rate is fixed;

(e) the production of incomplete items is possible because of the limit of the maximum cycle time; and

(f) idle time is possible because of starving, but blocking is not possible;

(g) the use of physical buffer stocks of items is not possible.

The fundamental difference between this type of line and the type described previously concerns the influence of preceding stations. Since the preceding station cannot encroach on the subsequent station, the cycle time is limited only by station length and feed rate, and is independent of the service time or completion time of the previous station.

Alternative (ii), in which only one item is available to non-overlapping stations, is less common. As before, workflow is regular and the feed rate fixed. Again, it is possible for incomplete items to be produced because of the limited cycle time and, furthermore, it is possible for station idle time or under-utilization to occur, but in this case the cause of idle time differs from that described previously. Here idle time or under-utilization can and will occur because, irrespective of the time required for work at a station (the service time), the item remains at the station for a fixed time (the cycle time). The obligation for a worker at a station to take a fixed time for each item and the resultant idle time which may occur can be likened to either starving or blocking, but, strictly speaking, it is quite a different phenomenon. On such lines pacing is with margin, and again it is, strictly speaking, different from the pacing experienced by workers on the other types of line because the maximum service time available for any station is the same for each cycle.

## COMPUTERS IN FLOW SYSTEM DESIGN

Much of the work in designing flow processing systems requires simple but repetitive calculations. The balancing of lines, particularly the balancing of mixed and multi-model lines, the determination of batch sizes, the sequencing of models, etc. are all relatively straightforward analytical procedures. Often these line design problems will be tackled infrequently, especially in the case of single-model flow processing systems. In designing these flow processing systems it is important that adequate solutions be found, since the introduction of inefficiencies will be costly. In other circumstances, in particular in the design of mixed-model and multi-model flow lines, line design decision will be made more often, perhaps at the change-over from one model to the next, change-over of shifts, etc. Again it is important that adequate solutions be found to the line design problems, and also that these solutions should be found relatively quickly and at minimum cost. All these requirements point to the advantages of using computer-based line design methods. Many computer programs are available for line balancing, for simulating different types of line operation, etc.

### Simulation

Many flow line design problems have been examined by means of computer simulation. The design of unbalanced lines, the provision and location of buffer stocks and the comparison of line balancing methods are amongst the problems which are best examined in this way. Many of the algorithms for use in flow system design have been tested and proved using simulation. More details on computer simulation are given in Appendix III.

EXAMPLE

## *TRW Inc.*

TRW Inc.'s Greensboro plant produces power steering gears for automobiles. Each production line consists of a chain conveyor that moves the work-in-progress through 16 assembly stations and four test points, i.e. a moving-belt, fixed items line, without overlap. After a shake-down period following construction of the plant, output was still below that of a comparable TRW plant. Meanwhile, TRW's management was looking for an opportunity to apply computer simulation modelling. TRW selected a modelling product from Istel Inc. called WITNESS. It runs on a standard PC with enhanced graphics. To generate hypotheses for the model, engineers considered increasing the conveyor travel and adding more pallets to the line. With the model, TRW has found that reducing the time spent moving pallets into stations can improve system performance. The model was also used to help TRW analyse its testing operations. By implementing changes verified in advance on the model, net output of each line rose 30%.

Source: Sayers, R. D. (1989) Simulation modelling at TRW provides insight on assembly line operations. *Industrial Engineering*, **21**(8), pp. 20–24.

## CHECKLIST FOR CHAPTER 15

### The nature of flow processing

### Flowline principles

Types of flow processing system
- Classes and varieties of flow line
  - Single-model lines
  - Multi-model lines
  - Mixed-model lines

### Design of 'simple' flow lines

Line balance
- Cycle time
- Service time
- Productive and non-productive work
- Precedence

Line balancing
- Objectives
- Methods
  - Kilbridge and Wester
  - Ranked positional weights
  - COMSOAL

Multi-model lines
- Nature
- Line balancing
- Batch sizes
- Batch sequencing

Mixed-model lines
- Line balancing
- Launching
  - Variable rate
  - Fixed rate
- Model sequencing

### Design of 'complex' flow lines

Human aspects
- Work time distributions
- Pacing
  - Rigid
  - With margin
- System losses

System loss problems
- Solutions
  - Cycle time choice
  - Buffer stocks

Complex line balancing

Types of manual flow line
- Non-mechanical lines

Moving-belt lines
- Removable items
- Fixed items
  - Station overlap
  - No station overlap

### Use of computers in flow process design

Line balancing programs

Simulation

## FURTHER READING

**Bhattacharjee, T. K. and Sahu, S. (1987)** A critique of some current assembly line balancing techniques. *International Journal of Operations and Production Management*, **7**(6), pp. 32–43.

**Ghosh, S. and Gagnon, R. J.** (1989) A comprehensive literature review and analysis of the design, balancing and scheduling of assembly systems. *International Journal of Production Research*, **27**(4), pp. 637–670.

**Rajamani, D. and Singh, N. (1991)** A simulation approach to the design of an assembly line: a case study. *International Journal of Operations and Production Management*, **11**(6) pp. 66–75.

**Savsar, M. (1989)** Production line simulator evaluates performance of system design alternatives. *Industrial Engineering*, **21**(5), pp. 60–63.

**Wild, R. (1972)** *Mass Production Management.* New York: Wiley.

## QUESTIONS

15.1 A multi-station flow line is to process a minimum of 6000 completed items per 40-hour working shift. Each item requires 25 elements of work together constituting a total work content of 11 minutes.

What is the minimum number of work stations for this line and what will the cycle time ($C$) ideally be?

15.2 What will the balancing loss be of the line, the requirements of which are given above?

15.3 The diagram to the right indicates the necessary precedence requirements of 12 work elements which together constitute the total work content of a simple service task.

Using the line balancing technique devised by Kilbridge and Wester, design a line (i.e. assign work elements to the required number of work stations) to produce as near as possible to, and no less than, three items per hour.

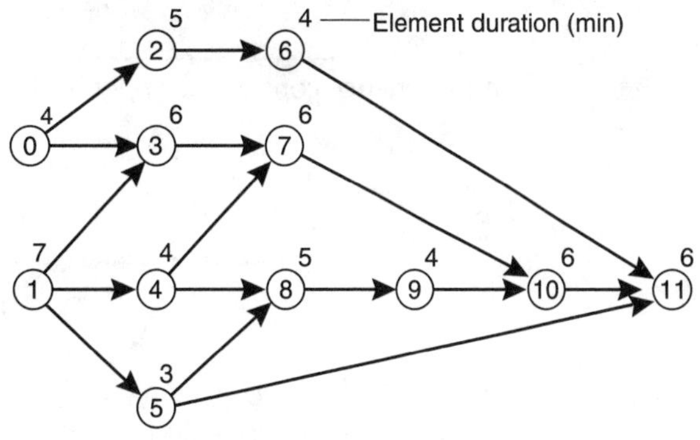


What is the balancing loss for the line that you have designed?

15.4 Use the Kilbridge and Wester line balancing technique to balance a simple line, with the minimum number of work stations, to process a minimum of 60 items per hour. The processing of each item consists of 21 work elements, some of which must be performed in a given order as shown by the precedence diagram below.

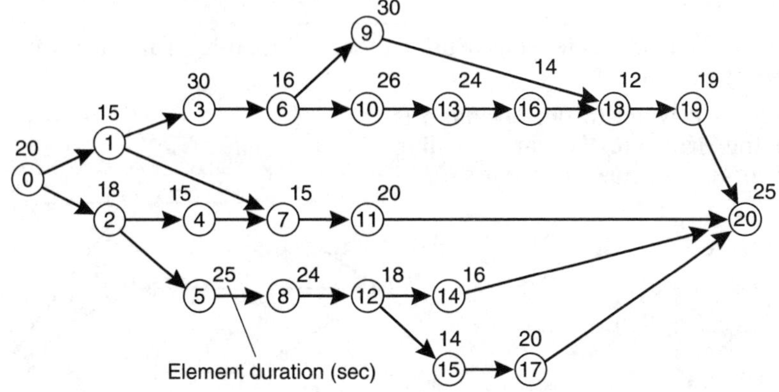

15.5 The work involved in assembling a small component can be described in terms of 11 minimum rational work elements whose element times are as follows:

| Element | Time (min) |
|---|---|
| 0 | 4 |
| 1 | 3 |
| 2 | 3 |
| 3 | 3 |
| 4 | 7 |
| 5 | 5 |
| 6 | 4.5 |
| 7 | 9.5 |
| 8 | 5 |
| 9 | 7 |
| 10 | 7 |

Certain precedence constraints apply to the work; these are shown diagrammatically below.

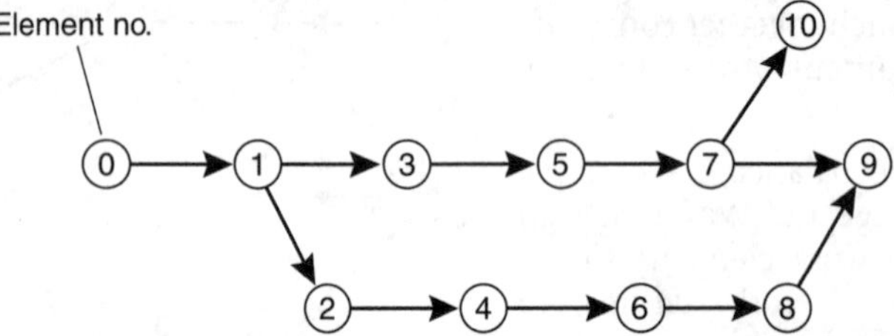


Furthermore, because of the nature of the work it is necessary to ensure that elements 0 and 3 *do not* occur at the same work station, elements 3 and 5 *do not* occur at the same work station, and elements 8 and 10 *do* occur at the same work station. Two assembly lines are to be designed (without buffer stocks), one producing components at a rate of 4.61 per hour and the other at a rate of 5.0 per hour.

Use the ranked positional weight method to assign work elements to work stations in order to minimize the number of work stations and the balancing loss on each line. Calculate the balancing loss in both cases.

Describe the heuristic device you are using to solve this problem and justify its use as a method of assembly line balancing.

15.6 The precedence diagram for an operation is shown to the right and the corresponding work element time is shown opposite.

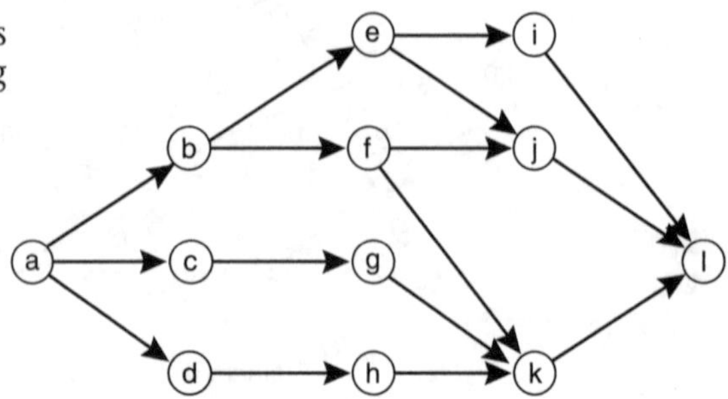

| Work element | Time (min) | Work element | Time (min) |
|---|---|---|---|
| a | 0.20 | g | 0.30 |
| b | 0.65 | h | 0.45 |
| c | 0.40 | i | 0.65 |
| d | 0.10 | j | 0.40 |
| e | 0.30 | k | 0.35 |
| f | 0.15 | l | 0.25 |

If there are three operators available for this work determine the maximum output that can be achieved by the line.

15.7 What is 'system loss', how is it caused, and how can it be reduced?

15.8 Analytical line balancing procedures are sufficient for the successful design of 'transfer lines' but are they adequate themselves for the design of mass production systems in which human operators are involved in executing the work?

What are the 'human' problems associated with the design and operation of mass production systems such as flow lines?

15.9 Determine the 'optimal' inter-station buffer stock capacities for a flow line consisting of six stations. Assume that the station work times are distributed normally with (a) a variance of 1.6 and (b) a variance of 3.2. The unit inventory cost per hour is £0.005 and the unit cost of the facilities per hour is £0.007.

Which formula have you used in calculating the optimal buffer capacity, and on what other assumptions does this treatment of the problem depend?

15.10 Describe briefly the following:

(a) a multi-model assembly line;

(b) a mixed-model assembly line;

(c) simple assembly line balancing;

(d) complex assembly line balancing;

(e) batch sequencing on assembly lines;

(f) model sequencing on assembly lines.

15.11 The matrix to the right shows the costs incurred through changing an assembly line from a set-up suitable for the production of one type of item to a set-up suitable for the production of a different type of item.

During each shift each of the five types of item must be produced once. A batch of item type A must be produced first. In what order must the batches of the five items be produced if the cost of setting up the line is to be minimized?

What is the total line set-up cost per shift?

| Cost ↗ | | Succeeding type | | | | |
|---|---|---|---|---|---|---|
| | | A | B | C | D | E |
| Preceding model | A | | 150 | 70 | 100 | 65 |
| | B | 100 | | 70 | 80 | 110 |
| | C | 50 | 100 | | 110 | 65 |
| | D | 75 | 65 | 75 | | 90 |
| | E | 125 | 110 | 80 | 70 | |

15.12 Two models (A and B) of a simple product are to be produced on a short 'manual' assembly line. Because of the nature of the demand for these items, it is preferable to design the assembly line for mixed production of the two models rather than for separate production in batches.

The line output for the two types, per 8-hour shift, must be:

A = 500 products

B = 250 products

The diagrams below show the precedence relationships of the work elements which constitute both models. Certain of the elements are common to both models, and the remainder are peculiar to each. (Common elements have the same numbers in both diagrams.)

Design an assembly line with the minimum number of stations and allocate work elements to stations.

What is the average balancing loss of your line over a period of one shift?

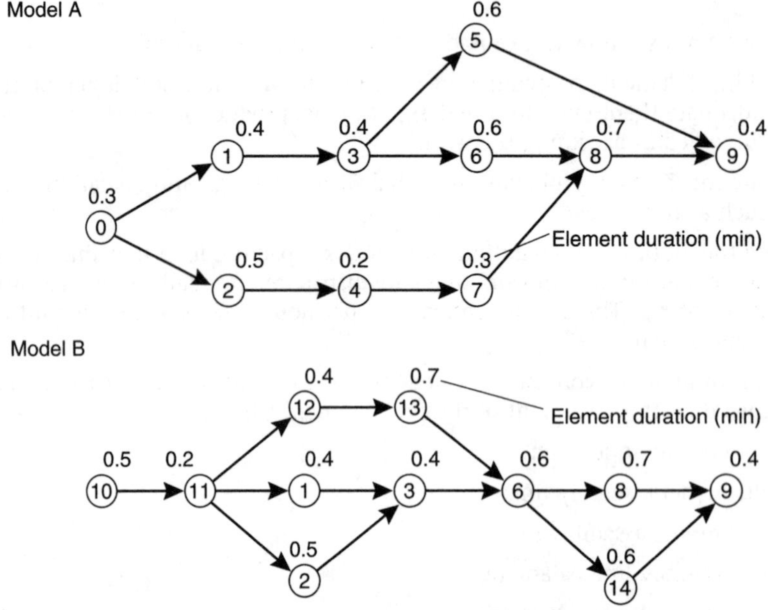


15.13 Four models of a product are to be produced on a 'mixed-model' line. The relative proportions of each of the models to be produced over any given period are given below. The model cycle times are also given below (i.e. cycle times for each model at each station).

| Model | Relative production (quantities required) | Model cycle times (min) |
|---|---|---|
| A | 0.2 | 0.6 |
| B | 0.3 | 0.3 |
| C | 0.3 | 0.4 |
| D | 0.2 | 0.7 |

The models must be launched onto the line at fixed intervals. Determine the sequence in which models must be launched onto the line to minimize congestion on the line.

15.14 'The minimization of balancing loss should be a secondary objective during the design of assembly lines, particularly mixed-model assembly lines.' Discuss.

15.15 The diagrams below indicate the precedence relationships for the work elements of two jobs. Certain of the elements are common to both jobs (i.e. elements 1, 2, 3, 4 6), while the remainder are peculiar to one job. At the moment product A is made on line A and product B is made on line B. The allocation of work elements to stations, and the line outputs, are also shown below.

Product A

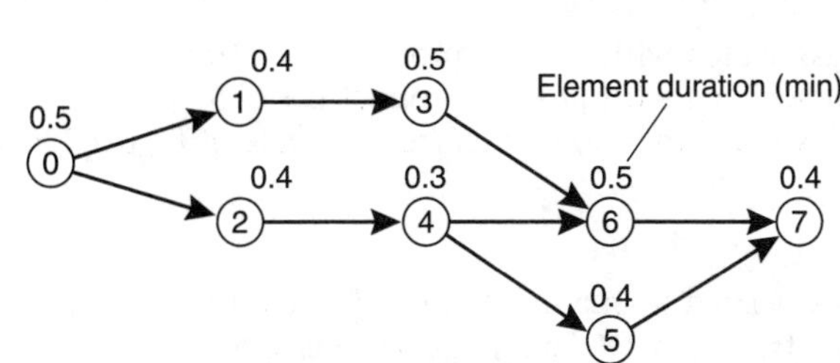


Output required = 60 per hour (i.e. cycle time = 1 min).

| Station | Elements | Work station time (min) |
|---|---|---|
| 1 | 0, 2 | 0.9 |
| 2 | 1, 4 | 0.7 |
| 3 | 3, 5 | 0.9 |
| 4 | 6, 7 | 0.9 |

Product B

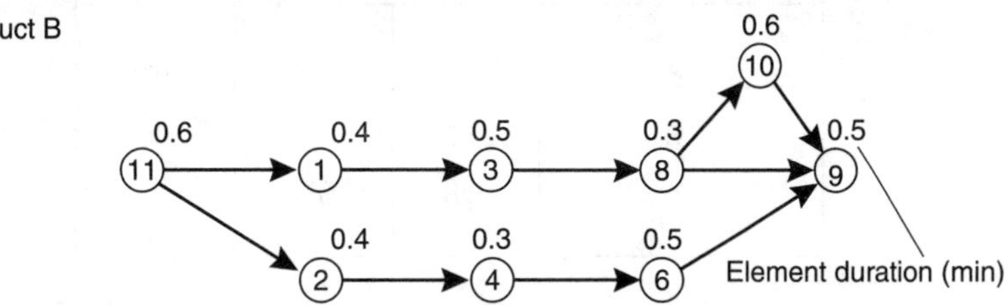


Output required = 50 per hour (i.e. cycle time = 1.2 min).

| Station | Elements | Work station time (min) |
|---|---|---|
| 1 | 11, 1 | 1.0 |
| 2 | 2, 3 | 0.9 |
| 3 | 4, 6, 8 | 1.1 |
| 4 | 10, 9 | 1.1 |

The company manufacturing these two products is anxious to evaluate the merits of three possible methods of manufacture:

(a) The manufacture of both A and B together on a mixed-model line.

(b) The manufacture of A and B separately in batches on an existing larger line which would also be expected to manufacture batches of another product, C.

(c) The present arrangement.

The evaluation of the three methods of manufacture is to be accomplished by comparing the total costs of each alternative, as follows:

Present situation:

Total cost =
Indirect costs: associated with line for product A = £100
: associated with line for product B = £75
+ Inefficiency costs: assumed to be incurred at a rate of £5 per 1% balancing loss per line

Alternative (a)

Total cost =
Indirect costs: associated with a mixed-model line = £150
+ Inefficiency costs: £5 per 1% balancing loss per line.

Alternative (b):

Total cost =
Indirect costs: addition to indirect costs for existing product C line = £50
+ Inefficiency costs: associated with balancing loss and calculated to be £50.
+ Change-over costs, incurred when the set-up of the multi-model line is changed between production of batches of two different products. The matrix below details such costs (assume the production of one batch of each model only and three line set-ups).

| Preceding product \ Succeeding product | A | B | C |
|---|---|---|---|
| A | – | 70 | 45 |
| B | 60 | – | 80 |
| C | 70 | 65 | – |

Which is the most economic method of producing products A and B in the quantities specified?

PART 7

# Materials management

Introduction to Part 7
Chapter 16 Materials management and supply chains
Chapter 17 Inventory management

## INTRODUCTION TO PART 7

Here we deal with the management of items, products and customers throughout the operating system, from inputs to outputs. We first identify different approaches to this task of materials management, and then consider those topics which are of particular and direct relevance to the operations manager.

Again, especially when dealing with inventory management in Chapter 17, we shall consider 'principal' or 'characteristic' operations management problem areas, i.e. problems which are influenced by the operating system structure and where the approaches employed are influenced by the operations objectives.

## STRATEGIC CONTEXT

The operations issues, problems and decisions considered in this part of the book exist within the broader strategic context of the organization. The main relationships are set out here as a preface to the details which follow.

### Influences of business policy decisions *(see Chapter 2, Figure 2.2)*

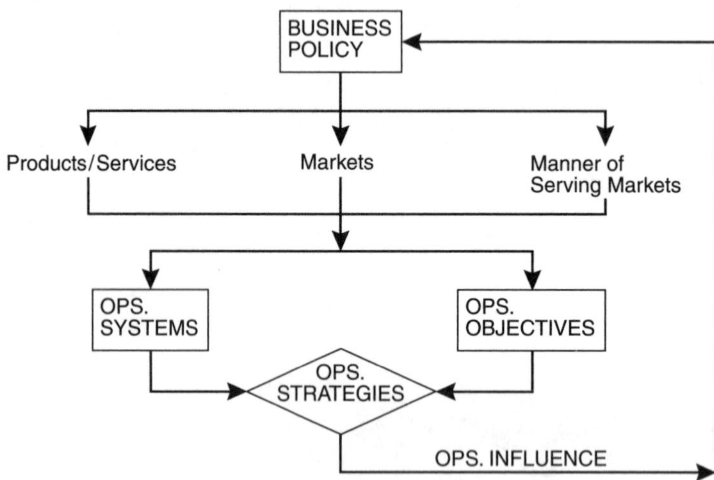


Much of what was identified in our discussion of the strategic context for scheduling must also apply here, for, to a large extent, effective materials management is also a matter of effective scheduling. This certainly applies in respect of supply chain management, purchasing/procurement and supply. So, business policies relating to the nature of the products/services to be offered, the markets and the manner in which these markets are to be dealt with must influence operating system structures (e.g. whether and where inventories exist) and objectives (i.e. the nature and relative importance of customer service and resource utilization objectives). These then are the two main 'drivers' influencing the way in which materials management and supply chains are dealt with.

Further, inventory management, a main element of materials management, will inevitably be influenced by the nature of the system structure, since that influences whether inventories exist, and where. Also, operations objectives, e.g. the importance to be attached to speed for service, may also influence whether stock of output goods or input queues of customers are used. As we have seen, both of these influences – structure and objectives – are in turn influenced by business policies. For example, if the policy of the business is to provide standard goods for a well-defined market, then output stocks may exist, and so the problems of maintaining those stocks at an adequate level must arise. If, in providing a standard service, the intention also is to compete on cost, then it is possible that input queues of customers may be allowed. So, there exists the problem of managing those queues (or customer inventories).

It follows that the existence of inventories in systems makes certain policy-related things more achievable and certain others less achievable. For example, output stocks of goods and input stocks of resources reduce the amount of time that might otherwise be required to deal with customers' orders. The absence of input queues of customers is likely to benefit speed of treatment, but may increase costs. These factors must be taken into account when setting or changing business objectives, for it will not be easy for operations managers to change existing strategies for managing materials and inventories.

## **Competitive advantage** *(see Chapter 2, Figures 2.6 and 2.7)*

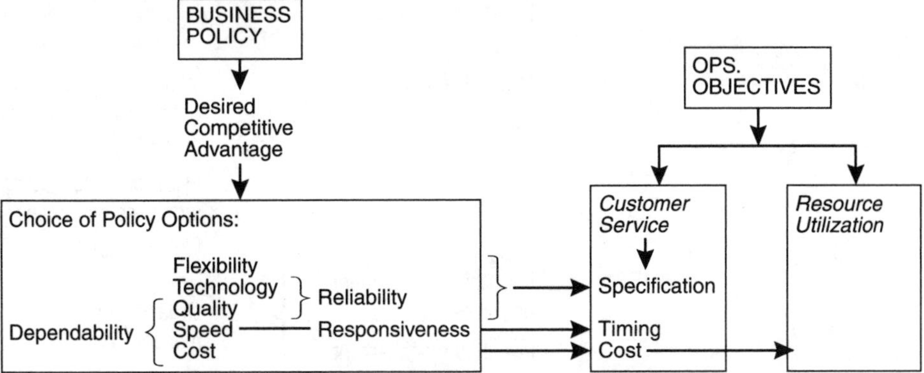


Focusing now on the relationships covered by the above model, we can identify the following principal relationships of policy options and materials management.

| **Business emphasis on:** | **Implications for operations:** |
|---|---|
| Flexibility | Low inventories required |
| | Flexible supply arrangements necessary |
| Speed | Low customer queues necessary |
| | Output inventories beneficial |
| | Low inventories/queues within the operating system desirable |
| | Adequate resource input inventories necessary |
| Cost | Low inventories desirable |
| Responsiveness | Low in-process inventories and queues desirable |
| | Adequate resource input inventories required |

## TOPIC MAP

| Topics in this Part | Chapter | Related topics in other chapters<br>Topic | Comments/aspects |
|---|---|---|---|
| Chapter 16 | | | |
| Integrated materials management | 1 | Operations management objectives | Impact of materials management on resource utilization and customer service |
| | | Operations system structure | Influence of system structure on materials management problems |
| | 3 | Marketing | Influence of marketing on organization of materials management |
| | 4 | Cost controls | Influence of materials management on materials costs |
| | 5 | Locational choice | Influence of location on materials management |
| | 7 | Materials handling | Influence of materials handling on materials management policies |
| | 12 | Scheduling | Influence of scheduling strategies on materials management |
| | 17 | Inventory management decisions<br>Inventory management systems | Organization of materials management |
| | 18 | Control of operations systems | Input factors for operations systems |
| | 19 | Management of quality | Control of quality of inputs |
| | 20 | Quality controls | Vendor controls |
| | 21 | Maintenance and repair | Supply of items for repair/replacement |
| Supply chain management | 5 | Locational choice | Influence of location on supply chain |
| | | Types of location problem | Multiple versus single locations and supply networks |
| | 17 | Inventory management | Management of inventories in supply chains |
| | 18 | Operations control | Control of supply systems |
| | 19 | Management of quality | Importance of input items to output and service quality |
| | 21 | Maintenance/replacement | Supply of replacement items |

## TOPIC MAP

| Topics in this Part | Related topics in other chapters: Chapter | Topic | Comments/aspects |
|---|---|---|---|
| *Chapter 16 continued* | | | |
| Purchasing and supply | 1 | Operations systems structures | Influence whether resources are stocked or obtained direct |
| | | Operations management objectives | Influence of purchasing on resource utilization and customer service |
| | 4 | Operations costs | Importance of purchasing to materials cost |
| | 5 | Locational choice | Proximity to suppliers |
| | | Types of location | Supply problems for single and multiple locations |
| | 12 | Scheduling | Need to schedule inputs |
| | 17 | Inventories | Need to replenish input inventories |
| | 18 | Operations control | Control of supply systems |
| | 19 | Management of quality | Importance of inputs for output and service quality |
| | 21 | Maintenance/repair/replacement | Need for replacement items for systems |
| Physical distribution and logistics | 4 | Operations costs | Contribution of PDM/logistics to costs |
| | 5 | Locational choice | Proximity to consumers |
| | | Types of location | Distribution problems for single and multiple facilities |
| | 12 | Just in time | Delivery/output requirement for JIT |
| | 17 | Inventory management | Management of in-progress and output stocks |
| | 18 | Kanban | Implementation of kanban controls |
| | 19 | Quality management | Need for effective distribution to ensure quality |
| Chapter 17 | | | |
| Nature and purposes of inventory | 1 | Operations management objectives | Influence on inventory management strategies |
| | | Operating system structures | (Influence on inventory management strategies) |
| | 4 | Operations costs | Costs of inventories |
| | | Cost control | Control of inventories |

## TOPIC MAP

| Topics in this Part | Related topics in other chapters: Chapter | Topic | Comments/aspects |
|---|---|---|---|
| *Chapter 17 continued* | | | |
| | 5 | Locational choice | Location of inventories in supply chain |
| | 6 | Layout planning | Need to accommodate inventories in layout |
| | | Automated storage and retrieval | Handling of inventory items |
| | 11 | Planning and control | Implications of inventories in planning |
| | | Capacity management | Use of inventories in managing capacity |
| | 12 | Scheduling | Influence of inventories on scheduling strategy |
| | | Scheduling techniques | Scheduling of inventory movements |
| | 15 | Flow process systems | Buffer stocks |
| | 16 | Materials management | Organization of inventory management |
| | | Supply chains | Inventories in supply chains |
| | | Purchasing and supply | Input inventories |
| | | Physical distribution | Output inventories |
| | 18 | JIT and kanban | Effect of JIT on inventories |
| | 20 | Reliability | Need for inventories for replacements |
| | 21 | Maintenance/repair/replacement | Need for inventories of 'spare' items |
| | 22 | Performance measurement | Measurement of use and performance of inventories |

Chapter 16

# Materials management and supply chains

## ISSUES

What is materials management?
What are the relationships of materials management, inventory management and logistics?
Should materials management be a centralized activity?
What is supply chain management?
How is effective purchasing managed?
What is the impact of JIT on purchasing?
How does an organization manage its distribution 'channels'?

## NOTATION USED IN THIS CHAPTER

| | |
|---|---|
| $B$ | Buffer or safety stock |
| $B_1$ | Buffer stock for location 1 |
| $B_n$ | Total buffer stock for $n$ locations |
| MRP | Materials requirement planning |
| $n$ | Number of stock locations at a given level in a customer channel |
| PDM | Physical distribution management |

## MATERIALS MANAGEMENT AND SUPPLY CHAINS

Materials management can be defined as the methods and principles by which we endeavour to plan, organize, co-ordinate, control and review the flow of materials throughout an organization. It offers, therefore, a means for the overall control of materials throughout an organization.

In the absence of a materials management approach within an organization, the management (i.e. the planning, organizing, co-ordinating, controlling and reviewing) of materials, materials stocks, materials flows, parts stocks, materials in progress and, where appropriate, the flow of customers will be the responsibility of several departments or individuals. This is the more decentralized approach.

Figure 16.1 shows the relationships and overlap between responsibilities for the management of materials for two different types of operating systems. It will be seen that the entire field can be subdivided into three main areas:

**Figure 16.1** The three stages of materials management – two examples

*Example 1. Manufacture from stock, to stock, to customer*

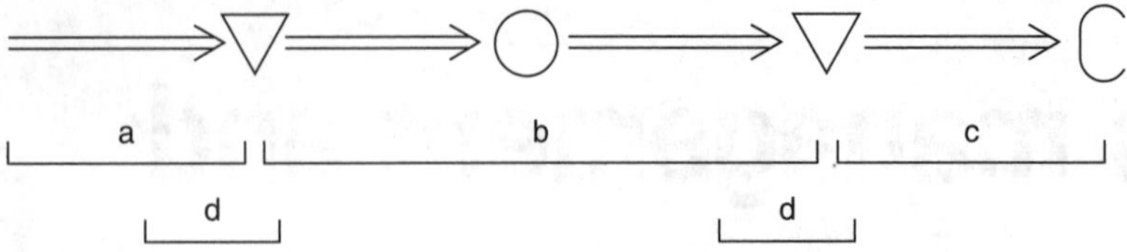


*Example 2. Service from stock, from customer queue*

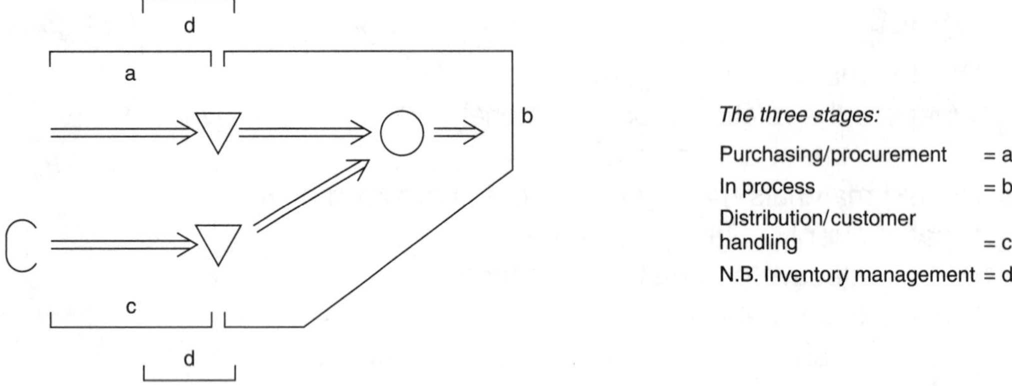


(a) purchasing or procurement, i.e. responsibility for obtaining and managing incoming materials through to input stocks;

(b) in-process materials management, i.e. the management of materials, items and, where appropriate, customers through the transformation process (see also Chapters 12–15);

(c) 1. In the case of manufacture and supply systems, distribution/logistics for the transfer of items, products, etc. to the customer from the system or from output stock;

  2. In the case of transport and service systems, customer handling, i.e. the management of customers joining the operating system or its input queue.

Within these areas of responsibility there will exist physical stock situations. In Example 2 in Figure 16.1 there are two stocks: (i) incoming materials, components, parts, products, etc.; and (ii) outputs. Similarly, in Example 2 there is an input stock of items from suppliers and also an input queue of customers. In many cases such stocks will be the responsibility of an inventory management function (see Chapter 17).

# INTEGRATED MATERIALS MANAGEMENT

Whether the management of the entire flow into, through and from the operating system should be treated as a single integrated function, or as separate activities, has been a matter of considerable debate. Initially the focus was on the merits of centralized and decentralized materials management. The benefits of a centralized (i.e. controlled from a single, central function, with little delegation of authority, or local autonomy) approach were seen to be:

(a) avoidance of problems of divided responsibility;
(b) avoidance of possible conflicting objectives and priorities;
(c) avoidance of duplication of effort;
(d) ease of communications throughout the organization;
(e) ease of, and better representation of, the materials management function at board/policy level;
(f) better career/development opportunities;
(g) economies of scale.

**EXAMPLE**

## *Centralized materials management in a national retail stationery organization*

This organization has several hundred retail shops throughout the country. Each shop sells stationery, records, some toys and some confectionery, but mainly magazines and popular books. It maintains a central national materials administration directorate operating from the corporate headquarters. The materials administration director and his staff are responsible for the acquisition of all products sold through the retail branches, their delivery to the three warehouses, their stocking in the warehouses, subsequent distribution to shops, retail stock at shops, point-of-sale display and local promotion of items. All the retail shops offer the same stock lines and all shops must obtain all their supplies from the company's warehouses. A catalogue is available offering a limited part of this range on mail order to customers. Such orders are satisfied directly from one of the warehouses through a mail order distribution function which is also the responsibility of the materials administration director.

The materials administration director has regional staff who liaise with retail branches in various areas. These staff operate from the warehouse locations. Their responsibility is primarily to advise local retail shop managers of merchandising policy, new lines which are to be introduced, local and point-of-sale promotion requirements, etc. The company maintains a centralized computer-based system for materials records. Point-of-sale returns are made directly from check-out machines to retail branch stock records and from there to warehouse records on a weekly basis. Deliveries are made to retail shops on a weekly basis.

A more decentralized approach might be seen to offer the following potential benefits:

(a) greater opportunity for functional specialization;
(b) greater flexibility;
(c) greater opportunity for materials managers to act as integral parts of geographically dispersed organizations (rather than being seen as separate head office/personnel staff).

The type of approach employed within an organization will depend on the relevance of the above advantages and the circumstances in which the organization is to work. For example, it might be argued (see Chapter 3) that a centralized approach might be more appropriate in 'static' situations subject to few uncertainties. In such situations the organization will face fewer changes in markets, demand, customer behaviour, supplier behaviour, technological change, etc., and thus it may be possible to implement and stick to relevant rules, procedures, etc. for materials management throughout the organization. Where there is a greater degree of uncertainty, e.g. because of demand changes, product changes, changes in the nature of the service and technological changes, particularly where these affect different parts of the organization in different ways, then there may be some merit in a decentralized approach which facilitates rapid response to their changing circumstances from different parts of the organization.

EXAMPLE

### Decentralized materials management in a college bookshop company

This organization runs about twenty bookshops on college and university campuses. It gives considerable autonomy to bookshop managers, in particular in respect of the books which they choose to stock and any point-of-sale advertising, promotion displays, etc. The quantities of items stocked in bookshops are also the responsibility of individual bookshop managers. However, the bookshop managers are required to order books through a company purchasing system; the system is run from the company headquarters, but deliveries are made from publishers directly to individual bookshops. Unsold books can be returned either to the publishers, depending on the conditions of their supply, or to a company 'clearing' inventory which either holds the items in stock against future occasional orders from individual bookshops or redistributes them to other shops where the demand might be greater. The smaller retail outlets are run, in some cases single-handed, by a local manager, possibly with a part-time assistant. He or she is responsible for receiving books into stock, displaying them, selling them and making his or her financial returns to the company. In the larger shops the retail manager will have staff responsible for ordering and stock-holding, for sales and for finance.

There are, however, other factors to consider. The approach to materials management must, for example, be influenced by strategic objectives – thus for many organizations the integrated management of flows into, through and from the operation is a prerequisite for achieving high-quality, rapid and low-cost provision for customers. Managing the supply chain is now, therefore, a major concern for organizations working in a 'just in time' (see Chapter 12) and 'total quality management' (see Chapter 19) framework.

## SUPPLY CHAIN MANAGEMENT (SCM)

There is increasing recognition that good supply chain management provides a major opportunity for organizations to improve efficiency and increase customer service. Supply chain management focuses on the organizing, integrating and operation of the complete materials management function. To this end an organization must:

1. define its strategy;
2. select an implementation;
3. resolve how to manage change;
4. identify the critical success factors that will measure SCM performance across the organization.[1]

EXAMPLE

### Du Pont, Australia

Du Pont (Australia) consists of many customer-focused operating departments. Printing Systems, one of these departments, supports a manufacturing facility at Girraween in Sydney that is one of the most technically advanced and cost-efficient plants in the company. The plant was under-utilized in servicing Australia and some small-scale exporting. It was appropriate therefore to consider a more integrated international strategy for film and chemistry – the products of the plant. The proposal to supply Southeast Asia with film and chemistry from Australia was one outcome of looking at the 'larger picture'. Using an integrated approach to the supply chain

[1] Battaglia, A-J. and Tyndall, G. R. (1991) Working on the supply chain. *Chief Executive*, April, pp. 42–45.

has meant that the system has been managed more closely. Customer service, manufacturing and distribution have not been considered in isolation from strategic planning. The information chain running alongside the supply chain and reporting back on the logistical function is the key to Du Pont's success.

Source: Blackshaw, D. (1989) Graphics arts film and chemistry to South East Asia: a case study. *International Journal of Physical Distribution and Materials Management*, **19**(10), pp. 27–33.

## The nature of the supply chain

The supply chain is shown in Figure 16.1, i.e. it is the complete flow system into, through and from the organization. Notice, however, that there are two flows – physical (as shown in Figure 16.1) and information. In general, information flows in the opposite direction to the physical flow.

So, managing this chain will normally involve dealing with the following:

(a) purchasing and supply;

(b) inventory management;

(c) operations schedules;

(d) distribution and logistics.

This, in turn, indirectly brings SCM into contact with other areas, e.g.

(e) facilities location and layout;

(f) capacity management.

All of this will be undertaken against a set of strategic and operational objectives which will involve achieving the necessary levels, and securing the appropriate balance between resource utilization and customer service.

## Developing a supply chain

A three-stage process can be identified[2] for developing an SC strategy, i.e.

1. ***Evaluation of the competitive environment.***

   This will normally involve the following:

   (a) understand the market characteristics;

   (b) examine current strategies;

   (c) decide on market-winning strategies (i.e. the policy options referred to in Chapter 2).

2. ***Review existing SC operations.***

   This will normally involve the following:

   (a) develop a cost model;

   (b) identify those activities which can have a significant impact on customers;

   (c) list improvement techniques for these activities.

3. ***Develop the supply chain.***

   The aim here is to develop an integrated supply chain to achieve the market-winning strategies – concentrating, if appropriate, on those key elements identified in (2) above.

[2] See Stevens, G. C. (1990) Successful supply chain management. *Management Decision*, **28**(8), pp. 25–30.

To develop an integrated supply chain requires consideration of functional, internal and external integration, i.e.

(a) ***Functional integration***

The aim will be to diminish or remove the separation between functions within the organization, e.g. by merging previously separate activities, e.g. Purchasing and receiving, Sales and distribution.

(b) ***Internal integration***

The aim now will be to improve the interfacing of the remaining activities, e.g. by reducing or eliminating inventories.

(c) ***External integration***

Finally, the objective will be to improve the input and output side interfaces of the organization, e.g. by removing inventories and improving information flows.

**EXAMPLE**

### *McDonald's*

Quality, service, cleanliness and value are the cornerstones of the McDonald's business, and the success of the supply and distribution functions can be attributed to this focus. Strict guidelines are applied to delivered quality and temperature, along with on-time performance and order reliability. McDonald's logistics approach includes the following principles: (1) the recognition that the end performance of delivering satisfaction to customers will only be as good as the weakest link in the supply chain; (2) the need to ensure that each link clearly understands the expectation of performance and why McDonald's has those expectations; (3) a constant monitoring or measuring of each critical element of the logistics function in accordance with predetermined criteria; and (4) the need to keep flexibility in the system to allow for growth and changing needs.

Source: Ritchie, P. (1990) McDonald's: a winner through logistics. *International Journal of Physical Distribution and Logistics*, **20**(3), pp. 21–24.

---

We can now examine the elements of the supply chain. Here the focus will be on purchasing/supply and on distribution/logistics, as scheduling and inventory management are covered in detail in other chapters.

## PURCHASING AND SUPPLY

Although rarely their sole responsibility, the purchasing or procurement function clearly concerns operations managers. Operations managers are responsible for providing goods or services of the right specification and quality, at the right time, in the right quantity and at the right price, and purchasing or procurement managers are, in the same terms, responsible for purchasing materials and items of the right specification and quality, at the right time, in the right quantity, from the right source and at the right price. Theirs, in other words, is the responsibility of obtaining those items required by the operating system. They are concerned with the input to the operating system, i.e. the flow of physical resources to the operating system.

### The objectives of purchasing

The main objectives of purchasing are as follows:

(a) 1. to supply the organization with a steady flow of materials and services to meet its needs;

2. to ensure continuity of supply by maintaining effective relationships with existing sources and by developing other sources of supply either as alternatives or to meet emerging or planned needs;

(b) to obtain efficiently, by any ethical means, the best value for every unit of expenditure;

(c) to manage inventory so as to give the best possible service at lowest cost;

(d) to maintain sound co-operative relationships with other departments, providing information and advice as necessary to ensure the effective operation of the organization as a whole;

(e) to develop staff, policies, procedures and organization to ensure the achievement of the foregoing objectives.

Reference (c) to the management of inventories raises the question of the relationship of purchasing to inventory management. Purchasing will, in some cases, be responsible for the provision of goods to input inventories (i.e. in those system structures in which inventories exist). In some cases this responsibility for supplying items and materials to input inventory will be linked with some responsibility for the maintenance of such inventories. In other situations inventory replenishment needs will be identified, to provide purchase requirements to be executed by the purchasing function. (We will assume the latter, i.e. separate purchasing and inventory responsibility.) We shall deal with inventory management in Chapter 17. The topics covered there are of relevance in purchasing, as indeed the topics covered here are relevant to inventory management.

Deriving from the above objectives, the following are the principal benefits to be gained from the effective management of the purchasing process:

(a) lower prices for materials and items used;

(b) faster inventory turnover;

(c) continuity of supply;

(d) reduced replenishment lead times;

(e) reduced transport cost;

(f) reduced materials obsolescence;

(g) improved vendor relationships;

(h) better control of quality;

(i) effective administration and minimization of organizational effort;

(j) maintenance of adequate records and provision of information for the operations managers.

The purchasing process is concerned primarily with obtaining physical items for use in, and conversion through, the operating system. Most operating systems need such items. Hospitals, for example, need a regular reliable supply of consumable items such as medicines and sterile equipment. Transport operations are dependent on an adequate supply of consumable materials such as fuel and tyres. Supply organizations naturally are dependent on an adequate, reliable and efficient supply of those items which are to be passed to customers, while manufacturing organizations are entirely dependent on the supply of consumable and non-consumable materials and items.

## The organization of purchasing

One major issue is the degree to which purchasing as a function should be centralized. In recent years there has been a trend towards the establishment of centralized purchasing functions. This has been particularly noticeable in health services and in local and central government supply, as well as in manufacturing. The principal benefits associated with central purchasing may be summarized as follows:

(a) the possibility of standardizing specifications and establishing common needs, as regards quantity, quality, specification, etc.;
(b) the possibility of more economic purchase through, for example, larger batch quantities;
(c) the reduction in administrative cost through the purchase of larger quantities on few occasions, possibly from fewer sources;
(d) the possibility of purchase staff specialization and thus increased knowledge of sources and supplies;
(e) the possibility of the use of more effective, detailed and accurate purchase information and records;
(f) the possibility of more detailed accurate and rapid budgetary and financial control procedures.

The principal advantages derive from the possibility of increased purchase volumes, from standardization and from specialization. Disadvantages of centralized purchasing, however, might include:

(a) difficulties of communication within the organization, deriving perhaps from geographical separation;
(b) slow response to new or unusual supply needs from the organization;
(c) possible increased dependence on a smaller number of suppliers resulting from increased volume and from standardization.

Thus the merits of centralized purchasing will depend on the possible financial savings through volume and variety considerations as against the possibility of reduced response times and flexibility.

## JIT purchasing *(see also Chapter 12)*

Summarizing, JIT can be defined as the processing of items or customers in the quantities required, when required. JIT, therefore, involves processing only as and when required rather than in anticipation of needs. One of the prerequisites for the effective implementation of JIT is vendor reliability. JIT involves the pursuit of low or zero inventory, so incoming goods and materials inventory is of particular importance. This inevitably affects the relationship between an organization and its vendor/supplier organization. Unless regular timely supplies of the requisite items with consistent quality can be assured, JIT is impossible. Some features of JIT purchasing are listed in Table 16.1.

Organizations which have pursued the JIT philosophy have identified the need to establish special relationships with vendors, the principal characteristics being:

(a) close relationships with few vendors/suppliers;
(b) long-term relationships with few suppliers;
(c) the establishment of an interdependence in the vendor–consumer relationship.

Effective JIT within an organization depends therefore on the organization's suppliers also adopting the JIT philosophy. The willingness to supply smaller quantities of items more frequently with assured quality is the principal requirement. To this end organizations have often found it necessary to help their suppliers develop JIT systems of their own, even to the extent of helping them develop their process technology, scheduling systems and management systems. In effect, organizations have, in many cases, come to regard vendors simply as extensions of their own organization. These issue will be of relevance here and in our discussion of quality in Chapters 19 and 20.

## Sourcing and suppliers

An important function of purchasing is the identification of suitable sources of supply. The systematic investigation and comparison of sources, the evaluation and monitoring of performance of supply sources and the development of appropriate procedures with suppliers are therefore of importance.

**Table 16.1 Some features of JIT purchasing**

**Suppliers**

- Few suppliers
- Nearby suppliers
- Repeat business with same suppliers
- Active use of analysis to enable desirable suppliers to be price competitive
- Cluster of remote suppliers
- Competitive bidding mostly limited to new items
- Suppliers encouraged to extend JIT buying to their suppliers

**Quality**

- Minimal product specifications imposed on supplier
- Help suppliers to meet quality requirements
- Close relationships between buyers' and suppliers' quality assurance procedures
- Suppliers encouraged to use control charts (see Chapter 20)

**Quantities**

- Steady output rate
- Frequent deliveries in small lot quantities
- Long-term contract agreements
- Minimal paperwork
- Delivery quantities variable from release to release but fixed for whole contract term
- Little or no permissible 'overage' or 'underage' of receipts
- Suppliers encouraged to package in exact quantities
- Suppliers encouraged to reduce their production lot sizes

**Deliveries**

- Scheduling of inbound deliveries
- Gain control by use of company-owned or contract delivery and storage where possible

*Source: Based on material from Schonberger, R. J. and Gilbert, J. P. (1983) Just in time purchasing: a challenge for US industry.* California Management Review, ***26****(1), pp. 54–68*

Vendor rating is discussed briefly below and in more detail in Chapter 20. Although market research will not be discussed in detail here, it will be appreciated that supplier market research is of importance in obtaining adequate supply sources for the organization.

Figure 16.2 outlines the procedure normally involved in selecting suppliers. The model suggests that the buyer, on receipt of a request to purchase, first checks whether the organization is currently committed to the particular supplier for the supply of such items and, if not, whether an existing source might satisfy the requirement. Repeat ordering with an existing source would be normal unless review is required. Such reasons might include recent price increases, recent extensions in supplier supply lead time, failure to meet specifications, decline in vendor rate performance, etc. Buyer source loyalty is a well-documented phenomenon and clearly offers benefits in terms of reduced administrative difficulty and improved vendor–buyer understanding and relationship. In fact, benefits accrue both to supplier and to vendor. Vendors tend also to give preference to existing customers.

Often an investigation of possible sources for the supply of new items and materials will reveal several alternatives, and hence the question of single or multiple sourcing often arises. Factors to be considered in this respect include the following:

(a) ***Effect on price***, i.e. single sourcing of increased quantities may reduce purchase price. Alternatively, in certain circumstances, multiple sourcing may in fact reduce price as a result of supplier competition for orders.

**Figure 16.2** Outline of procedure for selecting a supplier

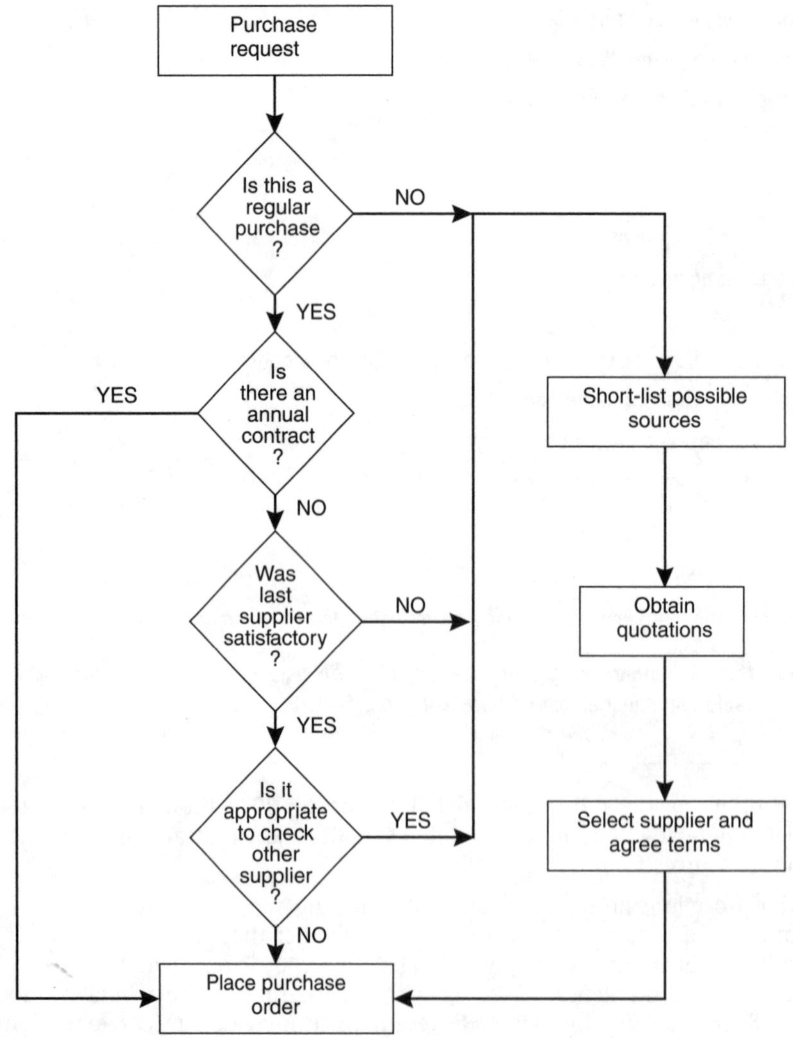

(b) ***Effect on supply security***, i.e. while organization of supply will be simpler with a single source, the organization will be dependent and thus at great risk as a result of any disruptions through, for example, strikes.

(c) ***Effect on supplier motivation***. Although the security resulting from regularly supplying large quantities to an organization might increase supplier motivation, and thus increase willingness to improve specifications, etc., undoubtedly in some circumstances increased motivation might also result from a competitive situation.

(d) ***Effect on market structure*** of single sourcing may in the long term result in the development of a monopolistic situation with the eventual elimination of alternative sources of supply.

The process of identifying and determining supply sources will often involve obtaining competitive bids and analysing such bids and proposals. The latter will often involve price and delivery comparisons, but in most cases more detailed analysis will be necessary. The following factors may be among those considered:

(a) price and cost factors, i.e. cost, delivery costs, insurance costs, price breaks, etc;

(b) delivery factors, including delivery lead times, delivery quantities and delivery frequencies;

(c) specifications factors and quality control/assurance practices;

(d) legal factors, e.g. warranty, in terms of condition, etc.

## Considerations in purchasing policy and procedures

Special considerations will apply in the purchasing of commodities in which the purchase of 'futures' and price forecasting are of importance. This specialist area will not be dealt with here.

Table 16.2 provides a checklist for the make or buy decision. Such decisions can be complex and therefore past, present and future market conditions will normally be analysed.

Documentation procedures for purchasing will not be considered here; however, it should be noted that, because of the often considerable amount of money involved in purchase and purchase decisions, adequate records must be maintained, and because of the often complex situations which exist, computer-based records and control procedures are normally essential. Such a system should cover all purchases, including bought-out equipment, standard parts, raw materials, subcontract work, repairs, services, commercial equipment and stationery. It should assist in the following functions:

(a) accumulation of the requirement to buy;

(b) printing of purchase orders;

(c) recording the progression of the purchase order;

(d) receipts;

(e) inspection;

(f) accumulation of the purchase history;

(g) supply analysis.

## Materials requirements planning *(see also Chapter 12)*

Although developed primarily for use in batch manufacturing situations, materials requirements planning (MRP) has potential in other manufacturing and non-manufacturing situations. The procedure is discussed in detail in Chapter 12 and will only be summarized here.

**Table 16.2 A make or buy checklist**

**If currently purchased from an outside source**

(1) Does capacity exist within own company?

(2) If so, is such capacity likely to be available for the planning period involved?

(3) Is the necessary raw material available now at economic rates?

(4) Will that material continue to be available at economic rates for the planning period?

(5) If tooling is involved: (a) what is the cost? (b) what is the expected life? (c) what is the delivery?

(6) Are we satisfied that the current suppliers are the most economic source?

(7) Is there a patent involved and thus the possibility of royalties to be paid?

(8) Is VAT chargeable?

(9) Are the current suppliers doing development work towards an improved version of the item?

(10) Have the current suppliers had difficulty with quality, quantity or time factors, and have their costs escalated as a result, thus affecting their selling price?

(11) If their quality has been affected: (a) has the suppliers' quality system been vetted? (b) what has been the extent of quality failures? (c) is our production department confident that the specification quality can be economically maintained in internal production? (d) are we over-specifying?

(12) If their other costs are escalating: (a) what are the reasons? (b) are we confident that we will not be affected in the same way?

(13) If the item is currently being imported, what is the cost breakdown? If duty is payable, what rates are applied? What duty, if any, will be payable on the relevant raw materials/components if they are imported?

**If currently being manufactured within the company**

(1) Is there a matter of secrecy to be considered?

(2) If the item is withdrawn from production, would redundancies result?

(3) If 'yes', what action would need to be taken by management regarding these redundancies?

(4) If tooling is involved, what is its condition? Can it be used by the prospective source?

(5) Will the machinery involved on current manufacture be fully utilized for alternative work if the part is withdrawn?

(6) Is there a possibility of development work being done on the part? If so, can this be done satisfactorily in conjunction with an outside supplier?

(7) Will the quantities involved interest an outside supplier?

(8) Do we know the true cost of alternative supply against manufacture (e.g. transport and handling costs) – present and forward?

(9) Is the item part of an integral production route involving several stages of manufacture? If so, can outside manufacture be satisfactorily co-ordinated with production schedules and machine loading in our shops?

(10) What is the forward market position for the item concerned for the relevant planning period?

(11) Are all drawings current?

(12) Is there any advantage in our supplying raw materials/components if a decision to buy is made?

(13) Can we indicate to the potential supplier the remaining life of the product?

(14) Can the potential supplier suggest ideas for taking cost out of the product?

*Source: Baily, P. and Farmer, D. H. (1985)* Purchasing Principles and Techniques. *London: Pitman. Reproduced with permission*

In batch manufacture, particularly assembly, certain components may be required in large quantities at infrequent intervals, i.e. to suit the batch assembly schedule. In many such situations, there will be little benefit in maintaining stocks of all parts and items at all times, since at most times these stocks will not be drawn upon.

If a procedure can be developed by which those items required for assembly are available at the times required and stocks of these items are not maintained, or are maintained at a far lower level, at other times the high cost of maintaining unnecessary stock is avoided but items will still be available when required. MRP provides such a procedure. It is based on the use of 'bill of materials' file and a production or assembly schedule. The bill of materials file provides information on all parts and materials required for all finished products and the production schedule provides information on the production or assembly schedule for all finished products.

Co-ordination of this information together with a knowledge of supply lead times permits the procurement of parts as and when required by the production/assembly schedule. MRP aims to keep inventories low in order to facilitate purchasing, to ensure a supply of parts and materials when needed and to highlight exceptions and priorities.

In non-manufacturing situations the MRP procedure may be of relevance, particularly when the system requires the acquisition of inputs specific to particular operations, jobs or outputs, i.e. when a batch processing procedure is employed. In, for example, certain supply operations where items are acquired against particular customer orders, it may be of value in providing an effective means of planning, controlling and monitoring the purchase of large quantities of a large range of items, to satisfy the requirements of a large number of customers each of whom has particular delivery or due date requirements.

# PHYSICAL DISTRIBUTION AND LOGISTICS

In manufacturing and supply systems the responsibility of distribution is that of getting goods to the customer. A similar responsibility exists in 'customer input' type systems (i.e. service and transport), where the responsibility is to get customers, whether they be people or things, into the system. In the simplest situation these responsibilities involve the organization in direct relationships with the customers. In more complex cases there will be intermediate stages.

In this section we shall deal with the management of both situations. The term 'customer channels' will be used to remind us that we are concerned with flows from or to customers.

## Physical distribution management (PDM)

PDM, concerned with the dynamics of distribution and with customer channel behaviour, may be defined in our context as the process by which appropriate quantities of items or customers are passed through the distribution channel to or from customers. This definition suggest that, given certain channels, the task of PDM is to make them work. However, it begs the question of 'influence' or 'control'. An enterprise may have a one-stage customer channel, i.e. dealing directly with its own ultimate customers, perhaps through a stock or customer queue over which it has some direct control. The manner in which it operates, i.e. its stock-holding, the service level provided to customers and its coverage of the market, can therefore be determined entirely by itself. If, however, more stages exist, e.g. there are intermediaries between the organization and its end customer, then each party may have some influence over such decisions. Figure 16.3 shows, diagrammatically, different types of customer channels, and gives examples for: A, service and transport organizations; and B, manufacture and supply organizations. The figure shows the channels as perceived by the organization. Notice that each stage in the channel might be viewed as a single input/output stage in the way shown in Figure 16.1, but here the emphasis is on multiple-stage channels.

**Figure 16.3** Types of customer channel for an organization, with examples

ULTIMATE CUSTOMERS OR CONSUMERS

(A) ① ② ③

Customer channels for service and transport organizations

Stage 1 / Stage 1, Stage 2

THE ORGANIZATION

THE ORGANIZATION

(B) ① ② ③ ④

Customer channels for manufacturers and supply organizations

Stage 1 / Stage 1, Stage 2 / Stage 1, Stage 2, Stage 3

ULTIMATE CUSTOMERS OR CONSUMERS

*Some examples*

| *Stages* | *Service* | *Transport* |
|---|---|---|
| 1 Stage (direct) | Dentist | Taxi service |
| 2 Stage | Hospital (Stage 1 = Doctors) | Charter airline (Stage 1 = Holiday company) |

*Some examples*

| *Stages* | *Manufacture* | *Supply* |
|---|---|---|
| 1 Stage (direct) | Specialist engineering products (e.g. civil engineering) | Retail shop |
| 2 Stage | Food manufacture (Stage 1 = Supermarket) | Wholesaler (Stage 1 = Retailer) |
| 4 Stage | Motor vehicle manufacture (Stage 1 = Overseas agent Stage 2 = Wholesaler Stage 3 = Retailer) | Importer (Stage 1 = Distribution centre Stage 2 = Wholesalers Stage 3 = Retailers) |

Ideally an enterprise would like to influence all stages in the distribution channel between itself and the final customer, and this is easily achieved for organizations with one-stage customer channels. The extent of the influence or the 'reach' of the enterprise along the customer channel will affect its PDM decision. An enterprise which controls its entire distribution channel to or from the final customer will make decisions affecting all stages in that channel, whereas an enterprise with less influence may make decisions affecting only a part of the channel.

## PDM decisions

The principal interrelated decision areas in PDM are as follows:

(a) the choice, design and implementation of a channel of distribution;

(b) the 'level of service' to be provided to customers;

(c) inventory decisions.

These are outlined in the following section, which can provide only an introduction to this subject. Notice that for single-stage channels the PDM decisions are principally (b) and (c) above, and in such cases the problem can be seen largely as one of inventory management. We shall be dealing with inventory management in this context in Chapter 17, so here we shall concentrate on the more complex PDM case of multi-stage channels where the approach required is somewhat different because of both (a) above and the more complex situations in (b) and (c).

## Channel decisions

We can identify four important questions:

(a) the question of ***level*** – the number of levels or stages which should exist in the channel;

(b) the question of ***type*** – which type or types of intermediary should be employed once the level has been decided;

(c) the question of ***intensity*** – how many of each type of intermediary are to be used;

(d) the question of ***control*** – what degree of control should the organization seek to exercise, and where appropriate what degree of control should it accept from others.

### *Level (or stages)*

Here we are concerned with the length of the customer channel, which to some extent will be influenced by the nature of the operation. For example, perishable items, those whose processing requires close liaison with customers, those delivered in bulk, those with high unit value, those which are urgent and those requiring particular services will all best be dealt with through short channels.

Markets which are temporary or which have limited potential will rarely justify the establishment of long channels, and small markets are often best served through short channels. Where communication and/or transportation is difficult or expensive, or where there are numerous 'sources' and 'destinations', an intermediary in the customer channels can reduce the total number of contacts in the manner shown in Figure 16.4. Where one customer represents a large proportion of total demand there will be pressure to establish relatively direct channels to that customer; conversely, where total demand is spread relatively thinly over many customers, the merit of intermediaries in reducing contact complexity is clear.

**Figure 16.4** The number of 'contacts' in a multiple source/destination table

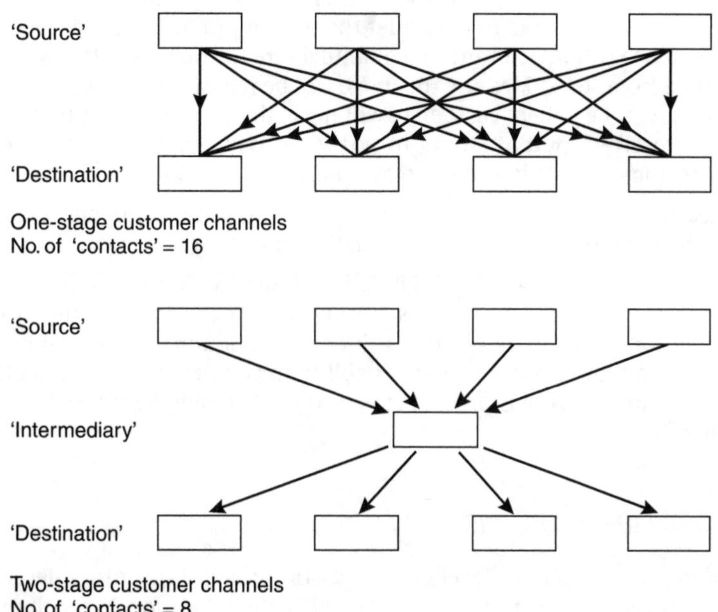

### Type

Which types of intermediary are most suited to particular channels? The nature of the 'end' market of customers should influence the choice of 'type' rather than vice versa. Items, transports or services must be available to 'end' customers where they expect to find them. It will therefore be difficult to break with tradition unless service to the end customer is clearly improved, although there are obvious examples of successful innovation, e.g. in new forms of retailing and in direct selling.

### Intensity and control

At one extreme there is the possibility of limited distribution through an exclusive channel, and a move from this situation will involve an organization in dealing with a greater number and range of intermediaries. This, however, may be justified where greater market coverage or 'presence' is required yet where the organization does not aspire to maintain close control over all intermediaries. The increased 'coverage' of the market might justify the use of more intensive distribution through multiple intermediaries at each stage with increased PDM costs. However, the use of a greater number of 'contact' points with the market will influence the stock levels required in order to provide a given level of service (see below).

## Service-level decisions *(see also Chapter 17)*

The level of service provided to end customers might be expressed in terms of:

(a) percentage of customer orders satisfied in a given period of time;

(b) average delivery or waiting time before a customer order is satisfied;

(c) percentage of customer orders which are satisfied after a quoted delivery or waiting time;

(d) percentage of total demand satisfied in a given period.

The type of measure employed in setting objectives for, and then in monitoring, customer service will depend on the type of organization, and in particular the type of product or service which is being provided. For example, (a) above will be relevant in a 'manufacture to stock' situation where the customer is normally to be satisfied from stock. Measure (b) above will be relevant where goods or service are provided against a specific order, i.e. where customers will normally expect to wait to be served, or where capacity is insufficient to create output stocks of goods or avoid input queues of customers, even though the nature of customer needs is known in advance.

Whatever the measure of customer service, normally the provision of higher levels of service will incur greater costs to the organization. The type of relationship shown in Figure 16.5 will often apply.

Clearly there is a cost penalty in providing high customer service, so the justification for aiming for high service must be demonstrable. The obvious reason is the need to conform to what customers expect, i.e. what competitors provide; indeed this will be essential unless some compensatory satisfaction is provided, e.g. through lower price. Equally, inability to compete in the market through price or specification will necessitate the provision of better service through better delivery, short waiting times, etc. (see Chapter 2).

## Inventory decisions *(see also Chapter 17)*

Where inventories of items exist, service-level decisions can influence inventory decisions in terms of not only the levels of inventory to be provided, but also their location throughout the customer channel.

**Figure 16.5** The relationship of customer service and cost

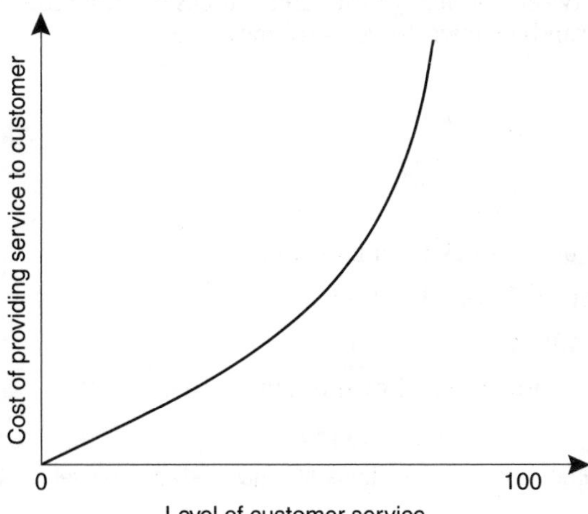


Chapter 17 will deal in detail with inventory management decisions. The emphasis there will be on the management of 'single-stage' inventories (e.g. the management of each stock in an operating system). Here we must consider inventories *throughout* customer channels. For example, in a three-stage distribution channel there may be three levels of inventory of the same type of items, with several different stock-holdings at each level.

Among other purposes, inventories provide service to the next stage in the channel. For example, an input stock of raw materials in a hospital helps to ensure that the medical activities of the hospital are not held up. An output stock in a manufacturing company helps to ensure that those directly served by that organization are able to get what they want when they want it. In other words, for each stock there is an immediate customer and a purpose of the stock is to provide service to that customer. We shall see in Chapter 17 that where demands on stock are uncertain, as is often the case, or when the time required to replenish stocks is uncertain, it is necessary to provide some buffer or safety stock to ensure that most customers get what they want most of the time, i.e. that 'stockouts' are normally avoided. Two related PDM questions, themselves related to the service-level question, therefore are what stock levels to provide and where to provide them.

The determination of safety (or buffer) stock levels to provide given levels of service will be dealt with in detail for the 'single-stage' problem in Chapter 17. These single-stage methods can be modified to deal with stocks in multi-stage systems. Here we shall consider only the basic principles to be remembered in making inventory decisions in multi-stage systems.

### *The number of stock locations at a given stage*

If one stock location is established from which demand throughout a given market is to be satisfied, then a safety stock must be provided in addition to a base stock. The base stock is that amount of inventory necessary to satisfy average demand during a given period of time, while the safety stock is that extra amount provided to protect against uncertainties. The way in which this safety stock can be determined is explained in Chapter 17. If we establish several stock locations *each* for a given sector of the market, e.g. a region, then base stock and safety stock must be provided at each. The sum of the base stocks for each stock location will be the same as the original single base stock, but the sum of the safety stocks at each location to provide the original level of service will exceed the safety stock required for the single location.

The general relationship between the sum of the safety stocks required for *n* stock-holdings and that required for a single holding can be shown to be as follows:

$$B_n = \frac{B_1(n)}{\sqrt{n}}$$

where $B_n$ = total safety or buffer stock for *n* locations

$B_1$ = safety or buffer stock for 1 location

$n$ = number of locations

The general nature of the relationship is shown in Figure 16.6.

**Figure 16.6** Safety stock v. number of stock locations at a given stage or level

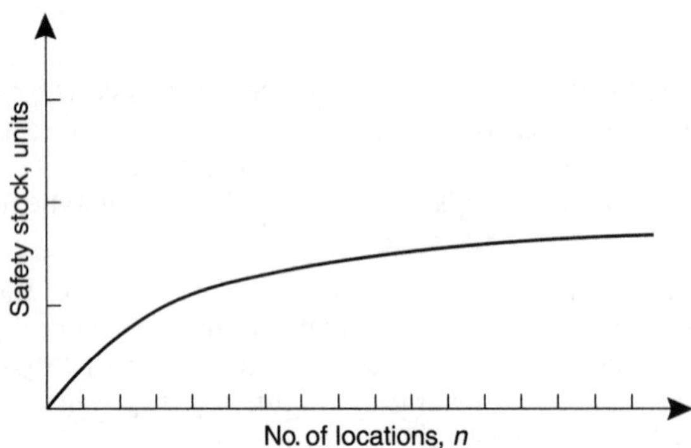


## Stock-holdings at different levels

In considering safety stock provision it should be noted that less total safety stock will be needed to provide a given level of end customer service if that stock is provided at a 'higher' level in the customer channel, provided of course that when required it can quickly be deployed to the end customer. For example, in a customer channel which has a wholesale and several retail stocks, safety stock provided at the wholesale level can protect against uncertain demand at all retail outlets, but since high demand at one can be offset by low demand at another, the safety stock-holding at the warehouse level will be less than the total safety stock required by all retailers if each is required to operate entirely separately in its own market sector.

The existence of stocks at 'higher' levels in the customer channel should not simply permit the duplication of stocks held at 'lower' levels, but should complement lower-level stocks. For example, low-usage and/or high-cost items should be stocked at higher levels to reduce cost, while high-usage/low-cost items should be concentrated in lower-level stocks since this permits high customer service at low cost.

EXAMPLE

## *Channel integration*

K-Mart, Kodak and Lee Apparel adopted a new approach to inventory management to co-ordinate the flow of product from the warehouse to the store floor. Known as 'channel integration', this process depends on retailers sharing information on sales at the store level with suppliers. This exchange of information enables suppliers to manufacture at the level of actual demand for a product and dispatch only the product needed. Channel integration allows both the supplier and the retailer to carry the minimum inventory in their warehouses. Both retailers and manufacturers benefit from channel integration by reducing inventory levels and lowering handling and transportation costs.

Source: Cook, J. A. (1992) Supply chain management – 1990s style. *Traffic Management*, **31**(5), pp. 57–59.

## CHECKLIST FOR CHAPTER 16

### *Materials management*

### *Integrated materials management*

Centralized v. decentralized

### *Supply chain management*

The nature of the supply chain
Developing a supply chain strategy

### *Purchasing and supply*

Responsibilities and relationship
Operations management
Objectives of purchasing
Benefits of effective purchasing
Organization of purchasing
- Centralized
- Decentralized
- JIT purchasing

Sourcing and suppliers
- Vendor rating
- Single or multiple sourcing: factors to be considered

Purchasing policy and procedures
- Make or buy policy
- Documentation and computer procedure
- Materials requirement planning

### *Physical distribution and logistics*

The role of distribution in materials management
Types of customer channel
- Examples of one-, two-, three- and four-stage channels

The role of PDM
- PDM decisions

Channel decisions
- Number of levels or stages
- Types of intermediary
- Intensity and control of distribution
- Service-level decisions
- Definition of service level
- Service level v. cost

Inventory decisions
- In single- and multi-stage channels
- Safety or buffer stocks
- Number of locations at a given stage
- Stock-holdings at different stages

## FURTHER READING


**Baily, P. and Farmer, D. H. (1985)** *Purchasing Principles and Techniques*, 5th edn. London: Pitman.

**Busch, H. F. (1988)** Integrated materials management. *International Journal of Physical Distribution and Materials Management*, **18**(7), pp. 54–68.

**Christopher, M. (1992)** *Logistics and Supply Chain Management*. London: Pitman.

**Leenders, M. R., Fearon, H. E. and England, W. B. (1985)** *Purchasing and Materials Management*, 8th edn. Homewood, Ill.: Irwin.

**Novack, R. A. and Simco, S. W. (1991)** The industrial procurement process – a supply chain perspective. *Journal of Business Logistics*, **12**(1), pp. 145–167.

**Schonberger, R. and Gilbert, J. (1983)** Just in time purchasing: a challenge for US industry. *California Management Review*, **26**(1), pp. 54–68.

**Stevens, G. C. (1990)** Successful supply-chain management. *Management Decision*, **28**(8), pp. 25–30.

## QUESTIONS

16.1 Discuss the merits of a centralized purchasing procedure for a chain of small retail domestic hardware stores.

16.2 What factors might influence the 'make or buy' decision for a manufacturing organization, and how might similar considerations operate in a transport or service organization?

16.3 'Materials requirements planning is little more than the extension of reverse scheduling from operations to the purchasing function.' Discuss.

16.4 Give examples of one-stage and two-stage customer channels for:

(a) a manufacturing organization;

(b) a supply organization;

(c) a transport organization;

(d) a service organization.

Explain why such channels are employed in these cases.

16.5 Select *one* of the following organizations and outline and explain the types of decision likely to be required in PDM in that organization (i.e. in the planning, management and control of flows through the customer channels):

(a) a book publisher dealing with college books;

(b) a microcomputer manufacturer.

## CASE STUDIES (from Part 9)

The topics covered in this chapter are relevant in the following (see Introduction to Part 9 and Table C.1 for further details):

| No. | Name | Country |
|---|---|---|
| 2 | Jograni Handicrafts | Bangladesh |
| 3 | Centre Hospitalier Reine Fabiola | Belgium |
| 7 | Pokhara Weavers | Nepal |
| 27 | Food Concept Sdn. Bhd. | Malaysia |

Chapter 17

# Inventory management

## ISSUES

What types of stock are there and where do they exist?
What are consumed items stocks?
How are stocks controlled?
What inventory management decisions are required?
What are the value and relevance of the many order quantity formulae?
How do we deal with uncertainty?
Where and how does MRP fit with inventory management?

## NOTATION USED IN THIS CHAPTER

| | | |
|---|---|---|
| $B$ | Buffer or safety stock | |
| $\sigma$ | Standard deviation of demand | |
| $C$ | Total cost of ordering and holding | |
| $C_1$ | Holding cost/item/unit time | |
| $C_2$ | Shortage or stockout cost/item/unit time | |
| $C_{11}$ | Fixed portion of $C_1$ | |
| $C_{12}$ | Variable portion of $C_1$ | |
| $C_{1A}$ | Variable holding cost/unit time, for one increment of storage | |
| $C_{1i}$ | Holding cost/item of item $i$/unit time | |
| $C_s$ | Ordering cost/order | |
| $C^*$ | Minimum total cost | |
| MRP | Materials requirements planning | |
| $N$ | Number of items ($i = 1 \ldots N$) | |
| $P(U)$ | Probability of usage $U$ | |
| $p$ | cost/unit | |
| $p_i$ | Price for order quantity $q_i$ | for discount price |
| $q_i$ | Order quantity | for discount price |
| $Q$ | Order quantity | |
| $Q_i$ | Order quantity for item $i$ | |
| $q$ | Delivery or production rate | |

| | |
|---|---|
| $Q^*$ | Optimum order quantity |
| $R$ | Reorder level |
| $r$ | Usage or demand rate |
| $r_i$ | Usage or demand rate for item $i$ |
| $S$ | Stock level after replenishment |
| $t$ | Order cycle |
| $t_i$ | Order cycle for item $i$ |
| $t^*$ | Optimum order cycle |
| $U$ | lead time usage |
| $\bar{U}$ | Mean lead time usage |

We discussed the management of inventories in the context of materials and supply chain management in Chapter 16. There we concentrated on multi-stage systems and the management of inventories throughout such systems. We noted that the management of multi-stage inventory systems was in some ways a different problem from that of managing single-stage inventories, i.e. single stock-holdings. Here we shall concentrate on the management of single-stage inventories. All of what will be discussed will be relevant in the management of the supply chain, since in some cases it will be appropriate to manage each stock-holding as a separate entity, and in some cases each stock-holding will be the property or responsibility of a different organization, so there will be little opportunity for co-ordinated control of inventories at different levels.

## THE NATURE AND PURPOSES OF SINGLE-STAGE INVENTORIES *(see also Chapter 1 and Chapter 11)*

Stocks will exist in operating systems if they are feasible, and if they serve some useful purpose. For example, it will be feasible to employ system output stocks in manufacturing or supply systems if the nature of future customer demand is known, i.e. if we know what future customers will want (see Chapter 1). In this case, therefore, such stocks will exist if they also serve some useful purpose, e.g. if they effectively protect the operating system from fluctuations in demand.

Similar considerations apply to all the stocks which might exist before, within and after any operating system. If they are feasible, they will be used if they are useful, and the latter will often depend on the capacity management strategy which is being employed (see Chapter 11).

For our purposes we can consider stocks to comprise either *consumed* or *non-consumed* items. Consumed items (e.g. materials or products) are utilized by the operating system or taken by the customer and must therefore be replaced. Non-consumed items (e.g. capital equipment and labour) are used repeatedly by the system and need repair and maintenance. In this chapter we deal only with consumed items, and therefore with three types of inventory:

(a) ***system output inventory*** (in manufacturing and supply systems), e.g. goods produced or provided by the operating system;

(b) ***system input resource inventory*** (in manufacturing, supply, transport or service systems), e.g. materials which will be consumed by the operating system;

(c) ***customer input queues*** (in transport or service systems), i.e. the input stocks of customers that will be processed through the system. (They are a resource which is input to the operating system, since the system cannot operate without them.)

Notice that 'work-in-progress' inventory, i.e. partially processed items or customers, is really the output stock of one part of the operating system and the input to the next. It is therefore contained within categories (a) and (b) above.

Inventory management is concerned essentially with the use and control of inventories. The need for inventory management is influenced by capacity management decisions, since the existence of inventories will, in part, be determined by the capacity management strategies which are to be employed. If inventories exist, they should serve some useful purpose, and therefore must be carefully managed. These 'purposes' might include:

(a) ***For output stocks*** (in manufacture and possible supply systems):

1. to provide good service to customers;
2. to protect the function from uncertainties in demand, e.g. permitting stable level of operating of function despite fluctuating demand;
3. to permit manufacture or supply of items in economic batches.

(b) ***For input resource stocks*** (in manufacture, supply, transport and service systems):

1. to permit favourable purchase/provision arrangements, e.g. price discounts and economic order quantities;
2. to protect the function from uncertainties in supply, e.g. permitting stable/undisrupted operation despite fluctuating/interrupted supplies.

(c) ***For customer input queues*** (in transport and service systems): to protect functions from uncertainties in demand, e.g. permitting stable level of operating of functions despite fluctuating demand.

# INVENTORIES OF CONSUMED ITEMS

## Output stocks

Certain operating system structures provide for output stocks. Customer demand is satisfied from such stocks, which in turn are replenished from the function. The information flows in the opposite direction to the physical flow; hence, in the case of intermittent stock replenishment, customer orders will be received at output inventory, depletion of which will give rise to the dispatch of replenishment orders to the function.

Stocks may be replenished *intermittently* or *continuously*, although in some cases the distinction is more evident in the type of inventory management decisions that are required than in the physical flow into stock.

For our purposes we can consider the nature of customer demand to be given; however, a knowledge or estimate of the nature of demand, in particular the demand level and fluctuations, will influence inventory management. The stock levels maintained and/or the amount of buffer (or safety) stock provided will reflect expected demand levels and fluctuation.

The complexity of the inventory management problem and the likely effectiveness of inventory management depend on the variability or unpredictability of stock input and output levels and also on the opportunities for, and the extent of, control. Thus, in certain systems, inventory management is likely to be more effective than in others simply because there is the opportunity for the exercise of closer control.

The classic stock control problem is that of establishing an inventory policy based on some *control over stock inputs* to satisfy unpredictable demand or output. Given a forecast output or usage rate per unit time and the variability of that output rate, the following inventory parameters might be established:

(a) For intermittent stock replenishment:

1. either reorder level *or* interval; and
2. order quantities.

(b) For continuous replenishment:

1. input rate; and
2. average stock level required.

## Input resource inventory

Certain systems require input stocks. The problem of managing the stocks of input resources closely resembles that of system output inventory management. Here, the function is the customer for input resource stocks, so, as with output stocks, demand is satisfied from stock, which in turn is replenished from supply. The activity scheduling function will be responsible for the manner in which the input stocks are depleted. Either consumable resources will be scheduled intermittently through the function or a regular throughput rate will have been fixed. In either case we can again consider the nature of demand on stocks to be given; however, a knowledge or estimate of the nature of demand, in particular demand level and fluctuations, will again influence input inventory management. As with output stocks, the amount of buffer (or safety) stock provided will reflect expected demand levels and fluctuation as well as the predictability and degree of control available over *inputs to stock*.

Again the following parameters might be established:

(a) For intermittent stock replenishment:

1. either reorder level *or* interval; and
2. order quantities.

(b) For continuous replenishment:

1. input rate; and
2. average stock level required.

## Customer input queues

Two operating system structures require input queues (or stocks) of customers (see Chapter 1). Here, customers, or items provided by them, are consumed resources. They are an input which differs from other consumed recourses only in being beyond the direct control of system management. In other words there is little or no control over the input or arrival of such resources, i.e. their input is unpredictable. Since there is little opportunity for control over inputs, such inventory is mainly managed through *control over the output*.

Given an estimate of the input rate and the variability of that rate, the following inventory parameters might be established:

(a) For intermittent depletion;

1. output intervals *or* the stock levels at which output is to occur; and
2. output quantities.

(b) For continuous depletion:

1. output rate; and
2. average stock level required.

# INVENTORY MANAGEMENT DECISIONS

Table 17.1 shows the two types of control referred to above – input and output – in relation to system structure and types of inventory. Table 17.2 summarizes the inventory management decisions required for these two types of control, and for the types of flow.

**Table 17.1 Control of inventories versus operating system structures**

| Type of control: Model | Type of control: Description | Application: System structures (see Chapter 1) | Application: Inventory |
|---|---|---|---|
| ⇒⧖⇒ ▽ ⇒ (Control on input) | Control of stock input | Function from stock to stock | Output |
| | | Function from stock to stock | Input |
| | | Function from stock to customer | Input |
| | | Function from stock from customer | Input |
| | | Function from stock from customer queue | Input |
| ⇒ ▽ ⇒⧖⇒ (Control on output) | Control of stock output | Function from source from customer queue | Customer input |
| | | Function from source from customer queue | Customer input |

The following example indicates the manner in which inventories are controlled in a particular situation. Some of the decisions required in this situation (Table 17.2) and the type of control situation which exists (Table 17.1) are seen to be influenced by the structure of the operating system, while the objectives to be achieved clearly influence the operations manager's decisions.

**Table 17.2 Inventory management decisions (consumed items)**

| Nature of flow | Location of flow control: On stock inputs | Location of flow control: On stock outputs |
|---|---|---|
| Intermittent | Determine stock replenishment level *or* interval | Determine stock levels *or* intervals at which output is to take place |
| | Determine input quantity | Determine output quantity |
| Continuous | Determine average (or safety) stock levels required | Determine average stock levels required |
| | Determine stock replenishment (input) rate | Determine stock output rate |

**EXAMPLE**

## *A hospital accident ward*

Inventories will exist on the input side of the function only and will consist of consumed and non-consumed resources. There will be no stocks of finished goods nor, ideally, stocks or queues of customers.

Taking first the consumed item input stocks such as medications, disposable items, bandages, etc., management will seek to control such inventory through control of input flow, such flow being either intermittent or continuous. In the case of intermittent flow, management will seek to establish either a replenishment level or a replenishment interval, and replenishment batch sizes. In the case of the control of continuous or almost continuous input flow, management will seek to establish a safety or average stock level sufficient to accommodate unexpectedly high demand. In contrast, non-consumed items will of course be all physical facilities, equipment, buildings, etc., together with labour, i.e. medical, nursing and administrative staff. Here replacement is almost certainly likely to be on an intermittent basis, the task again being to determine the timing of replacement, such replacement being either replacement of resources lost or the renewal of exhausted resources.

The objective in the management of such input resource inventories in the hospital accident ward will be concerned principally with the provision of adequate customer service. Here customer service will be considered satisfactory only inasmuch as the system structure is maintained, i.e. only inasmuch as customer queuing is avoided. A deterioration in customer service reflected in the queuing of customers will of course reflect a change in system structure. In the latter case somewhat different inventory management problems will occur.

## COSTS IN INVENTORY MANAGEMENT

Two sets of costs are of immediate relevance in inventory decision-making: inventory costs and customer service costs.

### Inventory costs

Items held in stock incur costs. *Holding costs* comprise the costs of storage facilities; provision of services to such facilities; insurance on stocks; costs of loss, breakage, deterioration, obsolescence; and the opportunity cost or notional loss of interest on the capital tied up. In general, an increase in the quantity of stocks held will be reflected in an increase in holding costs, although the relationships may not be linear. For example, costs of increasing stock-holdings may be in the form of a step function, since increased space is required when stocks reach certain levels. The cost of capital, insurance, etc. may also be discontinuous through the effect of price breaks or quantity discounts. Stock-holdings of a certain level may permit replenishment in quantities sufficient to attract quantity discounts. Other things being equal, higher costs of holding will result in lower stock quantities and vice versa. Certain *stock-change costs* apply particularly in intermittent flow systems, e.g. in input control systems change costs will consist of the cost of ordering replenishment and in some cases the cost of delivery of replenishment items and the cost of receipt, inspection, placing in stock, etc. In output control systems change costs will consist of the cost of ordering or initiating depletion and the cost of dispatch, etc.

### Customer service costs

Customer service considerations influence inventory decisions in operating systems in which output stocks exist. Here customer service might be measured in terms of the number of occasions over a given period in which orders cannot immediately be satisfied from stock, i.e. the number of '*stockouts*'. Equally, the probability of such stockouts might also provide a measure of customer service. In such a situation customers are in effect being starved by the system. In transport and service systems, customer service may be measured by the occurrence or duration of *queuing*. Where queuing is required, customer service may be measured by the average time spent in the queue or the number of items in the queue. Where queuing is not normally required, customer service may be measured by the probability that queuing will occur. In such situations customers are in effect being 'blocked' by the system. This customer service, whether in input or output control systems, has inventory cost implications, e.g. costs of shortage, loss of trade.

## WHICH ITEMS TO CONTROL

Many companies subject all items, purchased or produced, irrespective of their value, usage or quantity, to the same type of stock control procedure. Such a policy can be a waste of time and effort.

Although high usage rate does not necessarily mean high stock levels, fast-moving items, i.e. those for which the usage rate is high, and expensive items are likely to incur greater stock costs than slow-moving inexpensive items. Consequently we should aim to control the fast-moving/expensive items, since by doing so greater potential savings are possible.

The Pareto can be used in this context (see Figure 17.1). It helps show that a small proportion of the stocked items accounts for a large proportion of inventory cost or value. Their relationship is often referred to as the 80/20 'law', i.e. up to 80% of the firm's total inventory cost or value is accounted for by about 20% of items. This relationship encourages us to categorize inventory items into three classes, A, B and C. Category A would be those relatively few types of items which account for a relatively large proportion of total inventory cost or value, category B would be the slightly larger number of items which account for a smaller percentage of total cost, and category C would be that large proportion of items which account for a very small proportion of total cost.

Category A items should be closely controlled; category B items should be subject to less control; and for category C items a simple control procedure is probably sufficient.

**Figure 17.1** ABC chart (for the example on pp. 511–512)

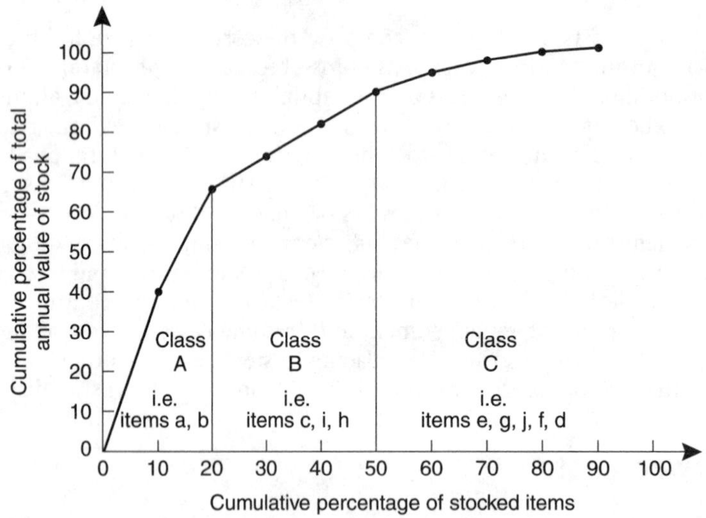

**EXAMPLE**

### *Tampa General Hospital*

Tampa General Hospital in Florida lost some $12 million in 1983. In 1984 organizational adjustments were made in materials management. The aim was to provide the basic foundations of efficiency, simplification, close interaction with finance, and a commitment to serve and support all areas of the institution. A master plan was developed that focused on the high departmental inventories, the numerous goods receiving areas and the slow turnaround of orders, among other problems. A new system was introduced through which supplies were delivered to theatres, etc. The aim was to improve control and stock utilization. By 1989, there had been a dramatic turnaround. For example, inventory turnover – a measure of the efficiency of the use of inventories – had improved from 2.2 in 1987 to 4.3 in 1989.

Source: Richardson, J. (1990) Material management in the operating room: a case study. *Hospital Materials Management Quarterly*, **12**(2), pp. 44–48.

---

The following example shows how an ABC curve can be constructed and items appropriate for category A, B and C treatment identified.

EXAMPLE

## *A clothing wholesaler*

The table below shows the bought-in price and annual sales of the set of different types of garments which are held in stock by a wholesaler. The aim is to construct an ABC chart for these items and identify which items should be treated as classes A, B and C.

*Inventory Management*

| Item type | Purchase price (£) | Annual sales (items per year) |
|---|---|---|
| a | 8 | 1250 |
| b | 18 | 450 |
| c | 30 | 75 |
| d | 25 | 10 |
| e | 3 | 280 |
| f | 4 | 80 |
| g | 18 | 45 |
| h | 7 | 250 |
| i | 12 | 150 |
| j | 26 | 30 |

*Solution*

Step 1: Calculate annual value:

| Item type | Annual value (£) |
|---|---|
| a | 10 000 |
| b | 8 100 |
| c | 2 250 |
| d | 250 |
| e | 840 |
| f | 320 |
| g | 810 |
| h | 1 750 |
| i | 1 800 |
| j | 780 |
| 10 | £26 900 |
| Total number of item types stocked | Total annual value |

Step 2: Order items by descending annual value and calculate cumulative percentage of total annual value:

Step 3: Draw ABC chart (see Figure 17.1).

| Item type | Annual value (£) | Cumulative percentage of £26 900 |
|---|---|---|
| a | 10 000 | 37 |
| b | 8 100 | 67 |
| c | 2 250 | 76 |
| i | 1 800 | 82.5 |
| h | 1 750 | 89 |
| e | 840 | 92 |
| g | 810 | 95 |
| j | 780 | 98 |
| f | 320 | 99 |
| d | 250 | 100 |

# INVENTORY MANAGEMENT SYSTEMS

We can now look more closely at the types of problems posed by the adoption of the inventory management strategies outlined in Table 17.2. We shall focus on the more usual case of intermittent flow/input control.

## Intermittent flow/input control

Most published treatments of inventory management deal with input control of intermittent flow systems, with the objective of satisfying a given output need or criterion. There are two basic approaches that might be adopted (see Table 17.2).

(a) fixed input level;

(b) fixed input interval.

The two approaches are compared in Figure 17.2.

**Figure 17.2** Input control inventory: types of control

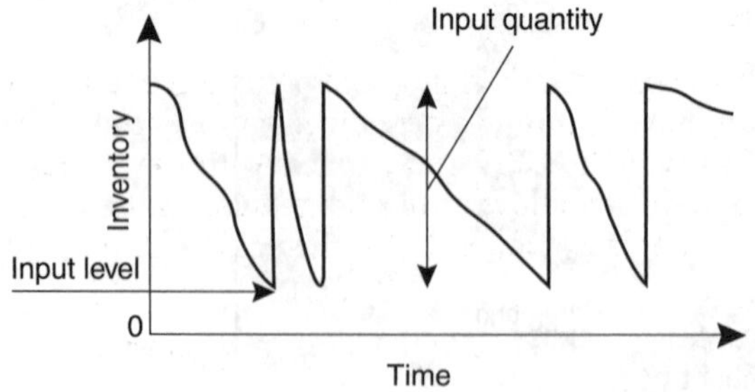


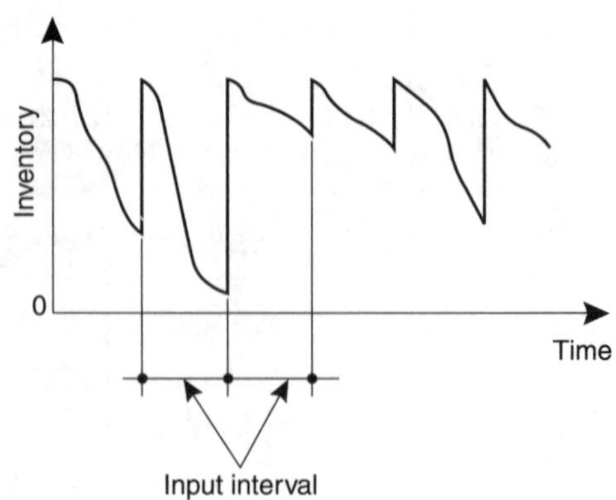

**Figure 17.3** Input control inventory – types of intermittent replenishment

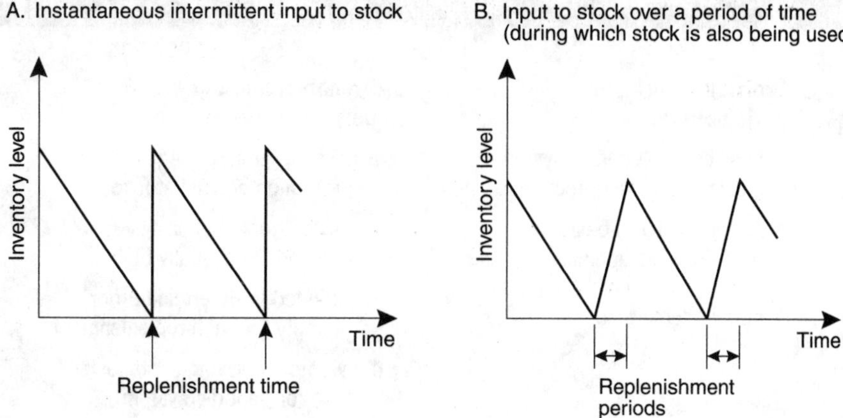


Fixed input level control relies on the replenishment of stock by a given input quantity, actuated at a given inventory level. In other words, inventory will fall to a reorder level when replenishment is initiated or takes place. This approach is sometimes known as the 'maximum–minimum' or 'two-bin' system.

The fixed input interval approach relies on the replenishment of inventory at fixed intervals of time. The replenishment quantity in such situations is often determined such as to replenish inventory to a given maximum level.

Replenishment of stock in input control/intermittent flow systems might take place instantaneously or over a period of time. The stock level 'traces' in Figure 17.2 rely on instantaneous replenishment, i.e. replenishment of stock by a whole quantity at one time. Figure 17.3 compares (a) intermittent input/instantaneous with (b) intermittent input/with usage. The latter relies on replenishment of stock intermittently yet over a period of time during which usage or output continues to occur.

The input level approach to inventory control is in effect a form of *perpetual* inventory management. Stock is replenished when it falls to a particular level, so it will be necessary to maintain some 'perpetual' monitoring of the inventory in order to ensure that action is taken when the appropriate stock level is reached. The input interval system is in effect a *periodic* inventory control system. There will be no need to check stock level except at the times when the replenishment order is to be placed. The type of system which is employed will depend largely on the circumstances. In some situations it will be very difficult, or expensive, to maintain a perpetual check on inventory levels in order to be able to operate the order level approach. However, where the number of transactions, i.e. the number of times the stock is depleted, is low compared with the annual usage, or where the unit cost of items is high, it may be more appropriate to use the perpetual inventory control system.

Table 17.3 compares the two systems. In many cases the cost of running a perpetual inventory control system (order level approach) will be greater than that of running a periodic inventory control system (order interval approach). However, the cost of carrying inventory may be less with the perpetual system than with the periodic system, especially where the periodic control system involves the replenishment of stock by a fixed quantity. As a guide, the order level approach, i.e. the perpetual inventory control system, may be more appropriate where:

(a) the number of transactions (i.e. stock depletions) is low compared with the annual usage;

(b) the processing cost of transactions is low compared with the ordering cost;

(c) the unit price of items is high;

(d) the required service level or degree of protection against stockouts is high;

**Table 17.3 'Periodic' (order interval) versus 'perpetual' (order quantity) inventory control systems**

| (Probable) merits of 'periodic' system | (Probable) merits of 'perpetual' system |
|---|---|
| 1. Less cost to operate system (i.e. less checking, recording, etc.) | 1. Less buffer stock required for protection against stockouts |
| 2. Administratively easier in multi-item situations, i.e. easier to place order for each item at same time | 2. Fewer stockouts when demand is unusually high |
| | 3. No need to determine order quantity for each replenishment |
| | 4. Inventory carrying costs lower than for periodic system |

(e) usage fluctuations are high and difficult to predict;

(f) inventory carrying costs are high;

(g) the use of a computer-based system permits frequent stock level updating (e.g. after every transaction), thus minimizing the disadvantage of the high operating cost of 'perpetual' inventory control.

Where demand is constant and replenishment is instantaneous or where the replenishment lead time is known, the fixed input level approach will resemble the fixed input interval approach. Only where either replenishment lead time or demand is uncertain will the adoption of each approach lead in practice to different inventory behaviour (e.g. Figure 17.2, in which the diagrams show the effect of each policy against the same demand patterns).

Virtually all inventory control quantitative models deal with intermittent flow and input control, i.e. batch ordering, and in most cases the objective is cost minimization, i.e the minimization of the total of holding and inventory change costs (see Figure 17.4). Most such models are deterministic, i.e. they assume a known constant demand and either known input rate with no lead time or instantaneous input and known lead time. In such deterministic situations (which rarely, if ever, occur) there will be no need for provision of buffer or safety stocks. Such stocks will be provided only to protect against uncertain demand and/or lead time (see below). Probabilistic models are available, as are models aimed at profit maximization, etc. Figure 17.5 provides a taxonomy of intermittent flow inventory models (models B, C and D are not discussed in the text).

**Figure 17.4** Costs in determining order quantities

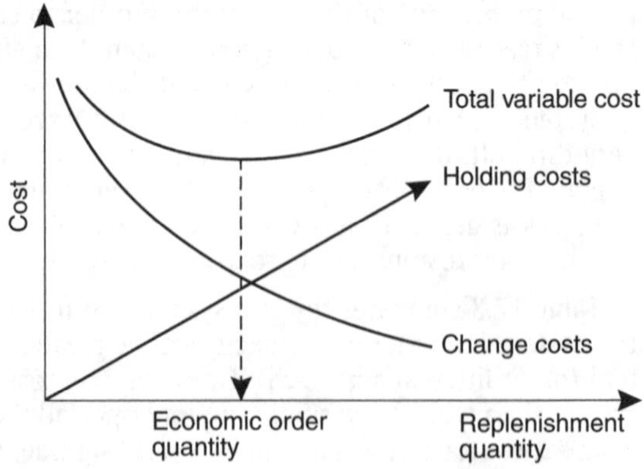


Although deterministic models make certain unrealistic assumptions, they are nevertheless of use in practice. Provided the uncertainties to be accommodated (e.g. demand uncertainties) are not too great, they can be dealt with through the provision of buffer stocks. So in practice the models discussed below may often be used to determine the order quantity or interval for use in conjunction with the type of approach developed in the section on probabilistic situations.

**Figure 17.5** Intermittent flow/input control inventory models (N.B. Letters refer to text)

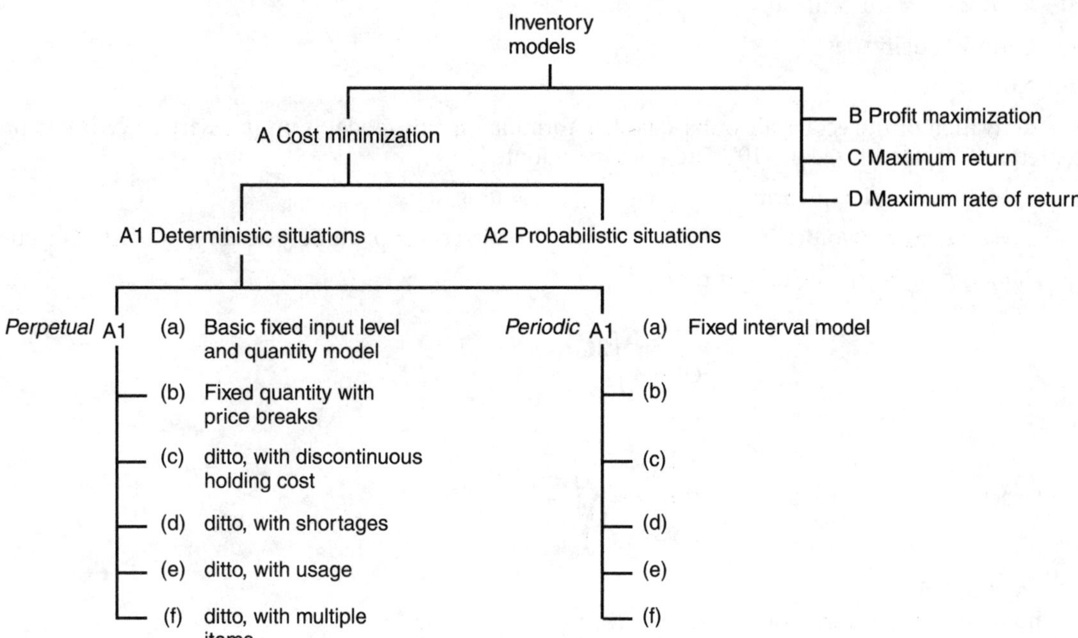


# A1 DETERMINISTIC SITUATIONS

## Perpetual control: the input level method

In this (the perpetual) inventory control method, two decisions must be made:

(a) What fixed input quantity will be used to replenish stocks?

(b) At what stock level will this replenishment order be made?

We shall first deal with the *order quantity* decisions.

### Order quantities

The act of replenishing inventories is often expensive. Such replenishment costs are normally proportionate only to the number of orders placed and not to the size of the orders.

The ordering cost is equivalent to the set-up cost considered during our discussion of batch quantities in Chapter 14.

The order quantity decision involves the determination of the most economical order quantity – the quantity which minimizes total variable costs. In graphical terms the problem is one of establishing the order or batch quantity corresponding to the lowest point on a total cost curve such as that shown in Figure 17.4. Various economic order quantity (EOQ) models have been developed. The following are those commonly adopted and of most value.

### Perpetual model A1(a)

The following are assumed:

(i) Known constant demand.

(ii) Complete deliveries.

(iii) No shortages.

The derivation of the economic order quantity formula for this model is unnecessary since it was presented in Chapter 14 (see p. 410). The notation adopted is:

$Q$ = optimal order quantity $\quad r$ = usage rate

$C_s$ = ordering cost/order $\quad p$ = direct cost per unit (price or manufacturing cost)

$C_1$ = holding cost/item/unit of time

EOQ = $$Q^* = \sqrt{\frac{2C_s r}{C_1}}$$

Order cycle $$t^* = \frac{Q^*}{r} = \sqrt{\frac{2C_s}{rC_1}}$$

Total ordering and holding cost per unit time $$C^* = \sqrt{2C_s r C_1}$$

### Perpetual model A1(b)

As model A1(a), *with price breaks*, i.e. bulk discounts on purchase price or reductions in cost of processing resulting from the use of larger order sizes.

To take advantage of such discounts we are encouraged to order a quantity larger than the economic order quantity.

Previously, the total cost equation for $C$ included only holding and ordering costs, since only these varied with order quantity. Now the price of the item, or its direct processing cost, $p$, is a function of order quantity and this must therefore be included in the cost equation, which is now as follows:

$$C^1 = \frac{C_s r}{Q} + C_1\left(\frac{Q}{2}\right) + rp$$

The problem is to find the order quantity $Q$ which leads to the minimization of this total cost $C^1$.

The item price $p$, is a constant within each quantity range, e.g. let price = $p_i$ apply for quantities $q$ where:

$$q_i \leq q < q_{i+1}$$

i.e. the price structure will be as follows:

| | | | | | |
|---|---|---|---|---|---|
| $p_1$ | for quantities $q_1 \leq q < q_2$ | | $p_{n-1}$ | for quantities $q_{n-1}$ | $\leq q < q_n$ |
| $p_2$ | for quantities $q_2 \leq q < q_3$ | | $p_n$ | for quantities | $q \geq p_n$ |
| $p_3$ | for quantities $q_3 \leq q < q_4$ | | | | |

A total cost function, $C^1$, for a system with price breaks is shown in Figure 17.6. Clearly, our problem is to find the minimum (lowest) point on such a curve. This will occur at *either* the lower end of one of the price/quantity ranges *or* at the point at which the continuous part of the curve is minimum.

**Figure 17.6** Total cost curve with price breaks

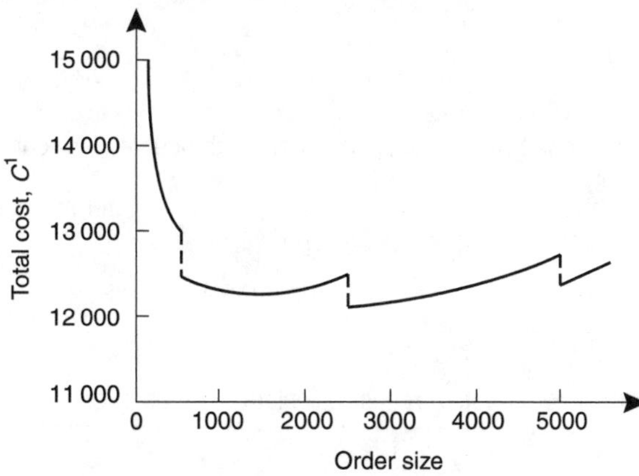

EXAMPLE

## A wine retailer

The retailer sells large quantities of bottles of a minor chateau-bottled Bordeaux wine. His purchase prices are shown below.

| Order quantity | 100–499 | 500–2499 | 2500–4999 | 5000 and over |
|---|---|---|---|---|
| Price per bottle | £5 | £4.75 | £4.6 | £4.5 |

Find the economic order quantity, given that the constant sales rate is 2500 units per year, the holding cost, expressed as a percentage of unit price, is 10% per unit per year, and the ordering cost is £100.

To determine the optimum order quantity we must first calculate the total cost associated with order quantities at the bottom of each price/quantity range, since one of these points may be the lowest on the curve, i.e.

Range 100–499 ($p = 5$)

$$C^1 = \frac{C_s r}{Q} + C_1\left(\frac{Q}{2}\right) + rp$$

$$= \frac{100 \times 2500}{100} + \frac{0.1\ (5)\ 100}{2} + 2500\ (5)$$

Ordering cost/year — Holding cost/year — Item cost/year

= £15 025 per year

*Similarly:*

Range 500–2499 ($p = 4.75$):

$C^1$ = £12 494

Range 2500–4999 ($p$ = 4.6):

$$C^1 = £12\,175$$

Range 5000 and over ($p$ = 4.5):

$$C^1 = £12\,425$$

Now we must look for the lowest point of the continuous part of the curve. This can be found by using the formula for economic order quantity:

$$Q = \sqrt{\frac{2C_s r}{C_1}}$$

but, since $C_1$ is now a function of item cost, we must calculate $Q$ for each price/quantity range, i.e.

Range 100–499 ($p$ = 5)

$$Q = \sqrt{\frac{2 \times 100 \times 2500}{0.1\ (5)}} = 1000$$

Range 500–2499 ($p$ = 4.75)

$$Q = \sqrt{\frac{2 \times 100 \times 2500}{0.1\ (4.75)}} = 1026$$

Range 2500–4999 ($p$ = 4.6)

$$Q = \sqrt{\frac{2 \times 100 \times 2500}{0.1\ (4.6)}} = 1043$$

Range 5000 and over ($p$ = 4.5)

$$Q = \sqrt{\frac{2 \times 100 \times 2500}{0.1\ (4.5)}} = 1054$$

Notice that only one of these values of $Q$ falls on the total cost curve, since there is only one minimum point to such a curve. The point in question is $Q$ = 1026, which is within the quantity range 500–2499. We must now calculate the total cost for this ordering policy and compare it with the minimum previously obtained.

For $Q$ = 1026

$$C^1 = \frac{C_s r}{Q} + C_1\left(\frac{Q}{2}\right) + rp$$

$$= \frac{100 \times 2500}{1026} + \frac{0.1\ (4.75)\ 1026}{2} + 4.75\ (2500)$$

= 244 + 243 + 11 875

= 12 362

This value is greater than the previous minimum of $C1$ = £12 175; consequently, in this case it is economically beneficial to take advantage of the quantity discount and order a quantity higher than might otherwise have been the case, i.e. $Q^*$ = 2500 bottles.[1]

The total cost curve shown in Figure 17.6 is plotted from the costs calculated above.

## *Perpetual model A1(c)*

As model A1(a), *plus holding costs*, a proportion of which vary with the order quantity.

We have so far taken the unit holding cost, $C_1$, as being a constant with respect to the order quantity, but there may be occasions where this relationship does not hold. For example, we have considered the holding cost (in the previous example) as being related to the price or value of the item being stored, but since the price is perhaps dependent on order quantity we ought logically to consider the case in which holding cost is a function of order quantity. Two such functions will be investigated, first the case where holding cost varies continuously and second the discontinuous variation of holding cost.

(a) *Continuous variation.* Notation as before, plus:

$C_{11}$ = The fixed portion of $C_1$ which is unrelated to order quantity

$C_{12}$ = The variable portion of $C_1$ which is a function of order quantity

Total cost of holding and ordering = $C$

$$= \frac{C_s r}{Q} + C_{11}\left(\frac{Q}{2}\right) + C_{12}Q$$

Ordering cost/unit time — Fixed holding cost/unit time — Variable holding cost/unit time

Differentiating with respect to $Q$:

$$\frac{dC}{dQ} = -\frac{C_s r}{Q^2} + \frac{C_{11}}{2} + C_{12}$$

Equating this to zero to obtain the minimum cost gives:

$$Q^* = \sqrt{\frac{2C_s r}{C_{11} + 2C_{12}}}$$

(b) *Discontinuous variation of holding costs.* When storage space is rented it is frequently possible to obtain space only in fixed increments. For example, if a company that rents space in a warehouse finds that more space is required because of its new stock-holding policy, it may be offered the use of another floor or department rather than the exact additional space required. In such cases the cost of holding varies discontinuously with order quantity, as shown in Figure 17.7. A similar

[1] This approach to determining order quantities is adequate where no safety stocks are held. Where safety stock exists the costs of carrying that stock must be considered. This will further encourage the use of order quantities sufficient to enable price discounts to be obtained.

**Figure 17.7** Holding cost varying discontinuously with ordering quantity

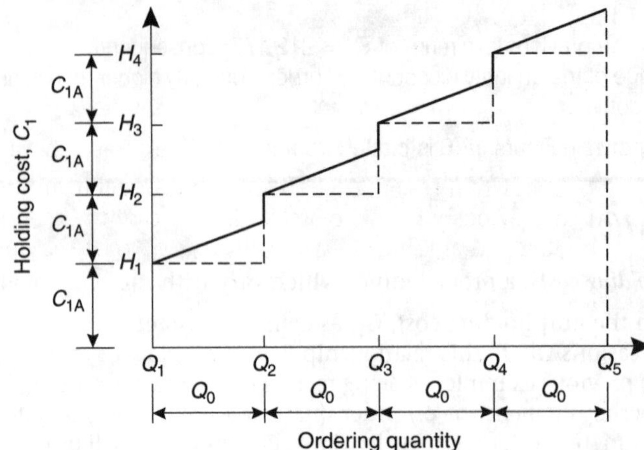


situation may apply where a company finds it necessary to build additional storage space, since again only certain increments can be added rather than the exact requirements. In the example shown in Figure 17.7, order quantities of size $Q_2$ or greater necessitate an increase in holding costs to level $H_2$. The same increase is necessitated for each increase in order quantity ($Q_o$).

If this variable holding cost associated with the cost per unit of time for renting one increment of storage is $C_{1A}$, while $C_{11}$ is the holding cost per item per unit of time which does not vary with order quantity, then the total cost of storage per unit of time, neglecting buffer stock, is:

$$C_1 = C_{1A}\left\{\frac{Q}{Q_o}\right\} + C_{11}\frac{Q}{2}$$

where $\left\{\frac{Q}{Q_o}\right\}$ is the next integer larger than $Q/Q_o$

**EXAMPLE**

## *A wine importer*

The company imports cases of wine from France. If storage space is available in increments each sufficient for 500 cases, the cost per year for each increment being £400, and if the fixed cost of holding is £1 per case per year, what is the total annual holding cost if the order quantity is 750 cases? There is no buffer stock.

$$C_1 = C_{1A}\left\{\frac{Q}{Q_o}\right\} + C_{11}\frac{Q}{2}$$

$$= 400\left\{\frac{750}{500}\right\} + 1\,\frac{750}{2}$$

$$= 400\,(2) + \frac{750}{2} = £1175 \text{ p.a.}$$

In such cases the total cost of holding and ordering, $C$ is given by:

$$C = \frac{C_s r}{Q} + C_{1A}\left\{\frac{Q}{Q_o}\right\} + C_{11}\left(\frac{Q}{2}\right)$$

Ordering cost — Variable holding cost — Fixed holding cost

A curve for total variable cost $C$ is shown in Figure 17.8. The economic order quantity can be determined in a similar manner to that used previously for price breaks. In this case the economic order quantity (i.e. the minimum point of the total variable cost curve) will occur *either* at the upper point of one of the holding cost increments *or* at the point at which the continuous part of the curve is at a minimum.

**Figure 17.8** Total variable cost with variable holding costs

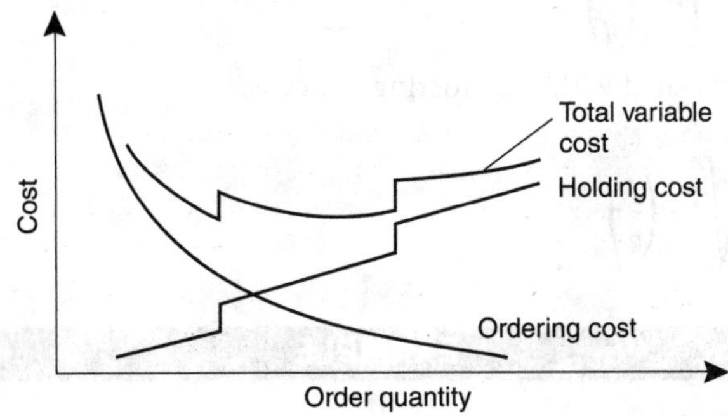


## *Perpetual model A1(d)*

As model A1(a) *except shortages allowed* (see Figure 14.4). Notation as before, plus:

$C_2$ = shortage or stock-out cost per item per unit of time

$S$ = stock level after replenishment

The derivation of $Q^*$ and $C^*$ for this model is given in Chapter 14 (see p. 412).

$$\text{EOQ} = Q^* = \sqrt{\frac{2rC_s}{C_1}}\sqrt{\frac{C_1 + C_2}{C_2}}$$

The total variable cost associated with this ordering policy is:

$$C^* = \sqrt{2rC_1C_s}\sqrt{\frac{C_2}{C_1 + C_2}}$$

## *Perpetual model A1(e) for fixed quantity with usage*

The following are assumed:

(i) Known constant demand.

(ii) Delivery of order at a known and constant rate.

(iii) No shortages.

(iv) Buffer stock.

Notation:

$Q$ = order quantity
$C_s$ = ordering cost
$C_1$ = holding cost/item/unit of time
$q$ = delivery or production rate
$r$ = usage or consumption rate

The derivation of $Q^*$ and $C^*$ for this model is given in Chapter 14 (see p. 414).

$$\text{EOQ} = Q^* = \sqrt{\frac{2C_s r}{C_1\left[1 - \left(\frac{r}{q}\right)\right]}}$$

The total variable cost associated with the ordering policy is:

$$C^* = \sqrt{2C_s r C_1}\sqrt{1 - \left(\frac{r}{q}\right)}$$

**EXAMPLE**

### A hospital sterile supply store

A hospital which uses a maximum–minimum stock ordering policy orders 2500 of purchased item A at a time. Its managers wish to determine what annual saving might be made by ordering this item in different quantities. An examination of previous stock records indicates that the annual usage of these items is constant at 7000. They further find that the cost of placing an order, which is independent of the order size, is £10. The purchase price of the items is £0.5 and the cost of holding stock is 7% of item price per item per year. The supplier undertakes to deliver the items at a constant rate of 50 per day.

$q = 50 \times 250$/year (assuming that there are 250 working days per year)
$r = 7000$/year
$C_s = £10$
$C_1 = 0.07\ (0.5) = £0.035$/item/year

$$\text{EOQ} = Q^* = \sqrt{\frac{2 \times 10 \times 7000}{0.07\ (0.5) \times \left(1 - \frac{7000}{12\,500}\right)}}$$

$Q^* = 3015$ units

Total annual variable cost $C^*$ associated with this policy:

$$= \sqrt{2 \times 7000 \times 10 \times 0.07\ (0.5)}\sqrt{1 - \frac{7000}{12\,500}}$$

$= £46.4$ p.a.

Total annual variable cost associated with present policy:

$$= \frac{C_1Q}{2}\left[1 - \left(\frac{r}{q}\right)\right] + \frac{C_s r}{Q}$$

$$= \frac{0.035 \times 2500}{2}(0.44) + 10 \times \frac{7000}{2500}$$

$$= £47.25 \text{ p.a.}$$

Potential annual saving on item A = £0.85.

## *Perpetual model A1(f) for multiple items*

Our previous models have related to the ordering of a quantity of a *single* product, but in practice there are many occasions when our ordering decision and our ordering cost cover quantities of more than one type of product. If, for example, the ordering cost consists mainly of the cost of transport of items by road from the suppliers, then the cost of ordering could be independent of both quantity of items and the number of different types of product (except, of course, that larger quantities may necessitate more journeys).

Consider such a situation in which there are $N$ different types of product to be ordered, where:

$C_s$ = ordering cost

$Q_1$ = order size for product $i$ ($i$ = 1, 2, 3, . . . $N$)

$r_i$ = usage or consumption rate for product $i$

$C_{1i}$ = holding cost/item $i$/unit of time

$t_i$ = reorder cycle for item $i$

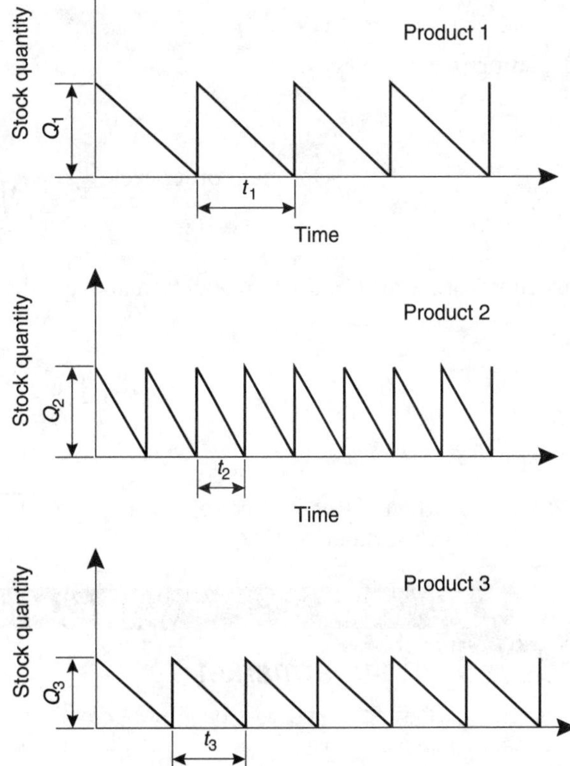


**Figure 17.9** Ordering systems for several products

Since ordering cost is independent of the number of items ordered, our objective, in order to attempt to minimize costs, must be to arrange the ordering policy so that as few orders as possible are made.

In Figure 17.9, the longest order cycle is for product 1 ($t_1$) and the shortest is for product 2 ($t_2$). If the order cycle for product 1 is reduced then the average stock is also reduced from the present level, $Q_1/2$. This in itself results in a reduction in the holding cost. Normally such savings would be offset to some extent by an increase in the costs of ordering due to the increase in the number of orders placed over a given period. However, in this case, if the order cycle is reduced so that it coincides with the order cycle for one of the other products, say $t_1 = t_2$, then since ordering cost is independent of order size and since no more orders are being placed than previously, ordering costs are *not* increased and total costs are decreased.

It follows, then, that for an optimum ordering policy, all ordering cycles should be of equal length and orders for different products should be made at the same time. Now:

The order size for each product $Q_i = r_i t$

Ordering cost/unit of time $= \dfrac{C_s}{t}$

Holding cost per unit of time $= \sum_{i=1}^{N}\left(C_{1i}\dfrac{Q_i}{2}\right) = \sum_{i=1}^{N}\left(\dfrac{C_{1i}r_i t}{2}\right)$

$\therefore$ Total ordering and holding cost/unit of time $C = \sum_{i=1}^{N}\left(\dfrac{C_{1i}r_i t}{2}\right) + \dfrac{C_s}{t}$

Differentiating with respect to $t$:

$$\frac{dC}{dt} = \sum_{i=1}^{N}\left(\frac{C_{1i}r_i}{2}\right) - \frac{C_s}{t^2}$$

Equating to zero gives:

$$\text{Optimum order cycle} = t^* = \sqrt{\frac{2C_s}{\sum_{i=1}^{N} C_{1i}r_i}}$$

By substituting for $t$ in the first equation above:

$$\text{EOQ} = Q_i^* = r_i\sqrt{\frac{2C_s}{\sum_{i=1}^{N} C_{1i}r_i}}$$

Notice that when $N$ (the number of different products) = 1, the equation for $Q^*$ reduces to EOQ equation for the basic model – A1(a).

**EXAMPLE**

## *A supermarket*

The table at the top of the next page gives data relating to three types of product which a supermarket purchases from a company.

The cost of ordering is £125 per order irrespective of its content. Items of each product are delivered to the shop by the supplier in complete orders. Neglecting buffer stock, what is the economic order size for each product and consequently the total order size? What is the order interval?

| Purchased product | Annual sales ($r_i$) | Holding cost/ item/year ($C_{1i}$) |
|---|---|---|
| A | 5 000 | 0.5 |
| B | 3 250 | 1.0 |
| C | 2 900 | 0.75 |

$$Q_i^* = r_i \sqrt{\frac{2C_s}{\sum_{i=1}^{N} C_{1i}r_i}}$$

| Product | $C_{1i}r_i$ |
|---|---|
| A | 2500 |
| B | 3250 |
| C | 2175 |
| $\sum_{i=1}^{N} C_{1i}r_i =$ | 7925 |

$$Q^*_A = 5000\sqrt{\frac{2(125)}{7925}} = 888 \qquad Q^*_B = 3\,250\sqrt{\frac{2(125)}{7925}} = 577$$

$$Q^*_C = 2900\sqrt{\frac{2(125)}{7925}} = 515$$

Total order size $Q^* = 1980$

$$\text{Order interval } t^* = \frac{Q_i^*}{r_i} = \frac{888}{5000} = 0.178 \text{ year}$$

## The reorder level

We decided earlier that in the fixed quantity (two-bin or order quantity) ordering system two questions must be answered: what is the fixed order quantity ($Q$) and what is the reorder level ($Q_1$)? We have decided how, in a few typical situations, the fixed order quantity can be determined and we must now look at the problem of reorder levels.

If the usage or consumption of items is perfectly constant and accurately known and if stock replenishment time is zero, then the stock order level may be zero and orders for stock replenishments can be placed when stock falls to this level. Thus in a deterministic situation the order level decision is easily made.

Unfortunately such an ideal situation rarely exists. In practice two complications can arise. First, the usage rate may not be absolutely constant and consequently there is the risk that stock may be prematurely exhausted. Even so, if replenishment of stock is instantaneous, no problems arise because exhausted stock can immediately be replaced. The second complication concerns replenishment. If this is not immediate, it becomes necessary to place orders some time before the items are needed and replenishment times may fluctuate. The occurrence of both these complications necessitates the maintenance of buffer or safety stocks.

If both these complications arise in any magnitude then we cannot reasonably use any of the ordering models discussed in the previous section, since all assume a static and deterministic state. However, if these fluctuations are not excessive then these models can be used, since only a slight, and usually tolerable, error is introduced.[2]

To summarize, then, the need to consider order levels other than zero arises because of uncertainty, i.e. the probabilistic nature of demand and/or replenishment lead time. Such uncertainty is alien to the ordering models we have discussed but they can nevertheless be used, with only minor error, provided demand and lead time vary only marginally. The approaches which might be employed are outlined in a discussion of probabilistic models later in this chapter.

## Periodic control: the fixed input interval method

If, to begin with, we again assume that usage or demand is constant and known, then this system of ordering is, in both practice and theory, identical to the maximum–minimum or order quantity system. In the maximum–minimum system, when stocks fall to a predetermined level (which can be zero if order delivery is instantaneous), a further predetermined quantity of items is ordered. In the order cycle system, at predetermined intervals a quantity of goods sufficient to restore stock to a given level is ordered. In the ideal conditions we have assumed both the order quantity and the order cycle would be the same, irrespective of the system we adopt. Consequently, for such cases the answers to our two basic questions – when to order and how much to order – can be found from the previous section, i.e.

$$\text{Order interval} = \frac{\text{Order quantity}}{\text{Usage rate}}$$

$$\text{Optimum order interval} = \frac{\text{EOQ}}{\text{Usage rate}}$$

i.e.

$$t^* = \frac{Q^*}{r}$$

So, for the models we examined in the previous section the optimum order intervals are given by the following formulae.

Periodic model A1(a):

$$t^* = \sqrt{\frac{2C_s}{rC_1}}$$

Periodic model A1(b):

$$t^* = \frac{Q^*}{r}$$

Periodic model A1(c):

$$t^* = \sqrt{\frac{2C_s}{r(C_{11} + 2C_{12})}}$$

---

[2] For example, Mabin, V. J. (1989) A practical near-optimal order quantity method. *Engineering Costs and Production Economics*, **15**, pp. 381–386.

Periodic model A1(d):

$$t^* = \sqrt{\frac{2C_s}{rC_1}}\sqrt{\frac{C_1 + C_2}{C_2}}$$

Periodic model A1(e):

$$t^* = \sqrt{\frac{2C_s}{rC_1\left[1 - \left(\frac{r}{q}\right)\right]}}$$

Periodic model A1(f) multiple items:

$$t^* = \sqrt{\frac{2C_s}{\sum_{i=1}^{N} C_{1i}r_i}}$$

It is only during conditions of uncertainty that these two methods of ordering differ. The fundamental characteristic of the order cycle system is that the stock status of each item is examined at regular and fixed intervals, at which time the following questions are asked:

(a) Should an order be placed to replenish stock now?

(b) If so, how many units must be ordered?

## A2 PROBABILISTIC SITUATIONS

All of the preceding discussion has assumed deterministic situations. The assumption has been made that demand, and the time required to replenish stocks, are known and constant, so problems of managing inventory have been minimized. In this section we shall deal with the more realistic situation in which there is some uncertainty to be accommodated. We shall deal with both the order quantity and the order interval approaches outlined above, and show how these two approaches can be adapted for use in circumstances where there is some degree of uncertainty.

Where there is some uncertainty in demand and/or in the time between the placing of an order and the receipt of that order to replenish inventories, it becomes necessary to use some safety or buffer stocks to try to prevent a stockout situation. Figure 17.10 refers to an order quantity method of inventory control and shows how variations in demand or usage rate, and/or replenishment lead time, might, unless buffer stock is used, result in a stockout situation.

The first case describes a situation in which the demand or usage rate is fixed but the replenishment lead time is variable. Here the ideal situation will occur where an order is placed at such time that items are received for replenishment stock when the constant rate of demand has depleted stocks to zero. However, it is possible that because lead time is greater than expected, the constant rate of demand has in fact reduced stocks to zero and a stockout situation thus exists before items are obtained to replenish stock. The second situation concerns a variable demand or usage rate and fixed replenishment lead time. Here again there is a possible stockout situation since, even though the lead time is fixed, demand during that period may be greater than expected, thus reducing stock to zero before replenishment. In the final situation both demand or usage and replenishment lead time are variable, so a stockout situation may occur because of the combination of the two situations described above.

**Figure 17.10** The effect of uncertainty of lead time usage (order level control system)

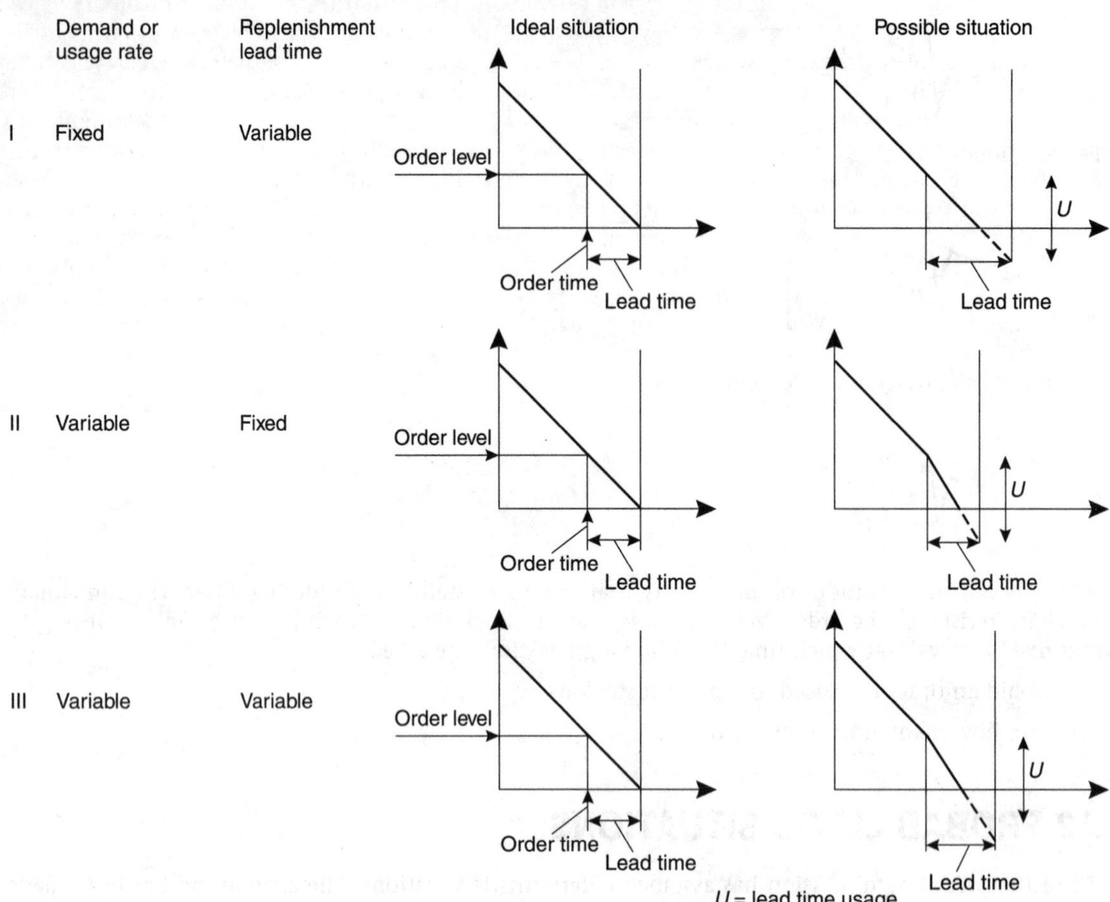


All three examples are in fact describing a situation in which usage or demand during the reorder lead time (*U*) is uncertain. Uncertainty on lead time usage necessitates the use of buffer stocks, i.e. the placing of a replenishment order earlier, or at a higher level of stock, than would have been necessary in a deterministic situation. In these circumstances the order level can be calculated as follows:

Reorder level = Average lead time usage + Safety stock

## Service levels and safety stock

The safety stock employed will be determined by the level of protection required against uncertainties in lead time usage. The required safety stock can be determined as follows:

(a) To provide a given risk of a stockout situation occurring, i.e. to provide a given risk that the actual demand between two replenishment orders will be greater than that expected, and thus that a stockout situation will occur before replenishment stocks arrive.

This probability of stockout is often expressed in terms of the 'service level' provided to the customer. Thus the lower the probability of a stockout occurring between replenishments, the higher the level of service to the customer. The 'service level' could, perhaps, be thought of in terms of the number of items delivered to customers compared with the total required over a period of time, or the number of customer orders which are satisfied in proportion to the number of orders placed over a period of time. The 'service level' provided to customers may also be seen in terms of the percentage of time during which stock is available to customers or the percentage of customer orders which can be satisfied immediately. These and other interpretations of 'service level' are common. The 'service level' is often expressed as a percentage, e.g. a 95% service level might indicate that 95% of all items requested during the period are delivered, or that 95% of all customer orders are satisfied, etc. In reality, however, in determining safety stock and reorder levels, we can deal only with the probability of actual demand between replenishments exceeding expected demand between replenishments. We must therefore fix safety stock and the reorder level to achieve a particular level of probability. Although we might choose, for convenience, to refer to a 95% service level, in practice this will generally mean a 95% chance that, between replenishments, actual demand will not exceed expected demand or, conversely, that there is a 5% probability that actual demand will exceed expected demand and thus a stockout will occur.

(b) To ensure a maximum number of stockout situations during a particular period of time.

This approach, which is more common when using a 'simulation' methodology, involves the fixing of safety stocks and therefore reorder levels in order to ensure that no more than a given number of stockouts occur during a given period of time.

(c) To minimize the cost of stockouts and stock-holding.

This approach again is common when using a 'simulation' methodology. If a stockout can be assumed to incur a certain cost, then this can be seen to be the penalty cost of holding insufficient stock, while the cost of stock-holding can be seen to be the penalty cost of holding too much stock. The safety stock and reorder level may be determined in order to minimize the sum of these costs.

(d) To minimize the cost of stockouts.

Here the cost is taken also to be a function of the number of items short during the stockout period, plus the cost of stock-holding.

The way in which the safety stock and reorder level is determined will to some extent depend on the information that is available. If, for example, uncertainties in demand or lead time, or both, can be expressed by probability distributions then a statistical approach can be employed, and in such cases the objective will be as described in (a) above, and will normally be expressed in terms of 'service level'. If, however, the uncertainties cannot be expressed by probability distributions, then an alternative approach will be employed. In these circumstances a 'simulation' methodology may be appropriate, as referred to above.

Both the statistical and the simulation methodology will be described below, where our discussion deals first with the order quantity inventory control systems.

## The order quantity method with uncertainty

The three examples below show how the three types of situation described in Figure 17.10 might be accommodated in those circumstances where demand, lead time usage or the lead time period can be considered to be distributed normally. The examples show how a reorder level can be calculated and, where appropriate, used in conjunction with a reorder quantity determined by one of the models described in the preceding sections (except model A1(d)). The first example deals with lead time variation, the second with demand variation during a known lead time, and the third directly with lead time and demand variations. In all cases service level is represented as a probability of actual demand between replenishments being less than or equal to expected demand.

EXAMPLE

## A garage selling accessories for cars

Demand rate for car batteries = 4500/month (constant)
Ordering cost = £150/replenishment order
Stock-holding cost = £3.75/item/year
Average stock replenishment lead time from supplier (assumed normally distributed) = 1 month
Standard deviation of replenishment lead time (from study of past data) = 0.2 months
Service level required = 95%

Determine:

(a) Reorder quantity
(b) Reorder level

Solution:

(a) $$Q^* = \sqrt{\frac{2 \times 150 \times 4500}{3.75/12}}$$

$= 2078$ items

(b) Reorder level ($R$) = Average lead time demand + Safety stock
N.B.: Safety stock = 1.64 × Standard deviation of lead time demand since for the normal probability distribution, 1.64 standard deviations above the mean excludes 5% of the distribution, i.e. equivalent to 95% service level.
Standard deviation of lead time demand = 0.2 (4500). Hence:

$$R = 4500\,(1) + 1.64\,(0.2 \times 4500)$$
$$= 5976 \text{ batteries}$$

EXAMPLE

## A garden centre selling sacks of fertilizer

Average demand = 10 sacks/day
Standard deviation of daily demand = 3 (assumed normally distributed)
Stock replenishment interval = 15 days (constant)
Service level required = 95%

Determine reorder level ($R$).

*Solution*

$R = 10(15) + 1.64$ (standard deviation of usage during replenishment lead time)
Standard deviation of lead time usage

$$= \sqrt{\sum_{i=1}^{n} \sigma d_i^2} \text{ (where each day's demand is independent)}$$

where $\sigma d_i^2$ = Variance of daily demand for $i$ = 1 to $n$ days ($n$ = 15)

$$= \sqrt{15(3^2)}$$
$$= 11.6$$

Hence $R = 10\ (15) + 1.64\ (11.6)$

$= 169$ sacks

**EXAMPLE**

## *A company manufacturing fertilizer*

Customer service required = 95%
Average manufacturing lead time to replenish stocks = 20 days
Average daily demand = 100 sacks
Standard deviation of demand during lead time = 200

Determine reorder level ($R$).

*Solution*

Reorder level ($R$) = Average lead time usage + Safety stock
= 20 (100) + 1.64 (200)

$R = 2000 + 328$
$= 2328$ sacks

These examples use the normal probability distribution to describe the various uncertainties. The use of the normal probability distribution is often appropriate where we are dealing with output or work-in-progress stocks in a manufacturing system. The use of a Poisson distribution is often more appropriate for retail stocks. The negative exponential distribution is often used for wholesale or retail stocks. In each of these cases statistical procedures similar to those described above can be used. Often, however, there will be no evidence to suggest that any particular probability distribution should be used, so in these cases it will be necessary to take a different approach. Such an approach is used in the following examples, in which historical lead time usage data are employed. The three examples show how the reorder level can be calculated to give:

(a) maximum number of stockouts/period of time;

(b) minimum cost of stockout + stock-holding;

(c) minimum cost of stockouts (where cost is a function of the number of items short during a stockout) + stock-holding.

**EXAMPLE**

## *A restaurant*

The annual usage rate of a purchased product is 5000. The cost of the product is 25p each, the cost of placing the order is £1.25 and the cost of holding stock is 10% of item price per year per item. Complete orders are delivered by the supplier.

An examination of the stock records indicates that lead time usage ($U$) varies from 32 to 40 as shown in the following table. Stockouts are permitted, but no more than one per year should occur.

What is to be the reorder level?

| $U$ | $P(U)$ | $P$ (actual usage > $U$) |
|---|---|---|
| 32 | 0.02 | 0.98 |
| 33 | 0.07 | 0.91 |
| 34 | 0.12 | 0.79 |
| 35 | 0.16 | 0.63 |
| 36 | 0.20 | 0.43 |
| 37 | 0.17 | 0.26 |
| 38 | 0.13 | 0.13 |
| 39 | 0.10 | 0.03 |
| 40 | 0.03 | 0.00 |

*Solution*

Using EOQ formula A1(a):

$$Q^* = 707$$

Hence number of orders per year is:

$$\frac{r}{Q} = \frac{5000}{707} = 7.07$$

Now buffer stock ($B$) can be defined as the difference between the reorder level ($R$) and the average lead time usage ($\bar{U}$). Hence, if in this case the reorder level is set at 37

$$B = R - \bar{U}$$
$$= 37 - 36$$
$$= 1$$

etc.

Now we can present all the information necessary for a solution in the form of a table:

| Reorder level, $R$ | 36 | 37 | 38 | 39 | 40 |
|---|---|---|---|---|---|
| Buffer stock, $B$ | 0 | 1 | 2 | 3 | 4 |
| Holding cost p.a. (10% × $B$ × 25p p.a.) | 0 | 2.5p | 5p | 7.5p | 10p |
| Stockouts: | | | | | |
| Probability per order | 0.43 | 0.26 | 0.13 | 0.23 | 0.00 |
| Expected no. per year (Probability × 7.07) | 3.04 | 1.83 | 0.92 | 0.21 | 0.00 |

Clearly from this table a reorder level of 38 must be used if no more than one stockout per year is to occur.

## EXAMPLE

As for the previous example but, instead of determining the reorder level to provide not more than one stockout per year, determine the reorder level to minimize stockout plus holding cost. An analysis of past records has shown that stocks of this product lead to a fixed cost of 50p per stockout period. Alternative reorder levels are examined in the following table.

Since the stockout costs dominate the holding cost of buffer stock, in order to minimize total cost it is clearly beneficial in this case to adopt a reorder level of 40, which corresponds, of course, to the maximum lead time usage.

| Reorder level, $R$ | 36 | 37 | 38 | 39 | 40 |
|---|---|---|---|---|---|
| Buffer stock, $B$ | 0 | 1 | 2 | 3 | 4 |
| Holding cost p.a. (1) (10% × $B$ × 25p p.a.) | 0p | 2.5p | 5p | 7.5p | 10p |
| Stockouts | | | | | |
| Number per year | 3.04 | 1.83 | 0.92 | 0.21 | 0.00 |
| Cost per year (2) (at 50p each) | 152p | 91.5p | 46p | 10.5p | 0p |
| Total cost per annum (1) + (2) | 152p | 94p | 51p | 18p | 10p |

## EXAMPLE

As for the first example, but in this case it has been found that the stockout costs depend not only on the number of times stockouts occur but also on the number of units short or required during the stockout periods. It has been found from records that the stockout cost is 5p per item.

To determine the reorder level which provides minimum cost we must calculate not only the number of stockouts per year at each reorder level but also the average number of units short during the stockout periods, i.e.

$$\text{Average stockout quantity} = \frac{\text{Average stockout per order during stockout periods}}{\text{Probability of stockout occurring}}$$

For reorder level $R$ = 36, the relevant data and calculations are shown in the following table:

| Actual usage ($U$) | Stockout quantity ($U$ - $R$) | Probability $P(U)$ | $P(U) \times (U - R)$ |
|---|---|---|---|
| 37 | 1 | 0.17 | 0.17 |
| 38 | 2 | 0.13 | 0.26 |
| 39 | 3 | 0.10 | 0.30 |
| 40 | 4 | 0.03 | 0.12 |
| | | 0.43 | 0.85 |

$$\text{Average stockout quantity} = \frac{0.85}{0.43} = 1.98$$

Similarly:

For $R$ = 37, average stockout quantity = 1.62
For $R$ = 38, average stockout quantity = 1.23
For $R$ = 39, average stockout quantity = 1.00
For $R$ = 40, average stockout quantity = 0.00

Now all the data necessary to compare the merits of different reorder levels can be presented in tabular form, as in the following table.

These figures indicate that the minimum cost reorder level is 39, which results in an average of 0.21 stock-outs per year.

| Reorder level, *R* | 36 | 37 | 38 | 39 | 40 |
|---|---|---|---|---|---|
| Average stockout quantity per stockout period | 1.98 | 1.62 | 1.23 | 1.00 | 0.00 |
| Buffer stock, *B* | 0 | 1 | 2 | 3 | 4 |
| Holding cost p.a. (1) | 0p | 2.5p | 5p | 7.5p | 10p |
| Stockouts: | | | | | |
| Number per year | 3.04 | 1.83 | 0.92 | 0.21 | 0.00 |
| Cost (number × quantity × 5p) (2) | 30.1p | 15p | 5.7p | 1p | 0p |
| Total cost per annum (1) + (2) | 30.1p | 17.5p | 10.7p | 8.5p | 10p |

## The order interval method with uncertainty

Under conditions of uncertainty in demand, order lead time, or both, a buffer stock must be maintained. But, unlike with the order level system, buffer stocks for the order interval system must protect against not only changes in lead time demand but also variations in demand at all other times. For example, consider the situation shown in Figure 17.11. The fixed order cycle is $t$ while lead time is constant at $l$. Usage during lead time $l_2$ conforms exactly to expectations; consequently an order for the fixed replenishment quantity $Q$ at this time eventually results in the replenishment of stock to the desired level $Q_2$. Usage remains constant during the following period and during the order lead time $l_3$ and again stock is replenished to the desired level. However, during the next lead time usage is greater than normal and consequently some of the buffer stock is consumed before replenishment can take place; therefore, unless a larger quantity is ordered, stock is replenished to a level less than $Q_2$. Usage during the entire next period is again greater than normal and further buffer stock is consumed. Again, unless a larger quantity of the product is ordered, the maximum stock level will fall since buffer stock must, as shown here, accommodate usage fluctuations throughout the entire period rather than just during lead time.

**Figure 17.11** The effect of usage uncertainty in an interval stock ordering system (using a fixed order quantity)

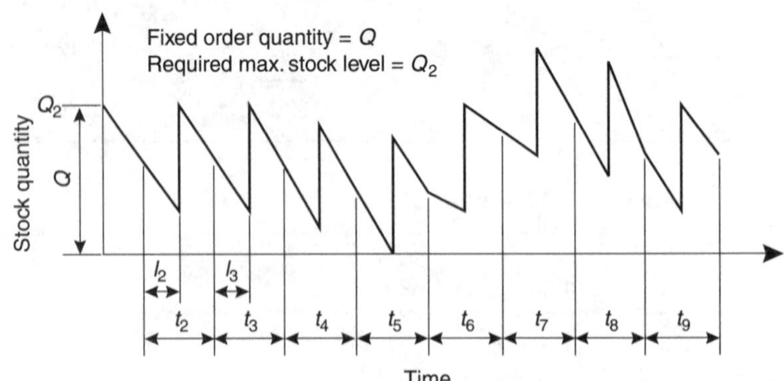

The following example will give some indication of the manner in which this type of problem can be tackled. It deals with the fixed order interval system where the order quantity is variable, which is the more common approach. The procedure adopted involves first establishing the fixed reorder interval based on economic reorder quantity calculations and then determining, at each order time, the quantity to be ordered to protect against demand fluctuations over the next period. It will be appreciated that the first part of this solution assumes constant demand rate, whereas the second part is explicitly concerned with dealing with varying demand rate. This might seem contradictory, but the approach *might* be appropriate where demand rate varies about an established mean rather than where substantial trends are evident.

**EXAMPLE**

## *A book publisher*

Retail demand for a book averages 100 books/week. There is no noticeable trend in demand, and the standard deviation of weekly demand has been found to be 15 books.

The publisher's stock-holding cost is £0.5/book/week and the reorder cost is £20 per batch.

It is intended to reprint the book, to replenish stock, in appropriately equal-sized batches at fixed intervals, and to do so in such a way as to try to ensure a 95% service level. Calculate the reorder interval and show how the reorder quantity might be determined.

*Solution*

A fixed reorder interval equal to the theoretical optimum reorder interval will be used, i.e.

$$t^* = \sqrt{\frac{2 \times 20}{100 \times 0.5}}$$

$$= 0.894 \text{ weeks}$$

The theoretical economic reorder quantity $Q^*$ for constant demand situation = $t^*(r)$ = 89.4 books, but this takes no account of demand uncertainty. If this quantity is ordered on every replenishment, a situation like that shown in Figure 17.11 may result. To protect against this it will be appropriate to determine the reorder quantity at the time of each replenishment.

If we assume that stock replenishment takes place, on average, at time intervals equal to the reorder interval $t^*$, then we must ensure that after each replenishment the stock in hand ($Q_2$) is sufficient to meet 95% of customers' orders during the following period $t^*$, i.e.

$$Q_2 = t^*(r) + 1.64\sqrt{\sum_{i=1}^{t^*} \sigma d_i^2}$$

$$= 0.894\,(100) + 1.64\ \sqrt{0.894\,(15^2)}$$

$$= 89.4 + 23.25$$

$$= 112.65 \text{ items}$$

Using this approximate approach the reorder quantity at each reorder point can be calculated as follows:

Reorder quantity (after a fixed reorder interval $t^*$) = $Q_2$ – (Stock in hand at the time of ordering)

## Uncertainties in batch quantities

Our discussion above has dealt with the situation where there is uncertainty about demand rate or lead time, or both. A third possible source of uncertainty is the delivered batch quantity. For example, in a purchasing situation it is possible that even though a particular batch quantity is ordered, a different quantity may eventually be received into stock. Where, for example, there are losses during delivery, there is a risk that a quantity less than the ordered batch quantity may be received to replenish stock. This uncertainty is not a major problem with the reorder level (perpetual) inventory control system, since the delivery of a quantity which is smaller than required will simply mean that the reorder level is reached more quickly than might have been expected, while the delivery of a larger batch than is expected results in the next order being placed later than might otherwise be expected. However, in the order interval system, since orders are placed to replenish stock to a particular level, the delivery of a quantity different from that which was ordered can increase the risk of a stockout before the next replenishment is received. If there is enough information on likely variation in delivered batch quantity, this risk can be taken into account when establishing the reorder quantity in the manner described above. In other circumstances it will be possible only to estimate the likely shortfall in delivered quantity and add that to the reorder quantity determined in the manner described above.

# CONTINUOUS FLOW/INPUT CONTROL

Conventional inventory control theory largely ignores the case of continuous, as opposed to intermittent, input flow, although a queuing theory approach may have some relevance. Assuming input control as a means of managing inventory to satisfy expected output needs, one problem for inventory management is the determination of an input rate (or average rate). Other problems will generally relate to the determination of average, minimum or safety inventory levels, and inventory capacity. Given deterministic output (or full control of output) and full control of input, input rate can be matched to output and inventory problems are obviated. Here, therefore, we must deal with problems deriving from probabilistic output and/or incomplete control of input.

The problem can be considered to be one of matching two probability distributions (i.e. for input and output rates). A mismatch may give rise to:

(a) ***output starving***, i.e. depletion of stock due to excess of demand over input (i.e. shortage, etc.):

(b) 1. ***input blocking***, i.e. insufficient space or capacity for inputs due to excess of input over output;
   or
   2. ***excess stock-holding***, if inventory capacity is not limited.

The required average inventory capacity will be influenced by input and output rate variability (mean input rate must equal mean output rate). The higher the variability, the greater the stock capacity required to accommodate short-term differences in input and output sales. Hence as a general rule of thumb, the greater the possible short-term difference between rates (i.e. assuming symmetrical distributions, the upper end of one distribution minus the lower end of the other), the greater the stock capacity required. For a given (known or forecast) output rate distribution, inventory levels can be determined for alternative input rate distributions, and vice versa. Simulation techniques will normally be employed.

A similar problem is encountered in the design of flow processing systems, where inventory must exist between successive stages in the system (e.g. buffer stocks between the stations on a flow line) (see Chapter 15).

## MATERIALS REQUIREMENTS PLANNING (MRP)
## *(see also Chapters 12 and 16)*

MRP was described in Chapter 12. It involves the scheduling of activities and impinges upon the control of inventories. MRP will normally be used in a situation where demand is dependent (see Chapter 12) and where activity scheduling is to be externally oriented. In such situations the end product demand may be known and thus it will be possible, by 'exploding' demand, to calculate with certainty the parts/components requirements to satisfy that demand. Where this certainty exists the MRP procedure can be used as the principal approach to activity scheduling, and the inventory control problem can be seen as a secondary problem. Thus at any one time the parts/components requirements of a system and the activities which are to be undertaken by the system are known with certainty and any inventories which are maintained are simply inventories of work-in-progress. The impact of a materials requirements planning system, used in this 'pure' fashion, on the management of inventory will be as shown in Figure 17.12.

**Figure 17.12** Comparison of inventory decisions for inventory control system and MRP

| Inventory decisions | Type of inventory control system | | MRP* |
|---|---|---|---|
| | Order level system ('Perpetual') | Order interval system ('Periodic') | |
| Order quantity | Fixed | Variable | Variable |
| Reorder level | Fixed | Variable | Variable |
| Reorder interval | Variable | Fixed | Variable |
| Buffer stock | Low | High | None |

* The use of MRP as the principal or sole means for the scheduling of activities and the management of inventories (i.e. without the use of economic batching procedures, buffer stocks, etc.) (see text).

In some circumstances, the end product demand will be forecast, and this forecast requirement will be exploded in order to estimate, for a given period, the parts/components requirements for the system. In these cases, i.e. when there is some degree of uncertainty, it will be appropriate to maintain inventories of parts/components and/or end products. Additionally it may be appropriate to maintain such inventories where there is some need to manufacture and/or purchase parts or components in economic batches. In these circumstances the gross requirements determined from the MRP procedure can be interpreted to a scheduling/inventory requirement as follows:

> Parts/components to be provided for a given period = Gross parts/components requirement for period – Opening inventory + Required closing inventory

Our discussion in Chapter 12 indicated the way in which an economic batch size approach and the use of buffer or safety stocks can be used alongside materials requirements planning. In this type of approach, therefore, MRP will be used alongside an inventory management procedure which might be developed in the way discussed above.

## COMPUTERS IN INVENTORY MANAGEMENT

Many computer software packages have been written, in whole or in part, to deal with inventory management. The rates of introduction of new packages and modifications of existing packages are high, so no listing can be complete or sufficient.

Many packages are derivatives of earlier software and are designed for implementation on computers. For example, MAPICS from IBM was derived from INVEN and other programs. In general such packages offer a wide range of facilities in addition to inventory management. Such commercially available packages often provide planning and control routines, purchase order processing, etc. as well as inventory management. Those designed for the manufacturing industries provide for full production/inventory management. Some of these programs (e.g. MAPICS) are built largely around MRP procedures. Some developed for distribution offer purchasing, warehousing, distribution and retail stocks control.

### Simulation

Computer simulation methods, as described in Appendix III, are of particular value in inventory management. Applications include the comparison of inventory policies, the determination of reorder levels, the location of stocks, etc.

**EXAMPLE**

#### *Waste control commission*

The Minnesota Metropolitan Waste Control Commission operates a warehouse containing about 21 000 items valued at $3.5 million. Inventory management has been computerized, and management wanted to remove much of the excess inventory carried over from the days of manual inventory control methods. It was found that the problem could be solved cheaply and efficiently by transferring the item movement history to a personal computer. Then a user-friendly database management system was used to formulate and test possible 'removal rules'. Warehouse management was able to formulate effective removal rules. In a pilot study, $244 000 worth of inventory saving was identified, concentrated in 20 items. A second, more extensive analysis was then undertaken, which indicated that at least $1 million worth of inventory could be eliminated from the warehouse.

Source: Jaede, E. K., Pettis, J. and Scotta, L. (1990) Personal computer tools for effective inventory management. *Industrial Engineering*, **22**(4), pp. 41–42.

## CHECKLIST FOR CHAPTER 17

*Single and multi-stage inventories*

*Purpose and role of inventories*

*Different types of inventory*

Consumed/non-consumed
Output
Input resource
Customer queues

*Decision parameters for different situations*

*Inventory management strategies*

*Costs in inventory management*

Inventory costs
Customer service costs

*ABC/Pareto analysis*

*Inventory management systems*

Intermittent flow/input control system
  Fixed input level (perpetual control)
  Fixed input interval (periodic control)
Merits of 'periodic' and 'perpetual' systems
Different inventory models

*A1: Deterministic models*

Input level method
  Order quantities
    (a) Constant demand/complete deliveries
    (b) As (a) with price breaks
    (c) As (a) with discontinuous holding costs
    (d) As (a) with shortages
    (e) Constant demand with usage
    Multiple items – otherwise as (a)
    Reorder level problem
Input interval method
  Multiple items

*A2: Probabilistic situations*

Lead time and demand uncertainties
Safety or buffer stocks
'Service' level
Order quantity and level method, with uncertainty
  Constant demand/variable lead time
  Constant lead time/variable demand
  Variable lead time demand
Order interval method with uncertainty
  Uncertainties in batch quantities

*Continuous flow/input control system*

Decisions

*Materials requirements planning*

*Computers in inventory management*

Simulation

## FURTHER READING

**Barker, T. and Steele, P. (1989)** *Essentials of Materials Management.* Maidenhead: McGraw-Hill.

**Cavinato, J. (1990)** Managing different types of inventory. *Distribution*, **89**(3), pp. 88–92.

**Close, D. J. (1989)** Inventory management – a comparison of a traditional vs systems view. *Logistics*, **10**(2), pp. 90–105.

**Jessop, D. and Morrison, A. (1991)** *Storage and Control of Stock*. London: Pitman.

**Rouen, D. (1983)** Inventory service measures – a comparison of measures. *International Journal of Operations and Production Management*, **3**(2), pp. 37–45.

**Tersine, R. J. (1987)** *Principles of Inventory and Materials Management*, 3rd edn. New York: Elsevier.

**Waters, C. D. J. (1992)** *Inventory Control and Management*. Chichester: Wiley.

## QUESTIONS

17.1 Describe the principles of maximum–minimum and order cycle systems of stock control. In what circumstances is the use of each of these types of system appropriate?

In what circumstances would the use of either system give rise to basically the same stock control system (i.e. the same ordering decision)?

17.2 In a certain situation, demand for goods is both known and stable. The goods are ordered from an outside supplier, they are delivered in complete batches and no quantity discount arrangements apply. No buffer stock is to be maintained.

Determine:

(a) the economic order quantity, given:

ordering cost per order = £20
holding cost per item per annum = £0.05
demand per annum = 10 000
price per item = £15

(b) the economic order quantity, given:

ordering cost per order = £20
holding cost per item per annum = 5% of item price
demand per annum = 10 000
price per item = £15

(c) the regular economic ordering interval, given:

ordering cost per order = £50
holding cost per item per annum = 5% of item price
demand per annum = 15 000
price per item = £25

17.3 Determine the economic order quantity for the following:

(a) $C_s$ (ordering cost) = £20
$C_1$ (holding cost per item) = £0.07/year
$r$ (demand) = 12 000/year
$p$ (price) = £25

(b) $C_s$ = £20
$C_1$ = £0.07
$r$ = 12 000

Purchase discounts as follows:

| Order quantity | 0–500 | 500–999 | 1000–2500 | Over 2500 |
|---|---|---|---|---|
| Price per item | £25 | £22 | £20 | £19.5 |

(c) $C$ = £20
$C_1$ = 10% of price/year
$r$ = 10 000/year

Purchase discounts as follows:

| Order quantity | 0–500 | 500–999 | 1000–2500 | Over 2500 |
|---|---|---|---|---|
| Price per item | £25 | £22 | £20 | £19.5 |

17.4 Determine the economic order quantity, given the following situation:

$C_s$ = £100
$r$ = 10 000/year

Holding cost per item per annum, a portion of which is fixed and unrelated to the order quantity, i.e. £0.05, and a variable portion which is related to the order quantity, i.e. £0.07.

17.5 Determine the cost of storage and ordering per annum for order quantities of: (a) 1000; (b) 2000; and (c) 3000 items, given the following:

$C_s$ = £150
$r$ = 12 000/year

Also, storage space is available in increments each sufficient for storing 1000 items. The cost per annum for each of these increments is £500 and the fixed cost of storage irrespective of quantity is £0.5 per annum. No buffer stock is required.

17.6 (a) Derive the formula used to determine economic order quantities in the following circumstances:

Stockouts permitted
Delivery of complete batches of ordered items
Deterministic and stable demand

(b) What is the EOQ given the following:

Ordering cost = £125
Annual demand = 7500 items
Shortage or stockout cost per item per month = £5
Stock-holding cost per item per annum = 10% of price
Price of each item = £50

17.7 A company uses 75 000 items of a certain type each year, which it purchases from an outside supplier under the following terms:

| Order size, units | Price per unit (£) |
|---|---|
| 1 to 999 | 0.60 |
| 1000 to 9999 | 0.54 |
| 10 000 upwards | 0.45 |

Each time an order is placed, office and handling costs of £5 and transport costs of £15 are incurred. The cost of storage, interest and deterioration is £0.08 per unit stored per year. No safety stock is held. If the components are used at a uniform rate, calculate the economic order size and the total annual cost to the company.

17.8 (a) The assembly section of a factory uses a certain component part at a rate of 40 units per day. The machine shop within the factory can produce the component at a rate of 200 per day. The associated set-up cost is £100, the manufacturing cost is £5, and the inventory holding cost is £0.1 per unit per day.

If management is prepared to tolerate an increase of up to 1% in the minimum total cost per unit, what flexibility does this give in the choice of batch quantities and what is the total cost per unit of the cheapest solution if, for technical reasons, production batches are restricted to multiples of 50 units?

(b) The component part can be purchased in any quantity from an outside source, the terms depending on the quantity supplies as shown in the table on the right.

| Order quantity (number of units) | Price per unit (£) |
|---|---|
| 0 to 249 | 5.5 |
| 250 to 499 | 5.2 |
| 500 or more | 5.0 |

If the ordering costs are £15 per order, what is the economic order quantity in this case? Is it cheaper to manufacture the component in the factory or purchase it from the outside supplier?

17.9 Quick Start Ltd are the 'manufacturers' of automobile batteries. They purchase four types of second-hand battery from a local company, which, after rebuilding, they sell to local dealers. Sales of each type of battery are stable. The cost of storage and the annual demand for the batteries are shown in the table to the right.

| Type of battery | Annual demand | Stock-holding cost of item per annum |
|---|---|---|
| Startrite | 5000 | £0.5 |
| Quickfire | 7000 | £0.7 |
| Longlife | 3500 | £0.7 |
| Highpower | 2750 | £0.4 |

Quick Start Ltd like to order all four types of second-hand battery from their suppliers simultaneously. The cost of ordering is £175. They do not believe in maintaining buffer stocks of batteries.

(a) What are the economic order quantities for each type of battery?

(b) What is the order interval?

17.10 A shoe shop takes delivery of Phrayle shoes once every three months. The shoes cost about £2 per pair and retail at £4. What recommendations on stocks would you make for the various sizes and fittings?

17.11 The Universal Manufacturing Co. purchases plastic 'U' bends from a local company. It uses the bends at a fairly constant rate of 2500 per year. The cost of placing an order for the bends is £15 and the stock-holding cost per bend per year is £0.10/year.

Unfortunately, the supplier of the 'U' bends is a little unreliable and, consequently, the lead time on orders (which are always delivered complete) varies. In fact, a study of the purchase and production records reveals that lead time varies from two to four days and that the usage of bends during the lead time varies from 15 to 25 with the probabilities shown to the right:

| Lead time usage of bends | Probability of usage |
|---|---|
| 15 | 0.02 |
| 16 | 0.05 |
| 17 | 0.07 |
| 18 | 0.10 |
| 19 | 0.16 |
| 20 | 0.20 |
| 21 | 0.17 |
| 22 | 0.14 |
| 23 | 0.06 |
| 24 | 0.02 |
| 25 | 0.01 |

The Universal Manufacturing Co. insists that on no more than one occasion per year should there be stockouts of 'U' bends.

(a) What should the order quantity and reorder level be?

(b) If the cost per stockout is found to be £0.25, what reorder level provides the minimum cost?

17.12 Calculate the order quantity and the reorder level to minimize costs given the following information:

| | |
|---|---|
| Annual usage | = 3000 |
| Ordering cost | = £150 |
| Price per item | = £50 |
| Stock-holding cost/item per annum | = 20% of item per annum |
| Fixed cost of stockout | = £1 |
| Maximum number of stockouts allowed per annum | = 1 |

| Lead time usage | Frequency |
|---|---|
| 20 | 5 |
| 21 | 15 |
| 22 | 22 |
| 23 | 32 |
| 24 | 40 |
| 25 | 32 |
| 26 | 22 |
| 27 | 15 |
| 28 | 5 |

17.13 With reference to the previous question, it has recently been discovered that the cost of stockouts depends not only on the frequency of stockouts but also on the number of items short during stockouts. The stockout cost has been found to be £1 per item short during the stockout period. Using the information provided in the previous question, determine the reorder level and order quantity which minimizes costs.

17.14 A hospital store stocks an item for which the annual average demand is 250. The demand during the lead time is normally distributed (mean = 15; std dev. = 4).

The item sells at £32.5 and is bought at:

£20 (if up to 39 are bought)
£18.5 (if between 40 and 99 are bought)
£16.5 (if 100 or more are bought in any order)

Inventory cost per year is taken as 20% of stock value. The goodwill loss for each item not supplied against customer demand is taken as £10 and the cost of an order to the suppliers as £1.15.

If a lot size/reorder point system is used, determine the best order quantity, reorder point, safety stock and the annual cost.

17.15

| Order quantity | < 500 | 500–2500 | > 2500 |
|---|---|---|---|
| Price per unit ($p$) | £5 | £4.75 | £4.6 |

$r$ = 2500 per year (constant)
$C_s$ = £100
$C_1$ = 0.1p/unit/year
Average replenishment lead time = 0.1 year
Standard deviation of lead time = 0.02 year
Service level required = 90%

*Determine*:

(a) reorder quantity;

(b) reorder level.

17.16 The demand for an item held by a retailer is 150/week on average. Demand is not seasonal and has not changed from this average for the past two years. From a study of two years' data it has been found that the standard deviation of weekly demand is 20 items.

The stock-holding cost is £0.4/item/week and the reorder cost is £17/order irrespective of quantity. A 90% service level is to be provided.

Design a 'periodic' stock control procedure and explain any assumptions or simplifications you make.

## CASE STUDY (from Part 9)

The topics covered in this chapter are relevant in the following (see Introduction to Part 9 and Table C.1 for further details):

| No. | Name | Country |
|---|---|---|
| 3 | Centre Hospitalier Reine Fabiola | Belgium |

PART 8

# The Control of Operating Systems


Introduction to Part 8

Chapter 18 Operations control principles

Chapter 19 Management of quality

Chapter 20 Quality control and reliability

Chapter 21 Maintenance and replacement

Chapter 22 Performance measurement

## INTRODUCTION TO PART 8

This section deals with control. The principal topics covered are the management of quality, and thus: the control of the quality of the goods or services provided by the operating systems and the reliability of those goods and services; the maintenance and/or replacement of the system, and its constituent parts; and the control of the system through performance monitoring.

The introduction chapter sets the scene for chapters on the three principal topics: quality; maintenance and reliability; and performance measurement. Two chapters are devoted to quality – the first dealing with important principles, and the second with controls.

## STRATEGIC CONTEXT

The operations issues, problems and decisions considered in this part of the book exist within the broader strategic context of the organization. The main relationships are set out here, as a preface to the details which follow.

### Influences of business policy decisions *(see Chapter 2, Figure 2.2)*

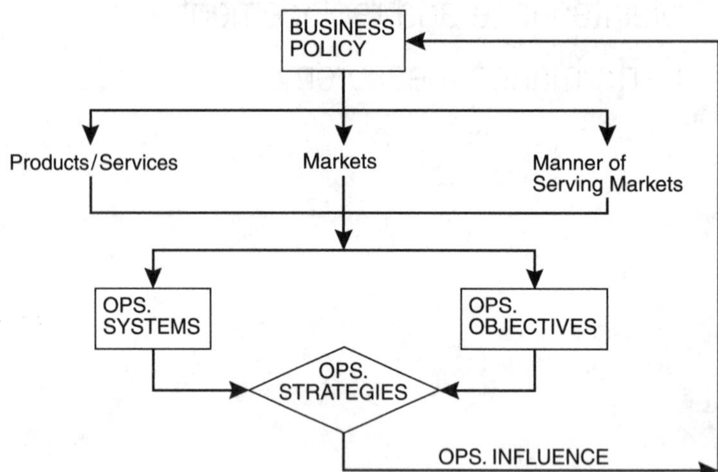

## Quality and reliability

These two interrelated topics are dealt with in this part. It is inappropriate to consider quality without also thinking of customers' requirements or expectations. Quality will normally be a major consideration when considering how a business will serve its markets. This in turn must influence the objectives that operations pursue, in respect of customer service, and this will influence the way in which operations are managed. So, operations managers will be charged with securing a customer service relationship in keeping with the business policy intentions. Of course, the nature of the products or services which are to be provided will have a major influence on how operations managers must set out to manage and ensure quality. For example, in service systems the achievement of high and consistent quality will depend to a large extent on the capabilities and management of the people in the system. The provision of a repetitive, standardized service, and also the provision of a standardized product range, will require a different approach to quality management than would be appropriate if repetition or standardization were low, and variety/change high.

Naturally, the levels of quality achieved by an organization, as well as the consistency or reliability of quality, must depend to a large extent on the type of resources used in the system – their capabilities, etc. – as well as the quality management procedures. Whilst it may be the intention continually to improve this quality capability, operations managers will wish to try to ensure that when business policies are under review, quality standards/expectations are not set so high as to be unachievable in the requisite time period, since otherwise formulated policies will not adequately be implemented. Equally, given a particular level of quality capability in operations, managers may not wish to see new policy objectives set which attach less importance to quality and, for example, greater importance to cost.

## Performance measurement

The final topic dealt with here is necessarily closely linked with business policy, for the measurement of the performance of the operating system or any of its parts must be made against a set of operations objectives which in turn must derive from business objectives. For example, a business which has chosen to seek competitive advantage through high customer service on quality will expect to measure the performance of its operations substantially against this criterion.

Here perhaps the policy–operations relationship is largely unidirectional. The priorities of the business will largely influence the manner in which operations performance is measured – or at least the emphasis in that measurement. Unlike other areas, the existence of particular performance measurement procedures in operations is unlikely to be a major factor when considering business policies or policy changes.

## TOPIC MAP

| Topics in this Part | Related topics in other chapters: Chapter | Topic | Comments/aspects |
|---|---|---|---|
| Chapter 18 | | | |
| Operations controls | 3 | Marketing | Relationship of marketing decisions to planning and control |
| | 11 | Operations planning and control | Relationship of planning and control |
| | 12 | Scheduling | Need for schedules against which to control |
| | | Scheduling techniques | Kanban |
| | | Balancing scheduling and control | |
| | | Effectiveness of scheduling | Need for control to compensate for scheduling inadequacies |
| | 13 | Project scheduling | Controls in project work |
| | 14 | Batch processing | Controls in batch processing |
| | 15 | Flow processing | Controls in flow processing |
| | 16 | Materials management | Control of supply, in-process and output flows |
| | 17 | Inventory management | Inventory controls |
| | 20 | Quality control | Control charts |
| | 21 | Maintenance/repair/replacement | Maintenance/replacement Scheduling and control |
| Control concepts | 3 | Finance/accounting | Financial controls |
| | 4 | Cost control systems | |
| | 8 | Work standards | Use of standards in control of work performance |
| | 9 | Technology | Automation and automatic control |
| | 10 | Payment by results | Payment systems and performance controls |
| | 12 | Operations scheduling | Balancing scheduling and control |
| | 13 | Projects | Need for control to complement scheduling (13–15) |
| | 14 | Batch processing | |
| | 15 | Flow processing | |
| | 16 | Materials management | Control of materials flows (Materials management, Supply chains, Purchasing and supply) |
| | | Supply chains | |
| | | Purchasing and supply | |

## TOPIC MAP

| Topics in this Part | Related topics in other chapters: Chapter | Topic | Comments/aspects |
|---|---|---|---|
| *Chapter 18 continued* | | | |
| | 17 | Inventory management | Inventory controls |
| | 19 | Quality control | Control charts; Acceptance sampling |
| | 22 | Performance measurement | Performance measurement and control |
| Control of operating systems | 12 | Operations scheduling | Balancing scheduling and control |
| | 13 | Projects | Need for control to complement scheduling |
| | 14 | Batch processing | Need for control to complement scheduling |
| | 15 | Flow processing | Need for control to complement scheduling |
| | 16 | Materials management | Control of materials flows |
| | | Supply chains | Control of materials flows |
| | | Purchasing and supply | Control of materials flows |
| | 17 | Inventory management | Inventory controls |
| | 19 | Quality control | Control charts; Acceptance sampling |
| | 12 | JIT | Kanban |
| Chapter 19 | | | |
| Nature of quality | 1 | Operations management | Quality in customer service |
| | 2 | Operations policy | Quality as a competitive advantage |
| | 3 | Marketing | Quality as a competitive advantage |
| | | Product/service design | Design for quality |
| | 4 | Operations economics | Quality influences operations costs |
| | 7 | Method study | Importance of worker and work methods in achieving quality |
| | 8 | Work measurement | Importance of worker and work methods in achieving quality |
| | 9 | Job design | Responsibilities for quality |
| | 10 | Payment by results | Rewards for quality |
| | 16 | Materials management | Importance of supplies for output and source quality |
| | 20 | Quality control | Need for quality control in context of TQM, etc. |

## TOPIC MAP

| Topics in this Part | Related topics in other chapters: Chapter | Topic | Comments/aspects |
|---|---|---|---|
| *Chapter 19 continued* | | | |
| | 21 | Maintenance/repair/ replacement | Need for reliable and adequate facilities |
| | 22 | Performance measurement | Need to measure operations performance against customer service and efficiency |
| Quality costs | 2 | Operations policy | Is quality a cost or a benefit? |
| | 3 | Marketing | |
| | 4 | Operations costs | |
| | 7 | Work systems | Labour and labour costs and their relationship to cost of quality |
| | 8 | Work systems | |
| | 9 | Work systems | |
| | 10 | Work systems | |
| | 11 | Capacity management | Impact of rework/rectification on capacity |
| | 12 | Operations scheduling | 'Need' to schedule rectifications (rework) repetitions |
| | 13 | Project scheduling | |
| | 14 | Batch scheduling | |
| | 15 | Flow processes | Sources of defects in flow processes |
| | 16 | Materials management | Need for input controls to avoid quality costs in process |
| | 17 | Inventory management | Costs of deterioration and damage |
| | 20 | Quality controls | Cost of controls versus benefits for quality |
| | 22 | Performance measurement | Importance of quality in customer service |
| TQM and standards | 1 | Operations management objectives | Customer service and quality assurance |
| | 2 | Operations policy | Quality as a competitive advantage |
| | 3 | Marketing | External standards and accreditation |
| | | Product/service design | External standards and accreditation |
| | 7 | Work systems | Worker and work system contribution to total quality |

## TOPIC MAP

| Topics in this Part | Related topics in other chapters: Chapter | Topic | Comments/aspects |
|---|---|---|---|
| *Chapter 19 continued* | | | |
| | 8 | Work systems | Worker and work system contribution to total quality |
| | 9 | Work systems | |
| | 10 | Work systems | |
| | 16 | Supply chains | Need to work with suppliers to ensure quality |
| | 20 | Quality controls | Need for controls even with TQM 'assurance' |
| | 22 | Performance measurement | Benchmarking |
| Behavioural and organization factors | 7 | Work systems | Worker and work system contribution to total quality |
| | 8 | Work systems | |
| | 9 | Work systems | |
| | 10 | Work systems | |
| Quality improvement programmes | 3 | Product/service design | Design improvement techniques |
| | 7 | Work systems | Worker and work system contribution to total quality |
| | 8 | Work systems | |
| | 9 | Work systems | |
| | 10 | Work systems | |
| | 22 | Performance measurement | Benchmarking |
| Chapter 20 | | | |
| Quality control and assurance | 4 | Cost controls | Control systems |
| | 7 | Work methods | Inspection tasks |
| | 8 | Work standards | |
| | 9 | Job design | Responsibility for quality control and assurance tasks |
| | 10 | Payment by results | |
| | 16 | Materials management | Vendor controls and assurance |
| | | Purchasing and supply | |
| | | PDM and logistics | Outgoing quality controls |
| | 18 | Operations controls | Control concepts |
| | 19 | TQM | TQM principles and quality controls |
| | 21 | Maintenance/replacement | Inspection and control activities |

## TOPIC MAP

| Topics in this Part | Related topics in other chapters: Chapter | Topic | Comments/aspects |
|---|---|---|---|
| *Chapter 20 continued* | | | |
| Quality control procedures | 16 | Materials management<br>Purchasing and supply | Vendor controls and assurance |
| | 21 | Maintenance/replacement | Inspection and control activities |
| Process capability | 3 | Product/service design | Achievability of standards |
| | 7 | Work systems | Worker performance as an aspect of process capability |
| | 8 | Work systems | Worker performance as an aspect of process capability |
| | 9 | Work systems | Worker performance as an aspect of process capability |
| | 21 | Maintenance/repair/ replacement | Condition of facilities and process capability |
| Chapter 21 | | | |
| The maintenance function | 1<br>2 | Operations management objectives<br>Operations policy | Reliability as a factor in customer service |
| | 3 | Product/service design | Need to relate to process design and maintenance |
| | 4 | Operations economics | Maintenance/reliability of facilities as a cost factor |
| | 5<br>6 | Location of facilities<br>Layout of facilities | Maintenance/maintainability as a location factor |
| | 7<br>8<br>9<br>10 | Work systems and job design<br>Work systems and job design<br>Work systems and job design<br>Work systems and job design | Roles and responsibilities in maintenance and repair |
| | 11 | Capacity | Maintenance and reliability of facilities and impact on real capacity |
| | 12 | Operations scheduling | Need to provide for maintenance and repair in schedules |

## TOPIC MAP

| Topics in this Part | Related topics in other chapters: Chapter | Topic | Comments/aspects |
|---|---|---|---|
| *Chapter 21 continued* | | | |
| | 13 | Operations scheduling | Need to provide for maintenance and repair schedules |
| | 14 | Operations scheduling | |
| | 15 | Operations scheduling | |
| | 17 | Inventories | Inventories and spares/ replacement items |
| | 19 | Management of quality | Role of maintenance in quality assurance |
| | 20 | Reliability | Influence of maintenance and replacement in reliability |
| | 22 | Performance measurement | Need to monitor maintenance performance |
| Maintenance decisions | 7 | Work systems | Role of worker in the scheduling of maintenance |
| | 8 | Work systems | |
| | 9 | Work systems | |
| | 10 | Work systems | |
| | 11 | Capacity | Influence of maintenance/ repair on capacity |
| | 12 | Scheduling | Scheduling of maintenance activities |
| | 13 | Scheduling | |
| | 14 | Scheduling | |
| | 15 | Scheduling | |
| | 16 | Materials management | Scheduling of supplier/items for maintenance/repair works |
| | 17 | Inventory management | |
| Inspection | 7 | Work systems | Role of worker in the scheduling of maintenance |
| Preventive maintenance | 8 | Work systems | |
| | 9 | Work systems | |
| | 10 | Work systems | |
| | 11 | Capacity | Influence of maintenance/ repair on capacity |
| | 12 | Scheduling | Scheduling of maintenance activities |
| | 13 | Scheduling | |
| | 14 | Scheduling | |
| | 15 | Scheduling | |
| | 16 | Materials management | Scheduling of supplier/items for maintenance/repair works |
| | 17 | Inventory management | |

## TOPIC MAP

| Topics in this Part | Chapter | Topic | Comments/aspects |
|---|---|---|---|
| | Related topics in other chapters | | |
| *Chapter 21 continued* | | | |
| Repairs/replacement | 2 | Business policy | Repair/replacement policy as an aspect of customer service |
| | 3 | Marketing | Repair/replacement policy as an aspect of customer service |
| | | Product/service design | Design to facilitate repair/ replacement |
| | 4 | Operations costs | Repair/replacement policy as an aspect of customer service |
| | 6 | Layout of facilities | Layout to facilitate repair/replacement |
| | 7 | Work systems | Design/specification and management of repair/ replacement work |
| | 8 | Work systems | Design/specification and management of repair/ replacement work |
| | 9 | Work systems | Design/specification and management of repair/ replacement work |
| | 12 | Scheduling | Impact of breakdown on schedules |
| | 13 | Scheduling | Impact of breakdown on schedules |
| | 14 | Scheduling | Impact of breakdown on schedules |
| | 15 | Scheduling | Impact of breakdown on schedules |
| | 16 | Materials management | Need for supplies and/or stocks or spares |
| | 17 | Inventories | (as above) |
| | 19 | Management of quality | Repair/replacement policies and quality assurance/control |
| | 20 | Reliability | Repair/replacement and relationship with reliability |
| Chapter 22 | | | |
| Customer service performance | 1 | Operations management objectives | Need to measure performance against objectives |
| | 2 | Operations policy | (as above) |

## TOPIC MAP

| Topics in this Part | Related topics in other chapters: Chapter | Topic | Comments/aspects |
|---|---|---|---|
| *Chapter 22 continued* | | | |
| | 11 | Capacity management | Impact on customer service |
| | 12 | Scheduling | |
| | 13 | Scheduling | |
| | 14 | Scheduling | |
| | 15 | Scheduling | |
| | 16 | Materials management and inventories | |
| | 17 | Materials management and inventories | |
| | 19 | Quality | |
| | 20 | Quality | |
| Resource utilization performance | 1 | Operations management objectives | Need to measure performance against objectives |
| | 2 | Operations policy | |
| | 8 | Work standards | For performance measurement |
| | 10 | Payment by results | Relationship to performance management |
| | 11 | Capacity | Measurement of capacity utilization |
| | 16 | Materials management | Measurement of materials utilization |
| | 17 | Inventory management | Measurement of inventory utilization |
| | 19 | Quality | Measurement of wastage/ rework, etc. |
| | 21 | Maintenance | Measurement of facility availability/downtime |
| Performance measurement and control | 1 | Operations management objectives | Need to set objectives for which performance management is possible |
| | 4 | Cost control | Cost control as an aspect of performance management |
| | 8 | Work standards | Uses in performance measurement |
| | 10 | Incentive pay | |
| | 18 | Operations control principles | |

## TOPIC MAP

| Topics in this Part | Related topics in other chapters: Chapter | Topic | Comments/aspects |
|---|---|---|---|
| *Chapter 22 continued* | | | |
| Performance audit | 1 | Operations management objectives | Need to set objectives for which performance management is possible |
| | 4 | Cost control | Cost control as an aspect of performance management |
| | 8 | Work standards | Uses in performance measurement |
| | 10 | Incentive pay | (Uses in performance measurement) |
| | 18 | Operations control principles | |
| Improvement and benchmarking | 1 | Operations objectives | Policies for continual improvement |
| | 2 | Operations policy | (Policies for continual improvement) |
| | | Competitive advantage | (Policies for continual improvement) |
| | 3 | Marketing | Information for benchmarking and improvement |
| | 7 | Work systems and job design | Responsibilities for improvements |
| | 8 | Work systems and job design | (Responsibilities for improvements) |
| | 9 | Work systems and job design | (Responsibilities for improvements) |
| | 10 | Payments | Rewards for improvements |
| | 16 | Materials management | Joint benchmarking/ improvement activities with suppliers |
| | 19 | Management of quality | Quality standards and benchmarks. Organization for continual improvement |
| | | TQM quality improvement programme | (Quality standards and benchmarks. Organization for continual improvement) |
| | 20 | Quality control and assurance | Information for benchmarking and improvement |

Chapter 18

# Operations control principles

## ISSUES

What is the relationship of operations planning and control?
Where and when is control important?
What are the requirements for effective control?
How are operating systems controlled?
What is kanban?

In Chapter 11 we distinguished between operations planning and operations control and chose to deal with the two aspects separately. Part 6 considered planning problems. In this chapter we consider operations control in a general manner before considering particular aspects of the control of operating systems in the remaining chapters in this section. The distinction that we are making between operations planning and control is again summarized, in Table 18.1.

Rarely within organizations will there be operations control departments. Normally the control function will be invested in departments alongside responsibilities for planning operations. For example, those responsible for inventory management decisions will be concerned with and responsible for both planning and control. Financial control will be exercised within most organizations;

**Table 18.1 Operations planning and control – some distinctions**

| | Planning | Control |
|---|---|---|
| **Time-scale** | Medium to long term (future time) | Short term and immediate (real/present time) |
| **Purpose** | Determine and schedule future activities | Monitor and adjust present activities |
| **Inputs** | Future demand requirements<br>Current capabilities and achievements | Current plans<br>Actual progress information |
| **Outputs** | Future schedules<br>Future resource requirements | Statements on past achievements |

however, again, those involved will be responsible for financial planning and budgeting as well as financial and cost control.

We have noted (in Chapter 11) that the general purpose of control is to ensure, as far as possible, the implementation of plans. Thus those involved in control, and those procedures established for the purposes of control, will, in general, seek to monitor activities with a view to ensuring that these activities correspond to some intended situation or state. Control derives from this process of monitoring activities and the comparison of actual and intended states. The need for control derives from the fact that rarely is it possible to ensure in advance that certain things will happen in a particular way at a particular time, etc. Control is necessary because of the existence of uncertainties. A purely deterministic situation is unlikely to necessitate control since, in such circumstances, planning in itself is sufficient. In practice such deterministic situations will rarely exist and thus control is an essential link in the circle or cycle which begins with planning and involves monitoring, action and correction, and possibly revision of planning for future events.

## IMPORTANCE AND EMPHASIS

The relative *emphasis* on planning and control in operations management will, to a large extent, be determined by the nature of the operating system. Consider, for example, the contrasting case examples discussed below.

*Case 1* This is the big 'one-off' planning project in a highly uncertain situation. Here planning cannot be perfect, and there will be little opportunity to replan. The emphasis, therefore, will be on the controls involved in using a given set of resources efficiently for different purposes. (Similar situations will exist in managing most one-off 'project' type situations, e.g. in the construction industry, hospital accident wards, expeditions, military operations.)

*Case 2* This is the repetitive situation where the (annual) requirements of the operating system(s) are known and where planning can therefore be accurate and certain. Here considerable effort will be put into establishing the system, and the subsequent problems of control will be minimized. If the system is properly planned there will be little need for decision-making in control, since there will be few exceptions to the norm. (Similar situations exist in managing most repetitive/process-type operating systems, e.g. mass production, regular/scheduled transport systems, customer banking services, routine medical and surgery services.)

The way in which planning and control are organized will depend on the emphasis which must be placed on the relative difficulty and frequency of occurrence of problems of planning and control. Where the emphasis is on planning, responsibility may be more centralized. Where the emphasis is on control, responsibility may be more decentralized. (Some of these issues are discussed in connection with organization structure in Chapter 3.)

**EXAMPLE**

### *Establishing and managing emergency services in a new town*

*Objective*

The operations manager must establish a comprehensive, integrated emergency service comprising ambulance, fire, health, evacuation, accommodation facilities, etc. for a new town. It must be able to cope with most conceivable local emergencies and disasters (e.g. major transport accidents, fires, floods, epidemics). The operations manager is then required to run the system.

*Planning problems*

The design and planning of a system to deal with a largely unknown demand is complex. The operations manager cannot know exactly what is required, and therefore must estimate and forecast, and try to establish a system which will cope with most needs for most of the time. Excess resources should be obtained if possible.

*Control problems*

The effectiveness of such a system, when established, will depend largely on the manner in which it is utilized. There will be flexibility in the system – alternative ways of deploying resources. The manner in which the system is used will differ on each occasion. No two emergencies will be the same. Thus effective control is paramount and the recurrent problem will be that of control, since the system cannot be redesigned frequently.

---

**EXAMPLE**

### *A college student accommodation unit*

*Objective*

The accommodation manager in a large college is required to provide on-campus accommodation (study bedrooms) for all first-year students. The number of students entering the college is subject to an upper limit, and all places are expected to be filled each year for the conceivable future period.

*Planning problems*

The required number of study bedrooms must be provided. The exact number is known. Support staff, e.g. cleaners, wardens, must be provided. Students from each college department must be allocated to each set of rooms. A small number of rooms must be provided with special facilities, e.g. ground-floor rooms for some disabled students. Some rooms must be kept in reserve in case others become unusable during the academic year.

*Control problems*

Apart from regular cleaning, the provision of security, the handling of occasional complaints and routine maintenance, there are few tasks which must be performed during the academic year. The nature of these tasks is similar each year.

---

## CONTROL CONCEPTS: REQUIREMENTS

The essential prerequisites for effective control are:

1. The purpose or objectives of the system to be controlled must be known.
2. Appropriate (level of detail, relevance and timeliness) information on system performance must be available.
3. A choice of actions must be possible and criteria for choice must exist.
4. There should be adequate speed, appropriateness and accuracy of system response.

Diagrammatically a control system may be represented in the manner shown in Figure 18.1. (This is an 'output' control system where output is monitored in order to assess the performance of the operation. In some situations it will be appropriate to employ a 'behaviour' control system where the behaviour of the operation itself is monitored; see Chapter 3.) It will be seen that there are four components:

**Figure 18.1** Feedback and control system (closed) (output control)

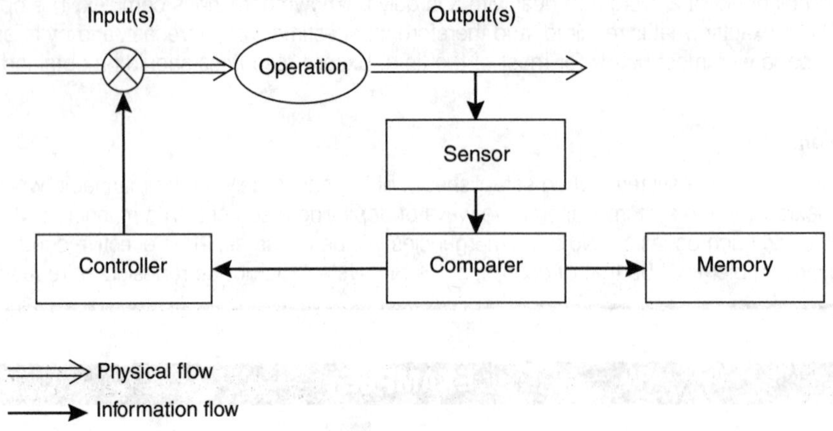


(a) a means of sensing output;

(b) a means of comparing actual output with intended output;

(c) a means of recording intended output (memory);

(d) a means of exercising control.

A *closed system*, as shown in Figure 18.1, is directly influenced by its own past behaviour. Its own outputs are monitored or observed in order that some purposeful control might be exercised over its inputs. The operation of the system is dependent on direct feedback of information. The normal domestic central heating system is an example of such control, since the thermostat monitors room temperature and controls the boiler to maintain a given room temperature.

In contrast, an *open system* exists where outputs have no direct influence over earlier parts of the system. In other words an open system does not react to its own performance. Its past actions have no influence over current or future actions. There is no feedback of information on its outputs for the control of its outputs. The simple clock is an example of such an open system.

In practice most operations control will be of the closed system type, although the mechanisms by which systems are closed will differ and will vary in their degree of sophistication. For example, in process control, i.e. the control of flow processes such as chemical processes using computers, several types of application exist, their principal differences being the manner in which information is fed back and control is exercised.

In a simple data logging system, a computer is used to scan rapidly and frequently the information secured from instruments connected to the process, e.g. flow meters, transducers, thermometers, etc., this information being recorded, processed and displayed, and used to calculate performance indices or guides which subsequently might be used by those concerned with the manual control of the process. Alarm systems are often incorporated, so the computer will signal the occurrence of faults or other unusual conditions in the process and also carry out simple diagnostic procedures using the input data to determine and indicate the cause of such conditions.

In contrast, a full control system will provide automated closed-loop control of the system. The efficiency of such systems depends on their being fed with the correct information, i.e. efficient data logging, and on the speed with which the control system works. Such systems must be carefully designed to accord with the characteristics of the process. The nature of the inputs must correspond to known and foreseeable disturbances of the process and the speed of the system to the nature of the process.

It is inappropriate here to enter into a detailed discussion of control theory. However, it is worth noting that in the development of feedback control systems, whether manual, automatic or mixed, it is essential that the feedback mechanism be matched to the characteristics and capability of the process. It is essential also that control be exercised at appropriate stages within the process and that each of the important variables be monitored for control purposes. In practice, therefore, control systems will often be complex, multi-stage and multi-level.

## CONTROL OF OPERATING SYSTEMS

Most control actions are *information dependent* in that they derive from the acquisition and use of information on the nature or state of the operating system. In Chapter 1 we modelled operating system(s) entirely in terms of physical flow. We should now note, however, that such systems are in effect 'covered' by information links so that, together, there is adequate information available for the control of activities and events at all stages in the system. For example, the control of physical flows in operating systems is exercised through a combination of activity scheduling and inventory control decisions. This situation can best be illustrated in the manner shown in Figure 18.2. The diagrams in this figure show the principal points in the system at which control of flow is exercised and the decision loops associated with such control. Thus in a 'function from stock to stock' system, information in terms of order or delivery requirements goes from the customer to a point equivalent to inventory output. Flow at this stage is monitored and information, through the inventory management system, passes to the flow control point on inventory input, from where, through the activity scheduling system, information passes to a flow control point on function input, and so on through to resource supply. A similar chain of information loops and a similar series of control points exist for all systems. For example, in a 'function from stock from customer queue' system, the customer influences the input to customer queues, which are monitored in order to ensure that appropriate decisions are made in respect of flow from customer queues through to the system. The flow into the system is monitored through the activity scheduling system so that the flow of resources to the system is appropriate. The flow in turn is monitored through the inventory management system in order to ensure that flow into (i.e. replenishment of) resource stocks is appropriate.

Flow control is an essential responsibility of operations management. Such flow control is associated with the inventory management system(s) and the activity scheduling system. Supplementing this flow control there will be a need to consider the *nature* of the items or customers which are flowing in the system, in order to ensure, for example, that intended quality levels are maintained and resources are utilized in the intended fashion. Chapter 17 dealt with control decisions relating to inventory management. In this part we shall consider control associated with activity schedules and quality control and also controls associated with resource utilization, i.e. with resource maintenance, replacement and repair. Finally, we shall take a broader approach and consider performance measurement, i.e. the way in which the performance of the whole operating system might be monitored for both planning and control purposes.

## THE KANBAN SYSTEM

The kanban system developed by Toyota in Japan as part of Toyota's JIT philosophy (see Chapter 12) provides a simple visible means of feedback control in the manner outlined in Figure 18.2. The system provides a basis for both operations and inventory control through simple manual/clerical procedures. Kanban is a simple flow control system, serving the purposes identified above.

### Kanban principles

The simplest kanban system utilizes pairs of cards (kanban is the Japanese for card). The cards are used to trigger movements between operations in flow systems where standard items are made in small batches against customer orders. More sophisticated systems can be developed for multi-product

**Figure 18.2** Operations control relationships

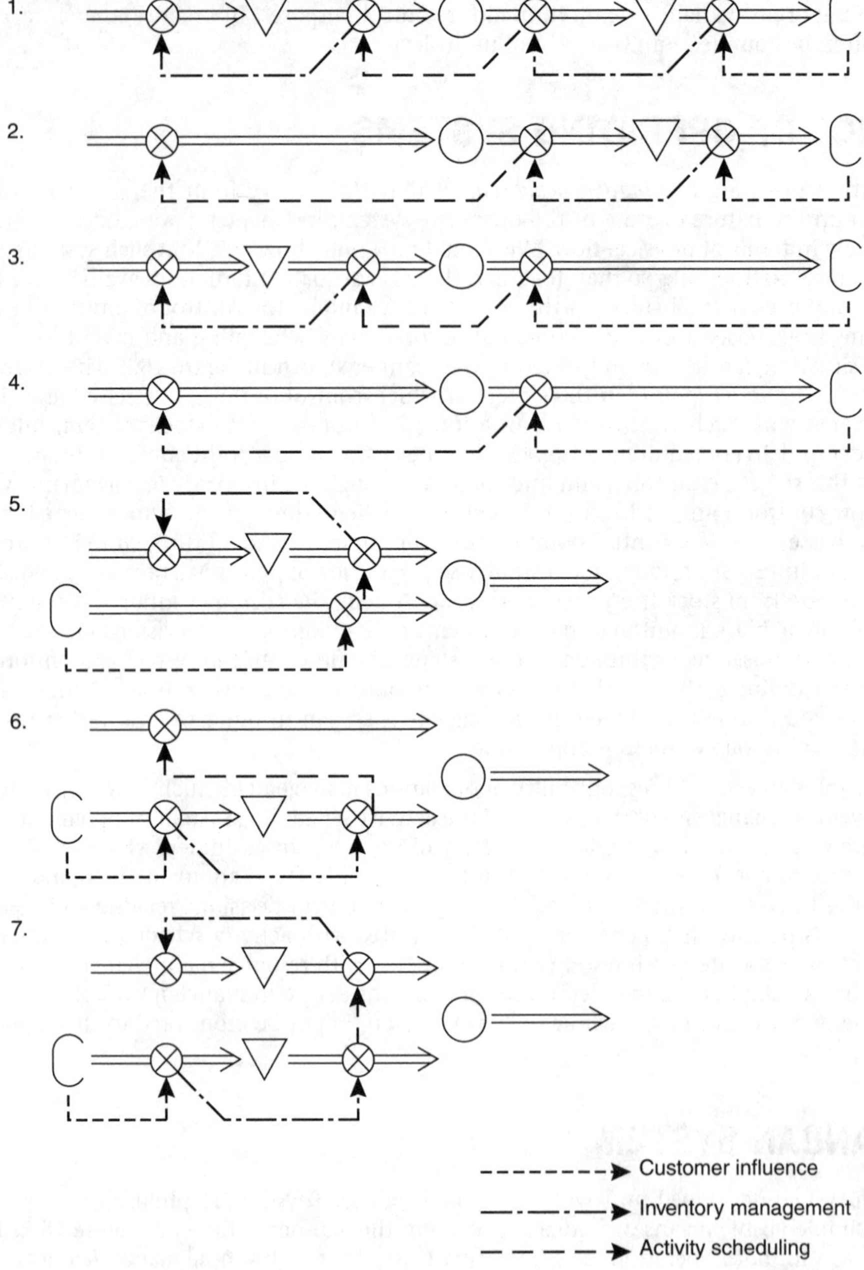


systems, but in all cases the flow through the system is triggered by demand from, or on behalf of, the customer as outlined in Figure 18.2.

A simple example will illustrate the principles of a two-card kanban system. Figure 18.3 shows how the system would work between two sequential processing operations. Operation 4, which supplies the customer, is in turn supplied by operation 3. Operation 3 has input and output stocks. Operation 4 has input stocks only and supplies directly to the external customer. The figure shows the

**Figure 18.3** The operation of a two-card kanban system

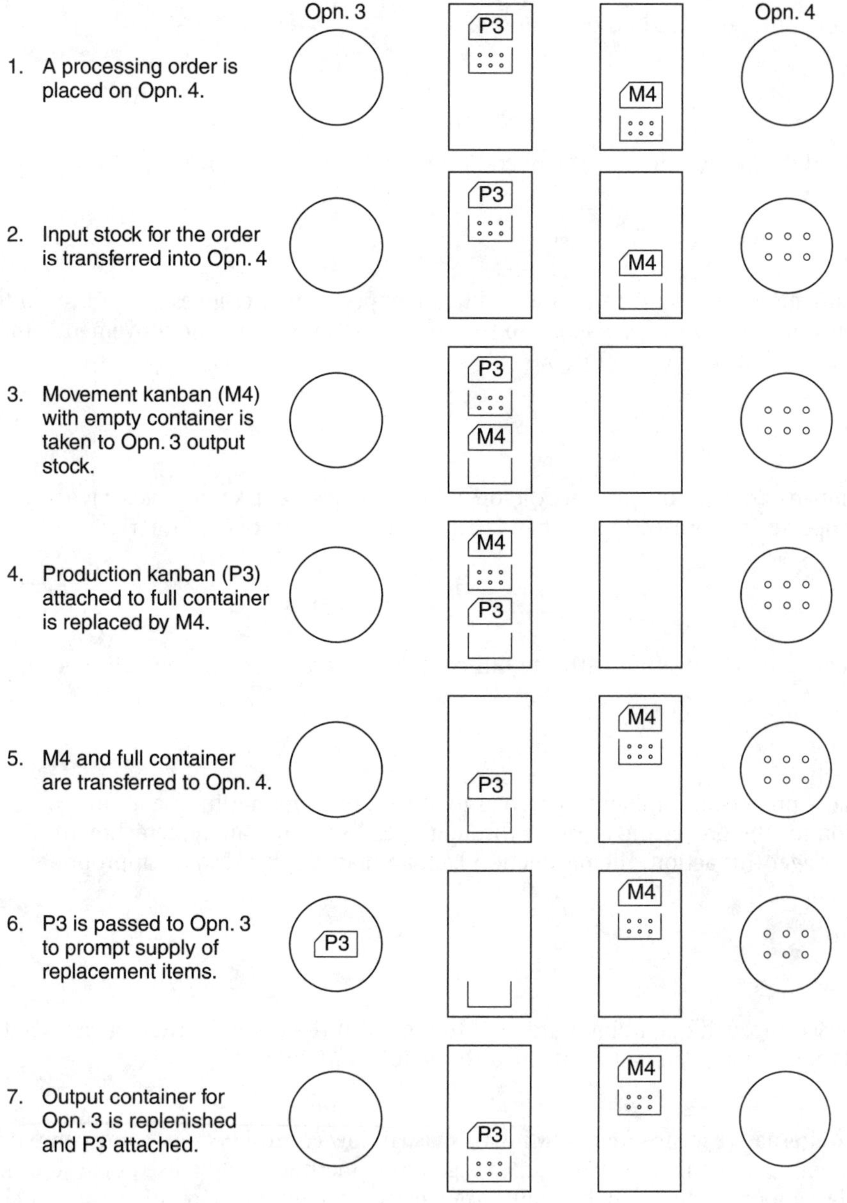


two intermediate stocks. Items are held in stock in standard containers – in this case each containing six items for processing. Each container has attached to it a kanban: either a *movement* kanban, or a *processing* kanban. Stage 1 shows a full container in both stocks, with their associated kanbans. The receipt of an order at operation 4 for completed parts gives rise to the following sequence of activities.

## Stage 1

The processing order is placed on operation 4.

## Stage 2

The items held in the container in the operation 4 input stock are transferred to operation 4.

## Stage 3

The fact that a movement kanban is attached to an empty container gives authorization for the movement of items from the preceding stage, so the empty container with the movement kanban is moved to the output stock area of operation 3.

## Stage 4

The two kanbans are exchanged; thus the operation 4 movement kanban is attached to the full container, and operation 3 processing kanban is attached to the empty container.

## Stage 5

The movement kanban together with the full container is transferred to operation 4 input stock.

## Stage 6

The fact that a processing kanban is attached to an empty container in operation 3 output stock gives authorization for the processing of items through operation 3 for the replenishment of the container. In order to trigger this action, the production kanban may be placed in an appropriate rack or display at operation 3.

## Stage 7

Items processed through operation 3 are used to replenish the empty container in operation 3 output stock and the processing kanban is attached to the full container.

There are alternative means for operating this visual flow control system. Some companies use a simpler system employing only one card. Other 'signalling' methods can be used instead of kanban cards; for example, coloured clips can be transferred between containers within stores, or flags can be attached to containers, etc. An alternative method is to mark out areas on racks or on the floor within store areas such that an empty area can operate as a trigger for the production of replacement items. The essential feature, however, of all such systems is that activities, e.g. the processing of items, are triggered only on demand. Requests, in effect, *pull* items through the sequence of operations.

Kanban-type flow control systems are an important part of JIT. The concept of processing only as and when required, coupled with the 'pull' system, are essential ingredients of JIT. The visibility of the system, e.g. the visibility of the movement of processed kanbans, is a further important characteristic of JIT.

Since the number of kanban cards operating within a system is directly proportional to the amount of work-in-progress in that system, changes in the number of cards will result in changes in in-process inventory. Thus operations management can control overall in-process inventory levels by the addition to or the subtraction of cards from the system. If, for example, management judges that a system can operate with less in-process inventory, then this is achieved simply by withdrawing kanban cards. Since such cards (or other 'triggering' devices) are readily visible, this has an immediate impact upon operations, so the system is highly responsive.

**EXAMPLE**

### *Kanban at Schlegel Corp.*

A kanban-based production control system was designed for a batch flow manufacturing facility for woven products at Schlegel Corp. The firm produces its products in more than 450 varieties. The main characteristic of the production process is that the weaving stage involves batched production with significant set-up and change-over times. Setting and maintaining the minimum finished inventory levels must accommodate the need to meet the target service levels for the customer. The production control system provides a framework for production planning and scheduling in addition to performance tracking and process improvements. One key element of the production control scheme is that the inventory at each part of the process is controlled.

Source: Groenevelt, H. and Karmarker, U. S. (1988) A dynamic kanban system case study. *Production and Inventory Management*, **29**(2), pp. 46–51.

## ACTIVITY CONTROLS

The control of activities associated with activity scheduling is one aspect of flow control within a system. Inventory control, the complementary aspect of flow control, has been dealt with in Chapter 17. Here, therefore, we shall deal briefly with the elements of activity control. Essentially there are three steps necessary in achieving control of activities: (a) monitoring and recording flows or activities; (b) analysing flows and/or progress by comparison with plans or schedules; and (c) control, that is, modification of plans or a rearrangement of schedules in order to conform as nearly as possible to original targets. To some extent the manner in which these steps are accomplished will depend on the nature and manner of activity scheduling and the nature of the activity schedules. Thus if schedules have been developed in order to achieve a particular flow or particular state at certain points in the system at particular times, then performance will be recorded and monitored by reference to these same points. The manner in which plans and schedules have been expressed and drawn up will influence the way in which step (b) above is achieved, i.e. the analysis of progress by comparison with plans and schedules. The extent and nature of control will of course depend on the variance identified between actual progress or flows and intended progress or flows. The manner in which this control will be achieved will depend to some extent on the nature of the system and the opportunities for the exercise of control. Thus, for example, if a particular procedure has been established for scheduling purposes then control will be linked to the use of the same procedure. If bar charts have been used then progress and monitoring will utilize such charts. If network analysis has been used then similar calculations and procedures will be employed for purposes of control. The latter application will be developed in a little more detail here by way of illustration.

When *network analysis* is employed, periodic feedback of progress information will be used to update the network. Updating is often carried out overnight or at weekends so that new information is available on the next working day. The procedure is as follows:

(a) Actual finish dates for jobs or estimated finish dates of partially completed jobs will be supplied to either the operations control or activity scheduling department on the departmental printout.

(b) All such information will be fed into the computer. (It is usually necessary to input only amendments or additions rather than the complete network, since the information from the previous run is normally stored.)

(c) These dates will then be used as a basis for a complete set of calculations for the remainder of the network.

(d) An updated set of figures will be printed out in the same format as before and distributed before the beginning of the next working week or shift.

## OTHER OPERATIONS CONTROLS

Although the relative emphasis will vary, where any form of planning is employed there must logically also be some form of control. For example, when setting business objectives it will be necessary to determine also the controls which will be employed to ensure that such objectives are achieved. It follows that wherever in this book we discuss planning we should also discuss control. In fact in most chapters both topics are implicitly covered, but in some cases separate chapters are devoted to one or other aspect. As a checklist Table 18.2 identifies some of the controls which will be of relevance to the operations manager, and gives cross-references to the relevant chapter in the book.

Table 18.2 Some operations planning and control tasks

| Area | Planning task | Control task | See: |
|---|---|---|---|
| Operations policy | Selection/formulation of objectives<br>Selection/choice of system structure<br>Selection/formulation of strategies | Monitor effective operation of system and achievement of objectives. | Performance Audit, Chapter 22<br>Cost Controls, Chapter 4 |
| Design/specification of product/service | Contribute to design/ specification of product /service | Monitor effectiveness of provision of product/service in order to ensure that specification and operating system are matched, i.e. that the system is capable of providing the product/service effectively. | Chapter 22 |
| Facilities location | Make/contribute to decision on location of facilities | Monitor effectiveness of location, e.g. through transport cost changes, effectiveness of communications, etc. | Chapter 22 |
| Facilities layout | Plan layout of all facilities | Monitor effectiveness of layout and control its use, e.g. through changes in routeing, traffic flows, etc., where traffic patterns/demand change | Chapter 6 |
| Work and job design | Design work methods, establish work standards, design workplaces, etc. | Monitor effectiveness of work, e.g. through measurement of output, labour costs, work performance, as well as indirect measures, e.g. labour turnover, absenteeism, etc. | Chapters 7, 8, 9 and 10 |

Table 18.2 continued

| Area | Planning task | Control task | See: |
|---|---|---|---|
| Capacity management | Determine capacity required and plan for its utilization | Monitor capacity utilization to ensure that appropriate capacity has been provided and appropriate strategies are being employed. Control capacity utilization through decisions on subcontracting, capacity changes, inventory levels, scheduling decisions, etc. | Chapter 11 and 12 to 16 |
| Scheduling | Determine what activities are to be performed at what time, in what order and at what place | Check completion of activities against scheduled dates to establish whether there is any lateness, excess queuing, excess congestion, work-in-progress, etc. Control activities through schedule changes, changes in priority rules, etc. | Chapters 12 to 15 |
| Inventory management | Determine locations of inventories, inventory levels, replenishment procedures, etc. | Control inventory through checks on inventory turnover rates, stock level changes, cost of obsolescence, deterioration, wastage and loss, etc. | Chapters 16 and 22 |
| Purchasing and supply | Determine sources of supply, purchase procedures, quantities, goods receiving procedures, etc. | Check on effectiveness of purchasing and supply through delivery performance, vendor rating, etc. | Chapter 17 |
| Quantity and reliability | Determine quality levels and reliability standards | Establish quality control procedures, e.g. acceptance sampling, control charts, and establish procedures for monitoring reliability and proper service performance. | Chapters 19 and 20 |
| Maintenance and replacement | Determine preventive maintenance and breakdown (repair) maintenance policies to include policies/schedules for inspection, preventive maintenance, etc. Establish replacement policies through life-cycle costing, etc. | Check effectiveness of maintenance through monitoring facilities availability, facilities downtime or maintenance costs. Check effectiveness of replacement policy through investment cost analysis, etc. | Chapter 21 |

## CHECKLIST FOR CHAPTER 18

*Distinction: planning and control*

Control and uncertainty

*Importance and emphasis*

Predictability v. uncertainty

*Control concepts*

Requirements of a control system
Closed- and open-loop control systems
Logging and control systems
Output and 'behavioural' controls

*Control of operating systems*

Information flows in operating systems
Control 'loops' in operating systems

*Kanban system*

Principles of kanban flow control
Kanban and JIT

*Activity controls*

In network analysis

*Other operations controls*

In operations policy
Design/specification
Location of facilities
Layout of facilities
Work and job design
Capacity management
Scheduling
Inventory management
Purchasing and supply
Quality and reliability
Maintenance and replacement

## FURTHER READING

**Cleland, D. I. and King, W. R. (1972)** *Management: A Systems Approach*. New York: McGraw-Hill.

**Eilon, S. (1971)** *Management Control*. London: Macmillan.

**Mize, J. H., White, C. R. and Brooks, S. G. H. (1971)** *Operations Planning and Control*. Englewood Cliffs, NJ: Prentice-Hall.

## QUESTIONS

18.1 Show diagrammatically, in the manner of Figure 18.1, the principal control 'loops' that will be used for the control of flows through the following systems:

(a) a small 'jobbing' engineering production works;

(b) a restaurant;

(c) a specialist retail delicatessen store.

18.2 Explain the main features of, and identify the difference between, a closed- and an open-loop feedback control system.

18.3 Consider one of the scheduling procedures outlined in the chapters in Part 6 and show how a related control system might work.

## CASE STUDY (from Part 9)

The topics covered in this chapter are relevant to the following (see Introduction to Part 9 and Table C.1 for further details):

| No. | Name | Country |
|---|---|---|
| 2 | Jograni Handicrafts | Bangladesh |

Chapter 19

# Management of quality

## ISSUES

Who defines quality?
What is quality and how is it achieved?
Why are attitudes and expectations important?
What are the main dimensions, or elements, of quality?
What are the main quality costs?
How do these costs relate to levels of quality?
Is quality expensive, or free?
What is TQM?
What are quality standards and why are they important?
Why are 'behavioural' and 'organization' considerations important?
What are quality improvement programmes?

Primarily we should think of quality from a customer's viewpoint. As consumers of *products* we expect our supplier (e.g. retailer) to provide only those goods which we find acceptable. This in turn requires suppliers to try to ensure that they themselves receive from manufacturers only goods or items which are acceptable, and that these items do not deteriorate or get damaged while being held by the supplier. Manufacturers in turn must ensure that they receive and use only materials and items which are of an acceptable quality, and that their manufacturing processes are used in such a way as to ensure that the goods that they produce are of a quality that is acceptable to their customers.

As consumers of *services* and *transports* we are again concerned with quality. For example, if we want to be transported by an organization we expect to be taken from an agreed place to an agreed destination, possibly by an agreed route, with an agreed duration. In being treated by a service system we expect the quality of the service to be acceptable. For example, in seeking accommodation in a hotel we expect to wait for only a relatively short period of time before being provided with a room of acceptable proportions with appropriate furniture, etc., and to be provided with facilities elsewhere in the hotel which are of an acceptable standard. Thus both transport and service organizations must ensure that they use items and products which are of an acceptable quality and that their operations conform to some acceptable standards so that we, the customers, when leaving the system, will express some satisfaction with the treatment that we have received there.

All customers will have some expectation of the quality of the goods or services which are to be provided. There will be an agreed *specification*. Agreement will have been reached with the organization. They will have accepted the specification which has been offered or there will be agreement from discussion and negotiation. Given an acceptable specification, customers will expect the product or service which is provided to *conform* to that specification.

These two factors – specification, which is to do with the 'design quality' of an item, and conformity, which is to do with the 'process quality' which is achieved – are of particular importance to customers. Ultimately they are the two factors which determine the quality levels provided by an organization to its customers. These two factors, however, are themselves determined by other factors, as shown in Figure 19.1. Consider first the specification. This will have been determined as a result of an organization's product or service policy, which in turn will result from decisions on its market policy, which in turn result from its consideration of the market or customer needs and requirements, and the activities of competitors. This is the process of *designing quality* into the product or service.

The degree to which the product or service conforms to the specification will be influenced by the capability of the conversion process. If the conversion process is incapable of providing products or services at the level specified, then it must follow that the products or services provided will be inferior to requirements. However, the fact that a conversion process is inherently capable of producing or providing products/services according to a specification will not in itself ensure that all products or services are of an acceptable standard, for some management control will be required to ensure that the conversion process is used in the appropriate fashion in order to ensure that the specification is achieved. This is all to do with the *management of process quality*, a topic that will be examined in detail in the next chapter, which deals with control and assurance procedures.

## THE NATURE OF QUALITY

Quality, cost and reliability are generally interrelated. We will look more closely at the relationships later. For the present it is sufficient to be aware that higher quality is usually associated with higher reliability, and that, where items are produced, or where services are provided, efficiently, some additional cost is usually incurred in attaining higher levels of quality, but some other costs are reduced.

**Figure 19.1** Factors influencing the quality of items/services as provided to customers

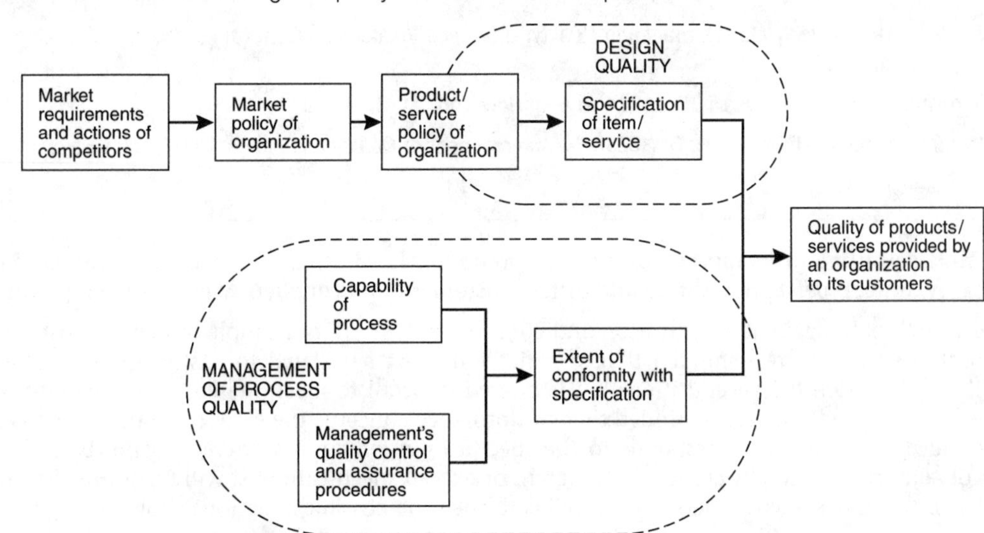

## Definitions

Some definitions of quality are given in Table 19.1. For our purposes we will begin with the following definitions:

> The quality of a product or service is the degree to which it satisfies customers' requirements.

This is influenced by:

> Design quality: the degree to which the *specification* of the product or service satisfies customers' requirements.
>
> Process quality: the degree to which the product or service, when made available to the customer, *conforms* to specifications.

**Table 19.1 Definitions of quality: attitudes and expectations**

Quality is:

(a) Fitness for purpose.

(b) The totality of features and characteristics of a product or service that bear on its ability to satisfy stated or implied needs.[a]

(c) The total composite characteristics through which the product or service in use will meet the expectations of the customer.[b]

(d) Quality's conformance with specification and price is a responsibility of the producer and a right of the customer.[c]

(e) Providing our customers, internal and external, with products and services that fully satisfy their negotiated requirements.[d]

[a] ISO 8402, 1991: *Quality Management and Quality Assurance Vocabulary*. Geneva: International Standards Organization, p. 17.

[b] Feigenbaum, A. V. *Total Quality Control*, 3rd edn. New York: McGraw-Hill.

[c] Sinha, M. N. and Willborn, W. H. O. (1985) *The Management of Quality Assurance*. New York: Wiley.

[d] Rank Xerox, UK.

Our simple definition of quality, whilst useful, should not be allowed to conceal a rather more complex reality. In fact, perceptions of quality differ. Customers' and suppliers' viewpoints might differ.

Figure 19.2 looks again at specification and conformance. It offers a simple model to illustrate several points. Firstly we are reminded that specification must be related to customers' requirements. Basically, and overall, the specification that is offered may fail to meet, match, or exceed customers' requirements. Secondly we are reminded that conformance concerns the extent to which what is actually provided to customers corresponds to the specification which was offered. Again, basically, the extent of conformance might fail to meet, match, or exceed specification. It will be of interest now to consider the attitudes of customers and suppliers to the nine possible situations shown in Figure 19.2.

**Figure 19.2** Possible attitudes to specification and conformance

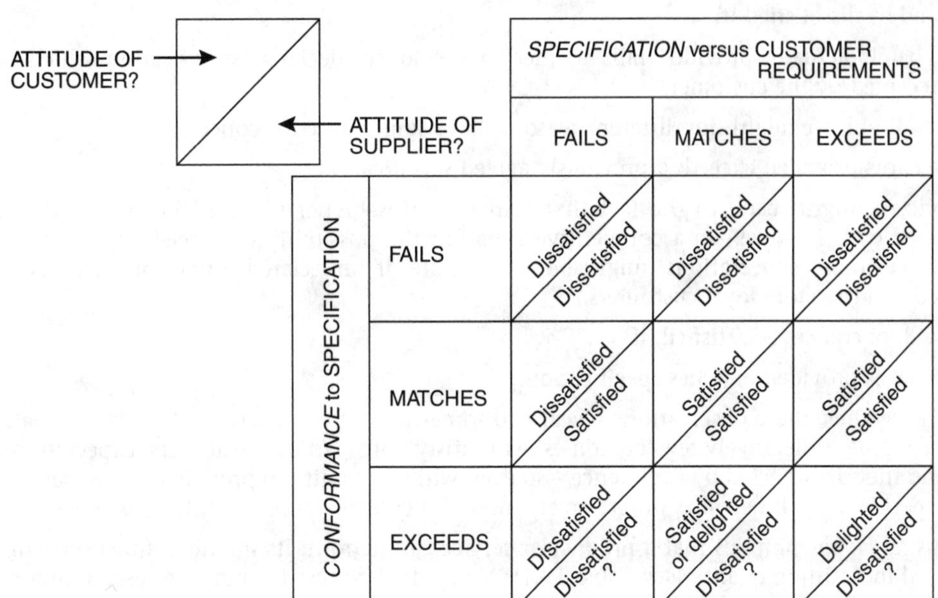


***1. From the customers' viewpoint***

Dissatisfaction will be caused by the following:

(a) failure of specification to meet requirements (irrespective of subsequent degree of conformance to that specification);

(b) failure to conform with specification which matches requirements.

But, in addition, dissatisfaction might also result when:

(c) what is provided fails to conform to a specification which exceeded requirements.

This latter situation might be the result of failure to receive items or services which meet new expectations, even though the specification was higher than would have been necessary, *or* failure to receive items or services which meet original requirements because of the extent of failure to conform to an even higher specification.

Customers will be satisfied if what is provided:

(d) matches an acceptable specification;

(e) matches a specification which exceeded requirements.

Where items or services actually exceed prior expectations, something stronger than satisfaction, e.g. 'delight', may result, i.e.

(f) provision of something which exceeds a specification which exceeded initial requirements, or even

(g) provision of something which exceeds a specification which matched initial requirements.

One point worth emphasizing, from the above, is that customers will have *expectations* – even to the extent of expecting a specification which exceeds their original requirements, if that is what is offered. Failure to meet these expectations will cause dissatisfaction; matching these expectations will give rise to satisfaction, and exceeding them may result in 'delight'.

***2. From the supplier's (operations) viewpoint***

We should be dissatisfied if:

(a) what is actually provided fails to meet a previously declared specification which has been accepted by the customer

but, in addition, we might, for different reasons, have some cause for concern if:

(b) what is provided exceeds a previously agreed specification.

This concern might relate to the fact that achieving this higher standard has incurred additional, unexpected cost. However, in a competitive situation the possibility of exceeding specification, and therefore customer expectations, might be a deliberate, if undeclared, intention in order to secure delighted and therefore loyal customers.

We will, of course, be satisfied, if:

(c) what is provided matches specification.

Taken together, these observations reveal two somewhat different sets of attitudes to quality. They are not congruent. Relatively few 'outcomes' will satisfy both parties. Customers' expectations are not fixed, and they are affected by experience – so even with the ability to provide items or services which exceed specification, it becomes progressively more difficult to secure delighted customers.

*Fitness for purpose* implies that a product or service can perform its intended function. This term is often used in defining quality (see Table 19.1). Notice that fitness for purpose results only when the specification is appropriate, and when conformity to specification is achieved. Notice again, however, that perceptions of customers and suppliers might differ. Four of the nine situations given in the matrix of Figure 19.2 may be seen to correspond to fitness for purpose – i.e. those situations in which specification matches or exceeds requirements, *and* where conformance matches or exceeds specification. Alternatively, just one cell (right at the centre of the matrix) might be regarded as the intention. Customers may tend towards the first view, whereas suppliers might have the second in mind. Whichever the view, it is, of course, essential that agreement is reached if the concept is to be of value in the management of quality.

## The dimensions of quality

Quality – as perceived by customers – is a multidimensional concept. We look for a variety of things in the products or services we receive; 'specification' can encompass many things.

Table 19.2 provides a simple set of 'core' dimensions, which will be of interest to customers and to suppliers. Each of these dimensions can be elaborated for particular types of product or service, but in most situations these five basic dimensions will be evident.

**EXAMPLE**

### *Airline service quality*

Five major airlines (and many others) fly the world's busiest long-haul route: London–New York. Competition is fierce for business class travellers, who, whilst in the minority, provide a major part of the revenue. Surveys have shown that such customers judge what these airlines offer on the following, the first three items being the most important:

(a) flight schedules – timing and frequency;

(b) airports used;

(c) price;

(d) terminal facilities;

**Table 19.2 Some 'dimensions' of quality**

| | Goods | Services |
|---|---|---|
| A. Functional dimensions | 1. Utility (i.e. what it does) | 1. Utility (i.e. what it provides) |
| | 2. Reliability<br>e.g. Continuity of operation<br>Availability for use<br>Consistency in use<br>Maintainability | 2. Reliability<br>e.g. Availability<br>Accessibility<br>Consistency of operation |
| | 3. Usability<br>e.g. Safety<br>Convenience<br>Comfort | 3. Serviceability<br>e.g. Safety<br>Convenience<br>Duration |
| B. Non-functional dimensions | 1. Design<br>e.g. Appearance<br>Performance | 1. Processes<br>(i.e. nature of interactions of system and customer) |
| | 2. Symbolic characteristics<br>(i.e. affecting image or self-image of user)<br>e.g. Availability/exclusivity<br>Novelty/rarity<br>Modernity<br>Price | 2. Symbolic characteristics<br>(i.e. affecting image or self-image of user)<br>e.g. Exclusivity<br>Novelty/rarity<br>Modernity<br>Customer group<br>Price |

(e) onward connections;

(f) luggage allowance;

(g) bonuses (e.g. free economy tickets);

(h) local transport (e.g. limousines/helicopters);

(i) in-flight service and facilities.

As the scope for airlines to compete in many of these factors is limited, intense competition exists on the nature of the in-flight services and facilities provided. Surveys have shown that six factors are important to customers in judging the quality of such services, the most important of which is seating. The four airlines differ on these factors.

| Quality factor | | Airline (differences) | | | | |
|---|---|---|---|---|---|---|
| | | American | British | Continental | United | Virgin |
| 1. Seat | (a) width | 19 inch | 19 inch | 20 inch | 20 inch | 22.5 inch |
| | (b) pitch | 40 inch | 40 inch | 55 inch (sleeper) | 40 inch | 55 inch (sleeper) |
| 2. Entertainment | | – | – | Individual video | – | Individual video |
| 3. Crew/passenger ratio | | 1 : 9 | 1 : 18 | 1 : 6 | 1 : 12 | 1 : 7 |
| 4. Food and drink | | – | – | – | – | – |
| 5. Facilities | | – | – | – | – | Massages and manicures |
| 6. Gifts (toiletries packs)* | | 3/10 | 6/10 | 8/10 | 4/10 | 9/10 |

Virgin Atlantic was voted 'best Business Class' service for 1992.

*Score out of 10.

Source: Sunday Times, *31 January 1993 (data as at 1 January 1993)*

## Determination of quality level

Quality may be a key policy option through which an organization seeks competitive advantage (see Chapter 2). Decisions relating to quality and consequently cost will therefore be influenced by the policy of the organization and by the policy and behaviour of competitors in the market (see Figure 19.1). Before launching a new product or service a company will investigate the quality and the reliability of others already on the market, and their objective may then be to better both their quality and/or price. There are circumstances in which such a procedure for establishing quality levels is unnecessary; for example, certain products must be manufactured to national or international standards. Adherence to such standards is often mandatory. Except on such occasions, price and quality decisions are often made empirically. Furthermore, both price and quality will often change as a result of market pressures.

The specification of the product or service will be established first. The operations manager must then seek to ensure conformity with this specification. Clearly, process capabilities should influence specification decisions, since there is little point in specifying something that cannot be achieved. Process capability is therefore of importance in determining quality levels. Similarly, the cost of ensuring conformity with specification must be taken into account.

# QUALITY COSTS

We must now look more closely at the nature of quality-related costs and then at the relationship of these costs to quality levels.

## Cost types and categories

Figure 19.3 shows diagrammatically, and in approximate sequential order, the principal quality-related costs. Three types of cost are identified.

(i) ***Systems*** costs, associated with setting up the operating system to aim to provide goods or services of appropriate quality.

**Figure 19.3** Quality-related costs

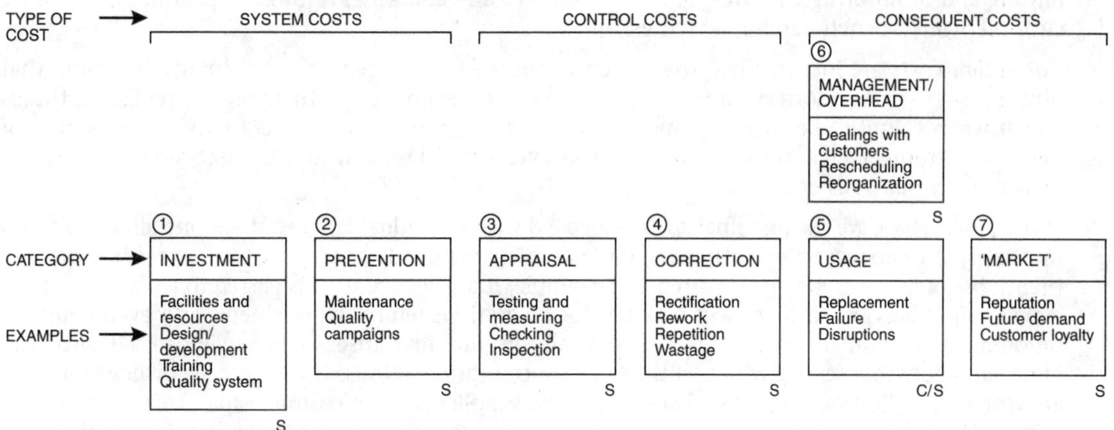


(i) ***Control*** costs incurred in monitoring, checking and correcting activities during the operations.

(ii) ***Consequent*** costs, incurred after completion of operations, i.e. after delivery of the goods, or completion of the service.

Two *categories* of cost are identified for each cost type, and in addition one category – management/overhead costs – is identified as being incurred after completion of operations.

We will examine these costs in more detail below, but some key points can be noted straight away, i.e.

(a) ***Sequential relationships***. There is general sequential relationship between these costs. The greater the effect, or the benefit gained, from system costs the less the need for control costs, and the lower the consequential costs. The greater the combined benefit of system and control costs, the less the consequent cost implication.

(b) ***Cost responsibilities***. Most of these costs will fall on the supplier. Certainly all of the costs of investment, prevention, appraisal, and usually all of the correction costs must be borne by the supplier, and also the consequent cost implications. Customers will normally bear some, but perhaps not all, of the usage costs – some of which may have to be met by the supplier.

## The nature of costs

1. ***Investment costs*** are incurred before operations begin. They are, essentially, concerned with the provision of appropriate facilities and systems, and also the design/development of the product or service. All this work will always be required, but here we are concerned with the additional costs which are incurred at the outset to try to ensure that an adequate quality level can be achieved and maintained. This expenditure, therefore, is intended to 'make life easier later'. The design of products or the specification of services to make it easier to achieve and sustain specified quality, the training of staff in quality procedures, the design and installation of facilities to make quality objects more easily obtainable, the establishment of arrangements with suppliers, and the quality management system are all examples of 'one-off' costs incurred in advance.

2. ***Prevention costs*** also relate to the operating system as a whole, but they are incurred repetitively, if not continually, over the life of that system. Examples include preventive maintenance of facilities, the running of quality campaigns to retain interest in and commitment to quality, the maintenance of supplier links, and regular quality improvement initiatives.

3. ***Appraisal costs*** are also 'on-going'. They include all costs associated with activities aimed at determining and monitoring current quality levels, including checking, testing, inspecting, monitoring customer views, benchmarking activities, etc.
4. ***Correction costs*** are incurred because the costs outlined above generally fail totally to ensure that nothing goes wrong. Correction involves doing things again (to get them right), replacing things which when found to be wrong cannot be rectified, the repetition of operations, the recycling of items or customers, etc., as well as costs of wastage, loss, scrap, and so on. These are often referred to as the '*internal costs of defects*'.
5. ***Usage costs.*** These are the principal costs associated with individual failures. If, despite all of the activities referred to above, an operating system fails to deliver goods or services to the specified quality, then subsequent costs may be incurred. For example, if a defective item is passed to a customer, then it may fail in service, so there will be a cost of disruption, return, replacement, and even compensation under warranty arrangements. On occasions disputes may arise, so there will be legal costs. The same can apply to a service which fails to meet specification. Whilst it may not be evident immediately on completion of the service – so neither the supplier nor the customer may be aware – failure to meet the specified quality standards may result in subsequent losses. For example, something may be damaged in transport, and only noticed later. Treatment in a hospital may be inadequate, resulting in recurrence of an illness. The food provided in a restaurant may be identified subsequently as having given rise to food poisoning, etc. In all such situations costs will be incurred for the customers and/or the supplier. These are often called the '*external costs of defects*'.
6. ***Management/overhead costs***. This category has been included in order to remind us that there are many, *more* indirect, costs associated with failure to achieve quality standards. Management may have to devote considerable time to customer relations in order to offset the effects of poor quality. Persistently poor quality, or major quality failures – even if infrequent – may cause loss of morale, motivation and commitment of staff, which must then be re-established. Activities may need to be rescheduled. Organizational changes may need to be introduced. Management and others may be distracted and other activities may be neglected or delayed. All of these are the indirect, managerial consequences of quality failures.
7. ***'Market' costs.*** Finally, the ability of an operating system consistently to provide goods or services at the required quality, or its inability to do so, will influence its reputation in the market. That reputation, or image, will in turn affect customer loyalty, and will influence future demand. A high reputation will facilitate and complement other marketing/promotional activities, and make them more cost-effective. A poor reputation will be an obstacle which may require extra efforts, and thus extra cost to compensate.

## Quality costs and quality levels

The relationship of these costs to quality levels is far more complex than has traditionally been assumed. Each cost may relate differently to quality in different situations. Furthermore, the costs themselves are interrelated, so simple cause and effect/cost and quality relationships may have little practical relevance. Despite this, it will be appropriate initially to consider each cost independently. Taking this approach, the following can be noted:

1. Increased ***investment*** should result in higher and consistent quality. Initially the 'returns' on investment may be great, but as the system becomes more sophisticated it will become increasingly difficult to achieve higher quality. In other words it will cost more to make a good system better than it will to make a poor system good. Since this is a 'one-off' cost, the greater the subsequent volume through the system over its working life, the lower the investment quality cost per unit.
2. Increased ***prevention*** cost should also increase quality levels and/or consistency. Again, there may be diminishing returns, as the system gets better, and of course in this case, since these are repetitive costs, there are no volume benefits.

3. Increased ***appraisal*** effort and cost will result in increased quality in certain situations. If the system is unstable, or unsophisticated, then, without on-going checking and monitoring, quality might suffer. More frequent or more widespread checking, measuring, inspection and monitoring will probably contribute to quality improvement, by drawing attention to weaknesses, areas in which performance is deteriorating or where special attention is needed, etc. Without such appraisal, quality is unlikely – *at this stage* – to get better, and with less appraisal it will probably get worse. Beyond a certain level, however, additional/further checking may contribute little, since it may simply draw attention more frequently to what is already known. Again, therefore, a 'diminishing returns' situation will apply.
4. ***Correcting*** things that are found to be wrong should improve the quality eventually delivered to customers. Greater expenditure here, therefore, will increase 'output' quality. Initially, if the system is unsophisticated a linear relationship may exist; i.e. proportionally, correction cost will give rise to greater quality. Eventually, however, saturation may occur. More and more correction effort may make it very difficult to adequately organize such work, so mistakes may occur, the level of attention may fall and the benefit will be diluted.
5. The cost of inadequate quality, or quality failure during ***usage***, will have a negative relationship to quality level. Higher costs will be associated with lower quality.
6. The same will apply to ***management overhead*** costs. They will be higher if quality is lower.
7. The cost implication associated with the ***market***, customer loyalty, subsequent demand, etc. is borne by the supplier. Lower quality will result in a lower or reduced reputation; lower, or lost, customer loyalty; and lower future demand. The cost implications for the supplier result from the need to compensate for these effects, e.g. by spending more on advertising, etc. So, 'market' costs to the supplier are inversely related to quality levels.

## 'Spending' and 'saving' on quality

We noted earlier that the quality costs are interrelated, and that there is a 'sequential' relationship between them. So, there is often a choice to be made as to how best to 'spend' in order to achieve required quality levels. Figures 19.4(a) and (b) show two alternatives. The approach shown in Figure 19.4(a) places emphasis on system cost expenditure, so that as expenditure here increases, the need for expenditure on control is reduced. This type of approach might be appropriate for large and complex systems providing complex products or services over long periods of time. In Figure 19.4(b) greater emphasis is placed on control expenditure to achieve higher quality, as system expenditure is not as high as before. In this case, therefore, to achieve higher quality, higher control costs are incurred. This type of approach might be appropriate where facilities are unsophisticated, change is frequent, and volumes are low.

**Figure 19.4** 'Spending' to achieve higher quality – two alternatives

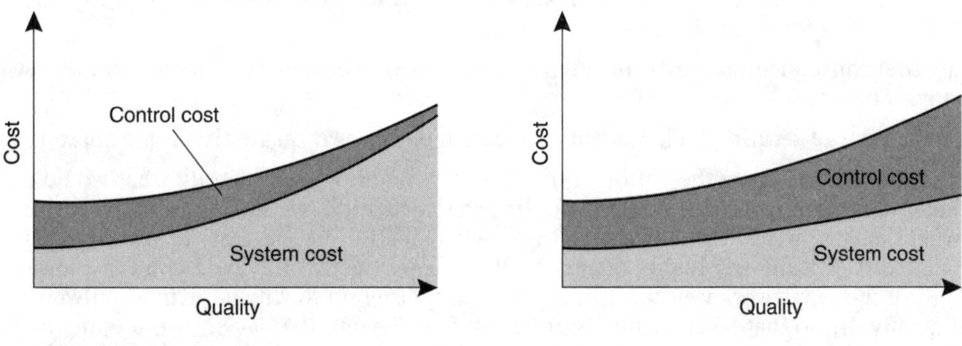


(a) Emphasis on system costs

(b) Emphasis on control costs

**Figure 19.5** 'Spending' and 'saving' on quality – the effect of cost levels

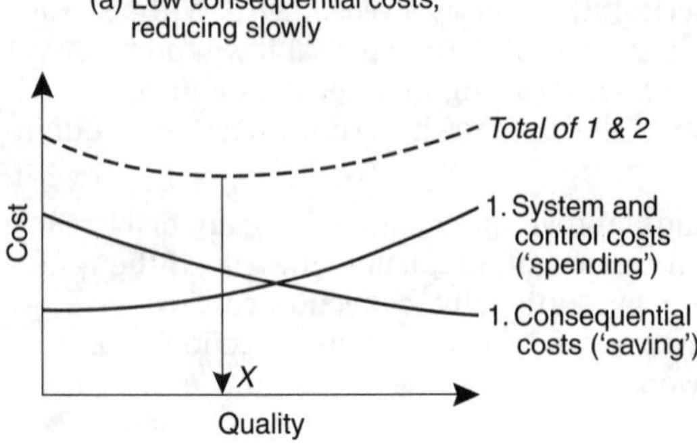


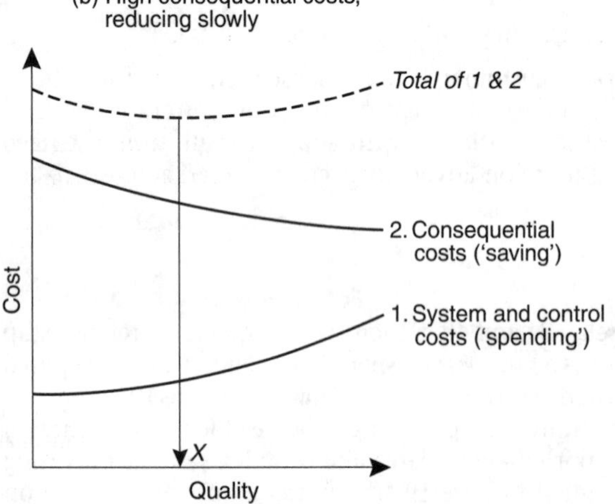


Greater effort to achieve quality (the greater expenditure on control costs plus system costs) should result in reduced consequential costs (i.e. usage, management and market costs). As 'spending' on achieving quality increases, so the 'savings' by reducing the costs consequent upon inadequate quality should also increase. Given these 'contra-directional' costs (one increasing and one reducing), it is possible that there exists a quality level at which the sum of the costs is at a minimum – and, if so, then it might be argued that this is the optimal quality level. This, theoretically at least, is true.

Consider the situation shown in Figure 19.5(a). Here the system plus control costs increase as higher quality levels are achieved, exactly as in Figure 19.4. The consequential costs reduce as quality increases, and the total of the two has a minimum at quality level *X*. Figure 19.5(b) uses exactly the same system plus control cost curve, but now the consequential costs of inadequate quality are higher, although they reduce at exactly the same rate as before. Again, the total cost curve has a minimum point at quality level *X*, but of course the minimum total cost is higher.

Now consider Figure 19.6(a). Here the system plus control cost curve is the same as before – but the consequential cost curve is different. Whilst the cost of inadequate quality starts high, as in Figure 19.5(b), it falls far more quickly. Here the total cost cover has a minimum at a higher quality level, *Y*. Finally, consider Figure 19.6(b), which uses the same consequential costs cure as Figure 19.6(a), but now the system plus control costs rise much more rapidly. Here the minimum total cost is reached at a lower level of quality, *Z*.

There are two important lessons to be learnt from these comparisons:

1. It is not the *levels* of the cost curves which influence the minimum total cost quality level, but rather the *shapes* of these curves. In other words, it is the relationship of cost to quality that matters, not whether costs are generally high or low.
2. (a) If the consequential costs of higher quality reduce rapidly, *higher* quality levels are appropriate.

   (b If the costs of securing higher quality increase rapidly, *lower* quality levels are appropriate.

Given the above, if we know the nature of the two cost curves, we can identify what would appear to be optimal (minimum cost) quality levels. So, in a static situation, we should aim for a higher quality level, where major savings can be achieved through reduction in the costs to us of quality failure. Where the costs of achieving higher quality levels increase steeply, we could aim for a lower quality level. Within this framework we can identify the quality level up to which 'savings' outweigh 'spending' on quality. Up to that level, quality is, in effect, free. Beyond that level, costs are incurred.

But this is a static view. In practice, attitudes to quality will change. We have noted that it is customers' expectations which influence their attitudes to the quality they receive. In general, as higher quality levels are achieved, expectations will increase – so as higher quality levels are provided, the cost of failing, subsequently, to repeat those levels also increases. In other words, the 'consequential' cost curve is not static.

This 'dynamic' situation is shown in Figure 19.7. Three consequential cost curves are shown. Curve (a) might initially apply, but it is replaced by (b), and then (c), as customers' expectations increase. This gives rise to three total cost curves, (a) being replaced by (b), and then by (c) – each with its minimum total cost and each therefore suggesting an 'optimal' quality level. In practice, of course, expectations shift gradually and continuously, so there are no discrete curves as shown in the figure; nevertheless, the effect is just the same.

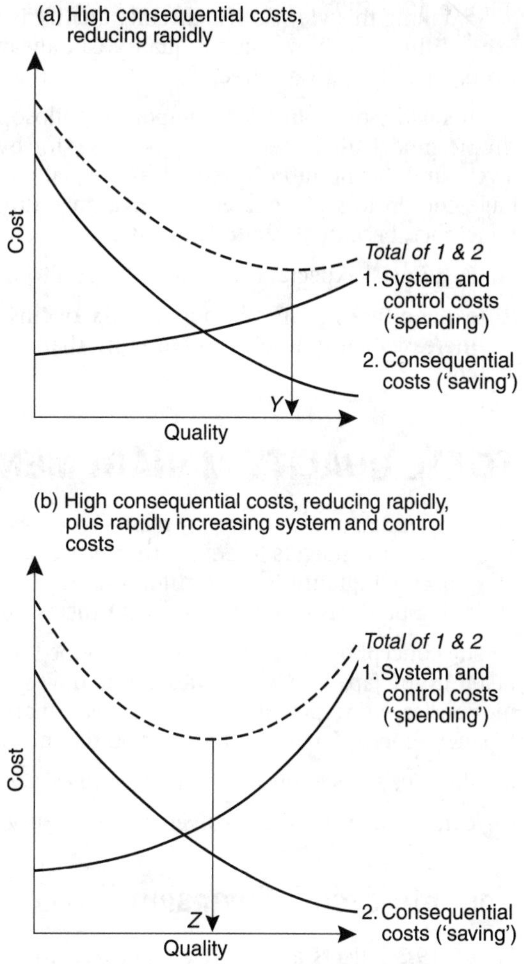

**Figure 19.6** 'Spending' and 'saving' on quality – the effect of cost curves

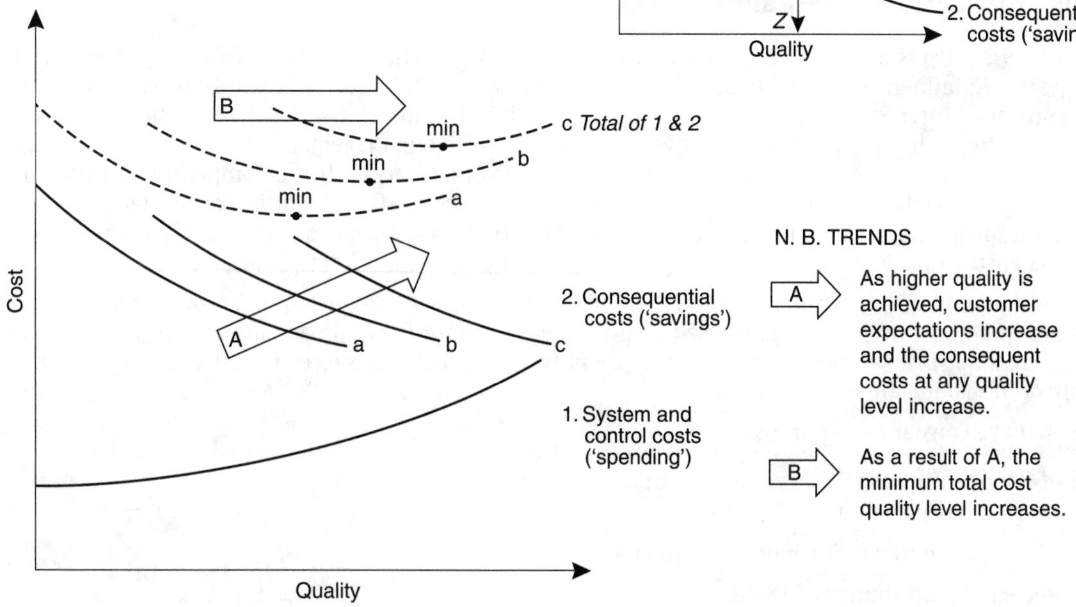

**Figure 19.7** 'Optimum' quality – an increasing target

So, taking this view to its extreme, quality is a moving target – the best level is usually higher, and expenditure to achieve higher quality can always potentially be matched by greater returns. In other words, quality is always free.

This is the prevailing 'contemporary philosophy' of quality. Ultimately it is no more true than the simple models discussed earlier, because, for example, there will often be physical limits to quality levels, and, furthermore, quality is not equally important to all organizations. Some, for example, may have chosen to seek competitive advantage on price (see Chapter 2). It is, however, a philosophy to remember, because it reminds us that:

(a) customers' expectations of quality tend to increase;

(b) expenditure on an appropriate mix of 'investment', 'prevention', 'appraisal' and 'correction' to increase quality levels is often more than offset by savings on 'usage', 'management' and 'market' costs.

## TOTAL QUALITY MANAGEMENT

The description above of quality management can be seen as a 'total' approach to quality management. The need for managers to ensure that processes within their organizations provide outputs or services of a specified quality is clearly important, but a total approach is concerned with the complete life-cycle of a product or service, not just process quality.

The concept of total quality was developed by Deming, an American consultant, in the 1950s. It was taken up by Japanese companies and is now seen as one of the principal Japanese management techniques, largely responsible for the transformation of Japanese product quality and the reputation of Japanese goods. There are, in fact, two distinctive dimensions to the philosophy:

(a) product/service *'life-cycle' quality management*;

(b) commitment to and involvement in quality assurance and control by the *whole organization*.

### The 'life-cycle' dimension

Figure 19.3 reflects a 'life-cycle' approach to quality management, i.e. the active management of all stages which influence the quality of the product or service which is received by the customer, followed by continued interest in the maintenance of the quality of items and services whilst 'in use' by the customer through service, repair, improvement, etc. The active management of quality in this 'longitudinal' manner is a major strategic commitment for the organization. It is a competitive instrument, an activity through which an organization competes with others. The recognition of this fact, together with the major commitment of resources which are required for total quality management (TQM), should ensure that organizations develop policies for, and then plan, their TQM activities.

The adoption of this strategic approach is one aspect about which Western organizations have learnt a great deal from the study of Japanese practice. The breadth of the approach adopted in Japan is captured in the list of key points identified by Deming as the basis for successful quality assurance and control in manufacture:

(a) Achieve constancy of purpose.

(b) Learn a new philosophy.

(c) Do not depend on mass inspection.

(d) Reduce the number of vendors (suppliers).

(e) Recognize two sources of faults:

1. Management and production systems;
2. Production workers.

(f) Improve on-the-job training.
(g) Improve supervision.
(h) Improve communication.
(i) Consider work standards carefully.
(j) Teach and use statistical methods.
(k) Encourage new skills.

## Organizational commitment

The above list brings us to the second dimension of TQM. With the TQM approach we cannot regard quality as the responsibility of a separate department. Quality is the responsibility of all: it is an organization-wide commitment, even to the development of a 'quality culture' within the organization. We shall return to some of these issues later in this chapter under 'Behavioural and Organizational Factors'.

EXAMPLE

### Dow-Corning

Dow-Corning (Australia) set up three pilot projects involving a range of different operational areas to train personnel in the application of seven basic total quality management tools to company operations. One year later, work groups were set up to allow employees working in the same area to meet on a regular basis to discuss, analyse and implement solutions to problems which they identified.

Later, technology-process groups were established where more complex technical improvement possibilities were analysed. The greatest benefits of this TQM implementation were seen to be the commitment and enthusiasm of management and staff.

Source: Chapman, R. L., Clarke, P. and Sloan, T. (1991) TQM in continuous-process manufacturing: Dow-Corning (Australia) Pty. Ltd. *International Journal of Quality and Reliability Management*, **8**(5), pp. 77–90.

## The introduction of TQM

Seven steps have been identified for the introduction and adoption of a TQM approach.[5] They serve to remind us, before we begin to discuss details, that the effective management of quality requires an organization-wide approach and commitment, and that TQM has an organization-wide impact.

1. ***Leadership.*** Make quality leadership a fundamental strategic goal to ensure that management energy is committed to the task. This requires a commitment throughout the organization and all of its activities.

   Recognize that quality levels are not permanent. The competitive stance of organizations in relation to the changing customer perception of quality creates a moving (upward) target.
2. ***Corporate-wide introduction***. Quality should firstly be defined in terms of all aspects of a product/service package, all benefits and supporting facilities. The next step is to implement all the necessary actions throughout the organization (not just in quality functions/departments).
3. ***Changing corporate orientation***. Reorient the corporate approach to quality, i.e.

---

[5] From L. P. Sullivan, in Chase, R. L. (1988) *Total Quality Management.* IFS/Springer/Verlag, pp. 11–19, as summarized by Hill, T. (1991) *Production/Operations Management*, 2nd edn. London: Prentice-Hall.

(a) Product/service orientation: move from a traditional 'control'-type approach which accepts, implicitly, that defects will occur.

(b) Process orientation: use appropriate statistical process control procedures and do not depend on checking outgoing items (see next chapter).

(c) Systems orientation: establish a quality structure which embraces all parts of a business and not just quality functions.

4. ***Motivation, education and training***. Create continuous motivation to achieve quality improvements, supported by appropriate education and training. Place emphasis on education to affect attitudes and motivation to achieving quality improvements.

   Support improvements with adequate resources to ensure that they are achieved within appropriate time-scales.

5. ***The robust function***. Recognize the need to build quality into the product/service at the specification stage.
6. ***Cost orientation.***

   (a) Optimizing product/service and process/delivery system design for improved quality and lower costs.

   (b) Use of the 'quality loss function' to quantify quality improvements in terms of cost and for use in design/specification.

7. ***Customer orientation.*** Apply quality control principles to design/specification activities to formalize the mechanism for ensuring that customer requirements are incorporated.

**EXAMPLE**

### *TQM at St Luke's Medical Center*

St Luke's Medical Center (Chicago) is using a TQM process to improve its operations. In addition to its principal urban, 983-bed facility, there are also two suburban hospitals, a health sciences university, a home health nursing service, a 'for-profit' subsidiary that markets health care products to corporations and other health care settings, and six occupational health clinics. To make the programme work, the organization is committing \$100 000 a year in direct operating expenses for the TQM programme. Another \$60 000–100 000 was initially spent on customer research to determine areas in need of improvement. The organization is already seeing a return on its investment. TQM has been credited with department improvement, such as:

1. decreasing the X-ray repeat rate in diagnostic radiology and reducing the department's absentee rate by 22.7% from 1987 to 1988;
2. reducing laboratory result turnaround time by an average of 25%, resulting in \$10 000 savings;
3. reducing the number of checks manually typed by the accounts-payable department by 25%.

Source: Koska, M. T. (1990) Case study: quality improvement in a diversified health center. *Hospitals*, **64**(23), pp. 38–39.

## QUALITY STANDARDS

National standards exist for many aspects of quality control and assurance, through from specific statistical techniques to the management of complete quality systems within organizations. In many cases these standards derive from those prescribed by governments for use in the defence industries.

BS 5750 (renamed BS EN ISO 9000 in 1994) was first introduced in 1979, replacing various others, which by that time had begun to proliferate. BS 5750 was designed as the single base standard for quality systems. In 1987 the International Standards Organization introduced ISO 9000 for the same purpose, and based very much on BS 5750.

Not only does the existence of such standards help organizations to design and implement effective quality management systems, but also the accreditation of an organization under such a standard provides assurance to customers, reduces their own control and assurance needs, and simplifies their procedures.

## BS and ISO standards

BS EN ISO 9000 dates from 1979, and ISO 9000 from 1987. The British standard derives from, and supersedes, others. Both are concerned with *quality systems*. They aim to define all relevant aspects of an organization's operations, procedures and systems concerned with identifying and meeting customers' requirements for quality products and services. Thus the standards aim to give customers an assurance that the quality of goods and services supplied to them meet their requirements, by specifying and regulating all the procedures which contribute to or affect quality.

The standards are of value in assisting organizations to develop quality systems, in helping organizations to help ensure quality inputs from suppliers, and as means for assessment for use by 'third parties'. Both standards were developed initially for engineering and manufacture, so the terminology relates to products, materials and items. However, both now find widespread use in service organizations, and accreditation under these standards is being examined by the customers of such organizations.

## The structure of the standards

The principal 'contents' of the two standards are outlined in Table 19.3. For the international standard, the principal elements are ISO 9001, 9002 and 9003 (BS equivalents are Parts 1, 2 and 3). The other documents are introductory and/or explanatory. ISO 9001 covers the situation where an organization has responsibility for design and development work and post-delivery work. ISO 9002 covers quality assurance during production and installation, whilst ISO 9903 deals with quality assurance at final inspection and test.

## An overview of the British standard Part 1/ISO 9000

The principal clauses of the standard are given in Table 19.4.[6] The list provides a summary of the requirements of the standard and the aspects to be dealt with in its implementation.

## Implementation and benefits

The benefits claimed for the use of such a standard for a quality system relate to:

(a) fewer complaints, fewer problems, greater co-operation;

(b) internal management, e.g. improved control, better discipline, reduced costs, greater awareness and commitment, improved working environment;

(c) 'third party' relationship, e.g. less need for external audits and monitoring.

However, to achieve such benefits implementation must be comprehensive and effective. This requires substantial and sustained effort over a period of time. Typical 'guidelines' for the introduction of the standard indicate the nature of the implementation task: [7]

---

[6] From: Dale, B. and Cooper, C. (1992) *Total Quality and Human Resources*. Oxford: Blackwell.

[7] Reported by Dale, B. and Cooper, C. (1992), ibid. and based on Long, A. A., Dale, B. G. and Younger, A. (1991) A study of BS 5750 aspirations in small companies. *Quality and Reliability Engineering International*, 7(1), pp. 27–33.

**Table 19.3 The British standard compared to ISO standards**

| British standard | ISO standards |
|---|---|
| | **ISO 8420** |
| | Quality vocabulary |
| **BS Part 0, Section 0.2** | **ISO 9004** |
| Principle, concepts and applications | Quality management |
| Guide to quality management and quality system elements | Quality system elements |
| **BS Part 0, Section 0.1** | **ISO 9000** |
| Principle, concepts and applications Guide to selection and use | Guidelines for selection and use of standards |
| **BS Part 1** | **ISO 9001** |
| Specification for design/development, production Production, installation and servicing | Model for design/development, installation and servicing |
| **BS Part 2** | **ISO 9002** |
| Specification for production and installation | Model for production/installation |
| **BS Part 3** | **ISO 9003** |
| Specification for final inspection and test | Model for final inspection and test |
| | **ISO 9004 Part 2** |
| | The services standard |
| **BS Part 4** | |
| Guide to the use of Parts 1, 2 and 3 | |

**Table 19.4 The requirements of ISO 9001/BS Part 1**

*Inspection, measuring and test equipment*

- Control, calibration and maintenance.
- Documentation and calibration records.
- Traceability to reference standards
- Handling and storage

*Inspection and test status*

- Identification of inspection and test status throughout all processes.
- Confirmation that tests and inspections have been carried out.
- Authority for release of conforming product.

**Table 19.4 (continued)**

*Control of non-conforming product*

- Identification and control to prevent unauthorized use.
- Review and decide on appropriate remedial action.
- Reinspection.

*Corrective action*

- Procedures and reporting.
- Investigation and analysis of causes.
- Elimination of causes and abnormalities.
- Preventive action.
- Corrective action control.
- Assignment of responsibilities.
- Changes to procedures, working instructions, etc.

*Handling, storage, packaging and delivery*

- Methods which prevent product damage and/or deterioration.
- Maintenance of product integrity.
- Use of secure areas and rooms to prevent damage and/or deterioration.
- Receipt and delivery of items into and out of storage.
- Procedures to ensure that the product is packed to prevent damage throughout the entire production-to-delivery cycle.

*Quality records*

- Adequate records to demonstrate achievements of product quality and effective operation of the system.
- Retention time for records.
- Storage, retrievability, legibility and identification.

*Internal quality audit*

- Audit plan and verification.
- Procedures to ensure that the documented system is being followed.
- Compliance and effectiveness.
- Reporting of results to personnel.
- Corrective action to bring activities and the quality system into agreement with the standard.

**Table 19.4 (continued)**

*Training*

- Assessment and identification of needs.
- Written job responsibilities and specification.
- Planned and structured training programme.
- Training records.

*After-sales servicing*

- Contractual specification
- Procedures for performing and verifying that needs and requirements are met.

*Statistical techniques*

- Process capability determination and acceptability.
- Product characteristic verification.

*Management responsibilities*

- Corporate quality policy development, statement, deployment, implementation, communication and understanding.
- Organization, structure, responsibility and authority.
- Management representative for quality.
- Management review of the system.

*Quality system*

- Documentation and implementation of procedures and instructions.
- Quality manual.
- Quality plans, work instructions, inspection instructions, etc.

*Contract review*

- Definition of customer (internal and external) needs and requirements.
- Contract and tender compatibility.
- Capability.
- Product belief and configuration.
- Information monitoring and feedback.

*Design control*

- Design and development planning.
- Identify and allocate resources.

**Table 19.4 (continued)**

- Definition and control of design inputs, outputs and interfaces.
- Design verification.
- Review, approve, record and control design changes.

*Document control*

- Formal control and review of all documents, procedures, specifications, data and standards, etc.

*Purchasing*

- Assessment and monitoring of suppliers/subcontractors.
- Formal written definition of requirements and specification.

*Purchaser-supplied material*

- Verification, storage and maintenance of 'free issue' or purchaser-supplied material.

*Product identification and traceability*

- Unique and positive identification of material, parts and work-in-progress during all processes.
- Demonstrated traceability and its recording.

*Process control*

- Identify and plan the processes.
- Work instructions.
- Monitor key characteristics and features during production.
- Process qualification.
- Processes undertaken under controlled conditions.
- Criteria for workmanship.
- Control of special processes.

*Inspection and testing*

- Inspection and testing of goods received.
- In-process inspection and testing.
- Final inspection and testing.
- Inspection and test records.

1. The implementation of a quality system should be managed as a major project.
2. The reasons for implementation must be clear (N.B. a single, specific reason, e.g. to satisfy a customer, is not normally sufficient).
3. A conducive and enthusiastic environment for implementation must be created.

4. A prior quality systems audit should be undertaken to identify the amount of work required and the time needed for implementation.
5. A steering committee representing senior management and chaired by the chief executive should be established.
6. Training should be provided at all levels in the organization.
7. Implementation of the standard should be the minimum aim.

**EXAMPLE**

### *Avant Hotel*

The Avant Hotel in Oldham in the UK is the first hotel to receive BS 5750. The BS certificate required management to establish quality specification for each product, to determine assignable causes of error, and identify ways of improving product performance. Initial work by the management, and a consultant, aimed at identifying operational objectives and quality standards. A quality manual was then developed and BS assessors visited the hotel to determine whether the manual is a true representation of the standard of the operation within the hotel. Routine assessments will take place about every six months. The benefits of the standard include a keener focus on staff training, reduced staff turnover, waste reduction and beneficial publicity.

Source: Callan, R. J. (1992) Quality control at Avant Hotels – the debut of BS 5750. *Service Industries Journal*, **12**(1), pp. 17–33.

## BEHAVIOURAL AND ORGANIZATIONAL FACTORS IN QUALITY MANAGEMENT

We have noted the importance of organizational and related factors in the implementation of TQM. Here we will consider some more specific factors.

### JIT and quality

Just in time (JIT) processing was discussed, in the context of inventory management, in Chapter 17. Here we will consider a related aspect – the influence of the JIT approach on quality assurance and control. We shall show how JIT facilitates, even necessitates, total quality management.

### The impact of lower batch sizes

The implementation of JIT leads to a reduction in batch sizes and inventory levels. One intention is to make the system more responsive by cutting waiting times and throughput times. One effect of this is that disruption at any stage in the system quickly has an impact on the subsequent stage – because there is less 'buffer' between them. A flow stoppage will lead quickly to a starvation at a subsequent stage when the intermediate buffer of inventory has been used up. Control of flow is therefore very important. Similarly, the production of a defective item at one stage, if noticeable at all, is soon evident at the next stage. It follows, therefore, that with an appropriate inspection and feedback system the production of defective items at some part in a system can more quickly be halted when a JIT approach is being used.

An examination of the extent of quality improvement in Japanese industry associated with the introduction of JIT gives some measure of the importance of this *rapid feedback* characteristic. The earlier recognition of defectives enables early rectification of the problem, reduced wastage and reduced cost.

**EXAMPLE**

### *Two-stage process*

(a) A two-stage processing system operates with a batch size of 10 units. The cycle time for each unit is 1 minute at each stage. All 10 units must be completed at the first stage, before work can commence on any of them at the next stage. Items are processed in random order.

Time for processing batch through one stage = 10 min.
Minimum time lag from production of one defective in a batch in stage 1 to identification at stage 2 $\simeq$ 0 min.
Maximum time lag $\simeq$ 9 min.
Average time lag $\simeq$ 4.5 min.

(b) As (a) but batch size = 2 units. Hence:
Minimum time lag $\simeq$ 0 min.
Maximum time lag $\simeq$ 1 min.
Average time lag $\simeq$ 0.5 min.

---

This is especially important where there is a risk that defective items might otherwise pass through several subsequent stages of processing, each adding cost, but with the likelihood that at the end of the process the output will be scrapped or costly to rectify.

This is just one of the quality benefits of JIT. Potentially more important is the *motivational* effect. The fact that poor-quality or defective items and their source are more immediately evident encourages those involved to strive for more consistent quality. There is, therefore, a greater motivation to do something about quality problems.

**EXAMPLE**

### *Mail order*

Telephone and postal orders received in a large sales office at a mail order company were entered by staff onto standard order forms which were collected together at the end of the day into batches by geographical customer area. The following day these orders were passed to warehouse staff who 'made up' the order package and sent them daily, in geographical batches, for dispatch. The company found that, of the orders received at the warehouse, 17% contained incomplete or insufficient detail and had to be returned to the sales staff for clarification.

A new system was introduced in which individual order forms, on completion, were passed directly to a warehouse clerk who checked them before passing them to 'make-up' staff. The clerk raised any queries on orders directly with sales staff. It was found that the percentage of orders queried or clarified by the warehouse fell to 5% and the average turnaround time from receipt to dispatch of order fell by 10%.

---

In this example the quality of the service received by the customer clearly improved in respect of response time. This, in part, was the direct result of the introduction of a JIT approach which reduced batch sizes and therefore the throughput time for order processing. A further improvement, however, possibly attributable to the increased concern for and attention to quality, was made possible by the new processing system. This would also improve response time, as well as helping to reduce 'defective output', i.e. the dispatch of incorrect items or incomplete orders.

So, the JIT approach, whether in manufacture or service-type industries, offers benefits for quality management through quicker identification and rectification of quality problems and greater awareness/involvement of staff. For this reason JIT is often accompanied by TQM, characterized by a 'whole organization' approach to quality embracing techniques such as quality circles (discussed later).

## People as inspectors

Inspection is an important activity in appraisal (see Figure 19.3). Despite the fact that increasing use is being made of automatic devices, the principal method of inspection, and hence of quality control and assurance, is still often the human inspector. What sort of decisions are inspectors asked to make? Essentially, there are two types: first, those connected with the inspection of variables (i.e. measurement); and second, those connected with the inspection of attributes (i.e. assessment).

In measurement, an inspector compares a characteristic of the item with a defined standard. Often this involves the use of a gauge or instrument against or within which the item is placed. Greater opportunity for error or mistake exists as the ease of comparison of characteristic and standard decreases.

A similar situation exists with respect to assessment. It is not too difficult to make decisions about the acceptability of certain noise levels, and of attributes such as brightness, because the inspector, conceptually at least, is able to compare such attributes with a known standard. In fact these could be considered as only slightly more difficult problems of *measurement* since it is possible to use decibel meters to measure noise levels and light meters to measure light levels. More difficult is the assessment of colour quality, since it is more difficult to define colour standards. The assessment of smell and taste is even more difficult because such characteristic standards are virtually impossible to define.

The more remote and ill-defined the standard the more difficult the comparison of characteristic and standard and, consequently, the more difficult and the more equivocal the decision. It should be clear, therefore, that in order to ensure adequate and consistent inspection procedures, instruments should be used which ensure easy and accurate comparison of characteristic and standard. Furthermore, standards for which instruments cannot be used should be clearly defined, e.g. colour shade cards might be used and inspectors could be trained and retrained to recognize standard noise levels, brightness levels, etc., in much the same way that time study practitioners are trained to recognize a notional concept of standard performance. Workplaces should be designed to permit and, preferably, emphasize the comparison of characteristic and standard.

The following notes will illustrate how the equipment and the situation might be designed to facilitate accurate and consistent inspection.

(a) Ideally the standard itself should be used during the inspection process.

(b) The standard, if not used during inspection, should be prominently displayed so that comparison of characteristic and standard is easy or, alternatively, so that inspectors might regularly refer to the standard in order to 'recalibrate their perception'.

(c) Where possible, inspection procedures might be 'reconstructed' as pattern recognition procedures. For example, in the design of instrument displays, dials are often arranged so that when each instrument is reading correctly all pointers appear horizontal or vertical. Consequently, when one instrument shows an unusual or wrong reading, the pattern is disrupted and recognition of the fact is made easier. In such a case the acceptable standard has been redefined, acceptability now being associated with consistency of appearance.

(d) Wherever possible the workplace conditions should be arranged to emphasize the characteristic being measured or assessed. For example, lighting might be arranged to emphasize irregularities or roughness of surfaces.

# QUALITY IMPROVEMENT PROGRAMMES

## 'Zero defects' programmes

The original 'zero defects' (ZD) programme was established by the Martin-Marietta Corporation in the USA around 1962. It was introduced to augment the established statistical quality control programme in order to try to improve product quality beyond that level which might economically be achieved by the statistical procedures. The programme was in large part a 'motivational' device which sought to organize and motivate direct and indirect workers to achieve higher levels of quality in their work. The slogan 'zero defects' was an important part of this motivational exercise.

This original ZD programme was considered to be highly successful, and the company was able to demonstrate significant improvements in product quality as a result of its introduction. This in turn led other companies in similar industries, e.g. defence and aerospace, to adopt this motivational/organizational approach to quality assurance and, in time, ZD programmes became well established. It has been suggested that the principal features of such programmes were as follows:[8]

1. A motivational package aimed at reducing individual operator-controlled defects. The contents of this package were such things as the 'Pledge Cards', 'Posters', 'Attention getters', 'Scoreboards', etc.
2. A prevention package aimed at reducing management-controlled defects. This package centred around 'error cause removal' (ECR) suggestions to be made by employers for subsequent analysis and action by supervisors. These suggestions were submitted to the supervisor on ECR forms which defined the probable error cause and proposed action.
3. Procedures to provide for prompt feedback to the worker.

Basic behavioural science principles and practices are the basis of ZD programmes. Such programmes are based on efforts to motivate workers, and the approaches employed, e.g. providing clear objectives, participation in decision-making and positive feedback on performance, are established principles which have widespread use in other applications. Thus the development of ZD programmes demonstrates a sensible application of established theories in a relatively new field.

Effective ZD programmes would probably involve the following:

(a) some method of establishing agreement on the quality problems, or quality goals to be achieved, or the reasons behind these problems and/or goals;

(b) the use of a well-structured approach to establishing a motivational programme aimed at solving these problems and/or achieving these goals;

(c) the participation of all those involved, i.e. all those who might in some way contribute to the solving of quality problems/achievement of quality objectives, in both the establishment and running of the programme;

(d) the setting of clear targets against which to measure improvements;

(e) the establishment of formalized, regular, simple procedures for reporting achievement on goals;

(f) the establishment of procedures for reinforcing effort in connection with the above;

(g) the organization of jobs, e.g. of workers, quality controllers, supervisors, management, etc., in such a way as to facilitate the above.

**EXAMPLE**

### *Zero defects at Lavelle Aircraft*

Lavelle Aircraft Company (Philadelphia) initiated a new 'zero defects' programme. It believed that, unlike such programmes in the past (which often relied largely on 'hype'), the new programme is solidly based on goals, measurements and cash incentives for employees and management. It also has some aspects of quality circles. Lavelle realized that, in order to make the programme work, it had to take into account the fact that today's younger workers were brought up in an instrumental and materialistic society. The 'zero defects' programme includes separate

[8] Juran, J. M. and Gryna, F. M. (1980) *Quality Planning and Analysis*, 2nd edn. Maidenhead: McGraw-Hill.

programmes for: (1) direct workers and (2) indirect workers, who are eligible for suggestion awards (maintenance, material handlers, etc.), and (3) indirect workers who are not eligible for suggestion awards (engineers, accountants, foremen, etc.). Since implementing the programme, Lavelle has found absenteeism to be down 31% compared to the same period in prior years. Lateness has been reduced 66% from the previous year, and the number of direct workers eligible for suggestion awards has increased about 55% from any prior year.

Source: Sklarow, G. (1989) Zero defects: old theme – new twist. *Industry Week*, **238**(14), pp. 35–38.

## 'Quality circles'

The quality circle[9] (QC) approach to quality assurance was widely established in Japan before being adopted in Europe and North America. Wherever employed, the QC approach rests upon the motivation of individuals and the organization of efforts to improve quality through error reduction, etc., and as such the procedure is designed to supplement conventional quality control procedure (see next chapter).

A quality circle comprises a group of workers and supervisors in a single area or department within an organization which meets regularly to study ways of improving quality and to monitor progress towards such goals. Thus it is a participative device, perhaps fundamentally more in tune with Japanese culture than with Western culture. A company will seek to establish quality circles largely on a voluntary basis. Those volunteering will often be up to half of the direct and indirect workers involved in the activities of a particular department. They are offered training in the analysis and identification of quality problems and problem-solving procedures. Once this training is completed, the circle is formed and is invited to tackle particular quality problems nominated by management or identified by the circle itself. Each quality circle will normally tackle a series of projects, one at a time, identifying quality problems and means of eliminating such problems and establishing targets (often financial targets) to be achieved through quality improvement.

There will be numerous quality circles within an organization and their work will be monitored and co-ordinated by company management, who will be responsible for establishing overall objectives and monitoring the progress towards the achievement of these objectives. Thus the quality control effort within the organization is diffused through all levels rather than being seen as the responsibility of managers and indirect, often specialist, staff.

The *original* concept of QC may be of relevance only in a Japanese type of culture. For example, originally most of the training for those involved in QC and the meetings of the circles themselves took place out of working hours and on a voluntary and often unpaid basis. Normally there was no financial incentive in the improvement of quality except that obtained indirectly through improvements in the performance and financial status of the organization as a whole. The only major incentive was that of obtaining further training and of recognition within the organization. This analysis, however, conceals the fundamental nature of the programme, i.e. that of motivating individuals through participation in decision-making and reinforcing by positive feedback of results. Fundamentally such an approach is 'culture free' and can possibly be employed with benefit in other situations where quality performance is largely a function of individual effort and attention. Certainly the use of QC in Europe and North America does not follow exactly the pattern established in Japan, and interest in this type of approach to quality 'assurance' is increasing.

Quality circles have some similarity to ZD programmes; however, the former is essentially a group approach and the latter individual. The QC methodology probably requires considerable effort to establish and sustain, and it is perhaps for this reason that those companies which have adopted the approach, especially in Japan, have tended to concentrate on this one concept, rather than trying to sustain several different types of programme or campaign.

---

[9] Originally, in Japan, referred to as 'quality control circles' but now generally abbreviated to 'quality circles' or QC in the West.

**EXAMPLE**

### *Quality circles in education*

The quality circle process introduced in the South Huntington School District on Long Island in New York, early in the 1980s, has gradually evolved and changed the schools from having a relatively autocratic management system to a far more participative one. Initially, staff identified work-related problems, put problem-solving techniques to work, researched data, reviewed findings and proposed solutions to the next higher level of management. Following the success of these first quality circles, joint decision-making groups were started for food-service workers, elementary-level teachers and students. Student quality circles have completed presentations on several subjects, including: (1) improving relations between students and bus drivers; (2) improving menu selection in the cafeteria; and (3) helping young people deal with peer pressure.

Source: Wilson, J. (1990) Investing in our futures: quality and participation for students and school staff. *Journal of Quality and Participation*, July/August, pp. 78–81.

## Taguchi method

Taguchi developed the concept of the 'quality loss function' (QLF). The QLF is a measure of the economic loss or penalty suffered by the customer when they receive an item (or service) which fails in any way, and to any extent, to meet the target-specified quality. Such losses would normally include increased maintenance costs, increased operating costs, adverse environmental costs, etc. Use of the QLF approach reminds us that any variation from a target specification incurs unexpected and unwelcome costs for the customer. In general, the greater the variation, the greater such costs. It is conceivable that an item may be judged to be satisfactory in that it exceeds a minimum required specification – however, failure to meet a higher target level imposes costs on the customer. So, the QLFs of two items may be different, even though both may have been judged acceptable.

The QLF provides a means to quantify quality improvements and thus to decide on where and how best to seek improved quality. (This is part of a broader approach which focuses on the design of inputs rather than the traditional approach of controlling outputs from the system.)

## Ishikawa (fishbone) method

Kaoru Ishikawa developed the quality circles approach described above. He also introduced the term 'company-wide quality control' (CWQC), for he felt that the TQM approach laid insufficient emphasis on the inputs of non-specialists within the organization. Ishikawa is also credited with the development of the 'fishbone' diagram as a means to identify quality problems and their causes, as a first step in quality rectification or improvement. Such a diagram is shown in Figure 19.8. It is in effect a 'cause and effect' diagram showing the various possible causes of a quality problem and their interrelationship.

**Figure 19.8** Fishbone (Ishikawa) diagram

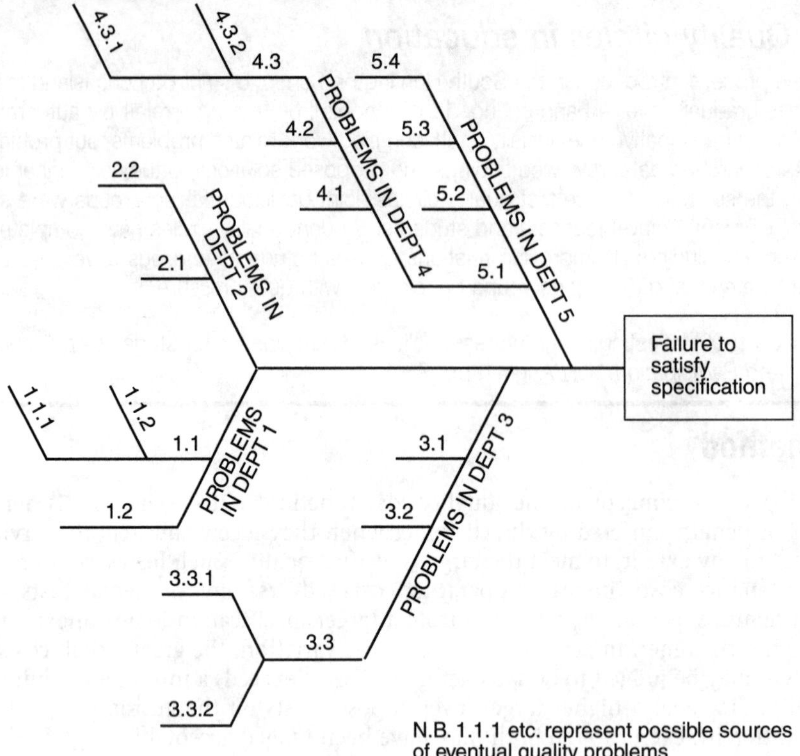

## CHECKLIST FOR CHAPTER 19

### Quality and the customer

Products
Services
Design or specification quality
Process or conformity quality

### The nature of quality

Definitions
Attitudes to, and expectations, of quality
- Customers' views, leading to:
  - Satisfaction and 'delight'
  - Dissatisfaction
- Suppliers' views, leading to:
  - Satisfaction
  - Dissatisfaction
- The importance of expectations
- Fitness for purpose
  - Different perceptions

The dimensions of quality
- Functional dimensions
- Non-functional dimensions

Determination of quality level
- Strategies
- Computation
- Capability
- Cost

### Quality costs

Cost types
- System
- Control
- Consequential

Categories
- Investment
- Prevention
- Appraisal
- Correction
- Usage
- Management/overhead
- Market

The nature of cost
Quality costs and quality levels
'Spending' and 'saving' on quality
- The effect of cost levels
- The effect of cost curves
- 'Optimal' quality
- Quality is 'free'?

### Total quality management

The life-cycle dimension
Organizational commitment
The introduction of TQM

### Quality standards

Nature
Benefits
BS EN ISO 9000/ISO 9000
- Nature
- Implementation
- Benefits
- Requirements
- Guidelines for introduction

### Behavioural and organizational factors

JIT and quality
- Batch sizes

People as inspectors

### Quality improvement programmes

Zero defects
- Quality circles

Toguchi method
Ishikawa method
- Fishbone diagrams

## FURTHER READING

**Adam, E. E. and Barker, E. M. (1987)** Achieving quality products and services. *Operations Management Review,* Winter, pp. 1–8.

**British Standards Institution (1987)** BS 5750. London: BSI.

**Dale, B. and Cooper, C. (1992)** *Total Quality and Human Resources.* Oxford: Blackwell.

**Ishikawa, K. (1985)** *What Is Total Quality Control?* Englewood Cliffs, NJ.: Prentice-Hall.

**James, G. (1992)** Quality of working life and total quality management. *International Journal of Manpower,* **13**(1), pp. 41–58.

**King Taylor, L. (1993)** *Quality – Sustaining Customer Service.* London: Century Books.

**Oakland, J. S. (1993)** *Total Quality Management,* 2nd edn. Oxford: Butterworth-Heinemann.

**Robson, M. (1982)** *Quality Circles – A Practical Guide.* Aldershot: Gower.

**Rosander, A. C. (1985)** *Quality Control in the Service Industries.* New York: Dekker.

**Rothery, B. (1991)** *ISO 9000.* Aldershot: Gower.

**Taguchi, G., Elsayed, E. A. and Hsiang, T. (1989)** *Quality Engineering in Production Systems.* New York: McGraw-Hill.

**Zeithaml, V. A., Parasuraman, A. and Berry, L. L. (1990)** *Delivering Service Quality.* New York: Free Press.

## QUESTIONS

19.1 Consider the 'dimensions' of quality (as summarized in Table 19.2). Identify, from a customer viewpoint, those quality features which might be important in the case of the following:

(a) a motor vehicle;

(b) an international passenger air journey.

19.2 Why do some quality-related costs, incurred after delivery of goods, or after completion of service, fall on the provider, rather than the customer? Give examples and explanations.

19.3 'Quality is free' – explain and discuss. Give examples.

19.4 What does 'total' mean in TQM?

19.5 Draw up a management 'action plan' for the achievement of ISO 9000 accreditation for one of the following:

(a) a road freight company;

(b) a motor-vehicle repair workshop.

19.6 Why are quality improvement campaigns sometimes necessary, and how can they be integrated with a TQM programme in an organization?

19.7 Use the Ishikawa method to show the principal possible causes for quality defects in one of the following:

(a) the provision of a meal in a restaurant;

(b) the provision of an item to a customer by a mail order catalogue organization.

## CASE STUDIES (from Part 9)

The topics covered in this chapter are relevant in the following (see Introduction to Part 9 and Table C.1 for further details):

| No. | Name | Country |
|---|---|---|
| 2 | Jograni Handicrafts | Bangladesh |
| 4 | Qormi Post Office | Malta |
| 9 | Malta MBA | Malta |
| 13 | The Shire of Corio | Australia |

Chapter 20

# Quality control and reliability

## ISSUES

What are the three stages of process quality control and assurance?
What procedures can be used in these three stages?
What are the roles of inspection and sampling?
What is acceptance sampling?
What are control charts?
Why is process capability important?
How is reliability measured or estimated?

## NOTATION USED IN THIS CHAPTER

| | |
|---|---|
| AOQL | Average outgoing quality level (as percentage defective) |
| AQL | Acceptable quality level |
| $\sigma$ | Standard deviation of individuals |
| $\sigma_{\bar{p}}$ | Standard deviation of proportions |
| $\sigma_x$ | Standard deviation of a sample |
| $\sigma_{\bar{x}}$ | Standard deviation of a sample means |
| $\bar{\sigma}_x$ | Mean standard deviation of several samples |
| $C$ | Acceptable number of defectives in a sample |
| $c$ | Number of defective items in a sample |
| $\bar{c}$ | Average number of defectives in several samples |
| LR | Lot rating |
| LSL | Lower specification limit |
| LTPD | Lot tolerance per cent defective |
| $N$ | Batch or lot size |
| $N_m$ | Number of lots submitted during a given month |
| $n$ | Sample size |
| $p$ | Proportion of defective items in a sample |
| $\bar{p}$ | Average proportion of defective items in several samples |

| | |
|---|---|
| $P$ | Probability |
| $P(a)$ | Probability of accepting a batch |
| PD | Actual percentage defective in batch or process |
| USL | Upper specification limit |
| $w_x$ | Range of a sample |
| $\bar{w}_x$ | Mean range of several samples |
| $\bar{x}$ | Mean of a sample |
| $\bar{\bar{x}}$ | Mean of sample means |
| $X$ | Dimension for an individual |
| $\bar{X}$ | Mean dimension for individuals |

In this chapter we deal, in detail, with some of the procedures which are available for controlling quality. We are, in effect, dealing with the implementation of one part of the quality management activity identified in Figure 19.3 in the previous chapter. Figure 20.1 shows the link. We are dealing with control activities and costs – in particular with appraisal, but also to some extent with correction. We will refer to the activities in this area as quality control and assurance, because it is necessary for us to make a distinction between two types of activities. Notice, however, that the assurance activities to which we will refer are not the same as those mentioned when we discussed investment and prevention costs in the previous chapter.

To a large extent the emphasis is on statistical procedures. This is the traditional territory of quality management. These procedures have been in use for many years. They have not changed much,

**Figure 20.1** The link between quality control costs and control and assurance procedures

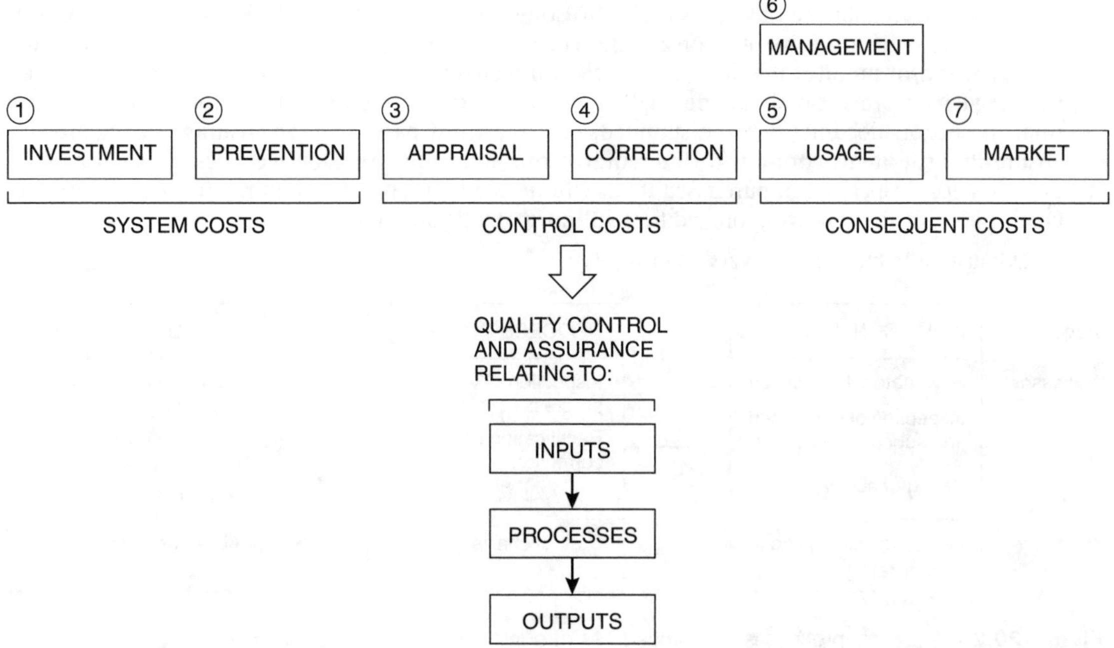

but what has changed is their role within the overall framework of the management of quality. These are important but subsidiary procedures which are used as part of the implementation of an overall or total managerial approach to delivering product or service quality. These procedures are not a sufficient means for the management of quality, but they have an important part to play within the framework set by the previous chapter.

In the final part of the chapter we consider reliability, again taking a largely statistical approach, and concentrating on the reliability of items.

# QUALITY CONTROL AND ASSURANCE FOR ITEMS

We will concentrate now on systems for ensuring conformity to specification, i.e. the management of process quality (see Figure 19.1). Throughout we will refer to items, i.e. physical entities, whether they be materials, parts, products or customers. Such items are the things which flow into, through and from conversion systems. We shall assume that the specification of the output, i.e. the item of primary interest to the customer, has been established, and that an appropriate process is available; hence it is now our task to ensure conformity to such specification.

To achieve this objective three stages can be defined. We must first ensure that only items which conform to the given specifications are accepted as inputs. Second, we must implement control procedures to attempt to ensure that during the conversion of these items only outputs which conform to the specifications are produced. And finally we must ensure that only those items which conform to the specifications are actually allowed to exit the system. These procedures are outlined diagrammatically in Figure 20.2 and discussed below. Examples are given in Figure 20.3.

## Control of inputs

An organization may adopt one or (usually) both of the following procedures in an attempt to ensure that it uses only items which fully conform to the required specifications and standards.

(a) Items used by the organization will be inspected. The items which are supplied to the firm will normally have been subjected by the supplier to some form of quality control. The purchasing firm will often also institute its own procedure, carried out in the receiving department on its own premises, and/or monitor the quality controls conducted by the supplier. It may ask to be supplied with regular information about the quality of items as they are prepared, ask for copies of all the final inspection documents to be supplied, or ask a third party (e.g. an insurance company) to ensure that the items conform to the required minimum quality. However, despite such precautionary steps, inspection of purchased items will normally be conducted on receipt, and before use. One or both of the following procedures will normally be adopted:

1. exhaustive inspection of every item received:

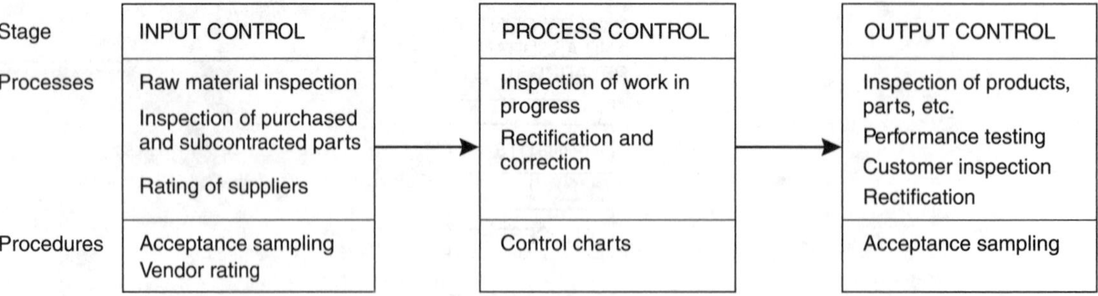


**Figure 20.2** The stages, processes and procedures of quality control and assurance

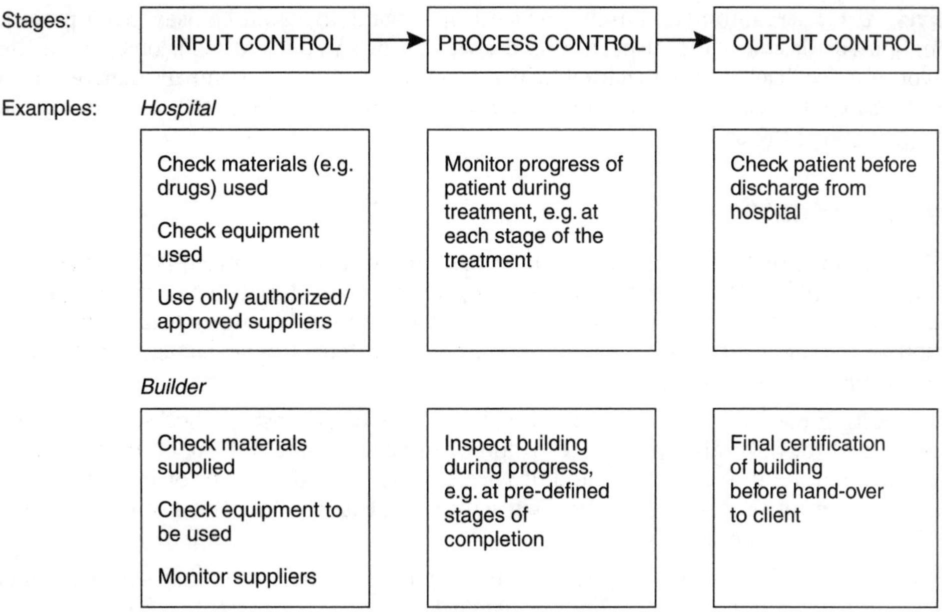


**Figure 20.3** Examples of quality controls on inputs, processes and outputs

2. an inspection of a sample of the items received – this procedure, which is commonly adopted, is referred to as *acceptance sampling* and is discussed in some detail later in this chapter.

(b) The organization will purchase only from those suppliers which are known to be likely to provide acceptable items. To ensure this the purchaser may undertake some form of *vendor rating* (VR), i.e. a comparative rating of suppliers taking into account quality-related factors such as:

1. percentage of acceptable items received in the past;
2. quality of packaging;
3. price;
4. percentage of warranty claims which can be traced to defective items provided by the vendor.

The commonest VR procedures will be discussed below.

## Control of process

Inspection of items between or during operations in the process is undertaken, not only to ensure that faulty or defective items do not proceed to the subsequent operations, but also in order to predict when the process is likely to produce defective items so that necessary preventive adjustments can be made. Quality control during the process often involves the use of *control charts*, which will be discussed in some detail shortly. The number and location of inspections should reflect both the probability of faults or defectives occurring and the consequences of such occurrences, as well as the cost of conducting inspection. Frequently, technical considerations determine the position and number of inspection operations, but nevertheless, within certain limitations, operations management is usually able to design the inspection procedure.

Well-defined procedures should be established for the selection and inspection of the items, for the recording and analysis of data, for reprocessing, rectifying or scrapping of defectives, and for the feedback of information. We have tended to assume that a group of people attached to a separate department within the organization is involved in these quality control procedures, but two other alternatives exist. First, automatic 'on-line' inspection or gauging could be used. Such procedures are increasingly used for automatic inspection and checking of variables (dimensions); often the equipment involves a 'feedback' to the machine, which is self-correcting. A second alternative is for workers to be responsible for checking and inspecting their own work. In such cases appropriate time allowances must be provided.

### Control of outputs

Quality inspection of output items is essential because unless defective output is identified by the producer it will be passed on to the consumer. Final inspection is unfortunate, since the purpose of all previous inspection has been to ensure that defective or faulty output is not produced. However, it is not a reflection on the ineffectiveness of earlier inspection, since items can be damaged at any time during the entire process.

Final inspection may involve only a sampling procedure, or exhaustive checks. Suitable procedures must be designed for the collection and retention of inspection data; for the correction, replacement or further examination of faulty items; and, if necessary, for the adjustment or modification of either previous inspection or processing operations to ensure that faulty items do not continue to be produced – at least not for the same reasons.

Inspection of output is normally conducted in a similar manner to the inspection of input items, the procedures being referred to as *acceptance sampling*.

## QUALITY CONTROL PROCEDURES

We have identified three basic stages in quality control (Figure 20.3), i.e.

(a) control of quality of input items;

(b) control of quality during the process;

(c) control of the quality of output items.

These three stages are complementary. Inadequate control at one stage will necessitate greater effort at subsequent stages. In the remainder of this chapter we shall focus on quality control procedures, and shall discuss three procedures:

(a) vendor rating
(b) acceptance sampling
(c) control charts

} involving the *inspection* of items.

Vendor rating is concerned with the monitoring of the performance and the selection of suppliers. Acceptance sampling is of relevance for the control of input and output quality. Control charts are of relevance for the control of quality during operations.

### Vendor rating *(see also Chapter 16)*

The supplies received by an organization are normally evaluated and used in purchasing decision-making. In vendor rating, this evaluation process is formalized to provide a quantitative measure of 'vendor quality'. Such ratings are meant primarily to provide an overall rating of a vendor for use in reviewing, comparing and selecting vendors. Vendor rating is therefore an integral part of a rigorous purchasing procedure, and an aspect of quality assurance for use alongside, or in some cases instead of, acceptance sampling.

It will often be difficult to create a single numerical quality/rating score because of the different factors which must be taken into account. These may include:

(a) the lot quality (number of lots rejected or number of lots inspected);

(b) the parts qualities (percentage of items defective);

(c) the 'characteristic' quality of items (e.g. percentage active ingredient, performance, etc.).

Because such factors differ in importance in different companies and for different items, the vendor rating method employed must be tailored for specific applications. However, in general such methods will fall into one of the following four categories:

(a) ***Categorical plan:*** a non-quantitative system in which those responsible for buying hold a periodic meeting to discuss vendors and rate each one, usually only as 'plus' , 'minus' or 'neutral'.

(b ***Weighted point plan:*** each vendor is scored on quality, price and service. These factors are weighted and a composite rating is then calculated for each vendor. An example is shown in Table 20.1.

(c) ***Cost ratio plan:*** compares vendors on the *total* cost involved for a specific purchase. This will include:

1. price quotation;
2. quality costs (e.g. repair, return or replacement of defectives);
3. delivery costs.

**Table 20.1** Example of a 'weighted point' vendor rating plan. A hospital purchases sterile supplies from three companies. Data are collected over a one-year period so that the three suppliers can be compared

| | Supplier A | Supplier B | Supplier C |
|---|---|---|---|
| 1. Lots received[a] | 60 | 60 | 20 |
| 2. Lots accepted[a] | 54 | 56 | 16 |
| 3. Percentage accepted[b] | 90.0 | 93.3 | 80.0 |
| 4. Quality rating ((3) × 0.4)[b] | 36 | 37.3 | 32 |
| 5. Net price[a] | 0.93 | 1.12 | 1.23 |
| 6. $\frac{\text{Lowest price}}{\text{Net price}} \times 100$[b] | 100 | 83 | 75.6 |
| 7. Price rating ((6) × 0.35)[b] | 35 | 29 | 26.5 |
| 8. Delivery promises kept[a] | 90% | 95% | 100% |
| 9. Service rating ((8) × 0.25)[b] | 22.5 | 23.8 | 25 |
| 10.Total rating (4) + (7) + (9)[b] | 93.5 | 90.1 | 83.5 |

[a] Data
[b] Calculations
*Note.* Here the relative importances of quality, price and service have been judged to be 0.4, 0.35 and 0.25.

(d) ***Quality only rating plans:*** the first three types of plan above recognize item quality in the rating of vendors but in no case is the rating restricted to quality alone. In the fourth type of plan *only* quality is taken into account. An example of a formula based only on quality is the Bendix vendor rating plan. The formula for the Bendix system is:

$$\text{Quality rating} = 70 + \left[ \frac{\sum^{N} \text{LR}}{N_m} - 70 \right] \sqrt{N_m}$$

where $N_m$ = number of lots submitted during a given month and

$$\text{LR} = 70 - 10 \left[ \frac{p - \text{AQL}}{\sqrt{\{\text{AQL}\ (100 - \text{AQL})/n\}}} \right]$$

where $p$ = percentage defective of the sample quantity inspected from a lot

LR = lot rating

AQL = acceptable quality level (%)

$n$ = sample size

With such a system each vendor starts out with a score which is considered to be average (in this case 70). Points are then added or subtracted to this to yield quality rating. The specific number of points added or subtracted in the formula is dependent on:

1. comparison of the percentage defective;
2. the number of lots submitted.

Hence 90 = quality significantly better than the AQL

50–90 = quality acceptable

50 = quality significantly worse than the AQL

The following is an example of the use of a vendor rating plan based only on quality.

**EXAMPLE**

## Domestic appliances

The following vendor rating and grading system is used for all suppliers of piece parts to an electrical company.

*Vendor rating* is based on points obtained covering five deliveries.
*Grade* is dependent on vendor rating achieved covering five deliveries.
Vendor rating and grading are reappraised every fifth consecutive delivery. Factors involved are as follows:

(a) total number of samples inspected over five deliveries;
(b) total number of rejects observed during sample inspection over five deliveries;
(c) total number of batches accepted over five deliveries;
(d) total number of batches received – five normally, but the system allows for more should the fifth delivery be overlooked, and in this instance the total number of batches involved becomes the common denominator.

*The system is divided into two sections:*

Section *one* carries a maximum of 60 points.
Section *two* carries a maximum of 40 points.
*Total* = 100 *points maximum*

*How vendor rating and grading are calculated:*

*Vendor rating:*
Section *one*:

$$\frac{\text{Total number of rejects}}{\text{Total number of samples}} \times 60 = Z$$

Therefore $60 - Z = A$

Section *two:*

$$\frac{\text{Total number of batches accepted}}{\text{Total number of batches received}} \times 40 = B$$

Therefore $A + B$ = Total points obtained

*Grading is based on total points obtained as follows:*

Grade A = 100 down to 90 points – Quality level acceptable
Grade B = 89 down to 70 points – Quality level requires some improvement
Grade C = 69 down to 40 points – Quality level requires considerable improvement
Grade D = 39 down to 0 points – Quality level requires immediate improvement or supplies terminated

*How the system operates between the company and the supplier:*
Suppliers falling into grades B, C or D on components supplied are notified by the company and requested to improve their quality level.
*Any supplier falling into grade D and remaining there for more than ten deliveries is dropped.*
Notification is given when improvement in quality results in *upgrading.*
Suppliers are vendor rated and graded on each component manufactured and supplied to the company.
*No notification will be given while supplier remains in grade A.*

---

Many such vendor rating systems exist. In selecting a system for a particular situation, a basic decision must be whether the rating will be based solely on quality performance or on additional considerations such as cost and delivery.

True vendor ratings (for the purpose of making decisions on retaining or dropping vendors) are published infrequently. These ratings are not to be confused with monthly publications of 'vendor performance', which serve mainly as product rating rather than vendor rating.

It is important that vendor ratings be used as an *aid,* and not as the sole criterion in vendor decision-making. It should be remembered that:

(a) A single index will often hide important detail.

(b) The specific purpose of the rating should be kept in mind.

Most vendor rating plans involve some degree of subjectivity and guesswork. The mathematical treatment of data in the plans often tends to obscure the fact that the results are no more accurate than the assumptions on which the quantitative data are based. In the final analysis, therefore, supplier evaluation must represent a combined appraisal of facts, quantitative computations and value judgements. In most cases vendor rating will be used along with an acceptance sampling plan.

Vendor rating is an important defect prevention device if it is used in an atmosphere of interdependence between vendor and customer. This means that the customer must:

(a) make the investment of time, effort and special skills to help the poor vendors to improve;

(b) be willing to change the specifications when warranted (in some companies 20 to 40% of rejected purchases can be used without any quality compromise).

Finally, in cases of consistently poor vendors who cannot respond to help, the vendor rating highlights them as candidates to be dropped as vendors.

## Inspection

In this section we shall consider both acceptance sampling and control chart procedures. Both procedures will involve the *inspection* of items so that a decision can be made on whether an item, or the batch from which a sample of items is drawn, is acceptable or not. The planning of inspection may involve deciding *where* to inspect. This will be dealt with first.

## The location of inspection

There will normally be some choice for the location of quality inspection points in operating systems. For example, we may choose to locate inspection before or after the inventories which exist in operating systems, or between an operation and its supplier, and its customer. This will provide a wide choice of locations, but, additionally, since most businesses are multi-stage, it will usually be necessary to decide where to inspect within a sequence of operations. Rarely will items be inspected formally after every stage in the system, since to do so would be expensive. The problem, therefore, is to locate inspection operations, taking into account the cost of inspection and the benefits of inspecting (or the risks of not inspecting).

In practice such decisions are often based on empirical and quantitative rules. For example, good 'rules of thumb' are:

(a) Inspect before costly operations in order to avoid high processing costs for defective items.

(b) Inspect before any series of operations during which inspection will be difficult and/or costly.

(c) Inspect after operations which generally result in a high rate of defectives.

(d) Inspect before operations which would conceal defects previously caused.

(e) Inspect before a 'point of no return', i.e. after which any rectification is impossible;

(f) Inspect before points at which potential damage may be caused, i.e. before the use of equipment which would be damaged through the processing of faulty items.

(g) Inspect before a change in quality responsibility, e.g. between departments.

A simple approach to the location of inspection stations is illustrated by means of the following example.

**EXAMPLE**

### *Food processing*

Consider a six-operation confectionery-making process where the expected proportion of defective items created at each operation and the processing cost per item for each operation are given in the following table.

| **Operation number ($j$)** | **1** | **2** | **3** | **4** | **5** | **6** |
|---|---|---|---|---|---|---|
| Proportion of defective items created at operation | 0.010 | 0.015 | 0.005 | 0.010 | 0.002 | 0.005 |
| Number of defective items per 10 000 items | 100 | 150 | 50 | 100 | 20 | 50 |
| Processing cost/item for station (£) | 1.00 | 0.50 | 1.00 | 1.00 | 0.60 | 1.10 |

The table below shows the processing cost of the defective items created at an operation through subsequent operations. For example, processing the 100 defective items created at operation 4 through operations 5 and 6 incurs a cost of £0.60 × 100 + £1.10 × 100, i.e. £60 for operation 5 and £110 for operation 6, a total of £170. Thus if an inspection station capable of identifying all passing defective items were located after operation 4, it would lead to the saving of this £170 and, in addition, it would save the remaining processing costs for defective items created at earlier operations, i.e. a total saving of £680.

| Operation number ($j$) | Number of defective items | | Cost of processing defective items created at operation $j$ through subsequent operations (£) | | | | |
|---|---|---|---|---|---|---|---|
| 1 | 100 | | 420 | 370 | 270 | 170 | 110 |
| 2 | 150 | | | 555 | 405 | 255 | 165 |
| 3 | 50 | | | | 135 | 85 | 55 |
| 4 | 100 | | | | | 170 | 110 |
| 5 | 20 | | | | | | 22 |
| 6 | 50 | | | | | | |
| | | Column sums (£) | 420 | 925 | 810 | 680 | 462 |

Thus the processing cost saving given by the location of a single inspection station after operation $j$ is given by the total of the figures in the column for operation $j + 1$ in the table. If we know the cost of inspection, we can use this method to assist in determining the location of inspection stations. For example, the best location of two inspection stations is after operations 2 and 4, i.e.

| | £ |
|---|---|
| Inspection after operation 2 saves | = 925 |
| Inspection after operation 4 saves £680 – (170 + 255) | = 255 |
| | £1180 |

This method of analysis relies on two basic assumptions. First, it is assumed that 100% inspection is used and all defective items are identified. Second, no account is taken of the accumulation of defects in items. For example, it is assumed that the 150 defective items created at operation 2 do not include any of the 100 created at operation 1 and thus that the total number of defective items produced by the system is equal to the sum of those produced at each operation. This is unlikely to happen in practice. The technique can be modified to take account of this fact, but the distortion of the results occasioned by this assumption is unlikely to be high, unless the proportion of defects produced at the operations is high.

## Acceptance sampling

Inspection of each critical feature of every item may be undertaken so that no defective items would pass unnoticed, except by a mistake or error in the inspection procedure. There are, however, several reasons why such a procedure may be uneconomical or even impossible:

(a) Inspection may cause damage or destruction of the items.

(b) The accuracy of inspection may be diminished after frequent repetition.

(c) Handling of the item may result in deterioration, or items may naturally deteriorate and lengthy inspection procedures would be undesirable.

(d) Inspection may be particularly expensive.

(e) Inspection may be hazardous.

For these reasons, some form of *sampling inspection* is often required. In acceptance sampling, decisions about the quality of batches of items are made after inspection of only a portion of those items. If the sample of items conforms to the required quality levels then the whole batch from which it came is accepted. If the sample does not conform to the required quality level, then the whole batch is rejected or subjected to further inspection. Adopting this procedure, decisions about the quality levels of items can be made fairly quickly and cheaply. However, a certain amount of risk is involved, since there is the possibility that the sample taken will not be of the same quality as the batch from which it came. A greater proportion of defectives in the sample will lead us erroneously to attribute a lower quality level to the batch and vice versa.

Several types of acceptance sampling plan may be used. Some necessitate taking a *single* sample from a batch, upon which a quality decision is made. Others may necessitate the use of *multiple* samples. Plans will also vary in the types of measurement that are involved. The most common, and simplest, type of inspection decision involves classifying items as acceptable or unacceptable. This is referred to as acceptance sampling by *attributes*. Less often, acceptance sampling by *variables* is utilized, in which the purpose of inspection is to obtain exact measurements for characteristics. We shall concentrate on the more usual procedure, which is *single acceptance sampling by attributes*.

Acceptance sampling by attributes not only is suitable for items whose critical features cannot easily be measured, but may also be used where inspection is concerned with dimensions, since such dimensions ultimately are either acceptable or not.

Customers would ideally like 100% of their items to be acceptable but this, as we have pointed out previously, is impractical. Therefore some lower quality level must, of necessity, be agreed. Even so, only by 100% inspection (and even then, only if there are no errors during inspection) can we be absolutely certain that a batch conforms to this agreed standard. In Figure 20.4, 100% inspection has been used, so we can be 100% certain that batches do, or do not, conform to the agreed quality level, which is a maximum of 20% defectives per batch (again assuming no mistakes during inspection).

A shape such as this is known as an *operating characteristic* curve and shows the probability of accepting batches with various percentage defectives. Operating characteristic (OC) curves can be calculated and drawn for any sampling plan if we specify:

(a) the sample size, $n$;

(b) the acceptance number, i.e. the allowance number of defects in the sample, $C$.

**Figure 20.4** The probability of accepting batches, with 100% inspection (acceptable percentage defective 20%)

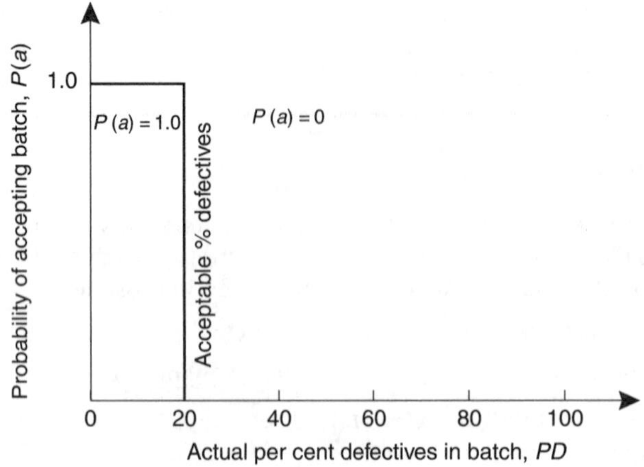

If the batches are large compared with the size of the sample, the construction of such curves is based on the use of the *binomial* probability expression, from which we can calculate the probability that a given number of defectives will be found when a sample of given size is drawn from a batch with a given proportion of defectives, i.e.[1]

$$P(r) = \frac{n!}{r!(n-r)!}\left(\frac{\text{PD}}{100}\right)^r\left(1-\frac{\text{PD}}{100}\right)^{(n-r)}$$

where $r$ = number of defectives found

$n$ = sample size

PD = percentage of defectives in batch

$P(r)$ = probability of finding $r$ defectives

**EXAMPLE**

## *Proofreading*

A sampling inspection procedure is used as a final check of the printing of a large encyclopedia. Ten pages are selected at random and checked for printing errors. The whole book is accepted if only one or zero pages with errors are found in the sample. What is the probability of acceptance of the book if the actual percentage of pages with mistakes in the book is 10%?

Sample size $n$ = 10

Acceptable number of mistakes $C$ = 1 or less

If actual percentage of mistakes in a book = 10%:

$$P(1) = \frac{10!}{1!\ 9!} \times 0.1^1 \times 0.9^9 = 0.39$$

$$P(0) = \frac{10!}{0!\ 10!} \times 0.1^0 \times 0.9^{10} = 0.36$$

$$\therefore P(\leq 1) = P(0) + P(1) \quad = 0.74 = \text{Probability of acceptance}$$

By performing similar calculations for different levels of actual percentage batch defectives, the OC curve shown in Figure 20.5 can be constructed for $n$ = 10 and $C \leq 1$.

Where the value of $n$ (sample size) is large, the use of this method of calculation becomes laborious, and it is fortunate therefore that in most cases it is possible to use an approximate yet adequate method of determining probabilities. It can be shown that when the expected number of defectives is small relative to the lot size, the *Poisson* distribution can be used as an adequate approximation to the binomial.[2] To simplify matters further in such circumstances the calculations may be performed with the assistance of the *Thorndike chart*. This chart, as shown in Figure 20.6, is in fact a set of cumulative

[1] $n! = n \times (n-1) \times (n-2) \ldots \times (n-(n-1))$
0! is taken to be 1.

[2] It is generally accepted that the Poisson distribution may be used where $N$ is large, where $N$ is over five times the sample size $n$ and where the proportion of defects, PD, is less than 10%. In cases where the batch or lot size is small, neither the Poisson nor the binomial distribution is satisfactory and use should be made of the hypergeometric distribution.

For both large $N$ and large $n$ and when PD is greater than 10% use of the normal distribution is satisfactory.

**Figure 20.5** Operating characteristic curve ($n$ = 10; $C \leq 1$)

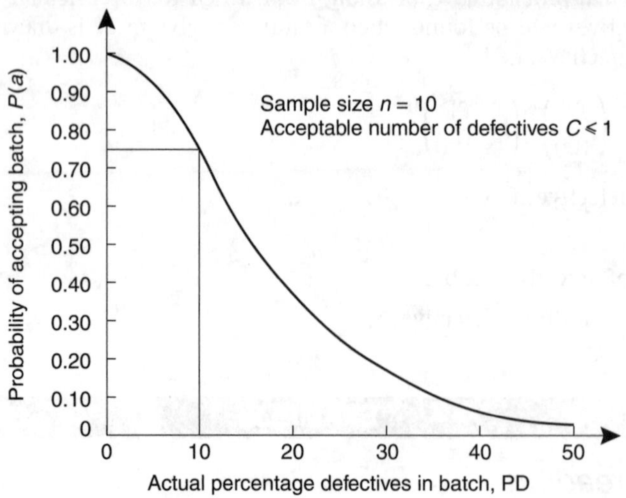


**Figure 20.6** Thorndike chart. Adapted with permission from Dodge, H. F. and Romig, H. G. (1959) *Sampling Inspection Tables*, 2nd edn. London: Wiley.

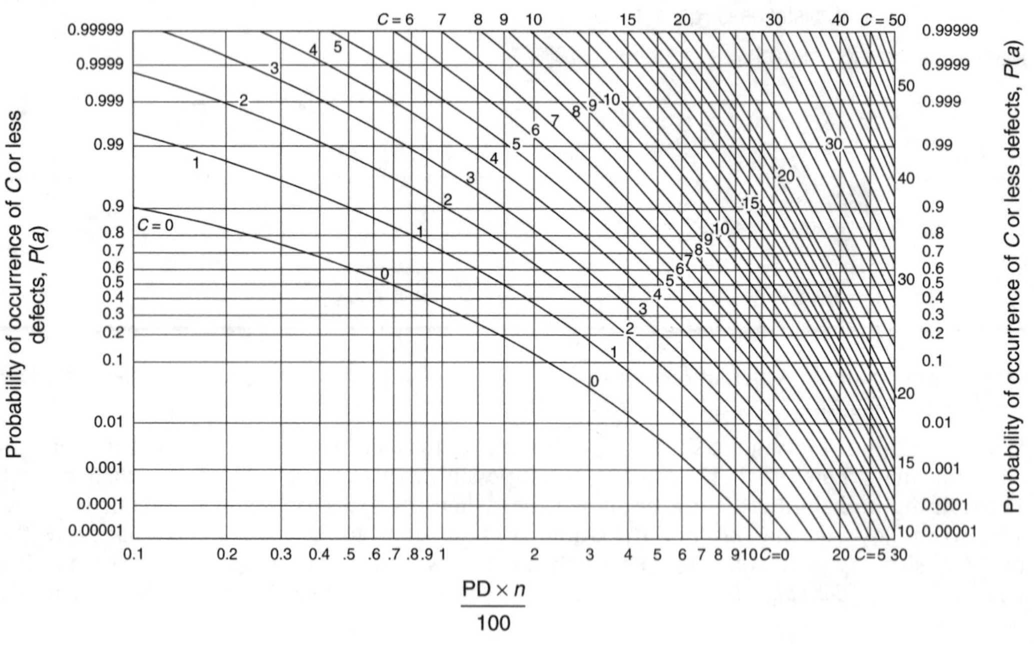


Poisson probability curves from which the probability of C or less defectives ($P(a)$ on the vertical axis) for given values of PD × $n$/100 (on the horizontal axis) can be determined, where PD = actual per cent defectives in a batch or lot and $n$ = sample size.

**EXAMPLE**

## *A restaurant*

A restaurant owner wishes to monitor the quality of the frozen beefburgers which are supplied in large quantities daily. Use the Thorndike chart to construct an operating characteristic curve for:

Sample size $n$ = 100/day

Allowable number of defective (e.g. misshapen) items per sample $C$ = 3

*Answer*

| Actual percentage of defectives in batch (PD) | $\frac{PD \times n}{100}$ | $P(a)$ |
|---|---|---|
| 1 | 1 | 0.98 |
| 2 | 2 | 0.86 |
| 3 | 3 | 0.65 |
| 4 | 4 | 0.44 |
| 5 | 5 | 0.26 |
| 6 | 6 | 0.15 |
| 7 | 7 | 0.08 |
| 8 | 8 | 0.04 |
| 9 | 9 | 0.02 |
| 10 | 10 | 0.01 |

These figures can now be used to plot an OC curve of the type shown previously.

The ability of a sampling procedure to distinguish between good and bad batches is primarily a function of the sample size. If three sampling processes are designed to test the quality level of batches of components for which the acceptable quality level is 1% or less of defectives, then the procedure using the largest sample will be more accurate than those using smaller samples, particularly where the actual percentage of defectives in the batch is high. Figure 20.7 shows three such OC curves, each of which is fairly accurate up to a percentage defective level just below the acceptable level, but above that point, *curve 3 is superior*. As the sample size is increased, the curves become steeper and begin to approach the perfectly discriminating OC curve given in Figure 20.4.

**Figure 20.7** Operating characteristic curves

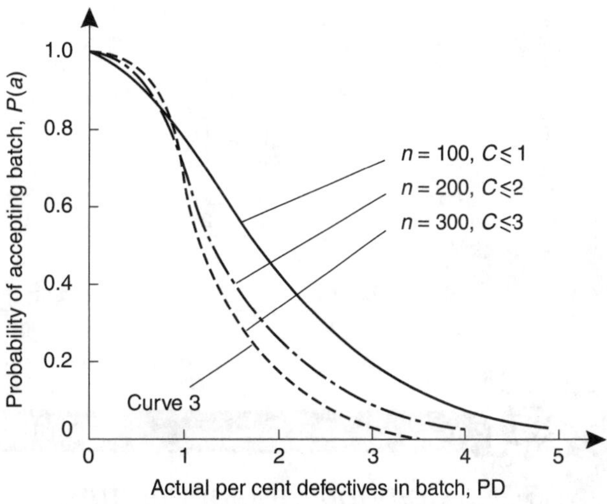

## The design of single acceptance sampling plans

The merit of any sampling plan depends on the relationship of sampling cost to risk. As the cost of inspection decreases and the cost of accepting defective items increases, then the merit of inspection increases and the more willing we are to use large samples. The OC curve shows, for any plan, both the probability of accepting batches with more than the acceptable number of defectives and the probability of rejecting batches with less than the acceptable number of defectives.

It is the consumer's desire to reduce the probability of accepting batches including too many defectives and the producer's desire to minimize the probability of rejecting batches including an acceptable number of defectives. These are called respectively the *consumer's risk* ($\beta$) and the *producer's risk* ($\alpha$). These two values are used to design acceptance sampling plans and, in addition, two further points are used:

(a) ***Acceptable quality level*** (AQL) – the desired quality level, at which probability of acceptance should be high;

(b) ***Lot tolerance per cent defective*** (LTPD) – a quality level below which batches are considered unacceptable, and a level at which probability of acceptance should be low.

These four values are shown on the OC curve in Figure 20.8. The consumer's risk ($\beta$) is usually specified at about 10% and the producer's risk ($\alpha$) at approximately 5%. Acceptable quality level is often around 2% and lot tolerance per cent defective around 10%. These four figures are specified in designing the sampling plan; all that then remains is to construct an OC curve which passes through the two points (AQL;$\alpha$) and (LTPD;$\beta$). This can be done by trial and error, selecting various values for the sample size ($n$) and acceptable number of defectives ($C$) and substituting into the binomial probability formula until an acceptable curve is obtained, or by use of the Thorndike chart.

**Figure 20.8** Operating characteristic (OC) curve and points specifying a sampling plan

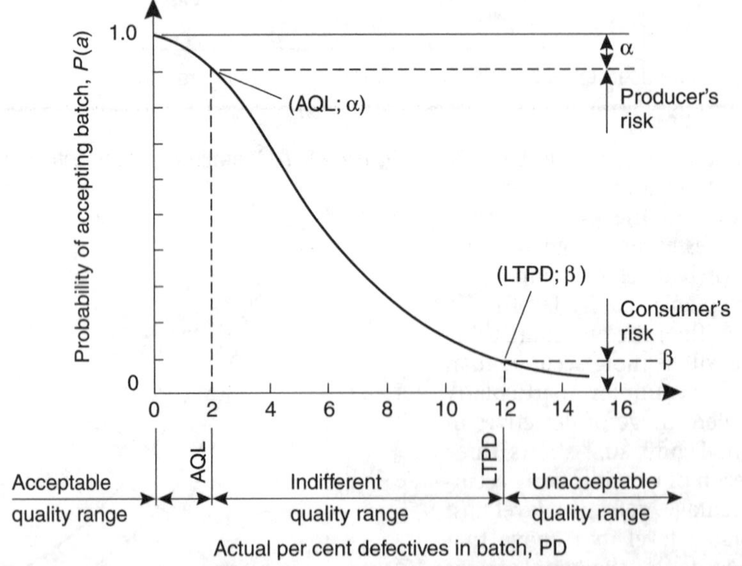

**EXAMPLE**

### *Component manufacture*

Use the Thorndike chart to construct an OC curve which as nearly as possible satisfies the following requirements, which have been agreed by the manufacturer and its major customer.

LTPD = 5% $\beta$ = 10%

AQL = 2% $\alpha$ = 5%

To specify the OC curve we must establish a value for *n* and for *C*. Consider first of all the point on the OC curve located by LTPD (5%) and $\beta$ (10%). Here the probability of acceptance, or *P*(*a*), on the Thorndike chart is 0.1. Reading along the *P*(*a*) = 0.1 ordinate, we can determine the value on the other axis, PD × *n*/100, for each value of *C*, i.e.

when *P*(*a*) = 0.1 ($\beta$ = 10%)

| C | $\frac{\text{PD} \times n}{100}$ |
|---|---|
| 1 | 3.9 |
| 2 | 5.3 |
| 3 | 6.7 |
| 4 | 8.0 |
| 5 | 9.3 |
| 6 | 10.5 |
| 7 | 11.8 |
| 8 | 13.0 |
| 9 | 14.2 |
| 10 | 15.5 |
| 11 | 16.7 |

Now consider the point on the OC curve located by AQL (2%) and $\alpha$ (5%). Here *P*(*a*) = 0.95, and hence the values of PD × *n*/100 can be determined as follows:

when *P*(*a*) = 0.95 ($\alpha$ = 5%)

| C | $\frac{\text{PD} \times n}{100}$ |
|---|---|
| 1 | 0.36 |
| 2 | 0.82 |
| 3 | 1.37 |
| 4 | 1.97 |
| 5 | 2.6 |
| 6 | 3.3 |
| 7 | 4.0 |
| 8 | 4.6 |
| 9 | 5.4 |
| 10 | 6.2 |
| 11 | 7.0 |

Now, in order to determine which OC curve best fits our requirements, we must use the two sets of PD × *n*/100 values. In the first set (*P*(*a*) = 0.1 or $\beta$ = 10%) we require a PD × *n*/100 value equivalent to the LTPD of 5%, while in the last set we require a PD × *n*/100 value equivalent to AQL = 2%. If we divide the pairs of PD × *n*/100 values for each value of $C$ we have in fact determined the value of LTPD/AQL, i.e.

| **C** | $\frac{\textbf{PD} \times n}{100}$ **for** $\beta$ **= 10%** | $\frac{\textbf{PD} \times n}{100}$ **for** $\alpha$ **= 5%** | $\frac{\textbf{PD} \times n/100 \textbf{ for } \beta = 10}{\textbf{PD} \times n/100 \textbf{ for } \alpha = 5} = \frac{\textbf{LTPD}}{\textbf{AQL}}$ |
|---|---|---|---|
| 1 | 3.9 | 0.36 | 10.8 |
| 2 | 5.3 | 0.82 | 6.46 |
| 3 | 6.7 | 1.37 | 4.89 |
| 4 | 8.0 | 1.97 | 4.06 |
| 5 | 9.3 | 2.6 | 3.58 |
| 6 | 10.5 | 3.3 | 3.18 |
| 7 | 11.8 | 4.0 | 2.95 |
| 8 | 13.0 | 4.6 | 2.83 |
| 9 | 14.2 | 5.4 | 2.63 |
| 10 | 15.5 | 6.2 | 2.50 |
| 11 | 16.7 | 7.0 | 2.39 |

In fact the ratio for LTPD/AQL specified in the question is 5/2 = 2.5, which corresponds to the ratio obtained for $C = 10$. It now remains only to determine $n$, which can be found as follows:

where $C = 10$ for $\beta = 10\%$

$$\frac{\text{PD} \times n}{100} = \frac{\text{LTPD} \times n}{100} = 15.5$$

$$\therefore n = \frac{15.5 \times 100}{\text{LTPD}}$$

$$= \frac{15.5 \times 100}{5}$$

$$= 310$$

Our OC curve is therefore specified by $C = 10$ and $n = 310$.

---

Defective items found in the *samples* will always be either rectified or replaced. If, during inspection, samples are drawn from the batch which include more than the acceptable number of defectives, then two alternatives are available:

(a) Reject and scrap the complete *batch*.

(b) Subject the complete *batch* to 100% inspection and replace or rectify all faulty items found in it.

The choice of alternative (a) or (b) will depend on the value of the items concerned and the cost of replacing or rectifying them, but often, in order to obtain a high quality level for batches with a minimum of inspection, the second alternative is adopted. In such a case we can represent our acceptance sampling procedure diagrammatically as shown in Figure 20.9. In this diagrammatic representation, a

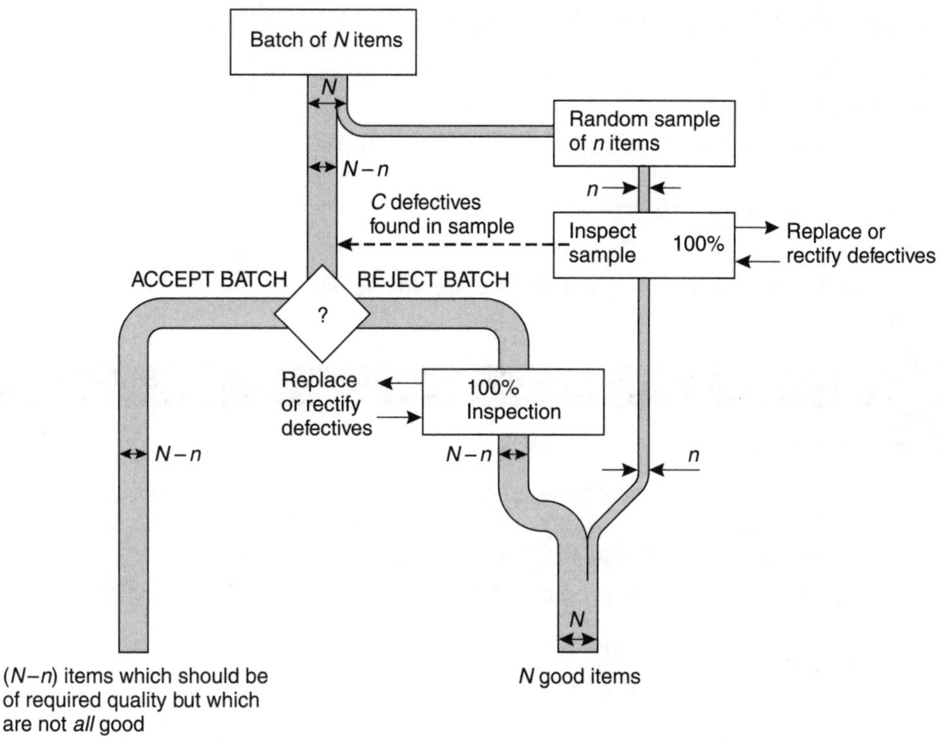


**Figure 20.9** Operation of a sampling procedure in which rejected batches are subject to 100% inspection

random sample of $n$ items is taken from the batch of $N$ items. The sample is inspected and $c$ defectives are found, which are then replaced or rectified. Depending on whether $c$ is greater than $C$ (the acceptable number of defects) the entire batch is either accepted or rejected. If the batch is rejected ($c > C$), the remaining $(N - n)$ items in the batch are all inspected, defective items being either rectified or replaced. In this case we can be certain (subject to inspection error) that we are left with $N$ good items. If, on the other hand, the batch is accepted because $c \leq C$ then we can be certain that the sample contains all good items, but of course some of the remaining $(N - n)$ items will be defective.

The *average outgoing quality* (AOQ) is the overall proportion of defective items in a large number of batches, when all batches are assumed to have the same actual percentage of defectives (PD) and when all batches are subjected to the type of inspection procedure described above. The AOQ percentage, which must be less than PD, can be found as follows:

$$\text{AOQ per cent} = \frac{\text{Number of defectives remaining}}{\text{Total number of items}} \times 100$$

$$= \frac{\text{Number of defective items in accepted batches each of size } N - n}{\text{Total number of items}} \times 100$$

$$\therefore \text{AOQ per cent} = \frac{P(a)(\text{PD})(N - n)k}{Nk}$$

where $P(a)$ = probability of accepting batch (from OC curve)

PD = actual per cent defectives in all batches
$N$ = batch sizes
$n$ = sample sizes
$k$ = large number of batches

$$\text{i.e. AOQ per cent} = \frac{P(a)(\text{PD})(N - n)}{N}$$

Curves showing the average outgoing quality level for any actual per cent defectives can be calculated quite simply.

**EXAMPLE**

### A hotel

A hotel is anxious to check the attitudes of its residents when they leave. Its staff take a sample of ten customers each day and ask if they were satisfied with the service. No action is taken if one or fewer customers in each sample complain (i.e. the OC curve in Figure 20.5 applies).

Construct the AOQ curve for this sampling plan where the batch size $N$ = 200 customers per day.

$$\text{AOQ per cent} = P(a)(\text{PD})\ \frac{N - n}{N}$$

$$= P(a)(\text{PD})\ 0.95$$

This AOQ curve is shown in Figure 20.10.

| $P(a)$ (from OC curve)[a] | PD per cent | AOQ per cent |
|---|---|---|
| 0.90 | 5 | 4.3 |
| 0.77 | 10 | 7.3 |
| 0.55 | 15 | 7.8 |
| 0.37 | 20 | 7.0 |
| 0.22 | 25 | 5.2 |
| 0.13 | 30 | 3.7 |
| 0.08 | 35 | 2.7 |
| 0.06 | 40 | 2.3 |

[a]See Figure 20.5

**Figure 20.10** AOQ curve

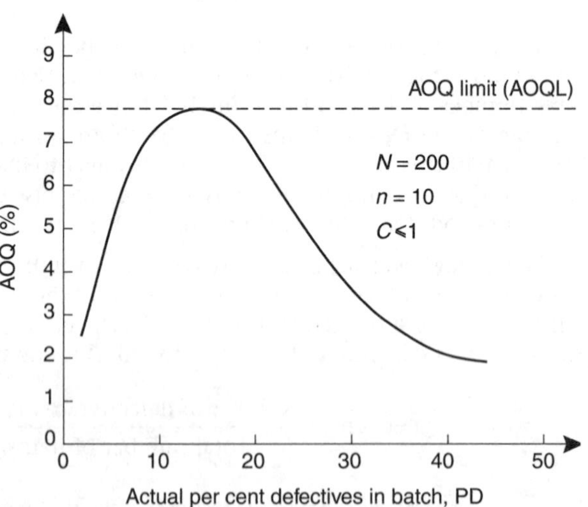


Using such a sampling procedure, not only is the AOQ better than the specified acceptable quantity level, but also a 'built-in' *limit* for the proportion of defectives – the average outgoing quality limit (AOQL) – exists. This limit represents the worst average quality which, over a large number of batches, we may expect to pass either to the customer or to the next production stage. Acceptance sampling plans may also be designed to provide a given AOQL.

## Summary of the design of single acceptance sampling plans for attributes

Sampling plans may be designed to provide:

(a) an average outgoing quality limit (AOQL);

(b) a given consumer or producer risk (LTPD and AQL).

AOQL plans are usually adopted where interest centres on the average quality level after inspection, whereas LTPD and/or AQL plans are used where a certain given level of risk is to be satisfied.

The basic steps involved in the design and use of an acceptance sampling procedure are as follows:

(a) Decide what features or characteristics of the items will be inspected:

1. if necessary, treat different characteristics with separate sampling procedures; but

2. wherever possible combine all characteristics which are the subject of the same kind of inspection (e.g. all characteristics necessitating visual inspection) and treat them all with the same acceptance sampling plan.

(b) Decide what, for the purpose of the sampling procedure, constitutes a batch, i.e.

1. a batch should, as far as possible, consist of homogeneous items from the same source; or

2. batches should be as large as possible to minimize inspection.

(c) Choose the type of sampling plan to be used, i.e. AOQL or AQL/LTPD plans, and determine suitable quality or risk figures to be used in the plan.

(d) Select a random sample from the batch and inspect appropriate characteristics on each item.

(e) As a result of the quality level of the sample, accept or reject the batch.

## Double and multiple sampling

The total amount of inspection required to obtain a certain output quality level can be reduced if *double* or *multiple sampling* is used.

In single acceptance sampling as described above, the decision to accept or to reject the batch of items is dependent on the inspection of a single random sample of size $n$ from that batch. In *double* sampling there is the possibility of delaying that decision until a second sample has been taken. A random sample of $n$ items is drawn from the batch, each item is inspected and the number of defectives ($c$) is counted. If this number is less than or equal to a given acceptance number ($C1$) then the batch is accepted. Alternatively, if it is greater than a larger given acceptance number ($C2$) the batch is rejected. If, however, the number of defectives in the sample falls between these two levels, then the result is inconclusive and a second sample is drawn from the same batch. Again, the number of defectives is counted and this number is added to the number of defectives found in the first sample. If the total number is less than $C2$, the batch is accepted, but if the total number is greater than $C2$ the batch is rejected.

*Multiple* sampling is a similar procedure, but here there is the possibility of taking more than two samples from the same batch. An initial sample is drawn from the batch and, depending on the number of defectives found, the batch is either accepted ($c \leq C1$) or rejected ($c > C2$), or a decision is deferred ($C1 < c < C2$). The number of defectives in the second sample is added to the number found in the first and the total is compared with two further acceptance numbers, the batch being accepted or rejected or the decision deferred as before. This procedure is repeated until a decision can be made. A multiple sampling plan is depicted diagrammatically in Figure 20.11.

*Sequential* sampling is a similar procedure but involves taking one at a time from the batch and basing acceptance or rejection decisions on the number of defectives accumulated.

Double or multiple sampling permits smaller-sized samples to be taken. Consequently, on the occasions when the items or material inspected are well within, or well beyond, acceptable quality levels,

**Figure 20.11** Multiple sampling plan (for batch sizes of 500 to 799 for 3% AQL)

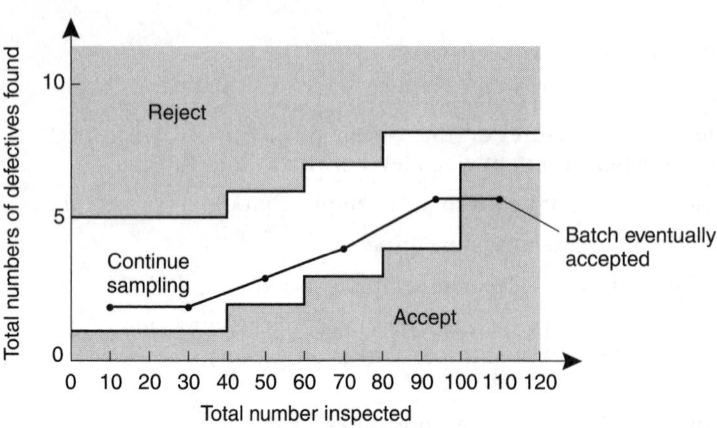


fewer items need be inspected. In such cases double or multiple sampling is more economical than single acceptance sampling.

## Acceptance sampling tables

In practice people responsible for the design and use of acceptance sampling rarely establish their sampling plans from first principles. More often one or more of the numerous sets of published charts or tables is used. For example, a widely used AQL scheme for acceptance sampling for variables was devised jointly in the USA, Canada and the UK, and is published in British Standard BS 6001 and in the USA as MIL-STD-105D. The UK Military Standard Attributes AS scheme is covered by Standard DEF-131-A, while in the USA an AS scheme for variables is given in MIL-STD-414. Another widely used set of tables was developed by Dodge and Romig at the Bell Telephone Laboratories.

The Dodge and Romig tables are of four types – each is concerned with attributes:

(a) single sampling lot tolerance tables (see Figure 20.12);

(b) single sampling AOQL tables (see Figure 20.13);

**Figure 20.12** Single sampling table for lot tolerance per cent defective (LPTD) = 5.0%. From Dodge, H. F. and Romig, H. G. (1959) *Sampling Inspection Tables*. London: Wiley. Reproduced with permission.

| Lot size | Process average 0 to 0.05% | | | Process average 0.06 to 0.50% | | | Process average 0.51 to 1.00% | | | Process average 1.01 to 1.50% | | | Process average 1.51 to 2.00% | | | Process average 2.01 to 2.50% | | |
|---|---|---|---|---|---|---|---|---|---|---|---|---|---|---|---|---|---|---|
| | *n* | *C* | AOQL % | *n* | *C* | AOQL % | *n* | *C* | AOQL % | *n* | *C* | AOQL % | *n* | *C* | AOQL % | *n* | *C* | AOQL % |
| 1–30 | All | 0 | 0.00 | All | 0 | 0.00 | All | 0 | 0.00 | All | 0 | 0.00 | All | 0 | 0.00 | All | 0 | 0.00 |
| 31–50 | 30 | 0 | 0.49 | 30 | 0 | 0.49 | 30 | 0 | 0.49 | 30 | 0 | 0.49 | 30 | 0 | 0.49 | 30 | 0 | 0.49 |
| 51–100 | 37 | 0 | 0.63 | 37 | 0 | 0.63 | 37 | 0 | 0.63 | 37 | 0 | 0.63 | 37 | 0 | 0.63 | 37 | 0 | 0.63 |
| 101–200 | 40 | 0 | 0.74 | 40 | 0 | 0.74 | 40 | 0 | 0.74 | 40 | 0 | 0.74 | 40 | 0 | 0.74 | 40 | 0 | 0.71 |
| 201–300 | 43 | 0 | 0.74 | 43 | 0 | 0.74 | 70 | 1 | 0.92 | 70 | 1 | 0.92 | 95 | 2 | 0.99 | 95 | 2 | 0.99 |
| 301–400 | 44 | 0 | 0.74 | 44 | 0 | 0.74 | 70 | 1 | 0.99 | 100 | 2 | 1.00 | 120 | 3 | 1.10 | 145 | 4 | 1.10 |
| 401–500 | 45 | 0 | 0.75 | 75 | 1 | 0.95 | 100 | 2 | 1.10 | 100 | 2 | 1.10 | 125 | 3 | 1.20 | 150 | 4 | 1.20 |
| 501–600 | 45 | 0 | 0.76 | 75 | 1 | 0.98 | 100 | 2 | 1.10 | 125 | 3 | 1.20 | 150 | 4 | 1.30 | 175 | 5 | 1.30 |
| 601–800 | 45 | 0 | 0.77 | 75 | 1 | 1.00 | 100 | 2 | 1.20 | 130 | 3 | 1.20 | 175 | 5 | 1.40 | 200 | 6 | 1.40 |
| 801–1000 | 45 | 0 | 0.78 | 75 | 1 | 1.00 | 105 | 2 | 1.20 | 155 | 4 | 1.40 | 180 | 5 | 1.40 | 225 | 7 | 1.50 |
| 1001–2000 | 45 | 0 | 0.80 | 75 | 1 | 1.00 | 130 | 3 | 1.40 | 180 | 5 | 1.60 | 230 | 7 | 1.70 | 280 | 9 | 1.80 |
| 2001–3000 | 75 | 1 | 1.10 | 105 | 2 | 1.30 | 135 | 3 | 1.40 | 210 | 6 | 1.70 | 280 | 9 | 1.90 | 370 | 13 | 2.10 |
| 3001–4000 | 75 | 1 | 1.10 | 105 | 2 | 1.30 | 160 | 4 | 1.50 | 210 | 6 | 1.70 | 305 | 10 | 2.00 | 420 | 15 | 2.20 |
| 4001–5000 | 75 | 1 | 1.10 | 105 | 2 | 1.30 | 160 | 4 | 1.50 | 235 | 7 | 1.80 | 330 | 11 | 2.00 | 440 | 16 | 2.20 |
| 5001–7000 | 75 | 1 | 1.10 | 105 | 2 | 1.30 | 185 | 5 | 1.70 | 260 | 8 | 1.90 | 350 | 12 | 2.20 | 490 | 18 | 2.40 |
| 7001–10,000 | 75 | 1 | 1.10 | 105 | 2 | 1.30 | 185 | 5 | 1.70 | 260 | 8 | 1.90 | 380 | 13 | 2.20 | 535 | 20 | 2.50 |
| 10,001–20,000 | 75 | 1 | 1.10 | 135 | 3 | 1.40 | 210 | 6 | 1.80 | 285 | 9 | 2.00 | 425 | 15 | 2.30 | 610 | 23 | 2.60 |
| 20,001–50,000 | 75 | 1 | 1.10 | 135 | 3 | 1.40 | 235 | 7 | 1.90 | 305 | 10 | 2.10 | 470 | 17 | 2.40 | 700 | 27 | 2.70 |
| 50,001–100,000 | 75 | 1 | 1.10 | 160 | 4 | 1.60 | 235 | 7 | 1.90 | 355 | 12 | 2.20 | 515 | 19 | 2.50 | 770 | 30 | 2.80 |

*n* = sample size; *C* = acceptance number
'All' indicates that each piece in the lot is to be inspected
AOQL = Average Outgoing Quality Limit

**Figure 20.13** Single sampling table for average outgoing quality limit (AOQL) = 2.5%. From Dodge, H. F. and Romig, H. G. (1959) *Sampling Inspection Tables*. London: Wiley. Reproduced with permission.

| Lot size | Process average 0 to 0.05% | | | Process average 0.06 to 0.50% | | | Process average 0.51 to 1.00% | | | Process average 1.01 to 1.50% | | | Process average 1.51 to 2.00% | | | Process average 2.01 to 2.50% | | |
|---|---|---|---|---|---|---|---|---|---|---|---|---|---|---|---|---|---|---|
| | $n$ | $C$ | $p_t$% | $n$ | $C$ | $p_t$% | $n$ | $C$ | $p_t$% | $n$ | $C$ | $p_t$% | $n$ | $C$ | $p_t$% | $n$ | $C$ | $p_t$% |
| 1–10 | All | 0 | | All | 0 | | All | 0 | | All | 0 | | All | 0 | | All | 0 | |
| 11–50 | 11 | 0 | 17.6 | 11 | 0 | 17.6 | 11 | 0 | 17.6 | 11 | 0 | 17.6 | 11 | 0 | 17.6 | 11 | 0 | 17.6 |
| 51–100 | 13 | 0 | 15.3 | 13 | 0 | 15.3 | 13 | 0 | 15.3 | 13 | 0 | 15.3 | 13 | 0 | 15.3 | 13 | 0 | 15.3 |
| 101–200 | 14 | 0 | 14.7 | 14 | 0 | 14.7 | 14 | 0 | 14.7 | 29 | 1 | 12.9 | 29 | 1 | 12.9 | 29 | 1 | 12.9 |
| 201–300 | 14 | 0 | 14.9 | 14 | 0 | 14.9 | 30 | 1 | 12.7 | 30 | 1 | 12.7 | 30 | 1 | 12.7 | 30 | 1 | 12.7 |
| 301–400 | 14 | 0 | 15.0 | 14 | 0 | 15.0 | 31 | 1 | 12.3 | 31 | 1 | 12.3 | 31 | 1 | 12.3 | 48 | 2 | 10.7 |
| 401–500 | 14 | 0 | 15.0 | 14 | 0 | 15.0 | 32 | 1 | 12.0 | 32 | 1 | 12.0 | 49 | 2 | 10.6 | 49 | 2 | 10.6 |
| 501–600 | 14 | 0 | 15.1 | 32 | 1 | 12.0 | 32 | 1 | 12.0 | 50 | 2 | 10.4 | 50 | 2 | 10.4 | 70 | 3 | 9.3 |
| 601–800 | 14 | 0 | 15.1 | 32 | 1 | 12.0 | 32 | 1 | 12.0 | 50 | 2 | 10.5 | 50 | 2 | 10.5 | 70 | 3 | 9.4 |
| 801–1000 | 15 | 0 | 14.2 | 33 | 1 | 11.7 | 33 | 1 | 11.7 | 50 | 2 | 10.6 | 70 | 3 | 9.4 | 90 | 4 | 8.5 |
| 1001–2000 | 15 | 0 | 14.2 | 33 | 1 | 11.7 | 55 | 2 | 9.3 | 75 | 3 | 8.8 | 95 | 4 | 8.0 | 120 | 5 | 7.6 |
| 2001–3000 | 15 | 0 | 14.2 | 33 | 1 | 11.8 | 55 | 2 | 9.4 | 75 | 3 | 8.8 | 120 | 5 | 7.6 | 145 | 6 | 7.2 |
| 3001–4000 | 15 | 0 | 14.3 | 33 | 1 | 11.8 | 55 | 2 | 9.5 | 100 | 4 | 7.9 | 125 | 5 | 7.4 | 195 | 8 | 6.6 |
| 4001–5000 | 15 | 0 | 14.3 | 33 | 1 | 11.8 | 75 | 3 | 8.9 | 100 | 4 | 7.9 | 150 | 6 | 7.0 | 225 | 9 | 6.3 |
| 5001–7000 | 33 | 1 | 11.8 | 55 | 2 | 9.7 | 75 | 3 | 8.9 | 125 | 5 | 7.4 | 175 | 7 | 6.7 | 250 | 10 | 6.1 |
| 7001–10,000 | 34 | 1 | 11.4 | 55 | 2 | 9.7 | 75 | 3 | 8.9 | 125 | 5 | 7.4 | 200 | 8 | 6.4 | 310 | 12 | 5.8 |
| 10,001–20,000 | 34 | 1 | 11.4 | 55 | 2 | 9.7 | 100 | 4 | 8.0 | 150 | 6 | 7.0 | 260 | 10 | 6.0 | 425 | 16 | 5.3 |
| 20,001–50,000 | 34 | 1 | 11.4 | 55 | 2 | 9.7 | 100 | 4 | 8.0 | 180 | 7 | 6.7 | 345 | 13 | 5.5 | 640 | 23 | 4.8 |
| 50,001–100,000 | 34 | 1 | 11.4 | 80 | 3 | 8.4 | 125 | 5 | 7.4 | 235 | 9 | 6.1 | 435 | 16 | 5.2 | 800 | 28 | 4.5 |

$n$ = sample size; $C$ = acceptance number
'All' indicates that each piece in the lot is to be inspected
$p_t$ = lot tolerance per cent defective with a Consumer's Risk ($P_C$) of 0.10

(c) double sampling lot tolerance tables (see Figure 20.14);

(d) double sampling AOQL tables (see Figure 20.15).

The LTPD tables provide values of $n$ and $c$ for a consumer's risk of 10% and for LTPDs from 0.5% to 10.0%. To use the tables the batch or lot size and the actual process average percentage defective must be known. The latter will usually be obtained from a pilot study. The LTPD tables also show in each case the AOQL which would result if rejected batches were subject to 100% inspection.

The AOQL tables provide values of $n$ and $c$ for a consumer's risk of 10% and for AOQLs from 0.1 to 10.0%. Again, to use these tables the batch size and the process average percentage defective must be known. The tables also give the LTPD which will result from each sampling plan.

## Control charts

Acceptance sampling is a method of quality control which is used to ensure that defective items are not accepted by the firm and to ensure that defectives are not output. It is concerned with both ends of the quality function but not (*at least not in this form*) with the middle. It is not concerned with controlling quality during the process. This problem, however, is particularly important, since it is during the process that steps may be taken to *prevent* the output of defective and substandard items. In fact, we can regard this as being the *quality assurance* function, as opposed to the *quality control* exercised by acceptance sampling. The procedure used during quality assurance is the *control chart*, which is a special application of statistical sampling techniques.

Irrespective of the capability of the process, the items produced will inevitably be subject to some variation. Not only *variables* such as length, weight, etc. will vary, but also other *attributes* which will be subject to some variations. These variations might be caused by several factors, which can be classified into two categories:

(a) ***usual*** or ***chance*** variations, which are likely to occur in a random manner and about which comparatively little can be done;

**Figure 20.14** Double sampling table for lot tolerance per cent defective (LPTD) = 5.0%. From Dodge, H. F. and Romig, H. G. (1959) *Sampling Inspection Tables*. London: Wiley. Reproduced with permission.

| Lot size | Process average 0 to 0.05% | | | | | | Process average 0.06 to 0.50% | | | | | | Process average 0.51 to 1.00% | | | | | |
|---|---|---|---|---|---|---|---|---|---|---|---|---|---|---|---|---|---|---|
| | Trial 1 | | Trial 2 | | | AOQL | Trial 1 | | Trial 2 | | | AOQL | Trial 1 | | Trial 2 | | | AOQL |
| | $n_1$ | $C_1$ | $n_2$ | $n_1 + n_2$ | $C_2$ | in % | $n_1$ | $C_1$ | $n_2$ | $n_1 + n_2$ | $C_2$ | in % | $n_1$ | $C_1$ | $n_2$ | $n_1 + n_2$ | $C_2$ | in % |
| 1–30 | All | 0 | | | | 0.00 | All | 0 | | | | 0.00 | All | 0 | | | | 0.00 |
| 31–50 | 30 | 0 | | | | 0.49 | 30 | 0 | | | | 0.49 | 30 | 0 | | | | 0.49 |
| 51–75 | 38 | 0 | | | | 0.59 | 38 | 0 | | | | 0.59 | 38 | 0 | | | | 0.59 |
| 76–100 | 44 | 0 | 21 | 65 | 1 | 0.64 | 44 | 0 | 21 | 65 | 1 | 0.64 | 44 | 0 | 21 | 65 | 1 | 0.64 |
| 101–200 | 49 | 0 | 26 | 75 | 1 | 0.84 | 49 | 0 | 26 | 75 | 1 | 0.84 | 49 | 0 | 26 | 75 | 1 | 0.84 |
| 201–300 | 50 | 0 | 30 | 80 | 1 | 0.91 | 50 | 0 | 30 | 80 | 1 | 0.91 | 50 | 0 | 55 | 105 | 2 | 1.00 |
| 301–400 | 55 | 0 | 30 | 85 | 1 | 0.92 | 55 | 0 | 55 | 110 | 2 | 1.10 | 55 | 0 | 55 | 110 | 2 | 1.10 |
| 401–500 | 55 | 0 | 30 | 85 | 1 | 0.93 | 55 | 0 | 55 | 110 | 2 | 1.10 | 55 | 0 | 80 | 135 | 3 | 1.20 |
| 501–600 | 55 | 0 | 30 | 85 | 1 | 0.94 | 55 | 0 | 60 | 115 | 2 | 1.10 | 55 | 0 | 85 | 140 | 3 | 10.2 |
| 601–800 | 55 | 0 | 35 | 90 | 1 | 0.95 | 55 | 0 | 65 | 120 | 2 | 1.10 | 55 | 0 | 85 | 140 | 3 | 1.30 |
| 801–1000 | 55 | 0 | 35 | 90 | 1 | 0.96 | 55 | 0 | 65 | 120 | 2 | 1.10 | 55 | 0 | 115 | 170 | 4 | 1.40 |
| 1001–2000 | 55 | 0 | 35 | 90 | 1 | 0.98 | 55 | 0 | 95 | 150 | 3 | 1.30 | 55 | 0 | 120 | 175 | 4 | 1.40 |
| 2001–3000 | 55 | 0 | 65 | 120 | 2 | 1.20 | 55 | 0 | 95 | 150 | 3 | 1.30 | 55 | 0 | 150 | 205 | 5 | 1.50 |
| 3001–4000 | 55 | 0 | 65 | 120 | 2 | 1.20 | 55 | 0 | 95 | 150 | 3 | 1.30 | 90 | 1 | 140 | 230 | 6 | 1.60 |
| 4001–5000 | 55 | 0 | 65 | 120 | 2 | 1.20 | 55 | 0 | 95 | 150 | 3 | 1.40 | 90 | 1 | 165 | 255 | 7 | 1.80 |
| 5001–7000 | 55 | 0 | 65 | 120 | 2 | 1.20 | 55 | 0 | 95 | 150 | 3 | 1.40 | 90 | 1 | 165 | 255 | 7 | 1.80 |
| 7001–10,000 | 55 | 0 | 65 | 120 | 2 | 1.20 | 55 | 0 | 120 | 175 | 4 | 1.50 | 90 | 1 | 190 | 280 | 8 | 1.90 |
| 10,001–20,000 | 55 | 0 | 65 | 120 | 2 | 1.20 | 55 | 0 | 120 | 175 | 4 | 1.50 | 90 | 1 | 190 | 280 | 8 | 1.90 |
| 20,001–50,000 | 55 | 0 | 65 | 120 | 2 | 1.20 | 55 | 0 | 150 | 205 | 5 | 1.70 | 90 | 1 | 215 | 305 | 9 | 2.00 |
| 50,001–100,000 | 55 | 0 | 65 | 120 | 2 | 1.20 | 55 | 0 | 150 | 205 | 5 | 1.70 | 90 | 1 | 240 | 330 | 10 | 2.10 |

| Lot size | Process average 1.01 to 1.50% | | | | | | Process average 1.51 to 2.00% | | | | | | Process average 2.01 to 2.50% | | | | | |
|---|---|---|---|---|---|---|---|---|---|---|---|---|---|---|---|---|---|---|
| | Trial 1 | | Trial 2 | | | AOQL | Trial 1 | | Trial 2 | | | AOQL | Trial 1 | | Trial 2 | | | AOQL |
| | $n_1$ | $C_1$ | $n_2$ | $n_1 + n_2$ | $C_2$ | in % | $n_1$ | $C_1$ | $n_2$ | $n_1 + n_2$ | $C_2$ | in % | $n_1$ | $C_1$ | $n_2$ | $n_1 + n_2$ | $C_2$ | in % |
| 1–30 | All | 0 | | | | 0.00 | All | 0 | | | | 0.00 | All | 0 | | | | 0.00 |
| 31–50 | 30 | 0 | | | | 0.49 | 30 | 0 | | | | 0.49 | 30 | 0 | | | | 0.49 |
| 51–75 | 38 | 0 | | | | 0.59 | 38 | 0 | | | | 0.59 | 38 | 0 | | | | 0.59 |
| 76–100 | 44 | 0 | 21 | 65 | 1 | 0.64 | 44 | 0 | 21 | 65 | 1 | 0.64 | 44 | 0 | 21 | 65 | 1 | 0.64 |
| 101–200 | 49 | 0 | 51 | 100 | 2 | 0.91 | 49 | 0 | 51 | 100 | 2 | 0.91 | 49 | 0 | 51 | 100 | 2 | 0.91 |
| 201–300 | 50 | 0 | 55 | 105 | 2 | 1.00 | 50 | 0 | 80 | 130 | 3 | 1.10 | 50 | 0 | 100 | 150 | 4 | 1.10 |
| 301–400 | 55 | 0 | 80 | 135 | 3 | 1.10 | 55 | 0 | 100 | 155 | 4 | 1.20 | 85 | 1 | 105 | 190 | 6 | 1.30 |
| 401–500 | 55 | 0 | 105 | 160 | 4 | 1.30 | 85 | 1 | 120 | 205 | 6 | 1.40 | 85 | 1 | 140 | 225 | 7 | 1.40 |
| 501–600 | 55 | 0 | 110 | 165 | 4 | 1.30 | 85 | 1 | 145 | 230 | 7 | 1.40 | 85 | 1 | 165 | 250 | 8 | 1.50 |
| 601–800 | 90 | 1 | 125 | 215 | 6 | 1.50 | 90 | 1 | 170 | 260 | 8 | 1.50 | 120 | 2 | 185 | 305 | 10 | 1.60 |
| 801–1000 | 90 | 1 | 150 | 240 | 7 | 1.50 | 90 | 1 | 200 | 290 | 9 | 1.60 | 120 | 2 | 210 | 330 | 11 | 1.70 |
| 1001–2000 | 90 | 1 | 185 | 275 | 8 | 1.70 | 120 | 2 | 225 | 345 | 11 | 1.90 | 175 | 4 | 260 | 435 | 15 | 2.00 |
| 2001–3000 | 120 | 2 | 180 | 300 | 9 | 1.90 | 150 | 3 | 270 | 420 | 14 | 2.10 | 205 | 5 | 375 | 580 | 21 | 2.30 |
| 3001–4000 | 120 | 2 | 210 | 330 | 10 | 2.00 | 150 | 3 | 295 | 445 | 15 | 2.30 | 230 | 6 | 420 | 650 | 24 | 2.40 |
| 4001–5000 | 120 | 2 | 255 | 375 | 12 | 2.10 | 150 | 3 | 345 | 495 | 17 | 2.30 | 255 | 7 | 445 | 700 | 26 | 2.50 |
| 5001–7000 | 120 | 2 | 260 | 380 | 12 | 2.10 | 150 | 3 | 370 | 520 | 18 | 2.30 | 255 | 7 | 495 | 750 | 28 | 2.60 |
| 7001–10,000 | 120 | 2 | 285 | 405 | 13 | 2.10 | 175 | 4 | 370 | 545 | 19 | 2.40 | 280 | 8 | 540 | 820 | 31 | 2.70 |
| 10,001–20,000 | 120 | 2 | 310 | 430 | 14 | 2.20 | 175 | 4 | 420 | 595 | 21 | 2.40 | 280 | 8 | 660 | 940 | 36 | 2.80 |
| 20,001–50,000 | 120 | 2 | 335 | 455 | 15 | 2.20 | 205 | 5 | 485 | 690 | 25 | 2.50 | 305 | 9 | 745 | 1050 | 41 | 2.90 |
| 50,001–100,000 | 120 | 2 | 360 | 480 | 16 | 2.30 | 205 | 5 | 555 | 760 | 28 | 2.60 | 330 | 10 | 810 | 1140 | 45 | 3.00 |

Trial 1: $n_1$ = first sample size; $C_1$ = acceptance number for first sample
'All' indicates that each piece in the lot is to be inspected
Trial 2: $n_2$ = second sample size; $C_2$ = acceptance number for first and second samples combined
AOQL = Average Outgoing Quality Limit

(b) ***unusual*** or ***assignable*** variations, which occur less frequently and can normally be traced to some 'external' causes.

'Usual' variations are normally smaller than 'unusual' variations and, since they result from some inherent process variability, they occur randomly and can be described by the normal probability distribution. Quality controllers define *limits* within which variations are acceptable and beyond which

**Figure 20.15** Double sampling table for average outgoing quality limit (AOQL) = 2.5%. From Dodge, H. F. and Romig, H. G. (1959) *Sampling Inspection Tables*. London: Wiley. Reproduced with permission.

| Lot size | Process average 0 to 0.05% | | | | | | Process average 0.06 to 0.50% | | | | | | Process average 0.51 to 1.00% | | | | | |
|---|---|---|---|---|---|---|---|---|---|---|---|---|---|---|---|---|---|---|
| | Trial 1 | | Trial 2 | | | $p_t$ % | Trial 1 | | Trial 2 | | | $p_t$ % | Trial 1 | | Trial 2 | | | $p_t$ % |
| | $n_1$ | $C_1$ | $n_2$ | $n_1 + n_2$ | $C_2$ | | $n_1$ | $C_1$ | $n_2$ | $n_1 + n_2$ | $C_2$ | | $n_1$ | $C$ | $n_2$ | $n_1 + n_2$ | $C_2$ | |
| 1–10 | All | 0 | | | | | II | 0 | A | | | | All | 0 | | | | |
| 11–50 | 11 | 0 | | | | 17.6 | 11 | 0 | | | | 17.6 | 11 | 0 | | | | 17.6 |
| 51–100 | 18 | 0 | 10 | 28 | 1 | 14.1 | 18 | 0 | 10 | 28 | 1 | 14.1 | 18 | 0 | 10 | 28 | 1 | 14.1 |
| 101–200 | 20 | 0 | 11 | 31 | 1 | 13.7 | 20 | 0 | 11 | 31 | 1 | 13.7 | 23 | 0 | 25 | 48 | 2 | 11.7 |
| 201–300 | 21 | 0 | 13 | 34 | 1 | 13.0 | 21 | 0 | 13 | 34 | 1 | 13.0 | 24 | 0 | 25 | 49 | 2 | 11.4 |
| 301–400 | 21 | 0 | 14 | 35 | 1 | 12.8 | 24 | 0 | 26 | 50 | 2 | 11.3 | 24 | 0 | 26 | 50 | 2 | 11.3 |
| 401–500 | 22 | 0 | 13 | 35 | 1 | 12.7 | 25 | 0 | 25 | 50 | 2 | 11.1 | 28 | 0 | 47 | 75 | 3 | 9.8 |
| 501–600 | 22 | 0 | 14 | 36 | 1 | 12.5 | 25 | 0 | 30 | 55 | 2 | 10.9 | 28 | 0 | 47 | 75 | 3 | 9.8 |
| 601–800 | 22 | 0 | 14 | 36 | 1 | 12.5 | 26 | 0 | 29 | 55 | 2 | 10.8 | 28 | 0 | 47 | 75 | 3 | 9.8 |
| 801–1000 | 26 | 0 | 29 | 55 | 2 | 10.8 | 26 | 0 | 29 | 55 | 2 | 10.8 | 29 | 0 | 46 | 75 | 3 | 9.6 |
| 1001–2000 | 27 | 0 | 33 | 60 | 2 | 10.5 | 27 | 0 | 33 | 60 | 2 | 10.5 | 33 | 0 | 72 | 105 | 4 | 8.3 |
| 2001–3000 | 27 | 0 | 33 | 60 | 2 | 10.5 | 30 | 0 | 50 | 80 | 3 | 9.3 | 33 | 0 | 72 | 105 | 4 | 8.3 |
| 3001–4000 | 27 | 0 | 33 | 60 | 2 | 10.5 | 31 | 0 | 49 | 80 | 3 | 9.1 | 33 | 0 | 77 | 110 | 4 | 8.2 |
| 4001–5000 | 27 | 0 | 33 | 60 | 2 | 10.5 | 31 | 0 | 49 | 80 | 3 | 9.1 | 36 | 0 | 94 | 130 | 5 | 7.6 |
| 5001–7000 | 28 | 0 | 32 | 60 | 2 | 10.3 | 31 | 0 | 49 | 80 | 3 | 9.1 | 36 | 0 | 94 | 130 | 5 | 7.7 |
| 7001–10,000 | 28 | 0 | 32 | 60 | 2 | 10.3 | 31 | 0 | 49 | 80 | 3 | 9.2 | 36 | 0 | 94 | 130 | 5 | 7.7 |
| 10,001–20,000 | 28 | 0 | 32 | 60 | 2 | 10.3 | 31 | 0 | 49 | 80 | 3 | 9.2 | 36 | 0 | 94 | 130 | 5 | 7.8 |
| 20,001–50,000 | 28 | 0 | 32 | 60 | 2 | 10.3 | 33 | 0 | 87 | 120 | 4 | 7.7 | 70 | 1 | 145 | 215 | 8 | 6.6 |
| 50,001–100,000 | 28 | 0 | 37 | 65 | 2 | 10.2 | 33 | 0 | 92 | 125 | 4 | 7.6 | 70 | 1 | 170 | 240 | 9 | 6.4 |

| Lot size | Process average 1.01 to 1.50% | | | | | | Process average 1.51 to 2.00% | | | | | | Process average 2.01 to 2.50% | | | | | |
|---|---|---|---|---|---|---|---|---|---|---|---|---|---|---|---|---|---|---|
| | Trial 1 | | Trial 2 | | | $p_t$ % | Trial 1 | | Trial 2 | | | $p_t$ % | Trial 1 | | Trial 2 | | | $p_t$ % |
| | $n_1$ | $C_1$ | $n_2$ | $n_1 + n_2$ | $C_2$ | | $n_1$ | $C_1$ | $n_2$ | $n_1 + n_2$ | $C_2$ | | $n_1$ | $C_1$ | $n_2$ | $n_1 + n_2$ | $C_2$ | |
| 1–10 | All | 0 | | | | | All | 0 | | | | | All | 0 | | | | |
| 11–50 | 11 | 0 | | | | 17.6 | 11 | 0 | | | | 17.6 | 11 | 0 | | | | 17.6 |
| 51–100 | 18 | 0 | 10 | 28 | 1 | 14.1 | 20 | 0 | 20 | 40 | 2 | 13.0 | 20 | 0 | 20 | 40 | 2 | 13.0 |
| 101–200 | 23 | 0 | 25 | 48 | 2 | 11.7 | 23 | 0 | 25 | 48 | 2 | 11.7 | 25 | 0 | 35 | 60 | 3 | 10.8 |
| 201–300 | 26 | 0 | 44 | 70 | 3 | 10.3 | 26 | 0 | 44 | 70 | 3 | 10.3 | 28 | 0 | 57 | 85 | 4 | 9.5 |
| 301–400 | 27 | 0 | 43 | 70 | 3 | 9.9 | 29 | 0 | 61 | 90 | 4 | 9.3 | 49 | 1 | 71 | 120 | 6 | 8.8 |
| 401–500 | 28 | 0 | 47 | 75 | 3 | 9.8 | 30 | 0 | 60 | 90 | 4 | 9.2 | 50 | 1 | 80 | 130 | 6 | 8.4 |
| 501–600 | 30 | 0 | 65 | 95 | 4 | 9.1 | 30 | 0 | 65 | 95 | 4 | 9.1 | 55 | 1 | 95 | 150 | 7 | 8.0 |
| 601–800 | 31 | 0 | 69 | 100 | 4 | 8.8 | 55 | 1 | 85 | 140 | 6 | 8.0 | 60 | 1 | 115 | 175 | 8 | 7.6 |
| 801–1000 | 32 | 0 | 68 | 100 | 4 | 8.7 | 60 | 1 | 100 | 160 | 7 | 7.8 | 85 | 2 | 120 | 205 | 9 | 7.2 |
| 1001–2000 | 60 | 1 | 90 | 150 | 6 | 7.6 | 65 | 1 | 150 | 215 | 9 | 7.0 | 95 | 2 | 210 | 305 | 13 | 6.5 |
| 2001–3000 | 65 | 1 | 115 | 180 | 7 | 7.2 | 90 | 2 | 170 | 260 | 11 | 6.8 | 125 | 3 | 265 | 390 | 16 | 6.0 |
| 3001–4000 | 65 | 1 | 140 | 205 | 8 | 6.8 | 95 | 2 | 205 | 300 | 12 | 6.4 | 185 | 5 | 350 | 535 | 21 | 5.5 |
| 4001–5000 | 70 | 1 | 160 | 230 | 9 | 6.5 | 100 | 2 | 255 | 355 | 14 | 6.0 | 220 | 6 | 410 | 630 | 24 | 5.2 |
| 5001–7000 | 75 | 1 | 190 | 265 | 10 | 6.2 | 130 | 3 | 265 | 395 | 15 | 5.7 | 255 | 7 | 495 | 750 | 28 | 5.0 |
| 7001–10,000 | 100 | 2 | 195 | 295 | 11 | 6.0 | 140 | 3 | 355 | 495 | 18 | 5.3 | 325 | 9 | 665 | 990 | 36 | 4.7 |
| 10,001–20,000 | 105 | 2 | 215 | 320 | 12 | 5.9 | 170 | 4 | 380 | 550 | 20 | 5.2 | 360 | 10 | 830 | 1190 | 43 | 4.6 |
| 20,001–50,000 | 105 | 2 | 245 | 350 | 13 | 5.8 | 205 | 5 | 485 | 690 | 25 | 5.0 | 415 | 11 | 1145 | 1560 | 54 | 4.3 |
| 50,001–100,000 | 110 | 2 | 295 | 405 | 15 | 5.6 | 245 | 6 | 610 | 855 | 30 | 4.7 | 510 | 14 | 1370 | 1880 | 65 | 4.2 |

Trial 1: $n_1$ = first sample size; $C_1$ = acceptance number for first sample
'All' indicates that each piece in the lot is to be inspected
Trial 2: $n_2$ = second sample size; $C_2$ = acceptance number for first and second samples combined
$p_t$ = lot tolerance per cent defective with a Consumer's Risk ($P_C$) of 0.10

they are either unacceptable or necessitate some examination. Such limits are called *control limits*. For example, for a normal probability distribution, 99.73% of all chance or usual variations would be expected to occur within limits placed three standard deviations larger, and smaller, than the mean value of a variable. Therefore any variation occurring beyond such limits would probably have resulted from some other unusual or assignable cause and would merit some investigation.

For example, after a pilot investigation of the length of rods produced by an automatic guillotine, we discover that the mean length ($\bar{X}$) is 100 cm, and that after excluding the faulty rods that were produced when the setting was accidentally altered, the standard deviation[3] ($\sigma$), which is a measure of the variability of the rods produced, was 2.1 cm. We could then set up a control chart with a mean of 100 and control limits of plus and minus three standard deviations. Such a chart (Figure 20.16) might then be used to test the quality of rods then produced. Rather than examine every rod, we take a sample rod every hour and examine it, and then plot our result on the control chart, and by so doing we are able to discover that the process, through initially 'in control', is now running 'out of control' and often producing rods which are too long.

**Figure 20.16** Simple control chart

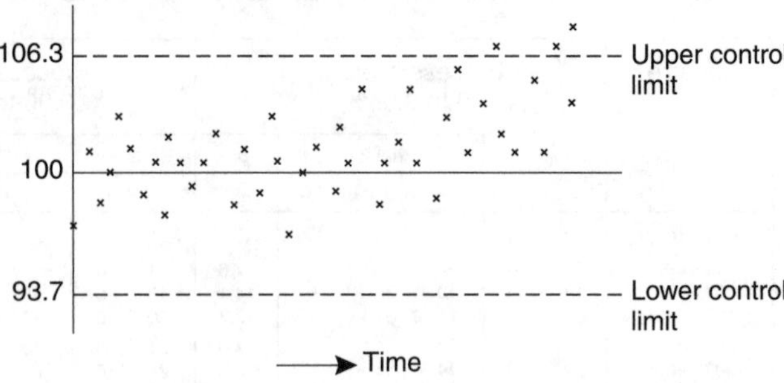


A process is considered to be statistically 'under control' or 'in control' if it regularly produces items whose attributes or variables fall within the acceptable or tolerable range, whereas a process is said to be 'out of control' if items are produced whose attributes or variables are beyond the acceptable or tolerable range. In this case (Figure 20.16) the process appears to have gone out of control because of a change in the mean value ($\bar{X}$).

This is only one of the three possible types of change which might occur in a process, i.e. in Figure 20.17 (1) has resulted from a change in the value of the mean, (2) has resulted from a change in the standard deviation, and (3) has resulted from a change in both of these characteristics. Each of these changes or disturbances in the process might lead to the production of defective items, but in each case the use of a control chart to monitor output will enable such items to be observed and action to be taken to prevent the production of defective items.

Control charts would therefore be used as follows:

*Step 1* Decide which characteristics of the items are to be controlled.

*Step 2* Conduct a pilot study of the process to determine the mean and the standard deviation of the characteristics.

*Step 3* Design the control chart(s) using these data.

*Step 4* Check the control limits to ensure that they are economically feasible and realistic.

*Step 5* Take samples of the process output and plot the characteristics on the control charts.

*Step 6* Whenever points fall beyond the control limits:

(a) investigate causes;

(b) take corrective action;

(c) inspect remainder of batch if necessary.

---

[3] The standard deviation ($\sigma$) is calculated using the formula:

$$\sigma = \sqrt{\frac{\Sigma(\bar{X} - X^2)}{\bar{N}}}$$

where $X$ = length of individual bar
$\bar{X}$ = mean length of all bars
$\bar{N}$ = number of bars

**Figure 20.17** Frequency distribution showing types of change which might occur in a process

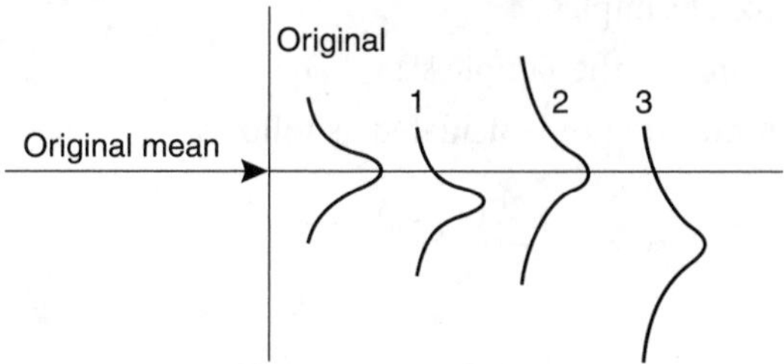


## Control charts for variables

Control charts for variables are usually based on the normal probability distribution and are usually designed to test the *means* of samples rather than individual measurements. The main reason why means are used is that, even when the actual distribution of a variable resulting from a process does not conform to the normal distribution, sample means will tend to be distributed normally. This is known as the central limit theorem of statistics. In practice, therefore, the dimensions of individual components are not plotted separately on control charts; only the *mean*, or average value, of the dimensions in the sample is plotted. Because we are now concerned with a distribution of means, the standard deviation ($\sigma_{\bar{x}}$) is calculated by a different formula, as follows:

$$\sigma_{\bar{x}} = \frac{\sigma}{\sqrt{n}}$$

where $\sigma_{\bar{x}}$ = standard deviation of mean values of samples

$\sigma$ = standard deviation of individuals

$n$ = sample size

Two upper and two lower control limits are normally used, these being referred to as the *upper and lower warning limit* and the *upper and lower action limit.* If points fall beyond the warning limits, this is taken to indicate that the process may be going out of control and that careful observation or additional sampling is required. Points falling beyond the action limits indicate the need to take immediate steps to establish and to eliminate the causes. Action limits are normally set so as to exclude only 0.2% of the points through usual or random variations. Warning limits are set so as to exclude 5% of the points through usual or random variation, i.e.

$$\text{Upper action limit} = \bar{X} + 3.09\sigma/\sqrt{n}$$
$$\text{Upper warning limit} = \bar{X} + 1.96\sigma/\sqrt{n}$$
$$\text{Centre} = \bar{X}$$
$$\text{Lower warning limit} = \bar{X} - 1.96\sigma/\sqrt{n}$$
$$\text{Lower action limit} = \bar{X} - 3.09\sigma/\sqrt{n}$$

where $\bar{X}$ = overall process mean value

In practice it is a little tiresome to calculate standard deviations for samples, and consequently the *range* is usually used as a measure of variability in place of the standard deviation. The *range* is merely the difference between the largest dimension and the smallest, and for small samples it has been shown that:

$$\sigma = \frac{\bar{w}_x}{d_n}$$

where $\sigma$ = standard deviation of individual items

$\bar{w}_x$ = mean range of several samples

$d_n$ = a constant depending on the sample size

Consequently, our control limits are now calculated as follows:

$$\text{Upper action limit} = \bar{X} + \frac{3.09(\bar{w}_x/d_n)}{\sqrt{n}}$$

$$\text{Upper warning limit} = \bar{X} + \frac{1.96(\bar{w}_x/d_n)}{\sqrt{n}}$$

$$\text{Centre ( = process mean)} = \bar{X}$$

$$\text{Lower warning limit} = \bar{X} - \frac{1.96(\bar{w}_x/d_n)}{\sqrt{n}}$$

$$\text{Lower action limit} = \bar{X} - \frac{3.09(\bar{w}_x/d_n)}{\sqrt{n}}$$

To simplify such calculations even further, tables for $3.09/\sqrt{n}d_n$ and $1.96/\sqrt{n}d_n$ can be used (see Table 20.2).

Even though the mean value is constant, we have seen how the process might produce defective items by an increase in variability (Figure 20.17). Consequently, a process cannot be said to be fully under control unless *both* mean and standard deviation are under control. We should, therefore, also construct a control chart on which to plot standard deviations but, for the same reasons as before, it is found to be easier to use the range as a measure of variability. In much the same way as for control limits for means, factors can be calculated from which control limits for ranges can be established. These are shown in Table 20.3.

**Table 20.2 Factors for calculating control limits for control charts for means**

| **Sample size** *n* | **Constant** $d_n$ | **Factors (*m*) for warning limits** $= \frac{1.96}{\sqrt{n}d_n}$ | **Factors (*m*) for action limits** $= \frac{3.09}{\sqrt{n}d_n}$ |
|---|---|---|---|
| 2 | 1.128 | 1.23 | 1.94 |
| 3 | 1.693 | 0.67 | 1.05 |
| 4 | 2.059 | 0.48 | 0.75 |
| 5 | 2.236 | 0.38 | 0.59 |
| 6 | 2.334 | 0.32 | 0.50 |
| 7 | 2.704 | 0.27 | 0.43 |
| 8 | 2.847 | 0.24 | 0.38 |
| 9 | 2.970 | 0.22 | 0.35 |
| 10 | 3.078 | 0.20 | 0.32 |

*Note:* To calculate control limits, multiply $\bar{w}_x$ by factor (*m*) and add or subtract from $\bar{x}$.

**Table 20.3 Factors for calculating control limits for control charts for ranges**

| Sample size $n$ | Factor ($R$) for warning limits | | Factor ($R$) for action limits | |
|---|---|---|---|---|
| | Upper | Lower | Upper | Lower |
| 2 | 2.81 | 0.04 | 4.12 | 0.00 |
| 3 | 2.17 | 0.18 | 2.98 | 0.04 |
| 4 | 1.93 | 0.29 | 2.57 | 0.10 |
| 5 | 1.81 | 0.37 | 2.34 | 0.16 |
| 6 | 1.72 | 0.42 | 2.21 | 0.21 |
| 7 | 1.66 | 0.46 | 2.11 | 0.26 |
| 8 | 1.62 | 0.50 | 2.04 | 0.29 |
| 9 | 1.58 | 0.52 | 1.99 | 0.32 |
| 10 | 1.56 | 0.54 | 1.94 | 0.35 |

Note: To calculate control limit, multiply $\bar{w}_x$ by the appropriate factor ($R$)

**EXAMPLE**

## *Bottling liqueur*

A process is used to fill bottles. Each bottle should contain 12 cl.

A random sample of five bottles is taken each hour, and for each sample the mean and range are calculated as shown in the table, right.

From an earlier pilot study the overall mean ($\bar{X}$) and the average range ($\bar{w}$) have been found to be:

$\bar{X} = 11.9994; \quad \bar{w} = 0.0091$

| Sample (size $n$ = 5) | Sample mean ($\bar{x}$) | Sample range ($w_x$) |
|---|---|---|
| 9.00 a.m. | 12.005 | 0.007 |
| 10.00 a.m. | 12.001 | 0.008 |
| 11.00 a.m. | 11.993 | 0.010 |
| 12.00 | 11.991 | 0.003 |
| 1.00 p.m. | 12.001 | 0.006 |
| 2.00 p.m. | 12.003 | 0.015 |
| 3.00 p.m. | 11.995 | 0.011 |
| 4.00 p.m. | 12.004 | 0.008 |
| 5.00 p.m. | 12.003 | 0.009 |
| 6.00 p.m. | 12.000 | 0.010 |
| 7.00 p.m. | 11.999 | 0.006 |
| 8.00 p.m. | 11.997 | 0.013 |
| 9.00 p.m. | 11.999 | 0.011 |
| 10.00 p.m. | 12.000 | 0.010 |
| *Total* | 167.991 | 0.127 |

Now, using the factors from Table 20.2 and 20.3, control limits for means and ranges can be calculated:

$$\text{Mean} \begin{cases} \text{UAL} = 11.9994 + 0.59(0.0091) = 12.0048 \\ \text{UWL} = 11.9994 + 0.38(0.0091) = 12.0029 \\ \text{Centre} = 11.9994 \\ \text{LWL} = 11.9994 - 0.38(0.0091) = 11.9959 \\ \text{LAL} = 11.9994 - 0.59(0.0091) = 11.9940 \end{cases}$$

$$\text{Range} \begin{cases} \text{UAL} = 0.0091 \times 2.34 = 0.0213 \\ \text{UWL} = 0.0091 \times 1.81 = 0.0165 \\ \text{Centre} = 0.0091 \\ \text{LWL} = 0.0091 \times 0.37 = 0.0034 \\ \text{LAL} = 0.0091 \times 0.16 = 0.0015 \end{cases}$$

The control charts can now be constructed using these figures and the individual sample means and ranges plotted (Figure 20.18). The charts indicate that the process is beginning to settle down. The means from early samples were probably unacceptable (see 'Control Limits and Design Limits' later in this chapter) but towards the end of the day the process was under better control.

**Figure 20.18** Control chart for means and for range

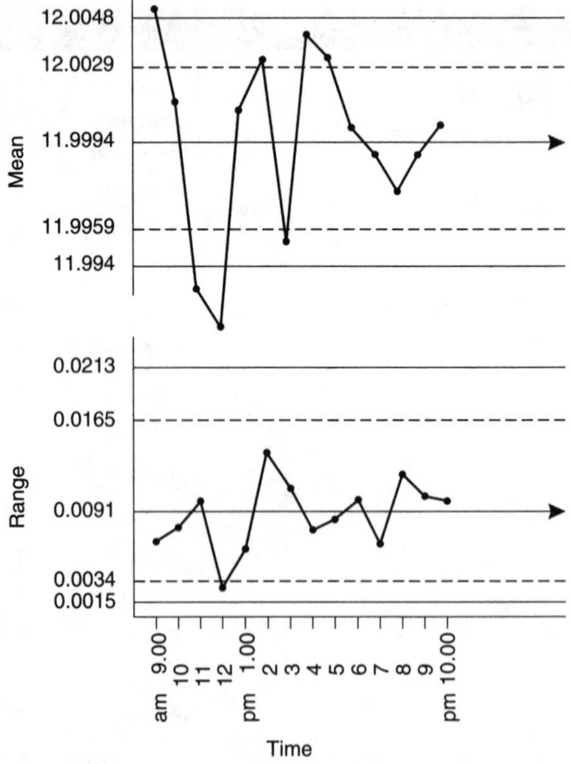

## Control charts for attributes

Often, as was the case in acceptance sampling, it is possible after inspecting items to classify them only as 'good' or 'bad', as 'acceptable' or 'not acceptable', and it is for reasons such as these that control charts for attributes have been devised. Such charts are developed in much the same way as were control charts for variables.

Two types of chart are most popular:

(a) control chart for *proportion* or *per cent* defective;

(b) control chart for *number* of defects.

The method of using the charts is similar to that outlined previously, except that in this case, rather than calculate the mean and range of all the items in each random sample, only the number or the percentage of defective items in the sample is calculated.

Control charts for *proportion* or *per cent defective* are known as *p-charts*. Control limits are constructed after a pilot investigation and if, during operation, the proportion of defectives in a sample falls within these limits the process is considered to be 'under control', whereas if the proportion of defectives in a sample falls beyond these limits this is taken to be a good indication that the process is, for some reason, out of control and that some investigation and corrective action are required.

An estimate of the proportion of defectives produced by the process is obtained after a pilot study consisting of several samples, i.e.

$$\bar{p} = \frac{\text{Total number of defectives in 10 to 20 samples}}{\text{Total number inspected}}$$

0.2% (and less frequently 5%) control limits are set in the usual way, i.e.

Action limits $= \bar{p} \pm 3.09\sigma_{\bar{p}}$

where $\bar{p}$ = proportion of defectives produced by the process

$\sigma_{\bar{p}}$ = standard deviation of this distribution

The statistical theory of the binomial probability distribution is used, by which it can be shown that:

$$\sigma_{\bar{p}} = \sqrt{\frac{\bar{p}(1-\bar{p})}{n}}$$

Consequently, the action limits are set at:

$$\text{Upper: } \bar{p} + 3.09 = \sqrt{\frac{\bar{p}(1-\bar{p})}{n}} \qquad (\text{where } \bar{p} < 0.1)$$

$$\text{Lower: } \bar{p} - 3.09 = \sqrt{\frac{\bar{p}(1-\bar{p})}{n}}$$

where $n$ = sample size

**EXAMPLE**

## Mail sorting

An automatic machine sorts letters in a large post office. A manual check is kept on the machine. About 200 letters are checked each hour to see if they have been sorted correctly. The data from one day's work are given below. Construct a *p*-chart and examine the data.

Throughput for previous week = 10 000

Number of defectives included in that throughput = 370

| Time of sample | Sample size ($n$) | Numbers in defectives in sample | $p$ |
|---|---|---|---|
| 9.00 a.m. | 205 | 12 | 0.0585 |
| 10.00 a.m. | 206 | 14 | 0.07 |
| 11.00 a.m. | 195 | 12 | 0.0615 |
| 12.00 | 200 | 15 | 0.075 |
| 1.00 p.m | 210 | 14 | 0.0665 |
| 2.00 p.m. | 195 | 12 | 0.0615 |
| 3.00 p.m. | 200 | 15 | 0.075 |
| 4.00 p.m. | 200 | 16 | 0.080 |
| 5.00 p.m. | 205 | 13 | 0.0635 |
| 6.00 p.m. | 195 | 14 | 0.0715 |
| 7.00 p.m. | 200 | 15 | 0.075 |
| 8.00 p.m. | 195 | 14 | 0.0715 |

The proportion of defectives produced by the machine can in this case be estimated from the figures given for the previous week's throughput, i.e.

$$\bar{p} = \frac{370}{10\,000} = 0.037$$

Therefore, upper action limit is: $\bar{p} + 3.09\sqrt{\frac{\bar{p}(1-\bar{p})}{n}}$

$$= 0.037 + 3.09\sqrt{\frac{0.037(0.963)}{200}}$$

$$= 0.0785$$

This action limit is shown on the *p*-chart given as Figure 20.19. The proportion of defectives in each of the 12 samples is plotted on the chart, from which it can be seen that, compared with the previous week's throughput, the proportion of defectives in the batches has increased, and the process is almost 'out of control'.

**Figure 20.19** *p*-chart

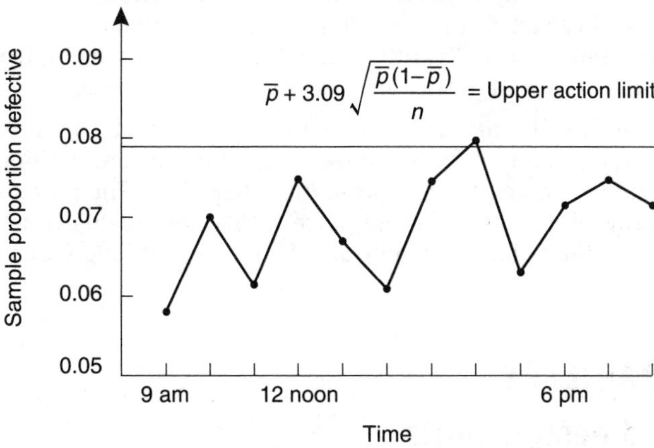


Since the control limits for a *p*-chart are a function of *n* (the sample size), when the sample size changes the control limits must also change (e.g. Figure 20.20). In the above example, the sample size was nearly constant, and hence a mean $n = 200$ was taken.

**Figure 20.20** A proportion defective control chart (*p*-chart) in which the sample size, *n*, has changed

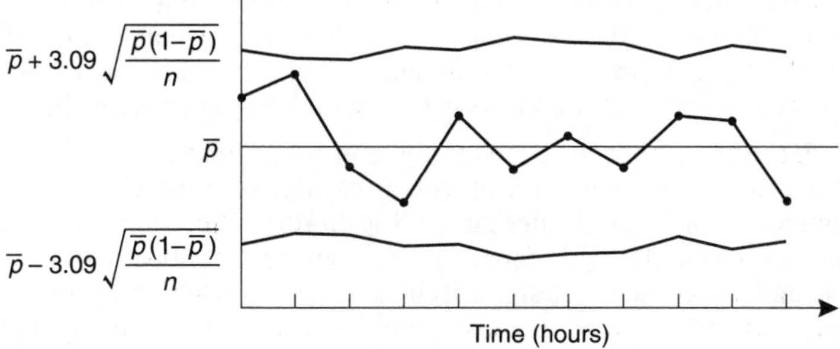


Control charts for *number* of defects are known as *c*-charts and are of particular value for controlling the number of defects in, or on, a particular unit, i.e. a single item, a group of items, or a part of an item. For example, the *c*-chart might be used to control the quality of cloth by counting the number of defects in a roll, to control the quality of a riveted structure by counting the number of faulty rivets, etc. Conditions such as these enable the Poisson distribution to be used. The symbol $\bar{c}$ is the average number of defects per unit obtained after a pilot investigation over several samples. The standard deviation of the Poisson distribution is given by $\sqrt{\bar{c}}$ consequently, the control limits are set at:

Upper action = $\bar{c} + 3.09\sqrt{\bar{c}}$ (where $\bar{c} < 15$)

Lower action = $\bar{c} - 3.09\sqrt{\bar{c}}$

The manner in which *c*-charts are constructed and used is very similar to the construction and use of *p*-charts.

## Cumulative sum techniques in quality control

The control chart is a useful and convenient method of recording successive readings, and it provides a clear presentation of historical data. The action limits are a convenient device for prompting corrective action, but unfortunately it is often difficult to detect small changes in the mean value of observations. In fact the control chart is basically a means of studying observations independently, rather than a method of studying trends in a series of observations. This insensitivity is to some extent overcome by the use of warning limits, but even so it is often desirable in quality control to use a procedure which is more sensitive to small changes in mean values.

The principal advantage of the *cumulative sum* (*cusum*) *chart*[4] is its ability to show such changes; indeed the cusum chart actually emphasizes changes in such mean values. Cumulative sum charts can also be constructed for ranges and number or proportion defectives. Their use, in the manner outlined above, maximizes the value of the data collected, since, unlike control charts, which concentrate attention on the latest figures, cusum charts promote an examination of long sequences of data.

## PROCESS CAPABILITY

### Control limits and design limits

The use of control charts permits us to determine whether a process is 'statistically' in control or not. By establishing action limits and plotting observations on a chart we can determine when to take appropriate remedial action or, using warning limits, appropriate preventive action. The positioning of these limits, however, is based on observations of the actual items received, or items output from a process. If we consider the latter, i.e. items produced by a process, then the establishment of the control chart involves us in considering the normal performance of the processes in order to establish limits beyond which output can be considered to be abnormal for those same circumstances. Thus if a process is highly reliable and extremely accurate, the control chart limits will be set relatively close to the mean. If, perhaps many years later, the same process becomes unreliable, the equipment worn, etc., then the normal variability in, for example, the dimensions of an item produced by the process will be greater, and thus the action and warning limits will be set further away from the overall mean.

It should be noted, therefore, that the limits set on control charts bear no direct relationship to the limits set in the specification for items. If a process is capable of producing items with considerable accuracy and extremely reliably, but the design specification for those items is very 'loose', then it is possible that, by using control charts designed in the manner described above, we will reject items which are acceptable under the original design specification. Conversely, if a process is not consistently capable of producing items to fine tolerances, yet the design tolerances for the item are very narrow, then it is possible, in using a control chart, to accept items which are not acceptable against the original design specification.

For these reasons we must consider the relationship between control chart limits and design or specification limits, and in doing so we must consider the question of *process capability*.

The use of the mean and range charts shows us whether a process is in statistical control or not, but does not necessarily given any adequate indication of whether individual items are acceptable within specification limits. Organizations are concerned primarily with ensuring that items are within the intended specification tolerance rather than being under 'statistical' control overall.

It will be recalled that in discussing the design of control charts for items we chose to use charts for mean values for reasons of convenience. Ideally we would have liked to set up control charts for individual observations in the manner shown below:

$$UAL_{\text{individuals}} = \text{Overall mean} + 3.90\sigma$$
$$LAL_{\text{individuals}} = \text{Overall mean} - 3.09\sigma$$

---

[4] See Appendix II.

We chose instead to set up a control chart for mean values as follows:

$$UAL_{means} = \text{Overall mean} + 3.09 \frac{\sigma}{\sqrt{n}}$$

$$LAL_{means} = \text{Overall mean} - 3.09 \frac{\sigma}{\sqrt{n}}$$

In fact the action limits for a control chart based on mean values are somewhat narrower than those that would be established for the same population of individuals. It follows, therefore, that if in using control charts based on mean values we are to be sure that individual items conform to design specifications, the design limits must be placed well beyond the action limits of a mean control chart. This relationship is shown in Figure 20.21. If the design limits are within the action limits for the means chart, or even just beyond those limits, then it is possible that, using the means chart, individual items will be accepted which do not conform to the specification limits.

**Figure 20.21** Comparison of action limits and possible specification limits

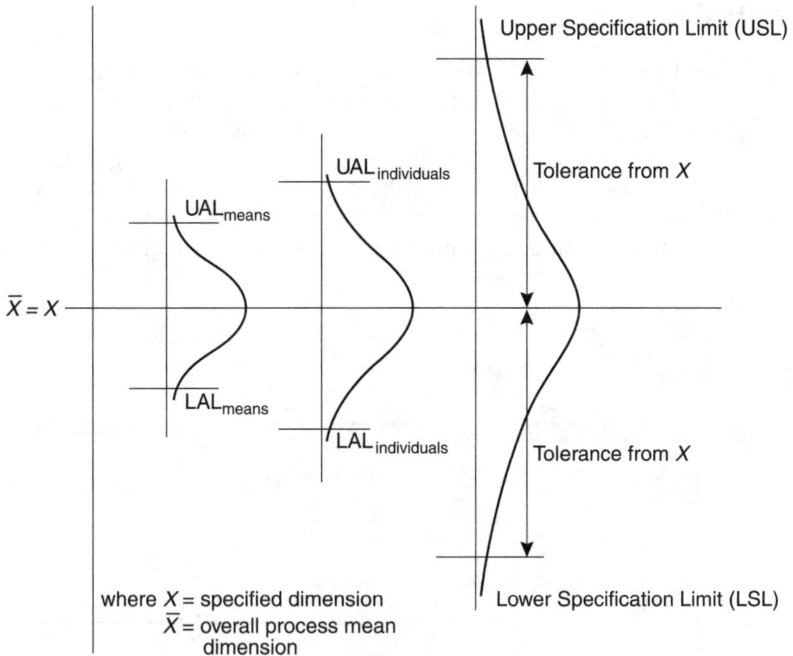


## Process capability measurement

In studying process capability we shall be concerned with the extent to which a process is capable of processing items that correspond to the design specification limits.

A measure of process capability can be obtained as follows:

$$PC = \frac{USL - LSL}{\sigma}$$

where PC = process capability
USL = upper specification limit
LSL = lower specification limit
$\sigma$ = standard deviation of individual items

Strictly, this measure of process capability applies only where the specification tolerances are distributed symmetrically about the intended dimension, and where the overall mean dimension produced by a process is the same as the intended dimension. In these circumstances, where the value of PC is less than 6, more than 2% of defective items will be produced, hence either the process variability must be improved or the specification tolerances must be increased. For a value between 6 and 11 the process may be controlled in the manner described above using a mean control chart. Where the value is greater than 11 then the use of a mean control chart may imply the use of a quality control procedure which is far tighter than is actually required. In these circumstances it may be appropriate to use modified action limits in the manner described later. Alternatively it may be appropriate, or indeed necessary, to retain action limits which are very much narrower than the specification limits in order to allow some 'drift' in the mean value, and in such cases the use of the dynamic control chart approach described below may be useful.

## Dynamic control charts

Another factor can now be considered. In many situations, because of the nature of the process, there will be a 'drift' in a variable over a period of time. For example, the size of manufactured items might increase because of tool wear, or the weight of items might reduce as working temperatures increase. In these situations we must seek to control the quality of items in a changing situation: this is feasible if the design limits on a variable are greater than the control chart limits. In these cases we can use a dynamic control chart of the type shown in Figure 20.22. Such charts are more easily used for the control of variable means. The original action limits must be set up just within one of the design limits

**Figure 20.22** 'Dynamic' control chart for mean

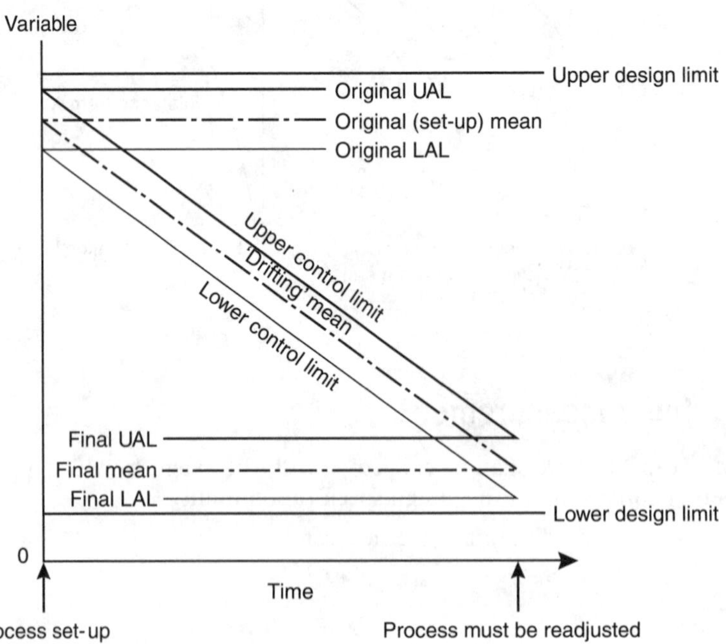

(either the upper or lower design limit, depending on the direction of the 'drift' which will take place). The final action limits, at the point at which the process must be readjusted, are just within the other design limits. Since the standard deviation is independent of the process mean we can join these extreme limits, as shown in Figure 20.22, to provide control limits for use with the 'drifting' mean over a period of time. To construct such a chart for use over a future period of time we must know the rate of change in the mean value, as otherwise we will not know what time-scale to use on the chart. If this is not known it will be necessary to construct the chart step by step, by calculating the new mean value from time to time. (This in turn may result in a 'stepped' chart.)

### Modified action limits

Where a process is inherently capable of producing items very consistently with very small variation in dimension, it may be possible to modify the control to provide wider action limits than would otherwise have been employed. This approach may be appropriate, since it can be unnecessarily expensive to try to maintain the process in statistical control if in fact items which fall beyond the control limits are still acceptable within broader specification limits. In these cases modified action limits can be established as follows:

$$\text{Modified UAL}_{\text{means}} = \text{USL} - 309\sigma + 3.09\frac{\sigma}{\sqrt{n}}$$

$$\text{Modified LAL}_{\text{means}} = \text{LSL} + 309\sigma - 3.09\frac{\sigma}{\sqrt{n}}$$

The use of such an approach again permits the process mean to change provided the sample mean values are within the modified action limits. The approach therefore is similar to that shown in Figure 20.22 except in this case the establishment of these broader modified action control limits permits the process mean to 'wander' whereas the 'dynamic control chart' is designed specifically to deal with the situation in which the mean drifts in a known direction.

## COMPUTERS IN QUALITY CONTROL

Many computer software packages are available for use in the broadly defined area of quality management.

A simple categorization of applications is as follows:

(a) ***data accumulation***, on item and process properties, i.e. the collection, organization and filing of data on quality levels, reject ratios, breakdown rates, customer complaints, etc. for use in decision-making on design, equipment replacement, pricing, etc.

(b) ***data reduction***, analysis and reporting, i.e. deriving from the above the analysis of data for presentation in, for example, graphical form;

(c) ***real time process control***, i.e. direct process monitoring and control to ensure the achievement of given quality requirements;

(d) ***automated inspection and testing***, perhaps associated with (c) above, but also to replace the manual monitoring of incoming or outgoing items;

(e) ***statistical analysis*** of data, e.g. of sample data to construct control charts and to make accept/reject decisions.

Item (e) above is of particular relevance to this chapter. Some examples of the use of computer-based quality control and assurance procedures are given in the following cases. Further sources of information are given in the Further Reading section for this chapter.

EXAMPLE

### 'OMAX+'

OMAX+ is a microcomputer-based quality improvement measurement system. It is a modified and enhanced version of the 'objectives matrix' approach for productivity and quality measurement, and is specifically designed for use by organizations engaged in total quality control (TQC). OMAX+ provides a useful measurement tool to quantify and monitor quality improvements. It is a self-contained program for PCs.

Source: Safford, R. R., Gobeli, D. H. and Suen, K. P. (1990) OMAX+: an advanced quality improvement measurement system. *Computers and Industrial Engineering*, **19**(1–4), pp. 267–271.

EXAMPLE

### SPC at ESNA

ESNA is one of the world's leading manufacturers of fasteners for the aerospace industries. Until recently, the company's quality assurance focused on, primarily, post-production inspection. A worker would prepare a machine for a production run, make a small sample of items, and then wait until a quality control inspector came to approve the set-up. At the end of the production run, an inspector would measure a sample and record data on a chart. This information was then plotted on control charts. Often it took several days to produce the charts. ESNA set out to implement a new statistical process control procedure. They installed several hand-held data collection terminals to give workers and QC staff almost immediate feedback on the quality of products and processes.

Source: Kendrick, J. J. (1990) SPC used to tighten fastener QC. *Quality*, **29**(10), p. 85.

EXAMPLE

### General Dynamics

Multi-level inspection sampling plans adopt the strategy that as the level of achieved quality increases, the sampling activity decreases. General Dynamics' Air Defense Systems Division in California incorporated such multi-level sampling into a program called the systematic process observation technique (SPOT). SPOT is used to audit individual part characteristics for conformance. With SPOT, a personal computer randomly selects a fraction of the available features for audit based on the sampling level that the process has achieved. A spreadsheet program is used to administer the sampling plans. With this approach quality control resources are more effectively and efficiently utilized. SPOT has reduced tedious 'output' inspection, replacing it with more effective, in-process, quality control audits. It has also improved quality feedback of process performance.

Source: Glaccum, J. F. (1991) Combining multilevel sampling plans and personal computers. *Quality Progress*, **24**(9), pp. 75–78.

## RELIABILITY OF ITEMS

The reliability of items was considered above in connection with the specification and achievement of quality. We have seen that quality, reliability and cost are linked, higher quality being associated with higher reliability and often some higher costs. In Chapter 21 we shall consider the maintenance and replacement of facilities. There again, consideration of reliability is relevant, since the higher the reliability the less the need for replacement and maintenance. We shall also have cause to mention reliability in a slightly different context in discussing performance measurement in Chapter 22.

Clearly, therefore, the reliability of items, products and facilities is an important consideration in design. It is of relevance to the user, and is a factor to consider in quality management and in maintenance and replacement. It merits some further consideration at this point.

## Failure

We tend to think of unreliability in terms of failure. An item which is prone to frequent failure will be considered to be unreliable. A reliable item would be one which is expected to operate for long periods of time without failure. However, we should not overlook the fact that the ways in which items fail may differ. Some items may suddenly cease to operate, while others may operate poorly or partially.

Failure is the termination of the ability of an item to perform its required function. We can consider failure in four classes, as follows:

(a) As to cause:

1. misuse failure;
2. inherent weakness failure.

(b) As to suddenness:

1. sudden failure;
2. gradual failure.

(c) As to extent:

1. partial failure (i.e. deviation from specified characteristics but not enough to cause total loss of function);
2. complete failure.

Hence:

(d) Catastrophic failure = (b)(1) + (c)(2)

Degradation failure = (b)(2) + (c)(1)

Clearly the cause, nature, manner and consequences of failure will vary. Thus in seeking to examine or in some way measure reliability of any item or process we must first be clear about what constitutes reliable operation and what constitutes a failure. Only having defined these terms, for our particular circumstances, can we then set out to study and/or measure reliability.

## Reliability characteristics and measures

The curves shown in Figure 20.23 are reliability distributions. They are different ways of illustrating the classic component reliability pattern which is found for some types of equipment. Each curve is in fact a different type of measure of reliability. The terms used in Figure 20.23 are defined in Table 20.4 and discussed below. The example on pp. 639–40 shows how the various reliability measures can be calculated. This example (and the descriptions below) concerns a situation in which a test has begun on a given number of items at time $t = 0$. In this test the number of items failing in each time period is counted, and from these data the various reliability measures can be calculated.

**Figure 20.23** Reliability distributions

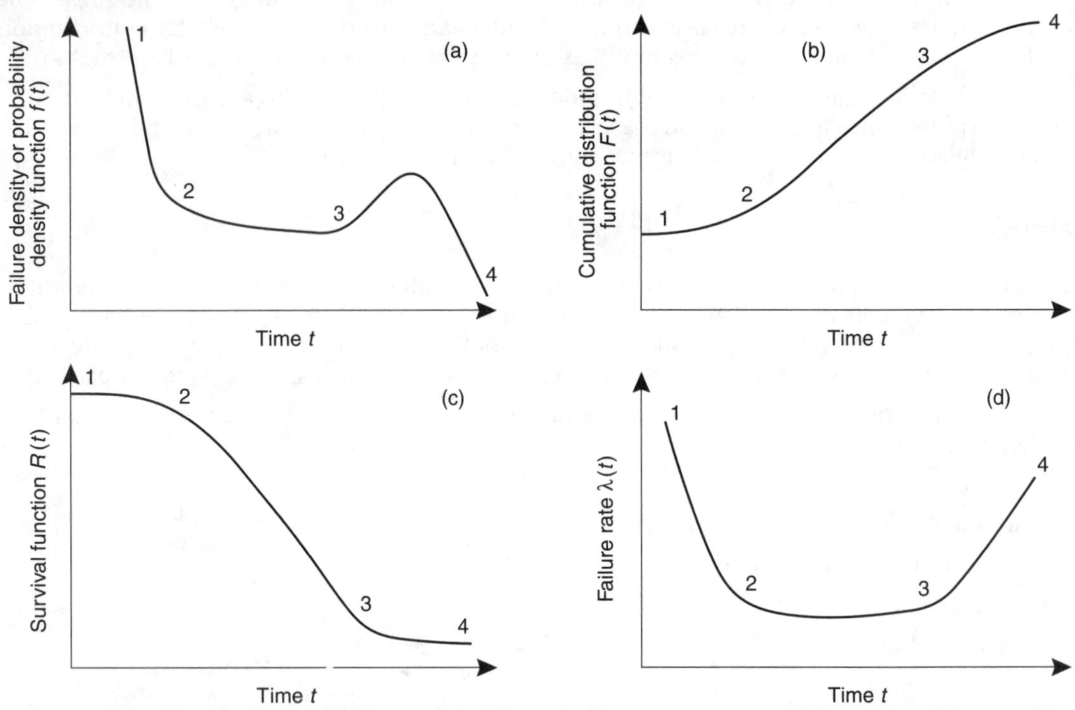


**Table 20.4 Reliability distribution terminology**

| Terms from Figure 20.23 | | Definition |
|---|---|---|
| Probability distribution (Failure density) | $= f(t)$ | Number of failures per unit time, expressed as a fraction of the original total number of parts under examination. |
| Cumulative distribution | $= F(t)$<br>$= \int f(t)dt$ | Cumulative number of failures up to any time $t$, expressed as a fraction of the original total number of parts under examination. |
| Survival function | $= R(t)$<br>$= 1 - F(t)$ | Cumulative number of survivors up to any time $t$, expressed as a fraction of the original total number of parts under examination. |
| Failure rate | $= \lambda(t)$<br>$= \frac{f(t)}{1 - F(t)}$ | Number of failures per unit time, expressed as a fraction of the number of survivors at the end of that time interval. |

## Failure probability ($f(t)$)

This gives, at any instant in time, the probability of the failure of an item which was working satisfactorily at time $t = 0$.

The curve shown in Figure 20.23(a) shows high probability of item failure in early life, falling for a period only to begin to rise again as items begin to wear out. The peak in the latter part of the curve (3–4) represents the mean 'wear-out' life of items. After this point we are left only with the more reliable items in operation.

## Cumulative failure probability ($F(t)$)

This is the cumulative measure of the probability of failure. It is in effect the probability of all items having failed after a given time (Figure 20.23(b)).

## Survival function ($R(t)$)

This is a measure of survival, i.e. the opposite of failure. It gives the cumulative probability of survival. It is in effect the probability of all items surviving after a given time (Figure 20.23(c)).

## Failure rate ($\lambda(t)$)

This is a measure of the probability that an item which was working satisfactorily at the beginning of a given time period will fail during that time period. It is, in effect, a measure of the risk that an item will fail during a particular period of time. The curve for $\lambda(t)$ shown in Figure 20.23(d) is the classic 'bathtub' pattern. It clearly shows the three phases of reliability, i.e.

1–2 'burn-in' or 'infant mortality' or 'early life' failure;
2–3 'random' or 'normal operating' or 'middle life' failure;
3–4 'wear-out' or 'old age' failure.

**EXAMPLE**

### *Reliability*

There were 100 items in use at the start of a test period. The items are checked every hour. The values of $f(t)$, $F(t)$, $R(t)$ and $\lambda(t)$ are to be calculated.

**Data**

| Time elapsed (h) | Failures (in past hour) | Cumulative failures | $f(t)$ | $F(t)$ | $R(t)$ | $\lambda(t)$ |
|---|---|---|---|---|---|---|
| 1 | 10 | 10 | 0.1 | 0.1 | 0.9 | 0.11 |
| 2 | 8 | 18 | 0.08 | 0.18 | 0.82 | 0.09 |
| 3 | 6 | 24 | 0.06 | 0.24 | 0.76 | 0.08 |
| 4 | 5 | 29 | 0.05 | 0.29 | 0.71 | 0.07 |
| 5 | 4 | 33 | 0.04 | 0.33 | 0.67 | 0.06 |
| 6 | 5 | 38 | 0.05 | 0.38 | 0.62 | 0.08 |
| 7 | 3 | 41 | 0.03 | 0.41 | 0.59 | 0.05 |
| 8 | 2 | 43 | 0.02 | 0.43 | 0.57 | 0.04 |
| 9 | 1 | 44 | 0.01 | 0.44 | 0.56 | 0.02 |

| Data | | | | | | |
|---|---|---|---|---|---|---|
| Time elapsed (h) | Failures (in past hour) | Cumulative failures | $f(t)$ | $F(t)$ | $R(t)$ | $\lambda(t)$ |
| 10 | 0 | 44 | 0.00 | 0.44 | 0.56 | - |
| 11 | 0 | 44 | 0.00 | 0.44 | 0.56 | - |
| 12 | 1 | 45 | 0.01 | 0.45 | 0.55 | 0.02 |
| 13 | 3 | 48 | 0.03 | 0.48 | 0.52 | 0.06 |
| 14 | 4 | 52 | 0.04 | 0.52 | 0.48 | 0.08 |
| 15 | 7 | 59 | 0.07 | 0.59 | 0.41 | 0.17 |
| 16 | 6 | 65 | 0.06 | 0.65 | 0.35 | 0.17 |
| 17 | 7 | 72 | 0.07 | 0.72 | 0.28 | 0.25 |
| 18 | 6 | 78 | 0.06 | 0.78 | 0.22 | 0.27 |
| 19 | 5 | 83 | 0.05 | 0.83 | 0.17 | 0.29 |
| 20 | 4 | 87 | 0.04 | 0.87 | 0.13 | 0.13 |

Two other measures of component or item reliability will often be encountered. The mean time between failures (MTBF) is the measure of the operating life of items between failures. The mean time to failure (MTTF) is, strictly, a measure of the operating life of an item up to its first failure. Strictly speaking these two measures are different. The MTBF should be used for items which are repaired on failure whereas the MTTF should be used for items which are replaced rather than repaired on failure. In practice the two terms have become confused and there is a tendency to use the MTBF measure for both repaired and replaced items. There is a tendency to use MTBF as a measure of reliability when the failure rate is approximately constant. However, strictly, MTBF is a function of time, particularly when we are concerned with the system which is dependent on the operation of many components. When the system is first operated with all new components the MTBF will be high. After that the mean time between failures may fluctuate until, after several failures and replacements, it will stabilize at a lower value, given by the following equation, which shows the relationship between MTBF and MTTF for a system comprising many components:

$$\frac{1}{\text{MTBF}} = \sum_{j=1}^{m} \frac{1}{\bar{T}_j}$$

where the system has $m$ components of different ages, each of which is replaced immediately following failure, and where $\bar{T}_j$ is the MTTF of the $j$th component.

In analysing item reliability we must consider each of the three phases of the reliability distributions shown in Figure 20.23. Following a period of decreasing failure rate during the 'infant mortality' period, the failure rate would be expected to remain relatively constant during 'middle age' and then to increase again during the old age period. Analysis of reliability during these periods necessitates the use of appropriate formulae to describe these three essentially different curves. The Weibull distribution is often used for this purpose. It is, in effect, a generalization of the exponential distribution and can be expressed, for the survival function, as follows:

$$R(t) = \exp\left[\frac{-(t-\gamma)^{\beta}}{\alpha}\right]$$

where $\gamma$ is the 'locating' constant on the time axis (origin of the distribution)

$\alpha$ is a 'scaling' constant ('characteristic life')

$\beta$ is a 'shaping' constant (Weibull slope)

Suitable choice of these three constants enables the Weibull distribution to be used to fit or simulate each of the three phases of the reliability curve.

## Reliability estimation

The Weibull formulation above may be used to estimate the reliability of items and products in service. Such estimates will be of value in design and in determining maintenance policies, etc.

First the three distribution constants $\alpha$, $\beta$ and $\gamma$ must be determined. This is most easily done by the use of Weibull probability graph paper, which has logarithmic scales. When $\gamma$ is zero, the cumulative percentage failures plotted on the graph will fall in a straight line,[5] the slope of which gives the value $\beta$, which in turn gives the shape of the failure distribution, which indicates whether failures are occurring during 'infant', 'middle age' or 'old age' periods.

If from such a plot $\beta$ is found to be less than 1, the failure pattern is likely to represent 'infant mortality'. If $\beta = 1$, the failure rate is constant, i.e. equivalent to 'middle age'. If $\beta$ is greater than 1, the failure rate is equivalent to 'old age' or wear-out.

A simple example will illustrate this and show how various other reliability measures can be estimated.

**EXAMPLE**

### *Domestic appliance testing by a consumers' association*

To estimate the reliability of a cooker, 25 products are chosen at random and tested. The results shown to the right were obtained.

The results are plotted on Weibull probability paper in Figure 20.24. They follow a straight line, from which $\beta$ is obtained by constructing a line perpendicular to the plot to meet the 'estimation point' marked on the graph paper. This line crosses the auxiliary scale, $\beta$, to give the value for $\beta$, i.e. in this case 1.45, suggesting that the failure pattern for the product corresponds to 'old age'.

The *characteristic life*, $\eta$, is the time after which 36.8% of products will be expected to have survived, i.e. 63.2% failed. In this case the characteristic life is at $16.5 \times 10^4$ cycles.

| Failure number | Cumulative percentage frequency | Number of cycles in operation ($\times 10^4$) |
|---|---|---|
| 1 | 4 | 2.0 |
| 2 | 8 | 3.1 |
| 3 | 12 | 4.0 |
| 4 | 16 | 4.9 |
| 5 | 20 | 5.9 |
| 6 | 24 | 7.0 |
| 7 | 28 | 8.1 |
| 8 | 32 | 8.9 |
| 9 | 36 | 10.0 |
| 10 | 40 | 10.9 |
| 11 | 44 | 11.6 |
| 12 | 48 | 12.7 |
| 13 | 52 | 13.6 |
| 14 | 56 | 14.3 |
| 15 | 60 | 15.0 |

10 products still operating at $15 \times 10^4$ operating cycles

[5] If, in plotting points, a straight line does not result, $\gamma \neq 0$. The value of $\gamma$ must then be determined and the points replotted against a new axis. For details of the procedure see Caplan (1978) in Further Reading.

**Figure 20.24** Weibull probability plot of failure rate

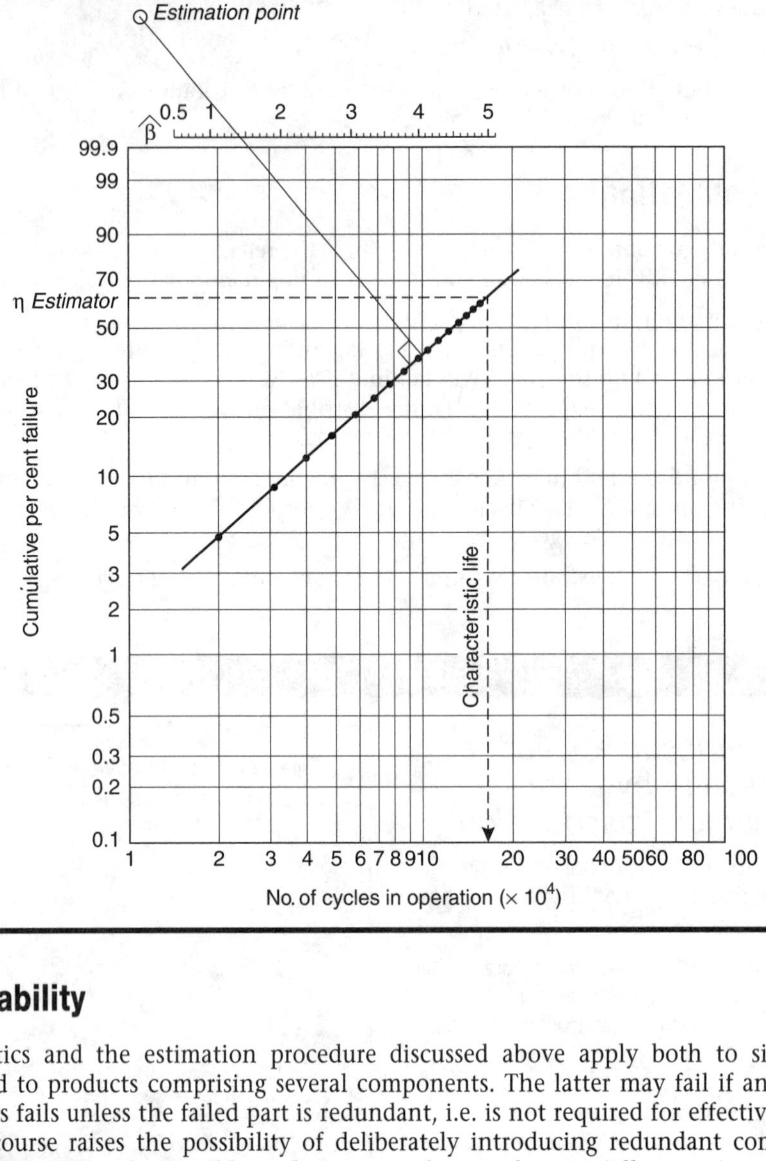

## System reliability

The characteristics and the estimation procedure discussed above apply both to single items or components and to products comprising several components. The latter may fail if any one of their component parts fails unless the failed part is redundant, i.e. is not required for effective system operation. This of course raises the possibility of deliberately introducing redundant components as a design feature. Thus it may be possible to design a product so that, initially, certain components are redundant and are brought into operation only when other components fail.

The reliability of complex products, or systems of components, is clearly a function of the number and the reliability of their components. Thus in a system without redundancy, which fails when any of its components A, B, C and D, fail:

$$R_{\text{SYSTEM}} = R_A \times R_B \times R_C \times R_D$$

For example, in a system comprising 10 components, each essential for satisfactory system operation (i.e. without redundancy), if component reliability is 0.99:

$$R_{\text{SYSTEM}} = 0.99^{10}$$
$$= 0.904 \text{ approximately}$$

Now if in this example, because of built-in-redundancy, five of the components would be replaced instantly by parallel components if they fail, the system might be shown as in Figure 20.25.

The reliability of components 1–5 = 0.99; the reliability of components 6–10 = 0.99; but since these are each arranged in parallel, the reliability of each pair is:

$$1 - (1 - R_{6,7\ \text{etc.}})^2$$

$$\text{Thus } R_{\text{SYSTEM}} = 0.99^5 \times (1 - (1 - 0.99)^2)^5$$
$$= 0.950$$

Such system reliability considerations are relevant in design and in planning maintenance and replacement.

**Figure 20.25** Diagrammatic representation of a ten-component system with redundancy

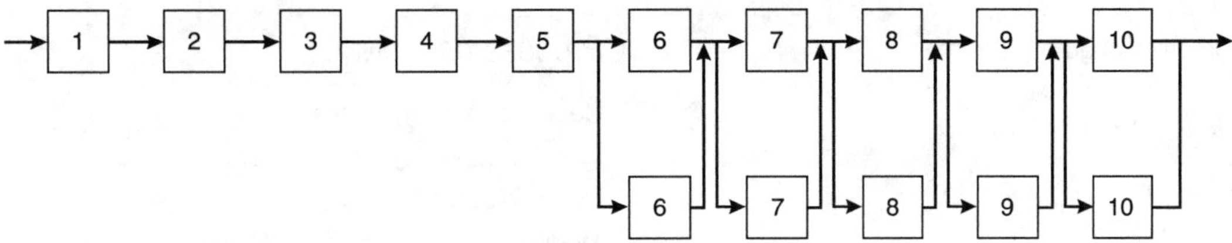

## CHECKLIST FOR CHAPTER 20

### The link between quality costs and control

The relevance of statistical control

### Quality control and assurance for items

Process (or manufacture) quality
- Control of input
- Process controls
- Output controls

Economics of quality control

### Quality control procedures

Vendor rating
- Categorical
- Weighted point
- Cost ratio
- Quality only

Inspection: where to inspect

Acceptance sampling (for attributes)
- OC curves
- Thorndike chart
- Design of single acceptance sampling plans
- LTPD and AQL
- AOQL
- Double and multiple sampling
- Tables

Control charts
- For variables
- Mean
- Range
- For attributes

Cusum

### Process capability

Control and design limits

Process capability measurement

Dynamic control charts

Modified action limits

### Computers in quality control

### Reliability

Failure

Reliability characteristics and measures

Reliability distributions

Reliability estimation

System reliability

## FURTHER READING

**Caplan, R. H. (1978)** *A Practical Approach to Reliability*, 3rd edn. London: Business Books. A comprehensive and comparatively easy-to-read treatment of reliability theory and management.

**Cox, D. R. (1990)** Quality and reliability: some recent developments and a historical perspective. *Journal of the Operations Research Society*, **41**(2), pp. 95–101.

**Dale, B. and Oakland, J. S. (1991)** *Quality Improvement through Standards*. Cheltenham: Stanley Thornes.

**Enrick, N. L. (1985)** *Quality, Reliability and Process Improvement*, 5th edn. New York: Industrial Press.

**Lloyd, D. K. and Lipow, M. (1990)** *Reliability: Management, Methods and Mathematics*, 3rd edn. Milwaukee: American Society for Quality Control.

**Oakland, J. S. (1986)** *Statistical Process Control*. London: Heinemann.

**Wolak, J. (1990)** Whither PCs in QC? *Quality*, **29**(6), pp. 25–27.

## QUESTIONS

20.1 (a) What is the purpose of acceptance sampling?

(b) What is an operating characteristic curve?

(c) Use the binomial probability expression to calculate the probability of finding two or fewer defectives in a sample of size 12, if the actual percentage of defectives in the batch from which the sample was drawn is 20%.

20.2 Construct an operating characteristic curve to show the probability of accepting batches of varying percentage actual defective levels if sample sizes of 80 items are drawn from the batches and if batches are accepted when two or fewer defectives are found in the samples.

20.3 Use the Thorndike or cumulative Poisson probability chart to specify an OC curve which can be used in a single acceptance sampling plan specified as follows:

| | | | |
|---|---|---|---|
| Lot tolerance percentage defective | 6% | Producer's risk | 6% |
| Acceptable quality level | 3% | Consumer's risk | 12% |

20.4 Construct an average outgoing quality curve and determine the average outgoing quality limit for the operating characteristic curve for n = 200, c ≤ 2 shown in Figure 20.7 and batch size of N = 2500.

20.5 An office machine processes 2000 items every day. From every lot processed a random sample of 100 is subjected to a visual quality check.

The defectives found in the samples are rectified or replaced and if more than one defective is found in a sample of 100 the entire lot produced is subjected to a quality inspection, during which all defectives are either rectified or replaced. If only one or no defectives are found in the sample the entire lot is accepted without further inspection.

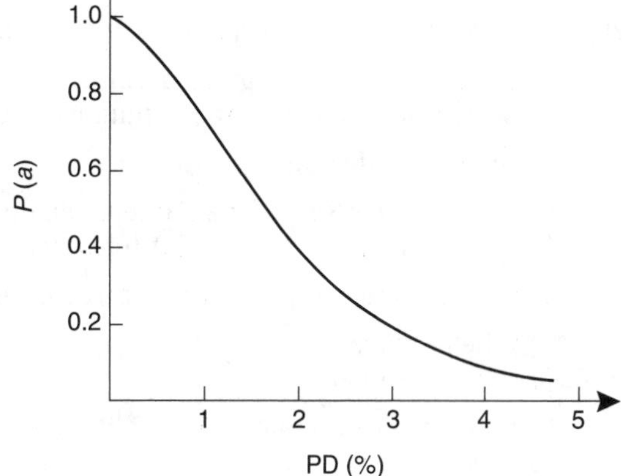


The diagram, right, is the OC curve for the sampling plan. It has been calculated using binomial probabilities.

(a) What is the average outgoing quality limit for this quality control procedure?

(b) Under what circumstances can the Poisson probability distribution be used to design the sampling plan? Note:

$$\text{Poisson probability } P(c) = \frac{e^{-pn}\,(pn)^c}{c!}$$

where $c$ = number of defectives in sample
$n$ = sample size
$p$ = actual percentage defective in lot

(c) Using the cumulative Poisson probability chart, design a single acceptance sampling plan to satisfy the following requirements.

| | |
|---|---|
| Producer's risk | = 0.050 |
| Consumer's risk | = 0.100 |

Acceptance quality level = 0.022
Lowest tolerance defective = 0.090

20.6 (a) Consider the output of a service system. Distinguish between and describe the use of double acceptance sampling and multiple acceptance sampling in this situation.

(b) Using the tables provided in the chapter (Figures 20.14 and 20.15) specify the sample size and the maximum acceptable number of defectives in the sample for:

Double acceptance sampling
Lot tolerance percentage defective = 5%
Batch sizes = 1500
Actual process percentage defective = 0.5–1.0%

(c) Using the tables provided, what is the average outgoing quality limit, given:

Single acceptance sampling
Lot tolerance percentage defective = 5%
Batch sizes = 2000
Actual process percentage defective = 0.5–1.0%

What is the lot tolerance percentage defective, given:

Single acceptance sampling
Average outgoing quality limit = 2.5%
Batch sizes = 750
Actual process percentage defective = 0.5–1.0%
Consumer's risk = 10%

20.7 Consider two single acceptance sampling plans specified as follows:

1. Sample size 50. Acceptable number of defects 1.
2. Sample size 100. Acceptable number of defects 2.

For each plan determine:

(a) the producer's risk for an acceptable quality level of 2%;
(b) the consumer's risk for a lot tolerance percentage defective of 5%.

Which of these two plans would be considered preferable by:

(i) the producer;
(ii) the consumer?

What is the average outgoing quality limit for each plan if in each case the batch sizes are equal to 1000? State the statistical assumptions you have made in arriving at your answers.

20.8 Refer throughout to supply, service or transport systems.

(a) Distinguish between quality assurance and quality control.

(b) Distinguish between quality control as regards the 'attributes' of items and the 'variables' of items.

(c) Distinguish between design limits and control limits.

(d) Distinguish between usual or chance variation and unusual or assignable variation in respect of quality control.

(e) Distinguish between warning limits and action limits in respect of control charts.

20.9 (a) A machine produces components at a rate of 100 per hour. Every hour a random sample of five components is taken and their lengths measured. After 10 hours the following data have been collected. Use these data to design control charts for the sample mean and range of the dimension concerned.

| Sample number | Measurements (cm) | | | | |
|---|---|---|---|---|---|
| 1 | 9.00 | 9.10 | 9.00 | 9.05 | 8.95 |
| 2 | 9.10 | 9.10 | 9.00 | 9.05 | 9.05 |
| 3 | 9.00 | 9.05 | 9.00 | 9.05 | 9.00 |
| 4 | 9.00 | 9.00 | 8.95 | 9.00 | 9.05 |
| 5 | 9.00 | 9.05 | 9.05 | 9.05 | 9.00 |
| 6 | 9.00 | 9.10 | 9.10 | 9.05 | 9.00 |
| 7 | 9.00 | 9.10 | 9.05 | 9.15 | 9.05 |
| 8 | 9.00 | 9.10 | 9.10 | 9.00 | 9.05 |
| 9 | 9.00 | 9.00 | 8.95 | 9.00 | 9.00 |
| 10 | 9.00 | 9.05 | 9.00 | 9.10 | 8.95 |

(b) Following the construction of the charts, the same sampling procedure is followed and the data shown below are obtained. Plot these data on the control charts and comment on the quality 'performance' of the process.

| Sample number | Mean length (cm) | Range | Sample number | Mean length (cm) | Range |
|---|---|---|---|---|---|
| 1 | 9.020 | 0.100 | 11 | 9.040 | 0.150 |
| 2 | 9.030 | 0.100 | 12 | 9.040 | 0.125 |
| 3 | 9.025 | 0.050 | 13 | 9.035 | 0.100 |
| 4 | 9.030 | 0.100 | 14 | 9.040 | 0.055 |
| 5 | 9.035 | 0.025 | 15 | 9.030 | 0.100 |
| 6 | 9.040 | 0.105 | 16 | 9.025 | 0.050 |
| 7 | 9.020 | 0.050 | 17 | 9.030 | 0.125 |
| 8 | 9.030 | 0.100 | 18 | 9.025 | 0.100 |
| 9 | 9.040 | 0.050 | 19 | 9.025 | 0.150 |
| 10 | 9.035 | 0.065 | 20 | 9.030 | 0.150 |

20.10 Using the data given overleaf, which have resulted from a study over a period of one week, construct a control chart and, on that control chart, plot the data given in the table below. Comment on the results.

Target throughput of items for period = 6250
Throughput of good-quality items = 5620
Total number of defective items = 99

$$\text{Percentage performance} = \frac{\text{Acceptable output}}{\text{Target}} \times 100 = 90\%$$

| Sample | Output | Sample | Numbers defective in sample |
|---|---|---|---|
| Mon. a.m. | 575 | 60 | 1 |
| Mon. p.m. | 600 | 60 | 2 |
| Tues. a.m. | 550 | 60 | 2 |
| Tues. p.m. | 550 | 60 | 1 |
| Wed. a.m. | 600 | 60 | 2 |
| Wed. p.m. | 650 | 65 | 2 |
| Thurs. a.m. | 625 | 65 | 1 |
| Thurs. p.m. | 590 | 70 | 2 |
| Fri. a.m. | 625 | 75 | 2 |
| Fri. p.m. | 490 | 60 | 1 |
| Sat. a.m. | 565 | 60 | 1 |

20.11 Phragyle Products Ltd supplies imitation glass decanters to the hotel trade. Because of the nature of the items, each decanter is expected to have some minor blemishes, most of which are completely invisible to the naked eye. These very minor blemishes may occur almost anywhere on the product and are not usually sufficient to lead to the rejection of the item. Nevertheless, the sales manager of Phragyle Products is anxious to investigate the effects of recent efforts that the manufacturers claim to have made to improve the manufacturing process and the quality of the products supplied to Phragyle.

Prior to the modifications to the process, each decanter had an average of five almost imperceptible blemishes. The table below shows the number of blemishes on every fifth decanter for a short period after the claimed improvement in manufacture. Comment on the success of the supposed adjustments to the manufacturing process.

**Number of blemishes per product: 6, 7, 6, 5, 6, 7, 7, 6, 8, 7, 7, 7, 6, 8, 9, 8, 7, 8, 9, 8, 8, 7**

20.12 (a) 'Even if 100% acceptance sampling is adopted, it is likely that a certain number of defective items will be accepted.' Discuss.

(b) What measures can be taken, and in what circumstances, to decrease the error rate of human inspectors?

20.13 Referring to Question 20.9 above, plot a cumulative sum chart of the 'mean' values given in the second table. Comment on the resulting chart and compare the results obtained with those obtained from the control chart previously constructed.

20.14 Three phases are often evident in the reliability of items. Describe them and explain the reasons for their existence. Use examples.

20.15 In order to estimate the reliability of an item, 20 items are taken at random and tested. The following results are obtained:

| Failure number | Percentage failures | Number of cycles in operation ($\times 10^4$) |
|---|---|---|
| 1 | 5 | 3.0 |
| 2 | 10 | 4.2 |
| 3 | 15 | 5.5 |
| 4 | 20 | 6.4 |
| 5 | 25 | 6.7 |
| 6 | 30 | 7.4 |
| 7 | 35 | 8.3 |
| 8 | 40 | 9.0 |
| 9 | 45 | 9.3 |
| 10 | 50 | 10.3 |
| 11 | 55 | 10.9 |
| 12 | 60 | 12.0 |
| 13 | 65 | 13.0 |
| 14 | 70 | 14.0 |
| 15 | 75 | 14.7 |

Five items were still operative after $14.7 \times 10^4$ cycles.

(a) Determine $\beta$ and comment on the result.

(b) Calculate the 'characteristic life' of the item.

## CASE STUDIES (from Part 9)

The topics covered in this chapter are relevant in the following (see Introduction to Part 9 and Table C.1 for further details):

| No | Name | Country |
|---|---|---|
| 2 | Jograni Handicrafts | Bangladesh |
| 9 | The Malta MBA | Malta |

Chapter 21

# Maintenance and replacement

## ISSUES

What is the relationship of maintenance, repair and replacement?
What is the role and purpose of maintenance?
Which items should be maintained?
How is maintenance organized?
How is preventive maintenance scheduled?
Can repair work be scheduled?
How can a replacement policy be established?

## NOTATION USED IN THIS CHAPTER

| | |
|---|---|
| $C_m$ | Cost/unit time of preventive maintenance |
| $C_s$ | Cost/unit time of repair |
| $E_n$ | Expenditure for year $n$ |
| $G$ | Value of the output of a facility (£/unit time) |
| $i$ | Annual rate of interest |
| $I_n$ | Income for year $n$ |
| $k$ | Constant |
| $K$ | Number of machines allocated to one maintenance team |
| $L$ | Life of equipment |
| $M$ | Number of maintenance teams |
| $N$ | Number of inspections/facility/unit time |
| NPV | Net present value |
| $S_L$ | Sale or scrap value at end of life, i.e. at year $L$ |
| $T_a$ | Average operating life without breakdown |
| $t_I$ | Time for an inspection |
| $T_m$ | Average time for a preventive maintenance operation |

$T_p$ Preventive maintenance interval
$T_s$ Average time for repair
$t_s$ Time for a repair
$T_T$ Total downtime

Our discussion of item quality in the previous chapter led us to consider the question of reliability. We noted that quality and reliability were related; in general, higher-quality items were likely to be more reliable. We noticed also that quality level and cost were related, so higher reliability is often associated with higher cost. Since few purchases were made irrespective of cost, most products or items in use will have less than perfect reliability. At some time most items will cease to function satisfactorily. On such occasions they will have to be repaired or replaced. To some extent, however, the need for repair or replacement may be reduced through effective servicing and maintenance. Thus:

(a) Most items will be inspected regularly, in order to detect any signs of reduced effectiveness or impending failure. And additionally:
(b) Items will normally be serviced regularly, also to try to ensure continued effective operation.
(c) Preventive maintenance will often be provided on a regular basis in order to try to sustain satisfactory operations of items or equipment. During preventive maintenance, items or parts which are liable to failure may be changed prior to the end of their working life. But nevertheless:
(d) Breakdown maintenance (i.e. repair) will normally be required so that items and equipment might be returned to satisfactory operation. And eventually:
(e) Replacement of items and equipment will occur when they are no longer capable of satisfactory operation and are beyond economic repair.

The relationship of these five activities is outlined in Figure 21.1. Points (a) to (d) above can be seen to be part of the maintenance function, while (e) is concerned with replacement. Initially in this chapter we shall consider maintenance, and then the problem of replacement.

## THE MAINTENANCE FUNCTION

Equipment of whatever type, however complex or simple, however cheap or expensive, is liable to break down. Thus in manufacture, supply, transport and service not only must procedures exist for equipment maintenance but also the possibility of breakdowns and disruption of operation must be considered during capacity planning and activity scheduling. The effective operation of any system is dependent on the maintenance of all parts of the system, e.g. machines, buildings, services. In this chapter we shall not deal with the maintenance of human facilities, although, in concept at least, the maintenance requirement also applies to workers. Indeed, company welfare or personnel practice may be designed partly as a maintenance activity, e.g. training and retraining to maintain the availability of appropriate skills, medical facilities to maintain human capacity, counselling to maintain interest and motivation. Here we deal only with the maintenance of inanimate items, e.g. equipment.

Large sums of money are wasted in business and industry each year, because of ineffective or badly organized maintenance. However, maintenance is just one element which contributes to effective operation during the life-cycle of a piece of equipment. It has an important part to play, but must be co-ordinated with other disciplines. Taken together, this approach – aimed at achieving economic life-cycle cost for an item – has been called 'terotechnology', and defined as:

> the multidisciplinary approach to the specification, design, installation, commissioning, use and disposal of facilities, equipment and buildings, in pursuit of economic life-cycle costs.

**Figure 21.1** Maintenance and replacement activities

**Figure 21.2** The operating life-cycle of a facility

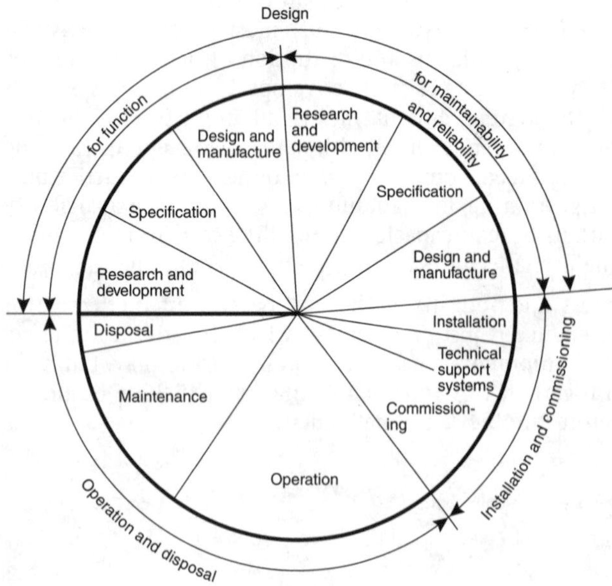


Figure 21.2 shows a typical life-cycle for a facility. The diagram indicates those activities required in conceiving, creating, providing, operating, maintaining and disposing of a physical facility. Taking maintenance from this set, it will be seen that many decisions and activities will affect the nature and amount of maintenance required. The design of the facility, both with regard to its design 'for function' and its design 'for maintainability and reliability', will influence operation, as will its installation and commissioning. The effectiveness of maintenance will influence the time available for and the time spent in operation. Thus the need for maintenance and the nature of the maintenance required are determined by a variety of factors. The maintenance function within an organization is therefore influenced by many other activities within the organization.

## The objectives of maintenance

The purpose of maintenance is to attempt to maximize the performance of equipment by ensuring that such equipment performs regularly and efficiently, by attempting to prevent breakdowns or failures, and by minimizing the losses resulting from breakdowns or failures. In fact it is the objective of the maintenance function to maintain or increase the reliability of the operating system as a whole.

Many steps can be taken to ensure that such an objective is achieved, but only a few of these are normally considered to be the responsibility of the maintenance department. For example, each of the following will contribute to the reliability of the operating system:

(a) improvement of the quality of equipment and components through improved design and/or tighter manufacturing standards;

(b) improvements in the design of equipment to facilitate the replacement of broken items and inspection and routine maintenance work;

(c) improvements in the layout of equipment to facilitate maintenance work, i.e. providing space around or underneath equipment;

(d) providing 'slack' in the operating system, i.e. providing excess capacity so that the failure of equipment does not affect the performance of other equipment;

(e) using work-in-progress to ensure that the failure of equipment is not immediately reflected in a shortage of materials or parts for a subsequent piece of equipment;

(f) establishing a repair facility so that, through speedy replacement of broken parts, equipment downtime is reduced;

(g) undertaking preventive maintenance, which, through regular inspection and/or replacement of critical parts, reduces the occurrence of breakdowns.

These points may be summarized in two overall objectives, which are:

(a) to attempt to ensure that breakdowns or failures do not occur ((a) and (g) above);

(b) to attempt to minimize the disruption or loss caused by the breakdowns which do occur ((b), (c), (d), (e) and (f) above).

Excluding the influence of improvements in equipment design and layout, discussion of which is not appropriate to this chapter, it is clear that two distinct facets of maintenance may contribute to the increased reliability of the operating system: preventive maintenance and repair.

We can, of course, draw the familiar total cost curve as shown in Figure 21.3, which demonstrates that increased effort in preventive maintenance should reduce the cost of repair. Were we able to define both of these curves, then it would be a simple matter to determine the minimum cost maintenance policy. However, the problem is not as simple as this, and consequently maintenance policy is substantially more difficult to determine.

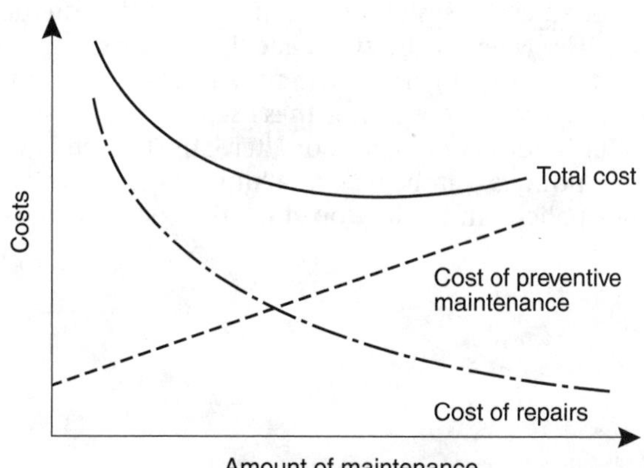


**Figure 21.3** Maintenance costs

## MAINTENANCE DECISIONS

It will be seen from the above that several decisions are required in the establishment of a comprehensive maintenance policy for any set of facilities. We can consider the establishment of a maintenance policy as comprising three necessary and interdependent decisions:

(a) Which items, facilities, etc., are to be maintained?

(b) What kind of maintenance will be applied in each case?

(c) How is this maintenance work to be organized?

### What is to be maintained?

Any maintenance activity incurs some cost. Inspection is costly in that it involves someone devoting some time to looking at an item or a facility, and that may mean that the operation of that facility has to be interrupted. Service work will be expensive and will not normally be possible while the facility is operating. Preventive maintenance will normally be undertaken while the facility is out of operation. To some extent all this work can be planned to take place at a time when the disruption caused by the inoperation of the facility is minimized, but of course breakdown maintenance can occur at any time and can be very disruptive, and can therefore be expensive in terms of both the direct effort involved and the time lost while the facility is repaired.

If the cost of any of this maintenance exceeds the cost benefits obtained, then it may be cheaper simply to dispose of items when they eventually break down. Indeed in some situations the way in which the items work and the conditions in which they are employed necessitate such an approach. There will, therefore, be situations in which it will be decided that some items will not be maintained, except perhaps through regular inspection and service to avoid safety and health hazards. Furthermore, the manner in which items break down or are subject to failure may make it difficult to develop an effective preventive maintenance strategy. And, if the cost per unit of time of undertaking preventive maintenance is greater than the cost per unit of time of repair, then there will be a tendency to rely on the latter.

Although in some cases preventive maintenance, and even breakdown maintenance, i.e. repair, may not be employed, in most cases facilities will require one or both of these approaches in addition to inspection and service. In these situations we must decide on the size of 'unit' to be maintained. Here there are three possible approaches:

(a) A large system comprising several interdependent facilities can be considered as one 'unit' for maintenance purposes.

(b) Single facilities can be considered to be the 'unit'.

(c) Parts or subsections of a particular facility can be considered to be the 'unit' for which maintenance must be planned.

For example, in transport an entire system may comprise all the interdependent and interlinked parts of a comprehensive vehicle, whereas the single-facility approach may involve the development of a maintenance plan for each separate part of that system. The third approach would involve the planning of maintenance for appropriate items of these separate parts. A complete computer installation can be considered as a 'unit' for maintenance, or alternatively each device in that system, e.g. the central processor, terminals, printers, can be seen as a 'unit' for the development of separate maintenance plans, or a maintenance policy can be developed for the components, e.g. the printed circuit boards, within certain facilities.

The extent to which the facilities within a larger system are interdependent, i.e. the extent to which the breakdown of one can cause disruption of the others, will influence the approach that will be employed. A system comprising similar facilities all installed at around the same time would perhaps be treated as an entire unit for maintenance purposes, whereas a system in which items, although linked together in some interdependent way, were installed at different times and have quite different reliability characteristics might encourage us to adopt the second approach. If an entire configuration of facilities operates continuously, then the entire system must be stopped when any part requires maintenance, and again there will be a tendency to see the entire system as the 'unit' for maintenance. On the other hand, where facilities operate intermittently, different facilities being idle at different times, then there will be a tendency to see each facility as a 'unit' for maintenance, since this provides the greatest opportunity for scheduling maintenance work. Where a system comprises several facilities, and where each facility has similar component parts, and where the reliability and/or breakdown characteristics of these parts are known, the third approach above may be appropriate.

## Types of maintenance

### Inspection

Facilities will normally be inspected at intervals in order to determine whether service and/or preventive maintenance is required or is likely to be required soon. Such work may involve visual inspection or the measurement of certain physical characteristics of a facility. Inspection may involve the whole facility or simply those parts which are known to be liable to failure. One of the problems in planning inspection is to decide on the *inspection interval*. This problem will be tackled in the next section.

### Service

This will involve the routine readjustment of equipment, etc. Such work will often be undertaken, if seen to be required, alongside inspection.

### Preventive maintenance

Preventive maintenance is precautionary and is undertaken to try to prevent or delay breakdowns, and therefore the need for repair. Preventive action may be undertaken according to a predetermined and regular schedule or when required. A regular schedule can be established for items which have known or fairly predictable reliability or breakdown characteristics. Preventive maintenance can be undertaken as and when required in circumstances where there is some evidence of deteriorating efficiency or impending breakdown. One of the problems, therefore, in planning maintenance is to identify the type of approach which will be suitable in particular circumstances.

### Repair

Breakdown maintenance or repair is remedial, taking place after an item has ceased to operate satisfactorily. The need for repair is not necessarily the result of inefficient or insufficient inspection, service and preventive maintenance, since in some cases the cost of repairs will be less than the accumulated cost of preventive work. One of the major problems in planning repair work is to decide on the amount of resources to be made available, since the larger the repair 'team' the shorter the repair time, but also the larger the amount of repair team idle time.

EXAMPLE

### Seattle city lighting

In Seattle, a typical maintenance area has about 5000 ducts, terminal poles and transformers for street lighting. Comprehensive maintenance is essential to avoid interruptions in the system. The programme covers inspecting, recording, maintenance and repairing. By determining the total number of items that must be inspected on a four-year cycle, the Authority found it a simple matter to prepare a rolling schedule to cover one-quarter of the inspections every year. With priorities set, the preventive maintenance inspections schedule is determined by the computer system, which provides an easy way to manage and track all the information that is generated by the maintenance programme. The system also supplies information in response to queries and requests from engineers and management.

Source: Kirkpatrick, D. (1990) Preventive maintenance programme is a three-step process – inspection, recording and repairing. *Transmission and Distribution*, **42**(7), pp. 58, 60.

## The organization of maintenance

Maintenance work can be performed by:

(a) the personnel who normally use the equipment;

(b) staff employed in a maintenance department by and within the organization;

(c) external maintenance personnel, e.g. under certain service contracts from equipment suppliers.

The first approach will often be employed for inspection and sometimes for service work. It may also be appropriate where preventive maintenance activities are relatively straightforward and are undertaken as and when required, i.e. where some urgent preventive action is required without prior warning. It may be employed for repair work where the facility operator has specialist skills and knowledge, perhaps acquired through the use of the facility, which are not available to other personnel.

More often an organization will maintain a specialist 'maintenance department'. The resources of this department will be employed in inspection, service, preventive maintenance and repair work, some of which can be undertaken on a scheduled basis. The main problems in organizing maintenance in this way are to decide on the size of the maintenance 'crew', the range of skills required, the amount of stocks to be held, the amount of standby equipment to be held in stock, etc.

Maintenance will be the responsibility of an external organization either where specialist equipment is involved or where a service or maintenance contract has been provided as a compulsory or normal part of the purchase contract for that equipment. This is normal for computer installations, etc. It may also be appropriate where maintenance work is highly specialized or hazardous, but infrequent, e.g. the maintenance of complex installations.

The planning of effective maintenance, however undertaken, will require collection and maintenance of certain data. For example, a complete list of all facilities in use, their date of purchase and their maintenance history to date will normally be kept. Statistics on operating life between failures, the time required to perform repair operations, etc., will be held so that decisions can be made about the scheduling of preventive work and the merits of preventive compared with repair maintenance.

The 'database' of information on each facility will be updated regularly so that appropriate statistics, etc. can be extracted. Often such data will be held on a computer-based system, such a system being used to schedule maintenance, allocate maintenance resources, etc. (These will be discussed towards the end of this chapter.)

# INSPECTION

Facilities will normally be inspected at intervals to determine whether maintenance is required or likely to be required in the near future. Often such inspection is disruptive, e.g. the operation of facilities may have to be halted while inspection is undertaken. On the other hand inspection might reasonably be expected to reduce the amount of time lost (downtime) through breakdowns. One problem, therefore, is to decide how much time to devote to inspection so that total downtime is minimized.

Let $T_T$ = total downtime per unit time

$t_I$ = downtime per inspection

$t_s$ = downtime per breakdown

$N$ = number of inspections per facility per unit time

$k$ = a constant for a particular facility

If the total time lost through inspection is a function of $t_I$ and $N$, and if we assume that the total time lost through breakdowns is a function of $t_s$ and inversely related to $N$, then:

$$T_T = t_I N + t_s \frac{k}{N}$$

Differentiating this equation with respect to $N$ and equating to zero will give the optimum value of $N$. If $t_I$ and $t_s$ are constants:

$$N \text{ to minimize } T_T = \sqrt{t_s \times \frac{k}{t_I}}$$

EXAMPLE

$t_s$ = 0.9 weeks

$t_I$ = 0.2 weeks

From experience it has been found that $k$ = 2. Hence:

$$N_{\text{opt}} = \sqrt{0.9 \times \frac{2}{0.2}} = 3 \text{ per week}$$

# PREVENTIVE MAINTENANCE

We want to perform the minimum amount of preventive maintenance, since maintenance even of this type will be expensive in terms of labour and material costs, and also the possible costs of disruption. Ideally, therefore, we would like to perform our preventive maintenance of equipment just before it would otherwise have broken down. Such a policy is possible only if either, because of the nature of the equipment, we receive some advance warning of impending failure or if failure of equipment is perfectly predictable. Rarely is warning of impending failure of value in practice, since either the warning is insufficiently in advance of failure or the warning is itself associated with some loss of efficiency or capacity in the equipment. Optimum preventive maintenance, therefore, depends on a situation such as that shown by *a* in Figure 21.4 in which the operating life of equipment between breakdowns is perfectly constant. Rarely will such a situation exist; indeed, it is more likely that one of the other curves shown in this figure will result, i.e.:

Curve *b* Random operating life, normally distributed about mean $T_a$.

Curve *c* Large probability of failure immediately after repair.

**Figure 21.4** Operating life curves

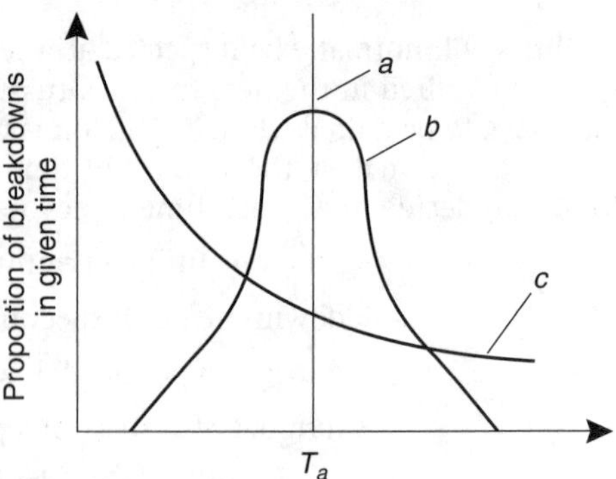


The design of maintenance programmes depends to a large extent on the operating life characteristics of the equipment, a thorough investigation of which should be made by equipment manufacturers or users prior to the determination of maintenance procedures. For convenience, such data are normally presented in the manner shown in Figure 21.5, such curves being referred to as *breakdown time distributions*. Obviously the nearer the actual breakdown time distribution approaches to the ideal distribution, *a*, the more appropriate and effective preventive maintenance will be.

In Figure 21.5 curve *a* corresponds to curve *a* of Figure 21.4, i.e. a situation in which the operating life between breakdowns is constant. Curve *b* also corresponds to *b* in the previous figure. It is worth noting at this point that the remaining curve, *x*, corresponds closely to the exponential distribution. This is important, since statistical queuing theory, which will be used shortly, depends to a large extent on the use of this probability distribution.

An important function of the maintenance department is to collect and record data so that breakdown time distribution curves can be kept for all pieces of equipment. Not only will the initial design of the maintenance policy depend on these data, but subsequent changes in policy may be required if, over a period of time, the breakdown characteristics of equipment change.

One other factor which determines the merit and hence the design of preventive maintenance is the cost required to conduct preventive, compared with breakdown, maintenance. If preventive maintenance costs as much as, or more than, breakdown maintenance, then, even where the breakdown time distribution for equipment permits the efficient adoption of preventive maintenance, it will still be

**Figure 21.5** Breakdown time distributions

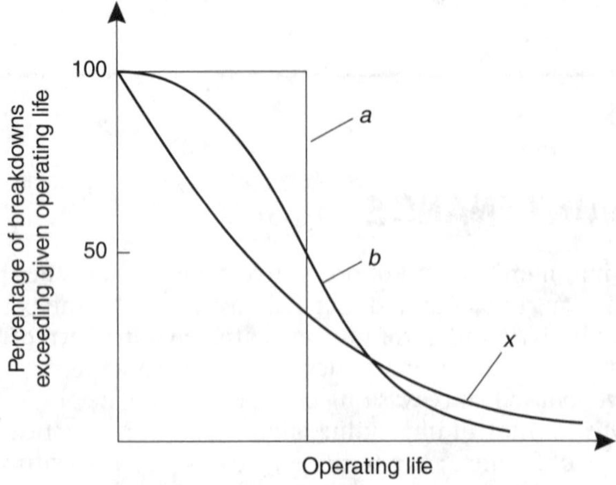

beneficial to rely on breakdown maintenance only. For example, Figure 21.6 indicates that even though preventive maintenance may result in fewer downtime periods, the total downtime and hence possibly the cost are greater than they would have been if breakdown maintenance alone had been used.

It is not enough, however, to consider only the time factor, since even though preventive maintenance operations may be comparatively time-consuming, they may be scheduled to occur at convenient times, such as during holidays, weekends, or periods during which the load on equipment is low. We should, therefore, compare the costs of maintenance in order to evaluate the benefit of preventive maintenance.

**Figure 21.6** Effect of maintenance durations.

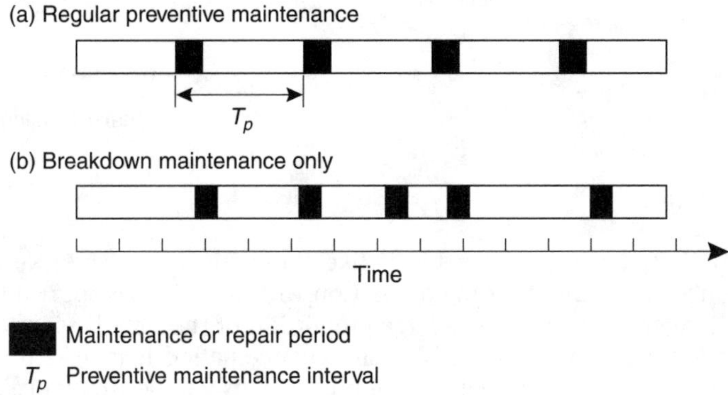


## The scheduling of preventive maintenance for a single machine

If the breakdown time distribution approaches the ideal one, then, if preventive maintenance is used effectively, one would expect comparatively few breakdowns to occur. On the other hand, if the distribution is more variable, then, even if preventive maintenance is used, breakdowns may still occur, i.e. a breakdown may occur before the next preventive maintenance operation is due.[1] If we let:

$T_p$ = fixed preventive maintenance interval, i.e. the time period between successive preventive maintenance operations on the same item of equipment

$T_m$ = average time required to perform a preventive maintenance operation

$T_s$ = average time required to perform a repair

$T_a$ = average operating life without breakdowns

and if we further assume that maintenance on a piece of equipment, whether it is preventive maintenance or repair maintenance, is equally effective in that both leave the equipment with the same probable operating life, then it has been shown that the operating efficiency of equipment, in terms of the percentage of time spent running, is a function of the ratio of the preventive maintenance interval to the average operating life, i.e. $T_p/T_a$.

[1] The approach presented here is based on that of Morse, P. M. (1958) *Queues, Inventories and Maintenance*. New York: Wiley.

For other approaches to some of these problems, see, for example: Olusoy, G. *et al.* (1992) Design and Implementation of a maintenance planning and control system. *International Journal of Production Economics*, **24**(3), pp. 263–272, and Olorunniwo, F. O. and Izuehukwu, A. (1991) Scheduling imperfect preventive and overhaul maintenance. *International Journal of Quality and Reliability Management*, **8**(4), pp. 67–79.

**Figure 21.7** Breakdown time distributions.

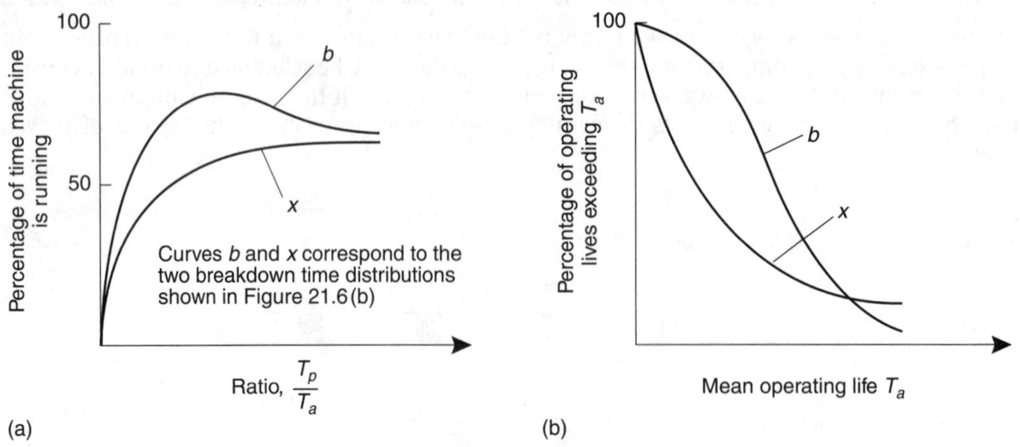


Using this relationship, curves can be drawn like those in Figure 21.7. Notice that where the preventive maintenance interval is short in comparison with the average operating life, the operating efficiency of the equipment is low because a large proportion of the time is spent in preventive maintenance. On the other hand, as the preventive maintenance period is increased in comparison with the average operating life, then a larger number of breakdowns will occur. Notice also that where the breakdown time distribution *does not* approach the ideal situation, operating efficiency continues to increase as the comparative length of the preventive maintenance interval increases, whereas in the situation shown by curve *b*, in which the operating life has low variability, the curve reaches a peak. In other words, the use of preventive maintenance enables equipment operating efficiency to be maximized only when the variability on equipment operating life is small. We can, as a general rule, consider that preventive maintenance leads to an optimal policy for breakdown time distributions which have variability less than the exponential distribution (curve *x*).

It has been mentioned previously that the merit of preventive maintenance also depends on the relative time required for preventive maintenance operations. Figure 21.8 shows how an increase in the size of $T_m$ (the time required for preventive maintenance) relative to $T_s$ (the time required for repair) reduces or eliminates the advantages previously offered by the preventive maintenance policy.

Clearly, if the breakdown time distribution for equipment is known, or can be obtained from records, then, using the method developed by Morse, the merits of a preventive maintenance policy, and the optimum preventive maintenance interval, can be established.

This is clearly not an appropriate place in which to study statistical queuing theory. It is, however, necessary to touch briefly upon the subject in order to deal more satisfactorily with preventive maintenance.

**Figure 21.8**

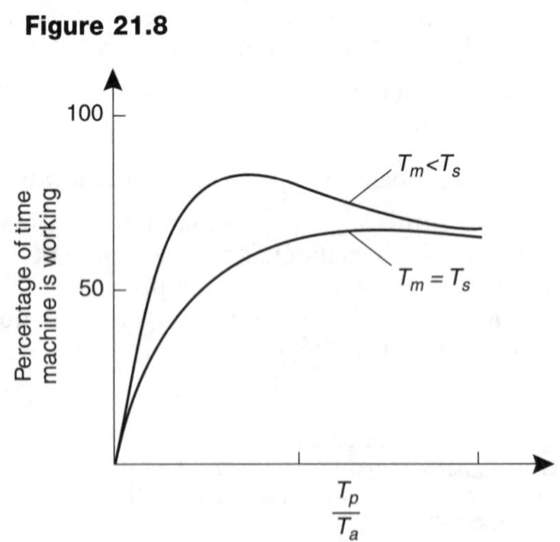


N.B. Both of these curves correspond to breakdown time distributions with low variability, i.e. curve *b* in Figure 21.7.

**Figure 21.9** Erlang breakdown time distributions. Adapted with permission from Morse, P. M. (1958) *Queues, Inventories and Maintenance*. New York: Wiley

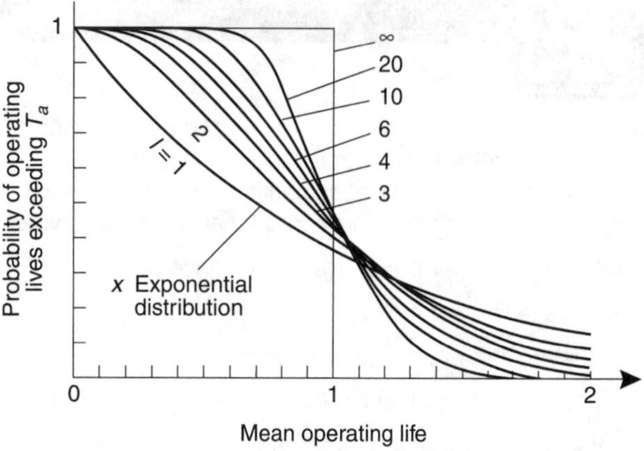


We have pointed out above that only where breakdown time distributions show comparatively little variability will preventive maintenance produce an optimal result. We should, therefore, discuss only those cases in which variability is less than that of the exponential distribution. The solution of the preventive maintenance planning problem depends on the use of queuing theory, and it so happens that useful queuing theory formulae have been developed for two types of situation which occur frequently in practice. The first deals with the exponential case mentioned above and the second deals with the case where the *Erlang* distribution applies. The precise nature of this distribution need not concern us here, and it is sufficient to say that the Erlang distribution covers those distributions which show variability equal to or less than the exponential. For example, curve $x$ in Figure 21.9, as well as being an exponential distribution, is also one of a family of Erlang distributions, as are the remaining curves in this figure. (The parameter $l$ is the only one which determines the variability of the distribution.)

If we adopt the following further notation:

$G$ = value of the output of the machine (£/unit of time)

$C_m$ = cost per unit time of preventive maintenance

$C_s$ = cost per unit time of repair

then the optimal value of $T_p$ – the preventive maintenance interval – can be obtained from the curves shown in Figure 21.10. To use these curves, the appropriate value of $l$ is found by comparing the breakdown time distribution with the Erlang distribution. The factor on the $y$ axis is calculated from known values of $T_m$, $T_s$, $C_m$, $C_s$, and $G$, and hence the ratio $T_p/T_a$ is obtained. From this, since $T_a$ is known, $T_p$ can be calculated.

**Figure 21.10** Curves for determining the optimum period, $T_p$, for preventive maintenance for different degrees of variability of breakdown time distribution (see Figure 21.9) and for different values of the ratio $T_m(G + C_m)/T_s(G + C_s)$ (explained in the text). Adapted with permission from Morse, P. M. (1958) *Queues, Inventories and Maintenance*. New York: Wiley

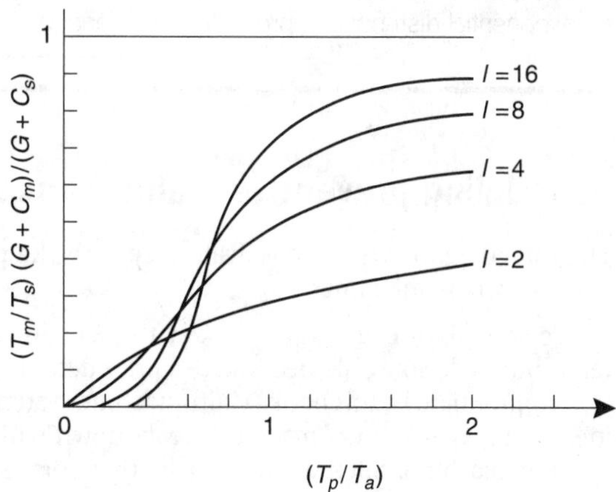

**EXAMPLE**

From data concerning a machine collected over a period of several years, it has been established that the average operating life between breakdowns is four weeks and that the breakdown time distribution corresponds approximately to an Erlang distribution with $l = 4$. Given the following information, determine the optimum regular interval at which preventive maintenance should be performed on this machine.

| | |
|---|---|
| Average time for preventive maintenance operation | = 2 hours |
| Average time for a repair | = 4 hours |
| Cost/hour of preventive maintenance | = £3 |
| Cost/hour of repair work | = £6 |
| Value of output of this machine | = £25/hour |

*Answer*

$$\left(\frac{T_m}{T_s}\right)\left(\frac{G + C_m}{G + C_s}\right) = \left(\frac{2}{4}\right)\left(\frac{25 + 3}{25 + 6}\right) = 0.452$$

From Figure 21.10, for $l = 4$:

$$\frac{T_p}{T_a} = 0.9$$

since $T_a = 4$ weeks, preventive maintenance interval, $T_p = 3.6$ weeks.

What would be the effect on the optimum preventive maintenance interval if:

(a) the average time for a repair was equal to the average time for a preventive maintenance operation;

(b) the breakdown time distribution corresponded to an Erlang distribution with $l = 1$?

*Answer*

(a)
$$\left(\frac{T_m}{T_s}\right)\left(\frac{G + C_m}{G + C_s}\right) = 0.901$$

hence for $l = 4$ there is no solution for $T_p/T_a$. In other words, in such circumstances there is no benefit in preventive maintenance.

(b) There is also no solution for $T_p/T_a$ for $l = 1$, i.e. because the breakdown variance is large (no better than the exponential distribution), preventive maintenance is not appropriate.

## Scheduling preventive maintenance for several machines

The foregoing discussion has dealt only with the planning, i.e. the scheduling, of preventive maintenance for single machines.

We should, of course, also look at the scheduling of preventive maintenance for multi-machine systems, but to do so would necessitate a prior detour through rather complex statistical theory which would be inappropriate in this book. Multi-machine systems differ from single-machine systems in that machine idle time may result if a machine breaks down while the maintenance team are engaged in the repair of another machine. Such a situation is, therefore, similar to the multi-machine assignment problem in which interference may occur (see Chapter 12). Indeed, were we concerned only with the repair of machines rather than repair *and* preventive maintenance, the two situations would be analogous. In the present context, however, we are concerned with the possibility of using regular preventive maintenance to reduce the occurrence of breakdowns. This, of course, adds considerably to the complexity of the situation. In the next section we shall consider the 'repair only' maintenance policy for several machines.

EXAMPLE

### *Oklahoma Gas and Electric*

In 1984, Oklahoma Gas and Electric Co. (OG&E) designed a computer-supported work management planning and scheduling programme to provide for the integrated scheduling, measuring and tracking of preventive maintenance for substation and transportation equipment. After a study of the information required for the programme, OG&E determined all resource requirements and the time needed to perform the PM work. The work measurement system selected was MOST, a well-known predetermined motion time system (see Chapter 8). These data are used in the programme, which provides definitions of all PM tasks and time requirements for such work. The computer-based programme provides a wide range of information to help manage transmission and distribution (T&D) operations. It has provided a significant reduction in the cost of maintenance in OG&E.

Source: Cinpak, D. M. (1991) OG&E reduces T&D costs with preventative maintenance. *Transmission and Distribution*, **43**(1), pp. 44–47.

## REPAIRS

Consider now the situation in which several machines of the same type are to be maintained. Furthermore, let us consider a policy which provides only for repair and not for preventive maintenance (a policy which might have been adopted because of large variability in breakdown time distributions).

Provided appropriate assumptions are made about the nature of breakdowns and repair time, the design of a maintenance system for such a situation can be accomplished by using conventional queuing theory.

Clearly, machine idle time caused by waiting for service by a maintenance team currently engaged on another machine can be reduced if the time needed to repair machines is reduced. Reduction in machine repair time, $T_s$, can normally be achieved by devoting more resources to maintenance, i.e. by increasing the size of the maintenance team. Such action, however, will increase costs; consequently the problem is one of achieving an acceptable balance between, on the one hand, the cost incurred by machine idle time due to breakdowns, and on the other hand the cost of the maintenance facility.

Let us first consider the case in which only *one maintenance team* looks after several identical machines. If we consider the breakdown time distribution to be exponential with average operating life $= T_a$, then it is reasonable that our maintenance policy should rely only on repairs, since preventive maintenance is unlikely to reduce costs. Let us further consider that the repair time is also exponentially distributed with an average of $T_s$. Such assumptions, which often correspond quite closely with reality, enable statistical queuing theory to be adopted. Using this approach Figure 21.11 can be calculated (see Morse, 1958). This shows the average number of machines running as a function of the ratio $T_a/T_s$ where $K$ is the number of machines allocated to one maintenance team.

An examination of this figure shows that for large values of $T_a/T_s$ the number of machines running differs only slightly from the total number of machines, $K$. For example, if $T_a/T_s = 10$, then if the

**Figure 21.11** Mean number of machines working: for $K$ machines and for the exponential distribution breakdown. From Morse, P. M. (1958) *Queues, Inventories and Maintenance*. New York: Wiley

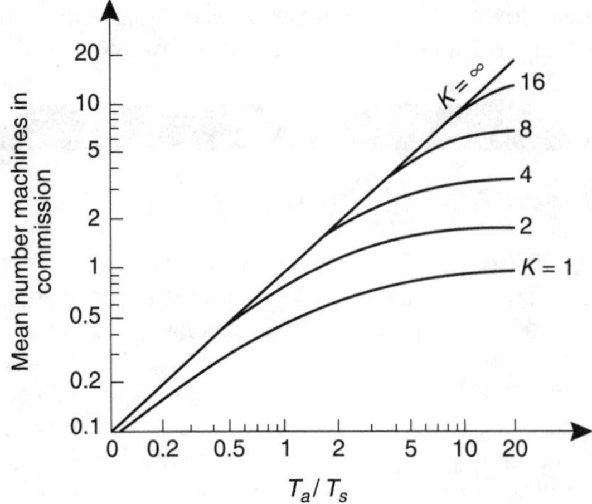


system contains four machines ($K = 4$) the average number running over a period of time is approximately 3.5. If, however, the ratio of $T_a/T_s$ falls, because of either reduced reliability of the machines or increased average repair times ($T_s$), then, naturally, the efficiency of the whole system falls. In fact it seems that, in order to maintain a reasonably efficient system, $T_a/T_s \geq K$.

This figure enables us to assess the cost of machine idle time due to breakdowns and time spent waiting for repair.

To assess the cost of the maintenance team, Figure 21.2 may be used. This shows the proportion of time that the maintenance team is busy, as a function of $KT_s/T_a$.

**Figure 21.12** Mean fraction of the time the repair team is busy: for $K$ machines and for exponential breakdown distribution. From Morse, P. M. (1958) *Queues, Inventories and Maintenance*. New York: Wiley

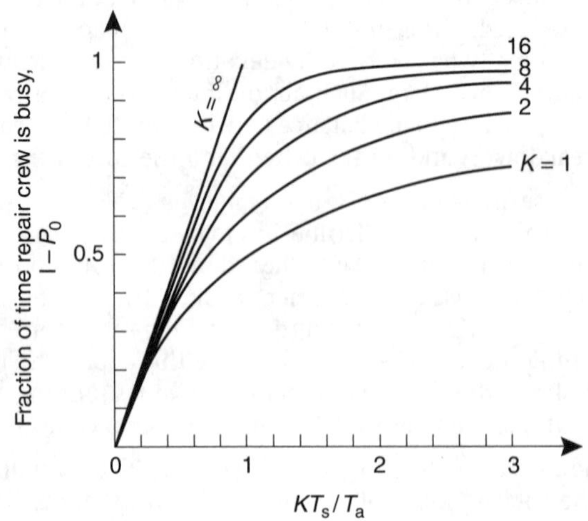

**EXAMPLE**

A single maintenance team is to be responsible for repairs to eight identical machines. It has been found from experience that the breakdown time distribution for the machines corresponds to the exponential distribution, as does that for the repair times. Because of a high and stable demand from customers, the operation planning department has scheduled operations making the assumption that the average number of machines that will be running is six. If the average operating life of the machines is seven five-day weeks, what average repair time should the maintenance department aim at providing, and how busy will the team be?

From Figure 21.11 the ratio $T_a/T_s$ corresponding to $K = 8$ and 6 on the $y$ axis is 7, i.e.

$$\frac{T_a}{T_s} = 7$$

$$T_s = \frac{7 \times 5}{7}$$

$$= 5 \text{ days}$$

$$K\frac{T_s}{T_a} = \frac{8 \times 5}{7 \times 5} = 1.14$$

Therefore percentage of time team is occupied = 82% (from Figure 21.12).

---

Now let us consider a situation in which there is more than one maintenance team responsible for the repair of a set of identical machines. Let us assume again both exponential breakdown characteristics and exponential service times for all maintenance teams. If the breakdowns are attended to on a 'first come, first served' basis, then curves such as those shown in Figure 21.13 can be constructed. One interesting point is evident from these curves. It can be seen that the use of one maintenance team performing the repair work twice as quickly as each of two teams is superior to the use of the two slower teams. For example, consider a situation in which there are four machines, where $T_a$ = 4 days. Suppose that there is a choice of using one quite large maintenance team which is capable of an average repair time of ½ day *or* two smaller teams each capable of average repair times of 1 day, then in both cases $MT_a/T_s = 8$, but it can be seen from Figure 21.13 that the use of one team ($M$ = 1) results in an average number of approximately 3.7 machines working, whereas the use of two teams results in an average of 3.5 machines working.

Clearly, if our objective is the reduction in machine idle time, then it is better, where possible, to use a single fast maintenance team rather than two or more slower ones.[2]

**Figure 21.13**

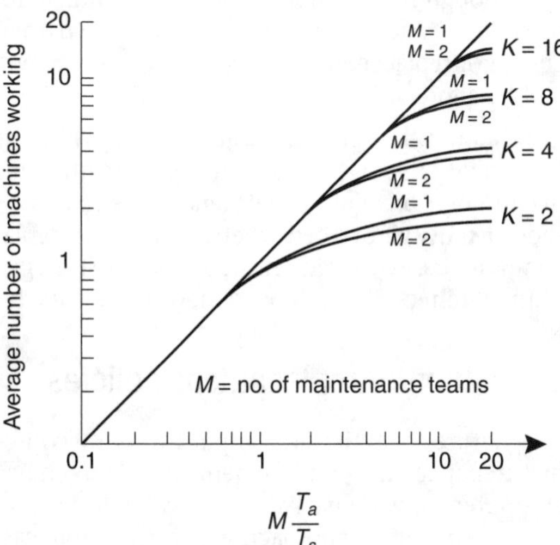


[2] See also: Ntuen, C. A. (1989) Forecasting maintenance crew size requirement based on periodic maintenance records. *Production and Inventory Management,* **30**(2), pp. 41–43.

# REPLACEMENT

## Replacement policies for items subject to sudden failure

When a machine stops because of the failure of one part, then the maintenance team may simply go along to the machine and effect a repair by replacing the failed item. An alternative strategy is to replace not only the broken component but also all similar components, on the assumption that since they have all been in service for some length of time, because one has already failed the others are also likely to fail in the near future. Or a third strategy might be adopted: the replacement of the broken component and *certain* of the similar components.

As an example, consider the problem faced by someone whose job is to replace, when necessary, the bulbs in the lights of every room of a multi-storey building. The replacement strategies may be as follows:

(a) Replace only those bulbs that fail. Such a strategy may involve an excessive amount of work, since replacing a bulb takes an average of 30 minutes erecting a ladder, obtaining new bulbs from stores, etc. Because of the difference between the comparatively low cost of a new bulb and the comparatively high cost of replacement, an alternative strategy may be preferred.

(b) When one bulb fails, replace *all* bulbs in that room or on that floor.

(c) Alternatively, as a compromise, replace the bulb that has failed *and* a proportion of other bulbs, perhaps those that have been in use for longer than six months, in other words those that are expected to fail fairly soon.

The problem then is to decide which of these strategies to adopt, a decision that must, of course, be made on the basis of cost considerations. The cost involved in replacement is dependent on the probability of component failure. In the case of strategy 1 the probable total cost of maintenance over, say, a year is given by the following:

$$\begin{matrix}\text{Cost of making a} \\ \text{single replacement}\end{matrix} \times \begin{matrix}\text{Probable number of failures} \\ \text{during year}\end{matrix}$$

In the case of strategy 2, the total cost is determined by the number of components replaced each time and the number of 'first failures' during the period. In the final strategy, 3, the cost would depend on the number of 'first failures' and the number of components at every replacement period which have been in use longer than a given time.

Although it is possible to develop formulae for the replacement problem in which items are subject to sudden failure, such formulae are often inadequate for the practical situation; consequently the choice of replacement strategy is often made with the aid of a simulation exercise, a procedure which will be adopted here.

It should be noted that, although we have spoken of the problem as being one of repair, similar considerations might apply during preventive maintenance. For example, if during the inspection of a machine for preventive maintenance purposes a component is seen to be likely to fail if left in service, then it must be decided whether or not to replace this component only, or some or all of the similar components. The logic behind the latter strategy is that, while some components do not yet show signs of impending failure, they are nevertheless likely to fail before the next scheduled maintenance period.

### Simulation of replacement policies

The nature, benefits and applications of computer simulation are outlined in Appendix III. Many maintenance and replacement problems have been examined using this approach and several computer software packages are available for use in this area. Here, as an example, we will look at one simple simulation approach which in simple cases can be implemented manually.

The Monte Carlo method of simulation is much used and essentially involves the use of random sampling from a distribution of variables. On several previous occasions we have made assumptions about the nature of distributions, often considering them to be normal, exponential, Poisson, etc., thus enabling us to develop statistical decision rules. When distributions of variables do not conform to one of these types then a simulation procedure must be adopted – often the Monte Carlo method in which use is made of the *actual* distribution of the variable rather than a convenient approximation to it.

## EXAMPLE

Consider the case of one machine which has four identical bearings, each subject to the same operating conditions.

The manufacturer is able to provide us with a probability distribution for the life of these bearings (Table 21.1), which does not, however, conform to any of the conventional types of statistical probability distribution.

Our own maintenance and costing departments are able to tell us, from an analysis of past work sheets:

(a) that the time required to replace these bearings is as follows:

- (i) to replace one bearing = 2 work hours;
- (ii) to replace two bearings = 4 work hours;
- (iii) to replace three bearings = 5 work hours;
- (iv) to replace four bearings = 7 work hours;

(b) that the relevant maintenance costs are as follows:

- (i) cost of bearing = £3 each;
- (ii) direct labour cost of maintenance = £2/worker/hour;
- (iii) cost of idle or machine downtime = £15/hour/machine.

We have to decide which of the three repair strategies to adopt for this particular machine.

First, we must construct a cumulative probability curve from the data given in Table 21.1. This is shown in Figure 21.14. Now we can use this figure to simulate the failure of bearings and to test the three repair strategies. To do this we also need random number tables.

The simulation is performed by first drawing any series of random numbers from random number tables, which are then used to enable us to take a random sample from the cumulative probability distribution in order to determine the simulated bearing operating life.

For example, consider bearing no. 1. If the first random number taken from four-figure random number tables is 2251, then since we wish to sample from a scale of 0 to 100 we consider this to represent 22.5% on the *y* axis of Figure 21.14. A horizontal line from this point cuts the cumulative probability curve at a point corresponding to 238 on the *x* axis, and hence the life of the first no. 1 bearing is taken to be 238 hours.

Similarly the life of the first ten no. 1 bearings might be found to be as in the table to the right.

| Random number | Operating life (hours) |
|---|---|
| 2251 | 238 |
| 7459 | 363 |
| 9380 | 450 |
| 2212 | 235 |
| 9237 | 440 |
| 3975 | 285 |
| 3278 | 270 |
| 1621 | 215 |
| 0413 | 125 |
| 3249 | 270 |

By drawing more random numbers, the probable life of several of all four bearings can be determined, as shown in Table 21.2. These figures can now be used in the simulation of the three repair strategies:

(a) Replace bearings individually on failure.

(b) Replace all bearings together whenever one of them fails.

(c) Replace the bearing that fails and at the same time replace those that have been in service for over 335 hours (the average operating life).

**Table 21.1 Probability of bearings failure**

| Bearing life (hours) | Number of failures | Cumulative number of failures | Cumulative percentage of failures |
|---|---|---|---|
| 0–49 | 0 | 0 | 0 |
| 50–99 | 1 | 1 | 1 |
| 100–149 | 3 | 4 | 4 |
| 150–199 | 5 | 9 | 9 |
| 200–249 | 9 | 18 | 18 |
| 250–299 | 16 | 34 | 34 |
| 300–349 | 24 | 58 | 58 |
| 350–399 | 20 | 78 | 78 |
| 400–449 | 13 | 91 | 91 |
| 450–499 | 6 | 97 | 97 |
| 500–549 | 2 | 99 | 99 |
| 550–599 | 1 | 100 | 100 |
| | 100 | | |

**Figure 21.14** Cumulative probability of failure of bearings. N.B. This distribution has been drawn using the 'discrete' data of Table 21.1. Since failure may occur at any time, probability of failure is a 'continuous' function, hence the continuous curve is used in the simulation.

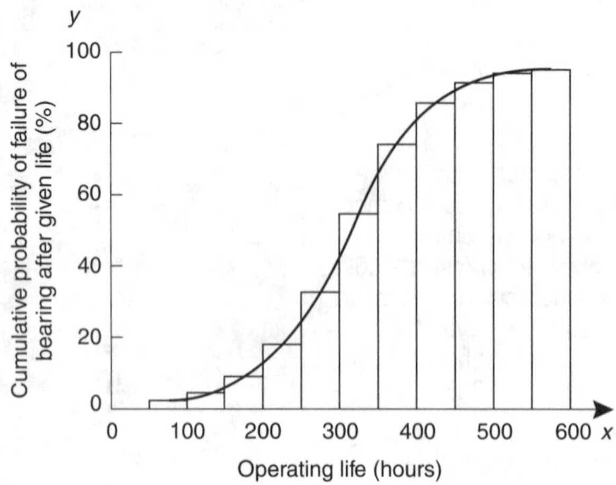

The simulation is shown by bar charts in Figure 21.15. For the first strategy the simulation merely consists of the operating life figures for the bearings taken from Table 21.2 arranged sequentially on a common time-scale.[3] For the second strategy each replacement is occasioned by the failure of only one bearing (shown by a solid line), the other three being replaced at the same time as a matter of policy (shown by dotted lines). The simulation for the third strategy is more involved. Initially bearings are replaced one at a time because, when each failure occurs, none of the others has been in service for more than the specified time (335 hours), and hence do

**Table 21.2 Simulated operating life for ten of each of four bearings**

| Bearing no. 1 | | Bearing no. 2 | | Bearing no. 3 | | Bearing no. 4 | |
|---|---|---|---|---|---|---|---|
| Random number | Life | Random number | Life | Random number | Life | Random number | Life |
| 2251 | 238 | 3711 | 280 | 2235 | 240 | 5761 | 325 |
| 7459 | 363 | 0347 | 115 | 0212 | 100 | 0983 | 175 |
| 9380 | 450 | 5034 | 310 | 3768 | 280 | 2236 | 240 |
| 2212 | 235 | 7816 | 375 | 6889 | 350 | 2250 | 240 |
| 9237 | 440 | 1385 | 200 | 2782 | 255 | 3053 | 265 |
| 3975 | 285 | 7823 | 375 | 3316 | 275 | 9938 | 550 |
| 3278 | 270 | 9942 | 550 | 8733 | 410 | 9360 | 450 |
| 1621 | 215 | 9019 | 430 | 1994 | 230 | 4558 | 300 |
| 0413 | 125 | 6307 | 335 | 6254 | 340 | 8015 | 380 |
| 3249 | 270 | 1873 | 225 | 0630 | 150 | 6104 | 330 |

**Figure 21.15**

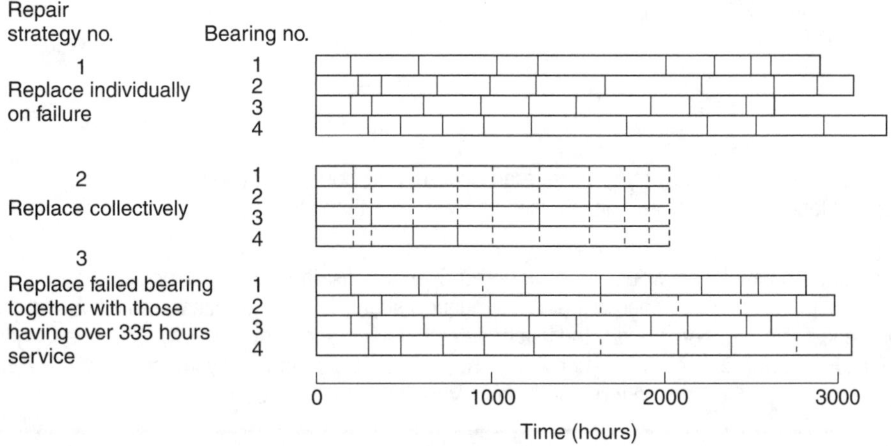


[3] Notice that, for reasons of simplicity, we have not attempted to include the comparatively short periods of time required for replacement on any of these charts.

not require replacing. However, on the fourth replacement of bearing no. 4 it is found that bearing no. 1 has already been in service for a period in excess of 335 hours. Consequently it is replaced.[4] A similar situation occurs on four other occasions (shown by dotted lines).

Now let us consider the maintenance cost incurred by each of these strategies. Let us consider a 2000-hour period and look first at strategy 1:

| | |
|---|---|
| Number of replacements | = 24 |
| Maintenance cost | = 24 × 2 hours × £2 |
| | = £96 |
| Cost of machine idle time | = 24 × 2 hours × £15 |
| | = £720 |
| Cost of bearings | = 24 × 3 |
| | = £72 |
| Total cost | = £888 |

Now consider strategy 2:

| | |
|---|---|
| Number of replacements | = 9 (each involving 4 bearings) |
| Maintenance cost | = 9 × 7 × 2 |
| | = £126 |
| Cost of machine idle time | = 9 × 7 × 15 |
| | = £945 |
| Cost of bearings | = 36 × 3 |
| | = £108 |
| Total cost | = £1179 |

Now consider strategy 3:

| | |
|---|---|
| Number of replacements | = 20 of 1 bearing |
| | 1 of 2 bearings |
| | 1 of 3 bearings |
| Maintenance cost | = 20 × 2 × 2 = 80 |
| | +1 × 4 × 2 = 8 |
| | + 1 × 5 × 2 = 10 |
| | = £98 |
| Cost of machine idle time | = 20 × 2 × 15 = 600 |
| | + 1 × 4 × 15 = 60 |
| | + 1 × 5 × 15 = 75 |
| | = £735 |
| Cost of bearings | = 25 × 3 |
| | = £75 |
| Total cost | = £908 |

The results of this simulation show that, considered over a 2000-hour operating period, it is economically advisable to adopt replacement strategy 1, since this incurs less cost than strategy 3 and substantially less than strategy 2.

In practice such a simulation would be conducted over a considerably longer period than the 2000 hours used here, since it is essential to ensure that the simulated situation has stabilized itself. By using the comparatively short period adopted here we run the risk of selecting a replacement policy which in the longer term may not be optimal. Furthermore, in practice such a simulation would be conducted with the aid of a computer, since manual simulation for a long time-period would be very tedious and time-consuming.

---

[4] In fact at this time bearing no. 1 has been in service for 379 hours, i.e. (325 + 175 + 240 + 240) – (238 + 363).

## Replacement policies for items which deteriorate

The cost of operating equipment and machinery normally increases with the increasing age of the equipment. Such increasing cost may be caused by: (a) the increasing cost of the maintenance necessary to obtain continuing reliability of the equipment; and (b) the obsolescence of the equipment, making its continued operation comparatively more costly when compared with the equipment which might be used to replace it. There comes a time, therefore, when it is not only economically justifiable to replace the present ageing equipment, but economically beneficial in order to obtain equipment which has greater output, reliability, etc.

Our present problem, then, is to decide at what time such equipment should be replaced. Such a decision must obviously be made on economic grounds, by a comparison of the net economic benefit of retaining present equipment and the net economic benefit of replacing present equipment.

As regards *present* equipment we must consider the following:

(a) its life;

(b) its current and future salvage or sale value;

(c) the revenue produced throughout the rest of its life;

(d) the expenditure incurred throughout the rest of its life.

As regards the *proposed* replacement equipment we must consider:

(a) the purchase price of the equipment;

(b) its life;

(c) the salvage or sale value at various times in its life;

(d) the revenue produced by the equipment;

(e) the expenditure incurred throughout its life.

In considering the replacement of equipment it is important to remember that money has a time value. For example, £100 is normally of more value to us now than it would be next year. The evaluation of the economic worth of equipment, therefore, depends on both its earning potential and time considerations. We must therefore make our replacement decisions by considering the *present value* of the net revenue associated with its use.

If $i$ = annual rate of interest, then £100 now is worth

$$\frac{100}{(1+i)^n} \text{ in } n \text{ years' time}$$

e.g. £100 is worth $100/1.1^2$ = £82.6 in 2 years' time.

Suppose that the investment of £10 000 in a new piece of equipment results in a net income of £5000 for each of the following three years. If we assume that the 'cost of capital' or the rate of interest which might have been achieved had the £10 000 been invested is 10%, then the *present value* of this income is £12 434, i.e.

$$\frac{5000}{(1.1)} + \frac{5000}{(1.1)^2} + \frac{5000}{(1.1)^3}$$

$$= £12\,434$$

The calculation of present values in this way, by *discounting* future sums of money at a given rate, is the basis of the *discounted cash flow* technique for investment appraisal.

When concerned with equipment replacement, this discounting procedure can be expressed by the following equation:

$$\text{NPV} = \left(\sum_{n=1}^{L} \frac{I_n - E_n}{(1+i)^n}\right) + \frac{S_L}{(1+i)^L}$$

where NPV = net present value
$I_n$ = income for year $n$
$E_n$ = expenditure for year $n$
$i$ = discount rate
$L$ = life of equipment or number of years being considered
$S_L$ = sale or scrap value at end of life, i.e. year $N$

Clearly, to be economically beneficial the net present value (NPV) must be equal to or greater than zero.

To assist discounted cash flow calculations, tables for $1/(1 + i)^n$ have been prepared (see Table 21.3).

The replacement decision normally takes the following form: whether to replace existing equipment now, or at a later date, up to and including the last year in the life of the existing equipment. The problem then is one of comparing, at *present value*, the cash flows associated with the use of the present and the proposed equipment over the common period from the present time to the end of the life of the present equipment. Naturally, cash flows that have already occurred do not enter into the decision – e.g. past operating costs of present equipment. We are concerned only with the cash flows that will result from the decision to retain the equipment and the decision to replace it, i.e. the operating costs, the revenues and the changes in disposal values.

**EXAMPLE**

## Replacement of a machine

The management of a company is anxious to determine whether or not to replace an existing machine with a new one of the latest type. The present machine has many years of useful service life left, but nevertheless it is thought that it may be better to obtain the new machine, which is known to have lower operating costs.

The cost of the new machine is £10 000 and its anticipated life is 20 years. The present machine is known to have a current disposal value of £5000 and an anticipated life of 16 years.

If the new machine is purchased an overhaul costing £2000 will be necessary after it has been in service for 10 years, and its disposal value after 16 and 20 years of service will be £500 and £200 respectively. If the present machine is retained, two overhauls will be required at 6 and 12 years, costing £2500 and £1500 respectively. Its disposal value after 16 years will be £150.

The net income (revenue less operating costs) which is expected to result from the use of the machines is shown in Table 21.4 along with the above data.

The net present value (using a discount rate of 10% per annum) of the cash flows over the 16 years for each machine is also calculated in Table 21.4. The NPV of the cash flow associated with decision 1 (replace present machine) is £2278. The NPV of the cash flow associated with decision 2 is £4061. Clearly, therefore, it is in the company's interest to retain the present machine rather than replace it.

---

It should be remembered, of course, that the discounted cash flow technique takes no account of the following, all of which may influence the replacement decision:

(a) risk, i.e. the uncertainty of factors such as operating life, repair costs, disposal values, etc.;

(b) inflation (except in that it relates to $i$);

**Table 21.3 Compound interest table ($1/(1 + i)^n$)**

| $n$ | $i$ = 1% | 2 | 3 | 4 | 5 | 6 | 7 | 8 | 9 | 10 |
|---|---|---|---|---|---|---|---|---|---|---|
| 1 | 0.9901 | 0.9804 | 0.9709 | 0.9615 | 0.9524 | 0.9434 | 0.9346 | 0.9259 | 0.9174 | 0.9091 |
| 2 | 0.9803 | 0.9612 | 0.9426 | 0.9246 | 0.9070 | 0.8900 | 0.8734 | 0.8573 | 0.8417 | 0.8264 |
| 3 | 0.9706 | 0.9423 | 0.9151 | 0.8890 | 0.8638 | 0.8396 | 0.8163 | 0.7938 | 0.7722 | 0.7513 |
| 4 | 0.9610 | 0.9238 | 0.8885 | 0.8548 | 0.8227 | 0.7921 | 0.7629 | 0.7350 | 0.7084 | 0.6830 |
| 5 | 0.9515 | 0.9057 | 0.8626 | 0.8219 | 0.7835 | 0.7473 | 0.7130 | 0.6806 | 0.6499 | 0.6209 |
| 6 | 0.9420 | 0.8880 | 0.8375 | 0.7903 | 0.7462 | 0.7050 | 0.6663 | 0.6302 | 0.5963 | 0.5645 |
| 7 | 0.9327 | 0.8706 | 0.8131 | 0.7599 | 0.7107 | 0.6651 | 0.6227 | 0.5835 | 0.5470 | 0.5132 |
| 8 | 0.9235 | 0.8535 | 0.7894 | 0.7307 | 0.6768 | 0.6274 | 0.5820 | 0.5403 | 0.5019 | 0.4665 |
| 9 | 0.9143 | 0.8368 | 0.7664 | 0.7026 | 0.6446 | 0.5919 | 0.5439 | 0.5002 | 0.4604 | 0.4241 |
| 10 | 0.9053 | 0.8302 | 0.7441 | 0.6756 | 0.6139 | 0.5584 | 0.5083 | 0.4632 | 0.4224 | 0.3588 |
| 11 | 0.8963 | 0.8043 | 0.7224 | 0.6496 | 0.5847 | 0.5268 | 0.4751 | 0.4289 | 0.3875 | 0.3505 |
| 12 | 0.8874 | 0.7885 | 0.7014 | 0.6246 | 0.5568 | 0.4970 | 0.4440 | 0.3971 | 0.3555 | 0.3186 |
| 13 | 0.8787 | 0.7730 | 0.6810 | 0.6006 | 0.5303 | 0.4688 | 0.4150 | 0.3677 | 0.3262 | 0.2897 |
| 14 | 0.8700 | 0.7579 | 0.6611 | 0.5775 | 0.5051 | 0.4423 | 0.3878 | 0.3405 | 0.2992 | 0.2633 |
| 15 | 0.8613 | 0.7430 | 0.6419 | 0.5553 | 0.4810 | 0.4173 | 0.3624 | 0.3152 | 0.2745 | 0.2394 |
| 16 | 0.8528 | 0.7284 | 0.6232 | 0.5339 | 0.4581 | 0.3936 | 0.3387 | 0.2919 | 0.2519 | 0.2176 |
| 17 | 0.8444 | 0.7142 | 0.6050 | 0.5134 | 0.4363 | 0.3714 | 0.3166 | 0.2703 | 0.2311 | 0.1978 |
| 18 | 0.8360 | 0.7002 | 0.5874 | 0.4936 | 0.4155 | 0.3503 | 0.2959 | 0.2502 | 0.2120 | 0.1799 |
| 19 | 0.8277 | 0.6864 | 0.5703 | 0.4746 | 0.3957 | 0.3305 | 0.2765 | 0.2317 | 0.1945 | 0.1635 |
| 20 | 0.8195 | 0.6730 | 0.5537 | 0.4564 | 0.3769 | 0.3118 | 0.2584 | 0.2145 | 0.1784 | 0.1486 |
| 21 | 0.8114 | 0.6598 | 0.5375 | 0.4388 | 0.3589 | 0.2942 | 0.2415 | 0.1987 | 0.1637 | 0.1351 |
| 22 | 0.8034 | 0.6468 | 0.5219 | 0.4220 | 0.3418 | 0.2775 | 0.2257 | 0.1839 | 0.1502 | 0.1228 |
| 23 | 0.7954 | 0.6432 | 0.5067 | 0.4057 | 0.3256 | 0.2618 | 0.2109 | 0.1703 | 0.1378 | 0.1117 |
| 24 | 0.7876 | 0.6217 | 0.4919 | 0.3901 | 0.3101 | 0.2470 | 0.1971 | 0.1577 | 0.1264 | 0.1015 |
| 25 | 0.7798 | 0.6095 | 0.4776 | 0.3751 | 0.2953 | 0.2330 | 0.1842 | 0.1460 | 0.1160 | 0.0923 |
| 26 | 0.7720 | 0.5976 | 0.4637 | 0.3607 | 0.2812 | 0.2198 | 0.1722 | 0.1352 | 0.1064 | 0.0839 |
| 27 | 0.7644 | 0.5859 | 0.4502 | 0.3468 | 0.2678 | 0.2074 | 0.1696 | 0.1252 | 0.0976 | 0.0763 |
| 28 | 0.7568 | 0.5744 | 0.4371 | 0.3335 | 0.2551 | 0.1956 | 0.1504 | 0.1159 | 0.0895 | 0.0693 |
| 29 | 0.7493 | 0.5631 | 0.4243 | 0.3207 | 0.2429 | 0.1846 | 0.1406 | 0.1073 | 0.0822 | 0.0630 |
| 30 | 0.7419 | 0.5521 | 0.4120 | 0.3083 | 0.2314 | 0.1741 | 0.1314 | 0.0994 | 0.0754 | 0.0573 |

where $i$ = annual interest rate
$n$ = number of years

(c) the timing of the cash flows in relation to opportunities for the use of the money elsewhere;

(d) the difficulty of raising money for the outlays;

(e) policy after the period considered;

(f) possible future development of improved equipment.

Table 21.4

| Year | $\frac{1}{(1+i)n}$ | (1) Machine is replaced | | | | (2) Machine is *not* replaced | | | |
|---|---|---|---|---|---|---|---|---|---|
| | | Outlays (£) | Net income (£) | Net cash flow | PV | Outlays (£) | Net income (£) | Net cash flow | PV |
| 0 | 1.000 | 10 000 | 5000 | -5000 | -5000 | | | | |
| 1 | 0.909 | | 1500 | 1500 | 1365 | | 1000 | 1000 | 909 |
| 2 | 0.826 | | 1400 | 1400 | 1155 | | 1000 | 1000 | 826 |
| 3 | 0.751 | | 1300 | 1300 | 980 | | 1000 | 1000 | 751 |
| 4 | 0.683 | | 1200 | 1200 | 820 | | 900 | 900 | 615 |
| 5 | 0.620 | | 1100 | 1100 | 685 | | 800 | 800 | 498 |
| 6 | 0.564 | | 1000 | 1000 | 565 | 2500 | 700 | -1800 | -1015 |
| 7 | 0.513 | | 900 | 900 | 460 | | 700 | 700 | 360 |
| 8 | 0.466 | | 800 | 800 | 374 | | 700 | 700 | 327 |
| 9 | 0.424 | | 700 | 700 | 297 | | 700 | 700 | 297 |
| 10 | 0.385 | 2000 | 600 | -1400 | -540 | | 600 | 600 | 232 |
| 11 | 0.350 | | 600 | 600 | 211 | | 500 | 500 | 175 |
| 12 | 0.318 | | 600 | 600 | 191 | 1500 | 400 | -1100 | -351 |
| 13 | 0.289 | | 600 | 600 | 174 | | 400 | 400 | 116 |
| 14 | 0.263 | | 600 | 600 | 158 | | 400 | 400 | 105 |
| 15 | 0.239 | | 600 | 600 | 144 | | 400 | 400 | 96 |
| 16 | 0.217 | | 600+500 | 1110 | 239 | | 400+150 | 550 | 120 |

$$\text{NPV} = \left(\sum_{n=1}^{16} \frac{I_n - E_n}{(1.1)^n}\right) + \frac{S_{16}}{(1.1)^{16}} = \mathbf{2278} \qquad \text{NPV} = \left(\sum_{n=1}^{16} \frac{I_n - E_n}{(1.1)^n}\right) + \frac{S_{16}}{(1.1)^{16}} = \mathbf{4061}$$

## COMPUTERS IN MAINTENANCE AND REPLACEMENT

Few other operations management responsibilities cover such a wide area as maintenance management. The maintenance manager will be concerned with the acquisition of equipment and parts, the planning of work, the control of work, costing, quality control, etc. To operate effectively the manager will need to collect, store and have access to a considerable amount of data. Additionally, complex decisions will have to be made about the planning of inspection, service work, preventive maintenance, etc., as well as the organization of repair and the planning of replacement. Given this range of tasks and the considerable amount of information required for the execution of these tasks, it is not surprising to find that maintenance departments are increasingly committed to computer-based maintenance management systems.

Computer-based maintenance management systems can be categorized as follows:

(a) maintenance records and documentation systems;

(b) maintenance records, documentation, decision-making and planning systems.

Many systems are available for simple applications, as in (a) above. They offer the opportunity of storing data on equipment and inventories, producing work schedules and requirements, analysing plant history, labour costs, etc. They are essentially data processing systems rather than decision-making systems. One such system will be described below. The approach required for (b) above involves such data processing but also provides for some decision-making. The use of such systems will enable preventive maintenance and inspection to be planned, replacement intervals to be determined, etc. This latter approach is, of course, more sophisticated, and offers the benefit of a more integrated computer maintenance management (CMM) approach. (See Further Reading for this chapter.)

**EXAMPLE**

### *Opmist*

Opmist (from Welcome Software) is a computer program designed to help managers reduce maintenance costs. The program covers four areas: (1) asset register; (2) maintenance procedures and documentation; (3) material inventory control; and (4) network (critical path) scheduling. It is arranged as a series of modules. They are related to each other since information is stored in relational database files. The Opmist data analysis module provides the tools to review and manipulate data available from the rest of the program. It includes a report generator for creating custom and graphic reports. The final module includes various utility functions – one set supplies tools for system management, while another deals with system variable functions.

Source: Brower, M. J. (1989) Maintenance management programme includes critical path method analysis. *Plant Engineering*, **43**(15), pp. 67, 70.

## CHECKLIST FOR CHAPTER 21

### The need for maintenance and repair

Types of maintenance activity and their interrelationships

### The maintenance function

Terotechnology and life-cycle costing

Objectives of maintenance

### Maintenance decisions

What is to be maintained?

Types of maintenance

Organization of maintenance

### Inspection

### Preventive maintenance

Nature

Operating life curves

Breakdown time distributions

Preventive maintenance for a single machine

Preventive maintenance for several machines

### Repair

Nature

Repair teams (crews)

Allocation/size of repair teams

### Replacement

Nature

Replacement policies

- Items subject to sudden failure
- Simulation method
- Items which deteriorate
- Discounted cash flow methods

### Computers in maintenance and replacement

## FURTHER READING

**Cho, D. I. and Parlar, M. (1991)** A survey of maintenance models for multi-unit systems. *European Journal of Operations Research*, **51**(1), pp. 1–23.

**Cordero, S. T. (1987)** *Maintenance Management Handbook*. Englewood Cliff, NJ: Fairmont Press.

**Kimmel, P. S. (1992)** From a maintenance to a management system. *Facilities Design and Management*, **11**(7), p.27.

**Mullin, R. (1992)** Maintenance software – the next generation. *Chemical Week*, **151**(8), pp. 33–34.

**Raouf, A. (ed.)(1994)** Maintenance management. *International Journal of Operations and Production Management*, **14**(7), pp. 2–80.

**Tombari, H. A. (1982)** Designing a maintenance management system. *Production and Inventory Management*, **23**(4), pp. 139–147.

## QUESTIONS

21.1 Define and differentiate between preventive maintenance and repair. What are the objectives of maintenance? In what circumstances is preventive maintenance particularly appropriate?

21.2 An examination of a machine operating history together with statistical information provided by the manufacturer has revealed that the breakdown time distribution approximates to an Erlang distribution with parameter l = 2. It has also been established that the average trouble-free life between breakdowns is 175 hours.

The maintenance manager estimates that the average time for repairs is 4.6 hours, and a study of the maintenance and service instructions for the machine indicates that the average time for preventive maintenance is 2.5 hours.

It has further been estimated that the costs of maintenance and repair are as follows:

Preventive maintenance £5/h

Repair £10/h

The average value of the output of the machine is £74.6/h.

(a) Determine the optimum preventive maintenance schedule.

(b) How would this schedule change if:

(i) the cost of repairs decreased to £5/h:

(ii) the average running life between breakdowns decreased to 75 h?

21.3 Referring to the previous question, i.e.

| | |
|---|---|
| Breakdown time distribution | = Erlang, l = 1 |
| Average life between breakdowns | = 175 h |
| Time for repair | = 4.6 h |
| Time per preventive maintenance | = 2.5 h |
| Cost of preventive maintenance | = £5/h |
| Cost of repair | = 10/h |

(a) Because of a change in the use of the machine the value of the hourly output changes. (All other figures above remain the same.) It is calculated that in the new situation the optimum preventive maintenance interval is 262 hours. What is the value of the hourly machine output?

(b) A work study team is engaged to study work methods during preventive maintenance, with the object of reducing the average time required for such maintenance.

For the data given initially, an average trouble-free life between breakdowns of 175 hours and an output value of £74.6 per hour, what is the optimum preventive maintenance interval if:

(i) both the cost and average duration for preventive maintenance are reduced by 25%?

(ii) the average duration of preventive maintenance is reduced by 50% but cost is increased by 25%.

21.4 If the average operating life, without breakdowns, of four similar machines is 4 weeks, and if the average time to repair a machine which has broken down is 6 weeks, what is the average number of machines working at any time? State what statistical assumptions you have made in arriving at your answer.

If one repair team is allocated to the repair of the above machines, what proportion of the time will this team be occupied? State what statistical assumption you have made in arriving at your answer.

21.5 (a) A single maintenance team is expected to effect repairs to several identical machines as and when necessary. Because of other, less important duties (which can be interrupted if necessary), the team can devote only 80% of their time to the repair of the machines. It is known that the breakdown distribution of the machines approximates closely to the exponential distribution and that the average time between breakdown is 75 hours.

(i) How many machines can the team attend if the repair time is exponentially distributed with mean = 15 hours?

(ii) What is the average number of machines in service at any time?

(b) An unlikely situation has arisen and a maintenance manager has a choice of allocating a repair team to look after one of three different groups of machines. The details of each group of machines are as follows:

Group of 'A' type machines:

| | |
|---|---|
| Number | = 8 |
| Average time between breakdowns | = 50 h |
| Average time to make repair | = 5 h |

Group of 'B' type machines:

| | |
|---|---|
| Number | = 6 |
| Average time between breakdowns | = 40 h |
| Average time to make repair | = 6 h |

Group 'C' type machines:

| | |
|---|---|
| Number | = 10 |
| Average time between breakdowns | = 20 h |
| Average time to make a repair | = 2 h |

Assuming that the breakdown time distribution and the repair time distribution are exponential:

(i) Other things being equal, which group of machines would keep the repair team busiest?

(ii) Which group should the repair team be allocated to if the criterion is the maximization of the average percentage of the total number of machines in service at any time?

21.6 Describe briefly how you would collect and analyse data in order to assist in the determination of a maintenance policy for a large computer installation in a bank.

Having determined the policy, what data would you collect regularly in order to ensure that the maintenance procedures were adjusted to conform to changes in the characteristics of the equipment?

21.7 (a) Determine the maximum average time required to perform a repair if two maintenance teams are to attend to two identical machines and if, on average, a minimum of one machine should be in service at any time. The repair time and the machine breakdown time are both exponentially distributed, and the average operating life of machines between breakdowns is 40 hours.

(b) What is the maximum average repair time if one maintenance team is to ensure the same performance of the machines?

21.8 A machine has three identical and rather complex mechanisms, each of which occasionally fails to operate satisfactorily. The cumulative probability of failure of a mechanism is given in the graph. It has been found from experience that the replacement of one mechanism takes 1 hour, while the replacement of two together takes 1.75 hours and the replacement of all three takes 2.5 hours. The costs associated with this operation are given below.

| | |
|---|---|
| Direct labour cost | = £8/h |
| Cost of replacement mechanism | = £10 |
| Downtime cost of machine | = £75/h |

Three replacement strategies are available:

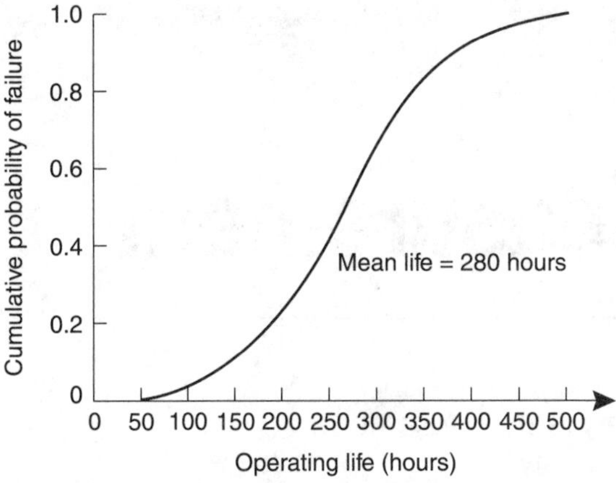


| Year | Revenue £ | Year | Revenue £ |
|---|---|---|---|
| This year | 1500 | 8 | 1800 |
| 1 | 2000 | 9 | 1600 |
| 2 | 2000 | 10 | 1500 |
| 3 | 2000 | 11 | 1500 |
| 4 | 2000 | 12 | 1000 |
| 5 | 2000 | 13 | 700 |
| 6 | 2000 | 14 | 500 |
| 7 | 2000 | 15 | 500 |

| Year | Revenue £ | Year £ | Revenue |
|---|---|---|---|
| This year | 1500 | 7 | 1000 |
| 1 | 1500 | 8 | 750 |
| 2 | 1200 | 9 | 750 |
| 3 | 1200 | 10 | 600 |
| 4 | 1100 | 11 | 500 |
| 5 | 1100 | 12 | 400 |
| 6 | 1000 | | |

(a) Replace each mechanism individually when it fails.

(b) Replace all three mechanisms every time one mechanism fails.

(c) Replace each mechanism when it fails and, at the same time, replace all other mechanisms that have been in service for longer than the known average operating life of the mechanism.

Using a simulation approach determine the minimum cost replacement strategy.

21.9 Profit Makers Ltd is considering the purchase of a machine to replace an ageing existing machine. The new machine would cost £6000 and is expected to have a life of 15 years during which it would earn revenue as shown to the left.

One major overhaul would be necessary in five years' time, costing £3750, and a second overhaul would be necessary in twelve years' time, costing £2500. It is anticipated that the realizable value on disposal of this machine would be £2500 at any time after the twelfth year and £5000 between the tenth and twelfth years inclusive. The existing machine is sound but technologically dated. Nevertheless, it has an expected life of a further twelve years. If it is retained it will be necessary to conduct minor maintenance work this year, at a cost of £1500, and every fifth year thereafter at a cost of £500 each time. Its disposal value is expected to be £500 and it is expected to earn revenue as shown in the second table, left.

The company is in the habit of evaluating future investment and revenues at present value, by means of a 10% 'discount' rate.

(a) Should Profit Makers Ltd replace the existing machine?

(b) What is the cost difference at present value between the two alternative strategies?

Chapter 22

# Performance measurement

## ISSUES

What is the purpose of performance measurement?
What should be measured?
How do we measure customer service?
How do we measure productivity, or resource utilization?
What is integrated productivity measurement?
How are performance measurements used?
What is a performance audit?

## NOTATION USED IN THIS CHAPTER

$AV$ Added value or net output
$C$ Operations cost
$Cx$ Indirect external expenses
$F$ Total factorial costs
$H$ Net earnings
$K$ Capital charges
$L$ Employment or labour charges
$M$ Materials throughput
$N$ Non-labour factorial cost
$P$ Profits
$R$ Internal expenses
$S$ Sales revenue or gross output
$T$ Total earnings
$X$ Total external purchases

In this chapter we shall consider briefly some aspects of performance measurement. This section of the book is concerned with control, and in Chapter 19 we noted that the measurement of operating system performance provides for control through the use of a feedback mechanism. Thus actual system performance might be compared with planned or intended performance, any resulting difference being used in determining appropriate action aimed at securing performance more closely corresponding to that intended. Performance measurement will of course have other uses, often associated with and resulting from its use for control. For example, present performance may be measured so that incentives, objectives and targets may be set or modified.

Two basic objectives for operating systems and operations management were identified in Chapter 1, i.e. the provision of customer service and adequate resource utilization. If operating systems are intended to achieve certain objectives in respect of both customer service and resource utilization, it is appropriate that system performance should be measured in respect of both objectives. Performance measurement in respect of resource utilization is common in operations management, but the measurement of performance in respect of customer service is less common.

Here we shall again consider the nature of both customer service and resource utilization and the manner in which objectives in each area are established and performance against them is measured.

## CUSTOMER SERVICE PERFORMANCE *(see also Chapter 1)*

To recap briefly on Chapter 1, the function of operating systems is the satisfaction of customer wants. This, therefore, is an objective of operations management. The items, movement or treatment provided by the operating system must match customers' needs if these customers are to be satisfied. The provision of customer service and the creation of customer satisfaction is a multi-dimension problem, three principal factors having been identified in Chapter 1 as follows:

(a) ***specification***, i.e. the provision of goods, movement or treatment as requested or specified by the customer, *or* to a standard but acceptable specification;

(b) ***cost***, i.e. the provision of goods, movement or treatment at a requested cost *or* at a standard but acceptable cost;

(c) ***timing***, i.e. (i) the provision of goods, movement or treatment at a requested time *or* at a standard but acceptable time, and/or at an acceptable delay, and (ii) in the case of movement or transport the provision of movement or transport having a requested duration *or* requiring a standard but acceptable duration.

An organization will seek to create customer satisfaction through the provision of adequate customer service by pursuing appropriate objectives in these three areas, and hence ultimately the effectiveness of the operating system can be assessed by considering the extent to which intended specification, cost and timing objectives are met.

### The measures of customer service: specification, cost and timing

These three customer service factors are general factors only; they each comprise several dimensions and in most cases it will be more practical and appropriate to assess or measure performance on these narrower dimensions.

(a) The *specification* of goods may be considered in terms of their design features and performance characteristics. Together these dimensions define what the item is and how it is intended to perform its purpose. Similarly the specification of a transport may be expressed in terms of its 'design' and performance. In this context design, i.e. the nature of the transport movement, may be expressed in terms of the origin, destination and route of movement. The performance can be considered synonymous with 'means', i.e. the means or method by which the movement is achieved. A service treatment may be defined in similar terms. The nature of the treatment can be considered to be the design characteristic or dimension, and the means by which the treatment is provided can be considered to be the performance characteristic.

Two main dimensions can therefore be identified for the specification of items, movement or treatment. They are the 'what' and 'how' dimensions. In designing an item, a movement or a treatment an organization will define these two characteristics. In assessing the performance of an organization the customer will again consider these two dimensions. They are summarized in Table 22.1.

**Table 22.1 The specifications of items, movement and treatment**

| **Dimensions for *specification*** | **Items** | **Movement** | **Treatment** |
|---|---|---|---|
| *Design*, i.e. *what* is the item, movement/ treatment? | e.g. comprising: *Appearance* and *dimensions* *Material* specifications Design and manufacture *quality* | e.g. comprising; *Source*, *destination* and *route* | e.g. comprising: *Nature* of treatment |
| *Performance*, i.e. *how* is the purpose achieved? – the means or method employed | e.g. comprising: *Operating* characteristics or performance characteristics or *operating principles* or means | e.g. comprising: *Means* of transport | e.g. comprising: Means of treatment or *procedures* employed, or *form* of treatment |

*Source: Wild, R. (1979)* Operations Management: A Policy Framework. *Oxford: Pergamon. Reproduced with permission*

(b) The general dimension of *cost* identified above may similarly be broken down into important components. The customer – theoretically at least – will evaluate an item of a given specification in terms of its total expected costs, i.e. acquisition price plus any necessary additional expenses associated with an item, e.g. installation, running and maintenance costs, all discounted to the present time in order to take into account cash flows over a period of time. Similarly the cost of a transport movement or service may be expressed in terms of the original price of acquisition plus any additional and necessary costs or expenses.

We can therefore distinguish, for our purposes, two aspects of costs, i.e. price and expenses. In seeking to provide customer service an organization will consider these two dimensions. In evaluating an organization customers will consider or respond to these two dimensions. These cost dimensions of customer service are summarized in Table 22.2.

**Table 22.2 The cost of items, movement and treatment**

| **Dimensions for *cost*** | **Items** | **Movement** | **Treatment** |
|---|---|---|---|
| *Price*, i.e. intended or quoted cost | e.g. comprising: *Purchase price*, or initial *cost* of good | e.g. comprising: *Cost of journey or fare* | e.g. comprising: *Cost of treatment or charge* |
| *Expenses*, i.e. expected additional costs | e.g. comprising: Cost of installation Cost of maintenance and replacement Running costs | e.g. comprising: Additional costs such as insurance, etc. | e.g. comprising: Additional costs such as insurance, etc. |

*Source: Wild, R. (1979)* Operations Management: A Policy Framework. *Oxford: Pergamon. Reproduced with permission*

(c) The third factor identified above – *timing* – may also be subdivided. Consider first the cost of goods. Customers will take into account the delay or wait between their expression of a want and the subsequent satisfaction of that want. This delay or wait will normally be evident as the period of time between placing an order and receiving the goods. This is clearly an important dimension of customer service, since delay greatly in excess of that which is acceptable will give rise to reduced overall customer satisfaction and loss of customers. Again this is a dimension which is, to some extent, within the control of the organization. It can, for example, set out deliberately to provide goods virtually on demand, or alternatively might choose to provide goods for which customers are expected to wait, perhaps for some considerable time. This delay dimension is also relevant in the provision of both transport and service. However, a further dimension is also important in these two functions. Both transport (i.e. movement) and service (i.e. treatment) are time-consuming. In both cases, therefore, the customers will consider their likely duration or the time required for their performance, i.e. to move from source to destination, or to be treated or accommodated. In assessing an organization the customer will therefore consider this dimension, and equally, in seeking to achieve customer service, an organization will seek to provide an appropriate or acceptable duration for its transport or services.

The timing factor can therefore be subdivided into the dimensions of delay and duration, summarized in Table 22.3.

**Table 22.3 The timing of the provision of items, movement and treatment**

| **Dimensions for *timing*** | **Items** | **Movement** | **Treatment** |
|---|---|---|---|
| *Delay*<br>i.e. intended or quoted delay or waiting time | e.g. comprising:<br>*Delivery time* or waiting time for delivery of goods | e.g. comprising:<br>Time spent waiting for transport | e.g. comprising:<br>Time spent waiting for treatment |
| *Duration*,<br>i.e. intended or quoted duration | | e.g. comprising:<br>Travel time or duration of journey | e.g. comprising:<br>Treatment time or duration of treatment |

*Source: Wild, R. (1979)* Operations Management: A Policy Framework, *Oxford: Pergamon. Reproduced with permission*

## The reliability factor

Customers, in appraising the *specification* of an item, will be aware that it may perform differently in practice from the way intended at design. Design and performance characteristics may therefore be seen as intended features. There will be some probability that items will perform unsatisfactorily. An item may fail to function as intended, i.e. to achieve its intended purpose. It may function, for some time and then fail, i.e. break down. It may break down regularly. It may function, but not at a desired level of performance. The customer must therefore consider the probability of an item satisfactorily achieving its intended purpose or continuing to achieve that purpose, i.e. its reliability. An organization must recognize this as a dimension of customer service and a characteristic of the product. The manner in which this reliability might be measured will depend on the nature of the item. It could, for example, be measured in terms of mean time between failures, or average operating life, or simply the probability that it will work at all. Similarly, in the specification of transport or service, it is necessary to consider reliability, the probability of the required destination being reached and the probability of the movement being achieved as intended.

The *cost* factor will also be seen in terms of its reliability. Price and expenses, as outlined above, can be considered to be quoted or intended costs. In practice actual costs may differ, and hence the probability of such changes will be an important customer service dimension and characteristic.

In considering the *timing* of goods, transport and service it is necessary to consider reliability issues. Both delay and duration, as discussed above, can be considered as intended times. The customer must consider the likelihood of the quoted or intended delay occurring and the likelihood of the quoted or intended duration occurring. In many cases in the provision of goods a delivery time is quoted, but both parties realize that there is a probability that in practice a longer delay will occur. Similarly, in the provision of transport, both parties will realize that while the normal intended or quoted duration for a journey may be *X* hours, owing to a variety of factors the actual duration may be greatly in excess of *X* hours. In this case, therefore, it is necessary again to consider reliability, i.e. the probability that the intended or quoted duration will in fact be achieved and the probability that the intended delay will be fact occur.

These three reliability dimensions (reliability of specification, cost and timing) are of major concern to operations management. The reliability of intended specification cost and timing will depend to a considerable extent on the effectiveness of operations management. Inadequate management of capacity and inventories and poor scheduling may give rise to cost, timing and specification changes. Poor resource utilization will add to costs, bring delays, and increase durations. Inadequate execution of design intentions may give rise to poor performance. Since achieving customer service in these three areas is primarily the responsibility of operations management, operations management must have a major influence on the formulation of objectives on these three reliability dimensions.

**Table 22.4 The principal dimensions of customer service**

| **Factors** | **Dimensions** | |
|---|---|---|
| *Specifications* | i.e. | |
| of goods, movement | 1. *Design* | 7. *Specification reliability* |
| or treatment | 2. *Performance* | |
| *Cost* | i.e. | |
| of goods, movement | 3. *Price* | 8. *Cost reliability* |
| or treatment | 4. *Expenses* | |
| *Timing* | i.e. | |
| of goods, movement | 5. *Delay* | 9. *Timing reliability* |
| or treatment | 6. *Duration* | |

**Table 22.5 Measures of customer service performance**

| **Customer service dimensions** | **Measures** |
|---|---|
| Specification reliability | Degree of conformity of goods, transport or service with specifications on design and performance (e.g. manufacture quality)<br>Number or proportion of goods, transports or services conforming to given and/or acceptable standards of design and performance |
| Cost reliability | Variance of goods, transport or service on price and expense specification<br>Number or proportion of goods, transports or services within given and/or acceptable price and expense range |
| Timing reliability | Variance of goods, transport or service on delay or duration specification<br>Number or proportion of goods, transports or services within given and/or acceptable delay and duration range (e.g. delivery performance) |

## The nine dimensions of customer service

Nine basic customer service dimensions can therefore be identified (Table 22.4). The intended specification, cost and timing of goods, transports and services will be largely determined by policy decisions within the organization. In some cases organizations will seek to maximize customer service on each of the six main dimensions, but in most cases different importance will be attached to each of these six dimensions. For this reason there can be no valid absolute measure of the performance of operations on design, performance, price, expenses, delay and duration. It is relevant only to measure the extent to which intended objectives are achieved, i.e. specification, cost and timing reliability.

Table 22.5 identifies some of the means of measuring and/or assessing operating system performance against these three customer service dimensions.

# RESOURCE UTILIZATION PERFORMANCE

Here we are on more familiar ground, for in most situations the intensity of the utilization of resources, i.e. resource productivity, will be accepted as a conventional measure of the performance of the operating system.

## Productivity measures

From the engineer's viewpoint, productivity and efficiency are synonymous and would be seen as the quotient obtained by dividing output by a factor of production, whether capital or raw material. Input generates output, and in a physical sense at least the quotient cannot exceed unity, although in a financial sense it must do so if the business is to secure a profit to survive.

An economist might take a different approach and might emphasize labour rather than capital productivity. Emphasis on the former encourages one to express inputs in terms of labour or labour equivalent, with attendant risks of estimation, averaging, etc. In an attempt to overcome this, the net output per employee can be used as a productivity measure, i.e.

$$\text{Net output per employee} = \frac{\text{Added value per annum}}{\text{Total number of employees}}$$

'Added value' represents the value added to materials by the process of production and from which wages, salaries, rent, rates, tax reserves and dividends, selling distribution and advertising costs have to be met.

An accountant might take yet another view. Many contemporary productivity measures are financially oriented because many firms evaluate the worth and effectiveness of their enterprise by using 'financial ratio analysis'. A variety of ratios might be developed but it is essential that those adopted are seen to be useful and relevant. The following are among those commonly employed:

(a) profit/capital employed;

(b) profit/sales;

(c) sales/capital employed;

(d) sales/fixed assets;

(e) sales/stocks;

(f) sales/employee;

(g) profits/employee.

In such an approach, an emphasis is placed on sales revenue and profit; however, it is possible that both are affected by supply and demand factors as well as being influenced by the efficiency of operations.

**Figure 22.1** Integrated productivity measurement model. Adapted with permission from Norman, R. G. and Bahiri, S. (1972) *Productivity Measurement and Incentives*. London: Butterworth

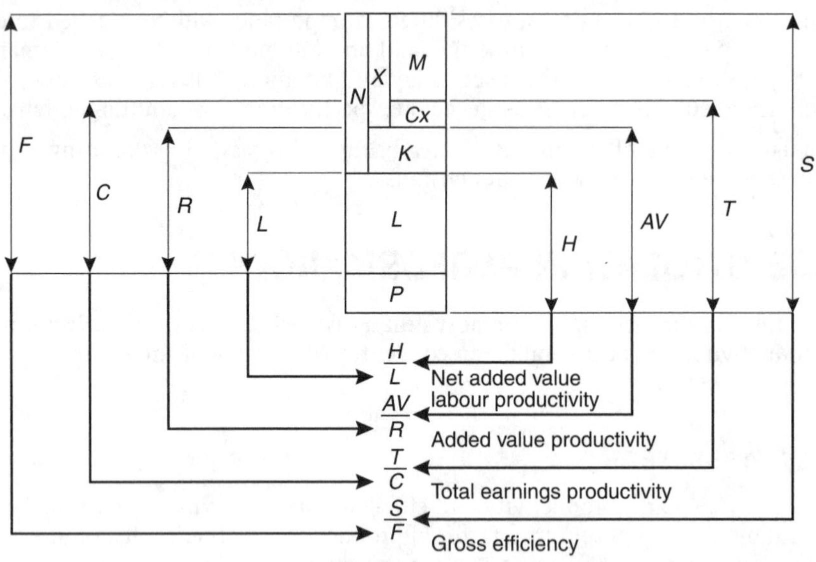


**Table 22.6 Notation for integrated productivity measurement model**

|  |  |
|---|---|
| *S* | = Sales revenue or gross output |
| *T* | = Total earnings |
| *AV* | = Added value or net output |
| *H* | = Net earnings |
| *M* | = Materials throughput |
| *Cx* | = Indirect external expenses |
| *X* | = Total external purchases |
| *K* | = Capital charges |
| *N* | = Non-labour factorial cost |
| *L* | = Employment or labour charges |
| *P* | = Profits |
| *C* | = Operations costs |
| *F* | = Total factorial inputs |
| *R* | = Internal expenses |

*Source: Adapted with permission from Norman, R. G. and Bahri, S. (1972)* Productivity Measurement and Incentives. *London: Butterworth*

### Integrated productivity measurement

Each of these approaches to the measurement of productivity may be seen as parts of a composite or integrated productivity model. Figure 22.1 presents such an integrated model through which can be identified various means of measuring the productivity of operating systems. The notation is given in Table 22.6. All inputs and outputs are measured in financial units, and though the model is particularly relevant in the measurement of resource productivity in conversion or creation systems, it can be modified for use in service and even non-profit systems. Referring back to the above, the engineer's measure of efficiency might be seen to be equivalent to a measure of total earnings productivity, i.e. $T/C$ in Figure 22.1. The economist's measure may be seen to be equivalent to added value productivity, i.e. $AV/R$, while the accountant's measure of productivity may be seen to be equivalent to the measure of gross efficiency shown in Figure 22.1, i.e. $S/F$.

### The 'physical' dimensions of resource utilization

The above integrated approach takes a largely financial view of resource utilization measurement. Returning, however, to the operations management objectives developed in Chapter 1, we might, in considering the three dimensions of resource utilization, take a largely 'physical' approach to the measurement of performance.

In Chapter 1 we identified three principal types of operating system resource: machines, labour and materials. Each of our three main physical resources must be used effectively, so we must consider performance on each of these three 'dimensions'. Table 22.7 (on page 688) outlines some objectives for each resource and some means of measuring performance against these objectives. In each case the achievement of high performance can be considered in terms of maximizing resource utilization or, of course, minimizing loss or waste. The precise objectives and hence also the performance standards employed will depend on the nature of the resource in each area, as will also the amount of detail necessary in both stating and measuring the achievement of objectives in these areas.

## OTHER PERFORMANCE MEASURES *(see also Chapters 5–17, 19 and 20)*

Finally it is worth reminding ourselves that we have in previous chapters dealt both directly and indirectly with the measurement of system performance-related factors and dimensions. In fact in most decision areas of operations management there will be means of either indirect or direct assessment of outcomes, and thus for the measurement not only of system performance in particular respects, but also of the effectiveness of operations management decisions. Table 22.8 reminds us of some of the performance measures which might be used in relation to each of the operations management decision areas.

## PERFORMANCE MEASUREMENT AND MANAGEMENT CONTROL

In Chapter 3 we noted that in seeking to exercise control over the parts of an organization, top management will use certain performance measurements. We identified two forms of measurement which might be employed in exercising management control of the operations function:

(a) the use of behaviour controls, in which the actual *behaviour of the system is measured* and compared with a required standard as a means of providing the management with control;

(b) the use of output control, in which the *output of the system is measured* and compared with a standard so that the system can be controlled.

**Table 22.7 Resource utilization and measurement**

| Resource | Utilization objectives | Utilization measures |
|---|---|---|
| *Machines*<br>i.e. all physical items, e.g. equipment, tools, buildings, space, directly and indirectly used by the system. | e.g.<br>*Maximize*<br>Output/distance/throughput/ machine hour<br>Proportion of total available time utilized<br>Effectiveness of utilization (e.g. capacity utilized)<br>Occupancy/space utilization | Output/distance/throughput/ machine hour<br>Time(s) used or percentage<br>Capacity used or percentage<br>Occupancy/space utilization or percentage |
| | *Minimize*<br>Idle time and downtime<br>Under-utilized/unoccupied space<br>Machine cost content | Idle time and/or downtime or percentage<br>Percentage utilized/occupied space<br>Machine cost content or percentage |
| *Labour*<br>i.e. those people who directly or indirectly necessarily provide or contribute to the operation of the system, e.g. manual labour, supervision. | e.g.<br>*Maximize*<br>Output/distance/throughput/ work hour<br>Proportion of total available time utilized<br>Effectiveness of utilization (e.g. capacity utilized) | Output/distance/throughput/ work hour<br>Time(s) used or percentage<br>Capacity used or percentage |
| | *Minimize*<br>Idle and ineffective time<br>Labour cost content | Idle and/or ineffective time or percentage<br>Labour cost content or percentage |
| *Materials*<br>i.e. those physical items directly or indirectly consumed or converted by the system. | e.g.<br>*Maximize*<br>Yield (i.e. output/distance/ throughput) per unit weight/ volume, etc. | Yield quantity, weight, etc. |
| | *Minimize*<br>Wastage, losses or scrap<br>Material cost content | Wastage, losses or scrap quantity or percentage<br>Rework/rectification quantity or percentage<br>Material cost content or percentage |

We noted that in some cases the use of either form of measurement is sufficient to provide full control of the operating system, but in some situations, because of the nature of the system and the manner in which it is managed, it will be necessary to use both types of control in order to ensure that the operations function achieves both its customer service and resource utilization objectives.

It is worth returning to this distinction at this stage so that we might be reminded that many of the performance measures discussed previously in this chapter will provide a basis for behaviour or output control. In general when the operating system is not 'buffered' from its customers by the existence of output stocks or input customer queues, where the scheduling of the activities of the system is entirely 'externally' oriented (i.e. where scheduling takes direct account of individual customers' timing requirements (see Chapter 12) and where the capacity management strategy does not require customer queuing, etc. in order to avoid capacity adjustment, then either an output or a behaviour performance measure will be sufficient to ensure conformity to both customer service and resource productivity objectives. However, where these circumstances do not apply then, by definition, the operating system is insulated or buffered from individual customer demands, and hence a behaviour measure concentrating on the actual internal behaviour of the operating system will be sufficient to monitor resource productivity performance, but an output measure will be required to investigate customer service performance adequately.

**Table 22.8 Some measures of operations performance**

| Operations decision area | Some typical performance measures |
|---|---|
| The location of facilities (see Chapter 5) | Transport costs |
| The layout of facilities (see Chapter 6) | Transport/movement costs<br>Physical throughput/unit of space (or value of turnover/unit of space) |
| Work methods and work standards (see Chapters 7, 8, 9 and 10) | Value added/work hour<br>Staffing required/unit throughput or output<br>Accident rates<br>(Labour absenteeism/turnover/rates and dispute levels) |
| Capacity management (see Chapter 11) | Percentage of full capacity normally available<br>Utilization of available capacity<br>Overtime, subcontract costs |
| Activity scheduling and planning (see Chapters 12, 13, 14 and 15) | Percentage work/jobs/customer delivered or dealt with on time (or conversely percentage late)<br>Percentage utilization of available capacity<br>Levels of work-in-progress<br>Average customer or input queue length or waiting time |
| Materials management and inventory management (see Chapters 16 and 17) | Inventory turnover rates<br>Rate of change of inventory levels<br>Capital tied up in stock<br>Occurrence/frequency of disruptions/delays in supply<br>Delivery performance<br>Customer queuing times |
| Quality management and reliability (see Chapters 19 and 20) | Reject rates<br>Rate of return of goods from customers/warranty claim<br>Rate of customer complaints on services<br>Percentage rejected batches<br>Rework/reject costs |
| Maintenance and replacement (see Chapter 21) | Facilities downtime or availability<br>Utilization of maintenance personnel<br>Operating life of equipment between breakdowns<br>Life-cycle cost of equipment |

EXAMPLE

## Computer software company

A small company develops, tests and sells software for a range of computers. The principal resources are the systems and programming staff, who use the company's computers to develop either standard program packages or software for specific customer requirements. The software is normally sold as discs, together with printed instructions, etc. for the use of the discs. The following provisional data are available for the company for the financial year just ended:

| | | |
|---|---|---|
| *L* | Total labour costs | = £50 000 |
| *K* | 'Straight line' depreciation charge against all capital items including equipment | = £30 000 |
| *M* | Cost of all materials consumed and sold to customers (including costs of discs) | = £10 000 |
| *S* | Total sales revenue | = £140 000 |
| *C* | Total operations cost | = £95 000 |

Company management uses certain performance measures to monitor the performance of the company. Figures are available for the previous financial year. How does performance for the year just ended compare with that for the previous year?

| | Previous year | Year just ended |
|---|---|---|
| Profits for year | £25 000 | 140 000 – (95 000 + 10 000) = £35 000 |
| Gross efficiency | 1.24 | 140 000 ÷ (95 000 + 10 000) = 1.33 |
| Net added value Labour productivity | 1.8 | (50 000 + 35 000) ÷ 50 000 = 1.7 |

*Comments on performance for year just ended*: Increased profits and gross efficiency but drop in VA labour productivity suggests an increase in labour costs, possibly partly offset by improvements elsewhere, e.g. increased profits from higher margins on product prices.[1]

Operations managers must ensure that the performance measures which are used by top management to monitor the performance of the operations function are adequate to measure performance against *both* objectives. The use of performance measures which emphasize only resource productivity will lead ultimately to a distortion in the operations manager's behaviour, so that the resource productivity objective is emphasized at the expense of the customer service objective. Equally, any performance measure which emphasizes customer service will lead ultimately to the pursuit of that objective at the expense of resource utilization. A balance must be achieved and it must be obtained between the two objectives, and the performance measures used must reflect and reinforce the balance. The two case examples which follow will illustrate this point.

EXAMPLE

## Public Services Ltd motel

Public Services Ltd owns several small companies specializing in service activities. One company, recently acquired, runs a small motel located in a prime site adjacent to a major highway. The motel has 15 bedrooms,

[1] Detailed figures for previous year were:

| | | | |
|---|---|---|---|
| Total labour cost | = £30K | Materials | = £10K |
| Depreciation | = £30K | Sales | = £130K |
| | | Operations costs | = £95K |

each of which has the usual facilities. Apart from a reception area, car parking and a limited number of vending machines, the motel offers no other facilities. It is managed entirely by a residential manager who is responsible for bookings, reception and the maintenance of the motel and who is assisted by one part-time person who does all the cleaning. There is no pre-booking arrangement for the motel, which depends entirely on trade from 'passing' customers. There is little repeat custom. Customers pay on entry, i.e. before occupying their bedroom. Public Services Ltd wish to introduce certain performance measures to ensure that the motel operates efficiently. It is their intention to give the manager considerable discretion and local responsibility, and to monitor his performance only through the performance measures. The following performance measures were proposed by the manager. The reasons for his proposals are given below.

*Resource utilization*

(a) Bedroom occupancy rate, i.e. percentage of total bedrooms occupied each month. (The manager considers this to be a sufficient measure of resource utilization since the labour cost is low and the principal resources are the bedrooms.)

*Customer service*

(b) The manager proposes to place in each room a *questionnaire* to be completed by residents and handed in before leaving. The questionnaire is designed only to establish whether customers are satisfied with the level of service provided at the cost charged. (The manager feels that this will be a sufficient measure of customer service since he is not concerned with those customers who do not register in the motel (e.g. on the few occasions when the motel is full) or with customers' attitude to price, since he believes that people use the motel only if the price is acceptable to them. There are few delays in registering in the motel, so he believes that the principal consideration should be the quality of service provided at the cost charged.)

The manager believes that in this service system these two 'internal' measures of performance (i.e. 'behaviour measures') will be sufficient to ensure control of the motel against the twin objectives of resource utilization and customer service. However, the parent organization, while accepting these measures, has also asked for the addition of a third measure so that the relative profitability of the motel might be evaluated against that of the other businesses run by the company:

(c) *Gross efficiency* = Total revenue ÷ Total operating cost, measured monthly.

**EXAMPLE**

## *Public Services Ltd. A private hospital* (see also Example in Chapter 3)

Public Services Ltd owns and runs a small private hospital. It has 30 beds in small wards, an operating theatre, a radiology and X-ray department, and a lounge. The hospital manager is responsible for a senior nurse and four assistant nurses. There is a resident doctor, and the hospital has a contract for up to 25% of the time of each of four medical/surgical specialists, and up to 50% of the time of an anaesthetist and a radiologist.

The hospital admits patients referred by a group of local doctors. The patients are all subscribers to a private hospital insurance scheme which meets the costs of treatment. The hospital has a waiting list for admissions and patients are admitted from the list as appropriate facilities become available. In many cases they are selected for admission by a form of 'batch processing', e.g. a set of patients are admitted, all of whom are thought to require the services of a particular surgeon. This facilitates scheduling in the hospital and makes better use of facilities.

Public Services Ltd currently monitors the performance of the hospital through use of the following statistics, which are collected monthly:

(a) *Bed occupancy*. In an average month 900 bed days are assumed to be available. Returns show the actual bed occupancy as a percentage of this 900 bed day capacity.

(b) *Length of patient stay*: The average length of patient stay in the hospital is calculated each month.

(c) *Patient bed days/member of staff*: The number of patient bed days is compared with the number of staff (nursing and medical) days worked each month.

(d) *Gross efficiency/month* = $\frac{\text{Total revenue}}{\text{Total operating cost}}$

Recently the hospital manager was able to demonstrate the inadequacy of this set of performance measures. She pointed out that the hospital's activities were largely 'internally' scheduled, that a queue of customers always existed, and that the capacity of the hospital was not adjusted to match changes in demand. She pointed out that the hospital had two sets of customers, and that because of the above factors internal (i.e. 'behaviour') controls could not be used to control the performance of the hospital in respect of the provision of adequate customer service. She persuaded the company that the following performance measures were also required:

(e) *Average time on waiting list*, i.e. the average time customers spend waiting for admission (calculated monthly for patients admitted during the month).

(f) *Doctors' attitudes to the service provided by the hospital*. A monthly sample survey of doctors' attitudes to the hospital, together with a monthly check on the number of referrals from each doctor.

# A PERFORMANCE AUDIT

The emphasis above is on performance measurement. The measurement of performance provides the opportunity to monitor achievements.

If the measurements are quite specific (as, for example, some of those in Table 22.8 are) then where performance is seen to be inadequate the type of remedial action required will be fairly clear. But where broader measurements are employed the specific causes of inadequate performance may be hidden, so it may not be clear how best to rectify the situation. For this reason it will often be appropriate also to employ a more diagnostic approach aimed at identifying the causes of inadequate performance and appropriate remedial actions. One broad-based diagnostic procedure, presented in the form of an 'audit', is described in Figure 22.2. It is derived from the type of approach introduced in this book and provides a simple but comprehensive tool.

**Figure 22.2** A performance audit framework. Reproduced with minor changes with the permission of B. Melville, University of Waikato, New Zealand

*1. MARKETS AND THE CUSTOMER INTERFACE*

| | *Questions* | *Comments* |
|---|---|---|
| (a) | What are the products?<br>(What is included? Excluded?)<br>What is the market?<br>(What is included? Excluded?)<br>Who are the customers?<br>(Why them?) | Productive systems exist to satisfy a demand. Analysis *must* begin by identifying the source and nature of that demand. |
| (b) | How do the customers get involved?<br><br>In particular, do they merely place an order, or do they need to supply a significant input to the production operation – either themselves or their property? | If the customers merely order the product, we are dealing with a manufacturing or supply operation.<br><br>If they must supply a significant input, we have a service or transport operation with special problems related to the quality, reliability and timeliness of the supply, all of which are outside our control, but which we must be capable of handling efficiently and effectively. |
| (c) | Is there any record of problems or complaints from the market? | Known problems may be 'swept under the carpet' but may provide very strong leads for change. |

**Figure 22.2** contined

*2. OPERATIONS STRUCTURE*

| *Questions* | *Comments* |
|---|---|
| (a) If manufacture or supply: What type of production system is indicated – flow, mass, batch or jobbing? Why that? What else? | Object here is to identify the basic structure or 'shape' of the operation. Production typing (flow, mass, batch, jobbing) is widely understood. But why is this type chosen here? (Flow and mass may be more efficient than batch or jobbing but are much less flexible–rethink the nature of customer demand.) |
| (b) Can we stock the inputs in advance? Or must we obtain them specially, or accept them when available without the option of deferral? | There are four possible structures for manufacture and supply:<br>⇒△⇒○⇒△⇒C<br>Buffered both ends.<br>⇒△⇒○═══⇒C<br>Make-to-order but from stocked resources.<br>═══⇒○⇒△⇒C<br>Direct input but making to stock.<br>═══⇒○═══⇒C<br>Special orders needing special resources.<br>Is the chosen structure logical? What alternatives? |
| (c) If service or transport: Will the customers wait or must they be served immediately, on demand? Can we expect to stock the resources needed to satisfy them, or must we obtain them specially? | As for (b), object is to define structure or 'shape'. There are three possible structures:<br>⇒▽⇘ ○⇒ / C⇗<br>Immediate service, but resources can be stocked.<br>⇒▽⇘ ○⇒ / C⇒▽⇗<br>Customer will wait and resources can be stocked.<br>⇘ ○⇒ / C⇒▽⇗<br>Customer will wait, but resources must be speciall' obtained.<br><br>(Defining structure identifies some significant features: where strategic stock control is needed, where queue disciplines must be established, what scheduling objectives are important, where immediate supply lines are needed. Note that there may be several, or many, structures in one firm.) |
| (d) What are the major influences on the structures identified in (b) and/or (c)? Under what circumstances might they change? | Usual problem is change in the supply/demand relationship – stocks may form or be depleted, queues may form or disappear. Can we handle that? |
| (e) Define the aspect of productivity which emerges as being the more important – efficiency, or customer service, i.e. just what are the productivity objectives? | Where stocks/queues exist, we have the luxury of planning for efficient operation. Otherwise, customer service (e.g. date required) will override and force lower efficiencies. |

**Figure 22.2** continued

3. *CAPACITY MANAGEMENT*

| | *Questions* | *Comments* |
|---|---|---|
| (a) | Obtain monthly/weekly output figures for at least one, probably two years. Graph them. Look for growth/decline; is it straight-line or is there a market growth curve?<br>Do it separately for products or product groups if appropriate. | Overall capacity level is fundamental to productivity. Too much means low efficiency. Too little means poor customer service. Question 3(a) shows how the balance between them is changing. |
| (b) | Identify seasonal peaks and troughs. What strategies have been used to cope? | A key issue. If marked peaks and troughs occur, two basic strategies are possible:<br>(i) adjust capacity to match – subcontract, buy in, defer maintenance, work overtime, rearrange shifts, employ more/fewer staff, use temporary staff, transfer labour, seek counter-seasonal products or counter-seasonal markets (export?);<br>(ii) eliminate the need to adjust – use stocks to buffer the peaks, maintain excess capability in troughs, alter prices in peaks, queue or lose customers in peaks.<br>(Choice is mainly by markets, customers, structure and productivity objectives.) |

4. *OVERALL PERFORMANCE AND MODUS OPERANDI*

| | *Questions* | *Comments* |
|---|---|---|
| (a) | Analyse wherever overall performance data exist: balance sheet, income statement, cost summaries, added value ratios. Match with all facts collected above and interpret. | Where is the money spent? Where is it stocked? Does that agree with above analysis or is it incongruous? What is changing? Especially, look for coincidental changes in two or more variables. Check what changes when volume increases or decreases. |
| (b) | Identify resource dependence and intensity. | Cost accounts will reveal which resource (labour, capital, materials) is most expensive.<br>Observation will show whether operation is labour or capital dependent in each area within the plant. (Key: can you increase output by increasing labour? If so, operation is labour dependent.) Thus, where is systematic work study best directed – at labour or machine efficiency? |
| (c) | Identify the objectives of current operations scheduling and control systems. Do they try to optimize labour or machine utilization? | Does this agree with 4(b)? |
| (d) | What is the underlying logic of physical layout – process, product, fixed position or site layout? | Does this match the operating system structure and production type? [2(a), (b), (c)]? Does it match the resource dependencies [4(b)]? |
| (e) | What methods are used to plan raw materials inventory? Maintain stock for random draw-off? (How are reorder points and quantities determined?) Or purchase to a specific production plan? (Does it work?) | Does this match with structure [2(a), (b) and (c)]? With overall performance [4(a)]? Inventory can be a key tactical issue: objective is not always to minimize it. |

*Note:* At this point in the audit, the principal issues affecting productivity should have been identified, and in particular any incongruities or mis-matches should be laid bare. Section 5 below depends on this having been done.

**Figure 22.2** continued

5. *DESIGN OF CHANGES NEEDED*

| | *Questions* | *Comments* |
|---|---|---|
| (a) | In each selected 'sensitive area' identified, dig for detailed performance data: material yields or scrap, labour performance, machine utilization, stockout frequency, late deliveries, labour turnover, absenteeism, quality performance, breakdown frequency, etc. Note that data will be in physical units, not financial. | Look for trends, patterns, coincident changes. Note especially what is *not* available. If these really are key areas, why not? Shortlist the main opportunities for change. They may be in new technology (plant, methods, layout, etc.), planning and control systems (capacity strategies, inventory and scheduling systems, quality control, labour or machine performance control, etc.), or organizational changes (new shift systems, supervisory structure, selection and training, financial rewards, etc.). |
| (b) | For each shortlisted change, think out what else it will affect and identify compensating changes that will be needed. | It is not possible to make a single isolated change in a productive system. If compensating changes are not identified now they will emerge as crises later. |

**EXAMPLE**

### *EG & G Inc.*

At EG & G Inc., performance measurement focuses on quality, cost-effectiveness and customer responsiveness at each level within the firm. The performance model has three parts: (1) a strategic summary statement of a unit's strategy; (2) a chart summarizing the major steps needed to achieve strategies; and (3) unit measurements in the general areas of cost-effectiveness, quality and responsiveness. EG & G requires managers to summarize their units' strengths and weaknesses as perceived by the customer. Competitive benchmarking is also used to measure a unit's products or services against its toughest competitors or those recognized as leaders in the sector.

Source: Fray, E. N. (1988) The evolution of performance measurement. *Industrial Management*, **30**(5), pp. 9–12.

## IMPROVEMENT AND BENCHMARKING

Much of what has been discussed in previous chapters was relevant to performance improvement in operations. Many of the procedures presented there, if effectively used, should contribute to improvements in operating performance. Now it is appropriate, in this final chapter, to reinforce this notion – that operations managers, in all that they do, aim to contribute to continual improvement in system performance. We will deal briefly with two specific aspects:

1. continual improvement;
2. benchmarking.

### Continual improvement

The Japanese have a term for the continuous, systematic effort to improve business, or system, performance – *kaizen*.[2] It means gradual, unerring improvement, and thus the setting and achieving of ever higher standards. There are two prerequisites for the effective use of this type of approach, i.e.

1. setting demanding, but achievable, objectives;
2. feedback of achievements against these objectives.

[2] Goddard, R. W. (1991) Kaizen! *Manage*, **42**(4), pp. 4–5, 21.

**Figure 22.3** Benchmarking process steps. Reproduced, with permission, from Camp, R. C. (1989) *Benchmarking.* Milwaukee, Wis.: Quality Press (Am. Soc. for Qual. Control).

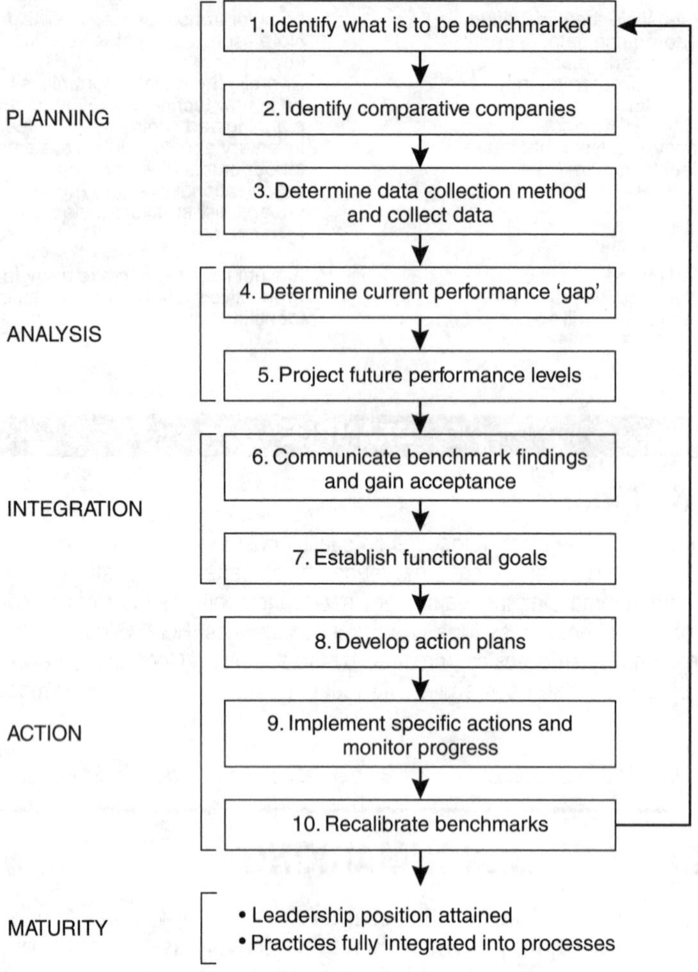


These in turn require other actions and/or conditions, e.g.

For 1. Objectives must relate to business strategies.
Objectives must be agreed by all parties.
Objectives must be relevant to the tasks of employees.

For 2. Feedback must be frequent and regular.
Opportunities for examination and analysis of achievements must exist.

In addition, the following will also generally be required:

(a) Remuneration will be related to performance.
(b) High achievement will be recognized by awards.
(c) Operations problem-solving procedures are required, so that obstacles to improvements in performance can be removed.
(d) A participative-process-oriented management style.

Kaizen is a philosophy and, of course, has much in common with total quality management[3] (Chapter 19).

## Benchmarking

Finally, we turn, logically, to benchmarking – a technique which enables organizations to compare performance to relevant and achievable standards and thus help secure continual improvement.[4]

Arguably, intermittent measurements of performance, such as output/throughput performance, provide little value to managers, but by measuring performance over time, managers can establish a record of performance and measure the rate of improvement. In order to judge the performance of operations effectively, therefore, managers should compare, or benchmark, performance with the outside world (see Figure 22.3). A benchmark can be an historical reference point that has already been passed or, more appropriately, a goal not expected to be reached for some time. Usually the benchmark reflects best-known actual performance for a sector, or the performance of a respected competitor. Obtaining benchmark data needed to create an external-based comparison of performance and improvement can be difficult since most organizations are secretive about internal measures of performance. However, procedures exist, using, for example, consultants, or survey organizations, to enable market-originated measures to be obtained, against which an organization can measure its own performance.

Thus, there are two basic complementary aspects of performance measurement – internal against company norms and standards, and external, against competitors' standards.

**EXAMPLE**

### *Rank Xerox*

Competitive benchmarking is closely tied to the RX 'Leadership through Quality' programme. The elements are as follows:

1. *Planning* Decide what is going to be benchmarked, and how to obtain information about that company. Care must be taken in securing information. Direct contact with competitors is not allowed. All information-gathering must be open. Systematic questioning of customers (of both RX and/or other suppliers) is the normal way, e.g. through surveys, questioning by service engineers, etc.
2. *Analysis* After the data are gathered, they must be analysed. The following questions would be relevant: 'Is the competition really better?' 'How much better?' 'What seems to make them better – what are they doing that we are not?' 'Could we do it?' 'Should we do it?'
3. *Integration* This step is to do with gearing up for change, i.e. on the basis of the data analysis, decide what changes are going to be made in the way work is done. If the changes involve other people, this step includes communicating to them what has been learned and what needs to change. Lists of functional goals can be established that take advantage of what has been learned from the competition.
4. *Action* In this step, action plans to achieve goals are developed, implemented and evaluated. Evaluation asks the question: 'Are we doing better as a result of this than we were doing before?'

If evaluation shows that there is still a gap between RX practices and those of the competitor, it will be necessary to go back and repeat the process.

Source: *Leadership through Quality*. Rank Xerox (UK) Ltd.

---

[3] Nandyal, R. K. and Welch, D. (1991) Goals-orientation, SPC, and incentives. *Quality*, **30**(6), pp. 12–14.
[4] Miller, J. A. (1992) Measuring progress through benchmarking. *CMA Magazine*, **66**(4), p. 37.

## CHECKLIST FOR CHAPTER 22

### The objectives of operations management

Customer service
Resource utilization

### Customer service performance

Measures of customer service
- Specification
- Cost
- Timing
- Reliability
- Measures of customer service performance

### Resource utilization performance

Productivity measures
Integrated productivity measurement
The 'physical' dimensions of resource productivity
- Machines: objectives and measures
- Labour: objectives and measures
- Materials objectives and measures

### Other performance measures

Location of facilities
Layout of facilities
Work methods and standards
Capacity management
Scheduling and planning
Inventory management, purchasing and supply
Quality management and reliability
Maintenance and replacement

### Management controls and performance measurement

'Behaviour'-type performance measures
'Output'-type performance measures

### A performance audit

Markets and customers
Operations structure
Capacity
Overall performance and modus operandi
Design of changes needed

### Improvement and benchmarking

Continual improvement
Kaizen
Benchmarking

## FURTHER READING

**Bailey, D. and Hubert, T. (eds) (1981)** *Productivity Measurement.* Aldershot: Gower.

**Camp, R. C. (1989)** Benchmarking: the search for industry best practices that lead to superior performance. *Quality Progress*, **22**(4), pp. 62–69.

Also, book of same title published in 1989 by Quality Press, Milwaukee (see caption to Figure 22.3).

**Chew, W. B. (1988)** No nonsense guide to measuring productivity. *Harvard Business Review*, Jan.–Feb., pp. 110–118.

**Didis, S. K. (1990)** Kaizen. *Internal Auditor*, **47**(3,4), pp. 66–69.

**James, G. (1980)** Total productivity measurement. *Management Services*, December, pp. 6–12.

**Norman, R. G. and Bahiri, S. (1972)** *Productivity Measurement and Incentives*. London: Butterworth.

**Wisner, J. D. and Fawcett, S. E. (1991)** Linking firm strategy to operating decisions through performance measurement. *Production and Inventory Management*, **32**(3), pp. 5–11.

## QUESTIONS

22.1 Describe and compare the customer service objectives which might be expected to influence the operation of the following systems:

(a) a small bespoke (i.e. 'made to measure') manufacturing tailor;

(b) a dentist's practice;

(c) a city bus service.

How might system performance in respect of these objectives be measured in each case?

22.2 Show how (a) added value productivity, (b) gross efficiency and (c) total earnings productivity would be measured in a small batch production to stock manufacturing organization.

22.3 Compare the notion of reliability introduced in this chapter with that discussed in Chapter 21. How might measures of item performance reliability and techniques for maintenance management be of value in performance measurement?

22.4 Identify and explain the types of performance measurement that might be employed in order to achieve adequate management control in the following types of operation:

(a) a dentist (see Example on p. 22 in Chapter 1);

(b) fire service (see Example on p. 276 in Chapter 11).

PART 9

# International Case Studies


Introduction to Part 9

| | | |
|---|---|---|
| Case 1 | Carreras SL | (Spain) |
| Case 2 | Jograni Handicrafts | (Bangladesh) |
| Case 3 | Centre Hospitalier Reine Fabiola | (Belgium) |
| Case 4 | Qormi Post Office | (Malta) |
| Case 5 | The Sahil Tea Garden | (Turkey) |
| Case 6 | Bourg Breton | (France) |
| Case 7 | Pokhara Weavers | (Nepal) |
| Case 8 | Malcolm Seal | (UK) |
| Case 9 | The Malta MBA | (Malta) |
| Case 10 | Airport building project | (India) |
| Case 11 | St John's Church | (UK) |
| Case 12 | FotoPrint Pronto | (Italy) |
| Case 13 | The Shire of Corio | (Australia) |
| Case 14 | Prince Philip Dental Hospital, Hong Kong | (Hong Kong) |
| Case 15 | The Textile Machinery Company | (UK) |
| Case 16 | America Burger and Pasta | (Brazil) |
| Case 17 | La Patisserie – A | (UK) |
| Case 18 | La Patisserie – B | (UK) |
| Case 19 | K&S (Israel) Ltd | (Israel) |

| | | |
|---|---|---|
| Case 20 | TAARUP Farming Machines Ltd | (Denmark) |
| Case 21 | Linden Christian Nursery School – A | (South Africa) |
| Case 22 | Linden Christian Nursery School – B | (South Africa) |
| Case 23 | Williams' College | (UK) |
| Case 24 | Winterthur non-life commercial insurance | (Netherlands) |
| Case 25 | European Foundation – group work | (Netherlands, Portugal) |
| Case 26 | The Open Polytechnic of New Zealand (TOPNZ) – 'The writing process' | (New Zealand) |
| Case 27 | Food Concept Sdn. Bhd. | (Malaysia) |

## INTRODUCTION TO PART 9

The material in this part of the book is intended to support that in Parts 1–8. These international cases – all but one of which were prepared specially for this text – are included here for use as study aids, as 'vehicles' for group discussion, and as bases for assignments, presentations, assessments, etc. Together they cover most of the topics dealt with in the previous chapters; however, as they deal with real, often complex situations, they do not, in general, focus exclusively on any single topic, and it is for this reason that they have been grouped together here rather than included at the end of chapters. (Notice, however, that suggestions are given below to relate cases to chapters.)

The cases have been prepared in order to illustrate or document practice in specific situations. They are not intended specifically to demonstrate good, or bad, practice. In most cases the situations to which the cases refer are undisguised in the cases. Identities are not, in general, concealed. In a small number of cases, some disguise is used – particularly where performance figures, etc. are used, which might be commercially sensitive. In no case has there been any major change of fact, function, nationality, etc.

## TOPIC MAP

Despite the comments above, it is appropriate to suggest which cases relate largely, or generally, to which topics/chapters. This will help the reader decide which case to study and when. Table C.1 is intended for this purpose. It brings together the suggestions made, for case work, at the end of the chapters.

**Table C.1 Case studies and chapter relationships**

| Case study no. | Relevant chapters | |
|---|---|---|
| | Principal | Also |
| 1 | 1, 11, 12 | 2 |
| 2 | 3, 16, 18, 19, 20 | 12, 17 |
| 3 | 16, 17 | 4 |
| 4 | 11, 12, 19 | 1, 2, 7, 8, 10, 20 |
| 5 | 6, 7, 9 | |
| 6 | 4 | |
| 7 | 6, 7, 15 | |
| 8 | 1, 11, 12 | |
| 9 | 19, 20 | |
| 10 | 6, 7 | |
| 11 | 3, 11, 12 | 13 |
| 12 | 5 | 2 |
| 13 | 19 | |
| 14 | 1 | 2, 6, 12 |
| 15 | 2 | 1, 11, 12, 16, 17 |
| 16 | 2 | 3, 4, 6, 7, 8, 10, 11, 16, 17, 18 |
| 17 | 1, 11, 12 | 2 |
| 18 | 2, 4 | 11 |
| 19 | 12 | 14, 15 |
| 20 | 12 | 17 |
| 21 | 13 | |
| 22 | 13 | 12, 4 |
| 23 | 13 | |
| 24 | 2 | 12 |
| 25 | 9 | |
| 26 | 9, 13 | 11, 12 |
| 27 | 2, 3, 16 | |

## Acknowledgements

I am grateful to the following in the preparation of these case studies:

| | |
|---|---|
| **Sheena Orr** | For providing the material on which the Jograni Handicrafts case is based, and for writing much of the case. |
| **Nick Meadows** | For providing the material on which the St John's Church case is based, and for writing much of the case. |
| **Katinka ten Ham** | For providing the material on which the Winterthur non-life commercial insurance case is based, and for writing much of the case. |
| **Roy Snaddon** | For writing and providing the Linden Christian Nursery A and B cases and the La Patisserie B case. |
| **Geoff Buxey** | For preparing and providing the Shire of Corio case. |
| **Henrique Correa** | For preparing and providing the America Burger and Pasta case. |
| **Ezey M. Dar-El and Pneena Sofer** | For preparing and providing the K&S (Israel) case. |
| **Jacques Lehmann** | For preparing and providing the Centre Hospitalier Reine Fabiola case. |
| **Barbara Morris** | For preparing and providing La Patisserie A case. |
| **Anthony Vella** | For providing the material on which the Qormi Post Office case is based, and for writing much of the case. |
| **Philip Newsome** | For preparing and providing the Prince Philip Dental Hospital case. |
| **Pascal Paoli and Hubert Kreiger** | For providing the material for the European Foundation case. |
| **Nevan Wright** | For preparing and providing the Open Polytechnic of New Zealand case. |
| **Khee Kin** | For preparing and providing the Food Concept case. |
| **Bendt Rorsted** | For preparing and providing the TAARUP Farming Machines case. |

Case study 1

# Carreras SL

Carreras SL is involved in making, packaging, distributing and selling wines, in the Levante region of Spain – i.e. the area around and inland from Valencia and Alicante on the Mediterranean coast (see Figure C1.1). It is an old-established organization which has grown substantially, and now faces decisions about its future development in the context of a rapidly changing Spanish wine industry,

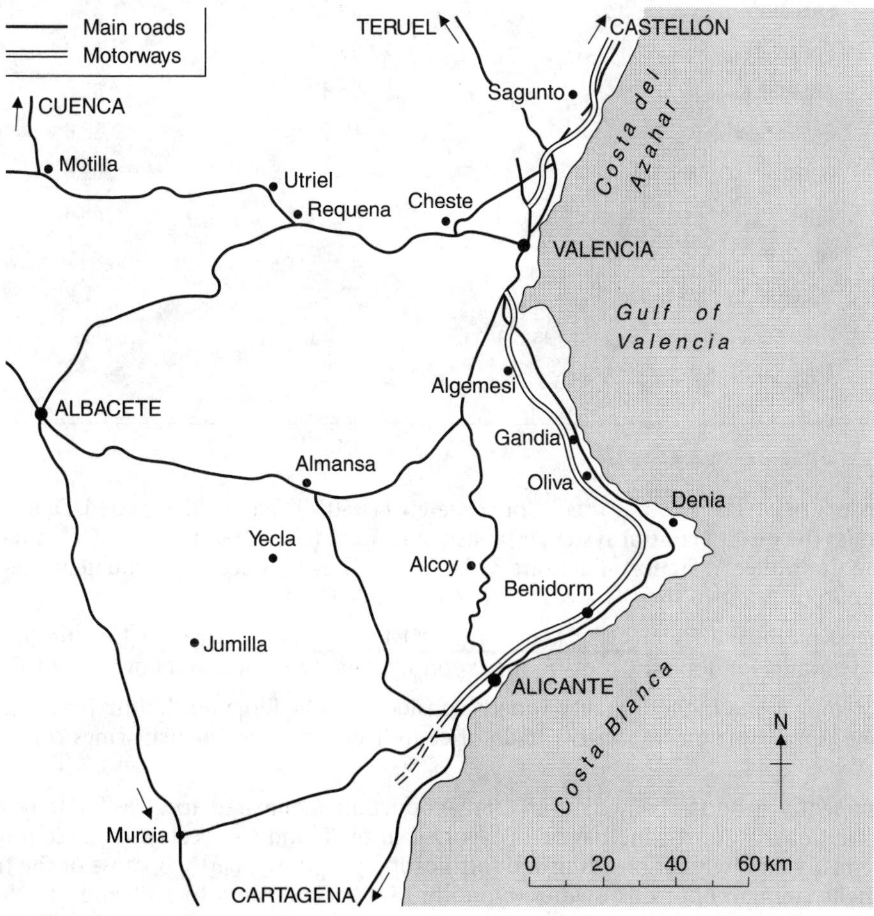


**Figure C1.1** The Levante region

# THE SPANISH WINE INDUSTRY

Spain has about 1 700 000 hectares (1 ha = 2.47 acres) of vineyards – the largest of any country worldwide. This compares, for example, with Italy – 1 400 0000 – and France – 1 300 000. However, Spain only produces about 33 million hectolitres of wine per annum or approximately 20 hl/ha, which compares to 70 million hl, for Italy – the world's largest producer – and 66 million hl for France.

Spain has a wine consumption per capita less than that of other large producer areas. Table C1.1 makes comparisons.

**Table C1.1 Per capita wine consumption (litres/person/year)**

| | 1990 | 1969 |
|---|---|---|
| France | 74 | 112 |
| Italy | 62.1 | 114 |
| Luxembourg | 58.3 | 31 |
| Portugal | 58 | 93.2 |
| Argentina | 55.8 | 87.5 |
| Switzerland | 49.9 | 38.6 |
| Spain | 47.4* | 62.5 |
| Chile | 35 | 48.9 |
| Austria | 32.9 | 32 |
| UK (26th by rank order) | 11.4 | 2.8 |

N.B. Rank order by 1990 figures.

*50% white, 25% red, 25% rosé.

More than 50% of Spain's vineyards (approximately (1 050 000 ha) are designated 'Denominación de Origen' under the quality control system established in 1972 (compared to 12% DOC in Italy and 15% Appellation Controllée in France). There are 39 DO areas. They produce approximately one-third of the total wine output. Some of the DO areas are listed in Table C1.2.

The largest producing region is La Mancha (4 DOs). The second largest is Levante (6 DOs). Table C1.3 shows outputs for domestic use and for export by wine type for several of the 32 DO areas.

The best-known and highest-quality wine is considered to be Rioja (excluding Jerez – sherry, a fortified wine). Approximate comparative trade price indices for some Spanish wines (Rioja = 100) are shown in Table C1.4.

Spain presently exports about 25% of total production (compared to 20% for Italy and 9% for France). Traditionally, most wine has been exported in bulk, and has been used in countries such as France, Germany and Italy for blending and fortification purposes – partly because of the traditionally high alcoholic strength of Spanish wines (typically 13–14% compared to 10% and 11% for Italy and France) but also because of their relative cheapness and the lack of a substantial market for Spanish wines *per se* (excepting Rioja and sherry). However, in recent years things have begun to change, exports have increased and the proportion of exports in bottles has grown substantially (Table C1.5).

**Table C1.2 Some DO regions – area**

| DO | | Area (000 ha) |
|---|---|---|
| Mancha | | 485 |
| Tarragona | | – |
| Rioja | | 44 |
| Jerez | | 11 |
| Cariñena | | 22 |
| Penedes | | – |
| Montilla-Moriles | | – |
| Navarra | | 23 |
| Huelva | | 19 |
| Utriel Requena | Levante | 50 |
| Valencia | Levante | – |
| Almanasa | Levante | 8 |
| Jumilla | Levante | 25 |
| Alicante | Levante | – |
| Yecla | Levante | 26 |
| All 32 DO areas | | 1050 |

# THE WINE-MAKING PROCESS

All that is required to convert grapes to wine is fermentation, which is the chemical process of changing sugar into alcohol and carbon dioxide brought about by yeasts – micro-organisms in the grape skins. This process can take place naturally provided the grape skins are broken. However, eventually fermentation will convert all the sugar, and so the wine will be dry and high in alcohol (e.g. about 15% by volume), so fermentation is often stopped by neutralizing the yeast or by filtering it out.

By using different grape varieties and by controlling the fermentation, different types of wine are produced.

The basic steps typically involved in wine making are:

1. grapes harvested (approximately October);
2. grapes crushed and (usually) de-stemmed (October);
3. grapes pressed and (for white wine only) skins removed (October);
4. fermentation in vat (up to 15 days) (October–November);
5. wine run off and filtered into barrels or larger containers (racking) (October–November);

6. re-racking and storage in barrels/tanks (November–June or longer for wine to be matured);
7. blending of wines (if appropriate) ( June, Year 2);
8. bottling (if appropriate) ( June, Year 2);
9. ageing in bottles (if appropriate) ( June, Year 2 onwards).

**Table C1.3 Some DO regions – outputs (hl 1988–1989)**

| DO | | White | Rosé | Red | Others |
|---|---|---|---|---|---|
| Montilla-Moriles | Domestic | 4 | 0 | 0 | 225 |
| | Export | 93 | 0 | 34 | – |
| La Mancha (4 DOs) | | 702 | 27 | 687 | 0 |
| | | 56 | 3 | 80 | 0 |
| Rioja | | 107 | 104 | 618 | 0 |
| | | 40 | 19 | 284 | 0 |
| Jerez | | 0 | 0 | 0 | 194 |
| | | 0 | 0 | 0 | 841 |
| Navarra | | 13 | 126 | 94 | 0 |
| | | 7 | 17 | 89 | 0 |
| Huelva | | 97 | 0 | 6 | 31 |
| | | 0 | 0 | 0 | 12 |
| Penedes | | 362 | 37 | 50 | 0 |
| | | 54 | 30 | 40 | 0 |
| Cariñena | | 79 | 65 | 150 | 0 |
| | | 1 | 1 | 5 | 0 |
| Valencia | Levante | 78 | 10 | 51 | 6 |
| | | 110 | 28 | 103 | 9 |
| Almanasa | Levante | 0 | 5 | 19 | 0 |
| | | 0 | 0 | 1 | 0 |
| Utriel Requena | Levante | 2 | 22 | 33 | 0 |
| | | 0.6 | 29 | 56 | 0 |
| Jumilla | Levante | 16 | 148 | 228 | 0 |
| | | 4 | 15 | 117 | 0 |
| Yecla | Levante | 1 | 1.5 | 3 | 0 |
| | | 0 | 1.5 | 3 | 0 |
| Alicante | Levante | 6 | 61 | 1 | 0 |
| | | 0 | 0 | 20 | 0 |
| Tarragona | | 289 | 8 | 37 | 3 |
| | | 10 | 4 | 29 | 1 |
| Total (32 DO areas) | | 2059 | 685 | 2288 | 1165 |
| | | 446 | 149 | 8631 | 1260 |

N.B. 0 = zero or negligible.

**Table C1.4 Wine trade price indices**

| DO | | Approximate price index | |
|---|---|---|---|
| Rioja | | 100 | (xx) |
| Rioja 'reserva' | | 125 | (xxx) |
| Rioja 'gran reserva' | | 200 | (xxxx) |
| Navarra | | 90 | (xx) |
| Mancha | | 80 | (x) |
| Jerez | | 125 | |
| Montilla-Moriles | | 120 | (xxx) |
| Cariñena | | 80 | (x) |
| Penedes | | 100 | (x–xxx) |
| Tarragona | | 100 | (x–xxx) |
| Huelva | | 100 | (x–xx) |
| Alicante | Levante | 60 | (x) |
| Valencia | Levante | 50 | (x) |
| Jumilla | Levante | 70 | (x) |
| Yecla | Levante | 60 | (x) |
| Utriel-Requena | Levante | 50 | (x) |
| Almanasa | Levante | 60 | (x) |

N.B. ( ) = Quality rating from recent wine guide (x–xxxxx).

**Table C1.5 Spanish wine exports**

| | 1981 | 1991 (approx.) |
|---|---|---|
| Table wine exports in bottle | 16% | 50% |
| Table wine exports in bulk | 84% | 50% |

| Destinations (1990) (% of total exports) | |
|---|---|
| Germany | 22 |
| UK | 19 |
| Netherlands | 13 |
| France | 4 |
| Denmark | 4 |
| Belgium | 3 |
| All EC | 66.5 |
| Switzerland | 12 |
| All EFTA | 19 |
| USA | 4 |

# CARRERAS SL

The organization began as a small business located in Requena, 70 km west of Valencia, the home town of the Carreras family, who have been involved in wine making for 35 years. Originally they made mainly red wines from their own vines in their own vinery, for sale locally and in Valencia. Over the following years, under the control of Sr Carreras, the business grew, mainly through certain key developments:

1. 1970 The extension and modernization of the family's wine-making facilities at Requena to create a modern 'cooperativa' with a capacity of 30 000 hl per annum. It was set up to serve not only the family's requirements but also the needs of the local growers in the Utriel-Requena area, many of whom could not afford, nor were big enough to justify, the investment in more modern wine-making and storage facilities.
2. 1975 The establishment of a road freight company to transport both bulk and bottled wine from the Requena Cooperativa.
3. 1975–1985 The acquisition of a controlling interest in five cooperativas in neighbouring DO areas, i.e.

   Valencia
   Jumilia
   Almanasa
   Yecla
   Alicante

   together, after modernization and extension, having a capacity of 200 000 hl per annum.
4. 1978–1988 The development of a chain of 'bodegas' providing retail outlets for wine, in major towns and tourist regions in the Valencia and Alicante provinces, mainly through acquisition from private operators.
5. 1983 The commissioning of a blending and bottling, packaging and warehouse facility in Valencia.

Through this development, the business (which was established as Carreras SL in 1985) grew into the largest of its type in the region, comprising, by 1991, the following:

(a) Las Cavas Levante – a company operating eight cooperativas (in the six DO areas);

(b) Bodegas Carreras – a company operating 15 retail wine stores;

(c) Transportes Vinos Levante – the transport company.

(d) Industria Carreras – the packaging and warehousing business.

The business overall is profitable, and still controlled entirely by the Carreras family. Carreras SL, the holding company, is headquartered at Requena. Las Cavas and Bodegas HQs are also at Requena. Transportes and Industria are based in Valencia. All four companies operate under their own management, each having a director and relevant staff. The four businesses, as they are now, are described below.

## Las Cavas Levante

Each cooperativa operates in a similar manner. They differ in scale, in produce/product mix and in the number of growers they serve.

All grapes are provided by local growers, who, if they choose to deal with the cooperativa, must opt, annually, for one of two contractual relationships:

1. Sales of grapes to the cooperativa, at the time of delivery, at the prevailing price – as determined by the cooperativa management for the relevant type, quality and quantity.
2. Contract, at a price agreed with the cooperativa, for the processing of the grapes for the production of wine which remains the property of the grower, who may, by July the following year, choose to remove the wine, sell it on to a third party, or sell it to the cooperativa at the prevailing price, as determined by the cooperativa management.

   N.B. Contract price for processing paid 50% on delivery of grapes and 50% by July the following year.

Negotiations between growers and the cooperativa typically take place in July, after prices are announced. Until such negotiations are finished, the cooperativa does not know how many suppliers it will have that September–October. The extent of the harvest, and thus the quantity and quality of grapes to be provided by contracted growers, is not known until September–October. The busy period in the cooperativa is September through to early November.

Each cooperativa has facilities to produce the wines appropriate for its area. Wines produced from different grower's grapes are not separated. Their rights to wine are determined in relation to their portion of the tonnage of the grapes used.

The cooperativa supplies wine in bulk from vats either into the customer's own containers, or into the cooperativa's own bottles or cubitainers (large plastic containers), labelled with the cooperativa's own label or left blank. The customers for such wine are:

(a) the local growers (contracted under (2) above);

(b) local retailers (e.g. shops, restaurants, etc.) and individuals;

(c) Industria Carreras.

Traditionally, several of the Carreras cooperativas also processed other crops – mainly olives and almonds – but such work has been largely phased out as the company has invested in the modernization and extension of the wine-making facilities.

Whilst growers without their own facilities are not obliged to use their local cooperativa (they can transport their grapes to other cooperativas in other towns), they are usually loyal to their local cooperativa provided the price they receive/pay is competitive.

The relationship of growers to the cooperativa, i.e. whether they choose (1) or (2) above, is influenced by the demand for their local wines, and their ability to sell their own brand wines. In general demand for local wines is higher in the higher-quality areas.

Some details of each of the cooperativas are given in Table C1.6.

## Bodegas Carreras

The 15 retail wine stores, whilst located throughout the region, are in general located in the larger or tourist towns, e.g. Alcoy, Gandia, Benidorm, Alicante, Denia, Valencia, Oliva, Javea, Algemesi. They are all now owned freehold by the company, and managed by a local manager, employed by the company. Each outlet stocks a full range of spirits, beers, soft drinks, waters, juices, milks, oils, fortified wines, table wines and certain foodstuffs (e.g. nuts and snacks). The wines stocked, whilst including the full range from Carreras, also include other brands. The Carreras wines are supplied by Industria Carreras and not directly from any of the company's cooperativas. The same Carreras wines are stocked by each bodega. A typical profile of a bodega is shown in Table C1.7.

**Table C1.6 Profiles of Las Cavas Levante**

| Cooperativa No. | DO Area | Processing capacity p.a. (hl) | Typical no. of growers p.a. | Approx. % of throughput under contract type (1) | (2) |
|---|---|---|---|---|---|
| 1 | Utriel-Requena | 33 000 | 120–170 | 85 | 15 |
| 2 | Utriel-Requena | 28 000 | 80–140 | 75 | 25 |
| 3 | Valencia | 100 000 | 180–240 | 75 | 25 |
| 4 | Jumilla | 85 000 | 100–150 | 30 | 70 |
| 5 | Jumilla | 70 000 | 90–140 | 35 | 65 |
| 6 | Almanasa | 8 500 | 30–40 | 60 | 40 |
| 7 | Yecla | 5 500 | 30–40 | 60 | 40 |
| 8 | Alicante | 27 000 | 170–220 | 70 | 30 |

Trade tends to be higher during the summer period, especially in the tourist areas, with other peaks around Easter and Christmas/New Year. In addition to 'over the counter' retail custom, all of the bodegas have trade customers (e.g. local hotels, bars, restaurants, etc.). In some areas this part of the business has grown substantially. However, each bodega does only deal with such customers in its area (i.e. there is no 'trade' competition between the 15 bodegas). Long-term large-scale supply contracts for large trade customers can be established directly between such customers and Industria Carreras (see below).

## Transportes Vinos Levante

The transport company is based in Valencia. At present the main vehicle fleet (excluding cars, service vans, etc.) is:

(a) Two Ebro 'L80 four-wheel rigid open trucks with canvas cover;
TARA (unloaded weight) 3730 kg
PMA (vehicle gross weight) 8000 kg

(b) Three Ebro 'L80' as tanker vehicle: 4000 litre capacity;

(c) Two Pegaso six-wheel rigid open trucks with canvas cover;
TARA 11 000 kg
PMA 26 000 kg

(d) Three Nissan 'Trade 2.8' four-wheel rigid vans;
TARA 2310 kg
PMA 3500 kg

Occasionally additional vehicles are hired and/or major transport jobs subcontracted.

The vehicles are engaged on the following principal tasks:

**Table C1.7 Profile of a typical Carreras bodega**

| Product | | Number of different brands or types | % of total turnover |
|---|---|---|---|
| Spirits | | 15 | 12 |
| Beers | | 3 | 9 |
| Soft drinks | | 15 | 8 |
| Waters | | 4 | 3 |
| Juices | | 10 | 3 |
| Milk | | 3 | 2 |
| Oils | | 4 | 2 |
| Fortified wines | | 10 | 12 |
| Table wines | | | |
| | Carreras | 10 | 18 |
| | Others | 10 | 21 |
| Other items | | | 10 |

(i) Deliveries from Industria Carreras to:

1. Las Bodegas Carreras (bottled and cubitainers)
2. Local retailers and trade customers (bottled)
3. Wine exporters (bottled, cubitainers and bulk wines)

(ii) Deliveries from Carreras Cooperativas to:

1. Industria Carreras (cubitainer and bulk wines)

General transport activities, e.g. of equipment, materials etc.

The work of Transportes Vinos Levante is the responsibility of a director, based at the Valencia headquarters.

## Industria Carreras

The company is responsible for the blending, bottling, packaging and warehouse facilities at a single-site location in Valencia. The activities undertaken are as follows:

(a) receipt of wine in containers or in bulk (tanker) from the company's cooperativas (June–September);

(b) storage of such wine;

(c) DO wine blending to the extent permitted by the regulations in order to provide Carreras branded wines for each of the DO source areas;

(d) table wine blending (non-DO) to provide Carreras branded table wines;

(e) bottling, labelling and casing of wines;

(f) supply of wines (bottle or container) to the company's bodegas;

(g) supply of wines (bottle) to other local (Levante region) retailers, wholesalers and other large trade customers (e.g. hotels);

(h) supply of wines (bottle or container or bulk) to exporters;

(i) storage of wines (bulk, container or bottle) either for stock and/or maturing.

The capacity available is currently as follows:

| | |
|---|---|
| Blending/bottling/packaging | 120 000 hl p.a. |
| Bulk storage | 100 000 hl |
| Bottle/cubitainer storage | 50 000 hl |

The company is managed by a director based at Valencia.

## THE MANAGEMENT OF CARRERAS SL

The company is controlled by the family. The President is still Sr Carreras. Other members of the family hold senior management positions. The directors responsible for Las Cavas Levante and Industria Carreras are members of the family. Recently a new Director General was appointed to run Carreras SL. This appointment attracted considerable interest in Spain. For example, translated extracts from an interview in the national news section of a leading regional daily paper are given below:

*You were appointed to the new post of Director General by the President of Carreras SL two months ago. However, you haven't worked in the family company, or in Spain, for nearly five years. Are you well prepared for this new job?*

Sra Carreras
I worked for what is now Carreras SL for four years after finishing at university in Madrid and before going abroad for postgraduate study. I married at the end of my course and we worked together for three years in the wine industry in France until we both decided to come here earlier this year. So I feel that I have relevant knowledge and experience for the job, and may be able to bring some different views.

*Do you believe that a new approach is needed in the company now?*

Sra Carreras
Certainly. The Spanish wine industry has changed dramatically since our entry into the EEC in 1986, but in both quality and efficiency we still lag far behind other European countries as well as the New World producers. There is a growing awareness of and market for Spanish wines in Northern Europe, but the output of many parts of Spain, including our region, is still largely unknown. We are still essentially a domestic industry struggling to modernize.

*But what approach will you adopt with your company, which is already in some respects the dominant wine business in this region, and what are the main problems you now face?*

Sra Carreras
One of our main problems is the lack of specialist and management skills. This is not a well developed region with strong industry and business. It is difficult to find good managers and technical people here, or to tempt them to come here. That is not likely to change, indeed it may get worse, so we need to have a better understanding of how we must manage each of our four businesses – which in many respects are quite different. If, for example, there are major similarities, then we can perhaps develop our own management talent or organize the businesses in such a way that we can manage with fewer people. However, if the four businesses need a different type of approach then we may have to decide whether we should be doing so many different things.

This company has just grown. We must now ask ourselves whether, managerially, we are in one business or four. Only then can we decide how to develop in the future and take advantage of the rapid changes which will undoubtedly continue in this industry. This will be my first priority.

*Yours was a very unusual appointment – especially in a country like Spain. How do you feel about it now that you have seen some of the critical reaction from elsewhere in the industry?*

Sra Carreras
Well I certainly do not agree with Cervantes's statement, 'An honest women and a broken leg are best at home', and I aim to prove my critics to be wrong!

Case study 2

# Jograni Handicrafts

Jograni is a medium-sized handicrafts co-operative based in Dhaka, Bangladesh. Its main function, at present, is to market the various items produced by its 53 member societies. The relatively few male societies concentrate mostly on wood-based products, whilst the women use their sewing, weaving and basket-work skills. Most of the societies comprise poor rural women or men.

Jograni currently has a turnover of 90 000 per annum. It runs two marketing outlets itself but more than 50% of its stock is sold through other outlets.

## PRODUCT SUPPLY

In some cases member societies will request a design input. More often than not this is prompted by Jograni staff, who are more in touch with the market-place and the need to provide variations on traditional products.

Once items have been made in any reasonable amount they are sent immediately to the central marketing warehouse, as few societies have any secure storage facilities. Also, with very little capital, a watchful eye must be kept on their cash flow.

Goods are stocked at the central warehouse after being given a brief check for flaws and tagged with a Jograni tag. They are held in stock to await being made up into orders for dispatch to retail outlets.

## PRESENT MARKETS

Jograni's market at present has three main segments:

(a) foreign tourists – pay premium price for items to be exported;

(b) local 'expatriates' – pay above average price for items mainly for use in Bangladesh;

(c) middle/upper class Bangladeshis – pay lower 'local' price.

The objective from the start has been to focus on the tourist and expatriate markets, but as this requires a significant degree of quality control, as well as relevant design work, the task has been long and arduous. With help from consultants, Jograni has, however, partly achieved its objectives. Currently, 6% of products are sold to tourists, 44% to local expatriates and the remaining 50% to Bangladeshis.

## FUTURE MARKETS?

Jograni is now having to consider future policy, particularly as the handicraft market becomes more competitive. Present government restrictions on the number of missions and aid agencies working in Bangladesh have raised the question of a diminishing market amongst expatriates.

The organization has grown steadily over the past 15 years but is now at a point where it needs to plan for the next 10 years. It has seen some of its stronger competitors go into the export business and is considering whether this is a viable option, given the problems that presently exist in producing quality items for the tourist market (where the quality demanded is virtually the same). On the one hand it is seen as the next logical step – simply an extension of current activities. Others argue that it will lead to some fundamental changes in the way in which the organization works, not least by altering the principal operational objectives which at present are dominated by resource and cost considerations, possibly to the detriment of aspects of customer service.

The tourist market has already shown Jograni that it needs to produce better-quality items. At present only 6% of turnover is derived from tourists, despite premium prices. A decision to export would mean new markets as well as better-quality goods with more emphasis on customer service.

Scheduling has been largely a function of how much producers send to the warehouse. With little way of controlling these arrivals, inventory levels can vary enormously and tend to peak dramatically around (Muslim) festival times when producers are desperate for money. Trying to produce 'seasonal' items for non-Muslim festivals, such as embroidered Christmas cards, thus becomes a rather hit and miss affair.

## FUTURE OPERATING PROCEDURES?

If Jograni is to achieve what is set out above, it is clear that certain changes will be necessary in the ways in which the organization operates. Amongst these implications are the following, which must now be considered by the management.

For *design* the current ad hoc system will probably have to be replaced. Systematic training and design input will probably be needed.

*Local manufacture* will still take place but some centrally supplied raw materials may be needed.

*Distribution* will perhaps undergo the biggest change. Research has shown that foreign buyers are particular in their orders and often specify minute changes to ensure originality. The implication is that a unique set of goods is produced for each overseas customer. In some cases raw materials may be supplied by the buyer to ensure adequate quality.

Overall *capacity* will probably have to increase in order to provide the volumes required for bulk ordering by overseas buyers. There is known to be some underemployment of facilities at present. However, estimating supply, as well as forecasting future demand, will be an important task. Further, since at present output stocks absorb some demand fluctuations, the move towards supplying against customer orders will necessitate a different approach to capacity.

*Stocks* will still be important for two reasons:

1. The home market will still be the 'cash cow' of the business and improvements in inventory management may help to improve this part of the business.
2. Foreign buyers often like to take back large samples with which to test their market. Competitors already have showrooms backed up by a wide range of stock. This enables a quick response to buyers' initial requests.

At present, each group procures its own materials. Central *purchasing* of some materials has, however, been considered, mainly for reasons of quality control (e.g. batik work, where it is difficult to know the quality of the dye being bought beforehand). Reduced cost through bulk buying would be an added advantage. But, for Jograni, it would mean additional storage space.

There are expected to be some major implications for *scheduling*. To a larger extent customers' requirements will determine the delivery dates rather than internal production schedules. This, in many ways, is seen to be the key to success in the export market, for even if the right quality of goods is produced, the delivery time, which will be linked to a 'movement' time (e.g. shipping arrangements), will be crucial to the whole process.

As a cultural aside it is worth pointing out that 'time' is much more 'fluid' in Asian cultures, and while the more Westernized Asian may appreciate the concept of a delivery date, conveying this idea to the rural producer is not just a question of introducing a new business concept but a whole new cultural viewpoint. Also, rural producers are rarely 'full-time' craft producers and will typically have more commitments. The priorities for them may not necessarily coincide with those of Jograni centrally, despite the fact that Jograni is attempting to work in their interests. In this respect it is also worth noting that those handicraft producers who have succeeded in breaking into the export market have all got the following in common:

1. centralized production centres near or in the capital city;
2. vertical integration of all activities to ensure schedules are met;
3. centralized purchasing of raw materials to some degree (usually more rather than less);
4. close ties with member groups, including additional services such as literacy, health and community development;
5. substantial design and technical input (invariably by foreigners).

Thus in the Bangladesh context, the handicraft market cannot be divorced from the wider cultural and societal values and norms. Overcoming and developing these are additional challenges on top of the operational ones.

*Quality* is considered to be the key to successfully establishing a position in the export market. For this reason, a number of 'options' must be considered, i.e.

1. ***Specifications*** for items will be more rigorous than for the home market. Fashion and colour considerations will also be important. The ability of producers to incorporate specific design features into the process will for most handicraft producers be a new concept. The emphasis for some products may change from making what comes 'naturally' to making for a market. In the initial stages special training will be important.
2. The variability and substandard quality of some ***inputs*** such as dyes for batik work raises the question of central purchasing. This is one way of introducing more control over the input materials.
3. Learning to ***inspect*** work at each stage will be an integral part of this. (In batik work, for instance, it is important to check for 'spotting' or 'cracking' wax which can ruin the desired effect. As dyeing is expensive, checking at the pre-dyeing stage can save costly errors. Likewise, checking the results of the dyeing before the wax is removed allows re-dyeing if necessary.)

If the above is effective, the need for inspection of products arriving at the central distribution centre should, in theory, be minimized. However, in the Bangladesh context, it will take a number of years to get consistent quality, and cultural differences will play a large role in the change process. Having to make changes to what local people see as perfectly functional items will at first be difficult to understand. Concepts of quality will also vary. What is regarded as quality to a rural group may not be the same as the quality required by foreign buyers.

Case study 3

# Centre Hospitalier Reine Fabiola

Mrs Demoulin is head pharmacist at the Centre Hospitalier Reine Fabiola located near Leuvain la Neuve in Belgium. Like her colleagues in other departments, she has been given the task of reducing costs. The evolution of medical technology, the cost of equipment, the increase of wages, etc. are such that, in the face of reducing contributions from the National Social Security Office (owing to reductions in people's contributions arising from higher unemployment, and the increase in the number of old persons) it is more and more difficult to maintain economical 'equilibrium' in hospitals. Moreover, the hospital cost increases are far ahead of the slowly increasing gross national product.

Purchases represent almost 25% of the total costs of a hospital. Among those, the purchases of pharmaceutical products are particularly important, being about 45% of the total purchase costs (Table C3.1).

The general categories of purchases are shown in Figure C3.1.

Structurally, Belgium may be considered to be divided into two main regions, according to the language spoken. The Reine Fabiola hospital is located in the French-speaking part; it belongs to the category of general hospitals where patients are accepted in the acute phase of their illnesses. Taking into account the number of beds and nursing units, the hospital is classified in the fourth category (cat. 1, 1–149 beds; 2, 150–249; 3, 250–349; 4, 350–499; 5, 500 beds and over).

In view of the value of the pharmaceutical inventory and of the annual amount of purchases, Mrs Demoulin aims to reduce the tied-up capital. In examining the problem, she chooses, initially, to limit her study to one category of articles: the surgical ligatures. These are a homogeneous group of articles by use, but, at the same time, are sufficiently differentiated by their material (linen, catgut, synthetic, etc.), the type of needle crimping the ligature, the number of units per packaging (each ligature is individually packed but the number of units is variable – but most often 40), and so on. They are mainly used for people who are in surgery and in maternity nursing units.

Relying on governmental data and on her contacts with colleagues, Mrs Demoulin has gathered financial information for the 15 hospitals in the region, including Reine Fabiola, in the different categories identified. A statistical analysis of these data shows that 67% of the variation of ligatures is explained by the number of beds in the surgery and gynaecology nursing units in the hospitals (Figure C3.2).

At present the hospital has 104 different ligatures on inventory. For each item, Table C3.2 shows the number of consumed packages and also the amount of the annual demand. The pharmacist notices that, in spite of previous actions she has taken, the number of different ligatures is increasing;

**Table C3.1 Financial data for a sample of 15 hospitals (in millions of francs)**

| Hospital | Total cost of expenses | Total cost of purchases | Ratio of purchases/ expenses (%) | Total cost of pharma- ceutical purchases | Ratio of pharma- ceutical to total purchases (%) | Total cost of ligature purchases | Ratio of ligature to pharma- ceutical purchases (%) |
|---|---|---|---|---|---|---|---|
| 1 | 1 774.50 | 391.00 | 22.03 | 175.00 | 44.76 | 4.42 | 2.53 |
| 2 | 1 301.90 | 314.23 | 24.14 | 124.24 | 39.54 | 5.62 | 4.52 |
| 3 | 750.00 | 162.40 | 21.65 | 88.20 | 54.31 | 3.30 | 3.74 |
| 4 | 6 938.00 | 2 755.00 | 39.71 | 671.00 | 24.36 | 36.15 | 5.39 |
| 5 | 456.70 | 83.80 | 18.35 | 55.50 | 66.23 | 2.50 | 4.50 |
| 6 | 1 967.90 | 637.70 | 32.40 | 377.36 | 59.17 | 10.50 | 2.78 |
| 7 | 1 096.30 | 346.10 | 31.57 | 96.77 | 27.96 | 2.81 | 2.90 |
| 8 | 1 220.90 | 261.20 | 21.39 | 140.50 | 53.79 | 4.00 | 2.85 |
| 9 | 2 366.70 | 510.00 | 21.55 | 136.50 | 26.76 | 8.20 | 6.01 |
| 10 | 1 310.00 | 251.00 | 19.16 | 70.00 | 27.89 | 4.17 | 5.96 |
| 11 | 628.60 | 153.50 | 24.42 | 82.90 | 54.01 | 4.53 | 5.46 |
| 12 | 1 399.40 | 231.00 | 16.51 | 86.98 | 37.65 | 2.03 | 2.33 |
| 13 | 1 050.00 | 209.00 | 19.90 | 94.50 | 45.22 | 2.29 | 2.42 |
| 14 | 722.60 | 189.50 | 26.22 | 81.00 | 42.74 | 3.52 | 4.35 |
| 15 | 361.80 | 102.45 | 28.31 | 75.23 | 73.43 | 2.07 | 2.75 |
| Total | 23 345.50 | 6 597.88 | | 2 355.66 | | 96.11 | |
| Average | 1 556.37 | 439.36 | 24 | 157.04 | 45.19 | 6.41 | 3.90 |

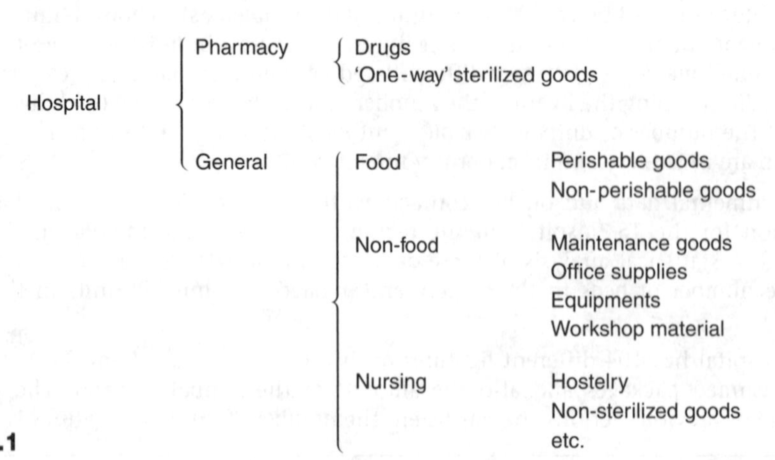


**Figure C3.1**

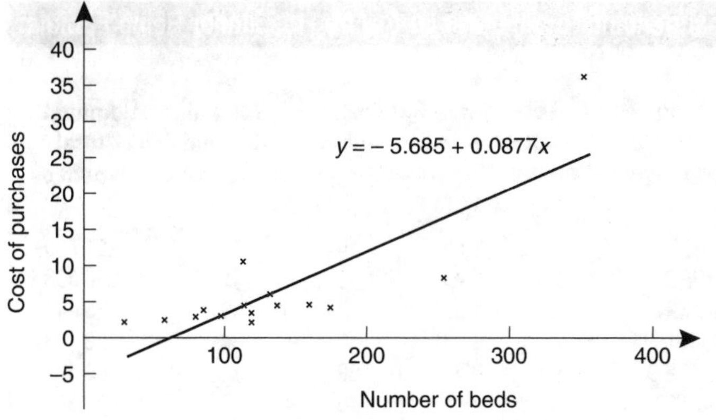


**Figure C3.2** Correlation analysis: cost of ligature purchases, number of beds

this increases not only the amount of tied-up capital but also the clerical work of her employees. She thinks that this tendency is due to the technological development in this kind of item, coupled with the fact that surgeons are not greatly concerned with cost and thus ask for new articles despite the fact that previous articles still exist. The demand for ligatures is relatively stable; peaks in spring and autumn are compensated with low points during the vacation period and the holidays; generally the demand for individual ligatures is fairly low. The number of suppliers is limited, the articles they sell belong to the same family and the minimum order quantity is limited by the size of the packaging. Some critical articles have a low demand and/or a low unitary price.

The purchase procedure is as follows: periodically – generally each Tuesday – the pharmacist places an order for one or more items from suppliers. Table C3.3 gives, for each supplier, the percentage of the monthly average demand. The buying frequency for each item is variable; so for some articles, it is three times a year, while for others, it may go up to once a month. The order quantity for each item varies; the number of units is calculated by the difference between a maximum value equal to six weeks' demand, less the inventory on hand.

The stocks are at present located in two places, the pharmacy and the surgical suite. Whilst every package delivered to the suite is considered as consumed, in fact stocks are spread about in the six operating rooms as well as in the suite. The average cost of the inventory at the surgical suite is 673 000 francs, while in the pharmacy it is 628 000 francs.

Each operating room is nominally dedicated to one of several types of operation:

1. maxillary and facial surgery, otorhinolaryngology;
2. gynaecology and plastic surgery;
3. orthopaedic surgery;
4. urology and blood-vascular surgery;
5. gastroenterological surgery.

However, when necessary, operations may take place in rooms other than the normal one.

Every day, a nurse supplies each operating room. When she judges that the number of ligatures left is too low, she takes new packagings from the central stock in the suite. Once a week the nurse responsible for the stock of the suite makes a check.

She notes, for each of the 104 articles, the number of packagings left, their identification code and the number of packagings needed in reference to a predetermined value. This requirement is sent to the pharmacy and the items are either directly delivered to the operating suite or ordered from a supplier. A deeper analysis has shown that, on average, the packagings at the suite contain 68% of the total number of ligatures. The ligatures are used on a first in, first out basis.

**Table C3.2 Analysis of the annual demand for ligatures at Centre Hospitalier Reine Fabiola**

| Number code | Order number | Wording | Rank | Price per pack-aging | Pack-aging | Annual demand | Annual total expenses |
|---|---|---|---|---|---|---|---|
| BV1058 | 35 | VICRYL 1 CRIMPED | 1 | 5835 | 40 | 38 | 221 730 |
| BV519 | 36 | VICRYL 1 CRIMPED | 2 | 5366 | 40 | 41 | 220 006 |
| JV517 | 43 | VICRYL2/0 CRIMPED | 3 | 4386 | 40 | 40 | 175 440 |
| FW775 | 71 | SOIE 2/0 CRIMPED RIGHT | 4 | 3428 | 40 | 36 | 123 408 |
| V516 | 45 | VICRYL 3/10 CRIMPED | 5 | 6398 | 36 | 14 | 89 572 |
| JV2015 | 46 | VICRYL 3/0 CRIMPED | 6 | 4825 | 40 | 15 | 72 375 |
| JV370 | 38 | VICRYL 0 CRIMPED | 7 | 4590 | 40 | 15 | 68 850 |
| JV457 | 47 | VICRYL 4/0 CRIMPED | 8 | 4386 | 40 | 15 | 65 790 |
| 35W | 104 | SKIN SUTURE CLIP | 9 | 2340 | 6 | 28 | 65 520 |
| JV360 | 32 | VICRYL 2 CRIMPED | 10 | 5671 | 40 | 9 | 51 039 |
| W996 | 99 | ETHIBOND 3/0 CRIMPED RIGHT | 11 | 1499 | 12 | 30 | 44 970 |
| JV473 | 39 | VICRYL 0 CRIMPED | 12 | 4488 | 40 | 10 | 44 880 |
| FW622 | 72 | SOIE 3/0CRIMPED RIGHT | 13 | 3186 | 40 | 14 | 44 604 |
| EW776 | 57 | ETHILON 2/0 CRIMPED RIGHT | 14 | 2261 | 40 | 19 | 42 959 |
| BN506 | 63 | ETHILON 6/0 CRIMPED CURVE | 15 | 615 | 10 | 60 | 36 900 |
| BV518 | 40 | VICRYL 0 CRIMPED | 16 | 4762 | 40 | 7 | 33 334 |
| EW788 | 58 | ETHILON 3/0 CRIMPED RIGHT | 17 | 2261 | 40 | 14 | 31 654 |
| F32028 | 98 | ETHIBOND 2/0 CRIMPED RIGHT | 18 | 2850 | 40 | 11 | 31 350 |
| EW319 | 61 | ETHILON 4/0 CRIMPED CURVE | 19 | 2100 | 40 | 12 | 25 200 |
| JV485 | 37 | VICRYL 0 CRIMPED | 20 | 4590 | 40 | 5 | 22 950 |
| V624 | 28 | VICRYL 3/0 BOBBIN | 21 | 3238 | 36 | 7 | 22 666 |
| FE4103 | 3 | CATG. NORM. 2/0 BOBBIN | 22 | 1667 | 20 | 13 | 21 671 |
| BC1123 | 7 | CATG. NORM. 2/0 CRIMPED | 23 | 3470 | 40 | 6 | 20 820 |
| BV1207 | 26 | VICRYL 0 BOBBIN | 24 | 2971 | 20 | 7 | 20 797 |
| JV1044 | 34 | VICRYL 1 CRIMPED | 25 | 6764 | 40 | 3 | 20 292 |
| BV1206 | 27 | VICRYL 2/0 BOBBIN | 26 | 2828 | 20 | 7 | 19 796 |
| FG2809 | 65 | ETHILON 9/0 CRIMPED CURVE | 27 | 4702 | 10 | 4 | 18 808 |
| FZ467 | 94 | PDS 0 CRIMPED RIGHT | 28 | 3750 | 30 | 5 | 18 750 |
| F1112 | 5 | CATG. NORM. 1 CRIMPED | 32 | 3856 | 40 | 4 | 15 424 |
| BC1124 | 6 | CATG. NORM. 0 CRIMPED | 38 | 3738 | 40 | 3 | 11 214 |
| JV524 | 42 | VICRYL 2/0 CRIMPED | 47 | 3978 | 40 | 2 | 7 956 |
| F1532 | 54 | MERSUTURES 2/0 CRIMPED | 48 | 2598 | 40 | 3 | 7 794 |
| FG129 | 15 | CATG. CHRO. 1 CRIMPED | 49 | 3791 | 40 | 2 | 7 582 |
| FG128 | 23 | CATG. CHRO. 0 CRIMPED | 50 | 3791 | 40 | 2 | 7 582 |
| ZH1503 | 103 | FDS BAND (RENFORT LIG.) 15 | 51 | 7530 | 3 | 1 | 7 530 |
| FE4105 | 1 | CATG. NORM. 1 BOBBIN | 52 | 1876 | 20 | 4 | 7 504 |
| FE4104 | 2 | CATG. NORM. 0 BOBBIN | 53 | 1745 | 20 | 4 | 6 980 |
| F1119 | 9 | CATG. NORM. 4/0 CRIMPED | 65 | 3688 | 40 | 1 | 3 688 |
| W202 | 68 | SOIE 3/0 BOBBIN | 70 | 941 | 12 | 2 | 1 882 |

**Table C3.2 (continued)**

| Number code | Order number | Wording | Rank | Price per packaging | Packaging | Annual demand | Annual total expenses |
|---|---|---|---|---|---|---|---|
| FE4102 | 4 | CATG. NORM. 3/0 BOBBIN | 71 | 1646 | 20 | 1 | 1 646 |
| W755 | 17 | CATG. CHRO. 1 CRIMPED | 72 | 1330 | 12 | 1 | 1 330 |
| FV321 | 74 | SOIE 2/0 CRIMPED CURVE | 73 | 650 | 10 | 2 | 1 300 |
| BP8390 | 86 | PROLENE 5/0 CRIMPED CURVE | 74 | 930 | 10 | 1 | 930 |
| BC1122 | 8 | CATG. NORM. 3/0 CRIMPED | 75 | 4000 | 40 | 0 | 0 |
| F4156 | 10 | CATG. CHRO. 2 BOBBIN | 76 | 2226 | 20 | 0 | 0 |
| F4155 | 11 | CATG. CHRO. 1 BOBBIN | 77 | 1876 | 20 | 0 | 0 |
| F2832 | 89 | PROLENE 6/0 CRIMPED CURVE | 100 | 7629 | 40 | 0 | 0 |
| Z443 | 91 | PDS 2/0 CRIMPED RIGHT | 101 | 4425 | 30 | 0 | 0 |
| Z460 | 92 | PDS 3/0 CRIMPED RIGHT | 102 | 3937 | 30 | 0 | 0 |
| Z305 | 93 | PDS 3/0 CRIMPED RIGHT | 103 | 2850 | 30 | 0 | 0 |
| Z984 | 95 | PDS 1 CRIMPED RIGHT | 104 | 3750 | 30 | 0 | 0 |
| TOTAL | | | 104 | – | – | 625 | 2 030 953 |

**Table C3.3 Average monthly demand per buyer (% of total)**

| Supplier | Average monthly demand |
|---|---|
| DG | 74.68 |
| ETH | 13.31 |
| BB | 5.67 |
| AUTO | 2.80 |
| WECK | 1.30 |
| ALC | 1.10 |
| IMPL | 1.02 |
| SSC | 0.12 |

Table C3.4 gives data for a family of ligatures from a single supplier.

More information has been secured by Mrs Demoulin:

1. For one item coming from one supplier, the supply lead time may be very different. Table C3.4 shows, that for a family of nine articles (CATG. NORM) from the same supplier, there may be variations in the annual number of purchases as well as in the lead time. The same data are available for other suppliers and show, overall, a range of 68 days with a mean of 16 days and standard deviation 19 days.

Table C3.4 Data concerning articles of a ligatures family CATG. NORM.

| Code number | Order number | Wording CATG. NORM. | Average weekly stock in packaging: Pharmacy Stock Av. | Val. | Surgical suite stock Room no. (1 = stock held) 1 | 2 | 3 | 4 | 5 | 6 | Total stock in rooms | Average weekly demand in packaging | Annual turnover rate (Annual demand / Av. inventory) | Lead time in days: Order no. lead time 1 | 2 | 2 | 4 | Variance on lead time |
|---|---|---|---|---|---|---|---|---|---|---|---|---|---|---|---|---|---|---|
| FE 4105 | 1 | 1 BOBBIN | 1.1 | 2060 | 1 | 1 | 0 | 0 | 1 | 0 | 3 831 | 0.08 | 1.32 | 8 | | | | – |
| FE 4104 | 2 | 0 BOBBIN | 1.2 | 2121 | 1 | 1 | 0 | 1 | 1 | 1 | 5 939 | 0.08 | 0.91 | 5 | 9 | | | 8.00 |
| FE 4103 | 3 | 2/0 BOBBIN | 1.7 | 2876 | 1 | 1 | 1 | 1 | 1 | 1 | 6 808 | 0.25 | 2.25 | 9 | 3 | 9 | 10 | 10.25 |
| FE 4102 | 4 | 3/0 BOBBIN | 1.6 | 2647 | 0 | 1 | 1 | 0 | 1 | 0 | 3 361 | 0.02 | 0.65 | 6 | | | | – |
| F 1112 | 5 | 1 CRIMPED | 2.3 | 8922 | 1 | 1 | 0 | 0 | 1 | 1 | 10 498 | 0.08 | 0.83 | 5 | 9 | 6 | | 4.33 |
| BC 1124 | 6 | 0 CRIMPED | 1.5 | 5790 | 1 | 1 | 0 | 0 | 1 | 1 | 10 177 | 0.06 | 0.74 | 6 | 15 | | | 40.5 |
| BC 1123 | 7 | 2/0 CRIMPED | 1.0 | 3606 | 1 | 1 | 0 | 0 | 1 | 1 | 9 447 | 0.12 | 1.68 | 5 | 6 | 9 | 9 | 4.25 |
| BC 1122 | 8 | 3/0 CRIMPED | 2.0 | 8000 | 0 | 1 | 0 | 0 | 1 | 1 | 8 168 | 0 | 0.00 | | | | | – |
| F 1119 | 9 | 4/0 CRIMPED | 0.9 | 3381 | 0 | 0 | 0 | 0 | 0 | 0 | 0 | 0.02 | 1.15 | 11 | 10 | | | 0.5 |

2. After discussion with the surgeons, they agreed that, given the number of ligatures and the possibilities to replace one by another, the service level should be 95% of the demand.
3. On the basis of evaluations or data given by the accounting department, the difference between the holding costs (opportunity cost of the capital, insurance, breakage, obsolescence, etc.) and the cost of the average total inventory is 16.75% whereas the ordering cost for an order (clerical and managerial costs) is calculated to be 125 francs, independently of the number of items bought simultaneously from the same supplier.

Mrs Demoulin must now decide what to do. She is required to put her proposals to the board of the hospital shortly.

Case study 4

# Qormi Post Office

The branch post office at Qormi, on the Mediterranean island of Malta, provides a postal service to a community of about 10 000 persons. It operates from a building which is located in a central position on the main road in the town. It comprises three main sections: a big sorting room where mail is stamped, sorted by locality and arranged for local delivery; a transport storage room where bicycles are kept; and a receipt and dispatch depot.

This local branch post office undertakes to collect letters and similar postal items (e.g. postcards, printed matter, etc.) in the town and deliver the same to addresses in the minimum time possible and also deliver, in the town, items sent from elsewhere. Items collected locally meant for addressees within the local area are 'processed' wholly within the branch, while other items addressed for outside the local area are date stamped, bundled and later collected by head office for onward transmission to destination. The Qormi Post Office operates only as a mustering room. It does not operate a counter service, so that it does not have the facilities to accept parcels and heavier items which need weighing, rating and certification prior to being accepted for posting, or the registration of letters which demand treatment (i.e. listing) upon acceptance. Nor does it have the facilities to sell stamps and advise people on postal tariffs and rates, or to offer any philatelic services like the special first day of issue date stamp. Local customers needing such services have to travel to the nearest large town, Valetta (the capital of the island).

## THE OPERATION

Collection of letters from the several post boxes laid out at strategic points around the town is made twice daily by postmen using bicycles as a means of transport, at 7 a.m. and again at 9 a.m. Once collected, letters are brought to the post office where they are date-stamped and sorted according to the locality postcode. Those letters addressed to the local area are immediately passed to the sorting room for sorting by postmen ready for delivery the same day. Postal items for outside areas are packed in bags for collection by head office.

Later on, mail from outside areas addressed to local addressees arrives by van from head office. The same van carries away local mail for 'foreign' destinations. The incoming mail is first sorted according to postal beats and immediately passed to the sorting room for re-sorting direct into the postmen's 'routes'. Upon completion of this, the postmen go out and start delivery of the mail. The inner town routes (or 'beats') are usually made on foot, while mail for outlying areas is delivered using bicycles for quicker transport.

Figure C4.1 shows the normal process of operation.

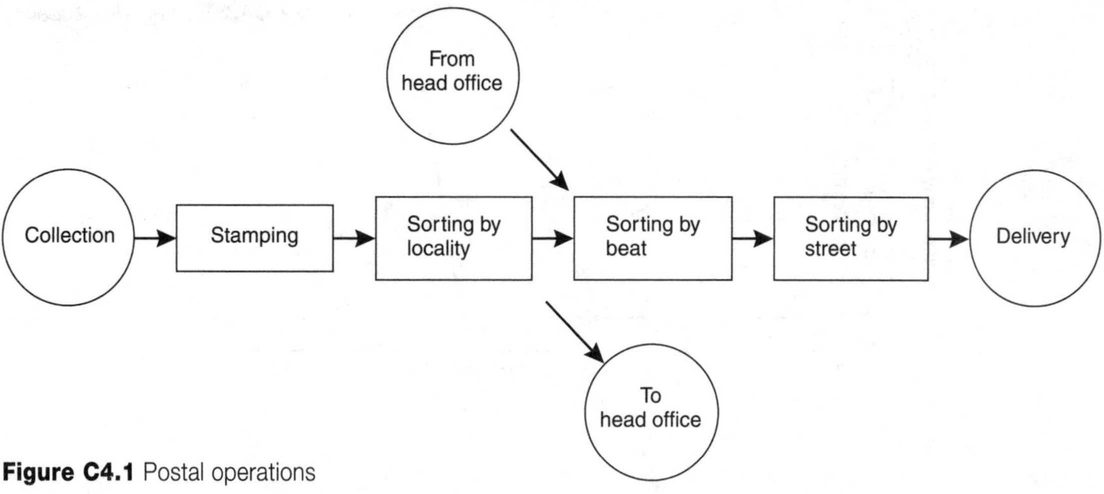


**Figure C4.1** Postal operations

It should be noted that although there are various levels of postal tariffs relating to the quality (i.e. speed) of service required (e.g. 1st class mail for closed letters or 2nd class mail for postcards and newspapers), all mail is afforded 1st class treatment in what is called an 'all up' service. Thus all mail is processed and delivered in one batch.

The staff employed consist of an officer in charge of the whole operation, plus seven postmen. There are five beats so that five of the postmen are totally dedicated to sorting and delivery. Another postman acts as a 'reliever', and stands in whenever another postman is absent, which is frequent as each postman is entitled to five weeks' vacation leave (there are no scheduled shutdowns) plus other absences due to illness, etc. The seventh postman takes care of the collection of letters from letter boxes, date stamping of letters and dispatch, and receipt of mail from head office.

## THE CUSTOMER

Post offices in Malta can deal with three sets of customers: the domestic consumer market, where the post office offers a service primarily aimed at collecting and delivering household mail (mainly letters); the business and industrial community, where the post office offers such services as fast transmission of documents and packages, bulk postings and reliable and fast commercial parcel service; and a 'niche' market, that only the post office could satisfy, and which concerns the needs of the philatelic enthusiasts.

Qormi branch post office deals mainly with the first 'market', although lately pressure has been mounting to extend operations so as to be able to accommodate demand from industry and philatelists.

## DEMAND

Demand for the postal service is typically uniform and stable, with a high peak during the Christmas festivities period when mail posting tends to double (Figure C4.2). Demand forecasting is therefore a straightforward affair, the more so since the Post Office, having a monopoly on the postal business, is not subjected to real competitive pressures (although some competition exists through alternative methods of communication, e.g. telephone, telefaxes and electronic mail).

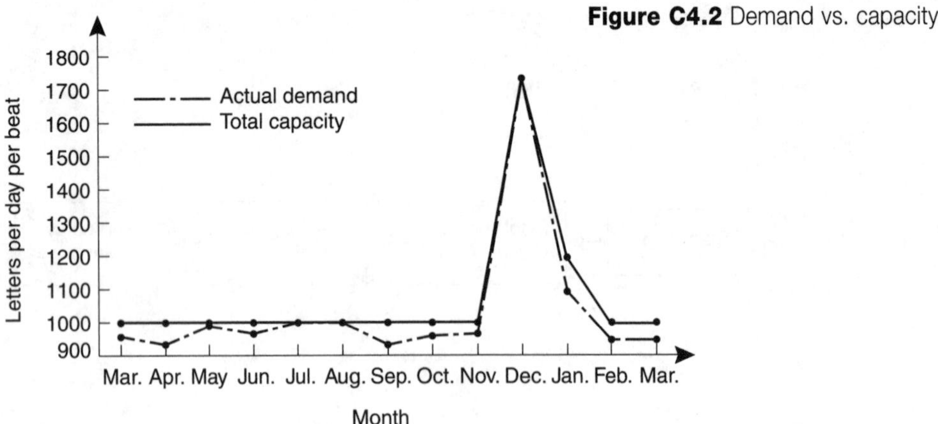


**Figure C4.2** Demand vs. capacity

## OBJECTIVES

The aim of the Malta post office service is to serve the community by offering a fast, reliable and cheap postal service. It commits itself to collect and deliver, within the island of Malta, all items posted up to a certain time (7 a.m.) on the very same day of posting. Items posted between 7 a.m. and 9 a.m. and addressed within the local area will also be delivered on the same day. Mail posted after 9 a.m. will get a next-day delivery. It also commits itself to deliver the articles intact and at the lowest possible prices. A very low level of complaints testifies to a high degree of customer satisfaction.

## RESOURCES

The most important resource employed is labour. Few materials are consumed in the process, and machinery/tools employed are minimal and comprise, besides the building, some bicycles, date stamps, racks, chairs, mailbags, tables and uniforms.

To solve the Christmas demand problem, the post office withholds all staff leave during December and introduces a double shift working arrangement at the peak demand period where postmen are required to collect, process and deliver mail a second time. (Temporary labour is not used because the use of inexperienced labour might lead to errors and a subsequent drop in quality, with the risk of complaints from customers. Moreover, inexperienced workers will be slow and thus costs will be higher.) Transfer of labour from other post office branches is also not feasible because other post office branches have the same seasonal demand situation.

## THE DEVELOPMENT OF THE QORMI POST OFFICE?

Although this branch post office has been operating very effectively, pressures have been mounting on the central post office management to extend the Qormi operations to be able to accommodate the growing demand from an expanding business community, especially since the setting up of an industrial area in the vicinity of the town. In addition to this, local philatelists have also been complaining about the problem of having to travel to another office in order to be able to satisfy their needs: they argue that a local branch with a customized 'first day of issue' date stamp would be a further service to philately and might increase demand. These 'public' demands have also been echoed in the press and by local politicians, and post office management has felt obliged to have the situation investigated, prior to considering whether to reformulate its business policy in relation to the Qormi branch. To do this it set out to:

(a) identify and forecast the level of expected extra demand that would be generated following the proposed change;

(b) identify any possible threats and risks (e.g. expected demand not materializing), whilst also:

(c) acknowledging the needs of the public as major stakeholders; and

(d) accepting the post office's responsibility as a public utility to cater for the requirements of society.

After some preliminary market research and an analysis of the Qormi branch operations, it was found that the level of expected demand was enough to warrant expanding the service. Moreover, it was noted that this presented an excellent opportunity to make use of available spare space on the premises and also to significantly improve utilization (which for most of the time was operating at less than maximum capacity). The decision was therefore taken to set up a counter section at the Qormi branch with the following objectives:

(a) to provide services to satisfy the needs of a variety of markets, in search of both greater market penetration (domestic market) and market development (business and philatelic communities);

(b) to make far greater use of available resources, thereby minimizing costs.

## BRANCH RESOURCES

The determination of the level of resources to be used for the new counter service depended on forecast demand for counter services. It was anticipated that demand will take some time to pick up, so that initially only one counter assistant was allowed by head office. Other resource requirements were considered to be minimal and amounted to some counter furniture and weighing scales and a limited stock of stamps (stocks of stamps were replenished from head office whenever they fell below a certain minimum amount).

Whilst this set-up in practice gave rise to some customer queuing, it was nonetheless thought to be minimal and considered by head office to be quite normal and acceptable in such situations.

## BRANCH ECONOMICS

Previously, resource utilization levels had enabled the Qormi Post Office to achieve its most economic level of operation at around 1000 letters processed per day, per beat (Figure C4.3). Any increase in output or demand will now involve an increase in costs (overtime) and will change the unit cost–output relationship.

In fact the new services increased demand significantly and generated a substantial rise of 45% in revenue (from Lm 19 000 to Lm 27 500). This was achieved at an increase in fixed costs of Lm 4000 and a smaller increase in variable costs (from Lm 2000 to Lm 4500 p.a.), mainly due to increased expenditure on overtime work and the employment of a counter clerk. This new situation lowered slightly the breakeven percentage capacity, which has been lowered from an estimated level of approximately 60% to 53% as illustrated in Figure C4.4.

## IMPACT ON CUSTOMERS

Given the new methods of operating, it is recognized that customer service could suffer. However, since the increased demand is not initially expected heavily to exceed the available capacity, it was reasoned

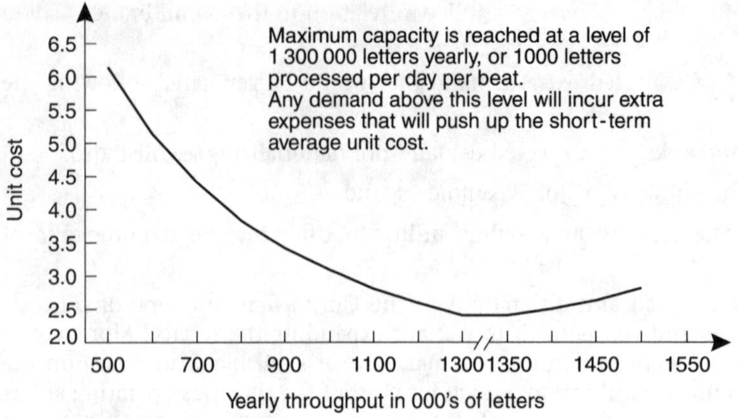


**Figure C4.3** Output/cost relationship

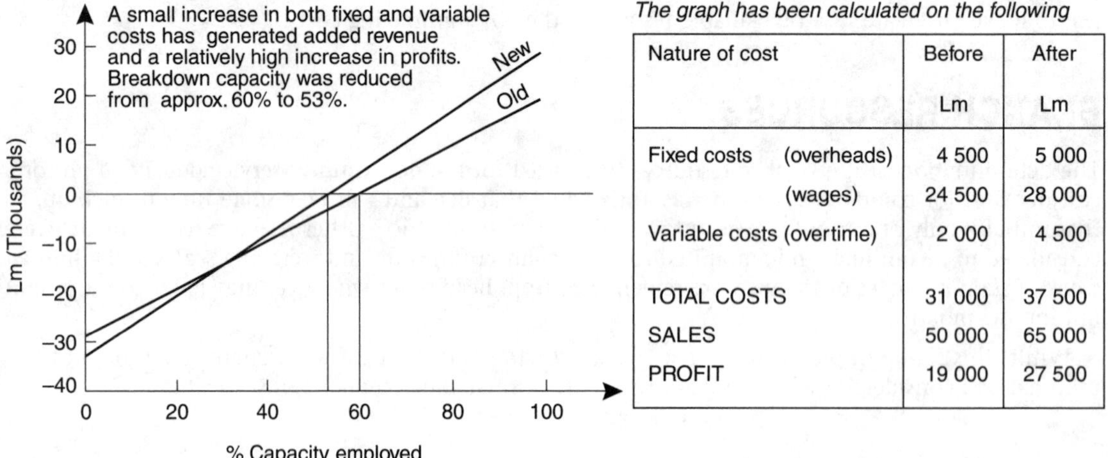


*The graph has been calculated on the following*

| Nature of cost | Before Lm | After Lm |
|---|---|---|
| Fixed costs (overheads) | 4 500 | 5 000 |
| (wages) | 24 500 | 28 000 |
| Variable costs (overtime) | 2 000 | 4 500 |
| TOTAL COSTS | 31 000 | 37 500 |
| SALES | 50 000 | 65 000 |
| PROFIT | 19 000 | 27 500 |

**Figure C4.4** Breakeven calculations

that any problems could easily be dealt with through the careful adjustment of capacity, as and when required, by overtime work. Certainly this seemed to be the only possibility, as central management was not prepared to consider employing additional labour which might be under-utilized at periods of normal demand. The manager, however, did consider other options available to deal with the problem, e.g.

1. ***Mechanization***, i.e. some form of mechanization to increase capacity, e.g. an automated stamp cancelling machine to release labour time to devote to other activities, or motorcycles instead of bicycles, to save time on collection and delivery rounds.
2. ***'Two-level' service***. Normally the 'all up' service has applied. However, now that available capacity may not always be enough to meet demand, the 2nd class type of mail could be left to 'queue'.
3. ***Revised scheduling***. Operating near to full capacity now means that the timing of activities becomes much more crucial. Demand for the new counter service is expected to be fairly stable and regular,

but will be highly differentiated since the counter will not offer just one product or service but a whole range of services and it will therefore be difficult to reliably forecast how demand will be structured.

The main effect of the new decision was to increase demand so as effectively to utilize available capacity all of the time. This, however, had implications for the quality of service through: (1) an inadequacy of the system on occasions to process all demand and therefore to ensure prompt delivery; and (2) a tendency to introduce mishandling and delivery errors in the various phases of the process through sheer pressure of work. Thus quality became a major concern for the branch manager, who took the view that provision of good-quality service is above all a result of a 'good' operating system and a 'quality culture'. Therefore, procedures and individual functions should be clearly defined so that responsibilities can be easily identified; commitment should be clearly visible from the operations manager downwards; work standards and specifications need to be emphasized; supervision and internal communication, coupled with a continuous on-the-job training, would also facilitate the quality process; the human aspect of ensuring quality through a satisfied workforce should also be highlighted through, for example, providing for work variety and allowing employees a degree of autonomy in determining methods of work and problem-solving; job rotation and job enrichment methods should also be studied.

In this context it was noted that the nature of the postal service has two particular advantages in that the postman comes in direct daily contact with his 'customers', thus developing a friendly relationship that not only helps to build a good image for the organization, but effectively motivates the postman to produce a quality service – for any errors on his or her part will have to be faced and explained directly to the customer. The other advantage is that the postal operation is a continuous and cascading mail sorting process, which immediately detects any errors that have been made in a previous stage, so that if, for example, a letter had been badly sorted by locality, it cannot be resorted by beat let alone by household order, and would be redirected to the previous sorting stage straight away. The chances of misdelivery are therefore much reduced.

Case study 5

# The Sahil Tea Garden

The Sahil Tea Garden (Sahil Çay Bahçezi) is at Kas – a small harbour village on the Mediterranean coast of southern Turkey. Kas has a normal population of 5000 but a 'seasonal' population of double that figure, for whilst it is undeveloped, unsophisticated and located a $3^1/_2$ -hour, difficult drive from the nearest airports (Dalaman and Antalya), it attracts holiday makers, mainly from Europe, through from June to September, and is a 'stop-off' for passing yachts and the occasional small cruise ship.

The Sahil Tea Garden, even by local standards, is a simple cafe/bar located along the pathway which runs immediately behind the rocky beach, to the west of the harbour. It is no more than an arrangement of tables under the vines and oleanders, together with a small kitchen, freezers, bar, chill cabinets, etc. It has seating for approximately 120 people around small tables. The layout is approximately as shown in Figure C5.1.

The Tea Garden is open for the full day during the period June–September inclusive and closed for the rest of the year. It provides breakfast from around 8 a.m. to late morning, lunch from 11 a.m. (approximately) to 4 p.m. (approximately) and then drinks and snacks for the remainder of the day. Breakfast typically comprises fruit juice, coffee, çay (tea), pastries, etc. Lunch offers a broader menu (see below) and thereafter the service is only soft drinks, beer, çay, coffee, ice cream, cakes, etc.

The most distinctive feature of the Tea Garden – well known to both locals and visitors – is evident at lunchtimes. Then the Tea Garden offers freshly made gözleme – a traditional Turkish nomad dish, being a cross between a pancake and a French crepe.

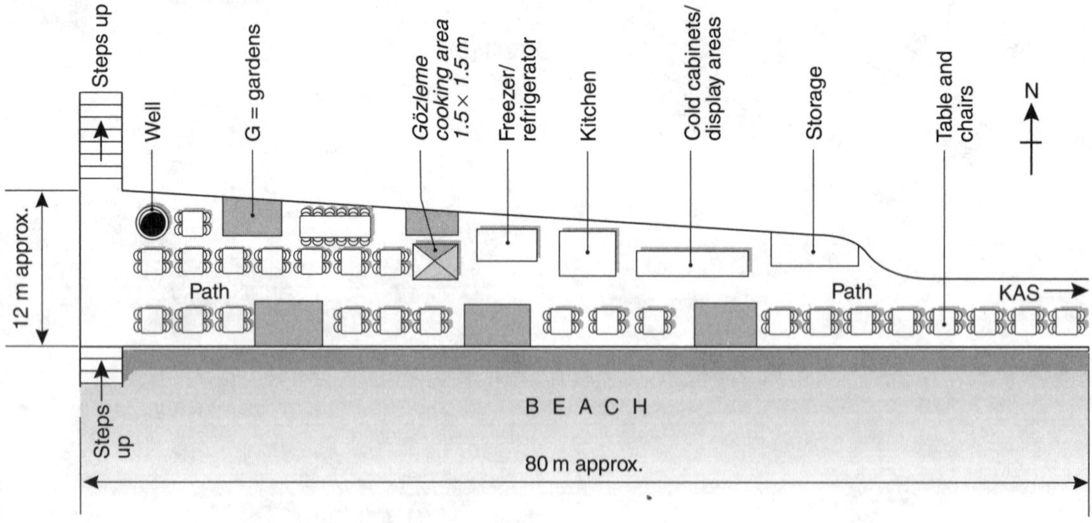


**Figure C5.1** Layout of the tea garden

The gözleme preparation process is outlined in Table C5.1. One person – normally the owner's wife, Hatice – is responsible for all the cooking for the entire 4–4.5-hour period. This is undertaken in the open in one area in the middle of the Tea Garden (see Figure C5.1) where the process attracts the attention of customers and passers-by alike. Whilst salads, bread, snacks and other dishes are served at lunchtimes, most customer order the gözleme with either herb and cheese, or herb and meat filling. With it they will often have beer, soft drinks, coffee or çay.

The staff of the Tea Garden at lunchtime typically comprises the manager (owner), wife/gözleme cook, another kitchen worker and two or three waiters. Staffing is much the same in the morning but fewer are involved in the evening.

The Sahil Tea Garden is a gathering/meeting place. In the morning customers take breakfast and read their newspapers. At lunchtimes, they meet friends and/or catch up on their reading or paperwork

**Table C5.1 Gözleme – preparation process**

**A Pre-work**

1. Prepare dough and store in basin, covered with cloth (keep in refrigerator until needed).
2. Prepare two fillings and store in dishes (keep in refrigerator until needed).

**B Preparation and cooking**

1. Small quantity of dough is rolled into a ball by hand, placed in centre of circular, floured, rolling board (approximately 0.7 m in diameter), sprinkled with flour and rolled to a 0.5 m diameter, very thin pancake with a round piece of wood (approximately 40 mm diameter and 0.8 m long).

   Approximate time required = 2 minutes.
2. Pancake is folded to approximate rectangle, filling is sprinkled on pancake, pancake is folded to a square (approximately 0.2 m) and edges sealed by pressing with fingers.

   Approximate time = 0.7 minutes.
3. Gözleme is placed on grill (approximately 0.5 m diameter, slightly convex, hot-plate, heated by gas burners), turned frequently (typically four times) and sides oiled with a brush dipped into bowl of oil, until cooked.

   Approximate time = 2.5 minutes.
4. Gözleme is removed to one of two plates awaiting serving.
5. Gözleme is removed from plate and placed on plate brought and taken by waiter as required.

N.B. Times for (1), (2) and (3) allow interruptions for (4) and (5).

**Equipment used**

Circular rolling board

Round rolling wood

Hot-plate (and gas bottle/burner)

Spatula to turn gözlemes on hot-plate, move off plate, serve, etc.

Containers with dough and two fillings

Container for oil

Brush for oil

Two plates for storage

(e.g. letter writing) and in the evening it is a place to meet, drink and smoke before going on to somewhere for a meal or going home.

Average table occupancy in July–August is as follows:

| | | |
|---|---|---|
| Morning | = | 30% |
| Lunch | = | 45% |
| Afternoon and evening | = | 35% |

Typical prices are shown in Table C5.2.

**Table C5.2 Prices (Turkish lira, 1992)**

| | |
|---|---|
| Gözleme | 6000 |
| Beer – glass | 6000 |
| Beer – bottle | 7000 |
| Salad (tomato) | 6000 |
| Çay (tea) | 1000 |
| Meze (starters) | 6000–8000 |
| (e.g. Russian salad, stuffed tomatoes, etc.) | |

This is one of 30 or so eating places in Kas, but is unlike many of the others in concentrating on lunchtime trade. Like all of the others, it is subject to some national regulations as regards health, etc. These regulations are enforced through inspection and the allocation of licences – renewable annually. The Sahil does not have a full restaurant licence but rather a bar/snacks licence, which permits the serving of all types of drink throughout the day and the preparation and serving of a limited range of 'snack'-type dishes.

Cold meze dishes (starters) are pre-prepared and served from a cold cabinet. The gözleme are cooked on site as required. Dishes such as salads are prepared on site as required. Coffee, tea, fresh fruit squashes, etc. are prepared on site as required also. The dough and fillings for the gözleme are prepared in the kitchen on site during the morning. Sufficient dough and filling are prepared for the day – dough left unused is thrown away. Any unused filling can be kept in the refrigerator and used the following day.

The renewal of the Sahil licence is due at the beginning of the summer season. A form must be filled out giving details of storage, serving and cooking facilities. A drawing showing the nature and layout of any cooking area must be included. Regulations are minimal but stipulate that food cannot be cooked where it can easily be touched by customers and that pre-prepared food awaiting serving must be behind glass, etc. The arrangement of the kitchen, cold cabinet, etc. is rarely changed. The main interest therefore is in the arrangement of the gözleme cooking area.

Case study 6

# Bourg Breton

Bourg Breton is a rural leisure centre located near the edge of the town of Châteaulin (population 6000), which is near the Atlantic coast of Brittany in north west France.

Five years ago it was a small farm. Now it is a 'Centre d'Equestre' and 'Centre d'Acceuil' providing facilities for local people and for visitors – mainly from other parts of Northern France. Many of the previously unused, and in some cases derelict, buildings have been converted. Some have been extended. Other buildings have been added. The access road, the original farmyard, and the surrounding paths and grounds have been improved. No farming activities now take place, although a great deal of the type of work associated with farming is still needed, e.g. the maintenance of fences, grass, hedge and tree cutting and so on.

## FACILITIES

The general layout of the centre is shown in Figure C6.1. The centre presently comprises the following main facilities:

(a) The ***original farmhouse***. This two-storey building is now unoccupied and unrenovated. It is used mainly for storage.

(b) ***Main buildings***. This is the largest facility. It comprises – on the ground floor – a large reception area, meeting rooms, offices, a large kitchen, two large dining rooms (with views over the countryside), services, etc. On the first floor there are mainly dormitory-style bedrooms (for 40 persons) and a small number of single bedrooms.

(c) ***Indoor arena***. This is a large enclosed barn now used for horse riding and jumping.

(d) ***Outdoor arena***. This open area at the side of the stables is set out as a horse jumping area.

(e) ***Stables***. These provide stabling for 18 horses.

(f) ***Games area*** (etc.). This comprises the reception/booking area for the mini-golf, a games room, cafe, locker room and similar facilities.

(g) ***Cottages***. The smaller cottage (1) is occupied by one of the full-time staff. The large cottage (2) is occupied by the owners of Bourg Breton.

(h) ***Gites***. The two gites are both converted farm outbuildings. They provide self-contained accommodation – each for up to four people.

(i) ***Storage building***. This open building is where the farm machinery, hay, etc. are stored.

(j) ***Games room 2***. This is simply an open-sided building used for table tennis, etc.

(k) ***Changing rooms***. This modern wooden building provides the main changing rooms, toilets, etc., outside of those in the other main buildings.

(l) ***Unconverted buildings***. There remains one original as yet unconverted farm building.

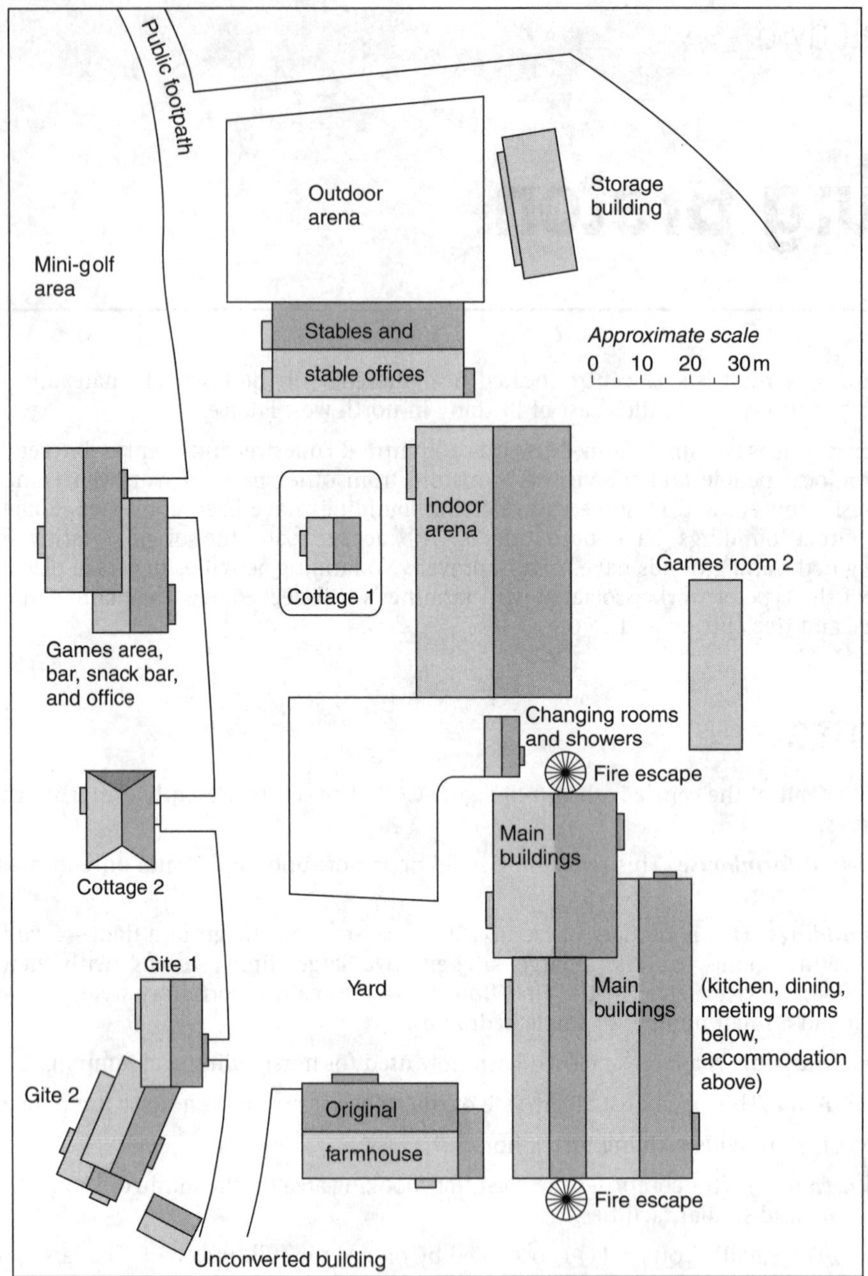


**Figure C6.1** Layout of centre

# ACTIVITIES

The principal current activities of the Bourg Breton are as follows.

## Centre d'Equestre

The stabling at the centre is presently sufficient for 18 horses (in residence). Stabling care and maintenance (pension) is provided for horses owned and used by others – currently there are eight such horses at the centre. Additionally, the centre owns and stables its own horses (currently seven). These are used by the centre to provide riding lessons, horse riding and horse jumping for its clients, either individually or in groups.

Horse riding and jumping tuition is also provided for those who stable their own horses at the centre. For the serious rider, tuition can take people up to examination/competition level. The centre occasionally organizes horse-jumping competitions for its own clients and visitors.

## Centre d'Acceuil

This is the basis for the principal residential use of the centre. Clients are mainly young people (15–18 years) who come in groups often organized by schools or community organizations. They stay at Bourg Breton, using it as their 'colonie de vacances', in the French tradition – usually for several weeks depending on the length of the school holidays. They come mainly from more urban areas in Northern France – often as far away as Paris – and use the full facilities of the centre, as well as other facilities in Châteaulin and the surrounding area. They are accompanied by supervisors (often their teachers), and in general these are the only adults who stay for long periods at the centre.

In addition to its main residential facility, Bourg Breton rents out two cottages – 'gîtes ruraux' – i.e. farm outbuildings converted into self-contained cottages. These are used by families on holiday – usually foreigners.

## Mini-Golf

Whilst advertised (e.g. on the signposts pointing to the centre) in this way, this is no more than a small 'crazy golf' course – i.e. a novelty putting facility with about 12 short 'holes' featuring hills, ramps, tunnels, obstacles, etc. It is used by residents, occasionally by tourists staying in the hotels in the town, and, less occasionally, by youths and families living locally.

## Other activities

The centre occasionally rents out its meeting rooms (the largest of which will accommodate 45 people), with or without meals, and will also, occasionally, cater (i.e. provide meals and dining facilities) for social, family or commercial events. The largest dining room can accommodate 50 people.

# RESOURCES

The centre is owned and managed by M. and Mme Penneneac'h. There is one full-time person employed, who lives on site. He has some supervisory responsibilities and deals mostly with the Centre Equestre activities. There are three other full-time employees, all of whom live in the area: two groundsmen (maintenance/building workers) and one 'horseman'.

All other employees are part or full-time and temporary. Their numbers depend on the season, and the level of activity of the centre. Typically, during a busy period, they will comprise:

Two stable workers;

Two cleaners;

Two dining room workers;

One horse riding instructor;

One horse riding 'attendant';

One labourer;

Two cooks.

## SEASONS

The centre is open for the whole year, but not for all activities.

The Centre Equestre operates for the full 12 months.

The Mini-Golf is open from March to October inclusive.

The residential facility is open from March to October inclusive.

The principal facilities associated with the Centre Acceuil are open from March to October inclusive (although meeting rooms and dining facilities can be hired 'out of season').

The gites are available for hire for the whole year.

## TARIFFS AND FEES

The currently advertised (1993) tariffs and charges for the centre's services are summarized in Table C6.1. They are in all cases 5% above 1992. All charges are inclusive of TVA (value added tax). It is normal to have to provide a commission of between 5% and 7% of the advertised rate for agency booking of large groups.

## WAGES AND COSTS

Table C6.2 summarizes the principal operating costs of the centre for 1992.

## PROPOSED DEVELOPMENT

Bourg Breton has developed to its present scale and form gradually over recent years. It has in effect been an extension to the 'hobby' interests of M. and Mme Penneneac'h – especially the Centre Equestre. In developing the facilities, e.g. in converting previously unused farm buildings, advantage has been taken of government grants. Some assistance has also been available from the Département (Finistère) Administration, as this is designated as a development area, with high unemployment, rural depopulation, etc.

The principal physical developments of the centre have been funded by M. and Mme Penneneac'h from revenues and from their own capital. A new project is, however, under consideration for which a loan will be required. Essentially, it comprises the conversion of the original farmhouse to provide a small auberge (or small hotel) – the intention being to use the rather better accommodation and facilities provided to support the equestrian activities by attracting people who would wish to stay in the hotel in order to horse ride, etc.

Plans have been drawn up and approved by the planning authority to create a six-bedroom facility in the farmhouse, without substantially altering its character. The total cost of conversion and fitting out (including furnishing) is estimated at F550 000.

M. Penneneac'h has already had discussions of his plans with the manager of his bank in town (Credit Agricole, Quai Jean Moulin). The manager was supportive of the proposals in principle but a decision to loan the amount required would need the authority of the regional manager in Quimper. In preparation for a meeting in Quimper, the Châtealin branch manager sought more information from M. Penneneac'h, for he wanted to know how his business as a whole was going, and to get some idea of its future prospects. He was interested in the profitability of the various activities, bookings for the coming year, etc. He wanted to be sure that if funds were to be advanced, they were best spent on adding a new facility rather than further developing the existing facilities.

Now M. and Mme Penneanac'h are prepared for their meeting at Credit Agricole in Quimper. They have in front of them the additional material shown in Table C6.3.

**Table C6.1 1993 Tariffs and fees (francs)**

| | Season | | |
|---|---|---|---|
| | Low | Mid (8 weeks) | High (8 weeks) |
| *Gite* rental (per week, per property) | 1500 | 2000 | 2500 |
| *Centre Equestre* | | | |
| Stabling of horse (per month) (6 months minimum) | | 600 | |
| Riding lesson (per hour) | | | |
| Group (of four) | | 100 | |
| Individual | | 300 | |
| Horse 'trekking' (per hour) | | | |
| Group (of four) | | 100 | |
| Individual | | 300 | |
| Horse jumping (per hour) | | | |
| Supervised use of facilities | | 200 | |
| Instruction | | 350 | |
| *Mini-Golf* | | | |
| Per person, per hour | 25 | 35 | 50 |
| *Centre Acceuil* | | | |
| Accommodation (dormitory) (with use of all facilities excepting Centre Equestre) per person, per week – full board | 1300 | 1600 | 2000 |
| Accommodation (individual) (for persons accompanying groups of six minimum only) at above rates + 20% (N.B. half board: subtract F60 per day) | | | |
| Riding lessons for residents and horse trekking for residents: at above group rates less 10% | | | |
| Conferencing/events: | | | |
| Catering: from F70 to F250 per person | | | |
| Meeting rooms, from F150 to F500 per hour | | | |

**Table C6.2 1992 Costs (francs)**

| | |
|---|---|
| Impots/Taxe d'habitation | 6 500 |
| Depreciation of assets[a] | 70 000 |
| Other fixed costs | 7 500 |
| *Salaries* (inclusive of pension contributions, ins.) | |
| For gites | 50 000 |
| For Centre Equestre | 590 000 |
| For Mini-Golf | 50 000 |
| For Centre Acceuil | |
| Accommodation | 480 000 |
| Conferences/events | 150 000 |
| Other | 140 000 |
| Non-attributed salary costs | 400 000 |
| (excluding 'salary' for M. and Mme Penneneac'h | |
| *Consumables* | |
| For gites | 30 000 |
| For Centre Equestre | 140 000 |
| For Mini-Golf | 10 000 |
| For Centre Acceuil | |
| Accommodation | 150 000 |
| Conferences/events | 50 000 |
| Other | 13 000 |
| Non-attributables | 50 000 |
| *Insurance* | 80 000 |
| | 2 467 000 |

[a] Includes all maintenance and repair work but not major new buildings. Excludes labour (excluding external contractors) and consumed materials.

**Table C6.3 Usage 1992 and 1993 (as at 1 April 1993)**

| | 1992 (actual) | | | 1993 (actual to date plus projections/reservations) | | |
|---|---|---|---|---|---|---|
| | Low | Mid | High | Low | Mid | High |
| *Gite* weeks | 8 | 6 | 7 | 10 | 7 | 7 |
| *Centre Equestre* | | | | | | |
| Stabling (horse months) | | 85 | | | 96 | |
| Riding lessons and trekking | | | | | | |
| Total hours (groups) | | 930 | | | 1100 | |
| Total hours (individual) | | 350 | | | 390 | |

**Table C6.3 (continued)**

| | 1992 (actual) | | | 1993 (actual to date plus projections/reservations | | |
|---|---|---|---|---|---|---|
| | Low | Mid | High | Low | Mid | High |
| Horse jumping | | | | | | |
| Facilities (total hours) | | 450 | | | 550 | |
| Instruction (total hours) | | 250 | | | 300 | |
| *Mini-Golf* | | | | | | |
| Total person hours | 100 | 170 | 280 | 60 | 190 | 300 |
| *Centre Acceuil* | | | | | | |
| Dormitory accommodation (person weeks) | 290 | 300 | 376 | 340 | 380 | 400 |
| Individual accommodation (person weeks) | 27 | 32 | 35 | 25 | 33 | 36 |
| Use of Centre Equestre (total hours) | | 1050 | | | 1100 | |
| Conferences/events (total) | | | | | | |
| Catering (no. of persons) | | 2200 | | | 2400 | |
| Average price/person | | 150 | | | 170 | |
| Meeting rooms: | | | | | | |
| Total hours | | 280 | | | 350 | |
| Average price/hour | | 350 | | | 360 | |

Case study 7

# Pokhara Weavers

Pokhara is a large lakeside town in central Nepal. Although its population is only 60 000, it is second in size and significance only to Kathmandu, the capital, 200 km to the east. The main crossroads in Pokhara is known as Prithvi Chowk. There, located virtually at the junction, is a group of people creating a variety of woven bamboo products. They occupy a piece of land about 10 x 10 m at the side of the road. In addition, they have a small area to display finished goods at the side of the road, at the junction. Goods, materials, etc. are stored, where necessary, in a hut at the rear of the main site.

The goods produced are mainly baskets of various sizes, and floor mats. Except for the final weaving operation, all operations are common, irrespective of the end product. The common operations together convert long pieces of bamboo into the raw materials for the final weaving process.

The description below focuses on the weaving of large floor mats, approximately 3 m square.

## THE OPERATIONS

Bamboo poles, cut locally, are brought to the site by hand or cart. They are typically 2.5 m long and 12 cm in diameter.

Usually it is necessary to cut off the solid end of the pole. This is done on the floor with a large, heavy knife, used as a hatchet.

The poles are then split lengthwise. They are first cut in half with a heavy knife driven down by blows from a piece of wood, until the pole splits into two. Each half is then split further by the same process, but now the knife can usually simply be pushed down the split pole. The number of splits determines the width of the final weaving material. Splitting each half into six (i.e. 12 pieces in total) produces pieces approximately 2.5 cm wide.

The next operation involves the cutting of thin flat strips from the split poles. Again this is done with a knife which is run along the poles but at right angles to the previous cut, i.e. producing strips at right angles to the radius, along the natural laminations of the bamboo. The material 'peels' quite easily in this way, but not always over the full pole length, so the strips produced are of different lengths. All but the strips from the outside of the pole are the same yellowish colour on both sides. The outer strip is green on one (the outer) side. All strips are approximately 2 mm thick.

The material is now ready for weaving. This – for mats – is done horizontally on the floor with considerable speed and dexterity, new strips being joined into the weave in either direction (along or across) as required, until a full mat is obtained. The green strips are used to introduce a squared pattern into the mat. Each mat is woven one quarter at a time, i.e. the first quarter is woven, then the second is added, to make a half mat, then the third and finally the last quarter to complete the square. Finally the strips are trimmed off, and all edges are bound.

There are other occasional operations, i.e. occasional sprinkling of water onto the waiting strips to keep them flexible; removal of finished products; removal of waste material; measuring of mats during weaving; and sharpening of knives.

## MANNING

During busy periods five people undertake the above operations as follows:

1 trimming ends and splitting poles;

1 making strips;

2 weaving products;

1 supervising, helping out, moving materials between workers and occasional jobs.

During quiet times, all operations are undertaken by two or three people. With full manning and making no other items, approximately five or six large mats could be made in one day.

Case study 8

# Malcolm Seal

Malcolm Seal is a graphic design business based in Henley on Thames in the UK. The company designs such things as letter headings, labels, posters and brochures. There is a small amount of product design work, and interior design where a client wishes their office or showroom to reflect a particular product image. The business caters for both the home and, increasingly, the export market.

Each job is individually tailored to the client's needs. Sometimes a budget for the design and production of the article has already been fixed and the design is limited by the money available. At other times, no prior financial limit is fixed and advice has to be given on the production and cost implications of the materials used in the design. Occasionally the client has no idea at all of the cost involved in producing the article once it has been designed and finds that the type of design he wants is too expensive. It thus becomes necessary for Malcolm Seal to explain the cost implications of the design specified by the client and to suggest alternatives.

The job is initiated by a client request, with the client sometimes visiting the business, and at other times the designer visiting the client. Some clients specify at this stage the material to be included in the design and provide photographs or other material. For other clients it is necessary for the designer to do some research on the company or product which is the design focus.

Having advised or consulted with the client on the materials to be used in the design, the designer produces a 'visual' (a rough design) for the client's approval. The visual is a simulated label or poster or other article indicating how the material will be arranged.

Once this is approved, a 'paste-up' of the design is produced. This is a full layout of the article exactly as it will look when produced. It involves obtaining any photographs, drawings and printed material required. Normally drawings are produced by Malcolm Seal but it may be necessary, with specialist materials, to commission a drawing from elsewhere. Photographic and photocopying work is subcontracted, as is the typesetting for the written material.

Normally, when the paste-up has been approved, Malcolm Seal's work is finished, apart from checking the proof copy from the printer before full production is started. Printing is subcontracted by the client. For some jobs, however, the firm is entirely responsible for both design and production. In these cases Malcolm Seal subcontracts the printing and retains full responsibility until the finished article is delivered to the client.

The staff of the firm consists of the designer, with office work and secretarial assistance provided by his wife. His wife does typing work for other people from the office and usually stays in the office to deal with clients when the designer has to go out to other clients. He tries to limit travelling away from the office because he feels other clients suffer if he is out. For this reason he prefers local clients although he does have some clients in London.

Demand is highly erratic; sometimes the designer has to work all night to cope with the work, and at other times he has little or no work. There is some predictable increase in demand just before holiday periods but there is not sufficient to justify taking on extra staff at these times, nor is other demand fluctuation sufficiently predictable to justify it. He feels it necessary to take on every job which he is technically capable of doing, even though at times this may over-stretch his resources. He feels that most clients are prepared to wait if he says he will do a job even though he may not be able to start immediately.

Scheduling the various phases of the work is difficult. Usually he estimates a date of completion when accepting a new job and feels he must meet this in order to create client confidence. Clients do not, however. always realize the costs and time involved. He is never sure how long it will take to collect any materials required from the client and has little control over how long it will take to obtain the client's approval of the basic ideas, the visual and the paste-up.

Standard design materials (paper, paints, etc.) are stocked and any special materials are bought in as required. At one time the designer had to go to London for photographic work, and any specialist illustrations, but all these services are now available locally, which has made control of subcontract work rather easier and quicker.

Case study 9

# The Malta MBA

The MBA (Master of Business Administration) degree programme was launched in Malta by the University of Malta in March 1991. Forty-six people entered the 'executive' level programme that year. Their average age was 35 years, all were in full-time employment, and all were supported on the programme by their employers.

Rather than develop its own local programme, the university's Department of Management Studies chose to work in conjunction with a UK management college to offer its international MBA programme on the island. The college is associated with a UK university, which accredits the course and awards the degree. The programme is also run, in this same manner, in 20 other countries throughout the world.

## PROGRAMME STRUCTURE

The basic structure of the programme is shown in Figure C9.1. It is based on a 'distance learning' programme design and is supported by comprehensive sets of audio, video, text and related materials. The UK university regulations permit the programme to be followed remotely by students, without the need for regular classes. However, the college has chosen to offer the programme in countries other than the UK in partnership with an appropriate local organization which is able to provide classes and tutor support suitable to the needs of the local students. In the UK, the college itself provides teaching and support for the MBA.

## THE PARTNERSHIP

The main steps in the establishment of the programme in Malta (and elsewhere) are outlined in Figure C9.2. Basically, the Maltese partner is responsible for all local activities, whilst the college (with the UK university) retains full control of the programme content, structure, materials, student entry, assessment, examinations and the award of the degree, as well as monitoring all the activities in Malta and, where appropriate, the resourcing of classes, the supply of tutors, the training of local staff, etc.

## STUDENT ENTRY

The main steps involved in the admission of students to the programme are given in Figure C9.3. All normal entry decisions are made by the college with delegated authority from the UK university. Exceptional cases are determined by the UK university.

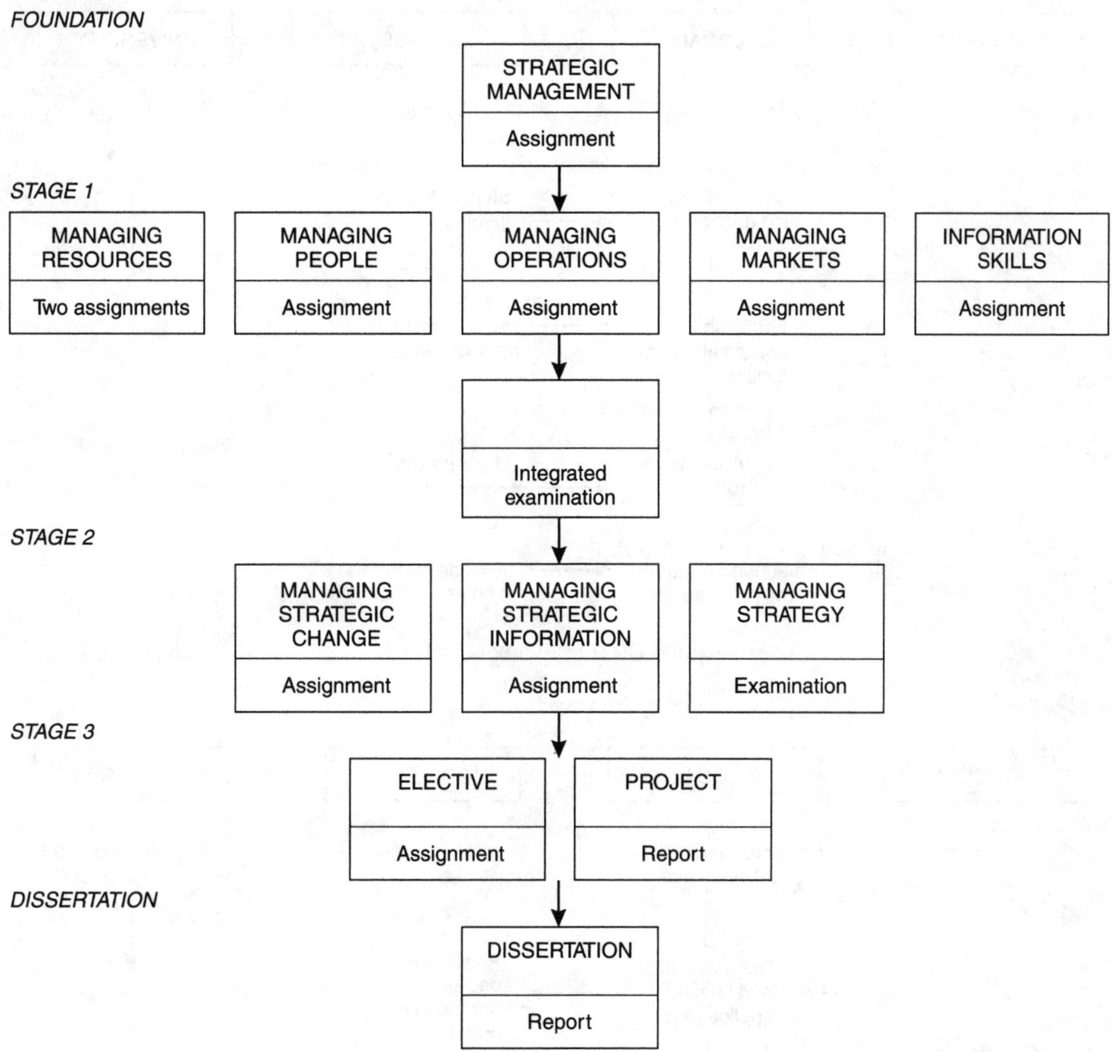


**Figure C9.1** Programme structure

# PROGRAMME DELIVERY

The manner in which the programme is delivered has been determined to suit local circumstances in Malta. A group of students enters every 18 months. Each student entry group is scheduled to proceed through the programme together, taking 18 months to complete the Foundation and Stage 1, then a further 18 months for Stage 2, etc. Students study one course at a time. In Malta the students are considered as students of the University of Malta and have full access to all normal facilities and resources. The teaching in Malta is organized mainly as 'workshops' and seminars, with tutorials sufficient to support students' individual studies in each course. Students attend 'classes' in groups of approximately 23

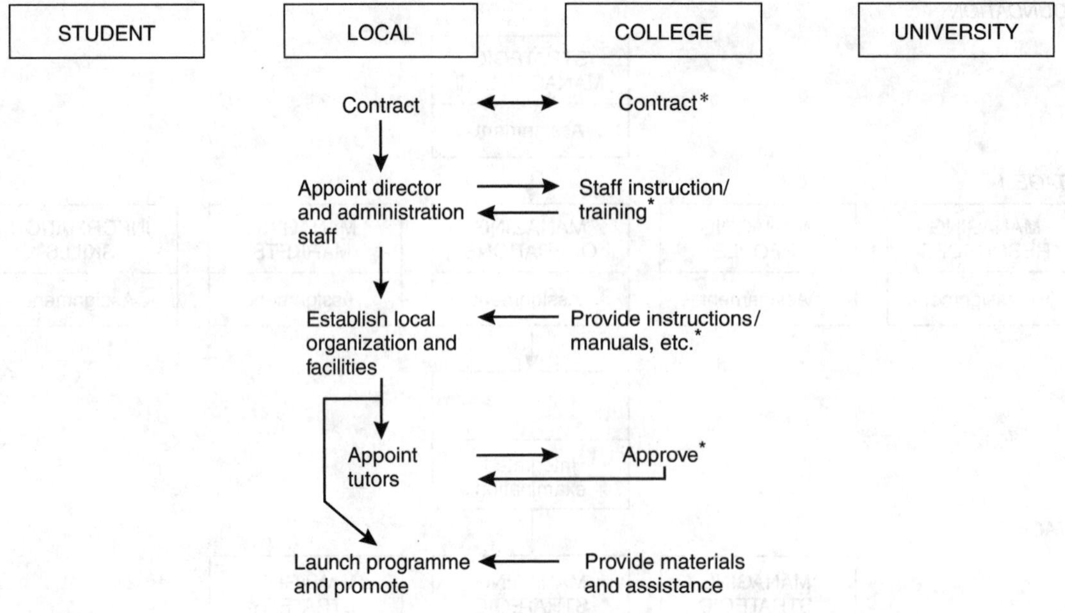


**Figure C9.2** Programme 'set-up'

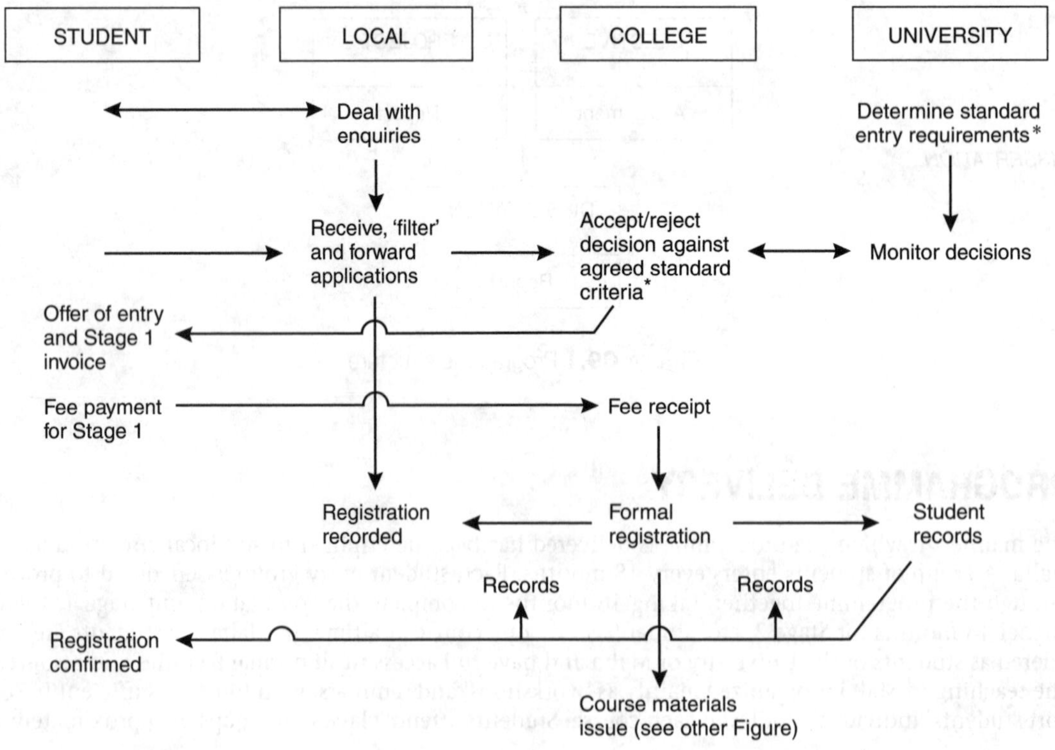


**Figure C9.3** Student registration

about twice per month. They receive around 12 formal class contacts per month and in addition are organized as small workgroups and encouraged and helped to work together in that way. Tutorial support is always available on an individual basis as required. (A computer-based conferencing system is also used for tutoring and support from the college.) An outline of the manner in which the programme operates in Malta and elsewhere is given in Figure C9.4.

## ASSESSMENT

Each course is assessed in the manner shown in Figure C9.1. Courses assessed by written assignment provide also for prior 'practice' assignments to be submitted for marking and feedback. All assignments are marked and then moderated by the college. Examinations are organized and invigilated in Malta, at precise times and according to procedures determined by the college with the UK university and with examination papers set by the college. All marking and moderation is then undertaken by the college. An examining board, working to UK university procedures, but meeting at the college four times per year, examines all students' assessment and examination marks and confirms results, thus permitting the students, where appropriate, to proceed to the next stage or to the dissertation. The award of

**Figure C9.4** Programme operation †

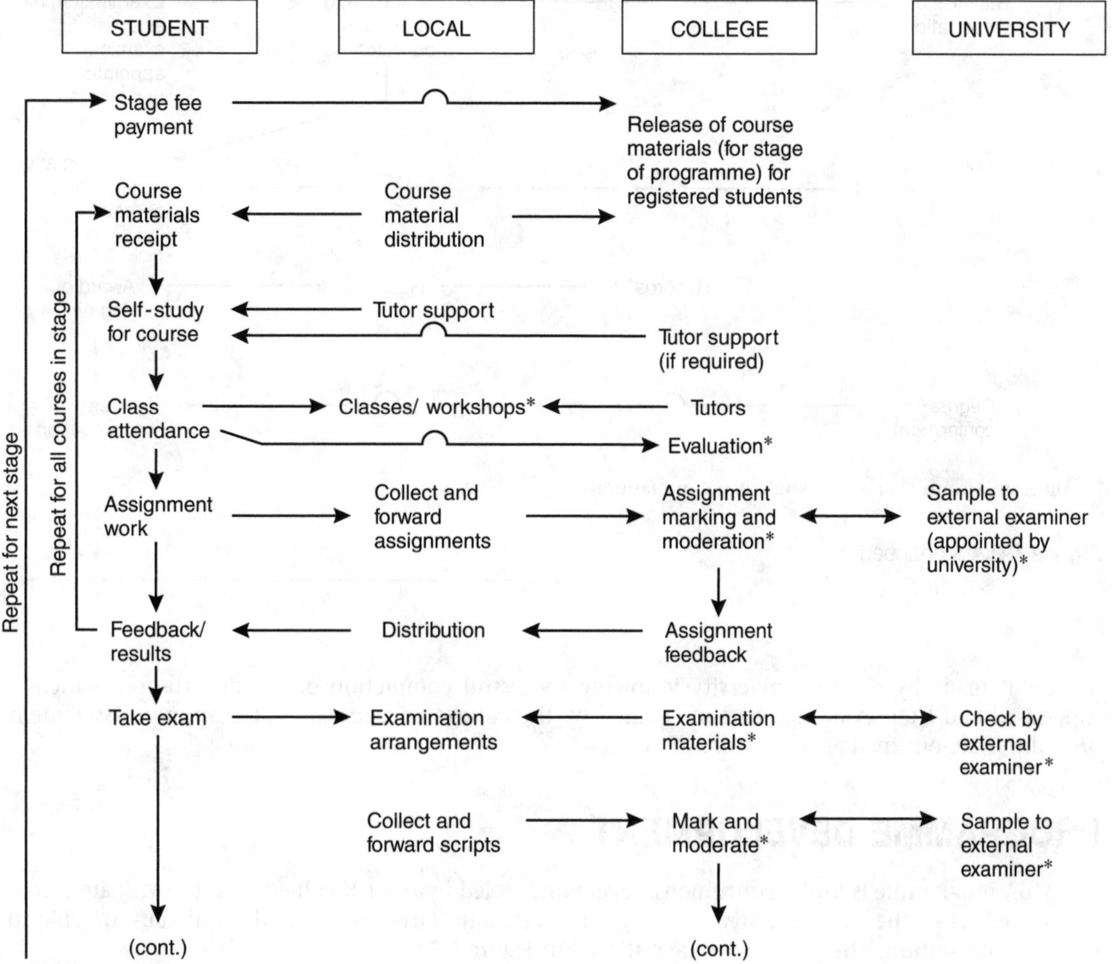

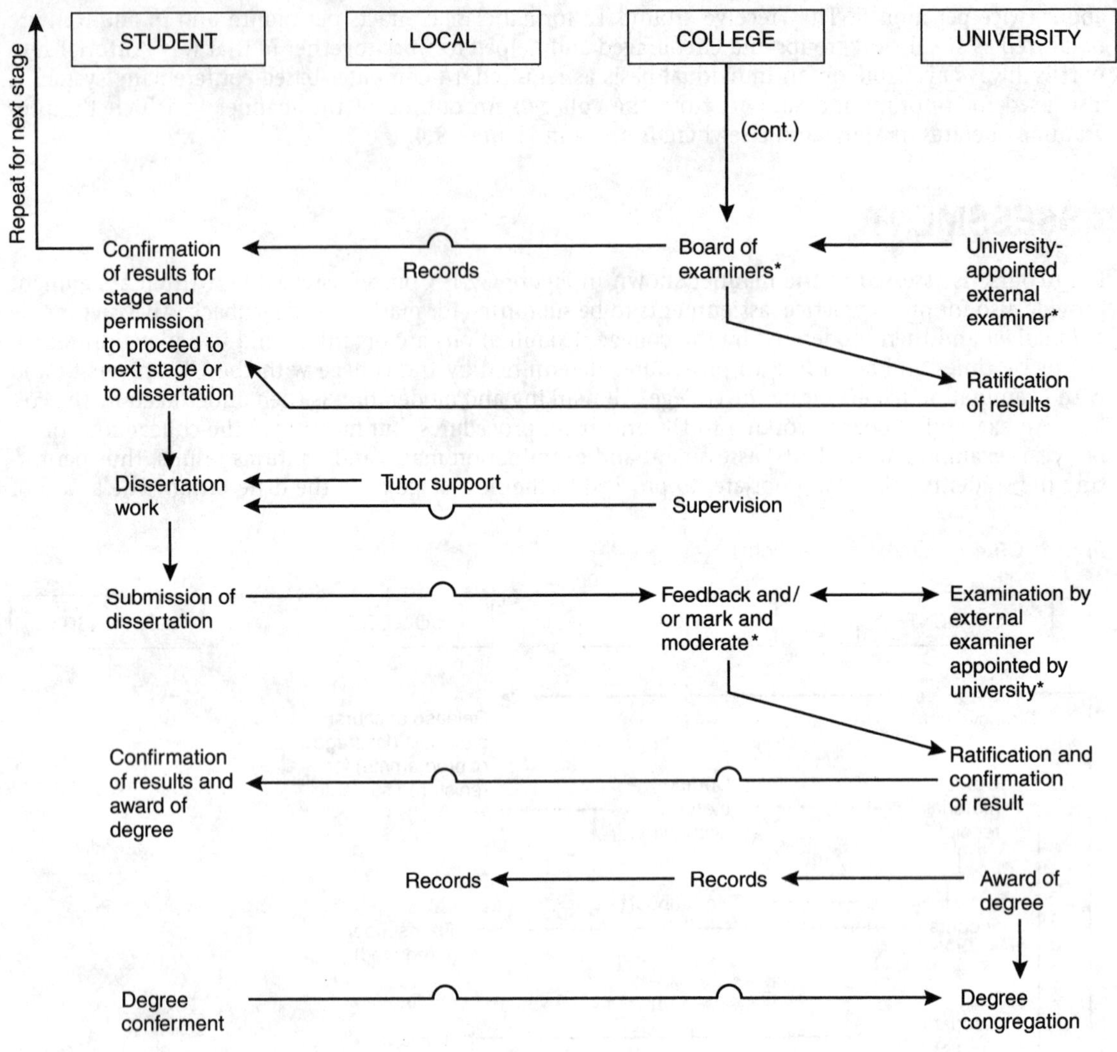


**Figure C9.4** (continued)

degrees is made by the UK university following successful completion of the dissertation, which is supervised and then examined and moderated by the college and an external examiner. Assessment procedures are outlined also in Figure C9.4.

# PROGRAMME DEVELOPMENT

The MBA programme is under continuous development, led by the UK college faculty (who are recognized teachers of the UK university). Through a Programme Advisory Council, local staff are able to make a contribution. The procedures are outlined in Figure C9.5.

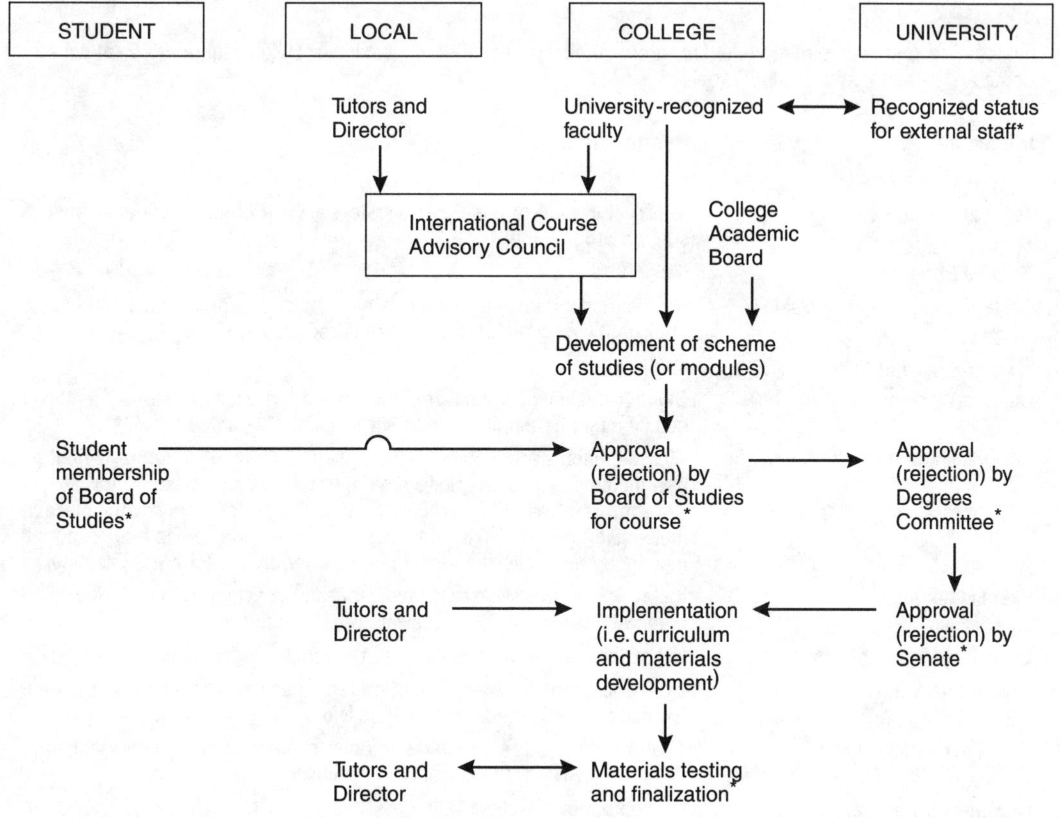


**Figure C9.5** Programme development

# STANDARDS AND QUALITY

The achievement and maintenance of high academic standards and high programme quality are vitally important, and of critical interest to all parties. Various procedures are built into the manner in which the programme is developed and run (Figures C9.2–C9.5). It is intended now to review all such procedures for the type of programme for which the Malta MBA is a typical example. The background and requirements of the review are outlined in the Memorandum, reproduced below.

To: MBA Programme Faculty

From: MBA Programme Director

**MBA PROGRAMME STANDARDS AND QUALITY**

Our programme has achieved an enviable reputation throughout the world. It is appropriate, however, that frequently we examine our standards and procedures. For this reason, I have asked a Faculty Group to review the situation. I have given them the following 'brief':

**Background**

The procedures used in our programme conform to the College and the University's requirements and follow best standard international practice. They are designed to ensure high academic standards and high programme quality. The principal, directly relevant, procedures are identified by asterisks (*) on Figures 2–5 (attached). Some are detailed, as a reminder, below:

| Procedure | Nature/Purpose |
|---|---|
| *Programme 'set-up'* | |
| Tutor approval | Approval of staff to ensure adequate standard of local academic staff to support programme. |
| *Student Registration* | |
| College accept/reject decision | To ensure conformity to University academic standards, and conformity to additional post-graduation experience requirement. |
| *Programme Operation* | |
| Classes/Workshops | Student evaluation forms are returned to the College, so that teaching quality might be monitored and action taken if required. |
| Assignment Marking & Moderation | All assignments are marked at the College by a marking tutor. All marked assignments are also moderated by the Subject Lead Tutor at the College. The Lead Tutor regularly receives a statistical review of each marking tutor's marks (i.e. average mark/standard deviation) to permit monitoring and action. A sample is reviewed by the External Examiner. |
| Exam Materials | Exam Scripts are set by College Staff and checked by others, including External Examiner. Model answers are prepared. |
| Examination arrangements | Examinations are run according to University Regulations. |
| Exam mark & moderated | Exams are marked, then moderated. Sample checked by External Examiner. Use is made of model answers. |
| Board of Examiners | The Board considers all marks to date for each student. External examiners are involved. Statistical data is available. |
| Dissertation Supervision | Carried out by a College Tutor |
| Dissertation | Marked and then separately moderated at the College before submission to the external examiner for accept/reject decision. |
| *Programme Development* | |
| Recognition of College Staff | Recognized Teacher status for College Faculty is awarded by the University Senate after examination by the Academic Staff Appointments Committee. |
| Board of Studies | The Board of Studies for the Course is a University Board, meeting at the College. It makes recommendations to the University. |
| Materials Testing | All materials are developed under the supervision of a course team and are thoroughly tested by external individuals. |

**Recent Developments**

Recent developments in the UK University system have led to the establishment of a National Academic Audit Committee which will audit the quality of courses. This and other developments are encouraging educational establishments to consider seeking full BS 5750/ISO 9000 accreditation. The College is intending to move in this direction.

**Needs**

There is a need now to have a broader and more comprehensive view of how we achieve, maintain and monitor quality. Each of the individual procedures (e.g. above) must be seen to be and treated as parts of a *Total System*. In order, adequately, to be able to explain our approach, its purpose and operation, we need to be able to describe the total system to those not directly involved, and then to identify each component part, its purpose, and those responsible for it. A short (4–5 page) document on 'Academic Standards and Programme Quality' should be sufficient to achieve this. In developing this document we should also be able to identify whether we wish to develop any of our existing procedures and/or add to them.

Case study 10

# Airport building project

The terminal building of a small rural airport at a town in the north of the Indian subcontinent is being extended. The present single storey L-shaped building has four rooms. A new room is now being added onto one end of the building.

The new – single-storey – room is approximately 6 x 8 metres. So far the foundations have been laid, the concrete floor laid, two of the three main walls have been built, and all the preparation work for the roof has been done. The next job is to finish the roof and then the final (non-load bearing) wall can be put in place and all the finishing work done.

The roof is to be reinforced concrete. The preparatory work has involved the erection of wooden scaffolding from the floor of the building to support the timber 'formwork' onto which the concrete will be poured for the roof. Above this formwork the steel reinforcing rods have been placed.

Timber scaffolding has also been erected at one corner of the new building to provide access for workers to the roof. Moveable 'walkways' made from wooden planks are used to allow workers to move about on the roof, above the steel reinforcements.

The ingredients for the concrete have already been delivered to the site, i.e. sand, gravel and cement. The sand and gravel are in two adjacent piles on the ground beside the building. The cement is in bags close by. Additional materials will be delivered when required. Water is available from a tap about 15 feet from the building.

The layout of the site prior to finishing the roof is shown in Figures C10.1 and C10.2.

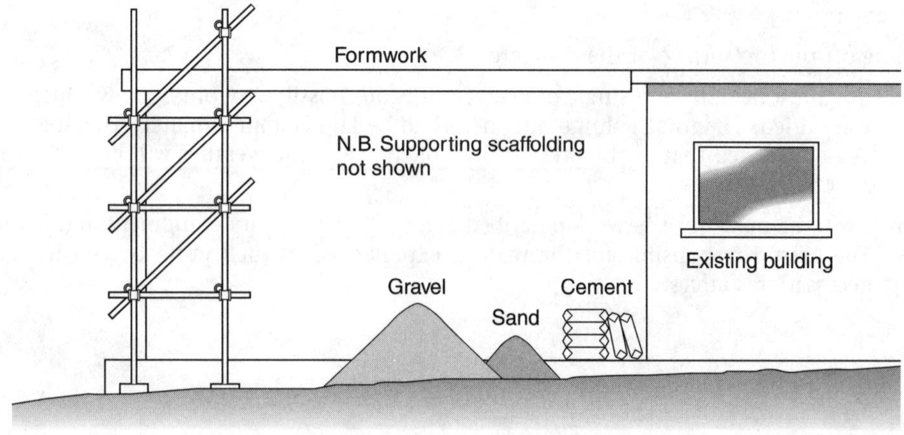


**Figure C10.1** Front elevation

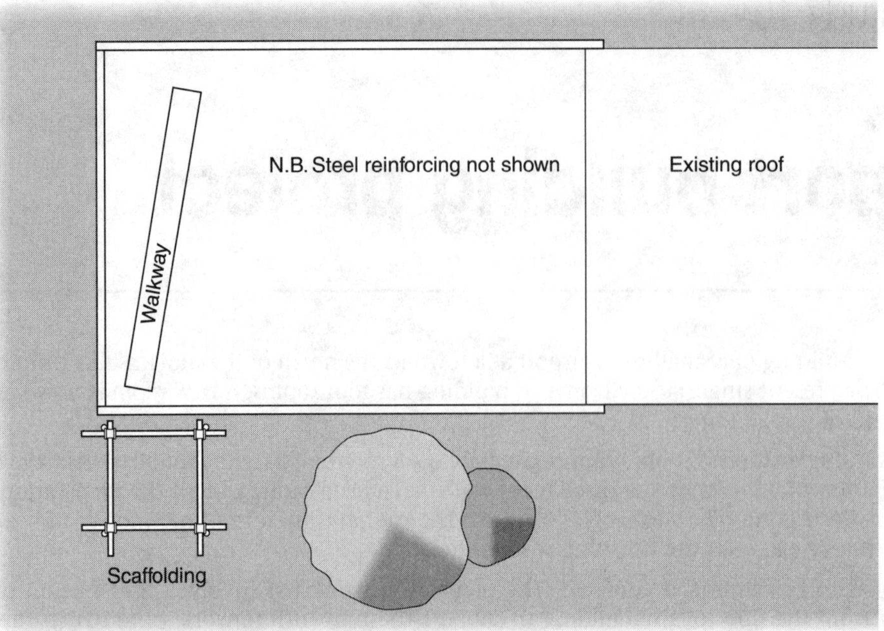


**Figure C10.2** Plan view

The immediate task now is to finish the roof. This will involve the following:

(a) mixing the dry ingredients for the concrete;

(b) adding water to mix the wet concrete;

(c) transporting concrete to the appropriate place on the roof;

(d) pouring concrete onto the roof formwork;

(e) pushing/knocking the concrete into place to ensure that it fills all corners, fully surrounds the steel reinforcement, etc.;

(f) smoothing off the top surface of the concrete.

This whole job must be done as a single project, for it is not possible to join up new concrete to that which has already dried. The total volume of concrete to be laid is approximately 10 cubic metres. It can confidently be expected that at the present time of the year, the weather will be dry with a mid-day temperature of 25°C.

Plans are now to be made for the work described above. Any necessary equipment and labour must be obtained. The person responsible for the work is experienced in such projects, and has adequate access to the necessary resources.

Case study 11

# St John's Church

St John's, an evangelical church, is situated near, and to the west of, a city centre. It is a satellite or 'daughter' of a large evangelical church nearby. The congregation of the mother church had become too large for the church facilities there, and in order to sustain its overall growth pattern it was decided to transplant approximately 100 members of the congregation to another site. This strategy would make room for new members, and give the daughter church, St John's, an opportunity to grow. The mother church would also send off a member of staff to lead the new congregation.

The building which accommodated St John's was at that time a shadow of its former self – a large, old, cold, gloomy and damp building with a roof in urgent need of repair, and with little else in the way of facilities. The remaining 12 of the original congregation were mainly elderly people who had staunchly kept the building open for the previous ten years or so without a pastor, and had so saved the Grade II listed building from the bulldozer and the planners. Apart from their keeping the building open every Sunday morning for regular worship, and ensuring the bank account was not in overdraft, there had been no other management controls.

The 12 had readily agreed to the influx of the 100, so from October that year, St John's became the spiritual home for the 112. At their first meeting, they appointed a new leadership team from their number to support the new full-time and paid pastor. Different functional leaders were appointed to ensure the smooth running of Sunday services – now both morning and evening. A manager (part-time, voluntary) was appointed and asked to head up a group to devise a strategy to achieve the agreed long-term objective of substantial growth, against a target of 600 in five years.

The manager was anxious because, in the short term, there was an expected level of service (e.g. pastoral care to the congregation, warm and welcoming church building) but limited resources with which to achieve that basic level of support. Winter was approaching and the building had no heating system. The pastor had to be paid. The manager devised an initial budget for the next 12 months to include the pastor's salary, a new heating system, minor repairs and decorations, office running costs, and a financial support budget, for those in need. The total came to £45 000. As part of the marketing plan to achieve growth, the pastor agreed to teach the congregation on giving and tithing. A gift day was set and approximately £30 000 was raised by the 112. The manager was then asked to consult with, and put out tenders to, heating specialists and to install a new heating system forthwith.

A room at the back of the church was re-wired and re-lit, fitted with storage heaters and quickly decorated. A coffee bar and small kitchen was built. Coffee could then be served after the Sunday services. The manager asked a member of the congregation to head up and supervise a kitchen rota for the next six months. At last there was one warm room for meetings. However, the room was not big enough for all the congregation to have coffee at the same time. The manager announced that the new heating system to the church would not be installed until the following February.

Existing members began to invite their friends to the Sunday services. These friends were invited to join an introductory eight-week, one night per week course, led by the pastor, on the tenets of the

Christian faith. Fifteen people signed up for the course. They were joined by six of the 112, to make 22 in total. Growth had started.

Over the next five years, the number of full-time staff grew from 1 to 12, including the manager, who also took on finance and other roles. Changing needs were identified and responded to, where possible. Courses were developed.

Toilets were built, a new roof was put on, the whole building was re-wired, re-lit and re-decorated, and a new sound system and telephone system were installed. A £300 000 project was then started, to excavate and redevelop the crypt of the building into extra offices, counselling rooms, facilities for children, youth groups and the elderly. All funds required were freely given by members of the congregation. During this period of reorganizing the plant, the manager ensured that the building was always open for Sunday services, and in a clean and presentable state. There were also changes in leaders and leadership roles.

On midweek evenings, the core of the church met in small home groups around the neighbourhood. Introductory courses were expanded to five per year and also included weekends away. A leadership programme was developed so that staff could pass on responsibilities to members of the congregation. Other special interest groups started to form, most of which needed to use the building and facilities at some time during the week.

Many times during this period, it seemed to the manager that the policy of 'go for growth' had outstripped resource availability.

Case study 12

# FotoPrint Pronto

Grazia Ceri has obtained the franchise to open and operate the only FotoPrint Pronto shop in her town – if she can convince the franchiser that she has found a commercially attractive site. She needs at least 75 square metres. There is plenty of space to let in the town. (A comparison of rents is given in Table C12.1.) Grazia has decided to take one of the shop areas in a new building soon to be opened on the Avenida Garibaldi – the main road which runs north–south through town from near the railway station to the sports stadium. Whilst some of the shops in the building are already let, there is still a choice left for her. She aims to choose the best shop for her purposes and then present her final proposals to the regional director of FotoPrint Pronto.

Further details of a typical FotoPrint Pronto operation are given in Table C12.2. The location of Grazia's chosen building is shown on the map (Figure C12.1). The layout of the three floors is shown in Figure C12.2. Further details of the building are given in Table C12.3.

**Table C12.1 Comparison of property rentals**

| Area | Rentals (compared to most expensive area) |
|---|---|
| Downtown retail area (around Avenida Garibaldi and north of the cathedral) | (most expensive area) |
| Industrial area 1 (north of autostrada) | 30% |
| Industrial area 2 (south and adjacent to autostrada) | 45% |
| Commercial area | 60% |
| Government area | 60% |

For locations see Figure C12.1.

**Table C12.2 A profile of a FotoPrint Pronto shop**

**Services offered**

A. *Photographic*

1. Development and printing of colour photographic film
2. Enlargements from colour prints or negatives

B. *Printing and binding*

1. Black and white photocopying (all sizes)
2. Colour photocopying from customers' originals (all sizes)
3. Binding (several methods)

C. *Other services*

1. Laser colour copying of originals (with enlargement/reduction, etc.)
2. Mounting and framing pictures, documents, etc.
3. Design and production of business cards, invitations, posters, etc. (black and white and colour)

D. *Retail items*

1. Sale of frames and framing materials
2. Sale of stationery
3. Sale of photographic film

**Typical activity profiles**

Typically, sales revenue is generated as follows:

| | |
|---|---|
| A (above) | 25% |
| B | 40% |
| C | 20% |
| D | 15% |

Typical customer profiles are as follows (by sales volume):

| | **Commercial/business customers** | **Individual/personal customers** |
|---|---|---|
| A | 10% | 90% |
| B | 85% | 15% |
| C | 65% | 35% |
| D | 10% | 90% |

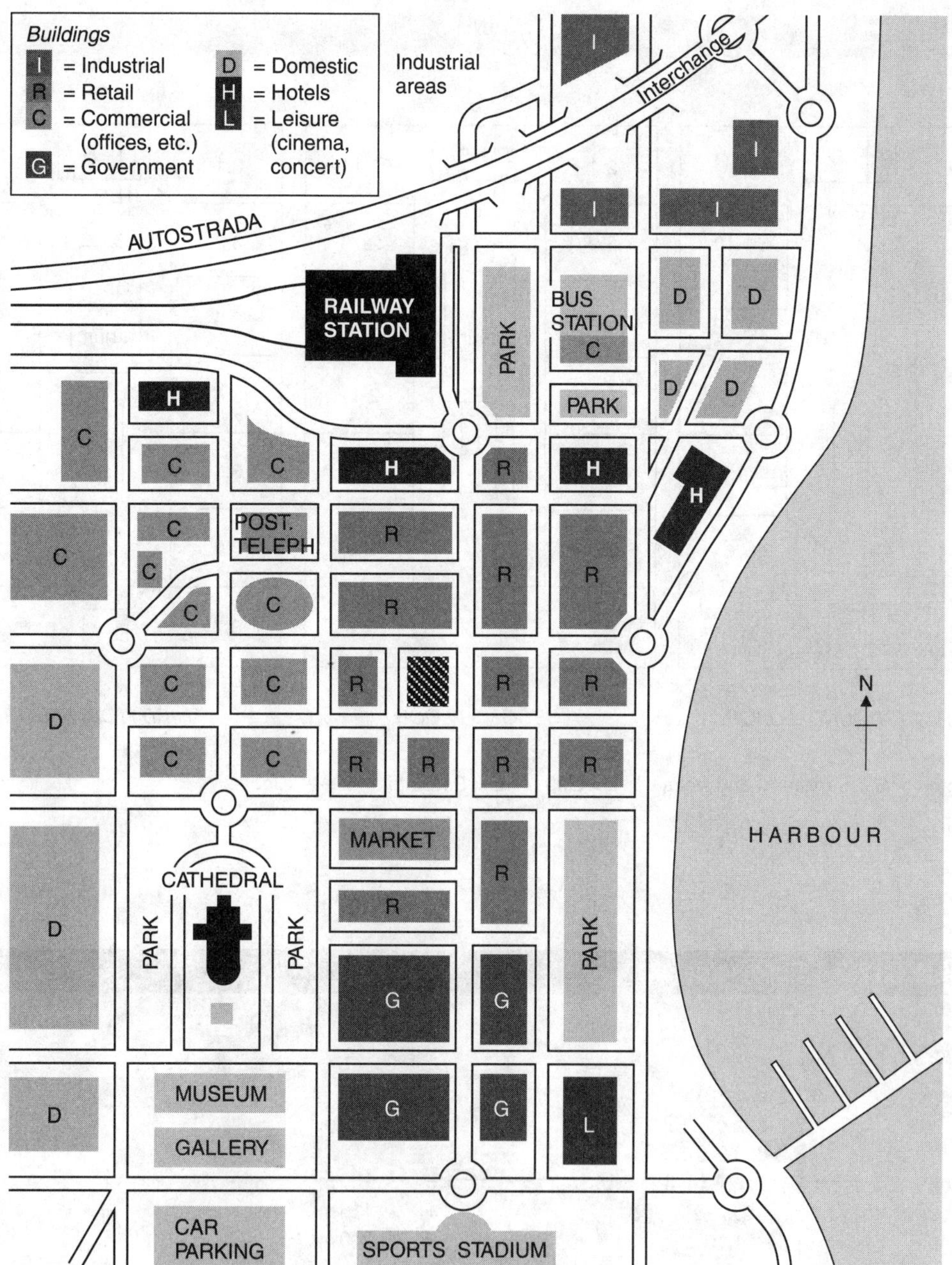
Buildings
I = Industrial
R = Retail
C = Commercial (offices, etc.)
G = Government
D = Domestic
H = Hotels
L = Leisure (cinema, concert)
Industrial areas
Interchange
AUTOSTRADA
RAILWAY STATION
PARK
BUS STATION
POST. TELEPH
MARKET
CATHEDRAL
HARBOUR
N
MUSEUM
GALLERY
CAR PARKING
SPORTS STADIUM

**Figure C12.1**

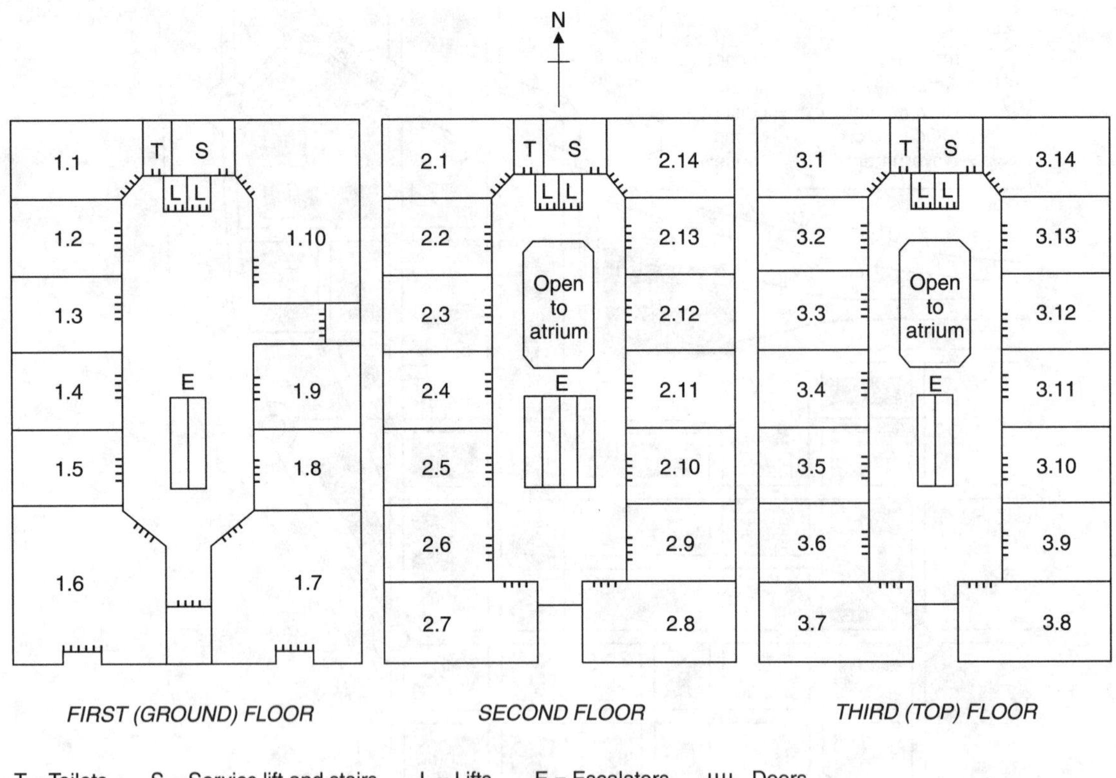


**Figure C12.2**

**Table C12.3 Building details**

**Floor area**

| | | | |
|---|---|---|---|
| Shops | 1.2–5; 1.8; 1.9; 2.2–6; 2.0–2.13; 3.2–6; 3.9–3.13 | = | 80 m$^2$ |
| Shops | 1.1; 2.1; 2.14; 3.1; 3.14 | = | 100 m$^2$ |
| Shops | 2.7–8; 3.7–8 | = | 115 m$^2$ |
| Shops | 1.6–7; 1.10 | = | 240 m$^2$ |

**Rental charges are quoted**

The cheapest shops are the single 80 m$^2$ units on the top floor. Comparative charges for all other units are as follows:

| Shops | Rental (if the cheapest) |
|---|---|
| 3.1; 3.14 | +10% |
| 3.7; 3.8 | +20% |
| 2.2–6; 2.9–13 | +10% |
| 2.1; 2.14 | +29% |

**Table C12.3 (continued)**

| | Shops | Rental (if the cheapest) |
|---|---|---|
| | 2.7; 2.8 | +30% |
| | 1.2–5; 1.8–9 | +30% |
| | 1.1 | +40% |
| | 1.6–7 | +380% |
| | 1.10 | +330% |
| **Shops already let** | | |
| | **Shops** | **Purpose/Nature** |
| | 3.4 | Travel agent |
| | 3.11 | Insurance agency |
| | 3.2 | Clothes (women) |
| | 3.13 | Clothes (men) |
| | 2.4 | Coffee shop |
| | 2.5 | Pottery/ceramics |
| | 2.6 | Hardware |
| | 2.9 | Gifts (general) |
| | 2.10 | Music |
| | 2.11 | Sports goods and wear |
| | 2.13 | Decorating |
| | 1.1 | Bank |
| | 1.2 | Toys |
| | 1.3 | Clothes (women) |
| | 1.6 | Fashions/clothes |
| | 1.7 | Restaurant |
| | 1.9 | Books/papers/stationery |
| | 1.10 | Food |

Case study 13

# The Shire of Corio

## GENERAL BACKGROUND

This municipality is 80 km from Melbourne in Victoria, Australia and takes in the northern ('blue-collar') suburbs of Geelong, Victoria's second biggest city. It has a heavy concentration of industry, companies of note being Ford (engines and body parts), Pilkingtons (automotive glass), Henderson's Industries (vehicle seats), Shell (oil refinery), Australian Cement, BHP Steel Wire Products, Aerospace Technologies of Australia (a recently privatized federal government facility which assembled and maintained FA/18A fighters for the RAAF and now has several contracts to provide major overhaul services for large international carriers), and Candy (a subsidiary of Pacific Dunlop making women's shoes). The Port of Geelong Authority operates several docks along the foreshore of Port Phillip Bay. However, more than two-thirds of the 700 km$^2$ area is rural, producing wheat, oats, barley, other cereals, and livestock, besides being home to five vineyards. Table C13.1 shows the wide range of property types.

The shire's population is 57 000 compared to 150 000 for the whole of urban Geelong. There are many low-income families and migrants from non-English speaking countries, and during the current recession unemployment has reached 35% in some districts. Geelong region comprises nine local government organizations. Corio is the largest, with a budgeted annual recurrent expenditure for 1992–1993 of A$29.9 million, whereas Geelong City's is A$15 million and Queenscliff's (a small coastal town) only A$2.7 million. Amalgamation is a hot political issue, following a recent change of state government, and proponents claim that it would allow rationalization of resources and economies of scale.[1] The Geelong Regional Commission exists to foster economic growth and co-ordinate the necessary activities, but has often been at loggerheads with the various councils.

Table C13.1 Distribution of property types

| Type | Number |
|---|---|
| Residential | 18 000 |
| Industrial | 875 |
| Shops/commercial | 445 |
| Small acres | 1 339 |
| Farms | 341 |

[1] Corio spends $18 million p.a. and has been prominent in the establishment of a purchasing syndicate (the Geelong Local Government Supply Group). The number of suppliers has been cut to 500 and increased buyer power has brought significant savings, e.g. A$21 000 per year on fuel costs alone.

## THE ORGANIZATION

The Shire Council consists of 12 councillors elected from four wards for three-year terms, and acts as a sort of board of directors, establishing policies, setting priorities, and allocating resources via the budget. There are 290 full-time staff, 260 part-time staff and 100 volunteers (mainly working in community services), of whom only 120 are based at headquarters (Osborne House). They represent over 50 different professions, and provide a diverse range of more than 200 services for residents and the general community. A list of the most important premises/sites under council management is given in Table C13.2. The various departments are assigned to one of five distinct programmes, whose principal activities/functions are listed in Table C13.3, along with incomes and expenditures for 1990–1991(Figure C13.4). Rates are the dominant sources of funds, and whilst Corio can adjust this levy on its 23 000 ratepayers, or cut certain services, in order to balance the books, these are politically sensitive issues.

In fact, it is the sole Victorian council to keep annual percentage rate rises below inflation for the past five years (the last two adjustments were 1% and 0%). Notwithstanding this, the variety and quality of services has increased. This period coincides with Brian Payne's appointment as general manager (GM) in 1988. He came from a Melbourne council and it was his first time in the top job. Since then a corporate philosophy has been developed (see Figure C13.2), along with a mission statement (Figure C13.3), now prominently displayed in the council chamber, the reception area at Osborne House, etc., and on the annual report and all job advertisements. Basically, council determines the corporate plan, after being presented with several options.

**Table C13.2 Main premises and sites**

Osborne House[a] (shire headquarters)

Operations Centre (newly constructed depot for fieldwork support)

Shopfront (at Corio Village shopping centre)

Leisuretime Squash and Sports Centre[b] (three stadiums, eight squash courts, eight outdoor courts, and several multi-purpose rooms)

Norlane Waterworld[c] (swimming pools and gymnasium complex)

Lara swimming pool

Elcho Park Golf Course

Deppeler Park pitch and putt (par 3) course

Libraries (three) and a mobile unit[d]

Tourist Information Centre

Community halls (five), neighbourhood centres, community health centres (two)

Parks, passive gardens, nature reserves and playgrounds (61)

Major football/cricket sports reserves (six)

[a] Australia's first naval college, now incorporating a naval museum and a National Trust historic building.

[b] 300 000 visits in 1991.

[c] 330 000 visits in 1991.

[d] More than 250 000 books and magazines.

**Table C13.3 The five programmes, principal activities, and executive responsibility**

**Management and development**

Collect rates and administer budget allocations
Invest funds
Develop and promote commercial activities and tourism
Quality
Training
Purchasing
Asset management (including plant maintenance and replacement)
Foster community relations (annual report, newsletters, calendars, etc.).
Conduct council elections, hold civic functions
Maintain (computerized) records office

**Community services**

Neighbourhood watch
Maternal and child health service (home visits, play groups, capsule hire, etc.)
Family care and children's services (day care,[a] four child care centres, kindergartens, after-school care)
Youth services (Youth Centre activities, vacation activity programmes)
Home care (assistance for the aged and disabled and emergency cases)
Senior citizens (clubs, 'meals on wheels', transport)
Neighbourhood centres (further education classes, community group activities, etc.)

**Health and environment**

Environmental Health Service (immunization,[b] head lice eradication,[c] pest control, food handlers' inspections)
Animal control (dog registrations, ranger and dog control, cattle pound)
Urban development (street sweeping, public toilets, rubbish and sanitary pan collections, recycling, tip operation[d])
Urban planning and control (issuing town planning permits[e] and processing building approval applications,[f] enforcing town planning regulations)

**Leisure**

Swimming (Waterworld, Lara pool)
Indoor sports (squash, racquetball, netball, basketball, soccer, volleyball, badminton, karate, aerobics, etc.)
Public halls (sports, functions, meetings)
Arts (libraries and naval museum)
Outdoor sports (sports ovals, golf and pitch and putt courses)
Playgrounds and passive gardens, nursery, landscaping, tree maintenance

**Transport**

Roadworks and line marking
Foot and bicycle paths
Traffic control (school crossings supervision, parking and street signs, traffic wardens)
Street lighting (installation and surveillance)
Drainage construction and maintenance
Works and services for ratepayers, clubs and organizations on a 'user pays' basis
Depot operations and administration

[a] In homes of registered care givers.
[b] 2000 schoolchildren and 6200 infants in one year.
[c] 15 000 children inspected by council's nurse in one year.
[d] Caters for most of Geelong, 230 000 $m^3$ deposited per year.
[e] 247 planning permit applications plus ten appeals in one year.
[f] 1197 building approvals granted in one year.

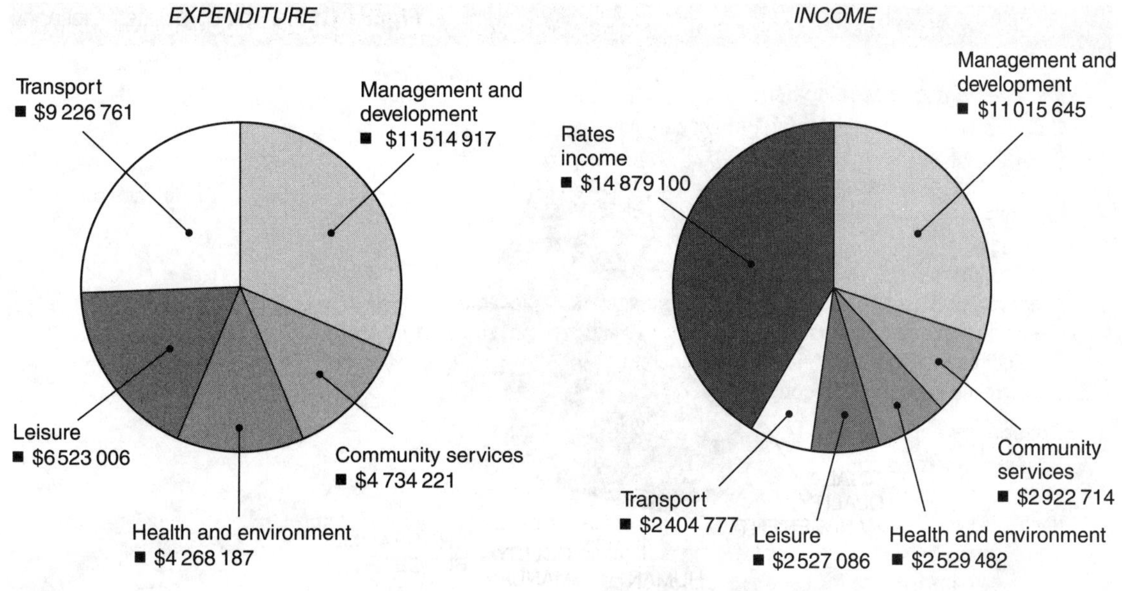


**Figure C13.1** Shire expenditure and income for year ended 30 September 1991

The GM is in charge of overall operations and acts as senior adviser to council. There are four functional divisions, headed by a director, completing the corporate management team (Figure C13.4). Departmental allocations correspond closely to the five major programmes except that 'leisure' is largely subsumed into the 'environmental services' portfolio and the 'management and development' programme is more or less split between the executives responsible for 'administration and community services' and 'corporate services'. Logically, the shire engineer is responsible for 'technical services', which consists mainly of 'transport', but includes the maintenance of all buildings and plant plus outdoor facilities. This is not the conventional structure, where the town clerk and shire engineer run two separate halves and report directly to council. There are even plans afoot to rotate executives, in the interests of innovation and teamwork, and it is fairly unusual to have a marketing manager and an economic and quality manager (Evan Sutton).

## TOTAL QUALITY MANAGEMENT

When Brian arrived he engaged an academic to give a session on teamwork and brainstorming to six management groups. Afterwards, a delegation suggested to him that supervisors were actually stifling ideas for improving operations. At the Geelong Business Club he heard a speaker from Enterprise Australia (Sydney) on TQM, and was then determined to build a quality culture and change the shire from a bureaucracy to a customer-oriented service. Corio has since pioneered the concept in Australian local government.

TQM commenced in 1989 when the executive visited Ford to get ideas and then advertised for a co-ordinator. After appointing their own data processing manager they looked for a suitable consultant. One job applicant was from Gas and Fuel Corporation of Victoria, also in the public sector, which had had good experiences with TQM, and their contribution has since proven invaluable.

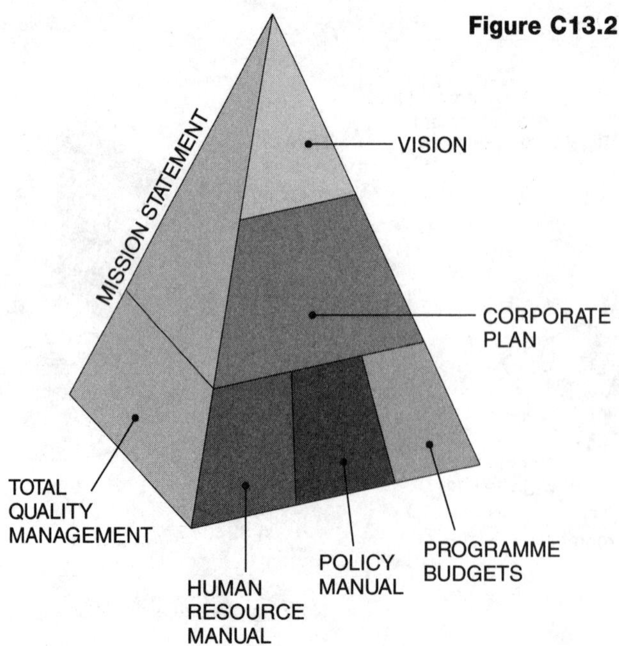


**Figure C13.2** The corporate philosophy

**Figure C13.3** The mission statement

Evan went to Enterprise Australia for two weeks and the executives attended a four-day course, whence a TQM committee was formed comprising the GM, two directors and three managers. It selected six (transitional) *cross-functional* teams, from different hierarchical levels, so that 'outsiders' would play devil's advocate. The teams received two days' training and were asked to generate potential improvement projects via 'brainstorming', but the committee made the final choice(s). There were some teething difficulties because the tasks tended to be too big for a 12 weeks completion target. For instance, 'parks maintenance' was only tractable when reduced to 'roundabouts' (there are 100). The successful groups tended to have strong leaders, so it was decided to train 12 'facilitators' who could be assigned to subsequent projects.

According to Brian the greatest obstacle was middle management. He said that generally they were products of the 1950–1970s who had received no formal management education. Their *modus operandi* was to check on people so as to catch them out, but now they must act as coaches, planners, facilitators and resource providers. After a TQM meeting, supervisors would imply that team members had been 'bludging'. To combat this, 96 staff, in groups of 16, participated in a five-day, in-house 'management course' which was TQM in disguise. The GM

COUNCIL

GENERAL MANAGER

**Byran Payne** Strategic planning

ADMINISTRATION AND COMMUNITY SERVICES

**Richard Metcalf**
- General administration
- Community services
- Child care services
- Maternal and child health

ENVIRONMENTAL SERVICES

**John Quirk**
- Building
- Town planning
- Health
- Local laws
- Leisure services
- Community development

CORPORATE SERVICES

**John Coggle**
- Finance
- Data processing
- Risk management
- Marketing
- Training
- Quality control

TECHNICAL SERVICES

**Roger Marsden**
- Engineering
- Construction and drainage
- Waste management
- Parks and gardens
- Maintenance of council properties

**Figure C13.4** The executive structure

introduced games and exercises he had obtained while studying for Melbourne University's MBA (he particularly enjoyed the TQM unit). This unearthed people with management potential. For example, a garbage truck driver became a TQM team leader and later a supervisor. Other measures included setting up a quality committee for each division, incorporating all its managers, and taking account of subordinates' contributions to TQM projects in their performance reviews. It is no longer sufficient to run a department efficiently – innovations and improvements are expected.

As TQM evolved, the emphasis switched to voluntary membership of quality circles. These are natural workgroups, which must have full control over processes they aim to improve, or gain the necessary co-operation. Once savings had been demonstrated (over A$1 million in 1990–1991 and A$4 million in total), Brian instigated two council-approved incentive schemes. Supervisors are empowered to give A$50 in gifts, tickets or vouchers to individuals (one per person per year) for a good idea, and quality circles can apply for another award worth up to A$5000 per team. All projects conclude with a report to council at a presentation dinner and the receipt of a framed certificate.

A representative sample of TQM projects is given in Table C13.4. Two of these, 'water usage' and 'recycling', are discussed at greater length in Appendices A and B respectively. They are both very topical subjects, related as they are to environmental concerns, so the teams were in effect breaking some

**Table C13.4 A sample of TQM projects**

| | |
|---|---|
| • roundabout maintenance | • depot relocation |
| • commercial garbage collection | • induction of new staff |
| • domestic garbage collection | • purchase order system |
| • recycling | • archiving |
| • street sweeping (Corio Village) | • disabilities and leisure |
| • water usage | |

new ground rather than merely trying to improve existing operations. The accounts illustrate how members of the general workforce can, when given the training and opportunity, collect and analyse data, calculate the costs of operations, and evaluate alternative strategies, technologies and methods. Above all, though, such exercises confer 'ownership' of the new work practices, and therefore facilitate the necessary, but often thorny, processes of change.

## CUSTOMER FOCUS

Ratepayers are encouraged to submit ideas for better services, and letter drop cards are distributed to particular zones asking for comments and suggestions to facilitate long-term planning. This tends to reveal major problems (e.g. inadequate drainage), whereas other statistics refer to symptoms (e.g. requests to unblock drains).

Amongst the new services is 'Corio Community Contact', available throughout the region to aged or disabled residents who live alone. It operates round the clock via a home unit connected to the telephone network. In an emergency the user squeezes a small pendant worn around the neck and the unit dials a switchboard at shire offices. After-hours calls are diverted to the Vital Call National Monitoring Centre in Sydney. Voice-to-voice contact is provided, which is especially reassuring when the caller is waiting for help to arrive. All Geelong's councils support the initiative, and a sponsorship campaign proved very successful. The costs of subscribing are further curtailed by using trained volunteers to man the switchboard, Lions club members to install the units, and friends and neighbours to respond to calls whenever it is appropriate.

On the industrial side, Evans runs a self-help programme for the embattled textiles, clothing and footwear sector, advocating TQM as a way of competing with cheap Asian imports. Better networking has resulted in transport sharing for deliveries to and from Melbourne, switching to local suppliers, etc. There has also been an 'awareness day' to promote local manufacturers. The public can be a resource too. Corio's 'adopt a park' scheme covers 61 reserves, and by providing free materials to community groups a higher standard of maintenance is achieved for the same cost.

A radical step occurred in 1991 when Corio Village Shopfront opened to make services more accessible. It is in the municipality's big shopping mall, whereas Osborne House is somewhat isolated and bereft of public transport. Links to the council's mainframe computer give terminals access to information on rates, property, electronic mail, diaries, etc., and the software relays customer requests and monitors response times. Shopfront now collects more rates payments than the main offices, the majority of postal votes in elections are lodged there, and there has been a general increase in inquiries.

Initially, over 80 staff (including the GM, gardeners, etc.) volunteered to man the shop, and even worked Friday evenings and Saturday mornings without pay for the three-month trial period. They undertook five days' training to familiarize themselves with the shire's operations and services. Once demand was established (90–150 customers per day) the hours were set at 9 a.m to 5 p.m. on weekdays plus 9 a.m to 1 p.m. on Saturdays, and Joanne Fields was appointed manager. A casual employee comes in for two hours per day to give her assistance and a lunch break, and some of the original volunteers put in one rotating four-hour shift per month. The shop advertises on local radio stations and in newspapers, emphasizing that Corio is the first council to introduce extended business hours.

A computerized payments system is used for rates, dog licences and parking fines, although most other transactions are manual. Joanne has learnt to cope with a great variety of demands and even redirects many clients to outside bodies such as the Commonwealth Employment Service, State Electricity Commission of Victoria (SECV), etc. Much of the required information is contained in brochures and leaflets, but if necessary keywords are input on a PC and text downloaded from central files and laser printed. However, certain areas, such as building applications, are sometimes difficult and the system user leaves an electronic message for the staff member responsible (an answer is expected within 24 hours). A similar procedure handles specific service requests, of which more than one-third relate to street tree maintenance, and by entering the appropriate urgency code number the next level of management is automatically notified in the case of non-compliance with the corresponding target response time. For an actual complaint a formal reply is expected within five working days. About five queries/requests per day are processed this way and a register maintained so that if any department is the subject of too many complaints an investigation will be carried out.

## INFORMATION TECHNOLOGY

Corio has been quick to adopt the latest technology, even though the old maxim 'roads, rates and rubbish' still applies. In 1989, the implementation of a computerized Land Information System began, based on the GIS (Geographical Information System) package, to provide a database on people and their properties. The raw mapping data were supplied on tapes by the SECV, and files have subsequently been created for each address. When this header is entered at a workstation's keyboard, a menu appears on the screen covering 'owner', 'titles', 'classification' (usage), 'rates', 'certificates' (building/planning), 'licences' (e.g. dog), 'requests', and 'works carried out'. The system can automatically project the right subdivision chart as it knows which properties are adjacent. This is particularly useful because ratepayers' 'requests' often concern neighbours' fences, overgrown gardens, building applications and suchlike. However, for other purposes it is better to be able to use (flexible) smaller scales, and now different layers (features) can be superimposed at the touch of a button. These include a blue inundation (flood) chart, the sewer network, and shire-owned land. Recently, a lot of people have asked about a proposed new waste disposal site in Staceys Road, and staff were able to call up a plan, hatched in red, overlaid on a suitable map.

Many departments deal with property but the old manual systems meant that they had to store and maintain their own paper maps even though much information was common. There was always a compromise between quality (currency) and the cost of making updates, and considerable time was also wasted trying to reconcile maps with subdivision charts. Now property services, rates, customer inquiries, engineering and accounting share the same database, and, apart from ensuring consistency, it facilitates one person rapidly obtaining all the details they (or a ratepayer) want, and not leafing through piles of charts and still having to request documents from other functions. Even then there were difficulties in matching up information from different sources, including numerous cases that straddled two adjacent maps. A microwave link, with satellite dishes, connects the central computer to terminals at the operations centre, Shopfront, Waterworld and Leisuretime. Without such modern technology these dispersed locations would have created yet more duplicate maps and records.

Richard Phillips, LIS officer, has been developing decision support systems, based on extracting the appropriate data and displaying their spatial characteristics. As 'requests' are logged against properties it is easy to highlight a service's 'black-spots'. For example, if drainage pipe failures are perceived to be excessive, the software allows the lengths of troublesome sections to be measured and estimates of the replacement costs made. The amounts spent on repairs are held in the database too, so the financial implications of these alternative maintenance procedures are clear. Similarly, the property file will soon contain details on trees. Then, complaints about street trees will be able to be analysed to see if particular species are unsuitable and should be substituted, or whether some neighbourhoods are too bare and need planting. Routeing/scheduling is another class of applications. New garbage collection rounds, 'home help' assignments, and 'meals on wheels' rounds can be designed more efficiently, by trial and error, on screen. If a volunteer driver for the latter service is absent, their clients can quickly be reallocated because times for the proposed additional journeys are instantly supplied.

A separate package is used for engineering survey, design and drafting because they require greater precision, although the files are fully compatible. Field measurements are recorded electronically and then transferred to the computer which automatically plots a survey plan. A drafting officer would use AutoCAD to superimpose a road design, and after completion produce a set of plans for use in the field.

## THE FUTURE

Despite a recent history of notable achievements, the Shire of Corio still faces an uncertain future. Not only is its very existence under threat as the Victorian government awaits a consultant's report on council amalgamations for the Geelong region, but also, in the current political climate, its monopoly position in regard to the provision of many services is likely to be challenged by privatization. Jobs will certainly disappear under an enlarged, and hopefully more efficient, local government authority, and entire functions may vanish too unless they can beat commercial organizations when quoting for tenders. The task that the GM must now undertake is to keep all the staff motivated in their dealings with the ratepayers, and focused on the long-term goals of the shire, notwithstanding these elements of insecurity, and to prevent any reversion to a 'public service' mentality. At the same time, he will be required to represent their best interests in the formation of any fledgling 'super-council', without losing sight of the economic rationale behind such a radical step.

## APPENDIX A

***The recycling Ragers*** (service improvement programme team): Irene Van Rooyen (leader), Boris Schanjko (facilitator), Gary Bowyer, Enzo Bruscella, Kevin Flynn, Anna Hughes, Les Vaughan.

Purpose: To provide Lara with a house-to-house recycling service suited to its needs.

This group convened in February 1992 and adopted the above task. Lara is a country town with 2400 tenements and 7400 inhabitants. At the time it just had two drop-off recycling centres (Kees Road Kindergarten for paper and the scouts in Rennie Street for glass), whereas the shire's city districts had a regular collection carried out by contractors. The Lara area was defined by its domestic garbage collection service, which takes place on Thursdays when three compactors and crews (one driver and two pick-ups) arrive from Corio suburb after finishing their rounds there.

The Ragers used brainstorming (about recycling), a herring-bone diagram, several flow-charts, field trips to look at other systems, and a customer survey. A questionaire and pre-addressed envelope were distributed to 2415 dwellings, and returns were accepted by post or at Osborne House, Shopfront or the operations centre. The ten questions covered present practices, awareness of current facilities, perceived needs and ideas for improving the recycling service, and there were 897 replies (27%). The major findings were that 45% of households used the existing (Lara) centres, the majority making monthly visits; 90% saw a need for a better recycling service; 93% preferred any upgrading to be based on a regular domestic collection; and 69% favoured a free bag over alternative containers. In addition respondents generally required monthly or fortnightly uplifts of the main categories of materials.

The principal recommendations were:

(a) a weekly house-to-house collection of all recyclables, coinciding with the Thursday waste removal, in order to simplify matters for residents;

(b) to collect steel cans, aluminium products, plastics, glass, and milk and juice waxed containers commingled in a bag, and separate bundles of cardboard and paper;

(c) to supply a free 1.2 x 0.6 m bag with Velcro seal, and to discourage putting it out half-empty. A seal should eliminate spillages, but decreases the usable volume. So, the bag is double the normal size to reduce incidences where it is filled and thereafter recyclables are thrown in the rubbish bin;

(d) use the council's direct labour force, not contractors;

(e) sell the commingled product for now, but examine the feasibility of operating a sorting facility;

(f) retain and promote the existing drop-off centres as the relevant community groups rely on this income;

(g) decision (d) rests upon amounts sold and the operations should be reviewed at the end of the financial year.

The proposed method calls for the parks department to loan two tray trucks and trailers, plus two staff (their drivers) and 16 cages. They would start to recycle Lara's *five-acre lots* at 6 a.m. whilst the shire's compactors work in Corio. After, each truck joins up with a compactor and commences their urban rounds. A team of five tackles the *densely housed areas*, consisting of one compactor with its driver and two pick-ups, and one recycle truck with a driver and one pick-up. Another team of four is assigned to lower-density areas and needs just one driver and pick-up per vehicle. The remaining compactor and crew of two remove garbage from the five-acre lots.

Firms were asked to quote for Lara, and 7¢ per household per week was the lowest tender, an annual fee of A$8736. The cost of 3000 bags per year, which allows for some loss and damage and then replacement for sanitary reasons, amounted to A$2450, and a promotional leaflet for each property added a further A$1200 to the cost of contracting out the job. If Corio's resources are used, the hourly hire rates for labour and equipment are known and the equivalent annual outlay was readily calculated. Estimating revenue from recyclables was not so straightforward, so three comparisons were made. The optimistic scenario assumed a 50% mean weekly household participation rate, from which quantities of commingled and paper could be extrapolated and multiplied by the relevant sale price. A figure of 25%, based on the current collection from urban areas of Geelong, was taken as worst case, and the breakeven point (36%) found to be more or less midway between. The shire faced a deficit in all cases, but initial confidence that the in-house option was cheapest stemmed from the facts that 74% of survey respondents already undertook some form of recycling, and 45% used the drop-off centres.

# APPENDIX B

***The H20 team*** (service improvement programme team): Barry Smith (team leader), Fran Norley (facilitator), Mick Jaensch (secretary), John Van Parreren, Andrew McInnes, Tony Wood, Milan Osolnik, Boris Littis, Peter Joynson, Jim Garlinge (guest).

A (fluctuating) team was established to address the rising costs of water usage, because the Water Board's impending switch to 'user pays'. It began by calculating the impact of this policy and found that an extra A$89 000 per year would be incurred, split more or less between new service fees (based upon connection sizes) and increases to actual consumption charges. Those accounts covering the council's golf courses, swimming pools and recreation reserves were particularly hard hit, generating a series of smaller projects.

## Elcho Park Golf Course

In year 1991–1992 more than 75 000 rounds were played at this popular public course, which used 80 000 kilolitres of water costing A$52 000. The TQM team aimed to retain sufficient water on site to meet total requirements, as it believed that in winter there is enough flow over and around the course to fill any catchment areas. A connection between the course dams and Gibbons Road was vital in this respect, and potential savings were as illustrated below:

| Kilolitres (town water) | Connection size (mm) | Cost (A$) |
|---|---|---|
| 100 000 | 100 | 66 100 |
| 90 000 | 100 | 59 900 |
| 80 000 | 100 | 53 700 |
| 60 000 | 50 | 38 225 |
| 40 000 | 50 | 25 825 |
| 20 000 | 32 | 12 820 |
| 10 000 | 32 | 6 610 |
| 0 | 25 | 164 |

Shire engineers estimated the existing reservoir's capacity at 17 000 kl, and the first proposal was to take in a tract of unused land going towards the eighteenth tee on one side and the driving range on the other and simultaneously increase the average depth from two to four metres, giving a revised volume of 72 000 kl. The preliminary costing was A$150 000 for the excavation of 42 000 m$^3$ of soil and its removal to the tip, plus A$60 000 for piping runoff from Gibbons Road underneath the course. However, a private contractor suggested a figure of A$130 000 for the complete earthworks, and the group considered that a spoon drain to the dam could be constructed for only A$5000 and would be adequate for the first few years, so the minimum total outlay came to A$135 000. For just A$50 000 the drain could be completed and the dam extended in one direction after removing 12 000–15 000 m$^3$ of earth, by spring, to give some quick payback over the first (dry) summer.

A strategy was also drawn up for commissioning two further dams, each of 15 000 kl capacity. The second priority was a new dam beside the sixth fairway because table drains already ran there from the main one and it could be filled from the overflow. After a pump had been installed, there would be an option either to water the surrounding holes directly, or send the water back as necessary for centralized distribution from the eighteenth. The lowest priority was to create a reservoir next to the twelfth tee. A marked water hazard existed here, although its state varied from marshy for most of the year to a dry cakebed in summer. Furthermore, it was the closest dam to Gibbons Road, so tunnelling would be relatively easy. The negative aspect was the difficulty of linking it with the other sites, but the work was deemed essential to improve the course's appearance.

The team held discussions with the Golf Course Committee and gained their approval. They then obtained A$25 000 from the Elcho Park Reserve fund and another A$25 000 from the Park's capital works budget in order to schedule the initial stage for 1992–1993.

## Computerized watering solutions

All the shire's watering was (originally) carried out by parks staff moving sprinkler hoses over a reserve, park, etc. This is labour intensive, and was done in normal working hours, which often wastes water. The H20 team investigated the possibility of converting to automatic watering. This needs underground reticulation, and accordingly A$10 000 worth of equipment was trialled at Windsor Park (an Australian Rules football/cricket oval), but has already been extended to include the golf course, Deppeler Park, and the operations centre's lawns.

The control system essentially consists of a central PC controller at the operations centre, a radio link, and satellite controllers, numerous valves, sprinklers, and water sensors distributed around the various grounds. The software enables an unlimited number of spray programmes to be initiated, depending on the weather (wind and rain), soil conditions, and local turf requirements, and satellites can be subject to manual overrides if desired. Sprinklers are normally activated in the middle of the night when it is cool and still, which also avoids interfering with recreational users. Different zones, such as greens, aprons and fairways on the golf course, or the forward pocket and centre-half forward patches on the 'footy' oval, can be both monitored and programmed independently.

During summer months staff used to manually operate 180 hoses on the golf course. The new automatic system cost A$300 000 in total and has 491 sprinklers linked to six satellite centres and makes use of rainwater. Elcho Park Golf Club made a joint financial contribution and members also helped by filling in and seeding trenches. The ongoing labour savings here and at the other sites allow more time to be spent on general parks maintenance.

## Solar watering systems

The shire had some median strips and roundabouts which were either watered by hand or by manually connecting a sprinkler, and many which received no watering at all. It is not practical to join them all to the electricity grid, so the group recommended that A$5000 be spent on a pilot in-ground irrigation system for the Cox Road/Anakie Road roundabout, to be activated by a solar-powered control box. This still triggers automatic watering at the optimum time of day, but as there are no ground sensors it is necessary to actually visit the site in order to change the set watering pattern.

Case study 14

# Prince Philip Dental Hospital, Hong Kong

## INTRODUCTION

The Prince Philip Dental Hospital was opened in 1982 and is the home of the Faculty of Dentistry of the University of Hong Kong. The hospital comprises seven floors almost entirely devoted to the study and practice of dentistry and employs over 500 people, of whom 238 are in clinical positions. The university's dental course is five years long, with around 50 dental surgeons graduating each year. After a first year of basic medical science the course concentrates on the clinical aspects of dentistry. The teaching system used within the hospital is based on small groups of six to eight students per group. The group forms the basic attachment for an individual student and the student accompanies the other group members through the weekly rotation of learning activities. The small student group is able to develop good relations with its teachers and also emphasizes the importance of teamwork and co-operation.

In 1992 over 125 000 treatment appointments were scheduled at the hospital, with 11 000 new patient registrations. Dental students learn through the treatment of patients in the various speciality departments of the hospital. Thus, they will learn about fillings and crowns in the Department of Conservative Dentistry, about surgical procedures in the Department of Oral and Maxillofacial Surgery, about the treatment of gum disease in the Department of Periodontology, and so on. Patients are not so easily compartmentalized though, and it is all too easy for students to lose sight of patients as whole beings who may present any number of different problems. It is the role of the General Practice Unit to bring together the teaching of the individual departments in one clinic and apply this knowledge in a setting that attempts to resemble a typical general dental practice as closely as possible.

## THE GENERAL PRACTICE UNIT

Dental students start to treat patients in the General Practice Unit in their final year of study. The philosophy of the unit has been defined as follows:

'The General Practice Unit will enable final year students and ancillary staff to experience the environment of a well-managed, high-quality general dental practice. Everyone in the unit will strive to form a better understanding of how best to meet patients' needs and will be expected to work together to (1) formulate and then (2) execute to a high standard, simple treatment plans within a friendly and co-operative atmosphere.'

The unit itself is housed within the Prince Philip Dental Hospital and comprises a reception area, 14 surgeries, one X-ray room and a dispensary/store plus offices for the teaching staff (Figure C14.1). Students arrange appointments directly with their own patients. The advantage of this arrangement is that students learn to appreciate the problems that receptionists face in scheduling patients, although the number of patients currently seen by students (two or three per session) means that such problems tend to be minimal. The disadvantage is that students may abuse the system, often to the detriment of patient service – e.g. cancelling patients at the last minute.

The dental students are assisted by trained dental surgery assistants who rotate around the various departments of the hospital every six months, so as to gain experience in all aspects of dentistry. One senior teacher administers the unit, with additional clinical supervision being provided by fully qualified general dental practitioners who usually work at the Dental Hospital on a part-time basis. The employment of such practitioners is encouraged because of their ability to provide a practical insight into dental practice.

As there are six groups of students the unit is fully operational only three days per week. The rest of the week the unit is largely unutilized.

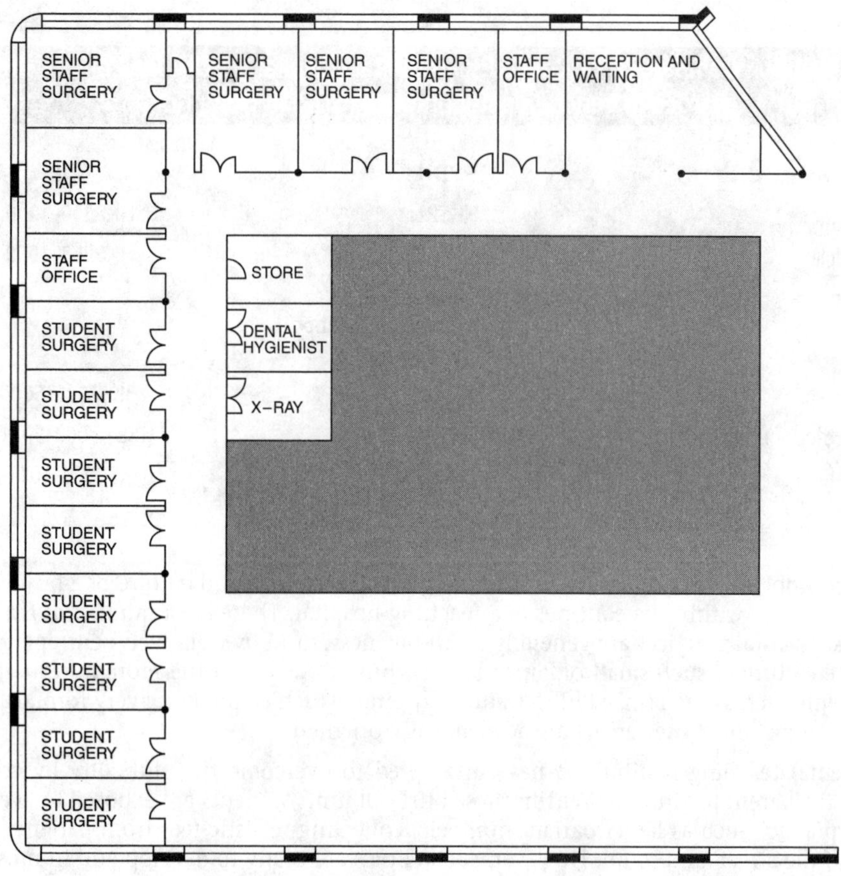


**Figure C14.1** General Practice Unit

# DISCUSSION

The General Practice Unit effectively serves two groups of 'customers'. These comprise external customers, i.e. patients, and internal customers, i.e. students. The unit therefore has to fulfil a dual role in the provision of services, firstly to its students (teaching) and secondly to its patients (care). This duality inevitably leads to a conflict between the differing needs of the two sets of customers. For example, students would ideally like patients who are always able to attend at a given time and often at very short notice, who are able to tolerate long appointments and who do not mind having their dental problems discussed openly in front of a number of people. The patient also has to put up with having to change 'dentist' every one or two years as students graduate and leave the hospital. The rotation of ancillary staff every six months adds to this lack of continuity; it is generally held that patients like to build up a relationship with support staff, who are often perceived as being more approachable than the dentist. In other words, ideal hospital patients are ones who do not mind putting up with any number of inconveniences in order to get their treatment done.

Most patients, on the other hand, would naturally like greater convenience in their dealings with the dentist in terms of scheduling, appointment duration and staff continuity. It is a widely held view, however, that patients attending the hospital are generally happy to put up with such inconveniences because treatment charges are much lower than those found outside the hospital in private practice (Table C14.1) (there is no state-subsidized health service in Hong Kong, and all dental practice is privately funded).

**Table C14.1** Comparison of Prince Philip Dental Hospital (PPDH) fees and 'average' fee charged in general dental practice (GDP) in Hong Kong

| Item of work | PPDH | GDP |
|---|---|---|
| Examination | HK$21 | HK$300–1000 |
| Simple filling | HK$105<br>(fee for full course of simple treatment regardless of number of fillings provided) | HK$250–1000 |
| Gold crown | HK$233 | HK$3000–5000 |
| Fixed orthodontic braces | HK$1240 | HK$12 000–20 000 |
| Full dentures | HK$310 | HK$5000–10 000 |

A further problem is the difficulty in recreating the atmosphere and culture of a busy, well-run general dental practice within the confines of a teaching hospital. There are a number of reasons why this should be so. Dental practices are generally small businesses run by (relatively) entrepreneurial professionals. The culture of such small organizations is thus at odds with the more bureaucratic nature of establishments such as the Prince Philip Dental Hospital, which is run along very formal and rigid lines and by teaching staff whose careers are academically oriented.

Some dental teaching institutions have attempted to overcome this difficulty by creating clinics away from the parent institution. Within these offshoot units students are exposed to everyday aspects of general practice such as larger patient numbers, collecting realistic fees from patients, dealing with patients 'off the street' and so on. However, such clinics are costly to develop and in most institutions training in aspects of general practice takes place inside the hospital either in a discrete unit (as with the General Practice Unit) or, worse still, as part of an existing department.

In the specialist departments within the Prince Philip Dental Hospital emphasis is placed on provision of treatment and the teaching of clinical techniques; the quality of service provided in terms of the softer, more intangible aspects of care is not overly emphasized. In a general practice setting, however, it is often these intangible factors that patients use to judge and differentiate between practices. While the treatment provided in the General Practice Unit is of the highest standard, dental surgeons manning the unit have encountered difficulty in convincing both students and support staff (receptionists, dental surgery assistants) of the importance of these intangible elements, simply because they are not stressed throughout the rest of the hospital. For example, there is no training programme for reception staff in such areas as dealing with complaints, answering the telephone, etc. Patients appreciate a reassuring phone call the day after treatment to confirm there are no after-effects following treatment. This can markedly improve the image of a practice and yet such a simple courtesy is seldom performed with patients at the hospital. Because these areas are given such low priority, students assume they are of little importance.

Students working in the General Practice Unit tend therefore to be shielded from the very elements that make up a typical general dental practice and in many ways leave the hospital unprepared for the 'real world'.

Case study 15

# The Textile Machinery Company

The principal plant of the Textile Machinery Company (TMC) is located in Accrington, an industrial town in Lancashire in England. The company is part of a larger engineering conglomerate whose products range through mechanical engineering, electrical engineering and specialist metal goods for the non-consumer industries. TMC manufactures textile machinery. It also manufactures in the USA and one other European country, and has factories in four other towns close to its principal plant. The principal plant employs approximately 800 personnel, of whom 400 are direct 'shopfloor employees', approximately 175 are staff and 225 in-direct 'shopfloor employees'. The factory makes parts for and assembles textile machines. Some of the items made in this plant are supplied as castings or fabrications from one of the company's other plants in the area. Some items are bought in. With these few exceptions the entire products are manufactured in the factory. This factory has been engaged in such work in this industry for over 100 years, although a series of mergers and takeovers has, since 1970, brought it within the present company and conglomerate. It is the major employer in the town.

## PRODUCTS

The textile machines made at the factory sell at between £20 000 and £50 000 each. They are electro-mechanical and most are developments of similar machines made on this site over the past 100 years. The factory basically manufactures two types of machine. The more recent version, developed over the past ten years, operates very much faster than the older machine and is able to produce output at a rate of three to four times the rate of the older machine. The older machine, however, is able to produce items of a far greater range than the new machine; in particular it is able to produce finer-quality products. The older machine costs about £20 000. The newer range of machines cost £40 000–£50 000. The newer machines also employ fewer castings, are more compact and are somewhat more automated.

The manufacture of both types of product involves machining, assembly, test, disassembly, packaging and dispatch.

## MARKETS

The products of this factory are marketed worldwide. There are no major competitors in the UK, although elsewhere certain major competitors do exist. An Italian manufacturer is a major competitor, whilst for the newer product a Czech manufacturer provides strong competition. Throughout the world there are approximately 20 competing companies. Demand for the products is cyclical, with an approximate four-year cycle. This derives from the four-year trade cycle which is an established pattern of the textile industry. Early delivery and also price are major factors in winning orders, and most companies are prepared to buy equipment from a variety of manufacturers, so supplier loyalty is not substantial.

Currently, of the total number of machines produced, approximately 60% are of the old types and 40% of the new type. The old type will be favoured by customers in developing countries where labour costs are low and where particularly high quality is required for a certain range of products. The new machinery will be favoured by companies seeking to maximize labour productivity (e.g. where labour costs are high) and to maximize output.

## MARKETING

The factory's products are marketed worldwide by a team of marketing personnel. These are backed up by a group of technical sales personnel located at the factory. The technical sales personnel tend to deal eventually with all prospective customers, since customers always require their machines to have specific features or characteristics. Often customers are provided with direct contact with company research/development and manufacturing personnel for this reason. Marketing personnel tend to quote a delivery time that has been previously agreed within the company by all key personnel. Currently that delivery time is 23 weeks from receipt of order. Marketing personnel quote a price based on a 'cost plus' procedure with a known minimum acceptable price for each product.

## PRODUCTION PLANNING/CONTROL

In general, orders are scheduled for manufacture on a 'first come/first served' basis, although in certain circumstances exceptions are made, e.g. for major established customers placing new orders with the prospect of major orders to follow. For production planning and control purposes the factory operates a form of order 'pipeline' or order book. The pipeline contains all orders which have been released to manufacture at a given time. When demand is high the pipeline contains firm, committed orders only, i.e. orders against specific customer requirements for delivery at agreed times at an agreed price. However, previously, when demand was lower, some speculative orders were released into this 'pipeline'. Available data were scrutinized at senior management meetings and decisions made as to which items to release speculatively into the order pipeline. The data included the orders placed, and in addition the possible orders anticipated by marketing personnel, i.e. the potential orders currently under discussion with potential customers. Given knowledge of customers from previous orders, the general level of demand in the industry, etc., management decided which of these orders to release speculatively into the order pipeline when the flow of firm orders was insufficient to occupy fully the available manufacturing capacity. In these circumstances the order pipeline might be similar to that shown in Table C15.1.

Only 20% of the manufactured content of the old product is common, i.e. required irrespective of the product specification demanded by the customer. Thus, in manufacturing speculative orders for the old machine, the factory must in effect manufacture entire products to the anticipated requirements of a potential customer. Because of the design of such machines it is not possible to manufacture, say, 80% of the machine and leave the remaining 20% to be completed when firm orders are received. In contrast, approximately 90% of the parts of the new machines are common, so there is less risk of manufacturing end products to inappropriate specifications when the speculative manufacture of new products is undertaken. The new machines will not, in the foreseeable future, completely replace the old machine, which continues to be in demand in certain parts of the world and for certain product ranges. A redesign of the old machine has begun – the intention being that the old machine be assembled in 'modular' form such that up to 80% of the items to be manufactured are common to all possible customer requirements, leaving only 20% of the content being made/assembled against specific customer needs.

In fact, for the past ten years the factory has been required to manufacture against a pipeline of orders comprising firm orders for old and new machines *and* speculative orders for these two products.

Table C15.1 Order pipeline (as at date ...)

| Customer (new,[a] previous[b]) | Actual/expected no. of units on order | Probability of receiving order | Delivery required (from above date) |
|---|---|---|---|
| A[a] | 50 | 1.0 (order received) | 14 months |
| B[b] | 48 | 1.0 (order received) | 6 months |
| C[a] | 35 | 0.5 | 10 months |
| D[b] | 15 | 0.90 | 12 months |
| E[b] | 75 | 0.80 | 7 months |
| F[a] | 105 | 0.65 | 7 months |
| G[a] | 25 | 0.70 | 9 months |

The balance between firm and speculative orders has varied depending upon the general level of demand experienced by the factory.

## POLICY DECISION

Recently, following a management change in the parent company, a new managing director has taken over at the Textile Machinery Company. He, an accountant, began a review of the company's activities because he was concerned, amongst other things, with the substantial increase in the capital tied up in finished but unsold products, the substantial overdraft required to fund such a stock, and its effect on the selling price of machines. This has now led to a major policy decision. It has been decided that, in future, the company will not manufacture goods of a particular specification against future anticipated orders, i.e. not build products to the specification required by customers with whom negotiations are currently proceeding but from whom firm orders have not yet been received.

## FACTORY ORGANIZATION

Overall responsibility for the factory lies with the plant manager, who reports to the managing director. Reporting to the plant manager are the personnel manager, the facilities manager (in effect the production engineer), the production manager responsible for the machine shops and assembly, the finance manager, the services manager responsible for production/control (with associated data processing) and, finally, the quality manager. The plant manager has held his job at this factory for the past 15 years.

The factory operates on a two-shift system. Currently no overtime work is undertaken.

Case study 16

# America Burger and Pasta

The partners in the Brazilian 'America Burger and Pasta' (AB&P) venture seemed to have the main characteristics it takes for a group of entrepreneurs who intend to start a successful restaurant chain. Helio Mattar got his PhD in Industrial Management and Engineering from Stanford University, USA. He is a former academic with a career in the fields of operations research, economics and strategic planning, having worked for some of Brazil's most prestigious business institutions. Dr Matter is AB&P's managing director. Artur Guimaraes and his wife, Maria Helena, were both considered to be 'cuisine artists' and have previous experience in the restaurant business, including seven years working for prestigious restaurants and studying with important 'chefs' in Europe. Luis Guelpi and Paula Maluhy both have previous experience in the restaurant and other businesses.

Unlike many other restaurant chains, which were originally planned to be a single restaurant and eventually, given the success, became chains, AB&P was from the beginning planned and created to be a chain of restaurants.

The inspiration for the creation of AB&P came from the 'American Diners', which serve quick meals, frequently working in old refurbished train wagons or caravans. The partners noticed that this type of restaurant had no equivalent in Brazil. On top of that, they also wanted to meet the needs of a very promising market niche in São Paulo: the young professionals.

According to Dr Mattar, the 'meal caterers' in São Paulo could be classified into five categories:

1. ***Fast food*** – which seek to serve the customers in the fastest, cheapest and most consistent (in terms of taste and service) way. They offer a limited variety of standard products. The great concern with cleanliness and service standardization, which this type of restaurant usually emphasizes, seeks to reinforce the customers' perception that 'they know exactly what they will get'. Broadly speaking, one of the important features of fast food restaurants is that the food is sold 'off the shelf', i.e. is ready waiting for the customer to consume it.
2. ***Sandwich shop*** – where the emphasis is also on quick meals, mainly sandwiches, but the variety of products is normally much broader, and customization (small changes in the way the products are made) is generally possible. The cycle times involved in the service are also more variable than in fast food systems and the consistency of the taste is not considered to be such a critical aspect.
3. ***Quick service*** – restaurants do not especially emphasize the speed of the service and do not sell only or mainly sandwiches. They also serve complete meals on the plate. The variety of products is usually larger than that of the sandwich shop. The service cycle times are also normally longer, but this is not regarded as a problem given that typical 'quick service' customers are not necessarily interested in the fastest service, but rather a service which takes the appropriate time – which should be sufficient for them to enjoy the ambience of the restaurant (which is therefore important). Normally, quick service restaurants take more care with ambience than the sandwich shops. Here the service dimension is similar to the traditional restaurants.

4. ***Traditional*** – most of the restaurants in São Paulo are in this category. The menu is varied and customers are able to specify the way in which the dishes are prepared. This makes the service cycle times longer and more variable than in quick service restaurants. As customers are expected to wait longer in the site, the restaurant usually takes greater care with the ambience and also provides some mechanisms to 'amuse' or occupy the customers (e.g. a bar) in order that their perceptions about the delay are reduced. Italian and Indian restaurants are good examples of this category.
5. ***Luxury*** – here ambience has maximum importance. Service is normally quite formal and the environment is designed to give an impression of sophistication, which requires that equipment (furnishings, etc.) is carefully chosen. Concern with service speed becomes secondary, since customers come for a pleasant time and a sophisticated environment.

## AB&P – ORIGINAL STRATEGY

It is not always easy to classify a restaurant, because the above categories are not completely self-contained. In fact they represent stages of a continuum. However, AB&P's partners noticed that there was a gap in the continuum in São Paulo at the 'quick service' stage. They also reckoned that the quick service type of restaurant would serve well the aim of establishing a restaurant chain rather than a single restaurant.

The partners noticed that to be in the quick service category, AB&P should have some of the characteristics of fast food, e.g. care with cleanliness and hygiene, and relatively quick service, but with great consistency in both quality of the products and service time. AB&P should also have some of the characteristics of the conventional restaurants, such as the higher quality of the food (deriving from special care with the quality of ingredients, the production process and the appearance of the dishes), the variety of the dishes served and the ambience.

The partners decided that, as distinctive or critical factors of AB&P's competitive strategy, they would emphasize the following:

1. ***Quality of the products served*** – they would have a distinctive taste and appearance, always creating the perception of 'quality food'.
2. ***Ambience*** – the emphasis would be on the 'modernity' of the ambience, which should always reflect 'AB&P's distinctive atmosphere'.

By analysing these strategic objectives, Dr Mattar decided that some critical operational factors should be emphasized:

1. ***The architectural and interior design of the shops.*** This would always emphasize 'modernity'. The interior design and decoration should always be 'clean', i.e. without unnecessary details. The decoration would always have style references to the train wagons, because of the original concept based on the American diners. Every piece of equipment and every object, such as plates, cutlery, chairs, table mats, etc., should also emphasize the concepts of 'modernity' and quality, even if this should mean higher costs. The partners were conscious that this would require an extra creative effort (e.g. finding sponsors to buy space for publicity in the menus) in order that they could achieve the project at the desired quality levels.
2. ***The quality of the recipes, ingredients and process.*** This would be distinctive. All the recipes would be developed in-house. The ingredients should also be of extra quality, and only supplied by previously tried and certified suppliers. As to the production process, as far as possible the dishes should only be 'finalized' in the shops. The components which most influence the perception of quality (e.g. pasta sauces and hamburgers) would be made in a central kitchen, where process control methods should be used to keep quality and methods standard.

3. ***Hygiene and cleanliness***. Emphasis would be put on employee training with regard to hygiene and cleanliness. They would be extremely important in establishing and consolidating the AB&P brand, as meaning *reliable quality* in all respects.
4. ***Informality, speed and consistency of services***. Waiters would not be as formal as in a conventional restaurant, but would be cordial, professional and very polite. This restricted, for example, the employment of 'part-time' staff. Priority would be given to professional waiters and maitres. The need for speed and consistency led to the development of a computerized service cycle time control system, and also to investment in the development of 'teamwork' and commitment among the employees.

From the beginning, the partners knew that they would face some of the usual problems in similar service activities in São Paulo and that some could jeopardize the achievement of their objectives. The main expected problems would be poorly qualified people in the labour market and the lack of consistency and quality of supplies.

To safeguard against these factors, Dr Mattar established rigorous criteria for selecting and hiring people. An intensive new employee training programme was established and special attention was given to the search for and approval of suppliers, together with the development of a quality control system for the bought-in ingredients. Eventually, in practice, worries about the difficulties with the human resources were justified. During the first three months of operation of the first shop, 50% of the employees had to be replaced because they were unable to meet (despite training) AB&P's needs. With regard to supplies, great managerial effort was always required to keep the product quality consistent.

# THE AB&P HISTORY

## The opening of the first shop: the start-up of the chain

The first AB&P restaurant opened in December 1985 on an important avenue in São Paulo, in a district where mainly upper middle class and young urban liberal professionals live. The choice of the site was based on visibility and on the type of local population.

In the first phase, the marketing strategy emphasized the restaurant as a 'trendy' place, aiming at establishing and developing the AB&P 'brand'. AB&P hired the services of experts in press and public relations in order to devise strategies to attract São Paulo's 'trendsetters'. This was successful but Dr Mattar knew that the 'trendsetters' are not necessarily loyal to places and brands, so a second phase was necessary. This would aim to broaden the range of customers. During this phase the image of 'modernity' would be consolidated, eventually replacing the 'fashion' image.

## The 'cruzado' governmental plan

In March 1986, when the second phase of AB&P's marketing strategy had just started, President Jose Sarney's government decreed the 'cruzado' economic plan (or 'package'). This froze all prices and salaries, at a time when inflation was at more than 20% per month. The price freeze helped AP&B keep its prices at a relatively low and stable level and helped attract new customers, cheered by the momentary economic growth (which would later be seen only as a deceiving demand 'bubble' rather than sustained economic recovery).

AB&P's turnover grew at the impressive rate of 150% in the first six months of operation. The management then became worried about the risk of losing consistency of quality, and decided to establish AB&P's first centralized industrial kitchen. It had 150 $m^2$ of space and capacity for the production of 32 different products, of those used in the menu. It was to start operating at the time of the opening of the second restaurant. The main objective of the central kitchen was to achieve tighter control over the products which most influenced customer perception of quality, and also to achieve scale economies in production through industrial-scale processing.

AB&P grew at the rate originally planned by the partners, making it possible to achieve their original goal of opening a new restaurant every year. The second was opened in November 1987 (together with the start-up of the central kitchen), the third opened in October 1988 and the fourth in March 1989.

Late in 1988 management noticed that the first central kitchen would reach its capacity limit at the time the fourth restaurant started operation, so they drew up plans to establish a new and larger kitchen. They decided to move on to a new location, an 800-$m^2$ plant, with modern and versatile equipment, capable of preparing 68 different products and with a capacity sufficient to support the operation of 20 restaurants. With the new kitchen, the original objective of only finishing the dishes in the restaurant sites could be achieved, thus ensuring levels of quality consistency of products and also improving the levels of consistency in the service cycle time, since less operations should be performed in the restaurants following customer order.

## The Collor economic plan

Everything was going well for the chain (despite the recession in the country) when in March 1990 the first freely elected president in 30 years, F. Collor, took power.

One of the first measures taken by the president, who inherited an inflation rate then reaching 80% per month (the freezing of prices and salaries of the 'cruzado' plan had been gradually relaxed since 1986), was a series of decrees (then called 'provisional measures') which became known as the 'Collor economic plan'. These included a new freeze of prices and salaries and also the 'arrest' of most of the means of payment of the economy, including current accounts, deposit accounts and investment accounts of companies and individuals. (The arrest would last 18 months, during which the major part of the means of payment were unavailable to the owners. From the nineteenth month on, the funds would be given back in 18 monthly instalments.)

The plan caused an initial euphoria, which soon turned into a nightmare that affected most of the sectors of the Brazilian economy: the final result was a severe deepening of the recession and high levels of unemployment. For example, it resulted in the reductions in AB&P's market shown in Table C16.1.

Given the new scenario, the partners were determined to reposition the AB&P chain, as profit margins could not support such a dramatic reduction in income. Additionally, some competitors, most of them single restaurants, were struggling to survive by competing, frequently in an unfair or at least uneven way. Many of them operated and dealt with their suppliers and employees in an 'informal' way, by not paying all the due taxes. As well as being 'irregular', such practices were impossible for an organization such as AB&P, because of the tighter controls the government kept on larger organizations.

**Table C16.1**

| Reduction in the: | AB&P | All restaurant businesses |
|---|---|---|
| Number of customers | 20% | 25–30% |
| Consumption per customer | 1–15% | 10–15% |
| Total turnover | approx. 35% | approx. 45% |

## AB&P's response to the deepening recession

AB&P's management decided to tackle the problem on three fronts:

1. By ***increasing productivity*** to reduce the breakeven level. They did not consider reducing their prices because the demand was not very price elastic (sufficiently to influence demand, the reductions in price would have to be around 30%, which would make AB&P unviable).
2. By adjusting the ***market strategy*** to win market share – mainly through promotions and by increasing the product line flexibility to secure new market niches such as the professional public (for the day-to-day lunch) and children (who would obviously bring their parents along).
3. By ***restructuring*** the chain management – to achieve greater economies of scale by centralizing suitable operations and to establish better management and financial control procedures (of paramount importance during periods of high inflation).

Some of the managerial actions now taken by AB&P's management in order to try to achieve these objectives, and, where known, the results obtained to date, are listed below.

## Increasing productivity

### *Productivity of the ingredients*

A thorough study was done on the required quantity of each ingredient per dish, to fix 'standard' portions, so that standards of 'productivity' per ingredient could be established. Also, a work study was carried out on the operations for preparing dishes, in order to eliminate waste. Standard containers for sauces and other ingredients were designed. Measures to standardize the meat cutting operation were adopted, and amongst others, exact measures for salads, chips and other side dishes were established and implemented.

Simultaneously, a computer system was developed to *control* the quantity of ingredients actually used, with the predetermined standards. The largest discrepancies could be identified and the appropriate actions to achieve productivity gains could be prioritized and performed. One of the findings of the system was that AB&P used twice as much sauce as it should have done (compared to standard portions). This increased costs and reduced margins.

### *Workforce productivity*

#### *Analysis of the jobs and tasks*

The aim was to reduce the amount of labour per restaurant. This analysis, together with a persistent drop in demand, gave the possibility of substantial reductions in personnel.

#### *New compensation and reward policy*

The aim was to motivate the workforce to fight waste. Here an unexpected phenomenon was identified. According to Dr Mattar:

> 'When we did the first analyses of the use of ingredients based on the standard portions, we found out that the levels of waste in the use of the premium meat we use to prepare the grilled rumpsteak was approximately 20%, caused either by careless cutting, misuse or theft. In other words, AB&P was spending 20% more on meat than was needed to make the grilled rumpsteak dishes. We then tried to introduce a new reward scheme, based on a positive reinforcement technique. In order to motivate the employees to reduce waste we offered the kitchen team 10% increased salaries if they were successful

in fighting waste. At the end of one month of this policy, the new levels of waste were measured and, disappointingly, we found the same 20%. We then thought that maybe the level of increase in salary was not enough to motivate the team, so we decided to offer them 15% instead. At the end of the following month we measured again the level of waste: once again we found 20%. Given the unchanged level and after double checking the standard portions we decided to change the policy. We decided therefore to try a negative reinforcement policy this time. AB&P would reduce the salaries of the kitchen team at the end of the month by the value found to be wasted with no reasonable explanation.'

### Development of multiple skills for kitchen employees

Through a system of training and reward, the aim was to develop a different approach to the usual Brazilian restaurant practice which, generally, has dedicated employees for specific tasks. By training the kitchen employees to perform several tasks it would be possible to maintain fewer people in the kitchen during off-peak hours. The adoption of the multi-skills policy, according to AB&P's management, would not be easy, again because of the low level of skills of the workforce.

## Productivity of the facilities

### The 'home free delivery' service

Through this, meals would be sold without the customer occupying AB&P's physical facilities. Additionally, AB&P might win a share of the market of those who usually prefer to eat at home. A measure was taken in order to try to guarantee that customers get the quality they expect when ordering dishes to be delivered. A simplified menu is given to customers to use for their phone orders. This gives information regarding which dishes are more or less subject to their taste/appearance being affected by the delivery. In this way AB&P aimed to manage the levels of expectation of the customer (who otherwise would tend to expect the dish at home to be exactly the same as that in the restaurant).

### Industrial catering

With the objective of increasing the utilization of the central kitchen, Dr Mattar is also considering going into the 'industrial catering' market. His concerns, however, relate to the possibility of losing the focus of the business, because competition in 'industrial catering' would be based on criteria which are substantially different from those with which AB&P is familiar. Although a different brand would be used for the new 'industrial catering' line, both lines of products would have to share the same facilities and most of the workforce. This could cause a whole new set of managerial problems.

### Coffee served in a separate restaurant area

The traditional short strong coffee after the meal (a preference of nine out of ten Brazilians) which normally accompanies long and relaxing chats (which can last up to 30 minutes) will be served in a pleasant, small and cosy 'winter garden', next to the main meal room. So, customers should leave the table sooner, freeing it for the use of other customers and therefore possibly increasing dining capacity or levels of utilization of the facilities.

### Discounts

The aim is to try to level up the demand, by attracting people in the off-peak periods in the day, and at the same time alleviating peak hour load, when either sales can be lost or the service level can drop (e.g. in terms of waiting time).

### *Work methods and procedures in the dining room*

The objective here is to increase the consistency of the 'waiting to be served' time, for two main reasons. On the one hand, increased consistency will improve customer perception of service quality. Also, an improved consistency will help keep the customer turnover within the planned limits. According to Dr Mattar, the work methods used by AB&P would make it possible to reduce customer waiting time substantially, but this is not necessarily desirable because, from assessment of customers' views (AB&P assesses customer satisfaction continuously, through questionnaires and direct contact) it was discovered that they do not want to be served quicker than a specific time (20 to 25 minutes between ordering and receiving the order). If the service is quicker, customers feel as if someone wants to get rid of them. This has focused management on the consistency of the service cycle time and has prompted the implementation of a computer system which follows up the times of the events (e.g. being seated, ordering, receiving the order, ordering the bill, receiving the bill, paying and leaving) for each customer during their stay in the restaurant. One aim is to operate between a lower control limit for ordering time – the minimum the customer requires (20 to 25 minutes) – and an upper control limit, influenced by the need for high customer turnover and, consequently, a high level of capacity utilization. With regard to the consistency of the service cycle time, AB&P innovated in the distribution of tasks among the staff who work in contact with the customer. A new function was created, called 'marchador', responsible for the liaison between the kitchen and the table. So, in future it will no longer be the waiter who takes the dish from the kitchen to the customer table, but the 'marchador'. In this way, the finished dish should not be kept waiting for the waiter to be free of his other tasks of seating customers and taking orders, making suggestions and checking the customer satisfaction.

## Marketing strategy

In order to broaden the range of customers and also to recover possible lost customers, AB&P made attempts to innovate in its marketing policies as follows.

### *Promotions*

A marketing professional was hired to be in charge of promotions. Some which are to be tried are the sponsorship of theatre plays and shows, and publicity in radios and cinema. A promotion was planned in which the customer could choose one of several AB&P postcards, write a message to someone and address it, and AB&P would send it to anywhere. Another promotion will be a competition where the customers are invited to suggest a new slogan for the restaurant. The winners will win prizes and trips.

AB&P also intend to reduce the price of one dish of each menu section (pasta, grilled, salads and so on) during one month. This discount would not affect all the dishes (which might affect viability) but it should allow 'professional' customers to spend less on their day-to-day lunch.

### *Menu flexibility*

The aim is to enable some dishes to be 'assembled to order' for the customer, from a variety of pasta, meat, salad and side dish types. The aim is to reduce the price paid by the customers and possibly to attract those customers who would otherwise consider AB&P to be too expensive for their day-to-day lunch. AB&P will also create a self-service buffet of salads, with a fixed price, cheaper than most of its dishes. AB&P will also try to secure a new market niche represented by children through promotions (e.g. simple puzzles printed in the children's dish paper mats), lower prices ('kid's menu') and simpler dishes more adequate to the children's taste. The idea behind this promotion is that there is always an adult accompanying a child and he or she will pay regular prices for his or her meal.

### *Role of the waiters in suggesting dishes*

The aim is to give waiters a more positive role but with the necessary subtlety in order to suggest dishes and drinks which result in higher profit margins (e.g. natural fruit juices instead of sparkling drinks). In this way AB&P aims to try to increase the margins per dish in order to offset the reduction in turnover.

## Restructuring

After the fourth restaurant was inaugurated, AB&P was reconstructed, by centralizing and, where possible, computerizing personnel control and payroll, accountability, stock control and management control systems. The objective was to reduce the overhead burden and improve efficiency. So, for example, for the opening of the fifth restaurant, in November 1990, the process was much smoother than with the first four restaurants, because 50% of the personnel for running the fifth restaurant were taken from the first four, and only 50% were newcomers, recruited in the market. The problem with turnover during the first months of operation was much simpler and easier to overcome.

# AB&P – FUTURE PLANS

AB&P opened its sixth restaurant in August 1991, so the original plan of growing at a rate of one new restaurant per year has been broadly achieved so far. Following the original plans, the capital for the opening of the last restaurants was attracted from the market, by admitting new partners, mainly 'capitalist' partners with no administrative role. The introduction of new partners bringing in capital is seen to be important, as AB&P's management has decided not to use the 'franchise' system because they are afraid of losing control over their critical competitive aspects such as quality.

The plan now is vigorously to pursue the actions taken since 1990, to build on successful actions and to look again at those which are less successful and to try, therefore, to follow the original expansion plan.

In the operation of the chain the emphasis will be on reducing waste of all kinds, automating and centralizing administrative activities for economies of scale, refining the computerized management control systems, and continuously seeking productivity gains without jeopardizing the desired levels of quality, service and product flexibility. On the marketing side, the intention is continuously to reassess and reposition AB&P's marketing strategy, in order to be able to respond well and quickly to the constant changes in the market.

Case study 17

# La Patisserie - A

La Patisserie is a small bakery and confectionery business operating from leased premises in a Thames Valley market town in England. The business is owned and managed by Mr Arnold, a master baker, assisted by his son, and it consists of a shop, where all the bakery products are sold, and the bakery itself, which is at the back of the shop out of the sight of customers.

The production of bread, pastries and confectionery is based on traditional methods, as Mr Arnold explained:

> 'We use a big traditional oven and make large batches of the different products. The oven takes a long time to heat up and so we heat it to the right temperature for the bread, which needs the highest temperature, and bake the bread first. Then the other products are baked in the residual heat as the oven cools down.'

This method is the most economical, but it is extremely time-consuming and expensive to have to go back through the cycle of bread, pastry and confectionery and therefore, once production of each product is complete, more of an earlier product cannot be produced. This method of operation means that it is necessary to decide in advance how much of each product is to be produced, and these amounts are fixed for each day's operations.

In addition to the traditional baking methods, the bakery employs traditional preparation and mixing. Three full-time bakers are employed, working overlapping shifts beginning at 4.30 a.m. and finishing at midday. Thus most of the products are ready for customers when the shop opens at 9.00 a.m. and the rest of the morning is spent preparing for the next day or making items which are made less frequently, such as malt bread, which is only made twice weekly. The bakers have assistants to carry out routine work such as cleaning, tin greasing and so on. Traditionally, master bakers do not carry out tasks of this nature; they are carried out by assistants learning the trade. None of the baking staff work in the shop.

The preparation and mixing of the various doughs is a skilled and time-consuming job. Bread dough, for example, takes three hours to mix properly and then has to be 'proved', which normally occurs overnight. High-speed mixers can be bought but the business does not have one.

The mixing and baking technology limits the rate of response to demand. It is possible to forecast demand reasonably well from past history, but once the day's production is decided it cannot be changed to cater for changes in demand. Because the goods are perishable, it is impossible in most cases to store them and hence the objective is to sell out. This can, however, mean failure to meet demand later in the day. It also means that it is difficult to allow for casual demand and since the town attracts a large number of tourists, casual demand can be high.

There is some fairly well-known fluctuation in demand for particular products throughout the week, and there is fairly well-known demand for seasonal products such as Christmas cakes. Hence the shop has a planned weekly production schedule, and production of seasonal items is added as necessary. Some items which are of a slightly less perishable nature such as malt bread can be held in stock for two or three days and do not have to be made daily. Malt bread, for example, is made twice weekly. Fruit bread is also made twice weekly because it requires a special oven temperature. This cannot be held in stock ready for sale since it is highly perishable but it responds well to freezing, and sufficient bread to meet daily demand is taken out for thawing and sale. Pastry is also made in large batches and much of the raw pastry frozen, with only sufficient for the day's production being taken out.

Items from the standard range can be ordered by customers, and the bakery will also produce items to customer demand. Normally all necessary stocks are held but special items will be bought in if required.

There is rigid demarcation between the jobs carried out in the bakery and those in the shop. Most of the counter staff work part time since the shop is fairly quiet in the mornings, and there are five boys and girls still at school who work on Saturdays and during holidays.

Because the business is small, the quantities of materials consumed are fairly small and the shop does not have sufficient space to stock large quantities. In addition, the materials are perishable so that the length of time for which they can be stored is limited. Mr Arnold, however, belongs to the London Bakers Buyers Association. This is a professional buying group owned by the bakers, which buys in bulk, and hence gives the smaller bakers the advantage of a bulk-buying discount without having to carry excessive stocks.

At the time of this study Mr Arnold had decided to purchase new premises in the town:

> 'You see, I'd like to update things a bit – buy some of the newer equipment. Finance is no problem: I'm my own boss and this is a good business; the beauty of that is that I can please myself what I spend the money on, provided the bank manager is satisfied, and he is. The problem is that I don't want to put the new equipment in here. I've rented for years but over the last few years the rent has shot up and I can see the time coming when it's just not economical to carry on here. I'd be a bit silly investing a lot of money here under those circumstances.'

Mr Arnold believed that there was enough business in the town to justify operating two retail outlets, but if the rent for the existing premises became excessive the entire business could be carried out from the new branch. He was undecided, however, about how to manage the two branches.

The new premises were about half a mile away and although Mr Arnold wanted both outlets to be reasonably independent, he thought there might be some merit in a certain amount of interdependence:

> 'The new shop will be managed by my son but we want it to have its own identity and customers, otherwise it will just take customers from the old branch and we shan't increase the overall business. On the other hand, the equipment we have at the old branch is capable of producing all the cakes and pastries for both branches and it seems silly to duplicate it at the new branch. What we'd like to do is buy a new high-speed mixer and an electric oven for the new branch. That combination would give us far more flexibility than we have at present because if we baked in small batches we could respond to demand almost as it happens. The high-speed mixer can produce a batch of bread dough in about an hour and we can change the temperature of the electric oven very quickly, so that we could bake small batches all day if demand seems to warrant it.'

Mr Arnold's proposal was that the existing branch should bake all the daily cakes and pastries for both branches whilst bread rolls and doughnuts should be introduced as new lines, baked at the new branch and taking advantage of the ability to respond flexibly to demand. Both branches would bake bread and seasonal products, such as Christmas and Easter cakes.

In principle this proposal seemed sound, but, as Mr Arnold said, there were a number of issues to be decided:

> 'If we are going to be so flexible in meeting demand we want it to be obvious to people that we are baking all the time and that, within reason, there is little chance of us being sold out by the mid-afternoon. In addition, if we are going to bake small batches we want to sell them almost as they come out of the oven; if we don't, stocks will build up and we'll finish up in the same situation as at the other shop with a day's supply ready for sale, but without the economies of baking in large batches. We also want to attract new customers and, in particular, the casual customers, because all this flexibility will be rather wasted if we don't. I think there may be something we can do with the layout of the bakery and the shop to attract people in.'

Mr Arnold is also well aware that his ideas are not compatible with the traditional working methods used at the old branch. Flexible response depends on the workers as well as the equipment and he is not sure how to get a flexible workforce.

Case study 18

# La Patisserie – B

Mr Arnold (junior), master baker, sat in the original Kings Street branch of La Patisserie reviewing the development of the business up to the situation today.

About 13 years ago his father had decided to open a second shop in Kings Street with electric ovens (see Case Study 17). He bought the Kings Street site and, about nine years ago, the original business was moved to a leased site close by in Book Street. The branches are no less than a kilometre distant from each other. The Book Street site has similar high-speed mixers. With these changes La Patisserie was, at both branches, able to be more flexible in making bread and pastries.

Since then, Mr Arnold (Jr) had taken over the firm, and his son Ricky joined seven years ago. Mr Arnold (Sr) had since died. During those years, La Patisserie had moved from making traditional English to French country food. They make quite a lot of French bread because it is a premium-priced product that can be made all day and it is one of the best profit generators. Another good profit generator is the doughnut. As Mr Arnold (Jr) said, 'The humble doughnut has been a cash cow all my life.'

Having two shops in the same town has worked very well, with many items, such as pastries, cakes, filled rolls and sandwiches, developing rapidly. At peak employment, Mr Arnold (Jr) had a staff of 25 people, which had now reduced to 15 in spite of producing about the same physical volume. Two years ago, his sales peaked at about £500 000 per annum, on which he made about £120 000 gross profit. The sales are currently running at £450 000 and physical volumes have decreased by 4% per year over the last two years. Records indicate that customers were shopping less frequently per week and there was no reason to expect a reversal.

During these general recessionary times (which have existed now three years) the Kings Street branch has been particularly hit by shops and offices closing nearby. Together with the shops and offices closing, there is a general increase in vehicles clogging the road outside. People find it unpleasant to walk around this area of town. As opportunities increased at Book Street, Mr Arnold (Jr) consolidated resources at that branch, further emphasizing the disparity between the shops.

Over the period manufacturing worked well but had been changed to a condition where one shop made bread and the other made cakes. Both shops sell the same product range and this worked well until the last four years. Over the past four years or so, Mr Arnold (Jr) could see that the shops were competing against one another: alternatively he was operating from two sites where one would be sufficient. He realized that moving to one site would cause a fall in sales.

Another change which had taken place was to buy in frozen puff, Danish and savoury pastry. The bought product was just as good as that which he made, and more consistent. The reliability of puff pastry delivery was also improved; as he said, 'frozen puff does not take a day off in a bank holiday week'.

At present La Patisserie makes small batches throughout the day. The final decision of how much to make is taken at about two o'clock in the afternoon. The policy of Mr Arnold (Jr) concerning trading is 'If we are here, we are open.'

Bakers start at between 4 and 4.30 a.m. and the door is unlocked. These bakers bake and serve until servers arrive at about 8.30 a.m. It is unlikely that the bakers can offer the full range early, but by 5 a.m. they can offer a cup of tea and something for early customers to buy. Trade increased because of this early opening, especially during summer. Mr Arnold (Jr) uses most of his manufacturing staff in selling during peak periods, including the fresh cream and sandwich makers. He maintains the delicate balance of the time spent by the bakers selling, and sometimes when sales are very high and pastries or bread are starting to diminish too quickly he says 'the wall is up – concentrate on the baking and if we cannot serve the customers, bad luck'.

Management at La Patisserie comprises three people: Mr Arnold (Jr), his son Ricky, and Alec. Mr Arnold (Jr) physically controls manufacturing and allows Ricky to concentrate on selling. He feels that Ricky is a better 'people manager' than he is. Ricky is likely to assign responsibility and ask 'why', where Mr Arnold (Jr) is likely to sympathize with staff. In addition, Alec comes in, on a part-time basis, to keep the computerized accounts and provide guidance as to the company's profitability. Alec is responsible for the payment of wages, accounts and banking. As there are virtually no debtors and little stock, quarterly comparisons are easily constructed.

The firm presently has two bakers beside Mr Arnold (Jr). This reduction has partly been brought about by bakers concentrating on specific lines. One baker concentrates on making bread, rolls and French bread, whilst the second concentrates on pastry. Mr Arnold (Jr) has measured the output of each baker over the last eight years and noted a doubling of output per baker over the previous five years. The bakers preferred the specialization but there were problems when bakers went on holiday. At such a time other bakers did not have adequate experience to bake at the same rate. When Mr Arnold (Jr) bakes himself, he finds that by ten o'clock in the morning he is an hour behind the other baker.

By doing baking himself, Mr Arnold (Jr) is able to experiment with small batches in a short time. With high-speed mixers and electric ovens, cycle times are short. Mixing lasts about two minutes and the bulk fermentation time of mixed dough is about two hours when quality reaches a peak. This dough is then placed in pans for baking. Mr Arnold (Jr) found that this method did not give adequate results for brown bread. He rediscovered, from early cookbooks, a superior method which he now employs. An example of his innovative ways was an accident when a baker dropped a sack of brown flour into a mix. This mix had to be changed to brown bread and some immigrants recognized this as the brown bread made in their country of origin. So, this is another variety of bread made to satisfy customer demand. The market for brown bread has grown continuously, even in the recession, and Mr Arnold (Jr) sees this market expanding as customers become more aware of health. Another product that La Patisserie introduced was bread without wheat to help those with allergies. As this bread was not made in a gluten-free environment, it was not suitable for people with coeliac disease but it helps to wean people from certain allergies. This had been formulated by a dietitian and it had taken about six months of experiments to develop an adequate seven-grain bread.

The quality of La Patisserie's products is considered by many customers to be excellent and Mr Arnold (Jr) is not concerned about supermarkets, like the Waitrose in town, entering his niche market. In general, supermarkets bake imported dough into products like rolls, which tend to have a heavy inside, a doubtful crust and a lack of volume. All of this leads to lower quality, and such products are unlikely to fool the many discriminating buyers around the town. In addition, La Patisserie concentrates on speciality items.

La Patisserie promotes the clean look. Outside, the white walls and glass contrast with other shops nearby, and the staff wear white caps and aprons to enhance the image. At present customers can see the bakers at work. Mr Arnold (Jr) wonders whether it is best to maintain this layout or to change back to baking in an environment 'which is mystical, out of sight, where customers can only get a glimpse'.

He sees that customers are becoming more conscious of hygiene and, as bakers work mainly by feel and touch, the public may be put off seeing bakers handling dough and other products. One particular example demonstrated this. After his sandwich maker started wearing gloves, sandwich sales doubled.

Regarding the future, Mr Arnold (Jr) wonders what he should do and he feels that timing is of the essence.

The lease on the Book Street branch comes to an end at the end of next year. One option is to lease the Kings Street site, which would yield about £20 000 per year. About half of this comes from the shop and half from two flats above the shop. He sees changes in shopping habits. A large Tesco supermarket is planned for the edge of the town. At present the supermarket, Waitrose, which is adjacent to his King Street shop attracts customers past his doors. Although Tesco is important he thinks that Waitrose's reaction will influence his sales more dramatically. Waitrose could expand to counter Tesco; could stay as it is; or close. Waitrose closing would be disastrous for him. The landlord of the Book Street branch of La Patisserie has been tardy in negotiating, and Mr Arnold (Jr) decided to wait to this point in time. His rental is about £24 000 per year at present and a commitment of another ten-year lease would be a poor decision if Waitrose closed. Mr Arnold (Jr) has spoken to a few of the managers at Waitrose and, although there was no comment, he knows that they are 'pretty miffed.'

Another option is to move everything to the Kings Street site and consider opening up in another town, not too distant. If he opens in another town the bakeries would have to be virtually independent. It could not be too distant for Mr Arnold (Jr) to maintain some physical control. A problem with moving to another town would be that different rules may operate and in that market people may not be prepared to pay for the product La Patisserie makes.

Case study 19

# K&S (Israel) Ltd

K&S (Israel) Ltd is a company that develops and produces machines for the microelectronic and semiconductor industry. It has about 300 employees, and manufactures three main product families, together with their associated requirements of spare parts.

## THE MAIN PRODUCTS AND MARKETS

The machine produced by the company are semi-automatic dicing and bonding machines. Only 50% of the machines sold by the company are 'standard' machines, and the rest are special applications, developed according to the client's needs and specifications.

The three main products are:

1. The ***wire bonding*** – an accurate bonding machine which uses metal wires for bonding in the hybrid industry. It is the simplest of the three products, and has the largest sales. Most of these sales are for standard machines, so it has relatively standard costs for manufacture.
2. The ***hybrid die bonder*** – a bonding machine for semiconductors. It is a fairly new product, with a low but steadily increasing sales rate.
3. The ***waffer saw*** – a very accurate saw for the cutting of chips. It is the most complex of the three machines, and has many complex versions.

The main markets for the company are the USA, Europe and the Far East. The market is very competitive, and the main factors that can increase sales are quality and shorter lead times.

## THE PRODUCTION PROCESS

Each of the products is an integration of several sub-assemblies and many components, numbering between 80 and 120, depending on the product. Some sub-assemblies are electronic, while others are mechanical, or both. Most sub-assemblies require a relatively short processing time (10 minutes to 1 hour); some go directly to integration while others are used in the next higher level sub-assemblies. About 80% of the sub-assemblies are made during the early stages of production.

There are six work stations in the production process:

st. 61 – electronic sub-assemblies, mainly of the early stages;

st. 64 – mechanical sub-assemblies;

st. 67 – quality control of sub-assemblies;

st. 27 – final integration and check of wire bonder;

st. 75 – final integration and check of waffer saw;

s.t 76 – final integration and check of die bonder.

The 'final integration' is a complicated process, whose times vary greatly around a mean of 50 hours.

Each sub-assembly is defined by its position in the production tree, its processing time, and the station that produces it.

A list of sub-assemblies in each product is given in Tables C19.1, C19.2 and C19.3.

Ordinarily, workers cannot be transferred between stations, since the work at each station is highly specialized. However, transfers together with some training have occurred in the past. The number of workers and typical overtime per week in each station are given in Table C19.4. Every work station has a work list, and gets kits with all the components needed for the items in the work list.

## THE PRODUCTION PLANNING PROCESS

The market requires short lead times, and therefore demand is known only for the very near future. However, raw materials have very long lead times (about three months) and should be ordered months ahead. Production planning is based on demand forecast, which considers a year ahead, but usually the actual demand does not match the forecast very well. The forecast is updated quarterly according to actual orders. Some machines are produced to orders while others are produced to stock, according to the demand forecast. A typical sales forecast for a quarter is given in Table C19.5.

The basic planning period for the company is a quarter. At each quarter, the production planner receives a report of the actual orders and the demand forecast for that quarter, and plans production accordingly. First, a master production schedule (MPS) is drawn by 'smoothing' the demand over the quarter, so that the number of machines completed each week is approximately equal. This is called the balanced 'macro' schedule, and is an input to both material requirement planning and production planning. While the MPS appears to give a balanced workload to the work stations over the quarter, in actuality it does not, since it does not consider the different resource requirements for the different machines at the various production stages.

The MPS is updated once a week, according to actual orders.

The next stage of production planning is the 'micro' schedule: the actual sub-assemblies required at each station for each week according to the 'macro' schedule. The production planning system does not consider the work capacity of the stations, and therefore may give a schedule requiring overtime in one week, while idle time occurs in the following week. In such cases, the user tries to alter the 'macro' schedule in order to find a better 'micro' schedule, but the change process is totally heuristic, lacking any knowledge on how to improve the outcome. However, the system does notify the user that capacity is exceeded, and that subcontracting or overtime is needed. The company restricts overtime for each employee to three hours at a time, and no more than twice a week. The separate planning in each quarter often causes a workload inbalance at the stations; i.e. towards the end of a quarter, all the planned machines must be completed, and therefore when a new quarter begins, there is plenty of machine time available.

The 'micro' schedule is planned so that sub-assemblies are transferred between work stations once a week, and this results in artificially long lead times, since a machine cannot be completed in less than four weeks, although the typical CPM network of the wire bonder shows that it can be manufactured in less than 60 hours. The only advantage in this weekly transfer method is in simplifying the kitting of sub-assemblies. The CPM networks of the products can be drawn according to the data in Tables C19.1, C19.2 and C19.3, which also include the slack time for each sub-assembly.

**Table C19.1 Wire bonder sub-assemblies**

| Catalogue number | Processing time (h) | Work station | Slack time | Predecessors |
|---|---|---|---|---|
| 9021 | 5.5 | 72 | 0 | 7300 0201 0403 |
| 7300 | 1.9 | 64 | 6.75 | 1840 |
| 1840 | 1.2 | 61 | 6.65 | |
| 0201 | 2.2 | 64 | 0 | 0211 0220 4320 7200 0001 0213 |
| 0211 | 1.9 | 64 | 4.25 | |
| 0220 | 0.5 | 64 | 4.15 | 11401 |
| 11401 | 3.4 | 61 | 4.15 | |
| 4320 | 1.65 | 61 | 4.4 | |
| 7200 | 0.7 | 64 | 4.3 | 1510 0555 |
| 1510 | 0.35 | 61 | 4.6 | |
| 0555 | 0.3 | 64 | 4.3 | |
| 0001 | 0.55 | 67 | 0.7 | 0110 |
| 0110 | 4.15 | 61 | 0.7 | |
| 0213 | 4.8 | 61 | 0 | 1210 |
| 1210 | 0.8 | 61 | 0 | |
| 0403 | 1.7 | 64 | 4.75 | 0460 0450 0420 0410 1837 0455 2300 |
| 0460 | 0.9 | 64 | 4.75 | 1730 |
| 1730 | 0.2 | 61 | 4.85 | |
| 0450 | 1 | 64 | 4.65 | 0452 |
| 0452 | 0.3 | 64 | 4.65 | 1710 |
| 1710 | 0.4 | 61 | 4.65 | |
| 0420 | 0.7 | 64 | 1.65 | 0427 0770 0040 |
| 0427 | 0.55 | 61 | 4.75 | |
| 0770 | 0.5 | 72 | 4.45 | |
| 0040 | 3.15 | 72 | 1.65 | 1000 |
| 1000 | 0.15 | 61 | 1.65 | |
| 0410 | 1.35 | 64 | 4.1 | 0412 |
| 0412 | 0.3 | 64 | 4.35 | 1500 |
| 1500 | 0.75 | 61 | 4.1 | |
| 1837 | 0.75 | 61 | 5.35 | |
| 0455 | 0.15 | 64 | 5.35 | 0555 1885 |
| 1885 | 0.1 | 61 | 5.4 | |
| 2300 | 0.25 | 64 | 4.75 | 3000 |
| 3000 | 1.55 | 61 | 4.75 | |

**Table C19.2 Die bonder sub-assemblies**

| Catalogue number | Processing time (h) | Work station | Slack time | Predecessors |
|---|---|---|---|---|
| 0571 | 0.2 | 64 | 12.5 | |
| 0593 | 0.2 | 64 | 11.8 | |
| 1300 | 3.9 | 61 | 8.1 | |
| 1601 | 1.0 | 61 | 12.1 | |
| 1602 | 0.5 | 61 | 13.1 | |
| 2620 | 3.6 | 61 | 8.5 | |
| 1110 | 0.75 | 61 | 1.85 | |
| 1130 | 1.5 | 61 | 0.0 | |
| 0570 | 3.95 | 64 | 11.6 | |
| 1502 | 1.4 | 61 | 11.7 | |
| 1503 | 1.1 | 61 | 12 | |
| 1950 | 1.5 | 61 | 12.3 | |
| 0800 | 0.16 | 64 | 16.4 | |
| 4120 | 2.1 | 67 | 18.6 | |
| 1504 | 4 | 61 | 17.2 | |
| 0200 | 5 | 76 | 8.1 | 0571 1300 1502 1601 1602 2620 |
| 0130 | 3.15 | 64 | 15.4 | |
| 1400 | 1.05 | 61 | 15.4 | |
| 0585 | 1.5 | 64 | 16.8 | |
| 1100 | 11 | 61 | 0.0 | 1110 1130 |
| 0301 | 4.5 | 76 | 11.6 | 0570 1503 1601 1950 |
| 2120 | 4 | 61 | 16.44 | 0800 |
| 0210 | 0.4 | 64 | 28.4 | |
| 0302 | 1 | 61 | 28.1 | |
| 0051 | 20 | 76 | 0.0 | 0200 0130 1400 0585 1100 0301 1504 2120 |
| 9003 | 30 | | 0.0 | 0210 0593 2302 0051 4120 |

**Table C19.3 Wafer saw sub-assemblies**

| Catalogue number | Processing time (h) | Work station | Slack time | Predecessors |
|---|---|---|---|---|
| 9006 | 49.5 | 75 | 0.0 | 3852 4350 0050 3850 |
| 3852 | 0.15 | 64 | 50.45 | |
| 4350 | 0.5 | 67 | 50.1 | |
| 0050 | 20 | 75 | 0.0 | 2010 0810 10130 2001 10200 11503 0526 0826 10514 |
| 2010 | 2.85 | 61 | 29.6 | |
| 0810 | 2.15 | 64 | 29.6 | |
| 10130 | 3 | 64 | 27 | 11601 |
| 11601 | 0.9 | 61 | 27 | |
| 2001 | 2.25 | 61 | 30.1 | |
| 10200 | 16.5 | 61 | 0.0 | 4027 11400 0806 1800 4340 10210 4541 4180 11100 11700 1701 |
| 4027 | 0.25 | 67 | 13.85 | |
| 11400 | 7.5 | 61 | 5.5 | 4400 |
| 4400 | 2 | 61 | 5.5 | |
| 0806 | 0.55 | 64 | 13.85 | |
| 1800 | 5.3 | 61 | 8.8 | |
| 4340 | 0.4 | 67 | 13.7 | |
| 10210 | 2.55 | 61 | 12.35 | |
| 4541 | 1.15 | 67 | 13.35 | |
| 11100 | 9.5 | 61 | 0.0 | 11110 |
| 11110 | 3.6 | 61 | 0.0 | 4510 |
| 4510 | 1 | 61 | 0.0 | |
| 11700 | 2 | 61 | 12.6 | |
| 4180 | 1 | 67 | 13.1 | |
| 1701 | 1.5 | 61 | 13.1 | |
| 11503 | 0.6 | 61 | 30 | |
| 0526 | 0.68 | 64 | 29.8 | |
| 0826 | 0.0 | 75 | 28.3 | 0726 |
| 0726 | 2 | 75 | 28.3 | 0825 |
| 0825 | 0.3 | 64 | 28.3 | |
| 10514 | 0.4 | 64 | 30.4 | |
| 3850 | 3.5 | 64 | 46.1 | 3841 3851 |
| 3841 | 1 | 64 | 46.1 | |

**Table C19.4 Number of workers in work stations**

| Station number | Workers | Typical weekly overtime (h) |
|---|---|---|
| 61 | 7–8 | 35 |
| 64 | 3 | 17 |
| 67 | 3–4 | 0 |
| 72 | 3 | 2 |
| 75 | 4–5 | 9 |
| 76 | 3 | 5 |

**Table C19.5 A typical recent sales forecast**

| Machine | January | February | March |
|---|---|---|---|
| Wire bonder | 4 | 3 | 4 |
| Wafer saw | 24 | 28 | 25 |
| Die bonder | 9 | 8 | 10 |

Case study 20[1]

# TAARUP Farming Machines Ltd

During the 1977–1987 decade, production volume at TAARUP Farming Machines Ltd, Kerteminde, Denmark was doubled, while the number of different machine models more than quadrupled through an increase from 45 to 210, as illustrated in Table C20.1. This development reflected the company's sales policy of increasingly satisfying the preferences of individual farmers as much as possible, but it did leave the company with average annual production volumes of each individual model reduced to less than half the previous volume.

Farming machine sales to the final customers – the farmers – obviously display a strong seasonality. Upward of 60% of annual sales are delivered during a three-month spring period, so production smoothing is an economic necessity and inventory build-up in anticipation of need is an inevitable consequence.

Some prediction of future need is possible, of course. The need for product 'function' may be predicted with some certainty because it is related to crops and acreage which change rather slowly from year to year. Some prediction of the demand for product type may also be made, although with less certainty. The change in size, type and power of tractors in use, for example, will reflect itself in the demand for different sizes of farming machines performing one specific function. At the lowest level of specification, however, it comes down to meeting the whims of each individual farmer needing a machine of a certain size for a certain function, and prediction of demand becomes almost impossible. Even the farmer himself may not have made up his mind about which model to choose before he is ready to buy.

When the model range was relatively limited, the production policy consisted of taking batches of machine models through to a completed machine inventory from which customers could be served immediately upon placing their orders. With limited uncertainty the company could adapt to the 'principle of speculation' which requires any changes in the specification of goods by customers to be made at the earliest possible time in order to reduce the costs of the production and marketing system. Some efforts were made to encourage machine dealers and import agents to place their orders early and thus shift the risk to independent distributor inventories.

As the model range increased, however, so did the risk of making wrong decisions. Obviously, it must be much more difficult to predict the demand for each of 210 different models than for each of 45 models, and so increasingly the company had to adopt the 'principle of postponement', which requires no production except to specific order and thus shifts the risks to the buyer – albeit with a longer delivery time, and the consequent risk to the company of competition with less cautious

[1] Translated and adapted from Danish material by graduate student Christian Lanng Nielsen and Professor Dr Bendt Rorsted, Institute of Management, University of Aarhus, Denmark.

manufacturers. Indeed, with the strong seasonality, total adherence to the principle of postponement would have to entail either a ruinous excess capacity or loss of sales to customers who would not tolerate the long delivery times necessary.

Thus a compromise had to be struck and the concept of a basic machine was developed. The basic machine would be the common content of several machine models, each of which would consist of the basic machine with the addition of a combination of supplementary parts and components (Table C20.2) (these are nine models of machine type DM 1500. Each model consists of a basic machine plus supplementary parts. Five of the models are identified in the table, i.e. 47, 002, 301–305).

**Table C20.1 Product variety: 1977, 1982 and 1987**

| Type | | | Number of different models of each type | | |
|---|---|---|---|---|---|
| | | | 1977 | 1982 | 1987 |
| DM | 1100 | Forage Harvester | 3 | 14 | 11 |
| DM | 1500 | Forage Harvester | – | 14 | 9 |
| NS | 1100 | Forage Harvester | 4 | 6 | 8 |
| S | 1250 | Forage Harvester | 4 | 6 | 8 |
| S | 1500 | Forage Harvester | 4 | 6 | 8 |
| BS | 1500 | Double Chop | – | 11 | – |
| DC | 1500 | Double Chop | 3 | 11 | 18 |
| 502 | | Fine Chop | – | – | 7 |
| 404 | | Fine Chop | – | – | 2 |
| 405 | | Fine Chop | – | – | 10 |
| DCE | 1500 | Precision Chop Forage Harvester | 5 | – | – |
| SE | 2100 | Precision Chop Forage Harvester | – | 8 | – |
| 602 | | Precision Chop Forage Harvester | – | – | 25 |
| 605 | | Precision Chop Forage Harvester | – | – | 6 |
| SK | 1500 | Flail Mower | 4 | – | – |
| SKB | 1800 | Flail Mower | 2 | 6 | – |
| SKT | 1500 | Flail Mower | 10 | 18 | 26 |
| SKT | 2100 | Flail Mower | – | 18 | 31 |
| SKT | 2150 | Flail Mower | – | 20 | – |
| SKT | 3000 | Flail Mower | – | 20 | – |
| TS | 1650 | Disc Mower | – | 10 | 10 |
| TSC | 2100 | Crimper | – | – | 7 |
| T3 | | Tipping Trailer | 6 | 10 | 21 |
| 107 | | Tipping Trailer | – | – | 4 |
| Total number of models – all types | | | 45 | 178 | 210 |

Table C20.2

# TAARUP Combination list DM 1500

| Date of issue: 27/03–92 | Price list for: | Price list No. | 1 |
|---|---|---|---|
| | **Specification** | Replaces price list No. | 0 |

| Part No. | Designation | Use | Combination – possibilities | | | | | | | | | Remarks |
|---|---|---|---|---|---|---|---|---|---|---|---|---|
| | | | 1 | 2 | 3 | 4 | 5 | 6 | 7 | 8 | 9 | |
| 47.276.000 | Basic machine | A | 1 | 1 | | | 1 | | | | | |
| 47.277.000 | Basic machine, Northireland | A | | | 1 | | | | | | | Incl. knives – pulleys – V-belts |
| 47.278.000 | Basic machine – IAM | A | | | | 1 | | | | | | Incl. knives – pulleys – V-belts |
| 47.341.000 | Grass attachment | B | 1 | | | | 1 | | | | | |
| 47.326.100 | Beet attachment | B | | 1 | | | | | | | | |
| 47.389.200 | Belt guard – open | C | 1 | | 1 | 1 | | | | | | |
| 47.461.100 | Belt guard – closed | C | | 1 | | | 1 | | | | | |
| 47.393.000 | Safety equipment | | | | | | 1 | | | | | Finland |
| 47.859.000 | Support wheel | | | | | | 1 | | | | | |

| Comb. No. | Remarks | Price |
|---|---|---|
| | | |
| | | |
| | | |
| | | |
| 47.002.305 | | |
| 47.002.304 | | |
| 47.002.303 | | |
| 47.002.302 | | |
| 47.002.301 | | |

There would be a basic machine for each overall size and function, roughly corresponding to each horizontal line in Table C20.1, and there would be a number of feasible alternative combinations roughly corresponding to the number in the last column of each horizontal line in Table C20.1.

Thus, as the prediction of the demand for basic machines could be relatively certain, while prediction of the demand for each individual model would be quite uncertain, inventory could now be shifted from completely finished machines for immediate delivery to basic machines for later final assembly with a relatively short delivery time reflecting the short time required to complete the model. Capacity utilization and resource productivity could be the primary objective in the production of basic machines, and customer satisfaction the primary objective of the last assembly process.

Formerly, the long winter build-up of finished machines inventory had enabled production with very comfortable working conditions up to the point in time when customer demand suddenly proved incompatible with inventory size, and immediate delivery of customer orders then became impossible. From this point onward there would be a mad rush to hurry supplementary machine batches through the entire production process before the start of the company's summer vacation which, incidentally, was often postponed by a week in order to clear the orders. The new concept would concentrate any rush to final assembly only, provided that sufficient intermediate inventory had been built up in time.

In order to facilitate the new way of thinking, the planning hierarchy was changed also, as illustrated in Figure C20.1.

Capacity planning was basically unchanged although substantial excess capacity in facilities and people had to be provided in final assembly. Summary activity scheduling for intermediate inventory was also basically unchanged as a due date planning process, but with decreasing significance of meeting due dates, since they were now primarily set for internal purposes.

The lowest-level planning, however, was entirely detached from the two higher levels. The objective now was to meet as best as possible all customer demand for delivery, even if inconsistent with original customer orders, subject to transportation options and availability of intermediate inventory.

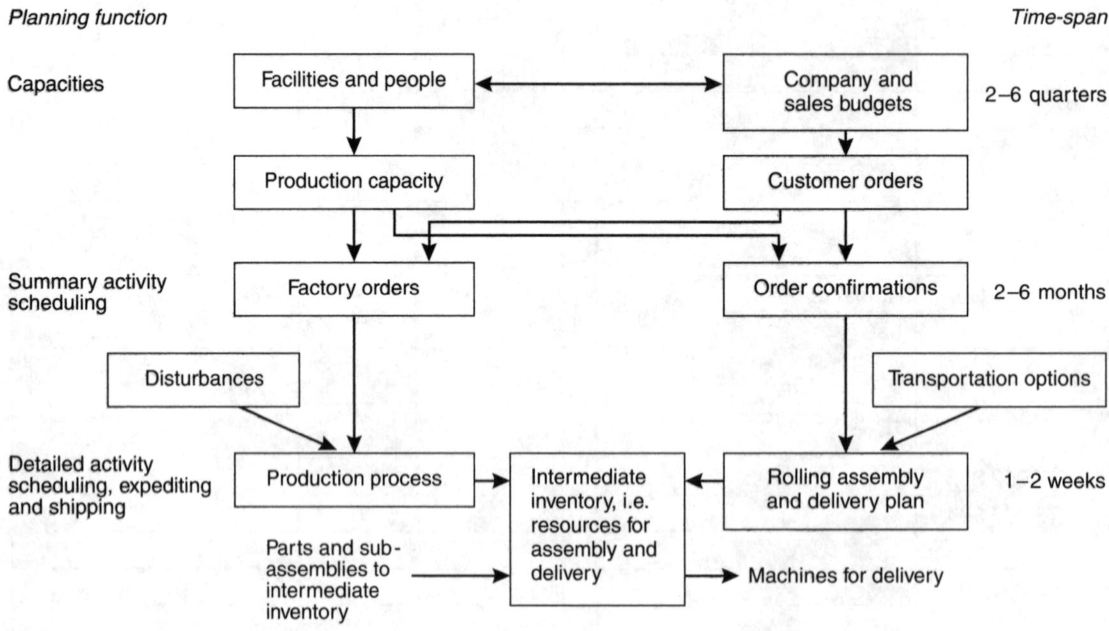


**Figure C20.1** Three levels of planning and scheduling at TAARUP

The time-span of two weeks was intended to be used in such a way that the outline for week 'plus two' would serve as information feedback to the factory, which could then, perhaps, provide any lacking parts of sub-assemblies during week 'plus one'.

Final assembly facilities, then, were rearranged in assembly line layout, with one line per basic machine surrounded by combination parts and with flexible manning.

In order to deal with all unusual circumstances such as delays and other disturbances, but also to take advantage of all opportunities, the lowest-level plan was intended to become the responsibility of a single experienced person.

Case study 21

# Linden Christian Nursery School – A

A subcommittee of the board of management of Linden Presbyterian Church (LPC) was meeting to consider tenders received for a contract. Roy, who chairs this subcommittee, recalled the history of the nursery school.

LPC is a small suburban church in the northwestern suburbs of Johannesburg, the largest city of South Africa. It serves a congregation of about 500 members.

Over the past few years LPC has bought two adjacent properties, which are now consolidated on a single property. The whole property is about 4500 $m^2$ in extent at the corner of 5th Avenue and 8th Street in the suburb of Linden (see Figure C21.1). On the northwestern portion of the property there is a sanctuary, halls and offices. On the remainder of the property there are the two houses and out-buildings. Doug Crawford, the minister, uses the house at the south corner as a residence (called a manse). On the east, 'Church House', as it is called, and the associated garage are shaded in Figure C21.1, and are used on Sundays only. Some members spotted the low level of utilization of Church House and suggested setting up a nursery school there. At that stage one member suggested that R10 000 would convert Church House to a nursery school.

The market for a nursery school depends on the demand by people who live in, commute through, or work in the area. Linden historically consists of detached residences. The congregation's home addresses are given in Table C21.1 and a map of the catchment area is given in Figure C21.2. The public transport in this section of Johannesburg is indifferent and most people use cars.

In outlying areas people are moving into the north and west, as the south and east are already settled and serviced. For example, there is a large Presbyterian church in Parkview. Developers are starting to erect flats (apartment blocks) and cluster (or town) houses in Linden that will lead to higher-density living. Flats and cluster houses are associated with young married couples and retired people.

In April the board of management commissioned a sketch plan and budget from John Duncan, an architect who has had considerable experience in church work. This showed that the original estimate of R10 000 was a gross under-estimate, because of both the state of the building and municipal requirements for converting Church House to a nursery school. John's budget for alterations to Church House was R108 000. As some members of the church felt strongly about the need for a nursery school, a meeting was held to attempt to cut the budgeted conversion costs. This meeting included the architect, John, likely teachers for the nursery school, including Monica, and selected members of the board of management, including Ernest, the chairperson, and Roy. During this meeting, members cut the budgeted expenditure on Church House from R108 000 to R73 300 by omitting anything not absolutely essential. The decision to proceed with the nursery school depended on special consent in

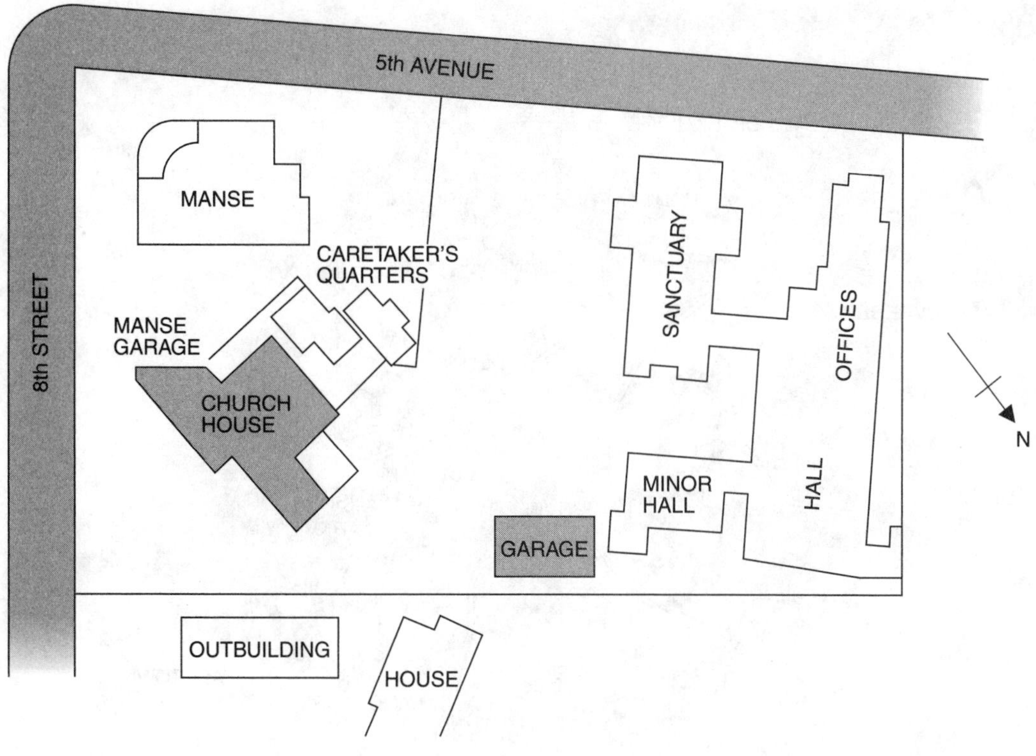


**Figure C21.1** Plan of LPC property

**Table C21.1 Distribution of congregation relative to LPC**

| Area | Suburbs | % |
|---|---|---|
| Central | Linden, Roosevelt Park, Northcliff, Montgomery Park | 26.6 |
| N to NE | Blairgowrie, Bordeaux, Robindale, Robinhills, Ferndale, President Ridge, Malanshof, Bromhof | 26.8 |
| N to NW | Randpark, Windsor, Fontainebleau, Aldara Park, Darrenwood, Cresta | 12.2 |
| W | Fairland, Valeriedene, Berario | 8.3 |
| Far W | Roodepoort, Weltevreden Park, Randparkridge | 5.9 |
| SE | Greenside, Emmarentia, Parkview, Parktown | 4.6 |
| S | Westdene, Auckland Park, Melville | 2.9 |
| Far N | North Rand | 2.7 |
| | other areas | 10.0 |

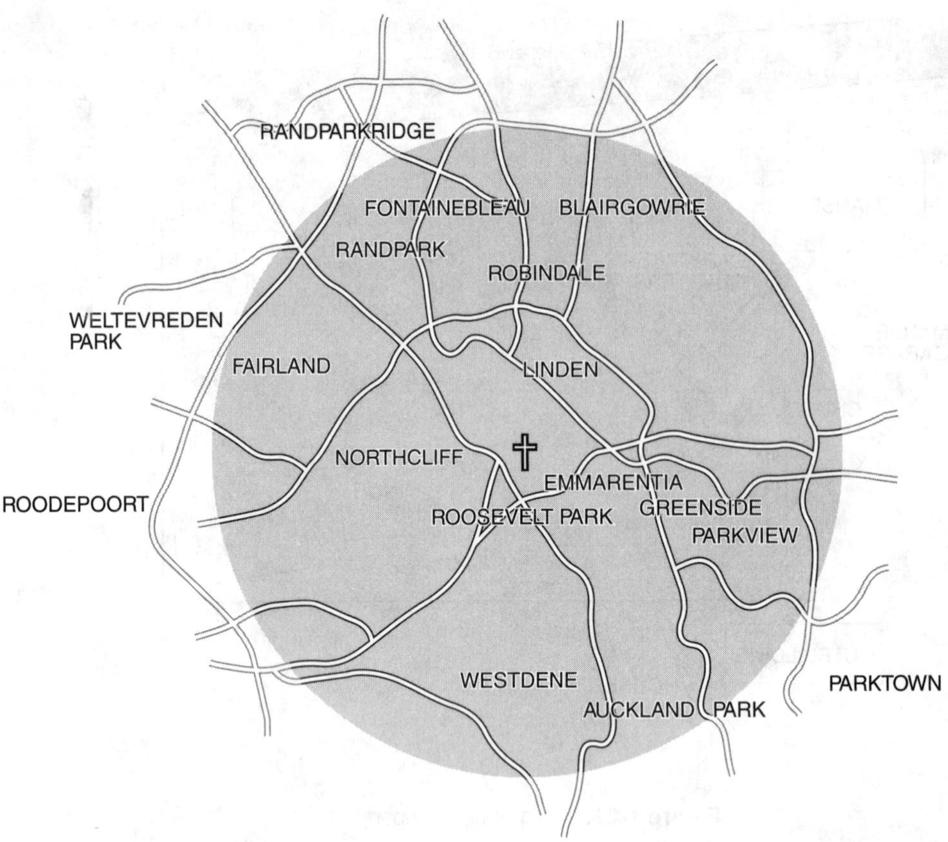


**Figure C21.2** Some suburbs and major roads near to LPC. The cross is LPC and the shaded circle designates a 5-km radius from the church

terms of planning regulations. As some people objected, there was a hearing and special consent was given to proceed with a nursery school. In addition the decision depended upon a plan to move the church or to stay in Linden. Both of these delayed the decision on the nursery school.

Some members of the LPC are qualified teachers and active in nursery school education. There are a few nursery schools in the area. A well-known nursery school for approximately 40 children is about half a kilometre away at a Methodist church. Informal discussion with the leader of this nursery school yielded the following information. Nursery school attendance had usually been strong, with demand always exceeding supply. During the past year, demand at this nursery school had slackened; changes in formal schooling have contributed to this.

In South Africa nursery schools provide a service for children up to 6 years of age, when formal schooling starts. The academic year starts in January, just after the long summer holidays.

Formal education in South Africa is undergoing changes. Changes imply that parents pay much more and have greater say in their children's education. Increases in fees of 50% with the changes are common. (One example of the fees increase is R850 in the year before changes, R1200 in the year of changes and R2000 the year after changes – the inflation rate was about 15% p.a. in these years.)

On 10 August the board of management decided to convert Church House and the associated garage to provide a nursery school opening at the beginning of the following year. As builders take their holidays in December, the deadline for undertaking such work was tight. Ernest asked Roy to chair a subcommittee which, amongst others, would manage providing physical facilities for the nursery school. Monica would head the day-to-day running of the nursery school with assistants and a capacity of 54 pupils.

During the next two weeks John worked at getting the plans and specification into a format acceptable to the municipality. This involved gaining acceptance from many branches such as the fire prevention committee, the sewerage branch, etc. He also had to make sure that the revisions would provide an adequate service for the nursery school. Part of the plan is given in Figure C21.3.

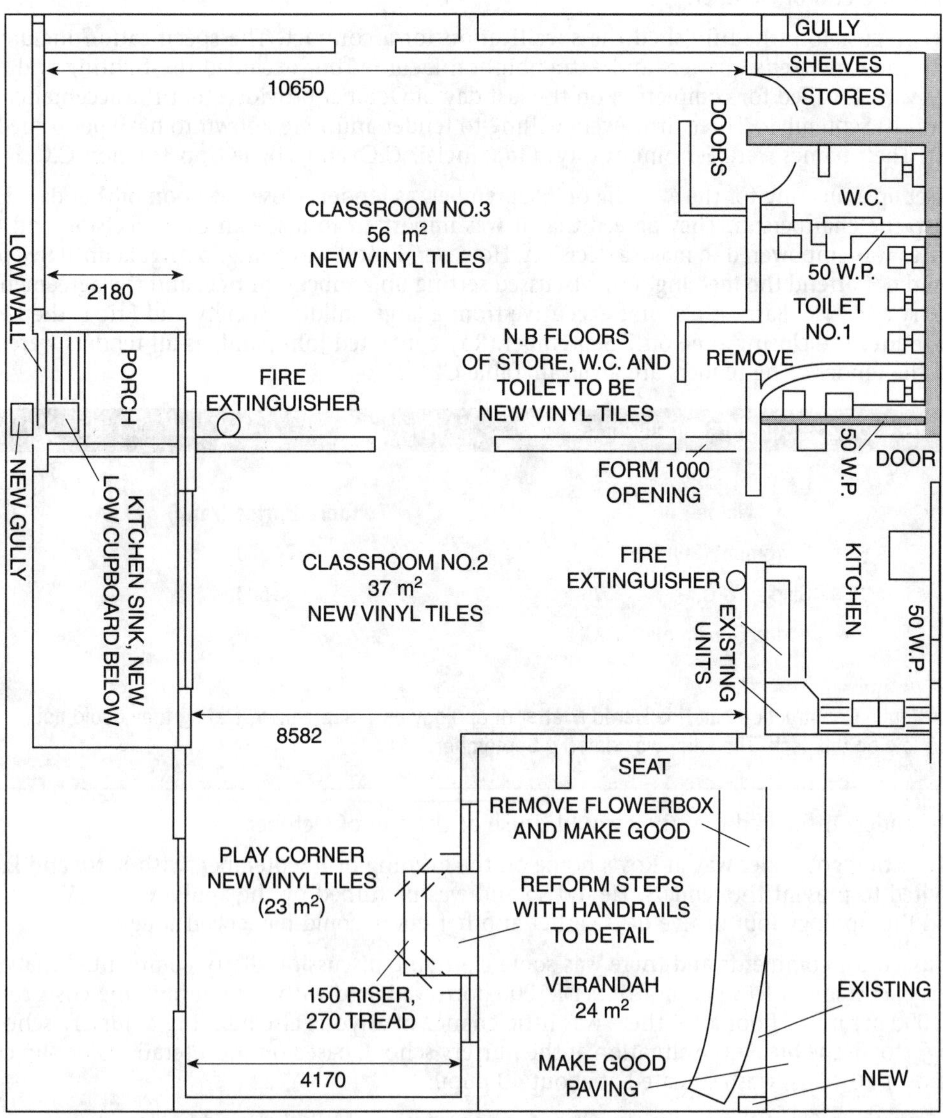


**Figure C21.3** Part of plan of alterations showing toilets, w.c., store and classrooms

John had to add extra work into the plan. The following changes were required, with the budgeted costs in parentheses:

1. The caretaker's quarters had to be altered to provide privacy from the nursery school (R6000).
2. Parking had to be provided with an extra entrance and driveway (R9300).
3. Extra ablution and washing-up facilities were required (R4150).
4. Fire-fighting regulations had changed and extra work was required (R6200).

John managed to lessen costs slightly in other areas by reduced painting, using standard gates at entrances, etc. John negotiated with officials in the various branches of local government to approve the design, talked with Roy, and got quotes from suppliers. Monica pointed out that, in order for the school to attract children, parents wanted to see what they were getting. For this she wanted completion by the end of October.

By 31 August John had finished the specification for a contract. The specification included alterations to the caretaker's quarters and extra ablution facilities but excluded fire-fighting and work for the driveway. It called for completion on the last day of October provided that the acceptance was on, or before, 10 September. Three firms were willing to tender and were known to have performed well in the past. Their names were Ferromont (Pty) Ltd, Sinclair C.C. and Vogue Construction C.C.

Roy set up a meeting for the evening of 7 September, as tenders closed at noon of that day. He spoke to Ernest, the chairperson. They agreed that it was important to make an early decision and the subcommittee was empowered to make a decision. However, Ernest was going to Angola until 9 September, and could not attend the meeting. Roy discussed setting up a subcommittee, and the agreement was to have Barry and Eric. Barry is a senior executive from a large building society and Eric is the LPC treasurer. Just after the closing time on 7 September, Roy contacted John, and, as all tenders were in, they opened the tenders. The tenders are given in Table C21.2.

**Table C21.2 Tenders received**

| Name | Tendered price (rand) |
|---|---|
| Ferromont (Pty) Ltd. | 74 500 |
| Sinclair C.C. | 88 500 |
| Vogue Construction C.C. | * |

* Vogue Construction hand-delivered a letter of apology on 7 September, stating they could not quote on this task. The letter was dated 4 September.

Both tenders intimated that they would finish at the end of October.

The meeting got under way at Roy's home on the evening of 7 September, with Barry and Eric. John was invited to present the tenders. He did so and was perturbed by the apology from Vogue. Had he received this apology four or five days earlier another quote could have been sought.

Roy asked for comments and there was some clarifying discussion. Barry commented that, as bond (mortgage) cost about R15 per month per R1000 borrowed, and with current building costs running at over R1000 per m$^2$ of floor area, there was little chance of anyone else building a nursery school. Even as things stood, the breakeven situation at the nursery school, based on the alterations, set-up costs and a bond over 20 years, was estimated at about 40 pupils.

Two questions faced the committee. What are the options? What should be done?

Case study 22

# Linden Christian Nursery School – B

This case must be read in conjunction with Linden Christian Nursery School – A.

The tender of Ferromont (Pty) Ltd was accepted subject to an OK by the chairperson, Ernest. When he arrived on 9 September, Roy saw him and secured approval. John, the architect, negotiated the usual financial terms of the contract.

On 10 September Ferromont started moving equipment on site ready to start work on 14 September. Immediately problems occurred. Standard materials such as window frames and door frames were difficult to obtain. The building recession and the approaching Christmas break meant that stockists were running their stocks as low as possible. The caretaker was aggrieved because he had been told that the builder would not start building until he had been informed. However, by 14 September both the caretaker and the builder were ready for the start. The contract explicitly stated that the caretaker would be in occupation during the work and would use the bathroom and kitchen of Church House until the caretaker's quarters were ready. In addition, the conversion of Church House into classrooms 2 and 3 had to be given priority for marketing the nursery school. Lastly, it was important to keep most of the site available, and safe, during Sunday activities. The complete area of caretaker's quarters, Church House and garage was rapidly taken over as the builder proceeded as people became available and material was delivered to site. The unskilled work of demolition and excavating proceeded relatively quickly but other work, e.g. plumbing and electrical, was only undertaken when skilled labour was on site and when suitable materials were delivered.

The Annual General Meeting of LPC took place on 23 September, and during this meeting the caretaker's quarters were raised as an area of concern. It was apparent that the caretaker was going to be without washing and toilet facilities at his quarters.

Roy alerted Eric, the treasurer, on 30 September that the builder would be likely to ask for his first progress payment on 1 October. Eric had facilities of up to R35 000. The builder handed his first progress payment request for R19 800 to John on 5 October. John discussed it with Roy. It was difficult to reconcile the progress payment with the budget for work done, because of part work complete. (See Appendix A for part of the budget and the architect's certificate for the provisional final account.) Substantial discussion followed. It included comments about the differences between the budget, which is estimated according to areas, and the building, which is estimated according to skill and resource availability. Finally, the amount was agreed as being reasonable. Roy passed the request and Eric paid the builder on 6 October (R19 800 less 10% retention = R17 820).

By 8 October, demolition was complete but rubble was still to be removed. Inside Church House internal brickwork and plastering were complete. The plumber had completed the laying of external pipes but trenches were still to be closed. The contractor was alerted to the length of time that trenches would remain open. Open trenches jeopardized safety, and so Sunday activities were relocated. The plumber had to start internal work. In Church House there was no start on the flooring. At the caretaker's quarters brickwork was in progress. In the garage, brickwork, plastering and glazing were completed. No electrical work was started.

By 16 October internal plumbing work was ready to start as the material was on site. Plumbing was not satisfactory, as the caretaker was without adequate washing and toilet facilities at his quarters. Backfilling of external trenches was still not complete, as the plumber tended to get people on site and then withdraw them. Fencing work commenced on 16 October and by 2 November the major part of the contract work was completed. On 2 November backfilling was complete and the rubble removed. Vinyl flooring was being installed. By 6 November, the contract was complete except for a list of defects and variations to contract. Defects included doors which did not close, and water drainage problems.

On 14 November church members cleaned the walls and on 21 November about 35 members of the church painted the nursery school. The next day the dedication service for the nursery school took place. This comprised speeches by John, Monica and the minister, Doug Crawford. After this the builder asked for final payment less retention monies for maintenance and defects. The nursery school was on track to open on 6 January. However, Roy wondered whether there were any lessons to be learned, and whether the project had been undertaken well. There had been no accidents reported to Roy and the contingency amount of R1800 had not been exceeded. John mentioned that the quality had been 'as good as you are likely to find these days'.

## APPENDIX A

This appendix shows the budget and the architect's certificate for the provisional final account.

The budget is undertaken in terms of areas, e.g. play corner and classroom no. 2, kitchen, external finishes, etc. The area for which a partial budget is given is the toilet no. 1, w.c. and store. This is shown in Table C22.1. (Part of the alterations are shown in a plan of Church House's conversion in case A, Figure C21.3.) The architect's certificate is in Figure C22.1.

Table C22.1 Budget – toilet no. 1, w.c. and store

| Items | Rand | Rand |
|---|---|---|
| Internal wall | 2800 | |
| Internal doors (four off) | 800 | |
| W.C.s (five off) | 4000 | |
| Basins (five off) | 3500 | |
| Floor tiling (14 $m^2$ at R42 per $m^2$) | 590 | |
| Skirting (13 m at R5 per m) | 65 | |
| Subtotal | | 11 755 |
| Other | | 71 695 |
| Total – contractual budget | | 83 450 |

Telephone : E. John Duncan
Architect No. 483

Postal address:

## LINDEN PRESBYTERIAN CHURCH NURSERY SCHOOL

**PROVISIONAL FINAL ACCOUNT**

| | | | | |
|---|---|---|---|---|
| Contract sum | | | | R74 500–00 |
| **DEDUCT** | Contingencies | R 1800–00 | | |
| | Vinyl floor tiles | 7200–00 | | 9 000–00 |
| | | | Subtotal | 66 500–00 |
| **ADD** | Vinyl floor tiles | R 5900–00 | | |
| | Vinyl tiles to caretaker's bathroom | 150–00 | | |
| | Topping to concrete outside caretaker's quarters | 140–00 | | |
| | Masonite covering over lower glass panels of double doors in lieu of plastic adhesive | N/C | | |
| | Plumbing extras (i) new manhole, (ii) new pressure valve, (iii) replace defective water main | R 1463–00 | | 7653–00 |
| | | | Subtotal | R73153–00 |
| | | Less previous payment | | 47995–20 |
| | | | | R25157–80 |
| | | Less 5% retention | | 1257–89 |
| | | Penultimate certificate | | R23899–91 |

**Figure C22.1** Architect's certificate for provisional final account

Case study 23

# Williams' College

Williams' College has 3500 students. It caters for many student populations but mainly:

(a) for those taking two-year courses prior to going to university. They typically enter Williams' at age 16, follow a course of study covering three or four subjects, and stay for two years.

(b) those aged 16 and over who are taking courses designed to prepare them for full-time employment two years later; and

(c) those taking courses on a part-time basis whilst in employment.

Throughout its existence, the college has been administered by a regional education authority. In addition to Williams', the authority has had responsibility for all, other than private, schools or colleges in its geographical area. The authority has had ultimate financial and legal control, has appointed and employed all staff, and has provided central services (e.g. personnel, accounting, maintenance, security, legal, etc.). Over two years ago, central government announced the intention to transfer all such colleges from authority control, and to establish them as self-managing units, with full managerial control vested in the college principals and college governors. Funding is to be provided from a colleges' funding council, and the manner of operation, etc. of colleges is to follow requirements set out by government and the council. There will be no remaining substantial links with the regional authorities.

## PREPARING FOR INDEPENDENCE

Following the government's decision, in effect, to re-create the colleges as independent but centrally funded and controlled establishments, all colleges were faced with the major task of preparing for independence. The government published many guidelines for the colleges which had to be followed. For example, governing bodies had to be re-established and various committees established. The funding council also stipulated many things relating to financial control and accountability. Further, the government appointed consultants to advise and monitor all colleges as they prepared for transfer. For example, there were to be audits of various aspects of the colleges to assess their preparedness for independence, and their subsequent progress, and finally there was to be an inspection on or near to the intended 'vesting date' – 1 April 1993 – to determine whether each college should be given independence, or whether further work was required. For each college, including Williams', the period up to April 1993 was to be a time of intensive activity.

## PLANNING FOR INDEPENDENCE

Amongst the several new senior staff members appointed to Williams' College in late 1990 was a Deputy Principal for Administration. That person was to have overall co-ordinating responsibility under the Principal and the governors for preparing for independence. The DPA was to prepare plans for the execution of all of the necessary tasks required by the government, the funding council and the governors. A schedule was also to be prepared for all of the work to be done, so that the Principal and the governors could allocate tasks and monitor progress.

## THE MAJOR TASK SCHEDULE

At a meeting of the governors in 1990 it was agreed that the first job to be done by the DPA was the preparation of a list of required key tasks and a schedule for those tasks. That schedule was to be put to the governors for approval in early 1991.

The DPA, who was new to Williams' College but not to education, after detailed consultation both in and beyond the college drew up the 'major task' list given in Table C23.1. The list identifies tasks and gives estimated times for their completion.

This list was agreed at a meeting of the college management group, so the DPA was then able to get on with the preparation of a schedule, using this information. A network-type schedule had been recommended in the government guidelines, so that was what the DPA prepared. It is shown in Figure C23.1. This also was discussed by the college management group and approved as the basis for any subsequent detailed planning.

**Table C23.1 Major tasks**

| | Estimated duration[a] (months) | | | |
|---|---|---|---|---|
| **Task (dept.)** | **Best** | **Probable** | **Worst** | **Comments** |
| A (1) | – | 2 | – | Fixed duration |
| B (1) | 5 | 6 | 7 | |
| C (1) | 1 | 3 | 5 | |
| D (1) | – | 4 | – | Fixed duration |
| E (2) | 2 | 3 | 4 | |
| F (2) | 1 | 3 | 4 | |
| G (2) | – | 3 | – | Fixed duration |
| H (3) | – | 6 | – | Fixed duration |
| J (2) | 2 | 8 | 14 | Uncertain duration because of dependence on subcontractor availability |
| K (2) | 2 | 5 | 6 | |
| L (4) | 3 | 4 | 10 | |
| M (4) | – | 4 | – | Fixed duration |
| N (4) | 3 | 4 | 10 | |
| O (4) | 5 | 6 | 7 | |
| P (3) | 1 | 4 | 7 | |
| Q (5) | – | 9 | – | *b* |
| R (5) | – | 4 | – | Fixed duration |
| S (2) | 1 | 2 | 3 | |

[a] Durations assume existing resource levels or resources proposed to governors.

[b] This task may not need to be undertaken, depending on outcome of progress audit.

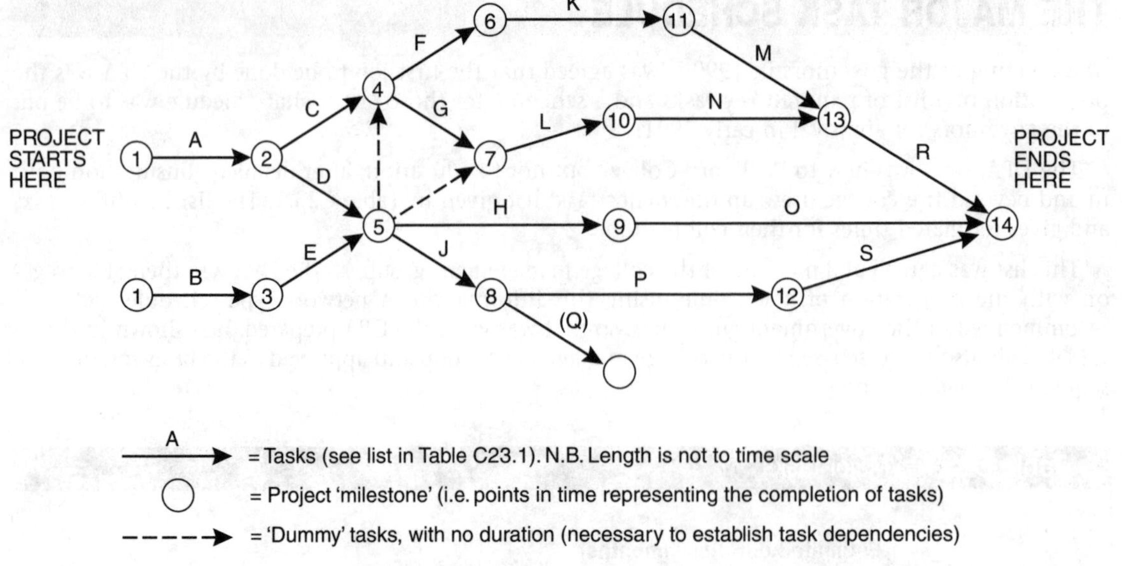


**Figure C23.1** Relationships of tasks

Finally, the DPA, using the information given in the table, and the figure, drew up a schedule for these tasks. Latest start dates were calculated, etc. The overall schedule showed that this series of tasks could be completed in 25 months, which was just enough time to meet the deadline of the 21 April 1993 inspection.

# GOVERNORS' MEETING – MARCH 1991

The main item on the agenda for the March meeting of the governors was a document from the DPA. The document, after outlining the intention of the plan, provided the information in Table C23.1 and Figure C23.1, together with the schedule shown in Table C23.2.

The following additional explanatory comments and observations were provided:

'The data from Table 1 and the information in Figure 1 have been used to prepare the schedule given in Table 2. The schedule indicates that the project can be completed by month 25, i.e. the end of March 1993, in time for the audit on or near 'vesting day' on 1 April. The critical tasks in the project, i.e. those which directly influence the overall completion date, are tasks B, E, F, K, M, R. It will be seen from Table 1 that three of these (E, F, K) will be the responsibility of one department (Accounts). However, as they will not occur at the same time, there should be no bottleneck in that department. It is not expected that task Q will be required, but it is included in the schedule for completeness (it will only be necessary if a mid-term audit produces unsatisfactory results).'

The report also provided certain further explanatory information, a recommendation that the 'major task' schedule be adopted as shown, and finally a list of specific actions now required in order that work might proceed as planned. These actions included such things as certain additional appointments, the establishment of various subgroups of governors to monitor progress, etc. It was clear that, whilst these or similar actions would soon be required, there need be no delay now in commencing the initial tasks.

**Table C23.2 Schedule for project**

| Project 'milestone' | Associated tasks Ending | Starting | Earliest date[a] | Latest date[a] |
|---|---|---|---|---|
| 1 (project start) | – | – | – | 0 |
| 2 | A | C, D | 2 | 5 |
| 3 | B | E | 6 | 6 |
| 4 | C | F, G | 9 | 9 |
| 5 | D, E | H, J | 9 | 9 |
| 6 | F | K | 12 | 12 |
| 7 | G | L | 12 | 13 |
| 8 | J | P, (Q) | 17 | 17 |
| 9 | H | O | 15 | 19 |
| 10 | L | N | 16 | 17 |
| 11 | K | M | 17 | 17 |
| 12 | P | S | 21 | 23 |
| 13 | M, N | R | 21 | 21 |
| 14 (project end) | R, O, S | | 25 | 25[b] |

[a] Month number from project start.

[b] Earliest completion of project.

Case study 24

# Winterthur non-life commercial insurance

Winterthur Insurance Company, Amsterdam (Holland) is part of the worldwide Swiss insurance group Winterthur Versicherungen, which employs 20000 people in 50 countries. The Winterthur non-life commercial insurance division in Amsterdam provides insurance services to companies to cover risks in areas such as product liability, property, accident insurances, etc.

## THE DUTCH NON-LIFE COMMERCIAL INSURANCE INDUSTRY

The Dutch commercial insurance market is characterized by a very strong position on the part of insurance brokers. Brokers are independent and do not represent any particular insurer. They analyse risks for their clients and obtain the best protection considering price and insurance coverage. For their services, brokers receive commission from the insurer(s) with whom they place the business.

In the Netherlands 73% of all commercial insurance goes through brokers. In no other European country is the percentage so high. Brokers have maintained their strong position by refusing to deal with insurers who seek also to deal directly with customers. They take the view that such direct contact should only exist when the customer demands it, and not when the insurer seeks it.

The advantage claimed for this arrangement is that Dutch insurance premiums are at least 25% lower than elsewhere in Europe, that competition is strong and that service to customers is good.

### Risk management

In order to secure insurance portfolios with clients who do not suffer regular losses but who require more than minimum premiums, insurers have developed engineering capability. Engineers provide a risk analysis and risk management advice so that insurers can avoid risky situations and continuity is more secured, both in premium and coverage. Brokers can offer the same risk management service. However, each insurance company has developed specialized technical and juridical knowledge relating to specific fields in trade and industry. The large brokers offer the same expertise in every possible field of trade and industry. Nevertheless, the insurer offers risk management service in line with the intermediance of brokers.

### Competition

Winterthur's main competitors are Royal, Zürich, and Gerling. Most insurers operating in the Dutch commercial insurance market are international. More mergers are likely. Research has suggested that the greatest percentage (approximately 50%) of recent merger activities in the service industry was in the insurance industry. There is also some new competitive pressure expected from Dutch insurers like Nationale Nederlanden, Aegon, Delta Lloyd, and Fortis.

### Multinationals

The negotiating power of corporate clients often depends on their size. If the insurance companies or the brokers are dealing with large companies (read: large premiums), then those clients can influence the terms of the insurance contract. Generally, insurers would not like to lose such an account. However, besides the premium, these accounts can also imply new risks. For example, a large chemical concern merges with another in order to expand research and development, and new products and innovative production processes may result. These might bring new risks with which the insurer has little experience.

## WINTERTHUR'S AIMS

Winterthur has a clear goal. It aims to acquire a leading position as an industrial insurer. It seeks to insure also companies with subsidiaries abroad. A worldwide network of subsidiaries has already enabled the group to develop an insurance programme with global coverage. So, Winterthur's objective is to penetrate those segments which offer the best prospects for growth and financial results.

## WINTERTHUR'S OPERATIONS

Winterthur Insurance Company, Amsterdam employs 250 people in the Netherlands. A managing director has overall responsibility. The non-life commercial division employs 35 people.

The commercial division secures clients typically as follows:

*Step 1:* Company asks broker for insurance coverage.

*Step 2:* Broker asks several insurers to make a tender to cover the risks.

*Step 3:* Insurance companies prepare tender and send to broker.

*Step 4:* Broker chooses best tender: normally, best coverage against lowest premium.

Clearly, the process can be time-consuming. The client has to wait a long time for the final insurance contract.

To speed up the whole process, Winterthur can only aim to provide quicker delivery of the tender for the broker. That process now takes five days on average. It has been suggested that this be reduced to two days on average. A strategic information plan has been developed which will also be of help in realizing this goal. The aim would be to provide a better service than competitors. This should be reflected in Winterthur's reputation and increased sales. However, competitors will probably follow. They will probably be forced to follow Winterthur, because the market is competitive.

Winterthur must now consider whether to implement the suggested change. Factors which will be considered must include whether the time to prepare tenders can be reduced, the benefits that might be obtained and the impact on the nature and management of the company's operations.

Case study 25

# European Foundation – group work

The European Foundation for the Improvement of Living and Working Conditions, based near Dublin, Ireland, is a tripartite (unions/employees, employers and government) organization involved in studies throughout the European Community. The Foundation, through its work, aims to contribute to the planning and development of the improvement of living and working conditions in Europe. To this end, it commissions and manages studies, organizes conferences and in other ways disseminates its findings.

## WORKGROUPS AND PARTICIPATION

One theme in the Foundation's work over several years has been 'group working and participation'. Several studies have been undertaken, by teams led by the two project managers, Pascal Paoli and Hubert Krieger.

For example, studies undertaken at organizations in five countries have recently been written up for publication in one of the Foundation's newsletters.[1]

Pascal and Hubert now aim to respond to a request to summarize the main findings of their work in order to present conclusions and thus guidance/advice in a new book on operations management. They aim to refer to several studies but to illustrate their contribution to the book mainly with two of the recent cases, and to focus their conclusions as practical guidelines for managers on the introduction and use of semi-autonomous group working. The two cases are presently written up as follows.

## TASK GROUPS AT EUROPE COMBINED TERMINALS

### by Willem Galama

**Personnel Manager, Europe Combined Terminals, Rotterdam, Netherlands**

Europe Combined Terminals bv (ECT) handled over 1.4 million containers and some 250000 cars in 1990, operating out of 12 km of quayside covering 355 hectares (887 acres). Based in the major Dutch port of Rotterdam, the company aims to place people first and foremost. Human resources policies are based on competitive salaries, a good health and safety record, and the provision of job training, opportunities for advancement and decent working conditions.

[1]*European Participation Monitor*, no. 5, 1993. European Foundation for the Improvement of Living and Working Conditions, Shankill, Co. Dublin, Ireland.

## Work organization

ECT employs a workforce of 2800 spread across its headquarters, nine terminals and the Rotterdam Harbour Pool (600). The company works 24 hours a day for 363 days of the year and so operates a daily three-shift system, with 18 gangs per shift on both waterside and landside containerized activities.

Waterside operations require a range of skills, including those of crane driver, lorry driver, deckman and groundman, whilst landside operations also require forklift truck drivers. Similar skills are needed in the barge and rail services. As a result, each operational employee combines between two and four tasks in his function – for example, lorry driver/groundman, or lorry driver/forklift truck driver/straddle-carrier driver. Job rotation has therefore always been a possibility, but has not always taken place because shortages of job functions do not allow it in practice.

## Experiment at ECT barge terminal

In 1986 an agreement between management and the works council introduced semi-autonomous workgroups at the ECT barge terminal under the slogan 'Running your own Shop'. The aim was to make barge terminal operations more efficient by establishing small gangs with fixed membership responsible for a wider range of tasks.

One problem, however, lay in how to deal with the unpredictable workload at the terminal. The answer was to set out priorities – if there was no work at the barge terminal, the gang was to move to the rail terminal, and if there was no work there, it was to move on to other activities within in its own job functions. In that way, the composition of the special barge terminal workgroups was maintained.

The next step was to set up the workgroups with as much self-supporting activity as possible. Each gang consisted of three workers: two crane drivers/groundmen, whose job rotated, and one lorry driver, whose job did not rotate. With five gangs in total at the barge terminal, they were responsible for their own workplans, operational activities and monitoring.

To ensure group cohesion, autonomy is supported by monthly meetings of the entire barge terminal group, including its departmental head. These meetings discuss the following subjects: workload figures for the previous month and forecasted figures for the coming month; performance indicators for barge operations; problems encountered and possible solutions; proposals for modifying equipment; training; contacts with other supporting departments; and visits to barge operators.

## Evaluation

Research designed to assess the results of the experiment shows improved job enrichment in terms of increased autonomy, self-regulation, motivation and quality of both social and functional communications. Problems centre on the isolation of the work area, continuation of 'them and us' attitudes, relationships with the heads of the other departments (including technical support) and 'the envy of colleagues'.

At the time of evaluation, productivity at the barge terminal had risen by an estimated 15%. It was therefore decided in 1992 to consolidate the experiment by introducing a second crane at the terminal and by enlarging gangs from the three to six members with total job rotation. In addition, it was decided to extend the workgroup concept to other parts of the company's operations, particularly to the development of ECT's new Delta/Sea-Land Terminal where it has become the leading idea for human resource management. Teams at the new terminal will enjoy full job rotation, greater responsibility for executing and co-ordinating tasks, and enhanced opportunities for promotion. There will be four levels of membership of the waterside and landside teams, depending on the number of functions (between two and four) which each member is trained to contribute. A similar system will also operate within the process control team at the terminal.

# TEAMWORK AT LEGRAND ELÉCTRICA


## by Maria Luisa Cristóvam

Universidade Autónoma de Lisboa, Lisbon, Portugal


When a company tries to improve its performance, changes in organization and human resource management are often fundamental since they may in turn determine the success of technological innovation. Teamwork has been increasingly viewed as a means of involving workers in the processes of industrial rationalization, not least in those cases where such innovation is constrained by a variety of social pressures.

## In search of performance

Legrand Eléctrica SA is a company which manufactures low-tension electrical equipment for the construction sector, and is the result of a merger in 1989 of the two largest and oldest Portuguese companies in this area of specialization, which began in the 1940s. Following the merger, senior management decided to improve the flexibility of the production process in order to retain market leadership.

Though the company is not considered high-tech – it has around 600 workers, the majority of whom are low-skilled – it could be included amongst the ranks of the more innovative or creative enterprises on account of its ability to meet customer requirements. The managing director defined 'customer satisfaction' as the principal goal; to achieve this goal, a programme was introduced to modernize plant and improve training and communications gradually. This included a quality strategy and the setting of management targets which required regular report-back to meetings. Teamwork was seen from the outset as a means of achieving both the humanization of work and a greater sense of responsibility amongst the employees. A belief in the intelligence of the workforce and their capacity to innovate was central.

## Teamwork

### 1. Rationalization

With the assistance of external consultants, an 'integrated line' was introduced for the production of a certain type of electrical plug. This experiment, by involving the workers concerned rather than imposing rules on them, built on a number of practices already in use which were designed to reduce production times and improve potential. These included an integrated system of 'just-in-time' production control which keeps work teams fully informed of stock levels, set-up times and lead times. Teams can thereby improve efficiency in relation to the utilization of equipment, materials and space and at the same time monitor their own performance.

### 2. Organization

The concept of production centres had been developed since 1989 to create interrelated but autonomous production units designed to foster 'team spirit'. Work then began to integrate plastics and metal products which had previously operated out of separate sites.

The creation of the first work teams in 1990 was therefore easier because of the learning processes initiated in the company's previous experiments involving basic training (such as courses in Portuguese, mathematics and so on) and specific training (in areas like teamwork, industrial management and quality control). These learning processes had also included participation in quality programmes – improvement groups with a brief taste of quality circles – since management believed that quality should become a 'state of mind'.

The teamwork project, which involved 84 workers from the total of 600, progressed through various stages:

- the *information and awareness stage* (October 1990) to ensure understanding of the concepts used; and
- the *implementation stage* (March 1991), which was itself broken down into substages including the following:
  - A competition to decide the slogan to launch the project.
  - Training in 'just-in-time'.
  - An event to mark the launch of the project, with the elimination of those aspects of the production line considered superfluous (equipment, materials and so on).
  - Introduction to the new work processes involved in the form of a game to which workers from other companies were also invited.

The first work groups, taking over a situation in which workers had been overspecialized and stocks excessive, developed a series of plans to rationalize production, including the formation of a 'kanban panel' (to disseminate information on production planning and control), the streamlining of production processes, the study of new installations and layouts and ways to propagate results.

## 3. Results

Project managers and teamworkers analyse production plans in advance every week and monitor their accomplishment. Production levels are assessed on a daily basis as well as quality, plans for the following days and any problems – for example over maintenance – requiring preventive action. There is total flexibility within *each* team and between 60% and 70% flexibility of members *between* teams. Difficulties have been encountered when different technologies are used – for example, plastics in contrast to metals – but these are being overcome. Quality is improving slowly (partly because it was already high) but overall assessment of the production centre is positive. Its performance has improved considerably mainly because of the training involved (40 hours per worker every year) and the ongoing consultation (30 minutes a day). However, the number of workers has been reduced from 84 to 72.

## 4. Extensions

The model was extended to other parts of the company's operations in January 1992. A general committee, comprising co-ordinator, project supervisors and a monitoring team, is now responsible for restructuring and increasing the number of teams. However, a number of questions are raised by the spread of teamwork concepts. The first teams emerged almost spontaneously amongst the most highly motivated – and efficient – workers, but will efforts to motivate other workers succeed? Existing teams are used to operating in stressful situations, but will management be able to sustain its support of all teams in such conditions? The spread of teamworking will require an intensification of networking throughout the company, but how will the company manage to direct it? Answers to these questions are not yet forthcoming.

# Industrial relations

All this reorganization carries implications for industrial relations within the company, for example in respect to worker representation and pay determination. Worker representatives did not become involved in creating the new framework even though the Economic and Social Standing Committee for Social Consultation (Conselho Permanente de Concertação Social), the body responsible for discussing industrial relations at intersectoral level, envisages their active role in initiatives of this kind. In fact, the company study revealed that the workers themselves did not see work reorganization as an issue for union negotiation. Worker representatives, they felt, should have a more active role in health and safety issues. As far as pay is concerned, wages comprise the basic contractual elements as determined on an individual basis. These relate to the achievement of agreed results. However, problems have been encountered in relation to social attitudes – for example, the traditional role of the 'boss' within the company – and the regrading of jobs in line with the improving qualifications of production workers. However, within the company's new participative framework, these issues are all in principle negotiable by workers' representatives.

Case study 26

# The Open Polytechnic of New Zealand (TOPNZ) – 'The writing process'

## THE BACKGROUND

Appendix A details the external environmental changes that The Open Polytechnic has had to face in recent years. It is based on an address given by Shona Butterfield, Chief Executive Officer of The Open Polytechnic of New Zealand, to the Australian Open Learning Conference of Australia held at Northern Rivers, New South Wales, in September 1992.

## THE SCENARIO

It is now 1989 and *you* are the newly appointed Principal and Chief Executive of TOPNZ. The Deputy Principal (Learning and Resources) is sitting opposite you. He has given you the writing plan for your approval. You note that he wants 379 new assignments to be written in 1989. Although you have not long been with TOPNZ you know that the teaching process revolves around assignments. An assignment consists of 30–40 pages of student learning material. Assignments also include exercises and assessment tests to return to tutors for marking and comment. It is important that assignments are well written and that the information given in them is current and technically correct.

You are surprised that such a large number, 379, need to be written. This seems to be an awful lot of writing, and you wonder whether the polytechnic has the capacity to cope and just how the work is to be allocated. You glance at the plan again and say 'OK, Fred, you want approval to write 379 assignments for 1989. How many did we write in 1988?'

Fred refers to his file and replies, '309 against an approved target of 355. That was pretty good under the circumstances.'

You think to yourself, 'There will always be circumstances.' Aloud, you say, 'Yes, but that is quite a shortfall, have there been shortfalls in previous years?'

Fred replies, 'There is always a shortfall. In 1987, the plan was to write 359 and only 314 were completed.'

You then ask, 'For those not completed – for example, in 1987, 45 were not completed – were these assignments no longer required or did we just fall behind? And if they were still to be written, would they be included in the 1988 writing plan?'

Fred says, 'Each year we fall behind by a similar amount. However, the courses still have to be completed. In some cases, most of the work has been completed and the writer is in the process of finishing off. The plan does not include assignments already approved in previous years.'

'This raises another question,' you say. 'How many of the 355 new assignments approved in the plan for 1988 were actually completed in 1988?'

Fred does not have this information, but he promises to provide it 'tomorrow'.

Next morning, Fred is again sitting in your office. 'These are the figures. In 1987, our plan was to write 355 new assignments in 1988. In 1988, we actually completed 309. Only 210 of these were 1988 assignments; the balance were the leftovers from 1987.'

You do some quick arithmetic and say, 'That means that if we completed 210 out of a target of 355, we had a shortfall of 145!'

Fred nods assent.

'What has it been like in previous years – 1987, for example?'

When you get the 1987 figures, you find that although the plan was for 359 assignments to be written, in fact only 215 of these were completed in 1987, a shortfall of 144. Admittedly, 314 were completed in total, but 101 of these were for previous years.

You recheck the figures. Something does not add up. If, in fact, there was a shortfall of 144 in 1987, surely the shortfall would have been carried over into the next period and completed in 1988. If so, of the 309 completed in 1988, then 144 really belonged to 1987. This would mean that only 165 of the 355 approved for 1988 had been completed in 1988. If you are right, there is now a balance of 190 to be carried forward to 1989. You explain these figures to Fred.

Fred thinks for a moment. Then he says, 'Yes, but some of the 1987 assignments had been withdrawn, and so the number to be carried forward is only 145.'

You could have asked Fred why assignments were put forward for writing if within 12 months they were no longer required. And what is the point of a writing plan if it is never achieved? You do not bother to ask these questions or several others that spring to mind. You now have enough information to know that a full study is needed.

## YOUR ANALYSIS

After Fred leaves your office, you make the following notes on the present situation (March 1989).

### What is to be done?

A plan was agreed in 1988 by your predecessor for the writing of 379 new assignments in 1989. There is still a backlog of 145 assignments from 1988 to be completed. However, some of these may not now be needed.

If none are withdrawn, the writing requirement for 1989 becomes 524 (379 + 145). For the last two years, the numbers of completed assignments were 309 and 314. Therefore, with the same number of staff, unless something drastic is done, the backlog by the end of 1989 will be over 200.

## How is the writing plan determined?

Tutors/supervisors recommend that assignments be written. These recommendations are considered for approval by the head of department. There are 14 heads of department. The head of department, after discussion with supervisors and tutors, prepares a list of new assignments for action by the Deputy Principal (Learning and Resources). This happens in September each year.

The Deputy Principal, who is responsible for vetting the list, actually does little more than add up all the requests and passes it to the Principal for approval. The previous Principal always approved the plan. In the past, the plan has been for about the same number each year and each year the target is almost achieved (that is, if you do not look too closely at the accumulated backlog).

## Who does the writing?

Tutors do the writing. Tutors are employed as subject specialists but also have to pass a writing test before being employed.

Tutors who are marking have a target of 12 assignments a day. The turnaround time aimed is three days from the time of receipt for each assignment. In addition to writing, many tutors are expected to carry some of the marking load as well as doing some technical editing. The target for writing is ten assignments per year.

Once writing of a new assignment is approved, each writer is assigned a technical editor. The technical editor works in tandem with the writer to make certain that the content is technically correct.

No tutor is expected to work more than 34 hours a week. Tutors keep time sheets and record their work in six-minute units. Tutors who work more than 34 hours in one week are encouraged by their union to take time off in the next week. This practice is known as 'glide time'. For many tutors, taking work home, or working above the mandatory 34 hours, just does not happen. Moreover, the buildings are locked at 5.30 p.m. on weekdays and closed over the weekends.

## What is an assignment?

A course usually consists of eight to ten assignments. Each assignment contains 30–40 pages, but some are longer (up to about 60 pages). Assignments include study material, self-assessment questions, and assessment tests to be returned to the tutor for marking and comment. In many courses, students need no further material – they can complete the course by studying the assignments. Some assignments are thinly disguised plagiarisms, with few acknowledgements of the original.

## Why is there such a need for new assignments each year?

Each year in August, tutors are urged to put forward a list of new assignments for writing. However, the rewriting is not meant to start until the next February. (Tutors have leave from the beginning of December until the beginning of February.) It is easy to be optimistic when planning for something you might start in six months' time, especially when you are looking forward to a two-month break before you begin! Also, at the time of the year (August) when tutors are being asked to put forward their writing plans, they are conscious of being assessed for promotion. Writing capabilities are an important factor in promotion considerations.

## How is progress of writing monitored?

Although there are strict guidelines as to how assignments are to be written – their style, layout, and self-assessment test questions, for example – there is no budget and no serious monitoring of progress. Once rewriting of a course (8–10 assignments) has begun, it is expected to be completed in 12 months. The lapsed time for writing an assignment is, at best, four weeks, but the whole process from writing to final printing always takes several months.

Appendix B shows the process in flow-chart form.

The writer/supervisor follows the assignment through all the stages of the process. The first delay faced is the availability of technical editors, who, like writers, are expected to give marking first priority. Likewise, at every stage delays will be experienced. Considerable rewriting or retyping is often required.

## How is the cost of an assignment calculated?

There is no mechanism for calculating the costs of delays or reworks. The cost of each assignment is not known.

# YOUR OBJECTIVE

You are now determined to examine the writing process for new assignments with a view to improving efficiency. You intend to present your recommendations in a report. You will analyse the present situation and make recommendations about:

(a) organizational structure;

(b) the production process;

(c) job design;

(d) motivation;

(e) control system(s).

(N.B. You can assume that the information given in the address in Appendix A was known to you in 1989. The address also gives an indication of some of the changes being contemplated at that time.)

# APPENDIX A: THE OPEN POLYTECHNIC OF NEW ZEALAND

## A brief history

Our institution was set up in 1946 as The New Zealand Technical Correspondence Institute (NZTCI). It began with the amalgamation of the Army's Overseas Education Service and correspondence courses for country apprentices which had been developed by the Wellington Technical College. Distance education was seen as suitable only for students in remote locations and was very much a second-best option. The NZTCI's national functions soon expanded as it became the primary provider of vocational education for the rural sector – a role it still performs today.

During the 1970s, the NZTCI increasingly provided apprenticeship, trades and technician training throughout the country. The 1980s saw rapid growth in professional courses, e.g. in accountancy, management, banking and legal studies. Other developments included the provision of flexible continuing education options for skills upgrading for re-entry to the workforce and for high school students taking 'taster' courses or first-level vocational courses.

By the end of the 1980s, NZTCI offered 8500 different study units in over 900 different courses. It had over 500 full-time staff, 400 of whom were teachers, and it serviced approximately 35 000 students. Tuition was virtually all by correspondence, with very little other student support.

The structure of the organization was very similar to that of a secondary school, with a principal, first and second deputies, 14 heads of teaching departments and a registrar, who was accountable for monitoring expenditure against budgets set by the Department of Education. All salaries, capital work and so on were managed directly by the Department of Education, not by the NZTCI.

By 1989, there were many in the Department of Education and in other institutions who felt that the NZTCI, as it was then known, had not 'kept up with the times', that other institutions could easily take on distance education functions, and that there might be no need for such a national institution. In May 1989, the Minister of Education announced a review which challenged our right to exist as an institution.

A number of reforms were being carried through by the government at that time which would allow considerably greater autonomy for tertiary institutions, with, of course, accompanying increased accountability. As well as justifying our existence, we had to prepare to be successful in the marketplace from 1 January 1990.

We had been funded for 45 years to teach the courses that were not viable because of tiny numbers in any one geographical area. Now we would have to survive on the same funding formula as other institutes. Of the over 800 courses on offer at that time, fewer than ten were really economically viable even with government funding. Thankfully, those few had large enrolments and have provided the base to get us through the transition. Needless to say, they are predominantly business and management courses.

To give you some idea of the magnitude of the change, in 1989 our institution had a budget of around $2 million, most of which was spent on paper and postage. None of the heads of department had any budgets, yet from 1 January 1990 we had to be capable of managing a $30 million budget and operating as a business. We had no central systems in place for management, and certainly not computerized ones – not even for enrolment. We knew how many students we had by asking teachers to do a manual 'head count' three times a year.

Another contrast is that while we were under the Department of Education we had a protected status in that other institutions were not funded to offer distance education courses. However, we were not permitted to enroll any student who lived within 16 km of another polytechnic without the written permission of that polytechnic principal; nor would the department provide any budget for advertising. The result of this was that although we serviced larger numbers of students than any other polytechnic, the institution did not have a high public profile or image at a national level which would support it in a competitive environment.

From this brief introduction, you will understand that our institution had to change. What I want to paint for you now is a picture of our organization as it is at this point of time. It is very different from just three years ago!

## The Open Polytechnic of New Zealand in 1992

### Shared beliefs

Our stated values are excellence, equity, responsiveness, integrity and professionalism. These are the base from which we operate and they certainly give us plenty of challenges in trying to live up to them.

### Strategy

The first thing is to put clients first. From an independent survey of all enrolled students last year, we learned that over 95% are satisfied with the service we offer and we now have a benchmark against which we can monitor progress.

We have a strong vision of what open learning means and how we want to be the leaders in that field. We say we want to be the client's *first-stop shop.* We do not set out to be all things to all people. Our first commitment is to ensure they get what they need or want. If we can only provide part of that, we *find a partner* who can help us to meet the full requirement, or we recommend another provider. We want people to come back to us again and again, and they will only do that if we serve them well.

We are trying to follow the tenets of open learning and provide our services when and where the clients want. We are not putting investments into buildings – we are investing heavily in *upskilling staff*, in ensuring *quality course production and learning support*, and in management of quality control systems which enable us to *respond flexibly* to client need.

We have *diversified our base of products and services*. From being only a correspondence teaching institution, we have moved to being an open learning business. The last word is important, because moving more towards a *business orientation* has been crucial for our survival. A key issue for staff is ensuring that this orientation does support *excellence in educational terms* – we cannot compromise our standing as an academic institution. Profit is *not* our objective, but staying in business most certainly is.

While we are trying to get more people wanting our existing products and services, we are also *developing new ones* but always within our core business of provision of open learning. For example, we now offer use of examination centres, management of external examinations, training needs analysis, workplace training, and student record systems for open learning, all on a commercial basis. One of our major 'earners' is our Instructional Design Unit, which is now providing services for outside organizations, including other polytechnics.

We have also put considerable investment into developing technologies for increasing delivery options. We offer freephone access for tutor help, audio conferencing, and audio and video letters; we are piloting audiographic teleconferencing; and we are producing videos as well as buying in when appropriate. At present we do not use broadcast TV, since for our students it is cheaper for us to pay for postage of the video cassette than pay for broadcast time.

In eight other polytechnics, we have student Learning Support Centres for our students, and we are now developing regional Open Learning Access Centres, beginning in Auckland next year.

All of these activities demonstrate our commitment to client choice. We have to provide the options.

## Style

It has been difficult to obtain commitment from staff to what is currently a highly centrally controlled system. Greater freedom will come as our systems become more robust. In my view, there is probably a cycle through central control and autonomy which is recurring – or at least a spiral, which does mean that you do progress with each swing.

With major changes, we do try to employ the key components of change management. While we have certainly used outside consultancy help, particularly where objectivity has been required, we have created our own future. We have not waited to have change imposed on us. It is our own staff who have made all key decisions and determined how these should be implemented. This has ensured that they understand better why and what is happening, and is probably the major reason why we have been able to achieve what we have.

## Structure

Our structure is now functionally derived, with a strong management team comprising three deans, five directors and me. We have three faculties – Commerce, General Studies and Technology. Directors cover Planning and Development, Marketing, Human Resources, Corporate Services and Education Services. This team leads the polytechnic. Although the accountability is mine, I believe that if I tried to implement any decision which did not have the support of this team, that decision would be unlikely to be successful. We need the collective wisdom of each of the perspectives on that team.

As well as their responsibilities for contributing to polytechnic management, each of the team leads and is accountable for the negotiated outputs for their faculty or branch.

Within faculties and branches, each dean or director can develop a structure that is most appropriate for them, provided that there are clear lines of accountability and that the span of control of each manager is not less than five and not more than 12.

Teachers have now begun to accept that there is a management role in each work area in the faculty – and that is a major change from the situation in 1989.

## Systems

We have developed disciplined systems and processes to help achieve our goals. These ensure that we assess our situation appropriately, plan well, focus people on doing things right the first time, give clear feedback on progress and performance, and evaluate the effectiveness of the system we use.

# APPENDIX B: PRODUCTION FLOW CHART WITH ESSENTIAL RESPONSIBILITIES

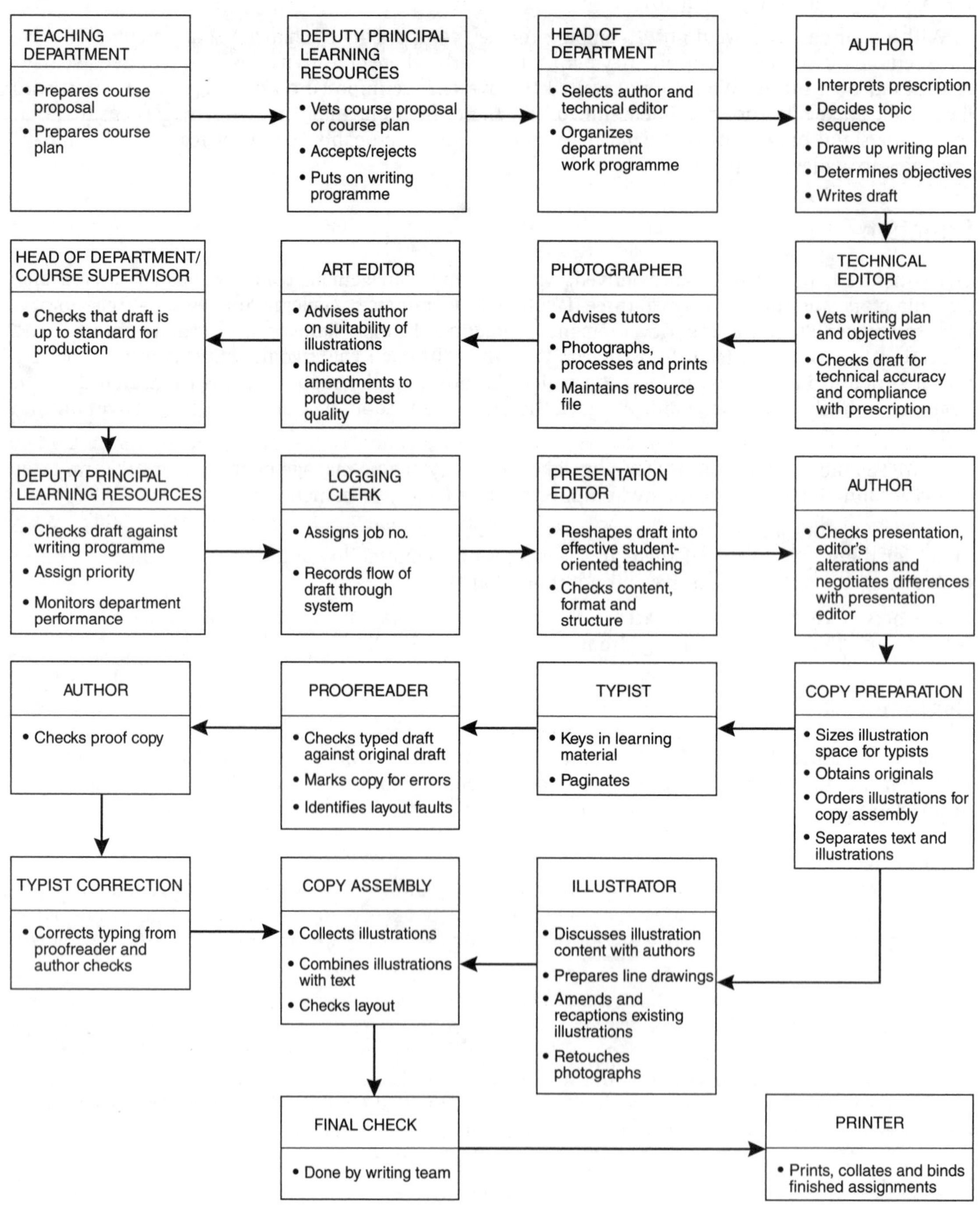

Case study 27

# Food Concept Sdn. Bhd.

## INTRODUCTION

Mr C. G. Cho was brought up in Taiping, which is about 150 miles away from Kuala Lumpur, the capital of Malaysia. Entrepreneurship is part of the family's tradition. Mr Cho's grandfather operated the largest pawn shop in Ipoh, which is about 60 miles away from Taiping, but it was closed down shortly after the Japanese occupation. Mr Cho's father is a businessman who owns two shops which sell clothing. During his schooldays, Mr Cho used to work in his father's shop after school. He recalls his father saying that to control one's destiny is to be 'on your own in wealth creation'.

After graduating with the BSc Degree in Electrical Engineering from National Taiwan University, Taipei, Taiwan in 1981, he worked as a programmer for over a year at the university's computer centre. Then he set out to acquire exposure in business operations and management and took a two-year MBA course in the USA. During that programme, he was working part-time as a marketing executive for Trimark in direct mail advertising, which provided a lot of opportunities for him to familiarize himself with and understand some of the operations of companies like KFC and McDonald's, as well as proprietary outlets like Korean and Japanese restaurants and jewellery shops. His experience inspired him to run his own business in a similar industry.

In 1985, on returning from the USA, in order to understand the Malaysian business environment he took up the post of marketing manager for CSA, a local computer company, for about nine months. Subsequent to that, he teamed up with a friend in an engineering company with the intention to set up a personal computer division; however, the project was abandoned. In 1987, he formed a company known as Prolog, selling PC solutions. At the same time, he saw an opportunity to open a food stall in Yaohan Shopping Mall in Kuala Lumpur, which marked the beginning of his food chain businesses.

## HISTORY

Mr Cho aims to transform the traditional hawker type of food stalls into an integrated food chain. With a capital of RM30 000 he started his very first food stall, known as Restoran Chili, in Yaohan Shopping Mall. With the success of the operation, he subsequently opened another three Restoran Chili outlets over a period of four years. They are located at Mutiara Court, Bangsar Shopping Centre and Lot 10 respectively.

Mr Cho's food stall business has been growing rapidly. At the same time, more and more shopping complexes are being built as the working population grows, particularly in Kuala Lumpur. Further, research indicates that most shoppers would also like to savour a variety of foods whilst shopping at their convenience. Mr Cho's aim is to establish his Food Concept Sdn. Bhd. business to incorporate Restoran Chili and other types of outlet; for example, the first Chili Food Court was opened at Lot 10 in October 1990 and it is also planned to open another one at Dataran Merdeka in mid-1993.

The overall aim is to operate an integrated food business. Having accomplished the first step, he has also ventured into the concept restaurant business with Cafe Galerie and Chili Restoran and Bar. The former was established in 1991 and located at Metrojaya Shopping Complex, while the later was established in late 1992 and located at Jalan Ampang.

## C. G. CHO'S BUSINESS PHILOSOPHY AND TRADE CONCEPT

'Business must grow and expand; if not, it will die.' Mr Cho has built his business to its present size on the basis of this maxim.

In line with his long-term vision, he has planned to open as many food stalls and food courts as possible in new and popular shopping complexes in order to recoup his investment within a short period, leveraging on the peak of the shopping complexes business cycle and at the same time sustaining profitability and maintaining market share.

With the success of the Cafe Galerie and Chili Restoran and Bar, he is now also looking into expansion into niche markets. Thus a Sogo Cafe is scheduled to be opened in January 1994.

To control and monitor his business closely, Mr Cho has centralized the following:

(a) purchasing and inventory control;

(b) preparation, cooking and quality control;

(c) distribution;

(d) administration and accounting.

He aims to ensure a net profit of 20%.

## PRODUCT LINES DEVELOPMENT

As at May 1993, there are three main product lines:

(a) fast food chain – Restoran Chili;

(b) food courts – Chili Food Court, Lot 10 and Dataran Merdeka;

(c) concept restaurants and cafes – Cafe Galerie, Chili Restoran and Bar, and Sogo Cafe.

With the centralized kitchen facilities, an outdoor catering service unit has also been established to cater for parties/functions, etc.

Mr Cho also wishes to venture into other types of restaurants, such as Korean, Japanese, Vietnamese and Chinese restaurants, and also entertainment outlets like discotheques and bars. For long-term product development, he wishes to invest in hotels and resorts, food processing and trading.

## ORGANIZATIONAL FRAMEWORK FOR OPERATIONS CONTROL

Restoran Chili, Cafe Galerie and Chili Restoran and Bar are wholly owned subsidiary companies of Food Concept Sdn. Bhd. They are all managed by Food Concept Sdn. Bhd.

Appendices A and B show the corporate profile and group organizational structure as at May 1993.

The group's operation consists of six major areas as follows.

1. ***Services***: Offer best customer services in the following areas:
   (a) attention to customer requests;
   (b) prompt service in order-taking and dispensing of foods.

2. ***Production***:
   (a) ensure availability of all items on the menu at all times;
   (b) maintain consistency of quality foods at all times;
   (c) ensure only fresh and quality foods to be served at all times;
   (d) ensure clean and hygienic preparation of all foods;
   (e) use of sophisticated equipment to cut down preparation time and hence increase productivity;
   (f) continue proper training and exposure for chefs to maintain leadership;
   (g) all new items in menu being fully tested before introducing to the public.
3. ***Distribution***:
   (a) timely and efficient delivery of goods from central kitchen to all outlets;
   (b) optimize scheduling and delivery.
4. ***Purchasing, inventory control and cost control***:
   (a) centralization of purchase for all outlets;
   (b) tendering exercise to ensure best pricing for bulk purchase;
   (c) optimize stock level;
   (d) primary and secondary suppliers policy to ensure a continued supply of all goods;
   (e) prompt, 'on the dot', payment according to terms to ensure best services from suppliers.
5. ***Promotion and advertisement***:
   (a) ensure corporate image and identity are all being considered and followed on all advertising and promotional exercises;
   (b) centralized co-ordination and planning for all outlets within the group.
6. ***Staffing***:
   (a) to provide on-going training and exposure to staff by visiting other establishments (local and overseas);
   (b) total trust is given when any staff are employed to ensure confidence/high motivation in work performance;
   (c) participative and flexible management style is being practised at all outlets;
   (d) internal promotion takes precedence over outside hiring;
   (e) provide better working environment, and office politics discouraged.

The organizational structure is shown in Appendix C (as at May 1993). The operating structure is shown in Appendix D (both as at May 1993). Financial highlights are presented in Appendix E.

## A LOOK TO THE FUTURE

The group has grown to such a stage that the management feels that it is high time to organize the business to optimize the operations and maximize profitability for future business expansion and diversification.

Better planning and control is also required in the six areas of the business.

## APPENDIX A: COMPANY PROFILE

Food Concept Sdn. Bhd. was founded in 1989, primarily to plan, design and manage the Chili Food Court (currently the most successful in Malaysia) at Lot 10, which opened on 10 October 1990. However, from its initial inception as a specialist in food court design and management, it soon ventured into other related businesses as a natural extension of skills acquired and opportunities identified. These include the chain of local fast food restaurants, food courts and concept restaurants.

The company now employs a team of highly competent professionals in various aspects of marketing, finance, operations, personnel development and training.

Food Concept Sdn. Bhd. is a holding company with special focus on food and beverage operations. It is well established and positioned in three major areas:

1. Fast food chain – local fast food restaurants strategically located at:
   Yaohan
   Mutiara Court
   Lot 10
   The Bangsar Shopping Centre
2. Food courts – innovative concept of food courts serving both local and international food fare:
   Chili Food Court, Lot 10;
   14 000 $ft^2$, 16 stalls

   Chili Food Court, Dataran Merdeka (mid-1993);
   10 000 $ft^2$, 12 stalls
3. Concept restaurants and cafes – Cafe Galerie Sdn. Bhd. Metrojaya;
   first of its kind, combining cafe and art gallery
   Chili Restaurant and Bar, 35 Jalan Ampang;
   located in an old colonial building more than 100 years old, the restaurant is tastefully decorated in the 1930s and 1940s style, with an ambience to complement the fine Malaysian cuisine

   Sogo Cafe (January 1994);
   a vibrant, contemporary cafe combining Eastern and Western cuisine

The companies which together cover these areas of activity are:

1. Food Concept Sdn. Bhd.
2. Restoran Chili Sdn. Bhd.
3. Cafe Galerie Snd. Bhd.
4. Restoran Chili (Jalan Ampang) Sdn. Bhd.

Group turnover: RM 5 million

Total staff strength: 150 persons

| Company | Date of incorporation | Principal activities |
|---|---|---|
| 1. Food Concept Sdn. Bhd. | 1989 | Independent management and consultancy company specializing in food court management |
| 2. Restoran Chili Sdn. Bhd. | 1987 | Local fast food chain |
| 3. Cafe Galerie Sdn. Bhd. | 1991 | Concept restaurant |
| 4. Chili Restoran and Bar | 1992 | Concept restaurant |

# APPENDIX B: CORPORATE STRUCTURE

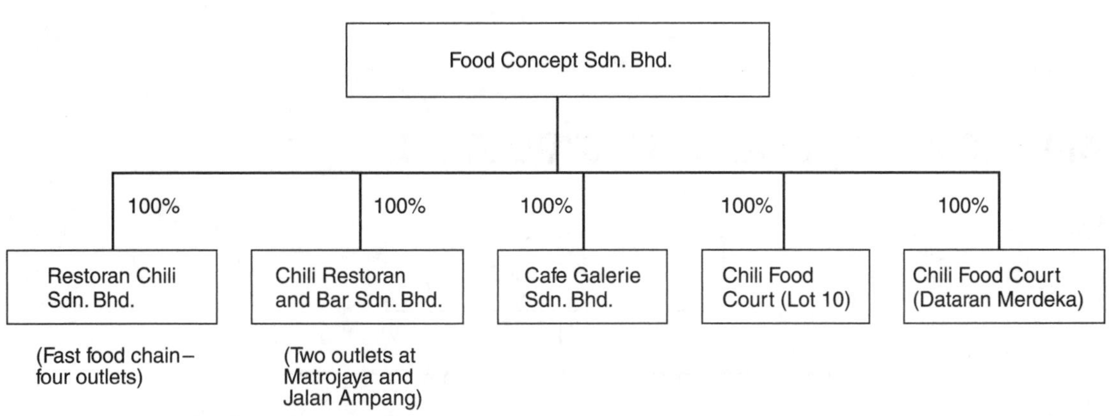

## APPENDIX C: ORGANIZATIONAL STRUCTURE

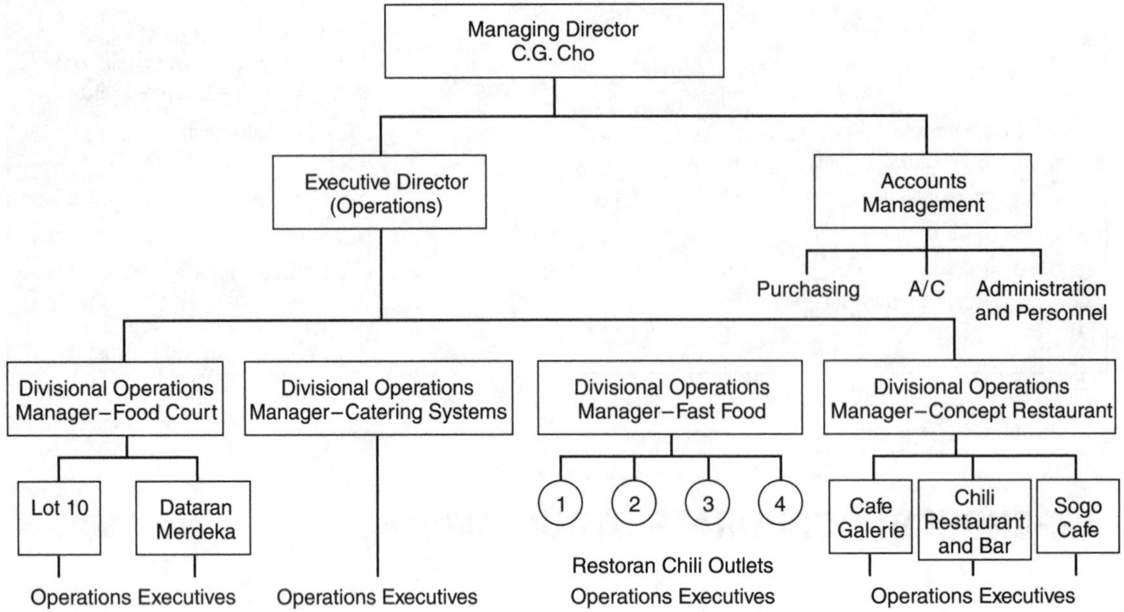


## APPENDIX D: OPERATIONAL STRUCTURE

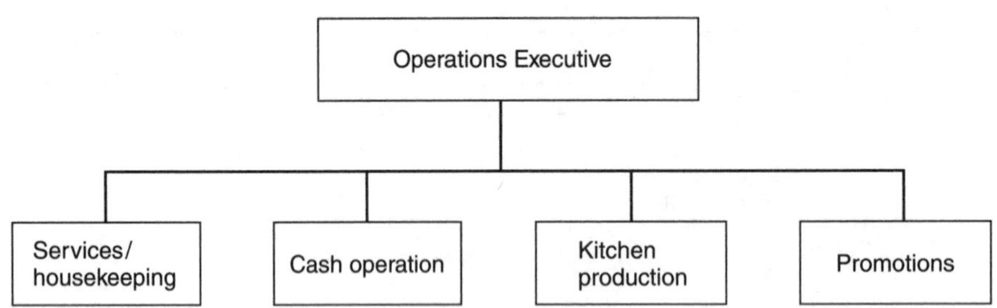

# APPENDIX E: FINANCIAL HIGHLIGHTS: NUMBER OF ESTABLISHMENTS AND REVENUE SUMMARY

| | 1987 | 1988 | 1989 | 1990 | 1991 | 1992 | 1993 |
|---|---|---|---|---|---|---|---|
| Fast food chain | 1 | 2 | 4 | 4 | 4 | 4 | 5 |
| Food courts | | | 1 | 1 | 1 | 1 | 2 |
| Concept restaurants | | | | | 1 | 2 | 2 |
| Total | 1 | 2 | 5 | 5 | 6 | 7 | 9 |
| Revenue (000s M$) | 200 | 400 | 1000 | 3000 | 4000 | 4500 | 5500 |

# Appendices

Appendix I Linear programming
Appendix II Forecasting techniques
Appendix III Computer simulation
Appendix IV Answers to odd-numbered analytical questions

Appendix I

# Linear programming

## NOTATION USED IN APPENDIX I

$a_i$ Capacity for source $i$
$b_j$ Requirement of destination $j$
$i$ Source ($i$ = 1 to $m$)
$j$ Destination ($j$ = 1 to $n$)
$x_{ij}$ Volume 'transported' from source $i$ to destination $j$

Consider the problem facing a firm making a range of different products. Each product is made in a different way, and for each product there exists a best or optimal method of manufacture. Unfortunately, there are insufficient resources to make each product in the best possible way, hence the problem is to decide which products to make, and in what proportions, in order to maximize profits, or minimize costs.

This is an *allocation* problem. Such problems arise whenever there are several activities to perform, but limitations on resources prevent the performance of each activity in its best way. For example, a manufacturer makes two types of product, A and B. Each product A requires 1 hour of machining, 5 hours of fabrication and 3 hours of assembly. Each product B requires 2 hours of machining, 4 hours of fabrication and 1 hour of assembly. In a given period of time there are only 720 hours of machining, 1800 hours of fabrication and 900 hours of assembly time available. How should the manufacturer use this capacity in order to maximize profit if the profit on each product A is £80 and on B £100?

Allocation problems such as this can be solved by means of linear programming, provided:

(a) the objective to be achieved can be expressed as a linear function in terms of the various activities;

(b) the limiting constraints can also be expressed in linear form.

## THE SIMPLEX ALGORITHM

The Simplex algorithm is best described by means of an example (based on the above manufacturing example).

## EXAMPLE I.1

### Maximizing

Two products, A and B. Manufacturing time required is shown in Figure I.1.

| | Machining | Fabrication | Assembly | Profit on product |
|---|---|---|---|---|
| A | 1 hour | 5 hours | 3 hours | £80 |
| B | 2 hours | 4 hours | 1 hour | £100 |
| *Total capacity available* | | | | |
| | 720 hours | 1800 hours | 900 hours | |

**Figure I.1**

Our *objective* in this case is to maximize profits. If $W$ = profit obtained, we wish to maximize $W$ where $W = 80A + 100B$.

Our *constraints* are as follows:

Machining capacity $A + 2B \leq 720$ (Total machining hours used cannot exceed 720)
Fabrication capacity $5A + 4B \leq 1800$
Assembly capacity $3A + B \leq 900$

We must express these constraints as equations rather than as the inequalities shown above. This can be done by introducing further variables (called *slack variables*) as follows:

$$A + 2B + p = 720 \quad (1)$$
$$5A + 4B + q = 1800 \quad (2)$$
$$3A + B + r = 900 \quad (3)$$

These slack variables ($p$, $q$, $r$) will, of course, represent either zero or positive figures.

The Simplex method is a procedure for solving a set of such equations simultaneously. The first step is to set down the data in a *tableau* or table form, as in Figure I.2. The first three rows of figures represent equations (1) (2) and (3). $P_o$ is the figure on the right-hand side of the equation, and $p$, $q$ and $r$ appear in the first column to indicate that they also feature in the equations. The fourth row is the objective function, but written in negative form.

The procedure by which the solution is achieved is known as the Gauss Jordan Complete Elimination Procedure.[1]

| | A | B | $p$ | $q$ | $r$ | $P_o$ |
|---|---|---|---|---|---|---|
| $p$ | 1 | 2 | 1 | 0 | 0 | 720 |
| $q$ | 5 | 4 | 0 | 1 | 0 | 1800 |
| $r$ | 3 | 1 | 0 | 0 | 1 | 900 |
| $W$ | −80 | −100 | 0 | 0 | 0 | 0 |

**Figure I.2**

[1] We shall use the procedure and show that an optimum answer results. The basis and development of the procedure and of the Simplex algorithm can be found in most operational research textbooks (see 'Further Reading' at the end of this appendix).

The steps in the procedure for obtaining an optimum solution are as follows:

1. Select the largest negative figure in the W row. In our case this is 100 in column B.
2. Find the figure in this column which gives the smallest positive figure when divided into $P_o$. In our case this is 2 in the first row, since 720/2 is smaller than either 1800/4 or 900/1.
3. Divide this row by this figure, enter the results as the equivalent row of a new tableau under W, and replace the slack variable letter on the left with the variable of the column concerned, as in Figure I.3.

| | A | B ↓ | *p* | *q* | *r* | $P_o$ |
|---|---|---|---|---|---|---|
| → *p* | 1 | (2) | 1 | 0 | 0 | 720 |
| *q* | 5 | 4 | 0 | 1 | 0 | 1800 |
| *r* | 3 | 1 | 0 | 0 | 1 | 900 |
| *W* | –80 | –100 | 0 | 0 | 0 | 0 |
| → B | $\frac{1}{2}$ | 1 | $\frac{1}{2}$ | 0 | 0 | 360 |

**Figure I.3**

4. Eliminate this variable from each of the other rows by multiplying the new row in turn by the negative values of the figures in the column and adding the result to the row concerned.

   Consider the second row. The negative of the figure in the second column is –4. Multiply all of the new row by -4 and add the result to the original second row, as in Figure I.4.

   Consider the third row. The negative of the figure in the second column is –1. Multiply all of the first row in the new tableau by –1 and add the result to the original third row.

   Do the same for the original *W* row, i.e. multiply the first row in new tableau by 100 (the negative of –100), and then add to original *W* row, as in Figure I.5.

5. Repeat the same procedure for the new tableau, i.e. largest negative in last row is –30. Select 3 in this column. Divide this row by 3 and write the new row into the third tableau, as in Figure I.6.

   Eliminate this variable from each of the other rows by multiplying in turn the new row by the negative value of the figure in the column and adding the result to the row concerned, i.e. for first row in new tableau multiply by -$1/2$ and add, etc. (Figure I.7).

6. Repeat until there are no further negative values in row *W*. Then the optimal solution has been obtained. In this case there are no further negative values in last row, so this last tableau represents the optimal solution.

| | A | B ↓ | *p* | *q* | *r* | $P_o$ |
|---|---|---|---|---|---|---|
| *p* | 1 | (2) | 1 | 0 | 0 | 720 |
| → *q* | 5 | 4 | 0 | 1 | 0 | 1800 |
| *r* | 3 | 1 | 0 | 0 | 1 | 900 |
| *W* | –80 | –100 | 0 | 0 | 0 | 0 |
| B | $\frac{1}{2}$ | 1 | $\frac{1}{2}$ | 0 | 0 | 360 |
| → *q* | 3 | 0 | –2 | 1 | 0 | 360 |

**Figure I.4**

**Figure I.5**

| | | A | B ↓ | $p$ | $q$ | $r$ | $P_o$ |
|---|---|---|---|---|---|---|---|
| | $p$ | 1 | (2) | 1 | 0 | 0 | 720 |
| | $q$ | 5 | 4 | 0 | 1 | 0 | 1800 |
| → | $r$ | 3 | 1 | 0 | 0 | 1 | 900 |
| → | $W$ | −80 | −100 | 0 | 0 | 0 | 0 |
| | B | $\frac{1}{2}$ | 1 | $\frac{1}{2}$ | 0 | 0 | 360 |
| | $q$ | 3 | 0 | −2 | 1 | 0 | 360 |
| → | $r$ | $\frac{5}{2}$ | 0 | $-\frac{1}{2}$ | 0 | 1 | 540 |
| → | $W$ | −30 | 0 | 50 | 0 | 0 | 36 000 |

**Figure I.6**

| | A | B | $p$ | $q$ | $r$ | $P_o$ |
|---|---|---|---|---|---|---|
| $p$ | 1 | 2 | 1 | 0 | 0 | 720 |
| $q$ | 5 | 4 | 0 | 1 | 0 | 1800 |
| $r$ | 3 | 1 | 0 | 0 | 1 | 900 |
| $W$ | −80 | −100 | 0 | 0 | 0 | 0 |
| B | $\frac{1}{2}$ | 1 | $\frac{1}{2}$ | 0 | 0 | 360 |
| $q$ | (3) | 0 | −2 | 1 | 0 | 360 |
| $r$ | $\frac{5}{2}$ | 0 | $-\frac{1}{2}$ | 0 | 1 | 540 |
| $W$ | −30 | 0 | 50 | 0 | 0 | 36 000 |
| – | – | – | – | – | – | – |
| A | 1 | 0 | $-\frac{2}{3}$ | $\frac{1}{3}$ | 0 | 120 |

The solution is interpreted as follows. The letters on the left of the tableau represent the variables which feature in the solution, i.e. in this case, variables B, A and $r$. In other words $p$ and $q$ have been lost, and hence our three equations are now as follows:

$$A + 2B = 720$$
$$5A + 4B = 1800$$
$$3A + B + r = 900$$

From these equations the values of A and B can be found. Alternatively, they can be read straight from the final tableau, i.e.

B = 300 ($P_o$)
A = 120 ($P_o$)
The profit $W$ = 80 (120) + 100 (300)
= £39600

| | A | B | $p$ | $q$ | $r$ | $P_o$ |
|---|---|---|---|---|---|---|
| $p$ | 1 | 2 | 1 | 0 | 0 | 720 |
| $q$ | 5 | 4 | 0 | 1 | 0 | 1800 |
| $r$ | 3 | 1 | 0 | 0 | 1 | 900 |
| $W$ | –80 | –100 | 0 | 0 | 0 | 0 |
| B | $\frac{1}{2}$ | 1 | $\frac{1}{2}$ | 0 | 0 | 360 |
| $q$ | (3) | 0 | –2 | 1 | 0 | 360 |
| $r$ | $\frac{5}{2}$ | 0 | $-\frac{1}{2}$ | 0 | 1 | 540 |
| $W$ | –30 | 0 | 50 | 0 | 0 | 36 000 |
| B | 0 | 1 | $\frac{5}{6}$ | $-\frac{1}{6}$ | 0 | 300 |
| A | 1 | 0 | $-\frac{2}{3}$ | $\frac{1}{3}$ | 0 | 120 |
| $r$ | 0 | 0 | $\frac{7}{6}$ | $-\frac{5}{6}$ | 1 | 240 |
| $W$ | 0 | 0 | 30 | 10 | 0 | 39 600 |

**Figure I.7**

**EXAMPLE I.2**

## *Minimizing*

It is often necessary to minimize a function such as cost. Minimization of an objective function can be achieved quite easily, since the objective *Min.* $W = x + y$ is equivalent to *Max.* $(-W) = -x - y$. Consequently a Simplex solution can be obtained in exactly the same manner as previously.

Minimize the following objective function: $W = 4A - 6B$ subject to the following constraints:

$$-A + 2B \leq 8$$
$$-3A + 4B \leq 12$$

The equivalent of minimizing $W$ is *Max.* $(-W)$, i.e.

Objective = *Max.* $(-W) = -4A + 6B$

The constraints can be expressed as equalities as follows:

$$-A + 2B + p = 8$$
$$-3A + 4B + q = 12$$

The initial tableau is shown in Figure I.8.

A solution is obtained as follows:

1. Select largest negative figure in $(-W)$ row, i.e. –6.
2. Find the figure in this column which gives the smallest positive figure when divided by $P_o$, i.e. 4.

| | A | B | $p$ | $q$ | $P_o$ |
|---|---|---|---|---|---|
| $p$ | –1 | 2 | 1 | 0 | 8 |
| $q$ | –3 | 4 | 0 | 1 | 12 |
| $(-W)$ | 4 | –6 | 0 | 0 | 0 |

**Figure I.8**

3. Divide this row by this figure, enter the result as the equivalent row of a new tableau, and replace slack variable on left, as in Figure I.9.

**Figure I.9**

| | A | B (↓) | $p$ | $q$ | $P_o$ |
|---|---|---|---|---|---|
| $p$ | –1 | 2 | 1 | 0 | 8 |
| → $q$ | –3 | (4) | 0 | 1 | 12 |
| (–$W$) | 4 | –6 | 0 | 0 | 0 |
| – | – | – | – | – | – |
| B | $-\frac{3}{4}$ | 1 | 0 | $\frac{1}{4}$ | 3 |

4. Eliminate this variable from each of the other rows by multiplying the new row in turn by the negative value of the figure in the column, and adding the result to the row concerned, as in Figure I.10.
5. Repeat this procedure for the new tableau until there are no more negative values in the (–$W$) row (Figure I.11).

**Figure I.10**

| | A | B | $p$ | $q$ | $P_o$ |
|---|---|---|---|---|---|
| $p$ | –1 | 2 | 1 | 0 | 8 |
| $q$ | –3 | 4 | 0 | 1 | 12 |
| (–$W$) | 4 | –6 | 0 | 0 | 0 |
| $p$ | $\frac{1}{2}$ | 0 | 1 | $-\frac{1}{2}$ | 2 |
| B | $-\frac{3}{4}$ | 1 | 0 | $\frac{1}{4}$ | 3 |
| (–$W$) | $-\frac{1}{2}$ | 0 | 0 | $1\frac{1}{2}$ | 18 |

**Figure I.11**

| | A (↓) | B | $p$ | $q$ | $P_o$ |
|---|---|---|---|---|---|
| $p$ | –1 | 2 | 1 | 0 | 8 |
| $q$ | –3 | 4 | 0 | 1 | 12 |
| (–$W$) | 4 | 6 | 0 | 0 | 0 |
| → $p$ | ($\frac{1}{2}$) | 0 | 1 | $-\frac{1}{2}$ | 2 |
| B | $-\frac{3}{4}$ | 1 | 0 | $\frac{1}{4}$ | 3 |
| (–$W$) | $-\frac{1}{2}$ | 0 | 0 | $1\frac{1}{2}$ | 18 |
| A | 1 | 0 | 2 | –1 | 4 |
| B | 0 | 1 | $1\frac{1}{2}$ | $-\frac{1}{2}$ | 6 |
| (–$W$) | 0 | 0 | 1 | 1 | 20 |

The solution is:

*Max.* (–$W$) = 20
*Min.* $W$ = –20
when A = 4
B = 6

## Inequalities of the form $x - y \geq N$

Suppose the constraints in a linear programming problem were as follows:

$$3x + y \geq 3$$
$$4i + 3y \geq 6$$

Then introducing slack variables gives:

$$3x + y - p = 3$$
$$4x + 3y - q = 6$$

where $p$ and $q$ are positive values or zero.

It is not possible, however, to use the Simplex procedure to solve equations such as these, since, with this method, only slack variables with positive signs are allowed. However, a solution can be achieved by introducing a further set of variables called artificial variables as follows:

$$3x + y - p + s = 3$$
$$4x + 3y - q + t = 6$$

Although we do not propose to describe the procedure, the Simplex method can now be used to obtain an optimum solution in a manner very similar to that described above.

## Equations

A similar situation to the above arises when constraints must be expressed as equations rather than inequalities. If, in our original example, it was essential that *all* of the machining capacity were used, our constraints would be:

$$A + 2B = 720$$
$$5A + 4B = 1800$$
$$3A + B = 900$$

Such a situation again necessitates the use of *artificial variables*, and a solution can again be obtained using the Simplex method.

# THE TRANSPORTATION ALGORITHM

The transportation algorithm is a special case of linear programming and is applicable to the special type of allocation problem in which both requirements and resources are expressed in terms of one type of unit. It can be used, for example, to minimize the total cost of distributing goods from $n$ dispatch points to $m$ receiving points, provided the following conditions are satisfied:

(a) The number of items to be dispatched from, and the number to be received at, each point is known.

(b) The cost of transportation between each pair of points is known.

Again the technique is best illustrated by means of a simple example.

**EXAMPLE I.3**

Three steel mills produce steel at the rate of:

A = 60 tonnes/h
B = 100 tonnes/h
C = 150 tonnes/h

Three factories require steel at rates of:

1 = 140 tonnes/h
2 = 120 tonnes/h
3 =  50 tonnes/h

The costs of transportation between steel mills and factories are given by the values in the cells in the matrix in Figure I.12.

Using all of this information we can construct our first transportation tableau for this allocation problem, where $x_{ij}$ is the amount of steel transported or allocated from mill $i$ to factory $j$ (Figure I.13).

The objective is to allocate steel to factories so as to minimize total transportation costs.

It is possible to obtain a solution to the problem by using what is known as the *North-west Corner* rule, which gives rise to the following procedure:

1. Start at the NW (i.e. top left-hand) cell.
2. If $a_i < b_j$, set $x_{ij} = a_i$ and proceed vertically.
3. If $a_i > b_j$, set $x_{ij} = b_j$ and proceed horizontally.
4. If $a_i = b_j$, set $x_{ij} = a_i = b_j$ and proceed diagonally.

**Figure I.12**

| | | Factories | | |
|---|---|---|---|---|
| | | 1 | 2 | 3 |
| Steel mills | A | 6 | 8 | 4 |
| | B | 4 | 9 | 3 |
| | C | 1 | 2 | 6 |

**Figure I.13**

| Mill ($i$=A,B,C) \ Factory ($j$=1,2,3) | 1 | 2 | 3 | Output per mill per hour ($a_i$) |
|---|---|---|---|---|
| A | $X_{ij}$ 6 | $X_{ij}$ 8 | $X_{ij}$ 4 | $a_A = 60$ |
| B | $X_{ij}$ 4 | $X_{ij}$ 9 | $X_{ij}$ 3 | $a_B = 100$ |
| C | $X_{ij}$ 1 | $X_{ij}$ 2 | $X_{ij}$ 6 | $a_C = 150$ |
| Requirements per factory per hour ($b_j$) | $b_1 = 140$ | $b_2 = 120$ | $b_3 = 50$ | |

5. Repeat until SE (i.e. bottom right-hand) cell is reached.

Adopting this North-west Corner rule and referring to our example, as in Figure I.14, the steps we would take are as follows:

**Figure I.14**

| | 1 | 2 | 3 | $a_i$ |
|---|---|---|---|---|
| A | **60** ↓ 6 | 8 | 4 | $a_A = 60$ |
| B | **80** → 4 | **20** ↓ 9 | 3 | $a_B = 100$ |
| C | 1 | **100** → 2 | **50** 6 | $a_C = 150$ |
| $b_j$ | $b_1 = 140$ | $b_2 = 120$ | $b_3 = 50$ | |

1. Start in cell A1 (the NW corner).
2. Since $a_i < b_j$ (i.e. 60 < 140), set $x_{ij}$ = 60 and proceed vertically to B1.
3. At B1, $a_i$ = 100 and $b_j$ = (140 – 60) = 80 (i.e. factory 1 required 140, but it has now been allowed 60 from steel mill A and therefore still requires 80). Set B1 = 80 and proceed horizontally.
4. At B2, $b_j$ is now 20 and $a_i$ = 120. Set B2 = 20 and proceed vertically.
5. At C2, $a_i < b_j$ (100 < 150). Set C2 = 100 and proceed horizontally.
6. Finally set C3 = 50.

This procedure gives us our first solution to this allocation problem, but this solution is unlikely to be the optimal solution and we must now try to improve on it.

In an attempt to improve on the solution we introduce the concept of *dispatch* and *receiving costs. The dispatch cost plus the receiving cost will equal the transportation cost for the route in question.*

To set the dispatch and receiving costs for mills and factories respectively, let us begin with steel mill A. If the dispatch cost here is 0 then the receiving cost for factory 1 must be 6, since the transportation cost for the route is 6.

Proceeding in an identical manner and using only the cells used in the first solution, we can now determine both dispatch and receiving costs for all the routes used by the first solution (Figure I.15).

**Figure I.15**

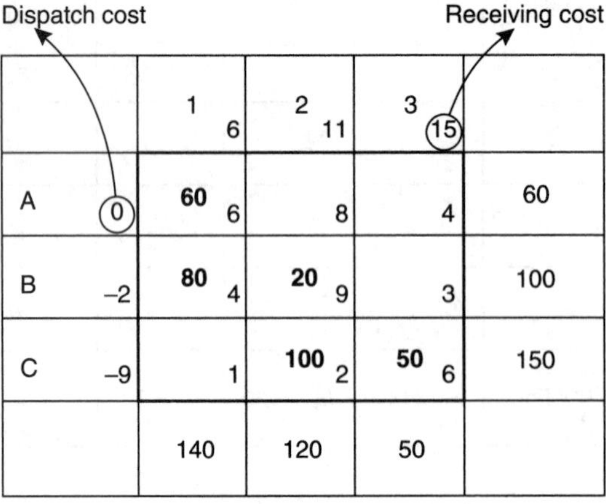


After setting the two costs for route A to 1, the receiving cost at 1 can be used to set the dispatch cost for B. This must be –2, so the total cost for the route will equal 4. This cost can now be used to set the receiving cost at 2, by considering route B2, etc.

Now let us look at the routes which were *not* used by the first solution. The 'costs' for these routes are the sum of the appropriate dispatch and receiving costs; for example, for route A2 the cost is 0 + 11 = 11. Now the difference between the *actual* cost for that route (i.e. 8) and the cost just calculated (i.e. 11) represents the saving which might be obtained by introducing this route into the solution (Figure I.16).

In our case the maximum saving will result from the use of route A3, so let us try to introduce this route into the solution.

Let us imagine that the quantity $\theta$ is allocated to that route. The total quantity transported by the other routes must be reduced by $\theta$ in order to balance out the allocation. The problem then is merely to *place $-\theta$ and $+\theta$ on the routes in use, so that the $\theta$s for both columns and rows cancel out* (see Figure 1.17).

From this tableau it can be seen that, in practice, the maximum value that $\theta$ can take is 20, since any quantity larger than this would result in the quantity for route B2 becoming negative, which is of course impossible.

We will therefore replace $\theta$ by 20, its maximum value, to produce a new tableau which represents an improved solution (Figure I.17).

**Figure I.16**

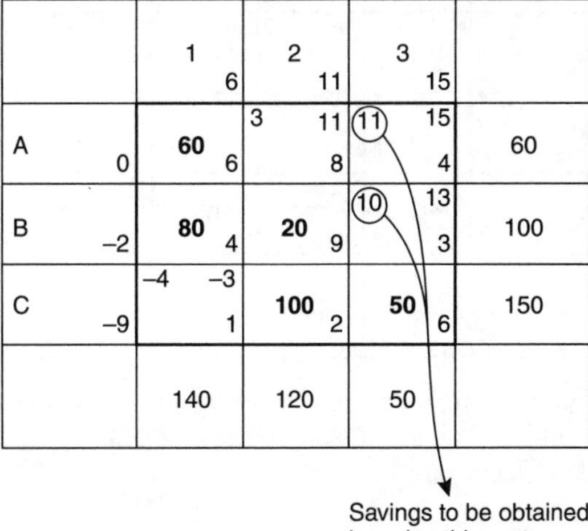

| | | 1 6 | 2 11 | 3 15 | |
|---|---|---|---|---|---|
| A | 0 | **60** 6 | 3 11 8 | (11) 15 4 | 60 |
| B | −2 | **80** 4 | **20** 9 | (10) 13 3 | 100 |
| C | −9 | −4 −3 1 | **100** 2 | **50** 6 | 150 |
| | | 140 | 120 | 50 | |



**Figure I.17**

| | | 1 6 | 2 11 | 3 15 | |
|---|---|---|---|---|---|
| A | 0 | **60 − $\theta$** 6 | 3 11 8 | (11) 15 $\theta$ 4 | 60 |
| B | −2 | **80 + $\theta$** 4 | **20 − $\theta$** 9 | 10 13 3 | 100 |
| C | −9 | −4 3 1 | **100 + $\theta$** 2 | **50 − $\theta$** 6 | 150 |
| | | 140 | 120 | 50 | |

**Figure I.18**

| | | 1 6 | 2 0 | 3 4 | |
|---|---|---|---|---|---|
| A | 0 | **40** 6 | −8 0 8 | **20** 4 | 60 |
| B | −2 | **100** 4 | −11 −2 9 | −1 2 3 | 100 |
| C | 2 | (7) 8 1 | **120** 2 | **30** 6 | 50 |
| | | 140 | 120 | 50 | |

Again we are not certain that it is the optimal solution, so we must once more attempt to improve on it by calculating dispatch and receiving costs to determine whether any of the other routes represent a cost saving (Figure I.18). Route C1 would result in a cost saving of 7; we must therefore introduce this into the solution by allocating $\theta$ to that cell and then balancing out as before (Figure I.19).

**Figure I.19**

| | 1<br>6 | 2<br>0 | 3<br>4 | |
|---|---|---|---|---|
| A<br>0 | **40– θ**<br>6 | –8 0<br>8 | **20+ θ**<br>4 | 60 |
| B<br>–2 | **100**<br>4 | –11 –2<br>9 | –1 2<br>3 | 100 |
| C<br>2 | (7) 8<br>θ<br>1 | **120**<br>2 | **30– θ**<br>6 | 150 |
| | 140 | 120 | 50 | |

The maximum value for $\theta$ is 30, and hence we can obtain a third solution. Again, we can attempt to improve on this solution, but since none of the figures in the unused cells is positive, no saving can be made, and an optimal allocation has been found (Figure I.20).

**Figure I.20**

| | 1<br>6 | 2<br>7 | 3<br>4 | |
|---|---|---|---|---|
| A<br>0 | 10<br>6 | –1 7<br>8 | 50<br>4 | 60 |
| B<br>–2 | 100<br>4 | –4 5<br>9 | –1 2<br>3 | 100 |
| C<br>–5 | 30<br>1 | 120<br>2 | –7 –1<br>6 | 150 |
| | 140 | 120 | 50 | |

The minimum total cost associated with this allocation is therefore:

10(6) + 100(4) + 30(1) + 120(2) + 50(4) = 930

## Complications

### Maximizing

Often the objective is to maximize rather than minimize a function. In such cases basically the same procedure is adopted. The first solution is obtained using the North West Corner rule, but improvements are sought from routes not in use by selecting the cell with the largest *negative* value in the top left-hand corner. For example, had we been maximizing in the previous case, an improvement to the first solution would be sought by introducing cell C1.

### Unequal supply and demand

In the above example the output from the three steel mills was equal to the requirements of the three factories. However, occasions may arise where such an equality does not exist, in which case a modified procedure is required:

(a) If total supply exceeds total demand an additional or 'dummy' column must be added to the matrix in order to accommodate this excess supply.

(b) If total demand exceeds total supply a 'dummy' row must be introduced in order to satisfy this excess demand.

In either case a solution is obtained in exactly the same manner as described previously, but in the case of (a) (supply in excess of demand) the allocations determined for the 'dummy' column (the imaginary consumer) represent the supply or production capacity not utilized, and in the case of (b) (demand in excess of supply), the allocations determined for the 'dummy' row represent the demands which are not satisfied.

## Degeneracy

When, as in the above example, a transportation solution, either intermediate or final, utilizes at least $m + n - 1$ routes or cells, it is possible to determine all 'dispatch' and 'receiving' costs (where $m$ = number of rows and $n$ = number of columns). However, if less than this number of cells are in use it is impossible to determine these costs by the procedure outlined above. Such a situation is said to be *degenerate* and this type of problem requires a slightly different procedure, a description of which can be found in the book given in Further Reading.

# THE ASSIGNMENT ALGORITHM

The assignment problem is a special case of the transportation problem.[2] It can be described as follows.

Given $\mu$ customers and $\mu$ facilities for processing those customers, and given the effectiveness of each facility for each customer, the problem is to allocate each customer to one facility so that a given measure of effectiveness is optimized.

In other words, in the assignment problem we are concerned with the allocation of one item only from each source and the assignment of one item only to each location. The measure of effectiveness of each job for each machine can be represented as before by means of a matrix (Figure I.21).

**Figure I.21**

| | | Customers | | | | |
|---|---|---|---|---|---|---|
| | | A | B | C | D | E |
| Facilities | 1 | 10 | 5 | 9 | 18 | 11 |
| | 2 | 13 | 19 | 6 | 12 | 14 |
| | 3 | 3 | 2 | 4 | 4 | 5 |
| | 4 | 18 | 9 | 12 | 17 | 15 |
| | 5 | 11 | 6 | 14 | 19 | 10 |

For example, the above matrix gives the cost associated with the processing of each of five customers (A–E) on each of five facilities (1–5). The problem therefore is to assign one customer to each facility so that the measure of effectiveness (total cost) is optimized. The problem therefore is a *minimization* one.

## The minimization problem

A solution to this type of problem can be obtained by means of the simple routine described overleaf:

---

2 The assignment problem is the completely *degenerate* form of the transportation problem.

1. Take out the *minimum* figures from each row, as in Figure I.22.

**Figure I.22**

| | A | B | C | D | E | *Minimums* |
|---|---|---|---|---|---|---|
| 1 | 10 | 5 | 9 | 18 | 11 | 5 |
| 2 | 13 | 19 | 6 | 12 | 14 | 6 |
| 3 | 3 | 2 | 4 | 4 | 5 | 2 |
| 4 | 18 | 9 | 12 | 17 | 15 | 9 |
| 5 | 11 | 6 | 14 | 19 | 10 | 6 |

2. Deduct each minimum figure from the figures in that row, as in Figure I.23.

**Figure I.23**

| | A | B | C | D | E |
|---|---|---|---|---|---|
| 1 | 5 | 0 | 4 | 13 | 6 |
| 2 | 7 | 13 | 0 | 6 | 8 |
| 3 | 1 | 0 | 2 | 2 | 3 |
| 4 | 9 | 0 | 3 | 8 | 6 |
| 5 | 5 | 0 | 8 | 13 | 4 |

3. Determine the least number of vertical and/or horizontal lines required to cover all zeros in the new matrix, as in Figure I.24.

**Figure I.24**

| | A | B | C | D | E |
|---|---|---|---|---|---|
| 1 | 5 | 0 | 4 | 13 | 6 |
| 2 | 7 | 13 | 0 | 6 | 8 |
| 3 | 1 | 0 | 2 | 2 | 3 |
| 4 | 9 | 0 | 3 | 8 | 6 |
| 5 | 5 | 0 | 8 | 13 | 4 |

$N = 2$

4. If the number of lines is less than the number of columns or rows (i.e. since $N = 2 < 5$) proceed to the next step.
5. Take out the minimum figures from each of the new columns, as in Figure I.25.

**Figure I.25**

| | A | B | C | D | E |
|---|---|---|---|---|---|
| 1 | 5 | 0 | 4 | 13 | 6 |
| 2 | 7 | 13 | 0 | 6 | 8 |
| 3 | 1 | 0 | 2 | 2 | 3 |
| 4 | 9 | 0 | 3 | 8 | 6 |
| 5 | 5 | 0 | 8 | 13 | 4 |
| *Minimums* | 1 | 0 | 0 | 2 | 3 |

6. Deduct each minimum figure from the figures in that column, as in Figure I.26.
7. Determine the least number of vertical and/or horizontal lines required to cover all zeros in the new matrix, as in Figure I.27.

**Figure I.26**

| | A | B | C | D | E |
|---|---|---|---|---|---|
| 1 | 4 | 0 | 4 | 11 | 3 |
| 2 | 6 | 13 | 0 | 4 | 5 |
| 3 | 0 | 0 | 2 | 0 | 0 |
| 4 | 3 | 0 | 3 | 6 | 3 |
| 5 | 4 | 0 | 8 | 11 | 1 |

8. If the number of lines is less than the number of columns or rows (i.e. since $N = 3 < 5$), proceed to next step.

**Figure I.27**

| | A | B | C | D | E |
|---|---|---|---|---|---|
| 1 | 4 | 0 | 4 | 11 | 3 |
| 2 | 6 | 13 | 0 | 4 | 5 |
| 3 | 0 | 0 | 2 | 0 | 0 |
| 4 | 8 | 0 | 3 | 6 | 3 |
| 5 | 4 | 0 | 8 | 11 | 1 |

$N = 3$

9. Identify *minimum uncovered element* in the new matrix, i.e. Min. = 1 (at E5).
10. (a) Subtract this number from all uncovered elements in the new matrix.
    (b) Add this number to those elements covered by two lines.
    (c) Do not change those elements covered by one line.
    (See Figure I.28.)

**Figure I.28**

| | A | B | C | D | E |
|---|---|---|---|---|---|
| 1 | 3 | 0 | 3 | 10 | 2 |
| 2 | 6 | 4 | 0 | 4 | 5 |
| 3 | 0 | 1 | 2 | 0 | 0 |
| 4 | 7 | 0 | 2 | 5 | 2 |
| 5 | 3 | 0 | 7 | 10 | 0 |

11. Determine the least number of lines to cover all zeros, as in Figure I.29.

**Figure I.29**

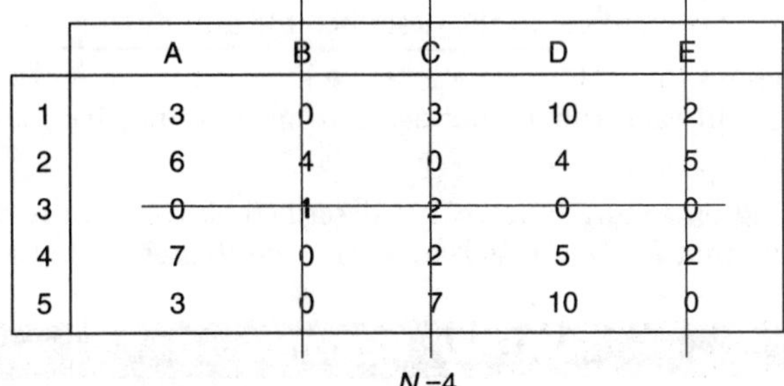

| | A | B | C | D | E |
|---|---|---|---|---|---|
| 1 | 3 | 0 | 3 | 10 | 2 |
| 2 | 6 | 4 | 0 | 4 | 5 |
| 3 | 0 | 1 | 2 | 0 | 0 |
| 4 | 7 | 0 | 2 | 5 | 2 |
| 5 | 3 | 0 | 7 | 10 | 0 |

$N = 4$

12. If the number of lines is less than the number of columns or rows, repeat steps 9, 10 and 11 until the number of lines is equal to the number of columns or rows, i.e. repeating step 9, Min. = 3 (at A5); repeating steps 10 and 11 gives Figure I.30.

13. The optimal assignment is obtained when the number of lines equals the number of columns or rows. The assignment of customers to facilities is given by the zeros in the matrix, as in Figure I.31.

**Figure I.30**

| | A | B | C | D | E |
|---|---|---|---|---|---|
| 1 | 0 | 0 | 3 | 7 | 2 |
| 2 | 3 | 4 | 0 | 1 | 5 |
| 3 | 0 | 4 | 5 | 0 | 3 |
| 4 | 4 | 0 | 2 | 2 | 2 |
| 5 | 0 | 0 | 7 | 7 | 0 |

$N = 5$

**Figure I.31**

| | A | B | C | D | E |
|---|---|---|---|---|---|
| 1 | [0] | 0 | 3 | 7 | 2 |
| 2 | 3 | 4 | [0] | 1 | 5 |
| 3 | 0 | 4 | 5 | [0] | 3 |
| 4 | 4 | [0] | 2 | 2 | 2 |
| 5 | 0 | 0 | 7 | 7 | [0] |

14. The cost associated with the optimal assignment may be calculated as follows:

| Assignment | Cost (from initial matrix) |
|---|---|
| 1–A | 10 |
| 2–C | 6 |
| 3–D | 4 |
| 4–B | 9 |
| 5–E | 10 |
| | Total = 39 |

## The maximization problem

The procedure for maximizing is identical to the described for minimizing, except for:

Step 1 The maximum figures for each row are extracted.

Step 2 Each of the figures in each row is subtracted from its respective maximum to produce the second matrix.

Thereafter the maximizing procedure follows that described above, i.e. the new matrix is modified by first subtracting the minimum figure for each row from the figures in that row, etc.

## FURTHER READING

**Hillier, E. and Lieberman, G. (1990)** *Introduction to Mathematical Programming.* London: McGraw-Hill.

## QUESTIONS

I.1 Given the following constraints, determine the values of $x$, $y$ and $z$ which minimize $W$, where $W = x - 3y + 2z$

$$3x - y + 2z \leq 7$$
$$-2x + 4y \leq 12$$
$$-4x + 3y + 8z \leq 10$$

I.2 A health 'retreat' is engaged in the treatment of two types of customers: type X and type Y. The retreat is capable of treating either 400 of type X or 800 of type Y per month but, because of a shortage of staff, it is restricted to treating at most 500 customers per month.

Each customer of type X requires four hours of 'infra-red' treatment, while each of type Y requires only half as many. There are only 500 hours of this treatment available each month. The merit of providing treatment for a type X customer is judged to be equivalent to an addition of £7 to the profit of the 'retreat', whereas that for type Y is rated as only £5. How many of each type of customer should be treated if 'merit', as defined here, is to be maximized?

I.3 A chemical company manufactures three types of fertilizer: *Grow, Quick Grow* and *Rapid Grow*. Each fertilizer contains the same maximum number of three ingredients, i.e. potash, peat and lime, but in different proportions as shown below:

| | **Potash** % | **Peat** % | **Lime** % |
|---|---|---|---|
| Grow | 40 | 40 | 20 |
| Quick Grow | 60 | 20 | 20 |
| Rapid Grow | 80 | 0 | 20 |

Each week up to 6000 kg of potash can be used in the manufacture of fertilizer and up to 3000 kg of peat is available, but there is no restriction on the lime that may be used.

The fertilizer is sold in 5 kg bags, the profit on each type being as follows:

Grow (G) 1p
Quick Grow (Q) 1.5p
Rapid Grow (R) 2p

How many bags of each type must be produced per week if profit is to be maximized and the maximum total output per week is 10 000 kg?

I.4 Solve the following minimization problem using the transportation algorithm.

| **Hotel** | **A** | **B** | **Customer** **C** | **D** | **E** | **Hotel capacity** |
|---|---|---|---|---|---|---|
| **1** | 23 | 27 | 32 | 30 | 43 | 115 |
| **2** | 15 | 15 | 20 | 16 | 35 | 65 |
| **3** | 14 | 19 | 25 | 21 | 37 | 100 |
| **4** | 35 | 44 | 47 | 45 | 60 | 35 |
| **Customer requirements** | 25 | 100 | 70 | 65 | 45 | |

I.5 The costs shown in the cells of the matrix given below relate to the cost of transporting one product between one of three factories (A, B, C) and one of three warehouses (X, Y, Z). Warehouses X, Y and Z must receive a total of 25, 5 and 35 products respectively from the factories A, B and C, which have capacities of 20, 15 and 30 products respectively.

Allocate the output of the factories to the warehouses in such a way that total transportation costs are minimized.

| | X | Y | Z |
|---|---|---|---|
| A | £9 | £8 | £6 |
| B | £3 | £2 | £5 |
| C | £10 | £7 | £11 |

I.6 A large garage wishes to buy four types of accessories in the following quantities:

| | |
|---|---|
| Standard | 25 |
| De luxe | 15 |
| Super | 10 |
| Super de luxe | 5 |

Quotations are received from three distributors who undertake to supply the garage with each of these accessories. The maximum quantities that the three distributors will supply are as follows:

A: 30 of all types combined
B: 30 of all types combined
C: 15 of all types combined

From the quotations, the financial manager of the garage calculates that the profit (£) on each accessory from each distributor is as follows:

| | Standard | De luxe | Super | Super de luxe |
|---|---|---|---|---|
| A | 10 | 11 | 12 | 15 |
| B | 9 | 12 | 15 | 15 |
| C | 5 | 7 | 13 | 20 |

The manager is confident that he can sell all accessories. How should he buy them, i.e. how many of each type from which distributors?

I.7 Each of five distribution depots is to supply one item to one customer. The costs involved in supplying customers are given in the matrix below. Find the 'assignment' of depot to customer which minimizes the total cost of supplying all five customers.

| | Customers | | | | |
|---|---|---|---|---|---|
| Depots | A | B | C | D | E |
| 1 | 2 | 5 | 4 | 3 | 7 |
| 2 | 2 | 6 | 5 | 4 | 6 |
| 3 | 5 | 6 | 5 | 3 | 7 |
| 4 | 3 | 4 | 7 | 2 | 4 |
| 5 | 7 | 5 | 6 | 2 | 1 |

I.8 A transport and general haulage company must send trucks to four cities in England. At the time in question there are six trucks vacant in different parts of the country. The matrix below indicates the costs associated with sending each of the available trucks to each of the four cities. If the company is to minimize the cost associated with redirecting these trucks, which two trucks will not be redirected, and where will the trucks presently at A and B be sent to?

| Present location of truck | City 1 | 2 | 3 | 4 |
|---|---|---|---|---|
| A | 3 | 8 | 2 | 6 |
| B | 7 | 1 | 4 | 5 |
| C | 3 | 8 | 5 | 8 |
| D | 6 | 4 | 3 | 6 |
| E | 5 | 2 | 5 | 3 |
| F | 5 | 7 | 6 | 2 |

Appendix II

# Forecasting techniques[1]

## NOTATION USED IN APPENDIX II

| | |
|---|---|
| $\alpha$ | Exponential smoothing constant |
| $a$ | Constant (intercept value) for linear regression line |
| $b$ | Constant in linear regression |
| cusum | Cumulative sum |
| $h$ | Decision interval in cusum technique |
| $n$ | Number of observations/values |
| $N$ | Number of periods in a moving average forecast |
| $r$ | Pearson product moment correlation coefficient |
| $S$ | Standard error of estimate of $Y$ and $X$ |
| $\bar{x}$ | Mean value of individual $x$ values |
| $\bar{y}$ | Mean value of individual $y$ values |

## FORECASTING BY PAST AVERAGE

If our objective is to forecast[1] or predict the sales of an item for the next sales period, then using this method:

Forecasted sales for next period = Average sales for previous periods

[1] Although our discussion of forecasting will focus on sales figures, the procedures considered are equally relevant for other applications.

**EXAMPLE II.1**

| Period | Sales |
|---|---|
| 1 | 6 |
| 2 | 4 |
| 3 | 8 |
| 4 | 7 |
| 5 | 4 |
| 6 | 7 |

Forecasted sales for period 7 = (6 + 4 + 8 + 7 + 4 + 7) ÷ 6 = 6.

Using this technique we might obtain data as shown in Table II.1. Clearly our forecast for period 7 was very accurate, as sales prior to this period had remained at much the same average level. But when sales began to increase in later periods, the accuracy of our forecast was reduced because the forecast was influenced too much by the early sales figures and consequently was unable to rise quickly enough to keep up with actual sales.

Table II.1

| Period | Actual sales | Forecast sales | Error in forecast |
|---|---|---|---|
| 1 | 6 | | |
| 2 | 4 | | |
| 3 | 8 | | |
| 4 | 7 | | |
| 5 | 4 | | |
| 6 | 7 | | |
| 7 | 6 | 6.0 | 0.0 |
| 8 | 8 | 6.0 | -2.0 |
| 9 | 9 | 6.25 | -2.75 |
| 10 | 10 | 6.55 | -3.45 |
| 11 | 12 | 6.9 | -5.10 |
| 12 | 13 | 7.35 | -5.65 |

## FORECAST FROM LAST PERIOD'S SALES

One obvious method of overcoming this is to eliminate the influence of old data and base the forecast only on the sales of the previous period. Had this technique been adopted, our forecasts would have been as in Table II.2. Now our forecast is less accurate during the early period because of the fluctuating sales, whereas in the later period the forecast is more accurate because of the *steady* rising sales.

Table II.2

| Period | Actual sales | Forecast sales | Error in forecast |
|---|---|---|---|
| 1 | 6 | | |
| 2 | 4 | 6 | +2 |
| 3 | 8 | 4 | –4 |
| 4 | 7 | 8 | +1 |
| 5 | 4 | 7 | +3 |
| 6 | 7 | 4 | -3 |
| 7 | 6 | 7 | +1 |
| 8 | 8 | 6 | -2 |
| 9 | 9 | 8 | -1 |
| 10 | 10 | 9 | -1 |
| 11 | 12 | 10 | -2 |
| 12 | 13 | 12 | -1 |

# FORECASTING BY MOVING AVERAGE

This method represents a compromise between the two previous methods, in that neither is the forecast influenced by very old data, nor does it solely reflect the figure for the previous period.

Consider the historical sales figures shown in Table II.3, which are to be used to construct a sales forecast for the next year. We must use a four-period moving average in this case, because it is clear from the graph (Figure II.1) that sales fluctuate on an approximate four-period cycle.

## Seasonal variations

The moving average forecast sales for the example in Table II.3 are compared with actual sales in Figure II.1. Clearly the effect of the moving average is to smooth the sales pattern, and it is therefore of more value in establishing trends. In this case, in order to make a useful forecast of sales, the seasonal variations must be taken into account. For example, for the four periods of 1974 the average sales were:

$$\frac{50 + 60 + 50 + 40}{4} = 50$$

The sales during periods 1 and 3 conformed to the average figure, but the sales during period 2 were high (20% high), while those during period 4 were low (only 80% of the mean for the year).

The percentage variation from the annual mean can be calculated for each period, as shown in Table II.4.

The average percentage variation from the mean for each period can now be used to modify the moving average forecast sales. For example, the forecast for 1977 period 1 would be 35 (moving average) × 102.7 per cent (average percentage variation) = 35.95. Of course this method of obtaining the average percentage variation can be justified only if, as in this example, the annual figures for each period do not differ substantially.

**Table II.3**

| Year | Period | Sales | Four-period moving average forecast |
|---|---|---|---|
| 1974 | 1 | 50 | |
| | 2 | 60 | |
| | 3 | 50 | |
| | 4 | 40 | |
| 1975 | 1 | 50 | 50 |
| | 2 | 55 | 50 |
| | 3 | 40 | 48.75 |
| | 4 | 30 | 46.25 |
| 1976 | 1 | 35 | 43.75 |
| | 2 | 45 | 40 |
| | 3 | 35 | 37.5 |
| | 4 | 25 | 36.25 |
| 1977 | 1 | 35 | 35 |
| | 2 | 45 | 35 |
| | 3 | 35 | 35 |
| | 4 | 30 | 36.25 |

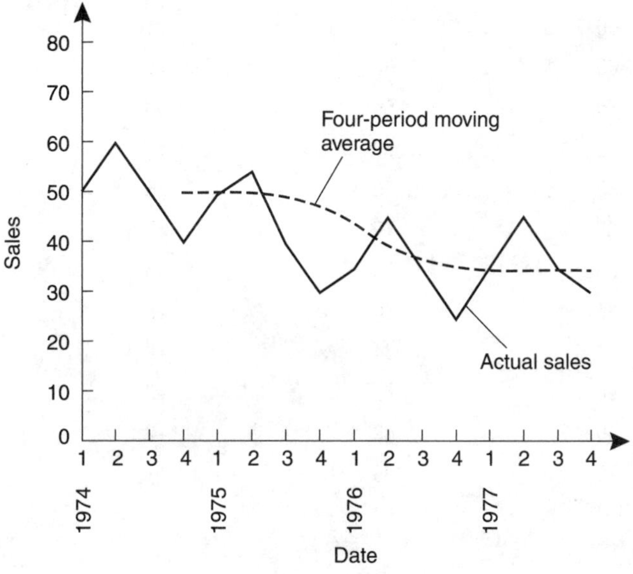


**Figure II.1** Comparison of moving average forecast sales (Table II.3) with actual sales

## Table II.4 Percentage variations calculated from annual means

| | (Values in brackets indicate the mean for the year) | | | | |
|---|---|---|---|---|---|
| Period | 1974 (50) | 1975 (43.75) | 1976 (35) | 1977 (36.25) | Average variation percentage |
| 1 | 100 | 114.2 | 100 | 96.6 | 102.7 |
| 2 | 120 | 125.7 | 128.5 | 124.0 | 124.6 |
| 3 | 100 | 91.5 | 100 | 96.6 | 97.0 |
| 4 | 80 | 68.7 | 71.4 | 82.8 | 75.7 |

## Table II.5

| Period | (a) Actual sales | (b) Five-period moving average | (c) Trend between successive moving averages | (d) Forecast moving average +3 (trend) |
|---|---|---|---|---|
| 0 | 50 | | | |
| 1 | 50 | | | |
| 2 | 50 | | | |
| 3 | 50 | | | |
| 4 | 50 | | | |
| 5 | 55 | 50 | | |
| 6 | 60 | 51 | +1 | 54 |
| 7 | 65 | 53 | +2 | 59 |
| 8 | 70 | 56 | +3 | 65 |
| 9 | 75 | 60 | +4 | 72 |
| 10 | 80 | 65 | +5 | 80 |
| 11 | 85 | 70 | +5 | 85 |
| 12 | 90 | 75 | +5 | 90 |
| 13 | 90 | 80 | +5 | 95 |
| 14 | 90 | 84 | +4 | 96 |
| 15 | 90 | 87 | +3 | 96 |
| 16 | 90 | 89 | +2 | 95 |
| 17 | 90 | 90 | +1 | 93 |
| | | 90 | 0 | 90 |

**Figure II.2**

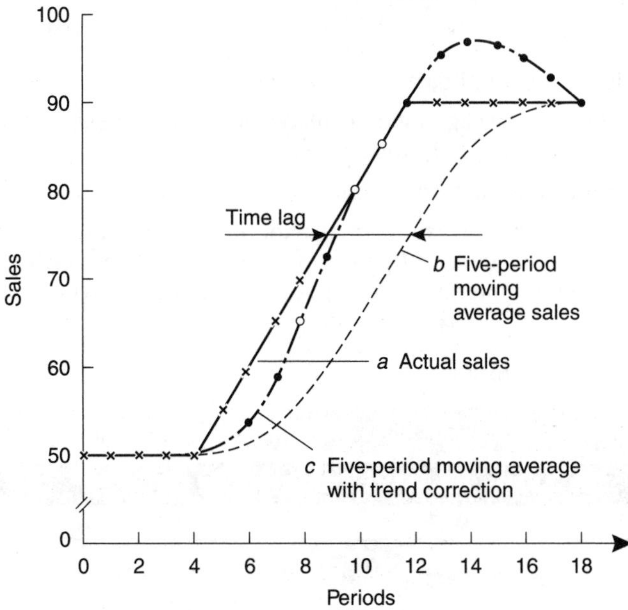


## Secular trends

A secular trend is one which causes sales steadily to increase or decrease. The use of simple moving averages is an adequate method of forecasting, provided sales are subject to neither seasonal variation (as we have seen in Table II.4) nor marked secular trends.

Consider, for example, the sales figures in Table II.5, for which a five-period moving average has been calculated (column (b)). Both actual sales and moving average forecast sales are plotted in Figure II.2 – curves *a* and *b* respectively – from which it can be seen that the forecast curve lags behind the actual curve. In fact the extent of the time lag is given by:

$$\text{Time lag} = \frac{\text{Time span or number of periods of moving average} - 1}{2}$$

But since the moving average is used as the forecast for the *next* period, the time lag is increased by one period, i.e.

$$\text{Actual time lag} = \left(\frac{\text{Time-span} - 1}{2}\right) + 1$$

In this case the time lag of the forecast is three periods. In order to overcome this disadvantage it is necessary to apply a *trend correction* to the moving average forecast. The difference between pairs of moving averages is a measure of the secular trend over one period (assuming that there is no seasonal variation in the data), hence the correction factor should equal this figure multiplied by the time lag, which in this case is three periods. The corrected forecast is given in column (d) of Table II.5.

Curve *c* in Figure II.2 shows how the corrected sales 'catch up' with actual sales after a brief lag period, then settle down to the new constant level after a brief overshoot period.

# FORECASTING BY EXPONENTIAL SMOOTHING

The main disadvantages of the moving average method are:

(a) the lengthy calculations involved;

(b) the need to keep quantities of historical data;

(c) the fact that the normal moving average method places equal weight on each of the historical figures used (equal weight on five figures in the above case);

(d) the age of the data, which increases with the number of periods used.

All these disadvantages are overcome by the exponential smoothing technique. With this technique it is necessary only to retain the previous forecast figure and to know the latest actual sales figures. The technique works by modifying the old forecast in the light of the new sales figure, i.e.

New forecast = $\alpha$ (latest sales figure) + $(1 - \alpha)$ (old forecast)

where $\alpha$ is known as the smoothing constant.

**EXAMPLE II.2**

| | |
|---|---|
| Forecast sales for last period | = 22 |
| Actual sales for last period | = 20 |
| ∴ Forecast sales for next period | $= \alpha(20) + (1 - \alpha)22$ |
| Let smoothing constant $\alpha$ | = 0.1 |
| ∴ Forecast sales for next period | = 0.1(20) + (0.9)22 |
| | = 2 + 19.8 |
| | = 21.8 |

The use of this technique permits the forecast to respond to recent actual events but at the same time retain a certain amount of stability. The amount by which the new forecast responds to the latest sales figure, or the extent to which it is 'damped' by the previous forecast, is, of course, determined by the size of the smoothing constant, $\alpha$. The size of $\alpha$ should be carefully chosen in the light of the stability or variability of actual sales, and is normally from 0.1 to 0.4.

The smoothing constant, $\alpha$, that gives the equivalent of an $N$-period moving average can be calculated as follows:

$$\alpha = \frac{2}{N + 1}$$

For example, if we wish to adopt an exponential smoothing technique equivalent to a nine-period moving average, $\alpha$ can be found as follows:

$$\alpha = \frac{2}{9 + 1} = 0.2$$

**EXAMPLE II.3**

| Week | Sales | Four-period moving average forecast | Error | Exponential smoothing forecast ($\alpha$ = 0.4) | Error |
|---|---|---|---|---|---|
| 1 | 10 | | | | |
| 2 | 12 | | | | |
| 3 | 8 | | | | |
| 4 | 9 | | | | |
| 5 | 10 | 9.75 | 0.25 | 9.45 | 0.55 |
| 6 | 14 | 9.75 | 4.25 | 9.67 | 4.33 |
| 7 | 15 | 10.25 | 4.75 | 11.00 | 4.00 |
| 8 | 14 | 12.00 | 2.00 | 12.60 | 2.40 |
| 9 | 10 | 13.25 | 3.25 | 13.25 | 3.25 |
| 10 | 8 | 13.25 | 5.25 | 11.95 | 3.95 |
| 11 | 6 | 11.75 | 5.75 | 10.37 | 4.37 |
| 12 | 10 | 9.50 | 0.50 | 8.62 | 1.38 |
| 13 | 12 | 8.50 | 3.50 | 9.17 | 2.83 |
| 14 | 8 | 9.00 | 1.00 | 10.30 | 2.30 |
| 15 | 15 | 9.00 | 4.00 | 9.38 | 5.62 |
| | | 11.25 | | 11.63 | |

## Secular trends and seasonal variations

When a secular trend is present the forecast sales obtained by the normal exponential smoothing method will lag behind actual sales, in just the same way as the moving average forecast did. As before, if we are able to estimate the magnitude of the trend in the data, we can apply a trend correction to the forecast to overcome the time lag.

Let us again estimate the trend by comparing successive pairs of forecast figures. In the example in Table II.6 any overall secular trend in the data is obscured by seasonal variations; consequently, in such cases, rather than just taking the difference between successive sales figures as an indication of trends, we must use an estimating procedure. In fact we can use the exponential smoothing method to estimate future trend, i.e.

Forecast trend over next period = $\alpha$ (latest trend figure) + (1 – $\alpha$) (old trend forecast)

The forecast trend can then be used as a correction factor by adding it to the exponential smoothing forecast in just the same way as the trend correction was added to the moving average forecast in the previous section. Hence:

Final forecast of sales = Normal exponential smoothing forecast
+ [(Time lag) × Exponential smoothing forecast of trend]

**Table II.6**

| Period | Sales | Exponential smoothing forecast | Trend in actual sales |
|---|---|---|---|
| 7 | 15 | 11.00 | |
| 8 | 14 | 12.60 | −1 |
| 9 | 10 | 13.25 | −4 |
| 10 | 8 | 11.95 | −2 |
| 11 | 6 | 10.37 | −2 |
| 12 | 10 | 8.62 | +4 |
| 13 | 12 | 9.17 | +2 |
| 14 | 8 | 10.30 | −4 |
| 15 | 15 | 9.38 | +7 |

### Adoptive forecasting

In employing the exponential smoothing technique in forecasting we must choose an appropriate value for $\alpha$. A large value of $\alpha$ will give considerable weighting to the latest actual values, and will be appropriate where a significant trend exists. While a small value of $\alpha$ will give more weighting to older data, and will therefore provide more smoothing in the forecast, the correct value of $\alpha$ will depend on the nature of the data. Ideally we should monitor the data and the forecast to check the errors in the forecast, and thus be able to modify the value of $\alpha$. This is the essence of adoptive forecasting, for which several well-established techniques are available, perhaps the best known being that derived by Trigg and Leach.[2]

## THE USE OF THE CUMULATIVE SUM TECHNIQUE

The cumulative sum method of examining data is of comparatively recent origin. It is conceptually extremely simple and has found widespread application, particularly in quality control and in forecasting. The cumulative sum chart is simply a plot of the cumulative total of a series of data, or a plot of the cumulative difference between each of the individual readings and a given constant quantity.

For example, consider the monthly sales figures shown in Figure II.3(a). From this figure it appears that sales over the 26 periods have fluctuated about a mean of 11. If, therefore, we consider 11 to be the mean or target value for these data, and subtract this amount from each of the months' sales, plotting the difference cumulatively, the cusum chart shown in Figure II.3(b) is obtained.

Notice that while the average value of the data is near to the target value, some of the differences between actual and target values will be positive and some negative, and hence the cumulative sum (cusum) chart will be more or less horizontal, but if the average value of the data rises then more of the differences between actual and target values will be positive and the cusum graph will rise. In Figure II.3(a) and (b), while a change in the average sales is barely perceptible in Figure II.3(a), it is very noticeable in the cusum chart, which rises markedly from about period 15. Had the average sales fallen, this would have been reflected in a noticeable negative (downward) slope of the cusum graph.

---

[2] Trigg, D. W. and Leach, D. H. (1967) Exponential smoothing with an adoptive response rate. *Operational Research Quarterly*, **18**, pp. 53–59.

**Figure II.3**

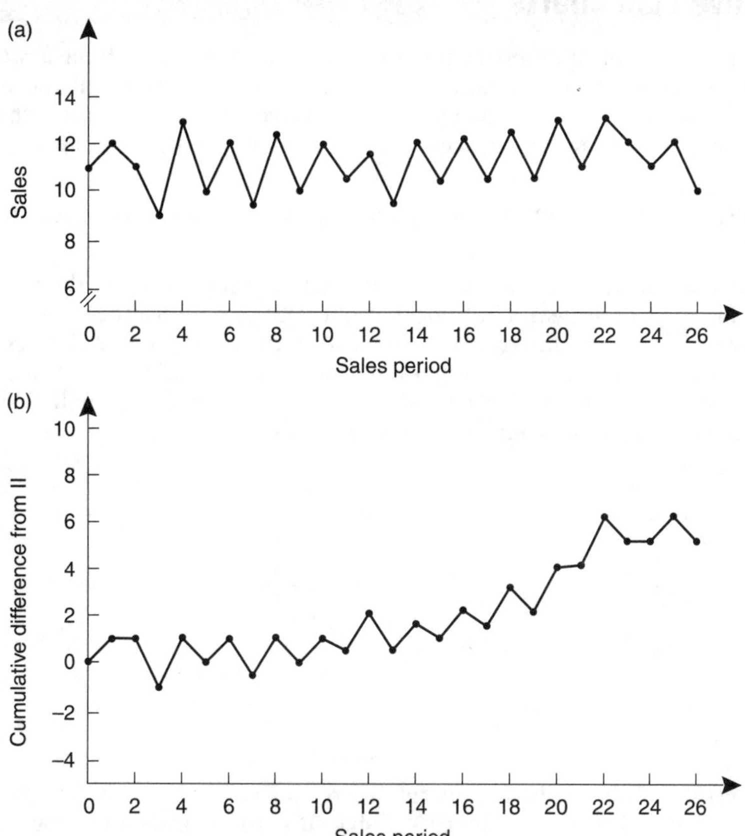


The great advantage of the cusum chart, therefore, is its ability to reveal clearly changes in the average level of data. The chart is interpreted solely on the basis of its slope, a horizontal graph indicating stability in the data, a positive slope indicating an increase in the data average, and a negative slope a decrease in the data average.

## Target or reference value and scale sizes

If the target value chosen is less than the average value of the data, the cusum graph will rise steadily, and vice versa. Should this happen, the chart can be restarted at zero, this time adopting a higher target value. Similarly, it is of value to restart at zero charts which have previously risen because of a change in the average value of the data. Unless this is done any subsequent change in average value may be less evident from the chart.

The choice of both the horizontal and vertical scales of the cusum chart is important, since the scale factors will influence the slope of the graph and hence its ability to show up changes in mean values. It has been suggested[3] that, considering the distance between successive readings on the $x$ axis as 1 point, a similar distance on the $y$ axis should equal $2\sigma$ units, where $\sigma$ is the standard deviation about the mean of the data in the short term. This scale factor enables significant variations in the data means to be deducted while random variations appear quite small.

---

[3] Woodward, R. H. and Goldsmith, P. L. (1964) *Cumulative Sum Techniques*, ICI Monograph No. 3. Edinburgh: Oliver & Boyd.

## Using cumulative sum charts

Cumulative sum charts are not appropriate for use against data which exhibit a steady trend, or data which exhibit a marked seasonal variation. Their main value, as has already been illustrated, is in determining the nature and extent of changes in mean values. The use of cusum charts, therefore, centres around a study of slopes, and in particular the decision of whether or not changes in slope are significant.

There are basically two methods of examining the slope of cusum charts in search of significant changes:

(a) ***The decision interval method.*** This method can be usefully adopted where the problem is one of studying either increases or decreases in slope, but not both. A significant increase in slope, necessitating corrective action, is considered to have occurred if the latest point of the chart is more than a given amount ($h$) below (or above) the highest (or lowest) point which has occurred on the chart since the last decision. The amount $h$ is termed the 'decision interval' (Figure II.4). This method is therefore analogous to the use of control limits in quality control.

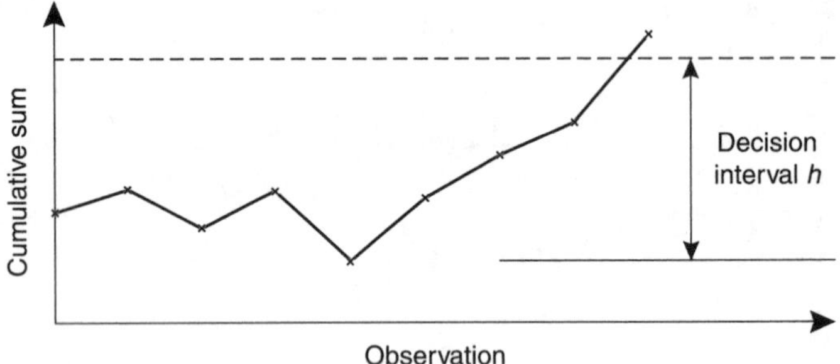


**Figure II.4** The decision interval method

(b) ***The masking method.*** This method is useful where the problem is one of examining simultaneously increases and decreases in slope. A V-shaped mask is made and superimposed on the cusum chart in such a way that if any of the points on the chart lie beyond the limits of the 'V' then it is considered that a significant change in slope has occurred (Figure II.5).

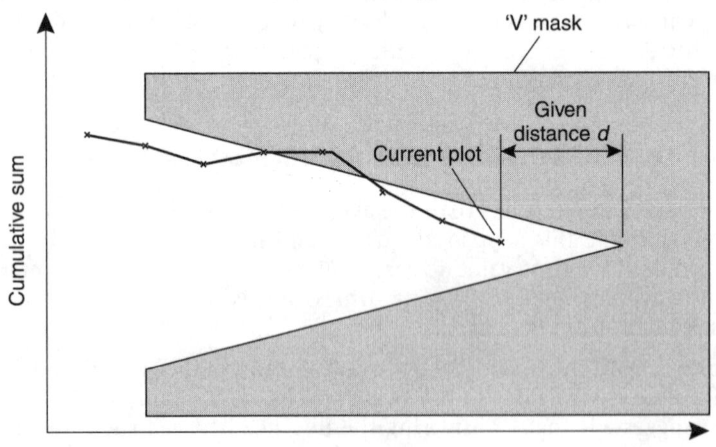


**Figure II.5** The 'V' mask method

Methods of calculating decision intervals and constructing masks are given in the Further Reading references listed at the end of this appendix.

The cumulative sum technique is of considerable value in both quality control and forecasting. It is invaluable as a means of detecting errors in forecasts, assessing the influence of price changes on demand, and so on.

# ASSOCIATIVE PREDICTIONS OR ECONOMIC INDICATORS

## Calculation of correlation coefficients

A correlation coefficient is a measure of the extent to which two variables are associated. In other words, a correlation coefficient is an indication of the extent to which knowledge of the value of one variable is useful for the prediction of the value of the other. This is the basis of a method of forecasting variously known as associative predictions or economic indicators.

For example, we may find that the weekly demand for a service is correlated to rainfall in the previous week; then, knowing the average rainfall, we may be able to forecast future sales. The strength or closeness of the correlation of variables is measured by the correlation coefficient, which varies between –1.0 and +1.0. It will be clear that to be of value in prediction or forecasting a correlation must be known to exist between a variable which can be measured, or is known *now,* and a variable for a future period; i.e. there must be a time lag.

Perhaps the most useful coefficient is the Pearson product moment correlation coefficient, which is calculated as follows:

$$\text{Coefficient, } r \text{, for two variables X and Y} = \frac{\Sigma(x - \bar{x})\,(y - \bar{y})}{\sqrt{\Sigma(x - \bar{x})^2\, \Sigma(y - \bar{y})^2}}$$

where $\bar{x}$ is the mean value of all the individual $x$ values
$\bar{y}$ is the mean value of all the individual $y$ values.

This formula measures linear correlation (Figure II.6).

**Figure II.6**

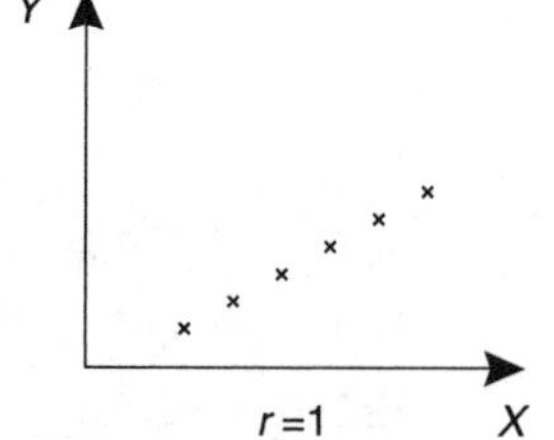


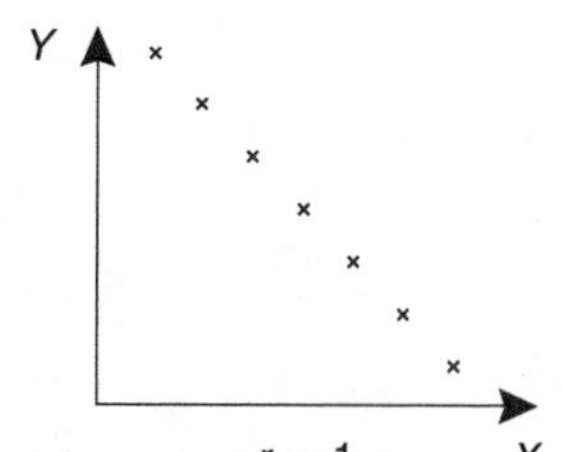


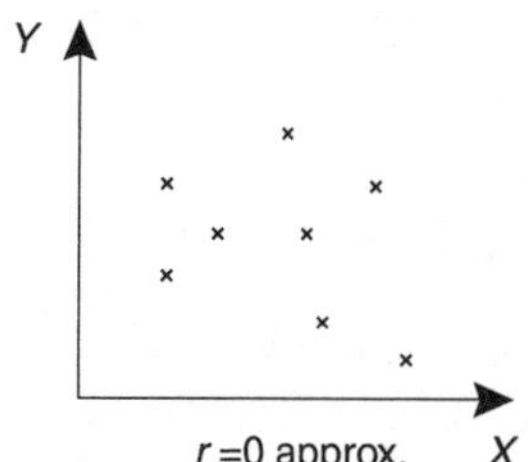

**EXAMPLE II.4**

Observation of two variables, $x$ and $y$, yields the following data. Calculate the linear correlation coefficient of $x$ and $y$. $x$ 1, 3, 5, 7, 11; $y$ 2, 4, 8, 9, 10

| $x$ | $(x-\bar{x})$ | $(x-\bar{x})^2$ | $y$ | $(y-\bar{y})$ | $(y-\bar{y})^2$ | $(x-\bar{x})(y-\bar{y})$ |
|---|---|---|---|---|---|---|
| 1 | –4.4 | 19.4 | 2 | –4.6 | 21.2 | 20.2 |
| 3 | -2.4 | 5.8 | 4 | -2.6 | 6.8 | 6.2 |
| 5 | -0.4 | 1.6 | 8 | +1.4 | 2.0 | -0.6 |
| 7 | +1.6 | 2.6 | 9 | +2.4 | 5.8 | 3.8 |
| 11 | +5.6 | 31.4 | 10 | +3.4 | 11.6 | 19.0 |
| $\Sigma x = 27$ | | 60.8 | $\Sigma y = 33$ | | 47.4 | 48.6 |
| $\bar{x} = \frac{27}{5}$ | | | $\bar{y} = \frac{33}{5}$ | | | |
| = 5.4 | | | = 6.6 | | | |

$$r = \frac{\Sigma(x - \bar{x})(y - \bar{y})}{\sqrt{\Sigma(x - \bar{x})^2 \Sigma(y - \bar{y})^2}}$$

$$= \frac{48.6}{\sqrt{60.8 \times 47.4}} = 0.91$$

## EXAMPLE II.5

A comparison of the monthly sales of an expensive item against the total number of visits made by sales representatives during the *previous* month yields the data shown in the table below. Is the correlation of the two variables good enough to enable the number of sales during a month to be adopted as an efficient indicator of sales during the next month?

| Month | Sales (x) | Visits made (y) | $(x - \bar{x})$ | $(x - \bar{x})^2$ | $(y - \bar{y})$ | $(y - \bar{y})^2$ | $(x - \bar{x})(y - \bar{y})$ |
|---|---|---|---|---|---|---|---|
| 1 | 11 | 605 | -1.46 | 2.132 | -52.7 | 2777.3 | 76.9 |
| 2 | 13 | 640 | +0.54 | 0.292 | -17.7 | 313.3 | -9.6 |
| 3 | 12 | 625 | -0.46 | 0.212 | -32.7 | 1069.3 | 15.0 |
| 4 | 12 | 630 | -0.46 | 0.212 | -27.7 | 767.3 | 12.7 |
| 5 | 10 | 630 | -2.46 | 6.05 | -27.7 | 767.3 | 68.1 |
| 6 | 12 | 645 | -0.46 | 0.212 | -12.7 | 161.3 | 5.8 |
| 7 | 13 | 655 | +0.54 | 0.292 | -2.7 | 7.3 | -1.5 |
| 8 | 14 | 680 | +1.54 | 2.37 | +22.3 | 497.3 | 34.3 |
| 9 | 12 | 660 | -0.46 | 0.212 | +2.3 | 5.3 | -1.1 |
| 10 | 14 | 680 | +1.54 | 2.37 | +22.3 | 497.3 | 34.3 |
| 11 | 11 | 675 | +1.46 | 2.132 | +17.3 | 299.3 | -25.3 |
| 12 | 11 | 670 | -1.46 | 2.132 | +12.3 | 151.3 | -18.0 |
| 13 | 13 | 670 | +0.54 | 0.292 | +12.3 | 151.3 | 6.6 |
| 14 | 14 | 690 | +1.54 | 2.37 | +32.3 | 1043.3 | 49.7 |
| 15 | 15 | 710 | +2.54 | 6.45 | +52.3 | 2735.3 | 132.8 |
| | $\Sigma x = 187$ | $\Sigma y = 9865$ | | 27.730 | | 11243.5 | 380.7 |
| | $\bar{x} = 12.46$ | $\bar{y} = 657.7$ | | | | | |

$$r = -\frac{380.7}{\sqrt{(27.73)\,(11\,243.5)}} = 0.681$$

The correlation between the number of visits during the previous month and the number of sales is 0.681, which is perhaps insufficient to justify its possible use as a method of short-term sales forecasting.

## Linear regression

We have seen that a linear relationship between two variables, $X$ and $Y$, is indicated by a high value of the correlation coefficient. However, this coefficient does not indicate the true relationship, and hence we are unable to estimate either a value of $X$ for a given value of $Y$, or vice versa. To do this a regression equation must be calculated, as in Figure II.7.[4]

The regression line for $Y$ on $X$ is the best line for calculating values of $Y$, and is obtained by minimizing the sum of the squares of the errors of estimation, i.e. the $y$ values in Figure II.7(a).

The regression line for $X$ on $Y$ is the best line for calculating values of $X$, and is obtained by minimizing the sum of the squares of the errors of estimation, i.e. the $x$ values in Figure II.7(b). The general equation for the regression line of $Y$ on $X$ is:

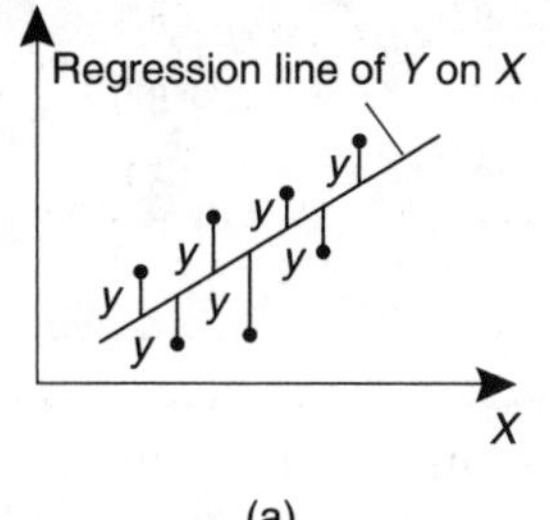


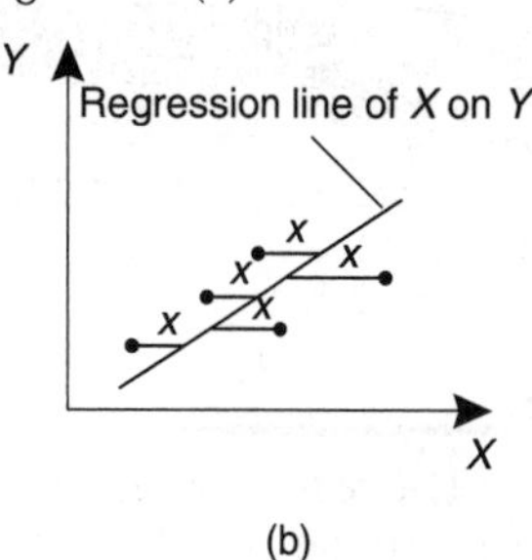


(a) **Figure II.7** (b)

$$Y = a + bX$$

where $a$ and $b$ are two constants. The values of these two constants are obtained by the following formula:

$$b = \frac{n\Sigma xy - (\Sigma x)(\Sigma y)}{n(\Sigma x^2) - (\Sigma x)^2} \qquad a = \frac{\Sigma y - b\Sigma x}{n}$$

Similarly, the general equation for the linear regression of $X$ on $Y$ is:

$$X = a + bY$$

where:

$$b = \frac{n\Sigma xy - (\Sigma x)(\Sigma y)}{n(\Sigma y^2) - (\Sigma y)^2} \qquad a = \frac{\Sigma x - b\Sigma y}{n}$$

### EXAMPLE II.6

The data in the following table relate to the weight of an item at a period of time and its growth at a future period. Find the regression line for predicting 'growth' and calculate the growth for a weight value of 52.

Let growth be variable $Y$

Let weight be variable $X$

$$b = \frac{7(1632) - (210)(51)}{7(7308) - (210)^2}$$

---

[4] We shall deal exclusively with linear regression equations, whereas in fact our data may be of a curvilinear form. A similar procedure to the one described here may be used to derive formulae for calculating non-linear regression equations. Furthermore, we shall be concerned only with the regression of two variables, whereas in practice two or more variables may be involved. In such cases a procedure similar to, if longer than, that described here can be adopted. Description of multiple and non-linear regression can be found in the books in Further Reading.

$$= \frac{714}{7056}$$

$$= 0.101$$

$$a = \frac{(51) - 0.101(210)}{7}$$

$$= \frac{29.79}{7}$$

$$= 4.26$$

$$x = 52$$

$$y = 4.26 + 0.101(52)$$

$$= 4.26 + 5.25$$

$$y = 9.51$$

| Weight ($x$) | Growth ($y$) | $x^2$ | $xy$ |
|---|---|---|---|
| 12 | 5.5 | 144 | 66 |
| 18 | 5.9 | 324 | 106 |
| 24 | 6.5 | 576 | 156 |
| 30 | 7.4 | 900 | 222 |
| 36 | 8.2 | 1296 | 295.2 |
| 42 | 8.9 | 1764 | 373.8 |
| 48 | 8.6 | 2304 | 412.8 |
| $\Sigma x = 210$ | $\Sigma y = 51.0$ | $\Sigma x^2 = 7308$ | $\Sigma xy = 1632.0$ |

The regression line provides only an estimate of the value of $Y$ on $X$. The uncertainty or accuracy of the estimate can be assessed by calculating the 'standard error' of the estimate of $Y$ on $X$ ($S_{Y,X}$):

$$S_{Y,X} = \sqrt{\frac{\Sigma(y - y^1)^2}{n - 2}}$$

where $y$ = actual value
$y^1$ = value calculated from regression equation

The standard error of the estimate of $X$ on $Y$ is given similarly by:

$$S_{X,Y} = \sqrt{\frac{\Sigma(x - x^1)^2}{n - 2}}$$

For example, in the above case:

| $y$ | $y^1$ | $= 4.26 + 0.101(x)$ | $(y - y^1)$ | $(y - y^1)^2$ |
|---|---|---|---|---|
| 5.5 | 5.47 | | 0.03 | 0.0009 |
| 5.9 | 6.08 | | −0.18 | 0.0324 |
| 6.5 | 6.68 | | −0.18 | 0.0324 |
| 7.4 | 7.29 | | 0.11 | 0.0121 |
| 8.2 | 7.90 | | 0.30 | 0.0900 |
| 8.9 | 8.50 | | 0.40 | 0.1600 |
| 8.6 | 9.11 | | −0.51 | 0.2601 |
| | | | | $\Sigma(y - y^1)^2 = 0.5879$ |

$$S_{Y,X} = \sqrt{\frac{0.5879}{5}}$$

$$S_{Y,X} = 0.343$$

$S_{Y,X}$ or $S_{X,Y}$ provides a measure of the 'closeness' of the relationship between the two variables. The smaller the figure, the closer the values are to the regression line and hence the more accurate the regression equation is for predictive purposes.

## FURTHER READING

**Jarrett, J. (1991)** *Business Forecasting Methods*. Oxford: Basil Blackwell.

**Wheelwright, S. C. and Makridakis, S. (1989)** *Forecasting Methods for Management*, 5th edn. Chichester: Wiley.

**Woodward, R. H. and Goldsmith, P. L. (1964)** *Cumulative Sum Techniques*, ICI Monograph No. 3. Edinburgh: Oliver & Boyd.

## QUESTIONS

II.1 The table below gives the monthly sales of a particular product over a 20-month period. Use (a) forecasting by previous average, and (b) forecasting from last period's sales, to forecast sales for period 4 onwards. Compare the accuracy of the two forecasts and comment on the practical implications of adopting these two simple methods of forecasting.

| Period | Sales | Period | Sales |
|---|---|---|---|
| 1 | 20 | 11 | 24 |
| 2 | 18 | 12 | 28 |
| 3 | 17 | 13 | 34 |
| 4 | 21 | 14 | 36 |
| 5 | 22 | 15 | 35 |
| 6 | 21 | 16 | 30 |
| 7 | 20 | 17 | 28 |
| 8 | 18 | 18 | 26 |
| 9 | 19 | 19 | 30 |
| 10 | 21 | 20 | 31 |

II.2 Plot the four years' sales figures shown in the tables below, along with the appropriate moving average sales figure.

| Year | Sales | Year | Sales |
|---|---|---|---|
| 1986 | 250 | 1988 | 260 |
| | 275 | | 295 |
| | 300 | | 320 |
| | 230 | | 245 |
| 1987 | 260 | 1989 | 245 |
| | 280 | | 290 |
| | 300 | | 315 |
| | 240 | | 230 |

How does the moving average sales graph compare with the actual sales, and what refinements are necessary before the moving average method can be used as an accurate technique for forecasting sales of this type?

II.3 Calculate the seasonally adjusted four-period moving average sales for the data given below:

| Year | Period | Sales (000) | Year | Period | Sales (000) |
|---|---|---|---|---|---|
| 1986 | 1 | 50 | 1988 | 1 | 54 |
| | 2 | 60 | | 2 | 70 |
| | 3 | 50 | | 3 | 56 |
| | 4 | 44 | | 4 | 50 |
| 1987 | 1 | 50 | 1989 | 1 | 54 |
| | 2 | 64 | | 2 | 60 |
| | 3 | 56 | | 3 | 52 |
| | 4 | 50 | | 4 | 50 |

II.4 Use the moving average technique with secular trend correction and seasonal adjustment to forecast quarterly sales of product X. The actual sales of product X over a five-year period are shown below. Calculate the forecasted sales over as much of this period as possible, and compare the forecasted sales with the actual.

| Year | Quarter | Actual sales (000) | Year | Quarter (000) | Actual sales |
|---|---|---|---|---|---|
| 1985 | S | 20 | | A | 40 |
| | S | 15 | | W | 35 |
| | A | 30 | 1988 | S | 30 |
| | W | 25 | | S | 25 |
| 1986 | S | 20 | | A | 45 |
| | S | 20 | | W | 35 |
| | A | 35 | 1989 | S | 30 |
| | W | 30 | | A | 25 |
| 1987 | S | 25 | | A | 50 |
| | S | 20 | | W | 40 |

II.5 The following figures show the actual sales of product Y which have occurred on each of 20 successive periods. Calculate the appropriate simple moving average sales (without seasonal adjustment) for as much of this period as possible and compare the difference between actual and moving average with the difference between actual and an exponentially smoothed equivalent to the moving average. Comment on the nature of your results.

| Period | Actual sales | Year | Actual sales |
|---|---|---|---|
| 1 | 10 | 11 | 10 |
| 2 | 12 | 12 | 13 |
| 3 | 12 | 13 | 14 |
| 4 | 10 | 14 | 12 |
| 5 | 8 | 15 | 9 |
| 6 | 10 | 16 | 10 |
| 7 | 13 | 17 | 13 |
| 8 | 12 | 18 | 14 |
| 9 | 9 | 19 | 11 |
| 10 | 8 | 20 | 10 |

II.6 Historical data for product Z indicate that there are both seasonal variations and a continuously increasing trend in sales. How can the simple exponential smoothing technique be modified to provide acceptable forecasts in such a situation?

Illustrate your answer by means of simple numerical examples of your own construction.

II.7 (a) Use the cumulative sum technique to examine the following sales data for any changes in average monthly sales.

| Month | 1987 | 1988 | 1989 |
|---|---|---|---|
| 1 | 10 | 10 | 9 |
| 2 | 11 | 9 | 12 |
| 3 | 10 | 10 | 11 |
| 4 | 12 | 11 | 13 |
| 5 | 8 | 10 | 12 |
| 6 | 10 | 12 | 11 |
| 7 | 12 | 13 | 10 |
| 8 | 9 | 12 | 11 |
| 9 | 12 | 10 | 10 |
| 10 | 7 | 9 | 9 |
| 11 | 9 | 11 | 10 |
| 12 | 10 | 12 | 11 |

(b) Comment on the value of this technique. How is its value affected by the choice of
(i) the reference value, and
(ii) the scale factor?

II.8 Explain the meaning of
(a) the decision interval, and
(b) the 'masking' method in the context of the cumulative sum technique.

II.9 Calculate the Pearson product moment correlation coefficient (*r*):
(a) of variables *X* and *Y*;

| X | Y | x | y |
|---|---|---|---|
| 15 | 0 | 1 | 5 |
| 16 | 2 | 2 | 6 |
| 17 | 4 | 3 | - |
| 18 | 6 | 4 | 12 |
| 19 | 8 | 5 | 11 |
| 20 | 10 | 6 | 13 |
| 21 | 12 | 7 | 16 |
| 22 | 14 | 8 | 16 |
| 23 | 16 | 9 | - |
| 24 | 18 | 10 | 19 |
| | | 11 | 23 |
| | | 12 | 22 |

(b) of a setting *x* and a reading *y*.

II.10 Calculate the linear regression of *Y* and *X* and, using the equation, calculate *Y* for the following values of *X*:

(a) 137;
(b) 95.

| Y | X | Y | X |
|---|---|---|---|
| 2 | 20 | 6 | 60 |
| 5 | 45 | 8 | 70 |
| 4 | 30 | 9 | 85 |
| 3 | 30 | 10 | 105 |
| 5 | 45 | 12 | 115 |
| 6 | 65 | 13 | 120 |
| 7 | 65 | | |

II.11 (a) Calculate the linear regression line for determining consumption from the gross national product.

(b) It is estimated that the GNP three years hence will equal £30 000. What is consumption likely to be four years hence?

| GNP (£) in year | Consumption for following year | GNP (£) in year | Consumption for following year |
|---|---|---|---|
| 20 200 | 13 900 | 22 500 | 16 000 |
| 20 800 | 14 500 | 23 600 | 16 600 |
| 21 200 | 14 600 | 24 400 | 17 000 |
| 21 600 | 14 900 | 24 600 | 17 300 |
| 21 700 | 15 300 | 25 500 | 18 000 |

Appendix III

# Computer simulation

The applications of computer simulation have been referred to in the course of the text. This appendix aims to provide further information by outlining the following:

(a) the nature of simulation;

(b) the nature of computer simulation;

(c) simulation languages;

(d) simulation model building;

(e) available computer simulation packages;

(f) simulation applications in production and operations management.

## THE NATURE OF SIMULATION

A general definition of simulation may be given as: 'a means of modelling a system in order to examine its behaviour over a period of time'. So, simulation enables systems to be examined without direct interference. In other words, experiments can be conducted without the need, directly, to manipulate the real system.

Simulation affords a means for experimenting without risk. It is also likely to be cheaper and safer to use a simulation model than to experiment with the real system. Simulation experiments may also, often, be completed in less time than would be necessary for actual experimentation, and since some simplifications can be incorporated into simulation models, the approach is a useful one where systems are too complex to examine mathematically.

### Forms of simulation

#### Analogue models

The earliest attempts to simulate systems involved the use of analogues, e.g. scale physical models, using mechanical, electrical or hydraulic models. Whilst this type of approach is still of value in certain specialist applications, it has now largely been replaced by computer simulation.

## Monte Carlo 'simulation'

One form of analytical simulation involves the use of random numbers to provide values of probabilistic parameters. The Monte Carlo method (see Chapter 21) is one classic procedure. Using random numbers, a probability distribution for a variable is sampled and the figures obtained are used in calculations in the simulation. The Monte Carlo method is strictly a method for sampling, although the term has become associated with the type of simulation which requires such sampling procedures. An alternative involves the generation of pseudo-random numbers using a computer. In effect, both approaches employ statistical distributions or expressions to provide data to describe uncertain activities (e.g. processing or queuing times) for use in a simulation of a system. They are really a means for generating data rather than types of simulation.

An alternative to this approach is the use of *empirical data* collected by observation and/or experiment.

## Computer simulation

Analog computers may be used to model complex systems, as described above. Here, however, we shall deal only with digital computer simulation. Whilst digital computers can be used to implement a Monte Carlo approach, true (digital) computer simulation has come to stand for a much broader and more comprehensive approach to the simulation of systems.

# THE NATURE OF (DIGITAL) COMPUTER SIMULATION

Computer simulation involves the use of a computer program written to model a system and to enable experiments to be conducted using that model. Thus a computer with appropriate software is used to model the system, perform the calculations which enable the system be 'run', make changes to the model or the conditions in which it is run, and collect and analyse data on the performance of the system.

## Types of computer simulation

### Continuous simulation

In a continuous simulation the system is represented by variables which change continuously over time. Such a simulation is often constructed using a series of differential equations. It is, of course, an appropriate means for examining a system which is dynamic and continually changing, e.g. the weather.

### Discrete simulation

Discrete simulation aims to deal with *events* (sometimes called *discrete event simulation* – DES), i.e. with variables which change discretely at specific times. The approach is the most appropriate one to use when we are interested in things which occur at particular moments in time, rather than continuously. For example, the simulation of a system to examine breakdowns would require a discrete simulation. DES is the more widely used and versatile methodology, and we shall deal exclusively with this approach.

This basic division of computer simulation methodologies is shown in Figure III.1. Computer software is available for both, though such software can be classified in more detail using the other terms in Figure III.1. These are explained below.

**Figure III.1** Classification of simulation software – type, application and structure

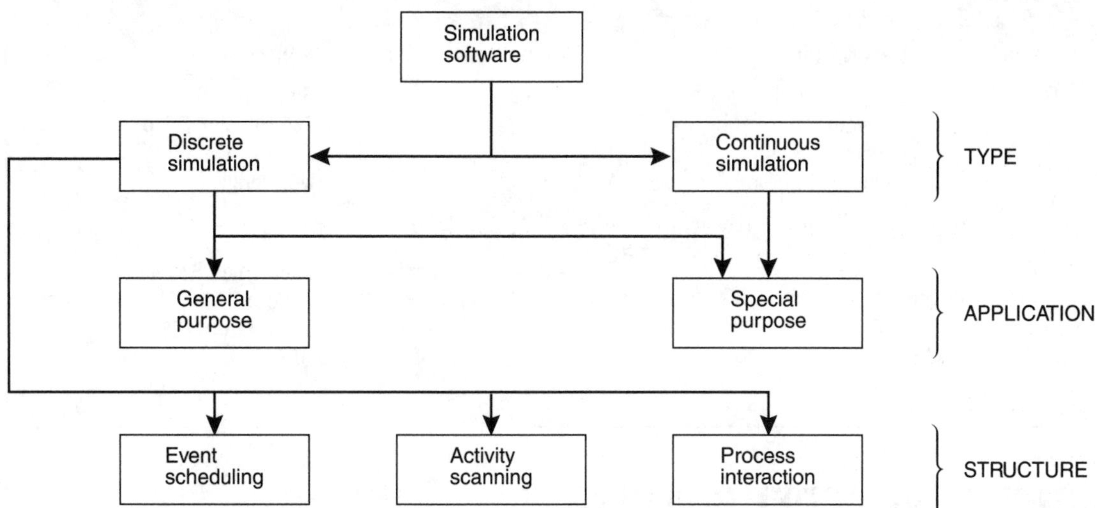


## General- and special-purpose applications

Special programming *languages* have been developed to facilitate the writing of simulation programs (see below). These are usually general-purpose languages, i.e. they can be used in writing programs to simulate any type of system.

At a higher level, software packages have been developed using these languages so that users do not have to write their own programs. These packages may be designed for general application, but are more usually designed for a particular purpose, e.g. modelling a factory or traffic system. Packages for continuous simulation are usually special purpose, whereas those for discrete simulation can be either general or special purpose.

### Discrete simulation structures

In a discrete simulation of a system, the state of the system changes only at event times and remains constant between events. The system can therefore be 'run' by moving simulated time from one event to the next.

DES can be constructed by defining the changes in state which occur at each event time, or by describing the activities in which the items of the system are engaged, or by describing the items in the system flow from entry to exit. These three approaches to constructing the simulation are known as:

(a) event scheduling (sometimes called three-phase modelling);

(b) activity scanning;

(c) process interaction.

# SIMULATION LANGUAGES

The principal simulation programming languages in which simulation packages are written are listed in Table III.1. Being 'high-level' languages developed for this application, they provide an easier means of preparing simulation programs than the more general-purpose programming languages.

Table III.1 Some simulation languages

| Name | Description | Computers | Source |
|---|---|---|---|
| GPSS | Language and software for general-purpose discrete modelling. N.B. Several implementations available, e.g. | Varies | Simulation Software Ltd 760 Headley Drive London, Ontario N6H 3V8 Canada |
| | GPSS/PC | PCs and compatibles | Minuteman Software PO Box 171 Stow, MA 01755 USA |

## SIMULATION MODEL BUILDING

After choosing a particular type of approach for the construction of the simulation, the simulation model will be constructed and tested in the manner outlined in Figure III.2.

In building the model, either a computer program will be written – probably using one of the languages listed in Table III.1 – or a computer model will be prepared using one of the many available simulation packages (or a combination of both). The use of a 'package' avoids the need for lengthy coding, but detailed knowledge of what is to be achieved will influence the choice of packages, as they offer many and varied features and capabilities.

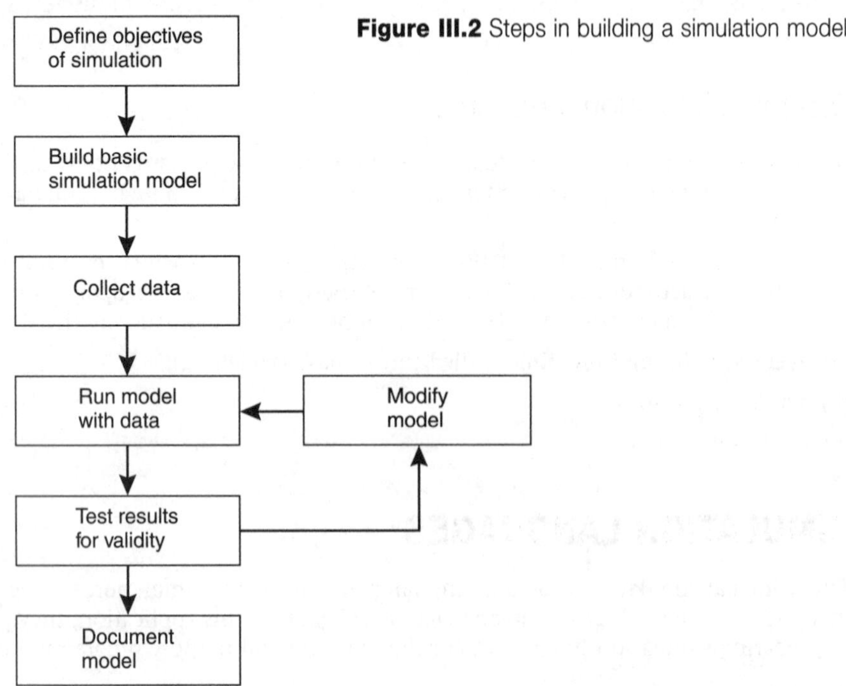


**Figure III.2** Steps in building a simulation model

**Table III.1 (continued)**

| | | | |
|---|---|---|---|
| SIMAN | Language and software for discrete and continuous modelling (with special applications for manufacturing) | PCs and others | Systems Modelling Corp.<br>PO Box 10074<br>State College<br>PA 16805<br>USA |
| SIMSCRIPT | Structured simulation language for discrete and continuous modelling | PCs and others | CACI<br>3344 North Torvey Pines Ct<br>La Jolla<br>CA 92037<br>USA |
| SLAM | Comprehensive simulation language | PCs | Pritsker & Assocs<br>1305 Cumberland Ave<br>PO Box 2413<br>West Lafayette<br>IN 47906<br>USA |

## SIMULATION PACKAGES

Some of the available discrete event simulation packages are described in Table III.2. Many packages are now available for use on personal computers, and many of these even provide for animation, i.e. animated pictorial representation of the system being modelled. This enables the characteristics of system operation and the effects of changes in system parameters to be observed more easily.

**Table III.2 Some computer simulation software packages**

| Name of package | Distributor | Computer system | |
|---|---|---|---|
| Beam/MAST/SPAR | Citroën Industrie UK<br>Leamington Spa<br>UK<br>and CMS Research Inc.<br>945 Bavarian Court<br>Oshkosh, WI 54901<br>USA | PCs | A set of three packages covering capacity planning and system simulation |
| Cinema | Calder Sq<br>PO Box 10074<br>State College<br>PA 16805<br>USA | PCs | A discrete general-purpose modeller with animation using SIMAN |
| HOCUS | P-E Consulting Group<br>Park House<br>Egham<br>Surrey TW20 0HW<br>UK | | Continuous and discrete models |

Table III.2 (continued)

| | | | |
|---|---|---|---|
| INTERACTIVE | Micro Simulation<br>50 Milk Street<br>Suite 1500<br>Boston, MA 02109<br>USA | PCs | Process interaction<br>for manufacturing<br>and inventory models |
| INTER-SIM | Decision Computing<br>3 St Edmund's Road<br>Canterbury<br>CT1 2PD<br>UK | PCs | Discrete event<br>scheduling with<br>visual interaction |
| MICRO-PASSIM | Dr C. Barnett<br>Department of Physics<br>Walla Walla College<br>College Place<br>WA 99324<br>USA | PCs | Discrete or<br>continuous three-phase<br>event scheduling<br>and process interaction |
| MICRO SAINT | Micro Analysis & Design<br>Colorado<br>USA | PCs | |
| PCModel | Simulation Software Systems<br>Simsoft UK<br>6 Selsey Close<br>Hayling, Hants<br>PO11 9SX<br>UK | PCs | Discrete event<br>scheduling for<br>assembly line models |
| SEEWHY | Istel Inc.<br>83 Cambridge Street<br>Burlington<br>MA 01803<br>USA | PCs | Discrete graphical<br>interactive simulation<br>for production systems |
| SIMFACTORY | CACI Inc.<br>La Jolla<br>CA 92037<br>USA and at<br>Richmond<br>Surrey TW9 1DL<br>UK | PCs | |
| SIMPLE | IPA-FhG<br>Schlosstr. 68<br>D-7000 Stuttgart 1<br>Germany | PCs | General-purpose<br>discrete or continuous<br>simulation |

**Table III.2 (continued)**

| | | | |
|---|---|---|---|
| SOLON | Y. J. Stephanedes<br>500 Pillburn Drive<br>Minneapolis<br>MN 55455<br>USA | PCs | Discrete graphical interactive simulation for transportation models |
| TESS | Pritsker & Assoc. Inc.<br>1305 Cumberland Avenue<br>West Lafayette<br>IN 47906<br>USA | PCs | A discrete modeller with animation using SLAM II |
| WITNESS | Istel (see SEEWHY) | | |
| XCELL | Pritsker & Assoc. Inc.<br>1305 Cumberland Avenue<br>West Lafayette<br>IN 47906<br>USA | PCs | Interactive Graphic |

**EXAMPLE**

## *Barber shop*[1]

This is an example of the simulation of a one-line, one-server queuing system using PCModel. A diagram of the system animation taken from the VDU is given in Figure III.3, and the program details are given in Table III.5.

The model assumes that customers arrive at a one-chair barber shop, receive a haircut (on a first come, first served basis) and then leave. The interarrival time of the customers is uniformly distributed over the range of 24 ± 6 minutes. Service time for the haircut is exponentially distributed with a mean value of 20 minutes.

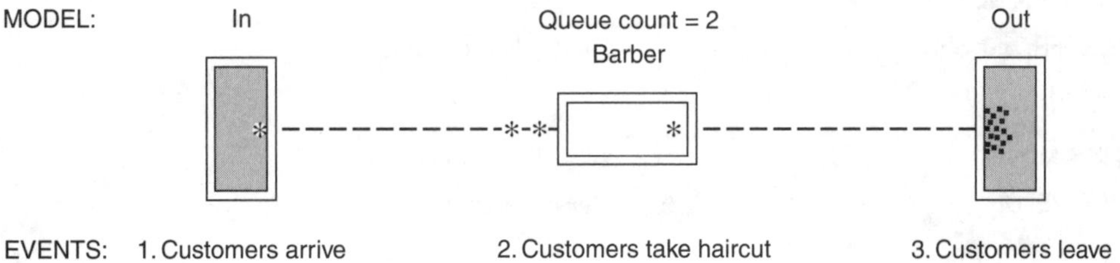


**Figure III.3** PCModel simulation of a one-line, one-server queuing system. Courtesy of Mr Sun Qi Zhi, Manufacturing and Engineering Systems, Brunel University.

[1] Courtesy of Mr Sun Qi Zhi, previously of Manufacturing and Engineering Systems Dept., Brunel University, UK.

**Table III.3 Program details**

```
1. DEFINITION
O = (BARBER)                      ; background file name is BARBER, OLY
@QUEUE = (0)                      ; record the number of customers in queue
% ARR = (0) % SER = (0)           ; random interarrival/service time
% M_ARR = (24:0)                  ; mean/deviation of interarrival time
%D_ARR = (6:0)
% M_SER = (20:0)                  ; mean value of service time
% MOVE = (0:30)                   ; move delay time
* ARRIVE = (XY(12,11))            ; arrival/service/leaving screen locations
* BARBER = (XY(38,11))
* LEAVE = (XY(63,11))
* Q_DISP = (XY(41,6))             ; location for displaying value of queue length
J = (1,*,1,0,0,1,500)             ; customers routeing, total 500 customers
U = (1, BARBER,*BARBER)           ; count utilization of the barber
2. ROUTEINGS
BR(1,*ARRIVE,%ARR)
                                  ; 1. CUSTOMERS ARRIVE
RV(U,%ARR, %M_ARR,
%D_ARP)                           ; generate random interarrival time
IV(@QUEUE)                        ; queue length increases 1
FV(*Q_DISP,@QUEUE)                ; display queue value
MR(23,%MOVE)                      ; move toward barber to get service
MA(*BARBER,O)                     ; 2. CUSTOMERS TAKE HAIRCUT
DV(@QUEUE)                        ; queue length decreases 1
PV(*Q_DISP,@QUEUE)                ; display queue value
RV(E,%SER,%M_SER)                 ; take a hair-cut time
WT(%SER)
MR(2S,%MOVE)                      ; 3. CUSTOMERS LEAVE
MA(*LEAVE, O)                     ; leave barber shop
ER
A:
```

*Courtesy of Mr Sun Qi Zhi, formerly of Manufacturing and Engineering Systems, Brunel University*

## CHECKLIST FOR APPENDIX III

### The nature of simulation

Definition of simulation
Purpose of simulation
Forms of simulation
- Analogue models
- Monte Carlo
- Empirical data
- Computer simulation
  - Analog
  - Digital

### The nature of digital computer simulation types

Continuous
Discrete
General purpose
Special purpose
DES structures

## FURTHER READING

**Chisman, J. A. (1992)** *Simulation Modelling using GPSS/PC.* Englewood Cliffs, NJ: Prentice-Hall.

**Wu, B. (1992)** *Manufacturing Systems Design and Analysis.* London: Chapman & Hall.

Appendix IV

# Answers to odd-numbered analytical questions

## Chapter 4

**4.5** (Employ option 1 for sales of 30.)

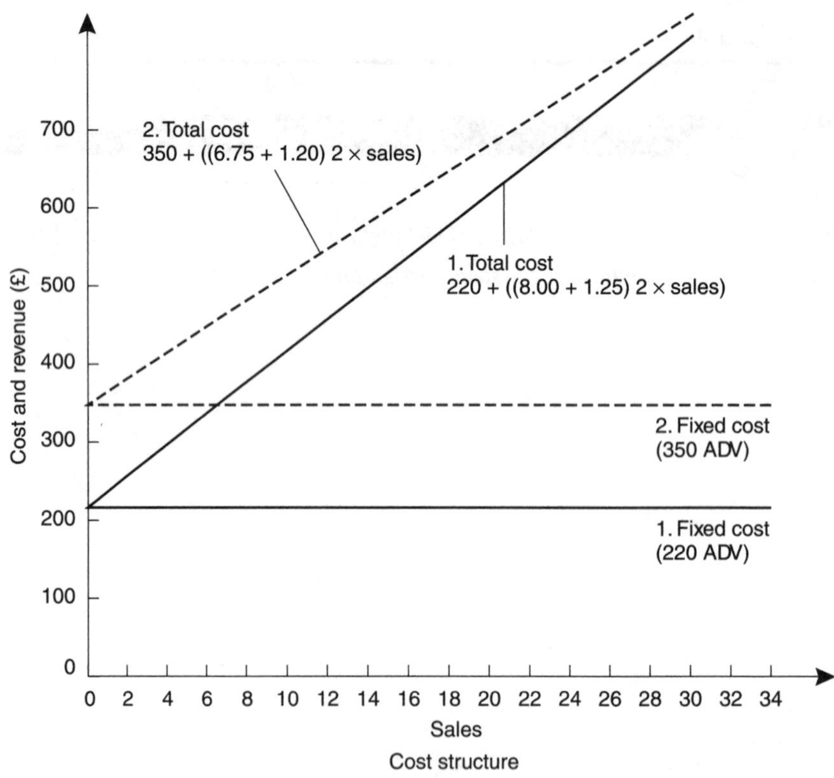

Cost structure

## Chapter 5

**5.3** About 95 km north-east of Birmingham.

**5.5** Sunderland

**5.7** Additional factory should be established at location D.
Total cost for ABD = £16 990/month.
Total cost for ABC = £17 240/month (assuming cost of excess capacity is zero).

**5.9** (a) Yes.
(b) Store at B.

## Chapter 6

6.1

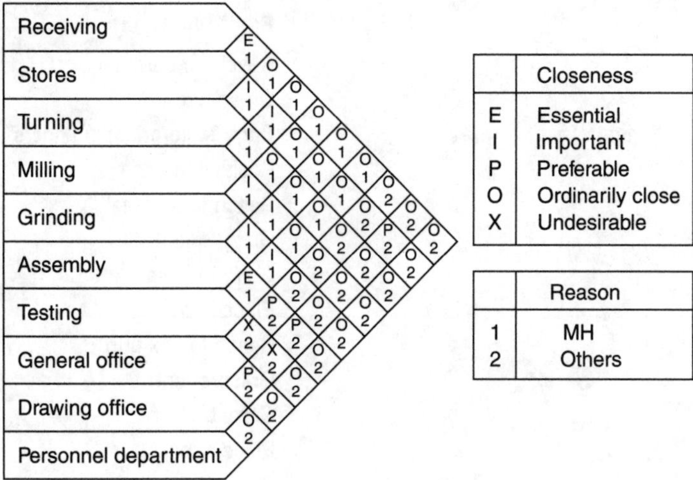


6.3 (This question is based on the example used by Buffa, E.S. (1955) Sequence analysis for functional layouts. *Journal of Industrial Engineering,* March/April, pp. 12–25.)

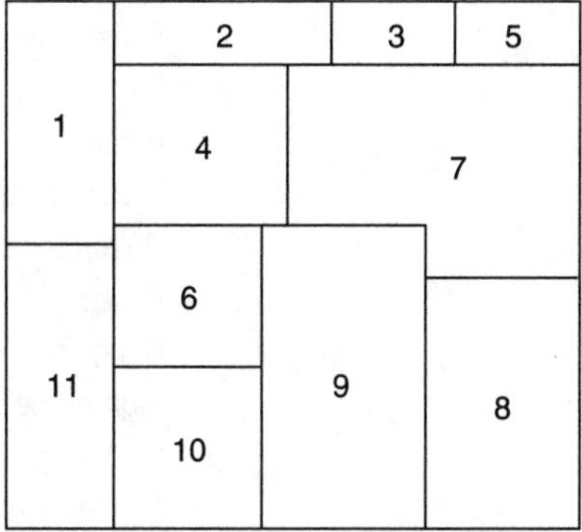


## Chapter 7

7.3

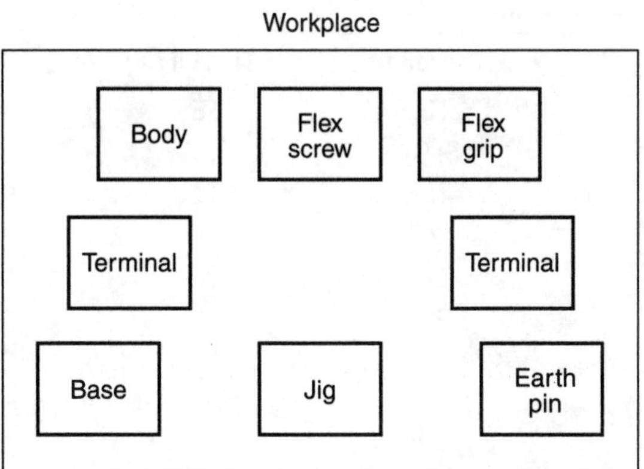

N.B. Screwdriver suspended over jig.

| **Left hand** | | **Right hand** | |
|---|---|---|---|
| Reach for base piece | ⇨ | Reach for earth pin | ⇨ |
| Grasp base | O | Grasp pin | O |
| Carry to jig/orient in fingers | ⇨ | Carry to jig/orient in fingers | ⇨ |
| Place in jig | O | Position in base | O |
| Reach to terminal | ⇨ | Reach to terminal | ⇨ |
| Grasp/orient | O | Grasp/orient | O |
| Carry to base | ⇨ | Carry to base | ⇨ |
| Place in base | O | Place in base | O |
| Reach to body top | ⇨ | Reach to flex grip | ⇨ |
| Grasp | O | Grasp/orient | O |
| Carry to jig | ⇨ | Carry to jig | ⇨ |
| | | Place in base | O |
| Place in jig | O | Reach to body screw | ⇨ |
| Grasp assembly | O | Grasp/orient | O |
| Remove from jig | O | Carry to assembly/orient | ⇨ |
| Place inverted on bench | O | Place screw in hole | O |
| Hold | O | Reach to flex screws | ⇨ |
| I | | Grasp two screws | O |
| I | | Carry | ⇨ |
| I | | Place one screw in hole | O |
| I | | Place second screw in hole | O |
| I | | Reach for screwdriver | ⇨ |
| I | | Grasp | O |
| I | | Carry to assembly | ⇨ |
| I | | Tighten body screw | O |
| I | | Tighten one flex screw | O |
| Grasp plug | O | Tighten second flex screw | O |
| Carry to bin | ⇨ | Return screwdriver | ⇨ |
| Release | O | Release screwdriver | O |

| **Left hand** | **Therblig** | **Therblig** | **Right hand** |
|---|---|---|---|
| Reach for bolt | TE | TE | Reach for nut |
| Select and grasp a bolt head | S, G | S, G | Select and grasp nut |
| Carry bolt to central position | TL | TL | Carry to central position |
| Position bolt | P | P | Position nut |
| Hold head | H | A | Assemble nut onto bolt |
| Release assembly | RL | G | Grasp assembly |
| Idle | | TL | Carry assembly to box |
| Idle | | RL | Release assembly into box |

## Chapter 8

**8.1** $N^1 = 9$, therefore sufficient observations have been made.

**8.3** 2262 pieces.

**8.5** Output per shift at standard performance = 200.
Production cost per piece = 9p.

**8.7** 10.2 SM

**8.11** Worker A El 1 BM = 0.09 } 0.23/item
El 2 BM = 0.14 }
Worker B El 3 BM = 0.15 } 0.20/item
El 4 BM = 0.05 }
Worker C El 5 BM = 0.20 0.20/item

(This question is based on an example given in Chapter 6 of Graham, C. F. (1965) *Work Measurement and Cost Control*. Oxford: Pergamon. This excellent little book gives a good description of the uses of rated systematic sampling).

## Chapter 10

**10.1** 2530p

**10.3** (a) 13500p
(b) 18000p
(c) 12150p
(d) 14000p

## Chapter 11

**11.1** The production plan is given by the following matrix:

| Week number | | 26 | 27 | 28 | 29 |
|---|---|---|---|---|---|
| 26 | Stock | 31 | 4 | | |
| 27 | Normal shift | | 35 | | |
| | Night shift | | 4 | 11 | |
| 28 | Normal shift | | | 35 | |
| | Night shift | | | 9 | 6 |
| 29 | Normal shift | | | | 33 |
| | Night shift | | | | |

**11.3** Total cost associated with this plan = £1501.

Since total demand in work hours exceeds total capacity, work will have to be subcontracted. For example, unless work is subcontracted, insufficient sub-assembly IIs will be available in May.

| Month | Shift | May I | May II | May III | June I | June II | June III | July I | July II | July III | August I | August II | August III | Stock I | Stock II | Stock III | Available capacity (work hours) |
|---|---|---|---|---|---|---|---|---|---|---|---|---|---|---|---|---|---|
| | 1 | 5 | 6 | 4 | 6.5 | 6.6 | 4.5 | 6.0 | 7.2 | 5.0 | 6.5 | 7.8 | 5.5 | 7.0 | 8.6 | 6.0 | 150 |
| **May** | 2 | 7 | 8 | 6 | 7.5 | 8.6 | 6.5 | 8.0 | 9.2 | 7.0 | 8.5 | 9.8 | 7.5 | 9.0 | 10.6 | 8.0 | 200 |
| | 3 | 7 | 8 | 6 | 7.5 | 8.6 | 6.5 | 8.0 | 9.2 | 7.0 | 8.5 | 9.8 | 7.5 | 9.0 | 10.6 | 8.0 | 200 |
| | 1 | | | | 5 | 6 | 4 | 5.5 | 6.6 | 4.5 | 6.0 | 7.2 | 5.0 | 6.5 | 7.8 | 5.5 | 200 |
| **June** | 2 | | | | 7 | 8 | 6 | 7.5 | 8.6 | 6.5 | 8.0 | 9.2 | 7.0 | 8.5 | 9.8 | 7.5 | 300 |
| | 3 | | | | 7 | 8 | 6 | 7.5 | 8.6 | 6.5 | 8.0 | 9.2 | 7.0 | 8.5 | 9.8 | 7.5 | 350 |
| | 1 | | | | | | | 5 | 6 | 4 | 5.5 | 6.6 | 4.5 | 6.0 | 7.2 | 5.0 | 250 |
| **July** | 2 | | | | | | | 7 | 8 | 6 | 7.5 | 8.6 | 6.5 | 8.0 | 9.2 | 7.0 | 300 |
| | 3 | | | | | | | 7 | 8 | 6 | 7.5 | 8.6 | 6.5 | 8.0 | 9.2 | 7.0 | 300 |
| | 1 | | | | | | | | | | 6 | 7 | 5 | 6.5 | 7.6 | 5.5 | 300 |
| **August** | 2 | | | | | | | | | | 8 | 9 | 7 | 8.5 | 9.6 | 7.5 | 250 |
| | 3 | | | | | | | | | | 8 | 9 | 7 | 8.5 | 9.6 | 7.5 | 250 |
| **Total demand** | | | | | | | | | | | | | | | | | 3050 |
| **numbers:** | | 20 | 50 | 30 | 40 | 65 | 25 | 25 | 75 | 50 | 40 | 72 | 32 | | | | |
| **work hours:** | | 100 | 350 | 150 | 200 | 455 | 125 | 125 | 525 | 250 | 200 | 504 | 140 | | 3124 | | |

## Chapter 12

12.1

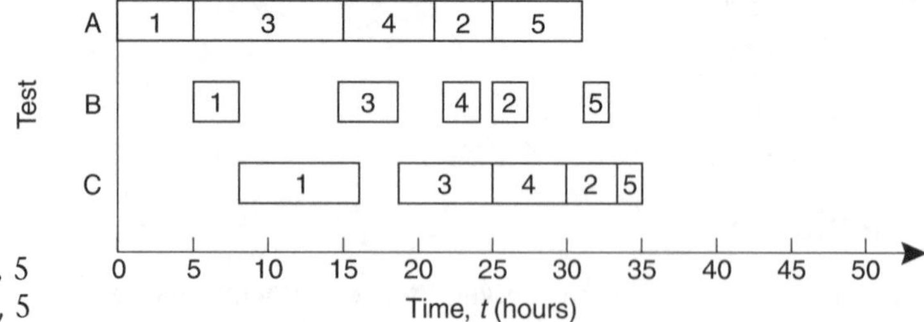


12.3 (a) Sequence = 3, 6, 2, 4, 7, 1, 5
or 3, 6, 2, 7, 4, 1, 5
(b) Sequence X = 3,2,5,6,1
Y = 4,3,2,5,6
(c) Several sequences give $T$ (throughput time) = 22, e.g. 3, 1, 4, 2; 2, 3, 4, 1; 1, 3, 2, 4; 2, 1, 3, 4; 3, 2, 4, 1 (obtained empirically since the special case of Johnson's rule does *not* apply)

12.5

| (a) Job | Priority rule 1 | 2 | 3 | 4 | 5 | 6 | 7 | 8 | 9 | (b) Job | Priority rule (+ FCFS) 1 | 2 | 3 | 4 | 5 | 6 | 7 | 8 | 9 |
|---|---|---|---|---|---|---|---|---|---|---|---|---|---|---|---|---|---|---|---|
| 1 | 4 | 4 | 4 | 3 | 7 | 4 | 3 | 7 | 1 | 1 | 4 | 4 | 4 | 3 | 7 | 4 | 3 | 7 | 1 |
| 2 | 1 | 1 | 1 | 5 | 3 | 1 | 1 | 4 | 10 | 2 | 1 | 2 | 1 | 8 | 6 | 1 | 1 | 4 | 10 |
| 3 | 5 | 4 | 8 | 3 | 7 | 5 | 3 | 9 | 2 | 3 | 5 | 5 | 8 | 4 | 8 | 5 | 4 | 9 | 2 |
| 4 | 2 | 1 | 2 | 9 | 2 | 2 | 2 | 6 | 4 | 4 | 2 | 1 | 2 | 9 | 2 | 2 | 2 | 6 | 4 |
| 5 | 3 | 3 | 3 | 1 | 9 | 3 | 6 | 3 | 9 | 5 | 3 | 3 | 3 | 2 | 10 | 3 | 6 | 3 | 9 |
| 6 | 10 | 8 | 9 | 5 | 3 | 10 | 8 | 7 | 3 | 6 | 10 | 8 | 9 | 5 | 3 | 10 | 8 | 8 | 3 |
| 7 | 8 | 7 | 10 | 1 | 9 | 8 | 3 | 10 | 5 | 7 | 8 | 7 | 10 | 1 | 9 | 8 | 5 | 10 | 5 |
| 8 | 5 | 6 | 4 | 10 | 1 | 5 | 9 | 2 | 8 | 8 | 7 | 6 | 5 | 10 | 1 | 7 | 9 | 2 | 8 |
| 9 | 5 | 8 | 7 | 5 | 3 | 5 | 7 | 4 | 6 | 9 | 6 | 9 | 7 | 6 | 4 | 6 | 7 | 5 | 6 |
| 10 | 8 | 10 | 6 | 5 | 3 | 8 | 10 | 1 | 7 | 10 | 9 | 10 | 6 | 7 | 5 | 9 | 10 | 1 | 7 |

**12.7**

| Order number | Number of products | A: I | A: Hours | B: I | B: Hours | C: I | C: Hours |
|---|---|---|---|---|---|---|---|
| 1 | 50 | 0.33 | | 0.67 | | 0 | 150 |
| 2 | 75 | 0.5 | | 0 | 150 | 1.0 | |
| 3 | 25 | 0.67 | | 0.33 | 100 | 0 | |
| 4 | 80 | 0 | 160 | 1.5 | | 1.0 | |
| | | | 175 (91%) | | 275 (91%) | | 175 (86%) |

**12.9** Minimize $C = 2(4Q_{1,A} + 3Q_{2,A} + 5Q_{3,A} + 2Q_{4,A}) + 3(5Q_{1,B} + 2Q_{2,B} + 4Q_{3,B} + 5Q_{4,B}) + 2.5(3Q_{1,C} + 4Q_{2,C} + 3Q_{3,C} + 4Q_{4,C})$

Subject to the following constraints:

$$Q_{1,A} + Q_{1,B} + Q_{1,C} = 50$$
$$Q_{2,A} + Q_{2,B} + Q_{2,C} = 75$$
$$Q_{3,A} + Q_{3,B} + Q_{3,C} = 25$$
$$Q_{4,A} + Q_{4,B} + Q_{4,C} = 80$$

$Q_{ij} \geq 0$ where $i = 1, 2, 3, 4$

$j = A, B, C$

where $Q_{ij}$ = quantity of order $i$ allocated to machine $j$.

**12.11** The production plan is shown below, assuming production during one month may be used to satisfy demand in the same month.

| | | | May A units | May B units | June A units | June B units |
|---|---|---|---|---|---|---|
| May | Factory 1 | Normal | 100 | 50 | | |
| | | Overtime | | 20 | | |
| | Factory 2 | Normal | | 80 | 90 | |
| | | Overtime | | | 20 | 20 |
| June | Factory 1 | Normal | | | | 100 |
| | | Overtime | | | | 5 |
| | Factory 2 | Normal | | | | 65 |
| | | Overtime | | | | |

Total cost = £2770 (assuming excess capacity has zero cost)

**12.13** (a) 65%

(b) Two lines

(c) (i) The probability of a line requiring service by the telephonist is independent of the time it has been used hitherto.

(ii) All service times are constant.

(iii) There is no priority system for answering calls on a line.

(iv) All lines have similar operational characteristics.

## Chapter 13

**13.1**

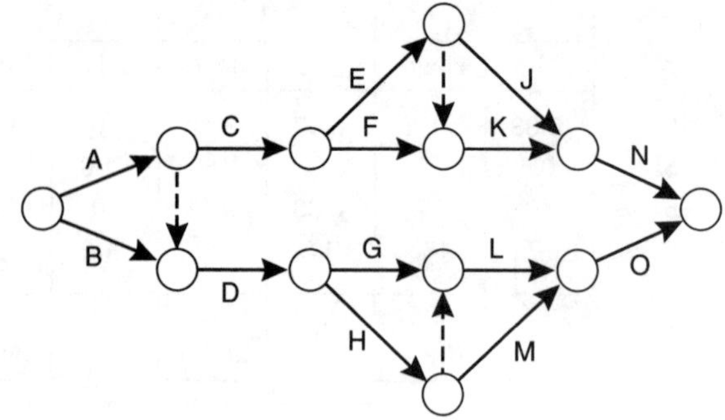


**13.3** Critical path = A, C, F, I

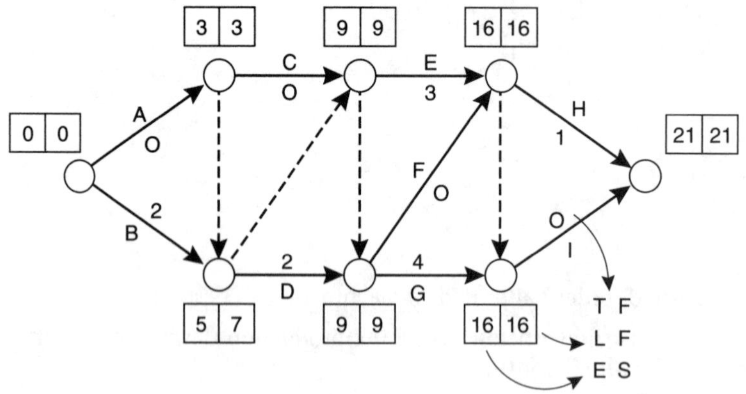


**13.5** Critical path = A, B, F, H, for which $t = 28$ and $\sigma^2 = 7.23$. From tables $P = 2\%$, i.e. considering critical path only, probability of finishing on or before 22.5 days = 2%. *But* minimum duration for path A, C, D, G = 2 + 9 + 5 + 7 = 23. Therefore actual probability = 0.

| Activity | TF | Activity | TF |
|---|---|---|---|
| 0–1 | 0 | 5–8 | 7 |
| 1–2 | 0 | 5–9 | 0 |
| 1–3 | 1 | 6–10 | 3 |
| 2–4 | 0 | 7–10 | 9 |
| 3–5 | 1 | 8–10 | 3 |
| 4–5 | 0 | 9–10 | 0 |
| 4–6 | 3 | 10–11 | 0 |
| 5–7 | 9 | | |

**13.7** (a) Critical path = 0, 1, 2, 4, 5, 9, 10 ,11

(b) (i) Delay project by 5 days.

(ii) The new critical path is 6, 10, 11, since these are the only activities in which delay will delay the project.

**13.11** (a) 31 days

(b)

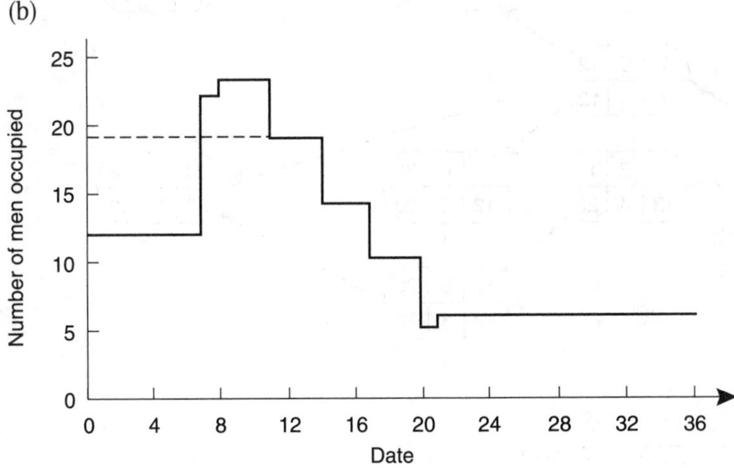


(c)

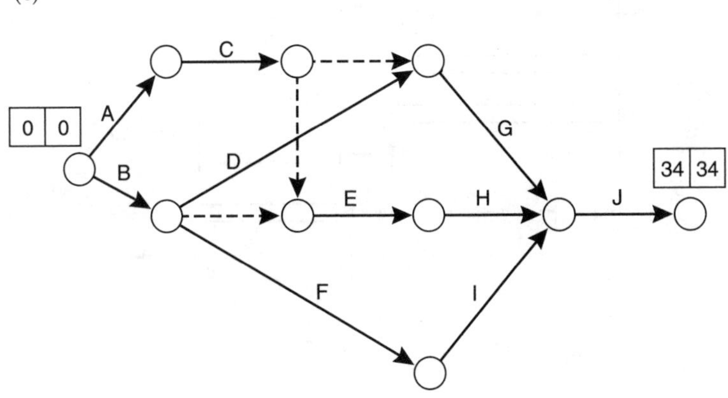


(d) Three days

**13.13** (a) Earliest completion = 27 days
Critical path = A, B, E, H, J
Total float: A = 0, B = 0, C = 5, D = 4, E = 0, F = 4, G = 4, H = 0, I = 4, J = 0, K = 8

(b)

| Days | Labour required | Days | Labour required |
|---|---|---|---|
| 0–2 | 4 | 11–12 | 16 |
| 2–5 | 9 | 12–15 | 17 |
| 5–6 | 3 | 15–19 | 18 |
| 6–9 | 16 | 19–27 | 7 |
| 9–11 | 15 | | |

**13.15**

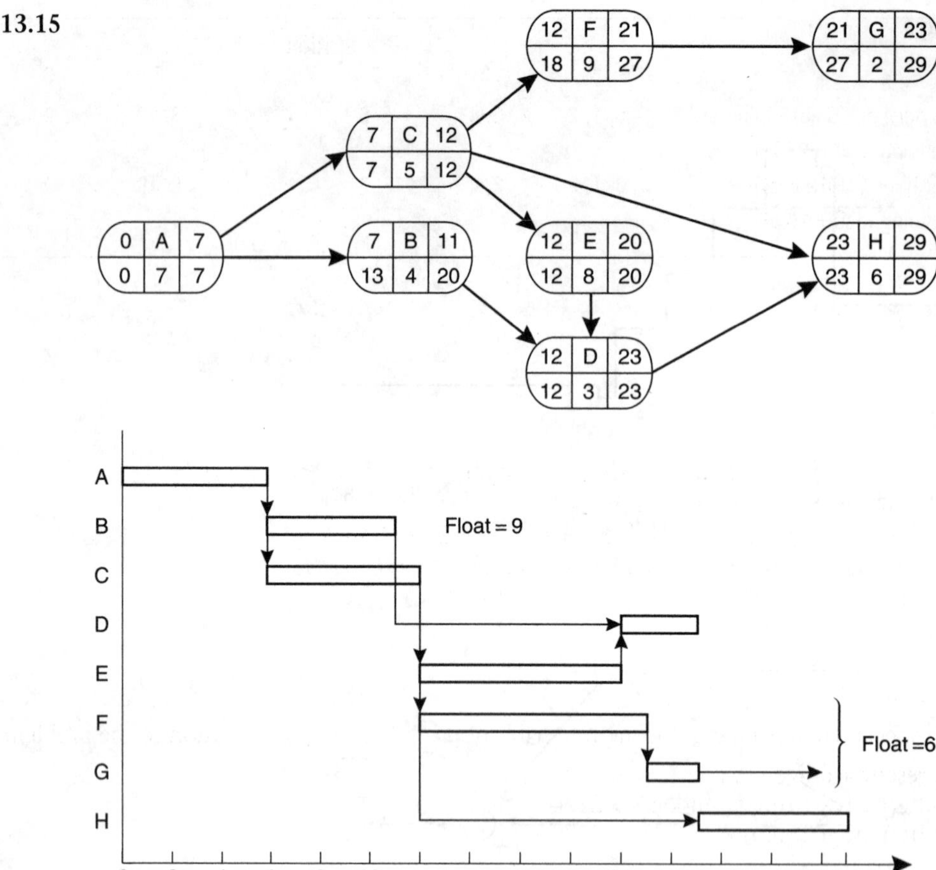


## Chapter 14

**14.3** 21 000 litres (equivalent)

**14.5** 14 100 to 31 200 litres (equivalent)

**14.7** (a) 1.2 months
(b) 1.22 months
(c) 1.26 months

**14.9** $Q_E = 4670$
$Q_V = 6670$
$Q_G = 10000$
$Q_M = 3330$
$N = 1.5$

## Chapter 15

**15.1** $n_{\text{min.}} = 28$
$C = 0.4$ minutes

**15.3** Cycle time = 20 minutes
Balancing loss = zero

| Station | Work elements | Station time |
|---|---|---|
| 1 | 0, 1, 2, 4 | 20 min |
| 2 | 3, 5, 7, 8 | 20 min |
| 3 | 6, 9, 10, 11 | 20 min |

15.5

| | Station | | | | | |
|---|---|---|---|---|---|---|
| | 1 | 2 | 3 | 4 | 5 | 6 |
| 4.61 per hour $C$ = 13 minutes | 0, 1, 2 | 3, 4 | 5, 6 | 7 | 8, 10 | 9 |
| Balancing loss = 25.7% | | | | | | |
| 5 per hour $C$ = 12 minutes | 0, 1, 2 | 3, 4 | 5, 6 | 7 | 8, 10 | 9 |
| Balancing loss = 19.6% | | | | | | |

**15.9** (a) 1
(b) 2

**15.11** A, E, D, B, C
£320

**15.13** Using the method described at the end of the chapter:
Fixed launching interval, $\gamma = 0.47$ minutes
Models must be launched in cycles as follows: A C A BA CC A CC
In other words, proportions of each model produced are as follows:

A = 0.40
B = 0.10
C = 0.50
D = 0.00

Except in special circumstances this method will not provide a complete solution to the problem.

**15.15** Cost of present arrangement = £323
Cost of Alternative 1 (mixed-model) = £224
Cost of Alternative 2 (multi-model) = £270
Use Alternative 1

## Chapter 17

**17.3** (a) 2620
(b) 2620
(c) 2500

**17.5** (a) £2550
(b) £2400
(c) £2850
$Q = 10000$
$C = £34300$

**17.9** (a) Startrite = 890
Quickfire = 1246
Longlife = 622
Highpower = 490
(b) 2.14 months

**17.11** (a) $Q^* = 862$
Reorder level = 21 items
(b) Reorder level = 21 items

**17.13** Reorder level = 24 items
Order quantity = 300 items

# Chapter 18

**18.1**

(a) *Jobbing engineering manufacture*

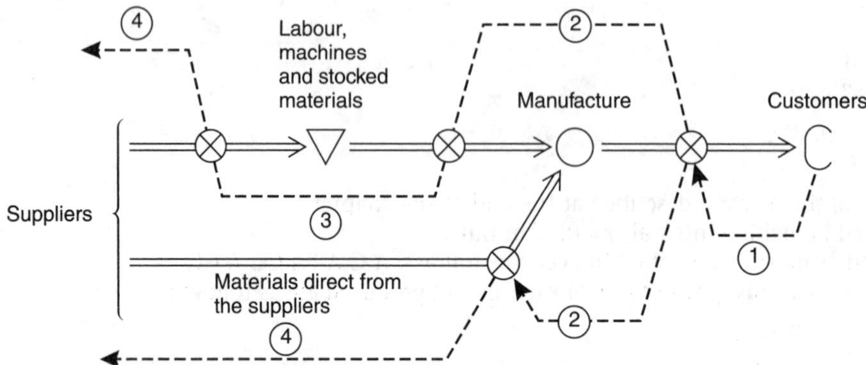


Controls: (1) Information on each customer's requirements: controls the flow out of the function
(2) Activity scheduling and control: controls the flow through the function or process in the system
(3) Inventory control: controls inventory levels and inventory inputs
(4) Purchasing control: controls input of resources from suppliers

(b) *A restaurant*

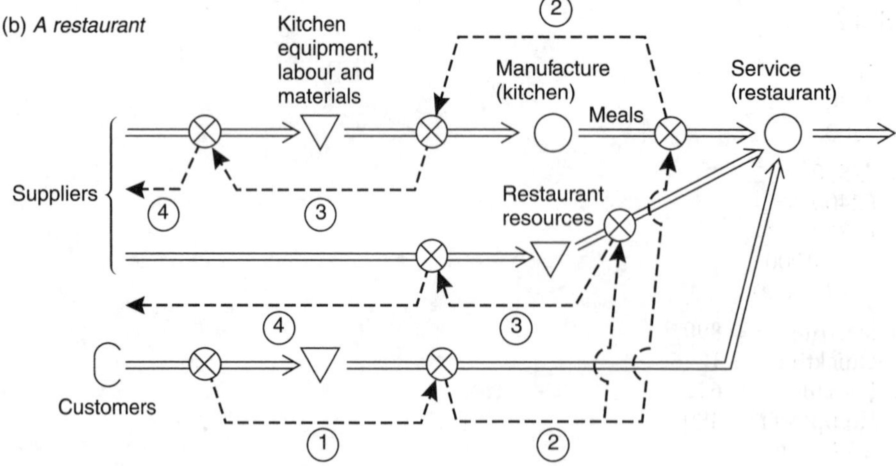


Controls: As for (a); however, the control of inventories (3) here involves the control of input stocks (through the control of levels and stock inputs), and also customer input queues (through the control of levels and queue outputs)

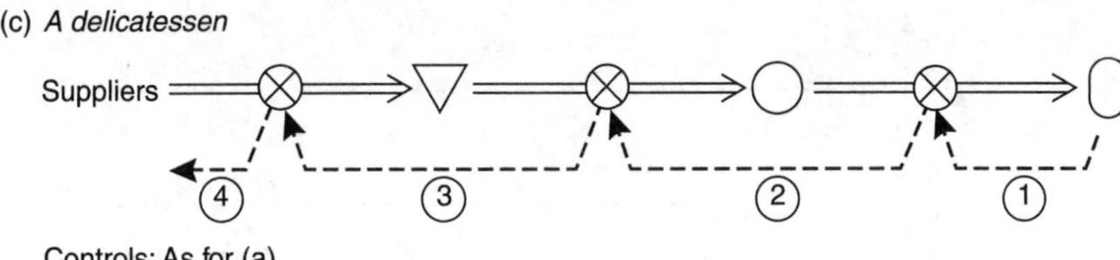


## Chapter 20

**20.1** (c) 0.56

**20.3** $C = 14$
$n = 317$

**20.5** (a) Approximately 0.82
(c) $n = 89$
$c = 4$

**20.7** (a) 1. $\alpha = 26\%$ 2. $\alpha = 33\%$
(b) 1. $\beta = 29\%$ 2. $\beta = 12\%$
(i) Plan 1
(ii) Plan 2
Average outgoing quality limit:
Plan 1 = 1.7 approximately
Plan 2 = 1.2 approximately

**20.9**

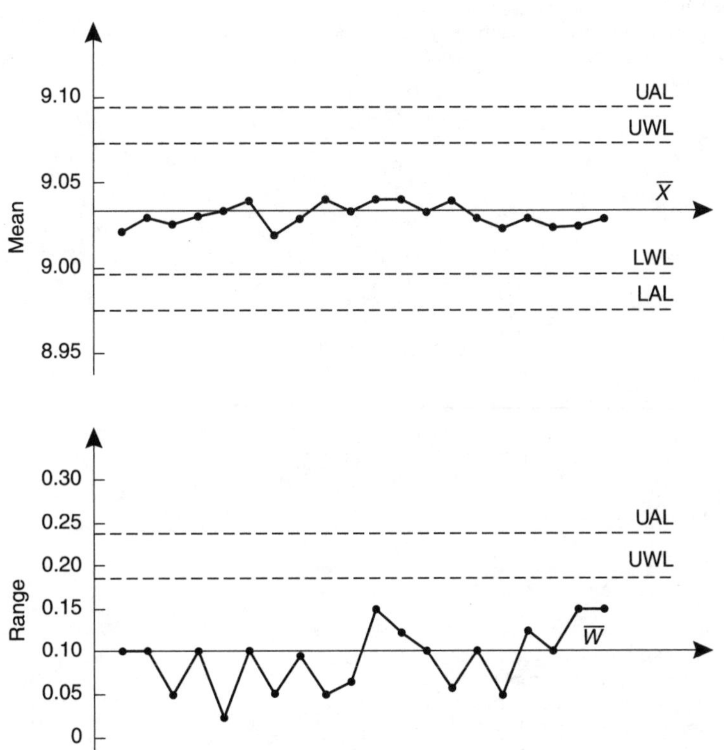

**20.11**

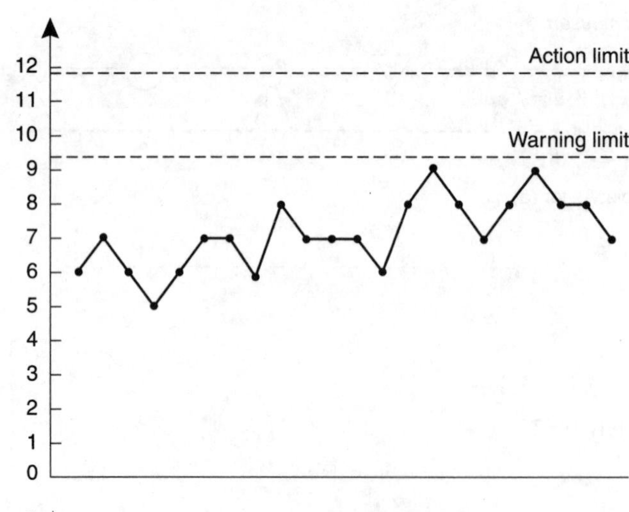


**20.13**

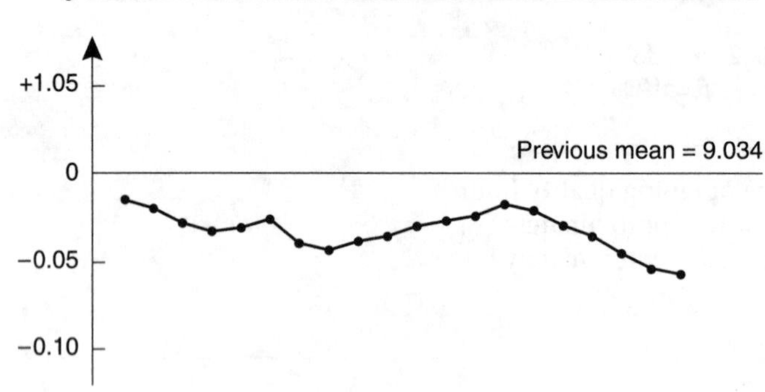


**20.15** (a) 2.2
(b) $12.4 \times 10^4$

## Chapter 21

**21.3** (a) £2.20/hour
(b) (i) 280 hours
(ii) 157 hours

**21.5** (a) (i) 6
(ii) 3.5
(b) (i) Group C
(ii) Group A

**21.7** (a) 47 hours
(b) 29 hours

**21.9** (a) Yes
(b) £18

## Appendix I

**I.1** $x = 4$
$y = 5$
$z = 10$
Min. $W = -11$

**I.3** Constraints:

$$2G + Q + p = 3000$$
$$2G + 3Q + 4R + q = 6000$$
$$G + Q + R + r = 10000$$

Max. $W = G + 3/2Q + 2R$

Solution R = 1500
Profit: $W$ = 3000p

**I.5**

| | X | Y | Z |
|---|---|---|---|
| A | | | 20 |
| B | 15 | | |
| C | 10 | 5 | 15 |

Minimum transportation cost = £465

**I.6**

| | Standard | De luxe | Super | Super de luxe |
|---|---|---|---|---|
| A | 25 | | | |
| B | | 15 | 10 | |
| C | | | | 5 |

Profit = £633

**I.7**

| | A | B | C | D | E |
|---|---|---|---|---|---|
| 1 | | | 1 | | |
| 2 | 1 | | | | |
| 3 | | | | 1 | |
| 4 | | 1 | | | |
| 5 | | | | | 1 |

Minimum cost = 14

## Appendix II

II.1

| Period | Actual sales | Forecast (a) | Error | Forecast (b) | Error |
|---|---|---|---|---|---|
| 1 | 20 | | | | |
| 2 | 18 | | | | |
| 3 | 17 | | | | |
| 4 | 21 | 18.3 | −2.7 | 17 | −4.0 |

| Period | Actual sales | Forecast (a) | Error | Forecast (b) | Error |
|---|---|---|---|---|---|
| 5 | 22 | 19.0 | −3.0 | 21 | −1.0 |
| 6 | 21 | 19.6 | −1.4 | 22 | +1.0 |
| 7 | 20 | 19.8 | −0.2 | 21 | +1.0 |
| 8 | 18 | 19.9 | +1.9 | 20 | +2.0 |
| 9 | 19 | 19.6 | +0.6 | 18 | −1.0 |
| 10 | 21 | 19.6 | −1.4 | 19 | −2.0 |
| 11 | 24 | 19.7 | −4.3 | 21 | −3.0 |
| 12 | 28 | 20.0 | −8.0 | 24 | −4.0 |
| 13 | 34 | 20.7 | −13.3 | 28 | −6.0 |
| 14 | 36 | 21.7 | −14.3 | 34 | −2.0 |
| 15 | 35 | 22.8 | −13.2 | 36 | +1.0 |
| 16 | 30 | 23.6 | −6.4 | 35 | +5.0 |
| 17 | 28 | 24.0 | −4.0 | 30 | +2.0 |
| 18 | 26 | 24.3 | −1.7 | 28 | +2.0 |
| 19 | 30 | 24.4 | −5.6 | 26 | −4.0 |
| 20 | 31 | 24.6 | −6.4 | 30 | −1.0 |
| | | 25.0 | | 31 | |
| Average error (neglecting sign) periods | | 4–20 | 5.20 | | 2.47 |
| Average error (neglecting sign) periods | | 4–10 | 1.6 | | 1.71 |
| Average error (neglecting sign) periods | | 11–20 | 7.72 | | 3.00 |

II.3

| Year | Period | Sales ('000) | Four-period moving average | Seasonally adjusted four-period moving average |
|---|---|---|---|---|
| 1986 | 1 | 50 | | |
| | 2 | 60 | | |
| | 3 | 50 | | |
| | 4 | 44 | | |
| 1987 | 1 | 50 | 51.0 | 48.5 |
| | 2 | 64 | 51.0 | 60.8 |
| | 3 | 56 | 52.0 | 51.0 |
| | 4 | 50 | 53.5 | 47.0 |
| 1988 | 1 | 54 | 55.0 | 52.5 |
| | 2 | 70 | 56.0 | 66.7 |
| | 3 | 56 | 57.5 | 56.2 |

| Year | Period | Sales ('000) | Four-period moving average | Seasonally adjusted four-period moving average |
|---|---|---|---|---|
| | 4 | 50 | 57.5 | 50.8 |
| 1989 | 1 | 54 | 57.5 | 54.7 |
| | 2 | 66 | 57.5 | 68.2 |
| | 3 | 52 | 56.5 | 55.3 |
| | 4 | 50 | 55.5 | 49.0 |
| | | | 55.5 | 52.8 |

II.5

| Period | Actual sales | Five-period moving average | Error | Exponential smoothing $\alpha = 0.33$ | Error |
|---|---|---|---|---|---|
| 1 | 10 | | | | |
| 2 | 12 | | | | |
| 3 | 12 | | | | |
| 4 | 10 | | | | |
| 5 | 8 | | | | |
| 6 | 10 | 10.4 | +0.4 | 10.4 | +0.4 |
| 7 | 13 | 10.4 | −2.6 | 10.3 | −2.7 |
| 8 | 12 | 10.6 | −1.4 | 11.2 | −0.8 |
| 9 | 9 | 10.6 | +1.6 | 11.4 | +2.4 |
| 10 | 8 | 10.4 | +2.4 | 10.7 | +2.7 |
| 11 | 10 | 10.4 | +0.4 | 9.8 | +0.2 |
| 12 | 13 | 10.4 | −2.6 | 9.9 | −3.1 |
| 13 | 14 | 10.4 | −3.6 | 10.9 | −3.1 |
| 14 | 12 | 10.8 | −1.2 | 11.9 | −0.1 |
| 15 | 9 | 11.4 | +2.4 | 12.0 | +3.0 |
| 16 | 10 | 11.6 | +1.6 | 11.0 | +1.0 |
| 17 | 13 | 11.6 | −1.4 | 10.8 | −2.2 |
| 18 | 14 | 11.6 | −2.4 | 11.5 | −2.5 |
| 19 | 11 | 11.6 | +0.6 | 12.3 | +1.3 |
| 20 | 10 | 11.4 | +1.4 | 11.9 | +1.9 |
| | | 11.6 | | 11.3 | |
| Average error (neglecting sign) | | | 1.73 | | 1.83 |

(taking period 6 exponential forecast as equal to period 6 moving average forecast)

**II.7**

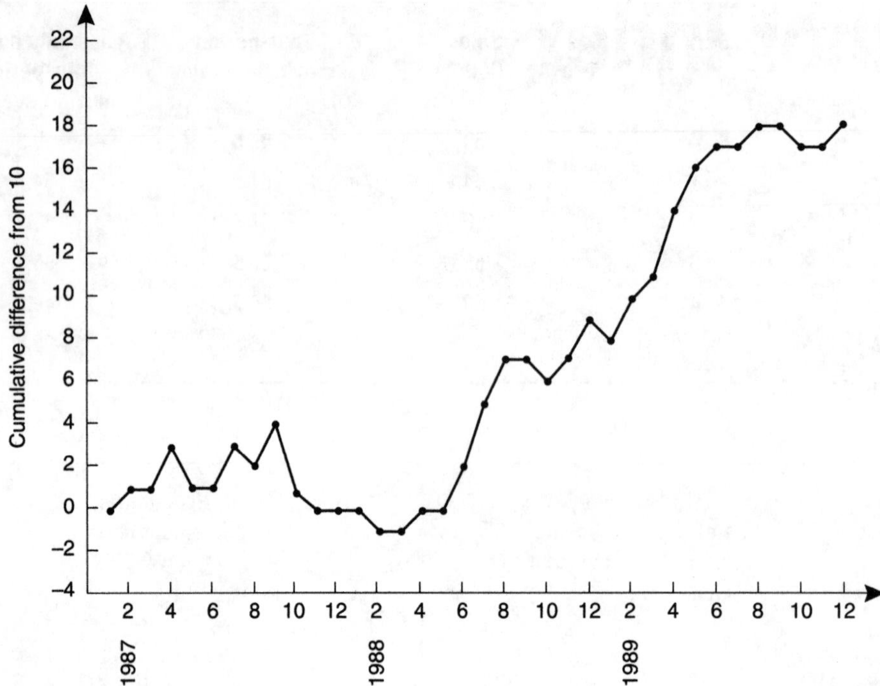


**II.9** (a) $r = 1.0$
(b) $r = 0.97$

**II.11** (a) $y = -1330 + 0.757x$
where $y$ = consumption
$x$ = GNP
(b) 20670

# Author Index


Adam, E.E. 598
Adams, P. 99
Agrawal, A. 198
Allenbach, R. 137
Ansoff, H.I. 43
Arcus, A.L. 442, 450
Armour, G.C. 136
Ashcroft 329–30, 331

Bahiri, S. 687, 699
Bailey, D. 698
Baily, P. 494, 502
Baker, K.R. 422
Barker, E.M. 598
Barker, T. 539
Battaglia, A.-J. 486
Beishon, J. 226
Berger, I. 455
Berry, L.L. 598
Berry, W.L. 50, 288, 346
Betts, J. 442
Bhattacharjee, T.K. 470
Birnie, D.P. 442, 447
Blackshaw, D. 487
Blank, L.T. 85
Blumberg, P. 229
Bourjolly, J.M. 455
Bowey, A. 240, 257
Bridgeman, P.W. 104, 116
Bright, J.G. 138
Brooks, S.G.H. 568
Brower, M.J. 675
Brown, J. 150
Buffa, E.S. 136, 889
Busch, H.F. 502
Butterfield, S. 825
Buxey, G. 762
Byrne, H.S. 80
Byrne, M. 432

Callan, R.J. 590
Camp, R.C. 696, 698
Campion, M.A. 230
Cannon, T. 74
Caplan, R.H. 641, 644
Cavinato, J. 539
Chang, Y.L. 318
Chapman, R.L. 583
Chase, R.L. 583
Chaykowski, R.P. 228
Chen, Chiu-Stveng 138
Chew, W.B. 698
Chisman, J.A. 887
Cho, D.I. 676
Christopher, M. 502
Cinpak, D.M. 663
Clark, K. 75
Clarke, P. 583
Cleland, D.I. 568
Close, D.J. 540
Conover, D.W. 214
Cook, J.A. 501
Cooper, C. 585, 598
Cordero, S.T. 676
Correa, H. 781
Costello, R. 345
Cox, D.R. 644
Cristóvam, M.L. 822
Cullen, J. 235
Currie, R.M. 178, 203

Dale, B. 585, 598, 644
Dar-El, E.M. 252, 254, 795
Das, B. 186, 188
Davidson, R.L. 251
Davis, L.E. 229
Davis, S.G. 420
Deckro, R.F. 442
Didis, S.K. 698
Dodge, H.F. 612, 620–3
Domschke, W. 117, 150
Doty, L.A. 178, 203
Drexl, A. 117, 150
Drury, C. 85

East, E. 389
Eilon, S. 288, 418, 568
Elsayed, E.A. 148, 598
England, W.B. 502
Enrick, N.L. 644
Evans, W.O. 135

Farmer, D.H. 494, 502
Fawcett, S.E. 699
Fawcette, J.E. 389
Fearon, H.E. 502
Feigenbaum, A.V. 572
Fein, M. 253
Fogel, L.J. 215
Foggarty, D.W. 27
Forger, G. 148
Fox, R.E. 345
Francis, R.L. 116
Fray, E.N. 695
Friedman, B. 257
Fujimoto, T. 75

Gagnon, R.J. 470
Galama, W. 820
Garvin, D.A. 50
Genaidy, A.M. 198
Ghosh, S. 470
Gilbert, J.P. 491, 502
Gilbreth, F. 169
Glaccum, J.F. 636
Gobeli, D.H. 636
Goddard, R.W. 695
Goldsmith, P.L. 869, 875
Gordon, J.R.M. 47
Gowen, C.R. 257
Graham, C.F. 891
Gray, C.D. 346
Gray, M.W. 244
Green, A. 345
Groenevelt, H. 565
Grossmann, J. 250
Gryna, F.M. 593
Guehi, W.G. 75

Hackman, S.T. 442
Haigh, R.W. 117
Hall, M. 203
Han, M.H. 148
Harrison, A. 345
Harrison, M. 50
Haus, K. ten 818
Hayes, R.H. 49
Heizer, J. 96
Helgerson, N.B. 442, 447
Hickson, D.J. 237
Hill, T. 50, 583
Hillier, E. 856
Ho, J.C. 318
Hoffman, T.R. 27, 442
Horngren, C.T. 85
Houshyar, A. 138
Hsiang, T. 598
Hubert, T. 698

Ishikawa, K. 595–6, 598
Izuehukwu, A. 659

Jacobs, J. 36
Jacobs, R.F. 340
Jaede, E.K. 538
James, G. 598, 698
Jarrett, J. 288, 875
Jessop, D. 540
Johnson, R. 137, 346
Johnston, K.J. 138
Juran, J.M. 593

Kaplan, R.S. 85
Kapstein, J. 237
Karmarker, U.S. 565
Kelly, J. 230
Kendrick, J.J. 636
Kengskool, K. 138
Kerzner, H. 389
Ketcham, R.L. 150
Khandwalla, P.N. 74
Kilbridge, K. 442
Kimmel, P.S. 676
Kin, K. 833
King, T.L. 598
King, W.R. 568


*Note*: most names are to be found in source notes or footnotes.

Kirby, J. 389
Kirkpatrick, D. 656
Koska, M.T. 584
Krieger, H. 820
Kumara, S. 115

Labban, J. 138
Landvater, D.V. 346
Laporte, G. 455
Lazarus, H. 235
Leach, D.H. 868
Lee, R.C. 135
Leenders, M.R. 502
Lehmann, J. 719
Lehtihet, A.L. 115
Levary, R.R. 452
Lieberman, G. 856
Lipow, M. 644
Lloyd, D.K. 644
Loizeaux, E. 345
Long, A.A. 585
Love, R.F. 116
Lovelock, C. 75
Lumsden, N.P. 432
Lyon, B.R. 217

Mabin, V.J. 526
McGregor, D. 229
McRoberts, K.L. 150
Magazine, M.J. 442
Mahomoud, K.I. 442
Makridakis, S. 875
Malstrom, E.M. 150
Meadows, N. 755
Melville, B. 276, 692
Meredith, J.R. 27
Milas, G.H. 455
Miller, J.A. 697
Min, H. 464
Mital, A. 198
Mize, J.H. 568
Moore, J.M. 135
Morris, B. 346, 789
Morrison, A. 540
Morse, P.M. 659, 661–2, 664
Mullin, R. 676
Mullins, P. 310

Nandyal, R.K. 697
Newsome, P. 774
Niebel, B.W. 178
Nielsen, C.L. 801
Norman, R.G. 687, 699
Novack, R.A. 502
Ntuen, C.A. 665

Oakland, J.S. 598, 644
O'Connor, T.F. 331
O'Grady, P. 432
Olorunniwo, F.O. 659
Olusoy, G. 659
O'Neal, K.R. 389
Ormsby, J.G. 343
Ormsby, S.Y. 343
Orr, S. 716
Owens, T. 256

Paoli, P. 820
Parasuraman, A. 598
Park, T. 458
Parlar, M. 676
Paulsen, K.M. 256
Peters, G. 226
Pettis, J. 538
P'Guin, M. 84
Pugh, D.S. 237
Pyke, D.F. 422

Rajamani, D. 471
Rangachari, S. 442
Raouf, A. 676
Rehder, R.R. 237
Render, B. 96
Renfro, M.D. 452
Richardson, J. 511
Ritchie, P. 488
Robson, M. 598
Romig, H.G. 612, 620–3
Rorsted, B. 801
Rosander, A.C. 598
Rothery, B. 598
Rouen, D. 540
Russo, T.J. 138
Ruthstrom, C.R. 343

Safford, R.R. 636
Safizadeh, M.H. 237
Sahu, S. 470
Salvendy, G. 237
Satem, M. 235
Savsar, M. 150, 471
Sayers, R.D. 469
Schember, J. 45
Schonberger, R.J. 491, 502
Schuring, R. 235
Scotta, L. 538
Seehof, J.M. 135
Shin, D. 464
Siegal, B. 73
Simco, S.W. 502
Singh, N. 471
Singleton, W.T. 428
Sinha, M.N. 572
Sizer, J. 82
Sklarow, G. 594
Skylar, J. 388
Slack, N. 50
Sloan, T. 583
Slotsve, G.A. 228
Sly, D. 138
Snaddon, R. 792, 806
Snead, C.S. 432
Sofer, P. 795
Solano, M.S. 250
Steele, P. 539
Stern, R.G. 148
Stevens, G.C. 487, 502
Stonebraker, P.W. 27
Streudel, H.J. 458
Suen, K.P. 636
Sule, D.E. 150
Sule, D.R. 135–6

Sullivan, L.P. 583
Sun Qi Zhi 885–6
Svestka, J.A. 137

Taguchi, G. 595, 598
Tamashunas, V.M. 138
Tarquin, A.T. 85
Taylor, A.J. 47
Taylor, F.W. 229
Tersine, R.J. 540
Thayer, P.W. 230
Tombari, H.A. 676
Tonges, M.C. 235
Tortorella, A.J. 138
Townroe, P.M. 92, 98
Trigg, D.W. 868
Turner, J.R. 355, 389
Tyndall, G.R. 486

Vella, A. 726
Vollman, T.E. 288, 346
Voss, C. 50, 432

Wang, P. 101
Waters, C.D.J. 27, 540
Watson, I.J. 185
Wee, T.S. 442
Weist, J.D. 378
Welch, D. 697
Werner, M. 137
Wester, L. 442
Wheelwright, S.C. 49, 875
White, C.R. 568
White, J.A. 49, 116
Whitmore, D.A. 203
Whybark, D.C. 288, 346
Wild, R.
  on capacity management 275
  on flow processing 471
  on international case studies 716, 726, 755, 818
  on payment and incentives 252
  on performance measurement 682–3
  on work measurement 183
  on work methods 163, 166
  on workers and conditions 222–4, 237
Willbom, W.H.O. 572
Willis, D. 198
Wilson, J. 595
Wisner, J.D. 699
Wolak, J. 644
Wood, L. 389
Woodson, W.S. 214
Woodward, R.H. 869, 875
Wright, N. 825
Wu, B. 887
Wygant, R.M. 198

Young, H.H. 464
Younger, A. 585

Zeithaml, V.A. 598
Ziai, M.R. 136, 150
Zygmont, J. 432

# Subject index


AB&P, *see* America Burger and Pasta
ABC (activity-based costing) 83–4
acceptable quality level 614, 616, 619–20
acceptance sampling 603, 604, 609–21
design of single plans 614–19
double and multiple samples 619–20
examples 611, 613, 614–15, 618
tables 620–1
accidents, industrial 220–1
accounting, *see* finance/accounting
active pricing 57
activity
-based costing 83–4
controls 565–6
on node diagrams, *see* scheduling *under* network
sampling 162, 182–91
examples 189–91
rated 189
scheduling 18, 296–7, 303–51, 354, 355
balancing scheduling and control 297, 344
control 562
dependent and independent demand 310–11, 312, 314
effectiveness 297, 343–4
network, *see under* network
problems 296, 311–12, 314
strategies for 296, 304–7
*see also* JIT; project management; techniques of activity scheduling *and also* uncertainty *under* demand
added value (AV) scheme 254–5
adjustment of system capacity 271–3
adoptive forecasting and exponential smoothing 868
advertising 59–60, 61–3
aggregation
capacity management planning 264, 265, 278
market 55
resource 383, 385
agriculture, *see* farming
AGVs (automatically guided vehicles) 430
airlines and airports
building case study 753–4
capacity management 267
facility layout 125
quality in manufacture 593–4
quality management 574–6
work study 161
alcohol
liqueur bottling 627–8
*see also* wine
ALDEP (Automated Layout Design Program) 135
allocation, resource 383, 385
allowances for interruptions in time study 187–8
ambulance 307
America Burger and Pasta case study (Brazil) 781–8
American Airlines 576
analogue visual displays, design of 211–12
analytical estimating and work measurement 162, 183, 198
analytical models and facility location 113–14
anthropometric data and workplace design 214–16
AOQ (average outgoing quality) 617–18
AOQL (average outgoing quality limit) 618–19, 620–3
appointments and demand uncertainty 313
appraisal in quality management 577, 578, 592
appropriateness 16
AQL (acceptable quality level) 614, 616, 619–20
Ashcroft numbers 330, 331
Asia, *see* Japan *and under* international case studies
ASR, *see* automated storage and retrieval
assembly lines 438–9
*see also* processing *under* flow
assessment, quality 592
assignable variations in quality 622
assignment (activity scheduling technique) 316, 324–32
facilities interference 328–32
index method 324–6
linear programming 326–8
assignment algorithm 853–6
maximizing 856
minimizing 853–6
associative predictions 269, 871–4
assurance for items and quality control 551, 602–4
ATM (automated teller machine) 99
attributes, acceptance sampling by 610
audit
internal quality 587
performance measurement 692–5
aural displays, design of 211–12
Australia
Corio Shire case study 762–73
facility location 98
materials management 486–7
quality management 583
Automated Layout Design Program 135
automated storage and retrieval (ASR) 90, 145–8
nature of 145–7
operating policies for 147–8
SR machines 146, 148
automated teller machine 99
automatically guided vehicles 430
automation, *see* work *under* technology
AV (added value) scheme 254–5
Avant Hotel 590
average
moving 862–5
outgoing quality 617–18, 620–3

bakery shops case studies 789–94
balancing
complex flow line 464–8
delay/loss 441
objectives 10–11
scheduling and control 297, 344
*see also* line of balance
Bangladesh: Jograni Handicrafts case study 716–18
banks and automation
activity scheduling 307
facility location 99
line balancing 452
payment 249
working conditions 223–4
barber shop 885–6
bar charts, *see* Gantt charts
bars, *see* restaurants and cafés
batch 6
batched orders 148
processing 298–9, 402–35
dealing with 298, 403–4
decisions on 404–7
examples 404
scheduling for 405, 419–26
sequencing 405, 407–8
*see also* sizes of batches
scheduling 317
bearings failure 667–70


*Note*: references are to operations management, which is therefore omitted as a qualifier.

behaviour
control 67, 68, 559, 686
quality management 551, 590–2
Belgium: Centre Hospitalier Reine Fabiola case study 719–25
Bell Telephone 620
benchmarking 556, 697
'Big Fry-Up' 47, 48
bill of requirements in MRP 337–8
body of worker
movement studied 192–6
shape and size and workplace design 214–16
use of 174
bonuses, *see* incentives
bookshop 486
bottleneck operation 333–5
Bourg Breton case study 735–41
brand 56
Brazil: America Burger and Pasta case study 781–8
breakeven analysis 129
breakeven point 80
brewing 161
Britain, *see* United Kingdom
British Airlines 576
British Standards
quality control (BS 6001) 620
quality management (BS 5750) 585–6, 590
work study and measurement (BS 3138) 160, 165–6, 182–3
budgeting 83
outline planning and 353, 354
*see also* costs
buffer (safety) stocks 59
activity scheduling 339
batch processing 415–16
flow processing 462–3, 465, 466
inventory management 527, 528–9, 532–4
materials management 499–500
building firms 15, 161
capacity management 268, 275–6, 277
buses 161
business policy 30, 33–43
choice of strategies 38
for competitive advantage 39–41
decisions and capacity management 260–1
delivery service example 35–6
formulation of 34–5
growth and development 41–3
implementation of 35
nature of 24–6
operations management decisions 36–9
*see also* policy

CAD and layout 138
cafés, *see* restaurants and cafés
calculations, network 361–9
float 363–7
matrix method 367–9
*see also* dates
Canada 228, 620
capacity
decisions and MRP 340
facility location 109
layout 131
management 18, 19–20, 259–91
building firm example 268, 275–6, 277
competitive advantage 261
computers 266
control 567
defined and described 262, 266–8
demand forecasting 268, 269–71
operations planning and control 262, 264–6
strategies for demand fluctuations 271–8
*see also* procedures *under* planning
opening in MRP 338
strategy and policy 48–9
cards, *see* kanban
Carreras SL case study 705–15
case studies, *see* international case studies
categorical vendor rating plan 605
cell layout 127–8, 130
'cellular' processing, *see* technology *under* group
centralization 64
Centre Hospitalier Reine Fabiola case study 719–25
certainty and batch size determination 409–14
chain management *see* SCM
chance variations in quality 621–3
change 16–17
*see also* time
channel decisions and PDM 496–8
charts
and layout 134
programme progress 425
quality control 603, 621–32
for attributes 629–31
cumulative sum techniques 631–2
dynamic 634–5
examples 627–8, 630–1
for variables 625–8
travel (cross) 133–4, 165, 428–9
Choice Hotels International: Sleep Inn 45
church case study 755–6
CIM (computer-integrated manufacturing environment) 430
cinema location 100, 105–6
city lighting 656
civil engineering 130
classification in group technology 427
cleaning firm 233
clerical PMTS 197–8
closed system 560
clothing wholesaler 511–12
coding in group technology 427
coefficients
learning curve 199–200
model, management 284
COMLAD II 135–6
company-wide quality control 595–6
compatibility 147
competitive advantage
business policy for 39–41
capacity management 261
design 72
materials management 479
policy 43, 49
scheduling 295
work study 155
competitive environment and materials management 487
competitive variables and marketing 53
complementarity 147
completion schedule in line of balance 424
complex flow line 301–2, 460–8
balancing 464–8
buffer stocks 462–3, 465, 466
human aspects 460–2
system loss 462
compound interest table 673
computers
banks, *see* banks and automation
batch processing 430
capacity management 266
computer-integrated manufacturing environment 430
Computerized Relationship Layout Planning 135
economics 80
flow line design 450, 452, 468–9
layout planning 134–9
location of facilities 113–15
maintenance and replacement 674–5
manufacturers and payment 244
materials handling, *see* automated storage and retrieval
network scheduling and analysis 386–8
performance measurement 690
project management 386–8
quality control and reliability 635–6
VDUs and keyboards, design of 215, 217–20
work measurement and standards 198
work study 177
COMSOAL (computer method of sequencing operations for assembly lines) 450, 452
concurrent activity in activity scheduling 328–9
conditions

performance rating 186–7
of work and job evaluation 243–4
configuration, organization 64
conflict of objectives 10, 11
conformity and quality 571
congestion and layout 123–4
consequent costs and quality management 577
consistency
performance rating 186–7
of policy 49
construction, *see* building firms
consumed items, inventories of 506–7
consumers' association testing 641–2
context of operations management 29–32
*see also* business policy; costs; economics; other business functions; policy
Continental Airlines 576
continuous digital computer simulation 880
continuous flow in inventory management 506, 508, 536
continuous variation in inventory management 519
contracting and project management 353, 354
control 17, 21, 545–6
capacity management 262, 264–6
costs 81–4, 577, 579–80
defined 264
finance/accounting 67–8
inventory management 506
limits 623, 632–3
and performance measurement 555–6, 686–92
planning, distinction between 557, 559
project management 353, 355, 356
quality management 577, 579–80
scheduling, balancing 297, 344
*see also* maintenance; performance measurement; principles of control; quality *and* quality control *under* charts
controls, design of 212–13
CORELAP (Computerized Relationship Layout Planning) 135
Corio Shire, case study (Australia) 762–73
correction in quality management 577, 578
correlation coefficients 270, 871–2
costs 9, 31–2, 76–8
accounts and MRP II 343
batch processing 403
capacity management 279, 282–3
control systems 81–4
customer service performance 681, 682, 684
facility layout 123
facility location 94–8
factors influencing 78
indirect 76–8, 577, 578, 579
inventory management 509, 519–21
manufacturing 654
marketing 53, 56–8, 62
network scheduling and analysis 379–83
payment 252
performance measurement 683
policy option 40, 43–4, 47
quality management 550, 576–82, 584
nature of 577–8
quality levels 578–9
'spending' and 'saving' on 579–82
types and categories 576–7
ratio vendor rating plan 605
uncertainties and batch size determination 414–15
*see also* budgeting; economics
CRAFT (computer program) 136–7
crafts, *see* handicrafts
crash activity and network scheduling 379–80
critical path
analysis 316, 565
float in network calculations 364
cross (travel) charts 133–4, 165, 428–9
Cummins Engineering 310
cumulative completion 424
cumulative graphs 279–81
cumulative sum techniques 868–70
customer service 8–10
costs 509
decisions and PDM 496, 498
performance 554–5, 681–5
cost 681, 682, 684
reliability 683–4
specification 681–2, 684
timing 681, 683, 684
safety stock 528–9
time 440
*see also* queue
customizing 47
cusum techniques 868–70
CWQC (company-wide quality control) 595–6
cycle time 440

data sensing and processing in worker–machine systems 225
databases, *see* computers
dates and network calculations 361–3, 365, 367–9
schedule 367–9, 371–5
*see also* time
decisions 3, 23–5
business policy for 36–9
capacity management 260–1
'decision tree' approach 276
facility location 114–15
interval method and cumulative sum techniques 870
inventory management 507–9
maintenance 553, 653–6
problems 3, 17–22
*see also* function *under* marketing
dedicated storage policy 147
degeneracy and transportation algorithm 853
delay 123–4, 441
delivery service example of business policy 35–6
demand
capacity management
curves 280
estimation/measurement 264, 265
fluctuations, *see* demand fluctuations
forecasting 268, 269–71
dependent 310–11, 312, 314
layout 131
life-cycle of 270
supply and transportation algorithm 852–3
uncertainty, managing 297, 312–13
appointments and reservations 313
'random arrivals' problem 313
demand fluctuations, strategies of 271–8
adjustment of system capacity 271–3
examples 275–7, 278
factors affecting choice of 273–8
democracy, industrial 229
Denmark: TAARUP Farming Machines Ltd case study 801–5
dentistry 15, 161
international case study 774–7
dependability 40, 43–4
dependent activity demand 310–11, 312, 314
design 17
control 566
limits and process capability 632–3
of products/services 20, 31, 69–73
make or buy decisions 71
process 69–71
purchasing 70–1
quality 70
simultaneous development 72–3
standardization 71
quality 571, 572, 575, 588–9
of tools and equipment 174
of workplaces 174, 214–21
*see also* planning
desirability 8, 16, 24–5, 274–5
desk, working at 215, 217–20
detailed operations schedule 265
deterministic determination of batch sizes 409–14
deterministic situations and inventory management 515–27
periodic control 526–7
*see also* perpetual control

development
  marketing 54, 55
  product 54
  research and 69
  sequential 72
  simultaneous, and design 72–3
  in work method study 162, 163, 173, 174
DHL Worldwide Express 36
diagrams, network 356–61
dialog management system in DSS 114
diary 164
differentiation, product 55
digital computer simulation 880–1
digital visual displays 211–12
dimensional analysis and facility location 101, 103–4
direct (prime) costs 76–7, 78
direct work measurement 162, 182, 184–91
  *see also* sampling *under* activity *and* study *under* time
discontinuous variation in inventory management 519–20
discrete digital computer simulation 880–1
discrete location problem 114
dispatching 315, 322–4
distribution, *see* supply; transport
diversification 54
*do* activities 173
domestic appliances
  manufacturer 307
  parts supplier 606–7
  testing by consumers' association 641–2
DOS (detailed operations schedule) 265
double acceptance sampling 619–20
Dow-Corning (Australia) 583
drinks company and batch processing 414, 418
Du Pont (Australia) 486–7
dummy activities and network diagrams 357–61
dynamic control charts 634–5
dynamic sequencing 318

earliest finish date 363, 365
earliest start date 361–2
earnings, *see* payment
economics 32, 78–81
  analysis of design 70–1
  breakeven point 80
  computers and 80
  economic indicators 871–4
  indicators and capacity management 269
  operating levels and capacity management planning 278–9
    of worker–machine systems 225
  *see also* costs

education and training
  international case studies 746–52, 806–13, 825–32
  quality management 584, 587, 595
EF (earliest finish) date 363, 365
efficiency and effectiveness
  activity scheduling 297, 343–4
  JIT 310
effort
  job evaluation 243–4
  rating 186–7
EG & G Inc 695
electricity 267
  international case study 822–4
electronic recording in time and motion studies 172, 185
elimination of unnecessary activities 173
emergency services in new town 558–9
employment, *see* work; worker
engine manufacturer 310
environmental factors
  variables and marketing 53
  worker–machine system 213–14, 218
equal pay example 244
ergonomics checklist 218–19
  *see also* worker–machine system
ES (earliest start) date 361–2
estimated monthly demand 280
Europe
  business and policy 35–6
  facility location 95
  Japanese firms in 72
  quality management 594
  *see also under* international case studies
European Combined Terminals case study 820–1
European Community directive on VDUs 217
European Foundation – group work case studies 820–4
evaluation, *see under* job
event dates 367
examination in work method study 162, 163, 172–3
excess stock-holding 536
expert systems 115
exploiters of technology 49
exponential smoothing 866–8
  adoptive forecasting 868
  demand forecasting 269
  seasonal variations and secular trends 867–8
Express Drinks Company 414, 418
external integration 488
external uncertainty 63–4
externally oriented activity scheduling 305–6, 311, 314
  *see also* JIT
eye travel and focus 192, 194, 196

facilities 87–90
  *see also* layout planning; location of facilities *and also* handling *under* materials
facilities interference method of assignment 328–32
FACLO 137
factor comparisons and facility location 101, 103
factory-flow analysis 138, 428
failure and quality control 639–41, 666–70
'families' of items processed 407–8
farming 531
  machinery case study 801–5
feasibility 8, 16, 23–4
  capacity management demand fluctuations 273–4
  studies and prototype work 353, 354
Federal Express (FedEx) 35–6
feedback 560–1, 590
fertilizer firm 531
filming, *see* video
final specification of design 70–1
finance/accounting 31, 67–9
  financial companies 388
    *see also* banks
  managerial and financial controls 67–8
  private hospital example 68–9
  *see also* costs
fire
  prevention and control 221
  service 15, 268, 276–7
fishbone (company-wide quality control) 595–6
fitness for purpose 573–4
fixed costs 80, 97, 98
fixed intervals of time 416–17
fixed position in layout 127, 130, 140
fixed quantity in inventory management models 521–2
flexible policy option 39–40, 43–4
flexible processing systems 299–300, 429–31
  *see also* FMS
'flicker' on VDU screen 218
float method of network calculations 363–7
flow
  control 561
  diagrams in work method study 164, 165, 167
  efficient, *see* JIT
  in inventory management, continuous 536
  processing 300, 436–76
    charts in work method study 164, 165–6, 167–9
    nature of 300–1, 437–8
  scheduling 317

flow line design
  computers and 450, 452, 468–9
  principles 301, 438–9
  *see also* complex flow line; simple flow line
FMS (flexible manufacturing systems) 403, 429–31
  *see also* robotics
food
  eating out, *see* restaurants and cafés
  processing 608–9
  retail 125, 130, 161, 524–5, 789–94
Food Concept Sdn. Bhd. case study 833–9
Ford Motor Company 6
forecasting 860–78
  associative predictions or economic indicators 871–4
  capacity management 269
  cumulative sum techniques 868–70
  from last period's sales 861–2
  past average 860–1
  *see also* exponential smoothing; moving average
FotoPrint Pronto case study 757–61
4M (motion time measurement) 197
France 95
  Bourg Breton case study 735–41
free float in network calculations 364
functional dimensions of quality 575
functional integration 488
functional layout 124–5, 128, 129, 130
furniture removal 178, 268

gainsharing 251–6
  calculations 253
  example 255–6
  experience with 256
  types of scheme 252–5
Gantt charts
  activity scheduling 315, 317–18
  network scheduling 384–5
garden centre 530–1
gas and electric company 663
geared incentive schemes 246–7
general costs 77
general-purpose digital computer simulation 881
Gibraltar savings 388
goods
  business policy 41
  development 54
  differentiation 55
  layout 126, 129, 139–40
  life-cycle 41
  marketing 53, 54–6, 62
  quality management 571, 575, 584, 589
  *see also* design; services
graphics firms 486–7
  design case study 744–5
group
  analysis 428
  incentives 250–6
    examples 251, 255–6
    profit sharing 251
    *see also* gainsharing
  layout 127–8, 130
  technology and batch size reduction 426–9
    facilities grouping 428–9
    parts families 427–8
    sequencing 429
  working and job design 234–5

hand motions 192–5
handicrafts 267
  case study 716–18
Hawthorne experiments 229
health and safety 220–1
  *see also* hospitals; medicine and health care
heat and VDU work 208
heuristic methods
  capacity management planning 284–5
  resource allocation program 378
holding costs and inventory management 509, 519–21
Hong Kong: Prince Philip Dental Hospital case study 774–7
hospitals 15
  capacity management 267, 286–7
  facility layout 130
  finance/accounting 68–9
  international case studies 719–25, 774–7
  inventory management 508–9, 522–3
  nursing 235
  performance measurement 691–2
  quality management 584
  scheduling 307
  work study 161
  *see also* medicine and health care
hotels
  facility layout 125, 130
  performance measurement 690–1
  policy 45
  quality control 618
  quality management 590
  work study 161
house builder, *see* building firm
human relations and human resources theories 229
hybrid, *see* mixed

IBM 538
idle time in activity scheduling 328–9
Improved Productivity Sharing (IMPROSHARE) 253
incentives 158, 245–56
  *see also* payment; PBR *and also* incentives *under* group
income, *see* payment
independent activity
  in activity scheduling 328–9
  demand 310–12, 314
independent float in network calculations 364
index method of assignment 324–6
India: airport building case study 753–4
indirect costs, *see* overheads
indirect work measurement 162, 182–3, 191–8
  analytical estimating 162, 183, 198
  synthetic timing 162, 182, 191
  *see also* PMTS
individual incentives, *see* PBR
information
  dependent control 561
  displays, design of 211–12
initial design 70
innovators 49
input
  blocking in inventory management 536
  control and quality control 602–3
  inventory management 506, 508
    control 512–26, 536
    fixed 526–7
    resources 507
  planning/control distinction 557
  *see also* queue
inspection
  maintenance 553, 655, 657
  quality 58, 589, 607–9
  sampling 610
installation in work method study 162, 163, 175–6
insurance company: international case study 818–19
integrated materials management 480, 484–5, 488, 501
integrated productivity measures 686, 687
interactive graphics 138
interference method of assignment 328–32
intermediate schedule date 367–8
intermittent flow in inventory management 506, 508
intermittent process 6, 512–15
internal integration 488
internal quality audit 587
internally oriented activity scheduling 305, 306, 312, 314
international case studies 701–839
  Asia
    Bangladesh 716–18
    Hong Kong 774–7
    India 753–4
    Malaysia 833–9
    Nepal 642–3
  Australia 762–73
  Brazil 781–80
  Europe
    Belgium 719–25

international case studies, Europe
—*cont.*
Denmark 801–5
France 735–41
Italy 757–61
Malta 726–31, 746–52
Netherlands 818–19, 820–1
Portugal 822–4
Spain 705–15
Turkey 632–4
UK 744–5, 755–6, 789–94, 814–17
Israel 795–800
New Zealand 825–32
South Africa 806–13
INVEN 538
inventory 18–19
batches 403–4
decisions
activity scheduling 340, 341–2
materials management 496, 498–500
holding costs 403
lack of, *see* JIT
management 481–2, 504–44
computers 537–8
consumed items 506–7
continuous flow/input control 536
control 562, 567
costs 509
decisions 507–9
examples 508–9, 510–12, 517–18, 520, 522–3, 524–5, 530–4, 535
items to control 510–12
MRP 537
nature and purpose of 481–2, 505–6
systems 512–15
*see also* deterministic situations; probabilistic situations
marketing 59
opening in MRP 338
strategy and policy 48–9
investment in quality management 577, 578
ISO 9000–9003 quality standard 585–9
Israel: K&S Ltd case study 795–800
Istel Inc. 469
Italy: FotoPrint Pronto case study 757–61

Japan 72, 310, 594
*kaizen* 695–6
*see also* JIT; kanban
JIT (just in time) 296, 307–10
batch processing 403, 429
benefits of 309
comparison with MRP 340, 341
elements of 308–9
example 310
philosophy 307–8
prerequisites for efficiency 310
purchasing and materials management 490
quality management 590–1
*see also* kanban
job 6
classification 242
costing 82
design
organization design 235
work organization 158, 229–34
enlargement 233
evaluation and payment 241–4
equal pay example 244
factor comparison 243
job classification 242
job ranking 241–2
points evaluation 242–3, 244
ranking 241–2
time and motion studies, *see* measurement *under* work
*see also* work
Jograni Handicrafts case study (Bangladesh) 716–18
just in time, *see* JIT

K&S (Israel) Ltd case study 795–800
K-Mart 501
*kaizen* 695–6
kanban 309, 310, 341, 561–5
keyboards, *see* VDUs
Kilbridge and Wester simple line design 442–7
Kodak 501

labour, *see* work; worker
languages, computer simulation 881–2
latest finish date 361–3
latest start date 363
Latin America, *see* Brazil
laundry 330, 332
Lavelle Aircraft 593–4
layout planning 21, 90, 122–42
basic types 90, 124–31
comparison and evaluation 141–2
computer-aided 134–9
control 566
fixed-position 140
methods 90, 132–4
need for 90, 122–3
objectives 90, 123–4
problems 90, 124
procedure 131–2
product 139–40
supply and storage 140–1
lead time 416, 424, 528
leadership and quality management 583
learning 156, 175–6
curve 175, 271
coefficients 199–200
work measurement and standards 157, 198–202
defined 176
factors influencing 175–6
principles of 176
Lee Apparel 501
Legrand Eléctrica case study 822–4
leisure
breaks during work 220
centre international case study 735–41
levelling system 186–7
LF (latest finish) date 361–3
library 130, 267
life-cycle
demand 270
facility 652
marketing 54–5
organization 42
product/service 41
project 353
total quality management 582–3
*see also* stages
lighting in workplaces 213–14, 218
Linden Christian Nursery School case studies 806–13
line analysis 428
line of balance 317
batch processing technique 422–6
simple line design 440, 441–52
COMSOAL 450, 452
Kilbridge and Wester design 442–7
ranked positional weights 447–50, 451
linear decision rule method 284
linear programming 842–59
capacity management planning 281–4
flow processing 453
method of assignment 326–8
sequencing by 322
*see also* assignment algorithm; Simplex algorithm; transportation algorithm
linear regression 873–4
liqueur bottling 627–8
LOB (line of balance) 317
location of facilities 20, 90, 91–121
computer methods 113–15
control 566
factors affecting 90, 94–9, 102
need for choice 90, 91–4
problems 90, 99–113
*see also* multiple-facility; single-facility
logistics of materials management, *see* PDM
long-term flexibility 431
loss, balancing 441
lot tolerance per cent defective 614, 616, 619, 621–2
LS (latest start) date 363
LTPD (lot tolerance per cent defective) 614, 616, 619, 621–2

McDonald's 488
machinery industry case studies 778–80, 801–5
mail, *see* post office
maintenance 22, 552–4, 650–70
  computers 674–5
  control 567
  decisions 553, 653–6
  examples 656, 663, 667–70, 672, 674
  function 552–3, 651–3
  inspection 553, 655, 657
  MRP II 342
  objectives 653
  preventive 553, 655, 657–63
  repairs 554, 655, 663–5
  in work method study 163, 176
  *see also* replacement
make or buy 71
  checklist 494
*make ready* activities 173
Malaysia: Food Concept Sdn. Bhd. case study 833–9
Malta
  MBA degree programme case study 746–52
  Qormi Post Office case study 726–31
Mamma Mia Pasta House 126, 437–8
management, *see* operations management
manual flow lines 464–8
manufacturing 5, 6–7, 9, 15
  batch processing 404–5, 410–11, 426–9
  capacity management 267–8, 272
  costs 84, 654
  design 72
  facility layout 124–9, 130
  facility location 96, 97, 100
  inventory management 531
  quality control 614–15
  quality management 570, 593–4
  scheduling 305, 307, 310, 353
  work study 161
  *see also* batch; output; process
MAPICS 538
market
  aggregation 55
  development 54
  penetration 54
  in quality management 577, 578, 579
  segmentation 55
marketing function and decisions 30, 52–63, 69, 342
  cost 56–8, 62
  distribution 53, 58–9, 62
  goods/services 53, 54–6, 62
  promotion 53, 59–61, 62
Martin-Marietta Corporation 592
masking method 870
mass production 6
  *see also* batch; process
master operations schedule 265
master production schedule 338
materials
  costs 77
  flow process chart for 166, 168, 170
  handling 21, 90, 142–52
    methods 143–5
    objectives 143
    *see also* automated storage and retrieval
  management 477–82, 483–503
    defined 483–4
    integrated 480, 484–5, 488, 501
    logistics, *see* PDM
    supply, *see under* purchasing
    *see also* SCM *and also* management *under* inventory
  requirement planning
    purchasing and materials management 493, 495
  requirements planning, *see* MRP
matrix method of network calculations 367–9
maximizing
  Simplex algorithm 843–6
  transportation algorithm 852
Maynard Operations Sequence Technique (MOST) 197, 663
MBA degree programme case study (Malta) 746–52
means, control charts for 625–6, 628
measured day work incentives 249
mechanization, *see* work *under* technology
medicine and health care
  facility layout example 148
  quality management 584
  *see also* hospitals
memomotion 165
memory 172
method study 131, 156, 162, 163–76
  *see also* recording work method
MICRO-LMS (Logistics Modelling System) 114–15
Middle East, *see* Israel
minimizing
  assignment algorithm 853–6
  Simplex algorithm 846–7
Minnesota Metropolitan Waste Control Commission 538
mixed layouts 128
mixed-model flow lines 439, 453–60
  balancing 454–6
  sequencing 456–60
MOCRAFT 137
MODAPTS (modular arrangement of predetermined time standards) 197
model management system in DSS 114
modifying existing layouts 138
MOS (master operations schedule) 265
Mosier Industries 255–6
MOST, *see* Maynard Operations Sequence Technique
motion/movement
  layout 132, 136–7
  moving averages and demand forecasting 269
  time measurement
    principles of motion economy 174
    *see also* PMTS; SIMO
motivation and quality management 584
motor vehicles 6
  ambulance 307
  assembly line 130
  carwash 130
  Japanese competition 72
  parts
    manufacture 469
    retail 530
  taxi 65–6, 267
  work study 161
movement, *see* motion
moving average 862–5
moving-belt flow lines 464, 465–8
  items fixed to 466, 467–8
  items removed from 465–7
  station overlap 466, 467–8
MRP (materials requirements planning) 316, 335–43
  batch sizes 339
  capacity, inventory and scheduling decisions 340
  comparisons 343
    with JIT 340, 341
    with OPT 340
  inventory management 537
  MRP II 316, 341–3
  principles of 336–7
  safety stock 339
  use of 337–9
MTM I and II (methods time measurement) 192, 193–5, 196–7
multi-factor incentives 249–50
multi-model flow lines 439, 452–3
multiple acceptance sampling 619–20
multiple activity records in work method study 165, 167
multiple time estimates 369–75
  probability of achieving scheduled dates 371–5
multiple-facility location problems 100, 109–13
  capacity 109
  distribution company example 109–13
  number of facilities 109
multi-project operations planning 384

Nepal: Pokhara Weavers case study 742–3

Netherlands case studies
European Combined Terminals 820–1
Wintherthur non-life commercial insurance 818–19
network
analysis 316, 565
location problem 114
scheduling and analysis 297–8, 356–401
computers 386–8
costs 379–83
Gantt charts 384–5
multi-project operations planning 384
network diagrams 356–61
probabilistic networks 385–6
resources 375–8, 383, 385
*see also* calculations, network; multiple time estimates
new town, emergency services in 558–9
New Zealand: Open Polytechnic case study 825–32
node diagrams, activity on, *see* scheduling *under* network
noise in workplaces 208, 214
non-functional dimensions of quality 575
non-mechanical flow lines 464, 465
normal activity and network scheduling 379–80
North America, *see* Canada; United States
nursing 235

objective rating 186–7
objectives 8
business policy 36–8
layout planning 90, 123–4
maintenance 653
materials handling 143
operations management 2–3, 8–11
policy 48
price variations 57
purchasing and materials management 488–9
OC, *see* operating characteristics
office
equipment manufacture 233
job evaluation 243–4
job and work measurement 189–90
Oklahoma Gas and Electric 663
one-for-one incentive schemes 245–6
Open Polytechnic of New Zealand case study 825–32
open system 560
opening inventory and capacity in MRP 338
operating characteristics curves 610, 612–13, 614–15
operating systems
costs and quality management 576, 577, 579–80
inventory control versus 508
inventory management 512–15
nature of 2, 4–7
output inventory 505
problems and decisions 3, 17–22
redefinition 6
reliability 642–3
structure of 3, 11–15, 16
operations control, *see* control
operations costs, *see* costs
operations economics, *see* economics
operations management 1–32
in action 22–3
decision-making 3, 23–5
defined 7
nature of 2, 7–8
objectives 2–3, 8–11
*see also* capacity; context; control; facilities; international case studies; materials; operating systems; scheduling; work
operations planning, *see* planning
operations policy, *see* policy
operator, flow process chart for 166, 168–9, 171
Opmist 675
opportunities 34–5
job 231, 232, 234
optimized production technology (OPT) 316, 333–5
bottleneck operation 333–5
comparison with MRP 340
'optimum' quality 581
order methods with uncertainty
interval 534–6
quantity 529–34
organization 30–1, 63–6
business policy 42–3
design and job design 235
life-cycle 42
purchasing and materials management 489–90
quality management 551, 590–2
taxi example 65–6
technology 63–5
total quality management commitment 583
work, *see under* job design
*see also* business policy; policy
orientation of scheduling 305–6, 311–12, 314
other business functions 30–1, 52–75
*see also* design; finance; marketing; organization
outline process chart 168
output
control 67, 557, 559–60
and performance measurement 686–7
and quality control 602, 603, 604
costs 79–80
inventory 505, 506–7
from MRP 338
planning/control distinction 557
profit sharing schemes 252–3, 254
and resource utilization 685–6
starving in inventory management 536
overheads 76–8, 577, 578, 579

PADS (in time and motion study) 197–8
parallel activities and network scheduling 357–8
passive pricing 57
past average forecasting technique 860–1
patient care, *see* hospitals
Patisserie, La: case studies 789–91
payment 21, 158, 239–58
by results, *see* PBR
systems 158, 239–44
structure 240–1
*see also* evaluation *under* job
*see also* incentives
PBR (payment by results) 158, 245–56
geared schemes 246–7
measured day work 249
multi-factor incentives 249–50
one-for-one schemes 245–6
piecework 247–8
premium payment scheme 249
p-charts (proportion or per cent defective) 629, 631
PDM (physical distribution management) 58–9, 481, 495–501
channel decisions 496–8
inventory decisions 496, 498–500
level of service 496, 498
penetration, market and price 54, 57, 58
people as quality inspectors 592
performance
measurement 22, 547, 554–6, 680–99
audit 692–5
computers 690
improvement 556, 695–7
*see also* service performance *under* customer *and* utilization *under* resources
rating 186–7
periodic control and inventory management 513–14, 526–7
perpetual control and inventory management 513–14, 515–26
models 516–25
order quantities 515
reorder level 525–6
personal selling 59–60, 61
PERT, *see* multiple time estimates
photocopier and work measurement 189–90
photographic shop case study 757–61

physical dimensions of resource utilization 686
physical distribution management, *see* PDM
piecework 247–8
planar location problem 114
planning 17
  capacity management, *see* procedures *below*
  and control, distinction between 557, 559
  defined 264
  materials requirements, *see* MRP
  procedures and capacity management 178–87, 262, 264–6
    aggregation 278
    cumulative graphs 279–81
    economic operating levels 278–9
    heuristic methods 284–5
    linear programming 281–4
    queuing theory 285–7
  *see also* design; layout planning; scheduling
PMTS (predetermined motion time systems) 162, 164, 169, 177, 183, 191–8, 202
  *see also* MTM
points evaluation 242–3, 244
Poisson distribution 611–12
Pokhara Weavers case study (Nepal) 742–3
policy 30, 43–5
  for ASR 147–8
  competitive advantage 43, 49
  control 566
  decisions 46–7
    capacity management 260–1
  examples 45, 47, 48
  growth, dealing with 46
  implementing 47, 49
  implications 44–5
  marketing 55–6
  *see also* business policy
port case study 820–1
Portugal: Legrand Eléctrica case study 822–4
positional weight 448–9
post office 161
  case study 726–31
  mail order 161, 591
  mail sorting 630–1
predetermined motion time systems, *see* PMTS
predictions, *see* forecasting
preference 8, 24, 25
premium payment incentive scheme 249
prevention
  accidents 221
  and maintenance 553, 655, 657–63
  in quality management 577, 578
pricing 57–8, 492, 516–18
prime (direct) costs 76–7, 78
Prince Philip Dental Hospital case study 774–7
principles of control 548–9, 557–69
  activity controls 565–6
  concepts and requirements 548–9, 559–61
  examples 558–9, 565
  importance and emphasis 558–9
  *see also* kanban
printing, *see* graphics
prioritizing 265–6
probabilistic determination of batch sizes 414–18
probabilistic networks 385–6
probabilistic situations in inventory management 527–36
  order interval method with uncertainty 534–6
  order quantity method with uncertainty 529–34
  service levels and safety stock 528–9
problems
  decisions 3, 17–22
  *see also* capacity; context; control; facilities; international case studies; materials; scheduling; work
procedures in quality control 552, 604–32
  inspection 607–9
  vendor rating 603, 604–7
  *see also* acceptance sampling *and* quality control *under* charts
process and processing 6
  automation 222
  batch sizes 417–18
  capability 552, 632–5
  charts, *see* process charts *under* flow
  control 589, 602, 603–4
  costing 82–3
  design 20, 69–71
  improvement formula 173
  layout by 124–5, 128, 129, 130
  quality 552, 571, 572, 575, 602, 603–4, 632–5
  *see also under* batch; flow
production
  range and batch sizes 417–18
  *see also* operations management
productivity, *see* output
products, *see* goods; services
profit sharing 251, 252–3, 254
project management 297, 353–6
  activity planning and scheduling 354, 355
  completion, evaluation and review 353, 355
  computer-based 386–8
  contracting 353, 354
  feasibility studies and prototype work 353, 354
  formulation and definition 353–4
  nature of 353–5
  outline planning and budgeting 353, 354
  role of 355
  scheduling and control 353, 355, 356
  *see also* scheduling *under* network
promotion, marketing decisions on 53, 59–61, 62
proofreading 611
proportion or per cent defective 629, 631
prototype testing 70–1
proximity maximization and layout 135–6
psychology, worker 229
publicity 59–60
publishing 343, 535, 611
purchasing
  control 567
  design 70–1
  materials management 481, 488–95
    JIT and 490
    make or buy checklist 494
    materials requirement planning 493, 495
    objectives 488–9
    organization 489–90
    sourcing and suppliers 490–3
  MRP II 342
  quality 589
*put away* activities 173
PW (positional weight) 448–9

QCs (quality circles) 594–5
Qormi Post Office case study 726–31
quality 21
  assurance, *see* quality control *under* charts
  circles (QCs) 594–5
  control 567
  control and reliability 546–7, 551–2, 600–49
    and assurance for items 551, 602–4
    computers 635–6
    examples 611, 613, 614–15, 618, 627–8, 630–1, 636, 641–2
    process capability 552, 632–5
    *see also* procedures in quality control *and* items *under* reliability
  design 70
  improvement programmes 551, 592–6
    Ishikawa's fishbone 595–6
    quality circles 594–5
    Taguchi's 'quality loss function' 595
    'zero defects' 592–4
  'loss function' 595
  management 549–51, 570–99
    behavioural and organizational factors 551, 590–2
    costs, *see under* costs

quality—*cont.*
determination of quality level 576
examples 574–6, 584, 590, 591, 593–4, 595
JIT 590–1
nature of 549–50, 571–6, 572–4, 574–6
standards 584–90, 592
total 550–1, 582–4, 591
*see also* improvement *above*
marketing 56
only vendor rating plan 606
policy option 40, 43–4
quantity and inventory management 529–34, 536
queue, customer input
activity scheduling 306
batch processing 406
capacity management planning 285–7
inventory management 505, 506, 507, 509

R & D 69
'random arrivals' problem 313
randomized storage policy 147–8
ranges, control charts for 625–8
Rank Xerox 697
ranked positional weights 447–50, 451
rapid feedback 590
recollection/memory 172
recording
quality 587
work method 162, 163, 164–72, 185
procedure 170–2
types of records 164–70
recreation, *see* leisure
redesigning 70–1
reference value and cumulative sum techniques 869
regenerative approach in MRP 339
regression equation 270
relationship charts and layout 134
reliability
curve 271
customer service performance 683–4
of items in quality control 636–43
characteristics and measures 637–42
estimation 641
example 641–2
failure 637–9
system 642–3
policy option 40, 43–4
quality 575
*see also* quality
removal firms 178, 268
remuneration, *see* payment
reorder level 59, 525–6
repairs 554, 655, 663–5
repetitive process 6
replacement 22, 554, 666–74
computers 674–5
items subject to sudden failure 666–70
items which deteriorate 671–4
*see also* maintenance
research and development 69
*see also* design
reservations and demand uncertainty 313
resources 5
allocation 383, 385
input, in inventory 505, 506, 507
network scheduling and analysis 375–8
requirements and layout 132
utilization 10
measurement 688
performance 555, 685–6
policy 48
*see also* capacity
responsibility
job evaluation 243–4
social, business policy and 34–5
responsiveness
policy option 40, 43–4
*see also* decision support systems
rest time 220
restaurants and cafés
capacity management 267
facility layout 125, 126, 130
flow processing 437–8
international case studies 732–4, 781–8, 833–9
inventory management 531–4
materials management 488
operating system 15
policy 47, 48
quality control 613
restructuring, job 229–30
results, payment by, *see* PBR
retail 15
capacity management 267
facility layout 125, 130
facility location 100, 105
international case study
bakery 789–94
photography 757–61
post office 726–31
inventory management 517–18, 524–5, 530–1
materials management 485, 486, 501
quality management 591
work study 161
retrieval, *see* automated storage and retrieval
revenue facility location 94–6
reverse scheduling 315, 317–18
rewards, *see* payment
road transport 161
robotics 228, 431
robust function 584
rough-cut capacity planning 265
routeing, SR machine 148
RPW (ranked positional weights) 447–50, 451
Rucker PBR scheme 252–3, 254

safety
health and 220–1
stock, *see* buffer (safety) stocks
Sahil Tea Gardens case study 732–4
St John's Church case study 755–6
St Luke's Centre 584
sales, *see* marketing
sampling inspection 610
'saving' on quality management 579–82
savings company 388
Scanlon PBR scheme 252–3, 254
schedule dates 367–9, 371–5
scheduling 19, 293–302
control 567
strategy and policy 48–9
*see also* batch; flow; network; planning; project management *and also under* activity
Schlegal Corporation 565
schools, *see* education
scientific management 229
SCM (supply chain management) 480, 486–9
described 484, 487
developing 487–8
examples 486–7, 488
screening, design 70–1
screens, *see* VDUs
Seal, Malcolm, graphic design case study 744–5
search decision rule method 284
seasonal variations
exponential smoothing 867–8
moving average 862–3, 865
Seattle city lighting 656
secular trends
exponential smoothing 867–8
moving average 864, 865
segmentation, market 55
selection
design 70–1
in work method study 163, 164
selling, *see* marketing
semiconductors industry case study 795–800
sequencing 315, 318–22
activities and network scheduling 357–8
batch 405, 407–8
dynamic 318
group technology and batch size reduction 429
by linear programming 322
mixed-model flow lines 456–60
sequential development 72
sequential relationships 577

Watertight Ltd 410–11
weaknesses in business policy 34–5
weaving, *see* textiles
Weibull probability 641–2
weighted cross chart 134
weighted point vendor rating plan 605
Welcome Software 675
Westinghouse rating system 186–7
wholesaling, *see* warehouses
Williams' College case study 814–17
wine firms
  import 520
  international case study 705–15
  retail 517–18
Winterthur non-life commercial insurance 818–19
WITNESS 469
work 21, 153–8
  control 566
  measurement and standards 156–7, 162, 180–209
    computer applications 198
    layout 131
    learning curve 157, 198–202
    *see also* direct work measurement; indirect work measurement; payment
  organization
    approach to 230–4
    examples 283
    job restructuring 229–30
  study 156, 159–79
    computer applications 177
    nature of 160, 161
    structure and purposes 160, 162
    *see also* method study
  technology, *see under* technology
  *see also* job; payment; worker; workplaces
worker
  costs 77
  involvement in JIT 309
  rating 162, 186–7
  -type flow process chart 168–170
  *see also* job; work; worker–machine system
worker–machine system 211–14
  controls 212–13
  environmental factors 213–14, 218
  functions allocated 225–7
  information displays 211–12
workflow uncertainty and organization 63–4
workplaces 157, 210–21
  design 174, 214–21
  ergonomics, *see* worker–machine system
writing process in New Zealand Open Polytechnic 825–32

xeroxing 697

'zero defects' (ZD) quality improvement programmes 592–4
zoning constraints and flow processing 440, 447